The *Writer's* Handbook

Edited by
SYLVIA K. BURACK
Editor, The Writer

Publishers   THE WRITER, INC.   Boston

Library of Congress Catalog Card Number: 36-28596
ISBN: 0-87116-148-6

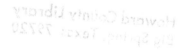

Printed in The United States of America

CONTENTS

PART I—BACKGROUND FOR WRITERS

CHAPTER

PART II—HOW TO WRITE: TECHNIQUES

GENERAL FICTION

SPECIALIZED FICTION

NONFICTION: ARTICLES AND BOOKS

PART III—EDITORS, AGENTS, AND BUSINESS

PART IV—WHERE TO SELL

THE WRITER'S HANDBOOK

1

EVERYTHING YOU NEED TO KNOW ABOUT WRITING SUCCESSFULLY—IN TEN MINUTES

By Stephen King

I. *The First Introduction*

THAT'S RIGHT. I know it sounds like an ad for some sleazy writers' school, but I really am going to tell you everything you need to pursue a successful and financially rewarding career writing fiction, and I really am going to do it in ten minutes, which is exactly how long it took me to learn. It will actually take you twenty minutes or so to read this essay, however, because I have to tell you a story, and then I have to write a *second* introduction. But these, I argue, should not count in the ten minutes.

II. *The Story, or, How Stephen King Learned to Write*

When I was a sophomore in high school, I did a sophomoric thing which got me in a pot of fairly hot water, as sophomoric didoes often do. I wrote and published a small satiric newspaper called *The Village Vomit*. In this little paper I lampooned a number of teachers at Lisbon (Maine) High School, where I was under instruction. These were not very gentle lampoons; they ranged from the scatological to the downright cruel.

Eventually, a copy of this little newspaper found its way into the hands of a faculty member, and since I had been unwise enough to put my name on it (a fault, some critics would argue, of which I have still not been entirely cured), I was brought into the office. The sophisticated satirist had by that time reverted to what he really was: a fourteen-year-old kid who was shaking in his boots and wondering if he was going to get a suspension . . . what we called "a three-day vacation" in those dim days of 1964.

I wasn't suspended. I was forced to make a number of apologies— they were warranted, but they still tasted like dog-dirt in my mouth—

and spent a week in detention hall. And the guidance counselor arranged what he no doubt thought of as a more constructive channel for my talents. This was a job—contingent upon the editor's approval—writing sports for the Lisbon *Enterprise,* a twelve-page weekly of the sort with which any small-town resident will be familiar. This editor was the man who taught me everything I know about writing in ten minutes. His name was John Gould—not the famed New England humorist or the novelist who wrote *The Greenleaf Fires,* but a relative of both, I believe.

He told me he needed a sports writer and we could "try each other out," if I wanted.

I told him I knew more about advanced algebra than I did sports.

Gould nodded and said, "You'll learn."

I said I would at least try to learn. Gould gave me a huge roll of yellow paper and promised me a wage of ½¢ per word. The first two pieces I wrote had to do with a high school basketball game in which a member of my school team broke the Lisbon High scoring record. One of these pieces was straight reportage. The second was a feature article.

I brought them to Gould the day after the game, so he'd have them for the paper, which came out Fridays. He read the straight piece, made two minor corrections, and spiked it. Then he started in on the feature piece with a large black pen and taught me all I ever needed to know about my craft. I wish I still had the piece—it deserves to be framed, editorial corrections and all—but I can remember pretty well how it looked when he had finished with it. Here's an example:

> Last night, in the ~~well-loved~~
> gymnasium ~~of~~ |Lisbon High School|, partisans
> and Jay Hills fans alike were stunned by
> an athletic performance unequalled in school
> history: Bob Ransom~~, known as "Bullet" Bob~~
> ~~for both his size and accuracy~~, scored
> thirty-seven points. He did it with grace
> and speed...and he did it with an odd courtesy
> as well, committing only two personal fouls
> in his ~~knight-like~~ quest for a record which
> has eluded Lisbon ~~thinclads~~ *is basketball team* since 1953...

4

When Gould finished marking up my copy in the manner I have indicated above, he looked up and must have seen something on my face. I think *he* must have thought it was horror, but it was not: it was revelation.

"I only took out the bad parts, you know," he said. "Most of it's pretty good."

"I know," I said, meaning both things: yes, most of it was good, and yes, he had only taken out the bad parts. "I won't do it again."

"If that's true," he said, "you'll never have to work again. You can do *this* for a living." Then he threw back his head and laughed.

And he was right: I *am* doing this for a living, and as long as I can keep on, I don't expect ever to have to work again.

III. *The Second Introduction*

All of what follows has been said before. If you are interested enough in writing to be a purchaser of this magazine, you will have either heard or read all (or almost all) of it before. Thousands of writing courses are taught across the United States each year; seminars are convened; guest lecturers talk, then answer questions, then drink as many gin and tonics as their expense-fees will allow, and it all boils down to what follows.

I am going to tell you these things again because often people will only listen—really *listen*—to someone who makes a lot of money doing the thing he's talking about. This is sad but true. And I told you the story above not to make myself sound like a character out of a Horatio Alger novel but to make a point: I saw, I listened, and *I learned*. Until that day in John Gould's little office, I had been writing first drafts of stories which might run 2,500 words. The second drafts were apt to run 3,300 words. Following that day, my 2,500-word first drafts became 2,200-word second drafts. And two years after that, I sold the first one.

So here it is, with all the bark stripped off. It'll take ten minutes to read, and you can apply it right away . . . if you *listen*.

IV. *Everything You Need to Know About Writing Successfully*
1. *Be talented*

This, of course, is the killer. What is talent? I can hear someone shouting, and here we are, ready to get into a discussion right up there

5

with "What is the meaning of life?" for weighty pronouncements and total uselessness. For the purposes of the beginning writer, talent may as well be defined as eventual success—publication and money. If you wrote something for which someone sent you a check, if you cashed the check and it didn't bounce, and if you then paid the light bill with the money, I consider you talented.

Now some of you are really hollering. Some of you are calling me one crass money-fixated creep. And some of you are calling me *bad* names. *Are you calling Harold Robbins talented?* someone in one of the Great English Departments of America is screeching. *V. C. Andrews? Theodore Dreiser? Or what about you, you dyslexic moron?*

Nonsense. Worse than nonsense, off the subject. We're not talking about good or bad here. I'm interested in telling you how to get your stuff published, not in critical judgments of who's good or bad. As a rule the critical judgments come after the check's been spent, anyway. I have my own opinions, but most times I keep them to myself. People who are published steadily and are paid for what they are writing may be either saints or trollops, but they are clearly reaching a great many someones who want what they have. Ergo, they are communicating. Ergo, they are talented. The biggest part of writing successfully is being talented, and in the context of marketing, the only bad writer is one who doesn't get paid. If you're not talented, you won't succeed. And if you're not succeeding, you should know when to quit.

When is that? I don't know. It's different for each writer. Not after six rejection slips, certainly, nor after sixty. But after six hundred? Maybe. After six thousand? My friend, after six thousand pinks, it's time you tried painting or possibly computer programming.

Further, almost every aspiring writer knows when he is getting warmer—you start getting little jotted notes on your rejection slips, or personal letters . . . maybe a commiserating phone call. It's lonely out there in the cold, but there *are* encouraging voices . . . unless there is nothing in your words which warrants encouragement. I think you owe it to yourself to skip as much of the self-illusion as possible. If your eyes are open, you'll know which way to go . . . or when to turn back.

2. *Be neat.*

Type. Double-space. Use a nice heavy white paper, never that erasable onion-skin stuff. If you've marked up your manuscript a lot, do another draft.

6

3. *Be self-critical*

If you *haven't* marked up your manuscript a lot, you did a lazy job. Only God gets things right the first time. Don't be a slob.

4. *Remove every extraneous word*

You want to get up on a soapbox and preach? Fine. Get one and try your local park. You want to write for money? Get to the point. And if you remove all the excess garbage and discover you can't find the point, tear up what you wrote and start all over again . . . or try something new.

5. *Never look at a reference book while doing a first draft*

You want to write a story? Fine. Put away your dictionary, your encyclopedias, your World Almanac, and your thesaurus. Better yet, throw your thesaurus into the wastebasket. The only things creepier than a thesaurus are those little paperbacks college students too lazy to read the assigned novels buy around exam time. Any word you have to hunt for in a thesaurus is the wrong word. There are no exceptions to this rule. You think you might have misspelled a word? O.K., so here is your choice: either look it up in the dictionary, thereby making sure you have it right—and breaking your train of thought and the writer's trance in the bargain—or just spell it phonetically and correct it later. Why not? Did you think it was going to go somewhere? And if you need to know the largest city in Brazil and you find you don't have it in your head, why not write in Miami, or Cleveland? You can check it . . . but *later.* When you sit down to write, *write.* Don't do anything else except go to the bathroom, and only do that if it absolutely cannot be put off.

6. *Know the markets*

Only a dimwit would send a story about giant vampire bats surrounding a high school to *McCall's.* Only a dimwit would send a tender story about a mother and daughter making up their differences on Christmas Eve to *Playboy* . . . but people do it all the time. I'm not exaggerating; I have seen such stories in the slush piles of the actual magazines. If you write a good story, why send it out in an ignorant fashion? Would you send your kid out in a snowstorm dressed in Bermuda shorts and a tank top? If you like science fiction, read the magazines. If you want to write confessions stories, read the magazines. And so on. It isn't just a matter of knowing what's right for the present story; you can begin to catch on, after awhile, to overall rhythms, editorial likes and dislikes, a magazine's entire slant. Sometimes your reading can influence the *next story,* and create a sale.

7. *Write to entertain*

Does this mean you can't write "serious fiction"? It does not. Somewhere along the line pernicious critics have invested the American reading and writing public with the idea that entertaining fiction and serious ideas do not overlap. This would have surprised Charles Dickens, not to mention Jane Austen, John Steinbeck, William Faulkner, Bernard Malamud, and hundreds of others. But your serious ideas must always serve your story, not the other way around. I repeat: if you want to preach, get a soapbox.

8. *Ask yourself frequently, "Am I having fun?"*

The answer needn't always be yes. But if it's always no, it's time for a new project or a new career.

9. *How to evaluate criticism*

Show your piece to a number of people—ten, let us say. Listen carefully to what they tell you. Smile and nod a lot. Then review what was said very carefully. If your critics are all telling you the same thing about some facet of your story—a plot twist that doesn't work, a character who rings false, stilted narrative, or half a dozen other possibles—change that facet. It doesn't matter if you really liked that twist or that character; if a lot of people are telling you something is wrong with your piece, it *is.* If seven or eight of them are hitting on that same thing, I'd still suggest changing it. But if everyone—or even most everyone—is criticizing something different, you can safely disregard what all of them say.

10. *Observe all rules for proper submission*

Return postage, self-addressed envelope, all of that.

11. *An agent? Forget it. For now*

Agents get 10% of monies earned by their clients. 10% of nothing is nothing. Agents also have to pay the rent. Beginning writers do not contribute to that or any other necessity of life. Flog your stories around yourself. If you've done a novel, send around query letters to publishers, one by one, and follow up with sample chapters and/or the manuscript complete. And remember Stephen King's First Rule of Writers and Agents, learned by bitter personal experience: You don't need one until you're making enough for someone to steal . . . and if you're making that much, you'll be able to take your pick of good agents.

12. *If it's bad, kill it*

When it comes to people, mercy killing is against the law. When it comes to fiction, it *is* the law.

That's everything you need to know. And if you listened, you can write everything and anything you want. Now I believe I will wish you a pleasant day and sign off.

My ten minutes are up.

2

TO BE A WRITER: WHAT DOES IT TAKE?

By John Jakes

You can answer the question two ways.

If you're an aspiring fiction writer, you might say something like, "It takes the ability to sense, imagine, and tell a strong story. It also takes talent for writing efficient dialogue that gives the illusion of reality and carries a lot of plot or characterization freight at the same time. Besides that, it takes good powers of description. . . ." You could spin out your answer to cover all the basic tools and techniques of the fiction writer's craft, and you would be right.

If you're an aspiring poet, you might mention meter and form first. A dramatist would think of structure and exposition. Those answers, too, would be right.

There's a second answer, though, equally correct but more fundamental. An answer that actually precedes the learning of technique, no matter what sort of writing you prefer.

By way of illustration, think about golf. I think about it a lot, because I love it, and I play badly. Obviously, good golf calls for certain skills. Strong, straight drives based on a good swing. Dependable putting. A keen eye for reading greens. Expert chipping to rescue your ball from a trap. But you can achieve none of that without certain broader fundamentals. Excellent hand-eye coordination and muscle memory (I don't have either one). Ability to concentrate. A liking for the game itself. All these underlie technique.

So, too, do certain attitudes underlie all the skills a writer must have. I call those attitudes states of being. During a professional career that spans thirty-seven years, I've thought about these states of being a lot. Added some, subtracted others. Finally distilled and described seven. I believe a writer must "be" all seven, even before taking the first steps toward technical mastery. Indeed, so crucial are these seven states of being, I believe that if you lack them, you will never be a professional, only an eternal novice.

Each of the seven is simple to describe, but profound in its impact on your life. Here they are, then . . . the seven "states of being" that support a writing career.

1. BE SURE. Do you really want to pay the price? It isn't small. Are you willing to isolate yourself day after day, session after session, year after year, in order to learn your craft the only way you can—by writing?

There are much easier, more pleasant ways to pass the time, though few so rewarding intellectually and spiritually. But it's no sin to be honest and admit it if you'd rather garden, fish, or socialize with friends than go it alone as a writer, with no guarantee of success. If you aren't sure you're up to all that writing demands of a person, go no further.

2. BE DETERMINED. This is a re-statement of one of my "three P's" of a writing career—practice. You must have guessed by now that I believe many parts of the writing process (though not all) can be learned, just as golf can be learned. It's true. You may never be a Fuzzy Zoeller or a Nancy Lopez—there are few out-and-out champions in any field—but, with determination and practice, you can probably become at least a part-time professional. To do it, however, you must write and keep on writing, trying to improve all the time.

3. BE PATIENT. This equates with the second of my "three P's," persistence. The writing profession is not, thank God, the record business. Idols are neither born nor made on the strength of a single three-minute album cut. A more substantial body of work is required. Nor do many stars emerge in the writing field at eighteen (only to be forgotten six months later). Except for a very few, a solid writing career usually arrives later in life.

Also, you must remember that publishing, like any other art that is part industry, changes constantly. Editorial people change jobs. A house or publication that rejects you this year may, under a new editor, say yes the next. Failure to realize this can increase your impatience to the danger point . . . the point at which you say, "What's the use?"

We live in an age of instant gratification. You won't get it writing . . . except for the joy in the work itself.

11

4. BE OPEN. This is the last of my "three P's"—professionalism. By being open, I mean being willing and eager to have all the flaws in your work exposed, so that you can fix them. I mean being anxious to have a working partnership with an editor who admires your strengths but won't spare you criticism of your weaknesses.

Don't let the editor do all the work, though. You must want to find the weak places for yourself, before the editor sees them. It is this rather cold-blooded attitude that sets most money-earning writers apart from dabblers and those who would rather talk about being a writer than do what it takes to be one. "No pain, no gain," runners say. It's the same with writing. Unless you're open to tough criticism and willing to do something about it, you'll never go the distance.

5. BE CURIOUS. Read everything you can read. Read widely, not merely in your chosen field of writing. Spend as much time as you can with your mouth shut and your eyes and ears open. Don't strive for attention . . . strive to go unseen in a crowd, on the beach, at a party. Watch people. Watch the sky. Watch a baby's repertoire of expressions. Watch the way sun puts shadow on a wrinkled garment. Nothing should escape your notice. Everything eventually contributes to what you write, even though the way it contributes is totally unknown to anyone, including you.

6. BE SERIOUS. Give unstintingly of yourself when you write. The kind of effort NFL players casually refer to as "110 percent." There's something to it.

Once again, if you dabble . . . withhold part of your energy . . . refuse to commit your whole mind and heart to the work . . . that will be reflected in a lackluster creative product. Give your work the best you have to offer at the moment you do it. Give it a clear head, and a body that's fit and rested.

On the other hand, while you're taking the work seriously, don't take yourself seriously. I abhor the kind of writer who can't laugh at himself . . . who can't avoid pretentious pronouncements (probably to cover a raging insecurity) . . . who carries "the gift" like a royal scepter and never stops waving it about for others to see.

Too many writers unwittingly play what I call Immortality Roulette. They get involved in worrying about their own reputations. How will they be remembered in a hundred years? They grow desperate, sometimes almost maniacal about it. They write nasty letters to harsh crit-ics—or at least talk about doing it. They are happy or sad depending on a few words from a total unknown (most reviewers). The result of all this is often compensation in the form of overweening self-importance.

The saddest cases are the most marginal . . . those very competent popular writers who probably will be largely forgotten, except by a few trivia scholars or aficionados, as time goes by. Since most of us can't answer questions about posterity—a Hemingway, acknowledged a gen-ius in his own lifetime, is a rarity—just do the best you can. No one can ask more, and what more can you logically ask of yourself? Posterity will take care of itself, with or without you.

7. BE YOURSELF. Above all, let who you are, what you are, what you believe shine through every sentence you write, every piece you finish. I don't mean preach. Just be natural. The originality and power of Tolstoy's *War and Peace* do not lie in the fact that he was the first to write a mammoth novel about Imperial Russia facing Napoleon. I don't know whether he was first or not. I suspect so; it doesn't matter. What matters is that he was unique, a singular person, and his great novel emerged from what *he* had to say about his homeland and its people in wartime. One of my favorite statements about writing, encountered so long ago I can't even acknowledge the source, is this:

"True originality lies not in saying what has never been said, but in saying what you have to say."

So there you are. Seven "states of being" you must achieve before you start your work in order to master the specific tools of your craft. Again, if you honestly feel these requirements are too tough—simply not for you—no one will blame or criticize you. But if you say, "Yes, I will be a writer because I can be all of those things . . . I am all of those things . . . or I'm willing to try to become them," then I predict eventual success for you.

Not enormous wealth, mind you. Not a best seller every year. Not immortality—just the solid satisfaction of being a *writer*. It's a proud and ancient profession . . . and it's a great feeling to achieve even a little success in the business of entertaining and enlightening millions with your own words. It's a calling very much worth the price.

13

3

DON'T THINK: WRITE!

By Madeleine L'Engle

When we write, for whom do we write? Or, as we would be more likely to ask, whom do we write for?

It sounds like an easy question to answer, and in some ways it is. But when it is applied to the matter of fiction, the logical answer—that we write for a specific audience—does not work. At least not for me.

Each year I teach at one or more writers workshops. I enjoy them for many reasons, not the least of which is the opportunity to meet other workshop leaders, often writers whose work I have long admired. Writing is a solitary profession, and a writers conference gives us a chance to get together. Another reason I enjoy the workshops is that I am forced to articulate what I have learned about the techniques of the craft of fiction writing; it is easy to get forgetful and sloppy. Having to explain imagery, simile, metaphor, point of view, is a way to continue to teach myself as well as the people who have come to the workshop.

At one workshop, I talked, as usual, about all the hard work that precedes the writing of fiction. Often there is research to be done. For my Time Trilogy I had to immerse myself in the new physics: first, Einstein's theories of relativity and Planck's quantum theory for *A Wrinkle in Time;* then cellular biology and particle physics for *A Wind in the Door;* and astrophysics and non-linear theories of time for *A Swiftly Tilting Planet.* For *The Love Letters* I had to learn a great deal more about seventeenth-century Portuguese history than I needed or wanted to know, so that the small amount needed for the book would be accurate. Before, during, and after research, the writer needs to be thinking constantly about the characters, and the direction in which the novel seems to be moving.

Does the story have the Aristotelian beginning, middle, and end? How do the events of the novel relate to me, personally, in my own journey through life? What are my own particular concerns at the time of writing, and how should they affect—or not affect—the story? When I actually sit down to write, I stop thinking. While I am writing, I am listening to the story; I am not listening to myself.

"But," a young woman in the class said in a horrified tone of voice, "my creative writing teacher says that we must keep the audience in mind at all times."

That is undoubtedly true for the scientist writing an article that is expected to be understood by people who have little or no scientific background. The writer will have to keep simplifying scientific language, explaining technical terms. Keeping the audience in mind is probably valuable for reporting in newspapers and magazines. The reporter is writing for the average reader; language should be neither so bland as to be insulting, nor so technical as to demand special knowledge.

As for lawyers, I assume they have each other in mind at all times as they write. Certainly they don't have most of us in mind. Their grandiosity appalls me. In a movie contract, I was asked to grant the right to my book to the producers, in perpetuity, throughout the universe. When I wrote in, "With the exception of Sagittarius and the Andromeda galaxy," it was accepted. Evidently the lawyers, who are writing to avoid litigation in a litigious world, did not anticipate a lawsuit from Sagittarius.

Of course I am being grossly unfair to many lawyers; I come from a family of fine lawyers. But the language used in a will or a contract is indeed a special language, and it is not aimed at the reader who enjoys stories, the reader of fiction.

Whom, then, does the writer of fiction write for? It is only a partial truth to say that I write for myself, out of my own need, asking, whether I realize it or not, the questions I am asking in my own life.

A truer answer is that I write for the book.

"But why do you write for children?" I am often asked.

And I answer truthfully that I don't. I haven't been a child for a long time, and if what I write doesn't appeal to me, at my age, it isn't likely to appeal to a child. I hope I will never lose the child within me, who has not lost her sense of wonder, of awe, of laughter. But I am not a child; I am a grown woman, learning about maturity as I move on in chronology.

A teacher, in introducing me to a class of seventh graders, said,

"Miss L'Engle has made it in the children's field, and she is now trying to break into the adult market."

I felt that I had better not explain to this teacher that I had no desire to break into the adult market and see my fiction in "adult bookstores." I am not interested in writing pornography. I did explain that my first several books were regular trade novels, which means that they were marketed for a general audience, not for children. And I explained that when I have a book that I think will be too difficult for a general audience, then we will market it as a juvenile book. It is a great mistake to think that children are not capable of understanding difficult concepts in science or philosophy.

A book that has a young protagonist will likely be marketed as a children's book, regardless of content. Since adolescents are usually more willing than their elders to ask difficult questions, and to accept the fact that the questions don't have nice, tidy answers but lead on to more difficult questions, approximately half of my books have young protagonists. But while I am writing, I am not thinking of any audience at all. I am not even thinking about myself. I am thinking about the book.

This does not imply anything esoteric. I do not pick up the pen and expect it to guide my hand, or put my fingers on the keyboard of the typewriter and expect the work to be done automatically. It is work. But it is focused work, and the focus is on the story, not on anything else.

An example of the kind of focus I mean is a good doctor. The good doctor listens to the patient, truly listens, to what the patient says, does not say, is afraid to say, to body language, to everything that may give a clue as to what is wrong. The good doctor is so fully focused on the patient that personal self-consciousness has vanished. Such focused listening does not make the doctor—or any of the rest of us—less ourselves. In fact, such focused listening makes us more ourselves.

The same thing is true in listening to a story as we write it. It does not make us any less writers, this strange fact that we do not think about writing as we are writing; it makes us more writers.

Then, of course, there is all the revising to be done. We do not always listen well. We do not always have our full attention on the story. Some scenes will need to be written and rewritten a dozen or more times before they work. We do have to revise with attention to infelicities of rhythm, flaw of syntax; there is, indeed, a great deal of conscious work to be done. But still, the writer is paying attention to the work itself, not the potential audience. I have, it is true, toned down scenes when the decision has been made to market a book as a "young adult" novel, because I know that young adult novels are read as often by nine- and ten-year-olds as by young adults. But such revisions are done long after the story has been listened to as attentively as possible, and cannot mutilate or betray the intent or integrity of the story.

It would be very inhibiting for me to have to keep an audience in mind. It would take a large piece of my mind off the story as it is unfolding, and I want all of my mind to be where it belongs: on the writing.

Have I had an audience in mind while I have been writing this piece? Not particularly. I'm telling myself things I need to remember. Nobody but someone interested in the writing of fiction is going to want to read this, so I am also writing for people who share my own concerns.

So, gentle reader (the Victorians seems to assume that all readers are gentle), give yourself the pleasure of forgetting earnestly to remember your audience at all times, and give yourself the fun of plunging deeply into your story, and having your mind focused on that, and nothing else. If the story that comes from this way of writing is a better story than the forcedly audience-centered story (and I am convinced it will be), it will have a wider audience. And isn't that what we hope for?—to reach as many people as possible, because we believe that what the story has to say is worth saying.

4

THE BEST TRAINING FOR REAL LIFE—FICTION

By Michael Korda

LITERATURE—good, bad and indifferent—shapes our lives. When we are young, it is the stuff of our dreams, fantasies and ambitions, not only an escape from the far less interesting real world around us, but also a way of learning about things that all too often can't be learned at home. A child of divorced parents and far-flung relatives, I made a family of the Rostovs, in *War and Peace,* because they were everything my own family was not—close-knit, emotional, living for each other.

Psychologists suppose that *life* teaches us what we know, for better or worse, but it's most often from fiction that we form our attitudes about life. If we waited for life to teach us about romantic love, for example, we might never learn anything about it at all—we pick that up, early on, from romantic novels, whether they're by Emily Brontë, Jane Austen or Danielle Steel. It's to books, movies and TV that we turn, in childhood and adolescence, for information about love, feelings, relationships in the adult world, and when we ourselves inevitably *become* adults, what we have learned from those sources becomes part of us, part of the way we see life—more important, part of the way we see *ourselves.*

A generation of young Americans modeled themselves after—or at least saw themselves reflected in—Holden Caulfield, or Franny and Zooey, in much the same way that ten years later the attitude of young Americans toward war was radically altered by reading *Catch-22,* or toward drugs was changed by reading *On the Road.* Books provide not only role models, they also teach us lessons we never forget about courage, sacrifice, ambition and desire, right and wrong, love and hate, war and peace.

All the lessons of life are there, buried in great books and great drama, and the interesting thing is that we absorb them without a sense of being *taught,* without effort, for at the same time we are being entertained. Time spent reading is therefore never, under any circumstances, time wasted, provided that what we're reading is worthwhile.

I'm sometimes astonished to realize how much of my own perceptions of life are filtered through literature. If I hadn't been exposed to Hemingway, T. E. Lawrence and Orwell at an early age, I wouldn't have left college in 1956 to go fight in the Hungarian Revolution, and if I hadn't been sustained there by the notion that what I was doing was essentially a romantic, literary act, I don't think I would have survived. If I hadn't read about the grandeurs of the military life, I would certainly not have joined the British armed forces when I was 17, nor been able to look upon that experience as interesting and significant, rather than a painful and time-wasting episode of three years duration, as my family viewed it.

When you come right down to bedrock, Shakespeare tells us more about jealousy in *Othello* than we are ever likely to find out by reading a modern nonfiction bestseller on the subject, and Dickens tells us more about families than we are ever going to learn from the works of modern family counselors. Literature is not an *escape* from life, it is a way of *experiencing* life, on a larger scale—a way of understanding that what we feel and experience has been felt and experienced before, that our problems are not unique but have been faced by other people, and overcome.

That, in the end, is the most important lesson of literature: that we are *not alone* in suffering the problems of childhood, or adolescence, or love, or marriage, or pain, or even death; that others over the centuries have gone through the same things and survived. In real life, it is hard to find people who can talk to us about such things—or at any rate who can talk to us sensibly, frankly and openly, beyond the usual clichés—but literature is full of just such experiences, from which anybody who can read, can *learn*.

In the end, great literature teaches us about *ourselves*. It does *not* offer us pat, ready-made solutions, like self-help books; it offers examples and life experiences that help us, in good times or bad, to face our own problems.

It is one of the ironies of our present age that increasingly we trust only what is new, based on "research," whereas the real truths almost always lie elsewhere. The works of self-help gurus, in the end, are thin fodder compared to Tolstoy, Dickens and Balzac, or their more modern

19

equivalents, to the extent there are any. How many people do we know in this new age of materialism (which in so many ways resembles the Twenties) who remind us of Gatsby, desperately trying to compensate for his inner emptiness with glitzy material success? I can never reread *Gatsby* without thinking of the number of people I know who are having a lousy time in the middle of their own prosperity and success today, and who don't know *why,* despite the fact that F. Scott Fitzgerald understood it perfectly, and wrote about it better than anyone else.

Circumstances change, customs and habits die out and are replaced by others, but human nature doesn't change, and hence literature is never out of date. That is why *King Lear* still tells us all we need to know about the perils of old age and pride, and why *Oedipus* still reads as if it had been written yesterday.

When I was a child, I was often told not to spend so much time sitting by myself with a book. How would I learn anything about life, I was warned, if I spent it reading? As a child, I took these warnings seriously, though I managed to keep on doing just what I wanted to do much of the time. But now, decades later, I can see that the advice was wrong. I learned far more about life from reading books than I would have from playing in the park or tossing a ball around with other children.

What lessons I did learn in the park and on the playing fields I have long since forgotten, or have been disproved by experience. The lessons I learned from books have stayed with me—and have invariably proved to be true.

5

SHOULD YOU COLLABORATE?

By Marcia Muller and Bill Pronzini

WHEN we mentioned to a fellow mystery writer that we had written a collaborative novel, he shook his head wonderingly. "And you're still *friends*?" he asked.

Indeed we are. In fact, we've since written a nonfiction book together, and are contemplating a second novel; and we've also done collaborative short stories, as well as co-edited several anthologies. It should be emphasized, however, that literary collaboration is *not* everyone's cup of tea. Most writers prefer to work alone. Of those who experiment with collaboration, many find it unsuccessful; a few have even suffered the loss of friendship because of it. It is not something to be entered into lightly.

But when a collaboration works, it can be highly rewarding for both partners, and in terms of their literary product. A successful collaboration is a work of fiction or nonfiction which is better than either party could have written alone. It is not the voice of one or the other, but a *third* voice created by the blending of two styles and visions.

There are other advantages to collaboration, as well. Writing, as we all know, is a lonely profession; working with a partner certainly alleviates some of that loneliness. (A warning, though: Any good collaboration is not half the work, as one might think, but usually *twice* the work.) Another advantage is the obvious one that two heads are better than one: Developing a fictional plot, for instance, can be a much easier chore for two people than for one.

There are various kinds of joint projects. One is ghostwriting. This is a partnership between a writer and a nonwriter who has special expertise, an unusual experience, or a specific story he wants to tell. The work may be fiction or nonfiction, and the nonwriter, rather than the writer, receives credit on the work. Closely akin to ghostwriting is

21

celebrity collaboration in which the writer and the celebrity work together to produce an account of the celebrity's life or experiences. Both receive credit; one or both may do the writing. (Ghostwriting and celebrity collaboration are areas open only to professionals.)

The third type is the two-author collaboration—our area of expertise and the type we'll confine ourselves to here. This type may take various forms, and may of course be fiction or nonfiction. In most cases, both writers' names appear on the work, although some teams may prefer a single pseudonym. And depending on the individual writer's strong points and abilities, the workload is broken up in various ways. In collaborating on a novel, one popular method is for the person who plots best to create the basic storyline, while the other does most of the actual writing. Another—which we use—is joint plotting and joint writing.

Our recent mystery novel, *Double,* which features Muller's Sharon McCone and Pronzini's "Nameless Detective," was a joint project in every way. The plot, which had to be complex in order to accommodate the skills of both series sleuths, was developed during many hours of discussion and planning. At first we considered setting it in San Francisco, the city in which both our characters live and work; but then we realized the dramatic possibilities inherent in using a different locale, one with which Sharon was familiar but "Nameless" was not. We settled on San Diego, her hometown and the place where her family still lives. How to get both of them to San Diego at the same time? They attended a private investigators' convention at a posh beach hotel, where an old friend of Sharon's is head of security. Once we had this basic premise, the various intrigues and relationships that make up the plot began to suggest themselves. But that was still only the beginning of our work. We then had to structure the book so that each of us (and each of our detectives) would share more or less equal worktime.

Because there were two of us on the project, the first draft was written rather quickly and easily—but the fact must be stressed that we did no writing at all until our plot was established and each of our characters was sharply delineated. Starting a collaborative project prematurely, before the authors have a clear idea of the direction the book will take, can produce disastrous results.

Before *any* work is done on a collaborative project, two vital elements must be present in the partnership. The first of these is *trust*. By this we mean that each person must have faith in the other's commitment to the project, writing abilities, and professionalism in following the work through to completion. In a way it is an implied contract. You know your collaborator will put his best efforts into the project, will support you whenever you need reassurance or help, and vice versa. This doesn't mean that every collaboration is a complete 50-50 sharing of the workload; often circumstances such as other commitments or differences in ability prevent that. But each partner must trust that the other will contribute a fair share throughout.

How do you know if you can trust your collaborator? It's the same as in any other personal or business arrangement. You make certain assumptions about how your collaborator will work and live up to responsibilities. If you know the person well enough, these assumptions will usually prove correct. In our case, we had been reading each other's works-in-progress for years; each of us knew how the other approached the craft of writing. Because we have similar styles and outlooks, each was able to offer helpful suggestions to the other. If you do not know your proposed partner well, if you cannot proceed on a firm basis of faith and trust, *do not* enter into a collaboration. Mutual enthusiasm for an idea is not enough on which to base weeks or months of difficult physical and mental labor.

The second essential element is *willingness to compromise.* Disputes will inevitably arise: one partner's dazzling plot twist may seem hopelessly contrived to the other; one's stylistic flourishes may seem embarrassingly purplish to his collaborator. The only useful method of settling such disputes is to discuss them rationally and to effect some sort of compromise satisfactory to both parties.

In the writing of *Double,* for instance, a problem arose with the plot: The "Nameless Detective" simply did not have enough to do. Muller yielded to Pronzini's judgment on this matter, even though it meant more work for her (sections had to be restructured and rewritten in order to integrate "Nameless" more fully into the story), because "Nameless" is Pronzini's creation and because Pronzini has more experience in plotting than Muller. Another dispute concerned fictionalizing and shifting a bit of San Diego geography, which also necessitated restructuring and rewriting. Pronzini yielded to Muller because she once lived in San Diego and had strong feelings on how to fictionalize that setting in a realistically acceptable way.

23

As we move on to the various methods of collaboration and the additional problems that may arise, we think you'll see how strongly the presence—or lack—of trust and the willingness to compromise can affect the quality of the final product. Indeed, how they can determine whether or not there *is* a final product.

The question we're most often asked is: *"How* do you collaborate?" There is no easy answer, for we have written together and with others in a variety of ways. It depends on the nature of the project—novel, short story, nonfiction book, anthology, article such as this one; and it also depends on the partners themselves. Pronzini has collaborated with some ten different writers over the past fifteen years, and each method of working was at least somewhat different. (And yes, Pronzini is still friendly with all ten of those authors.)

One of the easiest methods—the one we used in *Double*—is for each person to write alternate chapters. We were fortunate in that we were using two series detectives who were well-established and who had distinct first-person voices; it wasn't necessary to blend our styles, only to maintain a consistency throughout in Sharon's and "Nameless's" dealings with each other and with the various other characters. This method also works well for nonfiction and for non-series, third-person novels in which multiple viewpoint is employed (such as in Pronzini's recent collaboration with John Lutz, *The Eye*).

A variation on the above method is for each person to write alternate sections, rather than single chapters or scenes. This method worked well in another meeting of San Francisco sleuths, *Twospot*, in which Collin Wilcox's Lieutenant Frank Hastings and Pronzini's "Nameless" joined forces. *Twospot* is divided into four sections of some seven chapters each, the first section narrated by "Nameless," the second by Hastings, and so on. This is an advantageous approach in a novel whose plot requires a number of scenes involving one character before another character can be introduced.

A third method is for both collaborators to write from the point of view of the same character, or about the same things, dividing the work as they see fit, and then in a subsequent draft to rewrite each other's material in order to create a smooth flow—the "third voice" we spoke of earlier. Again, Pronzini has had success with this method in his several collaborations with Barry N. Malzberg. Muller and Pronzini have also used it successfully on a short story and on nonfiction projects, one of them being this article.

A few words should be said here about work habits. In any collaboration in which both parties do the actual writing, it is important that both maintain a steady output; and for both to read and discuss regularly what each has written. It is much easier to mediate a dispute and effect a compromise early on in a project, while it is in its first-draft stage. Waiting until a book or story is finished and then arguing about it does neither the collaborators nor the work any good.

No matter how confident you feel when you set out on a collaborative project, problems of one kind or another will surely develop. Some will be easily solved, others not so easily. But you should be aware of the pitfalls at the outset.

Ego. It is natural to have pride in your work; it is also natural to bristle when a collaborator says, "That scene doesn't work," or "That's a terrible metaphor; we'll have to cut it." But keep in mind that as often as not the collaborator is right. We are not always the best judge of our own work. Therefore your ego *must,* in many instances, yield to trust and compromise. If it doesn't, if it becomes a major stumbling block once a project has begun, the project should probably be abandoned. No decent collaborative work ever emerges from a battle of wills.

Snags. These usually concern work habits, and they come in all sizes and shapes. A common one is that elusive malady called "writer's block." One collaborator comes down with it and is unable to proceed, while the other remains as productive as ever. Another snag may occur when one person writes more quickly than the other and gets too far ahead. Still another is the interference of outside commitments, such as a bread-and-butter job or other, nonliterary projects. As soon as any kind of snag occurs, you should try to work out an immediate solution or compromise. Perhaps the partner not suffering writer's block can offer strong moral support, or take on some of his collaborator's workload. Perhaps the faster writer can regulate his pace to that of the other's. Perhaps the one without commitments can alter or adapt this schedule to accommodate his partner's.

Major snags. These concern such elements as the central premise of the work, important plot points, thematic statements. When they confront you, it can seem as if the entire project is doomed to failure. But they, too, can usually be remedied with enough discussion and compromise. We were not immune on *Double:* We had a draft finished, we liked it, we felt it worked well, and yet . . . there was a solution to one of several crimes that didn't seem to be well-motivated. The only alternative solution we could come up with required extensive rewriting, the addition of scenes and chapters. How did we deal with this? By going back to our typewriters, of course, and revising accordingly. When such snags develop, you'll find that your collaborator's willingness to undertake greater amounts of work is in direct proportion to his commitment to the project. And we were both 100% committed.

Collaboration is a unique opportunity for two writers to create something better than either could have accomplished alone. But this is only true if the partners remain in sync with each other on all fronts. Otherwise, each would be much advised to pursue individual literary careers.

Remember: No collaboration is worth the loss of a friend.

6

ON BEING A GOOD BOSS

By Katherine Paterson

RECENTLY I had lunch with a young writer whom I admire extravagantly. She has the kind of vision that can see exquisite, telling details which even Eudora Welty might miss and a voice whose clarity E.B. White would admire. Someday hers will be a name all of you will recognize. I'd be consumed with envy except for one thing. I don't think I could stand to work for her boss.

But, you say, that is ridiculous. If she is a free-lance writer, she is her own boss. Exactly. I do not believe for a minute that I am a better writer than my friend, but I know I have a better boss.

Now I haven't always had a good boss. When I started writing twenty years ago, I had an overcritical, demanding, sneering ogre at my elbow. But over the years, as I've learned more about how to write, I've also learned better how to manage my one employee. After all, if the writer is not working well, the whole company is in serious trouble. For those of you with poor labor/management relations, here are a few things I've discovered.

1. A good boss expects her worker to do the best she can and never compares her to someone else. Any boss who compares you to Leo Tolstoy would be laughed at, but how many of your bosses make snide comparisons between you and so-and-so who just got a $15,000 advance on *her* first novel?

2. A good boss sets realistic goals. Part of the job description for a manager is goal setting. Any goals set should, however, be attainable by work on the writer's part and not depend on the caprice of prize juries and even the decision of editors. It is all right, therefore, for the boss to say that the first draft of the novel will be mailed by October 3rd. It is not all right for the boss to say that it will be bought by November 3rd, published by June 3rd, and receive the Pulitzer Prize by the following

spring. In my company, the boss breaks up big goals into lots of little ones. On the calendar are dates when each chapter should be written (or revised) as well as the momentous day on which a project should be mailed. Also, because she is such an understanding manager, she builds in a cushion. Then if I have dental surgery or a sick child, I can still make the mailing deadline, and if nothing untoward occurs, I have the genuine delight of beating the targeted date by two weeks.

3. A good boss is understanding without being wishy-washy. She knows that there are days that you absolutely cannot get to the type-writer. But in all proper companies, sick leave and personal leave are carefully restricted. No good boss allows an employee simply to work whenever "inspired." A good boss know that a writer who writes only when she is inspired will work three or four days a year. Books do not get written in three or four days a year. On those terrible occasions when the writer is blocked, a good boss will not berate, but will gently insist that the writer go to work as usual. The last time I suffered one of these spells, my boss told me to write two pages before getting up from the typewriter and giving up for the day. On a number of days, the margins were suspiciously wide, but I continued to produce two mal-nourished pages each day, until, just as my boss had hoped, the log jam broke up, and the words began to flow normally.

4. A good boss reserves criticism for appropriate times. She knows that no one can work creatively and critically at the same moment. She never peers over your shoulder while you're on a first draft. In fact my boss doesn't come to work much while I'm on a first draft. I call her in for consultation, only after I've gotten through the whole story once. I have respect for her critical ability, but if I allow her to make remarks on my work when it is still tentative and fragile, she is likely to kill something before it has a chance to breathe properly. Later on, I don't mind how ruthless she becomes. She's a stickler, for example, on checking for accuracy, but if she makes me stop and do it in the middle of a thought, I may lose what I'm trying to say.

5. A good boss provides working conditions that are as congenial as she can possibly make them. She knows that if she does not take your work seriously, no one will. She regards your privacy as important, doesn't fuss when you don't clean up after yourself every day, and tries to keep up with supplies so that you don't run out of paper or need a new ribbon in the middle of a hard morning's work. A good boss doesn't

try to make you feel guilty about spending money that she knows will pay in the long run. My boss, for example, no longer insists that all first drafts be written on the back of Christmas letters, notices from school, and first drafts of earlier novels. She found that I work better on clean paper, even if it is only the first draft.

And finally, 6. A good boss makes the worker feel good about her work. My boss, in the old days, never missed a chance to sneeringly tell me how far short I fell of her vision. Now she knows that only makes me discouraged and reluctant to try again. So when I say, "How can I write another book? I don't even know where to begin," she says to me, "Sweetie, you can begin anywhere you want to. Just try something. Anything. It's not going to be engraved in stone. You can always throw it out tomorrow."

Sometimes my boss will pick up a book I wrote long ago and read a particularly felicitous passage. "Nice, huh?" It makes me glow all over. These days, she hardly ever goes back to point out the other less cheering examples. "What's the use?" she says. "It's too late to change it." Formerly, when reviews were painful, my boss would say, "See, they've caught on to you. That's just the fatal flaw I was telling you about. Whatever made you think you could write a book?" These days she just sighs and says, "Sweetie, haven't I told you never to read reviews? Good or bad, they just take your mind off the work you're doing now. And that is what's important. After all, *this* is going to be the best book we've ever written." See why I'm not about to trade the old girl in?

7

CREATIVE TRUST

By John D. MacDonald

The writer and the reader are involved in a creative relationship. The writer must provide the materials with which the reader will construct bright pictures in his head. The reader will use those materials as a partial guide and will finish the pictures with the stuff from his own life experience.

I do not intend to patronize the reader with this analogy: The writer is like a person trying to entertain a listless child on a rainy afternoon.

You set up a card table, and you lay out pieces of cardboard, construction paper, scissors, paste, crayons. You draw a rectangle and you construct a very colorful little fowl and stick it in the foreground, and you say, "This is a chicken." You cut out a red square and put it in the background and say, "This is a barn." You construct a bright yellow truck and put it in the background on the other side of the frame and say, "This is a speeding truck. Is the chicken going to get out of the way in time? Now you finish the picture."

If the child has become involved, he will get into the whole cut-and-paste thing, adding trees, a house, a fence, a roof on the barn. He will crayon a road from the truck to the chicken. You didn't say a word about trees, fences, houses, cows, roofs. The kid puts them in because he knows they are the furniture of farms. He is joining in the creative act, enhancing the tensions of the story by adding his uniquely personal concepts of the items you did not mention, but which have to be there.

Or the child could cross the room, turn a dial and see detailed pictures on the television tube. What are the ways you can lose him?

You can lose him by putting in too much of the scene. That turns him into a spectator. "This is a chicken. This is a fence. This is an apple tree. This is a tractor." He knows those things have to be there. He yawns. And pretty soon, while you are cutting and pasting and explaining, you hear the gunfire of an old western.

You can lose him by putting in too little. "This is a chicken," you say, and leave him to his own devices. Maybe he will put the chicken in a forest, or in a supermarket. Maybe the child will invent the onrushing truck, or a chicken hawk. Too much choice is as boring as too little. Attention is diffused, undirected.

You can put in the appropriate amount of detail and still lose him by the way you treat the chicken, the truck, and the barn. Each must have presence. Each must be unique. *The* chicken. Not *a* chicken. He is eleven weeks old. He is a rooster named Melvin who stands proud and glossy in the sunlight, but tends to be nervous, insecure and hesitant. His legs are exceptionally long, and in full flight he has a stride you wouldn't believe.

If you cannot make the chicken, the truck, and the barn totally specific, then it is as if you were using dingy gray paper for those three ingredients, and the child will not want to use his own bright treasure to complete the picture you have begun.

We are analogizing here the semantics of image, of course. The pace and tension and readability of fiction are as dependent upon your control and understanding of these phenomena as they are upon story structure and characterization.

Here is a sample: The air conditioning unit in the motel room had a final fraction of its name left, an "aire" in silver plastic, so loose that when it resonated to the coughing thud of the compressor, it would blur. A rusty water stain on the green wall under the unit was shaped like the bottom half of Texas. From the stained grid, the air conditioner exhaled its stale and icy breath into the room, redolent of chemicals and of someone burning garbage far, far away.

Have you not already constructed the rest of the motel room? Can you not see and describe the bed, the carpeting, the shower? O.K., if you see them already, I need not describe them for you. If I try to do so, I become a bore. And the pictures you have com-

31

posed in your head are more vivid than the ones I would try to describe.

No two readers will see exactly the same motel room. No two children will construct the same farm. But the exercise of the need to create gives both ownership and involvement to the motel room and the farm, to the air conditioner and to the chicken and to their environments.

Sometimes, of course, it is useful to go into exhaustive detail. That is when a different end is sought. In one of the Franny and Zooey stories, Salinger describes the contents of a medicine cabinet shelf by shelf in such infinite detail that finally a curious monumentality is achieved, reminiscent somehow of that iron sculpture by David Smith called "The Letter."

Here is a sample of what happens when you cut the images out of gray paper: "The air conditioning unit in the motel room window was old and somewhat noisy."

See? Because the air conditioning unit has lost its specificity, its unique and solitary identity, the room has blurred also. You cannot see it as clearly. It is less real.

AND WHEN THE ENVIRONMENT IS LESS REAL, THE PEOPLE YOU PUT INTO THAT ENVIRONMENT BECOME LESS BELIEVABLE, AND LESS INTERESTING.

I hate to come across a whole sentence in caps when I am reading something. But here, it is of such importance, and so frequently misunderstood and neglected, I inflict caps upon you with no apology. The environment can seem real only when the reader has helped construct it. Then he has an ownership share in it. If the air conditioner is unique, then the room is unique, and the person in it is real.

What item to pick? There is no rule. Sometimes you can use a little sprinkling of realities, a listing of little items which make a room unique among all rooms in the world: A long living room with one long wall painted the hard blue of Alpine sky and kept clear of prints and paintings, with a carved blonde behemoth piano, its German knees half-bent under its oaken weight, and with a white Parsons table covered by a vivid collection of French glass paperweights.

I trust the reader to finish the rest of that room in his head, without making any conscious effort to do so. The furnishings will be appropriate to his past observations.

How to make an object unique? (Or where do I find the colored paper for the rooster?) Vocabulary is one half the game, and that can come only from constant, omnivorous reading, beginning very early in life. If you do not have that background, forget all about trying to write fiction. You'll save yourself brutal disappointment. The second half of the game is input. All the receptors must be wide open. You must go through the world at all times looking at the things around you. Texture, shape, style, color, pattern, movement. You must be alert to the smell, taste, sound of everything you see, and alert to the relationships between the aspects of objects, and of people. Tricks and traits and habits, deceptive and revelatory.

There are people who have eyes and cannot see. I have driven friends through country they have never seen before and have had them pay only the most cursory attention to the look of the world. Trees are trees, houses are houses, hills are hills—to them. Their inputs are all turned inward, the receptors concerned only with Self. Self is to them the only reality, the only uniqueness. Jung defines these people in terms of the "I" and the "Not I." The "I" person conceives of the world as being a stage setting for Self, to the point where he cannot believe other people are truly alive and active when they are not sharing that stage with Self. Thus nothing is real unless it has a direct and specific bearing on Self.

The writer must be a Not-I, a person who can see the independence of all realities and know that the validity of object or person can be appraised and used by different people in different ways. The writer must be the observer, the questioner. And that is why the writer should be wary of adopting planned eccentricities of appearance and behavior, since, by making himself the observed rather than the observer, he dwarfs the volume of input he must have to keep his work fresh.

Now we will assume you have the vocabulary, the trait of constant observation plus retention of the telling detail. And at this moment—if I am not taking too much credit—you have a new

33

appraisal of the creative relationship of writer and reader. You want to begin to use it.

The most instructive thing you can do is to go back over past work, published or unpublished, and find the places where you described something at length, in an effort to make it unique and special, but somehow you did not bring it off. (I do this with my own work oftener than you might suppose.)

Now take out the subjective words. For example, I did not label the air conditioner as old, or noisy, or battered, or cheap. Those are evaluations the reader should make. Tell how a thing looks, not your evaluation of what it is from the way it looks. Do not say a man looks seedy. That is a judgment, not a description. All over the world, millions of men look seedy, each one in his own fashion. Describe a cracked lens on his glasses, a bow fixed with stained tape, tufts of hair growing out of his nostrils, an odor of old laundry.

This is a man. His name is Melvin. You built him out of scraps of bright construction paper and put him in front of the yellow oncoming truck.

The semantics of image is a special discipline. Through it you achieve a reality which not only makes the people more real, it makes the situation believable, and compounds the tension.

If a vague gray truck hits a vague gray man, his blood on gray pavement will be without color or meaning.

When a real yellow truck hits Melvin, man or rooster, we feel that mortal thud deep in some visceral place where dwells our knowledge of our own oncoming death.

You have taken the judgment words out of old descriptions and replaced them with the objective words of true description. You have taken out the things the reader can be trusted to construct for himself.

Read it over. Is there too much left, or too little? When in doubt, opt for less rather than more.

We all know about the clumsiness the beginning writer shows when he tries to move his people around, how he gets them into motion without meaning. We all did it in the beginning. Tom is in an office on one side of the city, and Mary is in an apartment on the other side. So we walked him into the elevator, out through the foyer, into a cab, all the way across town, into another foyer, up in the elevator, down the corridor to Mary's door. Because it was motion without meaning, we tried desperately to create interest with some kind of ongoing interior monologue. Later we learned that as soon as the decision to go see Mary comes to Tom, we need merely skip three spaces and have him knocking at Mary's door. The reader knows how people get across cities, and get in and out of buildings. The reader will make the instantaneous jump.

So it is with description. The reader knows a great deal. He has taste and wisdom, or he wouldn't be reading. Give him some of the vivid and specific details which you see, and you can trust him to build all the rest of the environment. Having built it himself, he will be that much more involved in what is happening, and he will cherish and relish you the more for having trusted him to share in the creative act of telling a story.

8

HOW TO FIND TIME TO WRITE WHEN YOU DON'T HAVE TIME TO WRITE

By Sue Grafton

EARLY in my writing career, I managed to turn out three novels, one right after another, while I was married, raising two children, keeping house, and working full time as a medical secretary. Those novels were never published and netted me not one red cent, but the work was essential. Writing those three books prepared the way for the fourth book, which *was* published and got me launched as a professional writer. Ironically, now that I'm a "full-time" writer with the entire work day at my disposal, I'm often guilty of getting less work done. Even after twenty-five years at it, there are days when I find myself feeling overwhelmed . . . far less effective and efficient than I know I could be. Lately, I've been scrutinizing my own practices, trying to determine the techniques I use to help me produce more consistently. The underlying challenge, always, is finding the time to write and sticking to it.

Extracting writing time from the fabric of everyday life is a struggle for many of us. Even people who are technically free to write during an eight-hour day often can't "get around" to it. Each day seems to bring some crisis that requires our immediate attention. Always, there's the sense that tomorrow, for sure, we'll get down to work. We're uncomfortably aware that time is passing and the job isn't getting done, but it's hard to know where to start. How can you fit writing into a schedule that already *feels* as if it's filled to capacity? If you find yourself lamenting that you "never have time to write," here are some suggestions about how to view the problem and, better yet, how to go about solving it.

First of all, accept the fact that you may never have the "leisure" (real or imaginary) to sit down and complete your novel without interruption. Chances are you won't be able to quit your job, abandon your family, and retire to a writers' colony for six weeks of uninterrupted writing every year. And even if you could, that six weeks probably wouldn't get the job done. To be productive, we have to make writing part of our daily lives. The problem is that we view writing as a luxury, something special to allow ourselves as soon as we've taken care of the countless nagging duties that seem to come first. Well, I've got news for you. It really works the other way. Once you put writing first, the rest of your life will fall into place.

Successful writers disagree about how much time is needed per stint—ranging anywhere from one to ten hours. I feel that two hours is ideal and not impossible to find in your own busy day. One of the first tricks is to make sure you use precious writing time for *writing* and not for the myriad other chores associated with the work.

"Writing" is made up of a number of sub-categories, each of which needs tending to. A professional doesn't just sit down and magically begin to create prose. The process is more complex than that, and each phase requires our attention. Analyzing the process and breaking it down into its components will help you understand which jobs can be tucked into the corners and crevices of your day. In addition to actual composition, writing encompasses the following:

Planning—initiating projects and setting up a working strategy for each.

Research—which includes clipping and filing.

Outlining—once the material has been gathered.

Marketing—which includes query letters, manuscript typing, Xeroxing, trips to the post office.

And finally, *follow-up* for manuscripts in submission.

All of these things take time, but they won't take *all* of your time, and they shouldn't take your best time. These are clerical details that can be dispatched in odd moments during the day. Delegate as much as possible. Hire someone for these jobs if you can. Have a teen-ager come in one day a week to clip and file. Ask your spouse to drop off a manuscript at the post office on his or her way to work. Check research books out of the library while the kids are at story hour. Use time waiting for a dental appointment or dead time at the laundromat to jot down ideas and get them organized. Take index cards with you every place.

Now take a good look at your day. Feel as if you're already swamped from dawn to dark? Here are some options:

1. *Stay up an hour later each night.* At night, the phone doesn't ring and the family is asleep. You'll have fewer distractions and no excuses. You won't drop dead if you cut your sleep by an hour. The time spent creatively on projects important to you will *give* you energy. Eventually, you can think about stretching that one hour to two, but initially, stick to a manageable change and incorporate it thoroughly into your new schedule before tackling more. I used to write from ten at night until midnight or one a.m., and I still find those hours best for certain kinds of work.

2. *Get up an hour earlier,* before the family wakes. Again, shaving an hour from your sleep will do you no harm, and it will give you the necessary time to establish the habit of daily writing. Anthony Trollope, one of my favorite writers, worked for most of his adult life as a postal clerk, on the job from eight until five every day. His solution was to get up at five a.m. and write 250 words every fifteen minutes till eight—three hours. If he finished a book before the time to go to work, he started a new project at once. In his lifetime, he turned out forty-six full-length books, most of them while he earned a living in another capacity.

3. *If you're employed outside your home, try working en route.* British crime writer Michael Gilbert wrote 23 novels . . . all while riding the train to his work as a solicitor. He used the 50-minute transit time to produce 2 to 2½ pages a day, 12 to 15 pages a week. Buses, trains, commuter flights can all represent productive time for you. Use those periods for writing, while you're inaccessible to the rest of the world.

4. *What about your lunch hour?* Do you go out to lunch every day to "escape" the tensions and pressures of the job? Why not stay at your desk, creating a temporary haven in your own head? Pack a brown bag lunch. It's cheaper, among other things, and if you limit yourself to fruit and raw vegetables, you can get thin while you pile up the pages!

5. *Look at your week nights.* See if there's a way to snag one for yourself. You'd make the time if you decided to take an adult education class. Invent a course for yourself, called "Writing My Novel At Long Last" and spend three hours a week in the public library. I heard about a writer who finished a book just this way, working only on Tuesday nights.

6. *Weekends generally have free time tucked into them.* Try Saturday afternoons when the kids are off at the movies, or Sunday mornings when everyone else sleeps late.

7. *Revamp your current leisure time.* Your schedule probably contains hidden hours that you could easily convert to writing time. Television is the biggest time-waster, but I've also realized that reading the daily paper from front to back takes ninety minutes out of my day! For a while, I convinced myself that I needed to be informed on "current events," but the truth is that I was avoiding my desk, squandering an hour and a half that I desperately needed to complete a manuscript. I was feeling pressured, when all the while, the time was sitting right there in front of me . . . literally. Recently, too, I took a good look at my social calendar. I realized that a dinner party for six was requiring, in effect, two full days of activity . . . time I now devote to my work. I still have friends. I just cut my entertainment plans by a third.

Now.

Once you identify and set aside those newly found hours, it's a matter of tailoring the work to suit the time available. This can be done in four simple steps:

1. Make a list of everything you'd like to write . . . a novel, a short story, a film script, a book review for the local paper, that travel article you outlined during your last trip.

2. Choose three. If you only have one item on your agenda, how lucky you are! If you have more than three projects on your list, keep the remaining projects on a subsidiary list to draw on as you complete the items on your primary list and send them out into the marketplace. I generally like to have one book-length project (my long-term goal) and two smaller projects (an article, a short story . . . short-term goals) on my list.

3. Arrange items on the list in the order of their true priority. Be tough about this. For instance, you might have a short story possibility, an idea you've been toying with for years, but when you come right down to it, it might not seem important enough (or fully developed enough) to place among the top three on your list. My first priority is

always the detective novel I'm writing currently. I work on that when I'm at my freshest, saving the smaller projects for the period after my first energy peaks. Having several projects in the works simultaneously is good for you psychologically. If you get stuck on one, you can try the next. As you finish each project, the feeling of accomplishment will spur you to renewed effort on those that remain. In addition, by supplying yourself with a steady stream of new projects, you'll keep your interest level high.

4. Once you select the three projects you want to work on, break the writing down into small, manageable units. A novel isn't completed at one sitting. Mine are written two pages at a time over a period of six to eight months. Assign yourself a set number of pages . . . 1 or 2 . . . and then meet your own quota from day to day. Once you've completed two pages, you can let yourself off the hook, moving on to the next task. By doing a limited amount of work on a number of projects, you're more likely to keep all three moving forward. Don't burden yourself with more than you can really handle. Assigning yourself ten pages a day sounds good on the surface, but you'll soon feel so overwhelmed that you'll start avoiding the work and won't get *anything* done. Remember, it's persistence that counts, the steady hammering away at the writing from day to day, day *after* day, that produces the most consistent work and the greatest quantity of it.

Essentially, then, all you need to do is this:

> Analyze the task.
> Scrutinize your schedule.
> Tailor the work to fit.

I have one final suggestion, a practice that's boosted my productivity by 50%. Start each day with a brief meditation . . . five minutes of mental quiet in which you visualize yourself actually sitting at your desk, accomplishing the writing you've assigned yourself. Affirm to yourself that you'll have a good, productive day, that you'll have high energy, solid concentration, imagination, and enthusiasm for the work coming up. Use these positive messages to block out your anxieties, the self-doubt, the fear of failure that in fact comprise procrastination. Five minutes of quiet will reinforce your new determination and will help you make the dream of writing real.

9

WHY?

By Michael Seidman

To A GREAT extent, I am what I am today because of what my parents did for me. Perhaps the most important thing is what they wrote in my autograph book when I was graduating from junior high school. On the left, my mother wrote, "Know thyself." On the right, my father wrote, "To thine own self be true."

As writers, you do it every day, don't you? Thousands *(thousands!)* of manuscripts—poems and essays, novels and synopses, articles and scripts—are sealed, stamped, kissed, and sent off, against all odds. Against all odds? Yes. Consider: Publishers (among themselves, certainly) will admit that only five to eight percent of what they publish supports the rest of their list. The average individual income from writing in the United States is $4,000 annually. Those are the odds. Writers face that, and increasing competition in almost every area for the space remaining. But you continue to write. Why?

Writing—craft, art, living—is not simply a matter of the sale. There is something else at work, something deeper. It is, I have found—over years of speaking as an editor at writers' conferences and workshops— something recognized but not generally acknowledged; something pushed aside as the recurring question is asked: What are you (as an editor) looking for?

What I am looking for is beside the point, and we both know it. Or should. My answer to that question, my advice, is always the same. Don't look for the bandwagon, create it. I can tell you what is selling *today*; if I knew, *if I knew*, what was going to sell *tomorrow*, I'd be wealthy. If I tell you that I'm looking for mysteries, and you—with no background in the genre—sit down and try to write one, we may both be wasting time. If you are already a mystery writer, fine. If not, why not continue what you do? At some point those of us on the other side of the desk, those of us reading the manuscripts in the slush piles, will see yours. It has long been said: Write what you know, write what you enjoy reading. That advice is far more important than knowing which side of the page your name and address go on. *Writing* is what you do, and it is more important than an immediate sale.

In this country, we are more often than not defined by and as what we do. I am an editor, which means different things to different people. You are a writer. What does that mean? On a blank sheet of paper you create universes. You populate them, create life, control the fates of your creations. You are as close to being a god as any mortal can hope to come. And you are more and other.

You are a shaman, the record-keeper. You record the history and mythology of the tribe; you are the perpetrator of the myths, the reporter whose commentaries will be used by later historians who try to define our age. Your role goes beyond earning a living: It is to excite the imagination of a reader, to inspire flights of fancy that may "alter and illuminate our times." As writers, you bear an awesome responsibility—to your contemporaries as well as your children. No matter what it is you write, you teach.

You teach through the sharing of experience, through the sharing of insights. The characters and situations you create are born of your vision, of your particular observations of a world, as only you, the individual writer, inhabit it. They bear your personal stamp, are a part of you. In one way or another, they are you. But when you emulate—begin to copy, borrow, appropriate the lives and situations of other writers— you are denying your readers the essence of yourself. Far more important, though, is another denial.

When you write with and to the constraints of marketing needs, when you set out to give some editors whatever you think they are looking for at a particular moment, you are deepening a tragic loss: the loss of spontaneity, the loss of faith in yourself and your vision. The loss, really, of trust. "I do not trust you to see what I see, and therefore I will try to see what you see," is what you are really saying. In that statement lies one even more frightening: "I do not trust what I see and will accept your vision."

"I do not trust what I see." If you cannot trust in yourself that far, into what other elements of your life will that loss of self creep, stealing your soul from you, stealing, finally, your self from you? Spontaneity is born of self-trust. Unfortunately, with trust and faith in yourself eroded,

instead of acting on faith, instead of trusting yourself and your vision, you bring other, irrelevant considerations to your work. "My agent says this is a bad idea, therefore I have to do something else; the market is soft on romances this month, I'd better write. . . whatever." You are no longer creating, no longer recording. You are playing back; you are parroting the vision of others.

Yes, you have to know what is being published and who is publishing it, just as you should learn, if you can, which agents specialize in a particular area, which editors are sympathetic to young writers, or specialize in a genre. But you must also remember that publishing is cyclical, that what is selling today may become tomorrow's returns. You must not write for the markets you find, but find the markets for what you write.

You are reading this because you are a writer. It would be wonderful if you were all selling writers, but if you bring your faith to your work, those of us on the other side of the editorial desks will catch up to you. Of course, if you are willing to become clones of whoever is on the bestseller list this week, that's your decision. You might make a sale sooner than someone else (and the book might even be a success).

But as a writer, your words are the legacy you will leave to future generations. All you know is yourself and your vision. If you deny them, you deny all.

It is not, ultimately, the goal that counts, it is the journey itself. You are a writer. Know thyself. You are a writer. To thine own self be true.

10

STRINGS THAT TOUCH THE SKY

By Jane Yolen

I come from a family of string savers and kite fliers. It is an easy connection: kites/strings. Taking what is left over and used up and making it touch the sky is a good metaphor for writing.

If I were a scientist, I would remind myself that matter can never be lost. If I were a gardener, I would call it the great recycle of life. If I had a religious vocation, I would call it the second coming. But I am a writer from a family of string savers and kite fliers, so I see my writing in terms of a series of loops. What you have researched and written about once, you can use again and again in brand new ways. Loop upon loop. A veritable cat's cradle of ideas. Let me give you an example.

I wrote a book about the Quakers, a biography of the founding father of the religion, entitled *Friend: The Story of George Fox.* And because it was successful, another publisher asked me to do a book about the history of the Shakers, for they were a bizarre and radical outgrowth of the Society of Friends.

Loop 1. Simple Gifts, the Shaker book, was built upon some of the history I had already researched for the Quaker book. The earlier work had also prepared me to understand the group religious mind as well as persecuted religious minorities and their behavior. However, as I researched this particular nonfiction book project, I kept thinking that there were surely many stories in that history. I had already found dozens of them in the journals of believers and apostates. One that interested me especially (probably because my then fourteen-year-old daughter was beginning to get interested in boys) was a Romeo and Juliet story set in a Shaker community, made more interesting by the central fact that Shakers were celibate! This led me to write a novel.

Loop 2. The Gift of Sarah Barker was that novel. Sarah greatly resembled my daughter in both looks and character: headstrong, passionate, self-doubting, but always questioning authority. Set *that* girl down in a community of would-be angels in nineteenth century Massachusetts, and there's bound to be an interesting explosion.

Loop 3. For that Shaker novel about Sarah, I used the great round barn of Hancock Shaker Village as the central meeting place for her and the boy Abel Church. I loved that barn and had spent many quiet moments meditating there when I was doing my research. I longed to make use of that peculiar, fascinating barn again. But how? I didn't want to write another Shaker book. For the moment, two were enough. But a year later, when I was in the midst of writing a science fiction novel, *Dragon's Blood,* the Shaker material surfaced again. *Dragon's Blood* takes place in the 24th century on an ex-penal colony planet called Austar IV. The dragon farm on which my young hero worked as a bond slave quite naturally began to resemble a Shaker farm community—*without* the celibacy. And the stud barn where the great cock dragons were kept was, not surprisingly, built around a round central mow. The description of the steam rising from the stored grasses in that mow comes directly from a period description of the Hancock barn.

Loop 4. Dragon's Blood grew into a trilogy. *Heart's Blood* is the second book. I'm currently writing the third, tentatively called *Dragon's Eyes.* I am thinking about new ways to transform all that I have learned in the writing of this particular series of loops, all involving Shakers in some way. Another novel about religious communities—this time the millennial kind who sit on mountain tops waiting for the predicted end of the world—is already beginning to take shape in my mind.

Loops within loops within loops.

Nothing is lost in research or writing, though it may take years before any one idea is rediscovered, disinterred. This is personal literary archeology.

English teachers in school writing classes always caution their students to "write about what you know." They always neglect to add (indeed they may not realize) that there are many ways to "know" something. By looping and re-looping, an author gets to know a lot of characters and settings in a very deep way. To reuse them, melting them down in the furnace of the heart and mind, then reshaping them into something new, is what writing is all about. We are, after all, craftspeople, and the heart-metal is tempered by that cooling process between books and stories.

Whether you call it crafting or the great recycle or the second coming or the fact that matter cannot be lost, it is the same. All writers are savers of string, and the best writers know instinctively that pieces of string tied together can make a line long enough, eventually, to touch the sky.

11

OWED TO THE PUBLIC LIBRARY

By Lesley Conger

YESTERDAY I fell in love with the public library all over again.

It was a mild, sweet day, not bright, not gloomy; faintly misty, but not wet. A perfect day, really. And because I had had an errand elsewhere, I approached the library from a direction I don't ordinarily use. It was like seeing a familiar, beloved face in a new and enchanting light. WALK, the traffic signal commanded me, but I stood bemused on the curb, just looking, until I found myself disobeying WAIT and loping across as the red turned green.

It's a middle-aged building, our library, rose brick and gray stone, built in a style that reminds me of some children's blocks I must have had when I was small, the kind that came with doors and windows and chimneys and arches. Georgian, Colonial? I don't know enough about architecture to tell you. But it's a lovely building, with tall windows arched at their tops, and broad stone steps leading up to the doors.

I usually take those steps two at a time. But yesterday I hesitated, and then I walked around the block. There are large elms lining the street, and on the inner edge of the sidewalk, a low concrete balustrade with a rail of the perfect width for young wall-walkers. Between the balustrade and the building grow rhododendron and other greenery, but along the walk concrete benches are set at intervals, each with a name chiseled upon its backrest: Henry Fielding, George Eliot, William Makepeace Thackeray. . . . On Henry Fielding an old man dozes, knobby hands resting on top of his knobby cane. Behind George Eliot, inside the balustrade, a young man sits on the grass reading. Charles Dickens, Charlotte Brontë, Victor Hugo. . . . There is a girl in a long patchwork skirt sitting on Victor Hugo; she looks at me through great, round, violet sunglasses, which she doesn't really need. Edgar Allan Poe, Mark Twain, Bret Harte . . . I wonder, do people always notice

47

whose lap they are occupying? Is the girl with the violet glasses waiting for someone, and did she say she'd meet him at the Victor Hugo bench? Oliver Wendell Holmes, Robert Louis Stevenson. . . . Can you remain utterly indifferent to Charlotte Brontë once you've sat leaning against her, eating an apple, feeling the spring sunshine?

Dumas, Hawthorne, Irving. Trollope, Sterne, Austen. . . . There are over twenty benches—twenty-two, I think. Sir Walter Scott, Charles Kingsley, James Fenimore Cooper. And if you approach from the southwest corner, the first two benches you see are Charles Reade and George Borrow. . . . Reade and Borrow, borrow and read. Yes, of course, that's what I'm here for!—and I stop to tie my shoe on Borrow's knee.

On the building itself there are more names, clusters of names, engraved large and clear high up on the gray blocks of the frieze. Not only writers, there, but inventors, musicians, explorers, scientists, painters, religious leaders. Palestrina, Aeschylus, Zoroaster, Copernicus, Raphael. I am dizzy, but less from looking up than from thinking of them: all of them, inside the library, waiting for me—all mine, all just for the asking!

Someone once wrote me to comment on my knowledge of literature. *Enviously.* But there is nothing to envy. The truth is that I never studied literature, certainly not in college, where for some mysterious reason I spent half my time grubbing about in exotic languages, most of which I haven't used since. My college education stands me in no good stead when it comes to writing this chapter—or anything else, for that matter.

Let me confess something—though, indeed, it's not a confession if confessing means admitting to something I'd rather conceal. When I write about books and writers, I am a great deal of the time writing about books and writers I have myself just that moment encountered, and the greatest part of my enthusiasm is the joy of recent discovery.

For finding out is the most delightful part of knowing. And fresh knowledge, even be it concerning things old to others, is my favorite commodity.

Not long ago I pointed out that writing is an occupation with free entry. You need no diploma, no union card, no previous experience. It doesn't matter who you are; everyone's eligible.

Well, unlike most colleges and universities, the public library doesn't care who you are, either. Victor Hugo doesn't care. Jane Austen doesn't care. Euripides doesn't care, and he is waiting there for you as much as he waits for me. To those who have asked me what kind of education a writer should have, and to those who have bemoaned their lack of an education, let me say that the best of *my* education has come from the public library—and still does, week after week. My tuition fee is bus fare and once in a while, five cents a day for an overdue book.

But despite the engraved names and despite the emotions they inspire in me, the library is not a pantheon, not some kind of temple dedicated to these gods of intellect and achievement, not a sterile memorial or a musty tomb. It holds not dry bones but still viable thoughts that can leap from a mind long dead to yours, through the agency of the printed page. And more—because of course it isn't Euripides that I seek out every time, or Thackeray, or Brontë or Poe. Last week it turned out to be Barbara Pym, Russell Baker, and John Updike; next week, who knows? Henry James, Jean Auel, and Shirley MacLaine? Or how about *The Cloister and the Hearth* (that's Reade) and *The Romany Rye* (that's Borrow)?

I rounded the block. Oh, it's a beautiful building, warm and mellow in the sunshine. For the sun is out now, and the girl with the violet glasses needs them after all. I look up at the frieze once more—Molière, Voltaire!—and I take the steps by twos and push my way through the heavy doors.

You don't need to know very much at all to start with, if you know the way to the public library.

12

SO YOU WANT TO WRITE A BESTSELLER?

By Barbara Taylor Bradford

When I'm on tour to promote a new novel, I meet many people in bookstores, TV audiences, and lecture halls, who tell me they want to be a bestselling novelist. They seek my advice. Generally, I tell them to sit down and do it, because that is the only way a book is ever written. However, I usually make a point of asking each one the same question: Why do you want to be a novelist?

Invariably they tell me that they want to make a lot of money and become a famous celebrity.

These are the wrong reasons.

There is only one reason to write a novel and that is because writing fiction is absolutely essential to one's well-being. It is to mine and it always has been. In other words, it is the work that really counts, the sense of creation that is the important thing to me.

Don't misunderstand me. Of course I want readers, every author does. But I have never sat down at a typewriter and told myself that I'm about to write a great bestseller. I have no idea if a book of mine is going to sell in the millions when I actually start it. How could I know, since I don't have a secret recipe? All I have is a story to tell about a number of characters who are very real people to me. I knew I wanted to be a novelist when I was a child in Yorkshire. I had no brothers or sisters so I invented playmates and told them stories. When I was ten, my father bought me a second-hand typewriter and I typed out these little tales and stitched them in a folder with a hand-painted title.

When I was 12 I submitted one—about a little horse, I think—to something called *The Children's Magazine* and it was actually published. I got ten and six for it. I have never stopped writing since.

The first novel I attempted was about a ballet dancer named Vivienne Ramage who lived in a garret in Paris! By this time I had managed to get a job on the *Yorkshire Evening Post* and had been to the Paris fashion shows with the women's page editor.

Paris totally overwhelmed me. I came back, and began this story. My ballet dancer was desperately poor and it was all terribly dramatic and suspiciously reminiscent of Dumas' *La Dame aux Camélias*! Anyway, I got to about page ten and suddenly thought: I've a feeling I've read this somewhere before.

I kept experimenting like that all though my girlhood. Being on a newspaper, doing the police beat, covering the coroners' courts, exposed me to life in the raw and taught me that you can't just write about the landscape or a room setting—a story is only interesting if it's about people. Their tragedies, their dramas, their joys.

That's what I'm dealing in now, human emotions. The hope is that I can get them down on paper in such a way as to touch a nerve in the reader so that he or she identifies and is moved. At 17 I was very much in love with being a newspaperwoman—a newspaper*man* I should say—even down to wanting a dirty trench coat. My mother accused me of having dragged it round in the street to make it grubby.

But my newspaper career didn't begin as a reporter. The only job I could get at the start was in the typist pool. First day I was still typing away long after everybody had gone home. As I was leaving I saw the wastepaper basket overflowing with the company's crumpled, vellum-like notepaper and I thought, I'm going to get fired for wasting their stationery. So I took a handful into the ladies' room, lit a match to it and threw it down the toilet.

Well, the blaze was so enormous I then thought: this way I'll be fired for being an arsonist! So I collected up the rest, smoothed it out and hid it in the bottom drawer of my desk.

For a week after that I took one of my mother's shopping bags to work with me and brought the telltale paper home in batches. I think I eventually got a job as a cub reporter because I was such an awful typist.

But I worked at getting moved, too—I did little stories and handed them in to my editor, who finally put me in the newsroom.

At 18, I became women's editor. When I was 20 I left Upper Armley, Yorkshire, for London and a job on *Woman's Own* as a fashion editor, followed by a stint as a reporter and feature writer on the *Evening News*.

51

Naturally, that was a job in which I met actors, film stars, novelists, screenwriters, politicians—people who were "achievers"—but I never expected to find success or be rich and famous myself. However, when I look back, I realize my mother always instilled in me a desire to do my best. I wanted to please her. She loved the theatre, movies, music and art and she got me my first two library tickets when I was still very small. When she died in 1981—only 5 weeks after I lost my father—I found those tickets in her purse.

I continued writing after I moved to the United States, where I have lived since my marriage in 1963 to a Hollywood film producer, Robert Bradford. I wrote non-fiction books between 1963 and 1974, mostly on interior design, and two books for children.

Between 1968 and 1974, when I was writing a syndicated column for American newspapers, I started four novels but discarded them all after a few hundred pages. One was set in Paris and North Africa. It was called *Florabelle*. I liked strong heroines from the start. That one was an actress.

Yet another novel was set in North Africa—I was smitten with Morocco at that time—and that tale was about a woman photo-journalist. My next was sited in the South of France. But the one I was writing when I thought of *A Woman of Substance* was called *The Jasper Cypher*. It was a Helen MacInnes-type suspense novel starting in New York and moving to Spain.

But obviously I was wrong, wasn't I? I should have been writing about Yorkshire, not Morocco. I got to chapter four and I thought, this is boring. I asked myself a lot of questions that day. It was like a dialogue with myself. I said: Well, what *do* you want to write about? What *sort* of book do you want to write? Where do you want to set it? And of course I knew, suddenly, that I really wanted to set it in England, specifically Yorkshire. Then I said: And I want to write about a strong woman.

So, having decided to write about a Yorkshire girl who emancipates herself and creates a big business empire, I could see it would be more effective if she were born poor and in an age when women were not doing these things, and to have her working for a rich family who falls as she rises.

After a couple of hours of thinking along these lines I had the nucleus of my plot and started to jot down a few notes and I thought, yes, she becomes a woman of substance. And I looked at that on my pad and thought, that's a marvelous title.

At a point like this I put paper in typewriter and tap out a few details. I might take two days experimenting with a name for the character. It has to have just the right ring. Then I create the other protagonists, maybe draw a family tree, listing names and ages, their relationships.

All the time I'm asking myself questions and answering them on paper. When is it going to start, how old is she, what is her background, what motivates her, why did this woman do what she did, become what she became? All my characters are totally analyzed, as if I were a psychiatrist.

I then transpose these notes onto index cards, and I maintain these character cards as if I'm dealing with real people—and they become very real to me. As I develop them, somehow the plot falls into place almost automatically.

Once I have title, characters and story line in note form, I divide the book into parts. It's a way to organize the material. In *A Woman of Substance* I got titles for the sections from the land—the valley, the abyss, the plateau, the pinnacle, the slope. It was a method of tracing the rise and fall of a life. In *Voice of the Heart,* I used the stage—overture, wings, Act 1, downstage right and so on. In *Hold the Dream,* the phases are entitled "Matriarch"—that's Emma Harte in old age—and "Heiress and Tycoon," which is the ascent of her granddaughter, Paula.

At this stage I write a piece like the copy on a novel's dust jacket, the bare bones of the story. Then I finish the outline, which is ten to 20 pages. That takes me about a week to ten days.

Once I get going on a novel, a good day is when I've written five finished pages. I usually start in longhand, using a fine nibbed pen (Sanford's Expresso, if you like to know that sort of thing) and then move to the typewriter.

Someone once asked me what a novel is and I said: It's a monumental lie that has to have the absolute ring of truth if it is to succeed.

It's easy to know when something is good and, in a way, it's easy to know when something is bad. But to know *why* it's bad, that's the thing. And how do you change it?

I've gone back and looked at my first attempts at fiction, and there wasn't too much wrong with them, except that I wanted basically to write about Yorkshire and didn't know it. So I wouldn't say to the would-be novelist: press on with *anything* you start. You could be on the wrong subject matter, as I was.

However, I now realize that as I labored, I was in effect honing my craft, teaching myself how to write a novel. I truly believe that learning the craft of fiction writing is vital and that you can't do that at classes. You can perhaps learn techniques—I borrowed library books on journalism when I was trying to become a reporter—but no one can teach you to write a novel. You have to teach yourself.

Basic writing ability is still not enough. A would-be novelist must also observe what I call the five Ds:

D for desire—the desire to want to write that novel more than do anything else.

D for drive—the drive to get started.

D for determination—the will to continue whatever the stumbling blocks and difficulties encountered on the way.

D for discipline—the discipline to write every day, whatever your mood.

D for dedication to the project until the very last page is finished.

Finally, there is a sixth D—to avoid! This is for distractions—perhaps the most important D of all, the enemy of all writers, whether would-be or proven.

Writing novels is the hardest work I've ever done, the salt mines, really. I sit long hours at my desk, starting out at six in the morning and finishing around six or seven in the evening. And I do this six and a half days a week, till my neck and shoulders seize up. I make tremendous social and personal sacrifices for my writing, but after all, I chose to be a novelist. Nobody held a gun to my head.

But in all truth, it's not possible to be a full-time novelist and a social butterfly, living the so-called glamorous existence of the bestselling novelist.

There's nothing which faintly resembles glamour about the work I do. I spend all of my working hours alone, facing a blank sheet of paper, and myself. For I have to dredge through my soul and my memories every day of my life.

When a book is finished I have to go on promotion tours. This may sound exciting. But it isn't. Taking a different plane or train every day and heading for another city is hardly my idea of fun; neither are crowded airports, poor hotels or bad food eaten on the run.

Then there are the fairytales. When reporters come to interview me they sometimes have a preconception. It's nothing to do with what they've learned about me, it's what they've decided without knowing me. They want to make me into Emma Harte. They want a rags-to-riches story. Somebody asked me the other day about my enormous change of lifestyle since I wrote a bestseller. Well, I started off simply enough but, to be truthful, my lifestyle changed when I married 22 years ago and went to live in Manhattan and also had an apartment in Beverly Hills.

But whatever I say, they're determined to write the story they want to tell. So the only thing I can do when I read a misleading story is smile and say, well at least they spelled my name right! But I'm not Cinderella, and never was.

Still, I admit that a bit of fiction about oneself is not much to put up with. I've been accused of dressing my Bichon Frisé puppy, Gemmy, in a diamond-studded collar and of wearing a £25,000 dress. I was due to go and stay with an old friend in Ripon and she roared with laughter when she read that. "Do I have to get a burglar alarm installed?" she kidded me. She knew a Yorkshire girl would never spend £25,000 on a dress, that she'd be doing something extraordinary if she paid £250!

So why do I go on? The answer is easy. I can't *not* do it. Writing is a means of self-expression for me, and it gives me great gratification. Especially when I know that a novel I have striven over truly works, not only for me, but for readers all over the world . . . readers who have derived enjoyment from my work, who have seen life through my angle of vision . . . who have been touched, enlightened and entertained. That is the greatest satisfaction of all.

And if you are a would-be novelist, hellbent on pursuing this career, then what better inspiration is there?

———————

Ten Questions for Would-Be Novelists

Let us assume that the would-be novelist has both ability and a talent for using words. What else is required in the writing of fiction? I think I would have to ask you these questions.

1. Are you imaginative?

If you create characters in your imagination that are interesting and different and yet with whom the reader can identify, then you have a good start. If you can picture scenes between characters you create and can also feel caught up in their emotions, that's what I call imagination.

2. Have you got insight?

A novelist must be able to understand what makes people tick. Insight is being able to weigh someone up, to understand why they do the things they do. You must have compassion, and be willing to understand all points of view.

3. Can you get under the skin of a character, express his or her nature?

You have to be able to put the feeling and thought processes of your characters on paper effectively. I think writing up character studies is helpful. It teaches you how to develop a *whole* person on paper, remembering that nobody is all good, nobody is all bad; we are all made up with many complexities in our nature.

4. Can you make readers care about your characters?

That depends on whether you can flesh them out so that the reader believes they truly exist. I've found reading biographies very useful since they are about real people.

5. Can you really tell a story?

If it's to be compelling, make the reader want to turn the page to find what happens next, a novel has to combine structure, plot and action in a way that produces narrative drive. I have what I call my "loving ears"—two girlfriends I can ring and say: May I read you these few pages? That's what I sometimes do if I'm trying to say something complex, and their reaction helps me know if I've refined it enough. Do they want to "hear on"? Some feedback is helpful if you're feeling unconfident.

Structure is very important. Studying favorite books is good homework here. The structure of *Tai Pan* by James Clavell, who also wrote *Shogun*, is marvelous. And Wilbur Smith did a trilogy, *Flight of the Falcon, Men of Men* and *The Angels Weep*, which are all well-constructed novels. And the classics of course. There's nothing better than studying Dickens. And Colette. Colette, by the way, said: Two things are important in life. Love and work. I like that. Yorkshire people have the work ethic. My mother was always polishing a chair or making a stew and I still feel I must work all day, every day, or God will strike me dead.

6. Have you a talent for plots?

Working out story lines and getting them down in, say, ten pages is the best way of finding out. For myself, an event will trigger a plot. For instance, a former friend who was dying and wanted to make peace with me and other friends she had once hurt led to my plot for *Voice of the Heart*. The story line may "unreel" in the bath or on a bus in anything from ten minutes to an hour.

I never use anything exactly as it has befallen me or my friends, but I've seen so much of what happens to people that I know my plots are not too far-fetched, not larger than life. Nothing is larger than life.

7. Can you create a sense of time and place, mood and atmosphere?

I rely on memory for scenes from nature but I have occasionally taken snapshots for interiors. For *Voice of the Heart*, I photographed a *schloss* in Germany, to help me keep the mood of the place in my mind. Note-taking is another helpful tool, and sensible for people who don't have photographic memories.

I can't explain how you create atmosphere. I mean, Stephen King, the "horror" writer who wrote *Carrie* and *The Shining*, among many others, is brilliant when he creates an atmosphere of horror, and I think he does it with his choice of words. Atmosphere is not something visual, it's a feeling, and it's conveyed by particular words, so I too feel I must find the *exact* word and I'll spend hours sometimes to arrive at it. But, having said that, it's hard for a writer to analyze how he or she writes: I always fear I might analyze it away!

8. Do you have the knack of writing dialogue?

Dialogue has to do several things. It has to move the plot along and provide information of some kind. It has to delineate the character of the person speaking—or somehow reflect his personality. It should add to the flavor of the book, convey emotion or feeling. So it has to be very structured, even though it must sound natural.

Ask yourself if the dialogue you have written does all of these things, and if in all honesty you have to answer "no" you will almost certainly find that you can throw it out without loss—indeed it will be an improvement—to your book.

Written dialogue is totally different from spoken dialogue—write down a taped conversation and you'll see it's unreadable.

9. Are you organized enough?

If you want your novel to have a feeling of authenticity, then you must write from strength, from knowledge—and that means research. But the important thing about research is to be able to throw it away! Put it all in and it slows down the narrative drive. I might do a day's research just for a few lines of dialogue but it has to be integrated so it's not apparent.

An efficient filing system is vital, as are good reference books and address books that record sources—or you will waste precious time and work in a muddle. I have a table next to my desk where I keep handy a large dictionary and the *Columbus Encyclopaedia*, along with a thesaurus, *Bartlett's Familiar Quotations*, a world atlas, and maps of England.

10. Do you have a sense of drama?

There's so much drama every day in the newspapers, surely everyone has. Reading plays, watching movies helps to sharpen a dramatic sense, teach you what makes a "story." A book I go back to time and again is *Wuthering Heights*. Every time I read it I find something I hadn't noticed before. It is extremely emotional to me, a very Yorkshire book—though structurally it's said *not* to be good.

13

REAL AND INVENTED PLACES

By Geoffrey Wolff

At the beginning of my novel *Providence,* there is an "Author's Note" that claims that "while the geography, neighborhoods, streets, and ancient history of my *Providence* are generally those of the New England city of Providence, Rhode Island, it is a place of the imagination. I have, for example, re-routed a river to suit my purpose, and every contemporary character who dwells within these pages is an invention; they who live and die here are not intended, should not be misunderstood, to be 'real.' "

Uh-huh. Sure. Tell us another. Hey, if that's the way you want it . . . Everybody knows about author's notes, those "purely coincidentals" attested to by writers dodging a lawsuit, or the cold-shoulder of kin, or—God forbid!—a bullet. Now, I'd hate to stand convicted of a want of cynicism, but let's just for the sake of amicable argument imagine that we have here an author's note that means exactly what it says, that the Providence of this book's title is a notion and region of one writer's dreams and inventions, a particular Providence, for better or worse singular, as different from the stories you build on the word providence as yours are different from your neighbor's.

If two people say "providence" and one thinks of a benign watchman while the other thinks of bad luck, those two will have a short and confusing conversation. They will not connect; neither will have what every storyteller wants and needs, an audience. If a writer makes a place called "Providence" and sets it in the high mountain ranges of Indiana, that whole-cloth creation, that fantasy, will assert its autonomy absolutely. That "Providence," as a setting, must create rather than inherit (and manipulate) a history, a context. No need in such a sci-fi "Providence" for an author's note, and no room for the Biltmore's Apogee, the Cheater's Club, the Turk's Head Building; no sense in naming the widest bridge in the world the Crawford Street Bridge.

Because the Providence I have made mine shares much geography but only some experience with the real city of Providence, Rhode Island, my novel may mislead, may disturb, may provoke skepticism in its citizens as to my motives, veracity, good will, and power to invent. Most of the questions such readers may raise about my novel are neither trivial nor stupid. Many of them drive directly to the heart of what fiction is and what it is not.

A couple of weeks ago I got a request from the producer of a local radio call-in talk show. She said the host of that show wished to interview me for a few moments in the early afternoon. I asked if her colleague had read the book, and she said he had not. That was O.K.: People are busy, and there are many books. To get a sense of this radio show I tuned in and learned from the host much about my book. He told his audience that while I had "disguised" it as a novel, *Providence* was no such thing. It was, he declared—his opinion unclouded by a reading of the novel—a "real book."

Well, he and I never did have our chat, but since then I have turned over in my mind, perhaps too obsessively, what in the world the fellow might have meant by the modifier "real" in his thumbnail sobriquet. Let's try to imagine his thoughts:

By "real" might he have meant true? If so, did he take into account the consequence on any narrative, in any mode, of point of view? I have in recent years written books of fact—a biography and an autobiography—and they taught me that the word truth, as meant by a scientist, a philosopher, or even a historian, is unavailable to literary narrative. Facts—the date of this person's birth, the address of that person's third house—may seem to be *there,* immutably, but they aren't. To be trivially plain, let me note that for a biographer to give a reader an industrialist's 1968 income on the "factual" evidence of that industrialist's 1968 1040 return is not necessarily to have written something true. More important, the storyteller's vantage, his partiality, conditions which facts live and which are suppressed. Art is above all a process of repudiation, whereby the chaotic thisness and thatness of life are shaped into a semblance of order, and this is as true of a "real" book—biography, let's say—as of an unreal book, like Henry James's *Washington Square,* Charles Dickens's *Tale of Two Cities,* Thomas Mann's *Death in Venice.*

But perhaps by "real" our radio host meant merely that he had heard tell that my *Providence* uses place-names that appear on city maps:

Benevolent Street, Atwells Avenue, Meeting Street. I have been asked if I fear being sued by the Biltmore for having set scenes in the downtown landmark. I hadn't considered the problem, frankly, any more than Scott Fitzgerald must have fretted about a lawsuit from New York's Plaza when he set that wonderful summer showdown between Gatsby, Tom and Daisy there. No reader thinks twice about finding Park Avenue in a New York novel, but for some Providence readers it has been a puzzling, perhaps irritating experience, to find *their* proper nouns in my damned book.

Why this might be so is not, for me, without interest, but let me indulge here in an aside about a place-name I am ashamed of, a place-name that my carelessness got wrong, and for me importantly wrong. You will find in my *Providence,* as you drive its pages east on Wickenden Street toward India, a place called "Fox's Point." Not a few people have remarked, with quite proper contempt, my pathetic adumbration of a real place, disfigured by my apostrophe *s,* called Fox Point. I'm irritated by my carelessness not because I got a "real" place wrong, but because I got a "right" word wrong. "Fox" Point is at least one hundred percent better than "Fox's" Point because it *sounds* better. A piece of writing, for me, *is* its sound. If the city of Providence has been in this book a principal character, my hero is the sound of the city's voices, its language, the expression of its singularity.

But I'm running ahead of myself, a little. I believe the reason some good citizens of Providence have felt proprietary about their city's proper nouns bears upon my license. I don't mean the liberties I have taken with the place, but my standing, my authority, my right to write about it. I am, after all, a newcomer, a relentless transient, California-born and raised in Florida, Seattle, Tennessee, Connecticut, here and there. My family moved here from Vermont, a ski town in the Mad River Valley.

I've got a theory about sightseers, self-serving, of course. My theory uses locutions like *sharp-eyed* and describes tourists like me as *putting their ears on.* Thing is, I believe this theory, because I know when we made our way to Providence six years ago I was astonished by it. It is one hell of a place, take the word of an outsider. Where it is beautiful, it is more beautiful than other cities of my experience. Its ugliness is in some places breathtaking. It has pizzazz, brass, presence, an idiom. Tell me if the place bores you. It has never bored me. I think one of the things the citizens of Providence have in common is a capacity for astonishment. And one of the sources of our astonishment is the imagination, energy and sublime stupidity spent by fellow citizens eager to have what they have not earned. I mean that we suffer preposterous crimes here, and that we also enjoy the most wonderful damned crime stories. I mean that as an outsider I was quickly robbed of many belongings, and just as quickly enriched, brought to life, by the extreme acts and speech of my near neighbors.

And here, again, comes the question of license. There is judgment in my words. I'd like to think of my impulse as discrimination in its best sense, a sorting of what matters from what does not, but some Providence readers have asked, with varying degrees of decorous restraint and plain anger, where I get off coming here from wherever the hell and holding their city up, holding my version of their city up, to the world's view? And don't they recognize some of those faces, a bit of that recent history? Of course, of course. Any novel—or any novel by me—is a synthetic composition fabricated of found art (who could improve on the nickname "Moron"?) and bits and pieces taken from a rag-bag of observation, memory, dreamy invention, willful creation. This character's jug-ears come from the guy a desk ahead in the 4th grade; that woman's "jeepers" was heard years ago at a Los Angeles drive-in restaurant, uttered by a waitress working on roller skates.

A corollary version of the question of license and civic responsibility, more forward-thinking, asks why I had to hang out all that dirty laundry—those crimes, rip-offs, pains, erotic fixations, sudden and lingering deaths—for public view? Why couldn't I have looked on the bright side, seen the Preservation Society's good works, lauded benefactors and savants? Why such a heavy cargo of low-lifes?

First off, let me say that I know enough about the world to realize that Providence has no monopoly on crime, corruption, bozos, prisoners of sex, the dead and dying. This is so obvious that to say it seems silly, but it's worth remembering that a novel, if it's good, is not written to deplore, or even to mend. It is written to expose, sure enough, but not in the way an investigative newspaper or television report exposes. It is written to expose our deepest apprehensions. (If there is solace in hoarding, miser-like, miserably and meanly, our most precious secrets, this solace is set inexorably against the writer's calling. I mean that ladies' and gentlemen's distrust of writers is well founded; writers are temperamental enemies of good-mannered decorous reticence, except as such verbal reserve might have formal properties useful to their work's purpose, the telling of secrets.) The fiction I admire is written to show through words—which *are* a novel's deeds—how seemingly small choices—whether or not to open that stranger's locked door—ramify out, touching the lives of the polity, the community, the neighborhood, the family asleep upstairs when that choice gets made.

Providence, city of two hills divided by a downtown river valley where we all meet in court or commerce or to send letters to the world, is substantial enough to resonate with the consequences of a long, long history of good and bad choices. It is small enough to hold us all, so the act of one truly touches the many. I have found the city to be like an apartment house with thin walls. Its voices, like those coming from John Cheever's "Enormous Radio," have been magically amplified. I hear the thuds and scuffles next door, the awkward motions of love. My novel is written from the premise that acts *matter,* that individual decisions *are* a city's history. The acts I have chosen to explore in my *Providence* may seem superficially to be extreme acts. Maybe they are extreme acts, but who here would gainsay their dailyness? My ambition was, in fact, to explore the limits my characters impose on one another, and more important, on themselves. Lisa will pass counterfeit tens, but not twenties. Skippy will rob the downstairs of a house, but will essay no upper invasion, until he does. Baby will kill the Moron but can't, despite himself, kill Skippy. Adam is a man of the law, until he breaks it. Tom, ditto. What does it take to push the limits?

It takes pressure. Fiction is *about* pressure. Nothing personal: my novel, like most, draws its heat not from the sun, but from friction, discord, opposition. In a novel of consequence, I believe, someone wants something from someone who does not want to give it. A bribe. A wallet. Love. Immortality. A kind word. And friction is made sensible, available to the heart through the senses, by language. Thus the idiom of my *Providence* attempts, by its simulation of lazy ease or frantic compression, whether trailing off fecklessly or sprung to the breaking point in its urgency, to enact will and friction. There is in my novel's language a kind of verbal aggression that *is* the battle waged by "little people" against their masters. It is by language that we even the odds against such bullies as bureaucrats, criminals, unloving beloveds, and death. And whatever its powers, excesses, and failures, this language— the coarse and fine music of a city in a time—I learned at *this* time, in *this* city. For which Providence, my thanks, "real" thanks.

14

THE MAGICAL WORLD OF THE NOVELIST

By Sidney Sheldon

ONE OF the questions I am frequently asked is, "How does one write a best seller?" My answer is that I don't know. If someone deliberately sets out to write a best seller, what he is really saying is that he is going to try to write a book that will appeal to everyone. In essence, he is looking for the lowest common denominator. I believe when you try to appeal to everyone, the result is that you end up appealing to almost no one. Every good writer that I know writes to please himself, not to please others. He starts with an idea that excites him, develops characters that interest him, and then writes his story as skillfully as he knows how. If one worries about quality rather than success, success is much more likely to follow.

How does one get started as a writer? The best advice I ever heard of came from Sinclair Lewis. After his Pulitzer Prize for *Main Street,* he was besieged by requests to speak to writing classes at various universities. He turned them all down until one day, after frantic importuning from an Ivy League college, he consented to speak. At the appointed time the auditorium was packed with eager would-be writers, waiting to hear words of wisdom from the master. Sinclair Lewis strode out on the stage and gazed upon his audience. He stood there for sixty seconds of absolute silence, and then said, "Why aren't you home writing?" And he turned and walked off the stage.

I started as a script reader in Hollywood when I was seventeen, then went on to write motion picture scenarios, Broadway plays and television series.

I was a producer at Columbia Studios when I got the idea for *The Naked Face,* my first novel. I contemplated writing it as a motion picture or a Broadway play, but hesitated because the plot called for a great deal of introspection on the part of the protagonist. Because so much of the story was cerebral, there seemed to be no way to let the audience know what the character was thinking. Then it occurred to me that if I wrote it as a novel I could do exactly that. Every morning from nine to twelve I dictated the book to one secretary, while another kept the outside world at bay. At twelve o'clock, I put on my producer's hat and worked on other projects until the following morning. The book was finished a year later. Irving Wallace sent me to his agent, who liked the book and sold it to William Morrow. Most of the reviews on *The Naked Face* were excellent, but the sales were minor. Since I had turned down other projects while writing the book, it proved to be an expensive experiment for me. It would have been easy to have returned to the dramatic rather than the narrative form of writing; but I was hooked. I immediately began another novel with no expectation that it would be any more rewarding financially than was *The Naked Face*. But I was not looking for financial reward. I had found something better: Freedom.

When you are writing for television, theatre or motion pictures, you have a hundred collaborators. There is the star who complains, "I can't read those lines. You'll have to change them"; the director who says, "That scene you wrote in the tea room—let's change it to having them climb the Matterhorn"; the cameraman who filters your story through his lens; the musicians who will finally create moods for your words with their music. I had been used to working with such collaborators all my professional life. It is part of the system. When a writer is under contract to a studio and he's told to change something, he changes it. He is an employee who receives a weekly check, just like the grips and the hairdressers.

Now, with my first novel, I had a taste of freedom—complete and total freedom. No one was looking over my shoulder, no one was telling me how or what to write, no one was second-guessing me. It was an exhilarating experience. I knew that what I wrote might fail, but at least it would be *my* failure.

My second novel was *The Other Side of Midnight,* and it turned out to be one of the ten best-selling novels of the past decade. *Turned out to be.* I did not set out to write a best seller. It began as an idea that I liked, and I went to work on it. Two and a half years later I turned it over to a publisher.

When I begin a book, I start out with a character. I have no plot in mind. The character begets other characters, and soon they begin to take over the novel and chart their own destinies.

A caveat: Even though it works for me, I strongly advise beginning writers not to write without an outline. Writing without some kind of blueprint can lead to too many blind alleys. (While writing *Bloodline*, I found that the character of old Samuel was taking over the book, and since he was not a major character, I had to throw 250 pages into the wastebasket to bring the story back into perspective.)

I dictate the first draft of my novels to a secretary. When the first draft is typed—and it usually runs between 1,000 and 1,200 pages—I go back to page one and start a rewrite. Not a polish—a complete rewrite. I will often throw away a hundred pages at a time, get rid of half a dozen characters and add new ones. Along the way, I constantly refine and tighten. When I get to the end of the book again, I go back to page one. I repeat this process as many as a dozen times, spending anywhere from a year to a year and a half rewriting and finally polishing, until the manuscript is as good as I know how to make it. When I have done my final polish, instead of sending it to the publisher, I start out at the beginning once more and cut ten out of every hundred pages so that the book will read ten percent faster.

The only one beside my secretary who sees my work while it is in progress is my wife, who is a brilliant editor. She reads the second drafts of my books, and I incorporate her comments into the following drafts. When the finished manuscript is ready, my editor and I meet to discuss any changes. He makes suggestions, but he emphasizes that they are *only* suggestions. If there is a difference of opinion, mine is allowed to prevail. Try that at MGM!

I think it is important to set up a disciplined schedule. If you write only when the muse sits on your shoulder, it is unlikely that your project will ever get completed. I work five or six days a week from ten in the morning to six in the evening, with a short break for lunch. I live with my characters, as they live with me.

There are two kinds of writers: Those who want to write and those who have to write. *Wanting* to write is not enough, for it is a painfully difficult profession filled with rejections, disappointments, frustrations. *Having* to be a writer is something else again. If that is the case with you, then I pity you and I envy you. I pity you because you are without a choice. There is no way for you to escape from the agonies and despair of creation, for you will find that what you write will never be good enough to satisfy you. You will always be striving to reach that impossible perfection. You will be Orpheus, using the music of your words to try to reach the unattainable Eurydice.

I envy you because you are going to reach heights that you never dreamed possible. You will create your own exciting worlds and people them with your own wonderful creatures. You will burden them with sorrows and disasters, fill them with joy, give them love, destroy them. What a fantastic and awesome thing it is to play God!

Perhaps, in this, is the clue to writing successfully. Make your characters live, make them real. If your readers do not empathize with your characters, your story, no matter how clever, must surely fail. Make them love your characters or hate them. Let the reader be envious of them or repelled or fascinated; but make the reader *believe*. There is only one way to do that: *You* must believe.

And when you have created that magic world, with characters that move and breathe and feel joy and sorrow, as you feel joy and sorrow, then, ah, then, you will have come as close as any mortal can to reaching out and touching the stars.

15

BUILDING TENSION IN
THE SHORT STORY

By Joyce Carol Oates

THE most important aspect of writing is characterization—does a character come alive, is he memorable in some way? But the means of disclosing character is also important, for if a story lacks a strong narrative line, an editor or reader might not be patient enough to discover even the most stunning of fictional characters.

Novels are complex matters; the density of interest has to go up and down. Short stories, however, are generally based on one gradual upward swing toward a climax or "epiphany"—moment of recognition. A good chapter in a novel should probably be based on the same rhythmic structure as a short story. The novel, of course, can be leisurely while the average short story must be economical. Certain modern stories are so economical that single words or phrases are used to reveal the story's meaning—for instance, John Collier's "The Chaser," which ends with the words "au revoir" and not "goodbye."

While I think the best kind of contemporary story is much more rich and complex and daring than the Chekhovian-type stories so fashionable a few decades ago, still the writer must be careful to limit the range of his "secondary" material—descriptions, background. If he succeeds in winning the reader's attention by dramatic means, then the more important aspects of his story will be appreciated. We have all written wonderful little stories that are "hidden" somewhere in overlong, awkward, unsatisfactory masses of words.

Here are two examples of short story beginnings, each leading into a different kind of story:

1) "Let me tell you something about the Busbys," the old gentleman said to me. "The Busbys don't wash themselves—not adequately. And especially not as they grow older."

67

2) Just around the turn, the road was alive. First to assault the eye was a pro-
fusion of heads, black-haired, bobbing, and a number of straw hats that
looked oddly professional—

The stories following these beginnings are to be found in *Prize
Stories 1965: The O. Henry Awards,* edited by Richard Poirier and
William Abrahams. The first story, "There," by Peter Taylor, invites the reader to listen in on a confidential, gossipy conversation:
the words "Let me tell you" are intriguing enough, but the surprise
comes in the second line. And we are introduced to a strange little
town, "There," where each family seems to have a peculiar trait all
its own—not washing properly, eating too much, narrow-minded
complacency—and dying. Peter Taylor, the author of many excellent short stories of a rich, complex type, builds tension in a highly
refined manner. We listen in on this old man's monologue, amused by
his portraits of people back "there," and gradually we become emotionally involved in the pathos of his love for a girl who belonged to
a family with a secret common trait—and then we find out, along
with the narrator, that this common trait is dying. The girl has died
young; the lover, now an aged man, has married someone else; there
is no tragedy here, everything is muted and understated. But the
story is unforgettable because Taylor has built so very gradually and
unobtrusively the tension that arises out of the girl's impending
death. Everything is past tense, but vitally alive.

The second beginning is from a story of mine, "First Views of the
Enemy." Beginning with a near-accident, this story relies on tension
building up within the main character's mind. A bus carrying mi-
grant fruit pickers has broken down at the roadside, and when a
young mother with her child drives by, one of the Mexican children
darts in front of the car to frighten her. The tension between the
young, American, rather materialistic woman and the socially-
marginal people is the theme of this story. The woman arrives home
safely, but she carries the image of this "enemy" with her into her
expensive home, which now seems to her vulnerable. Her realization
that she could lose everything she owns drives her to an orgy of selfishness as she locks things up, closes her drapes, even picks her most
beautiful flowers and forces food upon her child. The tension is psychological, not active; the "enemy" does not appear after the first

encounter. We see that the true "enemy" is the woman's hysterical selfishness, which she is forcing upon her child also.

Franz Kafka's classic, "The Metamorphosis," begins like this:

> As Gregor Samsa awoke one morning from uneasy dreams he found himself transformed in his bed into a gigantic insect.

Incredible, of course. Unbelievable. But Kafka's mild-mannered prose proceeds on as if an event of no great dimensions has taken place. You, the reader, find out about Gregor's metamorphosis at the same time he does. You are surprised, yes, but so is Gregor—a quite ordinary young man, devoted to his family and his work. This surrealistic story is much more "realistic" in its ability to convince and emotionally involve than most slick fiction with its easily-recognizable people. But Kafka thrives on tension. He builds it from his first sentence on. Kafka is always asking, "What happens next?" and then he asks, "After that, what happens?" Like Simenon, he drives his characters to extremes and tests them. "The Metamorphosis" is beautifully constructed in three sections, each dealing with the tense relationship between the stricken Gregor and his family, until Gregor dies in order to release his loved ones. Tension is achieved on the literal level—what is going to happen to the insect-man?—and on the symbolic level—what will be the outcome of the "love" between members of a family when one of them is mysteriously stricken and is no longer "human"?

These three stories, widely differing in technique, build up tension through an accumulation of detail. If violence erupts in fiction, it should be the outcome of tension; it should not come first, nor should it be accidental. Action stories are of interest to certain audiences, but quality stories usually refine action onto a psychological level. There is "action"—movement—but it takes place in a person's mind or in a conversation. If someone finally kills someone else, it is simply the climax of a rhythmic building of tension that lasts long enough to be convincing but is short enough to be interesting.

Remember that tension created for its own sake is cheap; no one will read your story more than once. The tension is part of your technique but technique is only a means to an end; it is never the end itself. That is why the French "new novel" is so boring—it has no capacity to move us—while older, stormy works like *Wuthering*

69

Heights (which could only be "camp" to today's *avant-garde*) will be interesting to all imaginable future generations. I think the stress placed today on technique is misleading. A writer should imagine his scenes dramatically, as if they were to take place on the stage. There, empty, wordy passages are found out at once. It isn't "words" or "style" that make a scene, but the content behind the words, and the increase of tension as characters come into conflict with one another. "Words" themselves are relatively unimportant, since there are countless ways of saying the same thing.

A final suggestion: be daring, take on anything. Don't labor over little cameo works in which every word is to be perfect. Technique holds a reader from sentence to sentence, but only content will stay in his mind.

16

THE USES OF AUTOBIOGRAPHY

By Gail Godwin

THE FIRST story I ever wrote was about a henpecked husband named Ollie McGonnigle. Leaving the house one morning, Ollie is so happy to be "escaping" that he forgets to look where he is walking and falls into an open manhole. As he is climbing out, a man comes along and says: "Why didn't you watch where you were going!" Ollie hits the man over the head with his umbrella. That night, Ollie comes home to find that his wife has invited company for dinner. The dinner guest turns out to be the man Ollie hit over the head with his umbrella. And, moreover, this man is also . . . THE MAYOR OF THE TOWN.

Now, when I wrote this story (I was eight or nine at the time), there was no man living at our house. I was being brought up by my mother and grandmother. I doubt that I had even met a henpecked husband, except for Dagwood Bumstead, or Jiggs, in the comic strips. But the reason I wanted to write that story, and the reason Ollie was my sympathetic character, was because Ollie McGonnigle was myself.

That slapstick little man, full of eagerness to be out on his own in the morning, so eager that he ignores that voice of authority whose favorite expression is, "Watch where you are going," was I. Ollie McGonnigle, who wanted to make his own mistakes, without anyone saying, "I told you so!" was I. And how gleefully I let him wield his umbrella against complacent authority, even though I knew it was his denouement to knuckle under by suppertime. And how did I know that? Because that was my fate, each evening, when I washed off what little dirt I had been allowed to pick up outdoors and sat down at the table with the authorities. And, on those few occasions when I didn't knuckle under, my grandmother always won by threatening to call her cousin Bill—who really *was* the mayor of our town.

It is revealing to me, to leaf through that file of childhood stories. Ollie the henpecked husband; the one about the rich and lonely little boy who lived behind a high ornate fence and waited each day for the perfect friend to come to play with him; the one about the dog on holiday—from the dog's point of view. What did I know about husbands, about being rich, about being a dog, about being a boy? Yet, behind each disguise, the protagonist was the young author, working out a problem in her life: how to coexist with the authorities; how to put up with solitude until you found the right friend who could get through that fence of perfectionism you'd built around yourself; how it would feel if you could take a vacation from civilization altogether, and get down on your four legs, and run off snarling and panting, to raise hell—even though you get smacked with a rolled newspaper at the end of your outing.

In adolescence, I came out from behind my male/animal disguise and began to write about women. There was a story called "A Sunday in Early New England," which began:

It was the year 1663 and the day was Sunday. All over the New World, people were getting ready to go to church. Prudence Purity was quite upset, however, as she prepared for the long walk with her father and mother and six brothers to the meeting house. The reason for her frustration was that she could not seem to tuck into her hat one bright curl which made her look like a Jezebel.

Looking back, I see clearly that the pressing theme behind all my teen-age stories with female protagonists was how to make peace with the social structure into which I was born—and yet salvage that one bright curl that refuses to tuck itself into the contemporary bonnet. I tried historical distance. In another story, I tried humor. I tried pathos in still another entitled, "I Broke the Code" (rejected by *True Confessions*). The bright curl led me on . . . and still does.

Another theme that surfaced, around high school time, was the theme of choices. The most unsubtle and badly executed of these stories was called "The Choice." It was about a girl who had to decide whether to spend her money to attend a gala where she would be able to shake hands with the world's most beautiful woman, or on a jar of a certain face cream that the beautiful woman used. My heroine chose the face cream.

My first published story, while I was in college, was about an old newspaper vendor who had gone without lunch for a week so he could pay the admission fee to a traveling Rembrandt show at the local art museum. But when he arrives at the museum, he discovers the fee has been raised for that particular show.

I try to recall the impetus for writing that story, over twenty years ago. I believe I wanted to write about how it feels to aspire to art and not know whether you'll have the price of admission when you get to the gates—a theme that has continued to haunt me, in life, as well as art. I was to confront this theme again, years later, in my novel about an artist called *Violet Clay*.

It is easy to look back through your juvenilia and say, "Oh, that's what I was doing. Those were my pet themes. Of course!" What is interesting is that, though the writing has improved, the old themes haven't changed very much. I'm still writing about the importance of salvaging and showing that bright curl, while coexisting with society at the same time; I'm still fascinated by the choices one has to make. And the aspiration theme continues to attract me, as does its dark counterpart: the thwarted aspiration theme! I combined the two of them in my novel, *The Finishing School*.

All of which is to say: I believe our lives shape our fiction just as much as our fiction gives shape to our lives. I'm most comfortable speaking for myself, but I'm convinced that I'm speaking for my favorite writers, as well. They wrote what they wrote, not "out of the blue," but because their lives made it necessary that they write just exactly what they wrote at that particular time. They wrote to discover, to work out, to test their ideas in the process of writing. As they worked on their novels, they worked on their lives: on their vision of life. They tested it, revised it, expanded it. They found—as Tolstoy found, as he worked on *Anna Karenina*—that they often began with one set of attitudes and gradually discovered, draft by draft; that there was quite another attitude beneath that one. They revised their judgments as they became more implicated with their characters, they stumbled on new connections, they watched new insights, and, as their characters grew and changed, they found themselves growing and changing, too.

"Let there be no question about it," writes Dickens's biographer, Edgar Johnson, "what a writer has not experienced in his heart, he can do no more than coldly image from without. Only what he has proved within emerges from those depths with irresistible power, and when new figures lighted in strong emotion force themselves into his imaginative world, they are a projection of that inward reality, no matter how thoroughly the mere surface details may have been changed and disguised."

I write what I write because I am attracted to a certain subject, a certain theme, a certain character I wish to send off on a mission for myself. I write because I need to re-examine some memory that just won't go away, because I need to re-imagine something until I can discover the real truth that lay behind the literal happening. I write because I want to know how it feels to be another kind of person who will do things I can't or won't do. I write to explore alternative choices, life patterns that may run parallel to mine for awhile, then deviate, on a track I cannot follow—except in my fiction.

I'm dubious when anyone tells me, "I never write autobiographical fiction," just as I'm dubious when someone says, "I've got to hurry and finish this story, because I'm afraid someone else will steal the idea." I want to respond, "How can anyone steal something that only you can write?" And if anybody else can write it, what's the point?

When I'm working best, I feel I'm writing something I have to write, something nobody else in the world can write. I feel everything in my life contributing to the destination of this work, determining even the shapes of the sentences. I am always afraid I'm going to die before I finish it.

When a story or novel dies on *me,* and, with a feeling of nausea and sadness, I put it away in a folder (I can't stand throwing out months of effort), I have come to know that the reason it died was that it didn't belong to me in the first place. People begin stories or novels for many reasons. "Wouldn't that make a good story?" someone says. Or someone hands you a clipping ("I cut this out of a newspaper just for you. It's *your* kind of story"), and when you read the clipping, you either catch fire or you don't. Or sometimes you catch fire and start to write and then realize that the anecdote *was* the story; you don't want to know any more. Sometimes I know as soon as I read a clipping that it just does not call out to me in any shape or form. It has no place in my mythology. If I were forced to write it, I suppose I could come up with a workmanlike story, but it would be, to quote Edgar Johnson, *"coldly imaged from without."* And that's not how I write.

I write because I'm looking for answers as well as the right questions.

Because I'm seeking consolation, but also revenge. Because it makes me feel better every time I come up with the precise sentence and the vivid image that expresses an aspect of life that attracts me or haunts me. Everything I have written since that long ago story about Ollie McGonnigle and the mayor of the town was written because I needed to find out what my characters knew, and because I was the only person in the world who could write their stories. All my protagonists—slapstick, allegorical, disguised by gender or species, occupation or social class, or hardly disguised at all—are parts of myself.

17

THE FACTS ABOUT FICTION
A Written Interview

WITH IRVING WALLACE

Q. *We've read somewhere that you draw your ideas for topical novels from the headlines. Is that true? If so, explain.*

A: What you've read is absolutely untrue. It must have been written by a journalist or critic who knows nothing about the making of books. Generally, if an author were to base his novels on daily headlines, he would write and publish books that were terribly dated, almost historical.

Let us presume you decide to base a book on today's major headline because you want to write about a current event. How would you do it? The headline has given you an idea for a theme, subject, background. You begin to develop it in your mind as a novel and you make notes. You evolve some fictional characters, decide where they came from, what they are going through, and where they are headed. Out of these characters and the overall theme you begin to develop a story line or plot. Once you have that, you begin to research the subject of your headline, read all you can about it, interview experts on it, even travel to the sites of the story to guarantee authenticity and get a feel for the background. In my case, this process takes six months to a year.

Now you are ready. You begin writing the first draft of the novel. For me, this creative part may take a half year of writing, writing daily—even Saturdays, Sundays, Mother's Day—at least five or six hours a day. With the first draft completed, you begin to rewrite and revise it, to delete scenes that do not work, to write new scenes that work better, to strengthen a character, to improve sentence structure. For my novel, *The Almighty,* I did six rewrites after I had a first draft. I don't mean I completely rewrote every page each time. But on every go-through I revised at least half the pages.

O.K. Now you have a finished book ready for submission to a publisher. Your literary agent reads it and comments. A publisher reads it, likes it, buys it, and prepares it for publication. Your editor will want some more revisions (because your novel may need revisions, or perhaps the editor must justify his or her job, or simply wishes to impose his or her point of view on the manuscript). With this done there follows copyediting (inconsistencies are spotted, semicolons inserted). Next, your book goes to the printer, and back come the first galley proofs, which your publisher and you collaborate on correcting, even revising some more. Finally, page proofs, which most writers don't see. To the printer, to the bindery, to the reviewers, to the bookstores, and certainly a bound copy to you. Publishers like to say this process takes eight months.

Remember, you wrote a topical book based on a headline. But here it is possibly two-and-a-half years since you saw that headline. Your topical book about a current event is no longer topical or current. No, that is definitely not the way to develop a topical book.

Q. *Well, if not from headlines, how do you get book ideas on subjects that will be current when the novel appears?*

A: By finding a subject of continuing and ongoing interest—a good example, *Space,* by James Michener. Another example, my novel *The Prize,* which deals in fiction with the behind-the-scenes story of Nobel Prize judges and Nobel Prize winners. The subject is in the news annually. It never dates. The other approach: By selecting a subject you sense and anticipate will be in the news and much on readers' minds three or four years from now.

Instinctively, I've used both approaches. A subject that is always news? The so-called Kinsey Report came out. Most people bought it but did not read it. It was too dense, too academic. People read *about* it. Some time after, I read another sex survey and was inspired to look into the subject. I learned there had been many sex surveys before Kinsey made them news. And there have been almost countless ones since. I wondered how a sex survey really worked, what kind of humans were involved in conducting it, why ordinary persons cooperated by giving personal answers, and how these answers affected them. So I researched the subject in depth. Along the way, I developed fictional characters. I blended facts with imagined fiction. The result was my novel, *The Chapman Report,* fortunately an international best seller. The central subject of the novel remains in the news constantly. Sex surveys are always news. More important, love and sex, the relationship between men and women, the emotions of the characters, remain timeless.

As to anticipating the news, can that really be done? I can only say that I have done it (and I can't say I'm psychic, although my daughter Amy—the co-author of *The Psychic Healing Book*—is). I don't know how you anticipate what readers will be interested in three or six or ten years from now. If you write about human emotions and problems, you are surely safe and will write a timely book. But we are discussing subject matter. Well, it has to do with reading, listening, thinking, imagining, above all *sensing* what you might be interested in and what future readers might be interested in some years from now.

When I published *The Man* in 1964, many persons, even in my publishing house, thought I was crazy. A black man who becomes President of the United States, even accidentally? Really crazy. I wrote the book because I had strong feelings about racism in America, and I felt such a novel could dramatize for millions of white readers what they were doing to the black minority. But I also sensed— anticipated—this would be an even more newsworthy or topical subject through the 1970's and 1980's and after.

I had the same instinct when I wrote *The Word,* published in 1972. It seemed to me that religion, faith, belief in a Supreme Being would be of growing interest in a confused world in the years to come. I guessed that my story, centered on the discovery of a previously unknown fifth gospel that might be added to the New Testament, could be an overall subject of continuing interest to me, as well as—hopefully—future readers. This proved to be true. The Born Agains are only one manifestation of the public's non-ending need for order, belief in something, belief in anything.

Q. *In your novel,* The Almighty, *you seem to have reached straight into the current news about terrorists for the subject. True, it is a continuously topical subject, but it was also a contemporary news subject. What do you say about that?*

A: *The Almighty* is not about terrorism. It is about the way the media misuse and manipulate the day-to-day news, and thus keep the reading public misinformed. I employ terrorists in the story largely to make my point and because this means of telling the story had a good dramatic feel to it.

Let me tell you how I got the inspiration for *The Almighty*. One evening, some years ago, I was watching the national network news on television. The anchorman was reporting some event concerning a subject upon which I was well informed at first hand. I realized that the news he was reporting was being utterly distorted, sensationalized, warped, to grab viewers and ratings. I was dismayed by the false picture of the world this was giving viewers. Then I thought about the hundreds of press interviews I had given this past decade in cities across the country, and how reporters who had interviewed me had exaggerated, omitted, rearranged statements I had made in order to produce more attention-getting features. More distortions. Immediately, I saw the subject for a new novel. The new publisher of a floundering Manhattan daily wants to top his competitors, wants to headline exclusive beats that no one else has. So he does the ultimate thing in manipulating the news: He invents it. He hires a terrorist gang to create front-page stories only for him. Until a woman reporter he has employed gets onto his trail. So you can see. My novel is not about terrorists. It is about the manipulation of events by the media. It was a statement I had to make. It was also a challenging drama to plot and write.

Q. *All right, let's talk about the use a novelist can make of fact in fiction. Several of your works of fiction have been called factions, because of the way you blend fact with make-believe. Why do you do it? How do you do it? How did you do it in* The Prize?

A: Novelists have always blended fact and fiction. Some were better at it than others. Charles Dickens was a past master. Leo Tolstoi and Stendhal were good at it, also. When I came to write novels, my experience as a writer had been largely in nonfiction. When I turned to fiction, I became fascinated by the technique of intermingling factual material with imagined material. It was, indeed, a technique. To thread fact through fiction was one more means of making the fiction absolutely believable, and even more colorful and interesting, as long as the use of facts did not obstruct the flow of story narrative. In *The Chapman Report* the members of the Chapman sex-survey team discuss

79

their fictional findings, but they also compare their findings to earlier real-life sex surveys I had researched and studied. In *The Prize* two fictional Nobel laureates from different countries, sharing the same scientific discovery, are at odds, antagonists, because one believes that the other has stolen his work and does not deserve to share the honor. I worried that readers might not accept this conflict as possible in real life, so to enable readers to suspend disbelief I had a wise Swedish official, who sensed the antagonism, relate to the pair some historical disputes and disagreements between famous Nobel laureates who did not like sharing the prize.

Actually, *The Prize* grew out of a visit I had made to Stockholm to write some articles on advances in Swedish science—and when one Swedish scientist, Dr. Sven Hedin, told me he was a judge on three different Nobel Prize committees, I was astounded. The reason I was astounded was that Dr. Hedin was not only pro-Nazi and pro-Hitler, but he was highly political, prejudiced, and utterly uninformed in certain areas in which he voted. (Since he was a judge for the literature award, I asked him whether James Joyce's name had ever come up as a contender for the Nobel Prize. Dr. Hedin said to me, "James Joyce? Joyce? Who's he?") This encounter led me to further research, interviews with other Nobel judges and even prizewinners, and they taught me about the human element in the annual prize-giving. That inspired me to write a work of fiction, *The Prize*, about the awards. It took me fifteen years before I found out how to write it, but write it I did, weaving incredible factual information with my fiction throughout. I even wrote a documentary book about how I wrote this work of fiction. It is called *The Writing of One Novel* and recounts in detail the whole process of how I used facts to underline and accent my fiction. Needless to say, in *The Word*, employing factual material I had obtained in interviews with clergymen, theologians, biblical scholars, I helped clarify and heighten the fiction I had written.

Q. *If, as many novelists believe, truth is too strange for fiction, how do you modify it to make it believable, real, true?*

A: You don't modify facts, you never tamper with them. A fact is a fact. Fiction *is* fiction. But the twain does meet, can meet. You use facts as support for your fiction, when helpful, when necessary. But you don't distort the facts. As my one-time agent, Paul R. Reynolds, used to say, "If truth is too unusual and strange, don't use it in fiction; use it only in nonfiction, where you can authenticate it with more facts."

Q. *Do you feel factual research is necessary for the writing of a novel?*

A: Of course not. We've been discussing fact in relation to a certain kind of novel. Most novels, some of the very best, require no research at all. The characters and plot come out of the author's own personal experiences, observations, readings, feelings. The trap here—in writing only about what you know or have experienced in your life—is that after a while, after many books, you can run out of first-hand material. You might tend to repeat yourself. You also limit yourself. I know one published author who always wanted to write a novel about an attorney, but he told me he simply couldn't because he wasn't an attorney and had never known one well. I told him that was no excuse. I told him to do some research on attorneys, meet some and interview them, find out about their professional and personal lives. I told him to research and broaden his horizon.

I remember when I was preparing my novel *The Seven Minutes.* It was about an attorney and an obscenity trial. I happened to know quite a few lawyers, and I questioned them closely about their lives and obscenity law and censorship. But I didn't know a thing about how an obscenity trial was conducted—this was to be the climax of my novel—and there were no trials in progress I could observe. So what I did was track down a copy of the transcript of the last great obscenity trial held in Los Angeles. It dealt with a Henry Miller book then banned. All transcripts had been destroyed save one, still in the hands of a court clerk at that trial. I rented his transcript and Xeroxed it. It came to twenty thick manuscript volumes, and I spent months studying these volumes to learn obscenity trial procedure. Several renowned attorneys, among them F. Lee Bailey, told me my resultant novel was the best trial book of its kind ever written and one without a single inaccuracy.

Another important value of factual research is that it gives you ideas for your fictional plotting. For *The Almighty,* I planned a fictional heist at the Dead Sea scrolls museum. I went to Jerusalem twice to research the scene and the scrolls. Just as I was leaving the museum on the second visit, I said casually to the expert who had been guiding me,

"Well, I guess this is just about the most valuable collection of authentic ancient documents on earth." And he said to me, "Not quite. The scrolls here aren't all authentic. One of them, the main one, is a phoney." This information was a stunner, and I was able to use it twice in *The Almighty*.

I had my protagonist write a feature story about the scrolls after he visits the museum:

> With reluctance Ramsey attended to his job, made notes for his story, noted everything from the fact that the museum's interior architecture was in the form of the cave in which the scrolls had been found to the fact that the scrolls were enshrined behind thick glass in ten display cases to the fact that the fragments of the main scroll, the Isaiah, were not the originals but clever photocopies, since the fragile real fragments might be destroyed by exposure to light in the building.

Later, when this tidbit is passed on to a terrorist leader on his way to attack and rob the museum, the leader instructs his cohorts:

> After the entrance hall and souvenir area in the museum, there's a tunnel with its lighted glass showcases. Ignore those. Don't bother with them . . . Those are not the great treasures. Go on past them into the main circular central hall. Avoid the elevated pedestal in the center of the room. It contains leaves of the Isaiah scroll, but these are photocopies, fakes, not the original. Go for the ten showcases around the room.

Q. *Is there one piece of advice you can give to an aspiring writer, one who wants to write but is finding it difficult to do so?*

A: There are many things I could say, but there is one thing I must say. The most difficult, even frightening, step for an aspiring writer is transforming the marvelous creative imaginings in his head into words on a blank sheet of paper. Somehow, the imagined words become clumsy and awkward when written down. Yet, writing them down is what writing is basically all about—putting black on white, as de Maupassant used to say it. The best way to ease into that is to keep a daily journal. I've kept a daily journal, one page a day, for many, many years. My children, David and Amy, used to watch me fill that journal. Eventually, both of them started keeping daily journals in their own manner. It was wonderful practice for them. It got them used to setting their thoughts down on paper. It made them comfortable about working with words. When it came to writing actual books, neither of them was blocked. To date, David has published more than ten books, and Amy has published more than six. Go thou and do likewise.

18

WHAT MAKES A FICTION WRITER?

By B. J. Chute

THE other day, an interviewer asked me, "What makes a fiction writer?" and I could only answer, "I have no idea." It is a time-honored and shopworn question, and there are as many answers to it as there are writers, because all writers are different.

The interviewer, being neither time-honored nor shopworn but, on the contrary, young and lively, changed her question to "What makes *you* a fiction writer?" I felt I could answer that question reasonably well, and I did so by offering such (time-honored and shopworn) reasons as a natural bent for storytelling, a life-long habit of reading, a love of words, and all the etcetera of halfway answers which I hope were useful to her but which really did not satisfy me.

Thinking now about her question, I have been turning it over and over in my mind until I arrived, like Alice, at my looking-glass destination by walking away from it. I do not believe I know what makes me a fiction writer, but I do believe that there are four qualities without which one cannot write fiction at all.

The first, of course, is *imagination*. Imagination is as necessary to a novelist or short-story writer as the spinning of webs is to a spider and just as mysterious. It defies analysis (either one is a spider, or one isn't), and it has been quite properly called "the creative impulse." It has also been called the Muse, and, when the Muse vanishes, that yawning void she leaves behind her is known as "writer's block."

Imagination cannot be created, but it can be fostered, and this fostering is part of the writer's duty. It is not enough to congratulate oneself on having been gifted (lovely word!) with imagination, though it is certainly a major cause for rejoicing. The imagination, like the intellect, has to be used, and a creative writer ought to exercise it all the time. There is no idea, however insignificant or vague it may be, that the imagination cannot touch to new beginnings, turning it around and around in different lights, playing with it, *listening* to it. One of the most marvelous things about spiders (and writers) is the way they will launch themselves into space on a filament so infinitely slender as to be nearly invisible, and, lo, there is suddenly a bridge flung over the chasm, across which any fly (or any reader) can walk with perfect confidence.

The second quality I believe to be essential for writing fiction is *empathy,* which the dictionary properly defines as "mental entering into the feeling or spirit of a person or thing." As with imagination, one is to a degree born with empathy; but, like imagination, it can be fostered. Writers of fiction write from inside themselves, but they also write from inside other people, and, again, this is a kind of gift. It is what produces strong and believable characterization. *Madame Bovary* was written from the inside out. Flaubert seems to know not only the passion, the boredom, the despair and the terrible loneliness of that pitiful woman, but he also seems to know the most trivial light or shadow that falls across her mind. Imagination could create her, and her world, and the people around her, but it is Flaubert's empathy that makes his unhappy Emma not just credible but totally real. This is Melville's "subterranean miner that works in us all," and, although we cannot expect to be Melvilles or Flauberts, we can mine what we have. And if we do that, with honesty and intensity, who knows what lode of treasure we may strike?

The third quality is *style.* In its simplest form, style in writing can be defined as the way. in which a thing is said. It is a much abused word, and it sometimes seems to me that it is woefully misunderstood by writers and readers alike. Style does not exist apart from the story, and, if five people tell an identical story, each one will tell it in a different style. The best style will produce the best story, and the listeners will turn to it even if they do not know why they turn. Style is a great preservative of writing, and no writer ought ever to think that a really good style is beyond his reach. But many writers do think so, and too many settle for second best when, in fact, they ought to be working all the time against any such preposterous limitation of their own capacities.

Once I ran across a description of style as applied to architecture, which is just as true of writing—"What is style? Clear thinking, really; the ability to use your head before you do anything with your hands." Sloppy thinking will produce sloppy style, and I am certain there is not a writer among us who has not stared hopelessly at the written page which reflects the muddy results. What to do? Go back, of course. Find out what you are trying to say, and, having found it, select the words that will make the reader see what you are seeing. Selection is vital to style. Because English is an incredibly rich language, there are many bad ways of saying something, and many good ways, but there is usually only one right way. This right way will be the writer's *own* way—in short, his style, or what Proust called "the underlying tune" which distinguishes one writer from another. This should represent the very best the writer has to offer. "Second best" will not do.

Take, as an example, a description from Nathaniel Hawthorne. He is introducing a minister, and all he wishes to say about him is that he is a serious person, wears a beard, and is dressed in the kind of dark clothes and tall hat that would have been affected by a clergyman of his time. There are perhaps a hundred ways of putting all these details together so that the reader can visualize the character sharply, and most such descriptions would probably take a paragraph, certainly several sentences. Hawthorne does it in seven words; his minister is "grave, bearded, sable-cloaked and steeple-crowned."

This is perfectly beautiful writing, and it is as exact as it is beautiful. The picture is instantaneous and vivid, and the tone is faultless. I do not know whether Hawthorne got those seven words right the first time, or whether he labored over them in rewrite after rewrite. Even successive drafts of his manuscript would tell us nothing, because the majority of a writer's work goes on in his mind. What matters is that every word in Hawthorne's description is the right one: *grave,* with its sonorous double meaning; *bearded,* just the simple piece of information to balance the poetic images that follow; *sable-cloaked,* concealing, mysterious, and darker than darkness itself; and, finally, the triumph of *steeple-crowned,* which makes us see not only the minister in his tall hat, but Church, Authority and Heaven as well.

It is true that the average writer is not a Nathaniel Hawthorne, but it is also true that none of these seven words is in the least obscure or recondite or self-conscious; each one would be available to any writer who was craftsman enough to persist in finding it. If a writer is willing to work all the time and in everything he writes to achieve the best style of which he is capable, the words will be there for him as they were for Hawthorne.

And this brings us, inevitably, to the fourth quality, which is *patience.*

Patience in a writer is many things, but most of all, I think, it is characterized by concern for the words on the page. The aim of this concern is "to see the thing and throw the loop of creation around it," as Joyce Cary said. (And notice how riveting the phrasing of that statement is; there's style for you!) What Cary calls "the thing" is the idea, the initial impulse, the product of imagination and empathy. The "loop of creation" is the finding of the right words that will make it possible for the reader to share the writer's special vision, and such words can be very evasive, very slow to come.

At rare and wonderful intervals, the stars in their courses do seem to join together, and the writer finds himself writing so effortlessly and with such precision that it almost seems as if he were taking dictation. These are the best of times, but they are certainly not ordinary. In ordinary times, the words on the page are merely adequate: they move the story along; the second draft will be easier; experience lends hopefulness. The worst of times are when the words will not come at all, and the writer feels as if he were floundering in a swamp or gasping for air in a desert. This can be really frightening, and it is here—in swamp or desert—that the quality of patience will spell the difference between disaster and survival.

In the dictionary, the second definition for the word *patience* is "calmness in waiting." I like this definition very much indeed, because there is a steadiness about it and a good deal of faith, and any writer needs both.

When the final draft of a manuscript is on paper, the words are all that really matter. Money, status, and fame are by-products; nice to have, but nothing permanent. If that statement seems idealistic, of course it is. It is meant to be. To call upon the dictionary once more, idealism is "the cherishing or pursuing of ideals, as for attainment." For the writer of fiction, the pursuit is through imagination and empathy, the cherishing is through style, and the attainment is through patience.

Excellence is simply idealism in action, and so high an aim is bound to fall short of the mark many times. I call to your attention the words of John Adams, written in February of 1776—"We cannot ensure success, but we can deserve it."

19

WRITING FROM LIFE

By Elizabeth Forsythe Hailey

WHEN the lawyer for my publisher read the manuscript of my new novel, *Joanna's Husband and David's Wife,* he called me to ask if we could count on my husband not to sue.

I admitted that the book, which traces the history of a marriage over twenty-five years, was often autobiographical. However, unlike cases where ex-spouses have threatened to stop publication, my husband, Oliver Hailey, to whom I'm still very much married, actually encouraged me to use the facts of our marriage as a springboard into fiction—much as I had used my grandmother's life as a starting point for my first novel, *A Woman of Independent Means.*

Only a man who was a playwright before he became a husband would give his wife that kind of creative license, but he's always believed that the best writing is close to the bone.

A basic maxim for writers is the seeming contradiction, "The more specific you are, the more universal." When I was writing *A Woman of Independent Means,* I was not sure anyone outside my family would be interested in this fictionalized version of my grandmother's triumphs and tragedies. However, the book seemed to strike a chord in readers of many different ages and backgrounds, who recognized elements of their own experience in this saga of an ordinary woman's life from childhood to old age.

Without the success of *A Woman of Independent Means,* I doubt that I would have dared draw so freely on my own marriage for *Joanna's Husband and David's Wife,* but I learned from that experience that by writing from the heart and revealing my private thoughts, I could connect on the most intimate level with readers I would never meet. I also discovered that life offers more original source material than anyone could ever invent.

In the early stages, *Joanna's Husband and David's Wife* was not nearly as autobiographical as it later became. What I was determined from the outset to use from my own marriage was the time frame. My husband and I were married in 1960 when roles were much more traditionally defined; we then had to face the challenge of keeping the marriage going as the rules changed. However, when I showed my husband the first hundred pages, he said, "You and I are a lot more interesting than these characters. Why don't you write about us?"

Once I began to trace the history of a marriage through the fictional diary of a wife whose feelings were at times uncomfortably close to my own, I realized how much I had to say about the difficulties of making a marriage work. And, of course, every time I described an incident that had actually happened, I could hear my husband talking back, adding his side of the story. I realized then that the only way to show a marriage from the inside was to allow both husband and wife to have a voice. From this the form of the novel slowly evolved.

I decided to tell the year-by-year story of the marriage through the journal Joanna starts the day she meets David. Later in the marriage, Joanna leaves the journal out for her older daughter, who is falling in love for the first time. But David finds it first and annotates it with his version of events.

While I was drafting the novel, I went back and read the one journal I had kept early in my marriage (oh, how I regretted not having written more). It reminded me of incidents I had completely forgotten, and I lifted a couple of entries almost verbatim for the novel.

However, in general, my own memories provided me with only the starting point for a scene, and each draft of the novel took me further and further into fiction. I had to imagine full-scale dramatic confrontations out of moments where just the seeds of conflict had been visible in real life.

For example, during a time when my husband and I were down on our luck in Dallas, Texas—following the failure of his first Broadway play—my mother's podiatrist, who had secret ambitions of becoming a playwright, dropped by for a visit, hoping to obtain professional advice. Oliver refused to see him, saying he had nothing encouraging to say to anyone who wanted to write for the theater, and so I had to deal with him. End of story in real life.

In my novel, however, I transformed the podiatrist into a psychiatrist.

Posing as a would-be playwright, he asks Joanna such sympathetic questions, she finds herself pouring out her heart to him:

Finally, after listening to me for almost an hour, the man said he thought he could help us—but he really had to see David too. Would I please ask him to come into the living room?

"What do you mean help us?" I demanded. "I thought you wanted David to help *you* write a play."

That was just an excuse to get through the door, he explained. He had no interest in the theater—frankly, he thought plays were boring compared to life. He was here because of my parents. They thought David needed help—in fact, they were afraid he was on the verge of a mental breakdown—but they knew he would never agree to see a psychiatrist, even if they paid.

"Is that what you are—a psychiatrist?" He nodded affirmatively. I would've screamed in outrage, but I was afraid David would hear me in the next room.

Not until he reads this diary entry—years after the fact—does David realize what happened that day:

My in-laws were trying to set a shrink loose on me? Thank God I never knew. It turns out Joanna is a better actress than I thought.

In looking for other ways to inflate incidents from my own life into drama, I remembered that Susan Cheever, in her book about her father, *Home Before Dark,* had discovered missing pages from his journal. I realized I could put this discovery to dramatic use in a fictional diary. David is stunned to find that Joanna has torn pages out of her journal and wonders what memories she was trying to erase:

I can't keep reading feeling like a victim of Joanna's view of our marriage. Those missing pages were torn from my life, too. I can't go on until I remember what happened that year—to both of us.

The first thing he remembers is the pink spring coat Joanna brought that year—a coat he hated and berated her for buying until, in despair, she dyed it black. This incident was taken—more or less—from life. But then fact gives way to fiction. As David searches his mind for what else went wrong between them that year, he remembers a trip Joanna took without him:

Did she have reasons of her own for making that trip to Texas? I remember that she had a doctor's appointment the week before she left. She said it was just a checkup, that everything was fine.

A thought keeps coming into my mind, and I can't get rid of it. Did the doctor tell her she was pregnant? She knew we couldn't afford a child. I'm making myself crazy staring at the binding, trying to see how many pages are missing, trying to imagine what she tore out of her life—our life—without a trace.

The suspicion grows in David's mind that Joanna had an abortion without telling him—something that could very conceivably happen to a young couple struggling to make ends meet. Writers are told to write about what they've experienced. I would amend that to "write about what you can *imagine* experiencing."

Actually, my struggle to write this book—taking events from my own marriage and heightening the conflicts to make drama—are described by my character Joanna, who, ten years into her marriage, decides to write a novel.

In my first draft, I had Joanna writing a novel about her grandmother, who is an important supporting character. She gives Joanna, through her own example, the means to maintain her independence and sense of self amid all the demands of family life.

I thought a fictional description of the writing of *A Woman of Independent Means* would be interesting to readers, but both my agent and my editor (and publisher) at Delacorte/Dell disagreed. They had displayed shrewd editorial instincts in the past, so when they both had the same reaction, I had to pay attention.

They argued that I had failed to take advantage of a potential source of conflict between Joanna and David—her decision to write a novel. He wouldn't have any reason to object if she wrote a book about her grandmother. But what if the book were about him and the effect he had had on her life from the day they met—challenging all the comfortable, middle-class values of her conventional upbringing?

The idea took root immediately, and when I began to write, I saw how threatened the marriage would be, first by Joanna's decision to write about David (I even allowed her to use the title of the book I always planned to write about my husband, *Disturbing the Peace*), then by the success of the book that turned their marriage inside out, exposing all the seams.

In describing Joanna's struggle to write honestly about her marriage, I was able to dramatize what I was going through transforming the facts of my own life into the fiction of *Joanna's Husband and David's Wife*. I was also able to share, through the advice David gives to Joanna, some of the lessons I've had to learn (and keep learning) as a writer:

91

I was fixing breakfast for the girls this morning, trying not to think about last night, when David suddenly appeared in his bathrobe and asked to speak to me privately.

Following him into the bedroom, I braced myself for what I knew was coming. He was going to tell me he couldn't live through the novel he was forcing me to write and wanted a divorce. I was wondering how we were going to tell the children when he suddenly pulled out his steno pad. "I woke up with a dozen ideas for your book," he said. "Now, sit down and let's go over them while they're still fresh in my mind."

I stared at him in amazement—and asked how he could separate himself so completely from his character in the book. He reminded me that I'm writing a novel, not a biography. Starting today, I have to forget that the characters are based on real people. What really happened is unimportant. Fiction has its own logic. "You have to face the truth first," he said, "but finally, you must free yourself from the facts and create a lie that tells a larger truth."

The breakthrough book for most novelists is usually autobiographical. So search your own life for the story that only you can tell. Write as truthfully as you can out of your own experience, using as many real details as you can recall. But then you must go that extra mile: forget what really happened and look for ways to make your story more dramatic, adding characters and incidents where needed. Above all, search for the hidden conflict in every situation. Fiction provides a wonderful second chance to say all the things you may have been too polite or too frightened to say at the time.

The best thing about writing from life is that you can be sure of using original material. And no research is needed beyond the time you spend looking deep inside your own heart.

20

THEME AND PLOT: THE DELICATE RELATIONSHIP

By Josephine Jacobsen

OFTEN, in fact usually, the short story is spoken of as though it were monolithic, as though certain principles applied to all kinds of short stories, excluding, of course, the specific genre stories such as fantasy or science fiction. As the writer well knows, there are short stories with quite different purposes. Aside from the fantasy and science fiction genres, there are primarily two other kinds of short stories, each difficult to accomplish with distinction, and each with a definite purpose and value, but grounded in different assumptions and produced by different techniques.

There is the story written purely as entertainment—and anyone who relegates such work to a level of inferiority is naïvely unaware of the true, urgent necessity for release into Once-Upon-A-Time. Entertainment is not only one of the universal joys, but at its best, it is not produced by the easy formulas many people assume are ready at hand.

But there is also another kind of short story, a story that appeals to a smaller audience, is more difficult to place, and does not necessarily leave the reader more refreshed and relaxed. Why is it written? Why read?

It is usually written because its writer has an irresistible desire to communicate a deeply-felt experience, one of those epiphanies which in some way, however minute, change the reader's own experience; and it is because of that tiny enlargement of true experience that it is read.

Stories of this kind are so diverse as to preclude any kind of generalization, but there are a few characteristics that are apt to be constant. The story will end, not according to the wishes of the reader, but according to the nature of the characters. It will neither begin nor end on the page; the reader will truly understand that these people have had lives before they appeared in the story. And the "end" of the story will be really the end of a particular section of that life: an incident, an action that will in some way permanently affect their minds, emotions and their future.

I like to believe that when the last word of my story has been read, the reader has been given choices for speculation, as in the lives of actual people, and can say, among the choices, "I think that things will now go this way."

This certainly does not mean that the story's plot can be a vague, shapeless section of the characters' time or circumstances. On the contrary, every single word must make its own contribution toward the climax the story will reach. Every move, by every character, must give to the reader an added knowledge of that character's implicit nature.

One of the fascinating aspects of this kind of story is that of the relation of theme and story line. Any theme worth its salt will be applicable to a great number of people—the enduring themes lie under everything. But whatever the theme—justice, loneliness, betrayal, fear, or the nature of power—it can be illustrated and given body by the most diverse plots. No one can possibly set out to produce a good story by determining to illustrate a theme, any more than one can fall in love upon an order.

I believe that what happens in most cases (certainly in mine) is that one becomes at some period haunted by a theme that knocks about in the consciousness or the unconscious for perhaps months; maybe even for a year or more. Then suddenly something unforeseen—a face, a gesture, an incident, a situation—turns out to have that theme as its very core, and you are off and running. Interestingly, the theme may be incarnated in a large or small subject, yet retain its own scale, untouched.

In a recent story of mine about whether a very attractive and endearing boy did or did not steal a wristwatch from a self-righteous stuffed shirt, the story line is small scale. Nothing here deals with matters of life or death. Practically speaking, the question involved is a single, minor, often-encountered situation.

In a second story, which takes up the thorny problem of how the sincere beliefs of an all-out pacifist can result in injury to others to whom such an attitude is inexplicable, the story line is large: A marriage, the nature of trust, and a young boy's entire future life are at stake.

It is the theme that gives the story its resonance, because in some fashion, the theme will apply to the reader as the plot may never do; it is the theme that leaves its echo on the reader's nerve. But the development of the plot is the very flesh and lifeblood of the story, and unless that carries conviction and interest, the theme will remain as cold and stiff as an admonition or a rule. Indeed, I feel that the theme should not be fully apparent until the end of the story—a discovery the reader makes with a shock of recognition, not by carefully-placed signposts that distinguish it en route.

An intriguing, and incidentally very useful, exercise for someone who hasn't yet consciously explored the relationship of plot and theme, is to take a dozen really fine short stories—preferably personal favorites— and separate theme from plot, as carefully and surely as one can separate whites from yolks. It will almost certainly be found that the size and weight of the plot may differ greatly from the size and weight of the theme. Then take one of the denuded themes, and locate it in other stories, where it is hidden in utterly different subject matter.

Certain rare writers (Tennessee Williams and Flannery O'Connor would be prime examples) are able to perform the miraculous juggling act of producing hilarity and pity or terror simultaneously. Humor— which is always based on a strict sense of proportion (how can it be distorted until it has been established?)—can carry a theme somber indeed. We need only think of Eudora Welty's "The Petrified Man," or Flannery O'Connor's "Revelation," or—in drama—Blanche DuBois's birthday dinner (in *A Streetcar Named Desire*), to see how possible this is, though one wrong movement would bring every ball to earth in disorder.

I think that a profound sense of reality (not necessarily a reality with which we are ourselves familiar) is the short story's basic necessity— even those details that don't enter the story verbally must be visible and familiar to the writer. If the writer sees, feels the weather, the setting, the time of day, the objects visible to the characters at that moment, those details will somehow infiltrate the story with a sense of actuality.

In a story of mine recently published, much of the dialogue takes place between two men of antipathetic temperaments, sitting over the enforced intimacy of pre-dinner drinks on the concrete porch of a small Caribbean boardinghouse. Before them is a garden in which a man is working, and behind him is a fence, and behind that is the cabin where he lives with his wife and child; his goat is tethered to a peripatetic stake. All these details are important to the story; but also present to me as I wrote were the clothes the two men were wearing, the variety of blooms in the garden, the quavering bleats of the goat, the shimmer of Caribbean heat. I know what sort of chairs the men were sitting on, what color of shorts the gardener wore, where the sun was, over the sea. And these last things, which in the story are not mentioned at all, are as important to the feel and taste and shape of the story as those details which are specified.

What all this really means is that the writer must, in her or his imagination, have actually lived through the story that is being told: There is no substitute for that identification.

The second great rule is that the story must grow out of the characters themselves, their reactions to each other, to the situation they are encountering. The story cannot be imposed upon them so that they lie, lopped, on a Procrustes bed. That is why the writer of this sort of short story often has the exciting experience of having a character move unexpectedly, right under the pen; assume an importance, show a side, which was never expected. In my story of two boys and the wristwatch, I had that happen. That confrontation, of natures and backgrounds, *was* the basis of the story; yet perhaps the most significant and lingering note turned out to be the conduct of the master who had to deal with the problem.

Any advice from writer to writer is at best so conditional, and should be so modest, that perhaps the summing-up of this piece on the "serious" short story (which can often be the hilarious short story of serious intent) would be three simple things, standing like warning guardians by the desk. Remember that the people are real enough to have previous or subsequent lives, and let your story offer valid glimpses of how their mind-sets or emotions may be altered by what has happened.

Live with and in your characters, so that you not only see what they see, hear what they hear, but are aware of all the peripheral surrounding life that forms part of their consciousness. And remember that if this is the sort of story you choose and need to write, you cannot aim it at a market as though it were a commodity, but must struggle to bring it to its own most complete life—and then let it take its chance on reaching out to human beings who recognize and believe in the validity of its existence. When it does so, it will be a friend to them and to you for a long time.

Stories of this kind are more difficult to place than more conventional work; they earn less money. But on them, as they are published, their author builds a reputation for a quality of work, and this effect is durable. Such stories have their widest welcome in the university quarterlies and in the more stable and respected of the "little" magazines, though they are encountered, like unexpected travelers, in publications generally given over to "pure entertainment." They are, obviously, in some ways, a lonely venture; but the obverse of this is the sense of intimacy shared with their congenial readers, and it is surprising how many an unexpected letter comes in to say what such a story has meant to one of its readers, or how such a story's crucial incident will be brought up, sometimes years later, in a strange place, by a stranger.

21

THE WILLING SUSPENSION OF DISBELIEF

By Elizabeth Peters

Although Coleridge coined the useful phrase, "the willing suspension of disbelief," it has been the goal of storytellers since the pre-literate dawn of time and of writers since fiction began. Writers of suspense fiction particularly depend upon this gesture of good will on the part of the reader, but successful achievement of that goal depends upon the writer as well as the reader. Presumably, the reader of thrillers or novels of suspense starts each book in the proper mood of suspended disbelief, but he cannot sustain this mood if the author taxes his intelligence too much. How, then, does the writer of suspense fiction create an aura of plausibility which will allow readers to accept his creation, "for the moment," as Coleridge adds?

The so-called Gothic novel is a sub-category of the novel of suspense. In most cases, the term "Gothic" is a misnomer, for the romantic, "damsel-in-distress" thrillers which publishers label "modern Gothics" are not Gothics at all. Their ancestors are not Mrs. Ann Radcliffe's *The Mysteries of Udolpho* or Horace Walpole's *The Castle of Otranto,* but Wilkie Collins' *The Moonstone* and Charlotte Brontë's *Jane Eyre.* The true Gothic novel requires an atmosphere of brooding supernatural horror and a setting that includes ruined castles and desolate moors. I don't consider my books to be true Gothics, but it would be pedantic of me to object to the term, which is certainly more succinct than more accurate designations. I may then be forgiven if I refer henceforth to this form of fiction as "Gothic."

The most important thing for a writer of Gothics to recognize is that the genre is inherently incredible, almost as unlikely as a fantasy novel. Personally, I find it as easy to believe in the green Martians of Barsoom as I do in the adventures of Gothic heroines. Some writers of Gothics seem to feel that because their plots are fantastic, they need not be logical. The converse is true. The more fantastic the plot, the more important are those factors that invite belief, or, at least, the suspension of disbelief.

What are these factors? Some may be seen in the three elements of plot, character and setting.

The plot of a Gothic novel must be tight, consistent, and logical —within the given framework. Like the fantasy novel, which starts with a single fantastic premise, the Gothic begins with what I like to call an "initiating coincidence." The heroine happens to overhear a conversation between two people who are planning a murder; or she happens to accept a job as governess in an isolated household whose inhabitants all suffer from severe neuroses. None of these situations is very likely, but we can admit one such fortuitous occurrence in order to get our plot moving. From that point on, however—no coincidences, no lucky accidents. If the hero is walking down Main Street at the moment when the heroine, cornered by the villain, screams for help, the hero must have a reason for being on Main Street at that vital moment. It will not suffice to explain that he keeps in shape by jogging down Main Street every fine afternoon. If the heroine is to be rescued—and Gothic heroines always are—the rescuer must be brought to the spot by hard work and/or logical deductions.

Plausibility of character is as important as consistency of plot. The two are related, of course. A stupid heroine's foolish behavior can lead to plot complications. Indeed, the plots of the poorer Gothics seem to depend wholly on the heroine's incredible naïveté, as she falls into one pitfall after another. But it is difficult for the reader to identify, or even sympathize, with heroines of such consummate imbecility. Admittedly, Gothic heroines have a propensity for getting into trouble. It is one of the important elements of the Gothic plot, but it can also be one of the great weaknesses of the genre. Critics justifiably jeer at the dim-witted girls who take nocturnal strolls around grim old mansions. If you must get your heroine out of her nice, safe, locked room in the middle of the night, after two murders have already been committed, do give her a good reason for leaving that security. (I cannot think of anything that would induce me to leave my room under those circumstances, except perhaps the voices of my children screaming for help.) Your heroine must have an equally pressing motive. Better yet, have her stay in her room and get into trouble in some less conventional manner. And no mysterious notes asking for a midnight rendezvous in the castle crypt, please. Critics sneer at that one, too. A heroine ought to have sufficient intelligence to check with the hero to make sure he actually sent the note before she ventures into a crypt.

The characters of Gothic novels are not profound or complex; in two-hundred-odd pages we do not have space for such luxuries, since we must spend a good deal of verbiage on plot and atmosphere. But if our characters are cardboard, they need not be absurd. They must not exhibit flagrant personality aberrations, or behave so idiotically that the reader begins to hope they will be murdered in the crypt, as they deserve to be.

Of course, the more fully developed and realistic your characters, the more plausible their actions will seem. One of the classics in the field, Daphne du Maurier's *Rebecca*, has a heroine who has always exasperated me by her timidity and docility; but she is believable, because she behaves in a way that is consistent with her background and her personality.

Atmosphere and setting are particularly important to thrillers of this type, and the same rule applies: the more unusual or exotic the setting, the harder you must work to give it an appearance of authenticity. In these days of jets and travel books, Samarkand is no more exotic than Paris or Rome. But you must make sure that your descriptions of these cities are accurate, and that you include enough details to convince the reader of the reality of the setting in which your heroine's wild adventures are to take place. I do not subscribe to the theory that a writer can write only about things he or she has personally experienced. I have personally visited all the cities and countries I have used in my books; but I could not have written about them without the aid of maps, photographs, and detailed notes taken on the spot. Perhaps a conscientious writer can do this with a city he or she has never seen—but it will require a great deal of work.

The rule holds even when you are inventing a setting. In one of my books, the action takes place in Rothenburg, a small German town I know fairly well, but for various reasons I decided to add an imaginary castle to that city instead of using an existing structure. I did almost as much research on the castle as I did on the city, reading about medieval castles and Franconian architecture, so that the description of my imaginary castle would agree with details of real structures of that period. If your characters do a lot of running around, draw floor plans. Readers love to spot discrepancies, and will write irritated letters if you have your heroine descend a staircase where no staircase can conceivably exist.

One useful trick to make sure that the reader will accept your devices of plot or of setting is to prepare him for them well in advance. A strategically located doorway, through which the hero gains entrance to the conference room—a secret passage whereby your characters can escape when danger threatens—these, and other devices, will seem more plausible if they are mentioned before you actually need them. Again, the more unusual the prop, the more carefully you must explain its presence. A secret passage in a medieval castle needs only a sentence or two of description, since the reader knows that medieval castles abound in such conveniences. A secret passage in a modern split-level house requires considerable explanation—and perhaps a brief character sketch of the eccentric individual who had it built.

Plot props require the same advance preparation. If the heroine's knowledge of Urdu is going to save her from a fate worse than death, or expose the master criminal, you must tell the reader early in the book that she is an expert in this abstruse language. If you do not, she will resemble Superwoman when she comes up with the information. And for pity's sake, if she or the hero is to be an expert in ichthyology or Egyptology, learn something about those subjects before you talk about them. I was once put off an otherwise readable Gothic because it involved a reincarnated Egyptian princess named Cha-cha-boom, or something equally absurd. No reincarnated Egyptian, fake or genuine, would have such a name, and the repetition of the inane syllables grated on me so strongly that I never finished the book. The author could easily have found an authentic ancient Egyptian name in the encyclopedia. I remember another book I never finished reading because the villain, a German sea captain, kept shouting "Grüss Gott!" in frenzied moments. If you do not know that "Grüss Gott" is a friendly greeting in southern Germany, have your villain stick to English.

You may think that few readers have much knowledge of Egyptology or other abstruse subjects. This would be a dangerous assumption. Archaeology is a popular field, and for some odd reason, which I mean to investigate one day, archaeology buffs seem to be especially addicted to thrillers. But that is not the important thing. The important thing is that plausibility depends upon the accumulation of consistent, accurate details. They really do add verisimilitude to an otherwise bald and unconvincing narrative. The reader may not consciously note all your errors; but a series of careless inconsistencies will tax the reader's willingness to accept your imaginary world, and a single glaring error may be enough to snap that fragile thread on which the suspension of disbelief depends.

Of course, you are bound to slip up occasionally, no matter how conscientiously you research your book. As I work through revision after revision, I come across howlers I can't believe I missed the first and second times. To my chagrin, a few of them escape me even in the third and fourth revisions and get into print, despite the additional efforts of my intelligent editors. In one of my books, written under another name, an integral plot prop was an old family Bible. Long after the book was published, a reader wrote to me inquiring how the Bible happened to survive the conflagration that had destroyed the equally ancient family mansion and most of its contents. "I can imagine several possible solutions," she added charitably, "but I do think you ought to have *told* us."

She was absolutely correct. I should have told her. And I would have done so, if I had noticed the discrepancy. However, errors of this sort are not in the same category as careless mistakes or poorly developed characters. An occasional gap in the plot or an error of fact will not be serious if the rest of the plot is as tight as you can make it, and if the other facts have been checked and rechecked.

I could go on, giving examples of the basic rule, but if you read many Gothics, you will spot plenty of other cases, of success and of failure. Of course there are some writers who seem to be able to break all the rules and get away with it. Don't bother writing to tell me about them. I know about them. I only wish I knew how they do it.

22

TURNING EXPERIENCE INTO A NOVEL

BY WILLIAM HOLINGER

WHEN I sat down one morning in January, 1979, to begin writing what eventually became my first published novel, *The Fence-walker*, I was certain of only one thing: What had happened to me and to others in Korea in 1968 and 1969 was worth writing about. That was all I knew. I didn't know whether I could make a good novel out of my experience; I didn't even know whether deep down I wanted to go through the painful process of dredging up those memories and shaping them into a novel. Still, the material was there—memories, images, overheard anecdotes, ideas, characters, voices—and I knew it was good material. So I began work on *The Fence-walker*.

While I wrote, I learned certain *principles* of fiction and developed a *process* of writing. The principles and the process stood me in good stead, and I set them down here with the hope that they'll be of use to others.

Principles

The art of fiction is the art of exaggeration. Fiction is reality heightened; and conversely, the unadorned truth is never publishable as fiction. Fiction is who we might have been, how we might have behaved: character and action, surely, but people and events more extreme and unusual than ordinarily encountered in "real life."

A friend of mine is fond of saying that fiction is all lies and storytelling. I think he's right. When I create fiction out of my own experience, I alter memory a great deal. I reshape experience in two ways: I exaggerate, and impose a structure. As my friend says: it's all lies and storytelling.

By "lies," I mean various acts of exaggeration. Novelists may begin with notes drawn from their lives and with memories, but as they develop a narrative, they exaggerate, using synthesis, invention, and other techniques that intensify the reading experience.

Characters, settings, action, dialogue, voice—these elements must be stretched to their limits, blown up, emphasized. Make them remarkable, clear, and engaging; write in technicolor, not black and white. The ordinary and the everyday seldom make interesting reading. When my internal editor whispers, "But that wouldn't happen in real life," or "But it didn't really happen that way," I take this as a sign not that I shouldn't write it that way, that I have to write it more convincingly.

Fiction often involves synthesis: like taking many gallons of sap and boiling them down to a quart of maple syrup. You might take three people you've known—say, three different people you've loved—and create a single character. Or create a small nuclear family out of all your relatives and friends. Or combine stories: make one scene out of three or four events from your past.

Then there's invention. Make up what you need. Approach your work with a sense of play; have fun with your imagination. Or try the "What if—?" game: That kid you had a fight with in the ninth grade wasn't hurt very badly when you punched him—but *what if* he'd died?

At some stage of the writing process, a great deal usually has to be cut, and this is especially true when fiction is being created from experience. "White noise" must be eliminated: unimportant characters, for example, and events that "really happened" and that may be interesting in and of themselves but that don't contribute to the plot, or central questions. Anything not essential to the narrative must go.

But how do you know what's essential? That's where storytelling comes in. By "storytelling," I mean structure. Most of life comes at us in unstructured form, so it's up to the writer to impose a structure, to arrange events in a sequence, a narrative progression. That is what plot is—structured action.

All narratives, including plays and films, have structure. Think of narrative structure as first a question, and then the answer to that question. The movie (first a novel) *Jaws,* for example, asks the question: Will Roy Scheider kill the shark? A good, complicated novel will ask (and answer) more than one question; but an overriding question must be asked in the opening pages, and answered at or near the end. We can call this the *major dramatic question.*

Conventional narrative structure, broken down into significant elements, begins with an *attack,* then moves through a series of *complica-*

tions to a *crisis*, which finally leads to a *climax,* or resolution. A brief *denouement* may follow the climax. Here's a detailed analysis of these five narrative categories:

The *attack* is the moment the major dramatic question is asked, the moment the reader gets hooked. The attack is order broken. Before the attack, there exists an established order; the attack sets in motion the events that will change that order forever. The major dramatic question is the reason the reader keeps on turning pages—unless the reader is an ideal one and goes on reading simply because your prose is compelling.

There may be any number of *complications,* perhaps one per chapter. These are other, minor "questions." Complications are characters, situations, conditions, or other elements; in a way, they are the story. They affect the way the story—the conflict(s)—will go. They exist for two fundamental reasons: to cause suspense, or tension; and to cause action. Example: the mayor quarreling with Roy Scheider and trying to keep the beaches open, when Roy and the audience know full well that the beaches should be closed, is a complication.

The *crisis* is a complication, but it's the biggest complication. It's also called the no-turning-back point; that is, after the crisis occurs, there is no turning back—the world can never again revert to its original order. The stakes have been raised exponentially. In *Jaws,* the crisis occurs when the shark almost eats Roy Scheider's son. That's when all reserve is shed, when the battle becomes fierce and personal, when we realize that either Roy or the shark is going to die before we walk out of the theater.

The *climax,* quite simply, is the answer to the major dramatic question. In *Jaws,* Roy Scheider kills the shark. The end.

Also called "falling action," the *denouement* in novels is usually very short these days; if one is written at all, a few lines, a few pages may follow the climax. It's nice to let the reader/theatergoer down slowly. A denouement ties up loose ends and shows the world being restored to some order. Not to its original order, though; that's impossible. The crisis made it so.

Principles are all very well—but how is one to apply them?

Process

Many writers outline a novel before beginning the actual writing, and properly so. But I didn't outline my first novel, *The Fence-walker,* before I began to write primarily because so much of it—setting, characters, scenes—was drawn from memory. Here is a description of the process I used.

I began by writing scenes. I wrote from memory, and eventually I made a list of all the scenes that I'd written and that I wanted to write, and then I continued writing scenes. I checked them off my list as I wrote them.

One day, I discovered I was avoiding writing the very big, important scenes. At first I wasn't sure why, but I realized after a while that it was because the experiences they were based on had been traumatic, and therefore writing about those experiences would be especially painful. Also, I knew that they were important scenes, so writing them involved more anxiety than writing less important scenes.

Once I got those fears reasonably under control, I began to work on the big scenes. Writing those six or seven key scenes took months. At the end of that time I had 400 to 500 very messy and unstructured pages scattered about in various notebooks. I had not only scenes, but also lists—lists of scenes, lists of characters, lists of questions and complications. Nothing was in any particular order.

This had been the "lying" stage. Most of the material was transformed beyond recognition. Now I had to set about telling a story. I knew that I had a big task on my hands. I had to organize, and I had to cut.

In my initial attempt to outline the book, I created a "chronology"—a timetable on which I entered each individual scene. This was a first step toward structuring, toward creating a logical sequence or progression of scenes, but it was difficult. The real breakthrough in this process, for me, came when I began to use 3″ × 5″ cards. I wrote a condensed version of each scene on a card and spread out the cards on the floor. This gave me a flexible structure, allowing me to move scenes around until the arrangement was structurally logical and satisfying. Now the story unfolded: The plot began with the introductory and moved toward the crucial, the violent, the radical. The first few scenes asked the questions; the last few answered them.

Even when I'd worked out the proper order for my scenes, however, I was only halfway there. Using the 3″ × 5″ cards as a guide, I put each scene onto a word processor in the proper order, and then began editing to make the chronology apparent and credible and to make the language flow consistently. The editing process involved rewriting, cutting, and writing new material.

106

This long process—from my early attempts at outlining, through the final editing—was "storytelling." I had to identify and then clarify the structural elements of the novel: what the major dramatic question was, which scene functioned as the crisis of the plot, which as the climax, and so on. It was a long and laborious stage of writing, and it involved making many difficult decisions, but then, doesn't all writing involve making countless decisions?

One evening, around the time I began writing *The Fence-walker,* I heard a colleague speak on a fiction panel. "The older I get," he told the audience, "the more I read to find out not what might be, but what *is.*" He was talking not about nonfiction, but about novels. His casual remark had a profound effect on me. I'd been fooled by the words "novel" and "fiction." I thought you had to make it all up.

You don't.

Don't be afraid to write about your own life. Fiction doesn't have to be entirely "made up," and the best fiction is always autobiographical to some degree. In fact, I believe the best work by any major artist is his or her most autobiographical work. Examples: Melville's *Moby Dick,* Hemingway's *The Sun Also Rises,* and O'Neill's *Long Day's Journey into Night.*

When writing fiction, try above all to tell a good story. Give your narrative a structure. If your material is based on experience, so much the better: The fiction will contain a loud ring of truth, and the passion you bring to it will infuse your work with energy and make it that much more powerful.

23

THE MAGIC INGREDIENT IN FICTION

By Joan Dial

WHAT is it that professional writers know and fledgling writers need to learn in order to sell that first novel? Is there a magic secret?

Not until I was struggling with my final draft of *Echoes of War* (St. Martin's Press) did it suddenly occur to me that there is indeed a magic, often missing, ingredient in fiction: *Your reader's imagination.* To create a believable fictional world, you must realize that your reader's imagination is almost as valuable to you as your own. Your reader will fill in all the details that you, as author, must leave out of your story if it is to be kept to a manageable length. If you were to include every single thing your characters did or said or thought or felt, or if you described your setting in minute detail, you'd produce a million-word manuscript (at least) that would be excruciatingly boring.

Think about your own reading habits. You visualize a person or a place from very little actual information. Your imagination creates the face that goes with the thoughtful hazel eyes, or the room that surrounds the littered Queen Anne writing desk.

Recently a well-known radio talk show host announced somewhat pompously that although he was about to interview a novelist, he—the host—never read novels; he read only non-fiction books, he said, because he wanted to *learn* something. He seemed inordinately proud of this, but in effect what he was telling his listeners was that he didn't have the imagination to enjoy or understand the fictional form. Nor had he realized that the readers of fiction are witnessing the contemporary scene, reliving historical events, and observing the forever fascinating range of human emotions in a way that no recitation of dry facts can ever recreate.

Insights into the human condition are often more vividly expressed in a dramatic scene in a novel than in a text by a historian or a psychologist. When we read a good novel, we say to ourselves, ah, yes, that's how life is, or how it could have been at that time.

108

Which makes the more poignant statement about the horrors of war, the famous World War I novel *All Quiet on the Western Front,* or a page of facts and figures listing the weapons, campaigns, and casualties of that war in the trenches?

Think how *Gone with the Wind* recreates in the reader's mind the austere years of the Civil War and its aftermath. Margaret Mitchell made you feel the hunger and deprivation by tapping into your imagination. Knowing, for example, that everyone has experienced hunger, she merely intensified the gnawing in your belly with a few reminders; the reader filled in the rest.

While trying to decide how much detail to include in a harrowing scene in *Echoes of War,* in which my heroine encounters the Gestapo, I realized that it always takes *two* imaginations to bring a novel to life.

I actually described very little in the Gestapo scene; it wasn't necessary to go into detail. I knew my reader's imagination would conjure up more horrors than I as author could ever possibly relate.

Later in my story, while creating a crucial scene set during the London blitz, I found myself swamping the reader with descriptions of the bombing, rather than using the raid as background to enhance the interaction of my fictional people.

Like writers, readers have a vast storehouse of information and memories to draw on. The novelist evokes those memories by using the significant detail, the emotion-producing word.

I wanted my characters' actions, not the air raid, to move the story forward. Therefore, I had to cut, condense, highlight, find the details that would get the reader's imagination working. Otherwise, I'd have a mammoth scene without dramatic impact. In the published book, the following brief paragraphs appear:

Searchlights crisscrossed the sky and an antiaircraft battery opened up somewhere close by. The taxi driver said, "I'm not sure how far we'll get, miss, before we're stopped."

"Try to make it to the station," Kate said.

"Trains mightn't be running, you know."

"Please, keep going."

Aircraft engines throbbed overhead and a flare burst into brilliant light, illuminating the empty street. There was a whistle of falling bombs and a fearful *crump.* Glass flew across the street in their path.

Swerving, the driver called, "What'll it be, miss, a shelter or the nearest pub?"

In less than a hundred words, the reader was brought into the middle of an air raid. With a few significant details, I started the reader's imagination working for me, painting a backdrop to the action. In the earlier draft, I had wallowed in so much description of the terrors of indiscriminate bombing that by the time I got to the heart of the scene, my fictional character's moment of truth, the reader would have been exhausted. It would be enough to jog the reader's imagination during the scene with brief reminders of the raid going on in the background:

The din of exploding bombs and staccato gunfire now sounded like a manic group of drummers pounding their drums in a closet . . .
Snowflakes of plaster drifted down from the ceiling . . .

In this way, I was able to devote more attention to the dramatic point of the scene, the events leading to my heroine's making a crucial choice that will influence her future, and, of course, the outcome of the novel.

I try to think my scenes through *before* I start to write, asking myself the following three questions:

• What emotions am I trying to arouse in my reader?
• What will the dramatic climax of this scene be?
• Which significant details or emotionally charged words will affect my reader's perception of what's going on? (In other words, *how do I tap into my reader's imagination?*)

As a novelist and an avid reader of fiction, I know that if I've given my readers a character they can care about, then during the course of the novel the reader will *be* that character, live those scenes, experience far more than the printed word suggests, through the magic of imagination.

The hero in *Echoes of War* is a Spitfire pilot. Although few of my readers flew in fighter planes in World War II, virtually all of them have flown in an airplane, or at least seen one.

Therefore the actual flying of the aircraft takes place in the reader's imagination, as in the following:

A squadron of Hurricanes, returning after presumably engaging the Luftwaffe formation Tony's squadron had missed, flew into view. They were several planes short and there was no "arse-end Charlie" to watch their rear. Tony maneuvered his Spitfire into position behind them to weave a protective path behind and above and around.
Within seconds he recalled the warning "Beware of the Hun in the sun." A yellow-nosed Messerschmitt 109 came out of the sun right at him, and, momentarily blinded, Tony had no time to go into an evasive roll or even to flip the button to the "fire" position. He watched, mesmerized, as bullets ripped along the starboard wing of his machine, felt the jolt of impact; then everything went crazily awry.

110

His plane was a blurred shape vanishing toward the dark blue of the channel below like a great wounded fish returning to the deep. Sunlight, and a sky scratched with tracers like the mindless scribbling of a child, spun into a dizzying kaleidoscope. The flash of flame and sudden agony of hands and face. Seared flesh meeting a welcome blast of cool air; then he was tumbling through space.

Carl Jung speculated that there is a deeper layer to the human personality that consists of residual memories of the entire human race, a "collective unconscious." These memories, he said, are based on the similar experiences of all peoples of all times and places since the dawn of human existence. Jung called these patterns archetypes, and theorized that a particular set of circumstances would cause us to identify with a particular archetype.

Whether or not we subscribe to Jung's concepts, the fact is that in literature many such archetypes have made a lasting impression on readers; for instance, the "wise old man" or the "earth mother" or the "hero."

Echoes of War and *Roses in Winter,* an earlier novel of mine with an anti-war theme, not only recreated the archetype of "the evil one" (the dictator, Hitler), who offers solutions to a country beset by economic woes, but also evoked the "hero" archetype with whom the reader could identify.

Knowing how to reach your reader's emotions, *through his imagination,* is your most effective tool as a novelist. But you should also use his imagination to get your fictional character from here to there. No need to say, "Harry pulled back the sheet and got out of bed and walked across the bedroom to the bathroom where he turned on the water and got into the shower and soaped and washed, then dried himself off, got dressed and went downstairs. . . ."

Your reader *knows* the process of getting up and showering. Or leaving his apartment and hailing a cab, or ordering a meal in a restaurant. Trust your reader to fill in the mundane details of your fictional people's lives and concentrate on giving your reader a fresh insight into your characters with a telling piece of action or dialogue, an important, memorable detail—*preferably all at the same time.*

In writing love scenes, especially, trust your reader's imagination. I've written my share of extremely explicit scenes, but I believe my most memorable ones were those in which I focused on what my characters were feeling and thinking, rather than on what they were

111

doing. We all know the mechanics of lovemaking, in itself a relatively simple act.

Again, from *Echoes of War:*

She felt a rush of emotion that had its origin in some hitherto untapped portion of her awareness. She felt a need to reveal more to him than her naked body. To tell him hopes and dreams and even fears and weaknesses. To know his. They hadn't had enough time; perhaps there'd never be enough.

The next time I'm asked to divulge the magic secret of selling a novel, I intend to say, the secret lies in trusting your reader's imagination. Get rid of the unnecessary clutter. Highlight, condense—everything: backdrops, dialogue, action. Concentrate on playing on your reader's emotions, and his imagination will fill in all you leave out.

24

LOVE FROM THE NECK UP

By Eva Ibbotson

I BEGAN my literary life in the fifties, as a writer of short stories for women's magazines.

To write those kinds of stories then was to accept the conventions that prevailed. If the hero and heroine kissed, they did so chastely, without physiological descriptions; they were presumed, at the end, to have come together in order to marry and, having done so, to live happily ever after. Love-from-the-neck-up-with-the-mouth-closed was the phrase I coined for their activities, mocking myself and making clear to my intellectual friends that I was well aware of the absurdity of what I was doing.

But secretly I very much enjoyed my work. I have always liked the discipline of working within limits and found total freedom hard to bear. (Consider the boredom one so often feels during "dream sequences" in musicals or films, where the rules of storytelling are suspended, and everything just goes on and on and on.)

And even more than limits, I liked love. I really loved love, from the word go. Romantic love with all its absurdities, its ludicrous determination of one man and one woman to commit themselves, each to the other, till the end of time. The forms this commitment has taken throughout history have been, for me, a never-ending source of fascination. Christian marriage, with its grandiloquent assumption that the partners can be all in all to each other till parted by death. . . . The orthodox Jewish tradition, in which a woman, shorn of virtually all legal rights, becomes—by the consent of those who love her—the kingpin, the lodestar (and frequently also the bane!) of her family. . . . The subtle, sensual delight that girls of the Orient took in serving their men. . . .

Of course, the feminists are right to be appalled by much of this, but I doubt if one can choose one's obsessions, and I—the child of parents who separated when I was three years old—was stuck with an abiding interest in this kind of love. Altogether, I think I'm with the Jesuits when they say that a child is there, *entire*, by the time it's seven years old. I'll bet that Tolstoy, trotting beside his nursemaid through the Russian forests, was already shaking his fist at God. I wouldn't be surprised if Charles Dickens was still in ringlets and knickerbockers when he began to grind his (milk) teeth at the fate of the poor. And I can see the elders of Venice hurrying by with averted faces to avoid the questions of that brat, Marco Polo, about what happened when one left the city and went East.

The fifties turned into the sixties. I wrote my stories, and the mouths of my heroines stayed closed. My own marriage was a happy one, my four children were a delight. There was nothing in England at that time to make romantic love seem obsolete. The hippies, the flower children, might not be much concerned with marriage, and when they loved, it was clear that they proceeded from the neck down and with the mouth open—but I felt in no way alienated from their world.

My stories sold. I wrote my way gradually "upwards" into anthologies and "proper" books; I published two novels for children. Then, as my own children grew up, I decided to write a full-length romantic novel. But not *only* romantic: the book was to be funny, well-researched and intelligently written, and if a man picked it up by mistake, I intended that he should go on reading.

A Countess Below Stairs took me two years to write. It's about a young Russian countess, Anna Grazinsky, who comes to work as a housemaid in an English country house after the Revolution. In it, I treated my reader to a number of my minor obsessions: for music, for ballet, for the landscape of the English countryside. . . . But, yes, the heroine does marry the earl who owns the house, and, yes, her bodice remains unripped, her mouth closed.

Here is an exchange between Anna and the earl after she hears him cry out in a nightmare (he has been wounded in the war) and has gone to his room to offer comfort:

"Do you realize if this were two hundred years ago I could keep you here? Exercise my *droit de seigneur.* What would you do then?"

"I should scream," said Anna, disengaging her wrist. She got up and went lightly to the door; then she turned and said, grinning, "I 'ope!"—and was gone.

This novel was published on the understanding that I write two more. Tessa, the heroine of *Magic Flutes* (set in Vienna in the twenties), has the same half-humorous awareness of her potential for passion, but she too remains chaste until the end. In my latest novel, *A Company of Swans*, Harriet, traveling to the Amazon with a ballet company at the time of the rubber boom, does go to bed with the hero, but if her mouth is open, it is rather with wonder and awe, and marriage follows. And, since to describe the act of love is to risk describing some complicated aerobic workout, I show Harriet's feelings afterwards as she tries to memorize the room in which the miracle of her "ruin" occurred:

> . . . Because she had to remember this room. It was Rom's own room to which he had carried her from the Blue Suite, and she had to remember every single thing so that years later she could come back here in her mind. Even on her deathbed, she must be able to come back here and walk across the deep white carpet . . . particularly on her deathbed . . .

The years rolled by. My daughter married; I was a grandmother. And with my contract for three books fulfilled, I woke up in the mid-eighties and looked about me at the world of entertainment.

I watched plays and films in which love prided itself on bringing about intricate cruelties and pointless betrayals, ensuring for everyone a miserable end. I watched thrillers in which the "goodies" perished horribly and the "baddies," as often as not, went merrily on. I read children's books in which teen-age sex and the shoddiness of adults were the main theme. (Great authors must of course deal with serious themes—with incest and murder as much as with glory and endeavor—but I'm talking about *entertainment*.)

I tried to fit in . . . started a novel about child abuse, another about abortion . . . and abandoned them both. "I'm finished," I said to my husband and to anyone else who'd listen. "I'm out of touch."

Out of touch—that dread phrase! How often I've heard it . . . on the lips of young people who thought they were not mature enough to matter as writers, or old ones who thought life had passed them by . . . from women who lived in the provinces and believed that "real" life happened elsewhere, or men whose religious faith isolated them in a world of rationality. . . . Now it was my turn.

I became quite seriously depressed, paid attention to my physical

115

ailments, and talked of giving up writing. I would keep chickens, run a bookshop, go to India and find a guru—anything except practice the craft I'd laboriously taught myself for thirty years.

What saved me was a girl called Shirlene.

On the train to York, on a visit to my mother, I sat opposite a homely woman of about my own age. Inevitably, we began to talk about our children. The woman had an only daughter, Shirlene, who was clearly the apple of her eye. Though a popular and friendly girl, "Our Shirlene" would never go out when they were showing old films on television. Shirlene loved these vintage movies; she liked the way there was a proper story and an end you could understand.

What sort of films, I asked, and Shirlene's mother said, "Oh, you know, Shirley Temple and Deanna Durbin and Fred Astaire. And those ones where James Stewart's putting things right. She likes things to be *nice*," said Shirlene's mother.

The train stopped at York and Shirlene was waiting on the platform. My image of her had been quite clear: one of those simple, homespun girls you still find in the north of England, wearing a tweed skirt and a cardigan. So the safety pin through her nose surprised me. Her hair surprised me too: puce on top and emerald green at the sides. Shirlene's ripped tousers were viciously studded, chains hung from her leather jacket.

And this was the girl who stayed home to watch Doris Day protect her maidenhood or watch Fred and Ginger waltz together in a cloud of tulle!

The scales dropped from my eyes. I remembered a number of things I'd heard and put out of my mind: A publisher telling me that those inordinately depressing and fashionable novels that win literary prizes are bought in quantity as Christmas presents but seldom actually read. . . . The experience of a friend who'd gone to see a much-hyped film about gang rape and found himself alone with an old bag lady who'd come to rest her feet. . . .

I remembered, too, a Jewish story of which I've always been very fond. An old rabbi is comforting a lost and bewildered member of his flock. "Remember, Moyshe," says the rabbi, "when you get up to heaven, God won't ask you if you've been Abraham or Moses; he'll ask you if you've been Moyshe Finkelstein. If you've been *you*."

I decided to be me: To have faith in the thousands of people all over the world who still want to read about men and women pursuing, with humor and tenderness, a high ideal of love. To be grateful for the lifting of taboos, the broadening out of topics, to use the new techniques that films and television have brought to us as writers, but to be true to my own vision of what it is that entertains.

So I started a new book. This time my heroine's mouth will almost certainly be open, because that's the way mouths are these days, and it will be nice for her. But for all her faults and frailties, she'll be concerned with fidelity and goodness—and in the end she'll have her reward.

And those of you who have also felt discouraged—who are "out of touch"—too young, too old, too far away—won't you please join me?

After all, we owe it to Shirlene!

25

WHERE CHARACTERS COME FROM

By Colby Rodowsky

THE one question that I'm asked most frequently—aside from "How old were you when you wrote your first book?"—is, "Where do your characters come from?"

For a while I tended to shrug, scuff my feet, and change the subject—which satisfied no one, including me. Then I came upon a quote by William Faulkner that seemed to sum up what I had been doing all along, without even knowing it. "It begins with a character, and once he stands up on his own feet and begins to move, all I can do is trot along behind him with a paper and a pencil trying to keep up long enough to put down what he says and does."

In the course of writing seven published novels, several failed efforts and false starts, I've done a lot of trotting along behind. But it's the character's initial standing up on his own two feet that I'd like to consider here. And as for the question, "Where do your characters come from?" I have come up with an answer that, if not profound, is at least obvious.

Characters—mine, at least—come from *anywhere* and *everywhere* and, at times, *nowhere*.

They come from a face in a crowd, a picture on a wall, an older brother I wish I'd had. They come from a story in a newspaper, a name in a book, a need to balance other characters already there, and from the deepest, innermost parts of myself.

And once they're here—standing on their own two feet, as it were—they frequently set off with an independence that astounds me, so that from time to time I have to catch up with them before I can determine where some of these people who stepped unbidden into my mind and my books came from.

There was the time, six or seven years ago, when I was at the beach. It

118

was a cold, cloudy day and I was reading in a downstairs room that had a sliding glass door opening onto a small boardwalk with a pier jutting out into the water. At the end of the pier a young boy was working on a boat. I thought at the time that he seemed to be puttering rather than working, as if shielding himself from something. His shoulders were hunched, and I'm sure his eyes, if I could have seen them, would have been what novelists call "hooded."

A neighbor went by and called to another neighbor on an upstairs porch, "Did you see in the paper that so and so was indicted today?"

There then followed much gesturing and mouthing of words so that I finally figured out that the boy working on his boat was the son of the man in the newspaper.

Now obviously that boy must have known he was the butt of all the pointing and whispering. This worried me, and for a long time afterwards I wondered how he felt about himself, about his father, and about the world in general.

Thadeus St. Clair, the boy I wrote about in *A Summer's Worth of Shame,* wasn't the boy on the pier. I don't even remember that boy's name. I didn't know him. But over the months I was working on the book I came to know Thad—and to know him very well.

Another time and another summer. A woman I met briefly was talking about her powers of ESP. She gave examples of things she had known, not always things she wanted to know. Because at the time this woman was taking care of her grandchild, I began to wonder what it would be like for a child living with a grandmother with extrasensory perception. This seemed to be a natural extension of my memory of an old woman—certifiably crazy—who wandered the streets of my grandmother's town picking things out of the trash and storing them away in her hodgepodge of a house until she was hauled off to the state asylum in Williamsburg.

The character of Gussie that I wrote about in *Evy-Ivy-Over* was not the old woman who roamed the streets of that small Virginia town. My Gussie—and Slug's Gussie, because how could she have a granddaughter named anything but Slug October?—did indeed have ESP. She did prowl the town garbage cans, not because she was crazy, but because she was searching for treasures for her son Brian, an artist who lived in the city and made collages.

There was another element in the character of Gussie: To me she was

119

the quintessential grandmother. I myself was blessed with two special grandmothers, and Gussie embodied all that was good in those relationships. The way Gussie felt about Slug—and Slug felt about Gussie—was the way my grandmothers and I felt about each other, though I've often thought that it would be difficult for those two very proper women to see themselves in a character who delighted in finding an empty milk of magnesia bottle or who knew how yellow felt all the way through.

As for Slug October, that points-and-angles child with the knobby knees and elbows, I don't know where she came from. I only know that she nags at me so that having written a book about her, I then gave her a cameo appearance in *H, My Name Is Henley,* and fully expect her to turn up again, older, changed the way we all change with the years, and ready to fill me in on what has happened to her since we last met.

Now, Nelson Trimper is another story. Nelson popped onto the scene because I needed a repulsive child, and there, from my childhood, was an odious red-haired boy whose mother had been a friend of my mother's. In the frequently misguided way of grown-ups, it was decided that this child and I should be friends. We weren't. In fact, he stuck pins in my best doll. So Nelson Trimper in *Evy-Ivy-Over* is, in a sense, my way of giving that other child his comeuppance.

Mrs. Prather, Slug's mean-spirited and wretched teacher, is indeed every mean-spirited and wretched teacher I, or any of my children, ever had. But if Mrs. Prather was a composite of the bad teachers, so Guntzie, the art teacher in *What About Me?,* was all the good, mind-broadening, imagination-stretching teachers I ever had, or wanted to have.

My husband and I have had different approaches when it comes to visiting museums. He is insatiable, moving from gallery to gallery, reading the cards, seeing, remembering. I, on the other hand, have a short attention span when confronted with what seem to be endless rooms of art. It is as if it were all suddenly too much, and I find that I wander aimlessly around until I come upon something special. Then I look, drift away, come back to look again, finally giving up and heading for the museum shop to get a postcard of the treasures I have found.

Several years ago at the National Gallery in London, I discovered a Murillo painting called "Peasant Boy Leaning on a Sill." I stopped and stared, moved on, then came back again, saying, "His name is Mudge and I'm going to write a book about him."

His name wasn't Mudge in the painting—but only in my mind, and later in *The Gathering Room*, the book I did write about him. There was, of course, nothing of that 17th-century peasant boy in my present-day book about a boy living with his parents in the gatehouse of a cemetery, but nevertheless, that painting had triggered something in me.

And the other characters in the book? There was Ned, Mudge's father, a psychologically bruised man, the result of the events that had threatened him and sent him fleeing to the security of that gatehouse. Serena, the mother, became the special laid-back kind of person it took to put up with that whole scene, and a passing fishing boat I saw one summer at the beach with *Serena* across the stern gave me, at least, her name.

Mudge's friends came as a result of my wanderings through cemeteries, both in person and in books. A bronze butterfly yielded The Butterfly Lady, though I am unable to explain her propensity for reciting the poems of Edgar Allan Poe. A newspaper article about unusual grave markers gave me Little Dorro, while the epitaph, "After Life's Fitful Fever She Sleeps Well," produced Frieda.

Two wordy and somewhat pompous eighteenth-century inscriptions produced The Captain and his aide-de-camp Jenkins, who, with a slight adjustment in time, became veterans of the War of 1812. The words, "He was a just judge and an honest man," resulted in the Judge.

Aunt Ernestus, who is somehow the catalyst for all that happens in the book, started out to be modeled after someone I knew—someone not known for her imagination or her flights of fancy. But Ernestus Stokes wouldn't hold still for that. Or maybe my own imagination wasn't big enough to create someone completely without any.

When *H, My Name Is Henley* came out, a friend wrote me about a book, closing with the questions, "Where *do* your characters come from?"

Sometimes the answer to that isn't clear, even to me, and it took a bit of thinking to sort it out. Booshie, I found, came from a woman I observed once in church during a long and boring sermon. She had the same spongy bosom; the blue-white mottled legs; the squishy arms that made me think, as Henley did in the book, that if I poked them my finger would disappear.

Aunt Mercy was an admirable character indeed, and something like one of my grandmothers. She was so admirable, in fact, that she caused my editor much grief, and as each new character trait emerged in the writing of the book, he would strike his brow, sigh, and say, "All this and she plays Chopin too."

The characters in *Keeping Time,* my most recent book, are a varied lot: a group of present-day street performers. There are Drew Wakeman and his father Gunther, his sister Betina, old Nicholas who juggles, and Kate, who lives and sings with them. And from another time, there is Symon Ives, an apprentice to a London wait in 16th-century England.

I'm still not sure where they all came from. They're too new, too raw, untried, though I do seem to remember Drew looking out at me from a group I saw singing one night down by the waterfront. I only know that while I was working on the book I went to London and walked the streets that Drew and Symon walked: along Cheapside, up to St. Paul's, onto Milk Street where Symon lived with Master Robert Baker. And it felt right to be there. Almost as if I might come upon them at any minute.

But I should be used to that by now. My characters have a way of intruding when I least expect it. Take my great-aunt Mildred's funeral, for example.

Several years ago, when she died at the age of ninety-four, we went to the funeral. It was in an old cemetery in the middle of the city—*my* cemetery. The one I had renamed Edgemount and wrote about in *The Gathering Room.*

It was a hot summer day. A lulling kind of day. The priest droned on, and I started to look around, casting quick surreptitious glances behind this angel, that vault or marble lamb. I knew, somehow, that they were all there. Mudge and his friends: Little Dorro, Frieda, The Butterfly Lady, the Captain and Jenkins. And of course Aunt Ernestus.

That's how real they are to me.

How real I try to make them to my readers.

26

HANDLING TIME IN FICTION

By Jonathan Penner

"BEGIN at the beginning," the King of Hearts commanded the White Rabbit in *Alice in Wonderland*. "Go on till you come to the end. Then stop."

In fiction, the arrangement of time is rarely so simple. Odd as it seems, not all stories stop at the chronological end. Some have circular patterns, concluding in the middle of the events they narrate. One or two even run backwards, starting with the final event and ending with the first.

But it's the beginnings of stories that present the most nettlesome problems. The very notion of a "beginning" is not philosophically secure. Everything comes *from* something, which in turn comes from something else. The selection of any starting point is a more or less violent imposition of order upon the flux of events.

A more practical problem is that once you've selected what feels like a beginning—someone waking up in the morning, or someone getting sick with the flu, or someone's first day on the job—you may find that it's dull stuff. And the start of a story is where you *must* be interesting. Though wonderful scenes may follow, the reader won't get to them if the opening is a bore.

Fortunately, what occurs first *chronologically* needn't come first *narratively*. You can begin your story partway through its chain of events, choosing material that's vivid, suggestive, amusing, tense. You can introduce your central character, and provide at least a thread-end of plot.

The opening is a huckster, a harlot. Engage the reader, charm him, seduce him, until he surrenders to your cause—until the critic in him concedes that he is going to finish this story. Then you can go back in time for relatively dull but indispensable background information.

In a few stories, of course, the handling of time presents no problem. These stories usually comprise a single scene, with little need for background. They may deal with a span of time no greater than that required to read them: perhaps ten minutes in a character's life.

But usually the author must choose where to launch into the river of events. And though his journey is with the current, at some point he must portage upstream to inspect the watersheds from which his story springs.

How far should you carry your story's first forward rush before providing a flashback? How long should the flashback continue before you return to the main story?

Each story will dictate its own rhythms. But a fair principle, albeit one easier to state than to apply, is to continue forward from your opening point until the reader's curiosity about the past outweighs his curiosity about the future.

You won't, in general, insert a flashback right in the middle of fascinating action. That merely frustrates the reader, who is trying to find out what happens next—not what happened a long time ago.

But at a certain moment he will *want* a flashback. He'll want to know how things got like this, what makes these people the way they are. He may require orientation: time, place, relationships. This is the moment—when the story has completed its first advance—to direct the reader's attention to such anterior matters.

Now: how do you move back and forth between the two time periods—the one that's *narratively* first (which we're calling, for convenience, the "main" time period) and the one that's *chronologically* first (the flashback material)?

The technique chiefly involves the use of appropriate verb tenses—complemented by indicators such as "now" and "back then"—to let readers know where they are in time.

A detailed example follows. At the start of our story, fifteen-year-old Cameron Pearl is going to have his hair cut. But we also want to include a flashback, dealing with Cameron's barbershop experiences when he was a little boy.

We begin in the *simple past* tense. (Yes, some stories are told in the present tense, and require slightly different mechanics.) Verbs in the simple past tense are *italicized*.

(1) One morning soon after his fifteenth birthday, Cameron Pearl *entered* Willy's Barber Shop, sliding around the half-open door as though he *hoped* nobody would notice his arrival. But the place *was* empty except for Willy himself, slowly pushing a broom. He *welcomed* Cameron with a toothy grin. "Into the chair, young fella." In no time at all, the familiar laundry-smelling sheet *was* around Cameron's neck, and he *heard* the rapid snip-snip-snip of the approaching scissors.

Suppose we insert our flashback right here. To let the reader know what's happening, we switch from the simple past tense to the PAST PERFECT tense (the "had" tense). Verbs in the past perfect tense are CAPITALIZED.

(2A) Cameron HAD BEEN coming to Willy for haircuts ever since first grade. In the early years he HAD ENJOYED it.

If that's enough flashback, and we want to return to the main story, we let the reader know it by returning to the simple past tense:

But now, staring at the eternally half-filled bottles aligned on the shelf below Willy's mirror, all he *felt* was boredom and irritation. "Leave it long in back," he *sighed*.

Smooth enough. But suppose we want a longer flashback? Won't page after page of the past perfect tense—"had done," "had said," "had thought," and so on—become a nuisance? It will indeed. A more graceful technique is to ease into the simple past as soon as we've gone far enough with the past perfect to establish that this is indeed a flashback.

Here's an example. In all that follows, verbs in the simple past are *italicized* and verbs in the past perfect are CAPITALIZED. Please reread paragraph (1) above. Then continue on with the following, and watch for the switch.

(2B) Cameron HAD BEEN coming to Willy for haircuts ever since first grade. In the early years he HAD ENJOYED it—paging through magazines while he *waited*, climbing into the throne-like chair, the tickle of the shears, the hot lather, and finally the cool air on his awakened neck when he *left* the shop. Because there *were* busy streets to cross, he always *came* with his father, who in those days *had* a full head of silver-blond hair. Cameron *thought* it so handsome that he *hated* to see the first locks of it fall to the floor.

125

His father always *entered* the chair first, and Cameron would pretend

(Note this "would" tense, which is often useful in flashbacks. It indicates habitual activity in the past.)

to read *Esquire* or the *Police Gazette* while he *listened* to the conversation of the men. Regulars, most of them: men like Mr. Hastings, from the candy store, and Dr. Albrecht, and Mr. Kutzko, who *owned* the shoe store. When they *talked* politics, Cameron *felt* proud—his father *knew* more than anyone, and they all *listened* with respect. But when the discussion *turned* to sports, Cameron *sat* in dread. His father's unconcerned ignorance about baseball *was* shocking—Cameron himself *knew* more—and he *prayed* silently that his father would say nothing at all.

See? We've finessed our way out of that awkward "had" tense and are now narrating the flashback in the simple past tense. We can stay in the simple past for the rest of the flashback—though if it were extremely long we'd look for ways to remind the reader, every so often, that it *is* a flashback, not the main story. That would prevent a jolt when the flashback ends.

Now, let's prepare to end our flashback, to get on with the story of fifteen-year-old Cameron and toothily grinning Willy. Can we go straight back to the simple past tense with which we began the story?

No—because we've just been giving the flashback, too, in the simple past tense. The reader wouldn't know where one ended and the other began. So we unobtrusively return to the past perfect tense to finish the flashback. Again, watch for the switch.

Fortunately, his father never *did*—he only *nodded* gravely at the recitations of statistics, the predictions and postmortems. And gradually Cameron HAD COME to understand that this *was* all that wisdom *was*—knowing what you *knew* and what you *didn't*. It *was* a discouraging insight, and once he HAD HAD it, he *lost* a degree of respect for his father. And it *was* then that he HAD STARTED enjoying his visits to the barber less.

By returning to the past perfect tense, we've reminded the reader that this is a flashback. Next we'll signal, with a shift from the past perfect tense to the simple past (and with the extremely useful word "now"), our return to the main story.

Now, staring at the eternally half-filled bottles aligned on the shelf below

126

Willy's mirror, all he *felt* was boredom and irritation. "Leave it long in back," he *sighed.*

From this point, the story will continue forward in the simple past tense to its conclusion—or until the next flashback.

I should like to make one more point about flashbacks, a point also illustrated by our tale of Cameron Pearl. Many writers are under the impression that, in order to go back in time, you have to have your central character *remember* past events.

This is emphatically not so. In fact, few devices of fiction are cornier or phonier than forcing bouts of nostalgia upon your central character.

Yes, people do sometimes remember things—but seldom with the coherence and completeness that flashbacks require. Yet many a character in fiction is made to relive the past regardless of psychological plausibility, regardless of what would more likely occupy his mind at the moment. Character is falsified for the sake of the reader's education. "Stanley stared out the window, letting his mind drift back—back— back to the time when . . ."

But if you keep that glassy stare out of Stanley's eyes, how will you enter the flashback?

The answer is that you simply *tell* us what happened in the past. No need for Stanley or anyone else to glaze over and remember. Just tell us. Telling is narration: as used here, the words are synonyms. This is one of the things narration, or narrative, is for.

I think there are two reasons many writers are uncomfortable with narrative—with telling. The first is that they were raised on movies and television, in which almost nothing *can* be told. In a visual medium, everything must be dramatized—shown.

The other reason is that some writing teacher, perhaps in high school, issued a commandment: "*Show,* don't tell." Misapplication of this excellent advice has caused incalculable mischief.

What the aphorism *does* mean is that you shouldn't (for example) tell us "Cameron's father was prudent" and expect us to believe it. Instead, you've got to present Cameron's father in such a way—for instance, by having him stay within his area of expertise when shooting the bull in the barbershop—that the reader himself comes to the conclusion that the man was prudent.

"Show, don't tell," does *not* mean that you can't narrate your story! Notice that we didn't make Cameron sit there in the barber chair

127

remembering his childhood. Fidelity to point of view requires that the flashback be limited to what Cameron *could* remember—it can't deal with material unknown to him—but not that he actually do the remembering.

We simply *told* the reader, "Cameron had been coming to Willy for haircuts ever since first grade." And our flashback continued from there.

27

FIRST PERSON SINGULAR

BY DONALD HAMILTON

LET US now consider the case of Ethelbert Hackworthy, one of the country's foremost producers of unpublished novels. With unquenchable optimism, Ethelbert is commencing a new book. In the opening scene, carefully planned to seize the reader's attention in a grip of iron, he brings his proud but impecunious young hero, John Pennywhistle, into the music room of rich old Senator Silverbuck's mansion, where pretty Mary Silverbuck is seated at the piano.

Ethelbert is going strong now; he's right in the groove. He has John look at Mary and think she's quite a dish. He describes Mary, tenderly, down to the last ruffle on her fashionable gown and the last freckle on her piquantly upturned nose. So far, so good. But now Bert realizes that something is missing. Great Heavens, he hasn't described John yet! Well, that's easy to fix; and he has Mary look up from her music. She sees John in the doorway, and thinks him a fine tall figure of a man, which leads naturally to a detailed description of John. . . .

Do you like this? Do you feel free to jump from character to character and from viewpoint to viewpoint whenever the fancy takes you? Well, I suppose that's your privilege. Certainly you have lots of company. Many very good, or at least very successful, writers operate in just this way; and after all, it's the way most movie and television scripts are constructed, isn't it, with the cameras cutting freely from one character to another? So what, if anything, is wrong with it?

As far as I'm concerned, everything is wrong with it. The typewriter—or word processor, if you're modernized to that extent—is not a camera, capable of recording only the surface of things, and people. Why throw away your ability to penetrate character and personality by using it as a mere photographic instrument? As a matter of fact, I hate this floating-viewpoint technique; in treating the reader to brief glimpses of all the people in a novel, it really presents a good look at none of them.

As a writer, I disapprove of it, which is O.K., since nobody's forcing me to use it. But more important, as an omnivorous reader, I detest it, because it cheats me out of a great deal of literary entertainment. Why? Just as I'm getting interested in a certain character, male or female, the fickle author switches his attention—and tries to switch mine—to a different character, female or male. As far as I'm concerned, this kind of jumpy writing (we might call it kangaroo writing, considering the way the viewpoint leaps around) is strictly expendable.

The corny scene with which I opened this article is one I actually wrote years ago to illustrate a literary piece I never managed to sell. At that time, I was naive enough to think that everybody shared my prejudice against writers who flitted from viewpoint to viewpoint. I took for granted that every sensible reader much preferred writers who stuck to one character through thick and thin. But the years have brought resignation, if not humility. I'm now hardened to the fact that a lot of readers and editors actually *like* the wandering viewpoint, and that a lot of fairly skillful writers employ it profitably. I will even admit that a truly good writer can get away with it, even with a cantankerous reader like me. But then, a truly good writer can get away with anything.

Even if you think it's perfectly fine to switch protagonists as the fancy moves you, you should be aware of the fact that there is another school of writing that's been around for quite a while. I seem to recall that Fielding stuck pretty tightly to Tom Jones; and Daniel Defoe concentrated on Mr. Crusoe, and didn't bother us much with Mr. Friday's intimate hopes and aspirations. So let's consider the alternative to the omniscient spy-in-the-sky kind of viewpoint treatment that's so popular today.

Some years ago I was very flattered when, reviewing several mysteries for a rather highbrow publication, Jacques Barzun referred to one of my early suspense novels as a first-person story. It wasn't, but the fact that he'd come away from the book thinking that it was showed that I'd achieved my goal. I'd put the reader into the mind of my character— one character—so firmly that the reviewer had laid the book down at the end with the impression that it had been narrated by that character, not by me. Which was exactly the effect I'd been striving for. Now I understand that many writers consider other techniques of viewpoint perfectly proper. I understand; but I don't necessarily agree.

But enough of my literary preferences. Let's just consider the problems of a single-viewpoint novel, as opposed to one written from multiple viewpoints. The basic problem is discipline. As you write about your single character, treating the rest of the cast as peripheral to him, or her, you'll be subjected to continual temptations. The plotting can be tough, if everything has to be filtered through the consciousness of one individual.

You'll hear seductive little voices whispering that the creative life would be much less laborious if, instead of sticking grimly to the thoughts and experiences of "he," for example, you just slipped next door for a minute and let the reader know what "she" or "they" were thinking and doing. Resist! Stay with it, work it out from the hero's viewpoint, if that's what you started with, and figure out how to tell him, and the reader, what the heroine or the villains were up to, while he was struggling desperately to free himself from the cruel bonds securing him to the rusty ringbolts in the wall of the secret cavern soon to be flooded by the rising tide. You know nothing that the hero doesn't know, you see nothing he doesn't see, you feel nothing that he doesn't feel.

The reward for such authorial self-discipline can be great: a kind of hypnotic intensity that leads the reader to identify himself completely with your character; an identification that can never be achieved if you spend two pages on this gent in Moscow followed by a couple of paragraphs about this lady in Washington followed by a whole chapter about this married couple—viewpoint shifting constantly between him and her, of course—in London.

There is a simple substitute for this difficult discipline: Just write your novel in the first person, and you won't be tempted to let the viewpoint wander. If your hero or heroine is "I" instead of "he" or "she," you'll never find yourself slipping into any other viewpoint accidentally, just because it makes the plot work out more easily. You're locked into one character for good or ill.

Many years ago when I asked an editor about the salability problem, I got the following answer: "I'd say there is no prejudice against first-person stories, but in general, first-person viewpoint is difficult to use successfully." The notion that first-person writing is tough in some mysterious way is held by many writers and editors, and that puzzles me tremendously. To me, it seems a very simple technique. It's self-policing. With only one viewpoint available to you, how can you goof? Of course, I've used it for well over twenty novels, so I should have mastered it by now; but I can't recall having any trouble with it even at the first.

There are just two hurdles to be surmounted when using first-person narrative. The first is the plotting, which, as I've already said, can be demanding whenever you stick to a single protagonist—whether you write in the first person or the third. Since your lone hero or heroine can't be everywhere, many things have to happen off stage, so to speak, and you have to avoid getting your book cluttered up with too many messages or messengers of doom, as your protagonist learns of dramatic disasters occurring elsewhere. But I've never found this a great handicap, and I don't see why you should.

More difficult to overcome for some writers is a second obstacle: If the story is to be narrated by the chief character in the novel, he or she has to be a fairly compelling character. An interesting author can write an interesting third-person novel about a dull character, enlivening the text with his own comments and observations; but a boring character is almost bound to tell a boring first-person story about himself. So consider your protagonist very carefully before you commit yourself to writing a whole book as told by or through him or her: Is he, or she, good enough, strong enough, intriguing enough, exciting enough, to carry it off?

Please understand, I'm quite aware that the multiple-viewpoint technique has a place in the literary scheme of things: Tolstoy would have played hell trying to write *War and Peace* through the eyes of a single character. For a truly big book, a panorama novel, it's obviously the way to go. But my feeling is that a lot of lazy writers use it, not because their books are so tremendous in scope, but simply because they can't be bothered to work out how to tell the story from a single point of view. For these writers, and for the beginner learning how to master the tools of the trade, planning and writing a whole novel about *one* character should be a valuable exercise, teaching the student many new things about the profession of writing.

I have a hunch that a novel so written might well turn out to be the best thing that author ever wrote. Of course I'm prejudiced.

28

MIDDLE-OF-THE-BOOK BLUES

Ten Ways to Get Your Novel Back on the Track

By Phyllis A. Whitney

Middle-of-the-book blues! I get them every time, and sometimes more than once along the way. The enthusiasm with which I started out has evaporated. The excitement of discovering and developing a new set of characters, a new setting and situations, lies in the past, and freshness is gone. Boredom is a dreadful state for any writer, and it must be dealt with promptly.

Nevertheless, forcing oneself to write is not the answer. Boredom is usually a warning that all is not well, so that the creative part of the brain is balking. Fortunately, I've been adrift on these becalmed waters before, so it's not as frightening as it was the first few times it happened. Now I pay attention to the warning and take several specific steps to turn myself around and rekindle interest in my work. You may develop a different set of steps for yourself, or adapt some of these for your own use.

1. When I find myself stopped, it is often because I'm not clear about where I am going next, or because I'm taking a mistaken direction, and my unconscious is alerting me. The first thing I do is to talk to myself on paper—whether in pencil or on the typewriter. I discuss the problems with myself, looking for leads that will help me understand what is wrong, and how I can start my imagination working again.

I jot down every stray idea that occurs to me that might be used in future action. I find that the mere act of setting something on paper can stir up the creative juices. Since this isn't really writing-for-keeps, there's no strain. At this point I take care not to be critical of any notion that comes my way. The sorting out, the judging can come later. Being critical too early may stop the flow.

2. Next I re-examine each character in turn, testing for ways in which

133

unforeseen action can be produced. Is there some hidden relationship between this character and that one—something I haven't thought of before? In one novel it suddenly developed that one of my important characters had been married years before to a secondary character in the story. Like me, my main character knew nothing of this marriage. The moment I discovered this, all sorts of possibilities opened up. My imagination stopped balking and went into action—because I had fed it something intriguing to work on.

Conflict and interest can grow endlessly out of our characters. I always keep in mind Brian Garfield's advice to "jolt the reader." Our characters are full of surprises if we give them half a chance. So I try to open up those past lives and develop new and unexpected turns for my plot.

3. Settings, interior and exterior, are always good sources for new plot possibilities. Each background is different and individual, and the setting itself will provide endless story material.

When I went to Sedona, Arizona, for the background of *Vermilion*, one of my first impressions of that stunning Red Rock country was of a line of tall rocks that reminded me of Egyptian statues. Some seemed to have faces carved into them by nature. I saw such "statues" in the red rocks a number of times, and I took color pictures of them. Later, when I studied these snapshots at home, the mystical possibilities began to stir in my imagination until I had part of the main theme of my story.

Exploring your setting again when you reach a static period can furnish new material that will make you eager to get back to your writing. Out of just such feeding of the imagination does inspiration grow.

Whenever I travel to find a new background for a novel, I am on the lookout for anything mysterious, any setting in which something nefarious might happen. West Martello Tower is an old Civil War fortress in Key West that I roamed through and knew that I would want to use in a novel at some point. It is now the home of the Key West Garden Club, and a variety of tropical plants and trees have been planted within the fort's enclosure. The fort is built against a hill, so that it is partly underground, and there are vaulted brick passageways and ceilings—all perfect for scenes of mystery! The setting itself was a challenge to my imagination.

4. It is important for my characters to interact with my settings. In

Vermilion my heroine is haunted by the faces in the rock. The mystical elements provided by the imaginary character, "Vermilion," are brought out all the more by the setting itself. Until setting *integrates* with character, I have only a travelogue.

When I was writing *Domino,* set in the Colorado Rockies, I wanted to use a tiny ghost town that was blowing away to dust. In the plotting, I devised ways in which this little town could affect the heroine's life and become so forceful a part of the story that the book could carry the town's name in the title.

For me, one of the most stimulating preparations for writing is this deliberate examination of character and setting, to find the ties that chain them together.

5. Of course, in the process of collecting background material, the real people I meet who live in a particular place are endlessly fascinating. I talk to everyone who will talk to me, though I'm not looking for *their* stories: I like to make up my own. Encounters with strangers provide take-off points for story ideas, though these may not come to me until later. For example, I saw a woman on a pier in Key West flying a spectacular kite, and I was able to use her to pick up a scene that was lagging.

In Carmel, California, an elderly sculptor whom I met in the Monterey Library invited me to see his beautiful home. Of course I jumped at the chance, since I always need to discover how people live in the setting I'm visiting and will want to write about later on.

All these elements make a rich stew of material and later, just going through pictures and brochures and reading the notes I've taken can set me off on interesting story trails.

However, not being able to travel doesn't mean that I can't write. When I had knee surgery, I had to forgo a trip to Newport, but I wrote a book about it anyway, leaning heavily on photographs and research material and finding someone who would check my manuscript for mistakes.

Wherever one lives, there are interesting corners, villages, city streets. When I couldn't take a long trip, I wrote about the place where I live, Cold Spring Harbor on Long Island, which became the background for my novel *Rainsong*.

6. In the planning stages, I always look for ways in which to make my main character's situation intolerable. Putting on emotional pres-

sure leads to conflict, explosions, action. In the opening of *Rainsong,* my heroine's husband—a famous pop singer—has died under mysterious circumstances. To escape the furor of the media, she accepts an invitation to an old Gold Coast mansion on Long Island. In the quiet of this huge house, she hopes to recover her talent for song writing. I asked myself how I could jolt my heroine and make her situation even more unbearable and frightening. One night she hears music playing in the supposedly empty house. Her dead husband's voice drifts up to her, singing the "rainsong" she had written for him. There are chills aplenty here, and the pressure is on.

Since *Jane Eyre,* the character hidden away and kept secret from the heroine is always fascinating, and possible variations for developing plots from this situation are endless. I never mind if a story idea or character has been used before, as long as I can give it a new twist. In *Poinciana,* my heroine becomes aware of the old woman living in a cottage on the grounds of her husband's Palm Beach house. By doling out a little information at a time, I fed the heroine's curiosity (and the reader's), until the confrontation scene between the old woman and the young one could furnish real jolts, and bring about the realization that the situation was intolerable for both my heroine and the old woman.

7. Since none of our characters leaps into existence full blown but must grow out of the events that have shaped them, it pays to look into past happenings, which may have a tremendous effect on the present. Of course, I do some of this in the plotting stages for my novel, but I can do so even more effectively when I know my story people and have seen them in action.

Characters who are dead before the story starts can be almost as important in the action as the live characters. There are always secrets in the past that still influence and affect the present and make a splendid source of new action. (*Rebecca* is an outstanding example.)

In writing *Dream of Orchids,* I found that the second wife of the heroine's father—dead a year before the novel begins—was still very much alive in the memories of the other characters, because of events she had set in motion. Jolts and surprises again—and a rich source of story action to pull me back on the track.

Force your characters to make decisions, for this always results in action. If you find that your main character is drifting along without much drive, you may have found one source for your lagging interest.

Not only the main characters, but other characters as well, need to make choices. Such decisions force characters to plan and act—often against one another.

8. Research in books and libraries can be an endless source of exciting ideas. When I started work on my Key West novel, *Dream of Orchids*, I had no suspicion that I would become interested in the subject of orchids, or in action that involved diving to a sunken Spanish galleon. I am not an orchid fancier, nor have I ever done any scuba diving. But after bringing home ten books on raising orchids, I could write about them with some assurance, and the orchids themselves gave me all sorts of plot material, including attempted murder. My research included a visit to an orchid greenhouse in my own locality— with a list of questions in hand.

My agent had suggested wreck diving as a subject I might use for the Key West background. I resisted at first, feeling that it had all been done too many times before, and I didn't know anything about scuba diving and wasn't interested anyway. She paid no attention to such nonsense and mailed me four issues of *National Geographic* with accounts of treasure brought up in recent years from Caribbean wrecks. Eventually, I was able to write those diving scenes with confidence. I was under water in my imagination, while my typewriter stayed dry.

A rule learned long ago: *If you don't know, find out.* Once you have your facts right, your imagination can take you anywhere you want to go.

9. I like to be specific about the questions I must find answers for before I begin to write. Very early in my plotting phase, I jot down all those questions for which I have no answers.

When I feel becalmed, I take out the list, cross off those that have been answered, and add others to the list. Since I never throw away any of my plotting material, but keep it all in labeled envelopes, I can give you examples of some questions that I wrote down when I was in the middle of writing *Emerald*. They will mean nothing to anyone else, but may give you a glimpse of the method I have found worked for me.

What action does Linda take to protect Monica from suspicion in Saxon's death?

What does Carol learn from Henry Arlen, without realizing until later what he has told her?

What about Linda's quarrel with Saxon? When? Where?

137

These go on and on, and when nothing else works, I turn to my question list and pick one of them to *think* about *at that moment*. This is the time for thinking, not writing. When the answers begin to come, my interest grows and I can push ahead.

10. Somewhere during this time, I may search back into my own life and emotions. What have I felt deeply about? What has angered me? What has made me happy? Parallels between our own emotions and those of our characters are always important. We can pull those feelings out of memory and apply them to the people in our stories.

Discouragement need never be permanent. It only feels that way while you are going through it. Stir up your imagination. Put in new combinations, new energy—open all those closed doors! Once you see what's out there, you won't be able to resist stepping through to make the novel in your typewriter even better.

29

LET YOUR DIALOGUE SPEAK FOR ITSELF

By Randall Silvis

LET US ASSUME that you know how to write good dialogue. This might be a dangerous assumption, but it is a necessary one; no one can train a tone-deaf writer to have a sharp ear for the rhythms and patterns of natural-sounding speech, for the infinitely rich music of the human language. Either you can carry that particular tune or you cannot. It is what is called talent, and talent, like blue eyes or a freckled nose, is a gift. Such gifts are not rare among us. What is rare is the drive to perfect the talent, the tenacity and compulsion that seem to grow stronger with each rejection.

What can and must be learned, then, is how to use your gift effectively to create realistic dialogue, how to make your characters' words an integral part of the story, so they serve a purpose other than padding or diversion—a mere fattening up of the story's physical dimensions.

Dialogue, like every other component of the successful piece of fiction, performs a function. It *does* something; that is why it is there. Dialogue can be used, in fact, to perform several functions—sometimes singly, often three or four simultaneously. But if too much of your dialogue goes nowhere, if your characters talk a lot but say nothing, your fiction is destined to hit a sour note.

One of the most important functions of dialogue is characterization. Through his own words, a character comes alive. You might have described him vigorously, or painted a wonderfully telling portrait of him, but not until that character speaks will he step off the flat page and into the multi-dimensional arena of the reader's imagination. Through his own words, a character defines himself and reveals who he is, whether he is trustworthy or deceitful, whether naturally ebullient or chronically depressed. His speech pattern will identify him as erudite or obtuse, an Okie or a New Englander, a stuffed-shirt or a clown. A few lines of well-chosen dialogue provide the perfect application of Hemingway's admonition that a writer must *show, not tell.*

In my novella, *The Luckiest Man in the World,* an adolescent Mexican revolutionary, Emiliano Fortunato, has returned to his mountain village as the only surviving member of an ill-fated regiment. Emiliano tells his mother:

> "You will never know, mama, how horrible it was for me. You will never know how bravely I fought. And all to no avail. I sometimes wish that I had not been successful in keeping myself alive."

Because it has already been established through a brief description of the one-sided battle that Emiliano survived not through heroics but through his own negligence, the reader immediately gains an insight into the boy's basic nature. How much better it is to allow Emiliano to reveal his true character in this way than to intrude with a mechanistic pronouncement such as: "Emiliano Fortunato was a liar and a braggart, and very often displayed a tendency toward self-pity." By employing dialogue I have *shown, not told* the reader what kind of person Emiliano is. Emiliano Fortunato will be a fuller, more believable creation because of it.

At the same time that dialogue is delineating character, it can be establishing the tone or mood of a particular scene. The manner in which characters address one another, for example—answering a question with another question; engaging in lighthearted repartee; exchanging caustic, guarded remarks—can draw a reader into the scene by making him "feel" its electricity and excitement, its dynamism. A long passage of dialogue, if handled skillfully, can keep the reader enthusiastically flipping the pages, because in his mind he smells the burning fuse that signals the inevitable explosion of accumulating tensions. Even a relatively brief passage can do much to invigorate a scene, just as a loud exclamation can in an instant silence and electrify a crowded room.

In this example from my story "Trash Man," Warren Schimmel, a trash collector, and his wife Sharon are about to begin the morning run. What we already know, through exposition, is that Sharon is driving the garbage truck today because Warren's helper has been accidentally injured, and that Warren holds himself responsible for the accident.

What we do not yet know is how Warren's sense of guilt has affected his relationship with his wife. In this scene, as Warren stands on the running board and clings to the side of the truck, Sharon asks him to sit in the cab until they reach the first pick-up point. Warren declines.

"What's the sense in freezing yourself to death?" she asked.
"Just drive," he said.
"You'd better get a hold of yourself."
"Just *drive*," he said.
"You've acting like a baby."
"For Christ's sake, Sharon," he said, leaning back wearily against the barrel-shaped hull, "can't you just shut up and drive?"

This simple and unexceptional exchange of remarks accomplishes two things: First, it contrasts Sharon's no-nonsense, practical nature with her husband's laconic, preoccupied attitude (i.e., it delineates character); secondly, by creating a tension between the two characters, it helps to establish the mood. The reader senses without being told that a resolution of one kind or another, either showdown or surrender, is inevitable.

If a passage of dialogue succeeds in animating a story, in making it come alive with a sense of imminent conflict, that dialogue also advances the plot and hones an edge on the tension, thereby bringing the reader more quickly to the story's climax. And the advancement of plot is a third function of dialogue.

It would not be difficult for a writer to tell his entire story through narrative alone. It would not be difficult, but it would not be very entertaining, either. Consider Hemingway's *A Farewell to Arms*. Instead of the teasing banter between Rinaldi and Frederick Henry, instead of the lovely, bittersweet, understated conversations between Henry and Catherine Barkley, the author could have condensed each passage into a few informative words:

After Catherine Barkley met Frederic Henry, she decided she liked him better than she liked Rinaldi.

Or this:

After rowing across the lake to Switzerland, Catherine and Frederick had breakfast at a small café. The café had no rolls. Catherine said she did not mind. Then they were arrested.

141

Fortunately, such uninspired summarization is not the task of the fiction writer. Fiction must live and breathe. Characters and situations must be made so vivid, so compelling, that for a short while the reader is able to ignore the growl of the neighbor's lawnmower, the children arguing, the nagging, bothersome banalities of his daily life. The reader immerses himself as beguiled spectator in a larger-than-life scenario, and it is the task of the fiction writer to keep him beguiled until the story achieves its natural end.

Although straight narrative can advance a plot faster and less circuitously, dialogue often does it more interestingly. Dialogue allows the reader to eavesdrop and observe. It is the difference between experiencing a summer lightning storm firsthand and having it described for you by someone else. Dialogue might slow down the pace of a story, but it also draws the reader closer to the action, *intensifying* it, letting the reader be surprised by the sudden flash of illumination and then instantly anticipate the crack of thunder, the scent of ozone. In other words, it allows him that vicarious pleasure of "being there," without which a story is mere journalese.

These two functions of dialogue—the advancement of plot and the changing of a story's pace—are quite often separate and yet inseparable. While it is possible to advance plot through dialogue without breaking an established stride, every sentence, whether used to quicken or retard the pace, must bring the reader that much closer to the story's resolution.

In the following two examples from *The Luckiest Man in the World,* dialogue is used to accomplish similar goals, but by different means. Although in both cases the spoken word advances the plot, one does so by speeding up the action, the other by slowing it down.

"Maria is having her baby!" Emiliano cried, breathless and redfaced, his hazel eyes wide with worry.

"Hurry, please!" Emiliano urged the doctor.

Sevilla smiled calmly. "Why?" he asked.

"Why? Sweet Jesus, I told you, Maria is having her baby!"

"So?" Sevilla said.

"What do you mean, so? Aren't you coming? She needs you!"

"The midwife can attend to her."

"I don't want that old witch near Maria! Please, doctor, I know you're angry with me, but can't you forget about it for now? I'm sorry I said what I did. Won't you please come? Maria needs you!"

142

"You're sorry?" Sevilla asked.
"Yes, truly, a hundred times!"

In the pages preceding this passage, the pace was leisurely, almost lethargic. But a few lines of dialogue can set the story off on a run again, imbuing it with a sense of urgency. Compare that effect to the following:

"Maria's crazy," Emiliano whispered to Rosarita, as though imparting a secret. "Her mind has been all stirred up like a sopa seca. We'll find another place for your mother to live, and then I'll move in with you. We will be the king and queen of Torrentino, guapa. You'll be the first mother, and I will be papacito grande."

Stretched out beside Rosarita, Emiliano nuzzled her neck and stroked her huge belly.

"You don't need to worry about our baby," he told her. "It's going to be a strong and healthy boy. You wait and see. It was only because of Maria and her stupidity that we lost the first one. But I've been lucky all my life and I can feel in my bones that this baby is going to be fine. He'll grow up to be just as handsome and brave as his father."

Besides adding evidence to what we already know about Emiliano—that he has a conceited, distorted opinion of himself; that he is guileful and hopelessly dishonest—this piece of dialogue provides the opening into a scene that is used as an interlude, a breather between two other scenes of rather frenetic activity. Interludes such as this, if not extended over too many pages, can actually *heighten* the pre-established tension by hinting at the climax, and then holding that climax in abeyance.

To sum up: It is not enough that your dialogue rings true, that it echoes the resonance and rhythms of actual speech, though this is a necessary beginning. But when that task is accomplished, you must ask yourself this: Does each passage of dialogue define or at least contribute to the delineation of character? Does it invigorate the scene with a tangible sense of mood, an enlivening tone of immediacy? Does it provide a change of pace where a change of pace is warranted, and in so doing, continue to advance the plot? If you can answer yes to at least one of these criteria, and preferably to two or more, give yourself a pat on the back. You are writing now with authority, with control. The "fictive dream," as John Gardner called it, has come alive; incorporeal characters have taken on bulk and density; they speak, they interact, they argue and laugh and make love as convincingly, as comically, as tragically as do the rest of us; and in so doing they have become more interesting, more *real* than reality itself.

143

In this manner, each passage of dialogue must justify its existence. When it has done so, there remains but one thing for you, the writer, to do. The advice is three hundred years old, but the truth of it ageless: *Trust on,* John Dryden said, *and think tomorrow will repay.*

30

POINT OF VIEW: EXPERIMENT IN LIVING

By Marjorie Franco

A few years ago I walked into a New York office, gave my name to the receptionist and sat down. The receptionist, a young girl, turned to me and inquired, "Are you an actress?" "No," I said, disappointing her, "I'm a fiction writer." I had the feeling she wanted me to be an actress—it's more glamorous, I suppose—and to make amends I said, "Inside many a writer lives an actor." Nodding agreeably, but clearly dissatisfied, the girl returned to her work. Had she been interested I could have explained that writing, like acting, is an experiment in living, and that the writer (and the actor), by lifting himself out of his own particular life, looks at life from another point of view.

What is point of view, and what does it have to do with writing, or acting, or the persons behind either of these creative arts? The dictionary says point of view is a "position from which something is considered or evaluated." All right; that seems clear. The writer takes up a position from which to tell a story. What position? A reader might say, "That's simple; he tells a story in either the first or third person." It might seem simple, but for the writer it is not.

There are at least six third-person viewpoints and five first-person viewpoints, some rarely used. To discuss all of these or to discuss technique without a story to hang it on can be confusing. Even though the writer has an intellectual mastery of viewpoint techniques, he may not create a good viewpoint character. Writers learn by doing. Did Chekhov sit down and ask himself, "Should I adopt the position of concealed narrator and third-person protagonist narrator restricted, or what?" Or did he simply write "The Kiss"?

This is not to say that it is unimportant to learn technique, for a writer needs to learn as much as he can about the tools of his craft. But tools are only a means to something more, and a preoccupation with them can lead to mechanical writing. Viewpoint, then, is not a matter of manipulation, of attaching oneself, willy-nilly, to a position, to a character, and then telling the story through that character's mind and feelings. Viewpoint is organic, and writers have in common with the actor the method to make it work.

An actor trained in the Stanislavski method knows the psychology of his character; he knows *how* he does things because first he knows *why*. The actor tries to put himself in his character's place, to enter his world, live his life, master his actions, his thoughts and feelings. His truth. It is not enough merely to think of an emotion. Abstract emotions don't come across, or they fall into clichés. It is better to imagine what a character might think or do in a *certain situation*. Then the emotion comes of itself.

A writer uses a similar method of organic viewpoint. He puts himself in his character's place, enters his world, indeed creates his world, suffers his pains and celebrates his joys. If a writer has never laughed or cried at his typewriter, then I doubt if he has ever been deeply inside a character.

Before a writer takes up a viewpoint position he might do well to consider his own temperament and personality and the limitations these impose on his choices. Fiction is personal, as personal as the writer's imagination and emotional experience. New writers are often told, "Write what you know." I would broaden that by saying, "Write what you know emotionally." Love, hate, anger, joy, fear—these are universal. They become unique when they are connected to experience. Our emotional experiences are stored within us. Filtered through memory and a well-developed imagination, they can be called up, made fresh and organized into the work at hand. Creative imagination is the writer's valuable gift, and even though it is somewhat limited by his experience, within that sphere of experience it is unlimited in variety and combination. Hopefully the writer is always enlarging his sphere, adding to his storehouse with outward experience in reality.

Out of the sphere of my emotional experience I wrote "The Poet of Evolution Avenue" (*Redbook*), the story of a young wife and mother who was, also, a bad poet. She believed her creative gift was being hampered by the intrusion of her family. She had neither the time nor the privacy to write a real poem. Time and privacy are practically forced on her in the form of a vacation alone in her father's California apartment, but it isn't until she is ready to go home that she is able to write a real poem, and then only because she doesn't want to go home empty-handed.

This story is based on the old Ivory Tower idea: a poet is more productive when isolated from the world. My poet discovered that she had been making excuses for herself, that her world was her stimulus, and that she had trouble producing poetry without it.

The idea for that story came out of my own emotional experience. Some years earlier I had gone to California to be near my father while he was in the hospital undergoing surgery. For three weeks I lived alone in his apartment, a large, tight-security building in which I rarely saw the other residents. I had brought my typewriter, thinking I would turn out a volume or two between hospital visits. It didn't work. I was accustomed to working with people around. Interruptions. Interruptions can be marvelous. They take the place of pacing, a necessary activity of some writers. I learned that I am not an Ivory Tower writer, ideal as that may seem; I need the stimulus of family and friends.

Every writer has his own voice, and it is up to him to find it and use it with authority. That voice comes through as male or female, child or adult, humorous or serious, but behind it, within it, is the author's brooding presence, his vision of life. He describes the world from his point of view. He is on intimate terms with his viewpoint characters. Henry James could imagine what his focal character (he is never named) in *The Aspern Papers* might think and do when he is forced to admit to the woman who loves him that he has been using her for his personal gain. But I doubt if James could have lived inside Bigger, as Richard Wright did in *Native Son*, and chased and killed the huge rat in a Chicago tenement. Who is to say one view is better or worse than another? Each is different, unique.

Recognizing his limitations, an author adopts a viewpoint position he can understand emotionally as well as intellectually. My story, "Miss Dillon's Secret" (*Redbook*), is about a teacher. I have never been a teacher, but teaching is within the sphere of my emotional experience. I have been a student, of course, and my hus-

147

band, now a principal, was once a teacher. His experiences have rubbed off on me. I believe that a natural teacher is born, not made, that the qualities in such a person work together to make learning exciting. The title character in my story, Miss Dillon, is drawn from a real person, an experienced teacher whose students come back to visit her with their husbands and wives and children and grandchildren.

I adopted the viewpoint position of a young teacher who had worked with Miss Dillon. There were more decisions for me to make. Will I place myself inside or outside the viewpoint character? And how far inside or outside? This can be a difficult choice, for each character has its own limitations, and the author, to keep his voice appropriate to the viewpoint, puts limits on his "knowledge" accordingly. He seems to know less than he does. Consider, for example, Hemingway's camera-eye view which limits his "knowledge" to what can be seen from the outside. Or, at the other extreme, Joyce's deep internalizing, which limits him in the other direction.

For my viewpoint character I adopted a position somewhere in between. With the story told in the third person, my character's problems are external, but her discovery of Miss Dillon's secret is internal, brought about by an emotional experience with one of her former students.

We might ask ourselves certain questions concerning viewpoint: 1) Who will be the narrator? author, in first or third person? character, in first person? or nobody (omniscient narrator)? 2) From what angle does the narrator tell the story? Above, center, front, periphery, shifting? 3) Where does the author place the reader? Near, far, shifting?

Sometimes an author adopts a viewpoint position instinctively, and all goes well. The voice flows from a stable position. At other times an author finds himself tangled in clumsy sentences and tedious explanations, surrendering his surprises too early, battling predictability, placing his best scenes offstage. When this happens, the problem could very well be the viewpoint he chose. He may be looking from the wrong angle. Usually I can tell by the way it "feels" if I'm in a good or poor viewpoint. But not always. Four years ago I wrote a short story called "The Boy Who Cooked." The title character, Benny, was the antagonist, and the viewpoint character was a woman protagonist whose name changed with each of the many versions I wrote. I couldn't sell the story. But I continued writing it, on and off, for four years, always keeping the boy, but frequently changing the characters around him, including the viewpoint character. The total number of pages devoted to that story runs into several hundred, which is some indication of my devotion to a character. But finally I gave up and put the story away.

Meanwhile, I had written and sold a story called, "No Such Thing as a Happy Marriage" (*Redbook*), in which the viewpoint character was a wife and mother named Jenny. Six months after that story was published, my editor, in a letter to me, mentioned Benny, the boy who cooked. Even before I had finished reading the letter, Benny, like Lazarus, rose from the dead. Why couldn't I write a new story for Benny? And why couldn't I surround him with the same cast of characters I had used in "No Such Thing as a Happy Marriage," with Jenny as the viewpoint character? I could, and I did. This time the viewpoint felt right; the voice flowed clearly from a stable position, and I wrote the story in a matter of hours. After four years of roaming through my typewriter, Benny had found his place, and his story, "The Boy Who Cooked," was published in *Redbook*.

The author's attitude toward a character (and his desire to create a similar attitude in the reader) can help determine the angle from which he views him. If the character is obviously sympathetic, the reader will identify. With some characters, however, the reader may feel only a tentative sympathy, until he is shocked into understanding by some revelation which allows him to feel complete sympathy. Sometimes, reader and character start out with a great distance between them. Perhaps their worlds are totally different. The author gradually pulls the reader into the character's world, and the reader ends by feeling sympathy. (I have this experience, as a reader, when I read Jean Genêt, for example.) A difficult relationship for an author to achieve is one in which the reader is forced to identify, perhaps unconsciously, with a character he dislikes. He is left wondering what there was about the story that fascinated him. What he may not realize is that, being human, we all have our share of unattractive qualities, and seeing them in someone else stirs our recognition. Playwright Harold Pinter frequently achieves this kind of relationship.

In my story, "An Uncompromising Girl" (*Redbook*), my aim was for tentative sympathy and eventual complete sympathy. As the author (concealed narrator), I speak in the third person through the focal character. The channels of information between author and reader are a combination of the author's words, thoughts, and perceptions, and the character's words, actions, thoughts, perceptions and feelings. I used the angle of the character attempting to see herself from the outside, but erring in her vision—a position which placed limits on my "knowledge" of the character.

Earlier I spoke of the writer's voice, which I related to his vision of life and which includes his entire personality. Now, to that voice I would add two more voices: the story voice, which is the pace, the music, the tone of the story; and the voice of the viewpoint character, since it is through his eyes that we see everything that happens. Actually, it is impossible to separate all these voices, fused as they are into a creation that has passed through a maturing process in the author's mind and found its way to the page, either in harmony or dissonance. But for the sake of clarity, let us for a moment consider the voice of the viewpoint character.

If a story is told in the first person through a character (and not the author), then that character's voice is ever-present, and the writer, like the method actor, must know the character's every thought, act, feeling and desire. He must know his truth, his conscious and unconscious life, what he wants, or thinks he wants, and the difference between the two. My story "Don't Call Me Darling" (*Redbook*), was written from such a viewpoint. I had to know my character's attitude toward herself as a woman pursuing a career. I had to know how she felt about women's rights in general. And how she felt about friendship and human communication. I had to understand her intellect, her ambitions, her habits, and her insights. When she spoke, she revealed herself as a careful individual, and this voice had to remain consistent throughout the story, even though some of her attitudes were undergoing a change.

When an author knows the details of action and speech in a

character, he is in control of his material. He can become more familiar with his character by spending time with him, engaging him in conversation or argument, as if he were a living entity. He may even want to get up from his typewriter to act out a detail, a gesture, or an entire scene, in order to visualize it more clearly in his mind. Creating characters, seeing them come to life, is an exciting experience.

The entire experience of a story, from start to finish—and it may cover a period of several years—is an exciting one, in spite of the hard work, frustration and failures. Not a small portion of that excitement lies in the discoveries that are made, for in any work of creative imagination one looks for insights. What does the story have to say? Does it reinforce a shallow view of life? Or does it open up new insights for the viewpoint character? When I write a story about a character who seems very real to me, am I not at the same time making a discovery about myself? Writing, like acting, is an experiment in living. It is looking at life from another viewpoint. And life can be exciting wherever it is lived, or re-created— on the stage, or on the page.

31

THE NOVEL SYNOPSIS
Your Best Selling Tool

By Serita Deborah Stevens

One of the most difficult problems in writing a novel may be preparing the synopsis, knowing just what it involves and what makes it different from a query, an outline, or a summary. Writing a good synopsis is a skill every novelist today must master.

Most editors, if interested in your novel on the basis of your query, will ask for your synopsis and opening chapters, often called a "partial." If that passes muster, you will then be asked for the complete manuscript. Established writers may be offered a contract on the basis of a partial, but a not-yet-published author will usually be required to submit the complete manuscript first.

The query

The query letter should indicate time, setting, and type of novel—especially if the company publishes more than one genre—and describe the major characters, their problems, their relationship to the other characters, and how the problems are resolved. The query should also include your qualifications and a summary of any special research you have done in preparing to write this novel. Indicate if the book is historical or contemporary. The query letter should be no more than two pages long.

Here is an example:

Dear Editor:
Enclosed find my partial of *Tame the Wild Heart,* a romance novel of about 85,000 words, which takes place in James II's court of Ireland.
Roxanna Alden, 19, niece of the great Irish general Patrick Sarsfield, hates James for what he did to her mother and vows her revenge in the only way she knows how—spying. She knows it would hurt her uncle, who supports James, if he found out, but she cannot let a man like James rule her beloved Ireland.

To her horror, she finds her assignment is to spy on Sebastian Steele, 30, her uncle's aide-de-camp.

Despite her own misgivings she is attracted to Sebastian. With the political intrigues of the day swirling about them, Roxanna must decide if she will betray the memory of her mother, or betray her heart.

In researching this book, I spent time in Ireland and at the British Museum in London.

My previous books are *This Bitter Ecstasy* and *A Dream Forever.*

Sincerely,

Sometimes you can use one or two sentences that sum up the story. For *Torrid January* I wrote: Will the D.A. prosecute the man she loves or will she first prove his innocence?

Also in your query tell the editor about your previous writing experience, whether, for instance, you've worked as a copywriter or done articles for a local newspaper, or related work. Also describe special knowledge that qualifies you to write about the subject. If your heroine is a dancer and you are, too—say so.

A query letter like the one above was my entrée to the Tapestry (Pocket Books) line. The editor then asked to see my partial, then my detailed synopsis.

Often "outline" and "synopsis" are used interchangeably, but they really mean two different things. The outline is only the barest of bones and is often used by the author in plotting the synopsis. I consider the outline for the author's use only; it states the facts but seldom gets into the emotional aspects of the story.

Here is a sample:

Chapter One: Roxanna learns of her new duty. Meets Sebastian as they both go into the castle together. He sees mud on her dress. Does he know where she has been? Will he tell her uncle?

Chapter Two: Attracting the eye of the King, she must fend him off. Sebastian helps her. She should be grateful, but she's angry he had to help her. She becomes ill at the ball. Uncle Patrick asks Sebastian to see her safely home to the manor.

Chapter Three: Waking after the fourth day of illness, she realizes Sebastian has been there taking care of her all the time. Has she said anything? She also realizes today is the day she must meet her contact. Can she ride back to Dublin in her ill state? She must.

Chapter Four: Sebastian finds her trying to leave and locks her in the room. She manages to get out and rides the following night.

This type of outline could go on for twelve chapters, or could be in

A.B.C. Roman numeral style. While writing, keep in front of you as a guide an outline listing each chapter and the scenes to go in it. But you must do a synopsis as well, and it is the synopsis of the full narrative that is sent to the editors.

The synopsis

The synopsis is often the first thing the editor reads, and it must be of sufficient interest to persuade her to read your first chapter.

Most beginning writers have trouble with the synopsis because they don't understand the necessity for immediacy, for action, for drawing the editor into a story. Instead, they philosophize for pages about the worthwhile objectives of their novel and the goals of their characters—without really touching the heart of the story.

Remember: The synopsis is your selling tool. It must hook your reader/editor just as your first chapter must in the next stage. The synopsis should show your writing at its best and prove to the editor that you know how to construct a fast-paced story. I know of several cases in which novels were bought or rejected, solely on the synopsis.

The hook I used in my synopsis of *Bloodstone Inheritance* follows:

After the sudden accidental death of her mother, Elizabeth Ann Larabee discovers a letter indicating someone other than Zebulon Larabee had fathered her. Who? Beset by curiosity, forced to sell off what she and her mother had, Elizabeth journeys to the thriving river town of Aberdeen, Illinois, to her mother's old home. She feels here she will find a clue to her natural father.

For *Spanish Heartland:*

Jersey Jordon couldn't believe her luck. Professor Tomas Ramirez, one of Spain's leading historical experts, had agreed to let her come study with him for the year, and to live with a Spanish noble family in Seville.

And for *Tame the Wild Heart:*

May, 1689, Dublin, Ireland:

Hating the English Catholic King James II and his court for what they did to her mother, Roxanna Alden has become a spy for the forces of William III. Being the niece of the Earl of Lucan, Patrick Sarsfield, a man highly regarded by James, Roxanna has no difficulty in getting information to pass on. The difficulty she does have is in keeping her feminine identity a secret from her contact and in coping with the nosey Sebastian Steele, Lord Bristol, her uncle's trusted aide.

On a misty, damp night, Roxanna is waiting for her contact on the bridge. There had been no time to change since she had to go straight to the ball that James was giving. She detests these parties as much as she detests James, but she does get good gossip there. . . .

In the beginning of all my synopses, I indicate who the heroine is and something of what the major problem will be, as well as the place and setting. To hook the reader (editor), think of the most crucial point of the story. This is usually where your novel starts (but not always); it comes at a point at which the heroine or hero is up against some problem or anxiously awaiting the outcome of a crucially important situation.

When the novel manuscript is first being considered by a publisher, the synopsis alone may be sent to several different people in a publishing house who decide if they want to read the whole manuscript. Seldom does a single editor have say over purchase of a book. The editor usually uses the synopsis in the sales meeting when she is trying to push for the acceptance of your book. It is the synopsis that is sent to the cover artists and blurb writers.

The synopsis is the outline with meat on it—just enough meat to give your skeleton form, but not enough to flesh it out fully. Making your synopsis too detailed will sometimes lead to a rejection. In one case, I made the mistake of mentioning in the synopsis that the heroine crossed herself at a crisis moment (since she was a good Irish Catholic). Immediately, I had a call from the editor. "We don't want religious books." The fact was, there was no religion in the book, but mentioning this incident in the synopsis made it seem so.

The synopsis should be in narrative form, usually in present tense (though some writers prefer past), including the premise of the story, and a bit about the characters. You want to get across not only who your characters are but their motives, emotions, and reactions. In these few pages, show the conflict that will develop between the characters, as well as the conflict that starts the novel moving. This building of tension is what will hook the editor. You should also include major turning points of your plot, as well as beginning, middle, and end. If the book is sexy, then sex should be mentioned in the synopsis.

Sometimes, I find it necessary to throw in a bit of dialogue or description, especially if I'm doing a historical novel. This will illuminate the character and her desires and will also give background for the story.

Editors have complained of writers ending their synopsis with: "Read the rest of this exciting novel to see what happens." I can almost guarantee you that this kind of come-on for an undisclosed ending will get your story rejected immediately. It's the mark of a novice. Editors want to know that all the loose ends are tied up and the story is brought to a satisfactory and satisfying conclusion.

Although the synopsis doesn't need to reveal all your secret twists and turns, include enough to catch the reader's interest. Don't be coy and cutesy, but do pack as much excitement and drama into these few pages as you can.

Not only must the synopsis open with a hook, but secondary characters who will be important to your story must be described and the viewpoint revealed. Give enough background about your characters to make them believable. If you're writing a suspense novel, requiring foreshadowing, mention the clues and indicate which are followed up and how. Action must be well spaced throughout the story. Because it is not necessary to put every scene into the synopsis, what you give the editor may not necessarily follow the chronological progression of events—but you should be clear on where each part of the story comes and how each scene fits, leading to a logical conclusion.

Some writers prefer to present their synopsis chapter by chapter—similar to what I did with the outline, only in much more depth. If so, write about four or five paragraphs per chapter—one for each major scene. Writers also sometimes complete the first three chapters and then synopsize the last part of the book in two or three pages.

I have found that this last method is not acceptable to most editors because, as I have said, they will usually read the synopsis first and send the synopsis around to other editorial readers. Doing a straight narrative rather than a chapter-by-chapter synopsis helps the story flow. If you want to do a chapter-by-chapter synopsis first, then by all means do so. You may then find it easier to make the synopsis tighter when you do it in narrative form.

In the sample one-page synopsis for my novel *For Love Betrayed* (see page 162), much of the first part describes events that had happened before the book opens, but are necessary to explain the story background and indicate what is happening to Montana McCormick, my heroine, *now*. Then I mention the major characters and two minor ones as well as three of the major turning points.

A lot happens in between those points, but I gave the editor only enough to hook her—enough, it turned out, to have her ask for the first few chapters and a more detailed synopsis.

The "mechanics"

As for "mechanics" of presentation, the majority of my synopses are single-spaced (since editors do no editing here), but I double-space between paragraphs. However, if you have elite type and the margins are small, you can double-space the entire synopsis for readability.

My synopsis can be as short as three pages or as long as twenty. There is no rule that applies to novels. Generally, the shorter your synopsis, the better. The average length for an 80,000-word book is six pages (single-spaced). As a guideline, I would say:

55–65,000—3–4 pages
75–90,000—5–6 pages
100–125,000—8–10 pages
150,000+—10–14 pages

Before you write your synopsis, it's important to have your plot worked out fairly well. That doesn't mean that in writing the novel you have to stick exactly to the synopsis. Often, as I start writing, the story changes because the characters take over, but if the editor has bought your novel on the basis of the synopsis, you're going to want to discuss any major changes with her. There are writers who can write super synopses but fail when it comes to writing the book, just as there are authors who can write great books but fail when it comes to doing a tantalizing synopsis. Professional writers must do both well.

Sample Synopsis. . . .

FOR LOVE BETRAYED

Montana McCormick is in love again but she is also scared. Her first marriage was a tragedy—more so than anyone knows. Shane Hunter tries to convince her to let go, to love him but he doesn't know the past that plagues her.

Having moved from a small Southern California town to the West Hollywood area, where she had hoped to "get lost," Montana found that she could not forget what had happened and the death of her husband. An abused wife, she had longed many times to take a gun to him but had not. Only when his mistreatment makes her lose her longed-for child, does Montana verbalize her threat—overheard by others.

Not wanting his property (wife) to leave, he comes after her with his gun. In self defense, Montana hits him with the fire stoker. He is knocked out. The stress and injury he had caused her make her faint.

She wakes in the hospital to learn that she is accused of her husband's death. Had she really killed him? She doesn't think so but he is dead and with his rich family, she is sure that she will be found guilty.

Escaping from the hospital, she goes to L.A. where she changes her name and finds herself falling in love with Shane. She wants to trust him with her past but doesn't know if he will love her or if he will treat her in the same way.

Shane's sister, who does not like Montana, finds out about the past. She tells Shane. He is shocked and wishes that she would have confided in him but wants to know what happened and wants her to know that he thinks she's innocent.

Going to her home, he finds that she has fled back to the town. Montana has decided that she cannot be free of the past until she learns what has happened. The house had not yet been sold so she goes there as she tries to reconstruct the events of that night.

She is surprised to find her brother-in-law, Holt, there. Holt has longed for her secretly for some time and admits that he had killed his brother because he could not stand what was happening to her. He wanted to follow her but could not find her. This is the first Montana has known of his love.

Shane comes and realizes what is happening. Holt realizes that Montana will not be his and tries to make her come with him by force. She cannot testify if she is married to him. Either that or he shoots her. If he cannot have her, no one can. Shane attacks him. In the struggle, the gun goes off and Holt is stunned. Shane goes to Montana to comfort her. Holt regains consciousness and gets the gun—but turns it on himself. He would rather die than face the charges of killing his brother and tells Montana how he loves her.

Shane and Montana return to L.A. to get married.

32

LEAVE THEM WANTING MORE

By Jean McConnell

THERE is an old adage in the theatre—always leave them wanting more. This might with profit be borne in mind by the writer of short stories. Perhaps the essential difference between the novel and the short story is that in writing novels you can meander—take time off to explore the byways—while in short story writing you must keep to the main road. But this could make for a pretty dull journey unless the way is enhanced by the writer's art.

So, the aim of the short story writer is to find the most economical way to convey an important point—a colorful image, at the same time moving the narrative forward. Sometimes it's just the choice of a single word: "The house was afire" does not conjure up the same picture as "The house was ablaze."

It is in dialogue that a writer can make points most speedily. We may laugh at a line like "You Jane . . . Me Tarzan," but in its context it puts across Tarzan's potential to learn to speak, the strong man's vulnerability, and his awakening sexuality.

It is an excellent test of a writer's ability to compress a sometimes complicated story line into short revealing speeches. Whereas in films the pictures provide the background detail, in the short story everything must be filtered in with no noticeable holdup in the main thrust of the plot.

How to do it? Where are the main opportunities?

It is in the opening paragraph of a story that the writer can make the most mileage. Often it is a good plan to begin the story where the action is already on its way, to plunge straight into a conversation. Here the dialogue must convey an idea of the setting and what has happened before, as well as some characterization and sufficient hint of conflict to make the reader want to know what is going to happen next.

Take the following example. This is from a short story of mine

159

entitled, "Remember Me?" The story had to reach quite a high peak of drama in a very little time; therefore, all relevant information had to be fed in speedily, yet without coming over as bald fact:

"Remember me?"
The voice was at my elbow. I turned. The blue eyes smiled up into mine, the pert nose wrinkled, the pale gold hair swung sideways, shimmering. Shorter. It had once been waistlength.
The other wedding guests surged around us. My awareness of them blurred. Only she, standing there before me, was in sharp focus.
"Remember me? Elizabeth?"
Yes. I remember you.
This was the girl who took from me my first love. Who can ever forget that girl? Who ever forgets that first love? Even now, so long after, in this crowded room—standing nearby a husband I had loved dearly for five years—even now the memory came back to me painfully.

We have the setup—a wedding—a sudden meeting of old friends. Note the description of Elizabeth: the detail in which our heroine assesses her is the first point of significance. Her immediate reaction is intensified by the use of italics. Then we get a basic fact—Elizabeth stole our heroine's first boyfriend. So when we learn that her husband is nearby, we are aware of the possible threat.

One could have described the heroine's looks, or what the bride and groom were like—whether they were friends or relations or whatever. But none of this is necessary. The whole of the story then happens in the few minutes it takes the two young women to exchange half a dozen sentences. It is a memory replayed in the heroine's head, only coming back to real life when she has to introduce her husband to the predatory Elizabeth and find he seems to know her. Again, the finale is brief but the heroine's relief is complete, and the outcome entirely satisfactory for her.

"Is that woman a friend of yours?" he asked.
"She was. Once," I replied carefully.
He opened the car door and I climbed in.
Why, John? Why? Why? Why?
At last it came out as a word.
"Why?"
"That's the woman who broke up Tom's marriage. Six weeks later she left him flat."
"Oh."
"She's—" He hesitated, seeking the word.

160

It was important he should find the right one. Important to me. Too weak a term could indicate saloon-bar gossip. Too strong might imply a former intimacy.

"She's—?" I prompted.

"Unkind," he said simply.

It was the right word.

"I'm sorry if she's an old friend, honey." He patted my hand.

"No," I assured him as we moved off. "I scarcely remember her."

Another important point is to make every word not only count in its own right and move the tale along, but reveal something useful about the situation or characters at the same time.

Take this opening of a story of mine called "Fresh Fields":

Beginning (a)

"Gilly, would you look after the farm for us while we're away?"

"But I've no experience with animals."

"Oh, there are only a few hens and ducks and pigs."

Beginning (b)

"I'd sooner you took over than anyone else, Gilly."

"But I've no experience with animals."

"Rover loves you."

"I mean the hens. And the ducks. And the pigs!"

In example (a) we have learned the heroine's name and the basic situation: a request for help on the farm.

In example (b) we have learned that our heroine is someone to trust. That she's warmhearted. That she's rather comically timid of farm creatures. Already the readers feel they know this nice girl and suspect the story is likely to be humorous. The number of words used is virtually the same, so it was much better to use example b, which immediately established the style in which I wanted to write the story and also implied a lot more than example a.

Setting the style of a story at the outset is important. Take this opening, for instance, which is from my story, "The Search":

There was hardly a depth of soil between the kitchen flagstones and bedrock to bury a few fingers, let alone the body of a full-grown man—even if he were of slender build. For that matter the tell-tale signs of recent disturbance were not present. The Inspector brushed back the small tuft of weak hairs which were all that remained of an unruly boyish forelock. Two weeks, he pondered, two

161

weeks the man had been missing. Not long. But long enough for a man who had said, "See you tomorrow night, Jack," to the barman at the pub. Too long for the man whose pedigreed Jersey cow had been due to calf at any moment. Long indeed for the daughter of the grocer who suspected she was carrying his child and believed he'd be pleased.

We know at once it's a crime story, and the remark about the fingers signals that it might be a gruesome one. The reference to "slender build" is also a plant for later—when the man is found sewn into a mattress. The description of the Inspector's hair engages the readers' sympathy and puts them on his side.

This story was only 1,100 words and all essential information was very usefully packed into the last three sentences of that first paragraph.

In writing a short story, the writer doesn't have much room to move, so he should go for the table and chairs and forget the cocktail cabinet and plant stand, by which I mean, concentrate on what is absolutely necessary and eliminate the trimmings—unless they are trimmings that are highly significant. Consider the following section from a story about a fairground stunt. A man is fasting to the point of death. He speaks to his wife.

"I'm finished."
"What ya talking about? Lyin' there with nothin' to do. You got it easy this time."
Easy, yes. Easy compared with holding a lighted candle to your flesh till the blisters rose. Easier than biting out the throat of a live chicken. He'd done these things to please the crowds. And the others for her private pleasure to earn the oblivion of the pinch of white powder she supplied in reward.

In a novel you might go on: "There was a time when . . .etc." But here there is no need—or time—to spell it out further. This particular story was called "All the Fun at the Fair," and the title itself added irony since it was a tragedy involving both murder and suicide.

Any author who has written stage plays recognizes that he must get the exposition over speedily and cleverly. Praise be for the invention of the telephone, whereby essential facts can be so swiftly imparted. The short story writer must also think along these lines, endeavoring to lay out his background entertainingly yet wasting no time in getting to the heart of the matter.

In a first draft, when you are finding your way through the plot, it is

162

inevitable that you overwrite. It is in the paring down that the challenge lies. Any story can be reduced to its fundamentals. What you are aiming at is compressing the length, while retaining the color, the flavor, the style. Things are easier if the matter is racy, light or humorous. Then a single word can jump-cut you along with good effect.

> "Come up for a nightcap," he said.
> "All right," I said.
> Madness.

Or take this passage from my story, "Spring Break":

> "What a marvelous break for you," everyone said.
> "Yes!" I responded, and smiled and smiled.
> Paul drove us to the dockside and his farewell was loving. As he waved from the quay, I thought I saw him glance at his watch. But perhaps not. I had to believe not.

The significance of the clock-watching—the impatience to be away—might have been dwelt on, but instead, the repetition of the word "not" works faster and surely better.

"Spring Break" was my original title for the story, but as published it was called "The Scent of Mimosa." My title had a double meaning: (a) a holiday and (b) the end of a love affair.

The magazine's title was perfectly relevant to the story and more romantic. In the end, it was just a matter of emphasis. Since it *was* a very romantic story, the magazine's choice was probably the right one.

However seductive, the descriptive passage is a space-waster unless it fulfills a secondary function of, say, implying the mood or attitude of a character. Consider the opening of "Spring Break":

> It's the wrong time to leave the city. The thought nagged me warningly. Despite the bleak wind whipping through the colorless buildings and the windowbox empty and dank, it was the wrong time. Because of her. She had come into my life only a month or two ago. The change in Paul had been gradual, but it signalled itself at last even to my resistant mind.

This can perfectly well be written:

> There was no doubt about it. It was the wrong time to leave the city. Because of her. She had come into my life only a month before. I knew it instantly. The change in Paul was obvious. I didn't want to understand. But I did.

Both examples are quite economical. The first takes time to establish a chillier mood. But the second gets straight to the point and thrusts the reader into the situation. It is for the writer to balance what he needs against what he has time for.

Often this task falls to the editor. And let it be said that the best of them are still highly skilled in this field and can cut to the bone yet still preserve the writer's original intention.

Nevertheless, the professional writer designs his piece to the correct length for the prospective market. And if it's to be the short story, then he must be fast on his feet. Ponder the fact that reducing the sauce usually enriches it. Let this be the objective.

Never forget that by confining yourself to the intriguing hint—the evocative word—you will have given your reader the infinite pleasure of using his imagination.

33

THE HIDDEN CENSOR

By Diane Lefer

Ten years ago, I had file cabinets full of fiction I'd written, and not a single page of it had ever seen print. Today, I make my living as a writer and, looking back, I'm convinced that the major turning points in my creative life had less to do with discovering tricks of the trade than with recognizing the personal attitudes and emotions that were standing in my way.

The first important lesson, which didn't come easily, was:

Don't worry about what people are going to think of you.

One day, about ten years ago, I read a novel by Chaim Potok called *My Name Is Asher Lev,* about a Jewish artist, from a deeply religious Hasidic family, whose breakthrough as a painter comes when he incorporates crucifixion symbolism into his work—not that he wishes to convert, but the Christian imagery helps him express his perceptions of life. The result: Asher Lev gains renown in the art world, but his family cannot understand or forgive what he has done. The moral: The artist must express his own truth, no matter how painful the consequences may be.

Most of us don't face as clear-cut and difficult a choice as Asher Lev. Our families may not always approve of our work, but they aren't going to turn away from us in shock, either. But Chaim Potok's novel shook me up anyway. For the first time, I recognized the hidden censor who'd been at work in my head, interfering with the words I put down on paper without my even knowing it.

I had heard, of course, about other writers' inhibitions. Marcel Proust, for example, couldn't write *Remembrance of Things Past* until after his mother's death; he was too concerned that what he said might hurt her. But I'd never thought I suffered from that kind of block. After all, I had been writing stories for years. And anyway, I didn't think I had anything to hide.

165

In fact, every time I sat down to write, somewhere in the back of my mind, I was worried about what my family, friends, neighbors, and people I barely knew would think of my morals, my attitudes, my mental health. I had not been writing the heart and guts into my stories; I'd been avoiding certain styles and subjects, as though I was afraid people might confuse me with my characters, or that a story rooted in deep emotion might be too personally revealing. Yes, I wanted people to read and like my work. But I also wanted them to like *me*.

And I finally became convinced that you cannot do good work until you stop worrying about being liked. If you really want to be a writer, you finally have to make up your mind to ignore the possible consequences and pull out all the stops.

Anyway, after reading *My Name Is Asher Lev*, I sat down and wrote what turned out to be my first published story ("Huevos," published in *Redbook*). The plot hinged in part on a sexual double entendre, and I awaited publication nervously, steeling myself in advance for what my parents might say. (Remember, no matter how old you may be, your parents can still make you jump through hoops!) To my relief, they liked the story very much.

My second published story was about a widow from Maine who moves down to New York City. No problem, I thought. But this time around, my father was very unhappy with what he read. He thought the story was weird and that people would think it was the product of a "twisted mind"—which was not the kind of mind he wanted his daughter to have.

My father's reaction had been impossible to predict. So even though it upset me, it also liberated me. Trying to avoid offending people not only hurt my work—it was futile, as well.

I'm not suggesting that you be utterly ruthless and trample on other people's feelings without a second thought. If your work is largely autobiographical, your accounts of real events may hurt real people. And writers do get sued for libel—though I've noticed that while people do recognize events they've been involved in, they are less likely to recognize characters based on themselves, especially when the portraits are not complimentary. So think carefully and make up your own mind about your view of ethics, loyalty, and privacy.

For my part, when I deal with material drawn from life, I try to be semi-ruthless. That is, I get it all down on paper, no holding back. I don't consider anyone's feelings till the piece is done. Then there's time enough to decide whether to send it out and face the possible consequences, or to revise it and change all the identifying details, or to withhold it from publication, at least for the time being.

But no matter how careful and considerate you may be, no matter how entirely you rely on your imagination instead of your experience, get ready to face the fact that you're bound to ruffle some feathers.

When my first Regency romance *Twice Bought Bride* came out (published under a pseudonym by Dell), my elderly aunt accused me of lifting characters and incidents from our family history. I cannot imagine anything more removed from our family experience than Regency romance, and so I denied the charge and asked Aunt Anna which sections and characters she had in mind. She refused to discuss it further and only gave me a very knowing smile.

Be a good parent to your characters.

After talking about my father, it's only fair that I confess my own wrongdoing.

After giving my characters life, I tend to forget that they then have minds of their own. Again and again, like a mother who insists her kid get all A's and become a doctor, I've tried to make my characters conform to my preconceived expectations and ideas, i.e., my plot.

In trying to move a story along, I've tried to force characters to phone people they had no desire to talk to, to avoid old friends without any reason, to go places they didn't want to visit, and even to commit suicide. I've been terrible. I recently tried to break up a marriage, but every time I headed this poor couple toward divorce, the dialogue became artificial, and the prose fell flat. I was manipulating my characters, moving them like puppets, putting them through their paces just to set them up for the next turn of the plot. No wonder it all rang false. The couple, as I had developed them up to that point, didn't want to be divorced. I was forcing this momentous event on them for my own purposes . . . and it didn't work. At last, I acknowledged their right to stay together, and I modified my story line to take their desires into account.

If you want your characters to ring true to the reader, they have to seem real. And you get that effect by treating them as if they are. When you invent a story, you may feel it's one place in your life where you have total control. Forget it! Like a good parent, provide your characters with an environment and stimulation, then try to stay open-minded. Let their words and actions flow from their personalities and don't arbitrarily interfere. Develop them—but with respect.

Get to know your enemies.

For me, the purpose of literature is to expand the limits of each person's particular world and experience, and by the use of imagination, to transcend the mental habits and assumptions of daily life. The writer, like the reader, needs to explore other worlds. But at the same time, we're constantly told to "Write about what you know." And so, many writers rely heavily on autobiographical material. This can be a real problem.

People often ask me to look at fiction they've written, drawn from real-life experience and based on their recent heartaches and problems—the inexplicable cruelty of a lover, the tyrannical attitude of a parent, the irresponsible or self-destructive behavior of a child. With a few shining exceptions, these stories tend to be long on self-pity and self-justification, and short on real understanding. This is no coincidence—if we really had any wisdom about our own situations, we wouldn't get into such terrible conflicts to begin with. When it comes to our own lives, we are often blind to true insight.

As time goes by, it becomes easier to look back on, say, the folly of youth. But if you are trying to write about pain you've recently suffered—because you think it's a dramatic story, or because it seems therapeutic to do so—my advice is not to write from your own point of view. You've probably spent enough time as it is, trapped within your own feelings. Instead, stretch your imagination, and try to get inside the head of the person who hurt you.

An example: Back at the end of the '60s, I wrote a novel (unpublished) about an idealistic young student who falls under the spell of a charismatic writer who visits her college campus. The man turns out to be a fraud, and his followers—including my heroine—suffer tragic consequences.

Well, at the time, I was an idealistic young college student, and I very much understood and knew the desire to believe in something and someone. I identified with my heroine and naturally chose to write the story in her voice and from her point of view.

Editors who read the manuscript didn't see what was so engaging about the villain and why my heroine was so impressed. So I rewrote and expanded, amplifying her obsession and explaining *her* and what she wanted to see in this man. Each revision was progressively worse. The heroine became progressively more desperate and pathetic. The bad guy became progressively more of a symbol and less of a person. Like the heroine and like me, the book was very intense and earnest. It was also very bad.

Several years ago, I came upon the manuscript in the back of my file cabinet. I cringed a bit when I reread it, but I still liked certain passages in the scene in which my student and false hero first meet. Maybe, I thought, a short story could be salvaged from the novel's wreck.

I had always realized that the young woman never understood the motivations of the man she chose to admire. But as I reread the pages again, I saw for the first time that he was a mystery to me, too. I didn't know what would make someone act the way he did. Totally identified as I'd been with the character who was most like myself, I hadn't been aware that I was every bit as blind as she.

It suddenly occurred to me to let this nasty but charming villain tell the story in his own voice. To do that, I would humbly have to give up my own values, transcend my own ignorance, and enter foreign terrain: the enemy's seemingly inexplicable mind.

When the resulting story, "Peonies," was published, I was satisfied that my charismatic bad guy had come to life. He was not a sympathetic character, but he had at last emerged as a complicated human being and not just a symbol of evil.

As writers, we aim to explore and illuminate areas of life, experience, and the human heart, so even as we work at developing our craft, we can fall short if we fail to seek new levels of insight or if we neglect our own personal growth.

When we summon up the strength to stand by our art and accept the consequences, when we learn to relinquish total, arbitrary control, when we develop empathy and learn to put ourselves in the shoes of characters who perplex us or threaten us, we may conceivably become better people. We will certainly become better writers.

34

TWENTY QUESTIONS TO ASK A CHARACTER

By Winifred Madison

Dig deeper! How many times does an author hear this advice? Characters are the life and breath of a story. Get your reader to care about what happens to them and you have won him over. But how do you do this?

First, most important of all, the character must seem alive to you, so very much alive that you feel as though you were inside his skin. This may happen instantly as you pass someone on the street or meet someone at a party and immediately you know something instinctively about this person and you feel you must use him in one of your stories. It may be a matter of luck that has no logical explanation. It simply happens.

The source does not matter so much as the *depth* and *insight* you develop. I get to know and understand my characters the same way I discover those individuals who come into my life. It's a mixture of first impressions, concrete factual knowledge, that mysterious "knowing" that comes about when you spend time with a person. Time is the key word.

Make up a dossier for each of your principal characters, either before you write your story or after you've completed the first draft. The twenty questions that follow will help you "dig deep," to probe the depths of your characters so you will get to know them.

1. Pretend you are walking down the street and you see your character for the very first time. Quick now—what word or phrase leaps to your mind? It may be one word: tyrant, drudge, darling, dreamer, flirt, macho, slob . . . anything at all. It may be a phrase, a warning, such as "Watch out!" or "Me first!" It could be a foolish giggle or a friendly hello or a plaintive, "I really wouldn't know . . ." No matter how far-

fetched or illogical this initial impact may be, it may prove a valuable insight into the essence of that particular person.

One day a young woman came to my door—attractive, blonde, smiling easily. The first words that filled my mind were "California, country sun, remarkably good health in every way." I made her sixteen years old, a capable 4-H girl, and she became the heroine of my young adult novel, *Dance With Me*. As I wrote it, that first impression stayed in my mind.

Some authors, attracted by a photograph or illustration in a newspaper or magazine, will clip it and use it as a model. A good idea.

2. Quickly following the initial impact will be the general physical impression of the person. Again, do not try to think of the words you may ultimately use when you write the story; let them come freely to your mind: "a burly block of a man," "a sunbeam," "a weed," "a wisp," "a full-blown cabbage rose about to shed its petals." The posture, the stance, the stride and rhythm of movement, possibly some body gestures, as well as the bulk and density of the physical build, will immediately give you clues to your character.

3. Are you reminded of an animal or an object? If a comparison happens to come to mind, explore it. Some people definitely resemble birds, cats, rodents, or monkeys, and in the case of inanimate objects such disparate things as a bus, or a feather duster, or a fragile wine glass. Be careful about clichés, the too frequent "birdlike woman" or the "China doll heroine."

4. Can you sense a color in your character, something beyond skin color or purely physical features? Certain psychics claim to see colors emanating from personalities. We cannot always go that far, but we may have the impression of an insistent color, a "brown personality," or a radiant red-gold, or a dismal blue-gray. One person may make you think of bright primary colors, while a subtle shifting of gray tones characterizes another.

5. What kinds of clothes does your character wear? Here is an important key to his psyche. Often people dress to conform to what they

believe is their social status: We all wear uniforms. However, we may be fooled, as individuals sometimes dress according to their fantasies and unconscious or unfulfilled desires—interesting and worthwhile for a fiction writer to explore. And use. For example, the middle-aged woman who wears too much makeup and designer jeans meant for her daughter or even for her granddaughter, may be saying she doesn't want anyone to know her age, or that she has a real dread of getting old and unattractive to young people (young men?), or that she wants to relive her youthful, romantic experiences. A businessman who wears western boots, shirt, and string tie and carries his attaché case to his big-city office is saying something important about himself and his dreams. It can be a defiance of convention or a yearning for a carefree youth he never had.

6. The person's voice is also revealing. Can you describe its tonal quality in one word, such as, soft, soothing, abrasive, enthusiastic, energetic, etc.? Does your character speak with an accent, a lisp, a certain eccentricity? How does he use words? What does he say, and what does he leave unsaid? As you learn more about this man, you should be able to imitate him, the quality of voice, the expression, suggest the very words he would use. Become an actor or actress as you write, saying out loud your character's speeches until you are convinced that is exactly how they must sound.

7. Where does your character live during the course of the story? How much of his immediate environment is forced on him and how much of it does he control? Does he like it? What does it mean to him? Is it possible he wants to leave it and if so, why?

You will not need and should not include in your story or novel every detail of your hero or heroine's life, but the more you know about it, the more you will understand some of the reasons for his or her actions.

8. Where and when was he born? Where did he live during his childhood? What country? What environment, i.e., a city, a small town, a rural area, mountains, the coast? How has this background shaped his personality? Was anything in particular happening historically?

9. What were the earliest and theoretically the most important influences? What of his parents, his siblings, relatives, friends, teachers, early loves? Here is where you will find many keys to the personality you are studying.

10. Every decade has new problems, changing standards, different moods. The forties are not like the fifties, nor are the fifties like the sixties, and so on. Does the one in which your hero formed his personality influence him in his actions and philosophy? Does he accept the standards of his time or does he rebel?

We have progressed beyond our first impression, although it should always stay with us. Can you imitate your character, walk like him, talk as he would, know exactly what he would think and how he would react to almost anything at all? If so, he is taking physical shape. Now try to get inside him. Know him better than he knows himself.

11. What is most important to him? What does he want more than anything else? Do you know his fantasies, his daydreams?

12. What is his conflict? If he has no problem, chances are he won't be interesting. Is his conflict imposed by circumstances, or does it emanate from within him? Suppose, for example, he is a young man who detests war and yet wishes to defend his country, a common dilemma for many young people today.

What of a woman who wants to get out and live by herself and yet fears she will lose her family if she does so?

Do you want your character to settle his conflict by himself, or will fate or circumstances do it for him?

13. How far will he go to get what he wants? Will he steal, commit a crime or perform an immoral act to achieve his goal? You may hook your reader by getting him to wonder about it along with you.

14. Here is a most telling question: What does your character fear the most? Does this keep him from achieving his ends?

15. More revealing areas. Cards, money, love. How much does winning matter to your character? How does he handle competition?

173

16. How does he react to children, and animals, foreigners, old people? How do you know? Would he kick his wife's dog if she weren't there to defend it? Would he carry a spider outside rather than kill it when it had crept into his bedroom? Would this woman refuse to rent a room to an oriental or a black or to someone who had children?

17. How does your character shape the plot? How does the plot shape him or her? Does he grow or change during the course of the story? If by any chance he remains the same, which should be unlikely, can you explain that?

18. How does this character interact with other members of the cast? Who acts as his foil? Who contrasts or complements your hero or heroine? Who or what threatens him?

19. By this time you've made quite a study of this character. Do you like him or her? What is undesirable or negative about him? What, no faults? Then such a character is likely to be b-o-o-ring. And not quite human. The same theory will hold for the villains of the piece. A person who is completely bad is only slightly less boring than one who is entirely good. Rembrandt used to advise mixing a little darkness in the light areas and a little light in the dark sections of a drawing. The same principle will make your characters more interesting.

20. Finally, what is there in your character that will make the reader care about what happens to him? Whether you are writing "the great American novel" or something more modest, your reader must be touched by your hero or heroine, or you have lost him. And what about you? Do you find yourself so involved that you hate to make your characters suffer? (Although you will have to do it anyway, because without suffering there is no story.)

A human being can be endlessly complicated. Twenty questions are only the first of many questions you will want to ask your character. What does he do on a stormy day? Does he cheat on his income tax? What does he like to eat? Where would he go on a vacation if he had a free choice and didn't have to think about money?

"Digging deeper" means living with your character day and night. It's one way of meeting interesting people!

35

THE LISTENING EAR

By Anne Chamberlain

"Dumb!" The unseen woman in the next booth exclaimed, "about as dumb as a coon in a tree, that's my opinion, and who knows better'n me?"

"You're the one as knows," an eager girlish voice supplied.

"More brains than you can shake a stick at, and turns them all the wrong way, that's my opinion. Why, let me tell you now what she done last Wednesday afternoon, nobody home, and in she snaked and I think she got into my parlor table drawer, read my postcards—my bills too, electric and the gas, she read, and that weren't the worst of it. Let me tell you . . ." The narrative slipped into a tantalizing whisper, incoherent to the casual listener. I was that listener, a traveler, enjoying a quick stopover meal at the village restaurant. Not having previously noticed the two women, I now realized that I probably wouldn't catch a good look if I left before they did. Fascinated, I lingered for a few minutes, and was rewarded with the suddenly loud, dramatic final line: "And then she ate the *whole* watermelon!"

Over the mountainous miles of the homeward drive, over the years since, this delectable tidbit remains one of the small treasures in my memory. A "treasure" it can be justly termed, for, with the intimate village atmosphere, the rural idiom and emphasis of the narrator, the avid (perhaps fawning?) attendance of her companion, this fragment limns a scene, hints at characterization, suggests numerous stories. What a sneaky, spiteful, absurd act, eating somebody's watermelon! And why would the marauder, obviously well known to the victim, indulge in so barbaric a feast? Were they feuding neighbors, rivals in quilting club contests, jealous sisters-in-law, or simply harborers of a longtime natural animosity? A humorous situation, certainly, which— as always with comedy—would be seasoned with sound psychological undertones. Over the countless possibilities, the listener/writer can muse, fantasize, and, in due time, select that which seems most suitable to his particular talents.

For me as an author, cultivating an astute ear for dialogue is a lifelong process. Having grappled with the task of presenting dramatic scenes on paper, of distilling ordinary speech for extraordinary effects, yet of preserving the tones and rhythm of natural talk, I have become a student, a collector, and a connoisseur. Mine is not a calculated eavesdropping. The phrases, fragments of discussion, and sometimes complete anecdotes that reach my ears by chance are tossed into the air wherever people gather and talk, free to any and all who pay attention. They are often delightfully unexpected, and in afterthought, may lend themselves to fascinating interpretations.

In restaurants, airports, stores, hotel lobbies, elevators, the listener finds rich fields to explore. Settings for arrivals and departures may be especially fruitful:

"Please," a woman clutches at the arm of her escort; they are standing in line at the airport, he with a gleaming briefcase, she—apparently—about to say goodbye: "I ask you once more, Arthur, please . . ." He does not answer, nor does he look at her. Her fingers tighten on his sleeve. "Arthur, I'm asking," she murmurs, her voice sinking into a whisper.

For what is she pleading? That he phone at the customary time tonight, forgetting this morning's argument? That he look up the wayward son, who in the city of the father's destination, has recently moved in with an objectionable girl friend? That he think more carefully before he accepts the promotion that will take them from the home and neighborhood she has learned to love? Is he usually "Arthur" to her or, in more relaxed moments, "Art"? Does he remain silent because he is angry, or merely bored?

The listener knows only that she is serious about something, that he is adamant. An alert ear learns the importance of inflection. How many dozens of ways there are of saying "please"! Politely, as a vocal punctuation, urgently, sardonically, savagely, humbly, sometimes a mixture of emotions pour into the single syllable. "It isn't what he said, it's the way he said it," is the frequent plaintive tagline of an anecdote, when the narrator remembers the direct quote but realizes that—in itself—this fails to capture the impact. It is the desperate, last-minute

176

quality of the airport woman's utterance, the breathlessness, the sleeve-clutching, the fading into a whisper that dramatizes her words. Were the writer to develop a story line from this episode, he would use the verbs, adjectives, and action detail to present the dialogue within its emotional context.

Perhaps Arthur is indeed expecting to be offered a promotion, his acceptance of which will take them and their children to a much larger city, a strange and—to Millicent, his wife—a frightening environment. It means transplanting their two youngsters, in sensitive early teen years, to more urban schools and (she suspects) more hazardous temptations. Ashamed as she is to admit it, she hates leaving the house she has cherished for years, the garden she has lovingly tended, the church and the women's clubs; oh, she loves him far more than any *place*, he surely knows this, but isn't she human, doesn't her own life, don't the lives of the children count? The present action, which seems to have evolved easily from Millicent's point of view, could be unfolded within the airport setting, as they arrive, check in, wait, continue the discussion that may have previously waxed into an argument, softened into mutual understanding, flared again into anger. Brief flashbacks, dramatizing the tensions, could be woven into the immediate scene, which builds to the last few minutes, as they stand in line. At this point, even though the situation may have been artfully developed, it would be temptingly easy to overwrite:

"Please," she begged wistfully, clutching at his sleeve, pouring her heart into this last minute entreaty, "I ask you once more, Arthur, please . . ."
Stone-faced, stubbornly silent, he stood, refusing to look at her.
"Arthur," tears surged into her voice. Her fingers tightened on his sleeve, as though she would hold him, draw him to her, fold him into her arms, "I'm asking . . ." Her voice sank into a whisper, a strangled sob.
He stared coldly and mutely into space.

This has too much trimming. Overembellishment is a weakness common to the writing of dialogue. If the author astutely employs other techniques, descriptions of characters and of setting, perhaps subjective delineation of the unspoken feelings of one or more of those concerned, the actual spoken exchange should need little adornment. Knowing Millicent and Arthur, through their airport wait and through the thoughts and the flashback episodes that have illuminated their tensions, the reader understands much of what is not spoken at their

177

parting. Seeing him board the plane, Millicent knows that some day she and the children will be boarding with him. Or she realizes, only dimly yet, as she turns from waving goodbye, that this time he is truly leaving, she is going home. One story possibility; airports bustle with them.

The listening author discriminates. It would impossible to hear, much less to heed, the countless words that may be spoken around one in the course of a crowded day. As a fiction writer, I have a built-in tape recorder, which, for my purposes, is more convenient and dependable than its mechanical counterpart. It receives constantly; it erases the superfluous; it may splice; it will store what seems worth keeping.

"I went downtown this morning—oh the loveliest day, I just can't tell you! Sunshine and breeze and spring everywhere, I danced, danced on my toes all the way, and right at the corner by the mailbox, you can't imagine who I saw, I ran right into her, I hadn't seen her for—you can't imagine how long!—centuries! And you'll never guess what she told me, she came right out with it—" the young woman babbles merrily to her hairdresser, a captive but not uninterested audience, "on the street, on the corner by the mailbox, I'll have you know, she told me, might have been saying, 'it's a nice day,' she was that nonchalant, she came right out with it—"

An individual's speech is as unique as his handwriting, his manner of dress, his voice, walk, gestures, his smile and his eyes. This woman talks in hyperbole, loves to prattle, and contrives through suspenseful hints to keep her audience attentive:

"She was divorced, that's what she said, cool as a cucumber, and then before I got over *that,* I mean I'd barely begun to digest it, she goes right on to say she's married again. Can you imagine! And all within five minutes, well no more than ten, and here I am, my jaw just dropping and she says, 'I thought you knew, didn't you know,' and I said no I didn't know, how could I, hadn't seen, hadn't heard a word about her in centuries and—" to a murmured question from the beautician, "didn't I tell you *who* she is? Well-l-l . . ." Into a genealogical chart she spins, spilling names, father, grandfather, uncle, aunts, first husband and, "a Hardquist, of course, and you do, well maybe you don't know the Hardquists but he, number one husband I mean, he was a chip off the old block, his father Jedson, *the* Jedson, and what I couldn't tell you, my dear, about Jedson Hardquist—"

Seated two chairs away in the beauty salon, I reflect that shocking news, delivered bluntly by a mailbox, might—for a minute or two— silence the babbler's torrential monologue. And I ponder over that woman, "as cool as a cucumber," with the mixed-up marital history. And what about Jedson? I will be hearing more, for I, too, am a captive audience.

In dramatizing the speech mannerisms of the babbler, who can rapidly become a loquacious bore, the writer must aim to convey her effect on others without producing a similar tedium in the reader. One quoted paragraph, like that above, can characterize her compulsive gushiness, and additional phrases will suggest all that is not on paper. While the incessant talker is particularly difficult to harness in dialogue, the need for pruning and culling applies to the speech of all characters.

"No, I didn't know about the Hardquists," the beautician interposes pointedly. She is tired of the monologue. Perhaps she dislikes scurrilous gossip; too much of it whirls around her shop. And is there, in the weary but gentle rebuke of her tone, a distaste for the whole carefree society, the smug, prosperous, much-married and divorced people about whom she hears so much? A story, a hundred or more stories could be written from the point of view of a skilled and patient beautician.

In contrast with the fluent monologuist, the terse speaker, who favors a form of verbal shorthand, poses a different challenge to the writer. Often his reticence can be dramatized through the speeches addressed to him. In the hotel lobby, I notice the young wife greeting her husband enthusiastically:

"How was your morning?"
"Same as ever." He kisses her amiably and takes her arm, steering her to the dining room.

She has come into town from suburbia. They will lunch together, and I reflect that she is hungry for excitement and news.

"Same?" She pouts, teasing him. "Oh, you, it's always the same, same, same," and pats his arm, "but what about Chalmers? Anything happen?"
He motions toward the hostess, they are conducted to a table, sit down, order cocktails.

From this overheard exchange, I spin an imaginative continuation, just enough to suggest more:

179

"You haven't told me about Chalmers. . . ."

"Fired," he lights a cigarette.

"Oh no! Oh how terrible, was he upset, how did he take it? Oh poor Lydia—"

He has opened the menu. "Think I'll have the steak."

"Did he come in? Did you see him? What did he *do?*"

"Yes," he smiles to the waitress, as she places the cocktails before them, "I think we'll order now."

With this taciturn man, who may have excellent reasons for not wanting to tell his wife about Chalmers, the problem is to convey what he does not choose to say; much can be achieved through action detail.

Fine stories have been written without a scrap of dialogue; others have consisted entirely of spoken words. Most authors use direct quotes at high dramatic points, emphasizing and advancing the narrative. Often, I become so absorbed with other aspects of the story that I do not give enough consideration to the question: Would this character say this in this way? By cultivating the listening ear, I am more aware of natural speech and more alert to those weaknesses that may be distilled into direct quotes.

I have learned to be wary of the overly structured sentence, the too complete and well-rounded paragraph. It is not inconceivable (in writing, nothing is!) for the anguished husband, leaving his wife, suitcase packed and hand on doorknob, to address her: "Much as I love you and always will, our marriage has become totally incompatible, is beyond the help of counselors, and is mutually erosive to our respective personalities." Not inconceivable, as this husband may be a person addicted to eloquence; one does imagine that, if he used such terms, his wife willingly opened the door for him. It is more likely that he would speak briefly, might shout, mumble, lunge out of the house. Under intense emotional pressure, a character's talk is usually jagged, sentences incomplete, feelings too deep for balanced, measured phrases.

A vehement discussion may go on for thousands of words, lasting a whole evening, and to report it literally would not only cover dozens of pages but would bury the story in the process. I am, therefore, aware that I must delete and, if I listen as an author may, I find myself deleting swiftly, editing what I hear, saving what is worthwhile.

"I told him in no uncertain terms," said the portly man at the bus stop, "that his attitude was depressing. demoralizing, and disappointing." He paused, groped for another alliterative adjective, exploded triumphantly, "destructive." He bit at his cigar. "Yes," I told him—"destructive!"

His companion nodded sagely and stroked his drooping moustache. "You told him off, Fred, you surely did. I wish I had your gift for language. But what'd he say? Fred, what *did* he say?"

The bus arrived, they climbed on together, still talking. . . .

The listening bystander will not know what he said. Or how he managed to be all of those adjectives, rolled into one, or were these faults pure imaginings of a pompous fellow worker? Was our denouncer guilty of the very accusations he so relished? A distinct possibility. A story? I muse.

Cultivating the listening ear is an educational process that helps me write dialogue I have never heard until I imagine the characters and what they are saying; it is also a rich source, an inexhaustible mine of material. Of perhaps a thousand tidbits that I overhear and speculate about, only one or two may combine within the ever mysterious creative self to produce a story. Constant entertainment is at my command. I can turn on that tape recorder which, in the depths of memory, is always waiting, brimming with ideas.

How did matters finally work out for Arthur and Millicent? Maybe he wasn't considering a promotion, after all. She might have been pleading because, in the city of his destination, there lived that former secretary, the golden-haired and lynx-eyed, the sly and determined, with whom Arthur was still in touch. He had said it would be stupid, plain unfriendly not to look her up, at least to telephone; why, she and Millicent had been on good terms, hadn't they? She had made the mistake of protesting and had lighted the match—or had the fire been simmering already? Another story.

The babbler in the beauty shop prates on. In the next chair may be Old Jedson Hardquist's third wife, young, sharp-eared, new to town, rapidly absorbing important information. Or the patient beautician, scissoring deftly, may have had, as her last client, the carefree "cool as a cucumber" woman who had met the babbler at the mailbox. Anything can happen; the listener can pick and choose.

How did poor Chalmers react to being fired? Will the eager wife ever learn details from her cautious husband? Was the portly man's unknown target actually "depressing, demoralizing, disappointing, and destructive"? Delectable, that phrasing, in its pompous smugness.

Come to think of it, how big was that watermelon?

181

36

VISUALIZING FICTION ON PAPER

By Dorothy Uhnak

WRITING began so far back in childhood that I literally cannot remember a time when I was *not* writing. I spent fourteen years of my adult life as a police officer in New York City. During all that time, I wrote continually, drawing on everything around me: the unique, exciting situations, the deadly boredom, the brutality, sadness, pain, humor (often macabre), the courage, cowardice, intelligence, stupidity, greed, anger, danger, and intense loyalty which characterize the working life of a police officer.

I was a capable police officer: I was promoted three times and awarded medals twice. I worked hard, was dedicated and earnest and concerned. Yet all the time, the writer in me was compiling events, feelings, atmosphere, emotions, situations for future use. *Policewoman,* semi-autobiographical, semi-fictional, was published during my tenure as a police officer and was my first attempt to set forth some things I had observed, learned, experienced, been a part of.

My first novel, *The Bait,* was published after I resigned from police work in order to devote myself more fully to writing and to continue my education. It was awarded the Edgar for the Best First Mystery of 1968, which I felt was somewhat ironic, for I never considered myself a "mystery writer." People are my main concern as a writer, and the task I set myself is to dig into the "mystery" of human behavior in given circumstances.

I have used the police world in all my books to date in order to explore certain events occurring between people, rather than to tell a "cop story" per se.

The Bait dealt with a sex murderer. On a deeper level, it explored the tormented world of a tragically demented man and his impact on a bright, sensitive young policewoman.

The Witness, second in my trilogy set in the Manhattan District Attorney's Squad, was a straightforward story about black organized crime and corruption. It was also a story about youthful idealism, hopes and energies that were misused and betrayed. It was part of the education-in-life of young Detective Christie Opara.

The Ledger, third in the trilogy, could be described as the story of the beautiful mistress of a crime lord. It was also a character study of two apparently opposite young women: one the worldly mistress, the other the idealistic Christie Opara. It was a probing of the painful, hidden truths each girl had to face about herself.

When I undertook my latest novel, *Law and Order*, I realized it was a radical departure from anything I had previously attempted. It was to span three generations, through four decades which have seen more social, political, moral upheaval than most of the rest of our history all put together. For one solid year, I did nothing but research. I probed back more than a hundred years to gain a fuller understanding of the immigrants who came to populate New York City, to lead and dominate not only the Police Department but the political and religious structure of the city for so many years. While the main characters are Irish, I also had to study all the important ethnic groups who comprise New York, to understand their aspirations, backgrounds, influences, self-image. I immersed myself in reading and discussion not only about politics, religious and ethnic history and folklore, but in economics and the effects of the Great Depression, World War II, the post-war world, the Korean War, Vietnam, the youth movement, generation gap, emergence of the drug culture.

I spent three weeks in Ireland wandering at random through that lovely tortured country: spoke to people, listened to them, read as much Irish writing as I could absorb until I could *feel* the rhythm of Irish thought and emotion. I allowed myself to get caught up and carried by the Irish idiom.

My characters grew out of the research. Certain strong characters began to dominate the other members of their family. And it was a "family" that grew into the story. They were at the hub and center of all the changing times of their city and their world. Through the three generations of O'Malleys, my aim was to present some of the social and moral questions with which we are confronted in these complex times. My hero, Brian O'Malley, is first introduced as a young, inexperienced boy of eighteen, faced with the sudden responsibility of caring for his mother, grandmother, brothers and sisters on the violent death of his policeman-father. The book ends when Brian is a fifty-two-year-old Deputy Chief Inspector in the New York City Police Department, dealing as best he can with forces of corruption, coming to terms with his own policeman son, a Vietnam veteran, trying to live in a rapidly changing and always puzzling world.

One of the·most exciting things about writing *Law and Order* was when the characters "took off" on their own. This hasn't happened to me as a writer very often. It is a rare, exciting, heady, exhilarating experience and occurs only when the characters are so well known, so well loved, that they can be trusted to act and react instinctively true to themselves.

The worst moment came when the manuscript was totally completed—all polished and ready to be set in galleys. I experienced the most dreadful sense of loss imaginable. All those warm, exciting, wildly active, strong and familiar people with whom I had shared my life for so long were suddenly taken from me, to be thrust out into the large and critical world.

The solution to this feeling of loss, for me at any rate, was to let a little time go by, enjoy the fruits of my labor, involve myself in other facets of the work, i.e., promotion and publicity—to relax, enjoy, take a deep breath, and begin the whole process all over again.

It must be admitted that no matter how many books I've written, how many characters created and lived with and let go, when I put the blank white paper in my machine, it is no easier for me to begin the written word than it ever has been. Publicity tours and best-seller lists, and book club and movie and TV sales are all very exciting and rewarding and lucrative. However, at the beginning of the day I am a pauper before the blank white paper. The trick is, I guess, just to keep at it from ground zero and to build on it during each session at the machine. Happily, it has started again for me; tentatively, fragilely, hopefully, I've begun a new book. Thankfully.

Since I've always been curious about other writers' work habits,

I will set down some of my own with hopes that my example will warn others to adopt other methods. Sometimes I wonder how in the world I've ever accomplished *any* body of work: I never seem to do all those things I'm positive a writer *should* do.

I've never kept notebooks filled with valuable phrases, impressions, observations. Oh, I've stacks of notebooks of all kinds—spiral ones with businesslike brown covers and spiral ones with pretty flowers on the cover. Somber little black looseleaf notebooks that fit into the palm of my hand and large ones that fill up my lap. They are all filled with empty pages, because I've never really known what to put in them. Once or twice, I've jotted down phrases which I conjured in the middle of the night, or en route somewhere on the subway, but somehow that never seemed pertinent to anything, and I spent too much time wondering what in the world I had in mind when I wrote them down in the first place. There are also pencil sketches of advertisements and some interesting doodles, not one of which is helpful.

A long time ago, I came to a strange conclusion relative to me and note-taking. Mysteriously, it has worked for me, but I do not recommend it to anyone else, merely report on it. If the thought, impression, idea, phrase, situation, or whatever is important enough for me to remember and use somewhere in my writing, I will retain it in cell x-y-or-z of my brain. If it isn't worth using, I will forget it. I don't remember how many flashing, brilliant thoughts might have been retained had they been jotted down. I do know that many conversations between characters in my stories give me a strong sense of *déjà vu*, because they were carried on in my head at some unconnected time in the past.

Another thing I don't do and feel I should: I don't have any work schedule. I mean, *I don't have any work schedule at all.* For a person who spent so many years in a structured work-situation, this leaves much room for feelings of guilt. I know I *should* sit at the machine and accomplish at least *that* much work each day, but I don't. I frankly don't know *when* I work. Sometimes, I leap out of bed at six in the morning, jump into my clothes, gulp my cup of tea and hammer out scene after scene after scene. Then, for days at a time, I avoid the top floor, which is where I work. At about three in the afternoon, the urge might hit again, and I hammer away at the

185

next scene. I will point out that no matter how remiss I am about regulating my work schedule, at least this much is structured: I work a scene through, beginning to end, whether it runs for four pages or forty, whether it takes twenty-three minutes or six hours. Maybe it's those six-hour binges that get the job done for me.

In between actually sitting and pounding the keys, the story does go on inside my head, regardless of what else I am, physically, doing. I rake the leaves, play with the dogs, feed the cats, forget to defrost the supper, stare at daytime television (which is a horrible admission, I realize). The saving grace is that the story process continues, sometimes in some subterranean, unknown manner, because solutions to story problems sometimes take place when least expected. For example: in the shower, riding in a car at night, folding laundry, dusting the furniture, painting a wall.

When I'm well into a manuscript—in fact, during all stages of the manuscript—I rarely if ever rewrite. Probably because I wait so long before actually sitting down to the task, forming sentences in the air before I form them on paper, by the time I actually *do* sit down to work (whenever that is!), the phrases are ready and generally come out the way I want them to. Not always, but more often than not.

Generally, I am amazed at the way the pages of a manuscript pile up, given a particular period of time, because although I complain continuously about working too hard, when it's all over, I have very little remembrance of having worked *at all*.

Given one magic wish as a writer, I would want to be gifted with some kind of power to transform the scene in my head immediately into a bound, printed form without the ever-present struggle to find the words to frame and form the thought. My constant struggle as a writer is to zero in on the exact words that will enable my reader to see, feel, experience a particular scene with as much concern and intensity as I experience while visualizing and writing it.

I don't know what advice to offer young writers. I'm not even sure anyone should presume to offer any advice beyond that one tormenting, beautiful, obvious, obscure, demanding, torturous ecstasy: WRITE. Don't talk about it, whine about it, rap about it, agonize over it, dissect, analyze, study or anything else: Just do it. WRITE.

186

37

ABOUT THAT NOVEL

By Evan Hunter

STARTING: If you haven't got an idea for one, forget it. If you haven't got an idea you want to express on paper, in words, forget it. If you prefer putting paint on canvas, or rolls on your pianola or in your oven, forget it. You're going to be with this novel for a long, long time, so you'd better have *thought* about it before you start writing it. When it's ready to be written, you'll know. You'll know because you can't get it out of your mind. It'll be with you literally day and night. You'll even *dream* about it, but don't get up and rush to your typewriter. Go back to sleep. Only in movies do writers get up in the middle of the night with an inspiration. The time to go to the typewriter is when you're fresh and ready to do battle. There *will* be a battle, no question, a siege that will seemingly go on forever. So sit down, make yourself comfortable, and begin.

No outline at first, except the loose one in your head, draped casually around the idea. The thing you are trying to find is the voice. This is the single most important thing in any novel. The voice. How it will *sound*. Who is telling the story? Why is he telling it? If you're sixty years old and writing in the first person singular about a sixteen-year-old high school student, beware of the voice. It may be your own, and that is wrong. If you're writing in the third person, you can change the *tone* of the voice each time you switch to another character, but the *voice* itself must remain consistent throughout. The voice is your style. Except in my mystery series, I try to change my style to suit the subject matter of any novel I'm writing. I've come a hundred pages into a novel using the wrong voice, and I've thrown those pages away and started a new search for the right voice. Don't worry about spending days or weeks trying to find a voice. It will be time well spent. You'll know when you hit upon it. Things will suddenly *feel* right.

Once you've found the voice, write your first chapter or your first scene. Test the water. Does it still feel right? Good. *Now* make your outline. First of all, determine how long the book will be. The average mystery novel runs about 200 pages in manuscript, but a straight novel can be something as slim as *Love Story* or as thick as *Gone With the Wind.* You are the only person who knows in advance what your story is about. You are the only one who can figure how many pages you will need to tell this story. Take out your calculator. Are you writing a 300-page novel? O.K., how many chapters will you need? The length of each chapter will be determined by how much you have to *say* in that chapter. If you're depicting the Battle of Waterloo, it might be a trifle difficult to compress it into ten pages. If you're writing about a man putting out the garbage, you probably have only a scene, and you'll need additional scenes to make a full chapter.

Outline the novel in your own way, never mind freshman high-school English courses. I've outlined a forty-page chapter with just the words "Father-son confrontation." The outline is you, talking to yourself on paper. Get friendly with yourself. Tell yourself what you, as the writer, want to accomplish in any given chapter. "O.K., now we want a big explosion in the garage, and we want to see all these goddamn flames, and smell the smoke, and we want neighbors running over with garden hoses. Bring the little girl in at the end of the scene, shocked by what she's done." Got it? *Talk* to yourself. You don't have to outline the whole book. Just take the outline as far as your invention will carry it. Later, when you've written all the chapters you've already outlined, you can make another outline of the *next* several chapters. If a chapter is needed between something that has happened before and something that will happen later, and you don't know what to put between those two slices of bread, just type in the words, SCENE MISSING. You'll come back to it later. You're going to be here awhile.

MOVING: Set yourself a definite goal each day. Tack it on the wall. Ten pages? Five pages? Two pages? Two paragraphs? It doesn't matter. *Set* the goal, make it realistic, and *meet* it. If you're writing a planned 400-page novel, it will seem impossible ever to get it finished.

400 pages may be a year away. But your daily goal is here and now, and it's important to set that goal and meet it so that you'll have a sense of immediate reward. At the end of each week, on your calendar, jot down the number of pages you've already written. Store your kernels. Watch the cache grow. Keep the thing moving. If it bogs down, if you're supposed to write a tender love scene and you've just had a fight with your accountant, put the anger to good use. Jump ahead and write the Battle of Waterloo chapter. *Don't stop writing!* It's easier to go fishing or skiing—but sit at that damn typewriter, and look at the four walls all day long if you have to. There is nothing more boring than looking at the walls. Eventually, if only to relieve the boredom, and because you've made a deal with yourself not to get out of that chair, you'll start writing again. At the end of the day, read over what you've written. If you think it's lousy, don't throw it away. Read it again in the morning. If it still looks lousy, do it over again. Or if it's still bothering you, and you don't know why, move on. Keep it *moving*. The nice thing about writing, unlike public speaking, is that you can correct all your mistakes later.

CHANGING: The only true creative aspect of writing is the first draft. That's when it's coming straight from your head and your heart, a direct tapping of the unconscious. The rest is donkey work. It is, however, donkey work that must be done. Whether you rewrite as you go along—taking that bad chapter from the night before and putting it through the machine again from the top—or whether you rewrite everything only after you've completed the book, you *must* rewrite. But be careful. You can hone and polish something until it glows like a diamond, but you may end up with something hard and glittering and totally without the interior spark that was the result of your first commitment to paper. You're only a virgin once, but try to bring to each rereading of your own material the same innocence you brought to it the first time around. You will be rereading it *twenty* times before you're finished. Each time, ask yourself what you intended. Do you want me to cry when I read this scene? Well, are *you* crying? If you're not, why aren't you? Find out why you aren't. Did someone say something that broke the mood of the scene? Is that field of daffodils too cheerful for the tone of the scene? Has your heroine stamped her foot when she should be tearing out her hair? Work it, rework it. When you yourself begin crying, you've got it.

ENDING: How do you know when you're finished? You're finished when you're satisfied. If a scene is right the first time around, leave it alone. Tell yourself, "Terrific, pal," and leave it alone. You'll know you're getting to the end because you'll suddenly slow down. When that happens, set smaller goals for yourself. Instead of those five pages today, make it three. Your pace is slower because you don't want to let go of this thing. You've been living together for a long, long time, you've let this smelly beast into your tent, and you've grown to love it, and now you're reluctant to have it gallop out over the sands and out of your life forever. The temptation is to keep it with you forever, constantly bathe it and scent it, groom it and curry it, tweeze its lashes and tie a bow on its tail. *Recognize* the temptation and recognize too that everything eventually grows up and leaves home. When you've done the best you can possibly do at this time (there *will* be other books, you know) put it in a box, give it a farewell kiss, and send it out into that great big hostile world.

SENDING: Where do you send it? Be exceedingly careful in choosing your agent or your publisher. Don't send the book to anyone who charges a fee for reading it or publishing it. In the real world of publishing, people pay *you* for your work. The Society of Authors' Representatives (if you decide to go the agent route) will send you on request a list of reputable agents in the United States. The address is P.O. Box 650, Old Chelsea Station, New York, NY 10113. Just write and ask, enclosing a self-addressed, stamped envelope. If you decide to submit your manuscript directly to a publisher instead, a long list of publishers looking for various kinds of novels appears in *The Writer* Magazine, or in the market list in Part IV of this volume. Although some book publishers today have given up reading unsolicited manuscripts, many others still maintain reading staffs, and their sole purpose is to search for publishing possibilities. Send the novel manuscript out. One publisher at a time. Multiple submissions are frowned upon except when an agent is conducting a huge auction, and then the publishers are made aware beforehand that the book is being submitted simultaneously all over the field. Choose a publisher who has previously published your sort of book. Don't shotgun it around blindly. If your novel espouses atheism, don't send it to a religious publisher.

WAITING: So now your monster is out roaming the countryside, trying to earn a living. No, there it is in the mailbox. Damn thing. Wish you hadn't given it life at all. Tear open the package. Nice little noncommittal note. Thanks a lot, but no thanks. Despair. Chin up, kiddo, send it out again. But here it is *back* again. And *again*. And *yet* again. Plenty of publishers in the world, just keep trying. Pack it, send it, wait again. Why? Why wait? Why set up a vigil at the mailbox? Why hang around the post office looking like someone on the Wanted posters? You should be *thinking* instead. You should be mulling a new idea. *Don't* wait. What you *should* be doing is—

STARTING: If you haven't got an idea for one, forget it. If you haven't got an idea you want to express on paper, in words, forget it. If you prefer putting paint on canvas, or rolls on your pianola or in your oven, forget it. You're going to be with this novel for a long, long time, so you'd better have *thought* about it before you start writing it. When it's ready to be written, you'll know.

Write it.

38

HOW TO BE YOUR OWN CRITIC

By Margaret Chittenden

ONE of our most difficult tasks as writers is to be objective about our own work. It's not easy to convince ourselves once a novel is finished that this is not necessarily the greatest story ever told. But we have to be honest with ourselves. We have to learn to criticize our manuscripts *constructively,* one step at a time. What should we look for?

From time to time, as I've read novel manuscripts by unpublished authors, I've discovered three main flaws that occur over and over again: the *beginning* is too slow, the *middle* is padded with irrelevant action, and the *ending* is either too long, or too unbelievable, or both.

Beginnings

The beginning of a novel should introduce your main characters, show where the story is taking place, and hint at the conflict. But none of these things should be revealed under static conditions. The story should get under way with the first word on the first page. The reader does not want to wade through a whole river of information and description of the characters before the story gets moving.

Yet many novel manuscripts that I've read either start out with long, long passages of exposition, or else they start with a paragraph of action and *then* go into long passages of exposition. It is not necessary to tell the reader everything about the main characters in the first chapter; you should hold back some of that information. Often, you can leave some of it out altogether. As the writer, you need to know everything there is to know about the main characters before you start writing the book, but you don't need to tell the reader right off about their parents, grandparents, ex-lovers, degrees they've earned in college, every happening in their lives that took place before the start of the story.

Usually, it's best to begin a novel with some kind of action going on, but not necessarily with the protagonist in an airplane circling the airport just before landing—a very popular opening that gives the main character lots of time for soul-searching. Instead, show the main character doing something, going somewhere, talking to someone. Make the opening *intriguing* and then continue with your characters in action, introducing *short* pieces of information that are essential. Later, you can weave in other essential acts through dialogue and in short quotes from the main character's thoughts. Be sure your reader can tell *where* the story is taking place. Don't open with pages of dialogue without giving at least a hint of the setting and who these characters are. Don't give the impression that the story is set in a drawing room and have it turn out to be in a car or an airplane.

Middles

The middle is the place where the novel should *develop*. Here again, writers often put in too much introspection on the part of the main character. Let your reader know what your main character has on his or her mind, but keep it brief. Also, when you write your original synopsis, make sure that enough *action* takes place in the middle section. Frequently, novel synopses by beginning writers have long beginnings and long endings, but the reader would have to take a giant leap between the two. The story doesn't grab the reader at the start and take him or her *suspensefully* to the end.

In plotting the middle, apply the law of cause and effect. Instead of simply asking, what comes next, ask yourself, what would happen as a *result* of this? When the synopsis is finished, go through and check for the *cause-and-effect*.

Here is an example from the synopsis of my novel, *This Dark Enchantment*. Karin has come to Quebec City to assist Charles in writing an architectural history of the city. *Because* of this she meets Doctor Paul Dufresne, whom she first sees being solicited by a seedy young man who looks as though he's on drugs. *Because* of what she sees, Karin suspects that Paul might be involved in drug dealing. *Because* of this, she is not receptive to his advances, and *because* of this . . . and so on. I don't write the synopsis this straightforwardly, but I do check to make sure it could read that way. Cause and effect—two much neglected, often forgotten words in novel writing.

Endings

If you have your causes and effects in proper sequence, the ending will be logical, though not too predictable. I try to sustain suspense in

193

the main plot while tying up any loose ends in the sub-plots, so that the reader will want to stay with me till THE END. But once I've reached the end, when resolutions or solutions are arrived at, I try to exit as rapidly as possible.

It's also necessary to strive for *believability* in the ending. For example, if you've had your hero being really nasty to the heroine in the beginning—which seems to be a popular thing to do—you can't suddenly have him be sweet and lovable at the end, unless you've shown cause and effect in the middle. Some of the manuscripts I've read in which the hero and heroine ended up at the altar would not convince the reader that any sane woman would want this man, or even want to speak to him again.

Now that you've checked the beginning, middle and end of your novel manuscript, it's time to look at it page by page, word by word.

Try going backwards through the manuscript, one page at a time, so you don't get caught up in the flow of the story. Look first for too many *wells, justs* and *verys,* and cross out most of them. Then check spelling and grammar, looking especially for mistakes in syntax. (In a recent novel manuscript, I read the following: "Her shoulders squared and left the room.")

Check to make sure the nouns are specific, that you have written, "the weeping willow" rather than "the tree," the "cocker spaniel" rather than "the dog."

Scrutinize verbs. Try to replace passive verbs with active verbs. "David hugged Joanna" is stronger than "Joanna was hugged by David."

Cut out as many adjectives and adverbs as you can, and check punctuation. (I have a tendency to forget commas.)

Once all this nit-picking is done, make yourself very comfortable, preferably in a recliner, then read the book from beginning to end, pretending it was written by a writer whose work you don't particularly enjoy. If you find yourself going to sleep, take a long, hard look at the passage that brought on your fatigue. Try to read straight through, as a reader would, making brief notes in the margins of anything obviously wrong—sections that seem slow or dull or unbelievable or trite. Mark scenes that don't seem *visual* enough, transitions that are too abrupt.

Once you've finished this initial reading, revise all the things you've marked. Then read the whole manuscript again. Check the movement

194

of the characters, so that you haven't had a character go off on a week's trip and then be present in a scene that takes place the next day. Check characterization. Have these invented people come to life? Can you see them—not just at the beginning, but all the way through? Do you *care* about them?

I try to check diligently to make sure my heroine has *acted*, not just reacted. I don't care for timid heroines. I want to be sure my young woman has done something for herself and not waited for the hero to initiate all the action. Has *your* heroine come through as a real, caring, compassionate, intelligent woman? If this is a romance novel, is she *worth* loving?

Take a close look at your hero. Is he a real human being with admirable qualities, or is he just an ad for jockey shorts?

Next, check on viewpoint. If the entire novel is told from the heroine's point of view, all of the action must be filtered through her point of view. The reader should not see, hear, learn or observe anything that the heroine cannot see, hear, learn or observe. Some editors have told me they don't mind seeing the viewpoint character from the outside occasionally, but I'm a purist about viewpoint. I try never to write, "Tears rolled down her beautifully sculptured cheeks." One: This sort of thing makes the heroine sound conceited. Two: Such a description jars the reader into looking at the heroine from the outside, instead of looking at everything through her eyes. When in doubt, I change the sentence temporarily into first person. I wouldn't write, "Tears rolled down *my* beautifully sculptured cheeks." So when I'm writing in her viewpoint, my heroine can *feel* her tears, but she can't *see* them. She can *look* at people, but she doesn't look at them with her "sparkling amethyst eyes."

If the writer presents the story from the main character's viewpoint, it's difficult to describe her completely, without using the trite device of having her look in the mirror, but it can be done. In my book *Song of Desire,* for example, Vicki's aunt tells her it's O.K. for her to look like an ad for sunshine and vitamins. Vicki herself complains that when people look at her they say, "Ah, a California Girl," and expect her to run around with a surfboard under her arm and not a thought in her head. Maintaining one viewpoint assures greater reader identification. It also gives unity to the emotions.

However, if your novel is written in multiple viewpoint, you still need to check to be sure that you haven't bounced in and out of several characters' minds in a short space of time. Viewpoint-hopping can be very confusing to a reader.

Once you are sure the viewpoint is consistent, make certain all the characters' actions have been properly motivated, so no one does anything without having a reason. Then ask yourself if any of the dialogue sounds stilted. Do the young people talk as young people do, or do they sound like senior citizens? "That's exceedingly kind of you," for instance, is not something a young person would usually say today.

Next, try to unravel the various threads in your story to make sure you haven't dropped any halfway through the novel, and that they are all tied up at the end. In *Song of Desire,* for example, one thread dealt with the hero's acting career, another with the heroine's career as an interior designer. A third thread dealt with the hero's young sister and her adventures, and a fourth with thefts from a hotel. In a multi-layered novel, it's easy to lose track of one of the threads, so this aspect of the manuscript must be carefully checked.

After all these questions have been answered and all necessary revisions are completed, read the whole manuscript again. By now you should be thoroughly sick of it, so if it still holds *your* interest, it should hold an editor's and a reader's. After this final reading, put the manuscript aside and think the story through, making sure you haven't missed anything significant.

Your aim in all this self-criticism is to produce the best book you can possibly produce. Before you send a completed manuscript to an agent or an editor, it should be the best work you can do. This is the writer's responsibility, the writer's task, the writer's joy.

39

SCIENCE FICTION TODAY

By Isaac Asimov

SCIENCE FICTION has changed enormously since I first began writing it, professionally, nearly fifty years ago.

When I submitted a story for the first time on June 21, 1938, there were three magazines in the field; only one of which, *Astounding Science Fiction*, was, in my opinion, quality. There was nothing else to speak of. An occasional amateur publisher put out a tiny printing of some poorly written science fiction novel. There were a few comic strips, notably *Buck Rogers* and *Flash Gordon*, and an occasional very primitive movie serial.

But now?

In the print media, science fiction novels are commonly found on the best-seller lists, both in hardcover and softcover. The book stores have shelves full of them. The movies and television find science fiction to be profitable blockbusters. Science fiction courses are taught in high schools and colleges. Short story anthologies exist by the hundreds. Science fiction is *big time*.

It might seem to you, then, that it must be a great deal easier to break into the science fiction field now than it was fifty years ago. After all, the target is so much larger now.

Unfortunately, I don't think that's so. Let us analyze the situation more closely. Fifty years ago, when sf consisted of three magazines and virtually nothing else, there were many other outlets for fiction. It was the heyday of the pulp-magazine craze. Every newsstand had dozens of them in every conceivable category: romance, mystery, western, jungle, war, horror, adventure. Some came out monthly, and some biweekly, and some even weekly. There were also "slick" magazines that published a great deal of fiction and paid much more than the pulps did.

Of them all, the science fiction magazines were the smallest in number, the least lucrative, the most specialized, and the least regarded

197

segment. Almost none of the myriads of young people who had the itch to write considered science fiction as a possible outlet. The science fiction magazines drew their new prospects from among their own long-time fanatic readers, who had been reading science fiction since they had learned to read and had no interest in anything else. They didn't care for either fame or wealth, but wanted only to write that wonderful stuff they were reading and see their name in print in a science fiction magazine. There weren't many of those fanatics (usually abbreviated as "fans"), but I was one of them. I had been reading science fiction avidly from the age of nine, and I was eighteen when I made my first sale.

Under those circumstances, it was not necessary to be a great writer, you understand. There were few science fiction writers of any kind in those days, and still fewer good ones. If you were eager to write science fiction, knew grammar and spelling, and had read enough science fiction to know a new idea from an old one, that was about all that was needed.

Nowadays, all that has changed also. In the first place, the fiction market has contracted violently in the last fifty years (a result of the coming of the comic magazine, and then, even more important, television). The pulps are gone. What slicks exist publish very little fiction. In fact, the only branch of popular fiction that has expanded wildly in the last half century has been science fiction. (Mysteries and romances have done no more than hold their own over the long run.)

This means that of all the youngsters who grow up with the itch to be writers, a sizable percentage tend to flood into science fiction in large numbers. There are hundreds of excellent science fiction writers today, whereas, half a century ago, there were mere dozens of not-so-excellent ones. In addition, many of those who entered the field years ago are still there. The "big three"—Isaac Asimov, Arthur C. Clarke, and Robert A. Heinlein—whose books are sure-fire best sellers today, have been writing steadily for nearly fifty years. Clarke and Heinlein, despite their advanced years, show no signs of slowing down and I, of course, am still a youngster.

What's more, all these writers tend to write novels. That's where the money and fame are. And novels are precisely what a beginner would find difficult to do. A novel has a complex structure, with interlocking plots and subplots, with room for characterization to be developed and dialogue to show a certain depth and wit. If a beginner throws caution to the winds and determines to tackle a novel anyway, he finds it represents an enormous investment of time and effort, all of which (the chances are) will be thrown away except for what good the writing experience will do him.

The natural way in which science fiction writers broke into the field in my early days was to turn out short stories for the magazines. (There was, after all, nothing else to do since, at most, two or three novels were published each year as magazine serials.) Clarke, Heinlein, and I all got our start as writers of science fiction short stories for the magazines. We worked our way up to novels by stages.

Well, then, are there not science fiction magazines that publish short stories today, to say nothing of science fiction anthologies?

Yes, but skip the anthologies. The vast majority of them include reprints—stories that have already appeared in the magazines. That leaves only the magazines.

Unfortunately, the magazines have not expanded along with the rest of the field. There are four magazines today that specialize in science fiction. In order of age, they are *Amazing Stories* (previously *Amazing Science Fiction Stories*); *Analog Science Fiction/Science Fact* (which had once been *Astounding Science Fiction*); *The Magazine of Fantasy and Science Fiction;* and *Isaac Asimov's Science Fiction Magazine.* In addition, there are a couple of other magazines, which publish some science fiction. Most notable of these is *Omni,* which publishes two or three stories in each issue. It pays much higher rates than the others do, and consequently seeks its stories from among the established writers. (And there are a number of little magazines in the field, a good place for beginning sf writers to try, though payment rates are low.)

The magazine field, therefore, is not much larger than it was fifty years ago, and the competition is keener. The level of writing in the magazines is consequently substantially higher than it used to be, and my 18-year-old self, if transported into the present with no more talent than I possessed then, might not have been able to break in.

However, all is not lost. In the old days, when a writer established himself as a science fiction short story writer, he stayed there having nowhere else to go, and left that much less room for newcomers. Nowadays, as soon as a science fiction writer begins to make a name for himself in the magazines and has gained the necessary expertise, he shifts to writing novels. The result is that the magazines are forced to be

199

on the continual lookout for new young writers. These new writers have to be good, to be sure—it is no longer enough that they feel warm to the touch—but the fact that they are unknown is not held against them.

But so what if the competition is keen? That makes the task the more challenging, and the triumph sweeter in the end. The rules are the same. You have to read a great deal of science fiction so that you gain some insight into what science fiction is and what makes it good. And you have to write a great deal of science fiction, because only by writing can you gradually learn the tricks of the trade. And you have to have an inhuman perseverance and develop a thick skin against disappointment and frustration. And don't think the world is picking on you. I suspect that Homer and Aeschylus had all the same experiences you had in getting started.

Perhaps something else occurs to you. It may seem to you that when I was just beginning (back in the Middle Ages) hardly anything was known about science and I could write freely about interplanetary travel and robots and all that stuff. Nowadays, however, we *have* interplanetary travel and robots, so what is there to write about? Hasn't science caught up to all the science fiction plots? Isn't science fiction dead?

Not at all! Nohow! The science fiction writer is tied to the front end of a locomotive that is speeding across the landscape. No matter how far and how fast the locomotive is going, the writer is looking ahead and sees an endless vista.

Scientific advance provides writers with fascinating new backgrounds. We used to think Mars had canals; now we know (not "think") it has extinct volcanoes. And we know Io has active volcanoes. And we know that Venus is as hot as hell—literally—and has no oceans. We can turn away from the tired old planets and make use of brand-new ones, and have the satisfaction of knowing that there's less guesswork and more knowledge now.

Again, we think of all the new concepts science has given us. We have neutron stars, and black holes, and quasars, and exploding galaxies, and big bangs. We have mesons, and hyperons, and quarks, and gluons. We have DNA and biogenetics. We have computers and microchips. We have jet planes and satellites of every kind and probes and shuttles. We have seen close-ups of Uranus and its satellites. We had *none* of that when I was starting out.

200

When I think of all these new scientific items there are to play around with now—and how little I had back in 1938—I am amazed that I was able to think up any stories at all in that medieval period.

Of course, we have to be careful of fashion. When I first started reading science fiction, it was all adventure and Sunday supplement science. It was written in primary colors and in jagged lightning streaks. It was ideal for a bright nine-year-old to get started on.

By the time I began to submit stories, however, it became fashionable to load them down with authentic science and to try to make the characters sound like real scientists and engineers. The 1940's and 1950's were the heyday of "hard science fiction" and that was my forte, and (to tell you the truth) I still write it even though it sounds old-fashioned today.

In the 1960's, there came a period of stylistic experimentation called "the new wave" which, it seems to me, made hard reading and wasn't very successful. However, it settled down into the literary style we have today.

So however much you may want to read the "old classics" (like Asimov) and however much you may enjoy them, you had better also read, and pay close attention to, the kind of material that is appearing in the magazines *now*. That is what you should be writing.

Of course, you may be asking yourself if you should be writing for the print media at all. Shouldn't you be breaking into movies and television, where the BIG money is?

Frankly, I don't know how that's done. I've never worked in the visual media myself except on two or three minor occasions when I was talked into it much against my will.

It is my experience that when you write for the print media, what you write is what gets published. If there is a need for revision, the editor asks *you* to revise, and the chances are even good that you will get to see a galley proof so that you can make sure that any last-minute editorial changes meet with your approval.

When you write for the visual media, however, you must apparently meet the requirements of the producer, the director, the various actors, the office boy, strangers who pass in the street, and the mother-in-law of any or all of these, each of whom changes your product at whim. If you are a real writer, money isn't going to compensate for never being free to write as you wish.

201

40

BUILDING WITHOUT BLUEPRINTS

By Tony Hillerman

IN MORE than thirty-five years of writing, I have accumulated two bits of wisdom that may be worth passing along.

First, I no longer waste two months perfecting that first chapter before getting on with the book. No matter how carefully you have the project planned, first chapters tend to demand rewriting. Things happen. New ideas suggest themselves, new possibilities intrude. Slow to catch on, I collected a manila folder full of perfect, polished, exactly right, pear-shaped first chapters before I learned this lesson. Their only flaw is that they don't fit the book I finally wrote. The only book they will ever fit will be one entitled *Perfect First Chapters*, which would be hard to sell. Thus Hillerman's First Law: NEVER POLISH THE FIRST CHAPTER UNTIL THE LAST CHAPTER IS WRITTEN.

The second law takes longer to explain. When I defend it, I'm like the fellow with his right arm amputated arguing in favor of left-handed bowling. However, here it is:

SOME PEOPLE, SOMETIMES, CAN WRITE A MYSTERY NOVEL WITHOUT AN OUTLINE.

Or, put more honestly: If you lack the patience (or brains) to outline the plot, maybe you can grope your way through it anyway, and sometimes it's for the best.

I was in the third chapter of a book entitled *Listening Woman* when this truth dawned. Here's how it happened:

I had tried to outline three previous mystery novels. Failing, and feeling guilt-ridden and inadequate, I finally finished each of them, by trying to outline a chapter or two ahead as I wrote. I had tried for weeks to blueprint this fourth book, sketching my way through about six chapters. At that point, things became impossibly hazy. So I decided to write the section I had blueprinted. Maybe then I could see my way through the rest of it.

I wrote the first chapter exactly as planned, an elaborate look at the villain outsmarting a team of FBI agents on a rainy night in Washington, D.C. I still feel that this chapter may be the best 5,000 words I've ever written. By the time I had finished it, I had a much better feeling for the key character, and for the plot in which he was involved. Unfortunately, this allowed me to see that I was starting the book too early in the chronology of the story I was telling. So this great first chapter went into the manila folder (to be cannibalized later for flashback material). Then I planned a new opening. This one takes place now on the Navajo Reservation at the hogan of an elderly and ailing Navajo widower named Tso. It is mostly a dialogue between him and a shaman he has summoned to determine the cause of his illness. The chapter was intended to establish time, mood, and the extreme isolation of the area of the Navajo Reservation where the novel takes place. It would give the reader a took at Tso, who will be the murder victim, and introduce the shaman, who would be a fairly important character. Finally, the dialogue would provide background information and—in its discussion of Navajo taboos violated by Tso—provide clues meaningless to the FBI, but significant to my Navajo Sherlock Holmes. Again, all went well, but as I wrote it I could sense a flaw.

It was dull. In fact, it was *awfully dull.*

I had planned to have the second chapter take place a month later. In the interim, Tso has been murdered offstage, and the killing is an old unsolved homicide. Why not, I wondered then, have the murder take place during the open scene? Because then either (a) the shaman would see it, tell the cops, and my novel becomes a short story; or (b) the murderer would zap the shaman, too, messing up my plot. At this stage, a writer who specializes in Navajos and has accumulated a headful of Navajo information searches his memory banks for help. Navajos have a terribly high rate of glaucoma and resulting blindness. Why not a blind old woman shaman? Then how does she get to the isolated Tso hogan? Create a niece, an intern-shaman, who drives the old lady around. The niece gets killed, and now you have a double murder done while the blind woman is away at a quiet place having her trance. You also have an opportunity to close the chapter with a dandy little non-dull scene in which the blind woman, calling angrily for her newly deceased niece, taps her way with her cane across the scene of carnage. The outline is bent, but still recognizable.

Early in chapter two, another bend. The revised plan still calls for introducing my protagonist, Navajo Police Lt. Joe Leaphorn, and the villain. Joe stops Gruesome George for speeding, whereupon G.G. tries to run over Joe, roars away, abandons his car and eludes pursuit. Two paragraphs into this chapter, it became apparent that Joe needed someone in the patrol car with him to convert the draggy internal monologue I was writing into snappy dialogue. So I invent a young sheep thief, handcuff him securely, and stick him in the front seat. He turns out to be wittier than I had expected, which distorts things a bit, but nothing serious goes wrong. Not yet. Leaphorn stops the speeder and is walking toward the speeder's car. As many writers do, I imagine myself into scenes—seeing, hearing, smelling everything I am describing.

What does Leaphorn see? His patrol car emergency light flashing red reflections off the speeder's windshield. Through the windshield, he sees the gold-rimmed glasses I'll use as a label for Gruesome George until we get him identified. What else? My imagination turns whimsical. Why not put in another pair of eyes? Might need another character later. Why not put them in an unorthodox place—peering out of the back seat of the sedan? But why would anyone be sitting in the back? Make it a dog. A huge dog. In a crate. So the dog goes in. I can always take him out.

Still we seem to have only a minor deflection from the unfinished, modified version of the partial outline. But a page or two later, in chapter three, it became obvious that this unplanned, unoutlined dog was going to be critically important. I could see how this ugly animal could give the villain a previous life and the sort of character I had to hang on him. More important, I could begin to see Dog (already evolved into a trained attack dog) could be used to build tension in the story. As I thought about the dog, I began to see how my unblueprinted sheep thief would become the way to solve another plot problem.

Since that third chapter of my fourth mystery novel, I have honestly faced the reality. For me, working up a detailed outline simply isn't a good idea. I should have learned that much earlier.

For example, in my first effort at mystery fiction, *The Blessing Way*, I introduce the Gruesome George character in a trading post on the Reservation. He is buying groceries while my protagonist watches, slightly bored. I, too, am slightly bored. So is the reader. Something needs to be done to generate a bit of interest. I decide to insert a minor mystery. I have the fellow buy a hat, put his expensive silver concha hatband on it, and tell the storekeeper that someone had stolen the original hat. Why would someone steal a hat and leave behind an expensive silver hatband? My protagonist ponders this oddity and can't think of any reason. Neither can I. If I can't think of one later, out will come the hat purchase and in will go some other trick to jar the reader out of his nap. But the hat stayed in. My imagination worked on it in the context of both the Navajo culture and my plot requirements. It occurred to me that such a hat, stained with its wearer's sweat, would serve as the symbolic "scalp" required at a Navajo ceremonial (an Enemy Way) to cure witchcraft victims and to kill witches. When my policeman sees the stolen hat (identified by the missing hatband) in this ritual role, it leads him to the solution of his mystery. (And the author to the completion of his book.)

I have gradually learned that this sort of creative thinking happens for me only when I am at very close quarters with what I am writing—only when I am in the scene, in the mind of the viewpoint character, experiencing the chapter and sharing the thinking of the people in it. From the abstract distance of an outline, with the characters no more than names, nothing seems real to me. At this distance, the details which make a plot come to life always elude me.

Another example: In *Fly on the Wall*, the principal character is a political reporter. He has been lured into the dark and empty state capitol building in the wee hours on the promise that doors will be left unlocked to give him access to confidential tax files. He spots the trap and flees, pursued by two armed men. Before I began writing this section, I had no luck at all coming up with an idea of how I could allow him to escape without straining reader suspension of disbelief. Now, inside these spooky, echoing halls, I think as my frightened character would think, inspired by his terror. No place to hide in the empty hallways. Get out of them. Try a door. Locked, of course. All office doors would be locked. Almost all. How about the janitor's supply room which the night watchman uses as his office? That door is open. Hide there. (Don't forget to dispose of the watchman.) A moment of safety, but only a moment until the hunters think of this place. Here are the fuse boxes which keep the hall lights burning. Cut off the power. Darken the building. Meanwhile, the readers are wondering, what's happened to the night watchman? Where is he? That breathing you suddenly hear over the pounding of your own heart, not a yard away in the pitch blackness, is the watchman, knocked on the head and tied up. Check his holster. Empty, of course. So what do you do? The hunters know where the fuse boxes are. They are closing in. Feel around in the darkness for a weapon. And what do you feel on the shelves in a janitor's storeroom? All sorts of stuff, including a gallon jug of liquid detergent. You open the door and slip out into the dark hallway, running down the cold marble floor in your sock feet, hearing the shout of your pursuer, dribbling the detergent out of the jug behind you as you sprint down the stairs.

In an outline I would never have thought of the janitor's supply room, nor of the jug of liquid detergent. Yet the detergent makes the hero's escape plausible and is a credible way to eliminate one of the two pursuers as required by the plot. Even better, it is raw material for a deliciously hideous scene—hero running sock-footed down the marble stairway, liquid soap gushing out behind him from the jug. Bad guy in his leather-soled shoes sprinting after him. Except for describing the resulting noises, the writer can leave it to the reader's imagination.

A big plus for working without an outline, right? The big negative is that I forgot Hero had removed his shoes and had no way to recover them. The editor didn't notice it either, but countless readers did—upbraiding me for having the hero operating in his socks throughout the following chapter.

I have learned, slowly, that outlining a plot in advance is neither possible, nor useful, for me. I can get a novel written to my satisfaction only by using a much freer form and having faith that—given a few simple ingredients—my imagination will come up with the necessary answers.

Those ingredients—not in any order of importance:

- *A setting with which I am intimately familiar.* Although I have been nosing around the Navajo Reservation and its borderlands for more than 30 years, I still revisit the landscape I am using before I start a new book—and often revisit it again while I am writing it. And then I work with a detailed, large scale map beside my word processor.
- *A general idea of the nature of the mystery* which needs to be solved, and a good idea of the motive for the crime, or crimes.
- *A theme.* For example, *The Dark Wind* exposes my Navajo cop to a

crime motivated by revenge—to which Navajos attach no value and find difficult to understand.

* *One or two important characters* in addition to the policeman-protagonist. However, even these characters tend to be foggy at first. In *Dance Hall of the Dead,* the young anthropology graduate student I had earmarked as the murderer turned out to be too much of a weakling for the job. Another fellow took on the role.

When I finish this, I will return to chapter eight of the present "work in progress." My policeman has just gone to the Farmington jail, where I had intended to have him interview a suspect. Instead he has met the suspect's attorney—a hard-nosed young woman who, as the dialogue progressed, outsmarted my cop at every turn. This woman did not exist in my nebulous plans for this book and has no role. But I have a very strong feeling that she will assume one and that it will be a better book because of her.

That's a good argument against outlines. Without one, I can hardly wait to see how this book will turn out.

41

WRITING REALISTIC WESTERN FICTION

By Elmer Kelton

IDEALLY, the only major difference between a Western and any other good, serious novel should be the subject matter, the setting. A good story is a good story, and a bad story a loser whether the setting is Paris or London, Cape Cod or Dodge City. The same general principles of characterization, plot and movement apply.

Being set in the West automatically bestows upon a story certain advantages and certain limitations. The main advantage is a loyal if sometimes-too-small readership receptive to the Western scene. The principal limitation is that it is unlikely to be taken seriously by most of the critical establishment, making it a stepchild in the literary family.

Because of this old prejudice—call it snobbery if you wish—much fine writing has been accorded the "averted gaze," ignored in favor of "relevant" material not half so well written.

The cliché view of the classic Western is a story built around a strong, unsmiling hero who stands seven feet tall and invincible against the worst of villainy, unselfishly sets all wrongs right, and then rides away into the sunset.

Certainly, such Westerns exist. They started in the days of Ned Buntline a century ago, and they continue to appear. There is an audience for the "utility Western," typical of the Saturday-matinee "B" Western film, in which the same frontier-town set and the same outdoor scenery are interchangeable, whether the story is set in Texas or Oregon.

But I am convinced there is a larger audience for a Western novel firmly and accurately grounded in history, the story growing out of conditions inherent in and peculiar to a specific time and place, its conflicts not falling neatly into black and white.

I made my first Western short story sale, to *Ranch Romances,* in 1947. Even so, after some fifty magazine stories and twenty-six published novels, I still consider myself a learner. I continually read and watch for a good story idea, for an interesting character I can interpolate into a novel.

Most of the rules that apply to other fiction apply to the Western. A writer who approaches the Western with a down-the-nose attitude is unlikely to get far in the field. Like any other form, the Western deserves the respect of its writer—respect for the rules of good storytelling and for the realities of history around which the story revolves.

Nothing turns me off faster than to get into a story and find anachronisms and inaccuracies about the time, the place and the people. Any serious writer of historical fiction studies the history that will be the foundation of his novel. The Western deserves no less. This study does not have to be drudgery. Doing the historical research is often the most pleasurable aspect of writing fiction. A writer who does not love history has no business writing about it.

A majority of my novels have been strongly grounded in history. Before I start to write, I study the setting of the story, the historical situations that will form the framework, and the people of the time and place, their problems, their beliefs. Old newspapers, diaries, and written reminiscences are invaluable.

Intricate plots have never been my long suit, though I admire writers who can bring them off. Rather, I rely upon characters and the historical situation to set the pattern. I like the story to grow out of the history to such an extent that the plot could not be transferred to some other time and place without radical surgery.

An example is an early novel of mine, *Massacre at Goliad,* still reprinted periodically in paperback. Two brothers emigrate to Texas from Tennessee some years before the Texas revolution against Mexico. They live through the situations and events that gradually build the atmosphere for revolution. In modern terms, one is a hawk, the other a dove. They become estranged because of their political differences. However, once the fighting begins, they are brought back together by their concern for one another.

My biggest historical novel has been *The Wolf and the Buffalo,* about the lives of a black cavalryman on the Texas plains in the 1870s and a Comanche warrior against whom he is pitted, the black man fighting the red man so the white man can have the land. This novel gave me an opportunity to dramatize the daily life of both the buffalo soldier and

209

his enemy. Gideon Ledbetter, the former slave now in uniform, is on a gradual ascent, while Gray Horse, the Comanche, is witnessing the twilight of his people's way of life.

It struck me that the two characters had a great deal in common. It was a temptation to have them realize it and perhaps come together in some way, but in real life it did not happen. The fact that it should have but did not is one of the ironies of history. I *did* let one black trooper in the story see the parallel and try to act upon it, deserting the army and riding out into Indian country with the idea of proposing an alliance against the white man. What happens to him is what would have happened in real life, more likely than not. The first Indians he encounters shoot him out of the saddle. They see him as an enemy, simply a white man with a black face.

At the end of the story the two characters come together in the only way they would in real life: in combat to the death.

This brings me to what I consider the most important element in a Western, or in almost any other type of fiction: characters.

I wrote the final scene of *The Wolf and the Buffalo* with tears in my eyes. Working with those characters for two years, I had come to care about them as real people. I gloried in their triumphs and felt deeply their personal tragedies.

Well-developed characters have a way of taking charge of a story and leading the writer in directions not anticipated. Often they change details, and sometimes they cause major alterations to the intended plot line. Usually I let them go their own way, for my unconscious is quietly telling me this is the natural and spontaneous thing for them to do.

In a recent question-and-answer session, a reader said she did not understand why I should let characters take over. "They are your creation," she declared. "You can make them do what you want them to."

But to force them into my preconceived plan makes the story seem mechanical and contrived. When in doubt, I follow the character. He knows himself.

In *Stand Proud,* I started with a young Texan forced into frontier service for the Confederacy late in the Civil War, carried against his will into an ill-considered Indian fight (a real one, incidentally) that gave him a wound he would have the rest of his life. Wherever other men led him, he invariably suffered. As the years passed, he increasingly resisted advice; he ignored any judgment not his own. His stubbornness caused him to make mistakes, a few with dreadful consequences. Not until almost too late in his life did he begin to acknowledge his dependence upon others.

Sound like a typical shoot-'em-up plot? I hope not.

These are not men seven feet tall and invincible. These are men five-feet-eight and nervous. They are vulnerable; they can lose, and the reader knows it.

What is more, their opponents, by and large, are not the dog-kicking villains of the old "B" Western. Often they can evoke a certain sympathy and understanding. Sometimes the reader is not sure how he wants the story to come out because he can feel empathy for both sides.

This brings up the question of conflict. The traditional image of the Western is a simple white-hat vs. black-hat yarn, a tall, strong, silent hero against a dyed-in-the-wool villain. It is an old war-horse plot, though one that a gifted writer can still make seem fresh and alive. I am not that gifted. When I have tried to use it, the old horse has shown all his ribs.

Somebody once suggested looking for plots at periods of traumatic change, when an old order is being pushed aside by something new. You can find these anywhere in history. We see them all around us today.

I like to use these periods of change as the basis for historical Westerns, for they set up a natural and understandable human conflict, often between honorable people, each side convinced that it stands for God and the right.

This type of conflict may be cataclysmic, like the clash of the Union and Confederate armies at Gettysburg. Or it may be small and intimate, like the conflict between a modern elderly couple who want to hang onto the family farm or ranch despite all of today's rural economic misery, and their grown children who want them to sell the homestead and retire to town.

At either extreme, the conflict is the same: change vs. resistance to change. It is the oldest plot in the world, and yet it is always fresh.

The conflict may be intensified when it is within the character himself as much as or more than between him and others.

There is a built-in hazard in doing a historical Western, or a historical novel of any kind: the possibility of losing the characters and the story amid all the spectacle. A few years ago we had a rash of 100th anniver-

211

sary celebrations of towns and counties in Texas. Many paid tribute to their past by staging historical pageants, parading costumed people, wagons, coaches, horses, mules, even Longhorn cattle and buffalo past the audience. The spectacle was grand, but with rare exceptions it was only that: a spectacle. The audience came away with little feeling for what it would have meant to be one of the historic personages represented. We saw them only from afar.

History provides the stage. The writer must provide the characters and make them walk and talk and breathe, feel joy and anger, exhilaration and despair. If he does not, he has simply a historical pageant, not a story.

A lot of myth surrounds the West, but the truth is there for the writer who wants to seek it out. The Western story does not deserve to be locked into any set pattern, any formula. It can be as varied as the land from which it springs.

It must be, if it is to survive in its second hundred years.

42

HORROR OF HORRORS

By Graham Masterton

You HAVE to make up your mind, of course, what terrible threat your characters are going to be obliged to face.

In my first horror novel, *The Manitou*, it was a three-hundred-year-old Indian medicine man, reborn in the modern age to wreak his revenge on the white man. In *Tengu*, it was a squad of Japanese zombies, invulnerable to almost everything including decapitation, who were trying to get their own back for Hiroshima.

Other terrors have included a sinister family who need other people's skin to keep themselves from growing old; a nasty religious cult who believe that the only way to get to heaven is to eat thy neighbor; and a demon who impregnates unsuspecting women in their dreams.

It isn't always necessary for your terrible threat to be totally original. Some of the finest horror novels have been fresh interpretations of well-worn themes. *'Salem's Lot*, Stephen King's breakthrough novel, was all about common-or-garden vampires; and *The Howling* by Whitley Strieber was a werewolf story.

You just have to make sure that no matter how wacky it is, your terrible threat is believable—at least for as long as it takes your reader to finish the novel. Unless it's believable, it won't be frightening, and if it isn't frightening, then you haven't delivered what your reader is looking for. And what your reader is looking for above everything else is fear.

Fear is the prime ingredient of all successful horror novels, although naturally you have to fulfil the terrible threat with which you have presented your characters. You can't write about vampires who never get around to sinking their fangs into anybody, or werewolves who don't tear anybody's lungs out, or zombies who stay in their coffins and don't shuffle around shopping malls dropping bits of themselves wherever they go.

But creating an atmosphere of fear is far more important (and far more difficult) than creating a moment of disgust. It is the atmosphere of brooding evil that will make your horror novel successful . . . the feeling that you implant inside your reader's reluctant mind that the terrible threat is hanging not only over your characters but over him, too.

If you succeed in making your readers sleep with their bedside lights on, then you've achieved something special.

Now, how do you go about creating this atmosphere of fear?

First of all, you mustn't ignore the principles of good storytelling. Your horror novel must have a beginning, a middle, and an end. Your characters should be believable and believably motivated—and that goes for your vampires and ghouls, as well as your heroes and heroines. No matter how outlandish the Threat From Beyond that you choose to visit on them, your characters should react the way that real people would react. If you're not sure how, go to a horror movie and watch the audience instead of the picture. You'll be fascinated by the responses you see in people's faces. And what you'll find particularly striking is how often people laugh with terror.

You should establish firm ground rules for yourself about what your Threat From Beyond can and can't do. Vampires can go out only at night; they're hypersensitive to crucifixes and garlic; they can be killed by a stake driven through their hearts. Werewolves can never remember what they were up to while they were werewolves and can be killed only with silver bullets.

Many of my Threats From Beyond have been based on ancient legends, and I have retained the characteristics that were described in the original folk stories. In *Tengu*, the evil mastermind of a horde of vengeful Japanese zombies was a diminutive dwarf called Kappa. I based him on cunning Japanese water-demons called Kappas, who drag men, women, children and livestock into lakes and suck their blood. The Kappas' one weakness is that they have concave, saucer-shaped heads which are filled with water, and this water gives them their strength. If you can persuade a Kappa to bow his head, the water will pour out, and he will lose his power. In *Tengu*, I adapted the legend to make Kappa a hydrocephalic who is eventually suffocated when his huge head drops forward, constricting his neck and suffocating him.

214

In *The Pariah,* a Mexican skeleton-demon called Micantecutli can be subdued by freezing; and the nasty family in *Picture of Evil* can be wiped out if their portrait is destroyed.

There must be a way in which your hero can eventually win out over the Threat From Beyond. How your hero finds out what it is, and how he attempts to carry it out, can be as desperate and as complicated as you like, and you can bluff and double-bluff to scare your reader even more: *Is that nice Mrs. Stephenson next door really a vampire or not? She's still wearing her crucifix, but . . .*

Similarly, your hero should be restricted by his morality and his conscience, and perhaps by other more mundane factors, too, like the fact that he simply can't afford to spend his time chasing demons, unlike the wealthy Duke de Richelieu in Dennis Wheatley's supernatural novels. Or maybe he's got a messy divorce to deal with, as well as the Thing That Eats Entrails.

Whatever kind of horror novel you're writing, never forget that you're still dealing with the fundamental struggle between Good and Evil, and for any struggle to be involving and meaningful, it has to be played out according to understandable rules. There is no tension in any confrontation if there aren't rules, whether that confrontation is chess, tennis, pro-football, or fighting malevolent demons from another dimension.

It isn't always necessary for your hero to overcome the Threat From Beyond completely. I often like to leave a tingling little element of doubt at the end of my horror novels. But it *is* necessary for the sake of the reader's satisfaction that Good should have proved itself during the course of the struggle to be superior to Evil. We all need to be reassured that honesty and purity and clean shining teeth will always win out over deceit and corruption and careless personal hygiene.

This needn't necessarily apply to short horror stories, some of the very best of which end up with the principal character facing the most hideous of extinctions. But a full-length novel requires very much more investment from your readers in terms of time and emotion and character identification, and they will feel frustrated and cheated if you feed your principal character to the Threat. Imagine the audience dissatisfaction if *Jaws* had finished off Roy Scheider instead of the other way around!

Having chosen your Threat and the general outline of your story, take a very close look at your characters. As a general rule, the more bizarre your Threat, the more ordinary your characters should be. In my award-winning novel *Charnel House,* the hero is a sanitary engineer working in San Francisco. He reacts and behaves like a sanitary engineer, all the way through the book, although his character is deepened and changed by his encounter with an age-old demon:

> The old man came into my office and closed the door.
> He said, almost apologetically, "It's my house. It's breathing."
> I picked up my ballpen. "Could you tell me your name, please?"
> "Seymour Wallis. I'm a retired engineer. Bridges, mainly."
> "Okay, and your problem is noise?"
> "Not noise," he said, softly. "Breathing."
> "Maybe you have a downdraft in your chimney," I suggested. "Sometimes the air comes down an old stack and finds its way through cracks in the bricks."
> He shook his head. "It sounds like some kind of animal breathing. I know it's hard to credit, but I've heard it for three months now, and it's quite unmistakable."
> I turned back from the window. "Are there any odors? Any unpleasant deposits? I mean, you're not finding animal excrement in your larder or anything like that?"
> "It *breathes,* that's all, like a German shepherd on a hot day. Pant, pant, pant. All night long, and sometimes during the day as well."

So, reactions are important. They have to be believable and consistent with your character's background and personality. I personally think that in horror fiction it's a mistake to make your principal character too brave. The gradual finding of courage within himself or herself, the discovery within his or her own personality of previously unrealized strengths, is an important part of making the character believable. And, if the character is believable, the horrors that he or she has to face are going to be all the more believable, too.

Your readers will also be able to identify with this growing sense of courage, and finish the novel feeling that they, too, have faced up to the Threat and come out on top.

Take a great deal of care with the location and general ambience of your horror novel. Some of the most frightening horror stories have been set in perfectly ordinary everyday locations, but there is something to be said for choosing a setting that is isolated or unusual. Various rural locations have worked well: Appalachian mountaintops

216

where none of the telephones work and most of the locals have near-together eyes and carry axes around with them, or downtrodden communities in the middle of the Texas plain where corrugated-iron doors bang monotonously in the wind and unseen eyes keep boring into the back of your head.

The purpose of choosing locations like these is to isolate your characters from the usual aids and comforts of civilization while at the same time not trying to be too Gothic and bizarre. Perhaps the finest creator of alarming rural locations was H.P. Lovecraft, who could frighten his readers just by describing his own invented New England landscape—and that was before he got on to the story itself:

When a traveler in north central Massachusetts takes the wrong fork at the junction of Aylesbury Pike just beyond Dean's Corners he comes upon a lonely and curious country. [Note the unsettling use of the word "wrong." You're only on the first sentence, and already you've been led astray.] The ground gets higher, and the briar-bordered stone walls press closer and closer against the ruts of the dusty, curving road. The trees of the frequent forest belts seem too large, and the wild weeds, brambles and grasses attain a luxuriance not often found in settled regions. When a rise in the road brings the mountains in view above the deep woods, the feeling of strange uneasiness is increased. The summits are too rounded and symmetrical to give a sense of comfort and naturalness, and sometimes the sky silhouettes with especial clearness the queer circles of tall stone pillars with which most of them are crowned.

Lovecraft did tend to overdo his forbidding settings sometimes. All his gorges are of "problematical depth," and all his houses have "rotting gambrel roofs." All his local characters have the "mental and physical stigmata of degeneracy and in-breeding." But his technique of leading his readers away into an unnerving country that is only just on the edge of the world we know is worth the appreciative study of anybody who wants to write horror.

John Farris uses the same technique to great effect in his novel *Wildwood,* in which "the town site had been laid out by a man with a talent for camouflage and misdirection" and in which the inhospitable and monotonous countryside is thick with "bog and bramble and bear wallow."

I used New England myself as a location for my novel *Picture of Evil,* but I tried to create the house in which the evil characters dwell out of glimpses and smells rather than straightforward graphic description:

217

They made their way cautiously along the darkened path. At length they reached a high red-brick wall, heavily overgrown with clematis, bare and brown now, and dripping with rain; and Maurice opened a rusted iron gate, which squeaked dolefully. Beyond the gate was a brick-laid yard and then the dark outline of a huge house. There were no lights at any of the windows, and as Laura followed Maurice toward the front porch, she could smell freshly turned earth, and drains, and damp.

At last we come to the horror itself: the moment when the Threat gets to chomp people, or mince them up, or drain their vital juices, or whatever your chosen Threat actually does. Just how much chomping or mincing or draining actually goes on (and how explicitly you describe it) will depend on what kind of readership you are aiming for. There is a dedicated category readership which will always buy books with plenty of vivid blood and guts—usually high school juniors, servicemen, blue-collar workers, and prison inmates. Then there is a more general but more demanding readership which will buy a horror story provided it is involving and well-written, rather than plain gory.

Choose your words very carefully when describing scenes of horror. The more matter-of-fact you are in your language and your treatment, the more goosebumps you can raise on your readers' skin without being tasteless. You don't need to gloat and lick your lips to make a bloodthirsty scene come alive. In fact, you may be in danger of losing your readers' sympathy if you do.

If you want to study moments of horror written in a hair-raising but completely acceptable way, you would do well to turn to the *Reader's Digest*, which regularly carries stories of the nasty things that have happened to real people. Here's a typical quotation from "Bear Attack," an article that appeared in a recent issue:

Shooting pains jerked Rollins back to reality. As the bears tried to get a better grip on his neck, he bit deep into the cold, damp earth. Now one bear was clawing at his back, while another gnawed at his skull . . . . As he lifted a hand to his head, his fingers slid under his warm, soggy scalp as if it were a hat.

What you can learn from the *Reader's Digest* articles is how people really react to horrific situations, and your fictional moments of true horror will become even more telling by the use of authentic descriptions.

There are few more telling compliments to the horror novelist than to have readers complain that his books are "stomach-churning," when in fact he has used no gruesomely graphic language whatsoever. Here is a scene from *Picture of Evil*, which a great many readers told me was "excessively bloody":

Vincent killed the girls, somehow. Such an act of violence was completely out of character. But he knew there was nothing left for him to do. It was like clubbing seals. Ermintrude knelt in front of him, and he beat her twice, so that her skull broke. Netty, he dragged from her wheelchair, and threw face down on the floor, and hit her as hard as he could on the back of the head.

It was, of course, the imagery of clubbing seals that made so many readers imagine that they had read about blood. If you choose your images well, you need never use the words "gore" or "guts" or even "blood." I'm not saying that I *never* do, but what I'm preaching is the powerful effect of restraint.

The horror novel is one of the most difficult and interesting of media. To my mind, it is still in its infancy, but the comparatively recent acceptance of the importance of horror fiction both as entertainment and literature bodes very well for any talented writer who wants to try his or her hand at it.

Read as much current and classic horror fiction as you can, from Poe on. Discover what has been tried before, and how well, or how badly. Then all you need is a sheaf of blank paper and the will to frighten your fellow human beings to death.

43

SUSPENSE WRITING

By Mary Higgins Clark

My publisher recently forwarded a letter to me from a man who had just read my suspense novels. It was brief and to the point. The reader also wanted to be a writer and he had a question for me: "About how many words and pages are required to turn out a best seller like your own?"

My immediate response was a smile, but it was quickly followed by a feeling of sadness. I don't think that particular aspiring writer will ever make it. And while his question is almost unbelievably naive, it's not the first time it's been asked.

For some reason, I find it difficult to put down advice in an organized manner. Telling someone how to turn out a marketable suspense novel is rather like dancing with an octopus. Which hand (or tentacle) do you reach for first?

However, I think that by attempting to answer the kinds of questions that pop up in my mail and by explaining how a story evolves for me, I might be able to pass along some useful suggestions.

Therefore, with the understanding between us that this will not be a precise blueprint or an annotated "how to," shall we begin?

Question: "I'm eager to write a mystery, but can't think of a plot. Where do you get your ideas?"

Obviously the plot, like the foundation of a house, is the structure on which all else is built. No matter how glib the writing, how enchanting the characters, if the plot doesn't work, or if it works only because of flagrant coincidence or seven-page explanations at the climax, I believe the book is a failure. But where to get the *idea?* Easy. Pick up your local newspaper. The odds are that on the first page or two it contains news of at least one homicide, an aggravated assault, a bank robbery, a mugging, a jailbreak. There also may be a recap on a criminal trial that merits national attention, an update on a series of unsolved murders, and an item about the child who has been missing six months. In other words, material for a dozen short stories or novels.

Now for your own plot. Select a case, one that for whatever reason sticks in your mind. Begin a file on it. Cut out every newspaper item that refers to it. *Know* that case. If a defendant is indicted, try to attend some of the trial sessions. And then—and here's the key—use that case as a nucleus for your story. You're a fiction writer; invent, go further, say to yourself, "What if?"

Several years ago I decided I wanted to try my hand at a suspense novel. Like everyone else, I was faced with the decision: What shall I write? At that time there was a celebrated case in New York in which a young mother was accused of murdering her two children. She stoutly denied her guilt. Two juries rejected her defense. The case fascinated me. I had five children, and the thought of losing any of them gave me nightmares. The thought of not only losing them but being accused of *murdering* them was beyond comprehension. A voice in my subconscious whispered, "And then suppose it happened again?" *Where Are the Children?* was in gestation. Let me reemphasize my point: *Where Are the Children?* was not based on the actual case. I took two ingredients: the young mother accused of infanticide; the frantic denials of guilt. With these in mind I began to build the story.

In my opinion time and place are essential contributors to a successful suspense novel. I chose to set *Where Are the Children?* on Cape Cod for a number of reasons. The Cape offers privacy. New Englanders and particularly "Capeys" do not intrude. The stranger who rents the big house off-season will not be the subject of idle scrutiny. The Cape has mists and fogs, churning surf, nor'easter storms, weatherbeaten captains' houses perched high on embankments above the sea. All these enhance the atmosphere of terror and gloom.

A Stranger Is Watching has as a principal location the bowels of Grand Central Station. Why? There you find dark, damp tunnels throbbing with the echo of rushing trains and groaning machinery; stray cats; underground people silently flitting by; abandoned storerooms, eerie with accumulated cobwebs and grime. I explored the area and knew it was right. And I loved the possibility of the juxtaposition of kidnap victims bound and gagged near a ticking time bomb while overhead thousands of commuters rush through the terminal.

Like the Greeks, I believe in the containment of time. *Oedipus Rex* starts in the morning with the king observing the problems of his stricken domain. It ends a few hours later with his wife a suicide, himself blinded, his world vanished. The swiftness of the action adds to the shock value.

221

I believe that if you write a book in which people are kidnapped and the villain plans to execute them at a specific time, the suspense is considerably greater than if the reader is only generally concerned about the victims' welfare. In *Where Are the Children?* the reader knows that the kidnapper is planning to throw the children into the rock-filled surf at high tide, seven P.M. In *A Stranger Is Watching,* the time bomb is set to go off at 11:30 A.M. Hopefully as zero hour approaches the reader is sharing the anxiety of the protagonists.

Question: "When I start to write, all my characters sound alike. What am I doing wrong?" That's another good inquiry and a valid problem. Through trial and error, I evolved something of a system that has helped me. The key phrase is *know your people.* Do a biography of them before you begin to write your story. Where were they born? Where did they go to school? What do they look like? What kind of clothes do they wear? Are they sophisticated, easy-going, observant? Are they married? Do they have children?

Think of someone you know or knew as a child who reminds you of the character you're trying to create. Remember the way that person talked, the expressions he or she used. When I was inventing Lally, the bag lady in *A Stranger Is Watching,* I combined two people from my childhood. One was our cleaning woman, who used to come up the street invariably singing "lalala"; the other the proprietor of a hole-in-the-wall candy store near my grammar school. She was one of the homeliest women I've ever known. The boys in my class always used to make jokes about calling her up for a date. Together the candy store proprietor and "Lala," as we nicknamed our cleaning woman, merged into Lally. But then to get the feeling of authenticity, I haunted Grand Central Station and chatted with real bag ladies. One of them became the prototype for Rosie, the other bag lady in *Stranger.*

There are hundreds of examples of fine books which contradict what I'm about to say, but here it is anyhow. I like to write about *very nice people* who are confronted by the forces of evil and who through their own courage and intelligence work their way through to deliverance. Personally, I'm not comfortable with the non-hero or non-heroine who is basically so bad-tempered or self-serving that in real life I would avoid him or her like the plague. I myself don't get emotional satisfaction out of a book in which the villain is so desperately attractive that I find my-

222

self rooting for him to beat the system. My villains are, and probably will continue to be, as evil, as frightening, as quietly vicious as I can dream them up. I know I'm on the right track if I'm writing at night and no one else is home and when the house makes a settling noise, I uneasily start looking over my own shoulder.

Another key element in creating characters is to *orchestrate* them. Within the framework of the plot try to have a variety of people in whom your readers will not only believe but with whom they can identify. Never, never throw away a minor character. Let your reader understand him, know what makes him tick. And make it a cardinal rule that every minor character must move the story forward. Suspense by its very nature suggests an express train or a roller coaster. Once on board, you cannot get off until the ride ends. I am committed to the belief that this kind of speedy action is essential to good suspense writing.

Question: "Do you do much research before you start writing?" Yes. Yes. Yes. And as I am working on the book I continue to research. My book, *The Cradle Will Fall,* is about an obstetrician who experiments on and sometimes murders his pregnant patients. I read everything I could get my hands on about artificial insemination, *in vitro* pregnancies, and fetal transplant experiments. I interviewed and picked the brains of a doctor friend who is a researcher in a pre-natal hospital laboratory. I proposed "what if" questions to obstetrician buddies. Then when the book was completed I gave a Xerox to one obstetrician friend. I was in New York. He was in Minneapolis. I was on a tight deadline: He stayed on the phone with me four hours. I had a list of all medical references in the book, e.g. page 2 top line, page 8 fourth paragraph, etc. Jack reviewed every one of them with me. On some he said, "That's fine." On others, he'd suggest changes. For example, near the climax of the book, a desperate search is going on for the gravely ill heroine. Jack said, "It's an emergency. Two doctors are talking. Don't have Richard say, 'She'll need a transfusion when we find her.' Put it this way, 'We'll hang a bottle of O-negative.' "

The Cradle Will Fall is set in New Jersey. The protagonist, Katie DeMaio, is a young assistant prosecutor. My daughter is an assistant prosecutor in New Jersey. She was my expert in police procedure. She went over every line that referred to the working of the court, the prosecutor's office, trials, witness statements, etc. For example, after a murder scene I had the homicide detective post a sign, CRIME AREA. POSITIVELY NO ADMITTANCE. I remembered having seen a sign like that somewhere. My daughter said, "No, that's wrong. In a suspicious death, we'd leave a cop guarding the premises until the apartment has been thoroughly searched." In another chapter, I had the prosecutor televise the interrogation of a witness. She corrected me. "In New York that's being done sometimes, but it's still not legal in New Jersey." The point is that authenticity of detail gives the ring of truth to a book.

Question: "How much rewriting do you do when you're working on a book?"

Plenty. But rewriting is a two-edged sword. I know too many people who've spent months working over the first chapter of the projected novel. That's wrong. Get it down. Bumble through it. Tell the story. Then when you have fifty or one hundred pages typed you've got something to work with. It may be at that point you'll start again from the beginning because the book has a fundamental flaw that has become obvious. I wrote fifty pages of *The Cradle Will Fall.* In that first version Katie DeMaio is the twenty-eight-year-old wife of a prominent judge. She is in a minor automobile accident while he is away, stays overnight in the hospital, and while sedated witnesses a crime.

I soon realized something was wrong. I couldn't get worried about Katie. The reason became obvious. Here she is married to an interesting, handsome man, a Superior Court judge. I just knew that when John DeMaio got home the next day, he'd make very sure that no one would hurt his Katie.

How to solve the problem? John had to go. Instead of the *wife,* Katie became the young *widow* of Judge John DeMaio. Immediately, she is infinitely more sympathetic—vulnerable and alone in the large secluded house she inherited from him. A great additional plus is that we now have room for a love interest. Doctor Richard Carroll, the provocative medical examiner, is very keen on Katie, and she has been holding him off. The reader, we hope, becomes emotionally involved in the potential romance and worries that Katie is sealing her fate because she does not let Richard know she is scheduled for minor surgery. The doctor who will operate on her is planning to kill her.

So there we have it. As I warned in the beginning I suspect this advice has a disjointed quality. I tend to offer writing hints the way an old

County Sligo cousin shared her recipe for Irish soda bread: "Take a handful of this, a fistful of that, a pinch of whatever . . . . Now taste it, love. Does it need more caraway seeds and raisins?"

Nevertheless if any of this advice helps anyone, I'm glad. There is surely no sweeter satisfaction to the suspense writer than to hear a heavy-eyed friend say accusingly, "You kept me up half the night reading your darn book!"

44

CREATING A SERIES CHARACTER

By Robert B. Parker

WHILE I have ventured outside the form upon occasion (*Three Weeks in Spring, Wilderness, Love and Glory*), it is the chronicle of a series character named Spenser that puts bread and Promise margarine on the table at my house.

Writing about a protagonist who has appeared before and will appear again presents some specialized problems. For instance, you have to find exposition tricks that will inform people who are reading you for the first time, without boring people who have read all your books in sequence. And, while both the writer and the reader are aware that the hero of a series is very unlikely to die, the hero doesn't know it. One has to be careful to render him as a man no less mortal than the rest of us.

But if there are problems in a series, there are also opportunities. If you create a character in one book that you like (Hawk, for instance, in *Promised Land*), you can use him again. And if you didn't get him right the first time, you have another chance, and another. Moreover, you have the chance to develop your hero over a sequence of books and during a span of real time. Thus Spenser, who first appeared when I was 41, can grow, as I have.

There are, then, a few things that are uncommon about writing a series of novels. But there is much more that is common to the craft. In each instance, series or not, I begin with what Henry James called a "treatment," a brief statement of story and locale and major characters. The treatment is normally about two pages in longhand. Don't be misled. This is the hard part. The treatment may take a month of sitting, several hours each day, thinking (my wife says thinking has always been especially trying for me, but one should pay her little mind. She once described me as looking like a Mississippi state cop). I

226

didn't have to think up the protagonist when I set out on my first novel (*The Godwulf Manuscript*). Spenser sprang fully conceived from my imagination where he had been lurking since I wrote my age in single figures. Because I don't have to imagine the hero, I always start with the scene, i.e., the place, the circumstances, the people that I can write about, the academic scene, for instance, or the book-tour-talk-show scene.

From the treatment, I develop a chapter outline, still in longhand, that lays out the sequence. It's not very fancy (a chapter might be outlined in a sentence, "Spenser drives to Smithfield and talks with the police chief"), and it partakes of none of those insistent curlicues that you learned in school (if there's an A, there has to be a B, etc.). The whole novel gets outlined in five or six pages. It is primarily for my emotional well-being. It saves me from rolling a piece of white paper into the typewriter and then staring blankly not knowing what to write. The outline is there, Linus; I need only look. Sometimes I don't look at all. The outline to *The Judas Goat* was there beside me on the desk every writing day, and I never so much as glanced at it. Sometimes I follow it closely, sometimes I stop mid-book and re-outline something I haven't been able to get right. But I always know pretty much what the story is when I begin to write it.

Then, the outline completed, I have only to write the book. I'm not being cute. Once the story is conceived, the hard part is over. If you have the ability, then executing the book is merely a matter of sustained (though hardly exhausting) effort. Discipline (though hardly of monastic intensity) is required.

If you have the talent without discipline, you'll have thirty pages of a swell novel in your desk for the rest of your life and you'll publish a couple of good short poems somewhere. If you have the discipline without talent you'll have ten unpublished novels in your closet. There's a third possibility, I suppose. You could have discipline, no talent, and a knack, and be Harold Robbins. Ideally, perhaps, all three would be best. But of one thing I am certain. Writers write, and one is not a writer until one has written.

I set myself a minimum number of pages, as a way to get from beginning, through middle, to end. The number of pages varies with circumstance. I have never set the limit lower than two pages a day, or higher than five. Unless I'm on a roll, I stop when I've written my quota. If there is time left in my writing day, I'll turn to something else, but by writing my quota I have fulfilled my responsibility to the book that day.

Since my typescript tends to equate one-to-one to the printed page, five pages a day will give me a two-hundred-page book in forty days of writing. That sounds mechanical, and it is. It is a large task broken down into many small ones. When I can, I try to follow Hemingway's advice to stop while you're hot so it will be easy to start up next day. But sometimes I'm not hot for weeks on end and then I just do my quota. If you wait to be hot you'll accomplish that thirty-page novel mentioned above.

I am not compulsive about writing. I don't work weekends. I don't work nights. If one of my sons is performing, I go and watch. If my wife will take a trip with me, I'll travel. I don't bring a typewriter. If my novel comes out three days later, or two weeks later, it makes small difference. Writing is my livelihood, not my life. And while I can't conceive of not writing at all, I'm not compelled to do it every day.

On the other hand, I do have to do it regularly. I would assume most writers who succeed in publishing any quantity of work do it regularly.

I have always been more interested in the protagonist than in the plot, which is, I suppose, one reason I write largely in the first person. If you're in doubt, I'd urge you to try first-person narration. It's the natural storytelling mode ("You shoulda seen what happened to me at Hampton Beach last night"), and it helps prevent inflated narrative language. If you tell your story in the first person, it is very handy to invent some people who can help you interpret your hero by offering some objective comment. In *The Great Gatsby,* Fitzgerald took that technique to the extreme by having Gatsby's story told to us by Nick Carraway. It is, of course, part of Gatsby's tragedy that he doesn't understand what happened to him. He couldn't have explained it. Carraway had to.

Spenser talks of himself, but for the parts he can't or won't speak of, Susan Silverman serves. She helps us understand him. She helps him understand himself. Hawk too helps illuminate Spenser. The ways in which Hawk and Spenser are alike, and the ways in which they are not alike, are crucial in imagining Spenser.

An interesting story about dull people may be possible, but I can't think of one. For me, the plot is in large part a frame, a series of occasions in which Spenser is able to demonstrate what he is, to enact himself. But to speak of the two, plot and character, as if they were separable is misleading. "What is character," James said, "but the determination of incident? What is incident but the illustration of character?"

The best books are always about more than the plot anyway. They have echoes and implications. They are informed by a sense of how life is, or ought to be. George Higgins wrote about cops and robbers. But his books are also about the thinness of the line between them, and about the way a man should behave, and about the relationships among men in groups. In *True Confessions,* John Gregory Dunne wrote about a murder investigation. But he also wrote about brothers, and hierarchy and autonomy and Catholicism, and Irish-ness. "The only reason for the existence of the novel," James said, "is that it does attempt to represent life." Aspiring writers should give their days and nights to Henry James (and me).

Writing isn't as hard as writers lead you to think it is, but it does not lend itself to shortcuts. Clichés are shortcuts; avoid them like the plague. But there are other more subtle temptations to cut across the field. I remember a manuscript in which the author used one description for two people, something to the effect that they were both huge and bald and menacing. That's a shortcut. The novelist attempting in some way "to represent life" must recognize that rarely in life are two people identical, even if they are minor characters.

A writer does that not because he's lazy, but because he's impatient. He wants to get on with it. It takes some understanding and some self-control to come to terms with the fact that the careful representation of life *is* getting on with it.

I have sometimes made the remark that I don't think writing very teachable. But if you are going to pursue writing instruction despite that admonition (no one has ever lost money rejecting my advice), be certain that your teacher has done what he/she/it teaches. Many people understand reading, but only writers understand writing. An intelligent reader can often say what's good or bad about a piece of writing, and there are critics who have helped me understand my own work better. But only a writer can tell you how (if it can be told): a writer who publishes; for money. I believe that there are very few good novels that don't get published. In fact I believe there are none.

There are, however, good novels that don't get finished. There is no one right way. Each of us finds a way that works for him. But there is a wrong way. The wrong way is to finish your writing day with no more words on paper than when you began. Writers write.

45

WRITING THE SUSPENSE-ADVENTURE NOVEL

BY CLIVE CUSSLER

I HATE to write.

Quite frankly, I see nothing blasphemous in admitting it. There are thousands of writers who find scribbling words on paper a colossal drag. Writing is a damned tough way to make a buck, at least to most people. I seethe internally when I hear or read about those Pollyannas who merrily peck away at their typewriters, whistling while they create, morning, noon and night, tossing off 20,000 words between coffee breaks.

I hate them, too.

On a good day of total effort, beginning at nine o'clock and ending at five (an old routine carried over from my advertising agency days), I'm lucky if I turn out four finished pages or 1,000 words. And then I have to take a long walk, indulge in a martini and take a snooze prior to dinner, before I'm mentally rejuvenated enough to return to the land of the living.

When I finally type THE END to a novel, the clouds part and the sun bursts through, flowers blossom across the land, angels sing along to harp music, and I deflate like an old balloon whose elastic is shot.

Therefore, because writing is so exhausting, to me at any rate, I plan and research each project thoroughly before hitting the proper keys to spell out CHAPTER ONE. My problem is that I can visualize my characters, backgrounds, and events as though I were standing in the middle of the action, so the difficult part is turning all these wonderful sights and sounds into mere words that place the reader amid the action, too.

To me the readers come above all else. I look upon them as guests who have gone out of their way to spend time and expense to indulge in whatever small enjoyment I can provide. My particular genre is suspense-adventure, so in order to get off the mark quickly, I must find a concept that grabs the reader's fancy before he turns past the title page. Within the realm of adventure there are thousands of subjects and tales that have great appeal. One of the trends in fashion at present is for novelists to write fiction based loosely on a non-fiction event. This often revolves around a "what if" principle. For instance, one day I asked myself, what if they raise the *Titanic*? The next question that entered my mind was why? Obviously the cost of salvaging the great liner from two and one-half miles down in the abysmal depths would be enormous. What reason would justify the effort and expense? Out of this pre-examination a plot was born.

Without a concept hook to hang your plot on, you have nothing. The swashbuckler of yesterday who chopped up the moustached villains and did little else but carry the insipid heroine off into the sunset at the finish won't cut the mustard today. The idea of having a blimp bomb the Superbowl as in *Black Sunday* was a good hook for a "what if" adventure. *Airport* and of course *Jaws* are other successful stories that embraced this principle.

More than ever, the reader who shells out for your novel is looking for an escape. It's a fact of life, that if you don't aim your talents at the market, you won't sell. If the reader isn't presold by an author's past reputation, or by word-of-mouth recommendation, or a blitz publicity campaign, he has no other reason to select your masterpiece except for one hell of an intriguing concept.

Assuming that you have the story the world is waiting to devour, you should now turn your energies to the next step in the adventure novel—structure.

Gotcha! I'll bet you thought I was going to say plot or perhaps characterization. Not so. Next to a mind-boggling concept, structure is the most important foundation for a novel. Whether you intend to write it in the first person or the third is elementary. You should take the path that makes you comfortable. First person allows you to probe the hero or heroine's mind in depth; you see only what they see. The third-person narration, on the other hand, gives a wider range of freedom to travel into areas the first person cannot follow. Seeing the action from the central character's eyes limits the writer to what I call the "Formula-A Structure." You travel with the narrator from pro-logue to epilogue, seeing only what he sees. This is a common practice among new writers because of its basic simplicity.

However, I do not mean to suggest that Formula A is mundane. Hardly. It has been used with great success by writers since man first scratched in the sand. The classical love stories, mysteries and, yes, horror stories, too, have taken advantage of its storytelling smoothness. Formula A also makes for a tight tale that involves the readers as closely in the action as though they were the parrot on Long John Silver's shoulder.

For writers who turn on to intricate plotting and a cast of hundreds, Formula B is the only way to fly. Here the third-person viewpoint throws open the floodgates of creativity, and you can pull the reader through a labyrinth of subplots, "sideplots," and "twistplots." You have the opportunity of setting the scene in a jet over the Arctic in one chapter and suddenly switching to a camel caravan crossing the Sahara in the next.

Leon Uris, Robert Ludlum, and Harry Patterson alias Jack Higgins are all masters of the complex structure. Instead of studying flowery prose and in-depth characterization as most writers are prone to do, you should examine quite closely the organization and precision the authors mentioned above weave throughout their stories. Harold Robbins, for example, used the epilogue as the prologue in *The Adventurers*, and then went on to slip his hero deftly in and out of first- and third-person narration.

Do you intend to utilize the advantages of a prologue to set up future conflicts? Will you need an epilogue to tie the ends together? Have you the guts to combine several plots into one? Have you considered dividing your novel into different parts? This is what we mean by structure.

There are no hard-and-fast rules for structuring the modern adventure novel. In Formula A, you must keep your hero believable and the action moving to keep readers turning the pages. With Formula B, the trick is to keep them second guessing and so involved with who's-doing-what-to-whom they can't put the book down. This is achieved by alternating your characters and their personal conflicts so that in the beginning there seems to be no comprehensible connection. Then as the plot unfolds, they're all irresistibly drawn together into an ever-heightening climax. I call this threading the needle. You've got to sew all your characters into the same pocket and thereby give your reader a satisfying conclusion.

A satisfying conclusion can never be stressed too strongly. How many books have you read that began like gangbusters and then fell to pieces in the end? The sad result is that you forget them damned quickly while a tale that has a smash ending stays with you.

All too often a writer will sit down with a blockbuster concept and barrel through the first half of the story only to fall off a cliff because he had no idea where he was going in the first place. You have to know what you're aiming at in the last chapter and then backtrack and work toward it. That's why planning your structure is so important. Creative blueprinting can't turn a bad book into a good one, but it sure helps.

When it comes to plotting, so much has been written by renowned authorities of mystery and adventure writing, I see no reason simply to repeat most of their well-known rules. I plot as I go. Many novelists write an outline that has almost as many pages as their ultimate book. Others knock out a brief synopsis. Again, do what is comfortable. If you have to plot out every move your characters make, so be it. Just make sure there is a plausible purpose behind their machinations. A good reader can smell a phony plot a block away.

In modern adventure writing, the trend seems to be to sacrifice great gobs of character-probing in favor of fast-paced action. Sad to say, most critics are still hung up on finely tuned character definition. but then critics only concern themselves with how well a book is written. The guy who actually lays down the cash for it is more interested in how well it reads.

Alistair MacLean, perhaps one of the finest adventure writers of the last several decades, favors rapid pace over character psychiatry. His people are sharply defined in their looks and mannerisms and come across very well, without pages of historical background.

The hero in my series is usually described through the eyes of other characters. These observations, usually in small doses, occur only when they appropriately add to a particular scene or action.

They don't make good heroes these days. The anti-hero seems to be currently in vogue, especially in detective and spy novels. But pure adventure is something else again. A Casper Milquetoast just won't do. Men readers want to identify with the shrewd, devil-may-care hero who surmounts every obstacle put up by the opposition and emerges victorious in the end. Likewise, women, in spite of the current hoopla about equality, still secretly yearn for the rugged he-man to sweep them off their feet. If you doubt this last statement, simply take a look at the staggering sales figures of the romantic novels by Rosemary Rogers and several other astute women writers.

In most dramatic genres, the reader likes to identify with the characters and to experience what they see and feel. In adventure, the reader runs along the sidelines, cheering everyone on—a prime reason for your characters to be bigger than life, but still believable. That's what's called walking the tightrope. On one hand, you run the risk of making some characters too ordinary. On the other, you don't dare allow them to become comic book Supermen or Wonderwomen.

If your hero must save the world, at least let him act human while he goes about it. He should still put his pants on one leg at a time, sneeze occasionally, blow his nose, and feel the urge to go to the bathroom. What man can identify with another who does none of these? Same with women. I like my girls to zing in a few four-letter words when they're angry or frustrated. Show me one who doesn't at least say "Damn!" after ramming a painted toenail through a pair of new pantyhose.

There is an old saying in the advertising business: "See what your competitors are doing, then do just the opposite." That's the whole idea of writing a book: You're telling a story no one else has told before.

When I decided to develop a series hero, I looked around the field and studied everyone from Sherlock Holmes to James Bond to Travis McGee. I figured the last thing the adventure arena needed was another private detective, spy or CIA agent. So I created a guy by the name of Dirk Pitt who is the Special Projects Director for NUMA (the National Underwater & Marine Agency). Fortunately, I stumbled onto a good thing. The mysteries that can be expanded upon in and around water are as boundless as the oceans themselves. I might mention that I chose the name Pitt partly because it is one syllable, thus making it easy to say, "Pitt did this, and Pitt did that," etc.

My final suggestion relates to what I said earlier about treating the reader as an honored guest. Every so often I'll stop and ask myself, what would the reader like to see at this particular moment in the story? Then I'll try my best to give it to him. I figure that since my

235

reader paid good money or took the time and trouble to check out my efforts from the library, the least I can do is place his interests above mine.

I don't cotton to writers who engrave on marble what *they* think should be read. My work is geared strictly to provide a few hours of enjoyable escape. I don't believe in imparting personal philosophy, social commentary, or hidden meanings between the lines. Some writers prefer to be called novelists, some storytellers, others spokesmen for the masses.

Me: I'm an entertainer, no more, no less.

46

ON WRITING SCIENCE FICTION

By Ursula K. Le Guin

I LOOK over my typewriter, out the study window, forty miles north to the mountain called "The Lady"—Mount St. Helens. Since the May 18, 1980 eruption and the May 25 ash-fall, people keep saying to me, "You're a science fiction writer—you should write a story about the volcano!" And I can only stare, and whimper, "But—But—"

I could attempt to describe what the eruption looked like from my study window. I could research and write up a history of the volcano. I could tell the true story of the old man who wouldn't leave his home at Spirit Lake (but that's been better done already in a country song). I could write poetry that has the volcano in it somewhere, some day. There's a great deal any writer could write about the eruption, and the ash-fall, and the people involved. But the one thing no writer could make of it, now, is a science fiction story. Science fiction is about what hasn't happened, but might; or what never will happen, but this is what it might be like if it did.

St. Helens happened. The Lady blew. Having seen that pillar of darkness towering seventy thousand feet above my city, I know that the most and best any artist could do with it is to try—and fail—to describe it.

Before May 18, a major eruption of St. Helens was an *idea*. Since then, it's an *event*. Science fiction works with ideas. It is basically an intellectual form of literature—with all the limitations, and all the potentialities, that go with the dominance of intellect.

I hear a polite mutter in my mind's ear: "The woman is nuts. Brainless heroes bashing brawny villains to rescue bronze-bra'd princesses while boring through Hyperspace towards Beta Bunthi, home of the Bug-Eyed Yrogs—this is intellectual?"

Well, no. But it isn't science fiction, either. It's space opera. Let me define my terms. As far as I can make out, "science fiction" and "speculative fiction" are the same thing—and so henceforth I'll call them SF, which nicely includes both. "Fantasy" covers all imaginative fiction, but may be used as a category including all imaginative fiction *except* SF and horror stories. It also includes "science fantasy." As for "space opera," in print or on the screen, it is to SF what "sword and sorcery" is to fantasy: the stuff produced for mass sales. Not steak, not hamburger, just baloney. Mindless, macho, and miserably imitative; but with a thirty-million-dollar budget it can be lots of fun and very pretty.

Space opera not only borrows hardware and gimmicks from SF, but also filches the great imaginative themes, such as space travel, time travel, alien beings, other worlds. But instead of using them as metaphors of the human condition, as SF does, space opera makes them into meaningless decorations. They are not part of the structure of the work, but serve instead to disguise it. You peel off the space suits and the tentacles, and guess what? Howdy, podner! Welcome to Hyperspace, Texas!—And, frankly, I miss the horses.

A real SF story, book, or film is fundamentally different. It starts with an act of the mind, a step from *is* to *if,* a reach of the imagination into the nonexistent. But it is not a leap into the impossible or the absurd. Indeed, SF dreads absurdity and loves logic almost as much as Mr. Spock does. In SF, the risky act of imagination is controlled by the thinking mind, the intellect. And therefore the discipline it accepts most naturally and gracefully is that of science. Real science: a respect for fact, and a sympathy with the patient way science arrives at fact.

Fantasy makes its connection to ordinary-daylight-outside-the-book-cover-reality through the emotions and through ordinary physical perception. (I could go on about that, but this chapter's about SF, not fantasy!)

SF makes its connection with ordinary-day-light-etc.-reality through ideas—principally the evidence of science and the speculations of the thinking mind. In SF, there is a reason for what happens, and it is a rational reason. The events of the story make sense in a cause-and-effect system. No matter how wildly imaginative they are, they don't happen just because the author likes it that way, or thinks it "feels right." Fantasy admits such reasons unknown to Reason. But SF doesn't. In SF, the questions "Why?" and "How?"—asked at any point in the story—should be answerable.

This doesn't mean that an SF story is an educational lecture with some fictional sugar-coating. Anything but! The ideas are the seed, not the tree—the blueprint, not the building. An SF story that hasn't *grown from* its ideas, but just flatly states them, is dull stuff.

A very few SF writers are practicing scientists, in such various fields as psychology, anthropology, biology, astronomy. Most are not. My impression is that the knowledge of science used by most SF writers comes from self-education—reading books and articles on subjects that interest them. (As for myself, the total of my formal training in science is one semester of anthropology and one of geology.) The point is, what's wanted is not a great mass of technical knowledge, but an attitude towards knowledge—an attitude of curiosity, above all. If learning facts and finding how events connect together bores you, then you probably don't read much SF, and certainly wouldn't enjoy writing it.

Let me try to illustrate this apparently paradoxical situation. Let's take a typical crazy SF invention: A five-hundred-foot-tall woman lands on Earth. Now, first of all, does she walk up Main Street, mashing a Honda at every step, and sit down for a rest on the First National Bank building?

In fantasy, she could. In the space opera movie, she does. In SF, she doesn't, because she can't. If she's really a woman just like us only a hundred times taller, she's too heavy to stand up, let alone walk. Crushed by her own weight—the gravitational pull of the Earth—the poor thing is lying there dying of internal injuries. We know that beings of our general type and mass cannot exceed a certain size, under our local conditions. Brontosaurus was at the limit for a land animal, and he wasn't any five hundred feet tall. Even Bill Walton has problems. And we are following Delany's Law. S.R. Delany, a most innovative writer of SF, put it this way: "Science fiction must not contradict *what is known to be known.*" And we know that it is known that solid 500-foot ladies are impractical.

But what if she's a projection of a five-foot Alien who is staying up in her space ship above the Earth until she finds if it's safe to arrive in person? She meant to beam down a five-foot projection, but the beamer got the size wrong. The technology involved—perhaps using holographic images—is not known to be impossible. Or, what if she really is five hundred feet tall, but, since she comes from a giant gas planet like Jupiter, she is made of airy, gauzy stuff, with almost negligible weight and mass? Realizing that she got the size wrong, she compresses herself into the shape of a five-foot woman weighing 3½ pounds, and walks briskly into the First National Bank building, holding her breath. . . . Well, this is

239

getting pretty hard to explain, but I'm not sure that we've contradicted anything that is known to be known. And so long as that rule is kept, SF is perfectly free to invent. It just has to make sure, as it goes along, that it doesn't contradict *itself*. The pieces must hang together.

Figuring out how it hangs together, all the where-why-what-and-whether, is half the fun of SF, for both the reader and the author. There's so much to know about our friend in the First National Bank Building—what life is like for someone as gauzy and compressible as a silk scarf, and what the weather is like on her home planet, and what kind of society her people might have, since they are all very fragile, very agile, and able to change size and shape at will. And what might have brought her here to Earth, and, as a matter of fact, what she's doing in the Bank. Madame, what are you up to in there?

"Prrswit frumbo rigpot thoom," she says into her Vox-Coder, which instantly prints out in English: * I * AM * GATHERING * MATERIAL * FOR * A * SEARINGLY * REALISTIC * STORY * ABOUT * BANK * TELLERS *

Fantasy and SF certainly overlap, but there is a real difference between them, and in general I believe they are best not muddled up together. A fantasy element—something rationally unexplainable—can be very annoying in an SF story, and often looks like what it is: a bit of laziness on the author's part, sloppy or wishful thinking. The reverse mix, SF intruding into fantasy, often occurs in books for young people by authors who are basically distrustful of the power of fantasy, and so try to explain away the whole thing—"But it was really all a dream!" That's a cheat, and the kids know it.

There is one more thing about SF that I feel I have to mention, but don't want to, because it is so undignified. In workshops I call it PSG. PSG stands for Pseudo-Scientific Garbage. It isn't meant as an insult, merely as a description. After all, the truth is that science fiction is not true. It isn't science. It's fiction. Although it starts from a known fact or an educated guess or at least a crazy but plausible hunch, and although it tries loyally not to contradict what is known to be known and not to stumble over its own internal logic—still, the whole thing is made up. And, especially if it's set in the future or on a different world, *all the details* have to be made up. Here's where the PSG comes in, and here's where the gift for SF may shine brightest.

For example: that Vox-Coder our Alien was using. I didn't explain that it's an instant translating machine, voice-activated. I didn't really have to. It's not a big step from the little hand-carried translator-computers we have right now. The Vox-Coder seems not only possible, but probable. Yet, the more you happen to know about language and translation, the less probable it may seem. Here evidence from one science (computer technology) contradicts evidence from another science (linguistic theory), and you have to take your choice. But your choice is warped by the fact that translators are so handy in SF. Without them, all the Aliens have to spend months learning English, or the Terrans have to painfully learn Voobish. So we gave our 3½-pound Alien a ¼-ounce Vox-Coder. And so I call it, with all due respect, a piece of PSG.

All interstellar space ships are PSG.

Much PSG is truly common property in SF. You learn it simply by reading SF. (Anybody who tries to write SF without having read it is wasting his time and ours.) There's a good deal of genuine sharing: the word "FTL," for example, meaning Faster Than Light. Anybody can fly an FTL ship. More often you don't borrow the name—Vox-Coder, phaser, pinlighter, etc.—but take the general idea and deck it out your own way. Of course you also are free to make up any gimmick or device you want or need, and this is fun. Much of the joyful inventiveness, the shock and beauty of SF is in its PSG. I think of Philip K. Dick's fully automated and highly verbose taxicabs, which tend to argue with their customers, sometimes becoming quite emotional. . . . Of Vonda McIntyre's gentle replacement of the hypodermic needle by the serpent's tooth. . . . Of H.G. Wells's lovely, shimmering Time Machine. . . . Of the pleasure I had trying to figure out what it would feel like to be a woman this month and a man next month and both/neither in between. . . . PSG, all of it. *Taxicabs don't talk!* Only if you're perfectly sure of that fact should you write a story about talking taxicabs.

In 1968 I wrote a book, *The Lathe of Heaven* (and in 1979 WNET/TV made a movie of it). At a climactic point of the book, Mount Hood erupts, and then the extinct volcano inside Portland city limits, Mount Tabor, erupts, and the whole Cascade Range goes off—except Mount St. Helens.

Why did I deliberately leave her out, knowing that she was in fact the likeliest to erupt? I can't explain. When I was writing the book I looked at her out the window, the "misty, blue-grey cone" which is in the story but not here in the real world any longer; and she must have whispered to me, "Sshh. Quiet. I have my own plans."

And I'm very glad I got it all wrong. My job's fiction. I'll leave the reality business to the Lady.

47

SEEING AROUND CURVES

By Martha Grimes

SOMETIMES I wonder if painters and potters are asked, "How far along are you?" with that portrait or vase, or "How much have you done?" with that landscape or bowl. Such well-intentioned inquiries into the progress of a novel make me feel a little cross and, in a way, slightly stupid, as if I, naïve traveler on the Orient Express, were asked to describe the Venetian canals before my feet had left the platform in Victoria.

People seem to grasp the idea that a painter does not see an orange or an ear floating in his mind's eye, and a potter does not see a neck or a handle. But perhaps because we all "write" in some sense, there is a certain familiarity about pages, and they think progress can be charted by counting them. Perhaps paintings and pots are seen spatially, as a whole, but stories and novels are seen as linear. An eye doesn't "follow" an ear in a portrait, but it's a dead cert that page two will follow page one in a book. And because of this, when I say "a hundred and fifty pages," my interrogator might answer, "Ah. Halfway through, then." No, definitely not, I tell him, no more than I'd have painted half a face if I had got down the eye and the ear.

But if one sees writing in this way—as linear—it is understandable that one might be more likely to look at it as a trip, with marked distances to go between colorful chapter stop-offs. And the mystery writer especially may lean toward this idea of inventing a sort of TripTic or map or other means of charting the territory he intends to cover, then peopling it with characters, and drenching it with atmosphere. Since it is true that in a mystery there should be no loose ends and no clues unaccounted for, it is likely that one might think all story plot problems are resolved in good time.

This assumption that the emphasis in the mystery novel is on eventful happenings or crises—like the murder itself, for it is most often murder—sometimes obscures the fact that the ax doesn't hang in the air, but must be dropped by someone's hands on someone's head. It also assumes that we who write it must know about Venice before we leave Victoria Station. Yet few people know exactly what their destination will look like before they get there or even if they will reach it. So we don't know where we are until we see what it looks like, and we don't know who we are until we see what we do. No one can see around curves no matter how far he sticks his neck out the window. Plot—the territory we want to chart—depends on the characters as much in a mystery as it does in any other novel; character directs the whole journey.

Many writers apparently do very well by mapping out the trip before they start, by sorting out what we might think of as the central elements of plot in a mystery—the perpetrator, the victim, the means, and the motive—and getting them into place by means of outlines, summaries, and synopses. On the other hand, there are writers who just go ahead and climb aboard the train, uncertain even of their destination, perhaps taking their chances that some unknown factor will keep the train from derailing.

I suppose I work this way because I find it so difficult to untangle plot from character, to invent crises for strangers. Nor do I think the device of the character sketch written ahead helpful, because what Tony had for tea when he was seven doesn't interest me unless at twenty-seven he's going to lace someone else's tea with cyanide. Plot, character, setting all seem one huge tangled skein when we set out to write. And because it's difficult to untangle the elements, you might think that the Grand Design should be set down before you have characters bumping into one another on the platform. Line them up and make them behave, for heaven's sakes! There goes the Colonel, making for the café. *Thwack!*

Now let's say that the sketches, the outlines, the synopsis, or the plot summaries are all approaches that you feel will at least get you aboard the Orient Express. You take your character-sketched people along and thus you and Sybil and Grimthorpe and the Colonel manage to get into the dining car (oddly lacking in ambiance since you would hardly have included that in your plot synopsis). The four of you are having a good gossip and being quite friendly, all of you with copies of the outline/sketch/synopsis before you.

243

You're all in a pretty good mood, except when the Colonel becomes rather churlish because he can't get the waiter's attention. Of course he can't because there is no waiter; he was not in the TripTic.

Now, Sybil, Grimthorpe and the Colonel read over the outline/sketch/synopsis. And there the trouble begins. Fortunately, the dining car is unpeopled—since the background passengers weren't in the synopsis—and the four of you can have a high old time:

Sybil is furious because you're having her marry Grimthorpe when the Orient Express hits Venice. Sybil claims she wants to marry Anthony.

Who's Anthony, you wonder? watching her dampen her finger and plaster a spit-curl to her cheek as she gazes out at the empty (truly empty) countryside.

"Sybil," you ask patiently, "*why* must you marry Anthony?"

"Well, *I* dunno, do I?" Then she rolls her eyes and adds, "I s'pose because he's ever so 'andsome. . . ." She swings her leg and twirls a cheap sequined bag. . . .

But Sybil's supposed to be a marchioness. Why is she coming on like a shopgirl?

Grimthorpe's mouth twitches as he looks down his knobby nose at Sybil and announces he wouldn't have her on a bet.

The Colonel's face is beet-red because he can't find a waiter, yell as he might.

You now realize something's wrong and wonder how the devil you're going to get out of this mess as the Orient Express chugs along to Paris. The only thing you're sure of is that they'll all detrain in Venice—

Until the train rolls into Paris, and Sybil just gets off. Anthony lives in Paris. . . .

The reader is certainly familiar with what is practically a cliché—that after a while the "characters simply take over." This is actually one of those wonderful remissions (or reprieves) for the writer, when everything seems to be on automatic pilot, and the people in your book "come alive," and appear to know what they're going to do and how they're going to do it. You would be willing to believe that the Muse indeed visiteth at such times. The Muse or Tinkerbell or Inspiration or something. But since you know that characters do not clear the mental compartments and take over themselves, it must be some other part of your mind doing it, and all of the scenario above is probably the unconscious ditching the lovely plot complications of the conscious mind. In other words, Sybil (part of you) has a reason for tuning out all of that highbrow marchioness stuff; you simply don't know what it is, any more than you can see around curves. But you will eventually know why, and eventually round the curve. That you will either go mad at worst or type away in a state of controlled hysteria (at best) is something writers like me have to put up with if they want to get to Venice.

All of this revolves pretty obviously around another question that makes me cross: "Where do you get your ideas?" *Idea* is a word that seems frighteningly all-encompassing and makes me think of Carl Sagan neatening up the cosmos. *Idea* really does sound as if the interrogator is asking you where you got your *plot*. And the whole point is—how on earth do you know what people are going to do (correction, what you're going to *have* them do) until you see what they've done so far?

Perhaps I'd opt for the word (if there must be one) of "notion." That sounds far more frivolous, something rather small and capable of being grasped. It could be *anything*. The "notion" for *The Man with a Load of Mischief* came purely from the name of a pub. That a pub would have such a strange name led me on the further notion that a mystery set in England and having something to do with pub names might be interesting. My original detective was an effete, snobbish aristocrat, whose only saving grace was the wit of Oscar Wilde. Unfortunately, I had to toss that one out, since I don't have the wit of Oscar Wilde. Anyway, this character ultimately became Melrose Plant, and by that time, Scotland Yard had insinuated itself into the mystery in the person of Richard Jury. Perhaps the reason I am so fond of British pub names is that the germ of an idea can be found in so many of them. *The Anodyne Necklace* was irresistible for this reason. The notion of someone's killing for a necklace with curative powers was all I climbed aboard with.

The initial "notion" might be anything concrete—scene, sound, smell. I think if you confuse "notion" with "theme," you are definitely on the wrong platform, and you'll be sitting on your suitcases forever. *Theme* is an abstraction; it is not a cause but an effect.

The notion for my novel *The Old Fox Deceiv'd* was nothing more than a mental image of a youngish woman walking along a dark and cobbled street. In this case, it was a setting that attracted me, and memories of the quintessential English fishing village called Robin Hood's Bay that I had visited ten years before. I was writing this plotless book when in one day I saw, in three different places, a woman dressed in black and white. It was Halloween, and one of them, in a black cape, was walking across a low-rising hillside. The three became a composite that begins the story:

> She came out of the fog, her face painted half-white, half-black, walking down Grape Lane. It was early January and the sea-roke drove in from the east, turning the cobbled street into a smoky tunnel that curved down to the water. . . . The wind billowed her black cape, which settled again round her ankles in an eddying wave. She wore a white satin shirt and white satin trousers stuffed into high-heeled black boots. The click of the heels on the wet stones was the only sound except for the dry *gah-gah* of the gulls.

Here, it was setting and atmosphere that intrigued me. I liked the idea of a young woman walking along the pavement of an English fishing village, and that someone be waiting in either a door- or alleyway, and that a knife come slashing down. I had no idea (1) who the girl was, (2) why she was being murdered, (3) who was murdering her. When I wrote the opening quoted above, the only additional thing I knew was that the young woman was either going to or returning from a costume party. That made me think of the various "disguises" and the endless possibilities arising therefrom for murder and mayhem.

I have probably used about every banal convention of the British novel of detection I can think of (hoping, of course, nothing appears to be banal in the end) simply because I like them. Bodies dumped in snow, letters dipped in vitriol, corpses stuffed in trunks. I have not actually used the near-holy device of the train schedule for some reason, but I imagine it will come up at some point.

When I sit down to write a book the only thing I'm sure of is that I'm there at the moment. Talent isn't guaranteed, but discipline is at least dependable, like any other habit. Fortunately, it's more productive than smoking and drinking. Flannery O'Connor said that although she might not come up with an idea for the allotted time she was there, at least she was there in case one happened along.

I have been asked (sometimes accusingly) why in the world I, an

American, would set her books in England. Like Sybil, "I dunno."
Probably I was on my way to Venice and got off, by some quirk, in
Little Grousdean, where I sit around in the local pub with Sybil and
Grimthorpe and the Colonel, arguing over train schedules and drinking
Old Peculier.

48

VILLAINS AND AVENGERS

By Suzanne Jones

I AM A newly published writer in the field of short mystery fiction, and as such, I was approached by the editor of this magazine some time ago to share with you some aspect of writing short mystery fiction. I enthusiastically accepted, only to come to a dismal conclusion: I had absolutely no idea of how to write it. Not only the article, mind you, the stories themselves. This was an unsettling realization, for if I didn't have a clue as to how I did it, the next frightening thought that occurred to me was how could I reasonably expect to do it again. And again.

While I mulled this over, I wrote another story and sure enough, it was very difficult to write. Fortunately, it was accepted, but it left me little wiser than before.

I am currently "writing" another story, "The Hooded Man" (most of my writing goes on in my head before I sit down with yellow ruled pad and black pen), so I resolved to pay more attention this time. I should say here also that I am more interested in the act of murder than in the deductive process of discovering the murderer, and that of course is reflected in the kinds of stories I write.

These stories I seem to produce the way hens produce eggs, that is, with considerable noise and angst, but with more or less predictable regularity. This is less inspiration than compulsion. Especially if you've never tried it, simply to decide to write a mystery story will suffice for "inspiration." How then to begin?

The easiest stories for me to write begin with the victim. Once I have decided to write about a violent death, I sort back through my experience until I find a likely candidate. I have lived a long time, and my experience teems with folk who are candidates for murder: waitresses who call me "honey," any gynecologist or dentist, bridge partners who pass forcing bids, evangelical friends who just quit smoking or drinking or eating fats or carbohydrates, or have been "born again," etc. One's relatives also present unusual opportunities for avenging past offenses, both real and imagined. My maternal grandfather was a villain in the classic sense, a drunkard out of melodrama, now completely lacking—courtesy of time and imperfect memory—any redeeming qualities, and a perfect candidate for murder.

I am not especially imaginative; I've killed my grandfather off in more than one story because he makes such a splendid villain. Villainy, by the way, raises the issue of justice, which is one element that I feel is critical to the success of my own stories. Killing off a sympathetic victim, an innocent person, would be almost as distasteful to me as reading yet another headline about one in the morning paper. The world is too full of innocent victims to add fictional ones as well. Admittedly, most of my victims are not as richly deserving as this particular grandfather, but murder victims should be deserving in some fashion.

The nature of the character of the victim should suggest to you the character of the murderer. In "The Hooded Man," though my victim is so vicious there were a number of choices as to his murderer, the one who hated him the most was a nine-year-old child. Children, I find, make surprisingly satisfactory murderers because they have almost no moral standards (not having had time I suppose to develop any) or inhibitions about removing a source of considerable pain. For them, punishment is the only real deterrent, so the problem becomes not a moral one but a practical one: How to do it and get away with it.

Although I begin the writing process with the victim, sometimes the focus of the story will be on the victim, sometimes the murderer. To date in my published stories, I'm running five to one for the perpetrator of the crime, since it is usually the murderer who has the problem that he or she is trying to solve. Once you have made the decision as to whose story it is, stay with it. Focus on either your murderer or victim. Don't muddle things by shifting back and forth. *Focus,* by the way, does not mean *point of view.* In "The Hooded Man," the focus is on the grandfather: It is he who must interest the reader, but the point of view is first person. The story is told by the adult the child has become.

When you have made your choice of murderer, the kind of person he or she is should also suggest to you the means of murder. My nine-year-old murderer has some considerable obstacles to overcome just because she is a child. Having decided to eliminate her grandfather for various good reasons that should become apparent to the reader in the beginning of the story, she must now devise a means of dispatch that can reasonably be expected to allow the crime to go unperceived. Even at her age she has enough social awareness to know that the blame for the murder might fall on one of her loved ones and add to the burden of her family rather than relieve it. This rules out choices that might be more practical, such as shooting or poisoning or stabbing or whatever method might otherwise be an effective means of destroying her victim. In this story, the child decides that drowning, while less horrible an end than her grandfather deserves, is one she might accomplish with a minimum of risk, and even should it fail, consequences for an unsuccessful attempt might possibly be avoided. The choice of victim and murderer will often suggest not only the means of murder, but the means in turn may dictate the setting. Thus, in my story the setting must be rural to allow easy access to an isolated stream.

The story then follows the efforts of the child to arrange for the grandfather to take her fishing—just the two of them. This will require ingenuity, deception, and low cunning because, as you might expect, the relationship leaves something to be desired. Of course, by the time they do get to the creek where the act is to take place, the grandfather has had to respond positively to the deceptive overtures of affection.

Ambiguities respecting the grandfather's character and motives are by now, if I'm doing my job, creeping into the reader's mind. This delicious villain is turning into a real victim. When he pushes the drowning child to safety, he in part redeems himself for a selfish and wasted life.

The child is not overmuch troubled by this, but the adult telling the story many years later is uneasy about the grandfather's act:

Did that hand I felt reach out so improbably and shove me to the safety of that muddy shore have purpose behind it, or was it the random flailing of a drowning man? If purposeful, was the force behind that act one of love or ultimate revenge? Or both?

That's how I do it (or at least, how I did it this time), but to emphasize a few points:

1. The selection of your victim should pretty much dictate your choice of murderer and the structure of the story. It literally will plot itself.

2. The story should satisfy a sense of justice. Not only should the

250

victim be ripe for killing, but if the murderer "gets away with it," as is sometimes the case, at least in my own fiction, there should be some inescapable consequence of the act. (Don't all acts have consequences?)

3. The problem (conflict, whatever) should be clearly stated early on. Once I baldly stated it in the very first sentence of my story "October Light" (*Ellery Queen's Mystery Magazine*):

Clarise Cole had two real problems. For one, she was dying. For the other, someone was trying to kill her.

While I normally try for a little more subtlety than that, the problem should be made clear. In "The Hooded Man," the child has a drunken, abusive, even dangerous grandfather who threatens the fabric of her family's existence. By story's end, she has solved that problem—though she may have raised others with which she is less well equipped to deal.

4. Focus on a single character, usually victim or murderer. Keeping him squarely in your sights will help you concentrate on the task at hand (dealing with his problem), and help you include what is important to his story and leave extraneous material for another day and another story.

5. Reading over the above, I find it solemn indeed and want to correct that impression by making one last point. I like to write the kind of stories I like to read, and I'm not much on "downers." I am optimistic concerning the essential nature of the human spirit, and I hope this will be reflected in the tone of the story I'm writing. You have to find your own tone for what *you* want to accomplish. While murder and violent death aren't very funny, people are, and humor I find most welcome in short mystery fiction.

Oh, yes. I now think I know why my last story was so difficult to write: I started with a lonely, isolated place I had come across in research for a book I was working on. I couldn't use the setting in the book, and I hate wasting things, so when I began to write the story, I had only the place—no victim, no murderer. And since I didn't know then what the key sequences of the writing process are I had belatedly to invent a murderer out of various parts of various people and a victim of pure convenience. I did a minimum of five drafts before I got one that "worked" (I normally do two), and throughout the whole experience, I was quite puzzled as to why I had no focus, no conflict, and no

251

resolution that was satisfactory. Eventually I got through the story, but it was too difficult to write. If writing were always that hard, I wouldn't do it.

One more word concerning murders. I think fictional murderers are a lot like you and me with a moral screw loose somewhere. Although *I* believe children are essentially amoral, I can't recommend setting loose a spate of children as murderers in short mystery fiction, since most people don't view children in that way. Whatever is perceived to be a bizarre choice requires a great deal of skill to pull off. Still, it's a choice I got to make for that particular story. It's *my* grandfather, after all. Go get your own victim and do him or her in however you please, via whatever method you choose, at the hands of whoever you decide is the most appropriate.

It can be a therapeutic experience, as well as a mildly profitable one.

49

CONSTRUCTING A SCIENCE FICTION NOVEL

By Roger Zelazny

THE LATE James Blish was once asked where he got his ideas for science fiction stories. He gave one of the usual general answers we all do—from observation, from reading, from the sum total of all his experiences, et cetera. Then someone asked him what he did if no ideas were forthcoming from these. He immediately replied, "I plagiarize myself."

He meant, of course, that he looked over his earlier works for roads unfollowed, trusting in the persistence of concerns and the renewal of old fascinations to stimulate some new ideas. And this works. I've tried it occasionally, and I usually find my mind flooded.

But I've been writing for over twenty years, and I know something about how my mind works when I am seeking a story or telling one. I did not always know the things that I know now, and much of my earlier writing involved groping—defining themes, deciding how I really felt about people and ideas. Consequently, much of this basic thinking accomplished, it is easier for me to fit myself into the driver's seat of a fresh new story than it once was. It may be the latest model, but the steering is similar, and once I locate the gearshift I know what to do with it.

For example: Settings. For me, science fiction has always represented the rational—the extension into a future or alien environment of that which is known now—whereas fantasy represented the metaphysical— the introduction of the unknown, usually into an alien environment. The distinctions are sometimes blurred, and sometimes it is fun to blur them. But on a practical, working level, this generally is how I distinguish the two. Either sort of story (I never tire of repeating) has the same requirements as a piece of general fiction, with the added necessity of introducing that exotic environment. Of the three basic elements of any fiction—plot, character and setting—it is the setting that requires extra attention in science fiction and fantasy. Here, as nowhere else, one walks a tightrope between overexplaining and overassuming, between boring the reader with too many details or losing the reader by not providing enough.

I found this difficult at first. I learned it by striving for economy of statement, by getting the story moving quickly and then introducing the background piecemeal. Somewhere along the line I realized that doing this properly could solve two problems: The simple exposition of the material could, if measured out in just the right doses, become an additional means of raising reader interest. I employed this technique to an extreme in the opening to my story "Unicorn Variation," in which I postponed for several pages describing the unusual creature passing through a strange locale.

A bizarrerie of fires, cunabulum of light, it moved with a deft, almost dainty deliberation, phasing into and out of existence like a storm-shot piece of evening; or perhaps the darkness between the flares was more akin to its truest nature—swirl of black ashes assembled in prancing cadence to the lowing note of desert wind down the arroyo behind buildings as empty yet filled as the pages of unread books or stillnesses between the notes of a song.

As you see, I was careful to tell just enough to keep the reader curious. By the time it became apparent that it was a unicorn in a New Mexico ghost town, I had already introduced another character and a conflict.

Characters are less of a problem for me than settings. People are usually still people in science fiction environments. Major figures tend to occur to me almost fully developed, and minor ones do not require much work. As for their physical descriptions, it is easy at first to overdescribe. But how much does the reader really need? How much can the mind take in at one gulp? See the character entirely but mention only three things, I decided. Then quit and get on with the story. If a fourth characteristic sneaks in easily, O.K. But leave it at that initially. No more. Trust that other features will occur as needed, so long as you know. "He was a tall, red-faced kid with one shoulder lower than the other." Were he a tall, red-faced kid with bright blue eyes (or large-knuckled hands or storms of freckles upon his cheeks) with one shoulder lower than the other, he would actually go out of focus a bit rather

254

than grow clearer in the mind's eye. Too much detail creates a sensory overload, impairing the reader's ability to visualize. If such additional details are really necessary for the story line itself, it would be better to provide another dose later on, after allowing time for the first to sink in. "Yeah," he replied, blue eyes flashing.

I've mentioned settings and characters as typical examples of the development of writing reflexes, because reflexes are what this sort of work becomes with practice—and then, after a time, it should become second nature and be dismissed from thought. For this is just apprentice work—tricks—things that everybody in the trade has to learn. It is not, I feel, what writing is all about.

The important thing for me is the development and refinement of one's perception of the world, the experimentation with viewpoints. This lies at the heart of storytelling, and all of the mechanical techniques one learns are merely tools. It is the writer's approach to material that makes a story unique.

For example, I have lived in the Southwest for nearly a decade now. At some point I became interested in Indians. I began attending festivals and dances, reading anthropology, attending lectures, visiting museums. I became acquainted with Indians. At first, my interest was governed only by the desire to know more than I did. Later, though, I began to feel that a story was taking shape at some lower level of my consciousness. I waited. I continued to acquire information and experience in the area.

One day my focus narrowed to the Navajo. Later, I realized that if I could determine why my interest had suddenly taken this direction I would have a story. This came about when I discovered the fact that the Navajo had developed their own words—several hundred of them—for naming the various parts of the internal combustion engine. It was not the same with other Indian tribes I knew of. When introduced to cars, other tribes had simply taken to using the Anglo words for carburetors, pistons, spark plugs, etc. But the Navajo had actually come up with new Navajo words for these items—a sign, as I saw it, of their independence and their adaptability.

I looked further. The Hopis and the Pueblo Indians, neighbors to the Navajo, had rain dances in their rituals. The Navajo made no great effort to control the weather in this fashion. Instead, they adapted to rain or drought.

255

Adaptability. That was it. It became the theme of my novel. Suppose, I asked myself, I were to take a contemporary Navajo and by means of the time-dilation effects of space travel coupled with life extension treatments, I saw to it that he was still alive and in fairly good shape, say, one hundred-seventy years from now? There would, of necessity, be gaps in his history during the time he was away, a period in which a lot of changes would have occurred here on Earth. That was how the idea for *Eye of Cat* came to me.

But an idea is not a science fiction novel. How do you turn it into one?

I asked myself why he would have been away so frequently. Suppose he'd been a really fine tracker and hunter? I wondered. Then he could have been a logical choice as a collector of alien-life specimens. That rang true, so I took it from there. A problem involving a nasty alien being could serve as a reason for bringing my Navajo character out of retirement and provide the basis for a conflict.

I also wanted something representing his past and the Navajo traditions, something more than just his wilderness abilities—some things he had turned his back on. Navajo legend provided me with the *chindi,* an evil spirit I could set to bedeviling him. It occurred to me then that this evil spirit could be made to correspond with some unusual creature he himself had brought to Earth a long time ago.

That was the rough idea. Though not a complete plot summary, this will show how the story took form, beginning with a simple observation and leading to the creation of a character and a situation. This small segment of the story would come under the heading of "inspiration"; most of the rest involved the application of reasoning to what the imagination had so far provided.

This required some tricky considerations. I firmly believe that I could write the same story—effectively—in dozens of different ways: as a comedy, as a tragedy, as something in between; from a minor character's point of view, in the first person, in the third, in a different tense, et cetera. But I also believe that for a particular piece of fiction, there is one way to proceed that is better than any of the others. I feel that the material should dictate the form. Making it do this properly is for me the most difficult and rewarding part of the storytelling act. It goes beyond all of the reflex tricks, into the area of esthetics.

So I had to determine what approach would best produce the tone that I wished to achieve. This, of course, required clarifying my own feelings.

My protagonist Billy Blackhorse Singer, though born into a near-neolithic environment, later received an advanced formal education. That alone was enough to create some conflicts within him. One may reject one's past or try to accommodate to it. Bill rejected quite a bit. He was a very capable man, but he was overwhelmed. I decided to give him an opportunity to come to terms with everything in his life.

I saw that this was going to be a novel of character. Showing a character as complex as Billy's would require some doing. His early life was involved with the myths, legends, shamanism of his people, and since this background was still a strong element in his character, I tried to show this by interspersing in the narrative my paraphrases of different sections of the Navajo creation myth and other appropriate legendary material. I decided to do some of this as poetry, some original, some only loosely based on traditional materials. This, I hoped, would give the book some flavor as well as help to shape my character.

The problem of injecting the futuristic background material was heightened, because I was already burdening the narrative with the intermittent doses of Indian material. I needed to find a way to encapsulate and abbreviate, so I stole a trick from Dos Passos' *U.S.A.* trilogy. I introduced "Disk" sections, analogous to his "Newsreel" and "Camera Eye" sequences—a few pages here and there made up of headlines, news reports, snatches of popular songs, to give the flavor of the times. This device served to get in a lot of background without slowing the pace, and its odd format was almost certain to be sufficiently interesting visually to arouse the reader's curiosity.

The evolving plot required the introduction of a half-dozen secondary characters—and not just minor ones whom I might bring in as completely stock figures. Pausing to do full-scale portraits of each—by means of long flashbacks, say—could be fatal to the narrative, however, as they were scheduled to appear just as the story was picking up in pace. So I took a chance and broke a major writing rule.

Almost every book you read about writing will say, "Show. Don't tell." That is, you do not simply tell the reader what a character is like; you demonstrate it, because telling will generally produce a distancing

257

effect and arouse a ho-hum response in the reader. There is little reader identification, little empathy created in merely telling about people.

I decided that not only was I going to tell the reader what each character was like, I was going to try to make it an interesting reading experience. In fact, I had to.

If you are going to break a rule, capitalize on it. Do it big. Exploit it. Turn it into a virtue.

I captioned a section with each character's name, followed the name with a comma and wrote one long, complex, character-describing sentence, breaking its various clauses and phrases into separate lines, so that it was strung out to give the appearance of a Whitmanesque piece of poetry. As with my "Disk" sections, I wanted to make this sufficiently interesting visually to pull the reader through what was, actually, straight exposition.

Another problem in the book arose when a number of telepaths used their unusual communicative abilities to form temporarily a composite or mass-mind. There were points at which I had to show this mind in operation. *Finnegans Wake* occurred to me as a good model for the stream of consciousness I wanted to use for this. And Anthony Burgess' *Joysprick,* which I'd recently read, had contained a section that could be taken as a primer for writing in this fashion. I followed.

Then, for purposes of achieving verisimilitude, I traveled through Canyon de Chelly with a Navajo guide. As I wrote the portions of the book set in the Canyon, I had before me, along with my memories, a map, my photographs and archaeological descriptions of the route Billy followed. This use of realism, I hoped, would help to achieve some balance against the impressionism and radical storytelling techniques I had employed elsewhere.

These were some of the problems I faced in writing *Eye of Cat* and some of the solutions I used to deal with them. Thematically, though, many of the questions I asked myself and many of the ideas I considered were things that had been with me all along; only the technical solutions and the story's resolution were different this time. In this respect, I was, at one level, still plagiarizing my earlier self. Nothing wrong with that, if some growth has occurred in the meantime.

From everything I've said, it may sound as if the novel was wildly experimental. It wasn't. The general theme was timeless—a consideration of change and adjustment, of growth. While science fiction often deals with the future and bears exotic trappings, its real, deep considerations involve human nature, which has been the same for a long time and which I believe will continue much as it is for an even longer time. So in one sense we constantly seek new ways to say old things. But human nature is a generality. The individual does change, does adapt, and this applies to the writer as well as to the characters. And it is in these changes—in self-consciousness, perception, sensibility—that I feel the strongest, most valid stories have their source, whatever the devices most suitable for their telling.

50

ONE CLUE AT A TIME

By P.D. James

FOR ME one of the keenest pleasures of rereading my favorite mysteries is their power to transport me instantly into a familiar world of people, places and objects, a world in which I feel at once comfortably at home.

With what mixture of excitement, anticipation and reassurance we enter that old brownstone in Manhattan, that gentle spinster's cottage in St. Mary Mead (never fully described by Agatha Christie but so well imagined), that bachelor flat in London's Piccadilly where Bunter deferentially pours the vintage port [for Lord Peter Wimsey], that cozy Victorian sitting room on Baker Street.

A sense of place, creating as it does that vivid illusion of reality, is a necessary tool of any successful novelist. But it is particularly important to the fabricator of the mystery: the setting of the crime and the use of commonplace objects help to heighten by contrast the intruding horror of murder. The bizarre and the terrifying are rooted in comforting reality, making murder more believable.

There is probably no room in crime fiction that we enter with a keener sense of instant recognition than the claustrophobic upstairs sitting room at 221B Baker Street. Baker Street is now one of the dullest of London's main thoroughfares, and it is difficult, walking these wide pavements, to picture those foggy Victorian evenings with the inevitable veiled lady alighting from her hansom cab outside the door of the celebrated Sherlock Holmes.

But we can see every detail of the room into which Mrs. Hudson will usher her: the sofa on which Holmes reclines during his periods of meditation; the violin case propped against the wall; the shelves of scrapbooks; the bullet marks in the wall; the two broad windows overlooking the street; the twin armchairs on each side of the fireplace; the bottle of 7-percent-cocaine solution on the mantel shelf; the desk with the locked drawer containing Holmes's confidential records; the central table with "its white cloth and glimmer of china and metal" waiting for Mrs. Hudson to clear away.

The mental scene has, of course, been reinforced countless times in films and on television, but what is remarkable is that so vivid a picture should be produced by so few actual facts. Paradoxically, I can find no passage in the books that describes the room at length and in detail. Instead, Sir Arthur Conan Doyle builds up the scene through a series of stories object by object, and the complete picture is one that the reader himself creates and furnishes in his own imagination from this accumulation of small details.

Few things reveal the essential self more surely than the rooms in which we live, the objects with which we choose to surround ourselves, the books we place on our shelves, all those small household goods that help reaffirm identity and provide comfort and a sense of security. But the description in crime fiction of domestic interiors, furnishings and possessions does more than denote character; it creates mood and atmosphere, enhances suspense and is often crucial to the plot.

In Agatha Christie, for example, we can be confident that almost any domestic article mentioned, however commonplace, will provide a clue, either true or false. A loose door number hanging on its nail; flowers that have died because no one watered them; an extra coffee spoon in a saucer; a picture postcard lying casually on the desk. In *Funerals Are Fatal*, we do well to note the bouquet of wax flowers on the malachite table. In *Murder at the Vicarage*, we can be sure that the tall stand with a plant pot standing in front of the window isn't there for nothing.

And in *The Murder of Roger Ackroyd*, we shouldn't be so intrigued by the corpse that we fail to notice how one chair has been strangely pulled out from its place by the wall.

All writers of mystery fiction use such devices, but few with such deceptive cunning. It is one of the paradoxes of the genre that it deals with that great absolute, death, yet deploys the trivia of ordinary life as the frail but powerful instruments of justice.

Because in a Christie mystery the puzzle is more important than either the characterization or the setting, she seldom describes a room in great detail. Hers is the art of the literary conjurer. How very different is the loving care and meticulous eye with which a novelist such as Margery Allingham creates for us her highly individual domestic interiors.

In *More Work for the Undertaker,* how brilliantly she describes every room of the eccentric Palinode family, so that the house itself is central to the plot, its atmosphere pervades the novel, and we feel that we know every secret and sinister corner.

But my favorite Allingham rooms are in *The Tiger in the Smoke,* with its opposing characters of the saintly Canon Avril and the psychopathic killer Jack Havoc. How simply described and how absolutely right is the Canon's sitting room. "It was the room he had brought his bride to 30 years before, and since then . . . nothing in it had ever been changed. It had become a little worn in the interim, but the good things in it, the walnut bookcase with the ivory chessmen displayed, the bureau with 13 panes in each glass door, the Queen Anne chair with the 7-foot back, the Persian rug which had been a wedding present from his younger sister, Mr. Campion's mother, had all mellowed just as he had with care and use and quiet living."

Right, too, in its very different style, is the sitting room of his dress-designer daughter, Meg, littered with its sketches of dresses and strewn with swaths of material and samples of braids and beads. "Between the demasked grey walls and the deep gold carpet there ranged every permissible tint and texture from bronze velvet to scarlet linen, pinpointed and enlivened with draining touches of Bristol blue."

This is a highly individual room in the grand manner but without pretentiousness, and I'm not in the least surprised that after a dubious sidelong glance, Chief Inspector Luke decided that he liked it very much indeed.

A room I like very much indeed is Lord Peter Wimsey's sitting room in his flat at 110A Piccadilly. We see it most clearly through the eyes of Miss Murchison in Dorothy L. Sayers's *Strong Poison.* She is shown by Bunter into a glowing, book-lined room "with fine prints on the walls, an Aubusson carpet, a grand piano, a vast chesterfield and a number of deep, cozy armchairs upholstered in brown leather.

"The curtains were drawn, a wood fire blazed on the hearth, and before it stood a table with a silver tea service whose lovely lines were a delight to the eye." No wonder Miss Murchison was impressed.

After his marriage, of course, Lord Peter honeymooned with his

Harriet at Talboys, an Elizabethan farmhouse in Hertfordshire that Lord Peter bought as their country retreat, complete with inglenooked fireplace, ancient beams, tall Elizabethan chimneys, erratic plumbing and the inevitable corpse in the cellar. Meanwhile, the dowager Duchess of Denver was busying herself collecting the chandeliers and tapestries for the Wimseys' town house in Audley Square and congratulating herself that the bride "was ready to prefer 18th-century elegance to chromium tubes." I am myself partial to 18th-century elegance, but I still feel more at home in that bachelor flat at 110A Piccadilly.

Incidently, Talboys was modernized and completely refurnished, including the installation of electricity and the provision of additional bedrooms, before the murderer of its previous owner had been executed—in England a matter then of only a couple of months. That was remarkably speedy even for the 1930's. Today I am doubtful whether even the son of a Duke would be able to command such speedy service.

I myself work in the tradition of Margery Allingham and share her fascination with architecture and domestic interiors; indeed, it is often the setting rather than a particular character or a new method of murder that sparks my creative imagination and gives rise to a novel.

In my last book, *The Skull Beneath the Skin,* the setting is a restored Victorian castle on a lonely offshore island. Here the owner, obsessed with violent death, has created his own private chamber of horrors, a study decorated with old woodcuts of execution scenes, Staffordshire figures of Victorian murderers, mourning regalia and the artifacts of murder.

Here I have used the setting to fulfill all the functions of place in detective fiction; to illustrate character, create atmosphere, provide the physical clues to the crime and to enhance that sense of unease, of the familiar and ordinary made strange and terrible, which is at the heart of detective fiction.

And it is surely the power to create this sense of place and to make it as real to the reader as is his own living room—and then to people it with characters who are suffering men and women, not stereotypes to be knocked down like dummies in the final chapter—that gives any mystery writer the claim to be regarded as a serious novelist.

263

51

ELEMENTS OF THE POLICE PROCEDURAL NOVEL

By Rex Burns

Given the development of the writer's sense of which words live and which don't — a development that for me comes as much through reading as through writing — I think the areas most pertinent to a successful police procedural are four: research, setting, plot, and character.

These divisions are, of course, artificial. As in any "recipe," the elements blend and influence each other; and in any art such as cooking or writing, the whole is greater than the sum of its parts. But though each writer must discover for himself this sense of life or wholeness, some of the basic elements contributing to it can be distinguished. Let's begin with research.

The kind of research I favor is quite basic: my main source for information is the daily newspaper. I figure that if a newspaper article about a crime interests me, it will interest other readers. Naturally, the newspaper story must undergo a metamorphosis before it comes out as fiction. For one thing, there are the questions of libel and plagiarism; and, for another, too great a reliance on the facts as reported can cause a story to become quickly dated.

More important is the question of a good yarn — an interesting newspaper article is only a germ, a bud. It provides a sequence of events and an indication of setting for the full-grown fiction. For example, the following paragraph from a UPI newswire release was the nucleus of a chapter of a novel I was working on: "The raids in Cordoba began when a small airplane, circling the city to apparently coordinate the attacks, threw a bomb that exploded without causing injuries near a provincial bank about 11 A.M." In short, a newspaper article can provide a rich source of actual whats, wheres, and whens. The whys and the whos are the novelist's responsibility.

A second good source of information for the police procedural writer is court records. Affidavits, depositions, and transcripts — in addition to the writer's sitting in on court hearings — help provide not only events and incidental tidbits for a story, but also the language of narration. Increasingly, a cop, especially a senior officer such as a detective, must understand the technology of the law. Every technology has it jargon, and this can be found in legal records and in courtrooms.

Both newspaper stories and court records are as valuable for what they leave out as for what they offer. To get some of that which is left out, read the story with the questions "how?" and "why?" in mind. For instance, that favorite phrase of reporters, "police, acting on a tip from an informant . . ." gives rise to such questions as: Which policeman? Who was the informant? What incentive did he have for informing? What kind of communication — telephone, written, conversational? Who believed the informant? Who didn't? How much time passed between the tip and the raid? These and similar questions come up when the novelist begins creating the fictional world which will embody any actual events he chooses to use.

Though the writer's imagination furnishes the answers to such questions as those asked above, that imagination can be stimulated by a third kind of research which I've found to be most beneficial: interviewing. A policeman, like almost everyone else, enjoys talking about his work, and most municipalities have programs for bettering police-community relations. And a writer — despite what his neighbors may think — is a member of the community. In a larger town, check with the department's public information office. Departments in smaller towns tend to be less formal, and I think somewhat less accessible, perhaps because their manpower tends to be insufficient and the training less professional, generating a defensive attitude. The prosecutor's office and the sheriff's office are also worthwhile avenues of approach. For me, this interviewing tends to be quite casual and takes place during a duty watch; there's a lot of time for conversation during eight hours of riding in a patrol car.

Armed with some specific questions derived from reading newspapers and reports, the interviewer can start filling in those blanks found in the documents. The answers don't have to be related to the same cases read about — in fact, I like it better if they aren't. The novelist deals with probability, and patterns of common behavior offer more freedom for the invention of particulars than does the mere reporting of facts, which is where the journalist ends and the novelist begins. Unlike what takes place on most television talk shows, an interviewer-novelist should be a good listener and, speaking for myself, a copious but surreptitious notetaker. It also helps to train your eye for such minutiae as manufacturer's labels, model numbers, organization charts — in short, anything that gives quick specific detail for your story's setting. Interviewing also provides the latest slang and technical jargon.

The manner of introducing those technical terms into the narrative varies. If a character honestly might not know what a particular device or procedure is called, he can simply ask someone in the story. The character and the reader become informed together. I use this device sparingly, since my characters in the Gabe Wager books are generally professional and well-trained. (Moreover, as a reader, I get damned irritated when a story's development is continually interrupted by some idiot who needs everything explained to him.) Another means of introducing technical terms is to use the phrase in normal dialogue and let the descriptive passage carry the explanation: " 'Let me have the Kell-Kit,' said Wager. Sergeant Johnston handed him the small body transmitter. . . ." Or, for variation, the equation may be reversed: " 'Let me have the body transmitter,' said Wager. Sergeant Johnston handed him the small Kell-Kit." I'm not sure if police departments have yet surpassed the federal government in the use of acronyms and arcane initials, but these are an essential part of bureaucratic jargon. It is a rule of thumb in writing first to use the full phrase, then, in the next sentence or two, the more common initials: "Wager turned to his little book of Confidential Informants. The first C. I. was. . . ." No explanatory passage is needed, and the action moves without interruption.

Research, then, is the foundation for the police procedural, and on that foundation are built in setting, plot, and character. Setting is, of course, easiest to create if it's well known to the writer. For the Gabriel Wager stories, that means Denver. Ironically, my editors more than once pointed out that a street which I invented wasn't on their map of Denver, or an odd-numbered address should be on the north rather than south side of a particular avenue. But the familiarity I mean is as much in flavor as in fact, and its manner of presentation is — for me — impressionistic. The single well-chosen detail that captures the flavor of the setting and gives focus and life to an otherwise sketchy scene is part of the economy I associate with the "grittiness" of a police procedural. A gothic, a novel that explores states of mind, or a sci-fi fantasy may call for more sweeping and panoramic descriptions to create a mood or sustain a romance. But I find harmony between a spare style and the realistic police story. Since this descriptive technique tends to emphasize action rather than setting, and since a police procedural is akin to a report — and a report is usually about "what happened" — the emphasis on concrete and concise detail feels right to me.

The concern with what happened brings us to plot. Plot is not just *what* takes place but *why* it takes place. The police procedural may or may not use the mystery as the basis of suspense. If the police do not know who the perpetrator is, then unraveling the mystery becomes the plot — i.e., the gradual revelation of motive and opportunity. But often, in life as well as in fiction, the police do know who the villain is, and the plot centers on gathering enough evidence for a viable court case. The manner of getting this evidence is quite tedious and even dull — questioning fifty or a hundred witnesses, long hours of surveillance, studying accounting records. The problem for the storyteller in the police procedural field becomes one of remaining true to reality without boring the reader. One technique that fits the police procedural is focusing attention on new methods of surveillance or on the ever-changing avenues of legal presentation. Here, research is indispensable. Another device is to give your detective more cases than one. This is by no means unrealistic, but a good story requires that the cases somehow work together toward a single conclusion. That's the old demand of art for unity, a unity seldom apparent in real life.

Another very familiar technique for maintaining interest is the foil — someone who offers byplay for the protagonist. A foil should serve a variety of purposes, all contributing toward the unity of the novel. The character used as a foil — a rookie, for instance — may be a device not only for explaining police procedure, but also for revealing the protagonist's character through his reaction to the foil's activities.

I try to make character as interesting as case. The strongest novels are those with living characters to whom the action is vital, and this holds true for any tale, even a plotless one. But whether it's a who-done-it or a how-to-prove-it, the police story is fundamentally an action story, and in it the development of character should not impede the action. Ideally, character development and action should coincide; but where they do not, I tip the balance in favor of action, possibly because I envision the Gabe Wager series as one long novel of perhaps fifteen volumes, and this view gives me plenty of room to let the character grow.

267

There are several other concrete devices that aid the quick presentation of character without interrupting the action. One device especially useful for creating secondary characters is the "signature" — a distinctive act, speech pattern, or habit of thought that identifies and distinguishes one character from another. This signature may be simple: one secondary figure from *The Alvarez Journal* smokes cigars, another has an old man's rumbling cough, a third speaks administrative jargon. Or, if the character is of more importance to the story, a combination of signatures may be used to flesh him out. At its worst, this device generates cliché characters — the western bad man with his black hat and sneer. At best, the signature makes the character become alive and individualized — the girth, thirst, and cowardice of Falstaff. The problem, of course, is to characterize without caricaturing — unless your aim is satire. The novelist's ability to create real characters can be improved by reading other writers who are very good at it: Shakespeare, Flaubert, Faulkner. Another means is "reading" friends and neighbors: What exactly is it that distinguishes one of your acquaintances from another? Given universal human qualities, what makes one individual different from another?

Minor and secondary characters, while absolutely necessary, do not give life to the action. Rarely can any story, police procedural or other, do without a protagonist. Again, because of the importance of action in police procedurals, the writer is faced with the need for an economical development of his main character. The technique I have chosen for my Gabe Wager series is by no means new: It's the familiar "recording consciousness" of Henry James, the restricted third-person point of view, in which every event and concept in the story is presented from the perspective of a single protagonist. I've found several advantages to this device: The action proceeds and the protagonist's character is revealed at the same time. The reader is faced with the same limitations of knowledge as the protagonist, and thus the element of suspense is heightened. Using third person rather than first person puts distance between the reader and the protagonist and offers another dimension to the story, which helps the reader through those necessary and authentic but often slow stages of a case's development.

This narrative technique also has shortcomings. The author can't give the reader any information that the protagonist does not have, thus leaving little chance for irony or depth. For this point of view to work, the author must also have a total understanding of the protagonist. While it may not be relevant to the story, it is nonetheless necessary if the character's actions are to be consistent.

First-person narration achieves many of the same results but brings an even closer identification between author and character. Think of the popular image of Mickey Spillane, for example. I prefer third person because it enforces objectivity and quite possibly because, unlike Gabe Wager, I'm not a good cop.

Focusing all the action through Wager's perspective, then, contributes to a unity of action and characterization in which action dominates but character development follows quite closely and, I hope, unobtrusively. I try to achieve this by placing a heavy emphasis on dialogue. By its very nature, dialogue is dramatic — the characters are onstage talking rather than being talked about by a narrator. Again, the signature is very important, and I play a little game of trying to see how many lines of dialogue I can put together without having to state who is speaking. The idea is that each character's voice should be distinct enough to indicate the speaker.

I place the police procedural in the category of literary realism. The contemporary, the probable, the routine, determine my choice of a realistic subject. Once I select my subject, the elements of research, setting, plot, and character are indispensable, and, in my Gabe Wager police procedurals, all of these elements must contribute to the action.

52

ERMINE OR RABBIT SKIN

Authenticity in the Historical Novel

BY URSULA ZILINSKY

SEVERAL years ago, while I was out for my usual morning run, I met three little boys. Their names were Toby, David, and Felix. Felix was dark and slight, with his eyes a little too close together. He spoke English well, but with a German accent. The other two were English and fair. The one called David was dazzlingly good-looking; had he worn the costume of an earlier period, he could have stepped into a Gainsborough with no one the wiser.

For the next four years of my life, and the next twenty of theirs, I watched them, listened to their talk, read their letters, and peeked in their bedroom windows. There were times when I begged them to go away and leave me alone, and times when they did and I pleaded with them to come back. They took up an unconscionable amount of my time, paper, and typewriter ribbon, led me on many a wild goose chase, shouldered aside my friends and family, gave me insomnia and turned me into a monomaniacal bore. And all of you who are working on your own novels are now saying, "So what? That's what writing a novel is like."

Of course, you are absolutely right. But my little boys presented me with a special problem. When I met them, they were admiring a garden bed planted with lobelias, geraniums and daisies in the shape of a Union Jack to honor the coronation of Edward VII, who became king of England in 1901. After having written several contemporary novels, stories, and a play for children, I had willy-nilly, without plan, forethought, or qualification embarked on an historical novel.

My first notion was to write an authentic Edwardian novel, what is loosely referred to as the 19th-century novel: a cast of thousands, lots of incident, weddings, parties, christenings, and of course a deathbed or two. I discovered almost at once that while historical accuracy was absolutely essential, authenticity was not possible. To write an Edwardian novel I could not afford to be Edwardian. I had to fake it.

A few years ago I saw an exhibit of the costumes used for the television series *The Wives of Henry VIII*. Anyone who saw that show on PBS will doubtlessly remember how sumptuous those velvets and ermines looked. Reality proved to be very different. Because the show had been filmed on a limited budget, the costume designer had contrived velvets of polyester, ermines of rabbit dipped in ink, jewels of rhinestones and colored glass. The great chains of office were toilet pull chains and plumbing washers. Yet it all somehow managed to look far more real than many recent American productions for which money was no object and fortunes were spent on "authenticity."

My own problem wasn't, of course, that I couldn't afford ermine and pearls for my characters. It is, after all, one of the chief pleasures of writing that generosity is so cheap. If you want your heroine to have a sable coat, you can give it to her and never be a penny the poorer. My problem was the reverse of that English costume designer's. In researching an exhaustively documented historical period, I could not give my characters the great wealth available to me or all the advantages of hindsight and modern sensibility.

Oh, those mountains of research. How fascinating it all was—that overripe, just-going-rotten time, which ended with its golden youth marching off to what was humorously referred to as the 4th Balkan War, until it disastrously grew into World War I. All those histories, letters, diaries, etiquette books, books on household management (bless Mrs. Beeton!), those newspapers and advertisements I'd studied. What did I get out of it? Accuracy of detail and a few telling incidents. Research, I discovered, is like fish spawn: Millions of eggs laid (or words read) and from this a few goldfish or, in a novel, what Conrad called "the accumulated verisimilitude of selected episode." Selected is the operative word.

I don't mean to speak slightingly of research. Titles, forms of address, the correct clothes and manner all matter. They matter a great deal. If they don't seem important, why bother with an historical setting? And you're bound to run into a reader who knows better. If I am that reader, you've lost me. Whenever I come across sloppy research in a novel, I can't help but conclude that the author didn't care, and if he didn't, why should I care to read his book?

But there is another reason that all those millions of eggs are necessary. The total immersion in another period, which comes with all that reading, allows us to write from the inside out rather than from the outside in.

This means that, having acquired all that knowledge, you have, in a manner of speaking, to disregard it. What was a matter of course to your characters can't continue to be a nine-days' wonder to the author, nor can their moral attitudes remain quaint or reprehensible simply because they seem so to us now. Edwardian views of women, the poor, and Jews frequently made me want to put one of my characters on a soapbox and tell everybody off, but since the people in my story were the kind who took such attitudes for granted (with the exception of a suffragette or two), I could not afford such luxury. And even if you do have a character who is at odds with his society, it is important not to have him express the author's view instead of his own. Suffragettes in the days before World War I, I found, had very little in common with the women's movement of the seventies; the anti-Semitism of the time, a pervasive but casual form of snobbery (more common in English writing than German, to my surprise), cannot be regarded in the same light in which we look upon anti-Semitism since the Holocaust.

My first setback in planning an authentic Edwardian novel came from my editor. Edwardian authors thought nothing of spreading themselves over 800 pages, and their readers would probably have been disappointed to get anything less. With the present cost of paper and printing, try to get an 800-page novel past your editor if your name does not happen to be James Michener!

Then there was the problem of authentic dialogue. Reading the popular fiction of the day, I discovered that it was totally unusable. English speech was florid enough ("The duke has most kindly offered to show me over the garden"), but German was so hedged with deference and politeness that it was nearly impenetrable. ("As the Herr Minister has had the condescension to remark, and if he will kindly permit me to agree with his ministership, it is a very nice day.")

I also had to cut back a good deal when dealing with forms of address and titles, most of which, if done authentically, would strike present-day readers as unbearably formal, or worse, humorous. Germans, especially, who think nothing of addressing someone in ordinary conversation as "Frau Lifeinsuranceactuarialistwidow," had all their lavish silks removed and were kept down to useful polyester instead.

It is easy enough to avoid the more obvious mistakes—letting your characters have "lifestyles" or "meaningful relationships"—using words that were not in existence then, or have since changed their meaning (square, gay), since such things can be looked up in Eric Partridge or the dictionary. What is more difficult is to judge just how much period slang to use. Characters in Edwardian novels tended to use a great deal of it, but I found that for me it worked best in small doses, mostly from children, servants and soldiers, who by Edwardian definition constituted an underclass.

As in real life, money and sex presented me with considerable difficulties. Had I stayed authentically in the minds of my characters, I would have mentioned merely what things cost and left it at that. But since I was dealing with foreign currencies (pre-inflationary ones at that), it would have been useless to say a character earned a hundred pounds a year. Was his employer a skinflint or incredibly generous? A present-day reader would have no way of knowing. I found it wisest not to be too specific unless the amount of money involved served to illustrate something about a character. When David gives five pounds to a soldier fallen on hard times to buy himself a civilian suit, and the soldier is shocked that there are people who actually spend as much as that on a suit, it tells both what five pounds would buy and that David tends to be careless about money. In present terms, that five pounds, incidentally, would be worth about $7.00. As Sylvia Townsend Warner remarked in regard to the price of gin then and now, it is a wonder any of us have the courage to write our memoirs.

As for sex, strictly speaking there shouldn't have been any. Of course, real Edwardians had a fair amount of it, some of it kinky enough to please the bluest noses, but in their books they had asterisks. I wasn't sorry to be able to avoid graphic sex scenes, which I hate writing in any case, since they always remind me of car repair manuals ("Push button Z, wind handle B. . . ."), but I realized I couldn't get away with pretending that all Edwardian babies were found under cabbages. I compromised by giving my characters some interesting kinks: one likes coachmen with high boots and whips; one likes little girls; one only fancies older women; and one is homosexual. But at crucial moments I

273

resorted to Edwardian asterisks, plus the trappings of Edwardian romance: glades of bluebells, white lilac, snow on a skylight, and if not a nightingale, a cuckoo, since the marriage that results from that particular seduction breaks up over an accusation of cuckoldry.

On the whole I enjoyed all that patching and contriving. I loved the research. I found it restful to be able to write about characters who belong to an established class structure, but what I liked best of all was that in a novel set in the past, the writer can endow the characters with some old-fashioned virtues that in a contemporary novel would sound nauseatingly goody-goody. Before World War I, idealism was not yet considered square—indeed "square" was a term of praise—and my young men could value loyalty, friendship, courage and decent manners without being regarded as wimps. They were rich, mostly, but not pampered. English plumbing and six years in that upper-class hell, the English public school, saw to that. They had been brought up to detest self-pity, and though all three of them were of an age to serve in a fiendish war, they did not suffer from anomie, anhedonia, or cosmic angst. This made them enjoyable to live with. Now that I am done with them I miss them. And if on one of the morning runs I should meet with a knight in clanking armor or a shepherd speaking in Virgilian hexameters who didn't object to considerable patching and contriving on my part, I might easily be tempted to bring him home and give him my next four years.

53

THE HISTORICAL NOVEL: BLENDING FACT
AND FICTION

By Thomas Fleming

First the good news. Writing an historical novel fuses factual research and the creative imagination in a way that is both exciting and meaningful.

Now the bad news. Making an historical novel work is the most difficult kind of writing I have ever attempted. As someone who has written formal history books, biographies, and contemporary novels, I think I can qualify as the voice of experience.

When I emphasize the difficulty, I presume a writer will take both fiction and history seriously. Taking fiction seriously means you have to have believable characters, whose motivations are intensely personal, whose individual lives are significant enough to make readers care.

Most of the characters in a serious historical novel are a blend of the writer's unconscious and his research. In my novel, *Liberty Tavern,* for instance, I discovered that before the American Revolution not a few British officers retired to the American colonies and went into business. Some bought taverns, a very lucrative operation in those days. Jonathan Gifford, one of the main characters in the novel, began to take shape in my mind. But his personal characteristics were formed by my enduring interest in conflict between strong taciturn fathers and idealistic sons—a conflict rooted in my own life experience.

The general ideas for my historical novels have always emerged from digging into the gritty, confusing tumultuous world of the past. There is simply no such thing as a dull era, if you get into the daily lives people led in other times, the things that worried them, obsessed them. But discovering the inner life of another time is not easy. You have to make an often mind-bending effort to grasp the way men and women felt about the large and small events that swept through their lives. I can assure you that nine times out of ten, it is not the way the formal history books tell it.

Take the Civil War, for instance. A crusade to free the slaves? Or at least to preserve the Union? Only about 50% true. Millions of northerners loathed the war and violently opposed it. To discover these forgotten voices in the past takes hours of reading diaries and letters, staring blearily at old newspapers on microfilm, plowing through articles in historical journals, devouring 700- and 800-page memoirs of politicians and pundits.

Here we come to an important principle in writing the historical novel. It should offer a fresh point of view about an historical experience, even a new interpretation of it, that says something significant to modern readers. My novel, *Liberty Tavern,* published in 1976, was set in the American Revolution—a long distance from our computerized, electrified, modern world. Yet it spoke to the concerns of post-Vietnam America. It portrayed the Revolution, as it was fought in New York and New Jersey, as a civil war that often pitted brother against sister, father against son, wife against husband. To a nation divided by the upheavals of the 1960's, riven by bitter conflicts between the generations about the meaning of America, *Liberty Tavern* reminded readers that even in the primary experience of the country's birth, Americans had had to deal with similar traumas.

Not all historical novels have to be set in the distant past. I considered my 1981 novel, *The Officers' Wives,* an historical novel because when I began it in 1979 it required the same techniques of massive research to exhume the attitudes and opinions of the 1950's when the book begins. I got the idea for this book while writing a history of West Point. In my four years of toil at the Military Academy, I got to know a lot of officers and their wives. I also read about the often grisly adventures of Army wives in other eras. Suddenly it occurred to me that no one had ever written a novel about the U.S. Army from a woman's point of view. Here was the new interpretation I feel is so important in an historical novel. I blended it with the twin agonies of Korea and Vietnam to give readers a picture of the post-World War II army from the inside.

Both these books offer other insights into technical aspects of the historical novel. *Liberty Tavern* dealt with the guerilla war side of the Revolution in New York and New Jersey—with experience that was too

276

scattered, undocumented, erratic, to appeal to the systematic mind of the historian. Guerilla encounters are minor events in history books, if they are mentioned at all. But they were not minor to the men who fought and died in them. More important, they were ideal material for me as a novelist, because they gave my literary imagination room to invent characters and events out of my knowledge of the period.

Similarly, in *The Officers' Wives*, by focusing on the women's experience in the Army, I instantly achieved the freedom to explore a world that official and formal histories never even mention. But it was (and is) a world intimately and intensely attached to the larger world of battles and policies in which the officers move. The oblique approach is highly recommended in writing historical novels. Coming at the big history from an unexpected angle can be the secret of a novel's success.

In these two novels, major historical figures—Douglas MacArthur in *The Officers' Wives*, George Washington in *Liberty Tavern*—appear on only one or two pages. The main stories are told almost entirely through the lives and passions of the imaginary characters. I know historical novels are written about great men and women (Gore Vidal's *Lincoln* is a recent example), but I have always felt uncomfortable about converting famous names into important fictional characters, inventing scenes and dialogue for them at length. To me this bespeaks either an indifference to the facts of history or a naïveté unbecoming to the serious historical novelist. Even moderately educated readers know too much about these people to give the literary imagination room to invent without blundering into outright distortion of the historical truth. The novelist should never confuse himself with the biographer.

Similarly I have never seen much point in historical novels that recreate the battles of Yorktown or Gettysburg or Midway. The novelist may make us feel these events with more intensity, but we learn nothing new from an historical point of view. These vast collisions can be—and have been—reported in exhaustive detail from known historical facts. I wrote a 320-page book, *Beat the Last Drum*, on the battle of Yorktown, without inventing a single character or line of dialogue.

Whether a book deals with major or minor events, one of the fundamental problems of the historical novel is the question of how much the writer can alter history as his research reveals it to him. In a brilliant discussion of the difference between fiction and the so-called new journalism, John Hersey laid down the principle that the fiction writer has a duty to invent while the nonfiction writer must never invent. This is a sound proposition, but it does not work for the historical novelist because he is consciously blending fact and fiction, telling a story set in another time, which has considerable historical importance (otherwise it's not worth telling) yet is invented. The historical novel exists in a border area between fiction and fact. This puts added strains on the artistic process and requires more than ordinary judgment from the writer.

Some writers have decided that this lack of clear-cut rules gives them the license to do almost anything with the historical facts. I disagree. If the historical novel is to be taken seriously as history—and I believe it can and should be—there are certain ground rules that should be observed. Major figures or events should never be altered in absurd or extreme ways. For instance, it would be ridiculous to portray George Washington as a homosexual, or tell your readers that the South won the battle of Gettysburg.

It is, on the other hand, perfectly permissible to have a jaundiced historical character of the second rank, such as Aaron Burr, portray Washington as an idiot, as the fictional Burr does in Gore Vidal's novel.

Remember, the imagination can invent anything. This is a boon if you are writing a novel set in the year 3500. But an historical novel requires the writer to anchor his imagination in a reality with discernible boundaries.

At the same time, the historical novelist should have the freedom to simplify certain aspects of the story he is telling. History is simply too confusing, too cluttered with extraneous characters saying or doing similar things, to be told exactly as it happened.

In my recent novel, *The Spoils of War,* one of the major characters becomes deeply involved in stealing the presidential election of 1876. This was a very complicated operation, involving at least two dozen people. I simplified it by focusing on two or three of the more interesting participants—my imaginary main character, Jonathan Stapleton, John C. Reid, the managing editor of *The New York Times,* and James Garfield, the future president of the United States.

Although the personal story must remain the primary focus, one of the chief reasons for writing an historical novel is to show the power, the impact of major events on peoples' lives. Here is where the novelist and the historian, artistry and research, should unite. It is too humdrum, too obvious, merely to show your characters getting thrown into the maelstrom of a war or a political upheaval. There has to be a personal dimension visible in their reaction to these major events.

In *The Spoils of War*, Jonathan Stapleton's son, Rawdon, is violently antagonistic to his father for the part he plays in the Civil War. Rawdon shares the feelings of the majority of the family, who opposed the war. It is also a neurotic wound, caused by the misery his father's participation in the war inflicted on his mother. In 1877 America was swept by stupendous strikes and riots. Many people feared it was the beginning of a revolution. Rawdon exultantly joined this radical upheaval, because he was eager to undo the status quo that his father and the men of his generation had established after Appomattox.

But Rawdon's wife, Genevieve, cannot join him because she has been wounded by history in another way. She lived in New York during the three nightmare days of the Draft Riots in 1863—a proto-revolution that was suppressed by Union troops, including a regiment commanded by her father. She cannot bear the thought of encouraging the mob to run wild in the city's streets again. She denounces Rawdon's recklessness, inflicting a wound on their marriage from which it never recovers.

I think—or at least hope—that readers watching these characters struggling with this blend of the personal and the historical will feel their personal anguish and simultaneously think and learn about the historical experience.

That is what makes the historical novel so exciting and so challenging—this need to appeal to both the reader's head and heart. For me, fiction makes history live with an intensity and reality usually lacking in the analytic prose of the modern historian. At the same time, history adds dimension to fiction. It makes the literary imagination more ambitious, more profound.

54

WRITE TO SELL

A 3-Point Checklist That Works

By Samm Sinclair Baker

Why do some writers make sales and collect sizable checks again and again . . . while others, perhaps you, are beaten back repeatedly by discouraging rejections? Is there some "magic" by which rejected writers can be transformed into published professionals? Is there immediate help for you if your work isn't selling?

Yes . . . the reasons for rejections are often surprisingly clear and simple—once you know how to identify and correct them for your own benefit. You'll gain some valuable eye-openers by applying these three basic checkpoints. They can open new pathways to selling what you write.

The primary reasons for failure to sell were affirmed vividly for me when I was the judge of a contest for beginning writers. Employing these practical insights has worked for me and for other selling writers. They're bound to work for you, if you'll follow through with them intelligently—*never giving up.*

Take advantage of these three checkpoints in analyzing any manuscript before you submit it for publication, and you'll uncover crucial, costly flaws. Making necessary corrections and revisions before you submit your article can mean the difference between sale and turndown.

First, study these recommendations; then apply them to the piece you've just finished—and to others that didn't sell. Concentrate on reading your article objectively, line by line, as though you were the editor. Now, as editor rather than writer, *you* must decide whether or not to buy the piece for publication. Be ruthlessly honest as you ask yourself, "Is the manuscript faulty, judged by any or all of the checkpoints?"

If yes, revise, rewrite—or start all over again. It often pays to discard the entire piece if it doesn't measure up. Finally, you'll be thrilled by the improvements you can readily make, once you realize exactly what is wrong. That's *self-help in action,* since you'll have a simple method to use profitably in planning and completing everything you write to sell from now on.

CHECKPOINT # 1
Will This Subject Interest Enough Readers?

The great editor of *Good Housekeeping,* John Mack Carter, enlightened me about editorial needs. He said that there are three subjects of outstanding interest to most women and many men today. Readers, he emphasized, are constantly seeking new, usable information about: *Diet . . . Sex . . . Money.*

If you write in the categories of these prime subjects—offering fresh, easily grasped approaches—you'll certainly have a better chance to sell than if your piece is about something as far-out as "The Prevalence of Fire Ants in Abyssinia." Obviously that's a wild exaggeration to make an essential point: *Write what interests most others, not just what pleases you.*

Of course, you don't have to confine yourself to those three basic themes. Yet, even within that seeming limitation, the possibilities for writing that sells are practically unlimited. For example, consider the many variations, such as:

DIET: "DROP POUNDS NOW WITH 12 DELICIOUS NEW RECIPES."

SEX: "ENCHANTING NEW HAIRSTYLES BOOST SEX APPEAL."

MONEY: "ADD INCOME WITH EASY NEW WORK-AT-HOME IDEAS."

It comes down to the old saw: Feed your pets what *they* want to eat, not what *you* like. Similarly, choose a subject that is of high interest to other people, realizing that editors are people, too. Analyze carefully in advance the interests of the specific reading audience you're trying to reach. Otherwise, you'll waste time and effort and invite discouragement and frustration. Smart subject selection is fundamental if you *write to sell.* Clearly, selling interests you. . . . or you wouldn't be reading this.

A common mistake of beginners is the I-I-I approach—writing about your personal experiences. That's relatively easy, but get it out of your head that anything that happens to you is of interest to others, unless it will appeal to a wide audience. Editors groan when a manuscript begins, "I remember Aunt Clara very well. I loved her deeply, and I'll always treasure sweet memories of her. . . ."

How many magazines readers care about your Aunt Clara or your Uncle Ted? How many of the same readers would be interested in an article that begins: "The weekend reducing spa business is booming, but what can a brief stay at a spa do for you realistically? Can it help you lose weight, keep on taking off pounds and inches, and stay slim from then on? For the answers, I interviewed five men and five women who had been to various weekend spas a month earlier. Here's what they reported. . . ."

Aren't your chances of selling the spa piece infinitely better? Checkpoint #1 is clear: Before you write on any theme, think of where you're going to aim for publication. Then consider the subject through the editor's eyes. Realize that, as editor, you must interest the largest possible number of your readers, so you'll buy only articles most likely to do that. To sell the articles you write, *you must fulfill the editor's needs.* For a men's magazine, for example, you would interview mainly men.

CHECKPOINT #2
Are Your Opening Lines "Reader-Grabbers"?

An editor of a mass circulation magazine (a neighbor) brought home for the weekend a huge briefcase loaded with articles submitted for publication. He said, "Before I take you sailing, help me weed out which of these pieces have possibilities for an issue coming up soon." I protested, "It will take me forever to get through these."

"You'll be finished in less than a hour," he assured me. "You can usually tell by reading just the first paragraph whether to discard it or go further. If the opening sentences don't hook you, reject it—the writing rarely gets any better."

Here are a couple of examples to show how much the opening sentences matter in the articles you write. Again, read them as though you're the editor examining the two following submissions on the same general subject. Based on the opening paragraphs alone, which manuscript would you have read with greatest attention?

(A) "Everyone in the neighborhood spoke well of Maryann Browne. She could usually be seen sitting in the old rocker on her front porch, swaying slightly as she knitted patiently hour after hour. We were all deeply shocked when we heard that her family doctor, whom we all knew, let it be known through the grapevine that she had cancer."

(B) "I'm a cancer patient, in the midst of that uneasy purgatory known as remission. After a year that would make the cast of *Dynasty* shake its collective head in disbelief, I am trying to get well. I *will* get well. That is, if people let me. The cancer may not kill me. But I'm not at all sure about the public."

The article that was bought, and appeared in a leading magazine, was "B." As a casual reader, I turned the pages rather idly, but the opening brief paragraph grabbed me. The writer telling flat out that she is afflicted with the dread disease led me on with the promise of hope in "remission." I was hooked further by the unexpected challenge in the surprising dramatic twist that "the public" might keep her from getting well. The public? That's *me!* Now *I* was involved. How could I stop reading?

It's obvious why I—or you—as editor, would, if offered a choice, probably reject "even without reading any further than that first paragraph. Why should I care or be particularly interested in someone I don't know—Maryann Browne—just because people "spoke well" of her? There's nothing very thrilling about a woman sitting in an old rocker on her front porch, knitting patiently hour after hour. Sure, I (and you) feel sympathy for anyone with cancer—but that's not enough to *compel* me to read more. Result: rejection. I'll bet that the discouraged writer never realized why her piece didn't sell—as you understand the reason now.

What's your next step? As an aspiring, determined writer, you'll gather all of your rejections for reexamination as soon as you can. You'll reread the opening paragraphs carefully, objectively, with fresh, clearsighted analysis—as if through the editor's eyes. Do your opening lines reach out and grip readers, pulling them into the rest of the article? If not, rewrite until you have created a solid reader-grabber, even if it means rewriting a dozen times. You'll have a far better chance of having your writing read and bought.

Here's one more self-teaching example to help you avoid rejection slips in the future, or turn your past rejects into sales: A fine professional writer wanted to sell an article on beauty care to one of the best-paying, top-circulation women's magazines. But she knew there was tremendous competition in the beauty article field, not just from other free-lance writers, men and women, but from the magazine's staff writers.

She put her creativity to work and sought out one of the most popular photography models, who agreed to coauthorship. There was just one problem, as she knew too well: Most women might feel that they couldn't learn from a model who started with "perfect features." So the writer tackled the dilemma head-on with this opening paragraph:

> You don't have to be born with perfect features to have a model's face. [Really? Tell me more. . . .] Many of the world's highly paid models are not necessarily natural beauties, but they do have the ability to put their best face forward. That means skin care and carefully applied make-up. I'd like to share with you some of the very special beauty secrets I've learned during my career as a model.

That's the hook—the grabber—the promise from a top model to share her beauty secrets with you. Possibly you're asking yourself, "Why didn't I think of a creative idea like that, and write an opening that would make the sale to an editor?" From now on, I hope you will.

I've reworked the opening paragraphs of my books up to twenty and more times, until I felt as sure as I could be that I'd fashioned an irresistible promise, the hook that would seize and hold the reader. One of the best examples I know is the start of the best-selling diet book of all time, *The Complete Scarsdale Medical Diet* (which I coauthored with Dr. Herman Tarnower). The opening proved a salesmaker.

The doctor is speaking:

> "I, personally, explain *The Complete Scarsdale Medical Diet*'s phenomenal popularity in two words: 'It works.' A slim trim lady said to me recently, 'Your diet is beautifully simple, and the results are simply beautiful.' I just say, 'It works.'"

A reader-grabber like that can work for you. Check your opening lines repeatedly to make sure they convey convincing promise of worthwhile reading ahead.

CHECKPOINT #3

Have You Done Enough "Self-Editing"?

"A superb cook knows when to take a dish out of the oven so it's neither underdone nor overcooked," an editor commented. "But most of the manuscripts I reject are either underwritten—not enough thought and work put into them—or overwritten—too many words to say too little, not enough careful cutting."

When I've been involved on the editing end, I've found that many 20-page manuscripts would have been more acceptable if cut to 15 or even 10 pages. Yet, when I've suggested this to earnest individuals, the reaction usually has been, "You want me to cut out what I've worked so hard to put in? The writing is good, isn't it?"

Yes, the writing may be good—but, as the cliché affirms, it can be "too much of a good thing." Any word that isn't effective and essential should be eliminated. Stop and think what "edit" means. According to dictionaries, "to edit" means "to make written materials suitable for publication." Next time you're about to send out a manuscript you've written, ask yourself . . .

• *Have I worked this over specifically, so it's "suitable for publication," saying exactly what the reader needs and wants to know?*
• *Have I been too lazy to go back and cut again and again?*
• *Am I too much in love with my own words to edit sufficiently?*

A big part of successful professionalism grows from enough self-editing. It pays to review and rework every page repeatedly, asking each time, "Is this word necessary?" This chapter was more than three times as long before I cut-cut-cut, to make it most understandable and useful for you. Yes, it hurts to cross out words, paragraphs, pages you've sweated over, but it's essential to successful editing.

After over thirty years of writing and seiling, I still check every piece according to all three of the preceding checkpoints. That discipline keeps working for me. There are other factors that can make or break a sale. Some, such as timing and a magazine's overstock, are often out of your control. Regardless of such unforeseeable obstacles, these three basic checkpoints can and will work remarkably for you—when you *write to sell.*

55

BETTER INTERVIEWING

By Dennis Freeland

INTERVIEWS—obtaining firsthand, "expert" quotes from primary sources—are at the heart of good nonfiction writing. As the magazine publishing market expands, so does the need for both topical and personality-oriented pieces.

I've been doing interviews for fifteen years and, although I began doing straight Q.-and-A. articles and extended my scope of writing to include articles on education and music, my approach to interviews and research hasn't changed much.

Whether you're interviewing someone for background or for an article—a profile centered around the subject—the style of the interview itself is not appreciably different.

To get a clearer picture of better interviewing, I decided to go straight to the horse's mouth by interviewing myself in my New Jersey office.

Q. *First of all, how do you find these people?*

A. That's the question most frequently asked of me. Finding an address for a noteworthy person is the easy part. In the arts, for example, each person has at least two business addresses which are public record. In ascending order of desirability and effectiveness, these are: Distribution and Management.

Q. *For example?*

A. Let's take the "Brat Pack" film from some time ago, *St. Elmo's Fire*. You could reach anyone connected to that film by writing to him c/o Columbia Pictures (Distribution). It is preferable to go through Management, though.

Q. *But how can you find out who handles whom?*

A. Let's use *St. Elmo's Fire* again. If I wanted to get in touch with its writer, John Hughes, I'd call the Los Angeles or New York office of The Writers Guild of America (WGA). All unions have people whose sole job is to look up agents' names for people who call. Screen Actors Guild (SAG) and the Directors Guild of America, same deal. *Who's Who in America* gives business addresses, too.

Q. *O.K. I've tracked down my subject. What do I say when I call?*

A. You don't call. Unless it's an urgent, pre-sold, deadline situation, you do not try to get these people on the phone. Let's face it—you're asking for a favor. In effect, you're asking them for money. Their time is valuable, and you hope to be paid for this interview. Usually, the subject's reward is less tangible.

It's less demanding of the subject if you ask him or her for an interview with a thoughtful, intriguing letter.

Q. *Intriguing?*

A. You're looking to establish a bond between subject and interviewer. The letter is the first step in that process. In initial contact, you want to pique your subject's interest, flatter him, show him you're capable of handling your craft better than the hundreds of others who are jockeying for a piece of his time.

Q. *How important is that first contact?*

A. How important is a good lead in a news story? It determines whether or not the piece will be read, right? If your letter doesn't "sell" you, it's all over.

Q. *That sounds rather mercenary.*

A. It isn't. Your letters have to be sincere, lively—even passionate.

Q. *But what if you don't have a "passionate" interest in the subject?*

A. Then you have no business asking for the subject's time. Next question?

Q. *What about "experts"—people who are not going to be the focus of an article, but whose expertise you need to make an article authoritative?*

A. Get their attention, show them you're qualified. For example, if you're asking a child psychologist for information about male nonreaders, you're talking to someone whose time is worth, literally, hundreds of dollars an hour. If you're asking for a lot of his or her time, you might *have* to pay his standard rate. It's preferable, though, just to point out that you'll use his name in the piece, double-check the galleys with him to assure accuracy, etc.

Another bit of advice: Treat famous people as if they aren't, and those who aren't famous as if they are. You don't have to grovel at your skin doctor's feet to get help with that story on acne for *Seventeen,* but treat him and all subjects respectfully, professionally.

Q. *What is the secret to good interviewing?*

A. The secret lies in establishing a rapport between interviewer and subject, to gain his or her trust *and* to establish this early in the interview.

Q. *How do you go about obtaining your subject's trust?*

A. Stage hypnotists have a very effective trick for getting volunteers from the audience to trust them. The hypnotist stands behind his subject and says, "Let yourself fall." Of course, he catches the person as he or she falls backwards. Instant trust.

There's something like that in interviewing, but it is not *instant,* unfortunately. You have to be willing to reveal a bit of *yourself* if you want the subject to give you "good quotes" by revealing him or herself.

Q. *How do you do that?*

A. By making your interview an exchange of ideas and experiences.

Q. *Isn't it a little narcissistic to presume that someone important enough to be interviewed would be interested in hearing interviewers talk about themselves?*

288

A. Not at all. Interviewees are delighted when the interviewer does more than nod impassively, and go on to the next question.

Q. *Why do subjects prefer participatory interviewers?*

A. A couple of reasons: 1) It takes the burden of work from the interviewee. 2) It reinforces the feeling that you're going to be fair when you write about him or her. 3) All of the important people I've met became prominent because they were interested in other people. Once they've become famous, ironically, they're often cut off from everyday life.

Q. *What should you do before an interview?*

A. Your homework. Find out as much as you can about the subject, from as many sources as possible—primary and secondary. Dig up clips, talk to the subject's friends and associates.

Q. *What about the theory that research biases the interviewer?*

A. Malarkey. You'll find a consensus of opinion regarding the person you're going to interview. Quite often it will be at least half-false. The subject *knows* how the press has made him or her look: How often do they get a chance to answer to these half-truths and misquotes that follow them around? If you go in with an open mind, you're doing the interviewee a favor.

Q. *You believe, then, in preparing questions beforehand?*

A. Absolutely. Interviews have a time limit, and a very specific function. You have to get a lot of information in a little time.

Q. *Where do you get questions?*

A. During research, keep the old "5W's and 1H" in mind—Who, What, When, Where, Why and How. Look for contradictions, gaps in information, things that are glossed over in previous interviews.

Update old things—bring up a couple of striking quotes and find out if the subject still feels the same way.

Q. *So, the interviewer's half of the interview is done before the interview takes place?*

A. Would that it were true. It isn't. An interviewer prepares the way a musician rehearses—but there's more to being a musician than playing the right notes. You have to be ready to go in whatever direction the subject takes. You can't just go down a list of questions in precise order.

Q. *How do you write questions down, then, if you're not going to ask them in the order you've prepared them?*

A. Group questions by topic. When I interviewed Jim Henson, for example, there was a group of "Muppet Show" questions, one on his early TV work in the 1950s and another on *Dark Crystal*, his non-Muppet film.

Also, don't write out word-for-word questions. For example: "Were you deeply hurt by the critical lambasting of your most recent book?" would become: "Neg. reviews/last book/hurt?"

Q. *Isn't it important to give the interviewee the feeling he or she is involved in spontaneous conversation?*

A. Sure. A good interview *is* spontaneous, but it is also planned, structured. Just because you're well prepared doesn't mean your interview will be stilted. I start this kind of "controlled spontaneity" before the interview starts.

Q. *How?*

A. I always devote some time to warmup. I go in with a few non-interview questions in mind, and toss them out while I'm settling in, turning on the tape recorder. For instance, I had just come from my agent's office when I went to meet Billy Joel, and we started discussing agents and managers. I knew it was a good warmup topic—Joel's experience with unscrupulous managers has been thoroughly documented in the rock press. It's also O.K. to say, "I see you fish . . ." if the subject's office is festooned with mounted trout and rod-and-reel sets. He's probably been waiting *years* for someone to say that.

Q. *You mentioned using a tape recorder. Journalism texts endlessly debate whether or not to use them.*

A. It's not a question anymore. Most major magazines won't print anything that's not on tape. Besides, people are far more used to tape recorders nowadays. You can't replicate a person's manner of speaking without it, either.

Q. *Then you don't believe in note-taking?*

A. I didn't say that. I always take notes—on topics covered (giving me an overview later), ambience, character quirks, etc.—but I do it inconspicuously, during interruptions (there are *always* interruptions). After the interview, I find a quiet spot and free-associate on paper, writing down whatever I think might help the piece.

A neat trick for taking notes during an interview is to leave a lot of white space on your question sheets, scribbling your notes on the margins as you go. It saves you from flipping pages, or carrying two pads.

Q. *Do any other "neat tricks" come to mind?*

A. Yes. While you're researching, look for "nuggets"—facts about the person that are eye-catching, but haven't been well publicized. Toss one in early in the interview. When I was doing background research on the late Harry Chapin, I discovered he'd sold a screenplay to Warner Brothers a few years earlier. In the first ten minutes of my interview with him I said, "Whatever happened with that screenplay—*The End of the World,* I believe it was called . . ."

Chapin said, "Hey—you did your homework," and he was visibly more at ease from that moment.

Q. *What other tips do you have?*

A. Dress is something people don't always consider. Bear the subject in mind when you're deciding what to wear. It's not an iron-clad rule—I wouldn't wear a wedding dress and black lace gloves to an interview with Madonna—but I also wouldn't wear a 3-piece suit to meet with Pete Seeger.

Promptness counts. You're dealing with a professional; act like one. Locale: If you can avoid interviewing in a public place, do so. If you have to interview over the phone, have more questions ready (the

291

answers will be shorter), and ask them faster (silence is death to a phone interview).

Q. *How do you end an interview?*

A. Often, the subject will do that—by just standing up or saying, "Anything else?" That's when you pull out your "ace-in-the-hole" question—one juicy, documented question to give that last note some resonance. You want your interview to end with a bang, rather than a whimper.

If you're the one who finishes up, however, the simplest way of wrapping up is the best: "Thank you for your time. Is there anything you wish I *had* asked, before I go?"

Q. *Anything else?*

A. Yes. *Smile.* The people who surround noteworthy people tend to behave as if life is a wake. Your subject will be grateful—and relieved—to be with someone who knows that life is too important to be taken seriously.

56

HOW TO WRITE A WINNING QUERY

BY LINDAANN LOSCHIAVO

A WINNING query letter is the key to getting a go-ahead on an article. Whether you're a novice or an established free lancer, it's usually a waste of time to propose your article ideas to an editor over the telephone—or to submit your finished product over the transom. Most editors don't like to be interrupted by calls unless you're already known to them and also if your topic is timely and urgent. And to write the whole piece without a preliminary nod from an editor is unwise. What if the magazine has just bought a piece on a similar subject? Even if that isn't the case, the "slush pile" piece is never considered as carefully as an article that's been assigned or requested on speculation.

To get that assignment or the agreement to read your work "on spec," sharpen up your query-writing techniques.

Hammering out the "hook"

An intriguing opening is called a "hook" because it *must* catch a busy editor's eye. Start off with your best. A great deal of material is rejected because its presentation is second-rate. However, if your proposed idea and style grab the *editors* right away, they'll be more willing to believe your final draft will grab their *readers*.

Here are some examples of my finely honed hooks, queries that brought positive responses from editors the first time out.

About eight million Americans wear contact lenses. Several million more wear eyeglasses. Now orthokeratology is making corrective lenses obsolete. Haven't heard of this new procedure? It's about time you did. ("Orthokeratology Is Making Things Perfectly Clear," *Ambassador Magazine*)

As you read this, several phones are ringing in the Greater New York area. A pregnant teen-ager is thinking about running away from home. A 30-year-old veteran has just been released from the hospital after his fourth operation—and he's contemplating suicide. A housewife's alcoholic second husband is beating up her preschoolers. A 72-year-old blind man is depressed and lonely. Who's at the other end of the telephone? A trained, para-professional counselor in a hotline crisis intervention center in one of the five boroughs, calming, advising, reassuring, *listening.* ("My Name Is Joseph. I'm Going to Kill Myself," *The New York Times Magazine*)

Most women diet before their weddings in order to look slim in their gowns and (ever after) in their wedding albums. What a shame then to ruin it because of poor eating habits during the honeymoon. Here's how your brides can enjoy themselves and *still* return home with no excess baggage around their hips. ("Staying Slim and Fit on Your Honeymoon," *Mode for Brides* [an Australian publication])

Now that you've read some good hooks, here are a few poor ones:

There are crisis intervention centers all over New York City. Listeners hear all kinds of exciting stories. I know your readers would find this provocative. (*Poor:* See why this flat-footed version is devoid of drama? Merely *telling* it's fascinating material, not demonstrating it by some heart-stirring vignettes, is unconvincing, boring, flat.)

I've been reading (name of magazine) for years. I think it's the best women's magazine on the newsstand. (*Poor:* This is amateurish and sounds like a fan letter, not a query.)

I've noticed you've never printed an article on _____, so I'd like to do one for you. (*Poor:* Maybe this is a taboo topic at that particular magazine. Even so, always make your lead *dance*—not limp along.)

Why were my three queries successful? Partly because their leads blended essential ingredients: instant reader identification, promises of help, and dramatic presentation. For instance, most airline passengers either wear glasses or know someone who does. Who would pass up a chance to improve his or her vision? Similarly, many New Yorkers would either sympathize with the troubled callers or identify with them and also want to know how to dial for hot-line help. Last, all brides go to great lengths to look their best on their wedding day.

There's a silent message as well. The hooks demonstrated that both my style and my subject matter would captivate an audience. Yours should, too.

Constructing the body of a query

This "silent message" in your hook or opening paragraphs should echo throughout the query. Your next few paragraphs must reveal that you (a) write well, (b) have a topic worth developing, and (c) can deliver what you're proposing. How? *Show*—don't just tell.

Highlight your preliminary research. *Poor approach:* "I'm planning to interview several therapists to learn about dealing with difficult people." *Good approach:* "Sometimes you can simply ignore difficult people. Sometimes you can't. Then what? 'It's not what you argue about with a difficult person—but *how*,' observes Vincent D. Foley, Ph.D., a New York psychologist." (A condensation of Dr. Foley's advice follows.) Promising to offer innovative tips or solutions is never as effective as serving up a tempting summary of lively direct quotes in a query.

Stress selling points. *Good phrases:* "Few people know about this unique procedure," "it saves consumers time and money," and so on. Are there news pegs? Is this timely? If possible, tie your article to the latest discovery, an anniversary, a holiday. If none of this is possible, emphasize why the audience of that publication would find your feature enjoyable or useful.

Describe your researching, interviewing, or writing methods. Setting these forth inspires confidence. *Poor approach:* "My article will cover the latest methods of whitening your smile." *Good approach:* "What's involved in the newest methods of whitening a smile through bleaching? Doctors Rudolph and Eisdorfer will explain—step-by-step—how it's done, how long it takes, how much it costs. They'll also discuss what's *not* involved: no pain, no drilling, no tooth reduction, no huge bills."

Emphasize your credentials

Conclude the query with your credentials. If you have published articles, list them with names and dates of magazines—tailored to this particular market or this topic, when possible. For example, if you're querying the editor of a men's fashion publication, stress that you've written for similar magazines. If you're proposing a self-help piece, note the other how-to features you've done and where they have appeared.

If you have no publication credits, emphasize some of your other qualifications. For example, if I were proposing an article "How to Run with Hand Weights"—and if I had no other exercise features ever printed—then I might say, "I've been jogging for three years, and I've taught a year-long seminar on using hand weights in aerobics. Also, I've been promised an exclusive interview by Leonard Schwartz, M.D., the Pittsburgh physician who invented Heavyhands." (Besides, if you master query writing, soon you *will* have plenty of credits to include.)

Whether or not you're a published author, if your query is well-crafted, competent, witty, appealing, the *product* itself gives you more authority than your *promises.*

Some General Guidelines for Your Query

- Type it single-spaced on good white bond or your letterhead.
- A clean keyboard and fresh typewriter ribbon make a good impression—on you.
- Keep your letter brisk, bright, and brief; a single sheet of stationery should suffice. (Exception: if the "Writer's Guidelines" indicate otherwise or if your idea requires a detailed, complex proposal.)
- Consider outlining your query first, a professional time-saver. Group the points that are most dramatic, salable, and pertinent. Then decide on the most effective arrangement. Model your letter on that skeleton.
- Avoid beginning with the pronoun "I" or starting too many paragraphs with it. Vary your syntax and sentence length until your text sounds rhythmic.
- Duplicate the magazine's *tone* in your query. Are their articles typically chatty, warm, urbane, arch? Demonstrate that your voice can chime right in with their regulars.
- Are you a novice? Conclude by offering to do the manuscript "on speculation," which means that an editor is agreeing *only* to read it—not necessarily to buy it.
- Write tightly and truthfully. Don't overstate, oversell, or overestimate an editor's patience.

57

TRICKS OF THE NONFICTION TRADE

By Donald M. Murray

UNDER the apprentice system still practiced in most crafts, a beginner has the opportunity to work beside an experienced worker and pick up small but significant tricks of the trade. Few of us, however, observe a writer at the workbench turning a phrase, cutting a line or reordering a paragraph so that a meaning runs easy and runs clear. Here are a few of the tricks I've picked up during more than forty years of trying to make writing look easy.

Before writing

An effective piece of writing is a dialogue between the writer and the reader, with the writer answering the reader's questions just before they are asked. Each piece usually has five or six questions that must be answered if the reader is to be satisfied.

I brainstorm and polish the questions first, then put them in the order the reader will ask them. For example, if I am doing a piece on diabetes, I list such questions as:

• What is diabetes?
• How can I tell if I have it?
• What's the latest treatment?
• Do I have to give myself shots?
• Where can I get that treatment?
• How dangerous is diabetes?

Then I reconsider, refine, and reorder the questions:

1. *Lead:* What's the latest treatment for diabetes?
2. How dangerous is diabetes?
3. What is diabetes?
4. How can I tell if I have it?

5. Do I have to give myself shots? No. New treatment.
6. Where can I get it?

As I write, I may have to reorder the questions if I "hear" the reader ask the question earlier than I expected, but that doesn't happen very often. It is also helpful to write these questions down before revising a draft—especially a confusing one. Just role-play a reader and put down the questions you would ask, combining them if necessary, and then put them in order. This trick will help you understand what readers want to know and when they want to know it.

Professional writers, however, don't wait until they have a completed draft to read what they have written. They learn to pay attention to lists, collections of information, partially drafted sentences and paragraphs, abandoned pages, notes, outlines, phrases, code words that constitute the kind of writing they do on the notebook page and in their heads before the first draft.

Reading those fragments, the writer discovers a revealing or organizing specific around which an article can be built, a pattern of action or argument on which a meaning may be hung, a voice that tells the writer what he or she feels about the subject and that may be used to communicate that feeling to the reader.

Many writers write everything at the same distance from the subject. It becomes an unconscious habit. Academic writers may stand too far back from the subject, so that the reader feels detached and really doesn't become involved with the content. Magazine writers usually move in close, many times getting too close, so that readers are lost in the details of a particular person and are not able to understand the significance of the piece.

The writer should use an imaginary zoom lens before writing the first draft and decide the proper distance for this particular article, the point from which the reader will see the piece clearly, understand its context, and care about the subject. The writer may stand back and put the winning play in the context of all Army-Navy football games or move in close and tell the story of the game in terms of the winning play itself, concentrating on the fifty seconds that made the difference.

Leads and endings

The first line, the first paragraph, the first ten lines of an article establish its direction, dimensions, voice, pace. "What's so hard about the first sentence is that you're stuck with it," says Joan Didion. "Everything else is going to flow out of that sentence. And by the time you've laid down the first *two* sentences, your options are all gone." It's worth taking time to get those sentences right.

The more complicated the subject the more time you may need to spend on the lead to make sure that you are giving the readers the information they need to become interested right away. You can't start too far back with background, and you can't plunge into the middle of the story so that the readers do not know what they are reading. You have to start at the right point in the right way, and the more time you spend drafting new leads, and then refining the leads you choose, the faster you will be able to write the whole piece. Most of the major problems in writing an article are solved when the right lead is found.

When I worked as writing coach at *The Boston Globe,* I found that the best writers usually knew where they would end. They had a quote, an anecdote, a scene, a specific detail with which they would close. It would sum up the piece by implication. The good writer has a sense of direction, a destination in mind. The best endings are rarely written to solve the problems of a piece that just trails off. The best endings are usually seen by the writer as waiting just ahead for the draft to take the writer and the reader there.

The right voice

Experienced writers rarely begin a first draft until they hear in their heads—or on the page—a voice that may be right. Voice is usually the key element in effective writing. It is what attracts the reader and communicates to the reader. It is that element that gives the illusion of speech. Voice carries the writer's intensity and glues together the information that the reader needs to know. It is the music in writing that makes meaning clear.

Writers keep rehearsing possible first lines, paragraphs, or endings, key scenes or statements that will reveal how what is to be said may be said best. The voice of a piece of writing is the writer's own voice, adapted in written language to the subject and audience. We speak differently at a funeral or a party, in church or in the locker room, at home or with strangers. We are experienced with using our individual voices for many purposes. We have to learn to do this same thing in writing, and to hear a voice in our head that may be polished and developed on the page.

The voice is not only rehearsed but practiced. We should hear what we're writing as we write it. I dictate most of my writing and monitor my voice as I'm speaking so that the pace, the rhythm, the tone support what I'm trying to say. Keep reading aloud as you draft and edit. To train yourself to do this, it may be helpful, if you use a word processor, to turn off the screen and write, listening to what you're saying as you're saying it. Later you can read it aloud and make the changes you need to develop a voice that the reader can hear.

Put your notes away before you begin a draft. What you remember is probably what should be remembered; what you forget is probably what should be forgotten. No matter; you'll have a chance to go back to your notes after the draft is completed. What is important is to achieve a draft which allows the writing to flow.

Planning allows the writer to write fast without interruptions, putting a space or TK (to come) in the text for the quote or the statistic that has to be looked up later. There are some writers who proceed slowly, but most of us learn the advantage of producing a draft at top speed when the velocity forces unexpected connections and makes language twist and spin and dance in ways we do not expect.

When you finish your daily stint or if you are interrupted during the fast writing, stop in the middle of a sentence so you can return to the text and start writing again at a point when you know what you have to say. It's always a good idea to stop each day before the well is drained dry, when you know what you'll try to deal with the next day. This is the best way to overcome the inertia we all suffer when returning to a draft. If we know how to finish a sentence, the chances are the next sentence will rise out of that one, and we'll be writing immediately.

Planning is important, but it isn't writing. You want to be free enough in writing a draft to say more than you expect to say. Writers do not write what they already know as much as they write to know. Edward Albee echoes many writers when he says, "I write to find out what I'm thinking about." Writing is an act of thinking, and the process of writing adds two and two and comes up with seven.

An effective article usually has one dominant theme or message; everything in it should advance that meaning. Other meanings collect around the dominant one, but in the process of revision, the writer must make sure that everything in the piece relates to the main idea, cutting what does not move the reader forward.

The inexperienced writer cuts a piece of writing by compression and produces a package of tight language that can be difficult to understand and is rarely a pleasure to read. The professional writer selects those parts that most efficiently and effectively advance the meaning and then develops them fully so that the reader understands the significance of the anecdote, the full strength of the argument.

Writing in which the meaning is not clear often occurs because writers bury the most important information. One way to make an article clear is to look at the most significant paragraphs and move the sections around so that the most important information is at the end of the paragraph, the next most important at the beginning, and the least most important in the center of the paragraph.

We need important information at the beginning to attract the reader, but what the reader remembers is usually at the end of the paragraph. This pattern doesn't work for every paragraph, and shouldn't. But it is a way of clarifying a complicated and significant paragraph, and the same rule may be applied to an entire piece of writing.

I find that I am a more efficient editor of my own draft if I read it three times and have a specific goal for each reading. *First,* I read it to see if I have all the information I need. Do I have the facts, statistics, quotations, anecdotes I need to construct an accurate, persuasive article? And do I understand that information? If I don't have the information or understand it I must stop my editing and deal with these problems.

Second, I read for organization. Does the article, as I have mentioned earlier, answer the readers' questions in the order they will ask them? Does the article flow naturally from beginning to end, with each part of the article fitting what has gone before and leading to what follows?

Third, I read the article line by line, listening both to what is said and how it is said, making sure, by reading it aloud, that my voice carries the meaning to the reader. I hope that my articles will be accurate and have the illusion of speech, the rhythm, music, and ease of an ideal conversation.

Those are a few of the tricks of the nonfiction trade. Try them out to see if they work for you. Collect others from your writer friends, and become aware of those devices that you have used to make your meaning clear, so that you will be able to call on them as you continue your lifelong course in learning how to write.

58

ARTICLE OUTLINES BRING SALES

By William E. Miles

"Put it before them briefly so they will read it, clearly so they will appreciate it, picturesquely so they will remember it and, above all, accurately so they will be guided by its light."

Give Joseph Pulitzer a prize for this nearly century-old advice to reporters! Although the publisher of the New York *World* was referring to newspaper stories, his remarks are just as applicable today to magazine article outlines. Brevity, clarity, color, accuracy—that's the gift-wrapping of the package you are inviting an editor to open when you submit an outline of a subject you hope will spark his interest in your article.

An outline should be kept as short as possible, preferably one page single-spaced. Sometimes, of course, the subject demands more detailed explanation—but try not to let it exceed two pages. Within this framework, fill it with enough colorful facts and figures to catch the editor's eye and indicate the authenticity of the material.

Typed on a separate page or pages, the outline should be accompanied by a brief covering letter and sufficient return postage. A sample covering letter might read like this: "Would you be interested in taking a speculative look at a 2,000-word article on the order of the attached outline? My articles have been published in . . ." (naming some of the magazines you have sold to or listing whatever other qualifications you may have). Then, paper-clipped to the covering letter, the outline itself. For example:

Pranks for the Memory

Practical jokes are probably so-called because they are practically never a joke to the victim—who often winds up on something funny as a crutch. Even Mark Twain, an inveterate practical joker much of his life, confessed in his later years that he "held the practical joker in limitless contempt."

303

The late Bennett Cerf, another humorist who held practical jokers "in low esteem," once waxed particularly indignant over the dirty trick perpetrated on a Chicago bridegroom. After passing out at a bachelor party, he awakened to find his right arm in a cast. His fun-loving friends told him he had broken it in a brandy-inspired brawl—forcing him to spend his entire honeymoon with a perfectly good arm in a painfully tight cast.

Such practical jokers, according to Cerf, are "under no circumstances to be confused with humorists." But American history, dating back to pre-Revolutionary War days, is filled with hundreds of other examples of more harmless exercises in hilarity that don't deserve the harshness of his critical verdict.

One of the earliest of these was conceived by General Israel Putnam, a hero of the French and Indian War, after being challenged to a duel by a British army officer. Putnam selected as his choice of weapons two powder kegs into which he bored holes and inserted slow fuses. When the fuses burned down to an inch of the kegs, the British officer beat a hasty retreat—from barrels filled with onions!

But some practical jokes turn out to be really practical—as in the case of a "green" engineer at the General Electric plant who was assigned by old-timers as a prank the "impossible" job of frosting light bulbs on the inside. Marvin Pipkin not only found a way but, at the same time, devised a method of strengthening the bulbs so they would last much longer—cutting the cost to consumers in half!

An article of mine, based on this outline, appeared in *Elks Magazine*. If this makes the outline approach to article sales sound easy, it isn't. An outline is only the bare bones of an article and no skeleton key guaranteed to unlock all editorial doors. For every idea that clicks, you may receive a dozen or more rejections. And sometimes the article itself is rejected after the outline has received a speculative O.K. For one reason or another, the article may just not live up to its billing.

But whether it does or not, outlines are not only attention-getters, but time-savers. A complete article can take a month or so to research and write and another month or so languishing in editorial offices awaiting a decison. An outline, on the other hand, requires only cursory research— enough to establish an intriguing lead and some supporting information. Only after the "go-ahead" (if you get it) do you need to start researching the subject in depth.

Editors also answer queries far more rapidly than they return articles—so even a rejection has its bright side. If the query is turned down, you've saved yourself unnecessary work in more ways than one. When outlines are returned, as they usually are, there's no retyping involved (except for another covering letter), if you decide to try elsewhere.

Another important aspect of an outline is that an editor, who likes the general idea, may have some suggestions of his own as to how he'd like it handled. An article I sold to *The Lion* is a good example of this. My original idea was to take a swipe at juries because of the way they were influenced by clever lawyers (and sometimes their own ignorance) into returning strange, far-out verdicts. I had no solutions to the problems in mind when I submitted the following outline to the editor:

The Trouble with Juries

FBI statistics show that 90 out of every 100 murderers are arrested, 50 receive some sort of punishment, and two are sentenced to death. This means that almost half of all accused killers are acquitted after their mandatory trials by jury in cases of first degree murder—presumably the guilty as well as the innocent.

This assumption was borne out by an investigation of the jury system in Pennsylvania which disclosed some juries had reached their verdicts by drawing straws or flipping coins. Other jurors were found to have rushed through their deliberations in order to get to a dance or a lodge meeting on time.

Although Thomas Jefferson described juries as "the best of all safeguards for the person, the property and the reputation of every individual," many legal experts regard them as outmoded relics in this modern age. Trial by jury stems from trial by oath in which the accused, swearing to his innocence, was supported by twelve "oath-helpers," or compurgators, who attested to their belief in his statements. This "jury of peers" was intimately acquainted with the defendant and the circumstances of the alleged crime. But in our day, as Dr. Joseph Catton points out, an attempt is made to select persons who know *nothing* about the offense. "There are those who believe," he adds wryly, "that today's jurors know nothing about anything."

Other criminologists contend that a modern jury is generally made up of persons unfamiliar with the law who often miss the significance of technical rulings by the judge. Even in cases where court rulings are simple and understandable, the jury sometimes ignores them. There is one actual case on record in which members of the jury, disregarding the evidence and the judge's charge, all knelt in prayer—and came up with a verdict!

The editor replied: "I'd be happy to consider your article 'The Trouble with Juries' with one important condition. I'd like to see the piece conclude with some constructive recommendations from authorities on how the jury system could be improved and/or replaced by better systems."

Further research incorporated his suggestions into the article whose whole thrust was changed, including the lead, when it appeared in *The Lion* under the new title, "Of Juries and Judgments."

The lead (aside from the idea) is probably the most important part of an outline, because it's the first thing to attract an editor's eye. One good means of accomplishing this is to tie it to a particular city or state even though the actual subject matter may range far afield. Here's an outline with just such a lead that resulted in a sale to the *Chicago Tribune Sunday* Magazine:

305

Chicago's long history of accomplishments includes the honor of being the first city to introduce what some engineering experts have called one of the ten most complex and ingenious inventions of the past hundred years. Back in 1893 it put the "zip" in the zipper when a sample of the original slide fastener was placed on display at Chicago's Columbian Exposition for use by the Fair's hootchie-kootchie dancer, Little Egypt, as a rapid skirt-release.

But it was the zipper, not the stripper, that caught the eye of a visitor to the Fair—Colonel Louis Walker of Meadville, Pa.—and he hired the inventor, Whitcomb L. Judson, to improve his original patent on a "locker or unlocker for automatically engaging or disengaging an entire series of clasps by a single continuous movement."

After years of experimentation, the device was finally perfected in 1913 and, four years later, a Brooklyn tailor made the fastener famous by attaching it to money belts which he sold to sailors at the Brooklyn Navy Yard. The Navy itself was soon using the fastener on flying suits. And during the depression, a dress company tried out the novelty as a sales booster—taking the industry by storm. Soon the zipper's long story of "ups and downs" was over. Its slide to success had begun!

Leads come in all shapes and sizes and there are dozens of other ways of writing that all-important first paragraph whose purpose is to sell a particular editor on a particular idea. For instance, the "striking statement" lead:

Lightning, the silent partner of thunder, has frightened more people—and killed fewer—than any other common danger. In fact, your chances of being killed by a lightning bolt are one in a million.

The editor liked this outline lead well enough to keep it intact when my article "Striking Down Lightning Myths" was published in *Wheels Afield.*

Another editorial eye-opener is the "news peg" approach—tying the article to a current happening or upcoming event—or the "anniversary angle" like this outline lead for my article "Meters By The Mile" that appeared in *The Rotarian* more years ago than I care to remember:

Ten years ago last October 1,500 parking meters went on trial in New York City. They were immediately found guilty by protesting motorists who charged that they interfered with their constitutional privileges of life, liberty and the pursuit of free parking space . . .

But why go on? The point is that, varied as they were, all of these leads had one thing in common—an ability to grab the editor's attention and keep him reading. From these examples, you can see that I like to write a lead (and sometimes an ending) that will be used more or less "as is" in the finished article if the outline receives an editorial O.K.

This gives the editor a good idea of what to expect—not only of the subject but of the style in which it will be written. For an outline must persuade the editor that you not only have a good idea, but possess the ability to handle it well.

59

WRITING ARTICLES FROM PERSONAL EXPERIENCE

By Rita Milios

WHEN I first began my professional writing career, I had the same goals as many other writers, amateur or pro. I wanted my work to be read by thousands of people in some of the nation's largest and most popular magazines. How could a novice writer achieve such dramatic results in a short period? I found that doors opened widest to me when I submitted one particular type of magazine article—the personal experience piece.

Many of my personal experience articles are what I call "emotional stories." Magazines are looking for more emotion, more real life. By filling this need, I have established a successful writing career. In just four years, my personal experience articles have been published in such magazines as *Reader's Digest, McCall's, Woman's World,* and many more.

The potential of a personal experience article lies not in the nature of the experience itself, but in the ability of the writer to turn an experience into an interesting, instructive, moving piece. "Slice-of-life" essays that reflect human nature are sought by many magazines, large and small; and the personal experience piece, because it requires no research, is one of the easiest articles to write.

Here are a few basic steps that I follow when writing personal experience articles, with good results:

STEP 1) *Begin your article at a dramatic point.*

A good way to hook your reader is with a dramatic lead that appeals to his or her emotions. However, I do not always begin with the *most* dramatic event. Instead, I start with the one that has true dramatic value and at the same time can provide a good lead into the rest of the article. Often this involves a flashback to fill in pertinent details. But once the flashback has been completed, usually by the end of the first or second page, my piece flows on in a steady forward progression to the end.

For example, I began "Our Bond of Love," which sold to *Lady's Circle*, with my thoughts as I lay in a hospital bed receiving news of my desperately ill newborn son.

> The doctor entered the room quietly, cautiously. His eyes held a look of concern and dread that betrayed his calm.
>
> "I'm sorry, Mrs. Milios," he said gently. "I'm afraid I bring more bad news." *No! Stop!* my mind cried. *I don't want to hear it. I can't take any more. Please, why can't you keep it from me? I can't change anything, and it hurts too much to know the truth. Why can't you just lie to me?* But I couldn't say that. "What is it?" I asked in a wooden voice.

Clearly, there is a crisis here, and the reader is hooked with both empathy and curiosity. What is the bad news? How will it affect the narrator? What will happen next? Once I had captured my reader's attention, I used a flashback to tell how I got into this situation and what possibilities lay ahead.

STEP 2) *Convey your thoughts and emotions.*

Since personal experience articles involve emotion and are written in the first person, if you're afraid to show your feelings, this type of writing might not be for you. But strong emotions elicit strong reactions. You have to try to relive the emotion of the experience, to create a scene that rings true and seems real. By recreating the scene complete with thoughts and emotions you can make your reader experience it, vicariously sharing with you all the intensity, insight, and understanding that the experience brings. And by sharing some of your "bad" feelings, you can create a bond with your readers and give them an unexpected "gift," helping them face negative emotions they may have repressed.

On several occasions, friends who have read "Our Bond of Love" have told me, "I had those same feelings and I felt so guilty," or, "Reading your story made me understand that those feelings are normal, that they're O.K."

STEP 3) *Choose an experience that readers can relate to.*

Not every reader has experienced a flood or a fire or catastrophe similar to the one you are writing about. Yet, most readers relate to these kinds of articles because of the emotion and the insights and understanding the piece provides. Readers look to the problems of others to find solutions to their own problems. And every reader has at some time faced fear, love, anger, and some kind of "life's-not-fair" situation.

But what about the lucky writer who has lived a relatively normal life? What personal experiences or everyday events can he or she successfully turn into articles? These can be as effective as a dramatic piece in eliciting a response from your reader. Most readers appreciate a simple anecdote about everyday life that uplifts or inspires them. In "Blackberry Pickin' Time," I used vivid descriptions to create a feeling of nostalgia in an anecdotal article for *Yesteryear* magazine:

I remember the day Mama dragged the old coal buckets down from the attic. They were black with soot and laced with cobwebs, for they hadn't been used since we moved into the new house with the modern oil burning furnace. But we scrubbed those buckets till they shined.
"We're goin' blackberry pickin'," Mama said.

Religious magazines often buy inspirational first-person anecdotes. "The Day God Rode the Bus," which sold to *Aspire,* was the story of a simple kindness from a stranger that had far-reaching effects.

"What can I ever do to repay you?" I asked the boy, certain that anything I could do would be inadequate.
He said, "Simply help someone else when they need you."

Normal, everyday experiences often provide the best insight into human nature. And it is these insights that editors and readers are looking for.

STEP 4) *Share with the reader the insights and lessons you have learned.*

Every crisis, every experience teaches you something about life. What insights or lessons did your experience give you that you can share with your readers to help them face and resolve a similar problem or to understand themselves better? Don't be afraid to spell it out.

My article, "What Did I Teach My Child Today?" written for *Living with Preschoolers,* is about setting good examples. All parents know that they should set a good example for their children, but how many of us realize the full extent to which our actions are mimicked? ("My children, little sponges that they are, soaked up everything that I said or did.") And how many fully realize the responsibilities of parenthood

310

until it is too late? (. . . "I suddenly realized that when I took on the job of parent, I also assumed the job of being a full-time adult, even though there are times when I don't feel big or strong or smart at all.") Sharing insights such as these bring reader and writer closer together, and add "significance" to your article.

STEP 5) *Marketing the personal experience article.*

You've finished your article, but can you sell it? Who will buy it? Almost any general interest, women's, or religious magazine, if you have written the article well. Is the emotion real? Can your reader relate to the feelings? Are they universal? Have you shared the lessons that you learned? If so, you are ready to choose the most suitable market for your story.

Go through the market listings and watch for such phrases as these: ". . . seeking meaningful stories of personal experience" (*McCall's*); ". . . looking for articles that give practical examples from real life" (*Christian Home & School*); ". . . want personal narratives that are true and have some universal relevance" *(Guideposts).*

A knowledge of individual magazine styles is important. For instance, I know that *Reader's Digest* likes narrow escapes. *Woman's Day* likes everyday situations with good insights and problem-solving techniques. *Redbook* likes "Young Mother's Stories," and *McCall's* often looks for medical miracles. Religious magazines like articles that inspire or uplift. The same experience might have to be written differently for each of these markets to fit in with the editorial style of the particular magazine. Gearing each personal experience article to the proper market requires careful study of each magazine, but it pays off. Good marketing skills mean fewer rejections.

Finally, when querying an editor about a particular personal experience article, make special note of its significance for the readers. Will your piece inspire them? Give them courage? Will it make them feel better to know that they are not alone in their feelings? Will it help them? If so, how?

When writing your personal experience article, make it *real.* Do your best to move your reader, inspire him, make him cry. Make your story *live.*

60

SO YOU WANT TO WRITE ABOUT SCIENCE

By Lorus J. Milne and Margery Milne

Editors continually need science articles to update their readers' understanding of their ever-changing world. Satisfying this hunger for scientific information and what it means can be an exciting and profitable activity for the scientist or the writer interested in science. Each week seems to produce new material that can be translated into significant articles an editor will buy—if they are written with accuracy and clarity in a way that connects with a reader's world.

A topic of interest

What interests you most may well interest others, and you have the advantage of a head start in recognizing your own enthusiasm. You may have found a fresh topic or a new angle on an old one. Relate everything to your subject, enhancing and clarifying it in an exciting way for the lay reader.

As you become a science writer, you learn to prepare lists, sentences, paragraphs, even phrases you would like to work into your piece, in draft form. A sentence you admire, quoted from some classic author not too far back in time, might well find a useful place. The secrets of science turn up in many different guises, because anything worth telling can be told in dozens of different ways.

Focus on a variety of related topics and try to expand your information by on-site observation and detailed reading. It is essential to write about what you know, even if your knowledge is quite new. You should serve as a strainer through which fine details can disappear while basic principles remain. Your own enthusiasm grows as you teach yourself. You might well speculate a little as a step toward making your readers care and want more. Science is particularly good for this because it is so open-ended. Rarely is anything final. More awaits discovery.

Keep exploring your subject, reading until you feel you have exhausted all the resources. When you are confident that you have a grasp of the subject, try explaining it to others and get them excited, too. Talking about the material gets you listeners who can respond. If their attention wanders, your idea or presentation needs improvement. If they keep asking questions that suggest new vistas to explore, you have something good.

This kind of unfolding experience followed a talk we gave in Halifax on animal behavior. As we drove home that stormy night, the positive reactions and lively questions from the group told us it was time to start to write. We studied the market and found that *Scientific American* runs an occasional article about animal behavior, so we sent off a query to the editor and, with his encouragement, prepared a manuscript. It included our own field observations and some new discoveries made by European scientists. It told of unusual family activity among small creatures. The science story that stirred us soon reached others.

Every article has its own origin. The spectacular valley of Jackson Hole, Wyoming, with its trusting moose browsing in a pond much closer to the Rockefeller hotel than to the snow-clad mountains in the background, focused our attention on its wildlife. For days we observed everything we could and learned about animal interactions in this idyllic setting. On our portable typewriter, we summarized our information in a few pages and boldly mailed them off without invitation as "Special to *The New York Times.*"

Back to the wilderness came a telegram, "Have you any pictures?" Everyone in the valley knew about that telegram before we did, for telegrams aren't delivered to campers in the bush. Yes, we had rolls of undeveloped black/white negatives, which we immediately sent off for the *Times* to process and inspect. A two-page spread in *The New York Times Magazine* showcased our article. Part of the text was selected for reprinting in a digest magazine.

The spark you need for an article may come from anywhere, even a paragraph or a news item in the paper. Read all you can find on the subject, and talk to people who are engaged in research on some aspect of it.

Research

Are science writers different from other writers? Must you develop special skills as well as endless curiosity to write about science?

You don't have to be a scientist to write science articles or even books. Your own curiosity should drive you to educate yourself until you become a self-taught expert. True dedication frees you from the need for college courses on the subject. By hunting up what we needed to know and without special training, we wrote *A Time To Be Born*, a 218-page book on animal courtship and parenting. Space limitations kept us from citing the 466 references on which we had relied.

You have the advantage of personal excitement in presenting details that are new to you. As long as you select subjects that lend themselves to rather simple research you can become a winner by getting your account of the topic published. You'll be astonished at the number of different outlets that turn up as you progress. While the topic ripens in your mind, your file folders fatten with notes. The real question is how much the topic intrigues you and keeps you alert to scientific work, as it appears in technical journals and newspapers.

In every scientific field, the volume of literature includes a greater range of discoveries and statements than almost anyone can recall unaided. On annotated file cards, record the articles and other references you find for your subject. Follow the format of bibliographies in some standard scientific journal. Alphabetize your list and have a copy ready under the heading "Sources." Unless you are writing about long-past events, as Stephen Jay Gould so often does, your references should mostly be from 1980 onward, only a minority from farther back. Recent work needs more publicity and gives a modern flavor to what you write.

Vocabulary

The first challenge in any scientific field is simplicity, both of presentation and vocabulary. Are you becoming involved with some aspect of natural science such as biology or geology, or of a physical science like physics or chemistry? Anyone who enjoys reading about physics will know what fiber optics are. Anyone with an interest in chemistry will recognize the symbols for elements and feel comfortable with a few simple formulae. Similarly, a person in sympathy with nature need not be told the difference between plants and animals, or that DNA and RNA are components of the mechanism of genetics and inheritance. Your role is to provide exciting and refreshing facts your readers will want to understand or know more about.

Broad as science is, one area of expertise is all you can consider in one topic. Within that area, choose the special vocabulary (the "jargon") that permits analysis and communication to be precise, without lengthy explanations. Readers might tolerate special words if you introduce them clearly, one at a time, and not more than one to a page. Keep others in mind for your own use in reading from journals. Spare your audience.

Contrast the following.

A) From the light focused on the retina the photosensitive molecules in the receptor cells absorb energy a quantum (photon) at a time, a molecule at a time, and trigger the sensation of sight.

B) The light energy focused on the sensitive cells in the eye is absorbed by special molecules. One molecule, excited by a single unit of energy, can trigger the sensation of sight.

A good basis for deciding which technical term(s) to include would be the frequency with which you find the word(s) in a national magazine or newspaper.

Readers on science topics may know the names of outstanding scientists and their accomplishments. These can be the guideposts within your article or book, helping you relate other scientific information to make it meaningful. You might find an analogy in something Charles Darwin attempted. What happened in North America or Europe during the years while Darwin was traveling around the world on *H.M.S. Beagle*? Wherever your curiosity leads you, dig out the facts, and let your readers know.

The scene around you can provide delightful anecdotes that are completely relevant. Puddles following a good rain in early June may be outlined in bright yellow, reminding you that the white pines are shedding their golden pollen and additional clouds of these dust-sized particles will billow forth if a lively squirrel shakes the branches. Even while jogging, be aware of your environment. Practice using your senses: sight, sound, smell, taste, touch. Think about what they detect and let you appreciate. These senses are the only avenues from the outside world to the brain. But environment affects the way we use them. In a city, we want privacy, and shut out the smell of onions cooking down the hall, the sound of buses starting up, fire sirens and garbage trucks. The country person, after going to the city, reacts to these sounds and smells. The city person in the country finds no sensory signals intense enough to crash through the protective wall, and wonders: Where is everything? Why is nothing happening?

The environment continually supplies you with two real advantages: it invites you to make your own observations, upon which you can count without quoting any authority, and it tends to be timeless, letting you safely combine information gathered from several different years.

Refining your article

Control your impatience, even while you wait for an editor to decide on the first version of the article you submit. Your time need not be lost, for the subject will ripen, letting you rethink paragraphs you wrote. Reread them with a critical eye. Substitute a better word or rearrange the sentence. Move an early sentence farther back (or forward). Expand if you need to. Keep it simple and show why it is relevant. Is that really the clearest way to express what you intended? Must the account read

> We know that, apart from encouraging the spread of forests, almost every change humankind makes in land leaves it drier. We have no wish to see in America the ultimate stage—the nearly irreversible alteration of valuable land into useless desert. In Africa, desertification has diminished space for human-kind at a frightening pace.

You could make that "pace" more specific by adding,

> "expanding the Sahara Desert during the past fifty years by an area twice the size of Spain." (*Country Journal*, vol. 7)

Honest science writing earns recognition. Even a rejection slip may point the way toward improvement, toward recognizing the needs of the market, or to the existence of other opportunities. Rewriting proves your P.Q. (Persistence Quotient), continually strengthening your science writing output and sharpening your reading and listening skills.

Rewards

Science writing has its rewards. Our awareness of the world's limited supply of fresh water led us to write a book on *Water and Life*. It brought us an invitation to discuss fresh water resources worldwide for a television program produced by the California Academy of Science. Our interview was even dubbed into Cantonese for re-broadcast from

Hong Kong. Still later the National Geographic Society sent us to North Africa, Israel, Kuwait and other places where water use must be limited because of their meager supply. Hoarding water was one of the unforgivable sins for an Egyptian pharaoh, equal in gravity to murder. Merely mentioning such a detail in your science article creates a sense of time and place.

Think of the editor who needs a new version of the science topic in which you have immersed yourself and made a central theme in the pages you have written. The time has come to test it out, to let one and perhaps thousands of people enjoy what you have found.

61

OUTLINES THAT SELL BOOKS

By Kenn Oberrecht

UNLESS you're new to the writing business, you probably know that publishers today offer book contracts on the basis of outlines and sample chapters. What might surprise you, however, is the possibility of getting contracts via outlines alone—sans samples. Of the eleven contracts offered me in eight years, seven were based solely on outlines.

The formula I use for writing salable outlines grew mainly out of trial and error and from no small amount of advice from editors, publishers, and others in the book business. If you're where I was a few years ago—on the brink of book publication—perhaps my methods will save you some time and frustration. There are few hard-and-fast rules for outlining, so take what I offer simply as the way one writer outlines and sells his books. The techniques work for me and might put you on the right track.

Page one

Page one is the most important part of my outlines, because this is where I hook or lose editors. It enables them to evaluate my proposal at a glance.

Page one is basically an outline of the outline. After typing my name, address, and phone number in the top left corner, I drop down several spaces and list the main elements of my proposed book. Headings for this list include *Working Title, Alternative Titles, Manuscript Length, Divisions, Completion Time,* and *Illustrations.* Let's examine each.

Titles. As a sales tool, the title is as important as dust-jacket design and paramount to everything else in the book. Spend some time thinking seriously about your title. Jot down the elements of your subject in as few words as possible. Then rearrange these into as many titles as you can think of. List published books in your subject area, both to avoid duplication and to improve on those titles.

318

Pick your best for a working title, then choose three to twelve others as alternatives, and keep your original list on file.

Manuscript length. If your subject has been written about before, or if you're writing a particular type of book (self-help, how-to, cookbook, biography, etc.), become familiar with related published books, and plan yours to be similar in length to the most successful. It is equally important to be aware of any publisher's current offerings. If a publisher is putting out books of one size, don't jeopardize your chances by offering something considerably longer or shorter.

My first sale was an angling book. Before submitting my outline, I studied other angling books and found that most ranged from 60,000 to 90,000 words. Concurrently, I examined the offerings of several publishers of fishing books and picked my primary target: a house that consistently published books of about 80,000 words. I proposed a book of 75,000 to 85,000 words.

Divisions. Most books are divided into chapters; some are further organized by grouping several related chapters into sections or parts. Your subject will dictate the best arrangement and suitable divisions.

Completion time. Only you can determine how long it will take to write your book, but be careful here, and allow yourself sufficient leeway. If you're an expert on your subject, have files full of supporting material, and can work full time on the project, you might be able to finish your book in a month. Then I would say you could give yourself a three-month deadline, but make it six for safety's sake.

If, on the other hand, you're faced with considerable research and can only work twenty hours a week, you might need six months or more. Add the fudge factor, and agree to deliver in twelve months.

Illustrations. If your book needs illustrations, handle them as you would the text. Find out what the competition is doing, determine what your target publishers want, and make your proposal along those lines. When doing my first book, I found that similar books had from 100 to 150 illustrations, usually black-and-white photographs. In my outline, I proposed 125 photographs.

Text of outline

Subdivisions of this main portion of the outline are grouped under several headings: *Project Description, Style, Length, Markets and Sales Potential, Competing Volumes,* and *Author's Qualifications.*

319

Project description. This section is next in importance to the page-one summary because, in two or three pages, you distill the essence of the proposed book. The writing must be tight and lively. Be positive and enthusiastic and try to convince the editor that your book will be the best ever written on the subject.

The soundest advice I can give you is to study blurbs on the other books in your subject area. What the blurb writer is trying to do to a potential reader is precisely what you're trying to do to an editor: sell a book.

Style. Each of us has his own style, but most of us work with several styles, adapting them to various subjects and audiences. If you're proposing a textbook, for instance, use an academic style suitable to the field. Psychology books differ in style from history books as much as thrillers differ from romance novels. Further, books on cooking, child rearing, gardening, home improvement, wine, travel, snakes, canoeing, and kazoo playing all differ stylistically, yet they share some similarities.

Keep in mind that popular nonfiction is normally written in an informal, conversational style. It should be grammatically correct, but friendly. Your proposal should clearly demonstrate your ability to write in the style appropriate for the book.

Two paragraphs covered the subject of style in my proposal for a book on the writing craft:

Although *Writing For Real* should prove suitable as a college textbook or supplementary text and will appeal as a popular how-to manual to writers and would-be writers everywhere, it will be neither a stuffy academic tome, nor a formula book written in the too-cute, gee-whiz style favored by some authors these days. Simply, the book will be carefully written and meticulously organized for easy reference.

The subject will be approached seriously and studiously, but not without colorful anecdotes and appropriate humor. Throughout, the purpose will be to inform and motivate the reader, and every effort will be made to entertain him as well.

Length. Mainly, this section deals with the finished book. It's important to envision your book as you will see it on a bookstore shelf. The editor will do so, too.

Take a closer look at some of the books you have already examined in your subject area. Keep in mind that design variations, format, and the

320

use of white space and illustrations can dramatically alter book size. But you should be able to give a reasonable estimate of length and format. Of course, the final decision will be the publisher's.

Markets and sales potential. Although publishers employ people who know more about marketing and sales than the average author does, don't be afraid to address this subject. Your ideas may call the editor's attention to sales possibilities he might otherwise overlook.

Suggest special-interest groups that you think will find your book valuable. Mention similar books that have been marketed successfully by direct mail. If your book seems a natural for one or more book clubs, name them. If you know that a similar book sold 60,000 copies in hardcover, was picked up by two book clubs, serialized in a major periodical, recently sold to a paperback publisher, and you're confident yours will be a better treatment, you can talk specifically, as I did in one of my proposals: "It's not unreasonable to expect hardcover sales to exceed 50,000 copies."

Competing volumes. Make at least one visit to your local library to check the *Subject Guide to Books in Print.* Then, armed with a list of those books most closely related to yours, read, evaluate, and briefly report on as many as possible in your proposal.

Be specific and concise. If you refer to a half-dozen or so books, summarize each in a sentence or two; then demonstrate how yours will excel or improve on them.

If there are no competing volumes, say so. Then explain why your book should be published to fill the obvious void. If you can offer examples of magazine articles on your subject and supporting opinions of well-known experts, all the better.

One of my fishing books was the first in its field. Anticipating criticism of over-specialization, I showed that my subject was as old as fishing itself, that numerous articles had been written about it, and I quoted seven well-known fishing writers. That list of quotations ended up on the back of the dust jacket and was used extensively in promotion and reviews. I'm sure those expert opinions were largely responsible for the contract offer.

Author's qualifications. Here's where you toot your own horn, but with all due modesty. When you're trying to sell a book, your best qualifications are previous books you've had published. But if you're peddling your first book, as all of us once had to, then you'll have to offer other credentials, such as magazine articles you've written, especially those related to your book's subject.

Whether or not you have published anything, be sure to discuss any applicable experience. If you're proposing a book on archery and won the National Field Archery Association Championship three years in a row, that could mean more than previous book sales. Cooking experience might count for more than writing experience in a cookbook proposal.

Everybody is an expert on something, and that expertise can go a long way toward convincing a publisher to offer a book contract.

Contents

Some writers include a table of contents in their outlines; some don't. On the assumption that no editor is going to object to its inclusion, but that some might frown on its omission, I always include one. I also try to outline each chapter in a short paragraph or statement of chapter topics. For example, one chapter of a photography book I currently have in outline form is described this way:

Chapter 20. Communicating With Photographs.
Emphasizes the important communicative aspects of editorial photography and gathers previously discussed principles into a cohesive philosophy. Further convinces the reader of the crucial role photography plays in modern journalism and stresses the ever-present need for effective photographs by magazine and book publishers.

Although my table of contents appears at the end of an outline, this is one of the first sections I start working on. When the project is organized into a workable list of chapters, I know I'm ready to write the outline and send it off to publishers.

Sample chapters

You might need to prepare a sample chapter or two, but that can wait. My feeling is that an editor who has no interest in my idea, or has something similar pending, isn't going to bother reading samples. So why waste money on extra photocopying and postage? And if the idea proves unsalable, preparation of sample chapters will have been a waste of time.

On the other hand, if my proposal sparks interest from the editor, he can always ask for samples. Better yet, he might offer a contract solely on the basis of my outline.

One question I've deliberately left unanswered until now is outline length. I've had good luck with outlines of 10 to 15 double-spaced pages. There's really no set rule for length, other than to make your outline only as long as it must be to cover the proposal and get an editor interested.

If you spend some time on your outline and put your best writing efforts into it, you might soon be doing the most important writing of all: putting your signature on your first book contract.

62

HAVING FUN WRITING HUMOR

By Gene Perret

IRONICALLY, writing and selling humorous magazine pieces follows the classic "good news-bad news" joke form. The good news is that editors want good, funny pieces. "We need good humor," or "We're constantly searching for people who can write humor," editors say. The bad news is that humor is one of the most difficult things to sell to those same editors.

That contradiction may seem as if it were created by a humorist, but it is logical. It's because magazine editors are so selective in buying humor that they're constantly in need of it. If humor were easy to write and sell, they'd have plenty.

Why are the editors so selective? First of all, comedy is an elusive art form. It is to writing what jazz is to music. It's innovative, often rebellious and more often than not, will break tradition rather than follow it. The standard rules might not apply to a humorous piece. Therefore, it can confuse and frighten editors.

With a conventional article, the editor can analyze the form and structure and can grade each piece, calculating whether it will hold the reader's interest. With humor, those hard-and-fast rules become only guidelines. The editor can only guess how effective the article will be.

The basis of judgment changes, too. It's no longer whether the article is well written and well constructed. It's whether the article is entertaining or not. Most editors are less sure of themselves on that ground. Consequently, they're more hesitant about buying.

Secondly, comedy is very subjective. A joke or story is funny only to the person hearing it. That person forms a picture in the mind. If that picture is amusing, the reader laughs; if it isn't, he doesn't. One article can be funny to reader A and not funny to reader B. Since editors are first of all readers, you can see the confusion.

I asked one managing editor how she bought humor for her magazine.

She said, "We pass it around to the various editors. If they all laugh, we buy it." If they ALL laugh! That's formidable veto power for a humorist to face.

None of this should discourage the aspiring comedy writer, though. Rather, it should be encouraging for several reasons:

1) Since humor writing is admittedly difficult to sell, it automatically cuts down the competition. If it were easy, everybody would be doing it. Lighter pieces may be a way of reaching editors who have their favorite writers for the more conventional articles.

2) There is a demand for humor. Those magazines that use it often admit that it usually finishes very high in their reader surveys. People enjoy a chuckle. They like comedy in the movies, on TV, and in their reading. And good humor is not easy to find. The demand is high, and the supply is low—that's a situation that every free lancer dreams of.

3) There is probably less rewriting demanded on light pieces than any other type of writing. Why? Because, again, it's an area that is foreign to most editors. They can strengthen a traditional piece with suggestions for rewrites or restructuring, but can they make something funnier? They're writers or journalists and usually not humorists. They leave that fine tuning to the wits. Also, there is less rewriting requested because the piece was basically amusing. If it weren't, it would have been rejected sooner.

4) Comedy is a rewarding type of writing. It's cathartic for the writer as well as the reader. It helps you get many little peeves out of your system and onto the paper. Humor also forces you, by definition, to search out the fun in any topic. Any time I suggest a humor project to a fellow comedy writer, regardless of whether it's a touch project or not, whether it has an unmeetable deadline or not, I always say, "Have fun with it."

Earlier I noted that humor writing was like jazz. It has rules, as jazz does. Music has mathematical rules of scales and rhythms, but sometimes the creativity comes from violating or bending those precepts.

It's difficult to define rules for writing humor. There are almost as many different forms of the art as there are humorists. Erma Bombeck is different from Art Buchwald is different from Stephen Leacock is different from H. Allen Smith. To limit one's style of writing is to restrict the innovation that creates the fun.

One way to create a humorous style is to read and study those humorists you enjoy. Then try to duplicate their style. Within a short time you'll be adding a flair of your own because humor demands that . . . it needs spontaneity. Soon you'll see that their style combined with your variations has created a new and different style.

A humor writer needn't be afraid of experimentation. Comedy has to be unpredictable. If it weren't, it wouldn't be as funny. People don't laugh as hard at a story they've heard before. The surprise element is part of the humor. It's fun writing that says to you, "Try anything."

While there may be few if any rules about the writing of lighter pieces, there are some universal truths about comedy that may keep your humorous writing more salable.

1) The best humor is based on truth. I used to write funny lines for Phyllis Diller. It's hard to imagine anyone more outlandish or bizarre than Phyllis. Yet she would say to me often, "Honey, if the jokes aren't true, don't send them to me." She knew what she was talking about.

Any humor you attempt should be based on a truthful premise. Like Phyllis Diller, you may then distort that truth. You can bend it, twist it, exaggerate it, carry it to extremes—even unbelievable extremes. The basic truth on which it was based remains.

To illustrate, suppose we do a comedy piece on where all the socks go that we lose in the wash. That's basically a truthful premise. Every household has had one unmatched sock show up after the family wash is done. For some reason the other one never does return. From that basic truthful premise you might hypothesize in your article that it goes down through the earth to Australia. You might conjecture that creatures from outer space feed on single socks. You might even suppose that they run off to join some sort of "sock circus." These are all wild, preposterous fantasies, but based on a totally believable, relatively truthful premise.

That's much more effective comedically than any humor based on a false, manufactured premise. For instance, suppose you were to do a hilarious treatise based on the fact that all people who own black dogs as pets are grouches. You may have some funny, plausible stories about people who own black dogs, but the basic premise is flawed. You created the premise to support your funny stories. Whereas in the first instance, you created the outrageous tales based on a believable premise.

Your humor will generally be stronger if it's based on truth.

2) Recognizable humor is usually more fun for a reading audience. Earlier I said that humor is graphic. A joke or story generates a picture in each reader's or listener's mind. If the picture is amusing, they laugh. If they can see themselves in that picture, they laugh harder.

In my lectures I tell the audience that humor is already around them. For example, I say, "If you see a man open the car door for his wife, you know right away either the car is new or the wife is." That line gets a quick response because so many listeners recognize themselves in that scene. The wives see their husbands, and the husbands see themselves. It has a high recognizability factor.

I once read a statement attributed to some vaudeville comic. I don't remember his name, nor do I know if he was a successful comic. I hope he was, because he knew what he was talking about. He said, "A good joke is saying what everybody else is thinking, only you say it better."

The best humor writers look at commonplace, everyday events from a fresh, oblique angle. The topic may be commonplace; the humorist's view of it is original.

3) Remember your readers. Again, the humorist can only suggest. The humorist paints the picture in the reader's mind. The reader then passes judgment on whether that scene is funny or not. You'll score higher if you know what your readers want to see. You do that by knowing who your readers are. Editors admonish us time and time again to "read the magazine." It applies as much in writing humorous pieces as it does in any other writing.

Since humor writing is different from conventional article writing, it also has some slightly different rules for marketing.

"Query first" is almost an absolute in dealing with magazine editors. It's not in selling humor. Editors have told me that they don't want to see a query letter or a proposal for lighter pieces. Why? Because they tell the editor practically nothing about how funny the piece will be. One writer may do a piece about the socks missing from the family wash and make it a masterpiece. Another may use the same premise and never generate a snicker. The value of a humorous piece is the humor. Editors can't tell how funny it is until it's written. So, humor writing will have to be submitted on speculation. Do the piece and then send it to the editors. It's wise to select subjects that have wide appeal—premises that would be of interest to many magazines. As an example, a piece on some aspect of cooking could be sent to all of the family and women's magazines. Then one rejection isn't catastrophic. It just means typing up a new submission envelope.

Try writing humor. The editors claim they want it and need it. We all know the world certainly could use a few more chuckles.

63

PUNS AND PARODIES PAY OFF

By Selma Glasser

MOST WRITERS are unaware of a short form of writing—puns and parodies—that can be a profitable pastime. I have used them to win fabulous awards in prize contests, to write light verse, greeting cards, and other short items. Payment for this type of writing is excellent when you consider how little time, energy, and how few words are required. Besides the amounts one can earn, writing puns and parodies is a delight—a really fun kind of creativity. Puns and parodies usually draw the largest readership, and because of their brevity, pointed revelations, and familiarity, they are long remembered.

What are puns and parodies? Very simply stated—one word or more altered (or not) for sound-alike, humorous, or double-meaning effects that depend heavily on multi-faceted meanings or recognizable qualities. They invariably involve combinations of similar sounds, alliteration, the same or different spellings and often different meanings of the identical word. Ideally, they should be humorous, strike a familiar note, be unique, and original.

You don't have to be quip-witted to compose puns and parodies (notice that "quip-witted" is a parody on the expression "quick-witted"). They're much easier to write than you might think. All that is required is an awareness of popular, recognizable phrases, double meanings of words, and a whimsical mind.

For example, let's take an expression like "Long time no see." Familiar to everyone, right? A sailor (retired) might say: "Long time no sea." An ex-golfer might state: "Long time no tee." And if your TV breaks down in the middle of your favorite show you might quip: "Wrong time no see." Are you beginning to catch on? If imitation is the sincerest form of flattery, why shouldn't takeoffs of popular phrases, words, and proverbs, or *double entendres* appeal to readers, editors, and sponsors of contests? In fact, they do!

329

My earliest initiation, exhilaration, and generous payoff from this form of writing came from a mere four words ending in a pun. A contest called for an answer to the question: "Why is a Stella D'Oro cookie like a trip to the Continent?"

My answer: "They both take dough."

For those few words, I won top prize—a trip to Italy and France.

Another sponsor asked contestants why they wanted to jump back into bed in the morning, I quipped: "Because I'm good for nodding!" Another cash award came my way. When the A.J. Funk Co. of Chicago asked contest entrants to describe their new cleaner, I called their product "funktional," thereby making a pun on the sponsor's own name. A radio show asked listeners to rename Engelbert Humperdinck to win a night on the town with him in New York City. My name was "Howie Sings" (how-he-sings). It was a delightful evening.

Puns are used more and more in greeting card writing. Sometimes even a single word with a double meaning can sell a card.

I liked the slang use of "pad" and thought it had a potential. Here's how I sold it to a major greeting card company:

OUTSIDE: For your birthday, how would you like to share my pad?
INSIDE: There was a real yellow pad enclosed, under which appeared the words: "Enjoy yourself and have a happy birthday."

I sold another card six months prior to St. Patrick's Day (a six-month lead time is standard for holiday and seasonal material). Here's how it went:

OUTSIDE: Know why the Irish parade on St. Patrick's Day?
INSIDE: Cause the calendar sez MARCH! Happy St. Patrick's Day.

For a juvenile market, I wrote this one:

OUTSIDE: Do you know the best way to pass a test?
INSIDE: Just keep walking.

A Bon Voyage card went like this: "I wish you a pleasant trip on your change of place."

A card for a new baby: "Congrats to your newlywet."

Lesson Three of my book, Glasser Guide to Filler Writing, called "Pun Fun," has seventeen pages of examples and illustrations. One

330

sample is the word "scales," which may be defined as weighing machines and also something found on fish. Then there are words like "appear," which can be humorously defined as where you fish (a pier), or "campaign" as stomach discomfort of a child at camp (camp pain).

Then there are the parodies or sound-alike words which make for amusing epigrams or definitions. For instance, we can define hayfever as "much achoo about nothing," or spring fever as "loaf at first sight." I once sold a group of puns from A to Z (26) to Hallmark Cards starting with: ALOHA = pullman berth (not an upper), and ending with ZEBRA = brassiere size for an elephant. You can imagine how "way out" the other puns on letters of the alphabet were. I employed a simple rundown on A to Z from ordinary words found in the dictionary, utilizing exaggerated, fun-sounding "take-offs"—and was paid extremely well.

Compiling time-worn clichés and *double entendre* words is the key to successful punning. Searching out these adaptable phrases is a fun sort of hobby in itself. They tend to start your creative juices flowing. The idea is to accumulate an inventory of usable words for unrestrained changes or "plays" on them, a sort of "think tank" that, when utilized productively, pays off.

I overheard a discussion on "problem drinkers," which is a very common phrase. From that one phrase came the title of a light verse I wrote about the newspaper advice-givers, which I titled, "The Problem Thinkers." For many years I listened to the weather forecasters. More times than they care to admit their forecasts are incorrect. After mulling that over in mind, I called my light verse "Weather Flawcasters" and ended it with the fact that they belong to a "Non-Prophet" group. In the summertime when green thumb gardeners are thriving, my garden is never surviving. One light verse I wrote was called "Home Groan." Another time, still on the subject of my failure as a horticulturist, I ended the verse with this line: "I'm thinking of taking REMEDIAL WEEDING."

Sometimes an entire poem or song can be done in parody form, which then would be a sound-alike of the original. Recognizing and appreciating the fact that it's familiar makes it work. For example, my parody of the song "Bye, Bye, Blackbird" (for a Vicks commercial contest) went like this:

> Pack up all my coughing woe,
> Vicks I know makes it go—bye, bye, sore throat.

and ended:

> Take my Vicks for coughing grief
> It assures quick relief, coughing, bye, bye!

This song parody won first prize and was the easiest, most fun of any writing I've done. And all I did was to imitate this well-known song. By adding a new dimension and substituting new words for the old, I came up with a winner.

Familiar phrases and songs are everywhere. My own files are packed with takeoffs on titles of TV shows or plays. Popular sayings, slang words, current expressions, and clichés keep my stock growing. Make your own list of current terminology. Be alert for titles of new books or movies, because the rewards for those puns and parodies can be fantastic, and the thrill of acceptance inestimable.

64

WRITING THE OP-ED ARTICLE

By George W. Earley

OPINIONS. We all have them, but the difference between yours and mine may well be that I get paid for putting some of mine on paper.

If you live in or near a major city, you've probably seen the market I'm hitting: the newspaper op-ed page.

So-called because its articles appear on the page *op*posite the *edi*torial page, the op-ed page is an ideal market for the beginning writer. But like any other market, it demands that the writer become familiar with editors' needs and requirements for submission.

For the beginning writer, local issues are the best ones to tackle first. Examples of local-interest items can be readily found by reviewing your paper's op-ed page. During one recent two-week period, my local paper, *The Hartford Courant,* carried a mix of serious pieces—abortion, drugs in schools, and state educational reform—and reminiscences— Grandpa vs. the dandelions, Sunday walks in the park, and the Governor's Foot Guard Band. All topics are suited to beginning local writers.

With that as preface, and bearing in mind that the market listing following this article covers specific needs and preferences of a number of papers, let's look at some general requirements.

First, know your market. Make a close study of several dozen local-issue op-ed articles your paper has run. Note the topics covered, the way the articles are structured, and their length. Op-ed pieces generally average about 750 words—a few are shorter and fewer yet are markedly longer. That's tight writing: You'll have to cut and cut and cut again when you first begin doing op-ed pieces. (And when you do get into print, reviewing the published piece against your original manuscript will help you edit your next article.)

Once you feel sufficiently familiar with your target market to be able to write for it, find a topic that's of strong interest to you. The op-ed

333

page is an *opinion* page; if you aren't strongly interested in your topic, it's going to show in your writing and you'll swiftly get a rejection slip.

As your study of them should reveal, op-ed articles generally follow a fairly straightforward three-part format. They open with a statement of opinion, usually on a topical issue, move on to arguments for and against the issue under discussion, and then close with a summing up of the points covered and a restatement of the writer's opinion. You will find variants among different papers; careful study should enable you to tailor this general pattern to your target market.

You don't need formal credentials in your topic . . . but you must have your facts straight! Nothing will kill your reputation as a writer faster than an error-ridden article. Your library can help you get the facts and figures needed to back up an opinion; letters or phone calls to local experts can also elicit useful information and often some good quotes.

With the article done, submission is the next step. Is a query letter needed? Not really. After all, why write a 400-word query letter about a 750-word article? Most papers (see the market listing for exceptions) accept unsolicited manuscripts. However, after you have made two or three sales to your local editor, you might want to ask him if you could discuss new ideas on the phone. I found it useful on several occasions to call my editor and briefly outline an article idea. The go-ahead I received was no guarantee of a sale, but at least I knew that my editor was interested and that no one else had approached him with a similar idea. And cultivating an editor in this way has another advantage. There were times when I sent in an article that was almost salable. Because my editor knew me, I received not a rejection slip, but a letter with comments and suggestions that enabled me to do a salable rewrite. Editors *are* approachable and I have found mine to be very helpful.

After you have developed your skills on local issues for your hometown paper—and especially if you have expertise or special knowledge that would lend itself to pieces submitted outside your local area—you might want to try out-of-town markets. You'll need to research those markets as you did your local ones; your local library, or that of a nearby college, should be able to provide you with a useful sampling of major city newspapers.

Every op-ed submission must be accompanied by a cover letter in which you briefly describe your piece, and indicate any special qualifications you have for writing it. You should also enclose self-addressed, stamped envelopes with all submissions. No SASE, no reply. But keep in mind that many editors will accept photocopied submissions. Just be sure to indicate in your cover letter that the manuscript you're submitting is a Xerox, and that the editor need not return it if he cannot use it. To learn the fate of your article, ask the editor to return a self-addressed postcard on which you've typed the name of your article and the paper to which you sent it. I've been using this submission method for some time now, and find that it works quite well.

One more thing about submissions: Always include your social security number and a daytime telephone number. Both should go on the first page of your manuscript, right below your name and address. Why? Your phone number on your manuscript lets an editor call you to clarify a point or two in an otherwise acceptable manuscript. You could lose a sale if an editor couldn't get in touch with you quickly.

How much will you be paid? Payments range from $25 to $150; the average is about $50, although some papers offer only a flat rate with no increase for subsequent sales. (*The Washington Post* does pay up to $500, but that is for a major [2,500-word] opinion piece.) When a paper lists a payment range of, say, $25 to $75, a first sale will usually bring the lower figure, but you should begin to get more if you continue to sell to that market.

A few other points in closing. Pay attention to those market listings. They're drawn directly from information supplied by the editors of those papers. Don't ignore taboos or seasonal lead times. To do so marks you as less than professional in your approach.

You'll also find that researching an op-ed piece will turn up more data than you can use when you write it. Save everything! Keep a separate file folder for each piece you write, whether it sells or not. Add to those folders any later information you find on your topics. (Also include your submitted manuscript and tear sheets of published pieces.) In time, you may accumulate enough material to do a longer opinion piece for a higher-paying magazine market.

Even rejection can be surmounted. When my op-ed piece on state lotteries was rejected by newspapers in both Connecticut and New York, I resubmitted it—adding a sidebar specific to the Connecticut lottery—to the *Connecticut Weekly* section of the Sunday *New York Times*. They bought it.

Opinions. Everybody has them. I get paid for some of mine, and you can, too!

For market list see page 654.

65

GETTING STARTED IN BOOK REVIEWING

By Lynne Sharon Schwartz

I LIKE to think of a new book as a mysterious geological treasure, a rock never before handled. The delighted discoverer's first, most natural response is, What have we here? I hold the rock in the palm of my hand to examine it: what are its colors, its contours, its special beauty (or ugliness)? Is it like others I've seen, enough like them, even, to fit into a generic category? Is it more or less beautiful than those of its kind? Or is it, though it bears a surface family resemblance, distinguished by intriguing, individual markings?

The "what have we here" approach will yield a reviewer fruitful results. Every book deserves this careful attention; every one is unique— though some uniquely bad—and demands to be judged for its intrinsic, living qualities. The opposite approach might be labeled "negative criticism." The negative critic appraises a book on the basis of what it has failed to accomplish, with the failings usually derived from the critic's own notion of how he or she would have handled the subject. Not only unfair but misleading, too. For a critic's job is to leave aside his own musings and try temporarily to share the author's view. What has the author set out to do? is the crucial question. (If you believe, however, that what the author has set out to do is not worth doing, better pass up that book. It deserves a fighting chance, and you as critic deserve a more worthwhile application of your talents.)

Now, it is far easier to be explicit about the goals of nonfiction than of fiction. When I reviewed a biography of Margaret Sanger, it was not difficult to decide whether or not the book gave an accurate, coherent, inclusive account of Sanger's life. (The larger question of how well it does so, compared to other efforts, is more complex.) Again, in *Visions of Glory,* Barbara Grizzuti Harrison set out to detail the history of the Jehovah's Witnesses and of her experiences among them. I became convinced of her thoroughness and accuracy and said so in my review. But it

337

is far harder to be unequivocal about fiction, since fiction at its best does not set out to prove or to do anything. To say that *Anna Karenina* "shows" what happens to an upper class nineteenth-century Russian woman who commits adultery would be literary blasphemy. Fiction is the working out of an inner vision; it is impossible to "judge" anyone's vision, and quite a delicate matter to evaluate its metamorphosis into words.

Still, books must be brought to the attention of readers, and a paid reviewer has certain obligations to an audience which sound exceedingly obvious yet are too often ignored. First, to tell the reader specifically what is in the book: to return to the rock analogy, describe its size, shape, color, texture and distinctive marks; the category it belongs to, its antecedents, its relative standing among others of its kind. If nonfiction, the premises on which it is based and the conclusions it reaches, the major issues and points raised along the way, the extent to which they are covered. If it is fiction, the themes, the areas and vicissitudes of life the author is preoccupied with. Plot summaries, as we all remember from school, should be minimal. But a dash of the reporter's standard questions—where, what, when, how, and why—will prove helpful. Above all, a discussion of the nature and interaction of the characters as they grow from the novel's inception through its development and close, is essential.

Secondly, an evaluation of style. Books, our fact-oriented age tends to forget, are made of words, in the best instances deftly laced together to create a texture that mirrors or complements its subject. Everyone, in the privacy of his brain, spins theories and fantasies. Only a writer labors to put the theories or fantasies into words. It is precisely for this labor with words, as much as for the quality of the content, that a book should be assessed. What is the flavor of the author's special idiom? Does the style aid or hinder the emergence of the themes? An even larger question, does the use of words enhance or detract from the richness and capacity of our common inherited language?

Finally—and here is what frightens many new reviewers—a personal judgment. In book reviewing, as in so much else, there is no way out of accountability for one's views. Certainly, don't review a book unless you have the courage and authority to state your convictions honestly. But once you do, don't shrink from the truth, pleasant or not; it is, after all, what the editor hired you for. (On the other hand, beware of using the seductive power of print for airing private grievances; if a book inspires you to invective or sarcasm for dubious personal reasons, better pass it up. Again, both you and the book deserve better handling.)

Since books are composed of words, ideally an astute, literate reviewer should be able to handle a book on any subject, and indeed some national magazines have successfully assigned books to critics outside the field. Practically speaking, however, as a beginning reviewer, you should get to know as thoroughly as possible the field you choose to work in.

When I started reviewing, I felt competent to write about current fiction because I was, after all, primarily a writer of fiction, besides having read it all my life and having taught literature at Hunter College. Nonetheless, with my first efforts I overprepared — not a bad thing to do, as it turned out. I made sure I was familiar with an author's earlier books so I could see the latest one in the context of a body of work. Naturally this meant more crammed reading and time spent in relation to money earned than was comfortable, but I felt I owed this to the author and my readers. I still do. (Anyone reading this is surely aware that reviewing is not one of life's more lucrative occupations.) Often, especially in brief reviews, hardly more than a sentence or two referring to the earlier works found its way into my final draft, yet I felt that the background knowledge improved my review and gave it a justified tone of authority.

I had trepidations for some time, though, about reviewing nonfiction. What could I claim to know about real facts in the real world? Nevertheless, intrigued by the advance publicity, I asked to review Ellen Moers' *Literary Women* for *The Nation*. Faced with the book's wealth of data, presented by someone who had evidently read every word penned by a woman over the past 200 years, I felt incompetent. Yet, as I read the book, not only did great forgotten chunks of my early studies return to me, but I found whatever else I needed to know on its pages. In my review, besides giving the usual information, I turned my attention partly to the controversy the book had engendered by its considering women authors apart from men, a controversy on which I had very definite and educated opinions.

Encouraged by that venture into nonfiction, I requested of *Ms. Magazine* Ann Cornelisen's *Women of the Shadows,* about the lives of Southern Italian peasant women. Here I worried that my ignorance of agricultural economy, of the difficulties of industrialization, and such, would hamper me. However, I had read other books on the region, and had lived in Italy and traveled through the areas Cornelisen wrote about. I hoped that this firsthand knowledge would stand me in good stead, and I believe it did. But I would hesitate to review a similar book on the lives of peasant women in Turkey or Morocco, places I know nothing about.

In brief, know your subject by study or by firsthand experience, or both. Then if, as occasionally will happen, you are given a book you feel overwhelmed by, stick to what you know and perceive, avoid grandiose generalities, and in the end, trust your instincts. Above all, don't attempt to sound authoritative when there is no basis for authority. I remember how pleased I was, as a beginner, to be offered a book by *The Chicago Tribune Book World,* but how distressed on opening the desired package to find a novel of World War II, filled with details of military strategy, sabotage, fortifications — subjects I knew nothing about and disliked besides. I turned to page one with a sense of duty. In the book itself, I found all I needed to know about strategy, and found in addition, to my pleasant surprise, that like all good novels, *Kramer's War,* by Derek Robinson, was about human beings working out their complex, connected destinies in a situation of great stress. I was able not only to review it but to enjoy it as well. Needless to say, I avoided undue discussion of strategy, fortifications, or deployment of troops.

The above remarks apply once you have the book in hand, but the novice reviewer is probably wondering, How do you get the books assigned? Timing is of the essence. Since newspapers' Sunday sections are prepared weeks ahead and magazines often months ahead, you need to know what titles are coming out well in advance of publication date. *Publishers Weekly,* the invaluable trade magazine, lists forthcoming books, as does *Library Journal.* From their brief and pithy descriptions you can find which books are suitable for you.

Getting the first assignment is difficult, yet a newcomer's prospects are not totally bleak. It's best to try your local papers or weeklies first, even if it means working for no pay temporarily—not advisable as a long-term habit, but worth the initial sacrifice. Send the editor a sample review, your best effort of course, with the names of several forthcoming books you'd like to try, and a few persuasive lines telling why you are especially qualified to review them. Don't be daunted if the first tries fail. The erosion technique—wearing down a solid, recalcitrant object by a light, steady trickle—has been known to work. Certainly competition is stiff, but if editors discover someone with a dash of originality, a capacity for felicitous use of language, a strong sense of organization and a willingness to work doggedly at improving, they will generally succumb. They also, incidentally, will be grateful for a readable, correctly spelled and punctuated manuscript, submitted on time.

Once you have established yourself locally you might try larger markets, sending around tear sheets of previous work. By all means follow up any leads from friends or colleagues. When book review editors send out the word that they're looking for new writers, they usually mean it.

It's extremely important to be aware of the tastes, readership, slants, if any, space limitations, and general tone of the magazine you're writing for. Your chances of impressing *The National Review* with an iconoclastic critique of capitalism are about as great as getting a laudatory review of Richard Nixon's memoirs into *The Village Voice*. In a realistic way, try to suit your review to the publication. If this requires too great a dislocation of your own values, better to try elsewhere. I have found it possible to write for varied periodicals without doing damage to my fundamental opinions about a book. When reviewing *Women of the Shadows* for *Ms.*, I stressed its feminist aspects more than I would have, say, for *The Nation*, where I might have dwelt more on the inequities inherent in the system of land tenure. Both themes were vital and important—the choice was a matter of emphasis, bearing in mind the concerns of prospective readers.

Once you are in the hard-earned position of writing fairly freely for a number of places (that is, once editors have come to trust you), you will find that magazines vary greatly in the way they handle review copy. Very few editors print every word as written. Some, like Emile Capouya, former Literary Editor of *The Nation,* make changes so small, subtle and apt that I, for one, never noticed them at first, only felt vaguely that my review was better than I thought. Others ask for extensive changes, either for style and coherence, or because of space limitations. In any case, it helps to be cooperative with editors, whose experience is usually vast and long. (Unless, of course, their requests involve distorting your opinions for extraneous reasons, which is unacceptable and happens, at least to my knowledge, thankfully seldom.)

Now, suppose you have won the coveted assignment and have the book in hand. How to proceed? The reading is often the hardest part of the job, very different from reading for pleasure. One reads at first with the unsettling sense of needing to remember everything, much like studying for an exam. This compulsion passes, but you do unquestionably owe the book and your audience an attentive reading. Authors frequently complain that their critics seem not to have read the book, or to have read some other book. There is no way of telling whether this is true, but at least new reviewers can avoid the imputation.

I usually read a book twice, once slowly, occasionally marking passages along the way, and the second time quickly, to get a sense of overall shape, flow, and pattern. One soon learns to read with pen in hand—but stopping for real notes fragments the experience of first reading. Note-taking during the second reading is more effective. Both readings are invariably accompanied by familiar conflicts which one learns to take in stride. If I am enjoying the book too much, I worry about losing objectivity, not paying enough attention to how the author achieves his or her effects and simply luxuriating in them. On the other hand, if I dislike the book, I make enormous efforts not to become resentful of my task and thus dislike it more than warranted. I try to look for good points that any one of my innumerable small prejudices may prevent me from noticing. In either case, it is hardly relaxing.

After the two readings I write down my general impressions with illustrations from the book, and organize them under several inclusive headings, which gives me a loose outline. I then proceed with the best intentions of working from this outline, but habitually write the piece straight on, barely glancing at the notes until later, to see that I've covered everything and to locate appropriate examples. It might be suspected that the extra reading, note-taking and outlining are wasted effort. Yet in the end it seems that the intense preparation is somehow needed for the rather swift, "thoughtless" writing process. Also, the outline exists as security in case I run dry halfway through. I don't presume that this method of total immersion, a valiant semblance of scholarly organization, and then an abandoned dash to the finish line can work for anyone else. I do offer it to demonstrate the devious, cumbersome and idiosyncratic ways that reviews get written.

Next come the patient correcting, revising, cutting and moving of parts, drudgery to be sure, but performed with the immense relief of knowing that the thing *exists*, in need only of tinkering. Always, when the review is typed in final form and on its way to the mailbox, I get wild flashes of insight informing me my work is all wrong: I should have kept in what I cut out and cut out what I kept in. These hand-on-the-mailbox insights are an inevitable part of the writing process and should be totally disregarded. (It may help to keep the finished review for a few days to give it a last check before mailing.)

There are, in addition, a few outside impediments to straight thinking that a novice reviewer should be aware of. One is an author's reputation. Depending on the murky depths of a reviewer's secret nature, he or she may be tempted to encourage or to attack new writers (regardless of the merit of the work), or to sustain or stab the reputation of well-known writers (also regardless of merit). To these temptations, the adage "Know thyself" is the best antidote; better still, "Guard against thyself or don't review the book at all." Reviewing books by friends or acquaintances—a common if doubtful practice—requires similar restraint or total abstinence.

Other reviews and publishers' blurbs are powerful obstacles as well. But while the first can be summarily dealt with (never read them till your own review is safely in the mail), advertising, jacket copy, or those ingratiating notes from the publicity staff telling how wonderful the book is, are less easy to avoid. What publicity people say should be regarded as a skillful pass in a complex ball game. The serious danger enters if the uninitiated reviewer's expectations are raised. "Smith's new novel relentlessly plumbs the depths of A, with brilliant insights into B, so that his style is reminiscent of C and D, though paradoxically echoing the uniqueness of E." Smith's book may in fact be a fine one, but a neophyte reviewer diligently in search of A, B, and C is sure to be disappointed, as well as blinded to the book's true worth.

The final questions that keep reviewers tossing in bed at night are, Have I praised a book that everyone will see immediately is idiotic? and Have I panned a masterpiece? The first is more easily dispensed with. It is unlikely that a competent reviewer, after years of reading, will fail to spot awful work. Moreover, it is probably more honorable to err on the side of generosity. But not to recognize genius is to be dull indeed, is it not? I had this experience reviewing a recent novel by a moderately well-known writer. I had read excerpts in a magazine and liked them, but after finishing the whole novel I realized it set enormous goals and failed to achieve them. The book turned out to be the focus of a good advertising campaign; other reviews appeared and were for the most part favorable. I considered retiring. First, though, I went back to the book dispassionately, my review already in print. It was still unsuccessful, and I was glad to have said so.

For one learns, after much time and ink and struggle, that there are no absolute standards of accomplishment, especially today when traditional and experimental modes rightfully flourish side by side. Reviewers' opinions will vary as much as readers'; the difference is that reviewers are expected to have the skill to articulate clearly what they think and why they think it. That is the most, in all conscience, that one can do, and it is no small task. Once it is done, let the reader be left to his own devices.

66

TRAVEL WRITING
FROM BOTH SIDES OF THE DESK

By Batya Moskowitz

Nothing sounds more enjoyable than traveling around the world visiting every exotic location you've ever dreamed of, returning home to write about it, seeing your words in print and receiving payment for it all. If it were only that easy. . . .

Travel writing requires hard work and a lot of time—researching, querying, waiting for a response from an editor, writing your article, and again waiting to see how the editor responds. There are ways to make the job simpler. If you know how to organize yourself and deal with your specialized editors, travel writing can be a warm wind if not a breeze. After 4½ years as an editor at *Travel & Leisure* Magazine, and now as a full-time free-lance writer, I have a viewpoint from both sides of the desk that I would like to share with you.

As a writer

There are a number of steps and procedures along the way for the beginning travel writer. First, you must familiarize yourself with the various types of travel articles you might write. The two most obvious are *destination-* and *establishment*-oriented. The former focuses on a particular place. It can be a town (Salem, Oregon), a city (San Francisco), a country (Bali), a museum (The Stephen Foster Center in Florida), a park (the San Diego Zoo), or similar places. *Establishment* pieces concentrate on one or more hotels, restaurants, cafés, sports arenas, nightclubs, antique shops, or other unusual shopping facilities. A new or renovated hotel would fit this category.

There are also *roundup* articles on such topics as the churches of Brooklyn or ethnic restaurants of Chicago. *How-to* articles can be about packing soft luggage, buying sweaters in Ireland, or choosing your berth on a cruise. *Fillers* and complete *service* articles are about specific new products, such as lightweight travel razors or magnetized games for children's travel. There are helpful and humorous *essays* (preferably upbeat) on reading maps or funny pieces on package tours. Any of these can address business, family, camping, adventure, foreign, domestic, upscale, budget, or other specific readership interests.

Also, familiarize yourself with the kinds of periodicals that publish travel articles. The trickiest part of travel writing, or any writing for that matter, consists of matching your idea to the needs of a publication. Study listings of magazines that specialize in travel and add general interest, regional, in-flight, business, men's, women's, and any other periodicals that have travel columns or special travel issues. Take a look at the markets that interest you most, and study the angles of the travel pieces they print. Remember that editorial policies change, so read recent issues.

How do you decide where to go? If you're just starting in the field, you'll have to reach your destination on your own and with your own money. Or you might start near your home or with vacation trips. Select a museum, a reconstructed landmark, a park with special hiking trails, an extraordinary restaurant or hotel, or a performing arts company. Local newspapers and magazines or even larger magazines that cover your region of the country might buy such a piece.

No matter how well you know a place, do some armchair travel and research it. Dig through your library and your travel agent's brochures. Keep track of references to local destinations in novels and stories, in biographies and news reports. Take notes on anything that strikes your fancy, even if it seems inconsequential. Often the smallest details are what make a travel article good reading.

After you've decided on your destination and the magazines that might publish your writing, send out a query letter. Some publications will give you a go-ahead for an article on spec; if you're willing to work on writing a piece with no guarantee of publication, these could be excellent markets for you. Beginners in the travel field should send proposals to those magazines, and later (after you've had some success) to those magazines that do make assignments.

What makes a good travel query? First, name the destination or establishment you want to write about. Second, the query should provide a feel for the location in fresh, lively language. Avoid clichés, overused adjectives, and superlatives. There is no *best* hotel, no *most wonderful* restaurant, no *most-amenities-for-the-money* resort.

The proposals that work well are those in which the first paragraphs could easily be expanded into an introduction for the article: They state the location, convey the ambience, and give evidence of your writing style.

Add to this the reason that *you* in particular should write the article for that particular magazine: give a little of your writing background; let the editor know if (and when) you visited the place, and describe what makes it special to you. If you've had any travel pieces published, include a few clips—two or three of your best will do. And if not travel articles, send tear sheets of any general nonfiction magazine pieces you've had published. Send only one or two proposals at a time, maximum of one to one-and-a-half pages each.

Get as much mileage from your travel as possible. Come up with as many angles as you can for as many publications as you can. Begin making notes of these before leaving for your trip, but remember to brainstorm as you travel. You might want to keep a separate page of your notebook just for ideas as you think of them.

While you shouldn't write different versions of the same story for competing magazines, you can use various topics from the same trip. For instance, you might write about a museum in Ibiza for *Signature,* the folkloric festival there for *Dance Magazine,* and three Balearic paella recipes for *Family Circle* or *Gourmet* (possibly as part of a feature travel piece).

Once you reach your destination, take as many notes as you can related to the ideas you already have. Also, jot down anything that intrigues you and might lead to an article in the future. I have an affinity for doll museums and always try to see at least one wherever I go. Someday, perhaps I'll write a roundup article.

I prefer to write as I go, making sure to get down on paper at least an outline of the relevant history and personalities, as well as legends and stories of the area. Dates and spellings (except for signposts) are often better taken from printed information than from someone's memory, even an expert's. But while it's important to get the facts down in your notebook, it is much more important to record your own impressions, observations, and reactions. You can always find a fact again, but if you didn't see the details of the Unicorn Tapestries at the Cloisters in New

York because you were too busy copying the descriptive tablets, your article will lack the personal touch that makes a travel writer successful.

Next point: Collect every scrap of paper, brochure, press kit, map, matchbook you can get your hands on, even if the topic of your article is right around the corner. Many magazines request these as checking backup. Facts and interesting items you missed can be gleaned from them. You should also get the names, addresses, and phone numbers of contact people—the general manager of a hotel, the shopkeeper (of antiques, special local items, or whatever), the education director of a museum, or whoever you think will enrich your material when you write it up later. On a long trip, I send a package of my papers, matchbooks, local newspapers, press materials, etc. (I usually hold on to my notes—they are irreplaceable) home to myself. This is a minor expense and saves me from carrying for a week or more the material I've collected.

You're now back home and ready to write. If you didn't submit proposals before you went, do it as soon after you return as possible, while you're still fresh and excited. Once you have the assignment or have decided to try a piece on speculation, read several issues of the magazine for which you're aiming. See if you can match the editorial focus of your piece to something already published there—something you like. Follow the style of that magazine. Don't use a lot of quotes if quotes are rare in the pieces you've read. Keep your article personal or formal, depending on the publication. What emphasis does the magazine seem to have? Some concentrate on people, some on scenery, some on history. Keep these priorities in mind for the particular article you're writing. And if you do have an assignment letter that spells out what the editor wants, try to follow it.

Many magazines require hard service information. They want addresses, phone numbers, costs, hours of operation, availability of transportation and schedules, reservation numbers, and the like. Contrary to popular opinion, such requirements were not created to torture writers but to help readers. If you have no patience for this sort of thing, be careful which publications you submit your ideas to. If not the most creative, it is actually the easiest part of the piece to write. Your sources will always give you directions, hours of operation, prices, and anything else you need. And try to keep it up to date.

When you have done the best possible job on your article and are ready to submit your manuscript, type it neatly, double- or triple-spaced. If you're working on a word processor, use a letter-quality printer. *This can't be restated enough.* Sloppy manuscripts not only cause editors eye strain, they also create a bad and lasting impression.

Editor's eye view

The first way to impress an editor is to address your query to the appropriate person *by name.* If you can't find a recent masthead, call the magazine. Most travel magazines divide editorial responsibilities geographically. Reaching the right person will save time and prove that you can do research.

For in-flight magazines (so named because they are distributed to travelers aboard the airlines that publish them), be sure to check the routing map (usually toward the back of the publication) before sending a proposal. In-flights cover only those destinations to which a particular airline flies.

Although editors are always looking for good new writers and fresh ideas, their publications have probably covered most locations in the world. Timely approaches and innovative views and angles are what catch their attention.

If the first two ideas you send don't bring a go-ahead from an editor, try another two. If you receive an encouraging rejection letter, keep trying. Go back and study the magazine again for contents, style, and focus. If, however, you've received three or more form rejections from a particular magazine, it might be a good idea to shift your efforts elsewhere. Not every writer fits every magazine. If *Northwest Orient* doesn't want your manuscript, you might try Delta's *Sky* or *National Geographic Traveler.*

Although you should look through the contents of your target periodical for the last six months or so, it is far more important to be familiar with its readership profile. While at *Travel & Leisure* (which reaches an upscale, service-oriented, mature audience), I received more than one proposal about traveling with children, RV vacationing, and "cheapest ways to get there." Not one of these was appropriate to *Travel & Leisure,* though if well written, any of these might have found publication in other periodicals. For example, *Camperways* publishes pieces on RV travel; *Chevron USA* zeroes in on family vacations; and

Travel Smart for Business concentrates on bargains for business travelers.

Let's assume the proper editor has your query and likes it. What happens next? At many magazines, the proposal is considered by a number of editors who give their suggestions, ideas, and comments. You might be asked to do the piece on speculation. Or the piece might be assigned in a different way from the one you presented. My best advice is to be flexible: The editor will appreciate your adaptability and be more willing to work with you in the future.

Whether you have a go-ahead on spec or a contractual assignment, read your letter from the editor carefully: You will be expected to produce what it asks for. I sent many first drafts back to authors asking them to give us what we had already asked for. If you are convinced the topic cannot be handled in the way the editor stipulated, drop him or her a note: Never assume that you can proceed with your version—or that the editor may not be persuaded to consider your approach.

Most travel magazines want you to entice their audiences to the destination, restaurant, hotel, or museum you write about. If problems exist, mention them in a light but honest manner. "The room becomes loud and lively at lunch hour, spacious and quiet after three," says the same thing as "Sheer havoc ensues during lunch." Warn readers about possible hardships: "The trail is steep and rocky; if you're not a dedicated hiker, take the bus to the other side."

Many major magazines prefer to have you concentrate on writing and leave the photography to them. If you're an accomplished photographer, however, you might want to click your shutters anyway. Fact checkers are known to appreciate photos (today's fact checkers are often tomorrow's editors), and even large magazines might need a picture of an out-of-the-way place. Smaller publications and newspapers, of course, are usually pleased to receive photographs to highlight your piece. (Send valuable photos registered mail; duplicate slides are safest.)

Finally, the most important thing a traveler can do is enjoy traveling. All the above is secondary. If you truly have a good time wherever you go, you'll be full of ideas, convincing in your proposals, and upbeat in your finished work. And fun, after all, is what travel is about!

67

HEADING FOR YOUR FIRST ROUNDUP

By Susan Purdy

As a writer, I wear many hats, both imaginary and real. I've worn a hard hat to get a story about the construction of a movie studio, a cap with MAP CLUB emblazoned in red letters to interview a man who provides maps to the real estate industry, and a plastic rain hat to protect me from the elements as I did field research for a piece on dentistry. But my favorite head covering is the imaginary, ten-gallon cowboy hat I wear while writing roundup articles.

To write a successful roundup article, you have to corral a group of people with an occupation, hobby, or characteristic in common—celebrities, show people, politicians, musicians—and ask them to respond to an interesting question. The roundup format appears in many of the largest national magazines—*Cosmopolitan, McCall's, Good Housekeeping*— which have run roundup articles in the past year on the following: Celebrities were asked, "What's the One Thing You Couldn't Live Without?" Several of the world's great cooks were asked how they diet. And for a roundup piece I wrote for *Good Housekeeping,* I asked some of New York's most influential and powerful men to talk about their mothers.

Roundup articles also appear in most newspapers, regional publications, town shopping newspapers, and Sunday supplements, and provide an easy way for writers to break into print. Editors know that their readers are always interested in what people prominent in a particular field have to say, and by familiarizing yourself with the magazine or newspaper, you can pose a provocative question and sell a roundup article.

How do I come up with a provocative question that will capture an editor's attention? How do I find the right people to ask?

Let's tackle the "question" question first. What piques your interest?

351

If you had the opportunity to ask almost anyone one question—and as a writer, you do—what would it be? You could ask your local politicians to tell you about the most influential person in their lives, or go down to your community college and ask women who are returning to school after raising a family how it has affected their marriage. You can read your local paper and ask residents how they feel about the sewage plant that is under consideration for their area, or do a roundup of your local clergy. You can find good questions everywhere, if you start thinking like a roundup writer. *Psychology Today* ran an article on "Super Sellers," men and women who are tops in their sales field. Who are the super sellers in your area? Why are they so good? Would the editor of your local paper or regional magazine be interested in them? While shopping for summer clothes this year, I began thinking about what items I should buy in the fall to update my winter wardrobe. (Writers have a tendency to think ahead because of the long lead time required by magazines.) I decided to ask the experts and wrote a roundup article for *Good Housekeeping* last year that included advice from Halston, Geoffrey Beene, and Mary McFadden. Your family and friends are great sources to tap, as are letters to the editor in newspapers, and such advice columns as "Dear Abby."

At a writers conference I attended in Manhattan, editors from national and regional magazines said they were always looking for seasonal material. Holidays like Thanksgiving, Christmas, Valentine's Day lend themselves especially well to roundup articles. Such questions as, "Have you ever spent Thanksgiving (or Christmas) alone?" "What was it like?" and "How did you spend the day?" provide a good focus for an article. Or you might interview the residents in a local nursing home: Elderly people have wonderful—or sad—stories to tell, and you could ask them about the first Christmas they can recall, how they feel the celebration of a holiday has changed since they were young, and other questions that would evoke responses that would be of interest to readers: "How did you trim the Christmas tree?" "Did you make your own ornaments?"—and if so, would they describe how?

A roundup piece for Valentine's Day could include such questions as "What was the most romantic gift you ever received for Valentine's Day?" "Do you think a single rose is more romantic than a bouquet?"

Roundup questions may be serious as well as light, instructive as well as amusing. You might ask lawyers in your city or town, "Do you think a newly married couple should make out a will? Why?" Or a roundup article could deal with such serious questions as, "How did you react when you learned that a member of your family had cancer?" "How did your children react when you and your spouse told them that you were going to be divorced?" "Do you think that a single parent can raise a family successfully?"

Teen-agers are an excellent source of roundup material. Parents as well as pre-teens and young adults might well enjoy reading about problems like, "How do you avoid peer pressure involving drugs, sex, or alcohol?" "If you could change one thing about adults in the world today, what would it be?"

Now you have dozens of questions in mind, and you can't wait to get started. At this point the second HOW comes into play. How do you get to politicians, celebrities, and the experts? Begin in your own backyard. First, query the publications in your area about doing a roundup article of local politicians, singers, theater groups, or business executives on a topic you think will be of interest to local readers. For *Business Connections,* a local magazine, I decided I wanted to question top executives from the banking world, public relations, the aircraft industry, computer sales, real estate, entertainment, and local politicians for a roundup article titled, "Long Island Business People Look Into the Future."

I did not know any of those people personally, but I kept in mind that most people feel flattered when asked for their opinions on a particular subject. For that article, I interviewed the people I'd selected directly, either at their offices or by telephone. That is not always possible. Especially when dealing with celebrities, it is best to go through their public relations or press representatives. For my article on New Year's resolutions—"Promises, Promises"—which appeared in *Good Housekeeping,* I wanted to include some local TV personalities. I called the publicity office of the television station, and identifying myself and the publication I was writing for, I described the questions I wanted to pose for my roundup piece and asked who might be available. (For future reference, I made a note of the name of the publicity person.) From the list she gave me, I chose those celebrities that I thought most suitable for my article.

She took down the question, asked me the deadline (which I always cut by two or three weeks to give me enough time to check and follow up). I always ask for an in-person interview, but if that's not possible, I ask the PR person to mail me the responses, in this way providing me with written proof that the people queried were aware that their responses were for publication.

It sounds simple—and it is—because people in the public eye want to stay there, and writers are an excellent source of free publicity.

I follow the same procedure for political figures, governors or mayors, always dealing with their press secretaries or public relations representatives, who know the officials' schedules and can judge whether they are likely to want to participate in the roundup. When I'm turned down, which happens on occasion, I thank the person I've been in touch with and say I'll call at what may be a more convenient time, leaving the door open for another article.

Some basic information to keep in mind when doing the roundup article:

1. Always get photos of the people you interview. Most people in the entertainment field have "head-shots," glossy 8 × 10 pictures that are available in their press kits. Or, with their permission, you can take your own photos, black and white, to submit with your article.

2. First asking permission, tape the interview, whether in person or over the phone. (You can buy a handy little gadget that attaches to your tape recorder for phone interviews.)

3. Remember, the people you are interviewing do not get paid for their answers. . . . the free publicity is reward enough.

4. Make sure that the publication that runs the piece sends a copy to each person quoted in the article. I always include their names and addresses on a separate sheet of paper when mailing in my roundups and often follow them up with a personal thank-you note.

Now that you have come up with some fantastic questions, have queried the people you wish to include in your article, the only thing left is to write it. *Yes, a roundup is written.* It is not just a compilation of quotes. You need an opening paragraph to prepare the reader for what will follow; lead-ins to the various people interviewed, identifying them and their position; and in most cases, a closing paragraph.

My opening paragraph for "Sons and Mothers" (*Good Housekeeping)* set the mood for the famous sons I interviewed to talk about their mothers:

Ralph Waldo Emerson wrote, "Men are what their mothers made them," and some of New York's most powerful men concur. A mother can help her son attain success by providing nurturing love, guidance, and in many cases, a strong sense of purpose he can emulate. The following men, tops in their fields, have taken time from busy schedules to tell us about this influential person in their lives.

I then led off the piece with New York City Police Commissioner Benjamin Ward, by giving his name, title, the fact that he was one of eleven children, and that his mother Loretta Ward was a great source of inspiration to him. I had interviewed Commissioner Ward in person, so I had pages of quotes to edit before I decided which would be most pertinent to the article.

That's another area in which you "write" the roundup. You must go through each interview and select only the heart. With this roundup, I had interviewed a dozen men, so my space was limited. I wanted the essence of how their mothers had influenced their lives and not pages of uninteresting material. I did not end that roundup with a closing paragraph, because the Governor of New York Mario Cuomo had provided me with an excellent closing quote, and I like to leave my readers with something special to take away when they finish the article. I find this works in most instances, as there is always one quote that lends itself to tying up the piece.

It doesn't matter whether you live in a big city or a small town, the roundup article can be written anywhere about anyone or anything, if you keep in mind that people love to be asked their opinions and are as close to you as a phone call or letter.

68

HOW TO SHOOT PICTURES TO ILLUSTRATE
YOUR ARTICLES

By Daniel R. Hopwood

I BELIEVE that almost any magazine article is more likely to sell if the writer can supply good photographs to illustrate that article, and that writers who do so make more money than writers who don't. It's cheaper, easier, and quicker for the editors to buy articles and photos as a package from one person than it is to assign a photographer to go take pictures or to search for stock photos.

Anyone wanting to do his own magazine photography will need the following things: a 35mm camera (or larger format) with a standard lens, a wide-angle lens, and a telephoto lens; a working knowledge of photography; and a supply of color transparency film (for color shots) and a good black-and-white film (such as Kodak Tri-X). There are hundreds of books about photography, and anyone having questions about the technical side of photography will find books that can answer their questions.

Creating photos is a highly personal form of expression. Your photos must speak to the readers just as your words do; they must convey a visual message to them. The following guidelines will help you present your photos and your articles as a unit, a complete expression of what you are trying to say. Use these twelve tips whenever you take pictures to illustrate an article:

1. *Tone.* Make your photos consistent with the tone of your article. If, for example, your article is about a serious subject like depression, obviously you shouldn't have smiling faces in your pictures. Instead, take pictures of cloudy, overcast days; a person crying; someone all alone; a cemetery, or anything else that says "depression" to you.

2. *When it's easy, don't make it hard.* Many articles are easy to illustrate: I recently did several articles on a sculptor named Peter Toth.

In honor of the American Indian, Toth is giving an Indian sculpture to each of the fifty states. When he was in Kentucky, I found three different magazines interested in an article on him and his work. To do the photos for all three magazines was easy: All I had to do was to follow Toth around for about two hours while he was working on his sculpture. I took over 100 photos all at the same location. I took pictures of Toth at work, his 35-foot-tall wooden sculpture, and shots of some smaller sculptures which he sells to support himself. I didn't need to go anywhere else or come up with any creative ideas to take enough shots for all three magazines. But it's not always that easy.

3. *Be creative.* Some articles just don't lend themselves easily to illustration. But this problem can usually be solved with a little creative thinking. I'm currently writing an article for *Police Product News* on Lizzie Borden, who in 1892 was accused but never convicted of murdering her father and stepmother with an ax. What can I take pictures of for this piece?

After a few minutes of creative thinking, here's what I'm planning: several pictures of a blood-stained ax (since I work for a blood center, this won't be any problem); an ax in a woman's hand; I could go to Fall River, Massachusetts, and take pictures of the house where the murders occurred—it still stands; I could go to Oak Grove cemetery in Fall River and take pictures of the tombstones of Lizzie and her parents; I can get my wife to dress up in one of her great-grandmother's dresses and take a silhouette of her wielding an ax. The possibilities for almost any article are limited only by your imagination.

4. *Slant.* When you take pictures for your articles, try to capture the slant that you are trying to convey. I did an article for *Grit* about Captain John Ritchie, pilot of the *Mississippi Queen* riverboat. The slant of "He's Santa of the *Mississippi Queen*" was that Ritchie, who has a long white beard, looks just like Santa and is constantly so called by the passengers. There were three elements I needed to capture in every picture: (1) Ritchie, (2) looked like Santa, and (3) worked on the riverboat. I shot Ritchie and his beard in the pilot's house, standing in front of the vessel, and holding children on his knee in the ship's library. But, if I shot the Captain driving his car, playing golf or shaving off his beard, I would have strayed from the slant of my article.

5. *Put people in your pictures.* Whatever you are writing about, try, if possible, to photograph people doing something related to the subject.

When I did an article on trouble-shooting the ignition system of the Ford Escort for *Motor Magazine*, I took pictures of ignition parts, spark plug wires and distributors, and I put people in—my wife and kids driving my Escort, my friend Rusty holding parts of the ignition system.

It's important to show that people are involved in the subject of your article. It's often the human element that adds interest to a story. Be sure to get anyone who poses for you to sign a model release, which you can buy at any photography store.

6. *Take many pictures.* Don't try to save money by taking one 12-exposure roll of film. Most professional magazine photographers would be lucky to get two or three publishable shots out of twelve. Many magazines use three or four photos per article. So, shoot two or three 36-exposure rolls for every article. Even if you're not that great with a camera, the law of averages should help you produce several good shots.

7. *Use a tripod.* Whenever you hand-hold a camera, your hand shakes at least some while you are taking the picture. The best way to make sure your photos will be sharp and clear, even in enlargements, is to use a tripod whenever possible. If carefully focused, your pictures will be clear and sharp. You never know when a magazine may want to blow up one of your shots and use it for the cover.

8. *Find the right angles.* Don't just stand in front of your subject and shoot. Stoop down and shoot up at it; climb above it and shoot down at it; go around it; get a close-up; back off and get a wide-angle shot. Finding an unusual angle can make an average shot into a great one.

9. *Think vertical.* Most cameras are made to take pictures horizontally. If you turn your camera ninety degrees, you are now taking a vertical picture. Almost all magazine cover shots and many inside shots are vertical in format. Professional photographers know that editors prefer vertical shots more than horizontal ones.

10. *Direct your photos.* Good marketable magazine photos do not happen by accident, though many beginning photographers act as if that were so. As the photographer, you must control all the elements that make up a picture. Pretend you are a motion picture director, and

tell everybody concerned with your picture what to do. If the background is cluttered, either remove the clutter or take the picture another place. If the lighting is bad, you must bring in better lighting (open the curtains, turn on more lights, use a flash) or go where the light is better. Tell the models what to do. Don't settle for anything less than perfection with your photos.

11. *Captions.* Before you send your photos in, write a caption for each one. A caption is simply a one- or two-sentence description of the picture, who is in it, or what is going on in the picture. Don't just say, "This is a picture of Norman Dyson." Tell the editor what Norman Dyson is doing. Keep your captions specific and to the point.

12. *Study the magazine.* This probably the most important tip of all: Look carefully through several back issues of the magazine you are aiming for to get a feel for the kinds of photos they use. Also, write and ask for their photographers' guidelines. What have they bought in the past is a key to what they will buy in the future.

The writer who also does photography has several advantages over the writer who just writes: He makes more money. He improves his chances of making a sale by supplying tailor-made photos to illustrate his article, rather than making the editor search for some photos that fit the piece. He expresses himself in both words and photography. And he gets a thrill from seeing his article *and* photography grace the pages of a national magazine. For the magazine article writer, it doesn't get much better than that.

69

HOW TO WRITE GOOD ARTICLE LEADS

By Marshall Cook

IF YOUR article lead doesn't catch the reader's attention immediately, your article doesn't stand a chance in the marketplace. That makes the first words of an article the most important ones you write. And it puts a lot of pressure on you to write them well.

First, your lead should issue a clear invitation to the reader by promising useful or interesting information and an enjoyable reading experience. Never try to trick your readers by promising more than your article will deliver. And there's no use trying to coerce them, either. You can't force your readers to participate in your visions. You can only show them how interesting and exciting those visions are.

Next, your lead should establish the focus of the article by introducing the subject and conveying the main idea or slant.

Finally, your lead should establish the tone of your article. If you plan to take a light, humorous approach, for example, your lead should provoke a chuckle.

Here are seven approaches that can help you create compelling leads.

The startling statement

"Your English teacher lied to you." That's how I started an article on advertising copy writing for an in-house publication. My point was not that English teachers are liars, but that good ad copy often breaks the sacred grammar rules we dutifully learned. "Ad copy often breaks grammar rules" didn't strike me as an especially effective lead, however, so I chose a statement that I hoped would generate more interest.

A study skills article I wrote for *Directions,* a regional college campus magazine, began, "The good grades don't necessarily go to the smartest students." They go, I pointed out, to those who have learned how to study most effectively.

The startling statement should convey the focus or slant quickly while evoking a positive attention and arousing curiosity.

The quote lead

It's often best to let the subjects speak for themselves. Quotation marks around a lead signal readers that the show is about to begin.

My profile of architect Kenton Peters for *Wisconsin Trails* magazine began with Peters' assertion, "We have the fundamental right not to be confronted by ugliness." I thought it a fine quote to lead with, because, though the words are easy to understand, the context isn't clear at once. It should pique the readers' curiosity without befuddling them.

Provide the context, along with attribution for the quote, as quickly as possible. If you leave your readers hanging too long, they may feel manipulated or become confused.

Sometimes the quote can be commonplace and close to home. For my humor piece, "Fraction Action," for *The Milwaukee Journal Green Sheet* (check your local newspapers as potential markets), I quoted my son:

"Hey, Dad. I need help with my homework."
Words to strike terror into any parent's heart.

Your best quotes come from your own sources, because they supply material that has never been in print. Occasionally, however, you may want the richness of allusion that a familiar quote can provide. I've used Mark Twain's, "If you can catch an adjective, kill it," and the immortal advertising slogan, "Plop, plop, fizz, fizz. Oh, what a relief it is," to bring the readers closer to my subjects.

The anecdotal lead

Perhaps the most effective but often the hardest to develop, the anecdotal lead shows rather than tells. The anecdote is a small, human story used to illuminate the point of the whole article.

I began my profile of a thriving acrylics company for *Business Age* magazine with the story of how Jim Lynn started the company with a $200 power saw and a few scraps of wood and plastic in the basement of his home. It provided a simple, human introduction to the complexities of the business and illustrated my theme, that a $2.2 million-a-year business could begin without planning and, indeed, almost by accident.

361

As with quotes, the best anecdotes come from your own sources. Probe for anecdotes in your interviews. When your subject gives you a generalization such as "You meet the most interesting people in my line of work," your response should be, "Describe some of those interesting people."

It's almost always best to keep yourself out of the article, but it may occasionally be effective to begin with a personal anecdote in order to make contact with your readers. I began my article "Holiday Hassles/ Holiday Happiness" for *Catholic Digest* by describing my 24-hour wait at the Milwaukee airport while my parents, snowbound in Denver, tried to get through for a Thanksgiving visit.

It's all right to make up an anecdote, as long as you make it clear to the reader that you're doing so. For my piece "Personal Publishing," I walked the reader through the experience of submitting a manuscript and having it rejected, to illustrate that the hardest work for the writer sometimes begins when the actual writing is done.

The cliché with a twist

Ordinarily, clichés have no place in your work, and especially not in the lead, where freshness is a must. But a good, hard twist can squeeze new life from a seemingly wrung-out phrase.

I began my article on physical fitness for *Directions* with an old saw with a couple of new teeth: "Caution: College may be hazardous to your health."

I've never forgotten the newspaper article on dieting that began, "Despite all the diets, pills and potions, heft springs eternal" or the baseball story that led with, "Things were so quiet in the Brewers clubhouse last night, you could hear a batting average drop."

Direct address

Often the best approach is the most direct one, a lead that puts the reader directly into the action.

I wanted to begin my description of a Mercury-Marine outboard motor plant for *The Yacht* magazine with the surprising fact that "Many yachts have their beginnings in an aluminum recycling plant in Fond du Lac, Wisconsin." I think I made the lead much stronger by rewriting it in direct address: "Your yacht may have begun as a mound of aluminum cans in Fond du Lac, Wisconsin."

One widely used variation on direct address is the question lead, but be careful here. Writers have overworked this technique, using it as an "if-all-else-fails" catch-all. Especially worn out is the "What do Sylvester Stallone, George Bush and Mother Theresa have in common?" format. Avoid it.

Avoid, too, the rhetorical question, one that clearly manipulates the reader into giving a predetermined response. "Do you want your children to have a good education?" (No, I want my kids to be illiterate bums!)

If the question provokes reader curiosity and introduces a genuine search for answers, it may be an excellent lead.

The narrative lead

For a long time, I thought there were two kinds of writing, "creative" (as in short stories and poetry) and "journalistic" (as in stuff you wrote for money). I've learned better. There are two kinds of writing, all right, writing that works and writing that doesn't. Effective writing uses any appropriate means to tell its story. If description and narration, primary tools of the fiction writer, work best in opening your nonfiction piece, you have both the right and the responsibility to use them.

I began an article on the old Boston Blackie television series for *Airwaves,* a public television programming guide, by describing the opening sequence of each episode, with the mysterious detective's silhouette looming ever-larger at the end of a darkened alley. I did so to try to evoke the rough charm of a 1950s low-budget production.

My profile of National Book Award winner Herbert Kubly for *Wisconsin Trails* began with a panoramic sweep, almost like the opening of a movie, panning from the tiny town of New Glarus, where Kubly grew up, out along a country road to the fourth-generation Kubly family farm. I wanted to show the author's tie to the land and the effect that tie has had on his writing. What better way than to describe that land?

Description for its own sake merely delays the true start of the article and makes the readers impatient—if it doesn't chase them away completely. Effective description must be thematic, revealing the focus of the article.

The comparison lead

Metaphor, simile, and analogy are effective tools for making sense out of nonsense and rendering the abstract concrete. Don't save them for later. Use them in the lead.

I've described a Wisconsin street as a carnival, compared a writer's query letter to a job interview, likened the process of scanning a magazine article to standing back to take in an entire mural before moving closer to study details, all to try to shine a light on the darkness of a new subject.

The effective comparison startles readers with new insights, makes them nod in agreement and murmur, "Ah-ha!" As with all good writing, it helps us to see familiar realities in new ways.

These seven lead categories often overlap. A metaphor may arrive wearing quotation marks. Direct address may also twist a cliché. Strict categorization isn't important. Finding the best lead for your article is.

Begin the search early. As you gather material, ask yourself, "What is unique about my subject?" Constantly and consciously look for quotes, anecdotes, and bits of thematic description that might illustrate this uniqueness in a memorable lead.

Trying to write the lead before you're ready can leave you staring into space, too worried about getting off to a good start to get off to any start at all. Work with the material you're comfortable with until lead possibilities begin to emerge.

When you're ready to tackle the lead, write not one but several. Let your imagination play with the idea. See how many possibilities you can generate. Don't be too quick to settle on one. The more choices you give yourself, the more likely you are to discover the best approach.

Finally, never impose a lead on your material. Let the lead emerge from the material.

It's worth the time and effort it takes to craft a compelling lead. It can make the difference between an article that never sees print and one that entertains and informs your readers.

70

WRITING FOR SYNDICATES

By Valerie Bohigian

Jack Anderson, Erma Bombeck, Richard Simmons, Sylvia Porter, and Ann Landers are syndicated writers. They write regular columns familiar to much of newspaper reading America, and they are well rewarded financially for their efforts. For every one of these writers, there are dozens of unknowns also earning steady, though more modest, dollars writing for syndicates. Some of them will build up the kinds of followings that will result in big earnings, book contracts, television and radio spots and lucrative speaking engagements. Other columns will be dropped as national trends and interests change, creating new openings that can be filled by writers who understand how syndicates work and know how to approach this market correctly with fresh, timely ideas. With the right information and the right idea, you can write one of these new columns.

Writing for a syndicate is different from writing for a magazine. A syndicate is not a publication. It is an agency that purchases columns, articles, comic strips, cartoons, photographs, horoscopes, jokes, puzzles, fillers, etc., and sells them to newspapers all around the country and the world. Contributors are paid a percentage—usually 50%—of total sales. (Syndicates occasionally pay a set fee.) Basically, a syndicate seeks to provide first-rate material at reasonable prices to as many newspapers as possible, and tries to stock a little of everything so that if a particular paper calls and asks for a travel column, or an etiquette column, or a humor column, the syndicate has it on hand and can fill the request.

The more newspapers that purchase your column, the more money you earn. Though wide distribution and circulation are important, other factors are equally so: Who buys your column is important. A major metropolitan newspaper will pay $100 for a column, whereas a Peoria paper will pay only $5. This means that if your column appears in such large papers as *The Boston Globe, The New York Daily News,* and *The Los Angeles Times,* you'll earn more than if it appears in fifty small-town papers.

Having your column appear in a small list of large newspapers can be more lucrative than having it appear in a large list of small newspapers. Of course, the ideal situation is to have your column sell to a large list of large and small newspapers. Once you get rolling this can happen. There are about 1,700 newspapers in the United States, and columns like Ann Landers' are bought by about 900 of them on a daily basis. Assuming she were to earn only $5 per paper (and she undoubtedly earns more), that's $4,500 per day!

Most syndicated writers do not earn anywhere near $4,500 per day. Rare is the column that sells to 900 newspapers per day; and rare is the columnist whose columns appear daily. However, there are several beginning columnists whose columns appear once or twice a week in about fifty newspapers. These writers are netting between $200 and $400 per week—not the big time yet, but not bad at all. Who are these people and how can you become one of them?

You have the best chance of becoming syndicated if you are an expert on a subject that is currently popular, not glutted with too many knowledgeable writers, and one that is growing in appeal. Certainly, it doesn't hurt to have an easily recognized name, but it is not crucial: The subject is. Ten years ago, for example, a syndicated column on plant care would not have sold, but now that plants are widely used in homes and offices as major decorating accessories, there are a few successful syndicated columns about plants. Though the authors are not "household names," the information and help they provide is read and used in thousands of households all over the country.

Columns showing people how to cope with various problems are popular today, and they are often written by individuals who have successfully solved these problems, rather than by theorists. For example, there is a lot of current interest in helping the handicapped care for themselves. A recent column on the subject, written by an invalid of many years, is selling widely. The author of this column passes along to her readers useful self-help ideas that she has discovered over the years, and that other disabled people have passed on to her. The handicapped, families of the handicapped, and people in professions relating to the care of the disabled are avid readers of this column.

How-to-cope columns need not deal with disabilities or tragedies; if you're coping successfully with a situation of wide interest, you may have a potential column in your hands. One of the major syndicates just took on as a columnist a mail order specialist who has learned not only how to deal with inflation, unemployment, job security, etc., but more specifically, how to do so by becoming an expert in mail order selling. The problems, pitfalls, and profits awaiting novice entrepreneurs in this field will be covered in this column. Another major syndicate, reflecting the growing interest in religion, has taken on a religion column geared to readers concerned with what they consider a current spiritual crisis in our society.

How-to material is also in demand today. If you know how to do something that most people would like to learn how to do or how to do better, you may have a salable column. Do you have a lot of good information to pass along in the fields of home entertainment, computers, home construction projects, knitting and crocheting, entrepreneurship, animal care? Right now the syndicates are looking for and buying columns in these areas.

Assuming you have a good idea and a concise (columns are generally only a few hundred words each) and readable style, how best to proceed? Though it is not the only way, the best way to begin is to develop a column for your local newspaper. Try to get your local paper to run it for awhile and then submit tear sheets of your columns to the syndicates, either through your local editor or directly. Syndicates respond well to columns that have proven popular in local newspapers.

Whether you're submitting to your local newspaper or to a syndicate, the procedure is the same: Submit an outline of what you have in mind, with six to eight sample columns that will demonstrate to the editors that you have more than just three good shots in your bag. A syndicate's editor can love your column, but its sales force can give it the kiss of death. Make sure, therefore, that your column reveals that it can help many thousands of readers who do not have easy access to the information you can provide, since it is a syndicate's sales department that must ultimately be able to place your work.

Don't get discouraged if you don't have a "hot" item for a column, or if it gets a cold response from a syndicate's editor. The best route to syndicate sales is through a careful study of what the syndicates seem to be selling, new subjects they seem to be taking on, and the writing styles and formats used. Familiarize yourself with all the syndicated newspaper columns you can find. (There are out-of-town newspaper stands in many cities; they can also be found in libraries.) Keep an eye out for trends, and list the specialized information you have to offer and what new ideas syndicates are using. See page 750 for information on the current market needs and requirements of the various syndicates. Also, at a large public library, consult *The Editors and Publishers Syndicate Directory*, which lists all syndicated columns, and *Literary Market Place*, which has a listing of syndicates.

While you're waiting for the right column idea to come along, or for your column to find a home, you might consider trying to sell "one-shots" to the syndicates. One-shots are reportorial pieces that some syndicates buy because they can easily be placed in several newspapers on a one-time basis. One-shots often draw fairly high fees (20¢ to 50¢ per word), and can be on any timely topic ranging from acrophobia to acupuncture. They can also be spin-offs from your already published magazine articles. One-shots not only produce income, but when your big column idea does come along, the editors will know you, and your material will receive special attention. Even though that alone won't make editors buy an unsalable column from you, they will be more likely to comment personally on why your idea won't work or on what you can do to make it more marketable.

Though big syndicates stock a wide variety of material, at a particular time one syndicate may be overstocked with business and fashion-advice columns, or because a key contributor didn't renew his contract, they may have a need for a record/music column. Another syndicate may be very much in the market for a column dispensing fresh business advice or offering money-saving tips. How do you know? You don't. Things change daily and timing can be very important. Unless you have a lot of already produced sample material on hand, or reason to believe that a particular syndicate is in the market for the kind of material you would like to provide, your time is probably best spent sending out a few queries to different syndicates, pitching your idea (for a one-shot or column). When a syndicate expresses interest, you can then follow up with a finished manuscript or several sample columns demonstrating your ability to produce quality with consistency. Always mention your specific qualifications.

The large syndicates sell material to hundreds of newspapers, large and small. There are also several smaller, more specialized syndicates you can try where you won't be competing with established professionals. Try them all, and don't be disheartened by rejections. Several widely syndicated features were turned down many times before being finally accepted. Yours may be, too.

71

FORM AND EXPERIMENTATION
IN POETRY

By Liz Rosenberg

THE WAR between poetic form and poetic license has been raging for a long time and continues to this day. In 1668 the poet John Milton threw down one gauntlet, in his blank verse poem *Paradise Lost:* "This neglect of Rhyme so little is to be taken for a defect, though it may seem so perhaps to vulgar Readers, that it rather is to be esteem'd an example set, the first in English, of ancient liberty recover'd to Heroic Poem from the troublesome and modern bondage of Rhyming."

Three hundred years later Robert Frost dropped the other glove in his now-famous scorn of unrhymed verse: "I'd as soon play tennis with the net down."

Rhyme has been the chief net over which the opposing sides slug it out, maybe because it is the most instantly noticeable musical aspect of English poetry and poetic form, though by no means the only formal element available to the poet. Anglo-Saxon poetry, which was highly regimented, depended upon a certain number of stressed beats per line, and alliteration. Chinese poetry uses pitch. Other formal elements have held precedence at various times—the controlled musicality of Sapphic verse, syllabics, cinquains, haikus, William Carlos Williams's "variable foot," and so on. Between structure and freedom the pendulum swings widely and regularly, one way, then another. We tend to think of our own time as the absolute reign of free verse: unrhymed, unmetered, personal, brief, as jumpy as a gesture by James Dean—yet there are already signs of a swing leading the other way, in poems one feels an urge to call "verse"—the formal, rhymed, structured and ornamented work of poets like Amy Clampitt, Philip Booth, Gertrude Schnacken-berg, and others.

As we draw closer to the end of the twentieth century, I suspect that the tendency both to poetic structure and poetic freedom will grow more exaggerated. Ends of centuries produce extremes, as witness

Alfred, Lord Tennyson on the one hand and Walt Whitman on the other, at the end of the nineteenth century. That these two poets had a great interest in and admiration for one another's work should come as no surprise. It's at both ends of the spectrum—extreme formal control, extreme poetic freedom—that the poet is pushing at boundaries, struggling to discover the necessities of the craft. It is exactly this pitched battle, *in extremis*, that produces great art, this pushing against limits, exploration of what is possible. The poet must write only according to internal necessity. The danger lies with those caught in the middle, like Dante's souls forever caught in the ante-chambers of hell, following first one flag and then another. This is the only mistake one can make in regard to poetic form: to allow the form to choose you. And it is as easy, as we have all lately discovered, to be the stooge of free verse as of formal verse. The worst one can do is to write in a particular form out of habit, intimidation, or laziness. There is an equal slackness in the doggerel rhyme of greeting cards or the nebulous free-form of Rod McKuen and his imitators. What one feels lacking in both is the tension of discovery, of necessity. And these are achieved only by a continual questioning of the status quo, by relentless experimentation and invention.

By "experimentation" I don't necessarily mean those finger exercises that are the stock in trade of many creative writing workshops. I'm not sure it's a good idea to get in the habit of just fooling around with poetry this way. It encourages a small kind of achievement; it puts a great emphasis on competence and cleverness, whereas great poetry is more like an explosion, built up under great pressure over a long period. One might practice with some of the tools of poetry—to sharpen musical and linguistic skills—but the poem, the thing itself, is not much good diluted.

Poets who practice with exercises must have a deep, nearly inexhaustible well of vital material. In this case, it will be impossible for anything the poet writes not to turn to poetry. But there is a frigidity in most poetic exercise, a sense of withholding that is deadly to real art. Poets shouldn't write villanelles or sonnets the way we are told we "should" write bread-and-butter letters or thank-you notes to Aunt Claire. This again is an encouragement to fall into the trap of thinking about form as somehow prescribed and habitual, as something one "really ought to do," rather than something one must do, having exhausted all other possibilities. It is only when this internal combustion

371

forces one into new forms that something strange and lovely takes place.

"New" forms proceed from an intuition of potentialities, of something lurking around the corner, a sense that what *is* is not enough. "Mine deeper, that's the ticket!" wrote Melville, and his remains the one true battle cry of all art. Experimentation is as natural to poetry as breathing is to life. If one were content with the old forms, with things-as-they-are, and with things-as-they-have-been-said, one could not write poetry at all.

Invention is the almost incidental by-product of this constant chafing against what is, an emergence into discovery. Invention need not be new to the world; it need only be genuinely new and fresh to the writer, who discovers his or her form alone, in solitude, after many failures and much self-doubt. It is absurd to imagine that Robert Frost did not grope his way toward the lyrical, rhyming, colloquially American language that evolved as his own. All of the so-called traditional or classical poets were wildly inventive and outrageous in their day. Milton, with his thundering blank verse, is only one example. Dante dropped from the "acceptable" elevated language of great poetry—Latin—to the mundane Italian spoken by street vendors, fishwives, soldiers, and farmers, and he did it against the advice and imprecations of his friends. Shakespeare careens from blank verse to formal sonnets to prose, all within a single play, and anyone who believes that his verse was written in strict iambic pentameter has a tin ear: "Howl, howl, howl, howl!" or "Bare ruined choirs, where late the sweet birds sang."

Invention is playful, but it is not merely play. My one objection to Frost's famous remark on free verse is that poetry seems to me an infinitely more important and complex "game" than tennis. Invention is the one true genius child of necessity, and it comes with the kind of passion and power that we may imagine first breathed life into the planets and spun them, the impulse that is always behind birth and creation. It is not strange, but familiar and fundamental to the very fact of our existence. Perhaps this is why great "new" poetry feels at the same time shocking and yet inevitable. There is nothing alien or rarefied about poetry, in whatever form. It is indeed at its best when it is closest to the mundane mysteries, when it is fresh with its own discoveries, with invention, and therefore brings us close to the common, creative wellspring of all being.

72

POETIC DEVICES

By William Packard

THERE is a good story about Walter Johnson, who had one of the most natural fast balls in the history of baseball. No one knows how "The Big Train" developed such speed on the mound, but there it was. From his first year of pitching in the majors, 1907, for Washington, Walter Johnson hurtled the ball like a flash of lightning across the plate. And as often as not, the opposing batter would be left watching empty air, as the catcher gloved the ball.

Well, the story goes that after a few seasons, almost all the opposing batters knew exactly what to expect from Walter Johnson—his famous fast ball. And even though the pitch was just as difficult to hit as ever, still, it can be a very dangerous thing for any pitcher to become that predictable. And besides, there were also some fears on the Washington bench that if he kept on hurtling only that famous fast ball over the plate, in a few more seasons Walter Johnson might burn his arm out entirely.

So, Walter Johnson set out to learn how to throw a curve ball. Now, one can just imagine the difficulty of doing this: here is a great pitcher in his mid-career in the major leagues, and he is trying to learn an entirely new pitch. One can imagine all the painful self-consciousness of the beginner, as Johnson tried to train his arm into some totally new reflexes—a new way of fingering the ball, a new arc of the elbow as he went into the wind-up, a new release of the wrist, and a completely new follow-through for the body.

But after awhile, the story goes, the curve ball became as natural for Walter Johnson as the famous fast-ball pitch, and as a consequence, Johnson became even more difficult to hit.

When Walter Johnson retired in 1927, he held the record for total strike-outs in a lifetime career (3409), and he held the record for total pitching of shut-out games in a lifetime career (110)—records which have never been equaled in baseball. And Walter Johnson is second only to the mighty Cy Young for total games won in a lifetime career.

Any artist can identify with this story about Walter Johnson. The determination to persist in one's art or craft is a characteristic of a great artist and a great athlete. But one also realizes that this practice of one's craft is almost always painstakingly difficult, and usually entails periods of extreme self-consciousness, as one trains oneself into a pattern of totally new reflexes. It is what Robert Frost called "the pleasure of taking pains."

The odd thing is that this practice and mastery of a craft is sometimes seen as an infringement on one's own natural gifts. Poets will sometimes comment that they do not want to be bothered with all that stuff about metrics and assonance and craft, because it doesn't come "naturally." Of course it doesn't come naturally, if one hasn't worked to make it natural. But once one's craft becomes second nature, it is not an infringement on one's natural gifts—if anything, it is an enlargement of them, and an enhancement and a reinforcement of one's own intuitive talents.

In almost all the other arts, an artist has to learn the techniques of his craft as a matter of course.

The painter takes delight in exploring the possibilities of his palette, and perhaps he may even move through periods which are dominated by different color tones, such as viridian or Prussian blue or ochre. He will also be concerned, as a matter of course, with various textural considerations such as brushing and pigmentation and the surface virtue of his work.

The composer who wants to write orchestra music has to begin by learning how to score in the musical notation system—and he will play with the meaning of whole notes, half notes, quarter notes, eighth notes, and the significance of such tempo designations as *lento, andante, adagio,* and *prestissimo.* He will also want to explore the different possibilities of the instruments of the orchestra, to discover the totality of tone he wants to achieve in his own work.

Even so—I have heard student poets complain that they don't want to be held back by a lot of technical considerations in the craft of poetry.

That raises a very interesting question: Why do poets seem to resist learning the practice and mastery of their own craft? Why do they

374

protest that technique *per se* is an infringement on their own intuitive gifts, and a destructive self-consciousness that inhibits their natural and magical genius?

I think a part of the answer to these questions may lie in our own modern Romantic era of poetry, where poets as diverse as Walt Whitman and Dylan Thomas and Allen Ginsberg seem to achieve their best effects with little or no technical effort. Like Athena, the poem seems to spring full blown out of the forehead of Zeus, and that is a large part of its charm for us. Whitman pretends he is just "talking" to us, in the "Song of Myself." So does Dylan Thomas in "Fern Hill" and "Poem in October." So does Allen Ginsberg in "Howl" and "Kaddish."

But of course when we think about it, we realize it is no such thing. And we realize also, in admiration, that any poet who is so skillful in concealing his art from us may be achieving one of the highest technical feats of all.

What are the technical skills of poetry, that all poets have worked at who wanted to achieve the practice and mastery of their craft?

We could begin by saying that poetry itself is language which is used in a specific way to convey a specific effect. And the specific ways that language can be used are expressed through all of the various poetic devices. In "The ABC of Reading," Ezra Pound summarized these devices and divided them into three categories—phonopoeia (sight), melopoeia (sound), and logopoeia (voice).

SIGHT

The image is the heart and soul of poetry. In our own psychic lives, we dream in images, although there may be words superimposed onto these images. In our social communication, we indicate complete understanding of something when we say, "I get the picture"—indicating that imagistic understanding is the most basic and primal of all communications. In some languages, like Chinese and Japanese, words began as pictures, or ideograms, which embodied the image representation of what the word was indicating.

It is not accidental that our earliest record of human civilization is in the form of pure pictures—images of bison in the paleolithic caves at Altamira in Northern Spain, from the Magdalenian culture, some 16,000 years B.C. And there are other records of stone statues as pure

375

images of horses and deer and mammoths, in Czechoslovakia, from as far back as 30,000 years B.C.

Aristotle wrote in the "Poetics" that metaphor—the conjunction of one image with another image—is the soul of poetry, and is the surest sign of genius. He also said it was the one thing that could not be taught, since the genius for metaphor was unaccountable, being the ability to see similarities in dissimilar things.

Following are the principal poetic devices which use image, or the picture aspect of poetry:

image—a simple picture, a mental representation. "That which presents an intellectual and emotional complex in an instant of time." (Pound)

metaphor—a direct comparison. "A mighty fortress is our God." An equation, or an equivalence: A = B. "It is the east and Juliet is the sun."

simile—an indirect comparison, using "like" or "as." "Why, man, he doth bestride the narrow world/Like a Colossus..." "My love's like a red, red rose."

figure—an image and an idea. "Ship of state." "A sea of troubles." "This bud of love."

conceit—an extended figure, as in some metaphysical poetry of John Donne, or in the following lines of Shakespeare's Juliet:

> Sweet, good-night!
> This bud of love, by summer's ripening breath,
> May prove a beauteous flower when next we meet...

SOUND

Rhythm has its source and origin in our own bloodstream pulse. At a normal pace, the heart beats at a casual iambic beat. But when it is excited, it may trip and skip rhythm through extended anapests or hard dactyls or firm trochees. It may even pound with a relentless spondee beat.

In dance, rhythm is accented by a drumbeat, in parades, by the cadence of marching feet, and in the night air, by churchbell tolling.

These simple rhythms may be taken as figures of the other rhythms of the universe—the tidal ebb and flow, the rising and setting of the sun, the female menstrual cycles, the four seasons of the year.

Rhythm is notated as metrics, but may also be seen in such poetic devices as rhyme and assonance and alliteration. Following are the poetic devices for sound:

assonance—rhyme of vowel sounds. "O that this too too solid flesh would melt..."

alliteration—repetition of consonants. "We might have met them dareful, beard to beard, And beat them backward home."

rhyme—the sense of resonance that comes when a word echoes the sound of another word—in end rhyme, internal rhyme, perfect rhyme, slant or imperfect rhyme, masculine rhyme, or feminine rhyme.

metrics—the simplest notation system for scansion of rhythm. The most commonly used metrics in English are:

iamb $(\smallsmile {'})$
trochee $({'} \smallsmile)$
anapest $(\smallsmile \smallsmile {'})$
dactyl $({'} \smallsmile \smallsmile)$
spondee $({'} {'})$

VOICE

Voice is the sum total of cognitive content of the words in a poem. Voice can also be seen as the signature of the poet on his poem—his own unmistakable way of saying something. "Only Yeats could have said it that way," one feels, in reading a line like:

That is no country for old men...

Similarly, Frost was able to endow his poems with a "voice" in lines like:

Something there is that doesn't love a wall...

Following are the poetic devices for voice:

denotation—literal, dictionary meaning of a word.

connotation—indirect or associative meaning of a word. "Mother" means one thing denotatively, but may have a host of other connotative associations.

personification—humanizing an object.

diction—word choice, the peculiar combination of words used in any given poem.

syntax—the peculiar arrangement of words in their sentence structures.

rhetoric—"Any adornment or inflation of speech which is not done for a particular effect but for a general impressiveness..." (Eliot)

persona—a mask, an assumed voice, a speaker pretending to be someone other than who he really is.

377

So far these are only words on a page, like diagrams in a baseball book showing you how to throw a curve ball. The only way there can be any real learning of any of these devices is to do endless exercises in notebooks, trying to master the craft of assonance, of diction shifts, of persona effects, of successful conceits, of metrical variations.

Any practice of these craft devices may lead one into a period of extreme self-consciousness, as one explores totally new reflexes of language. But one can trust that with enough practice they can become "second nature," and an enhancement and reinforcement of one's own intuitive talents as a poet.

73

LIGHT VERSE

By Robert Wallace

A few years ago, John Updike, heir to generations of great light verse poets (Dorothy Parker, Franklin P. Adams, Phyllis McGinley, E. B. White, Ogden Nash, Morris Bishop, Richard Armour among them) called light verse "a dying art." He added, "I write no light verse now." (It is hard to remember that Updike's first book was light verse.)

That glum conclusion was no great surprise to those who had watched the shrinking of markets to a mere handful—*The New Yorker* stopped printing light verse in the 1960's—and the dwindling of marketable forms to the clever, topical quatrains:

TAX HANG-UP

For those inclined to play
It fast and loose
Sometimes a tax loophole
Ends up a noose.

Light verse has been in the shadows for twenty years or more. It would be easy to see as its tombstone the fat anthology *The Best of Modern Humor* (Mordecai Richler, ed., Knopf, 1983), which is *entirely prose*. 542 big pages, going back to 1922, and not a shred, not even a single line of Dorothy Parker or Ogden Nash!

But, in Mark Twain's phrase, the report of its death would be "greatly exaggerated."

As long as there is laughter and as long as there is verse, someone will always be bringing the two together. Both fill deep needs. A comic tradition that includes Chaucer, Shakespeare, Pope, and Byron isn't about to vanish. What *has* happened, however, needs understanding before we can see the way ahead clearly.

We are victims, I think, of a distinction made in 1867 by an English light verse poet, Frederick Locker-Lampson. He distinguished between

379

"poetry"—that high, serious art—and what he called, coining the phrase, "light verse." He saw it as "another kind of poetry . . . which, in its more restricted form, has somewhat the same relation to the poetry of lofty imagination and deep feeling, that the Dresden China Shepherds and Shepherdesses of the last century bear to the sculpture of Donatello and Michael Angelo."

Though Locker-Lampson meant the term light verse as praise, this Victorian distinction has turned into a villainous Mr. Hyde, dividing poetry (seriousness) from mere light verse (humor). Joined to the Frankenstein of the twentieth-century's obsession with criticism (which essentially holds that no ordinary reader can really read a poem, novel, or play on his or her own), this distinction has been devastating. Laughter has been read out of the emotions proper for literature. Poetry, struggling under the weight of what can only be called *heavy* verse, has lost touch with the general reader. And light verse, isolated, trivialized, has fallen into the shadows. Ogden Nash doesn't even appear in the 1456 pages of that other could-be tombstone, *The Norton Anthology of Modern Poetry!*

Among the hopeful signs are three anthologies: *The Oxford Book of English Light Verse* (Kingsley Amis, ed., 1978), *The Oxford Book of American Light Verse* (William Harmon, ed., 1979), *The Penguin Book of Light Verse* (Gavin Ewart, ed., 1980). The magazine *Open Places* recently devoted a whole issue—222 pages—to humor, half of it verse. And there is *Light Year,* the annual of light verse and funny poems, which I edit. In its first three issues (totaling 626 pages) are poems by 306 poets, among them beginners as well as many of the finest writers in America: Richard Wilbur, Marge Piercy, X. J. Kennedy, Donald Hall, John Ciardi, May Swenson, Roy Blount Jr., Richard Armour—and John Updike!

And there is this most interesting straw-in-the-wind: as I write, Shel Silverstein's *A Light in the Attic* was on *The New York Times Book Review*'s hardcover best seller list for more than two-and-a-half years. That's a record. If only 10% of the "graduates" of *A Light in the Attic* can be persuaded to go on to other funny poems, there will be a very large, lively, paying audience once again. Perhaps there's gold in them thar hills.

Light verse—maybe we'd better call them *funny poems?*—is coming out of the shadows, and may well be in for a revival.

380

If I'm even partly right, what can a writer of funny poetry expect? What should he or she do differently, if anything? What will the funny poems of the immediate future be like? Here's some practical advice from the poet-and-editor's crystal ball:

Funny poetry will show a great variety in both subject and form, and will be more sophisticated, more honest, and—often at least—more serious. It will, in short, be more like what it really is: poetry.

1) Freed of the trivializing restrictions, it will find a range of subjects much broader than baldness, going on a diet, jogging, postal rate increases, and such foibles. It will be more topical, less moralizing, and often sillier and just plain merrier. There will be room again for things like Don Marquis's wonderful *archy & mehitabel*. It will, having the space, be peopled with more real and interesting characters. Look for poems like Katharyn Machan Aal's

HAZEL TELLS LAVERNE

last night
im cleanin out my
howard johnsons ladies room
when all of a sudden
up pops this frog
musta come from the sewer
swimmin aroun an tryin ta
climb up the sida the bowl
so i goes ta flushm down
but sohelpmegod he starts talkin
bout a golden ball
an how i can be a princess
me a princess
well my mouth drops
all the way to the floor
an he says
kiss me just kiss me
once on the nose
well i screams
ya little green pervert
an i hitsm with my mop
an has ta flush
the toilet down three times
me
a princess

2) Though epigrammatic quatrains will thrive—like Robert N. Feinstein's

381

THE OWL

Though I don't wish to seem too fanatical,
I consider the owl ungrammatical.
"To-whit, to-who" he sits and keens;
"To-whit, to-*whom*" is what he means.

—funny poems will often be longer, and both more varied and more daring in form. Look for more free verse, and for poems in complex forms like villanelle and sestina again. Whatever's happening in poetry will be happening in funny poetry. Visual poems, concrete poems, even funny "prose" poems like George Starbuck's

JAPANESE FISH

Have you ever eaten a luchu? It's poisonous like fugu, but it's cheaper and you cook it yourself.

You cut it into little squares as fast as possible but without touching the poison-gland. But first, you get all the thrill you can out of the fact that you're going to do it. You sit around for hours with your closest friends, drinking and telling long nostalgicky stories. You make toasts. You pick up your knives and sing a little song entitled "We who are about to dice a luchu." And then you begin.

3) It will be more sophisticated—often as corny, but probably cleverer. No doubt, sometimes, sexier. It will be less inclined to "nudge" the reader to be sure he gets the point. Titles will be less "cute," more functional, as in Michael Spence's

PROGRAMMING DOWN ON THE FARM

As all those with computers know,
Input-output is called I/O.
But farmers using these machines
See special letters on their screens.
So when they list a chicken fence
To "Egg Insurance and Expense,"
Into what file would it go?
Of course to EIE I/O.

4) It will be more honest and exact, more realistic. Puffy comic exaggeration—"[something or other] makes me tear my hair"—will vanish, as will banal (and untrue) generalities like "A man will stand for anything / Without a fight or fuss, / Except a lady or a lass / Upon a

382

crowded bus." Understatement will turn out to work better, as in Edward Willey's

FAMILY ECCENTRIC

Marie is bald and doesn't
give a damn. To prove it
she often spits in public
and hates to wear a hat.

I hope she changes
for the better before
she learns to talk.

5) It will often be closer to serious poetry, able to mingle the amusing with the lyrical, as in my

MYTH, COMMERCE, AND COFFEE
ON UNITED FLIGHT #622 FROM
CLEVELAND TO NORFOLK

Clouds, like bird-tracked snow,
spread to dawn-sun five miles below,

while businessmen (& poets) flow
on air streams, to and fro.

Now, of course, we know
Icarus *could* have made a go,

formed Attic Airways Co.,
expanded, advertised, and so

have carried Homer and Sappho
from Athens to Ilo

on reading tours—with, below,
clouds spread out like bird-tracked snow.

Or to mingle the amusing with the genuinely thoughtful—which is to say that it will have simply become poetry again!—as in Howard Nemerov's

POETICS

You know the old story Ann Landers tells
About the housewife in her basement doing the wash?
She's wearing her nightie, and she thinks, "Well hell,
I might's well put this in as well," and then
Being dripped on by a leaky pipe puts on
Her son's football helmet; whereupon
The meter reader happens to walk through

383

And "Lady," he gravely says, "I sure hope your team wins."
A story many times told in many ways,
The set of random accidents redeemed
By one more accident, as though chaos
Were the order that was before creation came.
That is the way things happen in the world:
A joke, a disappointment satisfied,
As we walk through doing our daily round,
Reading the meter, making things add up.

6) And one other, by no means the least consideration: funny poets may expect far more, and better paying, markets than they're used to. That's happening now.

74

PASSION AND THE MODERN POET

By Dick Allen

I KEEP coming back to passion. It is something all of us have felt, of course, but the severe and sustained passion of the poet is unique. The poet has a passionate need to create lines that seem to stand still but actually tremble and hover a lifetime in the mind: hummingbird lines.

"Batter my heart, three person'd God . . ." (John Donne). . . . "The seal's wide spindrift gaze toward paradise" (Hart Crane). . . . "Downward to darkness, on extended wings" (Wallace Stevens). . . . "You do not do, you do not do" (Sylvia Plath)—these and hundreds of other lines are in my mind daily. It is against them and the poems which sustain them that I measure my own work and the work of my contemporaries.

I do not mean to say that writing poetry is solely a matter of creating memorable lines, "touchstones" as Matthew Arnold called them. Rather, I am saying that the intensity of feeling they contain, their balance and art, is something toward which poets daily strive. The journey of the poet to a place and time when he may have a chance to write great poetry derives in large part from a passion of remembering. That is why the first test of a poet lies in the extent of his love for poetry itself. Virtually every publishing poet I know is a compulsive reader of past and present poetry. There is no quicker way to sort out hobbyist poets from poets who seem to have a chance at doing important work than by asking what they are reading.

The poet who answers that he regularly reads Shakespeare's sonnets, and such poets as Dante, Goethe, Pushkin, Keats, Whitman, Rilke, Akmatova, Montale, and Robert Lowell reveals that he honors and learns from the continuing tradition of poetry. The poet who reads his contemporaries, who subscribes to (or reads in libraries) such magazines as *Poetry, The Hudson Review, The New Yorker, The Atlantic*

Monthly, The American Poetry Review, and many large and small literary periodicals does likewise.

Let's assume that a poet sets out to read, say, the works of Robert Hayden and Adrienne Rich, Richard Howard's translation of Baudelaire's *Les Fleurs du Mal* and Anthony Hecht's *The Hard Hours*. What then?

The dominant mode of twentieth-century poetry is the short personal lyric, usually written in free verse. It is this mode that most college poetry workshops teach and that magazines most frequently publish. Learning to write a passable poem in this mode is not enormously difficult. Technique can be taught to any relatively talented poet. With technique, the poet can write and probably publish the standard contemporary American poem: a lyric that is essentially good, interesting personal journalism, written more or less rhythmically.

I don't mean to disparage such poetry. Just as writing the well-rhymed sonnet was a criterion for measuring a poet's ability in past generations, writing the intense and crafted personal lyric has become the late twentieth-century criterion. As in previous times, poets usually begin with trying to master a way of expression that seems most acceptable to the age in which they live.

The key technical principles for twentieth-century writers, poets included, are the two well-known admonitions of "Show, don't tell" and "Be specific." A great deal of the tension in modern verse derives from the poet's holding back what he or she would otherwise say outright, holding it back so that it will come into the reader's mind as a painting does, as does music, the thought or feeling seeming to have jumped distance and be born from the reader's own sensibility rather than impressed upon it.

"Be specific" forces the beginning poet really to observe the world around him or her and to search for precise words to describe what is seen. A passion for observation is also a passion for knowing and rendering life intensely. In fact, much of contemporary poetry has assumed—consciously or unconsciously on the part of poets—a duty to keep words alive and thus the ideas and feelings they evoke.

With "Show, don't tell" and "Be specific" in mind, the poet unlocks his or her experience. These admonitions intensify the poet's daily doings, meditations, conversations, and memories. What would otherwise be a dull walk on a gray day may turn into one in which the poet notices a small lightning bolt-shaped crack in a neighbor's kitchen windowpane, or how a haphazard arrangement of crocuses and tulips scattered on a suburban lawn makes it look as if the flower clumps were shot there by random cannon bursts. If the neighbor has been going through troubles recently, such imagery may connote it. To think vaguely of a past, lost love but then focus on the pattern of the towel wrapped around her as she stepped from a steamy shower makes that love seem alive in time.

My favorite definition of poetry comes from critic Fred B. Millett's *Reading Poetry:* "Poetry is language measured and supercharged." Supercharged relates to lyric poetry's intensity, which is a matter of many elements. "Language measured" reminds us that anyone serious about writing poetry should train himself in writing in a variety of meters. Knowledge of meter gives the poet maximum freedom; some poems wish to be iambic, or trochaic, or in lines of few or many feet. If a poet can write only free verse, that poet is cut off not only from the past, but from the challenge of writing in many of poetry's greatest traditional forms and modes.

Similarly, the poet who cannot write a decent rhymed poem is not one to be trusted as solidly grounded in the art. If you balk at this, remember that a prevalent kind of rhyming in our century is "slant" or "eye" rhyme. When the poet learns that "window" can be rhymed not only with "snow" but with "threw" and even with "now" or maybe even "blue," enormous possibilities open.

Since a contemporary poem is often valued for its interest—its interesting words, experiences—beginning poets who wish to do other than rake their lives to the coals in the "confessional" manner of Sylvia Plath are sometimes helped by being reminded that the contemporary personal lyric does not have to be an exact rendering of an actual event. "I" poems are not usually literal renderings; the "I" can easily be a persona.

If a poem comes from a train ride to Cleveland but works better when set on a train ride from Montreal, so be it. If "blue chair" works better than the "orange couch" on which a poet actually sat, the fictional aspect of writing allows use of the latter when it will create an emotionally truer and richer poem.

Based on actual experience or not, a great stress of contemporary poetry is on "honesty." The "honest" personal lyric is valued because,

387

reading it, we are reminded that no matter how formula TV shows would convince us differently, each different human life is a remarkably varied and vivid reflection on our own lives. Stereotypes and clichés are clumsy clay representations of the actual wonders and nuances to be seen and felt and heard by those who would truly know that living is more ripples than plains.

When a poet speaks of honesty, what she means is that the best lyrics contain elements that convince the reader that their feeling is not artificial. A poem must not seem to be a hiding place, or counterfeit the "proper" responses to situations with falsifying sentiment. The poet who writes only that she felt bad but resigned when she broke up with her boyfriend, yet does not show how she actually drew his picture in lipstick on her mirror and spat on it is not being honest with her readers. Her consequent poem will almost surely be hollow.

A continual lifetime involvement with reading poetry and with studying technique, as well as an open attitude toward writing poetry can take poets a long way; they cannot, however, give us much poetry that seems to matter ultimately. Good personal journalism and conversation written in free verse lyric poem form, fine descriptive vignettes—if the poet cannot do more she or he will remain at the best marvelously minor.

Everything else being equal, it is the content of the poem that causes it to change lives. In the twentieth century, a misplaced emphasis on "how a poem means" has misled too many poets into writing and teaching as if poetry were primarily a matter of aesthetics. Deep down, the best poets know it isn't, that their passionate intensity comes from a need to communicate deeply felt truths about the world or to tell stories concerning it in words, lines, images, musical throbs that simultaneously seem to hold still and vibrate.

Degrees of passion for subject material and the necessity to deal with ideas as well as feelings divide minor poets from major poets, and craftsmen from geniuses. Content crudely handled in verse has ruined hundreds of thousands of poems; yet without significant content a poet's work will be thin.

It is my conviction that contemporary poetry of the highest order—and who would strive for less?—requires a desperate need to be continually involved with the edges of experience, never to stop trying to write about the great subjects—love, religion, death, who we are, what is our purpose here, how shall we live; to have a living engagement with science and politics, and as many other matters as possible; and then to spend weeks, months, years honing individual works that laugh and shimmer, sob and stare.

75

EVERYONE WANTS TO BE PUBLISHED, BUT...

By John Ciardi

At a recent writers' conference I sat in on a last-day session billed as "Getting Published." Getting published was, clearly, everyone's enthusiasm. The hope of getting published will certainly do as one reason for writing. It need not be the only, nor even the best, reason for writing. Yet that hope is always there.

Emily Dickinson found reasons for writing that were at least remote from publication. Yet even she had it in mind. She seems to have known that what she wrote was ahead of its time, but she also seemed to know that its time would come. If Thomas H. Johnson's biography of her is a sound guide, and I believe it is, she spent her last ten years writing her "letters to the future." The letters, to be sure, were addressed to specific friends; yet they were equally addressed *through* her friends to her future readers. As Hindemith spent ten years composing his quartets and then ten more creating the terms by which they were to be assessed critically, so Emily spent ten years writing her poems (1776 of them, if I recall the right number), and then ten more years stating the terms for their reception.

Even she, then, had an audience (which is to say, publication) in mind. Nor do I imply that the desire to publish is an ignoble motive. Every writer wants to see himself in print. No writer, to my knowledge, has ever been offended when his published offerings were well received. The desire to publish becomes ignoble only when it moves a writer to hack and hurry the work in order to get it into print.

Poetry, of course, is relatively free of commercial motive. Every generation has its Edgar Guest. Ours, I suppose, is Rod McKuen. These are writers whose remouthing of sentiments catches some tawdry emotional impulse in commercial quantities. Yet such writers—or so I have long suspected—must come to believe seriously in the inanities they write. I doubt that they have sold out to the dollar sign: more tragically, they have sold out to themselves.

390

Such writers aside, it is hard to imagine that anyone would think to bribe a poet to write a bad poem. It would follow then (all temptation to cheat being out of the equation) that the only reason for writing a poem is to write it as well as one possibly can. Having so written it, one would naturally like to see it published.

I was, accordingly, in sympathy with the conference members—but I was also torn. For I had just spent days reading a stack of the manuscripts these people had submitted, and I had found nothing that seemed worthy of publication. I sat by, thinking that session on getting published was an exercise in swimming in a mirage. I even suspected a few of those present of drowning in their mirages.

Then one of the hard-case pros on the conference staff delivered a statistic. "You want to get published?" he said. "Fine. Look at the magazines. What are they publishing? The answer is, roughly, 98 percent nonfiction and not quite half of one percent poetry. Yet of the manuscripts submitted at this conference, seventy-six are poetry and only two are nonfiction." He paused. "Now you tell me," he said, "where are you going to get published?"

The hard case, as it happened, was a successful nonfiction writer for the large-circulation magazines; he had dismissed from consideration the literary quarterlies that do publish poetry, sometimes without payment, but sometimes with an "honorarium." To the quarterlies, I would certainly add our two excellent poetry tabloids, *The American Poetry Review* and *Poetry Now*.

For poetry does get published, though not on terms that would be attractive to the big-circulation pros. Poets *qua* poets do not run into serious income tax problems. So be it. If a little is all one asks, then a little is enough. I have never known of anyone who turned to poetry in the expectation of becoming rich by it. Were I to impersonate the hard-case pro at that conference, I could argue that a writer writes as an alcoholic drinks—which is to say, compulsively, and for its own sake. An alcoholic expects no special recognition for being helpless in his compulsion: Why should a poet expect money and recognition for his compulsion?

The fact is that the good poets do generally find their rewards and recognitions. Ego being what it is (and the poet's ego more so), any given poet may think his true merit has been slighted. For myself, whatever I have managed to make of my writing (and it has been a love affair, not a sales campaign), I have always felt that my own

391

satisfaction (or at least the flickering hope of it) was a total payment. Whatever else came has always struck me as a marvelous bonus. And there have been bonuses—grants, prizes, even a small, slow rain of checks. How could I fail to rejoice in that overflow of good? I wish it to every writer, and wish him my sense of joy in it.

But there is more to it. The hard case's manuscript count stayed with me. Can seventy-six poets and two nonfiction writers be called a writers' conference? He hadn't mentioned fiction, and I never learned how many fiction manuscripts had been turned in. But why, I asked myself, would seventy-six turn to poetry and only two to nonfiction? All writing is writing; all of it is part of one motion. I have enjoyed trying different sorts of writing. This present piece, for example, is nonfiction. It is part of the same exploration that poems take me on.

I asked myself the question, but I know I already had the answer —at least part of it—from the poems I had read and criticized. The poems had been bad, and I had fumbled, as one must, at trying to say why I thought they were bad. I wished on that last day that the conference were just starting and that I had ahead of me another chance to identify the badness of the poems. But perish that thought: I was emotionally exhausted.

Yet on that last day the reason so few of the conference members had turned to nonfiction seemed clear to me. Even to attempt nonfiction a writer must take the trouble of acquiring some body of information. The poems I had read lacked anything that could be called a body of information. The writers seemed to have assumed that their own excited ignorance was a sufficient qualification for the writing of poetry.

I wanted to go back and say to my conferees, "Your poems care nothing about the fact!" Isn't that another way of saying they were conceived in ignorance? Not one of the poets I read had even tried to connect fact A to fact B in a way to make an emotional experience of the connection. The writing lacked *thingness* and a lover's knowledge of thing.

Consider these lines by Stanley Kunitz (the italics are mine):

Winter that *coils* in the thickets now,
Will *glide* from the fields, the *swinging* rain
Be *knotted* with flowers. On every bough
A bird will *meditate* again.

392

The diction, the rhyming, the rhythmic flow and sustainment are effortless, but how knowledgeably things fall into place! Winter *coils* in the thickets because that snow that lies in shade is the last to melt, thinning down to scrolls of white by the last thaw. Winter will then *glide* from the fields—and what better (continuous, smooth) motion for the run-off of the last melt? The *swinging* rain (what word could better evoke our sense of April showers?) will then be *knotted* (as if) with flowers while birds (as if) *meditate* on every bough. The rain, of course, will not literally be knotted with flowers, nor will birds, literally, meditate. Yet what seems to be a scientific inaccuracy is of the central power of metaphor. Metaphor may, in fact, be conceived as an exactly felt error.

Metaphor is supposed to state the unknown in terms of the known. It is supposed to say X equals Y. Yet when we say "John is a lion," we do not think of John with a mane, with four clawed paws, nor with a pompon tipped tail. We extract from "lion" the emotional equivalent we need and let the rest go. The real metaphoric formula is X does-and-does-not-equal Y. Kunitz understands this formula. His knowledge of it is part of his qualification as a master poet.

There is more. More than can be parsed here. But note how the italicized words *hearken* to one another, each later term being summoned (by some knowledge and precision in the poet) by what went before. The italicized words form what I will dare to call a chord sequence by a composer who has mastered musical theory.

The passage, that is to say, is empowered by a body of knowledge of which I could find no trace in the poets I had been reading at the conference. My poets had been on some sort of trip. Their one message was "I feel! I feel!" Starting with that self-assertive impulse (and *thing* be damned), they then let every free association into the poem. They were too ignorant even to attempt a principle of selection.

I do not imply that I know what any given poem's principle of selection ought to be. To find the principle that serves best and to apply it in a way to enchant the reader is the art and knowledge of the poet. Everything in a good poem must be *chosen* into it. Even the accidents. How else could it be when one stroke of the pen will slash a thing out forever? All that has not been slashed out, it follows, is chosen in.

393

Ignorance, as nearly as I could say it (too late), was what had really stifled the poems I had read. The writers had not cared enough to learn their own art and use their eyes.

They will, I suppose, get published. Some of them somewhere. But have they earned the right to publication? I ask the question not to answer it. It is every writer's question to ask for himself.

76

WRITING POETRY FOR CHILDREN

By Myra Cohn Livingston

I NEVER intended to write poetry for children. It was a complete accident, and even today I marvel that it happened at all. I was eighteen, in college, and writing what I considered far more important—poetry about love! My instructor at Sarah Lawrence College, Katherine Liddell, had given us an assignment; we were to use alliteration and onomatopoeia. I turned in some verses. "These," she said to me in her converted closet-conference room, reeking with the odor of Sano cigarettes, "would be wonderful for children. Send them to *Story Parade*" (a magazine for boys and girls published by Simon & Schuster). I grudgingly followed her instructions—the accompanying letter, the self-addressed stamped envelope. Several weeks later the envelope came back. I threw it onto a pile of papers and three weeks later became so angry with Miss Liddell's folly, that I ripped it open to confront her with her error. I caught my breath. The editor had carefully clipped three of the poems, and there was a letter accepting these for publication.

It took me eleven years for my first book, *Whispers and Other Poems,* written when I was a freshman, to be accepted for publication by the same editor, Margaret K. McElderry, who had seen the manuscript when I was in college and encouraged me to continue writing. I know now that during the war years few new books were published, and certainly poetry for children was far down on the list of desired manuscripts. In those days, I read *The Writer* religiously, hoping to find someone who would want my work, and collected a sheaf of rejection slips.

But I did not write and never have consciously written *for* children. I cannot understand why the world appeared to me from the start as through the eyes of a child—of my own childhood—or why, even today, most of the poetry I write comes out that way. The only clue I have is that, even as an anthologist, I am drawn to (or write) those poems that speak to the subjects, emotions, and thoughts of children in a diction they understand.

My own poems have often been called "deceptively simple"; the first review of *Whispers* scathingly accused me of writing about "simple, everyday things," as though this were some sort of evil. Perhaps this is because many adults forget that to the child, these very things are what pique his curiosity, engage his attention. As the poet-in-residence for our school district, in my visits to schools and libraries throughout this country, and in teaching courses for teachers at U.C.L.A. Extension, I note that today's child is very different, in many respects, from the child I was, or that my children are, but that many things remain eternal. Children may know more facts, be more worldly wise, but the curiosity, wonder and fresh way of looking, the joys and pains and doubts, seem just as they always were.

I would like to suggest that anyone who wishes to write poetry that children might enjoy face up to a few basics about this vocation. The climate today is far more receptive to poetry than it was a number of years ago when the English—Walter de la Mare, Robert Louis Stevenson, and A. A. Milne—dominated the field. America has given us Elizabeth Madox Roberts, David McCord and Harry Behn, to mention but a few—and there are many exciting middle-aged and young poets publishing today whose work is excellent. We no longer have to take second place to the English, but we do have to recognize that poetry is still somewhat of a stepchild in juvenile literature. Children, themselves, are more apt to read a story in a picture book than to read poetry, for most adults and teachers feel uncomfortable about presenting it. Even Mother Goose is not as well known as once she was. And poetry demands an involvement of the emotions, whether it be laughter or wonder or a more serious way of viewing the world.

The crisis we seem to face now is the mistaken notion that *anyone* can write a poem. The Poets-in-the-Schools program, in many areas, has too often, in my opinion, fostered undisciplined writing, that which John Ciardi has called "a spillage of raw emotion." Any word or series of words written down are called "poems." This, as I see it, is a great disservice to the children who are falsely praised, but it also applies to older aspiring poets. Many of the high school and college students have had no real discipline. Metrical feet, scansion, forms are unknown. Of course, we do not want didactic, sing-song verse, the moralizing of a Henley's "Invictus" or the elusive fairies of Rose Fyleman. What we do need is true poetry that takes into account the interests and yearnings of the young and leads them toward a process of humanization.

In offering suggestions to the person who wishes to write such poetry, I would ask that he ask himself if anything of the child remains in him—a way of looking, tasting, smelling, touching, thinking; if he is in touch with the contemporary child and his way of viewing the world, if he is truly comfortable with children. I would also suggest that he make the commitment to learn the basics of writing in disciplined forms and meters. One cannot, for example, attempt a limerick without knowing how to use the iambus and anapest correctly, nor even free verse without knowing why it *is* free verse.

Another, and perhaps more elusive point, is that the writer understand and believe that poetry for children is not second-best; there is a tendency on the part of many to feel that a so-called children's poet is one who has failed in writing adult poetry, or that it is "easy" to do. The poet who writes for children exclusively is a sort of second-class citizen.

Although I have spent almost twenty years sharing with young people poetry ranging from Mother Goose to T.S. Eliot, it is difficult to give any definite answer as to what sort of poetry children like best. We know through experience that levity is always high on the list, and humor is important, for it counters the view of poems as soul-building messages in high-flown diction. But many a child prefers the more serious. The more a young person is exposed to poetry, the more refined is his taste in this, as in all arts. I would hope that any writer aspiring to publish poetry would not write for what he thinks is the juvenile market, but rather concentrate on his own strengths. The word-play of David McCord is something that comes naturally to his art; curiosity and a love for nature are intrinsic to Harry Behn's work; and Elizabeth Madox Roberts wrote about experiences of her own as a child.

My own poetry has gone through a series of changes. Trained in the traditional rhyme/meter school, I have at times broken away to free verse, knowing that the force of what I wished to say had to dictate the form. Yet I do not feel I could have made this break without a sure knowledge of the disciplines, taught to me by Robert Fitzgerald and Horace Gregory. I know that there are many who would take issue with me, who feel that anything one wishes to put down, if arranged in a certain order, is a poem.

This change may best be shown by contrasting my first published poem, "Whispers," to later work:

Whispers
    tickle through your ear
    telling things you like to hear.

Whispers
    are as soft as skin
    letting little words curl in.

Whispers
    come so they can blow
    secrets others never know.

Most of my verse in *Whispers, Wide Awake, Old Mrs. Twindlytart* and *The Moon and a Star* was written in traditional forms. But in *A Crazy Flight* (published in 1969), what I wanted to say suddenly refused to be confined by rhyme. The need to use repetition and a freer form of expression asserted itself in a poem that also picked up some current speech patterns of the children I was then teaching:

THE SUN IS STUCK

The sun is stuck.
I mean, it won't move.
I mean, it's hot, man, and we need a red-hot
    poker to pry it loose,
Give it a good shove and roll it across the sky
And make it go down
So we can be cool,
Man.

Yet, *The Malibu,* my poem inspired by the moon landing and America's concerns with litter, combined both the rhyming couplet and some elements of free verse:

398

ONLY A LITTLE LITTER

Hey moonface,
man-in-the-moonface,

do you like the way
we left your place?

can you stand the view
of footprints on you?

is it fun to stare
at the flags up there?

did you notice ours
with the stripes and stars?

does it warm you to know
we love you so?

moonface,
man-in-the-moonface,

thanks a heap for the rocks.

In *The Way Things Are,* the meter follows a child's pattern with a different rhyme pattern, in "Growing: For Louis."

It's tough being short.

Of course your father tells you not to worry,
But everyone else is giant, and you're just the
way you were.
And this stupid guy says, "Hey shorty, where'd
you get the long pants?"
Or some smart beanpole asks how it feels to
be so close to the ants?
And the school nurse says to tell her again how
tall you are when you've already told her.
Oh, my mother says there's really no hurry
And I'll grow soon enough.

But it's tough being short.

(I wonder if Napoleon got the same old stuff?)

But the rhymed couplet creeps up again and again in *4-Way Stop* (published in 1976):

OCEAN AT NIGHT

Mother Wave sings soft to sleep
the fish and seaweed of the deep

black ocean, and with quiet hands
pats to peace her tired sands,

her kelp and driftwood; fills her shoals
with gleaming tides, and gently pulls

across her bed the pale moonlight.
And this is night. And this is night.

Throughout these later books are outcroppings of free verse with which I am still experimenting, but there is an inherent pull that constantly draws me back to the containment of fixed forms. I have finally begun to tackle the haiku and cinquain, most demanding in their use of words:

Even in summer
bees have to work in their orange
and black striped sweaters.

Like any other poet, I feel that the most important factor in my poetry writing is not that I set out to write in any given form, but that I must find the right form for the subject matter. For this is when —and only when—the poem "comes right" for me.

What is right for me is not so for everybody. There are no surefire methods, although I do believe that one must know the basics and rules before breaking them. Even children need these rules, for without them, they flounder and grow dissatisfied with what they are doing. What we all have in common is that we are still learning, and, I hope, growing and changing.

77

THE EXPERIENCE OF THE POEM

By Ann Stanford

One may think of the ingredients of a good poem as an experience and a fresh perception of that experience. The experience need not be original or new, but the perception should be. Think of Gerard Manley Hopkins' delight in spring, a feeling old as humanity, couched in the freshest of images:

> Nothing is so beautiful as spring—
>   When weeds, in wheels, shoot long and lovely and lush;
>   Thrush's eggs look little low heavens, and thrush
> Through the echoing timber does so rinse and wring
> The ear, it strikes like lightnings to hear him sing;
>   The glassy peartree leaves and blooms, they brush
>   The descending blue; that blue is all in a rush
> With richness; the racing lambs too have fair their fling.

Hopkins' language is vital because his feeling about spring is intense and his own. He has taken the familiar ingredients of a poem about spring and made them into a new vision.

A contemporary example of a poem drawn from everyday experience is May Swenson's "Water Picture,"* which describes the reflection of objects in a pond; it begins:

> In the pond in the park
> all things are doubled:
> Long buildings hang and
> wriggle gently. Chimneys
> are bent legs bouncing
> on clouds below. A flag
> wags like a fishhook
> down there in the sky.

---

* From *To Mix with Time*. Charles Scribner's Sons. Copyright © 1963, by May Swenson.

The arched stone bridge
is an eye, with underlid
in the water. In its lens
dip crinkled heads with hats
that don't fall off. Dogs go by,
barking on their backs.
A baby, taken to feed the
ducks, dangles upside-down
a pink balloon for a buoy.

Seen in detail from a new angle, an ordinary experience becomes extraordinary and the substance of poetry. The fresh perception makes the old experience unique.

And the perception is conveyed through language. The words and combinations we choose must be carefully screened to see that they are not the old stereotypes through which we blind ourselves to the world. In his poems, e. e. cummings tore words apart and put the parts back into new combinations so that his language might reveal a new view of the world. Most of us will not follow his way, but we need to be sure we see what we see as it is, not as we think it is. There is a tree before you. What kind of leaves does it have? Are they alternating on the stem? Do they resemble plumes? Are they flat on the air like lily-pads in the water? Hopkins' journal frequently takes account of such phenomena:

Elm leaves:—they shine much in the sun—bright green when near from underneath but higher up they look olive: their shapelessness in the flat is from their being made . . . to be dimpled and dog's eared: their leaf-growth is in this point more rudimentary than that of oak, ash, beech, etc that the leaves lie in long rows and do not subdivide or have central knots but tooth or cog their woody twigs.

Such careful looking, such precision in visual perception, is a first step in writing poetry. If you cannot see what a tree looks like, it will be hard to tell anyone what a feeling feels like. Because in poetry we are dependent on the concrete manifestations of the world to use as symbols of our feelings and our experiences. This is especially true in lyric poetry. But apt suggestive details give credibility to narrative poems and character sketches as well. A good exercise in poetry is to record exactly what you see before you with no large statements about what is there. Simply describe it as if you are seeing it for the first time. An artist practices by carrying a sketch pad and drawing wherever he may be. In the same way, the result of the poet's sketch may not be a poem, but the practice will help develop a technique for handling a more complex subject when it does appear. Here is an example, a description of a shell done as an exercise:

> Being which is the size of my palm
> almost and fits the upcurled fingers
> flat-cupped the thirty-four fingers
> end in points set close together
> like the prongs of a comb
> sea-combing straining the waters
> they are printed on your back
> brown waves cutting light sand
> waves—merging inward
> lighter and lighter and closer
> whirling
> into the self-turned center
> of yourself.

Just as there are two kinds of perception—what is seen and what is experienced—there are two kinds of possibilities for exact or innovative language. And there are chances also for trite or easy observation on both levels.

A poem will not always die of a single cliché; indeed, a common observation can even be used for a deliberate artistic purpose. Only someone who has really mastered his craft, however, should dare to use a phrase which borders on the trite. Dylan Thomas sometimes uses old phrases but remakes them by small changes, so that they emerge as live word combinations like "once below a time." But I can think of no poetic situation in which a "rippling stream" or "glassy pond" can add anything but tedium. Worse than the cliché at the literal or visual level, is the cliché at the experiential level, the large abstract concept such as:

> Life, like time, moves onward.

The large concept gives the reader a stereotyped experience. Perhaps this is why some very bad poetry appeals to a number of undiscriminating readers: it repeats the stereotype of experience they have in their own minds and gives them nothing new to test it by. A good poem should jolt the reader into a new awareness of his feeling or his sensual apprehension of the world. One of the great mistakes is to make a poem too large and simple.

Poetry is an art which proceeds in a roundabout fashion. Its language is not chosen for directness of communication, for the passing on of facts, like "the plane arrives at five," or "today it is raining," although either of these facts could be a part of a poem. The truth that poetry attempts to communicate is reached by more devious means. Many of the devices thought of as being in the special province of poetry are devices of indirection: the metaphor or symbol, which involves saying one thing and meaning another; paradox, the welding of opposites into a single concept; connotations beyond the direct meaning of a word or phrase, and so on. When we think of the way things are in the world, we find that poetry is not the only area in which the immediate fact is disguised, distorted, or concealed. Poetry does this in order to reach a more complex truth. Other situations involve indirection for other reasons. Purpose determines the directness of statement. Take the guest telling his hostess he enjoyed the party. Did he really? But in saying this he is expressing some other feeling beyond the immediate situation. He may be expressing sympathy or long affection or any number of emotions rather than measuring the quality of his enjoyment of the moment. Take advertising, which often tries to pass along not so much a fact as a feeling about something. Take the art of the magician—the better the more deceiving. For the poet to speak too glibly may be to oversimplify his experience. The poet must constantly ask himself: "Is this the way it really felt? Is this the whole experience? Am I overlooking or suppressing part of it?"

As I write this, a living example has appeared before my eyes. I am looking at the tree just outside the window. If I should give you my visual experience at this moment, I should have to include a lizard that has climbed twenty feet up the trunk and is now looking at me. In my stereotyped picture of trees, birds sometimes come to rest, but not lizards. In my stereotype of the loss of a friend through death, there is sorrow, not anger. But I have felt anger at the death of a friend, and there is a lizard in this tree. The real includes these disparate elements. The poet must think of what he has really experienced. He gives certain real details, certain suggestions. The reader combines these into the experience intended by the poet, the real message of the poem, and so participates in its creation.

The poet uses three types of ingredients in his poem: at the first

404

level is what can be immediately caught by the senses—by sight, by hearing, tasting, feeling, smelling. I call this the literal level: the poet describes what is literally there. This poem of my own is written almost entirely at this level:

THE BLACKBERRY THICKET *

I stand here in the ditch, my feet on a rock in the water,
Head-deep in a coppice of thorns,
Picking wild blackberries,
Watching the juice-dark rivulet run
Over my fingers, marking the lines and the whorls,
Remembering stains—
The blue of mulberry on the tongue
Brown fingers after walnut husking,
And the green smudge of grass—
The earnest part
Of heat and orchards and sweet springing places.
Here I am printed with the earth
Always and always the earth ground into the fingers,
And the arm scratched in thickets of spiders.
Over the marshy water the cicada rustles,
A runner snaps sharp into place.
The dry leaves are a presence,
A companion that follows up under the trees of the orchard
Repeating my footsteps. I stop to listen.
Surely not alone
I stand in this quiet in the shadow
Under a roof of bees.

The sights and sounds caught by immediate sensation are described; the memories are of the same immediate quality. Even the ending of the poem is a literal description, although the reader may find there, if he likes, connotations that go beyond the literal.

Much of modern American poetry is written at this level. If not total poems as here, at least sections of poems. Most readers of modern poetry, many editors, look for this literal quality. Here, as I said earlier, the poet must look carefully and sensitively and report exactly. Notice, next time you read a poem, how much of it contains this literal looking and what details the poet has chosen to give the appearance of reality. Even an imagined experience should have some of this literal quality.

---

* From *The Weathercock*, by Ann Stanford. Copyright © 1955, by Ann Stanford. Reprinted by permission of The Viking Press, Inc.

The next level of poetry is the metaphoric, in which one thing is compared with another. The conventional poetic devices of simile, metaphor, symbol are part of this level. Comparison often mingles with the literal. In Elizabeth Bishop's well-known poem "The Fish," * exact description is aided by comparison:

> I looked into his eyes
> which were far larger than mine
> but shallower, and yellowed,
> the irises backed and packed
> with tarnished tinfoil
> seen through the lenses
> of old scratched isinglass.

The juxtaposing of two things that are not wholly alike but that are alike in some way is one of the ways that poetry creates a new view of the world. Comparisons or analogies can be used thus as part of description, or they can make a total poem. They can be either one-way or two-way comparisons. For example, the fish's eye can be said to resemble isinglass, but isinglass does not remind one of a fish's eye. It is not always necessary or desirable that the comparisons work both ways. Another example, Shakespeare's comparison of true love to a "star to every wandering bark," is effective even though within the poem he is not also comparing a star that guides to love. He is defining love in terms of a star, but not a star in terms of love.

However, often the poet uses a two-way analogy. The doubleness of the analogy is especially effective where the whole poem is in the form of comparison. Here is a poem of mine which satirizes the work of committees.

THE COMMITTEE †
by Ann Stanford

Black and serious, they are dropping down one by one to the top of the walnut
    tree.
It is spring and the bare branches are right for a conversation.
The sap has not risen yet, but those branches will always be bare
Up there, crooked with ebbed life lost now, like a legal argument.
They shift a bit as they settle into place.

---

* From *Poems: North and South*. Houghton Mifflin Company. Copyright © 1955, by Elizabeth Bishop.

† © 1967 The New Yorker Magazine, Inc.

Once in a while one says something, but the answer is always the same;
The question is, too—it is all *caw* and *caw*.
Do they think they are hidden by the green leaves partway up the branches?
Do they like it up there cocking their heads in the fresh morning?
One by one, they fly off as if to other appointments.
Whatever they did, it must be done all over again.

Here, what is said about the crows can be applied to a committee, but it is also true of crows, at least the ones I have observed in my neighborhood. This, then, is a two-way analogy.

There is another level at which poets sometimes work: the level of statement. Much of Wordsworth's poetry is statement, as:

This spiritual Love acts not nor can exist
Without Imagination, which, in truth,
Is but another name for absolute power
And clearest insight, amplitude of mind,
And Reason in her most exalted mood.

This is a hard and dangerous level for most poets. Much poetry, especially amateur poetry, constantly attempts statement without backing it up with the literal or analogic or comparative level. The poem which merely states, except in the hands of a master, falls flat because it does not prove anything to the reader. He is not drawn into the background of the statement. He is merely told. If his own experience backs up the statement, he may like the poem, but he likes it only because of his experience, not because of what the poem has done for him.

Masters of poetry, on the other hand, sometimes make one large statement and spend the rest of the poem illustrating or proving it. Hopkins does this with the statement "Nothing is so beautiful as spring—"; May Swenson does it in a more specific way in "Water Picture." William Carlos Williams in "To Waken an Old Lady" defines old age by describing a flock of birds in winter. His only reference to age at all is the first line, "Old age is." Without the first line to suggest the definition, the poem could be simply a nature description. Emily Dickinson often makes an abstract idea come to life by defining it in visual terms:

Presentiment is that long shadow on the lawn
Indicative that suns go down;

407

The notice to the startled grass
That darkness is about to pass.

It would be a rare poem which could exist on one of these levels—that of literal description, that of metaphor, or that of statement—alone. Poems usually combine these in varying proportions. There are dangers to the poetry, besides triteness, at all levels. Flatness, dullness, and poor selection of details menace literal description. Metaphor is endangered by irrelevance; a metaphor which does not contribute in tone or feeling may turn the reader away from the poem as a whole. Statement is most dangerous, for it must be proved.

A poem which succeeds may also have a fourth level—the transcendental level, where the connotations of the poem extend on beyond the limits of the poem. But the transcendental may hardly be striven for. We only recognize it when it shimmers in the exceptional poem.

Meanwhile the poet works at what he can. He looks for the whole significance of the experience. He renders it—even more, he understands it—through language built around his own view. His new seeing is what will make the experience of the poem worth telling once more.

78

TEN GOLDEN RULES FOR PLAYWRIGHTS

By Marsha Norman

Budding playwrights often write to ask me advice on getting started—and succeeding—in writing plays. The following are a few basics that I hope aspiring playwrights will find helpful.—M.N.

1. Read at least four hours every day, and don't let anybody ask you what you're doing just sitting there reading.

2. Don't write about your present life. You don't have a clue what it's about yet. Write about your past. Write about something that terrified you, something you *still* think is unfair, something that you have not been able to forget in all the time that's passed since it happened.

3. Don't write in order to tell the audience how smart you are. The audience is not the least bit interested in the playwright. The audience only wants to know about the characters. If the audience begins to suspect that the thing onstage was actually written by some other person, they're going to quit listening. So keep yourself out of it!

4. If you have characters you cannot write fairly, cut them out. Grudges have no place in the theatre. Nobody cares about your grudges but you, and you are not enough to fill a house.

5. There must be one central character. One. Everybody write that down. Just one. And he or she must want something. And by the end of the play, he or she must either get it or not. Period. No exceptions.

6. You must tell the audience right away what is at stake in the evening, i.e. how they know when they can go home. They are, in a sense, the jury. You present the evidence, and then they say whether it seems true to them. If it does, it will run, because they will tell all their friends to come see this true thing, God bless them. If it does not seem true to them, try to find out why and don't do it any more.

7. If, while you are writing, thoughts of critics, audience members or family members occur to you, stop writing and go read until you have successfully forgotten them.

8. Don't talk about your play while you are writing it. Good plays are always the product of a single vision, a single point of view. Your friends will be helpful later, after the play's direction is established. A play is one thing you can get too much help with. If you must break this rule, try not to say what you have learned by talking. Or just let other people talk and you listen. Don't talk the play away.

9. Keep pads of paper near all your chairs. You will be in your chairs a good bit (see Rule 1), and you will have thoughts for your play. Write them down. But don't get up from reading to do it. Go right back to the reading once the thoughts are on the paper.

10. Never go to your typewriter until you know what the first sentence is that day. It is definitely unhealthy to sit in front of a silent typewriter for any length of time. If, after you have typed the first sentence, you can't think of a second one, go read. There is only one good reason to write a play, and that is that there is no other way to take care of it, whatever it is. There are too many made-up plays being written these days. So if it doesn't spill out faster than you can write it, don't write it at all. Or write about something that does spill out. Spilling out is what the theatre is about. Writing is for novels.

79

THE S-N-A-P-P-E-R TEST FOR PLAYWRIGHTS

By Lavonne Mueller

Whenever I finish a play, I check to see that I have applied to it every point from what I call the "S-N-A-P-P-E-R Formula." Here is my "Snapper" checklist.

Secret

Everyone loves to hear a secret. Have the main characters in your play tell something about themselves that is revealing and intimate.

In my play *The Only Woman General,* Olive Wiggins tells us that when she was in combat, she couldn't tell the winning from the losing; all battles seemed the same.

The secret Anne reveals (but only to her diary) in *The Diary of Anne Frank* is the physical change in her body that turns her into a woman. Willy Loman, in Arthur Miller's *Death of a Salesman,* tells Ben about his life insurance policy and also what his funeral will be like:

They'll come from Maine, Massachusetts, Vermont, New Hampshire! All the old timers with strange license plates.

In Tennessee Williams' *The Glass Menagerie,* Laura tells the Gentleman Caller her secret humiliation when she was going to school with a brace on her leg:

My seat was in the back row. I had to go clumping all the way up the aisle with everyone watching.

How would *Death of a Salesman* change, for example, if Willy's secret was that he wanted to be an artist? How would *The Glass Menagerie* change if the secret Laura confides to the Gentleman Caller was that she had successfully hid from the world the brace on her leg?

411

Names

Give your characters interesting names. Names can define a character. They can also function ironically and humorously. A cowboy in my play *Little Victories* is called Double Ugly because he's been in a fight that cut his face in two places. In *The Only Woman General,* the woman general is ironically named Olive—olive for peace.

Big Daddy in Tennessee Williams's *Cat on a Hot Tin Roof* is the head of a wealthy household, and not only does he command obedience and servitude, but the humorous overtones of his name add an ironic dimension. Big Daddy's sons are Gooper and Brick—the first is simpering, the second headstrong.

How would *Cat on a Hot Tin Roof* change if Tennessee Williams had named Big Daddy Herbert or Leslie or reversed the names of his sons?

If you wrote a one-act play about a dermatologist, would you want to call him Sam Lumpkin?

Action

Every play must have action. Drama is like a boxing match. Two characters go at each other until one is shoved up against the wall. Or knocked out. The image of a boxing match is actually used by author Shirley Lauro in her excellent play, *Open Admissions.* Ms. Lauro states: "The audience's experience from the start should be as if they had suddenly tuned in on the critical round of a boxing match."

In *Little Victories,* Joan wishes to be a successful general. She has to convince her adjutants that she is competent. She is constantly being pressured by them. In desperation, she uses many tricks of common sense that she learned as a farm girl. Her main goal is always a source of action: Joan pulls soldiers out of mudholes with the same skill she used on her cows. Because she can't read, she uses the lines in the palm of her hand as a map. She struggles to win over her troops. Action.

Make sure your main character wants something, and make sure somebody is keeping him/her from getting it. In *Cat on a Hot Tin Roof,* Big Daddy wants a son from Brick. Brick is obstinate. They struggle. Action!

Props

Props can be very effective. They are visual messages to the audience, and they are an extension of the character's personality. Try to think of props that are genuinely important to the development of your play. You don't want to use a prop that is gratuitous.

In my play *Breaking the Prairie Wolf Code,* Helen, a pioneer woman, takes a tea set with her on the westward journey. At every wagon stop, she has tea to remind herself of a former gentility. As the trip progresses, parts of the tea set are broken and lost. I use this prop to show graphically the hardships of the journey.

Hamlet speaks to the skull of Yorick. The Moor in *Othello* uses a handkerchief as proof of his suspicions of Desdemona's infidelity. In *The Diary of Anne Frank,* Anne tapes pictures of movie stars on the wall of her small hiding space. In Eugene O'Neill's *Long Day's Journey into Night,* Mary's faded wedding dress is her one tangible connection to the past.

It's hard to imagine these plays without their classic props. What if Hamlet delivered his monologue to a rock instead of Yorick's skull? What if Anne Frank had pictures of food instead of movie stars on her wall?

Plot

Plot is as important to a dramatist as it is to a novelist. The attention of the audience is held by a clear, strong story line. Shakespeare is a master of storytelling. We want to know, for example, what will happen to Romeo and Juliet. What will happen to Lear after he's turned over his power to his children?

The plot is closely related to what we call "the dramatic question." This question is something an audience wants answered. In *Hamlet,* the dramatic question is: Will Hamlet avenge his father? The answer to that dramatic question keeps each person interested enough to come back after the intermissions.

The plot/dramatic question does not have to be complex. In *Little Victories,* the question is simply: How will Joan win the battle? In the musical *A Chorus Line,* the plot/dramatic question is simply: Who will get chosen for the chorus line?

If you think of a question to ask on stage, it becomes easier to structure a plot around it. In *Breaking the Prairie Wolf Code,* my question is simply: Will the wagon train get to California? After I came up with the question, I began to imagine all the things that could prevent this journey and make it more difficult. I invented obstacles and characters to "hang" on the story line of my dramatic question.

Ending

Give your characters a well-planned exit. They've come to the end of their tale, and it's very effective if they can leave the stage with some relevant words or actions.

Again, in *Little Victories,* the drama ends when Joan tells Susan that she must reach into the future and find somebody who can help her. Joan takes Susan's hand and points it to the audience, saying: "Take the dark."

In *Cat on a Hot Tin Roof,* Maggie says to Brick at the end of the play: "Oh, you weak, beautiful people who give up so easily. You need somebody to hand your life back to you like something gold."

Anne's father in *The Diary of Anne Frank* reads a last line from her diary entry: "In spite of everything I still believe that people are really good at heart."

How would *Cat on a Hot Tin Roof* change if the ending line were Brick's—perhaps saying that he didn't know if he had the strength to go on?

How would *The Diary of Anne Frank* change if her last diary entry were that people are basically corrupt?

Relatives

Let the characters tell us something about their relatives or background. It helps us to understand how they came to be the people they are.

Esther Bibbs, an ex-slave on the wagon train in *Breaking the Prairie Wolf Code,* tells us:

I used to make this pea soup for the Fenchler family. They were my marsters in Georgia. My folks was took to the South from Africa and sold into the Fenchler family, ya know. Course the North whupped the South and they made the Constitution signed. That's why I'm free—here in the west.

In *Death of a Salesman,* Willy tells us that his father lived for many years in Alaska and was an adventurous man. Willy adds: "We've got quite a little streak of self-reliance in our family."

414

Mary, in *Long Day's Journey into Night,* tells us that she was in a convent school for girls when she was young:

At the Convent I had so many friends. Girls whose families lived in lovely homes.

How would *Death of a Salesman* change if Willy's father had been a college professor? How would *Long Day's Journey into Night* change if Mary had gone to a public school?

Now you know the formula. It works for me, and it can work for you. Don't mail out your script until you give it the S-N-A-P-P-E-R test. And after you do so and send it off, begin immediately to think of your next play. Don't wait for the mail. Let your mind work on new ideas. The following test may help get your imagination rolling again. It is not meant to be an indicator of your creativity, but only a vector to point the way to your creative potential.

How's Your I. Q. (Imagination Quotient)?

(Give yourself 5 points for each YES answer. Give yourself 2 points for each SOMETIMES answer.)

1. When I see a person for the first time, I always observe the color of his eyes and hair.
YES   SOMETIMES   NO

2. I like to think about a person's name and how it is appropriate or not appropriate for that person.
YES   SOMETIMES   NO

3. I would definitely laugh (to myself) if I became acquainted with a Japanese man named John Smith.
YES   SOMETIMES   NO

4. When I look at a cloud in the sky, I often see more than just a cloud.
YES   SOMETIMES   NO

5. When I'm observing the behavior of animals, I am often reminded of certain human characteristics.
YES   SOMETIMES   NO

6. If I came across an empty food tray in a cafeteria, I would find it fun to *guess* by the leftovers what kind of person belonged to that tray.
YES   SOMETIMES   NO

7. If a person sits across from me on a bus or train or airplane for any length of time, I like to guess the occupation of that person by his appearance.
YES   SOMETIMES   NO

8. I find it fun to sit in an outdoor restaurant or park bench for long periods of time just to peoplewatch.
YES   SOMETIMES   NO

9. When I go into a person's house, I like to observe how that person added his own personality to the house by means of furniture, art objects, and color scheme.
YES   SOMETIMES   NO

10. If I see a person reading a particular book, I imagine what kind of person he is by the book he is reading.
YES   SOMETIMES   NO

11. If I observe a person carrying a large, wrapped box, I often imagine quite a few things that could be inside that box.
YES   SOMETIMES   NO

12. When someone I don't know is on the phone, I try to imagine what that person is like from the tone of his voice.
YES   SOMETIMES   NO

13. When I am at a large function such as a ball game, concert, or picnic, I often like to strike up a conversation with someone next to me because I find it interesting to know what they are thinking or what they might say to me.
YES   SOMETIMES   NO

14. If I see a movie I really like, I like to imagine what happens to the main character after the movie ends.
YES   SOMETIMES   NO

15. I always see variety in a rainy day. Rainy days are not all alike.
YES   SOMETIMES   NO

16. If I am outside and hear a jet going over, I like to imagine what the inside of the jet looks like and the people on it and what they might be doing at that instant.
YES   SOMETIMES   NO

17. I like to look at other people's picture albums and piece together their lives from the various photos.
YES   SOMETIMES   NO

18. I like to try strange and exotic foods just for the experience.
YES   SOMETIMES   NO

19. Whenever I go through a department store or grocery store, I have a strong desire to "touch" things so that I can feel as well as see objects.
YES   SOMETIMES   NO

20. An interesting smell such as that of perfume or food or flowers can suddenly bring back a memory to me.
YES   SOMETIMES   NO

WHAT IS YOUR IMAGINATION SCORE?

100–80 = Excellent
 79–60 = Very Good
 59–40 = Average
Below 40 = You need to be more observant about ways to improve your imagination.

80

WHY SCREENPLAYS GET REJECTED

By Bill Delaney

ARE THEY really *looking* for scripts in Hollywood?" I don't know how many writers have asked me that question or some variation such as, "Do they really *read* scripts in Hollywood?"

As a free-lance story analyst and script doctor, I have read hundreds of screenplays and treatments, as well as stage plays, novels, biographies, short stories, and all kinds of miscellaneous materials submitted as potential motion picture vehicles. And I can tell you: Yes, they really are looking for scripts and they really do read them. I, for one, read them.

Unfortunately, ninety-nine percent of the material I read ultimately gets "passed," as they say in the studios. The rejects often contain original ideas, clever dialogue, and challenging roles. But still they get passed, and most of the time the poor author is never told why.

The main reason screenwriters get so little feedback is that people in the industry tend to be picture-oriented rather than word-oriented. A publisher or editor may feel obligated or challenged to articulate his impressions; but this is rarely the case with movie people. Then again, the script may get read by the agent's secretary, the producer's girlfriend, or the star's chauffeur, people who, if they don't like a script, are apt to dismiss it with a few monosyllables (e.g., "I don't know, it's just sort of—you know—blah"). Big help!

So I would like to encapsulate here what I know about why scripts get rejected, as well as offer a few modest suggestions and perhaps air a few pet grievances.

No agent

Recently I was talking with an acquaintance who is an experienced writer but not an experienced *screen*writer. He had just finished a treatment of a story tailor-made for comedian Eddie Murphy. I suggested that my acquaintance get an agent, but he had a better idea. He knew someone who worked at the studio where Murphy is currently shooting a picture. That someone had offered to deliver the treatment to Murphy personally. And he did. Eventually it came back in the mail, still sealed in the original envelope, accompanied by a note saying that Murphy could not and would not read unsolicited manuscripts because of the legal problems involved.

Filmmakers are scared to death of lawsuits. That's why it's nearly impossible to get a manuscript read by anyone who counts, without going through an agent. They feel more secure dealing with professionals in their field. Frequently, producers are innocent victims of circumstances. For example, someone submits a screenplay or treatment on Amelia Earhart, and it just happens that the studio is in the process of developing a film about the ill-fated aviatrix. The script is rejected; the author sees a movie that has come out from the studio based on "his" subject and jumps to the conclusion they stole his idea.

Many times producers have paid for a screenplay or treatment they didn't need simply because it was too close to something they already have in the works. Obviously, no one wants to make a hit picture and then have some stranger tie up the receipts in court claiming the whole thing was based on his idea.

It's really not that hard to get an agent—if you have anything worth offering. This is a fact. The big agents are hard to approach, but there are smaller agents looking for new writers, and others are starting up all the time. Many are competent people who have broken away from bigger agencies. You can get a list of approved agents by mailing one dollar to Writers Guild of America West, Inc., 8955 Beverly Blvd., Los Angeles, CA 90048. (No SASE required.) The list indicates which agents will look at unsolicited material.

It's best to start with a query letter describing your script. And, if you're a newcomer, it should definitely be a completed script you are offering, not a treatment or a synopsis or a raw idea. You should do a mass mailing of your query in order to save time, because you'll be lucky to get a ten percent response. But if you write an intelligent letter and have a story with a chance of interesting a mass audience, you will get positive responses, because agents and producers are really and truly looking for movie material out here. In fact, that's all they ever talk about.

419

Be prepared to spend money on photocopies and postage. You'll need lots of copies of your script. It should, of course, be neatly typed and look thoroughly professional. Don't go overboard on camera instructions: just establish the scene and tell what the people say and do. The length should be very close to 120 pages, without being obviously stretched or squeezed by the typist. (There are plenty of good books on all of this, so I won't rehash it.)

Don't expect to get any of your scripts back. There's no point in including a stamped return envelope, because agents and producers rarely operate like Eastern book and magazine publishers. This is the Wild West out here. They may even take the brass doohickies out of your script and make photocopies of the photocopies to pass around. What protection do you have against your work getting stolen? That's kind of a broad question. Standard practice is to register the work with Writers Guild of America West, Inc. (same address as above) for $10 to non-members. This is to prove what you wrote and when you wrote it, in case you end up suing somebody—or vice versa. Producers would rather buy than steal, because they don't want even to *think* about lawsuits. Furthermore, they don't really feel they own a script unless they buy it; somebody might steal it from *them*.

When you finally get an agent, you should of course be loyal and give him a chance to prove his worth. You should also provide him with plenty of copies of your script to encourage him to send them out. He probably won't mind if you submit copies on your own, as long as you indicate on the front page that he is your representative.

Not cinematic

Unfortunately, a lot of the scripts agents receive are unsalable. I see too many that look like stage plays with a face-lift. Typically, these offerings call for a few indoor sets and tell the entire story through dialogue. Hollywood producers want scripts that *show* the story, not tell it. They hate what they call "talking heads"—that is, long-winded scenes in which the characters do nothing but yak at each other. The motion picture medium brings the viewer up close; that's what's so exciting and challenging for the writer. The viewer can see the gesture or look that tells everything. This seems to be the hardest single thing for aspiring screenwriters to grasp—and many never do.

A good example of talking heads is the kind of scene weak writers

420

really lean on in mediocre thrillers. They usually start with a good opener. A young woman, let us say, is walking down a deserted street. She hears footsteps. She walks faster. Suddenly she is confronted by a towering figure wrapped in an ulster. He's got a knife! She screams. Fade out. Enter the talking heads. We are in the police captain's office. He has a city map on the wall and is holding (so help me!) a pointer. He tells the hero: "For the past six months a homicidal maniac has been operating in our city. He has struck eight times, always in a different place. The crosses on the map indicate where the victims were found . . ." and on and on. It may be hard to avoid some of this, but more than a little is much too much. It is the kiss of death for many a screenplay, because it shows the author didn't understand writing for movies.

Alfred Hitchcock said that a good motion picture is one you could follow if the soundtrack were turned *off.* He felt there should be dialogue in movies because people do talk to each other, but that the dialogue should always be incidental. His opinion represents the dominant philosophy in contemporary filmmaking. As the great French director Francois Truffaut put it: "Whatever is *said* instead of *shown* is lost upon the viewer."

No third act

Every so often a reader gets hold of a screenplay that starts with a great idea and moves along at an exciting clip until he begins to think, "Wow! I've got a winner here!" And then around page 50 or 60, it falters and fizzles like a rocket that has run out of fuel. Why does this happen so often? There have been many books devoted to answering this question—and I might mention that the best I have ever read is *The Art of Dramatic Writing* by Lajos Egri. Essentially, a good motion picture story has a strong protagonist struggling with an equally strong antagonist over some "bone of contention," also known as a "MacGuffin." If a story fizzles, it usually does so because of one of a very limited number of basic dramatic flaws. Either the protagonist and antagonist are not evenly matched or not equally motivated, or the MacGuffin isn't adequate to justify their alleged motivations. If the protagonist is stronger than the antagonist or vice versa, you can guess who is going to win, and there is no suspense. A weak MacGuffin is frequently the fatal flaw in an unsatisfactory screenplay. You just can't

421

believe the principals would go to such trouble (including murder, risking prison, etc.), when you know you would behave differently in the same situation.

Writers who find themselves stuck with a de-escalating conflict often try to disguise the fact by writing a slam-bang finale that means little or nothing in the context of the story. Typically, this will consist of a chase or shoot-out or an explosion. Or else the sunbeam falls directly on the idol's eye precisely at dawn on Groundhog Day, and the temple crashes as the volcano erupts and the island submerges. These and related gimmicks won't get the scriptreader's blood pounding. They are a dead giveaway that the story is a bust because of something basically wrong with its conception.

A movie that could serve as a textbook model of outstanding dramatic construction is *Kramer vs. Kramer,* starring Dustin Hoffman and Meryl Streep. Here we have an estranged husband and wife fighting over custody of an adorable little blond MacGuffin. Mr. Kramer has a strong moral right to keep the boy because Ms. Kramer deserted both of them. However, she is the boy's mother, and how can anyone take a small child away from his mother? You can't foresee how this conflict will end, and the tension has to escalate because neither party will give in. They *can't* give in, because their love for the little boy is too strong. It's a primal motivation, and primal motivations are what make strong stories in books, magazines, or on the screen.

It's not unusual for a writer to get as much as $150,000 for his first screenplay. That kind of money naturally spurs competition. (Recently, in a single year, approximately 19,000 screenplays and related materials were registered with Writers Guild America West.) But a lot of the competition only *looks* like competition, a lot of scripts only *look* like scripts. When you look closer, you find they are full of sound and fury signifying nothing. Naturally, established writers have an edge, but they're only established because they work hard and have taken the trouble to learn how to turn out a solid product.

The best advice I could give a person who wants to write for Hollywood is this: Don't hold back. Give them your best, not your second-best. Don't send them a diamond in the rough; send them the diamond all cut and polished. Don't be paranoid about someone stealing your idea. Ideas are a dime a dozen. It is characterization and dramatic structure that are in short supply, and these are hard to steal.

And finally, it should be pretty common knowledge that everybody is looking for screenplays that will appeal to a youthful audience, because the overwhelming majority of the moviegoers and popcorn-buyers are under twenty-five. What interests a youthful audience? That's the question everyone in Hollywood is asking. The answer may be worth millions.

EPILOGUE

THE MOVIES have been one of the most important phenomena, if not *the* most important phenomenon, of our century. They have influenced all creative writers whether they know it or not. I believe there are many writers who would feel liberated if they switched from short stories and novels to screenplays because they could forget about long-winded descriptions of the weather and the landscape and all the "he saids" and "she saids" and other apparatus of fiction writing. The technical aspect of screenwriting is not hard to master; it is much easier than writing prose fiction. All you have to do is imagine people interacting. The writer rarely has to worry about things like close-ups and various kinds of camera angles. Scriptwriting has evolved radically in the past fifty years and has become very streamlined. The script the producer buys is not a "shooting script" but what might be called a "reading script," customarily referred to as a "first draft"—just something that allows the reader to visualize the story.

I believe that many writers are scared away from screenwriting because they think the technical aspects are overwhelming, when they can actually be learned in ten minutes. Motion picture making is, of course, a group effort, and the inexperienced writer may think he is responsible for a lot of details that are actually the province of the director, the cameraman, the wardrobe department, the music composer, or somebody else. It isn't easy to sell a screenplay for $150,000, but it isn't easy to sell a novel for $150,000, either. It isn't easy to sell *ten* novels for $150,000. A writer may work on a novel for years and end up getting a $1,500 advance and never see another cent.

Everybody is becoming picture-oriented rather than word-oriented. Schools and businesses are turning to audio-visual instruction more and more, because they really have no choice. Even if a writer cannot sell a movie script for $150,000, there are all kinds of training films

423

being made, as well as commercials and PR films. All of these require scripts. A lot of them get made in Hollywood, but others are being shot in all major cities.

Even if a fiction writer has no interest in writing for the movies, I'm sure there are very few who would object to having their work picked up for film adaptation. Which suggests that even prose fiction writers should have some knowledge of screenwriting. I wouldn't want to give the impression that it is easy, but I would like to convey my belief that it is a great deal easier than many people seem to think. If more good writers turned their attention and talent to writing screenplays, there would be more good movies and less trash.

81

CREATING TELEVISION STORIES AND CHARACTERS

By Stewart Bronfeld

CREATING stories and the characters in them is what script writing is really all about. The rest — the technology, the business, the timing and the luck—are also found in a thousand other activities of life. But when, in the matrix of a blank page, a story starts to emerge which never before existed, and characters are born and develop who never lived before that moment, something very special is happening. It is part craft, part art and (there's no other word) part magic.

The magic of the creative process remains basically mysterious, like any other kind of birth. The art is a product of the artist's personality and thus differs with each person. But the craft is based on experience, common sense and professional techniques and *can* be learned and practiced.

Principles and rules and fashions of playcraft change but one bedrock truth remains constant: *the basis of effective drama is conflict.* Learn this and you learn a lot. Sophocles knew it. Shakespeare knew it. And the writer of the script for that popular TV series you saw last Tuesday knew it. The conflict of man against man, man against woman, man against nature, man against himself—the clang of two opposing forces coming against each other makes for drama. The conflict may be Big and Important—the numberless masses tearing down the mighty regime of the Czar in *Dr. Zhivago*. Or it may be small and wistful—a fat, homely butcher and a plain neighborhood girl making a clumsy grab at a chance for love in *Marty*.

Consider one of the most successful motion pictures of all time, *Gone With the Wind*. Along with her skill for recreating a colorful time and place and sheer storytelling art, Margaret Mitchell built her story with such effective dramatic conflicts that both the book and the movie are still very much alive (and making money) today. While the Civil

War itself was not directly one of the conflicts (for conflict implies two opposing forces and the North almost never appears in her work), it served as a suitable backdrop for the interplays of strong dramatic conflicts with which the author fashioned her story and characters:

The Old South versus the emerging reality of a new and different world.

Rhett Butler, who could have any woman he wanted—*except* the one he wanted most.

Scarlett O'Hara, beautiful enough to attract any man *she* wanted—except the one she wanted most.

Ashley Wilkes, torn between wanting Scarlett and needing Melanie.

These characters, with their frustrations and longings, could have become no more than soap opera figures— just as *Macbeth* could have become no more than a murder melodrama. The difference, in both cases, was that the authors had the gift of imparting life to their characters and meaning to their conflicts. Thus audiences *cared;* they still do.

Examine any good story and you will discover the conflict that motivates the main character(s) and moves the plot along. One of Somerset Maugham's most enduring stories is *Of Human Bondage,* whose very title highlights the conflict of the young surgeon fighting against his imprisoning love for a worthless girl. But just as enduring, if not as deep, are Laura Lee Hope's children's books about the Bobbsey Twins, each of which gets the kids into some conflict which, happily, is resolved in the final pages.

Sometimes if you look carefully you find the same basic conflict in widely different stories. In *Tom Sawyer,* it is wanting to be good to a loved one (Aunt Polly) versus the pull of adventure with wilder companions. The same conflict (in a dog instead of a boy) is the basis for the drama in *The Call of the Wild.* And, in essence, nearly the same conflict is at the heart of the story of the opera *Carmen.*

The knowledge that conflict makes for drama is a nuts-and-bolts tool which writers can use—especially when they sit at their writing desk caught up in a conflict of their own, namely, "I've got a rough idea of a plot but I don't know what to do with it." First, *think of the plot in terms of the conflict or conflicts involved.* If you cannot identify any, you probably do not have the basis for a very strong story idea. This in itself is an accomplishment, for it can save hours of work, reams of paper and pangs of disappointment later.

426

What contributes drama to the plot is not the conflict itself, but rather what the character does and how he or she does it in response to that conflict. People are naturally more interested in people than they are in circumstances. What engages their attention is not so much the adventure as the adventurer, not the danger so much as how the people react to what is menacing them, not the surprise ending, but how the characters in the story are affected by, and respond to, the surprise.

This simple but fundamental fact that people are primarily interested in people is the basis for another important tool of scriptcraft: *characterization*, the development in a character of specific personality traits. Examine most successful movies and television series and you will find they often have one thing in common: a well-drawn central character (or characters) whose personality traits are clearly defined. These traits may be good ones or bad ones, but they are distinctive. Early in a movie, over the weeks in a TV series, these characteristics become familiar to the viewer. They add a dimension of depth and reality to the character. Another (and perhaps paramount) reason for the enduring success of *Gone With the Wind* is the author's skillful use of characterization; Rhett Butler and Scarlett O'Hara were so vividly conceived and depicted that millions of readers and viewers have found it impossible to believe they are not real people.

On television, the mortality rate of new programs is appalling. Not many new shows survive a season's journey through the ratings mine field. Half-hour comedies are especially popular with viewers, and so smoke pours out the stacks of the Hollywood fun factories day and night as they churn out an endless assembly line of new shows, in which "wacky" characters do "wacky" things—and get "wacky" ratings and disappear. Sometimes, before they expire, they are desperately switched from one time slot to another, scrambling around the network's program schedule like escaped hamsters.

Why do so few of them take root and prosper? The answer, I think, is that they are sitcoms, or situation comedies—which means their emphasis is on ever-zanier "situations," with the people in them seldom developed beyond the cartoon character stage. But there *are* half-hour comedies that become popular successes with longtime runs and high ratings. While they also may be called sitcoms in the trade, these shows might be more accurately called "charcoms," for their humor

427

comes not from artificially contrived "situations," but from artfully created characterization.

Among them was one of the most successful television series of all time, *The Mary Tyler Moore Show,* which ended only because the star grew tired of the weekly grind. The program immediately became a top success on the rerun circuit and established something of a record for the price paid for syndication rights. The secret of the show's success was clearly the effective characterization established by the original creators and skillfully followed by all the subsequent script writers. The funny situations almost always resulted from, or were related to, the regular cast's character traits, which were familiar to every viewer. Proof of the power of good characterization is the fact that no less than three of the show's characters were spun off into successful series of their own: Rhoda, Phyllis and Lou Grant.

What makes this kind of "charcom" so successful is also what makes many dramatic series attain great popularity while their competition regularly arrives and departs. This includes action-adventure shows. *Kojak,* for example, was a tremendous hit, and still is, in its syndication afterlife. But *Kojak* was never really about cops-and-robbers and drug busts; it was primarily about Lieutenant Theo Kojak.

Therefore, whether you are writing a script for a television series, a single original teleplay or a movie, a prime factor to consider is the importance of character creation. Even when you feel your plot is the paramount consideration in a particular script, your characters should never be mere puppets manipulated to suit it. It does not always take a full-scale portrait to make a character come alive; sometimes a few well drawn strokes can do it.

The best and strongest plots, however, are those that evolve naturally, even inevitably, out of the characterization. These stories have more impact, because they are more believable. There is good reason for this. In the lives of most of us, very few important things happen for totally external reasons; what happens to us is often the result of what we do—and what we do is often the result of what we are. That is true of you and me and your potential viewers. If it is also true of your characters in what you make happen to them, they will be perceived not as concoctions, but as living characters with a dimension of depth and reality. Thus your story will not merely gain the attention of the audience; it will make some impact upon them. There's a difference; it means they will *care* about what they are watching. And, as producers, directors and story editors well know, when an audience feels an involvement, it shows in the ratings and at the box office.

Let us see an example of plot developing out of characterization. Jane is a timid young woman, terrified of asserting herself, due in large part to her overbearing mother. She is constantly driven to gain her mother's approval, seldom succeeding. A situation arises at work wherein problems are causing the company's management to consider going out of business. Jane, who has a keen and analytic mind, has diagnosed the problems and feels she has a solution that may save the company. The frantic meetings of the managers behind closed doors are getting louder each day.

Conflict: Jane's desire to offer her solution, thus possibly becoming a heroine, getting her reward and making her mother proud of her— versus her inability to push herself into the councils of upper management and possibly be rebuffed and humiliated. It's not *Hamlet,* but it is the basis for an interesting human drama with which the audience can identify.

The point is that the characterization I created for Jane does not function merely as a kind of outer garment she wears as she makes her way through the plot; the plot evolves directly out of her characterization. If I changed the kind of person Jane is, my plot would no longer work. The two—characterization and plot—are welded together.

Some writers may have an intuitive ability to create a fully defined character as they go along; however, it cannot hurt (and will always help) to write a detailed sketch or profile of any major character first. Creatively, the more you "know" about a character the more you contribute to his or her reality in the script. Practically, facets of the character's personality will often strongly suggest plot ideas. (When one of my characters is especially well defined, I occasionally become aware that he or she is really writing the scene, while I follow along at the typewriter, interested and even curious to find out what will happen next.)

However, writers do vary in both their skill and their inclination for characterization. For some writers, formulating a plot is paramount, and the people caught up in the action are merely vehicles to advance the story line. Obviously, if a plot is compelling enough, viewers will be interested in what is happening even though they are not particularly interested in those to whom it happens. Many movies and television series attest to this. While I believe a more memorable story will evolve out of characterization, I would much rather see a script with an intriguing plot moving at a well-orchestrated pace even though with cardboard characters, than one with vividly sketched characters whose personalities are fascinating, but *nothing really happens.*

There is a test the script writer should apply to his or her work as it proceeds to be sure that there is a consistent plausibility to the characters and the plot. The test is *motivation.* Motivation makes the difference between actions seeming real or staged. People are not robots; they generally do what they do for a reason. Sensible people act from sensible reasons and fools act from foolish reasons. The writer looks at each action of the main characters and asks, "Would this particular person do this, in this particular circumstance?"

The movies of the thirties and forties, mostly ground out by writers on a weekly salary, were often written as fast as they were typed, and frequently had no time to bother with motivation. Now they live on mainly at 2:30 A.M. on television and there is a reliable way to identify them in the TV listings: the word *decides.* "An heiress decides to run off with her gardener . . ." "A millionaire decides to take a slum kid into his household . . ." Whenever you see the word *decides* in a movie listing, you know that the only motivation involved is that it was Thursday and the script was due in the producer's office by Friday. When you look over your script after a cooling-off period, try to be objective enough to note whether your character "decides" to do something just because, solely for plot purposes, you want him to. If he does, if proper motivation is lacking, it is a sign that the scene (or possibly a larger segment of the script) requires rethinking and rewriting.

There is another element in any kind of story, one not so susceptible to definite guidelines. I refer to *theme.* Writers generally are writers because they have an inclination (or perhaps an impulsion) to communicate. But the reason any individual writes any particular story must vary, not only with each writer but with each story he or she writes. We all have different interests, different outlooks on life and different matters we consider important; if these motivate us when we sit down to do our communicating—our writing—our work will reflect a theme.

430

In a story, plot is what happens. Theme is the larger framework of meaning in which it happens. Larger stories have larger themes, and lesser stories have lesser themes. In the powerfully written and expansively produced *The Godfather,* the theme was that evil is self-consuming. In a program I saw last night in a half-hour comedy series, the theme was the importance of good friends later in life.

Do not confuse a theme with a "message." The writer should not be trying to make a commentary on his or her theme, only to *air* it. Reflection on the meaning should rest with the viewer.

Do all writers have themes for their stories? The answer is, not all the time (and not always consciously). But a theme is an asset to any literary work. First, it elevates the story because there is some central meaning to it all. Then, it assures a better, more unified construction to the script, for it provides a general reference point to guide the direction of the plot and the development of the characters.

Herman Melville wrote, "To produce a mighty book, you must choose a mighty theme." You will find, however, that when it happens, it is more as though the mighty theme chose *you.*

82

GUIDELINES FOR
THE BEGINNING PLAYWRIGHT

By Louis E. Catron

YEARS OF teaching playwriting probably have been more educational for me than for my students. Several hundred young playwrights have taken one or more of my classes since I first started teaching at the College of William and Mary in 1966, and they have taught me that writing a play can be simplified—maybe not made "easy," but certainly "easier"—if certain boundaries are imposed.

We began experimenting with guidelines because so many playwrights were expending too much creative energy chasing nonproductive fireflies. We found that these limitations help playwrights over difficult hurdles. More, they are highly important for the overall learning process.

To be sure, for some writers the very idea of imposed limits appears to be a contradiction in significant terms. How, they ask, can I do creative writing if you fence me in?

Their objections have merit. Limitations often inhibit the creative mind, and many creative people expend a great deal of effort seeking clever ways of circumventing the rules. Certainly I've had students react to the guidelines with the fervor of a bull to a red flag and we've had to arm wrestle about the rules.

Nonetheless, imposition of limitations is a way of life in all creative arts. Theatre is no exception. As a play director, for example, I have found that one key portion of my job is establishing parameters of character for actors, holding these walls tightly in place during rehearsals, and encouraging the performers to create depth within those limitations.

We're talking about the contrast between the casual and sloppy meandering of a Mississippi River versus a tightly confined Colorado. The former changes directions so often that it confuses even experienced riverboat captains, but the latter is held so tightly in direction that it cuts the Grand Canyon. Discipline is essential for the creation of beauty.

432

The beginning playwright is encouraged to accept the following guidelines to write his or her first play. Later plays can be more free. Indeed, deliberately breaking selected guidelines later will help you better understand the nature of dramatic writing. For now, however, let these guidelines help you in your initial steps toward learning the art and craft of playwriting.

1. *Start with a one-act play.* A full-length play isn't merely three times longer and therefore only three times more difficult. And that a one-act is simpler doesn't mean it is insignificant. The one-act play can be exciting and vibrantly alive, as has been shown by plays such as *No Exit* (Sartre), *Zoo Story* (Albee), *The Maids* (Genet), *the Dumb Waiter* (Pinter) and *The Madness of Lady Bright* (Wilson).

Starting with the one-act lets the writer begin with a canvas that is easily seen at a glance, instead of a mural that covers such a huge space perception doesn't grasp it all.

The one-act typically has only a few characters, is an examination of a single dramatic incident, and runs about half an hour in length. It usually stays within one time frame and one place. Because there are fewer complexities, you'll be able to focus more upon the actual writing, and you'll have less concern about a number of stage problems which come with full-length plays.

2. *Write about something you care about.* Writing manuals usually tell the beginner to write "about what you know best." I think that can lead a beginner to think in terms of daily, mundane events. Better, I believe, is for the beginner to *care;* if the playwright is involved with the subject, that interest will pull an audience along.

3. *Conflict is essential to drama.* Quibble me no quibbles about plays which may not have conflict. For *your* first play, there should be conflict. Drama is the art of the showdown. Force must be opposed by force, person (or group) by person (or group), desire by desire.

If there's no conflict, the dramatic qualities are lost. The result may still hold the stage, but the odds against it are increased. More important, even if the one-act has no conflict and yet holds the stage, the playwright hasn't learned that all-significant lesson about showing conflict. You'll want to know that when you write more.

4. *Let there be emotion.* People *care,* in your first play, I hope; people feel strongly, whether it is love or hate, happiness or despair. If you are able to get them emotional, your characters more than likely are going to be active and going somewhere. The audience will care more about emotional people than those dull-eyed, unfeeling dramatic deadbeats.

5. *Stay within the "realistic" mode.* Realism deals with contemporary people, the sort who might live next door, in their contemporary activities, and with selective use of ordinary speech. It avoids the aside and the soliloquy. It is quite comfortable inside the traditional box set. Realism is selective, and sometimes critical, in its presentation of objective facts.

Realism is the familiar mode you've seen most often: it dominates television, and only a handful of movies break away from realism. No doubt you've also seen it on stage more than any other mode. Because you know it best, your first play will be easier to write if you stay in realism. Expressionism, absurdism, symbolism, epic: avoid these for your first experience with playwriting.

(Examples of realism would be full-length plays like *Ghosts* or *A Doll's House,* both by Ibsen, or one-acts like *Ile* and other sea plays by O'Neill. More recent plays tend to be eclectic—primarily but not totally realistic, like the full-length *Death of a Salesman,* by Arthur Miller, or the one-act *Gnadiges Fraulein* by Tennessee Williams.)

6. *Limit the number of characters.* Too many characters and you may lose some: they'll be on stage but saying and doing nothing, so you'll send them off to make dinner or fix the car while you focus on the remaining characters you like better. Consider eliminating those who are dead.

Strenuously avoid "utilitarian" characters—those people who make minor announcements (in older drawing-room plays they say little more than, "Dinner is served"), or deliver packages or messages (Western Union's delivery boy, remember, is as much a relic as the butler). Such characters tend to be flat and no fun for playwright, performer or audience.

Some utilitarians are confidants, on stage to serve as ears so the protagonist will be able to speak inner thoughts without resorting to the soliloquy. The confidant in this sort of case turns out to be about as vital as a wooden listening post.

Confidants, by the way, are easily recognized: their faces are covered with a huge question mark. They seem to be asking questions eternally, without any apparent interest in question or answer. The playwright uses the confidant to get to the answer. If such a person is necessary, let the character be more than a pair of ears.

Just how many characters should be in the play?

Three is a good number for the first play. The triangle is always helpful; three characters allow development of good action and conflict and variety. More, and there's the risk of excess baggage; less, and the characters may quickly become thin and tired.

7. *Keep them all on stage as long as you can.* All too often I've seen plays developing potentially exciting situations, only to be deflated by the exit of a prime character. The audience will feel let down—promised excitement evaporated through the swinging door.

A flurry of activity with entrances and exits is deceptive. There may be a feeling of action but in truth there's only movement of people at the door. The more such business, often the less the drama: in class we begin to comment jokingly about wanting a percentage of the turnstile concession.

The beginning writer needs to learn to keep all characters alive and actively contributing to the play's action. So, then, you need to try to keep them all on stage as long as you possibly can. If you have a character who keeps running out, perhaps he ought to be eliminated.

You needn't invent a supernatural force to keep them in the same room, by the way, although I've seen my student writers come up with fascinating hostage or kidnap situations and locked doors in order to justify keeping everyone present. All of that is clever, but all you need is action that involves all the characters.

8. *No breaks: no scene shifts, no time lapses.* Just as some playwrights have people leaving when stage action is growing, so also are there authors who cut from the forthcoming explosion with a pause to shift scenery or to indicate a passage of time. There is a break in the action and that always is disappointing. Such lapses are all too often barriers to the play's communication with the audience.

If you have in mind a play that takes place first in an apartment, then in a grocery store, then in a subway, you have let the motion pictures overly influence your theatrical concept. It just won't wash, not in a one-act stage play; with so many sets and breaks producers will shy away from your script. (Yes, yes, you can cite this or that exception, but we're talking about a beginner's first play, not a script by someone with an established reputation.)

Reduce the locales to the *one* place where the essential action occurs, and forget the travelogue. So also with the jumps in time: find the *single* prime moment for these events to take place.

Later you can jump freely in time and space, as Miller does so magnificently in *After the Fall*. Your first play, however, needs your concentrated attention on action, not on inventive devices for jumping around through time and space.

9. *Aim for a thirty-minute play.* One-act plays are delightfully free of the restrictions placed upon full lengths, and can run from only a few minutes to well over an hour. The freedom is heady stuff for a beginning writer.

Aim for around half an hour. Less than that and you probably only sketched the characters and action; much longer, and you might exhaust your initial energies (and your audience!). Your goal, of course, is to be sure you achieve adequate amplification; too many beginners start with a play only eight or ten minutes long, and it seems full of holes. Your *concept* should be one that demands around half an hour to be shown.

10. *Start the plot as soon as you can.* Let the exposition, foreshadowing, mood and character follow the beginning of the plot (the point of attack). Get into the action quickly, and let the other elements follow.

11. *Remember the advantage of the protagonist-antagonist structure.* Our era of the anti-hero apparently has removed the protagonist from the stage. Too bad. The protagonist is a very handy character indeed, and the protagonist-antagonist structure automatically brings conflict which, you recall, is essential for drama.

The protagonist is the "good guy," the one with whom we sympathize and/or empathize, the central character of the play. A better definition: *The one whose conscious will is driving to get a goal.* The antagonist stands firmly in the way. Both should be equal forces at the beginning of

436

the play: if one is obviously stronger, the conflict is over quickly and so should the play be.

(If you do not fully understand the personality of a true protagonist, look at Cyrano in Hooker's translation of Edmond Rostand's *Cyrano de Bergerac*. Cyrano is so strongly a conscious will moving actively that it takes several antagonists to balance him.)

12. *Keep speeches short.* Long speeches often grow boring. Sometimes they are didactic; the playwright delivering The Play's Message. Always they drag the tempo. But the worst sin of a long speech is that it means the playwright is thinking just of that one character and all the others are lying about dead.

Short speeches—quick exchanges between characters—on the other hand keep all of them alive and make the play appear to be more crisp and more vital. The play will increase in pace and you'll automatically feel a need to increase the complications.

How long is "short"? Let the dialogue carry but one idea per speech. Or, to give you another answer, let your ear "listen" to the other characters while one is talking, and see who wants to interrupt. A third answer: try to keep the speeches under, say, some twenty words.

One grants the effectiveness of the "Jerry and the Dog" speech in Albee's *Zoo Story*. It makes a nice exception to this guideline. But there are very few such examples, and there are many more examples of plays where the dialogue is rich and effective because the playwright disciplined the talky characters.

13. *Complications are the plot's heartbeat.* John wants Mary. Mary says fine. Her family likes the idea. Her dog likes John. His parrot likes Mary and the dog. So John and Mary get married. They have their 2.8 kids, two cars, a dishwasher, and they remember anniversaries. Happiness.

Interesting? Not very. Dramatic? Hardly.

John wants Mary. Mary is reluctant, wondering if John simply is in love with love. John is angry at the charge. Mary apologizes. John shows full romanticism. Mary worries again. Mary's grandmother advises Mary to take John to see what love really is by visiting Mary's older sis who everyone knows is happy in marriage. Mary and John visit. Sis and her husband Mike are having a violent fight; mental cruelty; damning accusations. Sis gets John to help her and he unwillingly does; Mike pulls John to his side; Mary yells at John for causing trouble.

That's the first ten minutes.

I think you'll grant it has more potential than the first sketch. *Complications* keep it vital, moving, alive. *A play depends upon conflict for its dramatic effect, and complications are the active subdivision of the basic conflict.*

So, then: the traditional baker's dozen—thirteen guidelines which will help you with your first play. They will help you avoid pitfalls which have lamed so many playwrights, and they will give you a basic learning experience which will help you with future plays.

83

HOW TO SELL YOUR TELEVISION SCRIPT

By Richard A. Blum

Marketing a television script requires strategy, determination, and a realistic understanding of the industry. The marketplace is extremely competitive, and even the best projects written by established professionals might end up on the shelf. Still, an *excellent* original script—submitted to the right person at the right time—might suddenly break through all barriers. The key word is *excellent*. It makes no sense to submit a script unless you feel that it is in the most polished form (even then it will be subject to rewrites), and that it represents the highest calibre of your creative potential. One might think producers are inclined to see the masterpiece lurking behind a rough draft script. More likely, they'll focus on the weaknesses, compare it to top submissions, and generalize about the writer's talents. So, if you feel uncertain about the professional quality of a work, hold off submitting it. Your next work might show you off to better advantage.

Since unsolicited scripts tend to be lost or "misplaced" by production companies, it's a good idea to have a sufficient number of copies. The *minimum* number you will need is three—one for your files, one for submission, and one for inevitable rewrites. More realistically, you'll probably want additional copies for two or three producers, an agent or two, and your own reserve file for unanticipated submissions. Incidentally, fancy covers and title designs are totally unnecessary. Three inexpensive brads can be punched through the left hand margins of the manuscript. Scripts are usually printed or photocopied to avoid the smudged look of carbons.

The Writers Guild

The Writers Guild of America protects writers' rights, and establishes minimum acceptable arrangements for fees, royalties, credits, and so on. You are eligible to join the Guild as soon as you sell your first project to a signatory company (one who has signed an agreement with the Guild). A copy of your contract is automatically filed and you will then be invited to join the membership. Before you sell the new project, you *have* to be a member of the Guild; otherwise, no signatory company can hire you.

The one-time membership fee for Writers Guild of America, West (Los Angeles) is $1,500, plus 1% of yearly earnings as a writer (or $25 quarterly, if you earn less than $1,000 as a writer). The membership fee for Writers Guild of America, East (New York) is $750. Dues are $50 per year, plus 1½% of annual earnings as a writer.

Any writer can register a story, treatment, series format, or script with the Writers Guild of America. The service was set up to help writers establish the completion dates of their work. It doesn't confer statutory rights, but it does supply evidence of authorship which is effective for ten years (and is renewable after that). If you want to register a project, send one copy with the appropriate fee ($15 for nonmembers; $5 for members) to: Writers Guild of America West, Registration Service, 8955 Beverly Blvd., Los Angeles, CA 90048, or Writers Guild of America East, Inc., 555 West 57th Street, New York, NY 10036.

You can also register dramatic or literary material with the U.S. Copyright Office—but most television writers rely on the Writers Guild. The Copyright Office is mainly used for book manuscripts, plays, music or lyrics, which the Writers Guild will not register. For appropriate copyright forms (covering dramatic compositions), write to: Register of Copyrights, Library of Congress, Washington, D.C. 20540.

The release form or waiver

If you have an agent, there is no need to bother with release forms. But if you're going to submit a project without an agent, you'll have to send to the producer or the production company for a release form—or waiver—in advance. (Addresses of selected production companies are listed at the end of this chapter.) Most production companies will return your manuscript without it. The waiver states that you won't sue the production company and that the company has no obligations to you. That may seem unduly harsh, but consider the fact that millions of dollars are spent on fighting plagiarism suits, and that hundreds of ideas are being developed simultaneously and coincidentally by writers, studios, and networks.

The waiver is a form of self-protection for the producer who wants to avoid unwarranted legal action. But it also establishes a clear line of communication between the writer and producer. So rest assured, if legal action is warranted, it can be taken.

The cover letter

When you prepare to send out your project, draft a cover letter that is addressed to a *person* at the studio, network, or production company. If you don't know who is in charge of program development, look it up in the trade papers, or telephone the studio receptionist. If she says, "Mr. So-and-So handles new projects," ask her to *spell* "Mr. So-and-So." That courtesy minimizes the chance of embarrassment, and maximizes the chance that the project will wind up at the right office.

The letter you write should sound professional. There's no need to offer apologies for being an unsold writer, or to suggest that the next draft will be ten times better than this one. If a cover letter starts off with apologies, what incentive is there to read the project?

Here's the tone a cover letter might have:

Dear_____

I've just completed a mini-series called FORTUNES, based on the book by Frank Tavares. I've negotiated all TV and film rights to the property, which is a dramatic adventure series about a family caught in the California Gold Rush. I think you'll find the project suitable for the mini-series genre. It's highly visual in production values and offers unusual opportunities for casting.

I look forward to your reaction. Thank you for your cooperation.

Sincerely,

The letter doesn't say I'm an unsold writer in the midwest or that Frank Tavares is my friend and let me have the rights for a handshake. Nor does it take the opposite route, aggressively asserting that it is the best project the studio will ever read. There's no need for such pretentions. The cover letter sets the stage in a simple and dignified manner. The project will have to speak for itself.

Submitting a script

Independent producers represent the widest span of marketing potential for the free-lance writer. If one producer turns down an idea, there are many others who might still find it fresh and interesting. However, the smaller independent producer is not likely to have the financial resources to compete with the development monies available at the network or studio.

Production companies do have that bargaining power. The distinction between smaller independents and larger production companies is their relative financial stability and current competitive strength on the air-waves. Production companies form and dissolve according to the seasonal marketing trends and network purchases. The more successful production companies have become mini-studios in their own right, with a great number of programs on the air and in development. Some of the more recognizable entities are M. T. M. Enterprises (Mary Tyler Moore), Embassy TV (Norman Lear), and Lorimar Productions (Lee Rich).

The major motion picture studios are in keen competition with production companies. Only six major film studios have aggressive and viable television divisions: Columbia Pictures—TV; Paramount Pictures—TV; Metro-Goldwyn-Mayer (M.G.M.)—TV; 20th Century-Fox—TV; Universal—TV; and Warner Brothers—TV. (Addresses at the end of this chapter.) They represent highly fertile ground for program development; strong deals can be negotiated by agents for the right project.

At the top of the submission ladder is the network oligarchy: ABC, CBS, NBC. Once a project is submitted at this level, there's no turning back. If a project is "passed" (*i.e.*, turned down), it's too late to straddle down the ladder to independent producers. *Their* goal is to bring it back up to the networks (who in turn must sell to the sponsors).

The closer the project comes to the network, the more limited the number of buyers. As the submission moves up the ladder, it faces stiffer competition and fewer alternatives. So you see that the marketplace is highly competitive, although not totally impenetrable. Your submission strategy will depend on knowing the marketplace trends and organizing a campaign to reach the most appropriate people and places.

There's no better way to stay on top of marketing and personnel changes than reading the trade papers—*Daily Variety* (1400 N. Cahuenga Blvd., Hollywood, CA 90028) and the *Hollywood Reporter* (6715 Sunset Blvd., Hollywood CA 90028). The trades reflect the daily

442

pulse of the entertainment industry on the West Coast. Moreover, each paper offers a weekly compilation of production activities ("TV Production Chart," "Films in Production," etc.), which lists companies, addresses, phone numbers, and producers for shows in work. A careful scrutiny of those lists will provide helpful clues to the interests and current activities of independent producers, production companies, and studios.

A similar resource is the "Television Market List," published regularly in the *Writers Guild of America Newsletter* (8955 Beverly Blvd., Los Angeles, CA 90048). It lists all current shows in production or pre-production, and identifies the story consultant or submission contact for each show. The WGA's market list states whether or not a show is "open" for submissions, and whom to contact for assignments. A careful reading of these and other publications, such as *Ross Reports Television* (40–29 27th St., Long Island City, NY 11101), a monthly magazine that lists new television programs and their producers, can help bring you closer to making knowledgeable and practical decisions about marketing your own projects and scripts.

In the network marketplace, you have a choice of submitting a script to a great number of places at the same time or sending it selectively to a few individuals. The specific strategy depends on the needs of the marketplace at the time. You should determine which producers and production companies are particularly interested in the type of project you have developed.

Options, contacts, and pay scales

If a producer is interested in a project he or she will propose a *deal, i.e.,* the basic terms for a contract. If you have no agent, now is the time to get one. *Any* agent will gladly close the deal for the standard 10% commission. An attorney would be equally effective, or if you have an appropriate background, you might want to close the deal yourself. The need for counsel depends on the complexity of the proposed deal, and the counter-proposals you wish to present.

On the basis of your discussions, a *Deal Memo* is drawn up which outlines the basic points of agreement—who owns what, for how long, for how much, with what credits, royalties, rights, and so on. The deal memo is binding, although certain points may be modified if both parties initial it. The *Contract* is based on the terms of the deal memo

443

and is the formal legal document. If you're dealing with a producer who is a signatory to the Writers Guild (most established producers are), the contract will adhere to the terms of the Minimum Basic Agreement (M.B.A.) negotiated by the Writers Guild of America.

A producer can either option your work, purchase it outright, or assign you to write new material. If the property is *optioned*, the producer pays for the right to shop it around (which means the project can be submitted by the producer to a third party, e.g., the network). During the option period, you can't submit the project to anyone else. Typically, option money is relatively small; perhaps $1,500 or $2,500 for a six-month period. But the writer will be paid an additional sum of money if the producer elicits interest and moves the project forward. If the producer fails to exercise the option (*i.e.*, if the option expires), the rights revert back to the writer.

A *Step Deal* is the most common form of agreement between producers and free-lance writers. It sets forth fees and commitments for story and teleplay in several phases. The first step is at the *story* stage. When the writer turns in a treatment, the producer pays for it—at least 30% of the total agreed upon compensation—but the producer does not have to assign that writer to do the script. If the writer *is* retained, the producer exercises the *first draft* option. When that draft of the script is turned in, the writer receives a minimum of 40% of the total agreed upon compensation. Now the producer has the final option—putting the writer to work on the *final draft*. Once that script is received, the writer is entitled to the balance of payment. The *Step Deal* is a form of protection for the producer who can respond to the quality of content, the inviolability of delivery dates, and the acceptability of the project to the networks. It also guarantees the writer that his or her work will be paid for, whether there is a cut-off or a go-ahead on the project.

How to get an agent

A good agent is one with a respectable track record, a prestigious list of clients, and a reputation for fairness in the industry. There is no magical list of good agents, although the Writers Guild does publish a lists of agents who are franchised by the Guild. (Send $1.00 to Writers Guild West, *Attn: Agency List,* 8955 Beverly Blvd., Los Angeles, CA 90048.) Names and addresses of literary and dramatic agents appear in *Literary Market Place* (Bowker), available in most libraries. A list of agents can also be obtained by sending a stamped, self-addressed envelope to Society of Authors' Representatives, 39½ Washington Square South, New York, NY 10012.

If you have no agent representing you, it's difficult to get projects considered by major producers. One of the best ways is to submit your work to an agent who already represents a friend, a professor, a long-lost uncle in the industry. If you are recommended by someone known to the agency, it makes you less of an unknown commodity. If you have no contact, make a list of possible agents for your project, and prioritize them in your submission status file. You might send the project to one top agency for consideration, or to a select number of agencies at the same time.

A brief cover letter might introduce you as a free lancer looking for representation on a specific project. If you don't get a response within six to eight weeks, you can follow up with a phone call or letter, and submit the project to the next agent on your list. Don't be discouraged if you get no response at first; just keep the project active in the field. If the script or presentation is good enough, you might eventually wind up with some positive and encouraging response from the agency.

If an agent is interested in your work, he or she will ask to represent it in the marketplace. If the work sells, the agent is entitled to 10% commission for closing the deal. If the work elicits interest but no sale, you have at least widened your contacts considerably for the next project.

The larger agencies offer an umbrella of power and prestige, but that elusive status is seriously undermined by the sheer size of the agency itself. Many clients inevitably feel lost in an overcrowded stable, and newcomers can hardly break into that race. In contrast, a smaller literary agency provides more personalized service, and is more open to the work of new talent. If you're going to seek representation, the smaller agency is the likely place to go. But don't be fooled by the label "small." Many of these agencies are exceptionally strong and have deliberately limited their client roster to the cream of the crop. In fact, many smaller agents have defected from executive positions at the major agencies. So you'll have to convince them you're the greatest writer since Shakespeare came on the scene—and that your works are even more salable.

How do you prove that you have the talent to be a star talent? It's all in the writing. If your projects look professional, creative, and stylistically effective, you're on the right track. Indeed, you can call yourself a writer. If the artistic content is also marketable and you back it up with determination and know-how, you might just become a *selling* writer. And that is the "bottom line" for success in the television industry.

Networks, Studios and Production Companies

(Note: New submissions should be addressed to the Head of Program Development.)

NETWORKS

ABC-TV
4151 Prospect Ave.
Los Angeles, CA 90027
or, 1330 Ave. of the Americas
New York, NY 10019

CBS-TV
7800 Beverly Blvd.
Los Angeles, CA 90036
or, 51 West 52nd St.
New York, NY 10019

NBC-TV
3000 W. Alameda
Burbank, CA 91523
or, 30 Rockefeller Plaza
New York, NY 10020

MAJOR STUDIOS

Columbia Pictures-TV
3000 Colgems Sq.
Burbank, CA 91505

MGM-TV
10202 W. Washington Blvd.
Culver City, CA 90230

Paramount Pictures-TV
5555 Melrose Ave.
Los Angeles, CA 90038

20th Century Fox-TV
10201 W. Pico Blvd.
Los Angeles, CA 90064

Universal Studios-TV
100 Universal City Plaza
Universal City, CA 91608

Warner Bros.-TV
4000 Warner Blvd.
Burbank, CA 91505

SELECTED INDEPENDENT
PRODUCTION COMPANIES

Embassy Television Corp.
100 Universal City Pl.
Universal City, CA 91608

Lorimar Productions
3970 Overland Ave.
Culver City, CA 90230

M.T.M. Enterprises
4024 Radford Ave.
Studio City, CA 91604

Aaron Spelling Productions
1041 N. Formosa
Los Angeles, CA 90046

84

REMEMBERING HOW IT WAS

By Lois Lowry

I REMEMBER hitting my daughter once. Swatting her right across the seat of her jeans with a wire coat hanger, when she was nine years old.

It was back in the days when little girls still wore dresses to school, and mothers still ironed them. I had ironed a whole week's worth of those cotton, starched, puffed-sleeved horrors, placed them on hangers, and asked her to take them to her room.

And she did. When I entered her room later, I found her sprawled on her bed with a book, and all seven freshly-ironed dresses in a heap on the floor where she had deposited them.

Naturally I swatted her on the behind with the nearest available weapon.

But my point is not confession or absolution. My point is this: recently I mentioned the incident to my daughter—who is now twenty-five and has a child of her own—and asked her if she remembered it.

"*Remember* it?" she replied. "How could I *not* remember the time my own mother beat me unmercifully around the head and shoulders with a blunt instrument?"

Memory, we should bear in mind, is a subjective thing.

It always amazes me when I hear people say, as many do, that they don't remember their own childhood. What time is my doctor's appointment? What was the name of the librarian I met at that last convention? Those things I forget. But childhood? I have only to press the mental key that calls up each year: 1941 (nursery school: I snitched a blue crayon and wrote my name on my cot during naptime; Pearl Harbor, and my father in uniform, letting me try on his major's cap; my green wicker rocking chair; a book about penguins); 1945 (the fourth-grade bully named Gene; the stain on the blanket under my cat after she gave birth to kittens in the attic); 1948 (the green jumper and white blouse I

447

wore, my first day in seventh grade; the three maids giggling together in the kitchen of our Tokyo home; "Kerria Japonica": the room I shared with my sister during a spring vacation in the Fujiya Hotel, where each room was named for a flower).

Each detail appears, and with it come back the emotions. Humiliation, at four, caught stealing a crayon. Anger at Allen, the boy across the street, who borrowed and lost my penguin book. Fear of the boy Gene, who terrorized the fourth grade. Sudden and frightening awareness, watching my cat lick her firstborn litter, that birth involves blood.

For me it is all there, and I can call it back. If that were not so, I could not write for children.

Some years ago, when working on an article about medical hypnosis, I interviewed a doctor who suggested that it would be helpful if he were to hypnotize me. I agreed, and sat there, relaxed, while he talked in a steady voice; I watched, feeling no pain, as he inserted a needle into the back of my hand.

Then he suggested that I would be regressing in age: now fifteen; now ten; now five.

"Now that you are five," his droning voice said, "where do you find yourself? What are you experiencing?"

"In my grandparents' backyard," I said without hesitation. "Barefoot, standing under the big pine tree; I can feel the dry needles under my feet. I can smell my grandmother's roses. I can hear a mourning dove."

"You're a good subject," he said, later. "Wasn't that amazing, how all those sensations came back from the time you were five?"

"But I do that all the time, without hypnosis," I told him. "If I'm writing about a five-year-old, I *remember* being five. And I can feel those pine needles, smell the roses, hear the mourning dove."

"Well," he said huffily, "somehow, then, you've mastered the art of self-hypnosis."

But I don't think it's self-hypnosis at all. For me it is simply memory, a phenomenon with which I seem to be richly endowed. And what a blessing it is for one who chooses to write for kids! Each day, sitting here at work, I call upon it constantly.

Anastasia Krupnik is a character who has now appeared in six of my books and is currently making her way through the manuscript pages of a seventh. She is fictional. She is not me. I never had her freckles, her astigmatism, her family, or what my mother would have referred to as her "smart alec mouth." But I have used my own memories again and again as I have created her and moved her through the incidents that appear on those pages.

Anastasia is ten in the first book, whose title bears her name. Writing it—specifically, writing a scene in her school classroom—I thought back, remembering my own anger at a supposed classroom injustice: for me, it was the day that the drawing of the class mural began. It was to be a mural across one entire wall, depicting a wagon train heading west.

I had looked forward to the mural so. At ten I prided myself on my drawing ability, and I had planned, in my mind, the creation of the stalwart pioneer figures: the gaunt sunbonneted mothers holding babies; the carefree children running beside the covered wagons, loyal dogs at their heels. I would draw a girl my own age, I would even make her look a little like me, skinny and blonde—turning with a look of irritated surprise as a brother pulled at her pigtails.

But my teacher took me aside in the midst of the classroom excitement as the paper was being unrolled and tacked across the wall, the art materials brought from the supply closet.

"You know," she said with a kind smile, "you draw better than anyone else in the class."

Of course I knew. But humility was appropriate, and I hung my head shyly. Inside myself, I glowed.

"And because of that," she went on, "I'm assigning you to the very hardest part of the mural."

A tiny gremlin of suspicion began to gnaw inside me where the glow had been, and I looked up at her.

"I want you to do all eight oxen for us," she explained. "All the children can draw people pretty well. But I know that no one but you will be able to draw oxen."

Oxen? Had I heard her correctly? Yes. Oxen.

And so I obediently, diligently, conscientiously, drew oxen for a week, while the other kids did the people. I researched oxen, practiced oxen, and completed oxen; and even today, forty years later, I'd bet you

449

anything that they were the best-rendered, most anatomically-accurate oxen any ten-year-old ever presented in crayon on a twenty-foot-long strip of white paper.

But oh, how I remember my resentment of the moment. Writing of Anastasia, I recreated not the moment itself, but the emotions of it. I had Anastasia's teacher, Mrs. Westvessel, assign the writing of a poem to her fourth-grade students. I tried to recapture the joy of the assignment:

. . . when Mrs. Westvessel announced one day in the fall that the class would begin writing poetry, Anastasia was the happiest she had ever been in school.
Somewhere, off in a place beyond her own thoughts, Anastasia could hear Mrs. Westvessel's voice. She was reading some poems to the class; she was talking about poetry and how it was made. But Anastasia wasn't really listening. She was listening instead to the words that were appearing in her own head, floating there and arranging themselves into groups, into lines, into poems.

. . . and the bitter disappointment of its outcome:

An F. Anastasia had never had an F in her entire life. She kept looking at the floor. Someone had stepped on a red crayon once; the color was smeared into the floor forever.
"Iworkedveryhardonthatpoem," whispered Anastasia to the floor.
"Speak up, Anastasia."
Anastasia lifted her head and looked Mrs. Westvessel in the eye. "I worked very hard on that poem," she said in a loud, clear voice.

In a later book, Anastasia is twelve. I punched my mental button to the memory section marked "12" and saw myself standing in front of a mirror, yanking a comb through tangled hair which seemed to have taken on, at puberty, characteristics of seaweed marinated in Wesson Oil. And I wrote:

. . . .Vaguely she remembered the fairy tale of Rapunzel, who had been locked in a tower, and who had hung her long hair from the window so that her lover could climb up. That was kind of neat.
But that Anastasia ran her fingers through her own hair, which had begun to be pretty long—halfway down her back—but she realized that it needed washing again. Yuck. If a lover tried to climb her greasy hair, he would slide back down.

Another book, and now she was thirteen. Almost unbidden (because surely I have repressed it; my mother is such a gracious and charming

450

lady now, at eighty) came this memory: me, thirteen, glaring at her as she appeared from her bedroom, dressed to attend a mother/daughter school event with me. I could hear my own voice: "You're not going to wear *that*, are you?" and see her look of surprise and hurt, as she stared down at her best dress. And I wrote:

"Well, I used to like you a whole lot. I thought you were really a neat mother. You used to be fun. But lately—"
"Yes? Go on. Tell me about lately."
"Well, your clothes, for example. They're embarrassing. You always wear jeans. I don't even like to walk beside you on the street because you don't look like a regular mother."

Now about the bludgeoning of my daughter. The details of memory, as I pointed out, are subjective. They are subjective because they depend upon the emotions. If my daughter remembers that I beat her mercilessly with a heavy wooden weapon, it is because she remembers not the weapon (and it *was* a wire hanger) but the overwhelming and terrifying astonishment of being physically attacked by a usually pleasant, soft-spoken mother.

And perhaps my fourth-grade teacher would be able to document that it was only six oxen, not eight; and that she let me draw a couple of people as well.

But in writing, it is not the veracity of the details that matters. As fiction writers, we lie about those anyway. The truth of the feelings is the only essential thing.

If you do not, or cannot remember those feelings, don't fake them; they're too strong, too powerful to be faked even by the best of tricksters at typewriters. And young readers are masters of phoniness-detection.

If your youth doesn't come back for you, call upon yesterday instead. Remember your rage and frustration standing at the Hertz desk in Boise after being told that they have no record of your reservation made three weeks before, and no car either? And then the clerk saying, "Have a nice day"? Use it, that memory. Apply that same pressure-cooker anger to your fictional adolescent who has just been cut from the basketball squad, or grounded for a month by his parents.

I use yesterday's—and this morning's—emotions myself, adding them to the stockpile of those that come from the past. Recently, for a short

451

story called "Splendor," I created two sisters, thirteen- and fourteen-years-old. Writing the scene where the younger has just acquired a very special new dress, I called back the old jealousies that I remembered from my own adolescent relationship with my own older sister, and wrote:

Back upstairs, she hung the dress carefully in her closet, and looked with pleasure at the burst of color it provided there in contrast to the clothes of her ordinary life. Beside it hung an outgrown brown jumper of Angela's, and next to that Angela's old plaid skirt. It was a closet full of leftovers, Becky thought, a *life* full of leftovers—until the dress changed everything.

But for a separate scene, I used other, more recent memories as well. I remembered a very few years back, when my husband, children, and I went every Thanksgiving to the home of a brother and sister-in-law. The sister-in-law was Wonder Woman. She could do anything, and did. Every Thanksgiving there were new accomplishments to admire: a hand-hooked rug, a newly papered room, a promotion in her professional field, a new and faster finish time in the Boston Marathon. Finally, one Thanksgiving, instead of the usual turkey, she had roasted a goose. Helping her clean up after dinner, I removed a pan swimming with goose grease from the oven.

"What would you like me to do with this?" I asked her, holding it carefully so that it wouldn't drip on the vinyl floor which she had, of course, installed herself.

"Why don't you take some of it home with you?" she suggested.

I stood there for quite a while, staring at several quarts of thick yellow grease, before I finally said, "What for? What would I do with it?"

She was hanging up a dish towel. It was probably handwoven. And she replied cheerfully, "Make soap."

I sulked all the way home, two hours by car. Every now and then I muttered, "Make soap."

I didn't. Didn't make soap, that is. And I didn't save the goose grease, either. But I saved the memory. And I used it when the younger sister, Becky, thrilled with her new, expensive dress, feels that same frustrating, antagonistic rivalry.

"Mine only cost ten dollars," Angela said smugly.
"Well, you *made* yours. Not all of us can sew," muttered Becky. Or sing, she

452

thought, or cook, or play the piano, or get all A's in school. Angrily she listed her sister's accomplishments in her mind. "Not all of us are perfect."

I suppose that psychologically, using painful memories fictionally is a way of getting over them. Personally, I think it's a good way of getting even. And pragmatically, it's a nifty way of getting published.

85

THOUGHTS IN THE RABBIT HOLE

By Anne Lindbergh

WHEN my niece was a little girl there were two Willys in her life: One was a friend of her father's, the other a dog. She answered the phone one day when her parents were out, and the voice at the other end instructed her to tell her father that Willy had called. "Willy the man or Willy the dog?" she asked.

The caller was Willy the man, but he could just as well have been Willy the dog, in which case my niece would have given the message unconcernedly except, perhaps, for remarking that it was the first time the dog had called on the phone.

I remember crossing a bridge over the railway tracks of the "Gare de Lyons" in Paris with my son, who lived in that city until he was nine. "What's down there?" he asked. "It's the 'Gare de Lyons'," I told him, "the Lyons station." He examined it carefully before saying, "I think you're wrong. It's a train station."

Small children come up with "cute" sayings all the time. We repeat them to our friends and laugh. They *are* funny, but what makes them funny is the key to a successful children's fantasy: a child's willingness to consider and eventually accept what most adults would reject as a preposterous situation.

I began to use fantasy more and more in writing my books for children as I became better acquainted with children. As a child, I loved reading *Alice in Wonderland, Mary Poppins,* E. Nesbit's trilogy *(The Five Children and It, The Phoenix and the Carpet,* and *The Story of the Amulet),* and later, C. S. Lewis's *The Lion, the Witch, and the Wardrobe,* followed by the further chronicles of Narnia. I read and reread them but didn't stop to ask myself why, or what they had in common. Now, raising my own children, listening to them and their friends, and hearing what children have to say about the books I write, I am beginning to find out.

454

Children have different tastes in their reading, of course, just as adults do. But the children who read the sort of books I used to read like them because they appeal to their credulity and their imagination at the same time. The characters and settings in the stories are familiar: The characters could be the readers themselves, and the stories could take place in their own homes. But the situation that is "impossible" in real life actually occurs in these books. The dog speaks on the telephone, lions are in the station, and the child in the story is only mildly surprised.

When Mary Poppins arrives at number seventeen Cherry-Tree Lane, lifted and blown by the east wind toward a very ordinary family, Michael Banks simply comments, "How funny! I've never seen that happen before!"

My favorite example of a child's accepting the preposterous is Alice. She is sitting outdoors with her sister on a hot day, feeling very sleepy and a little bored. A white rabbit runs by, talking to itself—in English. If Alice had been ten years older, she would have questioned her sanity, looked for the hidden mechanism, or for the ventriloquist. Instead, she decides to follow the rabbit because "it flashed across her mind that she had never before seen a rabbit with either a waistcoat pocket or a watch to take out of it." So down the rabbit hole she goes (a rash action, and one that worried me as a child), but does she leave reality behind when she slides into the dark tunnel? On the contrary, she takes time to inspect a jar of marmalade, consider altitude, longitude, and the distance to the center of the earth, and wonder if her cat, Dinah, will be fed at teatime. The only difference between Alice and today's reader on an ordinary trip is that the reader would be on a plane to California, while Alice was on her way to Wonderland.

The adventures in Wonderland were enthralling, but detached from my own world, and they seemed to function on a whole new set of rules. Who needed new rules? I was quite happy reading how a child differed from me only in that she had hit on a good thing, could bend or break the *existing* rules.

It would be dull if the child who has had the luck to find the rabbit hole, the mirror, or the magic picture, walked through to find a world no different from the one he or she had left behind. A few talking beasts liven things up, but the most endearing aspects of fantasy are usually those that relate to a child's everyday life. The child reader may not remember that Alice ran a caucus race with a mouse, two crabs, a duck, and a dodo, but rarely forgets the contents of Alice's pocket—a box of comfits (just enough to go around as prizes) and a thimble.

From talking to my readers, I have found that the details they relish are found in inventories, rather than in meticulous descriptions. Readers of my first book, *Osprey Island,* like the lists of supplies that Charles, Amy, and Lizzie took through the magic painting to camp on Osprey Island, or the contents of the trash cans in which August rummaged when he followed the rag-bag lady. A fourteen-year-old boy who lived next door, after reading the final version, commented, "It's still an O.K. book, but why did you leave out all those good parts about the food they ate?" He enjoyed reading how it felt and looked to be absorbed into a painting on the wall, and how time played tricks on children who played with magic, but he also wanted to know what Charles, Amy and Lizzie spread on their sandwiches.

Readers cling to familiar details in fantasy because these provide constant reminders that the readers are participating, that if they had the luck to find the magic painting, they would know what to wear, to put into their pockets, and pack for lunch. I think this is the basic difference between the fantasies I liked to read and later write, and the fairy tales that were read to me as a very young child. Seven-league boots and a cloak of invisibility are all very well in the land of giants and dragons, but if you have painted a "window" of a mountain lake on your bedroom wall and step through with the intention of camping there, what you really need are sensible shoes and a warm jacket.

I don't mean to imply that older children become less imaginative. On the contrary, they simply stop being apprentice imaginers who need the entire fantasy worked out for them, and go into practice. Given an invitation to step into the painting, they like to make out their own lists and pack their own knapsacks. For this reason, in the fantasies I write, I use magic primarily as a means, rather than an end. The painting of Osprey Island is a way of carrying my characters, all of whom could be my readers, into a new environment, where they will have to fend for themselves and use their own ingenuity, *without coaching from adults.* The children in *Osprey Island* could easily have been taken by boat to the island in Maine, equipped with tents, sleeping bags, and a collapsible cooking stove, but their parents would have done all the thinking. It wouldn't have been nearly as much fun, either for those children or for the readers.

"Fun" is a key word. Although I would like my readers to work out the practical problems of magic and time travel along with my characters, I believe that fantasy in children's books is primarily entertainment. It shouldn't be mindless entertainment (the reader is quickly bored when it is), but it should be fun.

Many children like to take off into a realm of fantasy and stay there, leaving their everyday lives behind until the end of the story, a little the way adults like to "get away from it all" on a vacation. But my favorite sort of vacation is one in which you stay at home and make short forays to museums and restaurants as if you were a tourist in your own life. That is the way I use fantasy in my books.

My characters travel back and forth—city, country, past, future—but they always keep in touch with home. A friend suggested to me that the children who prefer this treatment of fantasy are the ones who like to keep one foot in the door, and need the reassurance of an easily accessible home base. That may be true, but they are also the children who delight in the idea of flirting with magic and want as many opportunities as possible to do so in a story.

After stealing Mary Poppins's compass on "Bad Tuesday" and summoning North, South, East and West in one fell swoop, Michael Banks ends up in bed with a cup of warm milk. Reassuring, yes, but why not? As a child I wouldn't have bothered to reread the chapter if Michael had gone to the North Pole and stayed there.

In *The Story of the Amulet,* the final book of E. Nesbit's trilogy, the children travel in time as well as in space. First published nearly eighty years ago, this book added a new dimension to the genre: Not only could children go to the four corners of the earth and come safely home without having lost more than a few minutes of their time (there seems to be an unwritten rule in magical excursions that no matter how long you are gone, the hands of the clock have hardly moved when you get back home), but they could now travel into the past and even change it. For both the author and the reader, this was like being given a new toy. In their search for the missing half of the amulet, the children travel to 6,000 B.C., and Robert terrifies an entire Egyptian village with a cap pistol. After a lengthy and nearly disastrous visit, he and his brother and sister tumble back into their own time, where "Old Nurse met them with amazement. 'Well, if I ever did!', she said. 'What's gone wrong? You've soon tired of your picnic.' "

457

This last escapade (I keep wondering if it was inspired by Mark Twain's *A Connecticut Yankee in King Arthur's Court,* published seventeen years earlier, in which the appearance of gunpowder at Camelot creates much the same effect) represents a totally new and delightful way of flirting with magic, one which had since been used again and again by authors of children's fantasies. In *A Swiftly Tilting Planet,* Madeleine L'Engle sends Charles Wallace to "before this planet's Might-Have-Been" and has him work his way up to present time, rearranging events in order to prevent a nuclear disaster. In *The Shadow on the Dial,* the book I am working on now, a brother and sister go back to the beginning of the century and make a few changes to help their great-uncle find his Heart's Desire.

I remember being wildly excited as a child by the possibility of going back to rearrange the past. Ideas rushed into my mind, ranging from preventing Lincoln's assassination to marrying my maternal great-grandfather to someone nicer.

Then there's the future. I have noted that in "my kind" of fantasy, there is relatively little travel into the future. In fact, when there is too much of it, a book crosses the line to science fiction. Here and there in my books, a child has a glimpse of himself as an older child and adult (and usually doesn't like what he sees), but in general he sticks to the past and present. On the other hand, authors have had a wonderful time bringing characters out of the past into *their* future, which is usually the present for the children in the book. In *The Story of the Amulet,* Nesbit brings the Queen of Babylon to early twentieth-century London, where she tries to reclaim her jewelry from a display at the British Museum, and causes quite a disturbance. The author puts the child protagonist in a situation that is terrifying, irresistible, and screamingly funny.

Thinking about these books makes me want to go on a two-week binge and read each one of them over again, along with my other old favorites. Reading any well-loved book—fiction or nonfiction, adult or juvenile—is a little like falling down the rabbit hole or stepping through the arch of the amulet. You travel anywhere, to any time, and come back home for tea. But the story in which a child encounters magic not in outer space or fairyland but on his own street, in his own house, has an appeal that I have never found in other books.

Reading fantasy can be entertainment, escape, or even a form of tranquilizer, but its best side keeps the child alert and constantly on the watch. Few children expect to find a spaceship on the corner to speed them off toward the moons of Jupiter. But there is always a very slight possibility that one day they will open a door and find themselves in another country, or touch the seascape hanging on the wall to discover that the waves are wet and taste of salt.

86

WRITING NONFICTION BOOKS FOR YOUNG READERS

By James Cross Giblin

Where do you get the ideas for your nonfiction books?" is often the first thing I'm asked when I speak to writers. My usual reply is, "From anywhere and everywhere."

I've found a good place to start in the search for ideas is with your own interests and enthusiasms. It also helps if you can make use of personal experience. For example, the idea for my *The Skyscraper Book* (Crowell) really had its beginnings when I was a child, and loved to be taken up to the observation deck of the Terminal Tower, the tallest building in my home city of Cleveland.

Years later, after I moved to New York, I rented an apartment that was just a few blocks away from the Flatiron Building, one of the city's earliest and most striking skyscrapers. No matter how many times I passed the building, I always saw something new when I looked up at the carved decorations on its surface.

Although I had edited many books for children, I'd never thought of writing for a young audience until I was invited to contribute a 500-word essay to *The New York Kid's Book*. I chose the Flatiron Building as my topic because I wanted to find out more about it myself.

That piece led to an expanded magazine article (for *Cricket*) called "Buildings That Scrape the Sky," and then to *The Skyscraper Book*. In the latter I was finally able to tell the story behind Cleveland's Terminal Tower, the skyscraper that had fascinated me forty years earlier.

Besides looking first to your own interests and knowledge, you should also be open to ideas that may come your way by luck or chance. The idea of *Chimney Sweeps* (Crowell) literally came to me out of the blue when I was flying to Oklahoma City on business.

The plane stopped in Chicago and a tall, rangy young man carrying what I thought was a musical instrument case took the seat next to me. We started to talk, and I discovered that the man—whose name was Christopher Curtis—was a chimney sweep, and his case contained samples of the brushes he manufactured at his own small factory in Vermont. He was on his way to Oklahoma City to conduct a seminar for local sweeps on how to clean chimneys more efficiently.

Chris went on to tell me a little about the history of chimney sweeping and its revival as a profession in the last decade, because of the energy crisis. In turn, I told him I was a writer of children's books, and that he'd fired my interest in chimney sweeps as a possible subject.

We exchanged business cards, and a month or so later I wrote to tell him that I'd followed up on the idea and had started researching the book on chimney sweeps. I asked him if he'd be willing to read the manuscript for accuracy. He agreed to do so and volunteered to supply photographs of present-day sweeps that could be used (and were) as illustrations in the book.

According to an old English superstition, it's lucky to meet a chimney sweep. Well, meeting Christopher Curtis was certainly lucky for me!

Evaluating an idea

Once you have an idea for a book, the next step is to decide whether or not it's worth pursuing. The first thing I do is check R. R. Bowker's annual *Subject Guide to Children's Books in Print,* available in the reference department of most libraries, to see what else has been written on the subject. With *Chimney Sweeps,* there was nothing at all. In the case of *The Skyscraper Book,* I discovered that there were several books about *how* skyscrapers are constructed, but none with a focus on *why* and *by whom* they're constructed, which was the angle of the book I wanted to write. There may be many books on a given subject, but if you find a fresh or different slant, there'll probably be room in the market for yours, too.

Another thing to weigh when evaluating an idea is the matter of levels: A subject worth treating in a book usually has more than one. For instance, when I began researching *Chimney Sweeps,* I soon realized that besides the obvious human and social history, the subject also touched on economic and technological history. Weaving those different levels together made the book more interesting to write—and I believe it makes it more interesting for readers also.

461

A third important factor to consider is what age group to write the book for. That decision has to be based on two things: the nature of the subject and a knowledge of the market for children's books. I aimed *Chimney Sweeps* at an older audience, because I felt that the subject required more of a sense of history than younger readers would have. At the same time, I kept the text as simple and compact as possible, because I knew that there's a much greater demand today for children's nonfiction geared to the upper elementary grades than there is for Young Adult nonfiction.

After you've checked out your idea and decided what slant to take with it, and what age group to write for, it's time to begin the research. An entire article could be devoted to research methods alone. The one thing I feel it's safe to say after writing seven books is that each project requires its own approach, and you have to discover it as you go along.

When I was researching *The Scarecrow Book* (Crown, 1980), I came up against one stone wall after another. It seemed no one had ever bothered to write anything about scarecrows. Research became a matter of following up on the skimpiest of clues. For example, a brief mention in a magazine article that the Japanese had a scarecrow god led me to the Orientalia Division of the Library of Congress, where a staff member kindly translated a passage from a Japanese encyclopedia describing the god and its relation to Japanese scarecrows.

The Skyscraper Book presented the opposite problem. There was so much background material available on skyscrapers that I could easily have spent ten years researching the subject and never come to the end. Choices had to be made early on. I settled on the eight or ten New York skyscrapers I wanted to discuss and sought detailed information only on those. I did the same thing with skyscrapers in Chicago and other cities around the country.

Chimney Sweeps opened up the exciting area of primary source material. On a visit to the Economics Division of the New York Public Library, I discovered the yellowing transcripts of early 19th-century British investigations into the deplorable living and working conditions of child sweeps.

Fireworks, Picnics, and Flags: The Story of The Fourth of July Symbols (Clarion) introduced me to the pleasures of on-site research. I had spent two days at beautiful Independence National Historical Park in Philadelphia. I toured Independence Hall, visited the rented rooms nearby where Thomas Jefferson drafted the Declaration of Independence, and watched a group of third-grade youngsters touch the Liberty Bell in its pavilion. I won't soon forget the looks of awe on their faces.

Whenever I go out on a research expedition, I always take along a supply of 4 × 6-inch cards. At the top of each one, I write the subject for handy reference when I file the cards alphabetically in a metal box. I also write the title, author, publisher, and date of the book I'm reading so that I'll have all that information on hand when I compile the bibliography for my book. Then I go on to jot down the facts I think I might be able to use.

I try to check each fact against at least two other sources before including it in the text. Such double-checking can turn up myths that have long passed as truths. For instance, while researching *Fireworks, Picnics, and Flags,* I read two books that said an old bell-ringer sat in the tower of Independence Hall almost all day on July 4, 1776. He was waiting for word that independence had been declared so that he could ring the Liberty Bell.

At last, in late afternoon, a small boy ran up the steps of the tower and shouted, "Ring, Grandfather! Ring for Liberty!" The old man did so at once, letting all of Philadelphia know that America was no longer a British colony. It makes a fine story—but according to the third source I checked, it simply isn't true.

By no means will all of the facts I find appear in the finished book. Only a small part of any author's research shows up in the final manuscript. But I think a reader can feel the presence of the rest beneath the surface, lending substance and authority to the writing.

Picture research

With most of my books, I've gathered the illustrations as well as written the text, and this has led me into the fascinating area of picture research. On *The Scarecrow Book,* for example, I discovered the resources of the Prints and Photographs Division of the Library of Congress, where I located several stunning photographs of Southern scarecrows taken during the 1930s. Later, in a back issue of *Time* magazine, I came across a story about Senji Kataoka, a public relations officer with the Ministry of Agriculture in Tokyo, whose hobby was taking pictures of scarecrows. Over the years, the article said, Mr.

463

Kataoka had photographed more than 2000 examples in the countryside around Tokyo.

I decided to follow up on this lead, remote as it might prove to be. From the Japanese consulate in New York I obtained the address of the Ministry of Agriculture in Tokyo, and wrote Mr. Kataoka there. Six weeks later his answer arrived in neatly printed English, along with eight beautiful color snapshots of scarecrows. I wrote back saying I needed black-and-white photos for the book and Mr. Kataoka immediately mailed me a dozen, four of which were used in the chapter on Japanese scarecrows. Another appeared on the jacket. When I asked Mr. Kataoka how much he wanted for his photos, he said just a copy of the book.

Experiences such as these have taught me several important things about doing picture research. The first is: Never start with commercial photographic agencies. They charge high reproduction fees which are likely to put you in the red if your contract states that you are responsible for paying such costs.

Instead, try non-profit sources like U.S. government agencies, which provide photographs for just the cost of the prints; art and natural history museums, which charge modest fees; and national tourist offices, which will usually give you photographs free of charge, asking only that you credit them as the source.

Other good sources of free photos are the manufacturers of various products. Their public relations departments will be happy to send you high quality photographs of everything from tractors to inflatable vinyl scarecrows in return for an acknowledgment in your book.

Selling

Writers often ask me if they should complete all the research for a nonfiction book before trying to sell the idea to a publisher. That's usually not necessary. However, if you're a beginner you should do enough research to make sure there's sufficient material for a book. Then you'll need to write a full outline and draft one or two sample chapters. After that, you can send query letters to publishers and ask if they'd like to look at your material.

If a publisher is interested, you should be prepared to rewrite your sample chapters several times before being offered a contract. That happened to me with my first book, *The Scarecrow Book,* and looking back now I'm glad it did. For it helped me and my collaborator, Dale Ferguson, to sharpen the focus of that book.

Of course it's different after you become an established author. Then both you and your editors know what you can do, and generally a two- or three-page proposal describing your new book idea will be enough for the publisher to make a decision.

Once you have your contract for the book in hand, you can proceed with the writing of the manuscript. Some authors use electric typewriters, others have turned to word processors. I write longhand in a spiral notebook and mark in the margins the date each passage was drafted. That encourages me as I inch through the notebook, working mainly on Saturdays and Sundays and during vacations from my full-time editorial job.

Achieving a consistent personal voice in a nonfiction book takes me at least three drafts. In the first, I get down the basic material of the paragraph or section. In the second, I make certain the organization is logical and interesting, and I then begin to smooth out those spots where the style of the original research source may be too clearly in evidence. In the third draft, I polish the section until the tone and voice are entirely mine.

After I deliver to the editor the completed manuscript and the illustrations I've gathered, I may heave a sigh of relief. But chances are my work won't be over. The editor may feel that extensive revisions are necessary; sections of the manuscript may have to be reorganized, others rewritten. Perhaps the editor will want me to compile a bibliography, or a glossary of unfamiliar words used in the text.

At last everything is in place, and a year or so later—during which time the manuscript has been copyedited, designed, and set in type— the finished book arrives in the mail. That's an exciting moment, followed by a few anxious weeks as you wait for the first reviews to appear. The verdict of the critics isn't the final one, though. There's yet another stage in the life of any children's book: the reaction of young readers.

Perhaps a boy will come up to me after a library talk and tell me that he was inspired to find out more about the skyscrapers in his city after reading *The Skyscraper Book.* Or a girl will write to say that the chapter on a day in the life of a climbing boy in *Chimney Sweeps* made her cry. It's only then that I know I'm on the way toward achieving my goal—to write lively, accurate, and entertaining books for young people.

465

87

WRITING FOR YOUNG ADULTS

By Norma Fox Mazer

WRITING for young adults today is particularly satisfying. These young people are going through the most intensely felt time of their lives. They are a devoted audience and, once caught by one of your books, they will read all of them and wait impatiently for the next one to appear. To write for this audience, it's not necessary to know their slang or the latest fad. It is important to understand their fears, dreams and hopes, but it is vital to know your *own* point of view: what you, the writer, think, feel, fear, understand and believe. You cannot write a deeply felt, satisfying book without a point of view on your material.

The storyteller brings order to events that in life might be random, purposeless, even meaningless. It's this sense of orderliness and meaning that makes the novel so satisfying. But to create that order, the writer should be aware of certain rhythms and patterns. To begin with, a story needs those simple classic elements: a beginning, a middle, and an ending. Most books have a beginning and an ending of sorts, but a great many fall down in the middle. If the writer flounders, the reader gets the sense of the writer's despair: I've come this far—what do I do now?

There are two things I think will help the new writer. One is to work with a unity of opposites as the foundation for your story—two characters locked together but intent on opposite goals. In my novel *Taking Terri Mueller,* Phil and Terri are father and daughter; that is their essential unity. They are further united by the deep love between them, and this, in turn, is reinforced by their life style, which isolates them from other people. This is the background of the struggle that ensues between them. Terri is determined to know the truth about her past. Phil is equally determined that she should not. There they are, united, unable and unwilling to get away from each other, and wanting completely different things.

466

When you first come up with an idea for a novel, test it by asking yourself a few questions: What is the basic unity? (It does not have to be two people. The unity of a character and an animal, or a character and nature, such as a landslide or a hurricane, is just as valid.) What is the opposition? Can I put the idea of the story into a paragraph that will suggest the unity of opposites? *Taking Terri Mueller* began with a single sentence. "A girl has been kidnapped by her own father."

When a writer works with a powerful unity of opposites, there are scenes that almost demand to be written. Long before I knew how I would develop the story to the point at which a confrontation about Phil's lying takes place between Terri and Phil, I knew that scene had to be written. All I had to do was work my way through the story toward that point. This key scene comes about midway through the novel, when the reader has been fully engaged with Terri's struggles and her father's painful desire to keep her ignorant of the truth.

The second thing I find helpful in writing a novel is to think in threes. Three is a magic number. Human beings respond to threes. A story must rise and fall three times to satisfy the reader. When I'm planning, I often divide the book into three sections. Then each section can also be divided twice into three parts. And in most chapters, there is a threefold rise and fall. Let me give one illustration from the key chapter in *Taking Terri Mueller:*

Terri and her father Phil have a close, affectionate and trusting relationship. Her only other relative is her Aunt Vivian. Now it's time for Aunt Vivian's once-a-year visit, a wonderful event to which Terri looks forward all year.

She wants to make the most of the visit, yet it's marred almost from the beginning. Three things happen. First, Vivian dislikes Nancy, Phil's new girlfriend, creating a strained atmosphere. Secondly, Terri sees a wallet snapshot of her aunt, who is said to have no other family, with two young boys. And finally, Terri overhears a conversation between her father and her aunt that strongly suggests there are secrets between them.

There are other ways to use the rhythm of three. For instance, a working rule of thumb for fixing a character in the reader's mind is to repeat something about that character three times. Although it needn't be a physical characteristic, the obvious and old example is the mole on the nose. Use a bit of subtlety in repeating the detail—certainly don't

467

say it the same way each time—but within the first five or six chapters, working in the "mole" helps the reader visualize the character, especially if the detail can be used to shed light on the character's personality or state of mind.

In a description of Terri, I work on her appearance, but also on her state of mind.

> She was a tall girl with long hair that she sometimes wore in a single braid down her back. . . . She was quiet and watchful and didn't talk a lot, although she liked to talk, especially to her father, with whom she felt she could talk about anything.

The end of that description reveals something much more important than that Terri has long hair: her trust in her father. That he betrayed this trust is one of the central themes of the book. In the next chapter, Nancy thinks Terri is older than she is. Terri says, "You only thought so . . . because I'm tall." Thus, through dialogue, I repeat one of the points of Terri's description. And through narration we also learn that Terri is almost always the tallest girl in her class. But what's important here is not Terri's height, but her emotional maturity. And this is reinforced when Nancy says that it isn't Terri's being tall—but her poise—that made her think Terri was older.

In creating characters, remember that key word—create. You are not making a real human being, but an illusion of a human being. It would be impossible, confusing, and boring to put down on paper all the elements that go into any one actual person. Your job as a writer is to make your readers believe. Therefore, on the one hand your character needs a certain consistency, and on the other hand those very contradictions that are part of being human.

It's good to give your readers a sense of how your characters look, but what's basic are words and actions. What the characters say. What the characters do. I, the author, tell you, the reader, that Terri is a warmhearted girl, but if what you see her do is trip up a little old lady, then you know I'm lying to you. When I'm struggling with a character, I remind myself of the basic dictum: show, don't tell. I wanted to show Terri's longing for a family. Rather than say it, I showed Terri looking at a friend's family snapshots. Terri's interest and eagerness bring home to the reader her underlying sense of isolation and loneliness.

I've been speaking here of the young adult novel, and yet most of the things I'm saying should apply to any novel. Still, the young adult novel stands in a class by itself. Briefly, I'd like to mention what, in general, distinguishes the young adult novel from any other novel.

The first and most obvious point is the age of the protagonist. Nearly always, the main character is going to be a person the same age or slightly older than the people in your audience. In the young adult novel, there tends to be a very close identification between the reader and the protagonist. A reader wrote me recently, "I hope you know your book describes my life." Literally, it couldn't have, since story, setting, and characters were all products of my imagination. Yet this reader believed in the reality of the world I created. To achieve this sense of verisimilitude, when you write you cannot stand above or to one side of the character, you cannot comment as an older, "wiser" adult, but you must see and report the world through your protagonist's eyes. This limitation, more than anything else, makes the difference between a novel written for this audience and one written for an adult audience.

Although it's important to recognize who your audience is, it's simply death to allow a patronizing attitude to creep into your writing. Your readers deserve your best. The one time I focus on the fact that I'm writing for teenagers is in the early stages when I'm searching for the right idea. Clearly, some book ideas are better than others.

I consider this early stage of writing the novel, which is really an almost non-writing stage, the most important. Concept is all. A silly or unimportant concept can mean months of wasted work.

Questions: Is the idea about young people? Is there an opportunity for the characters to work out their own problems and destinies? Is there a chance for consideration of some serious subjects? Is there also a place for the playful scene or character? I like to achieve a balance. Even in *Taking Terri Mueller,* which is about the terribly serious problem of childnapping, there are a few funny scenes with her father, a scattering of amusing dialogues with her girlfriend.

There are rewards in writing for young adults. There is hardly a subject or an idea that can't be tackled. I have written short stories, serious realistic novels, a time fantasy and, in *Taking Terri Mueller,* a mystery.

Perhaps the first real lesson I learned about writing was that not only did I have something to say, but, whether I recognized it or not, it was there, inside me, waiting to be said. I'm convinced this is true for everyone. Each of us has a unique point of view on the world; the struggle is to get in touch with that uniqueness and bring it into our writing.

My method is to write a first draft in which I spill out everything. The inner censor is banished. I do not allow myself to ponder over the "right" word, to search for the felicitous phrase or struggle for the beautifully constructed sentence. For me, a first draft means putting the truth of a story before all else. It means digging down for all those unique, but what-if-no-one-else-agrees-with-me thoughts, bringing them into the light and onto paper.

Then there is your audience. Is there another group of readers who are quite so enthusiastic, who are ready to laugh and cry over your book, who will cheer you on and write to you in droves? What can compare with the thrill of receiving a letter like the one that came in my mail from a girl in Pennsylvania: "Once I began to read about Terri, I could not get my eyes away from the book."

Each time I approach the writing of a new young adult novel I wonder, "Can I do it again? Will I do this story justice? Will I write a book readers will enjoy? What does this story mean? And aren't there enough books in the world already?"

No, not as long as there are readers and writers. Not as long as there are people like me, like you, like all of us who, like the writer Katha Pollitt, believe that we "go to fiction for the revelation of character, the rich presentation of lived life and the daily clutter of things."

470

88

WRITING BIOGRAPHIES FOR CHILDREN

By Gloria Kamen

LAYER BY LAYER, stroke by stroke, the painter builds an image on canvas. A biographer does so with words, creating a portrait that either enhances, distorts, or defines. What both must never lose sight of is the essential character of their subject. It is careful attention to detail that helps do this.

If you are thinking of writing a biography for children, be prepared to go on a treasure hunt for details with special appeal to young readers. They may make the difference between an acceptable book and a *good* one.

Your starting place for research will be the library reference department, with *Books in Print,* which will show at a glance how many books there are on your subject, and when they were published. Then check the shelves for older books in both the adult and children's biography sections. If, as I did when researching the life of Charlie Chaplin, you find several substantial volumes about your subject, it would appear to be simply a matter of editing and condensing to come up with a 70-page children's book. But I was especially interested—and I believed my young readers would be also—in the events of Chaplin's childhood, for it was those events that later shaped his art and had a lot to do with his creation of "the little tramp." Most of the adult biographies about him either concentrated on his rise to fame or went into great detail about his films. But how did Chaplin feel when, for example, his mother was taken to an asylum, leaving him alone to roam the streets of Victorian London? What was it like to be in an orphanage, to be taken out of school to start working at age eight? Chaplin, I discovered, wrote most poignantly about all this in his autobiography. His own words were invaluable when I came to write about his childhood—which brings me to the subject of autobiographies as a primary source of information.

As reference material, autobiographies are extremely useful, *but* be

471

on guard against their pitfalls. Like a painter's self-portrait, an autobiography will tell you as little or as much as the author intended. It is up to you, the writer, to decide on the accuracy of the portrait. To do this, as with paintings or photos, one should compare them with those done by others. Chaplin, in his mid-seventies when he wrote his autobiography, did not have all his facts correct, and, as with most of us, had no desire to confess his faults or explain his failures in print. There were painful periods in his life that he either omitted or dismissed with a sentence. We learn little, for example, of the famous pantomimist's feelings about the introduction of sound to motion pictures, of his anxiety that it might mean the end of his movie career. He merely mentions that there was a seven-year gap in which he couldn't think of a scenario for a new film. *Modern Times,* the hybrid film, half silent, half talking, was his compromise.

When I read Fiorello La Guardia's autobiography, *The Making of an Insurgent,* I was disappointed to find the writing self-conscious and a little dull. Remembering him as the outspoken, wisecracking mayor of the New York City of my childhood, I had expected witty, lively anecdotes and a feisty, sardonic style. It was in the books written by his associates that I found the flavor of the man, who once told a reporter that "he had an obligation to get his facts straight *before* he distorted them." His own self-portrait was entirely misleading.

For my biography of Rudyard Kipling, I took copious notes from his book, *Something About Myself, For My Friends Known and Unknown.* As the title implies, he was trying to present what he considered to be an honest portrait of himself. The facts were there. His feelings and prejudices, on the other hand, could be found elsewhere: in his poetry, his fiction, and in his personal letters. Many of his letters were as free and informal as conversation, and, as such, useful in taking the place of made-up dialogue. Letters, particularly in the 19th century, were a kind of recorded dialogue between friends and family, replaced, alas, in today's world by voices on the telephone.

There was one letter Kipling wrote to his son in boarding school that was clearly meant to both amuse and reprimand him. It was reproduced in toto in the book, *O, Beloved Kids,* and went as follows:

HOW WOOD YU LICK IT IF I ROTE YOU A LETER AL FUL OF
MIS SPELT WURDS? I NO YU KNO KWITE WEL HOWE TO SPEL
ONLI YU WONTE TAIK THE TRUBBLE TO THINCK?

472

As I read it, the stiff-collared, walrus-moustached Kipling turned into a loving and concerned parent for me, and, I hope, for my readers.

How to use dialogue is a chronic problem for biographers, especially if the subject of the biography and those who knew him best are long since dead. If you have a strong commitment to veracity, as I do, there are ways of getting around the use of fake dialogue. Newspaper and magazine interviews may provide direct quotes, as I found, for example, when I discovered a report of Kipling's angry words about small-town small talk in America in an old Vermont newspaper. In his autobiography he recalled his parting words to his nursemaid and Hindu bearer when he left Bombay:

"Come back, baba," said Ayah, daubing her eyes.
"Yes, I will come back and I'll be a burra sahib bahadur," Ruddy answered in Hindi.

It was a touching piece of authentic dialogue that would have been all but impossible for me to make up. Without it, I would have described his departure and his feelings, those shared by any child in similar circumstances. Writing about emotions can be done without putting words in the person's mouth. Readers can accept joy, relief, or anxiety that is wordless. But hold onto those special quotes you come across, which will help enliven your book:

"Please, Ruddy," said Mrs. Kipling, "don't let Trix forget me." Kipling recalled his mother's words on his way to England, unaware that he and his sister, Trix, would not see their parents again for five years.
So each morning (on board ship) Ruddy asked three-year-old Trix, who answered, somewhat puzzled, that she "bemembered Momma."

Set yourself a reasonable limit for completing your research after which writing should begin. By putting your material in chronological order: birth and family, childhood, schooling, young adulthood, etc., you will have the facts ready to jog your memory as you go along. It is only after you begin to write that the gaps in your research will clearly show. Make a note of them, but continue to write while you seek out additional information.

It is easy to say *Begin* . . . but where? How? What should be kept in and what left out? For the writer of adult biographies, this last item may not be as crucial. It becomes primary when you write for children. You cannot indulge in the luxury of wordiness. The "on the one hand, but on the other" style of adult biographers will not do for juveniles. Information must also be made comprehensible and have some relevance to a child. Adult "gossip" of disappointing love affairs, nasty court cases, political squabbles don't belong in the book, unless they carry the story to some new conclusion or give some insight into the personality of the man or woman. I briefly mentioned Kipling's court case with his brother-in-law because it was the main reason for abandoning the house he loved in Vermont and moving to England. But I did not go into Chaplin's affairs or paternity court case.

The writer of juvenile biographies must squarely face the reason he chose that man or that woman as a subject. What will be conveyed through telling his or her life story? I do not mean a flat-out message, but rather the underlying one. The things you stress—courage, talent, persistence—should come through anecdotes, humor, and through glimpses of the person's strengths and shortcomings. It is then that I am most mindful of being a storyteller as well as a biographer, for biographies share many of the characteristics of novels. I like to think of them as novels coming directly from life, but with certain constraints: Characters and events are set out for you and cannot be changed. You are free as any writer, however, to interpret them. Like a novelist, you must breathe life back into your people and events. There were, no doubt, some crises, some resolutions, that made your subject interesting to you.

Keeping in mind the age level of your intended audience, you could begin your story with an event leading to this crisis, especially one happening at the age of your readers. Chaplin is twelve when my book begins. From here I used flashbacks to his infancy and his parents' early marriage. In the case of Kipling, I started the book just before he is to be sent halfway around the world to go to school. Some background on Ruddy's life as a little sahib in India was necessary to show the tremendous wrench this change had on him.

Because eight- to eleven-year-olds are expected to have only a limited knowledge of history or foreign cultures, it is necessary, somewhere along the way, to add the essential background information in your book. It must not slow down the narrative or be placed in indigestible

474

chunks inside the story. Researching this information may lead you to some interesting reading. You may find yourself absorbed in books on the history and religions of India, on Hollywood and the "silent film" era, or on New England fisheries. One thing leads to another, one subject, one idea to another . . . so, write on!

89

CLUES TO THE JUVENILE MYSTERY

By Joan Lowery Nixon

When I see the words 'mystery,' 'secret,' or 'ghost' in the title of a book for children," a librarian once told me, "I automatically order five copies, because I know the books will be read so eagerly they will soon be in shreds."

And when I announced to my family that I thought I'd switch from writing for adults to writing for children, one of my young daughters immediately said, "If you're going to write for children, you have to write a book, and it has to be a mystery!"

What are the magic ingredients of a mystery novel for the eight-to-twelve age group that draw young readers to it? What does a writer need to include in his story so that his readers won't be able to put the book down until they have come to the last page?

In a mystery story the idea is often the starting point. Sometimes this idea can come from a magazine article or news item. I once read an article about artifacts being smuggled out of Mexico that led to research on the subject and eventually to a juvenile mystery novel.

Sometimes the idea can come from experience. When we moved to Corpus Christi, Texas, we found ourselves in the middle of a hurricane. The eye of the storm missed our city, but the force of the rain, wind, and waves caused tremendous damage. The area had been evacuated, but I wondered what someone would have done who couldn't leave—who, for some reason, had been left behind in the confusion. The beach houses could not withstand the force of the storm, or stay intact, but what if high on the hill there stood a stone "castle," strong enough to survive the storm and to shelter its occupants? And what if this castle were known to have as its only occupant a ghost? Out of these questions came my book *The Mystery of Hurricane Castle*.

A study of the New Orleans French Quarter, with its legends of pirate treasure and its modern day fortune-tellers, grew into a mystery novel; and the idea of someone trapped on a cruise ship, or unwilling to leave when the "all ashore" is sounded for guests, because he thinks he has just overheard the plans for a murder, developed into *The Mystery of the Secret Stowaway.*

A mystery novel should give the reader an interesting background that will expand the child's horizons. Phyllis A. Whitney, in her excellent mystery novels for children, has taken her readers to many exciting and unusual foreign settings. But even the author who cannot travel can make a small town on the coast of Maine, or a truck stop in the middle of the Arizona desert, colorful and interesting to the child for whom this too is a new experience.

Deciding upon the main character is the next step in developing the mystery novel. It is his story. He (or she) will have to solve the mystery, and he will go about it in his own individual way.

It is important to make the main characters well-rounded, interesting and actively alive. The children who read the novel will want to identify closely with them and eagerly follow their adventures to the last page. They should have a minor fault or two—something with which children feel familiar. Maybe the boy's in trouble because he can't seem to remember to keep his room tidy, or perhaps the girl's impatient and plunges into things without thinking.

The main character preferably should be twelve or thirteen years old—at the top of this age group. Eight-year-olds will read about older children, but older children do not want to identify with younger children. Plots featuring boys and stories with girls as main characters are equally popular.

Once an editor told me, "Most of the mysteries I get take place during the summer vacation. I'd like to see one in which the main character was going to school." So in *The Mysterious Red Tape Gang,* I placed my main character right in the middle of the school year. His problem with turning in homework on time gave him a character flaw and added some humor to the story.

A little light humor can be a good ingredient in a mystery novel. I learned this lesson when I was writing my first mystery. I read chapters to my children, and my fifth-grade daughter would sometimes say, "It's scary for too long. Put in something funny." What she was telling me, in essence, was to break the mood of suspense occasionally. The author can't, and shouldn't, sustain tension in the story from beginning to end. It should have peaks of suspense and valleys—breathing space, one might say, and natural humor is a good ingredient to use for this purpose.

In order to make the main character more of a "real person," I think it's good to give him a personal problem to handle along with the mystery to solve. For example, in one story I let my character's fear of a neighborhood bully turn to compassion and a tentative attempt at friendship as he began to realize what made this boy behave like a bully. In another, I matched two girls as friends—one who thinks her younger brothers and sisters are a burden, and the other an only child who lives in an adult world. Each girl learns from the other, and each learns to appreciate her own family life.

The story must be told from the main character's viewpoint only, although if there are two characters traveling this mysterious road together—friends, brothers, or sisters—the viewpoint can include them both. You are telling the story through your main character's eyes, and it's important not to have anything happen of which he or she isn't aware. She may see an obvious clue and overlook it, thinking it's not important; or he may sidetrack his efforts, and thereby come closer to danger, thinking something is important that is not; but in either case, it is that main character's story alone and the author of the juvenile mystery must keep this in mind.

As to clues, children love the puzzle in a mystery. They love to find obvious clues which the main character seems to miss. They love to search for clues which the main character has discovered, but the readers haven't figured out. Both types of clues are needed in a mystery, but the hidden clues shouldn't be too well hidden. After the solution of the mystery is reached, at the end of the story, the reader should think, "Of course! I remember that! I should have known it all along!"

Sub-mysteries, which are complications, unexpected scary situations, or new questions raised, should be used throughout the story. They all tie into the main mystery, although some of them can be solved along the way. Each chapter, through action and suspense, moves the mystery closer to its solution, and each chapter should end with something tense or a little frightening—a cliff-hanger ending—so that the reader cannot stop at the end of the chapter, but must read on to see what happens. An example is this chapter ending for *The Mysterious Red Tape Gang:*

Linda Jean grabbed my arm and squeezed so tightly that the pressure of her fingers was painful. "Mike," she whispered, "those men might hurt my father!"
The same thought had occurred to me. I wanted to answer her; but my mouth was dry, and I tried to swallow.
Mr. Hartwell's face looked awful. He was like a trapped animal.
"Mike!" Linda Jean whispered. "You've got to do something!"

Children read for pleasure, not for all the reasons for which adults read—because the book is a best seller, or because one received it as a Christmas present. If a child doesn't like a book, after the first page or two, he puts it down and looks for something else to read.

Therefore, the story should immediately introduce the main character, lead into the mystery as soon as possible, and grab the reader. In the opening paragraphs of *The Mysterious Red Tape Gang,* I set the scene, established the mood of the story, introduced my main character, told something about the other characters who would be important, and gave the first hint of mystery to come:

My father gets excited when he reads the newspaper at the breakfast table. Sometimes a story makes him mad, and he reads it out loud to my mother. And all the time he reads, he keeps pounding his fist on the table.
Once, when his fist was thumping up and down, my little brother, Terry, carefully slid the butter dish over next to my father just to see what would happen. Terry had to clean up the mess, but he said it was worth it.
Sometimes my father reads a story to me, because he says a twelve-year-old boy ought to be aware of what could happen if he fell in with bad companions.
At first I tried to tell him that Jimmy and Tommy Scardino and Leroy Parker weren't bad companions, but I found out it was just better to keep quiet and listen.
"Michael," he said one morning, "listen to this! The crime rate in Los Angeles is rising again! People are being mugged, cars being stolen. A lot of it is being done by kids! Watch out, Michael!"
I nodded. What I had planned to do after school was work on the clubhouse we were building behind our garage, along with Tommy and Jimmy and Leroy. None of us wanted to steal cars. In the first place, it's a crime, and in the second place, we can't drive.

The mystery novel should have plenty of action. The old-fashioned mental detection type of story, with lots of conversation and little

479

action, is out of date even with adult readers. With children it's doubly important to include a great deal of action and excitement in mystery stories.

However, dialogue is important, too. Dialogue not only breaks up a page and makes the story look more inviting in print, but it draws the reader into the story in a way narrative description cannot do. A careful mix of dialogue with lots of action usually results in a fast-paced, suspenseful story.

The ending of a mystery novel is important to the writer, because it's one of the first things he must think about in planning his book. After he has mentally worked out the idea of the mystery, who his main character will be, and how the story will begin, he should decide how it will end. Once this is established, the middle will fit into place, with the clues planted and the direction of the action set. I find it helpful to make an outline, chapter by chapter, so vital clues and important bits of planted information won't be omitted.

A good mystery should always be logical, and the ending should be satisfying. It should never depend on coincidence. The main character must solve the mystery. If it's necessary to bring in adults to help out—such as the police or someone who could give advice—it must be the decision of the main character to do so.

The ending of a mystery novel should satisfy the reader, because it should present an exciting climax. The solution of the mystery should contain all the answers, so a drawn-out explanation of who-did-what-and-why isn't needed. Throughout the story the reader must be given reference points he can remember—well-planted clues. Just a page or two should be used to end the story and tie up all the loose ends concerning the main character's relationship with others in the book.

Stories for the reader of eight to twelve shouldn't be gory or horrifying: characters can be captured or threatened, but description should be kept within the bounds of good sense. The occult can be used in stories for this age, and can be left unexplained, if the author wishes, as the witchcraft in Scott Corbett's *Here Lies the Body*. At the author's whim, ghosts can be explained, or left forever to haunt future generations.

As for the title: Writers should remember the key words for which librarians look and make their titles mysterious or frightening. Some child who wants the pleasure of following a character through a scary adventure will reach for that book.

Mysteries for the readers of grades one to three, who are learning to read, have become increasingly popular with editors. These are "light" mystery novels—not as involved, and not as frightening as mystery novels for older brothers and sisters. The mystery tends to be more of a puzzle to solve than a threatening situation to investigate.

These stories are designed for 42 or 43 pages in a 48-page book. On each page, there are from one to eight lines, with six to eight words to a line. The vocabulary is not controlled, but is kept within the boundaries of common sense as to words a very young reader could read and understand.

As in the mystery for the eight-to-twelve-year-olds, the story opens with action and interest, and immediately introduces the main character. Within the limited number of words, the characters and the stories cannot be written with as much depth; but along with the mystery, the main character's relationship with others can still be shown. The plot should include a surprise kept from the reader, which sustains the suspense.

In *The Secret Box Mystery,* no one can guess what Michael John has brought to school in a box for his science project, even when it gets loose in the room. In *The Mysterious Prowler,* someone leaves a nose print on Jonathan's window, bicycle tracks across his muddy yard, and calls on the phone but won't speak; and Jonathan sets out to discover who the prowler is.

As in the eight-to-twelve novel, the solution of the mystery in books for beginning readers is in the hands of the main character, although he or she is allowed to have a little more help from friends.

90

STORYTELLING: THE OLDEST AND NEWEST ART

By Jane Yolen

SOME time ago I received one of those wonderful letters from a young reader, the kind that are always signed mysteriously "Your fiend." This one had an opening that was an eye-opener. It read:

Dear Miss Yolen:
I was going to write to Enid Blyton or Mark Twain, but I hear they are dead so I am writing to you...

Of course I answered immediately—just in case. After all, I did not want that poor child to think that all the storytellers were dead. Because that was what the three of us—Enid Blyton, Mark Twain, and Miss Yolen—had in common. Not style. Not sense. Not subject. Not "message or moral." The link was clear in the child's mind just as it was in mine. Blyton, Twain, and Yolen. We were all storytellers.

Nowadays most of the storytellers *are* dead. Instead, we are overloaded with moralists and preachers disguised as tale tellers. Our medium has become a message.

So I want to talk to you today about the art of and the heart of storytelling; about tales that begin, go somewhere, and then end in a satisfying manner. Those are the tales that contain their own inner truth that no amount of moralizing can copy. The Chinese, the *New York Times* reported in 1968, were recruiting "an army of proletarian storytellers" who were ordered to fan out into the countryside and "disseminate the thoughts of Chairman Mao." They told the kind of stories that end: "As a result, the evil wind of planting-more-watermelons-for-profit was checked." These tales waste no time in getting their message across. But they are sorry excuses for stories. As Isaac Bashevis Singer has said: "In art, truth that is boring is not true."

Storytelling may be the oldest art. The mother to her child, the hunter to his peers, the survivor to his rescuers, the priestess to her followers, the seer to his petitioners. They did not just report, *they told a tale.* And the better the tale was told, the more it was believed. And the more it was believed, the truer it became. It spoke to the listener because it spoke not just to the ears but to the heart as well.

These same stories speak to us still. And without the story, would the tale's wisdom survive?

The invention of print changed the storyteller's art, gave it visual form. Since we humans are slow learners, it took a while to learn that the eye and ear are different listeners. It took a while to learn the limits and the limitlessness of two kinds of tellers—the author and the illustrator—in tandem. And it has taken us five centuries, dating from Gutenberg, to throw away the tale at last.

Children, the last audience for the storytellers who once entertained all ages, are finding it hard to read the new stories. Their literature today is full of realism without reality, diatribes without delight, information without incantation, and warning without wisdom or wit. And so the children—and the adults they grow into—are no longer reading at all. The disturbing figure I heard only last month is that 48% of the American people read no book at all in the past five years.

And so I dare. I dare to tell tales in the manner of the old story-tellers. I do not simply retell the old tales. I make up my own. I converse with mermaids and monsters and men who can fly, and I teach children to do the same. It is the only kind of teaching I allow in my tales.

What of these stories? There is a form. First, a story has a beginning, an opening, an incipit. Sometimes I will use the old magi-cal words "Once upon a time." Sometimes I vary it to please my own ear:

Once many years ago in a country far to the East....

There was once a plain but goodhearted girl....

In ancient Greece, where the spirits of beautiful women were said to dwell in trees....

Once on the far side of yesterday....

In the time before time, the Rainbow Rider lives....

Once upon a maritime, when the world was filled with wishes the way the sea is filled with fishes....

483

But always a story begins at the beginning. That is surely a simple thing to remember. Yet my husband begins reading any book he picks up in the middle and, if he likes it, he will continue on. He says it does not matter where he begins, with modern books—and he is right. If stories and books no longer start at the beginning, why should the reader? And if, as Joyce Cary says, "... reading is a creative art subject to the same rules, the same limitations, as the imaginative process...," then a story that begins in the middle and meanders around and ends still in the middle encourages that kind of reading.

Now I am not saying that a story has to move sequentially in time to have a beginning. One does not have to start with the birth of the hero or heroine to start the story at the beginning. Still, there must be a reason, a discernible reason, for starting a tale somewhere and not just the teller's whim. The person who invented the words "poetic license" should have his revoked.

What of the story's middle? First it should not be filled with middle-age spread. But also, it should not be so tight as to disappear. Do you remember the nursery rhyme:

> I'll tell you a story
> About Jack O'Nory,
> And now my tale's begun.
> I'll tell you another
> Of Jack and his brother,
> And now my tale is done.

Where is the middle of that story? It should be the place in the tale that elicits one question from the reader—*what then*? The middle is the place that leads the reader inevitably on to the end.

Is that not a simple task? I run a number of writers' groups and conferences, and all persuasions of writers have passed through. There are the naive novices who think that children's books must be easier to write because they are shorter and the audience less discriminating. There are the passable writers, almost-pros who have had a story or two published in religious magazines and are ready to tackle a talking animal tale or—worse—a talking prune story where inanimate objects converse on a variety of uninteresting subjects. And there are the truly professional writers whose combined publications make a reasonable backlist for any publishing company. And they all have trouble with the middles of stories.

484

The problem is one of caring. Too few writers today care enough about storytelling. If they should happen in the throes of "inspiration" to come upon a beginning and an ending, then they simply link the two together, a tenuous lifeline holding two climbers onto a mountain.

Of course the middle *is* the mountain. It is the most important part of the book, the tale, the story. It is where everything important occurs. Perhaps that is why so few people do it well.

What of the end? Ecclesiastes says: "Better is the end of a thing than the beginning thereof." An overstatement perhaps. But if the end is not *just* right, and is not filled with both inevitability and surprise, then it is a bad ending.

Adults are quite willing to forgive bad endings. I saw only recently a review of an adult book that said, in essence, the ending is silly, unconvincing, and weak, but the book is definitely worth reading. Children will not forgive a weak ending. They demand a rounding off, and they are very vocal in this demand. I remember reading a story of mine in manuscript to my daughter, then age seven. It was a tale about three animals—a sow, a mare, and a cow—who, tired of men and their fences, decided to live together. When I finished reading, with great feeling and taking the dialogue in special voices, I looked up at my audience of one. She looked back with her big brown eyes.

"Is that all?" she asked.

"Well, that's all in this story," I said, quickly adding "Would you like another?"

She tried again. "Is that all that happens?"

"Well, they just...I mean they...yes, that's all."

She drew in a deep breath. "That *can't* be all," she said.

"Why?" I asked, defeated.

"Because if that's all, it's not a story."

And she was right. I have not yet worked out a good ending for that story, though I am still trying. G.K. Chesterton noted this about fairy tale endings, which are sometimes bloodier than an *adult* can handle. He wrote: "Children know themselves innocent and demand justice. We fear ourselves guilty and ask for mercy."

But lots of stories can still have a beginning, a middle, and an end and not be right. If they are missing that "inner truth," they are nothing. A tale, even a small children's tale filled with delight, is still saying something. The best stories are, in Isak Dinesen's words, "a statement of our existence." Without meaning, without metaphor, without reaching out to touch the human emotion, a story is a pitiable thing; a few rags upon a stick masquerading as life.

I believe this last with all my heart. For storytelling is not only our oldest art, it is our oldest form of religion as well; our oldest way of casting out demons and summoning angels. Storytelling is our oldest form of remembering; remembering the promises we have made to one another and to our various gods, and the promises given in return; of recording our human-felt emotions and desires and taboos. The story is, quite simply, an essential part of our humanness.

91

WRITING THE PICTURE BOOK STORY

By Mary Calhoun

You want to write for children. Picture books. You tell stories to your children or the neighbor's children, and they just love your stories. *And this is good.* If you're telling stories, you already have the first qualification for writing picture books: You are a storyteller. The person who can spin a yarn is the golden one who will fascinate the four-to-eight-year-olds.

Then why aren't the publishers snapping up your stories and publishing them in beautiful four-color editions? Just what I wanted to know when I first started writing down the stories I'd told my boys. Rejection notes from editors commented:

"Too slight."

"Not original."

"We've used this theme several times."

"Too old for the age group."

I can't tell you all the reasons editors reject picture book scripts—such as "might encourage kids to make mess in the kitchen," "might encourage kids to try this and kill themselves." You'll just have to experience some of the rejections yourself. However, these are the general heart of why picture books are rejected:

"Not enough body and plot."

"Idea not big enough."

"Not ready to be a book."

"Things happen to the hero rather than he making things happen."

"Action too passive."

"Basic situation not convincing."

And over and over, "Too slight."

Sound familiar? Use the rejection list to check your stories—my compliments. The thing is, there's a lot more to writing for children than reeling off a story.

Now about picture books.

First, definitions: A picture book is one with pictures and a story to be read to or by a child between the ages of three and eight. (Publishers usually say four-eight, but many a "mature" three-year-old can enjoy having a picture book read aloud to him.)

Of course, there are other picture books for young children. For the two- and three-year-old there are the counting books, the ABC books, the "see-the-cat" books. There are picture books with a very slim text line, books conceived by the artists mainly for the sake of the art work. (No, you don't have to supply the artist for your story; the editor will do that.) There are the "idea" books: non-fiction—exploring "what is night?", "what is time?"—and such books as *A Hole Is to Dig* and *Mud Pies and Other Recipes,* charming ramblings on an idea, but not stories.

Here let's concern ourselves with the traditional picture book, one with a story from which the artist gains his inspiration for the pictures.

What goes into a picture book story?

As I see it, the elements are four: idea, story movement, style and awareness of audience.

First of all, the *idea*. Without a good idea, the writer is dead. Most often, I'd guess, a picture book script is rejected because the idea isn't good enough. What's a good idea? Make your own definition; I suppose each writer and editor does. I'd say, though, that basically the hero is vivid, the basic situation and the things that happen in the story are fascinating to a child. And generally there is a theme, some truth you believe, such as "you can master fear." Not a moral tacked onto the story, but the essence of the story, the hero and events acting out the theme.

How do you come by good ideas? Perhaps in the long run only heaven can help you, but it seems to me that primary is rapport with children—and a strong memory of your own childhood feelings and reactions.

"Tell me a story" many times a day keeps the old idea-mill grinding. Many of my picture book and magazine stories grew directly from contact with my children.

One day I hugged Greg, saying, "You're an old sweet patootie doll." "What's a patootie doll?" asked Greg, so I launched on a spur-of-the-moment tale. The theme was (I discovered after I'd written down the story) "know who you are and be glad for it." *The Sweet Patootie Doll* was first published in *Humpty Dumpty's Magazine* and later became my first published picture book.

A magazine story, "Cat's Whiskers", came into being because Greg was always climbing into things and getting stuck—in buckets, under the porch, even in the washing machine. I coupled this with the idea that cats use their whiskers to measure whether they can get through openings; in the story the boy sticks broomstraws on his face for whiskers, and the story goes on.

However, here was a story idea too slight for a picture book. Not enough happened, really, and there was no real theme in the sense of a universal truth.

This brings us to a point valuable to beginning writers: If your story is rejected by book editors, try it on the children's magazines. The magazines have high standards, too, of course, but they can be your training ground and means of being published while you learn. It was my lucky day when a book editor said, "Not ready to be a book. Have you thought of sending it to a magazine?" My story, "Lone Elizabeth," went through many rewritings, but finally was published in *Humpty Dumpty's Magazine*. "Bumbershoot Wind" was termed "too slight" by a book editor but appeared in *Child Life*.

Actually, all of the elements of a story are tied into the idea, but let's go on to consider them in detail.

Story movement. I choose to call it this, rather than plot, for this suggests just what a story for children must do: move. Children like a story that trots right along, with no prolonged station-stops for cute conversation or description. Keep asking yourself (as the child does), "What happened next?"

In picture books there needs to be enough change of action or scenery to afford the artist a chance to make different pictures. Some stories are very good for telling aloud, but when you look at them on paper, you see that the scene hasn't changed much.

A book editor pointed this out for me on my "Sammy and the Something Machine." In this fantasy, Sammy makes a machine out of which come in turn mice, monkeys, mudpies, pirates and hot dogs. (It grew from my Mike's chant at play, "I'm making, I'm making!") This story went down on paper perfectly well in *Humpty*

Dumpty's Magazine, where there are fewer illustrations than in a picture book. But the scene doesn't change; there's that machine, over and over, turning out different things.

When your story is moving along vigorously, the scene changes will follow naturally—*if* the idea is storybook material. If the story moves but there's not much possibility for picture change (better let the book editors decide this), it may still be a fine story for some magazine.

Style. Of course, your style will be your own, and only you can develop it through writing and trying out and thinking about it and forgetting about it as you plunge ahead in the heat of telling a story.

The story content to some extent will indicate the style, that is, choice of words, length and rhythm of sentences. The story may hop joyously, laugh along, move dreamily, or march matter-of-factly. For study, you might read aloud folk tales and attune your ears to varieties in cadence: the robust, boisterous swing of a western folk tale; the rolling, measured mysticism of an Indian folk tale; the straightforward modern "shaggy dog" story; the drawling wry humor of the southern Negro folk tale.

If you already are telling stories to children, you're on your way to developing your style. However, "telling" on paper is slightly different from telling aloud, where the *effect* is achieved by a few judiciously chosen words and the swing of sentences.

I've had some success with one approach to the written story, and I've seen examples of it in other picture books. I call it "vividry." To me it's more vivid and succinct to say that than "vivid effect," and this explains what "vividry" is: words chosen with economy for their punch. For example, in a certain book I choose to say "little mummy mice." "Mummified mice" might be more proper, but to me it sounds textbookish. "Mummy mice" rolls off the tongue and seems a more direct idea-tickler for the child.

In college journalism courses, our bible was Rudolf Flesch's *The Art of Plain Talk.* From it we learned the value, in newspaper writing, of using sentences of short or varied length; strong verbs; short, strong nouns and many personal pronouns. Flesch might have been writing a style book for children's picture books.

We all know the delight in finding "the exact word" for a spot in a story. Never is this more effective than in children's books. Magazines for children generally have word-length requirements. Try putting a full-bodied story into 800 to 1,000 words. Every word counts. Writing for the magazines can be excellent training in choosing words and cutting out the lifeless ones.

I'm not saying, however, that big words have no place in a picture book script. Writing "controlled vocabulary" books for the young is a specialized art, and those books are used mostly by teachers and parents to stimulate a child's desire to read. Several book publishers now put out series of "easy-to-read" books. If you are interested in this field, read some of the books and query the editors on requirements. In the general picture book, though, I think children like to come upon an occasional delightfully new and big word. Haven't you seen a four-year-old trotting around, happily rolling out "unconditionally" or some other mouthful he's just heard? It's the *idea* of the story that the writer suits to the age group, not every given word in the story.

And this brings us to *awareness of audience*. I've mentioned rapport with children. If you're around them you know what they're thinking and wishing, what their problems are. And you'll know if a story idea is too old for the three-to-eight-year-olds or just plain wouldn't interest them.

With a small child underfoot or in tow, you see the details of the world that fascinate him: how a spot of sunlight moves on the floor; a cat's relationship with his tail (I used this one in "Tabbycat's Telltale Tail"); or the child's own shadow. (I haven't been able to make a good story of this; maybe you can.)

A child will watch a hummingbird moth at work in a petunia bed and report wisely, "He only goes to the red ones. White petunia must not taste good."

All of this, *plus awareness of the child's emotions, plus turning your mind back to remember how it was with you as a child*, tells you what to put into a picture book.

And then there's the other way to be aware of your audience: reading, reading all the good books and stories written for that age. Then you begin to see what has pleased children. You get the feel of what is suitable for that age group. You also see what has already been done, so that your own ideas can be fresh, not trite. You read "The Three Pigs," and the books about the Melops and you say to yourself, "Very well, but a story about a pig has never been told just in *this* way," and you start off on your own particular pig story. As you read (perhaps to a child to catch his reactions, too), you may begin to draw your conclusions of what is good in children's literature, what is slightly sickening, how the stories are put together, what has worked.

It has interested me, for instance, to notice how many of the traditional stories are built on what I call a "core of three." Three brothers, three mistakes, three attempts at a solution. "The Three Pigs" makes me wonder if the composer weren't slyly trying to see just how many times he could use three. Three pigs, three encounters with men carrying building materials, three houses visited by the wolf, "chinny-chin-chin," etc. In so many of the stories, the use of three attempts to solve the problem is effective in building intensity to the climax.

So there you have it: idea, story movement, style and awareness of audience. Study them, use them in your rewrites, let them sink into your subconscious.

And then don't worry about techniques as you tell the story. For the first, last and most important thing is: you must *like* the story! You're having a ball telling it. Right at this moment, it's the most wonderful story ever told to man or child.

That, finally, is what gives the story sparkle and makes editors say, "This will make a wonderful picture book!"

92

MESSAGES BELONG IN TELEGRAMS

By Connie C. Epstein

Sam Goldwyn, driving force of Metro-Goldwyn-Mayer, once said, "If you want to send a message, send a telegram." Although he is not usually thought of as a source of good advice for children's authors, his remark is one the aspiring writer for the young would do well to take to heart. Message writing is usually bad writing, and children's books appear to be especially vulnerable to it. In fact, it may be the reason children's writing is often considered a lesser art.

Katherine Paterson, a Newbery Medal winner, expressed her feelings about message writing very cogently: When an interviewer asked her, "What are you trying to do when you write for children?," he was clearly disappointed when she answered that she was simply trying to write as good a story as she possibly could. She concluded, "He seemed to share the view of many intelligent, well-educated, well-meaning people that while adult literature may aim to be art, the object of children's books is to whip the little rascals into shape."

What is message writing? After all, every writer has a point of view, and without it a book is boringly bland. My definition is that the message writer believes in one or more universal truths that hold for everyone, whatever the circumstances. The artistic writer, on the other hand, is interested in people as individuals, the way each behaves and why. She or he describes them as clearly as possible and then trusts the reader to draw the appropriate conclusions from the actions of the characters.

All kinds of messages have shown up in children's books ever since children's writing was first considered a form of its own. At first, proper manner, good habits, and virtuous behavior were a prime concern. Today's writers continue to worry about virtuous behavior, but the problems have changed. Instead of thumb-sucking, stories deal

493

now with the terrors of drug addiction. Or writers may feel they should instill proper attitudes toward social problems such as racism, sexism, and ageism.

Some of the early children's cautionary tales seem startling, to say the least, in this day and age. There is the famous *Struwwelpeter (Slovenly Peter)* by Heinrich Hoffman, published in Germany in 1845. It was considered a great advance in the development of children's books, for it used the technique of comic exaggeration, a largely missing ingredient until then. Still, to cure Little Suck-a-Thumb of his bad habit, the tailor cuts off his thumb with his shears. The illustration shows the blood dripping down, and the caption reads, "That made little Conrad yell."

I learned good table manners from a book that had dropped the violence but retained both the preaching and the humor. Certainly it pulled no punches when it advised on right and wrong. This Manual of Manners for Polite Infants was titled *Goops and How to Be Them* by Frank Gelett Burgess, first published in 1900, a collection of verses about a strange subculture of bald, round-headed beings. The opening poem read:

> The Goops they lick their fingers,
> And the Goops they lick their knives;
> They spill their broth on the tablecloth—
> Oh, they lead disgusting lives!
> The Goops they talk while eating,
> And loud and fast they chew;
> And that is why I'm glad that I
> Am not a Goop—are you?

We recited these lines in a chorus whenever any one of the three children in our family made a slip at the dinner table and, strangely, thought they were funny rather than irritating. Perhaps the silliness was a relief in contrast to the parental lecture. Anyway, the priggishness didn't offend us and apparently doesn't offend children today, for I find to my surprise that the book is still in print.

Humor, in fact, has saved many a morality tale. One that I was most closely connected with was *The Chocolate Touch* by Patrick Skene Catling, a modern variation on the legend of King Midas (Morrow). In it, everything the hero touches turns to chocolate, and it preaches the evils of greed unabashedly, but a number of the effects are really very funny. In retrospect, I think it was more popular with children than with critics, so much so that Morrow brought out a new reillustrated edition with considerable success.

Judging from the manuscripts submitted to children's book editors, I would say that the temptation to pass along a constructive message to children continues unabated. Everyone who cares about young people these days worries about the problems of addiction to alcohol and drugs. This topic turns up constantly. Sometimes the concern takes such precedence over characterization that we get dialogue like the following:

"If Sandy hadn't messed with drugs, she'd still be alive. . . ."
"Well, it won't ever happen to me," Tommy answered.
"I'm sure Sandy thought it would never happen to her."
"I guess you're right. After all, a lot of famous people have overdosed—Janis Joplin, Jimmy Hendrix."

I can't believe that any two teen-agers ever talked to each other this way, and I doubt that any other reader would be convinced, either. Unfortunately, drug addiction is not solved so simply, and this whole story loses credibility because the writer has clearly put the message before characters and plot, a reverse of writing priorities.

Because this writer has taken his message so seriously, the reader cannot take him seriously—certainly not as an author. Adult writing-in-progress rarely suffers from the disease of wishful thinking in quite so virulent a form, with the possible exception of religious work, in which the message is truly the medium. To master their craft, children's fiction writers must constantly guard against wishful thinking and not play their characters false, or they always will be considered lesser artists.

Some people are surprised that a topic as unpleasant as drug addiction appears in juvenile writing at all, but the extent of this modern plague has pretty well settled the question. Regrettably, it is part of the scene for teen-agers in most large urban areas. More to the point is the artistry with which the subject is handled. When believable characters and plot are created, the problem falls into perspective.

The danger is the "single-issue novel," narrated in first person so that it is limited to the scope of one, sometimes immature, sensibility. All too often, the characters in such a story are defined entirely in terms of their attitude toward the problem—in this case addiction. It is their only topic of conversation and the sole motive for their actions. If characters and plot are given proper priority, however, then the problem is only one part of the whole, and the story is probably not considered a problem novel at all.

The present-day problem novel seems to me simply the latest form of message writing. Even now when we smile about the Goops of the past, children's fiction is still afflicted with obvious messages.

Manuscripts written for little children usually do not get entangled with complicated social problems, but they sometimes try even more earnestly to instruct in good behavior. In one manuscript I saw last year entitled *The Little Ice Cream Truck Who Hated Snowballs,* a personalized truck explained to a group of children the dangers of throwing things at moving vehicles. Perhaps this concept would work visually as an animated television commercial for Good Humor sticks, but between covers it seems a thinly disguised tract.

Another recent example carried the title *Aunti-Pollution and the Bubble-Gum Mess.* Aunti-Pollution was a turtle who stepped on a wad of gum and needed the help of all her animal friends to make her clean again. Pollution is of crucial importance today, but presenting it in terms of do's and don'ts for the young runs the risk of turning them off with a lecture or, at the least, of making them always uncertain exactly how the word *anti* is spelled.

When messages dominate a story, all the characters are likely to be stick figures, but one type suffers especially: the villain. Adventure tales desperately need a good, credible villain to make them work properly, yet all too often the writer wants to shield child readers from evil and cannot bring himself to describe wrong-doing with conviction or, for that matter, with understanding. In fact, the villain in this kind of story may be more important to its success than the hero, and you should be sure to develop him or her with just as much or even more care.

Of course, citing examples of what not to do is much easier than offering advice on good technique. Recently the children's writer Beverly Cleary had the following to say about messages:

There are those who feel that a children's book must *teach* a child. I am not one of them. Children prefer to learn what is implicit in a story, to discover what they need to know. As a child I was tired of being taught when there was so much room for improvement in adults.

496

These remarks were made in acceptance of an award for her story, *Ramona and Her Mother,* in which Mrs. Cleary did reluctantly allow there was a message. She didn't know it was there until she had finished the book (which is a good thing to remember: let the characters grow naturally and the moral will emerge of itself), and then the message turned out to be for adults, not for children at all. Ramona learns at last that though she has done exasperating things like squeezing out an entire tube of toothpaste, her mother does love her. So Mrs. Cleary concluded, "If there are any adults in the audience who feel that a book for children *must* have a moral, here it is: Children need to be told in words that their parents love them."

In other words, the child's point of view should be paramount. Try to imagine how the *child* in your dramatic situation would feel, and relate adult reactions to this feeling. If you are truly seeing the world through the eyes of children, you can hardly send them a message about it at the same time. Perhaps the biggest challenge for the children's writer is the leap in point of view that must always take place. From memory, instinct, and observation, the writer is always re-creating another, slightly different sensibility. The adult writer is frequently able to take the far easier course of writing from his or her personal reactions and perspective.

Children's writing is said to have come of age in the United States since World War II, for in that period it came to be recognized as a distinct area of publishing with formal standards of its own. Those who care agree that children deserve the finest writing and resent the notion that it is in any way a lesser art. But until we remember to use Western Union, not children's books, for our messages, I suspect they won't be completely accepted in the mainstream. Sam Goldwyn was a smart man, and we should listen to him.

93

WRITING FOR YOUNG CHILDREN

By Charlotte Zolotow

Children's book writing includes fiction for children from picture books on up to the young adults, non-fiction—biography, autobiography and factual books—and of course poetry. In short, it includes every category of adult writing that exists, and everything that is true of distinctive writing for adults is also true of fine literature for children.

But there is in writing for children an additional skill required. It is easier to address our peers than those who are different from ourselves. And children are different from adults because they live on a more intense level. Whatever is true of adults is true of children, only more so. They laugh, they cry, they love, they hate, they give, they take as adults do—only more so. And this is what makes writing for children different from writing for adults.

One must first of all, over and above everything, take children seriously and take writing children's books seriously. Over and over I have met people who feel that writing for children is a first step to doing "something really good." A fairly successful, but undistinguished author of many children's books said to me one night, "Some day I'm going to do something really good. I'm going to write a novel or a play."

What this gentleman's abilities as an adult writer will be, I don't know. His children's books, however, lack something. There is nothing in them that would make a child put one down and say, "What else has this person written?" (A question children have asked many times after first reading a book by Ruth Krauss, Maurice Sendak, Else H. Minarik, Laura Ingalls Wilder, Margaret Wise Brown, E. B. White, Marie Hall Ets, E. Nesbit, P. L. Travers, Beatrix Potter— the great writers of children's literature.)

This remark of his made me understand why. *He doesn't respect what he is doing.* If he ever gets to his serious play or novel, it won't be that he came via children's books, but that he finally did take seriously what he was doing. I don't think writers of this sort should be writing for children at all. Children's books are an art in themselves and must be taken seriously. Anyone who regards them simply as a step along the way to "real" writing is in the wrong field.

I should make clear here that when I use the word *seriously* I don't mean *pompously.* I don't mean that every word is holy or that it should be heavy-handed. Some of the most delightful humor in books today is in the books for children. Some of the wildest kind of nonsense is there, too. But the writers are saying something seriously in their humor and in their nonsense—something that is real to them and meaningful to them—and they are saying it the best way they can without writing down to an audience whose keenness and perception they must completely respect.

There is a popular misconception about children's books that exists even among literate people. And it exists most particularly in the area of the picture book. A television writer once told me, "I never read my children what's in a picture book. I make up my own story to go with the pictures." He was quite pleased with himself—had no idea of the absurdity his smug assumption "that anyone can write a children's book" contained. He didn't realize that though his stories might amuse his own kids, delighted with the sound of his voice, the expression of his face, and the feeling of well-being his spending time with them gave them, a *published* story must be a finished, well-rounded work of art. In cold print, a story has to be good. The wandering, sketchy bedtime stories we tell our children have to be formed and shaped and sharpened before they can be printed, illustrated, bound in a book to be read over and over again to thousands of children who are strangers to the author's face and voice.

Some of my own books have indeed come out of stories I originally told my children, but years later, and after much thought, much reforming, reshaping, pruning, and in a voice or style that was a writer's, not a mother's. There is an immense difference.

In some picture books there are just a few words on a page. Certain immortal lyrics are four lines long. A sonnet has only fourteen lines. But the brevity doesn't mean they are "easy" to write. There is a special gift to making something good with a few words. The ability to conjure up a great deal just from the sound of a word and its relation to the other words in the sentence, the gift of evocation and denotation, is not only special to the poet but to children themselves. To say that he has had a good time at school that morning, a child may simply tell you, "The teacher wore a purple skirt." The recipient of this confidence would have to be close enough to the particular child to know that purple is her favorite color; that summing up a whole morning's events by that color is equivalent to having an adult say, "excellent wine"; that, in fact, in this child's vocabulary "purple" is a value judgment and the sign of a happy morning. And since children themselves so often use this oblique, connotative language, the writer who is fortunate enough to have retained his own childlike vision can speak to them in this special poetic shorthand that evokes worlds in a word.

A picture book writer must have this gift of using words carefully, of identifying with, understanding, projecting himself into the child's world. He must know and feel what they know and feel with some of the freshness of their senses, not his experienced adult ones. He must know what children care about a given situation. This is usually quite different from what an adult in a similar situation is thinking, wanting, seeing, tasting, feeling; and sympathy and empathy (and memory) are necessary, not condescension, not smugness, not superiority, not serious observation from an adult point of view.

And while the brevity of a picture book makes the author's use of words particularly selective, the rest of what I've said applies not only to picture books but to books going up in age group to the young adults. It is a question of experiencing at that particular level how the small or "middle-aged" child feels.

The best children's book writers are those who look at the world around them with a childlike vision—not childish, which is an adult acting like a child—but with that innocent, open vision of the world that belongs to the various stages of growing up, a clearer, more immediate, more specific, more honest, less judging vision than the adult one.

Children come fresher, with less cant, less hypocrisy, less guilt, to the world around them than even the most honest adults are apt to. Children smell good and bad things without inhibition. They taste, they hear, they see, they feel with all their senses and not so much interfering intellect as the adult, who will label things by applied standards, preconceived standards of good or bad—a good smell or a bad smell, a good taste or a bad taste. Children are realists of the first order. They have fewer preconceived ideas than adults. To them, flowers may smell bad. Manure may smell good. They have no fixed judgments yet. Most things are still happening to them for the first time. The first time water comes from a faucet, heat from a radiator, snow falls, the *real* itself is *magic*.

Because of this, children are open to belief in fantasy—fairies can exist if snow can fall, magic can happen if there are cold and heat, moon and stars and sun. Nothing is routine yet. They live more immediate lives than adults, not so much of yesterday or tomorrow. They are open to the moment completely. They respond to every detail around them completely. (That is why they are so often tiring to be with.)

I remember once the poet, Edwin Honig, came to visit us. He had never met our daughter Ellen, who was then four. They liked each other immediately. And when she offered to show him the house, he left his drink on the front porch and went off into the house with her. When I came in a few minutes later, he was holding her in his arms, and she was pointing into the living room.

"That is the fireplace where we have fires in winter.

That is the rubber plant where one leaf died.

That is the radio where we had the tube fixed.

That is the best chair but our dog sits in it." She might have invited him to see if he could smell the dog in the chair if I hadn't come in.

"You know," Honig said to me, "she's living everything here for me."

A poet could understand this. And in this sense that is what everyone who writes for children must be.

Always remember that the field of children's books is exciting and specialized. It is full of pitfalls that adult writing is free from, not the least of which is that a child's point of view is so different from that of an adult—more different at three than at six, and more so at six than at nine. And even when the child and adult reaction is identical—at any age level—in being hurt, in wanting, in hating, in loving, it is more intense. Adults are like a body of water that has been

501

dammed up, or channeled. Children haven't these constrictions yet on their emotions. They abandon themselves to emotion, and therefore everything from a cake crumb to an oak tree means more to them.

If you are to write for children, you must be absolutely honest with yourself and with them. Willa Cather once advised a young writer never to hold back on any idea or phrase when it fitted something he was writing, in the hope of using it later in something better. Never hold back on what fits the book you are writing for children either. Remember how you felt about things when you were a child; remember, remember that adults might laugh and say, "tomorrow he'll forget," but right then, at the moment, the child feels and believes in his pain or his joy with his whole being.

A famous children's book editor once said, "Young people can and will accept the very best truly creative people will give them." And in a *New Yorker* article about Maurice Sendak, one of the finest children's book artists and writers today, it was stated, "Too many of us . . . keep forgetting that children are new and we are not. But somehow Maurice has retained a direct line to his own childhood."

This is what anyone who wants to write for children must do.

94

ERASING THE BLUE-PENCIL BLUES

By David Petersen

I<small>F</small> <small>YOU'VE</small> ever felt that too many of the magazine articles you've strived so diligently to create have wound up getting edited too harshly, then I don't need to tell you about the Blue-Pencil Blues. You know the ailment well, even if you've not heard the term before. While I'd never say that you should consider this potentially debilitating malady a blessing, I *will* suggest that your writing can benefit from it.

During more than a decade of straddling the publishing fence as both a free lancer and a magazine editor, I've identified five nonfiction problem areas that I feel comprise the most common reasons editors bring out their blue pencils. The good news is that by learning to recognize and weed out these troublemakers, you can significantly reduce the need for editing and—a delightful spin-off—increase sales.

Here, then, are what I perceive to be the five primary reasons editors edit—along with a few tips to help you eliminate them from your writing.

1. Editors edit for grammar, punctuation, spelling, and all the other nuts and bolts that hold a manuscript together, but that too many free lancers too often fail to tighten.

Many aspiring wordsmiths feel so blessed with talent that they think they needn't bother with the more mundane details of the writer's craft—things such as submitting clearly typed manuscripts free of punctuation errors, pronouns that disagree in number, misspellings, and the like. Some of these writers do show budding talent, but anyone who believes that just a good yarn is enough to win consistently at the free-lancing game is setting himself up for a fall.

The reality is that few magazine editors have the time or inclination to take on serious cosmetic surgery, no matter how beautiful the hidden message may be. Sloppily prepared pieces, peppered with mechanical glitches that could easily have been caught and corrected by the writer, are rarely going to sell—and the few that do are bound to be heavily edited.

The self-evident remedy, therefore, is to make sure that your copy is road-ready; that nary a screw that you can detect is left jangling loose for an editor to spot and tighten. If *you* don't take care of the mechanical essentials and your editors have to, consider their tinkering a blessing rather than a curse.

2. *Editors edit for style.*

No two publications speak with exactly the same voice. A serious free lancer knows this and—while making no attempt to parrot every stylistic inflection of a magazine—will avoid submitting seriously off-key articles. You wouldn't, for example, use a stiff, academic style in an article bound for a magazine whose voice is as informal and conversational as *The Mother Earth News*, but many free lancers have—only to be rejected or heavily edited for their trouble.

A submission written in a voice that's gratingly off-key tells an editor that the writer a) hasn't bothered to familiarize himself with the publication (a cardinal and surprisingly common free lancer's sin); or b) is unable to recognize a magazine's style when he sees it. An off-key article is far less likely to sell and, if it does, is certain to be returned to bring it into editorial harmony. So, familiarize yourself with your target publication's voice, and pitch your style accordingly.

3. *Editors edit for length.*

When I queried one of my favorite magazines about an article idea not long ago, the editors gave me a green light to submit the piece on speculation, but stipulated that I hold the length to around 1,500 words. Had I sent them the 2,500 tome I generated on the first draft (rather than the 1,500 words I eventually trimmed it to), I could hardly have taken umbrage had they cut the piece to the requested length—or even rejected it. The moral: When an editor is helpful enough to indicate a preferred length for an article, don't exceed it.

But many times you don't have a specified length to shoot for. What then? Here's a procedure that has worked well for me as a free lancer—and *with* me as an editor.

Begin by studying a few recent issues of the target magazine to determine the average word count of several articles similar in style and scope to the one you plan to submit. Next, send an SASE for writer's guidelines (which will probably suggest minimum and maximum lengths for different kinds of articles). Finally, a query. And in that query, suggest a length for your article based on what you've learned by studying the guidelines and the magazine itself. This procedure will significantly improve your chances of getting a go-ahead from the editor. If the editor is interested in your proposal but wants more or fewer words than you've suggested, he can say so in his response.

4. *Editors edit for accuracy and completeness.*

Consider this scenario: You've written and submitted an article in which you quote a fellow named Stewart. The piece sells, is published, and all is well . . . until the day the publication's editor sends you a copy of a letter received from Mr. Stewartt (two t's). No matter that the extra "t" is a somewhat unusual spelling; Mr. Stewartt is upset that you got his name wrong—and the editors are also upset because they feel compelled to print Stewartt's letter along with an apology. How eager do you think they'll be to purchase more of your work?

The most common inaccuracies are dates, figures, quotations, professional titles, and the names of persons and places. The free-lancing war is won or lost through many small battles. Verify, verify, verify!

Hand-in-hand with accuracy goes completeness. Never assume that readers will have sufficient foreknowledge of your topic to fill in informational blanks for themselves. When in doubt, err on the side of providing too much detail rather than too little.

5. *Editors edit for clarity.*

Clarity is the cornerstone of effective communication—and effective communication is the foundation of good writing. To achieve clarity, polish each of your manuscripts until you think it shines, then ask a reliable friend who's willing to play the part of candid literary critic to read it and point out any hazy spots. If your critic is confused by a passage, fails to chuckle at a joke you thought was an absolute knee-slapper, or otherwise misses a point you've tried to make, it's a fair bet that other readers—including editors—will have the same trouble. (If you don't have someone to read your work for you, the next best critic is *time*. The longer you can afford to let a piece rest after you've "completed" it, the more objective you'll be when you return to it for further editing.)

505

Sure, a good editor can shine up your slightly hazy prose for you—that's part of what he's trained and paid to do. But a serious writer won't expect him to, won't want him to, won't give him the need to. To increase sales and minimize editing, polish your product until even the filmiest patches of fog disappear. Then polish some more.

And there you have it—the five kinds of problems that most frequently prompt editors to reject or heavily edit manuscripts . . . along with a few suggestions for eliminating them from your writing.

Of course, all this talk of how to minimize having your work altered assumes that you'll be dealing with competent editors. A fair assumption, I believe. Slovenly and unqualified editors are as scarce as fur on a fish and as ephemeral as Hailey's comet. In general, you can trust career blue-pencilers to be skilled professionals dedicated to making their publications the best they can be by making their free-lance contributors perform at their best. Both are essential.

When an editor improves my words without making them sound more like his than mine, I'm unabashedly grateful. But as much as I appreciate the help, I nonetheless set my sights on leaving no loose nuts and bolts to tighten, no fat to trim away, no murky prose to clarify, no inaccuracies to correct or blanks to fill in, and no off-key voice to bring my article into line with the magazine's style. I don't always succeed, but I always try. That's my duty as a writer.

And when I'm sitting on the other side of the editorial desk, I try to make every article I work with as good as it can be without destroying the writer's voice or betraying the style of my magazine. That's my duty as an editor.

I've never known a sadistic editor, and the unqualified are few and far between. In the majority of cases, therefore, the most effective way to avoid the feeling that your work is being edited too severely by others is to bear down a little harder with your own blue pencil.

95

INSIDE THE EDITOR'S OFFICE

By Patricia Tompkins

THE EDITOR'S OFFICE. If you've never been inside one, perhaps you've imagined what it is like: a plush, spacious room, with framed photographs on paneled walls; behind a vast teak desk and leather chair, a panoramic view of the city. Outside the door to this center of serene efficiency sits a secretarial sentinel. The elusive editor is out having lunch with a writer.

For the novice free-lance writer, the editor's office may seem like an inner sanctum, a place where only writers with the right password are admitted. But you'll be closer to reality—and closer to getting inside the office—if you imagine the following: a typewriter and possibly a word processor on a little table; mismatched chairs crowded around a gray metal desk, with calendars, memos, and page layouts taped on plaster walls; through the venetian blinds, a view of a parking lot. On the littered desk, alongside an overflowing in-box, are a salad in a plastic container and a mug of cold coffee. The phone rings while the editor is down the hall, trying to fix the photocopying machine. The editor's office, in short, is usually about as glamorous as that of a free-lance writer. (I'm writing this at my "desk"—a folding card table.)

Having set the scene, let's look at what the editor does in that office. First, understand that an editor is a working professional, often overworked and underpaid, in a wonderful, competitive business. That could describe a free-lance writer, too. Well, an editor is not so very different from you. But sometimes the mutual interests of writers and editors get lost in the shuffle of manuscripts. Aspiring contributors often forget that editors can be writers' greatest allies. The following guidelines, drawn from my experience as a copy editor for a monthly city magazine, apply to most publications and will enable you to improve your chances of selling articles. These three basics will help you reach your most important reader—the editor:

(1) Show your familiarity with the magazine to which you send your proposal or query.
(2) Communicate your enthusiasm for your subject in your query letter.
(3) Understand what an editor does and expects from free-lance writers.

The clues to what the editor is looking for appear in every issue. Study several recent issues of the magazine and obtain a copy of its writers guidelines. If your public library has back issues, you may also want to look at several copies from the past year and five years ago. Note any changes in format, content, and staff.

A thorough reading includes advertisements, which give a sense of the magazine's audience. And look at the staff list. The magazine I work for lists numerous contributing editors and identifies the subjects they cover. If there is already a regular columnist on wine, you may have a tough time selling your article on wine to the editor. But regular contributors are not necessarily permanent, and the magazine may buy free-lance material as well.

Once you've done your research and are confident your proposal suits the magazine, introduce yourself in your query letter. Remember: first impressions count, and you are competing with many others; to get the editor's attention, your letter must stand out. This doesn't mean typing in red ink on purple paper; it means writing an engaging, informative letter. Perhaps you're aiming at a local publication and are tempted to skip a letter and simply telephone the editor. Your idea is so good, you think, the editor will naturally say yes. And you'll save a month waiting for a reply by getting an instant assignment. No, you won't. The editor is not sitting around waiting for unsolicited proposals by telephone from unfamiliar callers. If you're a writer, write a letter; put your idea on paper so the editor can assess it at a convenient time.

Two weeks may pass before the editor has time to look at your letter. Why? Partly because most editors can't spend their days reading; they're busy putting out a magazine. Consider an average day in the editor's office: Arrives at nine o'clock; a glance through the mail reveals that two manuscripts due today didn't arrive. Assistant calls in sick. Editor writes final headlines and captions for three articles; associate art director asks for two lines to be cut from an article to fit layout. Desk

508

lamp burns out; no spare bulbs around. Appointment at ten with writer to discuss work needed on feature story. Meets with editorial staff at eleven to discuss possibilities for the next issue, three months away. Eats lunch at desk while returning phone calls. Writer delivers assignment and spends fifteen minutes pitching another article idea. Editor looks at an assigned article that arrived in the day's mail. Calls printer to find out why galleys are late; writer calls wanting to update her piece. Fact-checker brings in manuscript full of errors; copy editor asks how to handle a writer who refuses her suggested changes. Interview at four with potential summer intern. Discusses illustrations for cover story with art director. Selects five letters to the editor for inclusion in next issue. Leaves at six to spend half an hour at a press preview party.

Generally, the day doesn't allow time to read unsolicited manuscripts or queries. The editor I work for coordinates editorial production with two senior editors and manages a staff of two full-time assistants supplemented by six part-time helpers (free-lance copy editors and proofreaders, plus interns) in a noisy, crowded room next to her office. Rarely does she have ten minutes alone and uninterrupted at her desk— not exactly ideal reading conditions.

One assistant weeds out the inappropriate queries each week and passes along more hopeful prospects to the editor, who then reviews them, along with recent fiction submissions. When does she read? At home in the evening and on the weekends when, much as she loves her job, she wouldn't mind doing something else. Under these circumstances, she appreciates a clear, concise query, one with enthusiasm for and knowledge of the subject and the magazine.

Keep in mind that your query is one of dozens in limbo (make that hundreds or thousands for popular national publications). Although no one likes form rejection letters, they are time-savers. Unfortunately, they don't convey how close you may have come to acceptance. The difference between a positive and a negative response to a query is often a matter of timing and luck—good and bad. Once I proposed an idea for a new column in a monthly magazine; it seemed a natural, given the publication's audience. No, thanks. I still thought my idea was sound, so twelve months later, I tried again; this time the answer was yes. Why? The proposal was the same; so was the editor, but—unknown to me—he was planning a change in format, and my suggestion now solved a problem.

No can mean the editor already has a related story in the works. I've seen two pieces on the same subject arrive simultaneously; both took a similar approach to their subject. (The one chosen was by a writer long established with the magazine.) *No* can also mean the editor has a backlog of good material ready; she knows your article would sit on hold for many months—frustrating for the writer when payment is on publication, impractical for the editor when payment is on acceptance.

Suppose the editor says *yes*—on speculation—and gives you guidelines on the desired focus, length, and deadline. These guidelines are made to avoid wasting your time and the editor's. Follow them. The magazine's production schedule won't collapse if your piece is late, but the delay will be passed along to the copy editor, art department, printer, and proofreader. (The tendency to ignore basic directions is one reason editors ask new writers to submit work on speculation, rather than on assignment.) Turn your work in on time; it will save you the trouble of thinking up novel excuses for being late.

A problem even more common than missing deadlines is submitting a manuscript that is longer than requested. A maximum of 2,000 words doesn't mean that you should write 2,500 or 3,000. But isn't that the editor's job—to edit stories to the right length? No, it isn't. The right length is the requested or assigned length. The editor has other pieces competing for space and attention. Although the magazine may vary in length from issue to issue, the amount of advertising sold, not the length of articles, usually determines an issue's size. Holding to the assigned length can be an aid to keep your piece focused.

If you've done your job, the editor can concentrate on hers: critically examining the article and seeing if its parts work well together. Are the transitions adequate? Is the subject covered adequately, or is vital material missing? Does the piece start fast and finish slow? Will it inform or entertain readers? In asking such questions, the editor exercises her skills creatively, making murky prose lucid.

Once your article is accepted, the fact-checker, copy editor, and proofreader will be looking at your work closely. (With a small staff, one person may handle all three tasks.) The fact-checker verifies the statistics, the spelling of names, and the accuracy of quotes. These details are checked with primary sources when possible, usually not with the writer. Just a few misspelled names will cast doubt on your reliability;

substantial discrepancies and errors may put your piece in jeopardy. Check your manuscript for accuracy before submitting it.

The proofreader and copy editor will be alert to other types of errors. No one will reject a manuscript if it has a dangling participle and uses "which" where "that" is correct, but the fewer mistakes, the more professional you will look. The copy editor will ask for clarification of cryptic and confusing passages. If you're a local writer, include your home and work phone numbers, along with your name and address, on the first page of your manuscript so an editor can get in touch with you easily.

It's natural to assume your writing is perfectly clear when you know the topic. The copy editor helps ensure that everything will be clear to readers, too. I've found most writers appreciate careful editorial attention to their work, but some regard copy editors as meddlers and hacks, critics who can't write. Avoid this superiority complex and cooperate. All writers' work receives the same scrutiny. You might be surprised and encouraged if you saw the deletions and revisions on most manuscripts by the time they're ready for the typesetter. Only rarely does what appears in the magazine exactly match what the editor received in manuscript form. An acceptable manuscript doesn't have to meet impossible criteria of perfection before an editor will accept it, but the less time the editorial staff has to spend cutting and polishing your manuscript, the better they'll like it.

When you have the published version of your work in hand, compare it with your original copy. Over a period of several weeks or months between writing and publication, you may be better able to see alterations as improvements. Think of editing as a writing lesson. If you're pleased with the results, send a note of thanks to the editor.

At its best, the editor-writer relationship is a partnership of peers. If you use common sense and courtesy and treat the editor as an ally, you'll be two steps ahead of the crowd.

96

BREAKING INTO THE BIG MARKETS

By Sondra Forsyth Enos
Executive Editor, *Ladies' Home Journal*

WHEN James B. Conant was president of Harvard University, he kept among other objects on his desk a statuette of a turtle, on whose base was the inscription: "Consider the turtle. He makes progress only when he sticks his neck out." There could perhaps be no more fitting admonition to free-lance writers than that one. I have a great deal to share with you about the business of selling what you write, but what I would like most of all is to inspire you, to instill in you the conviction that you can and will succeed—in short, to give you the courage to stick your neck out.

To start with, let me debunk the long-standing myth that unsolicited queries from unknown, unagented writers are never read with much attention or consideration. That's simply not true. I have been on the staff of three major national magazines, and I've discussed this subject with editors at many other magazines. The consensus is that while we all receive reams of so-called slush submissions—as many as five hundred pieces of mail a week at *Ladies' Home Journal,* for example— someone on each staff opens and reads every single submission. You see, we all *want* to discover new talent "over the transom," or to include in our stables established writers who have not yet worked for us. Believe me, it is a thrill to find in the morning's mail a sparkling query by a clearly gifted writer, who has come up with an idea that is just right. When that happens, I lose no time contacting the writer, even if he or she has no publishing credits at all. I would have to give a rank beginner a go-ahead on spec—speculation—of course, not a firm assignment, but that's an opportunity no one should turn down. Editors don't ask to see pieces on spec unless they are serious about wanting them to work out.

But that's enough of a pep talk for the moment. Let's get on to the nuts and bolts of breaking into the big markets.

Rule Number One: *Read your target markets.* If you want to sell me an article, go to the library and read every issue of *Ladies' Home Journal* for the last year or two. Try to absorb the tone and style, and decide who the average reader must be. Learn to think the way we, the editors, think. I am often asked what sort of manuscripts we buy, and this amazes me, because what we buy is out there on the newsstands every month for anyone to see.

Rule Number Two: *Offer ideas that are as fresh and unique as possible.* Editors read and research a lot, trying to come up with ideas and stay a jump ahead of the readers. We clip items, spot trends, and meet to share what we have gleaned. The result is that if there is, say, a rise in the rate of Caesarean deliveries, we're going to know about it right away, and if we decide we want a piece on the topic, we'll surely call one of our regular writers and assign the piece that afternoon, before your query on the subject, however compellingly written, can even reach us.

What's a writer to do, then? My suggestion is that you forget national topics for the moment, and look instead in your own backyard. For instance, suppose your hometown newspaper carries the story of a brave family coping with a gravely ill child, who has a rare and perhaps incurable disease, and let's say the family has inadequate medical insurance, so theirs is a double tragedy. Now there is a story of human courage which I would never know about unless you brought it to my attention. And if you had done your homework, reading *LHJ* from cover to cover, you'd know that we run at least one such "ordeal story" in almost every issue. You would also have noticed that we frequently run fact-filled boxes along with such articles, detailing where people in similar straits can get help or find support groups or financial assistance. Knowing all that, you would then send me a query, preferably noting that the people involved had agreed to give you an interview. If your query were exemplary, I'd surely bite. In fact, I did, when Beverly Jacobson of Scarsdale, New York, sent me a query on this very case. The result was a much-loved article, "The $300.00 Medical Bill," which ran in our August 1982 issue.

Rule Number Three: *When you stick your neck out, make the best impression possible*. Of course, I wouldn't have responded positively to Beverly Jacobson's query if it hadn't been so thoroughly professional, with a warm, attention-grabbing lead that could actually have been the lead for her story, and then a crisp summation of the facts in the case. She kept her query to under two pages, and she let me know that she had already approached the people involved and that they were willing to be interviewed and photographed, and that they would agree, for an honorarium, to give the story as a magazine exclusive to *Ladies' Home Journal*. Beyond that, successful writers know that neatness counts. You don't need a fancy letterhead or a word processor, but do spring for a fresh typewriter ribbon, and remember to include your full name, address, and telephone number.

Rule Number Four: *Don't send a completed manuscript*. There are a few exceptions to this rule—for example, short humor pieces, essays, fillers and anecdotes—but in most cases editors prefer to read brief queries. Even if you have written the entire piece, please follow this rule.

Rule Number Five: *Don't phone a query*. If you are a writer whose work I know, you may break this rule. Otherwise, you need to show me how you write by sending a written query.

Rule Number Six: *Send a resume and clips, if you have them*. Naturally, if you have no previous publishing credits, you'll have to take your chances and hope your query is a stand-out. It will not automatically be passed on to a top editor, as it would be if you had clips, but if it's good, I can guarantee you that the slush readers *will* pass it on.

Rule Number Seven: *Don't worry about getting an agent*. I know that the phrase "literary agent" has a certain glamour to it, conjuring up visions of lunching at the Four Seasons or La Cote Basque. But it is really not necessary to be represented by an agent when you are submitting nonfiction to magazines. If you also write books, you and your agent can decide whether or not he or she will also handle your magazine work.

514

Rule Number Eight: *Meet your deadlines.* This is most important if an editor is planning to use your piece for a specific issue. On the other hand, don't be disappointed if you do get your story in on time, and then it's bumped from the issue and put on hold for a future issue. Scheduling each issue of a magazine is a delicate task, and we always have a sound reason for whatever changes are made.

Rule Number Nine: *Send full names and addresses of all your sources.* Thi. is true for your experts and your case history people as well, so that we can fact-check quickly. Also send a bibliography for secondary sources, and keep all of your notes and tapes on file in case we need to go back to them.

Rule Number Ten: *Expect to be edited.* The best writers always seem to be the ones who are the most eager to cooperate in the editing process, recognizing that it is a joint venture designed to polish and clarify their work. So be available by phone throughout the editing process, and read your copy of the edited manuscript the minute it reaches you, so that you can call with any changes.

There you have them: my ten rules for getting out of the slush and into print. But just to make sure you really go for it, let me close with my all-time favorite break-in-over-the-transom story. Some years ago there was a young Michigan woman who wanted to be a published writer. She wrote all the time, and she read *The Writer* religiously every month, but she never put anything in the mail because she was afraid to stick her neck out. She was afraid of getting rejection slips, of being out of her league. Then one summer, she was on the island of Crete with her new husband. They had dinner at an intimate little taverna on the Mediterranean in a tiny town on the south coast, called Ierapetra. It wasn't a tourist town, and they were the only Americans at table that evening. The food was delicious and the atmosphere enchanting. "You ought to write an armchair travel piece about this place for *Gourmet*," her husband suggested. She was touched by his faith in her writing, and so the next day she borrowed the only English language typewriter in town, from the schoolmaster, and she wrote a query and sent it off to *Gourmet*. A few weeks later, she got a go-ahead on spec. Breathlessly, she wrote the story, sent it off, and waited. She was rewarded in a month with a lovely acceptance letter and a $300 check. She had broken in over the transom!

I was that young woman. I'm glad I stuck my neck out. You will be, too.

97

THE EDITOR'S SIDE

By Olga Litowinsky

I HAVE written books as well as edited them, and know full well the many frustrations a writer can experience. I remember waiting six months for a check due on acceptance of a manuscript on which I had labored over a year. My books were also not promoted enough, went out of print too soon and did not make me rich and famous (ah, there's the rub!). Obviously, this was the publisher's fault. We all know that.

On the other hand, I am forever grateful to the editor of my first novel, who returned the manuscript looking as if a chicken had wandered delicately over every page. I resented every change she tactfully suggested, but after some thought, duly made all but one. I resisted that one only because I had to take a stand *somewhere*. My next editors were charming. Even though one of them insisted a passage was unintelligible to her no matter how many times I told her it was perfectly clear, we are still friends (I did make the change). The other editor was sorry there weren't more ads for the book, and I remain embarrassed at the outrage I directed toward him, even though it wasn't his fault.

Now let's discuss some points from the editor's side of the desk:

1. *Time.* Since every writer considers him/herself the *only* writer an editor has, of course the editor should take the new manuscript home and spend the evening (or weekend) reading it. We get paid about the same as schoolteachers. While we know teachers are underpaid, they at least get lots of time off. Editors get standard corporate vacations, go to conventions on weekends, and are expected to keep up with the flow of manuscripts. Reading manuscripts is *work* when read during one's *leisure* time.

2. *Form rejection slips.* How nice if we could write a thoughtful note to each of the authors of the 5000 manuscripts we receive. The form

rejection slip has turned out to be the kindest and quickest way to say no thank you. When an editor does offer a gentle criticism to a promising writer of a mediocre work ("You might consider developing the characters a wee bit more"), we are usually branded as insensitive louts. It's a no-win situation.

3. *The flow of words.* Is an editor to allow murky or ungrammatical passages to go out to the world? Reviews are of the writer's work, not of the editor's; rarely have I seen a book criticized for being poorly edited, often for being poorly written. Am I wrong to think one of my functions as an editor is to aid the writer in presenting the best face possible to the world? I admit that when I was younger, I did overedit as a means of satisfying my ego, of making the book "mine" in a way it did not have a right to be. I still remember Ben Bova's question to me: "Is this book mine or yours? Perhaps you should try writing one of your own." It was a valuable lesson in keeping my mitts off when it *wasn't* necessary. Since then I learned to trust my writers more.

Editors are not perfect (surprise!). Yet there is no one else an author can trust to be impartial and honest about his or her writing. Husbands, wives and friends are either "too busy" or too adoring; other writers are often jealous; reviewers may have private axes to grind. Editors sit between the virgin manuscript and the public. We are the first real reader the book is exposed to, and like a kindly parent, we are the first to say "your slip is showing." Writers—even the very best—are not perfect either; they can have blind spots. I was mortified recently when an editor returned an article I had done, asking me to "please change all the passive voices to active." How many times have I asked my writers to do the same?

4. *Editing on a word processor.* Like most editors I know, I've never done it and don't want to have to squint at a screen all day long. I'm not sure I trust the dang things yet. When it becomes inevitable, I guess I'll do it, but for now I like my Blackwing pencils.

Because I am a writer as well as an editor, I've become more sensitive to my writers' concerns. But being a writer doesn't change for me some of the fundamental defects in the editorial and publishing process. Too much work, not enough staff, not enough money. We will all say we do what we do because we love it, although recently quite a few potential editors have gone off to become lawyers, doctors and M.B.A.s because they don't believe in taking vows of poverty.

But what bothers me most is that it's a rare writer who ever says thank you to the person who's worked hard (and anonymously) to make the writer look good. Turnabout, they say, is fair enough. The next time a writer is between books, why doesn't he or she spend a few months at the publisher's office to get a better idea of what it's like on this side of the desk? Perhaps if writers and editors were more sympathetic to each other's problems, we could dispense with petty resentments and back-biting and get on with the work.

98

WHAT EVERY WRITER NEEDS TO KNOW ABOUT LITERARY AGENTS

By Ellen Levine

Q. *At what stage in their careers should writers look for an agent— or will a good agent find them?*

A. Most agents prefer to begin a working relationship with a writer when there is a book-length work to market, rather than articles or short stories. Some agents prefer writers who already have publication credits, perhaps magazine publication of shorter work. However, a writer who has never published before, but who is offering a book which deals with a unique or popular topic may also have an excellent chance of securing an agent. Quite a number of agents are actively looking for new writers, and they comb the little magazines for talented writers of fiction. They also read general interest and specialty magazines for articles on interesting subjects, since they might contain the seeds for books. Some agents visit writers conferences and workshops with the express purpose of discovering talented authors who might be interested in representation.

Q. *How does a writer go about looking for a legitimate agent?*

A. Writers can obtain lists of agent members from two professional organizations—The Society of Authors' Representatives (SAR) or The Independent Literary Agents Association (ILAA)— by writing to these organizations at (for SAR) 39½ Washington Square South, New York, New York 10012 and (for ILAA) 21 W. 26th St., New York, NY 10010. Writers can also obtain a more complete list of agents by checking the "Agents" section of *Literary Market Place* (LMP), available from R. R. Bowker, 205 E. 42nd St., New York, NY 10017, or as a reference work at the local library. Finally, the Authors Guild at 234 W. 44th St., New York, NY 10036 will supply a list of agents.

Q. *How important is it for an agent to be a member of SAR or ILAA?*

A. It is not essential for a good agent to belong to either organization, but membership is very helpful and adds credibility and professionalism to the agency. These organizations schedule meetings to discuss issues and problems common to the industry and their members work together to solve them. Expertise is often shared; panels and seminars are regularly scheduled, often including key publishing personnel. There are also certain codes of professional ethics, which members of each group subscribe to. This, of course, is to the writer's advantage.

Q. *Do literary agents specialize in particular types of material— novels, plays, nonfiction books, short stories, television scripts? Are there some categories that agents could not profitably handle that could better be marketed by the authors?*

A. Most of the agents' listings in LMP specify which kind of material the agency handles. A few agencies do have certain areas of specialization such as screenplays, or children's books, as well as more general fiction and nonfiction.

Q. *Should a writer query an agent (or several agents) before sending him or her his manuscript(s)?*

A. It is acceptable for a writer to query more than one agent before sending material, but it should be made clear to the agent that the writer is contacting several agents at one time. It is even more important for the writer to clarify whether he plans to make multiple submissions of a manuscript. Most agents prefer to consider material on an exclusive basis for a reasonable period of time, approximately four to eight weeks.

Q. *What do agents look for before accepting a writer as a client?*

A. An agent usually takes on a new client based on his or her enthusiasm for that writer's work and a belief that it will ultimately be marketable.

Q. *Once an agent has agreed to take a writer on as a client, what further involvement can the agent expect and legitimately ask of the writer?*

521

A. It may take longer to place the work of a new author, and the client should be patient in the process. If the writer has made contact with a specific editor or knows that there is interest in the work from a specific publisher, he or she should inform the agent. The writer should feel free to continue contacts with book editors with whom he or she has worked, and to discuss ideas with magazine editors.

Q. *Do most agents today ask for proposals, outlines, synopses, etc., of a book-length work before taking on the job of reading and trying to market the whole book? Do agents ever prepare this type of material, or is that solely the author's function?*

A. This varies among agents. A popular procedure for consideration of material from a prospective client is the request of an outline or proposal and the first 50 or 100 pages. If the book is complete, some agents might request the completed manuscript. It is common practice to submit a nonfiction work on the basis of one or more chapters and a synopsis or outline. The extent of the sample material needed is often based on the writer's previous credentials. It is generally the author's job to prepare the outline and the agent's to prepare the submission letter or the "pitch."

Q. *When, if ever, are multiple queries or submissions allowable, acceptable, desirable? By agent or by author?*

A. If an author is working without an agent, multiple submissions to publishers are acceptable only if the author informs the publisher that the book is being submitted on that basis. However, this can sometimes backfire since those publishers who will read unsolicited manuscripts may not care to waste the staff's reading time on a manuscript that is on simultaneous submission to five other publishers. Multiple queries with one-at-a-time submissions upon receipt of a favorable reply are probably more effective for a relatively new author. However, if a writer has a nonfiction project that is obviously very desirable or timely (an inside story, a current political issue), it is of course expedient to proceed with a multiple submission. This should be done carefully, informing all the participants of the deadline, ground rules, and so on. Agents must judge each project individually and decide on the appropriate procedure. If more than one publisher has expressed an interest in a specific writer or project, a multiple submission is not only appropriate, it is fair and in the author's best interest if there are competitive offers. If a book is very commercial, an auction may well be the result of a multiple submission. If other factors, such as a guaranteed print order or publicity plans are important, a multiple submission without the necessity of taking the highest bid may bring the best results. If an agent routinely makes multiple submissions of all properties, credibility may be lost. If this practice is reserved for the projects which warrant it, the procedure is more effective. It is usually not appropriate to send out multiple copies of a promising first novel. It may be for the inside story of last week's Congressional investigation.

Q. *What business arrangements should a writer make with an agent? Are contracts common to cover the relationship between author and agent? How binding should this be and for what period of time?*

A. Author-agent business arrangements vary among agencies. Some agents will discuss commission, expenses, and methods of operation with their authors, and this informal verbal agreement is acceptable to both parties. Others will write letters confirming these arrangements. Several agencies require contracts defining every detail of the business arrangements, and others require formal, but less extensive contracts. Written agreements often contain a notification of termination clause by either party with a period varying from 30 days to a full year. A few of the agency agreements require that the agency continue to control the subsidiary rights to a book even after the author and agent have parted. Most agents include what is known as an "agency clause" in each book contract the author signs, which provides for the agency to receive payments for the author due on that book for the complete life of the contract, whether or not the author or agent has severed the general agency agreement. In a few cases this clause will contain the provision mentioned above (compulsory representation of the author's retained subsidiary rights). It is important for a writer to discuss these and all aspects of the agency's representation at the beginning of the relationship. In addition to understanding clearly commission rates and expenses he or she will be required to pay, a writer might want to discuss such matters as expectations for consultation on marketing, choice of publishers, the number of submissions to be made, frequency of contact with agent, and so on. *Poets and Writers, Inc.* at 201 West

523

54th Street, New York, NY 10019 has published a helpful handbook entitled *Literary Agents: A Writer's Guide* ($5.95), which addresses these issues. Commissions vary among agents. The range is often between 10% and 20%. Some agencies may vary the commission for different rights, charging 10% or 15% for domestic sales and 15% or 20% for foreign sales. Certain agencies have different rates for different authors, depending upon the length of time the author has been with the agency, the size of the publishing advance, or the amount of editorial and preparatory work the agent must do before marketing the book. Some agents work more extensively in an editorial capacity than others and may make detailed suggestions and ask for revisions before marketing a work.

Q. *Can a writer express a preference to the agent concerning the particular publishing house or kind of house he would prefer for his book?*
A. Writers should share with their agents any preferences or ideas they may have about their work, including which publishers would be most appealing, and in which format they envision their books. However, writers should not be dismayed if their agents feel in some cases that a particular preference may be unrealistic or inappropriate.

Q. *How much of the business side of publishing does the writer need to deal with, once he is in the hands of a competent agent?*
A. An agent acts as a writer's business representative for his publishing affairs. Most agents do not act as a writer's overall financial manager, and if an author begins to earn a substantial income, he or she may be well-advised to consult with a C.P.A. and/or tax attorney. The prudent writer, while entrusting his business affairs to his or her agent, will want to stay informed about these matters.

Q. *How much "reporting" can a writer legitimately expect from the agent who has agreed to handle his work?*
A. This would depend on the agent's individual style and the writer's need and preference. Many agents keep clients informed about the progress of submissions by sending copies of rejection letters; others do not, and will give the writer a summary periodically. A writer

should be kept informed of all important events and conversations with editors and co-agents about his or her work; for instance, a favorable *Publishers Weekly* review that has come in, a substantial delay in publication, a paperback auction date that has been set. On the other hand, writers should not expect daily contact with an agent as an established routine.

Q. *What involvement, if any, should a writer have in the contract that the agent makes with a publisher? Does he have the right, responsibility to question the terms, change them, insist on higher royalty rates, advertising, etc., or is this left entirely to the agent, along with the sale of substantial rights?*

A. It is the agent's responsibility to consult with the author before accepting any of the basic terms of an offer such as the advance, royalties, subsidiary rights, and territories granted. If the author has any particular reasonable requests which he or she would like to include in the contract, such as approval or consultation on the jacket design, it is the author's responsibility to let the agent know before the start of negotiations. The choice of an agent should imply the author's trust and confidence in the agent's expertise in negotiating the contract and securing the best possible financial and legal terms for the author. Authors should read contracts carefully and ask questions about any provisions, if necessary. However, it is not reasonable for an author to ask for changes in every clause or expect provisions that are extremely difficult to obtain, particularly for authors who have not had best sellers. For instance, advertising guarantees in contracts are not common for new authors. If the author has chosen a skillful agent, he or she should have confidence in the agent's explanation of what is or is not feasible in a contract with a particular publisher.

Q. *If an agent feels that he cannot place a manuscript and the author feels that it is marketable, or, at least, worthy of publication, can the author try to sell it on his own?*

A. If this happens on occasion and the agent has no objection, the author should feel free to try after discussing what he or she plans to do. The agent will want to be informed so that no prior obligation, such as an option requirement, is breached. If the author's agent repeatedly

525

feels that the author's manuscripts cannot be placed, perhaps it is time for the author and agent to re-examine their relationship and discuss a change.

Q. *What services, other than the marketing of the manuscripts, negotiating the terms of their publishing contracts and related business arrangements may authors reasonably expect from their agents?*

A. In addition to marketing manuscripts, agents often help authors in formulating book ideas, passing along book ideas from editors when appropriate, and making introductions to appropriate editors if the author is between projects and free of contract obligations. Agents also follow up on various details of the publication process, such as production schedules, publicity, promotion, suggestions of other writers who might offer a quote for the jacket. The agent should also disseminate reviews, quotes, and information on subsidiary rights sales such as reprint and book club sales. Agents also examine royalty statements and, when necessary, obtain corrected statements.

Authors should not expect an agent to act as a secretary, travel agent, or bank. On the other hand, it is inevitable that a more personal bond may often form in the author/agent relationship, and in certain cases, agents do become involved to varying extents in friendships with their clients. In fact, hand-holding, "mothering" and counseling are not unfamiliar to many agents in dealing with certain authors. This is really a function of the agent's personality and often a conscious decision about how personally involved with his or her clients that particular agent wishes to be. A client should not expect that agent to solve his or her personal problems routinely.

Q. *How would you sum up the major role the agent plays in selling an author's work?*

A. If a manuscript is marketable, a good agent can short-circuit the random process of submissions by knowledge of the market, publishers, and the tastes and personalities of specific editors. However, an agent cannot place unsalable work. An agent can also be effective in the choice of marketing strategy for a particular work—should the book be sold as a trade paperback? Is a "hard-soft" deal best for the project? Would the author best be served by an auction, or would select individual submissions with editorial meetings be best?

99

LITTLE MAGAZINES: NO SMALL THING

BY SANDRA SCOFIELD

A FEW years ago I had a stack of unpublished short stories eight inches high, a novel manuscript nobody would read, a shoe box of impersonal rejection slips, and a rapidly diminishing store of confidence. Then I discovered "little" magazines and found an audience for my work. Also, as the result of a single story in *Ploughshares,* I acquired an agent, heard from editors asking to see my work, and received a citation in *Best American Short Stories.*

If you have been trying to sell your short stories, you already know how slim your chances are in magazines like *The Atlantic.* What you may not know is how satisfying and professionally important it can be to join what I think of as the small press community of dedicated editors, writers, and readers.

Is it worth your time and postage to send stories to these markets? You bet it is. Many first-rate fiction writers value the readership they find in the little magazines and literary journals and the opportunity these publications offer them to explore new themes and techniques.

You will find lists of these magazines in writer's marketing guides, an annual listing in *The Writer,* and in monthly marketing news. The most comprehensive guide is *The International Directory of Little Magazines and Small Presses* (Dustbooks). One I found very helpful was *The Writer's Guide to Magazine Markets: Fiction* (Plume), for its thorough discussion of 75 literary journals. Once you have such guides on hand, you may find yourself overwhelmed by the choices. Here are some suggestions to help you identify the right markets for your work. If you follow them, you will save yourself time, and you will do something else that is very important—you will support the small presses. Remember that readers (subscribers!) keep writers afloat.

1. *Analyze your own work.* You should probably do this twice, once before you study the markets, and again after you have become thor-

oughly acquainted with editors' jargon. If you do it first you will avoid the urge to fudge, to make your story *sound* as if it fits a market you like. Ask yourself:

Is this story good enough to publish? This is not a silly question! Separate your devotion to an idea and your critical sense of what is your best work. *Antaeus* editors have said that stories are mostly rejected because they aren't well written or interesting. Other editors also decry the trivial, the too familiar, the imitative. Some stories are learning experiences. Period. Little magazines consider themselves the guardians of quality.

What kind of story is this? Think in terms of style: is it experimental or traditional? Does it have a strong plot or is it focused on the inner life of a character? Does it belong to a specific genre, such as science fiction, erotica, or fantasy? Is your perspective identifiable as ethnic, lesbian, feminist, working-class, or "of color"? There are many markets giving preference to such orientations. Is your work polemic, political, or "socially-involved"? Some journals won't touch it, while others identify themselves as "left-wing" (*Another Chicago Magazine, The Minnesota Review*). *Know your own work.* Later you can compare it with stories published in potential markets.

2. *Study the descriptions of the little magazines* in market lists. Cross out ones you know you'd never read (for example, "demonic and macabre" doesn't interest me). List or star ones that seem interesting and possible, but *make no submissions yet.*

Many market listings give the price of sample copies. If the price is not included, send the editor a post card asking the price of a sample copy. Specify that you are interested in fiction (some magazines alternate fiction with special poetry issues), and ask for writers' guidelines. If you live near a university or a large public library, you will find some of the major little and literary magazines in their reading or periodical rooms. If not, be sure to buy one or two leading little magazines, such as *Antaeus, Ploughshares, TriQuarterly,* so that you can read top-quality stories. Generally, magazines with circulation of 2,000 or more—that pay—are hardest to break into. Be sure to read some less lofty ones, too; you may be pleasantly surprised, and you won't be scared off.

3. *Read each magazine.* More than once. Do you like it? This is probably the most important criterion. Don't make the decision on the basis of looks. Some journals that I like very much, with readership I would like to reach, are mimeographed rather than printed.

Watch for theme-centered issues; if you like the journal, write and ask for future themes. (*Calyx, Chelsea,* and *13th Moon* organize this way.)

Check the listings again. It is amazing how contradictory editors can be! One says, "Submit short bio." *(Arizona Quarterly).* Others say "Don't bother." *(Croton Review, Prairie Schooner).* Pay strict attention to length. Long stories (over 2,500 words) are the hardest to place. Note deadlines; many magazines don't read in the summer.

4. *Make your best guess, and submit. Be patient.* Well-known journals may get as many as 5,000 submissions a year. (Take heart; most are absolutely unpublishable, the editors say.) Editors are unpaid; many are students or professors. Three months is a reasonable time to wait before querying, so keep track of your submissions. If your follow-up query (with a self-addressed, stamped post card) gets no reply, submit elsewhere.

5. *Learn from your rejections.* Small press editors are idiosyncratic. A story of mine that won second place in *Nimrod's* Katherine Anne Porter Fiction Contest was rejected by another journal as "static and ageist." A story one magazine rejected as "disgusting" was accepted with high praise by *The Missouri Review.* On the other hand, one editor, who took the time to tell me why my well-crafted story (she compared it to James Agee) failed to "give her anything new," made a real contribution to my development as a story writer.

The printed slip without a comment is probably telling you something, too. My experience, with more than three dozen submissions, has been that most editors who respect your writing will say something even if they turn you down. They will say, "not right for us," or "send us something in the fall; we're overstocked," or "sorry we kept this so long, it was a tight choice at the end." You will have pangs, but you will know to keep sending the story around. Magazines that don't bother to pen a few words are crossed off my list, even if I love them. They didn't like my *writing,* not just this story.

6. *Read carefully books of short stories* published by the best of the small presses, as for instance, the annual prize anthologies of Pushcart Press (P.O. Box 380, Wainscott, NY 11975). Again, libraries are likely to carry these collections.

Also, buy current issues of the literary magazines. They are often found in large paperback bookstores and in university or public libraries.

Every few months I send for sample copies of a few magazines I am not familiar with. Then, I subscribe to three or four little or literary magazines a year, rotating among the ones I like best. Finally, *I subscribe to any publication that published my work.*

Little magazines may not make you rich (but one paying sale can buy a year's postage!) and they may not make you famous (though some wonderful writers got their first attention this way). Your nonwriting friends may not be impressed with a publication in *CutBank* or *Prairie Schooner* (they should be!), but you will have the satisfaction of *being read,* and you will read wonderful work you might otherwise never have seen.

Small magazines are a big opportunity.

100

THE 10% SOLUTION

By Anita Diamant

EACH time that I have had the privilege of talking to a group of writers, the consensus seems to be that it is harder today to find a good agent than a publisher. True? Well, legitimate agents work on a 10% commission basis, and of the manuscripts submitted to an agent by new writers only a very small percentage will prove to have sales potential. The agent will have spent time and energy in appraising these materials with no certainty of any income. After all, 10% of nothing doesn't really help to pay the rent!

But does this mean that in the field of book publishing, a new writer, or even a once-published writer, must attempt to sell a work himself? Not necessarily. There is no question about the fact that an agent can be enormously helpful to both an experienced and a new writer, depending upon the kinds of personalities involved and the type of relationship that can be established. While an agent is primarily the writer's business representative, it would be most unusual if a personal relationship between them did not come into being. I like to feel that my writers are not only my clients but also my friends, based upon our mutual interest and respect for each other.

It is important, however, for the writer to understand the function of a literary agent — what to expect from the agent and what a literary agent either can or cannot be asked to do. I feel that I can help my clients, not just by selling what they write, but also by advising them about the potential markets for the work they are planning and assisting them in smoothing out problems of plot and treatment in their manuscripts. Writers may expect agents to be so experienced that the advice they give their clients would be invaluable. But it is unrealistic for a writer to expect the agent to act as a publicity director, to handle bookstore sales, to act as a banker, or to offer psychiatric advice.

531

How can a writer obtain the services of a suitable agent? Although our agency is not eager to take on any number of unpublished writers, we do read and answer every letter of inquiry sent to us. It is extremely helpful for a prospective client to tell us something about his or her work, background, and why he or she feels he has a salable work in progress. We are frequently tempted to ask for sample chapters and an outline of the proposed book, and in many instances, we have found salable manuscripts in this way. The cliché, "Write, don't telephone," applies here, because our office time is taken up largely with numerous telephone calls from our clients, publishers, and editors, and we simply cannot take additional time to answer telephone queries from new writers.

When my assistant was asked what literary agents really do, he answered simply, "They talk on the telephone and go out to lunch." And while this may seem simplistic, frankly this kind of activity takes up much of our time. Lunches are important, for this is when agents meet editors and publishers to discuss projects. It is so much easier to sell a book on a personal, eyeball-to-eyeball basis, and any good agent can, through the dramatic presentation of an idea, create enormous interest on the part of an editor. (Of course, there are times when a writer does not fulfill that excitement in the presentation of the material!)

You are probably aware of the fact that legitimate literary agents do not advertise for writers, any more than legitimate publishers advertise for book properties. Then how does one go about finding an agent? The best way, of course, is through recommendation. If a writer has a friend who has had a book published, he can ask this person for the name of his agent. He then may write a letter to the agent, mentioning the recommen-

Agents are listed in *Literary Market Place,* published by R. R. Bowker Company, and the Society of Authors' Representatives (P.O. Box 650, Old Chelsea Sta., New York, NY 10113) also publishes a list of members, which will be sent if a stamped, self-addressed envelope is enclosed. In addition, a newer group of agents, the Independent Literary Agents Association (21 W. 26th St., New York, NY 10010) will send a list of members to those enclosing a stamped return envelope. Any agent listed in these three sources would be knowledgeable and reputable and would have a grasp of the markets and the requirements of various publishers today.

There are times when a new writer may be able to start on his own, and in the case of specialized books, such as books on crafts, juveniles and certainly academic subjects, a writer may find it relatively easy to make a direct contact and sell a manuscript. Many publishing houses, however, will not read manuscripts that come "over the transom," and consequently, if at all possible, a writer should attempt to find an agent. Also, there are some editors who find it difficult to deal directly with a writer and prefer to talk to an agent about business matters. (We have even had to shift a successful author from one large publishing house to another because of an unfortunate relationship between the writer and the editors at the first house.) The agent should always negotiate for the client and should run interference between editor and writer, when necessary.

When a writer complains — and not always unreasonably — about the lack of promotion and publicity for his book and the fact that it cannot be found in major bookstores, the agent takes up the complaint with the publisher. Acting as the intermediary, the agent, who is most apt to know when the complaint is justified, either telephones or makes a personal call on the publisher to straighten out the problem.

The agent frequently assumes the role of arbiter between two writers working together, since many collaborations, I find, begin happily and end disastrously.

An agent is most important to a writer in reading and working out the details of a book publisher's contract. While there are standard clauses that can rarely be changed in any publishing contract, still, the agent is more likely than the writer to know the customs and mores of the business and will be able to determine just what is negotiable and what will have to remain intact. At a writers' conference at which I was a speaker, I found that many writers were curious about the comparable benefits of using a lawyer against those of using a literary agent. There are many attorneys who specialize in literary properties and who can be extremely helpful in advising their clients about specific clauses in a contract. But the average lawyer has had little experience in this highly specialized form of legal document and may "make waves" that may not be beneficial to the writer's interests. On one occasion I sold a book manuscript to a major publisher for a new client who in turn had her lawyer read the contract. He made changes in minor clauses that worked against the author's interests!

533

In negotiating contracts, agents make every effort to retain subsidiary rights, such as first serial excerpt, foreign rights, television, motion picture, and so on, for these in many cases bring the authors larger sums than the initial book publication. But agents are aware that in the case of new writers, publishers will not yield on the usual 50-50 split in the proceeds from the sale of paperback or book-club rights. Also, many of the clauses that refer to the author's liability are difficult to alter, and here again, agents know just how far they can go in requesting changes in the contract.

Apart from benefiting from the agent's know-how in negotiating contracts, a writer also benefits from the agent's knowledge of the kind of publisher to whom a particular work should be submitted, and the form in which the material is most likely to be sold. For example, when I read a novel manuscript, I must determine at once whether it would be best to submit it for hardcover publication, or whether it should go directly to a paperback publisher. There is, of course, a difference: Though many books on the hardcover best-seller list are similar in style to paperbacks, a book must be fast-moving and filled with incident to appeal to the paperback audience. Also, I have to make the same kind of decision in deciding where to submit a nonfiction book idea for what we term the "oversize paperback," instead of a standard rack-size. The oversize paperback is a new and very profitable market today, and it has opened up many possibilities for nonfiction writers.

The work of literary agents has become so specialized that they have to decide not only which publisher would be best for a manuscript, but also which editor would offer a relationship that might be most *simpatico* for the author. If possible, I like to have my client and the editor meet at the very outset, so that they can work together without having any misunderstandings later on. This, of course, works most effectively when the contract for a book is signed before the book is completed.

At times, the agent is also faced with the important decision of whether to auction a manuscript or just to offer it on a multiple-submission basis. It should be stressed that auctions and multiple submissions are techniques that can be used *only* by agents, not by writers themselves. These are techniques by which we try to get a quick response from a publisher. In the case of a multiple submission, we send out several copies of the proposal or manuscript simultaneously to various publishers. But the whole purpose of this lies in telling each publishing house that a multiple submission is being made: Each house understands that it is in competition for the property offered. The same procedure is followed with an auction, but in this case the agent informs the publishers that there is a "floor" — a minimum advance that the author will find acceptable. Each house is then given a brief period to make an offer over the "floor." Although such auctions have received wide publicity recently, these are highly competitive techniques and should be used only very rarely — and then only by professionals.

This is another instance in which an agent's experience in professional matters is useful in making decisions for the benefit of the author. And that is why it is so important for a writer in selecting an agent to feel that he or she can place complete trust in the judgment of such a representative. Agents can make mistakes, of course, but they are likely to make fewer if they are dealing from knowledge and experience.

An agent receives a 10% commission on all domestic sales of manuscripts, including all rights, such as sales to magazines, television, syndicates, films, cassettes, and so on. However, in the case of British sales, we charge 15%, and on other foreign sales, a 20% commission. The increased commissions are charged because we all have representatives abroad who in turn have to be compensated for their work.

Is it worth 10% of a writer's income to have an agent? I am prejudiced, of course, but I sincerely think so. After all, an agent's function does not cease when a writer becomes established, witness the fact that such top authors as Irving Wallace, Arthur Hailey, Harold Robbins, and Erica Jong are all represented by agents. And I feel certain that all these successful writers would agree that they are more than reimbursed by the "10% solution."

PART IV

Where to Sell

Editors, publishers, and producers look to free-lance writers for a wide range of material, from fiction and articles to play scripts, opinion essays, and how-to books. This year's edition of THE WRITER'S HANDBOOK includes an extensive list of markets, completely revised and updated, offering an encouraging number of opportunities for writers at all levels of experience.

Beginning free lancers will find that one of the best magazine markets remains the field of specialized publications, including travel, city and regional publications, and those covering such fields as science, sports, hobbies and crafts, personal finance, and health. Since editors are always seeking authoritative articles, writers with a special interest, expertise or hobby—whether it's gardening, chess, car repair, knitting, or teaching—will find their knowledge particularly helpful, as there is usually at least one publication devoted to every one of these areas. Such interests and activities can generate more than one article, if a different angle is used for each magazine and the writer keeps the audience and the editorial content firmly in mind.

One nonfiction field that has grown considerably in the last few years is the market for technical, computer, and health writing, with articles on these topics appearing in almost every publication on the newsstands today, from general-interest monthlies to more specialized science publications; personal finance articles are in demand at a variety of publications, as well. For these subjects, editors are looking for writers who have an ability to translate technical material into lively readable prose, providing authoritative articles on complex and constantly changing subjects.

While some of the more established markets may seem difficult to break into, especially for the beginner, there are thousands of lesser-known publications, where editors are receptive to submissions, and are willing to consider the work of first-time free lancers. City and regional publications offer some of the best opportunities, since these editors generally like to work with local writers, and often use a wide variety of material, from features to fillers. Many newspapers accept op-ed pieces, and are most receptive to pieces on topics not covered by syndicated columnists (politics, economics, and foreign affairs); pieces with a regional slant are particularly welcome here.

It is important for writers to keep in mind the number of opportunities that exist for nonfiction, because the paying markets for fiction are somewhat limited. Many general-interest and women's magazines do publish short stories; however, beginners will find these markets extremely competitive, with their work being judged against that of experienced professionals. We highly recommend that new writers look into the small, literary, and college publications, which always welcome the work of talented beginners. Payment is usually only in copies, but publication in literary journals can lead to recognition by editors of larger circulation magazines, who often look to the smaller publications for new talent. A growing number of regional, specialized and Sunday magazines use short stories, and are particularly receptive to local writers.

The market for poetry in general-interest magazines continues to be tight, and the advice for poets, as for fiction writers, is to try to get established and build up a list of publishing credits by submitting material to literary journals. Poets should look also to local newspapers, which often use verse, especially if it relates to holidays or other special occasions.

New playwrights will find community, regional and civic theaters and college dramatic groups offer the best opportunities for staged production in this competitive market. Indeed, many of today's well-known playwrights received their first recognition in regional theaters, and aspiring writers who can get their work produced by one of these have taken a dramatic step toward breaking into this field. In addition to producing plays and giving dramatic readings, many theaters also sponsor competitions or new play festivals.

Though a representative number of television shows are included in this section of the HANDBOOK, writers should be aware of the fact that this market is inaccessible without an agent, and most writers break into it only after a careful study of the medium, and a long apprenticeship.

While the book publishing field remains competitive, beginners

538

should be especially encouraged by the many first novels published over the past few years, with more editors than ever before receptive to fiction submissions. And with an increasing number of publishers broadening their nonfiction lines, editors at many hardcover and paperback houses are on the lookout for new authors, especially those with a knowledge of or training in a particular field. Small presses across the country continue to flourish, and writers may find these an attractive alternative for their manuscripts.

All information in these lists concerning the needs and requirements of magazines, book publishing companies, and theaters comes directly from the editors, publishers, and directors, but editors move and addresses change, as do requirements. No published listing can give as clear a picture of editorial needs and tastes as a careful study of several issues of a magazine, and writers should never submit material without first reading through several back issues of a publication. If a magazine is not available in the local library, write directly to the editor for a sample copy (often free or sent at a small cost).

ARTICLE MARKETS

The magazines in the following list are in the market for free-lance articles of many types. Unless otherwise stated in these listings, a writer should submit a query first, including a brief description of the proposed article and any relevant qualifications or credits. A few editors want to see samples of published work, if available. Manuscripts must be typed double-space on good white bond paper (8½ x 11), with name, address, and telephone number at the top left- or right-hand corner of the page. Do not use erasable or onion skin paper, since it is difficult to work with, and always keep a copy of the manuscript, in case it is lost in the mail. Submit photos or slides only if the editor has specifically requested them. A self-addressed envelope with sufficient postage to cover the return of the manuscript or the answer to a query should accompany all submissions. Response time may vary from two to eight weeks, depending on the size of the magazine and the volume of mail it receives. If an editor doesn't respond within what seems to be a reasonable amount of time, it's perfectly acceptable to send a polite inquiry. Many publications have writer's guidelines, outlining their editorial requirements and submission procedures; these can be obtained by sending a self-addressed, stamped envelope (SASE) to the editor. Also, be sure to ask for a sample copy: Editors indicate the most consistent mistake free lancers make is failing to study several issues of the magazine to which they are submitting material.

GENERAL-INTEREST PUBLICATIONS

ACROSS THE BOARD—845 Third Ave., New York, NY 10022. Nancy Boas, Assoc. Ed. Articles, to 5,000 words, on a variety of topics of interest to business executives; straight business angle not required. Pays $100 to $750, on publication. Query.

ALCOHOLISM & ADDICTION—P.O. Box 31329, Seattle, WA 98103. Neil Scott, Ed. Articles on all aspects of alcoholism: treatment, legislation, education, prevention, and recovery. Send SASE for guidelines. Pays after publication.

ALLIED PUBLICATIONS—1776 Lake Worth Rd., Lake Worth, FL 33460. Mark Adams, Ed. Articles, to 800 words, on business careers, management, foreign travel, fashion, beauty and hairstyling. Photos; cartoons. Pays 5¢ per printed word, extra for photos and cartoons, on publication. Editorial guidelines available.

THE AMERICAN LEGION MAGAZINE—Box 1055, Indianapolis, IN 46206. Michael D. LaBonne, Ed. Articles, 750 to 1,800 words, on current world affairs, public policy, and subjects of contemporary interest. Pays $100 to $1,000, on acceptance. Query.

AMERICAS—OAS, General Secretariat Bldg., 1884 F St., NW, Washington, DC 20006. A. R. Williams, Man. Ed. Features, to 2,500 words, on life in Latin America and the Caribbean. Wide focus: anthropology, the arts, travel, science and development, etc. No political material. Query. Pays from $200, on publication.

AMTRAK EXPRESS—140 E. Main St., Suite 11, Huntington, NY 11743.

Christopher Podgus, Ed. General-interest articles on business, health, books, sports, personal finance, lifestyle, entertainment, travel (within Amtrak territory), technology, and science for Amtrak travelers. Submit seasonal material three to six months in advance. Pays on publication, $300 to $700 for 1,800- to 3,000-word manuscripts; $250 to $600 for department pieces of 1,500 to 2,500 words. Query with published clips.

THE ATLANTIC—8 Arlington St., Boston, MA 02116. William Whitworth, Ed. In-depth articles on public issues, politics, social sciences, education, business, literature, and the arts, with emphasis on information rather than opinion. Ideal length: 3,000 to 6,000 words, though short pieces (1,000 to 2,000 words) are also welcome. Pays $1,000 to $7,000, on acceptance.

BETTER HOMES AND GARDENS—1716 Locust St., Des Moines, IA 50336. David Jordan, Ed. Articles, to 2,000 words, on home and family entertainment, building, decorating, food, money management, health, travel, pets, and cars. Pays top rates, on acceptance. Query.

CAPPER'S—616 Jefferson St., Topeka, KS 66607. Dorothy Harvey, Ed. Articles, 300 to 500 words: human-interest, personal experience for women's section, historical. Pays varying rates, on publication.

CHATELAINE—Maclean Hunter Bldg., 777 Bay St., Toronto, Ont., Canada M5W 1A7. Mildred Istona, Ed. Articles, 3,000 words, for Canadian women, on current issues, personalities, medicine, psychology, etc. Pays $750 for personal-experience pieces, from $1,000 for articles, on acceptance.

THE CHRISTIAN SCIENCE MONITOR—One Norway St., Boston, MA 02115. Roderick Nordell, Feature Ed. Articles on arts, travel, education, food and lifestyle; interviews; literary essays, to 800 words, for Home Forum; guest columns, to 800 words, for editorial page. Pays varying rates.

CLASS—27 Union Sq. W., New York, NY 10003. D. Alex Harris, Ed. Articles, to 2,500 words, of interest to the Third World population living in the U.S., and inhabitants of the Caribbean Islands. Pays 5¢ to 20¢ a word, after acceptance. Query.

COSMOPOLITAN—224 W. 57th St., New York, NY 10019. Helen Gurley Brown, Ed. Guy Flatley, Man. Ed. Articles, to 4,000 words, and features, to 2,500 words, on issues affecting young career women: jobs and careers, male-female relationships, sex, emotions, health, money matters, and first-person experiences. "We insist that writing be concise, not soupy or watery. The tone of voice should be conversational, but never cutesy; authoritative (quote real experts), not merely chatty. Writers should avoid repetition of works, phrases, and sentence structure. Definitely avoid clichés. Case histories to illustrate a point should be numerous but *short*." Pays $1,500 to $2,000 for full-length articles, less for features, on acceptance. Query first.

COUNTRY JOURNAL—Box 870, Manchester Center, VT 05255. Tyler Resch, Ed. Articles, 2,500 to 3,000 words, for country and small-town residents: practical, informative pieces on contemporary rural life. Pays about $400, on acceptance. Query.

COUNTRY PEOPLE—5400 S. 60th, Greendale, WI 53129. Dan Johnson, Assoc. Ed. Articles, 500 to 1,000 words, for a rural audience. Fillers, 50 to 200 words. Taboos: tobacco, liquor, and sex. Pays $125 to $200, on acceptance. Query.

DAWN—628 N. Eutaw, Baltimore, MD 21201. Bob Matthews, Exec. Ed.

Illustrated feature articles, 1,500 words, on subjects of interest to black families. Pays $100 on publication. Query.

EASY LIVING—9965 Valley View Rd., Eden Prairie, MN 55344. Articles, 1,000 to 1,800 words, for customers of financial institutions, on personal finance, lifestyle, consumerism, money, and some foreign travel. Pays $250 to $600, on acceptance. Query.

EBONY—820 S. Michigan Ave., Chicago, IL 60605. Herbert Nipson, Exec. Ed. Articles, with photos, on blacks: achievements, civil rights, etc. Pays from $150, on publication. Query.

ELLE—551 Fifth Ave., New York, NY 10176. Joan Harting, Sr. Ed. Articles, varying lengths, for fashion-conscious women, ages 20 to 50. Topics include beauty, fashion, careers, fitness, travel, and lifestyles. Pays top rates, on publication. Query required.

EM: EBONY MAN—1270 Ave. of the Americas, New York, NY 10020. Alfred Fornay, Exec. Ed. Articles of interest to black men. Mostly staff-written; query required.

EQUINOX—7 Queen Victoria Rd., Camden East, Ont., Canada K0K 1J0. Frank Edwards, Exec. Ed. Articles, 4,000 to 8,000 words, on popular geography, biology, astronomy, sciences, the arts, industry, and adventure. Department pieces, 300 to 500 words, for "Nexus" (science and medicine) and "Habitat" (man-made and natural environment). Pays $1,000 to $2,000 for features, $100 to $200 for short pieces, on acceptance.

ESQUIRE—2 Park Ave., New York, NY 10016. David Hirshey, Articles Ed. Articles, 250 to 4,000 words, for intelligent adult audience. Pays $250 to $1,500, on acceptance. "We prefer receiving a query letter with some published feature writing samples rather than a finished manuscript. However, writers who have not been published as yet should send the finished article."

ESSENCE—1500 Broadway, New York, NY 10036. Susan L. Taylor, Ed.-in-Chief. Provocative articles, 1,500 to 3,000 words, about black women in America today: self-help, how-to pieces, careers, health, celebrity profiles and political issues. Short items, 500 to 750 words, on work and health. Pays varying rates, on acceptance. Query for articles.

FAMILY CIRCLE—488 Madison Ave., New York, NY 10022. Susan Ungaro, Articles Ed. Articles, to 2,500 words, on child care, consumer affairs, changing lifestyles, health and fitness, jobs, money management, food, travel, gardening, true-life dramas. Query required. Pays on acceptance.

FORD TIMES—One Illinois Center, 111 E. Wacker Dr., Suite 1700, Chicago, IL 60601. Thomas A. Kindre, Ed. Articles for a family audience, particularly geared to ages 18 to 35: topical pieces (trends, life styles); profiles; first-person accounts of unusual vacation trips or real-life travel adventures; unusual sporting events or outdoor activities; food and cooking; humor. Bright, lively photos desired. "Road Show" and "Glove Compartment": travel and dining anecdotes; pays $50, on publication. Payment for articles, 1,200 to 1,500 words, is $550 to $800; $400 for 800 to 1,200 words; and $250 for short pieces (500 to 800 words), on acceptance. Query with SASE required for all but humor and anecdotes.

FRIENDLY EXCHANGE—Locust at 17th, Des Moines, IA 50336. Adele Malott, Ed. Articles, 1,000 to 2,500 words, for young, active families who live in the western half of the U.S. Subjects include domestic travel, camping, health, culture, personal finance, consumer information, and food. No poetry, fiction, cartoons. Photos. Pays $400 to $800, extra for photos. Query preferred. Writer's guidelines available.

FRIENDS—30400 Van Dyke, Warren, MI 48093. Herman G. Duerr, Exec. Ed. Active life style articles and upbeat subjects of general interest, for owners of Chevrolet vehicles. Photos required. Pays from $300, extra for photos. Query Karel Bond.

GENTLEMEN'S QUARTERLY—350 Madison Ave., New York, NY 10017. Eliot Kaplan, Man. Ed. Articles, 1,500 to 4,000 words, for a male audience, on politics, personalities, life styles, trends, grooming, sports, travel, business. Columns, 1,000 to 2,500 words: "Male Animal" (essays by men on life); "All About Adam" (nonfiction by women about men); "Games" (sports); "Health"; and "Humor"; also columns on fitness, nutrition, investments, music, wine and food. Pays $750 to $3,000, on acceptance. Query with clips.

GLAMOUR—350 Madison Ave., New York, NY 10017. Ruth Whitney, Ed.-in-Chief; Judith Coyne, Articles Ed. Articles on careers, health, psychology, interpersonal relationships, etc.; editorial approach is "how-to" for women, 18 to 35. Fashion and beauty material staff-written. Pays from $1,000 for 1,500- to 2,000-word articles, from $1,500 for longer pieces, on acceptance.

GLOBE—5401 NW Broken Sound Blvd., Boca Raton, FL 33431. Donald McLachlan, Ass't. Ed. Factual articles, 500 to 1,000 words, with photos: exposés, celebrity interviews, consumer and human-interest pieces. Pays $50 to $1,500.

GOOD HOUSEKEEPING—959 Eighth Ave., New York, NY 10019. Joan Thursh, Articles Ed. In-depth articles and features, 1,200 to 5,000 words, on controversial problems, topical social issues; dramatic personal narratives about unusual experiences of average families; sharply-angled pieces about celebrities; research reports on news of interest to women, for "Better Way." Pays top rates, on acceptance. Query. Guidelines available.

GRIT—208 W. Third St., Williamsport, PA 17701. Alvin Elmer, Assoc. Ed. Articles, to 500 words, on religion, communities, jobs, recreation, families and coping. Pays 12¢ a word, extra for photos, on acceptance.

HARPER'S BAZAAR—1700 Broadway, New York, NY 10019. Anthony Mazzola, Ed.-in-Chief. Articles on topics of interest to women: food, career, finance, beauty, health, and travel. Pays top rates, on acceptance. Query required.

HARPER'S MAGAZINE—666 Broadway, New York, NY 10012. No unsolicited articles or queries. Considers manuscripts submitted through an agent only.

HOUSE AND GARDEN—350 Madison Ave., New York, NY 10017. Louis O. Gropp, Ed.-in-Chief. Shelley Wanger, Articles Ed. Articles on decorating, architecture, gardens, the arts. Query. Rarely buys unsolicited manuscripts.

HOUSE BEAUTIFUL—1700 Broadway, New York, NY 10019. Carol Cooper Garey, Dir. Copy/Features. Service articles related to the home. Pieces on beauty, travel and gardening mostly staff-written. Pays varying rates, on acceptance. Send for writer's guidelines. Query with detailed outline.

INQUIRER MAGAZINE—*Philadelphia Inquirer,* P.O. Box 8263, 400 N. Broad St., Philadelphia, PA 19101. David Boldt, Ed. Local-interest features,

500 to 7,000 words. Profiles of national figures in politics, entertainment, etc. Pays varying rates, on publication. Query.

IRISH AMERICA—34 E. 29th St., New York, NY 10016. Patricia Harty, Man. Ed. Articles, 1,000 words, of interest to Irish-American audience; preferred topics include history and politics. Pays 7¢ a word, after publication. Query.

LADIES' HOME JOURNAL—3 Park Ave., New York, NY 10016. Articles on contemporary subjects of interest to women. Personal experience and regional pieces. Queries only (with SASE) to Exec. Ed. Jan Goodwin or Beth Weinhouse and Roberta Grant, Sr. Eds. Not responsible for unsolicited manuscripts.

LIFE—Time-Life Bldg., Rockefeller Center, New York, NY 10020. Dean Valentine, Articles Ed. General-interest articles, 3,000 to 5,000 words. Pays varying rates, on acceptance. Query. Rarely buys free-lance material.

McCALL'S—230 Park Ave., New York, NY 10169. A. Elizabeth Sloan, Ed. Anne Cassidy, Articles Ed. Interesting, unusual and topical first person essays, narratives, reports on health, home management, social trends relating to women of all ages, 1,000 to 2,500 words. Humor. Human interest stories. Pieces for VIP-ZIP and regional sections: consumer, travel, crafts. Pays top rates, on acceptance.

MADEMOISELLE—350 Madison Ave., New York, NY 10017. Kate White, Exec. Ed. Articles, 2,000 to 3,000 words, on subjects of interest to single women in their 20's. Pays from $1,750, on acceptance. Query.

MARRIAGE & FAMILY LIVING—St. Meinrad, IN 47577. Kass Dotterweich, Man. Ed. Articles, to 2,000 words, on husband-wife and parent-child relationships. Pays 7¢ a word, on acceptance. Query.

MBM: MODERN BLACK MEN—1123 Broadway, Suite 802, New York, NY 10010. Sharon Breland, Man. Ed. Articles, 1,200 to 2,500 words, for black American professional men, aged 25 to 54; high quality fiction, 2,500 to 5,000 words; fillers, 100 to 1,000 words. Pays $15 to $200, on publication. Query.

MD MAGAZINE—3 East 54th St., New York, NY 10022. A. J. Vogl, Ed. Articles, 750 to 2,500 words, for doctors, on the arts, history, other aspects of culture. Fresh angle required. Pays from $200 to $700, on acceptance. Query.

METROPOLITAN HOME—750 Third Ave., New York, NY 10017. Service and informational articles for metropolitan dwellers in apartments, houses, co-ops, lofts, and condominiums, on real estate, equity, wine and spirits, collecting, etc. Pays varying rates. Query.

MODERN MATURITY—3200 East Carson St., Lakewood, CA 90712. Ian Ledgerwood, Ed. Articles on careers, workplace, human interest, living, finance, relationships, and consumerism, for persons over 50 years, to 2,000 words. Photos. Pays $500 to $2,500, extra for photos, on acceptance.

THE MOTHER EARTH NEWS—105 Stoney Mt. Rd., Hendersonville, NC 28791. Articles, with photos, on alternative life styles, for rural and urban readers: home improvements, how-to's, indoor and outdoor gardening, family pastimes, etc. Also, self-help, health, food-related, ecology, energy and consumerism pieces. Profiles. Pays varying rates, on acceptance. Send for writer's guidelines.

MOTHER JONES—1663 Mission St., San Francisco, CA 94103. Adam

Hochschild, Ed. "We specialize in our own brand of investigative reporting, which focuses on corporate and government cover-ups. We also publish human-interest pieces, profiles, interviews, political essays, economic analysis, and coverage of the arts. The best guide to the kinds of material we're interested in is to read several recent issues of the magazine." Pays $750 to $2,000, after acceptance.

MS.—119 W. 40th St., New York, NY 10018. Address Manuscript Ed. Articles relating to women's roles and changing lifestyles; general interest, how-to, self-help, profiles. Pays varying rates, on acceptance. Query with SASE required.

NATIONAL ENQUIRER—Lantana, FL 33464. Articles, of any length, for mass audience: topical news, the occult, how-to, scientific discoveries, human drama, adventure, personalities. Photos. Pays from $325. Query; no unsolicited manuscripts accepted.

NATIONAL GEOGRAPHIC—17th and M Sts. N.W., Washington, DC 20036. First-person, general-interest, illustrated articles on science, natural history, exploration, and geographical regions. Half staff-written; half written by professionals and scholars. No unsolicited manuscripts accepted; send 500-word query (with SASE) to Sr. Ass't. Ed. Study back issues and index before submitting. Pays on acceptance.

NEW WOMAN—215 Lexington Ave., New York, NY 10016. Pat Miller, Ed. "Read the magazine in order to become familiar with our needs before querying." Articles on new lifestyles. Features on financial and legal advice, building a business, marriage, relationships, surviving divorce, innovative diets. Pays varying rates, on acceptance. Query.

THE NEW YORK TIMES MAGAZINE—229 W. 43rd St., New York, NY 10036. Address Articles Ed. Timely articles, approximately 4,000 words, on new items, forthcoming events, trends, culture, entertainment, etc. Pays $350 to $500 for short pieces, $1,000 to $2,500 for major articles, on acceptance. Query with clips.

THE NEW YORKER—25 W. 43rd St., New York, NY 10036. Address The Editors. Factual and biographical articles, for "Profiles," "Reporter at Large," "Annals of Crime," "Onward and Upward with the Arts," etc. Pays good rates, on acceptance. Query.

NEWSWEEK—444 Madison Ave., New York, NY 10022. Phyllis Malamud, My Turn Ed. Original opinion essays, 1,000 to 1,100 words, for "My Turn" column: must contain verifiable facts. Submit manuscript with SASE. Pays $1,000, on publication.

OMNI—1965 Broadway, New York, NY 10023-5965. Patrice Adcroft, Ed.-in-Chief. Articles, 2,500 to 3,000 words, on scientific aspects of the future: space colonies, cloning, machine intelligence, ESP, origin of life, future arts, lifestyles, etc. Pays $750 to $2,500, less for short features, on acceptance. Query.

PARADE—750 Third Ave., New York, NY 10017. Fran Carpentier, Articles Ed. National Sunday newspaper supplement. Factual and authoritative articles, 1,000 to 1,500 words, on subjects of national interest: health, education, consumer and environmental issues, science, the family, sports, etc. Profiles of well-known personalities and service pieces. No fiction, poetry, games or puzzles. Photos with captions. Pays from $1,000. Query.

PENTHOUSE—1965 Broadway, New York, NY 10023-5965. Claudia Val-

545

entino, Man. Ed. Peter Bloch, Exec. Ed. General-interest or controversial articles, to 5,000 words. Pays from 20¢ a word, on acceptance.

PEOPLE IN ACTION—Box 10010, Ogden, UT 84409. Frank J. Cook, Ed. Features, 1,200 words, on nationally noted individuals in the fine arts, literature, entertainment, communications, business, sports, education, etc.: must exemplify positive values. Manuscripts should be accompanied by high-quality color transparencies. Query. Pays 15¢ a word, on acceptance.

PEOPLE WEEKLY—Time-Life Bldg., Rockefeller Center, New York, NY 10020. Hal Wingo, Ass't. Man. Ed. Considers article proposals only, 3 to 4 paragraphs, on timely, entertaining, and topical personalities. Pays good rates, on acceptance. Most material staff written.

PLAYBOY—919 M. Michigan Ave., Chicago, IL 60611. John Rezek, Articles Ed. Sophisticated articles, 4,000 to 6,000 words, of interest to urban men. Humor: satire. Pays to $3,000, on acceptance. Query.

PRIME TIMES—Suite 120, 2802 International Ln., Madison, WI 53704. Joan Donovan, Assoc. Man. Ed. Articles, 500 to 2,500 words, for dynamic, young- to middle-aged audience. Departments, 850 to 1,000 words. Pays $125 to $750, on publication. Query.

PRIVATE CLUBS—AA Magazine Publications, P.O. Box 619616, DFW Airport, TX 75261-9616. Gary Hardee, Man. Ed. Articles, 1,200 to 1,500 words, for members of city, country, and athletic clubs, on a wide variety of topics. Pays from $400, on acceptance. Query required.

PSYCHOLOGY TODAY—1200 17th St. N.W., Washington, DC 20036. Address Manuscripts Ed. Most articles assigned to researchers in the social sciences. Query.

READER'S DIGEST—Pleasantville, NY 10570. Kenneth O. Gilmore, Ed.-in-Chief. Unsolicited manuscripts will not be read or returned. General-interest articles already in print and well-developed story proposals will be considered. Send reprint or query to any editor on the masthead.

REDBOOK—224 W. 57th St., New York, NY 10019. Annette Capone, Ed.-in-Chief. Gini Kopecky, Articles Ed. Articles, 1,000 to 3,500 words, on subjects related to relationships, sex, current issues, marriage, the family, and parenting. Pays from $750, on acceptance. Query.

ROLLING STONE—745 Fifth Ave., New York, NY 10151. Magazine of modern American culture, politics, and art. Query; "rarely accepts free-lance material."

SATELLITE ORBIT—P.O. Box 53, 9440 Fairview Ave., Boise, ID 83707. Rick Ardinger, Sr. Ed. Television-related articles, 1,500 to 2,000 words; personality profiles; and articles of interest to the satellite TV viewer. Query with clips. Pays varying rates, on acceptance.

THE SATURDAY EVENING POST—1100 Waterway Blvd., Indianapolis, IN 46202. Ted Kreiter, Exec. Ed. Family-oriented articles, 1,500 to 3,000 words: humor, preventive medicine, destination-oriented travel pieces (not personal experience), celebrity profile, the arts, and sciences. Pieces on sports and home repair (with photos). Photo essays. Pays varying rates, on publication. Submit written query or complete manuscript.

SATURDAY REVIEW—214 Mass. Ave., N.E., Suite 460, Washington, DC 20002. Frank Gannon, Ed. Interviews; profiles; and reviews of events and books, 800 to 1,500 words. Pays varying rates, after publication.

SAVVY—3 Park Ave., New York, NY 10016. Annalyn Swan, Ed.-in-Chief. Service articles for women executives, 500 to 3,000 words, on business politics, finance, entrepreneurs. Pays $300 to $1,000, on publication. Query.

SELF—350 Madison Ave., New York, NY 10017. Valerie Griffith Weaver, Ed. Articles for women of all ages, with strong how-to slant, on self-development. Pays from $700, on acceptance. Query.

SIGNATURE—641 Lexington Ave., New York, NY 10022. Peter Young, Articles Ed. Highest quality literary and journalistic articles, 2,000 words, and columns, 1,300 words, for successful, affluent business people on all aspects of "living well": travel, dining, sports, art, music, acquisitions, fitness, etc. Query with published clips. Pays from $700, on acceptance.

STAR—660 White Plains Rd., Tarrytown, NY 10591. Topical articles, 50 to 800 words, on human-interest subjects, show business, lifestyles, the sciences, etc., for family audience. Pays varying rates.

SUCCESS—342 Madison Ave., New York, NY 10175. Scott DeGarmo, Ed.-in-Chief. Profiles of successful individuals, executives; entrepreneurs; psychology, behavior, and motivation articles, 500 to 3,500 words. Query.

SUNDAY—*The Chicago Tribune,* 435 N. Michigan, Chicago, IL 60611. Mary Knoblauch, Ed. General-interest articles, to 5,000 words. Pays on publication. Query.

TOWN & COUNTRY—1700 Broadway, New York, NY 10019. Address Features Dept. Considers one-page proposals for articles. Rarely buys unsolicited manuscripts.

TRAVEL & LEISURE—1120 Ave. of the Americas, New York, NY 10036. Pamela Fiori, Ed.-in-Chief. Articles, 800 to 3,000 words, on destinations and leisuretime activities. Regional pieces for regional editions. Pays $600 to $3,000, on acceptance. Query.

TROPIC—*The Miami Herald,* One Herald Plaza, Miami, FL 33101. Tom Shroder, Ed. Essays and articles on current trends and issues, light or heavy, 1,000 to 4,000 words, for sophisticated audience. Pays $200 to $1,000, on publication. Query.

TV GUIDE—Radnor, PA 19088. Andrew Mills, Ass't Man. Ed. Short, light, brightly-written pieces about humorous or offbeat angles of television. Pays on acceptance. Query.

US MAGAZINE—745 Fifth Ave., New York, NY 10151. Chris Connelly, Sr. Ed. Articles, 800 to 3,000 words, on timely general interest, entertainment, life style, and related topics. Pays from $500, on publication. Query with published clips required.

USA WEEKEND—P.O. Box 500W, Washington, DC 20044. John Walter, Sr. Ed. Marcia Bullard, Man. Ed. Short, lively articles on celebrities, health, personal finance, money management, and fitness. Pays from $200, on acceptance. Query.

VANITY FAIR—350 Madison Ave., New York, NY 10017. Tina Brown, Ed. Articles. Pays on acceptance. Query.

VILLAGE VOICE—842 Broadway, New York, NY 10003. Robert Friedman, Ed. Articles, 500 to 2,000 words, on current or controversial topics. Pays $75 to $450, on acceptance. Query.

VOGUE—350 Madison Ave., New York, NY 10017. Amy Gross, Features

Ed. Articles, to 1,500 words, on women, entertainment and the arts, travel, medicine and health. General features. Query.

VOLKSWAGEN'S WORLD—Volkswagen of America, Troy, MI 48099. Ed Rabinowitz, Ed. Articles, 600 to 1,000 words, for Volkswagen owners: profiles of well-known personalities; inspirational or human-interest pieces; travel; humor. Photos. Pays $150 per printed page, on acceptance. Query. Guidelines on request.

WASHINGTON POST MAGAZINE—*The Washington Post,* 1150 15th St., NW, Washington, DC 20071. Stephen L. Petranek, Man. Ed. Personal-experience essays, profiles and general-interest pieces, to 4,000 words, on business, arts and culture, politics, science, sports, education, children, relationships, behavior, etc. Pays from $250, after acceptance.

WEEKDAY—20 N. Wacker Dr., Chicago, IL 60606. Informative articles, 200 to 1,000 words, on solutions to everyday problems: consumer affairs, legal and community issues, real estate, etc. Pays $20 to $50, on acceptance.

WEEKLY WORLD NEWS—600 S. East Coast Ave., Lantana, FL 33462. Joe West, Ed. Human-interest news pieces, about 500 to 1,000 words, involving human adventure, unusual situations. Pays $125 to $500, on publication.

WISCONSIN—*The Milwaukee Journal Magazine,* P.O. Box 661, Milwaukee, WI 53201. Beth Slocum, Ed. Trend stories, essays, humor, personal-experience pieces, profiles, 500 to 2,000 words. Pays $75 to $500, after publication.

WOMAN'S DAY—1515 Broadway, New York, NY 10036. Rebecca Greer, Articles Ed. Articles, 500 to 3,500 words, on subjects of interest to women: marriage, education, family health, child rearing, money management, interpersonal relationships, changing lifestyles, etc. Dramatic first-person narratives about women who have experienced medical miracles or other triumphs. "Reflections": short, provocative personal essays, 1,200 to 1,500 words, humorous or serious, dealing with concerns of interest and relevance to women. Pays $2,000 for essays, top rates for articles, on acceptance.

WOMAN'S WORLD—177 N. Dean St., Englewood, NJ 07631. Stephanie Saible, Sr. Ed. Articles, 600 to 1,800 words, of interest to middle-income women between the ages of 18 and 60, on love, romance, careers, health, psychology, family life, travel, dramatic stories of adventure or crisis. Pays $300 to $750, on acceptance. Query.

WORKING WOMAN—342 Madison Ave., New York, NY 10173. Anne Mollegen Smith, Ed. Articles, 1,000 to 2,500 words, on business and personal aspects of working women's lives. Pays from $400, on acceptance.

YANKEE—Dublin, NH 03444. Judson D. Hale, Ed. Articles, to 3,000 words, with New England angle. Photos. Pays $100 to $700 (average $450 to $550), on acceptance.

CURRENT EVENTS, POLITICS

AFRICA REPORT—833 U.N. Pl., New York, NY 10017. Margaret A.

Novicki, Ed. Well-researched articles by specialists, 1,000 to 4,000 words, with photos, on current African affairs. Pays $150 to $250, on publication.

AMERICAN LAND FORUM—5410 Grosvenor Ln., Bethesda, MD 20814. Sara Ebenreck, Ed. Well-researched articles, 3,500 words, on U.S. land issues. Commentaries, 1,000 words. Pays $150 to $500 for articles, $75 for opinion pieces, on acceptance. Query first.

THE AMERICAN LEGION MAGAZINE—Box 1055, Indianapolis, IN 46206. Michael D. LaBonne, Ed. Articles, 750 to 1,800 words, on current world affairs, public policy, and subjects of contemporary interest. Pays $100 to $1,000, on acceptance. Query.

AMERICAN POLITICS—810 18th St., NW, Suite 802, Washington, DC 20006. Grant Oliphant, Ed. Articles, 1,200 to 2,500 words, on issues, trends and figures in American politics; political perspectives on business, entertainment, science, and health. Pay varies, 30 days after acceptance. Query.

THE AMERICAN SCHOLAR—1811 Q St., N.W., Washington, DC 20009. Joseph Epstein, Ed. Non-technical articles and essays, 3,500 to 4,000 words, on current affairs, the American cultural scene, politics, arts, religion and science. Pays $450, on acceptance.

THE ATLANTIC—8 Arlington St., Boston, MA 02116. William Whitworth, Ed. In-depth articles on public issues, politics, social sciences, education, business, literature, and the arts, with emphasis on information rather than opinion. Ideal length: 3,000 to 6,000 words, though short pieces (1,000 to 2,000 words) are also welcome. Pays $1,000 to $7,000, on acceptance.

COMMENTARY—165 E. 56th St., New York, NY 10022. Norman Podhoretz, Ed. Articles, 5,000 to 7,000 words, on contemporary issues, Jewish affairs, social sciences, community life, religious thought, cultural activities. Pays about 20¢ a word, on publication.

COMMONWEAL—15 Dutch St., New York, NY 10038. Peter Steinfels, Ed. Catholic. Articles, to 3,000 words, on political, social, religious and literary subjects. Pays 3¢ a word, on acceptance.

THE CRISIS—4805 Mt. Hope Dr., Baltimore, MD 21215. Fred Beauford, Ed. Articles, to 1,500 words, on civil rights, problems and achievements of blacks and other minorities. Pays from $75.

DOSSIER—3301 New Mexico Ave., NW, Washington, DC 20016. Nancy F. Smith, Ed. Features with a Washington, D.C. slant. Sophisticated investigative pieces, personality profiles, service articles, etc., 1,000 to 2,500 words. Pays 10¢ to 20¢ a word, on acceptance. Query.

ENVIRONMENT—4000 Albemarle St., N.W., Washington, DC 20016. Jane Scully, Man. Ed. Articles, 2,500 to 6,500 words, on environmental, scientific and technological policy and decision-making issues. Pays $75 to $300, on publication. Query.

FOREIGN POLICY JOURNAL—11 Dupont Circle, N.W., Suite 900, Washington, DC 20036. Charles William Maynes, Ed. Articles, 3,000 to 5,000 words, on international affairs. Honorarium, on publication. Query.

FOREIGN SERVICE JOURNAL—2101 E St. N.W., Washington, DC 20037. Stephen R. Dujack, Ed. Articles on American diplomacy, foreign affairs and subjects of interest to Americans representing U.S. abroad. Pays 2¢ to 10¢ a word, on publication. Query.

THE FREEMAN—Foundation for Economic Education, Irvington-on-Hudson, NY 10533. Brian Summers, Sr. Ed. Articles, to 3,000 words, on economic, political and moral implications of private property, voluntary exchange, and individual choice. Pays 10¢ a word, on publication.

INQUIRER MAGAZINE—*Philadelphia Inquirer,* P.O. Box 8263, 400 N. Broad St., Philadelphia, PA 19101. David Boldt, Ed. Local-interest features, 500 to 7,000 words. Profiles of national figures in politics, entertainment, etc. Pays varying rates, on publication. Query.

MIDSTREAM: A MONTHLY JEWISH REVIEW—515 Park Ave., New York, NY 10022. Joel Carmichael, Ed. Articles; reviews. Pays 5¢ a word, on publication.

MOMENT—462 Boylston St., Boston, MA 02116. Sophisticated articles, 2,000 to 4,000 words, on Jewish political, social, literary, and religious issues. Pays from $100, on publication. Query.

MOTHER JONES—1663 Mission St., San Francisco, CA 94103. Adam Hochschild, Ed. Investigative articles, political essays, cultural analyses. Pays $750 to $2,000, after acceptance. Query.

THE NATION—72 Fifth Ave., New York, NY 10011. Victor Navasky, Ed. Articles, 2,000 to 2,500 words, on current issues. Pays about 5¢ a word up to $150, on publication. Query.

THE NEW YORK TIMES MAGAZINE—229 W. 43rd St., New York, NY 10036. Address Articles Ed. Timely articles, approximately 4,000 words, on new items, forthcoming events, trends, culture, entertainment, etc. Pays $350 to $500 for short pieces, $1,000 to $2,500 for major articles, on acceptance. Query with clips.

THE NEW YORKER—25 W. 43rd St., New York, NY 10036. Address The Editors. Factual and biographical articles, for "Profiles," "Reporter at Large," "Annals of Crime," "Onward and Upward with the Arts," etc. Pays good rates, on acceptance. Query.

NEWSWEEK—444 Madison Ave., New York, NY 10022. Phyllis Malamud, My Turn Ed. Original opinion essays, 1,000 to 1,100 words, for "My Turn" column: must contain verifiable facts. Submit manuscripts with SASE. Pays $1,000, on publication.

NUCLEAR TIMES—298 Fifth Ave., New York, NY 10001. Renata Rizzo, Man. Ed. Terse, timely news articles, to 1,500 words, on the nuclear disarmament movement, the arms race, nuclear weapons and nuclear war. Pays 12¢ a word, on publication.

PRESENT TENSE—165 E. 56th St., New York, NY 10022. Murray Polner, Ed. Serious reportage and political journalism, 2,000 to 3,000 words, on contemporary developments concerning Jews worldwide. Pays $100 to $250, on publication. Query.

THE PROGRESSIVE—409 E. Main St., Madison, WI 53703. Erwin Knoll, Ed. Articles, 1,000 to 3,500 words, on political, social problems. Light features. Pays $75 to $300, on publication.

PUBLIC CITIZEN MAGAZINE—P.O. Box 19404, Washington, DC 20036. Bimonthly. Elliott Negin, Ed. Investigative reports and articles of timely political interest, 500 words to feature length, for members of Public Citizen: consumer rights, health and safety, environmental protection, safe energy, tax reform and government and corporate accountability. Photos, illustrations. Pays to $500.

THE ROTARIAN—1600 Ridge Ave., Evanston, IL 60201. Willmon L. White, Ed. Articles, 1,200 to 2,000 words, on international social and economic issues, business and management, human relationships, travel, sports, environment, science and technology; humor. Pays good rates, on acceptance. Query.

TROPIC—*The Miami Herald,* One Herald Plaza, Miami, FL 33101. Tom Shroder, Ed. Essays and articles on current trends and issues, light or heavy, 1,000 to 4,000 words, for sophisticated audience. Pays $200 to $1,000, on publication. Query.

VFW MAGAZINE—Broadway at 34th, Kansas City, MO 64111. Magazine for Veterans of Foreign Wars and their families. James K. Anderson, Ed. Articles, 1,000 words, on current issues, solutions to everyday problems, personalities, sports, etc. How-to and historical pieces. Photos. Pays 5¢ to 10¢ a word, extra for photos, on acceptance.

VILLAGE VOICE—842 Broadway, New York, NY 10003. Robert Friedman, Ed. Articles, 500 to 2,000 words, on current or controversial topics. Pays $75 to $450, on acceptance. Query.

THE WASHINGTON MONTHLY—1711 Connecticut Ave., N.W., Washington, DC 20009. Charles Peters, Ed. Investigative articles, 1,500 to 5,000 words, on politics, government and the political culture. Pays 10¢ a word, on publication. Query.

WASHINGTON POST MAGAZINE—*The Washington Post,* 1150 15th St., NW, Washington, DC 20071. Stephen L. Petranek, Man. Ed. Personal-experience essays, profiles and general-interest pieces, to 4,000 words, on business, arts and culture, politics, science, sports, education, children, relationships, behavior, etc. Pays from $250, after acceptance.

REGIONAL AND CITY PUBLICATIONS

ADIRONDACK LIFE—P.O. Box 97, Rt. 86, Jay, NY 12941. Jeffrey G. Kelly, Ed. Features, to 3,000 words, on outdoor activities: hiking, camping, canoeing, etc.; arts and crafts, wilderness, business, life styles, and history in the upstate New York region. Pays $100 to $400, on publication.

ALASKA—Box 4-EEE, Anchorage, AK 99509. Tom Gresham, Ed. Articles, 1,500 words, on life in Alaska and northwestern Canada. Pays on acceptance. Write for guidelines.

ALOHA, THE MAGAZINE OF HAWAII—828 Fort Street Mall, Honolulu, HI 96813. Rita Ariyoshi, Ed. Articles, 1,500 to 4,000 words, on the life, customs, and people of Hawaii and the Pacific. Pays 10¢ a word, on publication. Query first.

AMERICAN WEST—3033 N. Campbell Ave., Tucson, AZ 85719. Mae Reid-Bills, Man. Ed. Articles, 2,500 to 3,000 words, and department pieces, 900 to 1,000 words, that celebrate the West, past and present. Pays $200 to $800, on acceptance. Query required.

ARIZONA HIGHWAYS—2039 W. Lewis Ave., Phoenix, AZ 85009. Merrill Windsor, Ed. Articles, 2,000 words, on travel in Arizona and environs; pieces on adventure, nature, arts and crafts, humor, life style, nostalgia, history, archaeology, and Western nonfiction romance. Pays 35¢ to 50¢ a word, on acceptance. Query first.

ARKANSAS TIMES—Box 34010, Little Rock, AR 72203. Mel White, Ed. Articles, to 6,000 words, on Arkansas history, Arkansas people, travel, politics. All articles *must* have strong AR orientation. Pays $100 to $300, on acceptance.

ATLANTA—6255 Barfield Rd. Atlanta, GA 30328. Neil Shister, Ed. Articles, 2,500 words, on Atlanta subjects or personalities. Pays $600 to $1,000, on publication. Query.

THE ATLANTIC ADVOCATE—P.O. Box 3370, Gleaner Bldg. Prospect St., Fredericton, N.B., Canada E3B 5A2. Harold P. Wood, Ed. Well-researched articles on Atlantic Canada and general-interest subjects. Pays to 8¢ a word, on publication.

ATLANTIC CITY MAGAZINE—1637 Atlantic Ave., Atlantic City, NJ 08401. Jill Schoenstein, Ed. Lively articles, 500 to 5,000 words, on Atlantic City and Southern New Jersey: casinos, business, personalities, environment, local color, crime, for locals and tourists. Pays $100 to $600, on publication. Query.

AUSTIN—Box 1967, Austin, TX 78767. Hal Susskind, Ed. Articles, 800 to 1,500 words, on Austin. Photos; cartoons. Pays varying rates, on publication. Query.

AVENUE—145 E. 57th St., New York, NY 10022. Michael Shnayerson, Ed. Articles, 2,000 to 2,500 words, for Upper East Side New Yorkers, and residents of affluent suburbs around the country. Profiles of Upper East Siders in business and the arts, food, fashion. Pays $400 to $500, on publication. Query.

AVENUE M—100 E. Walton, #36A, Chicago, IL 60611. Bob Williams, Ed. Articles, 500 to 1,000 words, on lifestyles, finance, and travel, for residents of Near North area of Chicago. Profiles. Pays $25 to $50, on publication. Query preferred.

BALTIMORE MAGAZINE—26 S. Calvert St., Baltimore, MD 21202. Alan Sea, Man. Ed. Articles, 500 to 3,000 words, on people, places, and things in the Baltimore metropolitan area. Consumer advice, investigative pieces, profiles, humor, and personal experience pieces. Payment varies, on publication. Query required.

BOSTON MAGAZINE—300 Massachusetts Ave., Boston, MA 02115. David Rosenbaum, Ed. Informative, entertaining features, 1,000 to 4,000 words, on Boston area personalities, institutions and phenomena. Pays $250 to $1,200, on publication. Query.

BUFFALO!—See *Living Publications.*

BUFFALO SPREE MAGAZINE—Box 38, Buffalo, NY 14226. Johanna Shotell, Ed. Articles, to 1,800 words, with regional slant. Pays $75 to $100, $20 for poetry, on publication.

BURLINGTON MAGAZINE—444 S. Union St., Burlington, VT 05401. Tim Etchells, Ed. Articles, fiction, poetry, humor, related to Burlington. Pays on acceptance. Query first.

CALIFORNIA—11601 Wilshire Blvd., Los Angeles, CA 90025. Lisa Blansett, Asst. to Man. Ed. Features with a California focus, on politics, business, environmental issues, ethnic diversity, and sports. Service pieces, profiles, and well-researched investigative articles. Pays $500 to $2,500 for features, $250 to $500 for shorter articles, on acceptance. Query first.

CALIFORNIA LIVING—See *Image.*

CAPITAL DISTRICT—See *Living Publications.*

CAPITOL, THE COLUMBUS DISPATCH SUNDAY MAGAZINE—Columbus, OH 43216. T. R. Fitchko, Ed. General-interest, first person, and humorous articles, 3,000 words. Pays varying rates, on publication.

THE CENTER MAGAZINE—745 W. Main St., Louisville, KY 40202. Terry Parsons, Ed. Articles, 500 to 1,500 words, related to events at the Kentucky Center for the Arts. Pays $100 to $300, on publication. Query.

CENTRAL FLORIDA MAGAZINE—P.O. Box 7727, Orlando, FL 32854. Rowland Stiteler, Ed. Articles on business, sports, travel, cars, and other regional topics; profiles. Pays 5¢ to 10¢ a word, on publication. Query first.

THE CHARLOTTE OBSERVER—Box 32188, Charlotte, NC 28232. Cynthia Struby, Features Ed. Newspaper features and travel articles, 500 to 1,000 words, with NC and SC slant. Pays $25 to $75, on publication.

CHESAPEAKE BAY MAGAZINE—1819 Bay Ridge Rd., Annapolis, MD 21403. Betty D. Rigoli, Ed. Articles, 8 to 10 typed pages, related to the Chesapeake Bay area. Profiles. Photos. Pays $65 to $85, on publication. Query first.

CHICAGO—303 E. Wacker Dr., Chicago, Il 60601. Don Gold, Ed-in-Chief. Articles, 1,000 to 5,000 words, related to Chicago. Pays varying rates, on acceptance. Query.

CHICAGO HISTORY—Clark St. at North Ave., Chicago, IL 60614. Timothy C. Jacobson, Ed. Articles, to 4,500 words, on urban political, social and cultural history. Pays to $250, on publication. Query.

CINCINNATI ENTERTAINER—18 E. 4th St., Suite 601, Cincinnati, OH 45208. Susan Conner, Ed. Interviews, profiles, articles, on entertainment; columns, 750 words. Pays $15 per printed page, and copies.

CINCINNATI MAGAZINE—35 E. Seventh, Suite 300, Cincinnati, OH 45202. Laura Pulfer, Ed./Pub. Articles, 1,000 to 3,000 words, on Cincinnati people and issues. Pays $75 to $100 for 1,000 words, on acceptance. Query with writing sample.

CLINTON STREET QUARTERLY—Box 3588, Portland, OR 97208. Lenny Dee, Ed. Articles on politics, culture, humor, and art in the Portland and Seattle region. Pays $50 to $200, on publication.

COASTAL JOURNAL—Box 84, Lanesville Sta., Gloucester, MA 01930. Joseph Kaknes, Ed. Articles, to 2,000 words, on the New England coast, past, present and future trends, current events, personalities and nautical history. Photos. Pays $100 to $150, on publication.

COLORADO BUSINESS—5951 S. Middlefield Rd., Littleton, CO 80123. Warren Smith, Ed. Articles, to 1,500 words, on banking, real estate, transportation, manufacturing, etc., in Colorado. Pays 10¢ a word, on publication. Query.

COLORADO HOMES & LIFESTYLES—Suite 154, 2550 31st St., Denver, CO 80216. Joseph Kim Bella, Exec. Ed. Articles on topics related to Colorado: travel, fashion, design and decorating, gardening, luxury real estate, art, lifestyles, people, food and entertaining. Pays to 20¢ a word, on acceptance. Query.

COLORADO SPORTSTYLES MAGAZINE (formerly *Colorado Sports Monthly*)—P.O. Box 3519, Evergreen, CO 80439. Robert J.Erdmann, Ed. Articles, 1,500 to 2,000 words, on individual participant sports in Colorado. Pays varying rates on publication. Query.

COLUMBUS HOMES & LIFESTYLES—P.O. Box 21208, Columbus, OH

553

43221. Features for upscale readers, 35+ years, on history, nostalgia; interviews and profiles; photo features, with a central Ohio slant. General-interest articles on interiors, gardens and landscaping, and collectibles. Pays $50 to $200, or 6¢ a word, on publication. Query with clips.

CONNECTICUT—636 Kings Hwy., Fairfield, CT 06430. Sara J. Cuneo, Ed. Articles, 1,500 to 2,500 words, on Connecticut topics, issues, people and life styles. Pays $500 to $800, on publication.

CONNECTICUT TRAVELER—2276 Whitney St., Hamden, CT 06518. Elke P. Martin, Man. Dir. Articles, 500 to 1,200 words, on travel and tourist attractions in New England. Photos. Pays $50 to $175, on publication. Query.

CORPORATE MONTHLY—105 Chestnut St., Philadelphia, PA 19106. Bruce Anthony, Pub. and Ed. Articles of interest to the Philadelphia business community, 1,500 to 2,000 words. Pays varying rates on publication. Query required.

COUNTRY—See *Mid-Atlantic Country.*

THE COVENTRY JOURNAL—P.O. Box 124, Andover, CT 06232. Bill Cisowski, Ed. Monthly newspaper. Folklore, legends, tales of New England, to 2,000 words. Family-oriented, Connecticut Yankee, farm articles. Articles, to 2,000 words, on New England history and Eastern Connecticut. Photos. Pays $50 to $100, on acceptance.

CRAIN'S DETROIT BUSINESS—1400 Woodbridge, Detroit, MI 48207. Peter Brown, Ed. Business articles, 500 to 1,000 words, about Detroit, for Detroit business readers. Pays $75 to $150, on acceptance. Query required.

D—3988 N. Central Expressway, Suite 1200, Dallas, TX 75204. Ruth Fitzgibbons, Ed. In-depth investigative pieces on current trends and problems, personality profiles, and general-interest articles on the arts, travel, fashion, and business, for upper-class residents of Dallas. Pays $350 to $500 for departments, $800 to $1,200 for features. Written queries only.

DALLAS CITY—*The Dallas Times Herald* Sunday Magazine, 1101 Pacific Ave., Dallas, TX 75202. Steven Reddicliffe, Ed. Articles, 2,500 words, and short essays, 500 to 750 words, on contemporary topics of interest to people living in the Dallas/Fort Worth area. Department pieces. Pays $100 to $750, on acceptance. Query required.

DALLAS LIFE—*The Dallas Morning News,* Communications Center, Dallas, TX 75265. Melissa East, Ed. Well-researched articles and profiles, 750 to 2,000 words, on contemporary issues, personalities, or subjects of strictly-Dallas related interest. Short Dallas-oriented humor features, 750 to 1,000 words. Pays from 25¢ a word, on acceptance. Query required.

DALLAS MAGAZINE—1507 Pacific Ave., Dallas, TX 75201. D. Ann Shiffler, Ed. Features, 2,500 words, on business and businesses in Dallas. Department pieces, 1,500 words. Pays $100 to $600, on acceptance. Query required.

DELAWARE TODAY—P.O. Box 4440, Wilmington, DE 19807. Peter Mucha, Ed. Service articles, profiles, news features, on topics of local interest. Best bets for out-of-state writers are articles on finance, high-tech consumer items or cars. Pays $75 to $125 for department pieces, $125 to $300 for features, on publication. Query required; enclose writing sample.

DETROIT MAGAZINE—*Detroit Free Press,* 321 W. Lafayette Blvd., Detroit, MI 48231. Articles, to 2,000 words, with a Detroit-area or Michigan focus, on issues, lifestyles. Personality profiles; essays; humor. Pays $100 to $500.

DETROIT MONTHLY—1400 Woodbridge, Detroit, MI 48207. Martin Fischoff, Ed. Articles on Detroit-area people, issues, life styles and business. Payment varies. Query with clips required.

DOWN EAST—Camden, ME 04843. Davis Thomas, Ed. Articles, 1,500 to 2,500 words, on all aspects of life in Maine. Photos. Pays to 10¢ a word, extra for photos, on acceptance. Query.

ERIE & CHAUTAUQUA MAGAZINE—Charles H. Strong Bldg., 1250 Tower La., Erie, PA 16505. Mary J. Brownlie, Ed. Feature articles, to 2,500 words, on issues of interest to upscale readers in the Erie, Warren, and Crawford counties (PA), and Chautauqua (NY) county. Investigative pieces. Pays $35 per published page, on publication. Query preferred, with writing samples. Buys all rights. Guidelines available.

EXECUTIVE REPORT—213 S. Craig St., Pittsburgh, PA 15213. Charles Shane, Ed. Articles, 1,000 to 4,000 words, covering business news in western Pennsylvania. Pays 10¢ a word, on publication. Query first.

FLORIDA GULF COAST LIVING—1311 N. Westshore Blvd., Suite 109, Tampa, FL 33607. Milana Petty, Ed. Articles, 750 to 1,200 words, for the active home buyer on the Gulf Coast: home-related articles, moving tips, financing, etc. Pays 7¢ to 10¢ a word, on acceptance. Query preferred.

FLORIDA KEYS MAGAZINE—Box 818, 6161 O/S Hwy., Marathon, FL 33040. Address David Ethridge. Articles 1,000 to 4,000 words, on the Florida Keys: history, environment, natural history, profiles, etc. Humor. Photos. Pays varying rates, on publication. Query preferred.

FLORIDA SPORTS—Placeo Publishing Corp., Box 18694, Tampa, FL 33679. Tony Hill, Ed. Profiles of state sports personalities; topical pieces, 1,000 to 2,000 words. Pays $25, on publication. Queries are preferred.

FLORIDA TREND—Box 611, St. Petersburg, FL 33731. Richard Edmonds, Ed. Articles, to 2,000 words, on Florida business and businesspersons. Photos. Query.

GEORGIA JOURNAL—Agee Publishers, Inc., Athens, GA 30603. Jane M. Agee, Ed. Articles, 1,200 words, on people, events, travel, etc. in and around GA. Pays $20 to $35, on acceptance.

GO: THE AUTHENTIC GUIDE TO NEW ORLEANS—1033 Pleasant St., Suite D, New Orleans, LA 70115. Katherine Dinker, Ed. Articles, 2,000 words, on local events of interest to visitors. Pays $150, on publication. Query.

GOLD COAST LIFE MAGAZINE—4747 N. Ocean Dr., Ft. Lauderdale, FL 33308. Tina Loeftler, Ed. Articles, from 1,000 words, on life styles of southeastern Florida. Pays $50 to $200, on publication.

GOLDEN YEARS—233 E. New Haven Ave., Melbourne, FL 32902-0537. Carol Brenner Hittner, Ed. Controlled-circulation monthly for Florida residents over the age of 50. Pieces on health, nutrition, and travel, 500 words. Pays 8¢ a word, on publication.

GULFSHORE LIFE—3620 Tamiami Trail N., Naples, FL 33940. Anita Atherton, Ed. Articles, 950 to 3,500 words, on personalities, travel, sports, business, investment, nature, in southwestern Florida. Pays $50 to $300. Query.

HIGH COUNTRY NEWS—Box 1090, Paonia, CO 81428. Ed Marston,

Managing Ed. Articles on environmental, land management, energy and natural resource issues; profiles of western innovators; pieces on western politics. B & W photos. Pays $2 per column inch, on publication, for 750-word roundups and 2,000-word features. Query first.

HONOLULU—36 Merchant St., Honolulu, HI 96813. Brian Nicol, Ed. Features highlighting life in the Hawaiian islands—politics, sports, history, people, events are all subjects of interest. Pays $250 to $400, on acceptance. Columns and department pieces are mostly staff-written. Queries are required.

HUDSON VALLEY MAGAZINE—Box 425, Woodstock, NY 12498. Joanne Michaels, Ed. Profiles, investigative articles, and features on the businesses, arts and resources of the region. Pays $40 to $50, on publication, for features of 1,200 to 1,500 words; queries are required.

ILLINOIS ENTERTAINER—Box 356, Mount Prospect, IL 60056. Guy Arnston, Ed. Articles, 500 to 1,500 words, on local and national entertainment and leisure time activities in the greater Chicago area. Personality profiles; interviews; reviews. Photos. Pays 3¢ to 5¢ a word, on publication. Query preferred.

ILLINOIS TIMES—Box 3524, Springfield, IL 62708. Fletcher Farrar, Jr., Ed. Articles, 1,000 to 2,500 words, on people, places and activities of Illinois, outside the Chicago metropolitan area. Pays 4¢ a word, on publication. Query required.

IMAGE (formerly *California Living*)—*The San Francisco Examiner,* 110 Fifth St., San Francisco, CA 94103. Susan Brenneman, Ed. Articles, 1,500 to 2,500 words, on lifestyle, leisure activities, business, history, jobs, people, etc., in northern California. Photos are a plus. Pays $200 to $500.

INDIANAPOLIS MAGAZINE—32 E. Washington St., Indianapolis, IN 46204. Nancy Comiskey, Ed. Articles on almost any topic—health, business, sports, people, etc.—must have a regional tie-in. Lengths vary (to 12 pages). Pays $40 to $300, on publication.

INDIANAPOLIS MONTHLY—8425 Keystone Crossing, Indianapolis, IN 46240. Deborah Paul, Ed.-in-Chief; Steve Bell, Assoc. Ed. Articles, 1,000 words, on health, sports, politics, business, and Indiana personalities. All material must have a regional focus. Pays varying rates, on publication.

INQUIRER MAGAZINE—*Philadelphia Inquirer,* 400 N. Broad St., Philadelphia, PA 19101. David R. Boldt, Ed. Articles, 1,500 to 2,000 words, and 3,000 to 7,000 words, on politics, science, arts and culture, business, life styles and entertainment, sports, health, beauty, psychology, education, religion, home and garden, and humor. Short pieces, 200 to 800 words, for "Our Town" department. Pays varying rates. Query.

THE IOWAN MAGAZINE—Mid-America Publishing Corp., 214 9th St., Des Moines, IA 50309. Charles W. Roberts, Ed. Quarterly for educated, affluent Iowans. Articles, 1,000 to 3,000 words, on the business, arts, people and history of Iowa, with photos, if available. Query first. Pays $100 to $400, on publication.

ISLAND LIFE—P.O. Box X, Sanibel Island, FL 33957. Joan Hooper, Ed. Articles, 500 to 1,200 words, with photos, on unique or historical places, wildlife, architecture, fashions, home decor, cuisine, on barrier islands off Florida's S.W. Gulf Coast. Pays 5¢ a word, on publication. SASE necessary.

ITHACA—See *Living Publications.*

JACKSONVILLE MAGAZINE—P.O. Box 329, Jacksonville, FL 32201. Caralyn Carroll, Ed. Articles of interest to the Jacksonville business community: strong regional slant a must. Pays $100 to $300, on acceptance. Query required.

KANSAS!—Kansas Dept. of Economic Development, 400 W. 8th Ave., 5th fl., Topeka, KS 66603. Andrea Glen, Ed. Quarterly. Articles of 5 to 7 typed pages on the people, places, history and events of Kansas. Color slides. Pays $75 to $150, on acceptance. Query.

LAKE SUPERIOR PORT CITIES—325 Lake Ave. S., Meierhoff Bldg., Suite 510, Duluth, MN 55802. Paul Hayden, Ed. Articles with unusual twists on regional subjects; historical pieces that highlight the people, places and events that have affected the Lake Superior region. Pictorial essays; humor. Pays to $200, after publication. Query first.

LIVING PUBLICATIONS—Office Complex, DeWitt Bldg., Ithaca, NY 14850. Jill Hartz, Marina Todd, Eds. Publishes five bimonthly upstate city magazines: *Rochester, Syracuse, Buffalo, Capital District, Ithaca.* Articles, 1,200 to 4,000 words, with black and white or color photos, of interest to urban professionals, including cultural, educational, historical, political, humorous topics. Pays $50 to $400, on publication. Query with bio and writing sample.

LONG ISLAND HERITAGE—132 E. Second St., Mineola, NY 11501. Christine Hellmer, Ed. Articles, 500 words, on the history and crafts of Long Island; local artists, collectors, architecture. Query.

LONG ISLAND'S NIGHTLIFE MAGAZINE—1770 Deer Park Ave., Deer Park, NY 11729. Bill Ervolino, Ed. Articles, 1,000 to 2,500 words, on entertainment, leisure, personalities. Photos. Pays $50 to $200, on publication. Query preferred.

LOS ANGELES MAGAZINE—1888 Century Park E., Los Angeles, CA 90067. Lew Harris, Exec. Ed. Articles, to 3,000 words, of interest to sophisticated, affluent southern Californians, preferably with local focus on a life style topic. Pays from 10¢ a word, on acceptance. Query.

LOS ANGELES READER—8471 Melrose Ave., Los Angeles, CA 90069. Dan Barton, Ed. Articles, 1,000 to 3,000 words, on subjects relating to the Los Angeles/Southern California area; special emphasis on entertainment, feature journalism, and the arts. Pays $25 to $300, on publication. Query preferred.

LOS ANGELES TIMES MAGAZINE—Times Mirror Sq., Los Angeles, CA 90053. Michael Parrish, News Features Ed. General-interest news features, photo spreads, profiles, and interviews focusing on people and events in Southern California, to 3,500 words. Pays to $2,000, on acceptance. Query required.

LOUISVILLE—One Riverfront Plaza, Louisville, KY 40202. Betty Lou Amster, Ed. Articles, 1,000 to 2,000 words, on community issues, personalities, and entertainment in the Louisville area. Photos. Pays from $50, on acceptance. Query; articles on assignment only. Limited freelance market.

MAGAZINE OF THE MIDLANDS—Omaha World-Herald, World Herald Sq., Omaha, NE 68102. Tim Anderson, Ed. General-interest articles, 800 to 2,000 words, and profiles, tied to Omaha. Photos. Pays $25 to $150, on publication. Query.

MAGNETIC NORTH—c/o Thorn Books, Franconia, NH 03580. Jim McIntosh, Ed. Well-researched, off-beat articles, 500 to 1,500 words, for residents of and visitors to New Hampshire's White Mountains. Pays $50 to $150, on publication. Query with SASE.

557

MAINE LIFE—8 St. Pierre St., Lewiston, ME 04240. Bradbury D. Blake, Assoc. Pub. Articles, 150 to 3,000 words, about traveling, places to see, and things to do in Maine. Short, breezy, upbeat pieces, to 1,000 words, on people, trends, enterprises, and events, for "Omnibus" section. Pays 8¢ a word, on publication. Query.

MARYLAND—Dept. of Economic and Community Development, 45 Calvert St., Annapolis, MD 21401. Bonnie Joe Ayers, Ed. Articles, 800 to 2,200 words, on Maryland subjects. Pays varying rates, on acceptance. Query preferred. Guidelines available.

MAUIAN—P.O. Box 10669, Lahaina, Maui, HI, 96761. Joe Harabin, Ed. "We seek informative, thought-provoking, upbeat articles (500 to 5,000 words, with an indication of available photos) about any aspect of life and times on Maui—past, present, or future. Our audience is threefold: vacationers, residents, and the business community." Pays $50 to $500, $15 to $25 for photos, on publication.

MEMPHIS—Towery Press, Box 370, Memphis, TN 38101. Kenneth Neill, Ed. Articles, 1,500 to 4,000 words, on a wide variety of topics related to Memphis and the Mid-South region: politics, education, sports, business, etc. Profiles; investigative pieces. Pays $75 to $1,000, on publication. Query. Guidelines available.

MIAMI/SOUTH FLORIDA MAGAZINE—P.O. Box 140008, Coral Gables, FL 33114-0008. Rick Eyerdam, Man. Ed. Features, 1,500 to 2,500 words, and department pieces, 900 to 1,300 words, on a variety of subjects related to South Florida. Short, bright items, 200 to 400 words, for the "Big Orange" section. Pays $75 to $400, 15 days before publication.

MICHIANA—*The South Bend Tribune,* Colfax at Lafayette, South Bend, IN 46626. Bill Sonneborn, Ed. Articles, 300 to 3,000 words, on the people, places, and events in the Northern Indiana and Southern Michigan area. Photos. Pays $50 to $125, on publication. Query.

MICHIGAN BUSINESS—Cranbrook Center, Suite 302, 30161 Southfield Rd., Southfield, MI 48076. Ron Garbinski, Ed. Business news and features on Michigan businesses. Queries are preferred. Pay varies, on publication.

MICHIGAN: THE MAGAZINE OF THE DETROIT NEWS—Evening News Assn., 615 W. Lafayette Blvd., Detroit, MI 48231. Lisa Velders, Ed. Clifford A. Ridley, Asst. Man. Ed. Articles, from 750 words, on business, politics, arts and culture, science, people, sports and education, etc., with a Michigan slant. Cover articles, to 3,000 words. Pays $200 to $650, on publication. Query preferred.

MICHIGAN LIVING—17000 Executive Plaza Dr., Dearborn, MI 48126. Len Barnes, Ed. Travel articles, 500 to 1,500 words, on tourist attractions and recreational opportunities in the U.S. and Canada, with emphasis on Michigan: places to go, things to do, costs, etc. Color photos. Pays $100 to $350, extra for photos, on acceptance.

THE MICHIGAN WOMAN—P.O. Box 1171, Birmingham, MI 48012. Sue McDonald, Ed. Articles, 750 words, highlighting the achievements and contributions of Michigan women and helping others enjoy more fulfilling careers and personal lives. Pays 10¢ a word, on publication. Query first.

MID-ATLANTIC COUNTRY—P.O. Box 246, Alexandria, VA 22313. Philip Hayward, Ed. Articles, 2,000 words, related to life in the Mid-Atlantic region:

travel, outdoor sports, gardening, antiques, history, architecture, environment, etc. Photos. Pays $3.50 per column inch, on publication. Query.

MILWAUKEE—312 E. Buffalo, Milwaukee, WI 53202. Charles Sykes, Ed. Profiles, investigative articles, and historical pieces, 3,000 to 4,000 words; local tie-in a must. Pays $300 to $500, on publication. Query required.

MONTANA MAGAZINE—P.O. Box 5630, Helena, MT 59604. Carolyn Cunningham, Ed. Where-to and what-to-do items, 300 to 500 words, directly related to Montana. B & W photos and photo essays. Pays $100 to $300, on publication. Query first.

MPLS. ST. PAUL—12 S. 6th St., Ste. 1030, Minneapolis, MN 55402. Sylvia Paine, Man. Ed. In-depth articles, features, profiles and service pieces, 400 to 3,000 words, with Minneapolis-St. Paul focus. Pays to $600.

MYRTLE BEACH—P.O. Box 1474, N. Myrtle Beach, SC 29598. Cynthia L. Clemmer, Ed. Features, 1,500 to 2,500 words, and department pieces, 500 to 1,500 words, on the Myrtle Beach area. Articles must be geared to residents, not tourists. "Please review the magazine before submitting material," says Ms. Clemmer. Submit query with clips, if available. Pays from $35 for short pieces, from $75 for main features, on publication. Pay for photos (B&W or color) varies.

NEVADA—Capitol Complex, Carson City, NV 89710. Caroline J. Hadley, Ed. Articles, 500 to 700 or 1,500 to 1,800 words, on topics related to Nevada— history, profiles, travel, and places—with photos. Pay varies, on publication.

THE NEVADAN—*The Las Vegas Review-Journal,* Box 70, Las Vegas, NV 89125-0070. A.D. Hopkins, Ed. Feature articles, to 3,000 words, on social trends in Southern Nevada. Pieces, 2,000 words, on history in Nevada, Southwest Utah, Northeast Arizona, and Death Valley area of California, accompanied by B & W photos. Pays $75 to $125, on publication.

NEW ENGLAND GETAWAYS—21 Pocahontas Dr., Peabody, MA 01960. Patricia Burns Fiore, Associate Pub. Articles, 1,500 to 2,000 words, on travel destinations and events in New England. Articles include specific information on travel times, photos, calendar of events, etc. Queries are required. Pays $150 to $300, on publication.

NEW ENGLAND MONTHLY—P.O. Box 446, Haydenville, MA 01039. Daniel Okrent, Ed. Articles on politics, arts, business, education, crime and nature; a regional angle is a must, and a strong accent on reportage is preferred. Pays, on acceptance, $150 to $200 for short items (600 to 800 words) and from $1,000 for features (3,000 to 4,000 words). Include published clips with query.

NEW HAMPSHIRE PROFILES—90 Fleet St., Portsmouth, NH 03801. Rae Francoeur, Ed. Articles, 500 to 1,500 words, on New Hampshire people, events, arts, and life styles. Pays $100 to $300, on publication. Query in writing.

NEW JERSEY LIVING—830 Raymond Rd., RD 4, Princeton, NJ 08540. Marie C. Turi, Asst. Pub. General-interest articles, 2,500 to 3,000 words, about New Jersey. Pays $50, on publication. Query.

NEW JERSEY MONTHLY—7 Dumont Place, Morristown, NJ 07960. Larry Marscheck, Ed. Reportorial and service pieces, 2,000 to 3,000 words, and department pieces, 1,200 to 1,800 words, with a strong regional slant. Some "think" pieces and humor of general interest. Pays $35 to $75 for short pieces, $350 to $2,000 for features, on acceptance. Query first.

NEW JERSEY REPORTER—The Center for Analysis of Public Issues, 16

Vandeventer Ave., Princeton, NJ 08542. Rick Sinding, Ed. In-depth articles, 2,000 to 6,000 words, on New Jersey politics and public affairs. Pays $100 to $250, on publication. Query required.

NEW MEXICO MAGAZINE—Bataan Memorial Bldg., Santa Fe, NM 87503. Address Ed. Articles, 250 to 2,000 words, on New Mexico subjects. Pays about 12¢ a word, on publication.

NEW ORLEANS MAGAZINE—Box 26815, New Orleans, LA 70186. Sandy Sciacca Shilstone, Ed. Articles, 3 to 15 triple-spaced pages, on New Orleans area people and issues. Photos. Pays $50 to $300, extra for photos, on publication. Query.

NEW YORK—755 Second Ave., New York, NY 10017. Edward Kosner, Ed. Laurie Jones, Man. Ed. Feature articles of interest to New Yorkers. Pays $350 to $3,500, on acceptance. Query required; not responsible for unsolicited material.

NEW YORK ALIVE—152 Washington Ave., Albany, NY 12210. Mary Grates Stoll, Ed. Articles aimed at developing knowledge of and appreciation for New York State. Features, 3,000 words maximum, on business, lifestyle, education, history and the arts. Department pieces for regular columns, including "Great Escapes" (travel ideas) and "Expressly New York" (unusual places, products or events in New York). Pays $200 to $350 for features, $50 to $150 for departments. Query preferred.

NEW YORK FAMILY—420 E. 79th St., New York, NY 10021. Susan Ross, Ed. Articles on parenting in New York City. Pays $50 to $100 for manuscripts of varying lengths, on publication.

NORTH DAKOTA HORIZONS—P.O. Box 2467, Fargo, ND 58107. Sheldon Green, Ed. Quarterly. Articles, about 3,000 words, on the people, places and events that affect life in North Dakota. Photos. Poetry. Pays $75 to $300, on publication.

NORTHERN LIGHTS—Box 8084, Missoula, MT 59807-9962. Dan Whipple, Ed. Thoughtful articles, 500 to 1,500 words, about the West. "We're open to virtually any subject as long as it deals with our region (the Rocky Mountains) in some way." Pays up to 10¢ a word, on publication. Query.

NORTHWEST—1320 S.W. Broadway, Portland, OR 97201. Sunday magazine of *The Sunday Oregonian*. Jack R. Hart, Ed. Articles, to 3,000 words, on Pacific Northwest issues and personalities: regional travel, science and business, outdoor recreation, and lifestyle trends. Personal essays. Local angle essential. Pays $75 to $800. Query first.

NORTHWEST LIVING (formerly *Northwest Edition*)—130 Second Ave. S., Edmonds, WA 98020. Archie Satterfield, Ed. Lively, informative articles, 400 to 1,000 words, on the natural resources of the Northwest: natural science and history, homes, gardens, people, travel, etc. Color photos essential. Pays to $400, on acceptance. Query required.

OHIO MAGAZINE—40 S. Third St., Columbus, OH 43215. Ellen Stein, Managing Ed. Profiles of the people, cities and towns of Ohio, and short pieces on its institutions (schools, police departments, etc.). Lengths vary; pay varies. Query preferred.

OKLAHOMA TODAY—Box 53384, Oklahoma City, OK 73152. Kate Lester Jones, Managing Ed. Articles, 1,000 to 3,000 words, on interesting aspects of life in Oklahoma, with an emphasis on travel. Pays $200 to $300, on publication. Query required.

ORANGE COAST—245-D Fisher, Suite 8, Costa Mesa, CA 92626. Katherine Tomlinson, Ed. Articles of interest to educated, affluent Southern Californians. Pieces, 1,000 to 3,000 words, for regular departments: "Profile," "Coasting" (op-ed), "Media," "Business" (hard news about the regional business community), and "Nightlife." Feature articles run 3,000 to 5,000 words. Query. Pays $150 for features, $100 for columns, on acceptance. Guidelines are available.

ORLANDO MAGAZINE—P.O. Box 2207, Orlando, FL 32802. Nancy Long, Features Ed. Articles and profiles, 1,000 to 1,500 words, related to Central Florida. Photos a plus. Pays $50 to $150, on acceptance. Query required.

PD—*St. Louis Post-Dispatch,* 900 N. Tucker Blvd., St. Louis, MO 63101. Robert W. Duffy, Ed. Profiles, personal-experience pieces and investigative articles, 3,000 to 4,000 words: politics, science, life styles and entertainment, psychology, etc. Humor. Pays $125 to $150, on publication. No unsolicited manuscripts. Query.

PENNSYLVANIA MAGAZINE—Box 576, Camp Hill, PA 17011. Albert E. Holliday, Ed. Quarterly. General-interest features with a Pennsylvania tie-in. Pays 10¢ a word, usually on acceptance. Query preferred.

PHILADELPHIA—1500 Walnut St., Philadelphia, PA 19102. Bill Tonelli, Articles Ed. Articles, 1,000 to 5,000 words, for sophisticated audience, relating to Philadelphia area. Pays from $150, on publication. Query.

PHOENIX BUSINESS JOURNAL—1817 N. 3rd St., Suite 100, Phoenix, AZ 85004. G. Chambers Williams III, Ed. Articles on leading and innovative businesses and business people in the Phoenix area. Photos. Pays $2.75 to $3.75 per column inch, extra for photos, on publication.

PHOENIX MAGAZINE—4707 N. 12th St., Phoenix, AZ 85014. Fern Stewart Welch, Ed. Dir. Articles, 1,000 to 3,000 words, on topics of special interest to Phoenix-area residents. Pays $75 to $300 for features, on publication. Query.

PITTSBURGH—4802 Fifth Ave., Pittsburgh, PA 15213. Bill Van Wyngarden, Ed. Articles, 850 to 3,000 words, with western Pennsylvania slant. 3- to 4-month lead time. Pays after publication.

THE PITTSBURGH PRESS SUNDAY MAGAZINE—*The Pittsburgh Press,* 34 Blvd. of the Allies, Pittsburgh, PA 15230. Ed Wintermantel, Ed. Well-written, well-organized, in-depth articles of local or regional interest, 1,000 to 3,000 words, on issues, trends or personalities. No hobbies, how-to's or "timely events" pieces. Pays $100 to $400, extra for photos, on publication. Query.

PITTSBURGH PREVIEW—1112 S. Braddock Ave., Suite 203, Pittsburgh, PA 15218. Kimberly Flaherty, Ed. Career-oriented articles, geared to women, preferably with a local slant. Pays $25 to $300, on publication. Query required.

PORTLAND MONTHLY—638 Congress St., Portland, ME 04101. Colin Sargent, Sr. Ed. Articles on people, fashions, trends, and events in the Portland area, to 2,500 words. Queries are preferred. Pays $150, on publication.

ROCHESTER—See *Living Publications.*

RURAL LIVING—P.O. Box 15248, Richmond, VA 23227-0648. Richard G. Johnstone, Jr., Ed. Features, 1,000 to 1,500 words, on people, places, historic sites in Virginia and Maryland's Eastern Shore. Family-oriented fiction, 1,000 to 1,500 words. Family humor, 100 to 250 words. Queries are preferred. Pays $150 for articles, on publication.

561

RURALITE—P.O. Box 557, Forest Grove, OR 97116. Address Editor or Feature Editor. Articles, 1,000 words, of interest to a primarily rural and small-town audience in Oregon, Washington, Idaho, Nevada, and Alaska. Upbeat articles; biographies, local history and celebrations, self-help, etc. Humorous articles and animal pieces. No sentimental nostalgia. Pays $30 to $100, on acceptance. Queries are preferred.

SACRAMENTO MAGAZINE—P.O. Box 2424, Sacramento, CA 95811. Ann McCully, Man. Ed. Features, 2,500 words, on a broad range of topics related to the region. Department pieces, 1,200 to 1,500 words, and short pieces, 500 words, for "City Lights" column. Pays to $200, on acceptance. Query first.

SAN ANTONIO MAGAZINE—Chamber of Commerce, P.O. Box 1628, San Antonio, TX 78296. Sandy Brown, Ed. Articles on San Antonio area. Pays $75 to $300, on publication. Query.

SAN DIEGO MAGAZINE—4206 W. Point Loma Blvd., P.O. Box 85409, San Diego, CA 92138. Winke Self, Man. Ed. Articles, 1,500 to 2,500 words, on local personalities, political figures, life styles, business, history, etc., relating to San Diego area. Photos. Pays $350 to $700, on publication.

SAN DIEGO READER—P.O. Box 80803, San Diego, CA 92138. Jim Mullin, Ed. Articles, 2,500 to 10,000 words, on the San Diego region. Pays $250 to $750, on publication. Query preferred.

SAN FRANCISCO—950 Battery St., San Francisco, CA 94111. Virginia Butterfield, Ed. General-interest articles, 1,000 to 3,000 words, related to the Bay area. Pays from $100 to $500, 30 days after publication.

SAN FRANCISCO FOCUS—680 Eighth Ave., San Francisco, CA 94103. Mark Powelson, Ed. Service features, profiles of local newsmakers, and investigative pieces of local issues, 2,500 to 3,000 words. Pays $250 to $750, on publication. Query required.

SHREVEPORT—P.O. Box 20074, Shreveport, LA 71120. Peter H. Main, Ed. Articles, 800 to 1,500 words, focusing on business and economic development in the Shreveport area business community: managing a business, small businesses, money management, commercial activity, reports on the economy, success profiles, business new briefs, and pieces on offbeat and amusing topics for "Observer." Pays $90 to $250, on acceptance.

SIERRA LIFE—699 West Line St., Bishop, CA 93514. Marty Forstenzer, Ed. Articles, 1,000 to 2,500 words, dealing with the history, personalities, environment, or recreational opportunities of the Sierra region. Pays 4¢ a word, on publication.

SOUTH CAROLINA WILDLIFE—P.O. Box 167, Columbia, SC 29202. Tom Poland, Man. Ed. Articles, 1,000 to 3,000 words, with regional outdoors focus: conservation, natural history and wildlife, recreation. Profiles, how-to's. Pays from 10¢ a word.

SOUTH FLORIDA HOME & GARDEN—P.O. Box 140008, Coral Gables, FL 33114-0008. Rosemary Barrett, Man. Ed. Features, 800 to 1,000 words, and department pieces, 400 to 800 words, about South Florida interior design, architecture, landscaping, gardening, cuisine and home entertaining. Must focus on the Key West to Melbourne area. Pays $50 to $300, before publication.

SOUTHERN—P.O. Box 3418, 201 E. Markham, Suite 200, Little Rock, AR 72203. Linton Weeks, Ed. "Our goal is to explore all facets of the contemporary

South—with an eye toward making some sense out of what it means to 'be Southern.' We're looking for main pieces of 1,000 to 6,000 words: hard journalism; profiles; articles; essays; first-person adventure; history; and personal-services features. We also use fiction and humor, and material for our departments, including politics, sports, business, food and drink, etc. In all cases, we look for a strong Southern angle. Our rates range from $50 and up for departments to approximately $2,000 for major pieces, on acceptance."

SOUTHERN OUTDOORS—Bell Rd., Montgomery, AL 36141. Larry Teague, Ed. How-to articles, 2,000 words, on hunting and fishing, for fishermen and hunters in the 16 southern states. Pays 15¢ a word, on acceptance. Query.

SOUTHWEST ART—9 Greenway Plaza, Suite 2010, Houston, TX 77219. Susan McGarry, Ed. Articles on the artists, museums, and galleries west of the Mississippi. Particularly interested in representational or figurative arts. Pay rates start at $250, on acceptance, for manuscripts of 1,800 to 2,200 words. Query.

THE STATE: DOWN HOME IN NORTH CAROLINA—P.O. Box 2169, Raleigh, NC 27602. W. B. Wright, Ed. Articles, 600 to 2,000 words, on people, history, and places in North Carolina. Photos. Pays $15 to $50, on acceptance.

SUNDAY—*Chicago Tribune*, 435 N. Michigan Ave., Chicago, IL 60611. Bob McVea, Man. Ed. Articles, 2,000 to 3,000 words, on politics, arts, health, travel, etc., for Chicago and Midwestern readers. Query.

SUNDAY MAGAZINE—*Providence Sunday Journal*, 75 Fountain St., Providence, RI 02902. Thomasine Berg, Ed. Profiles, personal-experience pieces, 1,000 to 1,500 words. Pays $75 to $200, on publication. Query.

SUNSET MAGAZINE—80 Willow Rd., Menlo Park, CA 94025. William Marken, Ed. Western regional. Queries considered but not encouraged.

SUNSHINE MAGAZINE—The News/Sun-Sentinel, P.O. Box 14430, 101 North New River Dr. E., Ft. Lauderdale, FL 33302. John Parkyn, Ed. Articles, 1,000 to 4,000 words, on topics of interest to South Floridians. Pays to 25¢ a word, on acceptance. Query.

SUSQUEHANNA MONTHLY MAGAZINE—Box 75A, RD 1, Marietta, PA 17547. Richard S. Bromer, Ed. Articles, 1,000 to 4,000 words, on regional (SE PA, DE, MD, DC) history, ecology, arts, etc. Pays to $75, on publication. Query with SASE required.

SYRACUSE—See *Living Publications.*

TALLAHASSEE MAGAZINE—P.O. Box 12848, Tallahassee, FL 32317. William Needham, Ed. Articles, 800 to 1,100 words, with a positive outlook on the life, people, and history of the North Florida area. Pays 10¢ a word, on publication. Query.

TEXAS HIGHWAYS MAGAZINE—State Dept. of Highways and Transportation, 11th and Brazos, Austin, TX 78701. Frank Lively, Ed. Texas history, scenic and travel features, 200 to 1,800 words. Pays $150 to $600, on acceptance, extra for photos. Guidelines.

TEXAS REAL ESTATE—4665 Sweetwater Blvd., Suite 100, Sugar Land, TX 77479. Donald L. Pierce, Ed. Articles, interviews, profiles, and guides, 1,000 to 4,000 words, for people who lease, develop, build or broker real estate in Texas. Developer briefs, 150 to 500 words. Pays $50 to $1,000, after acceptance. Query.

THIRD COAST—P.O. Box 592, Austin, TX 78767. Kate Berger, Man. Ed. Articles, 1,000 to 1,500 words, on business, arts, architecture, growth, politics, education, etc., in Austin. Some fiction, with an Austin slant. Pays from 10¢ a word, after publication. Query.

TIMELINE—1985 Velma Ave., Columbus, OH 43211-2497. Christopher Duckworth, Ed. Articles, 1,000 to 6,000 words, related to the history, pre-history, and natural history of Ohio; topics of regional and national focus will be considered. Shorter, sharply-focused vignettes, 500 to 1,000 words. Photos. Pays $100 to $900, on acceptance. Query. Guidelines.

TOLEDO MAGAZINE—*The Blade,* Toledo, OH 43660. Sue Stankey, Ed. Articles, to 5,000 words, on Toledo area personalities, news, etc. Pays $50 to $500, on publication. Query.

TORONTO LIFE—59 Front St. E., Toronto, Ont., Canada M5E 1B3. Marq De Villiers, Ed. Articles, 1,000 to 4,500 words, on Toronto. Pays $500 to $2,000, on acceptance. Query.

TROPIC—*The Miami Herald,* One Herald Plaza, Miami, FL 33101. Gene Weingarten, Ed. General-interest articles, 1,500 to 3,000 words, for South Florida readers. Pays $300 to $600, on acceptance. Send SASE.

TROPICAL ISLAND LIVING—P.O. Box 7263, Arlington, VA 22207. Dennis Wilmeth, Ed. Newsletter for people who live or vacation on islands in the Caribbean, Hawaii, or South Pacific. Articles, 200 to 1,000 words, about living or vacationing on a tropical island. Pays $50 to $100, on publication.

TULSA—6 E. Fifth St., Suite 410, Tulsa, OK 74103. Lynn Rollins Price, Man. Ed. Factual, business-oriented articles, and human interest articles of local interest, 1,000 to 2,500 words. Pays $100 to $250, on publication. Query.

TWIN CITIES READER—600 First Ave. N., Minneapolis, MN 55403. Deborah L. Hopp, Ed.-in-Chief. Articles, 2 to 4 printed pages, on cultural phenomena, city politics, and general-interest subjects, for local readers aged 25 to 44. Pays to $3 per inch, on publication.

ULTRA—2000 Bering Dr., Suite 200, Houston, TX 77057. Barbara Dixon, Ed. Articles for upscale Texans, 1,000 to 1,500 words, with a regional "good living" focus: arts, personalities, health, travel, etc. Pays $500 to $1,500, on acceptance. Query required.

VALLEY MAGAZINE—16800 Devonshire, Suite 275, Granada Hills, CA 91344. Anne Framroze, Ed. Articles, 1,000 to 3,000 words, on celebrities, issues, education, health, business, dining and entertaining, etc., in the San Fernando Valley. Pays $100 to $500, within 8 weeks of acceptance.

VERMONT LIFE—61 Elm St., Montpelier, VT 05602. Tom Slayton, Editor-in-Chief. Articles, 500 to 3,000 words, about Vermont subjects only. Photos. Pays 20¢ a word, extra for photos. Query required.

THE VIRGINIAN—P.O. Box 2828, Staunton, VA 24401. Hunter S. Pierce, IV, Man. Ed. Articles, 2,000 words, relating to VA, WV, and MD.

WASHINGTON MAGAZINE—1500 Eastlake Ave. E., Seattle, WA 98102. David Fuller, Man. Ed. Articles, varying lengths, on the people and places of Washington State. Payment varies. Query required.

WASHINGTON POST MAGAZINE—*The Washington Post,* 1150 15th St., NW, Washington, DC 20071. Stephen L. Petranek, Man. Ed. Personal-experience essays, profiles and general-interest pieces, to 4,000 words, on business, arts and culture, politics, science, sports, education, children, relationships, behavior, etc. Pays from $100, after acceptance.

THE WASHINGTONIAN—1828 L. St. N.W., Suite 200, Washington, DC 20036. John Limpert, Ed. Helpful, informative, interesting articles, 1,000 to 4,000 words, on Washington-related topics. Pays 20¢ a word, on publication. Query.

THE WEEKLY, SEATTLE'S NEWS MAGAZINE—1931 2nd Ave., Seattle, WA 98101. David Brewster, Ed. Articles, 700 to 4,000 words, with a Northwest perspective. Pays $75 to $800, three weeks after publication. Query required.

WEST MICHIGAN MAGAZINE—7 Ionia St. SW, Grand Rapids, MI 49503. Dottie Clune, Ed. Articles, to 2,000 words, on the people, places, and events of the region. Pays varying rates on publication.

THE WESTERN BOATMAN—16427 S. Avalon, P.O. Box 2307, Gardena, CA 90428. Ralph Poole, Ed. Articles, to 1,500 words, for boating enthusiasts from Alaska to Mexico, on subjects from waterskiing and salmon fishing to race boats and schooners. Pays on publication. Query preferred.

WESTERN SPORTSMAN—P.O. Box 737, Regina, Sask., Canada S4P 3A8. Red Wilkinson, Ed. Informative articles, to 2,500 words, on outdoor experiences in Alberta and Saskatchewan. How-to's, humor, cartoons. Photos. Pays $40 to $325, on publication.

WESTWAYS—Box 2890, Terminal Annex, Los Angeles, CA 90051. Mary Ann Fisher, Ed. Articles, 1,000 to 1,500 words, and photo essays, on western U.S., Canada, and Mexico: history, contemporary living, travel, personalities, etc. Photos. Pays from 20¢ a word, extra for photos, 30 days before publication. Query.

WISCONSIN—*The Milwaukee Journal Magazine*, Newspapers, Inc., Box 661, Milwaukee, WI 53201. Beth Slocum, Ed. Articles, 500 to 2,000 words, on business, politics, arts, science, personal finance, psychology, entertainment, health, etc. Personal-experience essays and investigative articles. Pays $75 to $500, on publication. Query.

WISCONSIN TRAILS—P.O. Box 5650, Madison, WI 53705. Susan Pigorsch, Man. Ed. Articles, 1,500 to 3,000 words, on regional topics: outdoors, life style, events, adventure, travel; profiles of artists and craftsmen, and regional personalities. Pays $100 to $300, on acceptance and on publication. Query first.

WORCESTER MAGAZINE—P.O. Box 1000, Worcester, MA 01614. Michael G. Bingham, Ed. Articles, to 1,500 words, on the arts, entertainment, fashion, events, and issues specific to Worcester County. Pays $1.00 to $1.50 per column inch, on publication. Query required.

YANKEE—Dublin, NH 03444. Judson D. Hale, Ed. Articles, about 2,500 words, on New England and residents. Pays about $600 for features, $750 for fiction, on acceptance.

YANKEE HOMES—Main St., Dublin, NH 03444. Georgia Orcutt, Ed. Articles on New England real estate, 200 to 1,500 words. Pays $50 to $500, on acceptance.

YANKEE MAGAZINE'S TRAVEL GUIDE TO NEW ENGLAND—Main St., Dublin, NH 03444. Elizabeth Doyle, Ed. Articles, 500 to 2,000 words, on unusual activities, attractions, places to visit in New England. Photos. Pays $50 to $300, on acceptance. Query with outline and writing samples.

TRAVEL ARTICLES

AAA WORLD—8111 Gatehouse Rd., Falls Church, VA 22047. Clyde T. Linsley, Jr., Man. Ed. Published in 12 regional editions, with appropriate regional material. Articles, 600 to 1,500 words, on general travel-related concerns. Pays $200 to $800, on acceptance. Queries preferred.

ACCENT—Box 10010, Ogden, UT 84409. Robyn C. Walker, Ed. Articles, 1,200 words, about destinations in the U.S. Must include transparencies. Pays 15¢ a word, on acceptance. Query first.

ADVENTURE MAGAZINE—P.O. Box 1190, Kirkland, WA 98083. Pam Sather, Ed. Articles, 1,000 to 2,000 words, for members of a national campground association. Topics include outdoor living, history, hobbies, sightseeing, profiles, and RV life styles. Pays $100 to $200, on publication. Query. Guidelines available.

ADVENTURE ROAD—Citycorp Publishing, 641 Lexington Ave., New York, NY 10022. Deborah C. Thompson, Ed. Official publication of the Amoco Motor Club. Articles, 1,500 words, on destinations in North America, Mexico, and the Caribbean. Photos. Pays $400 to $850, on acceptance. Query required.

AIRFAIR INTERLINE MAGAZINE—25 W. 39th St., New York, NY 10018. Ratu Kamlani, Ed. Travel articles, 1,000 to 2,500 words, with photos, on shopping, sightseeing, dining, for airline employees. Prices, discount information, and addresses must be included. Pays $75, after publication.

AMERICAS—OAS, General Secretariat Bldg., 1884 F St., N.W., Washington, DC 20006. A. R. Williams, Man. Ed. Features to 2,500 words on travel in Latin America and the Caribbean. Pays from $200, on publication. Query.

ARIZONA HIGHWAYS—2039 W. Lewis Ave., Phoenix, AZ 85009. Richard G. Stahl, Man. Ed. Informal, well-researched travel articles, 2,000 to 2,500 words, focusing on a specific city or region in Arizona and environs and including anecdotes, historical references, etc. Pays 35¢ to 50¢ a word, on acceptance. Query required. Guidelines available.

BRITISH HERITAGE—P.O. Box 8200, Harrisburg, PA 17105. Gail Huganir, Ed. Travel articles on places to visit in the British Isles, to 2,000 words. Include detailed historical information with a "For the Visitor" sidebar. Pays $100 to $200, on acceptance.

CALIFORNIA HIGHWAY PATROLMAN—2030 V St., Sacramento, CA 95818. Travel articles, 2,000 words maximum, focusing on places in California and the West Coast. Pays 2½¢ a word, extra for black-and-white photos, on publication.

CARIBBEAN TRAVEL AND LIFE—616 N. Washington St., Alexandria, VA 22314. Veronica Gould Stoddart, Ed. Lively and informative articles, 500 to 2,200 words, on all aspects of travel, recreation, leisure, and culture in the Caribbean, Bahamas, and Bermuda. "We have a special need for pieces with a unique approach, personal point of view, unusual angle." Include both background and "how-to" information on a destination. Pays $75 to $550, on acceptance. Query.

CHARLOTTE OBSERVER—Box 32188, Charlotte, NC 28232. Doug Robouchek, Travel Ed. Travel articles on North and South Carolinas and the Southeast—how-to pieces (what to pack for a trip, etc.), roundup articles (ethnic restaurants of Charlotte, for instance), and destination pieces that focus on specific places or cities in the region. Pay rates start at $25, on publication.

CHARTERING MAGAZINE—P.O. Box 1933, Jensen Beach, FL 33457. Antonia Thomas, Associate Ed. Articles on chartered yacht vacations, 1,000 to 1,800 words. Query first. Pays varying rates, on publication.

CHEVRON USA ODYSSEY—P.O. Box 6227, San Jose, CA 95150. Mark Williams, Ed. Quarterly. Articles, 700 to 1,600 words, on travel and leisure activities in the United States and Canada. Travel anecdotes, 50 to 250 words. Color slides. Pays about 25¢ to 30¢ a word for articles, $25 for anecdotes, on acceptance; $125 to $400 for slides, on publication.

COLORADO HOMES & LIFESTYLES—Suite 154, 2550 31st St., Denver, CO 80216. Barbara Baumgarten, Man. Ed. Travel articles on cities, regions, establishments in Colorado; roundups and travel pieces with a how-to focus, 1,200 to 3,000 words. Pays 10¢ to 25¢ a word, on acceptance. Query.

CONNECTICUT TRAVELER—2276 Whitney St., Hamden, CT 06518. Elke P. Martin, Man. Dir. Articles, 500 to 1,200 words, on travel and tourist attractions in New England. Pays $50 to $175, on publication.

CONNECTIONS—P.O. Box 6117, New York, NY 10150. Jeanine Moss, Ed. First-hand, detailed travel articles, varying lengths, for women executives who travel frequently. Specific costs, details and advice a must. Pays from $50, on publication. Query required.

CONSUMERS DIGEST—5705 N. Lincoln Ave., Chicago, IL 60659. Robin C. Nelson, Ed. Articles, 500 to 3,000 words, on subjects of interest to consumers: automobiles, travel, etc. Pays from 30¢ a word, on publication. Buys all rights. Query with resume and published clips.

DISCOVERY—Allstate Motor Club, 3701 W. Lake Ave., Glenview, IL 60025. Mary Kaye Stray, Ed. Articles, 1,000 to 2,500 words, on travel topics that explore continental North America and its people. Photos on assignment only. Pays $500 to $850, on acceptance. Query and published samples required.

DIVERSION MAGAZINE—60 E. 42nd St., Suite 2424, New York, NY 10165. Stephen N. Birnbaum, Edit. Dir. Articles, 1,200 to 3,000 words, on travel and entertainment, for physicians. Pays from $350, on publication. Photos. Query.

EARLY AMERICAN LIFE—Box 8200, Harrisburg, PA 17105. Frances Carnahan, Ed. Travel features about historic sites and country inns, 1,000 to 3,000 words. Pays $50 to $400, on acceptance. Query.

EUROPE FOR TRAVELERS!—408 Main St., Nashua, NH 03060. Carol Grasso, Ed. Quarterly. Travel articles of varying lengths. Especially interested in unusual modes of travel (barge, balloon, bike, horse and wagon, etc.) and out-of-the-way destinations. Include information on hotels, restaurants, shopping, etc. Pays up to $100, on publication.

EUROPEAN TRAVEL AND LIFE—755 Second Ave., New York, NY 10017. David R. Breul, Ed.-in-Chief. Articles, 1,500 to 3,500 words, for sophisticated American travelers. Pay starts at $750, on acceptance. Queries are required.

FAMILY CIRCLE—488 Madison Ave., New York, NY 10022. Susan Ungaro, Articles Ed. Travel articles, to 2,000 words. Destination pieces should appeal to a national audience and focus on affordable activities; prefer area roundups, theme-oriented travel pieces or first person family vacation stories. Pay rates vary, on acceptance. Query first.

FAMILY MOTOR COACHING MAGAZINE—8291 Clough Pike, Cincinnati, OH 45244. Pamela S. Wisby, Ed. Publication of the Family Motor Coach Association. Travel articles, including information about RV accommodations and peculiar road conditions. Articles covering technical information on mechanics, coach housekeeping, the latest RV products and accessories, etc. Photos. Pays on acceptance: $100 to $200 for standard travel features; $100 to $300 for technical articles; $200 to $250 for coach reviews; and $50 to $200 for all others. Queries are preferred; length requirements are about 1,500 words.

FARM FAMILY AMERICA—1999 Shepard Rd., St. Paul, MN 55116. George Ashfield, Ed. Quarterly travel and recreation magazine for American farm families. Articles, 1,000 to 1,500 words. Pays $250 to $500, on acceptance. Query.

FORD TIMES—One Illinois Center, 111 E. Wacker Dr., Suite 1700, Chicago, IL 60601. Thomas A. Kindre, Ed. Articles to 1,500 words on current subjects, profiles, places of interest, travel, humor, outdoor activities. Main focus is on North America. Pays from $500, on acceptance. Query with SASE.

FREQUENT FLYER—888 Seventh Ave., New York, NY 10019. Coleman Lollar, Ed. Articles, 1,000 to 3,000 words, on all aspects of frequent business travel, international trade, aviation, T & E, etc. No pleasure travel or personal experience pieces. Pays $100 to $500, on acceptance. Query required.

GO GREYHOUND—Greyhound Tower, Phoenix, AZ 85077. Juanita Soto, Asst. Ed. Pieces, 500 to 800 words, on historic, scenic, entertainment attractions that can be reached by Greyhound Bus. Must be accompanied by 12 color transparencies. Pays $350, on acceptance. Query first.

GULFSHORE LIFE—3620 Tamiami Trail, N., Naples, FL 33940. Destination-oriented travel articles, 1,800 to 2,400 words. Payment negotiable, on publication. Query.

INTERNATIONAL LIVING—824 E. Baltimore St., Baltimore, MD 21202. Francine Modderno, Ed. Newsletter. Short pieces and features, 200 to 1,000 words, with useful information on living abroad, investing overseas, and unusual travel bargains. Pays to $200, on acceptance.

KIWANIS—3636 Woodview Trace, Indianapolis, IN 46268. Chuck Jonak, Exec. Ed. Magazine of the Kiwanis Club. Travel articles, 2,000 to 3,000 words, of interest to an intelligent male audience. Pays $400 to $1000, on acceptance. Query first.

MICHIGAN LIVING—Automobile Club of Michigan, 17000 Executive Plaza Dr., Dearborn, MI 48126. Len Barnes, Ed. Informative travel articles, 500 to 1,500 words, on U.S., Canadian tourist attractions and recreational opportunities; special interest in Michigan. Photos. Pays $100 to $300, extra for photos, on acceptance.

MID-ATLANTIC COUNTRY—P.O. Box 246, Alexandria, VA 22313. Jim Scott, Ed. Travel articles, 1,200 words, on destinations and establishments in the Mid-Atlantic region (VA, MD, DE, WV, NC, NJ, PA); how-to pieces and humorous essays on travel-related subjects, with a regional slant. Pays $3.50 per column inch, on publication. Query.

THE MIDWEST MOTORIST—12901 N. Forty Drive, St. Louis, MO 63141. Jean Kennedy, Man. Ed. Articles, 1,000 to 1,500 words, with photos, on travel, transportation and consumerism. Pays $50 to $200, on acceptance or publication.

NATIONAL GEOGRAPHIC—17th and M Sts., N.W., Washington, D.C.

20036. Wilbur E. Garrett, Ed. Publishes first-person articles on human geography, exploration, natural history, archeology, and science. Does not review manuscripts. Send SASE for guidelines.

NATIONAL GEOGRAPHIC TRAVELER—National Geographic Society, 17th and M Sts., NW, Washington, DC 20036. Joan Tapper, Ed. Articles, 1,500 to 4,000 words, that highlight specific places. Query with 1–2 page proposal, resumé, and published clippings required. Pays $1 a word, on acceptance.

NATIONAL MOTORIST—One Market Plaza, Suite 300, San Francisco, CA 94105. Jane Offers, Ed. Illustrated articles, 500 or 1,100 words, for California motorists, on motoring in the West, car care, roads, personalities, places, etc. Photos. Pays from 10¢ a word, extra for photos, on acceptance.

NEW WOMAN—215 Lexington Ave., New York, NY 10016. Armchair travel pieces; personal experience and "what I learned from this experience" pieces, 2,000 to 3,000 words. Pays $500 to $2,000, on acceptance. Query required.

THE NEW YORK TIMES—229 W. 43rd St., New York, NY 10036. Michael J. Leahy, Travel Ed. Considers queries only; include writer's background, description of proposed article. No unsolicited manuscripts or photos. Pays on acceptance.

NORTHWEST—1320 S.W. Broadway, Portland, OR 97201. Travel articles, 800 to 1,000 words, that focus on the central overall psychological experience—the article should give the reader an idea of what unique experiences he might encounter by taking the trip. All material must pertain to the Northwest (Oregon, Washington, Idaho, and Montana). Include details about where to go, what to see, plans to make, with specific information about reservations, ticket purchases, etc. Pays $150 to $250, on acceptance. Query. Guidelines available.

OFF DUTY MAGAZINE—3303 Harbor Blvd., Suite C-2, Costa Mesa, CA 92626. Bruce Thorstad, U.S. Ed. Travel articles, 1,800 to 2,000 words, for active duty military Americans (aged 20 to 40) and their families, on U.S. regions or cities. Military angle essential. Pieces with focus on an event or activity, with sidebars telling how-to and where-to. Photos. Pays from 13¢ a word, extra for photos, on acceptance. Query required. Send for guidelines. European and Pacific editions. Foreign travel articles for military Americans and their families stationed abroad. Send SASE for guidelines.

OHIO MOTORIST—P.O. Box 6150, Cleveland, OH 44101. F. Jerome Turk, Ed. Articles, 750 to 1,500 words, with photos, on domestic (preferably in Ohio) and foreign travel, automotive subjects. Pays to $300, on acceptance. Query required.

SACRAMENTO MAGAZINE—P.O. Box 2424, Sacramento, CA 95811. Cheryl Robo, Ed. Destination-oriented articles in the Sacramento area (or within a 6 hour drive), 1,000 to 1,500 words. Pay varies, on acceptance. Query first.

SIGNATURE MAGAZINE—641 Lexington Ave., New York, NY 10022. Barbara Coats, Ed. Articles on travel in U.S. and abroad; features on leisure and entertainment topics: food, wine, sports, the arts, etc. Pays good rates, on acceptance. Query.

TAKEOFF—20 William St., Wellesley, MA 02181. Norman J. Groh, Ed. Private pilots' travel, recreation, and lifestyle magazine. Articles of varying lengths on travel and adventure, resorts, restaurants of interest to men and women who fly for business and recreation. Include information on airports, ground transportation, and hotel accommodations. Photos—color slides or black and white prints. Pays $100 to $350, on publication.

TEXAS HIGHWAYS MAGAZINE—State Dept. of Highways and Transportation, 11th and Brazos, Austin, TX 78701-2483. Frank Lively, Ed. Travel, historical, cultural, scenic features on Texas, 1,000 to 1,800 words. Pays $400 to $700, on acceptance, extra for photos. Guidelines available.

TRANSITIONS ABROAD—18 Hulst Rd., Box 344, Amherst, MA 01004. Martha Yoder, Man. Ed. Articles, to 1,500 words, with B/W photos, for long-stay travelers abroad: work, study, travel. Include practical, first-hand information: travel deals, work and study opportunities, etc. Pays on publication. Send SASE for guidelines and editorial schedule.

TRAVEL AGE WEST—100 Grant Ave., San Francisco, CA 94108. Donald Langley, Man. Ed. Articles, 800 to 1,000 words, with photos, on any aspect of travel useful to travel agents, including names, addresses, prices, etc.; news or trend angle preferred. Pays $1.50 per column inch, after publication.

TRAVEL AND LEARNING ABROAD—P.O. Box 1122, Brattleboro, VT 05301. Douglas I. Grube, Ed. Articles, to 1,750 words, for people of all ages participating in or planning learning trips (exchange or study abroad programs), as well as independent international travel. Pays varying rates, on publication. Query. Guidelines available.

TRAVEL & LEISURE—1120 Ave. of the Americas, New York, NY 10036. Pamela Fiori, Ed.-in-Chief. Articles, 800 to 2,500 words, on destinations and leisuretime activities. Regional pieces for regional editions. Pays $600 to $2,000, on acceptance. Query; articles on assignment.

TRAVEL HOLIDAY—Travel Bldg., Floral Park, NY 11001. Scott Shane, Ed. Informative, lively features, 1,600 to 1,800 words, on foreign and domestic travel to well-known or little-known places; featurettes, 800 to 1,000 words, on special-interest subjects: museums, shopping, smaller cities or islands, special aspects of destination. Pays from $250 for featurettes, $400 for features, on acceptance. Query with published clips.

TRAVEL SMART—Dobbs Ferry, NY 10522. Short pieces, 250 to 1,000 words, about interesting, unusual and/or economical places: give specific details on hotels, restaurants, transportation, and costs. Pays $100, on publication.

TRAVEL SMART FOR BUSINESS—Dobbs Ferry, NY 10522. H. J. Teison, Ed. Articles, 200 to 1,000 words, for company executives and business travel managers, on lowering travel costs and increasing travel convenience. Pays on publication.

VISTA/USA—Box 161, Convent Station, NJ 07961. Exxon Travel Club. Kathleen M. Caccavale, Ed. Travel articles, 2,000 words, on North America, Hawaii, Mexico and the Caribbean. Pays from $600, on acceptance. Query with writing sample and narrative outline. Limited free-lance market.

VOLKSWAGEN'S WORLD—Volkswagen of America, Inc., Troy, MI 48099. Ed Rabinowitz, Ed. Travel articles on unique places, to 1,000 words. Pays $150 per printed page, on acceptance. Query.

WESTWAYS—P.O. Box 2890, Terminal Annex, Los Angeles, CA 90051. Ann Fisher, Ed. Travel articles on where to go, what to see, and how to get there, 1,500 words. Domestic travel articles are limited to Western U.S., Canada, and Hawaii; foreign travel articles are also of interest. Quality color photos should be available. Pays 20¢ a word, 30 days before publication.

YANKEE MAGAZINE'S TRAVEL GUIDE TO NEW ENGLAND—Main St., Dublin, NH 03444. Elizabeth Doyle, Ed. Articles, 500 to 2,000 words, on unusual activities, restaurants, places to visit in New England, for tourists. Photos. Pays $50 to $300, on acceptance. Query with outline and writing samples.

INFLIGHT MAGAZINES

Inflight magazines are published by commercial airlines for their passengers, and use a wide variety of general-interest articles, as well as travel pieces on the airlines' destinations.

ABOARD—North-South Net, Inc., 777 41st St., P.O. Box 40-2763, Miami Beach, FL 33140. Ana C. Mix, Ed. Inflight magazine of eight Latin American national airlines. Articles, with photos, on Chile, Panama, Paraguay, Dominican Republic, Ecuador, El Salvador, Bolivia, and Venezuela. Pieces on science, sports, home, fashion, and gastronomy, 1,200 to 1,500 words. Pays $150, on acceptance and on publication. Query required.

AMERICAN WAY—P.O. Box 619616, MD 2G23, DFW Airport, TX 75261-9616. Judy Steinbach Brown, Man. Ed. American Airlines' inflight magazine. Features, 1,500 to 1,750 words, on health, business, the arts, etc.; profiles of people and places. Short pieces, 700 words, for "American Observer." Photos. Pays $100 for shorts, from $450 for full-length pieces, on acceptance. Query articles editor.

ECHELON—12955 Biscayne Blvd., N. Miami, FL 33181. Chauncey Mabe, Ed. Inflight magazine for corporate executives flying on Butler Aviation aircraft. General-interest articles, 2,000 to 3,000 words. Pays $200 to $1,000, on acceptance. Query first.

INFLIGHT—P.O. Box 10010, Ogden, UT 84409. Marjorie Rice, Ed. Articles, 1,200 words, for high-income business travelers. Personality profiles. Photos. Pays 15¢ a word, on acceptance. Query.

NORTHWEST ORIENT—East/West Network, 34 E. 51st St., New York, NY 10022. Northwest Airlines' inflight magazine. Features, 2,000 to 3,000 words, on travel, business, lifestyles, sports, and entertainment. Profiles. Pays from $400 for articles, on acceptance.

OZARK—East/West Network, 5900 Wilshire Blvd., Los Angeles, CA 90036. Laura Doss, Ed. Ozark Airlines in-flight magazine. Uses mostly freelance material. Query. Same address for Pacific Southwest *PSA Magazine,* Republic Airlines *Republic,* Western Airlines *Western's World,* and Southwest Airlines *Southwest.*

PACE—338 N. Elm St., Greensboro, NC 27401. Leslie Daisy, Ed. Piedmont Airlines inflight magazine. Articles of interest to business travelers; economic reports, business management and communication. Travel pieces to Piedmont destination cities. Pays varying rates, on acceptance.

PAN AM CLIPPER—East/West Network, 34 E. 51st St., New York, NY 10022. Richard Kagan, Ed. Monthly inflight for Pan Am Airlines. Interviews, profiles, and travel pieces on Pan Am destinations, 2,500 words. Detailed query required. Very limited market. Pays varying rates, on acceptance.

PEOPLEXPRESSIONS—Halsey Publishing Co., 12955 Biscayne Blvd., N.

Miami, FL 33181. Debra Silver, Assoc. Ed. Inflight publication for People Express Airlines. Articles 1,000 to 1,500 words, on a wide variety of topics. No religious or political material. Humor and cartoons. Pays $200 to $600, on acceptance. No unsolicited manuscripts accepted; query required.

PRESIDENTIAL AIRWAYS MAGAZINE—338 N. Elm St., Greensboro, NC 27401. Davis March, Ed. Bimonthly inflight magazine for Presidential Airways. Articles, 3,000 to 4,000 words, on business, travel, leisure, the Southeast, and golf. Pays on acceptance. Query first.

PSA MAGAZINE—See *Ozark.*

REPUBLIC SCENE—See *Ozark.*

SKY—12955 Biscayne Blvd., North Miami, FL 33181. Lidia de Leon, Ed. Delta Air Lines' inflight magazine. Articles on business, lifestyle, high tech, sports, the arts, etc. Color slides. Pays varying rates, on publication. Query.

SOUTHWEST—See *Ozark.*

UNITED MAGAZINE—East/West Network, 34 E. 51st St., New York, NY 10022. Jonathan Black, Ed. United Airlines' inflight magazine. Profiles of unusual or upscale Americans. Travel pieces on United destinations. Interviews. Pays varying rates, 60 days after acceptance. Query.

USAIR—600 Third Ave., Suite 2700, New York, NY 10016. Richard Busch, Ed. Inflight magazine of USAir. Articles, 1,500 to 3,000 words, on travel, business, sports, entertainment, food, health, and other general interest topics. No downbeat or extremely controversial subjects. Pays $350 to $800, on acceptance. Query.

WESTERN'S WORLD—See *Ozark.*

WOMEN'S PUBLICATIONS

THE ALLURE WOMAN—22 E. 41st St., 3rd Floor, New York, NY 10017. T. Rose Murdock, Ed. and Pub. Articles "for the full-figured woman who loves beauty and style": 700- to 900-word travel pieces (U.S. vacation spots, cruises, resorts, spas, etc.) and food articles (food trends and technology, low-calorie and ethnic foods, etc.). Food pieces should include 4 to 6 recipes. Payment for food and travel articles: $200 to $300. Also uses health, fitness and nutrition articles on sports, cardiovascular fitness, diet and exercise, psychology, sexuality, etc. Nutrition and fitness pieces, 800 to 1,000 words (payment $250); general health articles, 1,500 to 2,000 words (payment $300 to $500). Payment is on publication.

BEAUTY DIGEST—126 Fifth Ave., New York, NY 10011. Diane Robbens, Ed. Reprints of book and magazine pieces, 2,500 to 3,500 words, on beauty, health, exercise, self-help, for women. Pays varying rates, on publication.

BRIDAL GUIDE—5225 N. Ironwood Rd., Milwaukee, WI 53217. Eveline Kohl, Man. Ed. Features, 500 to 2,500 words, on wedding planning, remarriage, honeymoons, ethnic traditions, as well as unusual and celebrity weddings. Photos. Pays $100 to $300, on acceptance. Query.

BRIDE'S—350 Madison Ave., New York, NY 10017. Address Copy and Features Dept. Articles, 1,000 to 3,000 words, for engaged couples or newlyweds, on communication, sex, housing, finances, careers, remarriage, stepparenting, health, birth control, pregnancy, babies, religion, in-laws, relationships. Pays $300 to $800, on acceptance.

CAPPER'S—616 Jefferson St., Topeka, KS 66607. Dorothy Harvey, Ed. Articles, 300 to 500 words: human interest, personal experience, historical. Letters on women's interests, recipes, hints, for "Heart of the Home." Jokes. Children's writing and art section. Pays varying rates, on publication.

CHATELAINE—Maclean Hunter Bldg., 777 Bay St., Toronto, Ont., Canada M5W 1A7. Mildred Istona, Ed. Articles, 2,500 words, on controversial subjects and personalities of interest to Canadian women. Pays $750 for personal-experience pieces, from $1,000 for articles, on acceptance.

CHOICES—2311 Pontius Rd., Los Angeles, CA 90064. Rieva Lesonsky, Ed. Articles, 1,500 to 2,000 words, for women in business. Shorter pieces, 350 to 500 words, on news, travel, entertainment and product tips of interest to business women. Pays $75 to $350, on publication. Query required.

COMPLETE WOMAN—1165 N. Clark, Chicago, IL 60610. Attn. Suzanne Merry, Assoc. Ed. Articles, 800 to 1,800 words, with practical advice for women, on careers, health, personal relationships, etc. Inspirational profiles of successful women. Pays varying rates, on publication.

COSMOPOLITAN—224 W. 57th St., New York, NY 10019. Helen Gurley Brown, Ed. Guy Flatley, Man. Ed. Roberta Ashley, Exec. Ed. Articles, to 4,000 words, and features, to 2,500 words, on issues affecting young career women. Pays from $1,500 for full-length articles, on acceptance.

ELLE—551 Fifth Ave., New York, NY 10176. Joan Harting, Sr. Ed. Articles, varying lengths, for fashion-conscious women, ages 20 to 50. Subjects include beauty, health, careers, fitness, travel, and life styles. Pays top rates, on publication. Query required.

ESSENCE—1500 Broadway, New York, NY 10036. Susan L. Taylor, Ed.-in-Chief. Provocative articles, 1,500 to 3,000 words, about black women in America today: self-help, how-to pieces, careers, health, celebrity profiles and political issues. Short items, 500 to 750 words, on work and health. Pays varying rates, on acceptance. Query.

THE EXECUTIVE FEMALE—1041 Third Ave., New York, NY 10021. Susan Strecker, Man. Ed. Features, 6 to 12 pages, on investment, money-savers, career advancement, etc., for executive women. Articles, 6 to 8 pages, for "More Money," "Horizons," "Profiles," and "Entrepreneur's Corner." Pays varying rates, on publication. Limited freelance market.

FAMILY CIRCLE—488 Madison Ave., New York, NY 10022. Susan Ungaro, Articles Ed. Ellen Stoianoff, Eleanore Lewis, Features Eds., Nicole Gregory, Books Ed. Articles, to 2,500 words, on marriage, family, child-rearing, consumer affairs, social and political issues, travel, humor, etc. Pays on acceptance. Query required.

FARM WOMAN—P.O. Box 643, Milwaukee, WI 53201. Ruth C. Benedict, Man. Ed. Personal-experience, humor, service-oriented articles, and how-to features, to 1,000 words, of interest to rural women. Pays $40 to $250, on acceptance.

FLARE—777 Bay St., Toronto, Ont., Canada M5W 1A7. Dianne Rinehart, Man. Ed. Service articles, 1,500 to 3,000 words, on health, careers, relationships, and contemporary problems; articles on home decor, food, and entertaining for Canadian women aged 18 to 34. Profiles, 750 to 1,500 words, of up-and-coming Canadians. Pays on acceptance. Query.

573

GLAMOUR—350 Madison Ave., New York, NY 10017. Ruth Whitney, Ed.-in-Chief. Barbara Coffey, Man. Ed. Rona Cherry, Exec. Ed. Judith Coyne, Articles Ed. How-to articles, from 1,500 words, on careers, health, psychology, interpersonal relationships, etc., for women aged 18 to 35. Fashion and beauty pieces staff-written. Pays from $1,500.

GOOD HOUSEKEEPING—959 Eighth Ave., New York, NY 10019. Joan Thursh, Articles Ed. Naome Lewis, Fiction Ed. In-depth articles and features on controversial problems, topical social issues; dramatic personal narratives with unusual experiences of average families; new or unusual medical information, 1,200 to 5,000 words. Ideas on subjects of practical interest to women for "Better Way." Pays top rates, on acceptance.

HARPER'S BAZAAR—1700 Broadway, New York, NY 10019. Anthony Mazzola, Ed.-in-Chief. Articles 1,500 to 2,000 words, for active, sophisticated women. Topics include the arts, world affairs, food, wine, travel, families, education, personal finance, careers, health, and sexuality. No unsolicited manuscripts; query first with SASE. Pays top rates, on acceptance.

LADIES' HOME JOURNAL—3 Park Ave., New York, NY 10016. Myrna Blyth, Ed.-in-Chief. Articles of interest to women. Send queries with outlines to Jan Goodwin, Exec. Ed.; Roberta Grant and Beth Weinhouse, Sr. Eds.

LUTHERAN WOMEN—2900 Queen Ln., Philadelphia, PA 19129. Terry Schutz, Ed. Articles, with photos, on subjects of interest to Christian women. No recipes, homemaking hints. Pays to $50 on publication.

MCCALL'S—230 Park Ave., New York, NY 10169. A. Elizabeth Sloan, Ed. Articles, 1,000 to 3,000 words, on current issues, human interest, family relationships. Pays top rates, on acceptance.

MADEMOISELLE—350 Madison Ave., New York, NY 10017. Kate White, Exec. Ed. Articles, 1,200 to 3,000 words, of interest to women in their 20's. Pays $750 to $1,750, on acceptance.

MODERN BRIDE—One Park Ave., New York, NY 10016. Mary Ann Cavlin, Man. Ed. Articles, from 1,500 words, for bride and groom, on wedding planning, financial planning, juggling career and home, etc. Pays on acceptance.

MS. MAGAZINE—119 W. 40th St., New York, NY 10018. Address Manuscript Editor, specify fiction, nonfiction, or poetry. Articles relating to women's roles and changing lifestyles; general interest, self-help, how-to, profiles; fiction. Pays varying rates. Query with SASE. Accepts very little freelance material.

NA'AMAT WOMAN—200 Madison Ave., 18th fl., New York, NY 10016. Judith Sokoloff, Ed. Articles on Jewish culture, women's issues, social and political topics, and Israel, 1,500 to 2,500 words. Pays 8¢ a word, on publication. Query.

NEW BODY—888 Seventh Ave., New York, NY 10106. Norman Zeitchick, Ed. Lively, readable service-oriented articles, 1,000 to 2,000 words, by writers with background in health field: exercise, nutrition, and diet pieces for women aged 18 to 40. Pays $250 to $500, on publication. Query preferred.

NEW WOMAN—215 Lexington Ave., New York, NY 10016. Pat Miller, Ed. "Read the magazine in order to become familiar with our needs before querying." Articles on new lifestyles. Features on financial and legal advice, building a business, marriage, relationships, surviving divorce, innovative diets. Pays varying rates, on acceptance. Query.

574

PARENTS—685 Third Ave., New York, NY 10017. Elizabeth Crow, Ed.-in-Chief. Articles, 2,000 to 3,000 words, on growth and development of infants, children, teens; family; women's issues; community; current research. Informal style with quotes from experts. Pays from $450, on acceptance. Query.

REDBOOK—224 W. 57th St., New York, NY 10019. Annette Capone, Ed.-in-Chief. Karen Larson, Senior Ed. Articles for women ages 25 to 40. Pays from $1,500 for short stories; $850 for short shorts, 1,400 to 1,600 words. Pays $750 for personal-experience pieces, 1,000 to 2,000 words, on solving problems in marriage, family life, or community, for "Young Mother's Story." SASE required. Query for articles over 12,000 words.

SAVVY—3 Park Ave., New York, NY 10016. Annalyn Swan, Ed.-in-Chief. Service articles for women executives, 500 to 3,000 words, on business politics, finance, entrepreneurs. Pays $300 to $1,000, on publication. Query.

SELF—350 Madison Ave., New York, NY 10017. Valerie Griffith Weaver, Ed. Articles for women of all ages, with strong how-to slant, on self-development. Pays from $700, on acceptance. Query.

SUNDAY WOMAN PLUS—King Features Syndicate, 235 E. 45th St., New York, NY 10017. Merry Clark, Ed. General-interest articles, 1,000 to 1,500 words, and profiles, 1,200 to 1,500 words, on a wide range of topics. Study magazine before querying. Pays from $50 to $500, on acceptance.

TODAY'S MARRIAGE—Dell Magazine Group, 245 E. 47th St., New York, NY 10017. Genevieve Landau, Ed. Dir. Articles, 2,000 to 3,000 words, on any aspect of married life—including physical and mental health, community and family relations, food and nutrition, beauty and fashion, travel and entertainment, work, money, education, pregnancy, and infant care. Articles should be upbeat, thoughtful but not preachy, and geared to young married women. Pay varies, on acceptance. Query with outline and a few opening paragraphs.

VIRTUE—P.O. Box 850, Sisters, OR 97759. Becky Durost, Ed. Articles, 1,000 to 1,500 words, on the family, marriage, self-esteem, working mothers, opinions, food, decorating. Pays 10¢ a word, on publication. Query required.

VOGUE—350 Madison Ave., New York, NY 10017. Address Features Ed. Articles, to 1,500 words, on women, entertainment and the arts, travel, medicine and health. No unsolicited manuscripts. Query first. Pays good rates, on acceptance.

WEIGHT WATCHERS MAGAZINE—360 Lexington Ave., New York, NY 10017. Nelly Edmondson, Articles Ed. Psychological pieces on weight control; health, fitness, and nutrition; inspirational weight loss stories, 1,200 to 1,500 words. Pays from $250, after acceptance.

WOMAN—1115 Broadway, New York, NY 10010. Sherry Amatenstein, Ed. Personal-experience pieces, 1,000 to 2,000 words, for women who want to better their relationships, careers or lifestyles. Profiles of women business owners for "Be Your Own Boss." Short interviews with successful women for "Woman in the News," and "Bravo Woman." Short medical and legal news items for "Let's Put Our Heads Together." Pays $25 to $125, on acceptance. Query.

WOMAN'S DAY—1515 Broadway, New York, NY 10036. Rebecca Greer, Articles Ed. Eileen Herbert Jordan, Fiction Ed. Human-interest or helpful articles, to 3,500 words, on marriage, child-rearing, health, careers, relationships, money management. Dramatic narratives of medical miracles, rescues, etc. Quality short stories. Pays top rates, on acceptance. Query for articles.

WOMAN'S WORLD—177 N. Dean St., Englewood, NJ 07631. Stephanie Saible, Sen. Ed. Articles, 600 to 1,800 words, of interest to middle-income women between the ages of 18 and 60, on love, romance, careers, medicine, health, psychology, family life, travel, dramatic stories of adventure or crisis. Pays $300 to $750, on acceptance. Query.

WOMEN IN BUSINESS—9100 Ward Parkway, Box 8728, Kansas City, MO 64114. Margaret E. Horan, Ed. American Business Women's Assn. Features, 1,000 to 1,500 words, for working women between 35 and 55 years. No profiles. Pays on acceptance. Written query required.

WOMEN'S CIRCLE—Box 337, Seabrook, NH 03874. Marjorie Pearl, Ed. Success stories of home-based entrepreneurs. How-to articles for craft and needlework projects. Unique money saving ideas and interesting hobbies. Pays varying rates, on acceptance.

WOMEN'S CIRCLE HOME COOKING—Box 1952, Brooksville, FL 33512. Barbara Hall Pedersen, Ed. Food-related articles, to 1,200 words; humorous fiction, to 400 words. Pays to 5¢ a word, on publication.

WOMEN'S SPORTS AND FITNESS—310 Town and Country Village, Palo Alto, CA 94301. Mariah Nelson, Ed. How-to's, profiles, and sports reports, 500 to 3,000 words, for the active woman. Health, fitness, and sports pieces. Photos. Pays from $50, on publication.

WORKING MOTHER—230 Park Ave., New York, NY 10169. Olivia L. Buehl, Ed. Well-thought-out articles, 1,500 to 2,000 words, for working mothers: child care, home management, the work world, single mothers, etc. Pays around $500, on acceptance. Query, with detailed outline.

WORKING WOMAN—342 Madison Ave., New York, NY 10173. Julia Kagan, Ex. Ed. Articles, 1,000 to 2,500 words, on business and personal aspects of working women's lives. Pays from $400, on acceptance.

HOME AND LIFESTYLE

THE AMERICAN ROSE MAGAZINE—P.O. Box 30,000, Shreveport, LA 71130. Harold S. Goldstein, Ed. Articles on home rose gardens: varieties, products, etc. Pays in copies.

AMERICANA—29 W. 38th St., New York, NY 10018. Michael Durham, Ed. Articles, 1,000 to 2,500 words, with historical slant: restoration, crafts, food, antiques, travel, etc. Pays $350 to $600, on acceptance. Query.

BETTER HEALTH AND LIVING—800 Second Ave., New York, NY 10017. Laura L. Vitale, Man. Ed. Articles, 2 to 35 manuscript pages, on healthful living; shorter items and tips. Pays $50 to $100 for short tips, to $1,000 for features, 90 days after acceptance. Query preferred.

BETTER HOMES AND GARDENS—1716 Locust St., Des Moines, IA 50336. David Jordan, Ed. Articles, to 2,000 words, on home and family entertainment, building, decorating, money management, food, health, travel, pets, and cars. Pays top rates, on acceptance. Query.

BON APPETIT—5900 Wilshire Blvd., Los Angeles, CA 90036. Barbara Fairchild, Sr. Ed. New and unusual ideas about food and cooking techniques: menu articles, dessert articles and general food features. Any topics that are not food-related should be avoided. Features run 500 to 700 words. Query first, with examples of published work. Give a clear and concise outline and detailed descriptions of recipes. Editorial guidelines are available. Payment varies.

THE CHRISTIAN SCIENCE MONITOR—One Norway St., Boston, MA 02115. Roderick Nordell, Features Ed. Hattie Clark, Living/Children's pages. Phyllis Hanes, Food Ed. Articles on lifestyle trends, women's rights, family, parenting, consumerism, fashion, and food. Pays varying rates, on acceptance.

THE COOK'S MAGAZINE—2710 North Ave., Bridgeport, CT 06604. Articles on trends in home and restaurant food and cooking, and food-related articles for food and cooking enthusiasts. Query with three- to four-sentence outline, published clips, and sample recipe (for writing and recipe style). Pays $200 to $375, 60 days after publication. SASE required.

COUNTRY JOURNAL—Box 870, Manchester Center, VT 05255. Tyler Resch, Ed. Articles, 2,500 to 3,000 words, for country and small-town residents: practical, informative pieces on contemporary rural life. Pays about $400, on acceptance. Query.

COUNTRY PEOPLE—5400 S. 60th, Greendale, WI 53129. Dan Johnson, Assoc. Ed. Articles, 500 to 1,000 words, for a rural audience. Fillers, 50 to 200 words. Taboos: tobacco, liquor, and sex. Pays $125 to $200, on acceptance. Query.

FARM & RANCH LIVING—5400 S. 60th St., Greendale, WI 53129. Bob Ottum, Man. Ed. Articles, 2,000 words, on rural people and situations; nostalgia pieces, profiles of interesting farms and farmers, ranches and ranchers. Poetry. Pays $15 to $400, on acceptance and on publication.

FARMSTEAD MAGAZINE—Box 111, Freedom, ME 04941. Heidi N. Brugger, Man. Ed. Articles, 700 to 2,500 words, on organic home gardening, country living, livestock and marketing for the small farmer, wood heat, how-to, and homestyle recipes. Pays 5¢ a word, on publication. Query preferred.

FLOWER AND GARDEN MAGAZINE—4251 Pennsylvania, Kansas City, MO 64111. Rachel Snyder, Ed.-in-Chief. How-to articles, to 1,200 words, with photos, on indoor and outdoor home gardening. Pays 7¢ a word, on acceptance. Query preferred.

FOOD & WINE—1120 Ave. of the Americas, 9th fl., New York, NY 10036. Ila Stanger, Ed.-in-Chief. Warren Picower, Man. Ed. Current culinary or beverage ideas for dining and entertaining at home and out. Appropriate "F.O.B." essays. Submit detailed proposal.

FRIENDLY EXCHANGE—Locust at 17th, Des Moines, IA 50336. Adele Malott, Ed. Features, 1,000 to 2,500 words, for young, active families who live in the western half of the U.S. Subjects include domestic travel, camping, health, culture, personal finance, consumer information, and food. No poetry, fiction, cartoons. Photos. Pays $400 to $800, extra for photos. Query preferred. Writer's guidelines available.

GARDEN—The Garden Society, Botanical Garden, Bronx, NY 10458. Ann Botshon, Ed. Articles, 1,000 to 2,500 words, on botany, horticulture, ecology, agriculture. Photos. Pays to $300, on publication. Query.

GARDEN DESIGN—1733 Connecticut Ave., NW, Washington, DC 20009. Kenneth Druse, Ed. Articles, 500 to 1,000 words, on classic and contemporary examples of residential landscape, garden art, history and design; interviews. Pays $300, on publication. Query.

577

GARDENS FOR ALL NEWS—See *National Gardening Magazine.*

HARROWSMITH/USA—The Creamery, Ferry Rd., Charlotte, VT 05445. Tom Rawls, Man. Ed. Investigative pieces, 2,000 to 4,000 words, on ecology, energy, health, and the food chain. Short pieces for "Pantry Arts" (culinary arts and food preservation); "Benchmarks" (do-it-yourself projects); "Screed" (opinions); and "Gazette" (news briefs). Pays $500 to $1,500 for features, from $50 to $750 for department pieces, on acceptance. Query required. Send SASE for guidelines.

THE HERB QUARTERLY—P.O. Box 275, Newfane, VT 05345. Articles, 2,000 to 10,000 words, on herbs: practical uses, cultivation, gourmet cooking, landscaping, herb tradition, unique garden designs, profiles of herb garden experts, practical how-to's for the herb businessperson. Include garden design when possible. Pays on publication. Send for writers' guidelines.

HOME MAGAZINE—140 E. 45th St., New York, NY 10017. Channing Dawson, Ed. Articles of interest to homeowners: remodeling, decorating, how-to's, project ideas and instructions, taxes, insurance, conservation and solar energy. Pays varying rates, on acceptance. Query, with 50- to 200-word summary.

THE HOMEOWNER—3 Park Ave., New York, NY 10016. Jim Liston, Ed. Articles, 500 to 1,500 words, with photos, on do-it-yourself home improvement and remodeling projects. Pays $100 to $150 per printed page, on acceptance. Query.

HOMESTYLES MAGAZINE—6800 France Ave. S., Suite 115, Minneapolis, MN 55435. Anne Welsbacher, Ed. Informative, lively articles, 800 to 1,800 words, on new homes, ownership, and lifestyle. Photos. Pays $200 to $600, after acceptance. Guidelines available.

HORTICULTURE—755 Boylston St., Boston, MA 02116. Steven Krauss, Managing Ed. Authoritative, well-written articles, 1,500 to 3,000 words, on all aspects of gardening. Pays competitive rates. Query first.

HOUSE & GARDEN—350 Madison Ave., New York, NY 10017. Louis O. Gropp, Ed.-in-Chief. Shelley Wanger, Articles Ed. Articles on decorating, architecture, gardening, the arts. Query required.

HOUSE BEAUTIFUL—1700 Broadway, New York, NY 10019. Carol Cooper Garey, Features Dir. Service articles related to the home. Pieces on design, travel and gardening mostly staff-written. Pays varying rates, on acceptance. Send for writer's guidelines. Query with detailed outline.

HOUSTON HOME & GARDEN—5615 Kirby, Suite 600, P.O. Box 25386, Houston, TX 77265. Nancy F. Smith, Ed.-in-Chief. Articles on interior design, regional gardening, cooking, art, architecture, health, fitness, and travel. Limited freelance market. Query.

METROPOLITAN HOME—750 Third Ave., New York, NY 10017. Service and informational articles for metropolitan dwellers in apartments, houses, co-ops, lofts and condos. Pays varying rates. Query.

MICHIGAN WOMAN—P.O. Box 1171, Birmingham, MI 48012. Susan Sajdak, Ed. Articles, to 750 words, that highlight the achievements of Michigan business women. Fillers, to 200 words. Pays 10¢ a word, on publication. Query required.

MILITARY LIFESTYLE MAGAZINE (formerly *Ladycom*)—1732 Wisconsin Ave., N.W., Washington, DC 20007. Hope Daniels, Ed. Articles, 800 to 2,000 words, for military families in the U.S. and overseas, on lifestyles; pieces on issues of interest to military families; fiction. Pays $75 to $500, on publication. Query.

THE MOTHER EARTH NEWS—105 Stoney Mt. Rd., Hendersonville, NC 28791. Bruce Woods, Ed. Articles on country living: home improvement and construction, how-to's, indoor and outdoor gardening, crafts and projects, etc. Also self-help, health, food-related, ecology, energy, and consumerism pieces; profiles. Pays from $100 per published page, on acceptance. Address Submissions Ed.

NATIONAL GARDENING MAGAZINE (formerly *Gardens for All News*)— 180 Flynn Ave., Burlington, VT 05401. Ruth W. Page, Ed. How-to articles on food gardens and orchards, general-interest pieces for gardeners, 300 to 3,000 words. Pays $40 to $300, extra for photos, on acceptance. Query preferred.

NEW AGE—342 Western Ave., Brighton, MA 02135. Articles for readers who take an active interest in social change and personal growth, health and contemporary social issues. Features run 2,000 to 4,000 words; columns, 750 to 1,500 words; short news items, 50 words; and first-person narratives, 750 to 1,500 words. Payment varies. Query first.

NEW HOME—Village West, Country Club Rd., Guilford, NH 03247. Laurence E. Oberwager, Ed. Articles, 1,000 to 4,000 words, for homeowners, on kitchen, bath, energy matters, security, decorating and design, and outdoor living. For "Back Porch" section, pieces on an individual's feelings about his home. Pays varying rates, on acceptance.

NEW SHELTER—See *Practical Homeowner.*

THE OLD-HOUSE JOURNAL—69A Seventh Ave., Brooklyn, NY 11217. Patricia Poore, Ed. Articles, 1,200 to 3,500 words, by free lancers with experience in restoration, architecture, or building maintenance. How-to pieces for "do-it-yourselfers." Pays $100 per printed page, on acceptance. Query.

1001 HOME IDEAS—3 Park Ave., New York, NY 10016. Ellen Frankel, Ed. General-interest articles, 500 to 2,000 words, on home decorating, furnishings, antiques and collectibles, food, household tips, crafts, remodeling, gardening. How-to and problem-solving decorating pieces. Pays varying rates, on acceptance. Query.

PRACTICAL HOMEOWNER (formerly *New Shelter*)—33 E. Minor St., Emmaus, PA 18049. Articles on contemporary home management: how-to, total home design, home improvement, with emphasis on energy efficiency, new products, materials and technologies. Query with SASE required; address Articles Ed.

RODALE'S ORGANIC GARDENING—33 E. Minor St., Emmaus, PA 18049. Steve Daniels, Exec. Ed. Articles, to 2,500 words, on building soil, growing food and ornamental plants, new developments in horticulture, plant breeding, etc. Pieces on food preparation, storage, and equipment for "Gardeners' Kitchen." Photos. Pays $300 to $750, extra for photos, on acceptance. Query required.

RSVP—828 Fort St., Honolulu, HI 96816. Cheryl Tsutsumi, Man. Ed. Articles, 1,500 to 2,000 words, on investments, acquisitions, lifestyle, and manners. Query.

SELECT HOMES—2000 Ellesmere Rd., Unit 1, Scarborough, Ont., M1H2W4 *or* 382 W. Broadway, Vancouver, B.C. V5Y 1R2, Canada. Mike McVean, Eastern Ed./Pam Miller Whithers, Western Ed. Articles, 1,000 words, on home improvement, maintenance, decorating and finance, with Canadian tie-in. Profiles of decorators and projects. Tips on decorating. Humor about home ownership for "The Back Porch," 650 words; home energy topics for "Home Energy." Pays $250 to $600, on acceptance. Query first with clips. Send international reply coupons for guidelines.

THE WORKBASKET—4251 Pennsylvania, Kansas City, MO 64111. Roma Jean Rice, Ed. Instructions and models for original knit, crochet, and tat items. How-to's on crafts and gardening, 400 to 1,200 words, with photos. Pays 7¢ a word for articles, extra for photos, on acceptance; negotiable rates for instructional items.

WORKBENCH—4251 Pennsylvania, Kansas City, MO 64111. Jay W. Hedden, Ed. Illustrated how-to articles on home improvement and do-it-yourself projects, with detailed instructions, energy conservation and alternatives, manufactured housing. Pays from $125 per printed page, on acceptance. Send SASE for writers' guidelines.

YOUR HOME—Box 10010, Ogden, UT 84409. Marjorie H. Rice, Ed. Articles, 1,200 words, with color transparencies, on home decor, construction, remodeling, management and ownership. Pays 15¢ a word, on acceptance. Query.

SPORTS, OUTDOORS, RECREATION

AAA WORLD—AAA Headquarters, 8111 Gatehouse Rd., Falls Church, VA 22047. George Ashfield, Ed. Automobile and travel concerns, including automotive travel, maintenance and upkeep, 750 to 1,500 words. Pays $300 to $600, on acceptance. Query preferred.

AERO—P.O. Box 6050, Mission Viejo, CA 92690. Dennis Shattuck, Ed. Articles, 1,000 to 4,000 words, for owners of high performance single- and twin-engine planes, relating to ownership, piloting, and use; pieces on favorite fly-in travel spots. Photos. Pays $75 to $250, on publication.

THE AMATEUR BOXER—P.O. Box 249, Cobalt, CT 06414. Bob Taylor, Ed. Articles on amateur boxing. Fillers. Photos. Pays $10 to $35, extra for photos, on publication. Query preferred.

THE AMERICAN FIELD—222 W. Adams St., Chicago, IL 60606. William F. Brown, Ed. Yarns about hunting trips, bird-shooting; articles to 1,500 words, on dogs and field trials, emphasizing conservation of game resources. Pays varying rates, on acceptance.

AMERICAN FORESTS—1319 18th St., N.W., Washington, DC 20036. Bill Rooney, Ed. Well-documented articles, to 2,000 words, with photos, on recreational and commercial uses and management of forests. Photos. Pays on acceptance.

AMERICAN HANDGUNNER—Suite 200, 591 Camino de la Reina, San Diego, CA 92108. Cameron Hopkins, Ed. Semi-technical articles on shooting sports, gun repair and alteration, handgun matches and tournaments, for lay readers. Pays $100 to $500, on publication. Query.

AMERICAN HUNTER—1600 Rhode Island Ave. N.W., Washington, DC 20036. Mike Hanback, Man. Ed. Articles, 1,400 to 2,000 words, on hunting. Photos. Pays on acceptance.

580

AMERICAN LAND FORUM—5410 Grosvenor Lane, Ste. 205, Bethesda, MD 20814. Sara Ebenreck, Ed. Well-researched articles, 3,500 words, on U.S. land issues, achievements; leadership profiles or land use topics. Commentaries, 1,000 words, on U.S. land issue, experience or idea. Pays $150 to $500 for articles, $75 for opinion pieces, on acceptance. Query first.

AMERICAN MOTORCYCLIST—American Motorcyclist Assn., Box 6114, Westerville, OH 43081-6114. Greg Harrison, Ed. Articles and fiction, to 3,000 words, on motorcycling: news coverage, personalities, tours. Photos. Pays varying rates, on publication. Query.

THE AMERICAN RIFLEMAN—1600 Rhode Island Ave., N.W., Washington, DC 20036. Bill Parkerson, Ed. Factual articles on use and enjoyment of sporting firearms. Pays on acceptance. Query.

ARCHERY WORLD—11812 Wayzata Blvd., Suite 100, Minnetonka, MN 55343. Richard Sapp, Ed. Articles, 1,000 to 2,000 words, on all aspects of bowhunting, with photos. Pays from $100, extra for photos, on publication.

THE ATLANTIC SALMON JOURNAL—1435 St. Alexandre, Suite 1030, Montreal, Quebec, Canada H3A 2G4. Joanne Eidinger, Ed. Material related to Atlantic salmon: conservation, ecology, travel, politics, biology, etc. How-to's, anecdotes, cuisine. Articles, 1,500 to 3,000 words; short fillers and poetry, 50 to 100 words. Pays $100 to $350, on publication.

BACKPACKER MAGAZINE—1515 Broadway, New York, NY 10036. John A. Delves, Ed. Articles, 250 to 3,000 words, on backpacking, technique, kayaking/canoeing, mountaineering, alpine/nordic skiing, health, natural science. Photos. Pays varying rates. Query.

THE BACKSTRETCH—19363 James Couzens Hwy., Detroit, MI 48235. Ruth LeGrove, Man. Ed. United Thoroughbred Trainers of America. Feature articles, with photos, on persons involved with thoroughbred horses. Pays after publication.

BASEBALL ILLUSTRATED—See *Hockey Illustrated.*

BASKETBALL ANNUAL—See *Hockey Illustrated.*

BASSIN'—15115 S. 76th E. Ave., Bixby, OK 74008. Andre Hinds, Exec. Ed. Articles, 1,200 to 2,000 words, on how to and where to bass fish, for the average fisherman. Pays $175 to $250, on acceptance.

BASSMASTER MAGAZINE—B.A.S.S. Publications, P.O. Box 17900, Montgomery, AL 36141. Dave Precht, Ed. Articles, 1,500 to 2,000 words, with photos, on freshwater black bass and striped bass. "Short Casts" pieces, 400 to 800 words, on news, views, and items of interest. Pays $200 to $400, on acceptance. Query.

BAY & DELTA YACHTSMAN—2019 Clement Ave., Alameda, CA 94501. Dave Preston, Ed. Humorous features, satire and cruising stories. Must have Northern California tie-in. Photos and illustrations. Pays varying rates.

BC OUTDOORS—#202, 1132 Hamilton St., Vancouver, B.C., Canada V6B 2S2. Henry L. Frew, Ed. Articles, to 1,500 words, on fishing, hunting, conservation and all forms of non-competitive outdoor recreation in British Columbia, Alberta, and Yukon. Photos. Pays from 10¢ to 15¢ a word, extra for photos, on acceptance.

BICYCLE GUIDE—711 Boylston St., Boston, MA 02116. Theodore Costantino, Ed. "Our magazine covers all aspects of cycling—racing, touring, sport riding, product reviews, and technical information—from an enthusiast's perspective. We depend on free lancers for touring articles and race coverage." Queries are preferred. Pays varying rates, on publication.

BICYCLING—33 E. Minor St., Emmaus, PA 18049. James C. McCullagh, Ed. Articles, 500 to 2,500 words, on recreational riding, training, equipment, racing, and touring, for serious cyclists. Photos, illustrations. Pays $25 to $600, on publication. Guidelines available.

BIKEREPORT—Bikecentennial, P.O. Box 8308, Missoula, MT 59807. Daniel D'Ambrosio, Ed. Accounts of bicycle tours in the U.S. and overseas, interviews, personal-experience pieces, humor and news shorts, 1,200 to 2,500 words. Pays $25 to $65 per published page.

BIRD WATCHER'S DIGEST—P.O. Box 110, Marietta, OH 45750. Mary B. Bowers, Ed. Articles, 600 to 2,500 words, for bird watchers: first-person accounts; how-to's; pieces on endangered species; profiles. Cartoons, fillers. Pays to $50 for articles, $25 for reprints, $5 for fillers, $10 for cartoons, on publication.

BOAT PENNSYLVANIA—Pennsylvania Fish Commission, P.O. Box 1673, Harrisburg, PA 17105-1673. Articles, 200 to 2,500 words, with photos, on boating in Pennsylvania: motorboating, sailing, waterskiing, canoeing, kayaking, and rafting. No pieces on fishing. Pays $50 to $200, on acceptance. Query.

BOATING—One Park Ave., New York, NY 10016. Doug Schryver, Ed. Illustrated articles, 1,000 to 2,000 words, on power boating. Pays good rates, on acceptance. Query.

BOW & ARROW HUNTING—Box HH, 34249 Camino Capistrano, Capistrano Beach, CA 92624. Roger Combs, Ed. Articles 1,200 to 2,500 words, with photos, on bowhunting; profiles and technical pieces. Pays $50 to $300, on acceptance. Same address and requirements for *Gun World*.

BOWHUNTER MAGAZINE—3808 S. Calhoun St., Fort Wayne, IN 46807. M. R. James, Ed. Informative, entertaining features, 500 to 5,000 words, on bow and arrow hunting. Fillers. Photos. Pays $25 to $300, on acceptance. Study magazine first.

BOWLERS JOURNAL—875 N. Michigan Ave., Chicago, IL 60611. Mort Luby, Ed. Trade and consumer articles, 1,200 to 2,200 words, with photos, on bowling. Pays $75 to $200, on acceptance. Query.

BOWLING—5301 S. 76th St., Greendale, WI 53129. Dan Matel, Ed. Articles, to 1,500 words, on amateur league and tournament bowling. Profiles. Pays varying rates, on publication.

CALIFORNIA ANGLER—179 Roymar Rd., Suite C, Oceanside, CA 92054. Tom Waters, Ed. How-to and where-to articles, 2,000 words, for freshwater and saltwater anglers in California: travel, new products, fishing techniques, profiles. Photos. Pays $50 to $300, on acceptance. Query first.

CAR AND DRIVER—2002 Hogback Rd., Ann Arbor, MI 48105. Don Sherman, Ed. Articles, to 2,500 words, for enthusiasts, on car manufacturers, new developments in cars, etc. Pays to $1500, on acceptance.

CAR CRAFT—8490 Sunset Blvd., Los Angeles, CA 90069. Jeff Smith, Ed. Articles and photofeatures on unusual street machines, drag cars, racing events; technical pieces; action photos. Pays from $150 per page, on publication.

582

CASCADES EAST—716 N.E. 4th St., P.O. Box 5784, Bend, OR 97708. Geoff Hill, Ed./Publisher. Articles, 1,000 to 2,000 words, on outdoor activities (fishing, hunting, backpacking, rafting, skiing, snowmobiling, etc.), history, and scenic tours in Cascades region of Oregon. Photos. Pays 3¢ to 10¢ a word, extra for photos, on publication.

CHECKPOINT—P.O. Box 660460, Dallas, TX 75266. T. Pfiffner, Ed. Articles, 400 to 800 words, on automotive and safety topics; how-to's. Pays to 10¢ a word, on publication. Query.

CHESAPEAKE BAY MAGAZINE—1819 Bay Ridge Ave., Annapolis, MD 21403. Betty Rigoli, Ed. Technical and how-to articles, to 1,500 words, on boating, fishing, conservation, in Chesapeake Bay. Photos. Pays $85 to $125, on publication.

CITY SPORTS MAGAZINE—P.O. Box 3693, San Francisco, CA 94119. Maggie Cloherty, Ed/Northern California. Peg Moline, Ed/Southern California, 1120 Princeton Dr., Marina Del Rey, CA 90291. Articles, 1,700 to 3,000 words, on sports for active Californians. Pays $50 to $450, on publication. Query.

CORVETTE FEVER—Box 44620, Ft. Washington, MD 20744. Pat Stivers, Ed. Articles, 500 to 2,500 words, on Corvette repairs, swap meets, and personalities. Corvette-related fiction, about 700 lines, and fillers. Photos. Pays 10¢ a word, on publication.

CRUISING WORLD—524 Thames St., Newport, RI 02840. George Day, Ed. Articles on sailing, 1,000 to 2,500 words: technical and personal narratives. No fiction, poetry, or logbook transcripts. 35mm slides. Pays $100 to $600, on acceptance. Query preferred.

CYCLE GUIDE—20916 Higgins Ct., Torrance, CA 90501. Jim Miller, Ed. Articles on motorcycling. Pays $125 to $2,500, on acceptance. Query required.

CYCLE MAGAZINE—780-A Lakefield Rd., Westlake Village, CA 91361. Paul Gordon, Exec. Ed. Articles, 6 to 20 manuscript pages, on motorcycle races, history, touring, technical pieces; profiles. Photos. Pays on publication. Query.

CYCLE NEWS WEST—2201 Cherry Ave., Box 498, Long Beach, CA 90801. John Ulrich, Ed. Technical articles on motorcycling; profiles and interviews with motorcycle newsmakers. Pays $2 per column inch, on publication. Query.

CYCLE WORLD—1499 Monrovia Ave., Newport Beach, CA 92663. Paul Dean, Ed. Technical and feature articles, 1,500 to 2,500 words, for motorcycle enthusiasts. Photos. Pays $100 to $200 per page, on publication. Query.

CYCLING U.S.A.—U.S. Cycling Federation, 1750 E. Boulder St., Colorado Springs, CO 80909. Josh Lehman, Ed. Articles, 500 to 1,500 words, on bicycle racing. Pays 10¢ a word, on publication. Query first.

CYCLIST—20916 Higgins Ct., Torrance, CA 90501. John Francis, Ed. Articles on all aspects of bicycling: touring, travel and equipment. Query required.

THE DIVER—P.O. Box 249, Cobalt, CT 06414. Bob Taylor, Ed. Articles on divers, coaches, officials, springboard and platform technique, training tips, results, and upcoming events. Photos. Pays $15 to $40, extra for photos, $5 to $25 for cartoons, on publication.

DIVER MAGAZINE—#295, 10991 Shellbridge Way, Richmond, B.C.,

V6H 3C6, Canada. Neil McDaniel, Ed. Well-illustrated articles, 1,000 to 2,000 words, on dive regions, with up-to-date service information, for scuba divers in the NW U.S. and Canada; features on aquatic life, history, equipment, underwater photography, interviews, personal experience, humor, and travel destinations. Pays $2.50 for column inch, extra for photos, after publication. Query first with international reply coupons.

EASTERN BASKETBALL—Eastern Basketball Publications, West Hempstead, NY 11552. Rita Napolitano, Man. Ed. Articles on college and high school basketball in the Northeast. Pays $75, on publication. Query.

ENVIRONMENTAL ACTION—1525 New Hampshire Ave., NW, Washington, DC 20036. News and features, varying lengths, on a broad range of political and/or environmental topics: energy, toxics, self-sufficiency, etc. Book reviews; environmentally-related consumer goods. Pays 7¢ to 10¢ a word, extra for photos, on publication. Query required.

FAT TIRE FLYER—Box 757, Fairfax, CA 94930. Charles R. Kelley, Ed. Articles, 700 to 2,000 words, related to "fat tire" or mountain bikes. B/W photos or drawings. Pays 5¢ to 10¢ a word, on publication.

FIELD & STREAM—1515 Broadway, New York, NY 10036. Duncan Barnes, Ed. Articles, 1,500 to 2,500 words, with photos, on hunting, fishing. Fillers, 350 to 900 words, for "How It's Done." Cartoons. Pays from $500 for articles with photos, $250 to $350 for fillers, $100 for cartoons, on acceptance. Query in writing on articles.

FINS AND FEATHERS—401 N. Third St., Minneapolis, MN 55401. Dave Greer, Ed. Articles, 2,000 to 2,500 words, on a wide variety of recreational activities, including hunting, fishing, camping, and environmental issues. Pays $100 to $500, on publication. Query.

FISHING WORLD—51 Atlantic Ave., Floral Park, NY 11001. Keith Gardner, Ed. Features, to 2,500 words, with color transparencies, on fishing sites, technique, equipment. Pays $300 for major features, $100 for shorter articles. Query preferred.

THE FLORIDA HORSE—P.O. Box 2106, Ocala, FL 32678. F. J. Audette, Publisher. Articles, 1,500 words, on Florida thoroughbred breeding and racing. Pays $100 to $150, on publication.

FLY FISHERMAN—Box 8200, Harrisburg, PA 17105. John Randolph, Ed. Articles, to 3,000 words, on how to and where to fly fish. Fillers, to 100 words. Pays from $35 to $400, on acceptance. Query.

FLYING MAGAZINE—One Park Ave., New York, NY 10016. Richard Collins, Ed.-in-Chief. Articles, 1,500 words, on personal flying experiences. Pays varying rates, on acceptance.

FOOTBALL DIGEST—Century Publishing Co., 1020 Church St., Evanston, IL 60201. Michael K. Herbert, Ed. Profiles of pro stars, "think" pieces, 1,500 words, aimed at the pro football fan. Pays on publication.

FOOTBALL FORECAST—See *Hockey Illustrated.*

FUR-FISH-GAME—2878 E. Main St., Columbus, OH 43209. Tom Glass, Ed. Illustrated articles, 800 to 2,500 words, preferably with how-to angle, on hunting, fishing, trapping, dogs, camping or other outdoor topics. Some humorous or where-to articles. Pays $40 to $150, on acceptance.

GAME AND FISH PUBLICATIONS—P.O. Box 741, Marietta, GA 30061.

Publishes outdoors magazines for 37 states. Articles, 2,000 to 2,500 words, on hunting and fishing. How-to's, where-to's, and adventure pieces. Profiles of successful hunters and fishermen. No hiking, canoeing, camping, or backpacking pieces. Pays $150 for state-specific articles, $200 to $300 for multi-state articles, on publication.

GOAL—500 Fifth Ave., 34th Fl., New York, NY 10110. Stu Hackel, Ed. Official magazine of the National Hockey League. Player profiles and trend stories, 1,000 to 1,800 words, for hockey fans with knowledge of the game and players, by writers with understanding of the sport. Pays $100 to $200, before publication. Query.

GOLF DIGEST—5520 Park Ave., Trumbull, CT 06611. Jerry Tarde, Ed. Instructional articles, tournament reports, and features on players, to 2,500 words. Fiction, 1,000 to 4,000 words. Poetry, fillers, humor, photos. Pays varying rates, on acceptance. Query preferred.

GOLF ILLUSTRATED—3 Park Ave., New York, NY 10016. Al Barkow, Editor. Lee Schreiber, Managing Ed. Golf-related features, 1,000 to 2,000 words: instruction, profiles, photo essays, travel, technique, nostalgia, opinion. Pays $750 to $1,500, on acceptance. Query preferred.

GOLF JOURNAL—Golf House, Far Hills, NJ 07931. Robert Sommers, Ed. U.S. Golf Assn. Articles on golf personalities, history, travel. Humor. Photos. Pays varying rates, on publication.

GOLF MAGAZINE—380 Madison Ave., New York, NY 10017. James Frank, Exec. Ed. Articles of 1,500 words, with photos, on golf. Shorts, to 500 words. Pays $500 to $1,000 for articles, $75 to $150 for shorts, on publication.

THE GREYHOUND REVIEW—National Greyhound Assn., Box 543, Abilene, KS 67410. Tim Horan, Man. Ed. Articles, 1,000 to 10,000 words, pertaining to the greyhound racing industry: how-to, historical, nostalgia, interviews. Pays $40 to $150, on publication.

GUN DIGEST AND HANDLOADER'S DIGEST—4092 Commercial Ave., Northbrook, IL 60062. Ken Warner, Ed. Well-researched articles, to 5,000 words, on guns and shooting, equipment, etc. Photos. Pays from 10¢ a word, on acceptance. Query.

GUN DOG—P.O. Box 35098, Des Moines, IA 50315. Bob Wilbanks, Man. Ed. Features, 1,000 to 2,500 words, with photos, on bird hunting: how-to's, where-to's, dog training, canine medicine, breeding strategy. Fiction. Humor. Fillers. Pays $50 to $150 for fillers and short articles, $150 to $350 for features, on acceptance.

GUN WORLD—See *Bow & Arrow Hunting.*

GUNS & AMMO—8490 Sunset Blvd., Los Angeles, CA 90069. E. G. Bell, Jr., Ed. Technical and general articles, 1,500 to 3,000 words, on guns, ammunition, and target shooting. Photos, fillers. Pays from $150, on acceptance.

HANG GLIDING—U.S. Hang Gliding Assn., P.O. Box 66306, Los Angeles, CA 90066. Gilbert Dodgen, Ed. Articles and fiction, 2 to 3 pages, on hang gliding. Pays to $50, on publication. Query.

HOCKEY ILLUSTRATED—355 Lexington Ave., New York, NY 10017. Stephen Ciacciarelli, Ed. Articles, 2,500 words, on hockey players, teams. Pays $125, on publication. Query. Same address and requirements for *Baseball Illustrated, Wrestling World, Pro Basketball Illustrated, Pro Football Illus-*

585

trated, Basketball Annual (college), *Baseball Preview, Baseball Forecast, Pro Football Preview, Football Forecast,* and *Basketball Forecast.*

HORSE & RIDER—Box 555, 41919 Moreno Rd., Temecula, CA 92390. Ray Rich, Ed. Articles, 500 to 3,000 words, with photos, on Western riding and general horse care: training, feeding, grooming, etc. Pays varying rates, before publication. Buys all rights. Guidelines.

HORSEMAN—5314 Bingle Rd., Houston, TX 77292. Michael Rieke, Ed. Instructional articles, to 2,500 words, with photos, for Western trainers and riders. Pays to $350, on acceptance.

HORSEMEN'S YANKEE PEDLAR—785 Southbridge St., Auburn, MA 01501. Nancy L. Khoury, Pub. News and feature-length articles, about horses and horsemen in the Northeast. Photos. Pays $2 per published inch, on publication. Query.

HORSEPLAY—Box 545, Gaithersburg, MD 20877. Cordelia Doucet, Ed. Articles, to 3,000 words, on eventing, show jumping, horse shows, dressage, driving and fox hunting, for horse enthusiasts. Pays 9¢ a word, after publication.

HOT BIKE—2145 W. La Palma, Anaheim, CA 92801. Tod Knuth, Ed. Articles, 250 to 2,500 words, with photos, on motorcycles. Event coverage on high performance street and track and sport touring motorcycles, with emphasis on Harley Davidsons. Pays $50 to $100 per printed page, on publication.

HOT BOAT—P.O. Box 1708, Lake Havasu City, AZ 86403. Jay Koblenz, Ed. Articles, 850 to 2,500 words, on motorized family water sporting events, personalities: general interest, how-to, and technical features. Humor, 600 to 1,000 words. Pays $85 to $300, on publication. Query.

HOT ROD—8490 Sunset Blvd., Los Angeles, CA 90069. Patrick Ganahl, Ed. How-to pieces and articles, 500 to 5,000 words, on auto mechanics, hot rods, track and drag racing. Photo-features on custom or performance-modified cars. Pays to $250 per page, on publication.

HUNTING—8490 Sunset Blvd., Los Angeles, CA 90069. Craig Boddington, Ed. How-to articles on practical aspects of hunting. At least 15 photos required with articles. Pays $250 to $400 for articles, extra for color photos, on acceptance.

INSIDE RUNNING & FITNESS—9514 Bristlebrook Dr., Houston, TX 77083. Joanne Schmidt, Ed. Articles, fiction, and fillers on running and aerobic fitness in Texas. Pays $35 to $100, $10 for photos, on acceptance.

KEEPIN' TRACK OF VETTES—P.O. Box 48, Spring Valley, NY 10977. Shelli Finkel, Ed. Articles of any length, with photos, relating to Corvettes. Pays $25 to $200, on publication.

KITPLANES—P.O. Box 6050, Mission Viejo, CA 92690. Dennis Shattuck, Ed. Articles, geared to the growing market of aircraft built from kits by home craftsmen, on all aspects of design, construction and performance, 1,000 to 4,000 words. Pays $75 to $250, on publication.

LAKELAND BOATING—1921 St. John's Ave., Highland Park, IL 60035. Brian Callaghan, Ed. Articles for powerboat and sailboat owners on the Great Lakes and major inland rivers, on long distance cruising, short trips, maintenance, equipment, history, and environment. Photos. Pays 10¢ to 20¢ a word, on publication. Query first. Guidelines.

MICHIGAN OUT-OF-DOORS—P.O. Box 30235, Lansing, MI 48909. Kenneth S. Lowe, Ed. Features, 1,500 to 2,500 words, on hunting, fishing, camping and conservation in Michigan. Photos. Pays $15 to $60, on acceptance.

MID-WEST OUTDOORS—111 Shore Dr., Hinsdale, IL 60521. Gene Laulunen, Ed. Articles, 1,500 words, with photos, on where, when and how to fish in the Midwest. Fillers, 200 to 500 words. Pays $15 to $35, on publication.

MOTOR TREND—8490 Sunset Blvd., Los Angeles, CA 90069. Mike Anson, Ed. Articles, 250 to 2,500 words, on autos, racing, events, and profiles. Photos. Pay varies, on publication. Query.

MOTORCYCLIST—8490 Sunset Blvd., Los Angeles, CA 90069. Art Friedman, Ed. Articles, 1,000 to 3,000 words. Action photos. Pays varying rates, on publication. Query.

MOTORHOME MAGAZINE—29901 Agoura Rd., Agoura, CA 91301. Bob Livingston, Ed. Articles, to 2,000 words, with color slides, on motorhomes; travel and how-to pieces. Pays to $500, on acceptance.

MUSCULAR DEVELOPMENT—Strength and Health Publishing, P.O. Box 1707, York, PA 17405. Jan Dellinger, Ed. Articles, 5 to 10 typed pages, on competitive body building and powerlifting for serious weight training athletes. Pays $50 to $200, extra for photos, on publication. Query.

NATIONAL PARKS MAGAZINE—1015 31st St., NW, Washington, DC 20007. Michele Strutin, Ed. Articles, 1,000 to 2,000 words, on natural history, wildlife, outdoors activities, travel and conservation as they relate to national parks: illustrated features on the natural, historic and cultural resources of the National Park System. Pieces about legislation and other issues and events related to the parks. Pays $100 to $400, on acceptance. Query. Send for guidelines.

NATIONAL RACQUETBALL—P.O. Drawer 6126, Clearwater, FL 33528. Lydon Kuhns, Ed. Articles, 800 to 1,200 words, on health and conditioning. How-to's. Profiles. Fiction. Material must be related to racquetball. Pays $25 to $150, on publication. Photos.

NATIONAL WILDLIFE AND INTERNATIONAL WILDLIFE—8925 Leesburg Pike, Vienna, VA 22184. Mark Wexler, Man. Ed., *National Wildlife*. Jon Fisher, Man. Ed., *International Wildlife*. Articles, 1,000 to 2,500 words, on wildlife, conservation, environment; outdoor how-to pieces. Photos. Pays market rates, on acceptance. Query.

NAUTICAL QUARTERLY—Pratt St., Essex, CT 06426. Joseph Gribbins, Ed. In-depth articles, 3,000 to 7,000 words, about boats and boating, U.S. and foreign. Pays $500 to $1,000, on acceptance. Query.

NORTHEAST OUTDOORS—P.O. Box 2180, Waterbury, CT 06722-2180. Deborah Neally, Ed. Articles, 500 to 1,800 words, preferably with B/W photos, on camping in Northeast U.S.: recommended private campgrounds, camp cookery, recreational vehicle hints. Stress how-to, where-to. Cartoons. Pays to $80, on publication. Send for guidelines.

NORTHEAST RIDING—209 Whitney St., Hartford, CT 06105. Paul Essenfeld, Pub. Motorcycle-related articles, 500 to 1,000 words, for motorcyclists in the Northeast. Pays negotiable rates, on publication.

OCEAN REALM—6061 Collins Ave., Suite 19 C, Miami Beach, FL 33140. S. M. George, Ed. Articles, 1,200 to 1,800 words, on scuba diving and ocean science and technology. Department pieces: adventure; technology/medicine;

587

instruction; photography and marine life. Photos. Short items, 100 to 500 words, for "FYI": up-to-date news items of interest to the diving community. Pays $100 per published page, $5 for FYI, on publication. Query with SASE.

OFFSHORE—220 Reservoir St., Needham Hts., MA 02194. Charles J. Doane, Man. Ed. Articles, 1,000 to 3,000 words, on boats, people, and places along the New England coast. Photos. Pays from 5¢ to 10¢ a word, on acceptance.

ON TRACK—17165 Newhope St., "M," Fountain Valley, CA 92708. Jeremy Shaw, Edit. Dir. Features and race reports, 500 to 2,500 words. Pays $3 per column inch, on publication. Query.

OUTDOOR AMERICA—1701 N. Ft. Myer Dr., Suite 1100, Arlington, VA 22209. Quarterly publication of the Izaak Walton League of America. Articles, 1,500 to 2,000 words, on natural resource conservation issues and outdoor recreation; especially fishing, hunting and camping. Pays from 15¢ a word, for features, on publication. Query Articles Ed., with published clippings.

OUTDOOR LIFE—380 Madison Ave., New York, NY 10017. Clare Conley, Ed. Articles on hunting, fishing and related subjects. Pays top rates, on acceptance. Query.

OUTSIDE—Continental Bank Building, 1165 N. Clark, Chicago, IL 60610. High-quality articles, with photos, on sports, nature, wilderness travel, adventure, etc. Pays varying rates. Query.

PENNSYLVANIA ANGLER—Pennsylvania Fish Commission, P.O. Box 1673, Harrisburg, PA 17105-1673. Address Editor. Articles, 250 to 2,500 words, with photos, on freshwater fishing in Pennsylvania. Pays $50 to $200 on acceptance. Must send SASE with all material. Query.

PENNSYLVANIA GAME NEWS—Game Commission, Harrisburg, PA 17105-1567. Bob Bell, Ed. Articles, to 2,500 words, with photos, on outdoor subjects, except fishing and boating. Photos. Pays from 5¢ a word, extra for photos, on acceptance.

PERFORMANCE HORSEMAN—Gum Tree Corner, Unionville, PA 19375. Miranda Lorraine, Articles Ed. Factual how-to pieces for the serious western rider, on training, improving riding skills, all aspects of care and management, etc. Pays from $300, on acceptance. Query.

PGA MAGAZINE—100 Avenue of the Champions, Palm Beach Gardens, FL 33418. Bill Burbaum, Ed. Articles, 1,500 to 2,500 words, on golf-related subjects. Pays $300 to $500, on acceptance. Query.

PLEASURE BOATING—1995 N.E. 150th St., North Miami, FL 33181. Robert Ulrich, Ed. Articles, 1,000 to 2,000 words, on fishing and recreational boating, covering the coastline from Texas to New York harbor. Pays varying rates, on publication. Query first. Study sample copies.

POPULAR LURES—15115 S. 76th E. Ave., Bixby, OK 74008. André Hinds, Exec. Ed. Articles, 1,200 to 1,500 words, on tackle and techniques for catching all freshwater and saltwater fish, primarily bass, trout, catfish, crappie, walleye and salmon. Pays $175 to $225, on acceptance.

POPULAR SCIENCE—380 Madison Ave., New York, NY 10017. C. P. Gilmore, Ed.-in-Chief. Factual articles, 300 to 2,000 words, with photos and illustrations, on advances in science and technology, new products in electronics, cars, tools; recreational or do-it-yourself projects for home, shop, and yard. Pays varying rates, on acceptance. Query.

POWERBOAT—15917 Strathern St., Van Nuys, CA 91406. Mark Spencer, Ed. Articles, to 1,500 words, with photos, for powerboat owners, on outstanding achievements, water-skiing, competitions; technical articles on hull developments; how-to pieces. Pays about $300, on publication. Query.

PRACTICAL HORSEMAN—Gum Tree Corner, Unionville, PA 19375. Miranda D. Lorraine, Articles Ed. How-to articles on English riding, training, and horse care. Pays on publication. Query.

PRIVATE PILOT—P.O. Box 6050, Mission Viejo, CA 92690. Dennis Shattuck, Ed. True-experience pieces and technically-based aviation articles, 1,000 to 4,000 words, for aviation enthusiasts. Photos. Pays $75 to $250, on publication. Query.

PRO BASKETBALL ILLUSTRATED—See *Hockey Illustrated.*

PRO FOOTBALL ILLUSTRATED—See *Hockey Illustrated.*

RIDER—29901 Agoura Rd., Agoura, CA 91301. Tash Matsuoka, Ed. Articles, with photos, to 3,000 words, with emphasis on travel, touring, commuting, and camping motorcyclists. Pays $100 to $500, on publication. Query.

ROAD RIDER MAGAZINE—P.O. Box 6050, Mission Viejo, CA 92690. Bob Carpenter, Ed. Articles, to 1,500 words, with photos or b&w illustrations, on motorcycle touring. Pays from $100, on publication. Query.

THE RUNNER—1 Park Ave., New York, NY 10016. Marc Bloom, Ed. Features, 3,000 to 4,000 words, and columns, 900 to 1,500 words, for runners. Pays varying rates, on acceptance.

SAIL—Charlestown Navy Yard, 100 First Ave., Charlestown, MA 02129. Keith Taylor, Ed. Articles, 1,500 to 3,500 words, features, 1,000 to 1,500 words, with photos, on sailboats, equipment, racing, and cruising. How-to's on navigation, sail trim, etc. Pays $75 to $1,000, on publication. Writer's guidelines sent on request.

SAILING—125 E. Main St., Port Washington, WI 53074. William F. Schanen, III, Ed. Features, 700 to 1,500 words, with photos, on cruising and racing; first-person accounts; profiles of boats and regattas. Query for technical or how-to pieces. Pays varying rates, 30 days after publication. Writer's guidelines sent on request.

SAILING WORLD (formerly *Yacht Racing & Cruising*)—111 East Ave., Norwalk, CT 06851. John Burnham, Ed. Articles, 8 to 10 typed pages, on sailboat racing and cruising, regatta reports, equipment, techniques. Photos. Pays $150 per published page, on publication. Query.

SAILORS' GAZETTE—337-22nd Ave. N., Suite 110, St. Petersburg, FL 33704. Alice N. Eachus, Ed. Articles, 500 to 1,500 words, with photos, on Southeastern sailing. Emphasis on cruising, racing, destinations, and how-to's. Pays to 6¢ a word, extra for photos, on publication.

SCORE, CANADA'S GOLF MAGAZINE—287 MacPherson Ave., Toronto, Ont., Canada M4V 1A4. Lisa A. Leighton, Man. Ed. Articles, 800 to 3,500 words, on travel, golf equipment, golf history, personality profiles of prominent professionals. Fillers, 25 to 100 words. Pays $10 to $25 for fillers, $125 to $600 for features, on assignment and publication. Query with published clips.

SEA—1760 Monrovia Ave., Suite C-2, Costa Mesa, CA 92627. Cathi Douglas, Man. Ed. Articles, 200 to 900 words, about cruising destinations, profiles o boating personalities, nautical navigation and seamanship. News and features, 800 to 3,500 words, on the marine environment, for West Coast boaters. Query. Payment varies, on publication.

SEA KAYAKER—1670 Duranleau St., Vancouver, BC, Canada, V6H 3S4. John Dowd, Ed. Articles, 400 to 2,000 words, on ocean kayaking. Fiction. Pays 10¢ a word, on publication. Query with sample clips. Include international reply coupons.

SHOTGUN SPORTS—Box 340, Lake Havasu City, AZ 86403. Frank Kodl, Ed. Articles with photos, on trap and skeet shooting and hunting with shotguns. Pays $25 to $200, on publication.

SIERRA—730 Polk St., San Francisco, CA 94109. James Keough, Ed. Articles, 1,000 to 2,500 words, on environmental and conservation topics, hiking, backpacking, skiing, rafting, cycling. Book reviews and children's dept. Photos. Pays $200 to $500, extra for photos, on acceptance. Query.

SKI MAGAZINE—380 Lexington Ave., New York, NY 10017. Dick Needham, Ed. Articles, 1,300 to 2,000 words, for experienced skiers: profiles, humor, "it-happened-to-me" stories, and destination pieces. Short news items, 100 to 300 words, for "Ski Life" column. Equipment and racing articles are staff written. Query first (with clips) for articles. Pays from $200, on acceptance.

SKI RACING—Box 1125, Rt. 100, Waitsfield, VT 05673. Gary Black, Jr., Pub. Interviews, articles, and how-to pieces on national and international nordic and alpine ski competitions. Photos. Pays varying rates.

SKIING—One Park Ave., New York, NY 10016. Bill Grout, Ed. Personal adventures on skis, from 2,500 words (no first-time-on-skis stories); profiles and interviews, 50 to 300 words. Pays $150 to $300 per printed page, on acceptance.

SKIN DIVER MAGAZINE—8490 Sunset Blvd., Los Angeles, CA 90069. Bonnie J. Cardone, Exec. Ed. Illustrated articles, 500 to 2,000 words, on scuba diving activities, equipment and dive sites. Pays $50 per published page, on publication.

SKYDIVING—P.O. Box 1520, Deland, FL 32721. Michael Truffer, Ed. Timely news articles, 300 to 800 words, relating to sport and military parachuting. Fillers. Photos. Pays $25 to $200, extra for photos, on publication.

SNOWMOBILE—11812 Wayzata Blvd., Suite 100, Minnetonka, MN 55343. Dick Hendricks, Ed. Articles, 700 to 2,000 words, with b&w and color photos, related to snowmobiling: races and rallies, trail rides, personalities, travel. How-to's; humor; cartoons. Pays to $450, on publication. Query.

SNOWMOBILE WEST—P.O. Box 981, Idaho Falls, ID 83402. Steve Janes, Ed. Articles, 1,200 words, with photos, on snowmobiling in the western states. Pays to $100, on publication.

SOCCER AMERICA MAGAZINE—P.O. Box 23704, Oakland, CA 94623. Lynn Berling-Manuel, Ed. Articles, to 1,000 words, on soccer: news, profiles, coaching tips. Pays $25 to $100 for features, within 60 days of publication. Query.

SOUTH CAROLINA WILDLIFE—P.O. Box 167, Columbia, SC 29202. John E. Davis, Ed. Articles, 1,000 to 3,000 words, with regional outdoors focus: conservation, natural history and wildlife, recreation. Profiles, how-to's. Pays on acceptance. Query.

SPORT MAGAZINE—119 W. 40th St., New York, NY 10018. Neil Cohen, Ed. Query.

THE SPORTING NEWS—P.O. Box 56, 1212 N. Lindbergh Blvd., St. Louis, MO 63132. Tom Barnidge, Ed.-in-Chief. Articles, 1,000 to 1,500 words, on baseball, football, basketball, hockey, and other sports. Pays $150 to $750, on publication.

SPORTS AFIELD—250 W. 55th St., New York, NY 10019. Tom Paugh, Ed. Articles, 2,000 words, with quality photos, on hunting, fishing, natural history, personal experiences, new hunting/fishing spots. How-to pieces; humor; fiction. Pays top rates, on acceptance.

SPORTS AFIELD SPECIALS—250 W. 55th St., New York, NY 10019. Well-written, informative fishing and hunting articles, 2,000 to 2,500 words, with photos, with primary focus on how-to techniques; include lively anecdotes, and good sidebars, charts. Pays to $450 for features, on acceptance. Query.

SPORTS ILLUSTRATED—1271 Ave. of the Americas, New York, NY 10020. William O. Johnson, Articles Ed. No unsolicited material.

SPUR MAGAZINE—P.O. Box 85, Middleburg, VA 22117. Address Ed. Dept. Articles, 300 to 5,000 words, on Thoroughbred racing, breeding, polo and steeplechasing. Profiles of people and farms. Historical and nostalgia pieces. Pays $50 to $250, on publication. Query.

STOCK CAR RACING—P.O. Box 715, Ipswich, MA 01938. Dick Berggren, Ed. Articles, to 6,000 words, on stock-car drivers, races, and vehicles. Photos. Pays to $350, on publication.

SURFER MAGAZINE—Box 1028, Dana Point, CA 92629. Steve Pezman, Pub. Paul Holmes, Ed. Articles, 500 to 5,000 words, on surfing, surfers, etc. Photos. Pays 10¢ to 15¢ a word, $10 to $600 for photos, on publication.

SURFING—P.O. Box 3010, San Clemente, CA 92672. David Gilovich, Ed. Bill Sharp, Assoc. Ed. First-person travel articles, 1,500 to 2,000 words, on surfing locations; knowledge of sport essential. Pays varying rates, on publication. Query.

TENNIS—5520 Park Ave., P.O. Box 0395, Trumbull, CT 06611-0395. Alex McNab, Ed. Instructional articles, features, profiles of tennis stars, 500 to 2,000 words. Photos. Pays from $100 to $500, on publication. Query.

TENNIS U.S.A.—3 Park Ave., New York, NY 10016. Pamela Stites, Man. Ed. Articles, 750 to 1,000 words, on local, sectional, and national tennis personalities and news events. Pays $25 to $75, on acceptance. Query; uses very little free-lance material.

TENNIS WEEK—6 E. 39th St., Ste. 800, New York, NY 10016. Eugene L. Scott, Pub. Robin Serody, Ed. In-depth, researched articles, from 1,000 words, on current issues and personalities in the game. Pays $100, on publication. Query.

THREE WHEELING—Box 2260, Costa Mesa, CA 92628. Bruce Simurda, Ed. Articles, 1,000 to 1,500 words, relating to three- and four-wheel, all-terrain vehicles. Pays $60 per printed page, on publication. Query.

TRAILER BOATS—16427 S. Avalon, P.O. Box 2307, Gardena, CA 90248. Jim Youngs, Ed. Technical and how-to articles, 500 to 2,000 words, on boat, trailer or tow vehicle maintenance and operation, skiing, fishing, cruising. Fillers; humor. Pays 7¢ to 10¢ a word, on publication. Query.

TRAILER LIFE—29901 Agoura Rd., Agoura, CA 91301. Bill Estes, Ed. Articles, to 2,500 words, with photos, on trailering, truck campers, motorhomes, hobbies and RV lifestyle. How-to pieces. Pays to $500, on acceptance. Send for guidelines.

TRI-ATHLETE—6660 Banning Dr., Oakland, CA 94611. William R. Katovsky, Ed. Articles, 1,500 to 3,500 words, on triathlons and training. Pays 5¢ to 10¢ a word, on publication. Query required.

TURF AND SPORT DIGEST—511-13 Oakland Ave., Baltimore, MD 21212. Allen L. Mitzel, Jr., Ed. Articles, 1,500 to 4,000 words, on national turf personalities, racing nostalgia, and handicapping. Pays $75 to $200, on publication. Query.

ULTRASPORT—711 Boylston St., Boston, MA 02116. Chris Bergonzi, Ed. Articles about any participant athletic endeavors; profiles and descriptive pieces; athletics-related fiction, to 3,500 words. Humor, to 1,500 words. Pays $800, on acceptance. Query.

VELO-NEWS—Box 1257, Brattleboro, VT 05301. Barbara George, Ed. Articles, 500 to 2,000 words, on bicycle racing. Photos. Pays $2.75 per column inch, extra for photos, on publication. Query.

VOLKSWAGEN'S WORLD—Volkswagen of America, Troy, MI 48099. Ed Rabinowitz, Ed. Articles, 1,000 words, related to Volkswagen cars and their owners. Color slides necessary. Pays $150 per printed page, on acceptance. Query.

WASHINGTON FISHING HOLES—502 E. Fairhaven, Burlington, WA 98233. Address Brad Stracener. Detailed articles, with specific maps, 800 to 1,500 words, on fishing holes in Washington. Local Washington fishing how-to's. Photos. Pays on publication. Query. Send SASE for guildelines.

WASHINGTON WILDLIFE—c/o Washington State Game Dept., 600 N. Capitol Way, Olympia, WA 98504. Janet O'Mara, Ed. Articles, 300 to 2,500 words, on fish and wildlife management and related recreational or environmental topics. Fillers, to 150 words. Photos. Pays in copies. Query.

THE WATER SKIER—P.O. Box 191, Winter Haven, FL 33882. Duke Cullimore, Ed. Offbeat articles on waterskiing. Pays varying rates, on acceptance.

THE WESTERN BOATMAN—16427 S. Avalon, P.O. Box 2307, Gardena, CA 90218. Ralph Poole, Ed. Articles, to 1,500 words, for boating enthusiasts from Alaska to Mexico, on subjects from waterskiing and salmon fishing to race boats and schooners. Pays on publication. Query preferred.

THE WESTERN HORSEMAN—P.O. Box 7980, Colorado Springs, CO 80933. Randy Witte, Ed. Articles, around 1,500 words, with photos, on care and training of horses. Pays from $150, on acceptance.

WESTERN OUTDOORS—3197-E Airport Loop, Costa Mesa, CA 92626. Timely, factual articles on fishing and hunting, 1,500 to 1,800 words, of interest to western sportsmen. Pays $300 to $500, on acceptance. Query. Guidelines.

WESTERN SALTWATER FISHERMAN—See *California Angler.*

WESTERN SPORTSMAN—P.O. Box 737, Regina, Sask., Canada S4P 3A8. Rick Bates, Ed. Articles, to 2,500 words, on outdoor experiences in Alberta and Saskatchewan; how-to pieces. Photos. Pays $75 to $325, on publication.

592

WIND SURF—P.O. Box 561, Dana Point, CA 92629. Drew Kampion, Ed. Articles on all aspects of windsurfing. Pays 10¢ to 20¢ a word, on publication.

WINDRIDER—P.O. Box 2456, Winter Park, FL 32790. Nancy K. Crowell, Ed. Features, instructional pieces, and tips, by experienced boardsailors. Fast action photos. Pays $50 to $75 for tips, $100 to $250 for features, extra for photos. Send for guidelines first.

THE WOMAN BOWLER—5301 S. 76th St., Greendale, WI 53129. Bill Krier, Ed. Profiles, interviews, and news articles, to 1,000 words, for women bowlers. Pays varying rates, on acceptance. Query with outline.

WOMEN'S SPORTS AND FITNESS—310 Town and Country Village, Palo Alto, CA 94301. Mariah Nelson, Ed. How-to's, profiles, and sports reports, 500 to 2,500 words, for active women. Fitness, recreation, adventure-travel, psychology, nutrition and health pieces. Pays from $25, on publication.

WRESTLING WORLD—See *Hockey Illustrated*.

YACHT RACING & CRUISING—See *Sailing World*.

YACHTING—P.O. Box 1200, 5 River Rd., Cos Cob, CT 06807. Deborah Meisels, Assoc. Ed. Articles, 2,000 words, on recreational power and sail boating. How-to and personal-experience pieces. Photos. Pays $250 to $450, on acceptance.

YOGA JOURNAL—2054 University Ave., Berkeley, CA 94704. Stephan Bodian, Ed. Articles, 1,200 to 3,000 words, on holistic health, consciousness, spirituality, and yoga. Pays $50 to $150, on publication.

AUTOMOTIVE PUBLICATIONS

AAA WORLD—AAA Headquarters, 8111 Gatehouse Rd., Falls Church, VA 22047. George Ashfield, Ed. Automobile and travel concerns, including automotive travel, maintenance and upkeep, 750 to 1,500 words. Pays $300 to $600, on acceptance. Query preferred.

AMERICAN MOTORCYCLIST—American Motorcyclist Assn., Box 6114, Westerville, OH 43081-6114. Greg Harrison, Ed. Articles and fiction, to 3,000 words, on motorcycling: news coverage, personalities, tours. Photos. Pays varying rates, on publication. Query.

AUTOBODY AND THE RECONDITIONED CAR—431 Ohio Pike, Suite 300, Cincinnati, OH 45230. Fran Cummins, Assoc. Ed. How-to articles for bodyshop technicians, 1,000 to 2,000 words. Shop tips, 50 to 100 words. Pays $150 to $200 for articles, $10 for tips, on publication. Query.

CAR AND DRIVER—2002 Hogback Rd., Ann Arbor, MI 48105. Don Sherman, Ed. Articles, to 2,500 words, for enthusiasts, on car manufacturers, new developments in cars, etc. Pays to $1,500, on acceptance.

CAR CRAFT—8490 Sunset Blvd., Los Angeles, CA 90069. Jeff Smith, Ed. Articles and photofeatures on unusual street machines, drag cars, racing events; technical pieces; action photos. Pays from $150 per page, on publication.

CORVETTE FEVER—Box 44620, Ft. Washington, MD 20744. Pat Stivers, Ed. Articles, 500 to 2,500 words, on Corvette repairs, swap meets, and personalities. Photos. Pays 10¢ a word, on publication.

CYCLE GUIDE—20916 Higgins Ct., Torrance, CA 90501. Jim Miller, Ed. Articles on motorcycling. Pays $125 to $2,500, on acceptance. Query required.

CYCLE MAGAZINE—780-A Lakefield Rd., Westlake Village, CA 91361. Paul Gordon, Exec. Ed. Articles, 6 to 20 manuscript pages, on motorcycle races, history, touring, technical pieces; profiles. Photos. Pays on publication. Query.

CYCLE WORLD—1499 Monrovia Ave., Newport Beach, CA 92663. Paul Dean, Ed. Technical and feature articles, 1,500 to 2,500 words, for motorcycle enthusiasts. Photos. Pays $100 to $200 per page, on publication. Query.

HORSELESS CARRIAGE GAZETTE—P.O. Box 1000, San Gabriel, CA 91776. Bradley Haugaard, Ed. Articles, 1,200 to 2,000 words, on pre-1916 cars, and related topics. Pays $50 to $70. Photos essential.

HOT BIKE—2145 W. La Palma, Anaheim, CA 92801. Tod Knuth, Ed. Articles, 250 to 2,500 words, with photos, on motorcycles. Event coverage on high performance street and track and sport touring motorcycles, with emphasis on Harley Davidsons. Pays $50 to $100 per printed page, on publication.

HOT ROD—8490 Sunset Blvd., Los Angeles, CA 90069. Patrick Ganohl, Ed. How-to pieces and articles, 500 to 5,000 words, on auto mechanics, hot rods, track and drag racing. Photo-features on custom or performance-modified cars. Pays to $250 per page, on publication.

KEEPIN' TRACK OF VETTES—P.O. Box 48, Spring Valley, NY 10977. Shelli Finkel, Ed. Articles of any length, with photos, relating to Corvettes. Pays $25 to $200, on publication.

MOTOR TREND—8490 Sunset Blvd., Los Angeles, CA 90069. Mike Anson, Ed. Articles, 250 to 2,500 words, on autos, racing, events, and profiles. Photos. Pay varies, on publication. Query.

MOTORCYCLIST—8490 Sunset Blvd., Los Angeles, CA 90069. Art Friedman, Ed. Articles, 1,000 to 3,000 words. Action photos. Pays varying rates, on publication. Query.

NORTHEAST RIDING—209 Whitney St., Hartford, CT 06105. Paul Essenfeld, Pub. Motorcycle-related articles, 500 to 1,000 words, for motorcyclists in the Northeast. Pays negotiable rates, on publication.

POPULAR SCIENCE—380 Madison Ave., New York, NY 10017. C. P. Gilmore, Ed.-in-Chief. Factual articles, 300 to 2,000 words, with photos and illustrations, on advances in science and technology, new products in electronics, cars, tools; do-it-yourself projects for home or shop. Pays varying rates, on acceptance. Query.

RESTORATION—P.O. Box 50046, Tuscon, AZ 85703-2201. Walter R. Haessner, Ed. Articles, 1,200 to 1,800 words, on restoration of autos, trucks, planes, railroads, etc. Photos. Pays varying rates—from $50 per page—on publication. Query first.

RIDER—29901 Agoura Rd., Agoura, CA 91301. Tash Matsuoka, Ed. Articles, with photos, to 3,000 words, with emphasis on travel, touring, commuting, and camping motorcyclists. Pays $100 to $500, on publication. Query.

ROAD RIDER MAGAZINE—P.O. Box 6050, Mission Viejo, CA 92690. Bob Carpenter, Ed. Articles, to 1,500 words, with photos or b&w illustrations, on motorcycle touring. Pays from $100, on publication. Query.

SPORTS CAR GRAPHIC—8490 Sunset Blvd., Los Angeles, CA 90069. John Hanson, Ed. Articles, 500 to 1,000 words, on modified sports cars; technical how-to pieces. Pays to $500, on acceptance. Guidelines available.

STOCK CAR RACING—P.O. Box 715, Ipswich, MA 01938. Dick Berggren, Ed. Articles, to 6,000 words, on stock-car drivers, races, and vehicles. Photos. Pays to $350, on publication.

THREE WHEELING—Box 2260, Costa Mesa, CA 92628. Bruce Simurda, Ed. Articles, 1,000 to 1,500 words, relating to three- and four-wheel, all-terrain vehicles. Pays $60 per printed page, on publication. Query.

TURBO—9568 Hamilton Ave., P.O. Box 2712, Hamilton Beach, CA 92647. Bud Lane, Ed. Articles, 750 to 2,500 words, related to turbo-charged autos. Fillers. Pays about $75 per published page, on publication.

VOLKSWAGEN'S WORLD—Volkswagen of America, Troy, MI 48099. Ed Rabinowitz, Ed. Articles, 1,000 words, related to Volkswagen cars and their owners. Color slides necessary. Pays $150 per printed page, on acceptance. Query.

FITNESS MAGAZINES

AEROBICS & FITNESS—15250 Ventura Blvd., Ste. 310, Sherman Oaks, CA 91403. Peg Angsten, Ed. Articles, 500 to 1,500 words, on exercise, health, sports, nutrition, etc. Cartoons. Pays $60 to $120, 30 days after publication.

AMERICAN HEALTH: FITNESS OF BODY AND MIND—80 Fifth Ave., New York, NY 10011. Joel Gurin, Ed. Lively, authoritative articles, 1,000 to 3,000 words, on scientific and lifestyle aspects of health and fitness; 100- to 750-word news reports. Pays $150 to $2,000, on acceptance. Query required.

BETTER HEALTH AND LIVING—800 Second Ave., New York, NY 10017. Laura L. Vitale, Man. Ed. Articles, 2 to 35 manuscript pages, on healthful living; shorter items and tips. Pays $50 to $100 for short tips, to $1,000 for features, 90 days after acceptance. Query preferred.

INSIDE RUNNING & FITNESS—9514 Bristlebrook Dr., Houston, TX 77083. Joanne Schmidt, Ed. Articles, fiction, and fillers on running and aerobic fitness in Texas. Pays $35 to $100, $10 for photos, on acceptance.

MUSCULAR DEVELOPMENT—Strength and Health Publishing, P.O. Box 1707, York, PA 17405. Jan Dellinger, Ed. Articles of 5 to 10 typed pages on any aspect of competitive bodybuilding and powerlifting, for serious weight training athletes. Photos are a plus. Pays $50 to $200, on publication. Query.

NEW BODY—888 Seventh Ave., New York, NY 10106. Norman Zeitchick, Ed. Lively, readable service-oriented articles, 1,000 to 2,000 words, by writers with background in health field: exercise, nutrition, and diet pieces for women aged 18 to 40. Pays $250 to $500, on publication. Query preferred.

SLIMMER—3420 Ocean Park Blvd., Santa Monica, CA 90405. Lori Berger, Ed. Articles, 2,500 words, and columns, 1,000 words, on nutrition, fitness, beauty, skin care, diet, exercise, fashion, travel, and sports, for women aged 18 to 40. Pays $300 to $400 for features, $100 to $150 for columns, 30 days after acceptance. Query required.

WEIGHT WATCHERS MAGAZINE—360 Lexington Ave., New York, NY 10017. Nelly Edmondson, Articles Ed. Psychological pieces on weight control; health, fitness, and nutrition; inspirational weight loss stories, 1,200 to 1,500 words. Pays from $250, after acceptance.

WOMEN'S SPORTS AND FITNESS—310 Town and Country Village, Palo Alto, CA 94301. Mariah Nelson, Ed. How-to's, profiles, and sports reports, 500 to 2,500 words, for active women. Fitness, recreation, adventure-travel, psychology, nutrition and health pieces. Pays from $25, on publication.

YOGA JOURNAL—2054 University Ave., Berkeley, CA 94704. Stephan Bodian, Ed. Articles, 1,200 to 3,000 words, on holistic health, spirituality, yoga, and transpersonal psychology; "new age" profiles; interviews. Pays $50 to $150, on publication.

CONSUMER/PERSONAL FINANCE

BETTER HOMES AND GARDENS—1716 Locust St., Des Moines, IA 50336. Margaret V. Daly, Money Management, Automotive and Features Ed. "We run ten to twelve articles on finance each year. They cover any and all topics that would be of interest to our audience of eight million households, primarily homeowning, family-oriented, middle-income people. Some of the articles we've run are 'Health Insurance: Seven Common Gaps,' 'Fifteen Mutual Funds That Let You Start Small,' and 'Answers to the Questions Most Asked of Financial Planners.' We prefer to see queries first, but will look at complete manuscripts (750 to 1,000 words). Payment runs roughly from 75¢ to $1.00 a word, on acceptance. We buy all rights."

COMPLETE WOMAN—1165 N. Clark, Chicago, IL 60610. Suzanne Merry, Associate Ed. Articles, addressed to a general audience, which cover broad-based financial planning (for taxes, retirement, etc.) rather than highly specific investment vehicles. Readers are working women, 25–50, who want to improve and enrich all aspects of their lives. Query first. Payment rates for articles of 1,800 to 2,000 words vary, on publication.

CONSUMERS DIGEST—5705 N. Lincoln Ave., Chicago, IL 60659. Robin C. Nelson, Ed. Articles, 500 to 3,000 words, on subjects of interest to consumers: products and services, automobiles, travel, health, fitness, consumer legal affairs, and personal money management. Photos. Pays from 30¢ a word, extra for photos, on publication. Buys all rights. Query with resume and published clips.

DIVERSION MAGAZINE—60 E. 42nd St., New York, NY 10165. *Diversion* is a monthly travel and leisure magazine read by 180,000 physicians across the country, and editors welcome proposals, 100 to 150 words in length, for articles on investing. Enclose samples of published work when submitting article ideas. Articles run from 1,000 to 1,200 words; payment is $350, on publication. Send for a copy of the editorial guidelines.

FACT: THE MONEY MANAGEMENT MAGAZINE—305 E. 46th St., New York, NY 10017. Daniel M. Kehrer, Ed.-in-Chief. Articles for a sophisticated audience on all aspects of personal investing. Queries for manuscripts of 1,000 to 2,000 words are required since this is a limited market for free lancers. Payment ranges from $50 to $150, on acceptance.

FAMILY CIRCLE—488 Madison Ave., New York, NY 10022. Susan Ungaro, Articles Ed. "We publish a money management feature in every issue, and are particularly interested in well-written, easy-to-understand articles on investing, real estate and financial planning. Articles should be geared to our typical reader: an educated, middle- to upper-middle class woman in her 30s, 40s, and 50s, who is a home owner looking for other ways to invest her spare cash. Fifty-four percent are working women. 'Should You Refinance Your Mortgage Now,' 'How to Cut Car Insurance Costs,' and 'Twelve Ways to Secure Your Financial Future' are a few of the recent articles we've run. Always send a query with sample clips before submitting complete manuscripts (1,000 to 2,000 words). Payment rates are $1.00 a word, on acceptance."

GEICO DIRECT—1999 Shepard Rd., St. Paul, MN 55116. Jane A. Kennedy, Managing Ed. "We have a department titled 'Money-Wise,' in which we use four to five capsule pieces on various money matters. The topics are general, and each runs about five paragraphs. Our audience is made up of government and military employees, as well as general insurance policy holders. We prefer to be queried first; payment is made on acceptance."

GOLDEN YEARS—233 E. New Haven Ave., Melbourne, FL 32902-0537. Carol Brenner Hittner, Ed. "We consider articles on pre-retirement and retirement planning and real estate—topics of particular interest to our readers, most of whom are over 50 and affluent. Payment for manuscripts (to 500 words) is 10¢ a word, on publication.

THE KIWANIS MAGAZINE—3636 Woodview Trace, Indianapolis, IN 46468. Chuck Jonak, Exec. Ed. "Although the majority of our readers are older small-business owners and professionals—or retirees from the same areas—we also have a large percentage of younger readers, so we'd like to see articles on financial planning for younger families in a variety of areas, as well as pieces on financial planning for retirees and small business owners. Articles should be in the 2,500- to 3,000-word range; a 300-word sidebar is always helpful. Payment, on acceptance, is $400 to $1,000. Query first."

MARRIAGE & FAMILY LIVING—St. Meinrad, IN 47577. Kass Dotterweich, Managing Ed. In demand here are articles, 2,500 to 3,000 words, on taxes, retirement planning, real estate, or other financial matters of interest to young married Christian women with children. Payment is 7¢ a word, on acceptance. Query first.

MODERN MATURITY—3200 E. Carson St., Lakewood, CA 90712. Ian Ledgerwood, Ed. "We consider queries from free-lancers on a wide range of financial topics—almost anything is a possibility, but it mustn't be too technical. Articles (1,500 to 2,000 words) should be directed to our readers, who are age 50 and over. Payment ranges up to $2,500 for 2,000-word manuscripts."

MONEY—Time-Life Bldg., New York, NY 10020. Landon Jones, Man. Ed. Articles on personal finance: how to earn more money, invest more profitably, spend more intelligently and more pleasurably, save more prudently, and enhance your career. Pays on acceptance and publication. Query.

THE MONEYPAPER—Two Madison Ave., Larchmont, NY 10538. Vita Nelson, Ed. and Pub. "*The Moneypaper,* 'A Financial Publication for Women,' covers all aspects of money and money management. We do consider complete manuscripts. Payment is $75 on publication."

MONEYPLAN MAGAZINE—3500 Western Ave., Highland Park, IL 60035. Margaret Mucklo, Ed. "Ninety-five percent of our magazine is written by free lancers. We use articles on taxes, insurance, real estate, retirement, automobiles, leisure, and employment—all with a financial planning/money management slant. The magazine is purchased by financial institutions to distribute to their high-balance and multi-account customers. Articles should not advocate specific investments, especially those not offered by banks and savings & loans institutions. Our purpose is to provide practical financial planning information to a general audience, so articles must cross age and education lines and emphasize the broad application. Articles run from 375 to 600 words or 1,000 to 1,200 words, 1,300 to 1,600 for cover stories. Query first, with a brief description of the article idea and credentials. Payment is made 30 days after acceptance; rates range from $100 to $600."

SAVVY—3 Park Ave., New York, NY 10016. Address Kelly Walker. "We are looking for articles on women in finance-related jobs (banking, brokerages, insurance, etc.), and personal money management. Topics covered in the money management column range from accounting quirks in annual reports to how to buy the best auto insurance. Recent issues featured a stock investment column on Nike, Inc., an article on how to get a second mortgage, and a Q & A piece on the questions most frequently asked about IRAs. We always prefer to see queries first. Payment (for 800- to 1,000-word manuscripts) is made on acceptance and varies, depending on the writer's abilities and experience—usually starting at $650 an article."

SELF—350 Madison Ave., New York, NY 10017. Pamela Bayless, Sr. Ed., Money/Careers. "We seek articles on money strategies for our readers, most of whom are women in their 20s and 30s. More than half of them are single, nearly three-quarters have some college education, and most are employed—about 40% in secretarial/clerical occupations. In recent months, we've published 'Four New Options in Banking,' 'A Snap Course in Mutual Funds,' 'How to Profit From Our Cheaper U.S. Dollar,' and 'A Shy Shopper's Guide to Bargaining.' Always query first, keeping it to one page whenever possible; read back issues first for content and style. Payment for articles of 1,500 to 2,000 words is on acceptance and varies with the writer's experience. A writer's first piece for *Self* might earn him $800; rates would escalate for subsequent sales."

SUNDAY WOMAN PLUS—235 E. 45th St., New York, NY 10017. Merry Clark, Ed. Articles on financial planning and personal money management that would interest the broad range of people who read *Sunday Woman,* the weekly newspaper supplement distributed throughout the U.S. and Canada. Recent issues carried pieces on how to make money at home, and women and retirement planning. Submit query or completed manuscript (1,000 to 2,000 words). Payment—$50 to $500—is on acceptance.

SUPER SHOPPER—2929 S. Industrial Rd., Las Vegas, NV 89109. Howard Bernard, Ed. Articles, 200 to 1,000 words, that will help readers in their budgeting and shopping activities. Pays $50 to $100.

WOMAN'S DAY—1515 Broadway, New York, NY 10036. Rebecca Greer, Articles Ed. "We use free-lance articles that are fresh and authoritative and that do not conflict with our 'Money Facts' column. Pieces should appeal to a broad range of women, as do our recent articles 'How to Pay Holiday Bills in 30 Days' and 'Forty Ways to Cut Vacation Costs.'" Ms. Greer prefers to see queries for articles of varying lengths (to 3,000 words). Top rates are paid, on acceptance."

PROFESSIONAL/TRADE PUBLICATIONS

ACCESSORIES MAGAZINE—22 S. Smith St., Norwalk, CT 06855. Reenie Brown, Ed. Dir. Articles, with photos, for handbag, accessory and women's footwear buyers, on store displays, merchandising, retail promotions; profiles. Pays $75 to $100 for short articles, from $100 to $250 for features, on publication. Query.

ALTERNATIVE ENERGY RETAILER—P.O. Box 2180, Waterbury, CT 06722. Jon Swebilius, Ed. Feature articles, 2,000 words, for retailers of alternative energy products—wood, coal and fireplace products and services. Interviews with successful retailers, stressing the how-to. B/W photos. Pays $200, extra for photos, on publication. Query first.

AMERICAN BANKER—One State Street Plaza, New York, NY 10004. Patricia Standza, Features Ed. Articles, 1,000 to 3,000 words, on banking and financial services, human resources, management techniques. Pays varying rates, on publication. Query preferred.

AMERICAN BAR ASSOCIATION JOURNAL—750 N. Lake Shore Dr., Chicago, IL 60611. Robert Yates, Assoc. Ed. Practical articles, to 3,000 words, that will help lawyers in small firms better their practices. Pays from $500 for features, $25 for shorts, on acceptance. Query.

AMERICAN BICYCLIST—80 Eighth Ave., Suite 305, New York, NY 10011. Konstantin Doren, Ed. Articles, 1,500 to 2,800 words, on sales and repair practices of successful bicycle and moped dealers. Photos. Pays from 9¢ a word, extra for photos, on publication. Query.

AMERICAN CLAY EXCHANGE—P.O. Box 2674, La Mesa, CA 92044. Susan N. Cox, Ed. Thoroughly-researched articles to 1,000 words, for collectors and dealers of American-made pottery, with emphasis on antiques and collectibles. Pays $5 for fillers, from $100 for features, on acceptance.

AMERICAN COIN-OP—500 N. Dearborn St., Chicago, IL 60610. Ben Russell, Ed. Articles, to 2,500 words, with photos, on successful coin-operated laundries and dry-cleaners: promotion, decor, maintenance, etc. Pays from 6¢ a word, $6 per B & W photo, two weeks prior to publication. Query. Send SASE for guidelines.

AMERICAN DEMOGRAPHICS—P.O. Box 68, Ithaca, NY 14851. Cheryl Russell, Ed. Articles, 1,500 to 3,000 words, on demographic trends and business demographics for strategists in industry, government, and education. Pays $300, on publication. Query.

AMERICAN FARRIERS JOURNAL—P.O. Box 700, 20 Central Ave., Ayer, MA 01432. Joanne Lowry, Ed. Articles, 800 to 5,000 words, on horse handling, hoof care, tool selection, business practices, maintenance techniques, etc. Pays $50 per published page, on publication. Query.

AMERICAN PAINTING CONTRACTOR—2911 Washington Ave., St. Louis, MO 63103. Paul B. Stoecklein, Ed. Technical articles, to 2,500 words, with photos, on industrial maintenance painting and management of painting business, for contractors and architects.

THE AMERICAN SALESMAN—424 N. Third St., Burlington, IA 52601-9989. D. Ruschill, Pub. Dir. Barbara Boeding, Ed. Articles, 900 to 1,200 words, on techniques for increasing sales. Pays 3¢ a word, on publication. Query.

ANTIQUES DEALER—1115 Clifton Ave., Clifton, NJ 07013. Nancy Adams, Ed. Articles, 1,500 words, on national and international trends and news in antiques business. Features by authorities in specific fields. Fillers, 750 words. B/W photos. Pays on publication. Query.

THE APOTHECARY—895 Cherry St., Petaluma, CA 94952. Susan Keller, Man. Ed. Articles, 2,000 to 4,000 words, for pharmacies, on management and marketing techniques, and computer topics. Pays $250, on publication. Query.

ARCHITECTURE—1735 New York Ave., N.W., Washington, DC 20006. Donald Canty, Ed. Articles, to 3,000 words, on architecture, urban design. Book reviews. Pays $100 to $500, extra for photos. Query.

AREA DEVELOPMENT MAGAZINE—525 Northern Blvd., Great Neck, NY 11021. Tom Bergeron, Ed. Articles for top executives of manufacturing companies, on industrial and office facility planning. Pays $40 per manuscript page. Query.

ART BUSINESS NEWS—60 Ridgeway Plaza, P.O. Box 3837, Stamford, CT 06905. Jo Yanow, Ed. Articles, 1,000 words, for art dealers and framers, on trends and events of national importance to the art industry, and relevant business subjects. Pays from $75, on publication. Query preferred.

ART MATERIAL TRADE NEWS—6255 Barfield Rd., Atlanta, GA 30328. Charles C. Craig, Ed. Articles, from 800 words, for dealers, wholesalers, and manufacturers of artist materials. Fillers. Pays to 15¢ a word, on publication. Query.

ATTAGE—11754 Jollyville Rd., Austin, TX 78759. Wendell Watson, Ed. Articles, 1,000 to 3,000 words, on computer/telecommunications solutions to problems in business, industry, and research. All material should be related to the role of AT&T in the market; readers are business managers, data processing professionals, and others interested in the impact AT&T has on the information automation industry. Pays 10¢ a word, on publication.

AUTOMATION IN HOUSING & MANUFACTURED HOME DEALER—P.O. Box 120, Carpinteria, CA 93013. Don Carlson, Ed. Articles, 500 to 750 words, on various types of home manufacturers and dealers. Query required. Pays $300, on acceptance, for articles accompanied by slides.

AUTOMOTIVE EXECUTIVE—8400 Westpark Dr., McLean, VA 22102. Gary E. James, Man. Ed. National Automobile Dealers Assn. Articles, 750 to 2,500 words, on management of automobile and heavy-duty truck dealerships and general business and automotive issues. Photos. Pays on acceptance. Query.

BARRISTER—American Bar Assn., 750 N. Lake Shore Dr., Chicago, IL 60611. Anthony Monahan, Ed. Articles, to 3,500 words, on legal and social affairs, for young lawyers. Pays $200 to $700, on acceptance.

BARRON'S—200 Liberty St., New York, NY 10281. Alan Abelson, Ed. National-interest articles, 1,200 to 2,500 words, on business and finance. Pays on publication. Query.

BETTER BUSINESS—235 East 42nd St., New York, NY 10017. John F. Robinson, Pub. Articles, 10 to 12 double-spaced pages, for the small business/minority business markets. Pays on publication. Query.

BLACK ENTERPRISE—130 Fifth Ave., New York, NY 10011. Earl G. Graves, Ed. Articles on money, management, careers, political issues, entrepreneurship, high technology, and lifestyles for black professionals. Profiles. Pays on acceptance. Query.

BOATING INDUSTRY—850 Third Ave., New York, NY 10022. Olga Badillo-Sciortino, Ed. Articles, 1,000 to 1,500 words, on marine management, merchandising and selling, for boat dealers. Photos. Pays varying rates, on publication. Query first.

BUILDER—Hanley-Wood, Inc., 655 15th St., N.W., Suite 475, Washington, DC 20005. Frank Anton, Ed. Articles, to 1,500 words, on trends and news in home building: design, marketing, new products, etc. Pays negotiable rates, on acceptance. Query.

BUSINESS AGE—4060 N. Oakland, P.O. Box 11597, Milwaukee, WI 53211. Margaret Brickner, Ed. How-to business articles, 1,000 to 2,000 words, for small business owners and managers. Department pieces run 500 to 1,000 words; shorts, 100 to 300 words. Pays from $200 for features, from $50 for departments, on publication. B&W or color photos desired. Writer's guidelines available.

BUSINESS AND COMMERCIAL AVIATION—Hangar C-1, Westchester Co. Airport, White Plains, NY 10604. John W. Olcott, Ed. Articles, 2,500 words, with photos, for pilots, on use of private aircraft for business transportation. Pays $100 to $500, on acceptance. Query.

BUSINESS ATLANTA—6255 Barfield Rd., Atlanta, GA 30328. Barre S. Rissman, Ed. Articles, 1,000 to 4,500 words, with Atlanta or "deep South" business angle, strong marketing slant that will be useful to top Atlanta executives and business people. Pays $300 to $800, on publication. Query with clippings.

BUSINESS MARKETING—220 E. 42nd St., New York, NY 10017. Bob Donath, Ed. Articles on selling, advertising, and promoting products and services, for marketing executives. Pays competitive rates, on acceptance. Query only.

BUSINESS SOFTWARE MAGAZINE—M & T Publishing, 501 Galveston Dr., Redwood City, CA 94063. Nancy Groth, Man. Ed. Software applications for business-oriented audience; tips and techniques using popular software; reviews of new products; case studies of corporate users. Pays to $500, before publication. Query.

BUSINESS SOFTWARE REVIEW—9100 Keystone Crossing, Indianapolis, IN 46240. Dennis Hamilton, Ed.-in-Chief. Articles, 300 to 3,000 words, on the computer business, centering on management software: productivity, profitability, return-on-investment. Pays $50 to $500, on publication. Query.

THE BUSINESS TIMES—544 Tolland St., E. Hartford, CT 06108. Mark D. Isaacs, Ed. Articles on Connecticut-based businesses and corporations written for executives. Pays $2 per column inch, on publication. Query first.

BUSINESS TODAY—P.O. Box 10010, 1720 Washington Blvd., Ogden, UT 84409. Robyn C. Walker, Ed. Articles, 1,200 words; profiles of businessmen and women. Pays 15¢ a word, $35 for color photos, on acceptance. Query.

BUSINESS VIEW—P.O. Box 9859, Naples, FL 33941. Eleanor K. Sommer, Pub. Innovative articles and columns, 750 to 1,500 words, on business, economics, finance; profiles of business leaders; new trends in technology and advances in management techniques. Real estate and banking trends. Southwest Florida regional angle a must. Pays $75 to $200, on publication. Query.

BUSINESSLIFE—8100 Penn Ave., S., Minneapolis, MN 55431. Terry White, Ed. Articles, 350 to 1,400 words, for Christian business and professional people. Fillers, anecdotes, case studies and cartoons. Pays 10¢ a word, on pub'ication. Query.

CALIFORNIA BUSINESS—4221 Wilshire Blvd., Suite 400, Los Angeles, CA 90010. Margaret Hart, Ed. Articles, 1,200 to 1,500 words, on business and econometric issues in California. Pays varying rates, on acceptance. Query.

CALIFORNIA HORSE REVIEW—P.O. Box 2437, Fair Oaks, CA 95628. Jennifer Forsberg Meyer, Ed. Articles, 1,000 to 3,000 words, for professional horsemen, on training; how-to pieces, features. Pays $50 to $125, on publication.

CALIFORNIA LAWYER—555 Franklin St., San Francisco, CA 94102. Thomas K. Brom, Ed. Articles, 2,500 to 3,000 words, for attorneys in California, on legal subjects (or the legal aspects of a given political or social issue); how-to's on improving techniques in law practice. Pays $250 to $750, on acceptance. Query.

CAMPGROUND MANAGEMENT—11 N. Skokie Hwy., #205, Lake Bluff, IL 60044. Mike Byrnes, Ed. Detailed articles, 500 to 2,000 words, on managing recreational vehicle campgrounds. Photos. Pays $50 to $200, after publication.

CASHFLOW—6255 Barfield Rd., Atlanta, GA 30328. Richard Gamble, Ed. Articles, 1,250 to 2,500 words, for treasury managers in public and private institutions: cash management; investments; domestic and international financing; credit and collection management; developments in law, economics, and tax. Pays $125 per published page, on publication. Query.

CERAMIC SCOPE—3632 Ashworth N., Seattle, WA 98103. Michael Scott, Ed. Articles, 800 to 1,500 words, on retail or wholesale business operations of hobby ceramic studios. Photos. Pays 10¢ a word, extra for photos, on publication. Query.

CHEESE MARKET NEWS(formerly *Dairy Record*)—Gorman Publishing Co., 8750 W. Bryn Mawr, Chicago, IL 60631. Jerry Dryer, Ed. Articles, to 2,500 words, on innovative dairies, dairy processing operations, marketing successes, new products, for milk handlers and makers of dairy products. Fillers, 25 to 150 words. Pays $25 to $300, $5 to $25 for fillers, on publication.

CHEMICAL WEEK—1221 Ave. of the Americas, New York, NY 10020. Patrick P. McCurdy, Ed.-in-Chief. News pieces, to 200 words, on chemical business. Pays $11 per column inch, on acceptance. Query.

CHIEF FIRE EXECUTIVE—33 Irving Place, New York, NY 10003. William Porter, Ed. For volunteer and paid fire chiefs, fire protection engineers and architects. Factual articles, 200 to 3,500 words, on the management of fire departments and community fire protection systems. Payment varies, on publication. Query required.

CHINA, GLASS & TABLEWARE—P.O. Box 2147, Clifton, NJ 07015. Amy Stavis, Ed. Case histories and interviews, 1,500 to 2,500 words, with photos, on merchandising of china and glassware. Pays $50 per page, on publication. Query.

CHRISTIAN BOOKSELLER—396 E. St. Charles Rd., Wheaton, IL 60188. Karen Tomberg, Ed. Articles, with photos, on all phases of Christian bookstore operation: new ideas, news reports, store profiles, industry analyses, gift and music merchandising, how-to's, etc. Pays $10 to $100, on publication. Query. Send SASE for guidelines.

CHRISTIAN BUSINESS LIFE DIGEST—3108 W. Lake St., Minneapolis, MN 55402. Terry White, Ed. Articles, 500 to 1,200 words, for Christian business and professional people. Fillers; anecdotes. Pays 5¢ a word, on publication. Query for features.

CLEANING MANAGEMENT—15550-D Rockfield, Irvine, CA 92718. R. Daniel Harris, Jr., Pub. Articles, 1,000 to 1,500 words, on managing efficient cleaning and maintenance operations. Photos. Pays 10¢ a word, extra for photos, on publication.

COLLEGE STORE EXECUTIVE—P.O. Box 1500, Westbury, NY 11590. Catherine Orobona, Ed. Articles, 1,000 words, for college store industry only;

news; profiles. No general business or how-to articles. Photos. Pays $2 a column inch, extra for photos, on acceptance. Query.

THE COMICS JOURNAL—4359 Cornell Rd., Agoura, CA 91301. Kim Fryer, Man. Ed. Criticism, essays, interviews with comics professionals; 700 to 4,000 words. Include graphics. Pays 1½¢ per word, on publication.

COMMERCIAL CARRIER JOURNAL—Chilton Way, Radnor, PA 19089. Jerry Standley, Ed. Factual articles on private fleets and for-hire trucking operations. Pays from $50, on acceptance. Query.

COMPUTER CONSULTANT—208 N. Townsend St., Syracuse, NY 13202. Articles, to 2,500 words, on innovative sales techniques, and tips for increasing profitability for computer consultants. Pays varying rates, on publication. Query required.

COMPUTER DEALER—Box 1952, Dover, NJ 07801-9060. John Blackford, Ed. Articles, 1,700 words, for dealers and distributors of computers. Pays on publication. Query first.

COMPUTER DECISIONS MAGAZINE—10 Mulholland Dr., Hasbrouck Hgt. NJ 07604.Mel Mandell, Ed. Articles, 800 to 4,000 words, on generic uses of computer systems. Pays $30 to $100 per printed page, on acceptance. Query.

COMPUTER GRAPHICS WORLD—119 Russell St., Littleton, MA 01460. Tom McMillan, Man. Ed. Articles, 1,000 to 5,000 words, on computer graphics technology, applications and products. Photos. Pays $100 per printed page, on publication. Query.

COMPUTING FOR BUSINESS (formerly *Interface Age*)—7330 Adams St., Paramount, CA 90723. Les Spindle, Ed. Articles, 1,000 to 5,000 words, on microcomputer applications in the business field. Reviews of new products and computer programs. Pays $50 to $80 per published page, on publication.

CONCRETE INTERNATIONAL: DESIGN AND CONSTRUCTION—Box 19150, 22400 W. Seven Mile Rd., Detroit, MI 48219. Robert E. Wilde, Ed. Articles, 6 to 15 double-spaced pages, on concrete construction and design, with drawings and photos. Pays $100 per printed page, on publication. Query.

CONTACTS—17 Myrtle Ave., Troy, NY 12180. George J. Yamin, Ed. Articles, 300 to 1,500 words, on management of dental laboratories, lab techniques, and equipment. Pays from 7¢ a word, on acceptance.

CONTRACTORS MARKET CENTER—Box 2029, Tuscaloosa, AL 35403. Claude Duncan, Ed. Articles about heavy equipment-using contractors; success stories, 500 to 1,500 words. Pays $10 to $50, on acceptance.

CONVENIENCE STORE NEWS—254 W. 31st St., New York, NY 10001. Denise Melinsky, Ed. Features and news items, 500 to 750 words, for convenience store owners, operators, and suppliers. Photos, with captions. Pays $3 per column inch, extra for photos, on publication. Query.

COOKING FOR PROFIT—P.O. Box 267, Fond du Lac, WI 54935. Bill Dittrich, Ed. Practical how-to articles, 1,000 words, on commercial food preparation, energy management; case studies, etc. Pays $75 to $250, on publication.

CRAIN'S CHICAGO BUSINESS—740 Rush St., Chicago, IL 60611. Dan Miller, Ed. Business articles about the Midwest exclusively. Pays $9.50 per column inch, on acceptance.

CREDIT AND COLLECTION MANAGEMENT—Bureau of Business Practice, 24 Rope Ferry Rd., Waterford, CT 06386. Russell Case, Ed. Interviews, 500 to 1,250 words, for commercial and consumer credit managers, on innovations, successes and problem solving. Query.

D & B REPORTS—299 Park Ave., New York, NY 10171. Patricia W. Hamilton, Ed. Articles, 1,500 to 2,500 words, for top management of smaller businesses: government regulations, export opportunities, employee relations; how-to's on cash management, sales, productivity, etc.; profiles of innovative small companies and managers. Pays on acceptance.

DAIRY HERD MANAGEMENT—P.O. Box 67, Minneapolis, MN 55440. Sheila Widmer Vikla, Ed. Articles, 500 to 2,000 words, with photos, on techniques and equipment used in well-managed large and medium dairy operations. Pays $100 to $200, on acceptance. Query.

DAIRY RECORD—See *Cheese Market News.*

DEALERSCOPE MERCHANDISING—North American Publishing Co., 401 N. Broad St., Philadelphia, PA 19108. Neil Spann, Ed. Articles, 750 to 3,000 words, for dealers and distributors of audio, video, personal computers for the home, office; satellite TV systems for the home; major appliances on sales, marketing and finance. How-to's for retailers. Pays varying rates, on publication. Query with clips first.

DENTAL ECONOMICS—P.O. Box 3408, Tulsa, OK 74101. Dick Hale, Ed. Articles 1,200 to 3,500 words, on business side of dental practice, patient and staff communication, personal investments, etc. Pays $100 to $250, on acceptance.

DESIGN GRAPHICS WORLD—Communications Channels, 6255 Barfield Rd., Atlanta, GA 30328. James J. Maivald, Ed. Articles, 1,500 to 2,000 words, on news, trends, and current methods of engineering, architecture, computer graphics, reprographics, micrographics, and related design fields. Pays varying rates, on publication.

DOMESTIC ENGINEERING—135 Addison St., Elmhurst, IL 60126. Stephen J. Shafer, Ed. Articles, to 3,000 words, on plumbing, heating, air conditioning, and process piping. Photos. Pays $20 to $35 per printed page, on publication.

DRAPERIES & WINDOW COVERINGS—P.O. Box 13079, North Palm Beach, FL 33408. Katie Renckens, Ed. Articles, 1,000 to 2,000 words, for retailers, wholesalers, designers and manufacturers of draperies and window coverings. Profiles, with photos, of successful businesses in the industry. Pays $150 to $250, after acceptance. Query.

DRUG TOPICS—680 Kinderkamack Rd. Oradell, NJ 07649. Valentine A. Cardinale, Ed. News items, 500 words, with photos, on drug retailers and associations. Merchandising features, 1,000 to 1,500 words. Pays $100 to $150 for news, $200 to $400 for features, on acceptance. Query for features.

DUN'S BUSINESS MONTH—875 Third Ave., New York, NY 10022. Arlene Hershman, Ed. Articles, 1,500 to 2,500 words, on trends in corporation management, the economy, finance, and company performance. Pays from $500, on acceptance.

EARNSHAW'S INFANTS & CHILDREN'S REVIEW—393 Seventh Ave., New York, NY 10001. Christina Gruber, Ed. Articles on retailers, retail promotions, and statistics for children's wear industry. Pays $50 to $200, on publication. Query. Limited market.

ELECTRICAL CONTRACTOR—7315 Wisconsin Ave., Bethesda, MD

20814. Larry C. Osius, Ed. Articles, 1,000 to 1,500 words, with photos, on construction or management techniques for electrical contractors. Pays $90 per printed page, before publication. Query.

EMPLOYEE SERVICES MANAGEMENT—NESRA, 2400 S. Downing, Westchester, IL 60153. Joan Price, Ed. Articles, 800 to 2,500 words, for human resource, fitness, and employee service professionals.

ENGINEERED SYSTEMS—7314 Hart St., Mentor, OH 44060. Robert L. Schwed, Ed. Articles, case histories, on business management and legal issues related to hvac engineering systems in large buildings or industrial plants. Pays $4.75 per column inch, $12 per illustration, on publication. Query.

THE ENGRAVERS JOURNAL—26 Summit St., Box 318, Brighton, MI 48116. Michael J. Davis, Managing Ed. Articles of varying lengths on topics related to the engraving industry. Photos and drawings are used. Pays, on acceptance, $60 to $175. Query.

ENTRÉE—7 E. 12th St., New York, NY 10003. Terence Murphy, Ed. Articles, 100 to 2,500 words, on trends and people in better housewares industry, both retailers and manufacturers. Pays $400, on acceptance. Query.

ENTREPRENEUR—2311 Pontius Ave., Los Angeles, CA 90064. Articles giving advice for independent business owners and those aspiring to own businesses on running a business: advertising, business techniques, and new business ideas. Pays $100 to $400, on acceptance. Query first.

EXECUTIVE REPORT—Riverview Publications, Bigelow Sq., Pittsburgh, PA 15219. Charles W. Shane, Ed. Articles, 1,000 to 3,000 words, on business news and issues in western Pennsylvania. Pays 10¢ a word, on publication. Queries are required.

EXPORT MAGAZINE—386 Park Ave. South, New York, NY 10016. Robert Weingarten, Ed. Articles, 1,000 to 1,500 words, on the business of agents and distributors who import products (primarily consumer durables) in foreign countries. Pays $300 to $350, with photos, on acceptance. Query preferred.

FACT: THE MONEY MANAGEMENT MAGAZINE—305 E. 46th St., New York, NY 10017. Daniel M. Kehrer, Ed.-in-Chief. No unsolicited material.

FARM JOURNAL—230 W. Washington Sq., Philadelphia, PA 19105. Practical business articles on growing crops and producing livestock. Pays $50 to $500, on acceptance. Query required.

FENCE INDUSTRY/ACCESS CONTROL—6255 Barfield Rd., Atlanta, GA 30328. Bill Coker, Ed./Assoc. Pub. Articles on fencing and access control industry; interviews with dealer-erectors; on-the-job pieces. Photos. Pays 10¢ a word, extra for photos, on publication. Query.

THE FISH BOAT—P.O. Box 2400, Covington, LA 70434. William A. Sarratt, Ed. Articles on commercial fishing, seafood marketing and processing. Short items on commercial fishing and boats. Pays varying rates.

FITNESS MANAGEMENT—P.O. Box 1198, Solana Beach, CA 92075. Edward H. Pitts, Ed. Authoritative features, 750 to 2,500 words, and news shorts, 100 to 750 words, for owners, managers, and program directors of fitness centers. Content must be in keeping with current medical practice: no fads. Pays 8¢ a word, on publication. Query.

FLORIDA CONSTRUCTION INDUSTRY—P.O. Drawer 520, Maitland,

FL 32751. Carolyn Kaiser, Ed. Articles on the construction industry in Florida, 250 to 1,000 words. Pays $50 to $250, on acceptance. Photos. Queries are preferred.

FLORIST—29200 Northwestern Hwy., P.O. Box 2227, Southfield, MI 48037. Susan Nicholas, Man. Ed. Articles, to 2,000 words, with photos, on retail florist business improvement. Photos. Pays 8¢ a word.

FLOWERS &—Teleflora Plaza, Suite 260, 12233 W. Olympic Blvd., Los Angeles, CA 90064. Marie Moneysmith, Exec. Ed. Articles, 1,000 to 3,500 words, with how-to information for retail florists. Pays from $400, on acceptance. Query first.

FOOD MANAGEMENT—747 Third Ave., New York, NY 10017. Donna Boss, Ed. Articles, on foodservice in healthcare, schools, colleges, prisons, business and industry. Trends and how-to pieces, with management tie-in. Pays to $500. Query.

FOREIGN TRADE—8208 W. Franklin, Minneapolis, MN 55426. John Freivalds, Ed. Articles, 1,700 to 2,100 words, on any topic related to international trade, examining problems managers have faced and how they were dealt with. Pays $200, on publication.

THE FOREMAN'S LETTER—24 Rope Ferry Rd., Waterford, CT 06386. Carl Thunberg, Ed. Interviews, with photos, with top-notch supervisors and foremen. Pays 8¢ to 12¢ a word, extra for photos, on acceptance.

GARDEN DESIGN—1733 Connecticut Ave., NW, Washington, DC 20009. Susan Frey, Ed. Association of American Landscape Architects. Articles, 1,500 to 2,000 words, on classic and contemporary examples of residential landscape, garden, art, history, and design. Interviews.Pays $300, on publication. Query.

THE GENERAL LEDGER—The Wethersfield Group, 78 Wethersfield St., Rowley, MA 01969. Shirley E. Doherty, Ed. Newsletter. Articles, to 600 words, on bookkeeping, accounting, office and personnel procedures. Short humor, to 50 words, about office environment. Queries are preferred. Pays 8½¢ a word, on acceptance; $5 for fillers, humor, and jokes.

GLASS DIGEST—310 Madison Ave., New York, NY 10017. Charles Cumpston, Ed. Articles, 1,200 to 1,500 words, on building projects and glass/metal dealers, distributors, storefront anᵈ glazing contractors. Pays varying rates, on publication.

GLASS NEWS—P.O. Box 7138, Pittsburgh, PA 15213. Liz Scott, Man. Ed. Articles, to 1,500 words, on developments in glass manufacturing, glass factories, types of glass. Personality profiles. Pays 5¢ to 10¢ a word, on publication. Query with SASE.

GOLF SHOP OPERATIONS—5520 Park Ave., Box 395, Trumbull, CT 06611-0395. Nick Romano, Ed. Articles, 200 to 800 words, with photos, on successful golf shop operations; new ideas for merchandising, display, bookkeeping. Short pieces on golf professionals. Pays $175 to $250, on publication. Query with outline.

GRAPHIC ARTS MONTHLY—875 Third Ave., New York, NY 10022. Roger Ynostroza, Ed. Technical or business-oriented articles, 1,500 to 2,000 words, on printing industry. No profiles. Pays 10¢ a word, on publication. Query.

GREENHOUSE MANAGER—P.O. Box 1868, Fort Worth, TX 76101. Jim Batts, Man. Ed. How-to articles, success stories, 500 to 1,800 words, accompanied by color slides, of interest to professional greenhouse growers. Profiles. Pays $50 to $300, on acceptance. Query required.

HARDWARE AGE—Chilton Way, Radnor, PA 19089. Rick Carter, Man. Ed. Articles on merchandising methods in hardware outlets. Photos. Pays on acceptance.

HARDWARE MERCHANDISER—7300 N. Cicero Ave., Chicago, IL 60646. Pamela C. Taylor, Ed. Articles, to 1,000 words, with photos, on merchandising in hardware and discount stores. Pays on acceptance.

HARVARD BUSINESS REVIEW—Harvard Graduate School of Business Administration, Soldiers Field Rd., Boston, MA 02163. Query Editors on new ideas about business management, of interest to senior executives. Pays on publication.

HEALTH FOODS BUSINESS—567 Morris Ave., Elizabeth, NJ 07208. Mary Jane Dittmar, Ed. Articles, 1,500 words, with photos, on managing health food stores. Shorter pieces on consumer trends, alternative therapies. Interviews with doctors and nutritionists. Brief items for "Quote/Unquote" (include source). Pays on publication. Query. Send for guidelines.

HEATING/PIPING/AIR CONDITIONING—2 Illinois Cntr., Chicago, IL 60601. Robert T. Korte, Ed. Articles, to 5,000 words, on heating, piping and air-conditioning systems in industrial plants and large buildings; engineering information. Pays $60 per printed page, on publication. Query.

HIGH TECH MARKETING—1460 Post Rd. East, Westport, CT 06880. Candace Port, Ed. Feature-length articles, 9 to 15 pages, on the marketing of high-tech products. Pays 20¢ to 30¢ a word, on acceptance. Query required.

HOSPITAL GIFT SHOP MANAGEMENT—7628 Densmore, Van Nuys, CA 91406. Barbara Feiner, Ed. Articles, 750 to 2,500 words, with managerial tips and sales pointers; hospital and merchandise profiles. Pays $10 to $100, on acceptance. Query required.

HOSPITAL SUPERVISOR'S BULLETIN—24 Rope Ferry Rd., Waterford, CT 06386. Janice Endresen, Ed. Interviews, articles with nonmedical hospital supervisors on departmental problem solving. Pays 12¢ a word. Query.

HOSPITALS—211 E. Chicago Ave., Suite 700, Chicago, IL 60611. Frank Sabatino, Ed. Articles, 500 to 800 words, for hospital administrators. Pays varying rates, on acceptance. Query.

INC.—38 Commercial Wharf, Boston, MA 02110. George Gendron, Ed. Feature articles about how owners and managers of small companies solve common problems. Pays to $1,500 on acceptance. Query.

INCOME OPPORTUNITIES—380 Lexington Ave., New York, NY 10017. Stephen Wagner, Ed. Helpful articles 1,000 to 2,500 words, on how to make money full or part-time; how to run a successful small business, improve sales, etc. Pays varying rates, on acceptance. Query.

INDUSTRIAL CHEMICAL NEWS—633 Third Ave., New York, NY 10017. Irvin J. Schwartz, Ed. Articles, 500 to 2,000 words, on technical and professional issues of interest to chemists working in industrial labs. Pays $150 to $600, on acceptance. Query.

INDUSTRIAL DESIGN—330 W. 42nd St., New York, NY 10036. Annetta Hanna, Man. Ed. Articles to 2,000 words, on product development, design management, graphic design, design history, fashion, art, and environments for designers and marketing executives. Profiles of designers and corporations that use design effectively. Pays $250 to $500, on publication.

INFOSYSTEMS—Hitchcock Bldg., Wheaton, IL 60188. Wayne L. Rhodes, Ed. How-to articles, 6 to 8 pages, for managers in the data processing field. Pays negotiable rates, on publication. Query.

INSTANT PRINTER—P.O. Box 368, Northbrook, IL 60065. Dan Witte, Ed. Articles, 5 to 7 typed pages, for owners and/or managers of printing businesses specializing in retail printing: case histories, how-to's, technical pieces, interesting ideas. Opinion pieces, 1 to 2 typed pages. Photos. Pays $150 to $200 ($25 to $50 for opinion pieces), extra for photos, on publication. Query preferred.

INTERFACE AGE—See *Computing for Business.*

INTV JOURNAL—80 Fifth Ave., Suite 501, New York, NY 10011. William Dunlap, Man. Ed. Features and short pieces on trends in independent television. Pays to $500, after publication. Query.

KIDS FASHIONS—71 West 35th St., Suite 1600, New York, NY 10001. Larry Leventhal, Ed. Articles, 1,000 to 2,000 words with photos, on retailing and merchandising of children's apparel, in larger specialty stores, specialty chains, better department stores. Pays from $250 for articles with photos; from $150 for how-to and consultation pieces, on acceptance. Queries preferred.

LASERS & APPLICATIONS—23868 Hawthorne Blvd., Torrance, CA 90505. Tom Farre, Ed. Controlled-circulation publication for the laser electro-optics industry. News articles, 2 to 3 manuscript pages, with significant scientific content. Pays $100 per published page, on publication.

LOS ANGELES BUSINESS JOURNAL—3345 Wilshire, #207, Los Angeles, CA 90010. David Yochum, Ed. Feature articles on specific industries in the five-county Los Angeles area, stressing the how-to, trends and analysis. Pays on publication.

LOS ANGELES LAWYER—Box 55020, Los Angeles, CA 90055. Susan Pettit, Ed. Journalistic features, 12 to 16 pages, and consumer articles, 8 to 12 pages, on legal topics. Pays $200 to $600, on acceptance. Query required.

LOTUS—P.O. Box 9123, Cambridge, MA 02139. Steven E. Miller, Ed. Articles, 1,500 to 2,000 words, for business and professional people using Lotus software. Query with outline required. Payment varies, on acceptance.

LP-GAS MAGAZINE—131 W. First St., Duluth, MN 55802. Zane Chastain, Ed. Articles, 1,500 to 2,500 words, with photos, on LP-Gas dealer operations: marketing, management, etc. Photos. Pays to 15¢ a word, extra for photos, on acceptance. Query.

MACHINE DESIGN—1100 Superior Blvd., Cleveland, OH 44114. Robert Aronson, Exec. Ed. Articles, to 10 published pages, with information of practical use to design engineers. Payment is negotiable, on publication.

MAGAZINE DESIGN & PRODUCTION—4551 W. 107th St., Suite 343, Overland Park, KS 66207. Maureen Waters, Man. Ed. Articles, 6 to 10 typed pages, on magazine design and production: printing, typesetting, computers, layout, etc. Pays $100 to $200, on publication. Query required.

MANAGE—2210 Arbor Blvd., Dayton, OH 45439. Doug Shaw, Ed. Articles, 1,500 to 2,200 words, on management and supervision for first-line and middle managers. Pays 5¢ a word.

MANUFACTURED HOMES MAGAZINE—P.O. Box 354, Bremerton, WA 98310. Sandra E. Haven, Ed. Dir. Articles on manufactured homes, for manufactured home buyers and owners. Practical information on selection, purchase, protection, maintenance, and enjoyment of living in today's mobile, modular, and panelized homes. Pays to 10¢ a word, on acceptance. Good B&W or color photos are helpful. Humorous reflections and "Reader Projects" (200 to 500 words).

MANUFACTURING SYSTEMS—Hitchcock Bldg., Wheaton, IL 60188. Tom Inglesby, Ed. Articles, 500 to 2,000 words, on computer and information systems for industry executives seeking to increase productivity in manufacturing firms. Pays 10¢ to 20¢ a word, on acceptance. Query required.

MEDICENTER MANAGEMENT—1640 5th St., Santa Monica, CA 90401. Rebecca Morrow, Ed. Articles, 1,500 to 3,000 words, on the business of practicing medicine. Payment varies, on acceptance. Query required.

MEMPHIS BUSINESS JOURNAL—4515 Poplar, Suite 322, Memphis, TN 38117. Barney DuBois, Ed. Articles, to 2,000 words, on business, industry trade, agri-business and finance in the Mid-South trade area. Pays $80 to $200, on acceptance.

MINIATURES DEALER—Clifton House, Clifton, VA 22024. Geraldine Willems, Ed. Articles, 1,000 to 1,500 words, on advertising, promotion, merchandising of miniatures and other small business retailer concerns. Pays to $200, on publication.

MIX MAGAZINE—2608 Ninth St., Berkeley, CA 94710. David Schwartz, Ed. Articles, varying lengths, for professionals, on audio, video, and music entertainment technology. Pays 10¢ a word, on publication. Query required.

MODERN HEALTHCARE—740 N. Rush St., Chicago, IL 60611. Clark Bell, Ed. Features on management, finance, building design and construction, and new technology for hospitals, health maintenance organizations, nursing homes, and other health care institutions. Pays $7 per column inch, on publication. Query.

MODERN TIRE DEALER—P.O. Box 5417, 110 N. Miller Rd., Akron, OH 44313. Lloyd Stoyar, Ed. Merchandising management and service articles, 1,000 to 1,500 words, with photos, on independent tire dealers and retreaders. Pays $200 to $250, on publication.

MONEY MAGAZINE—Time & Life Bldg., New York, NY 10020. Landon Jones, Man. Ed. Articles on various aspects of personal finance and investment. Welcomes article suggestions. Pays $2,500 and up for major articles.

MONEY MAKER—5705 N. Lincoln Ave., Chicago, IL 60659. John Manos, Ed. Informative jargon-free articles, to 4,000 words, for beginning to sophisticated investors, on investment opportunities, personal finance, and low-priced investments. Pays 25¢ a word, on acceptance. Query for assignment.

THE MONEYPAPER—2 Madison Ave., Larchmont, NY 10538. Vita Nelson, Ed. Financial news and money-saving ideas, especially those of interest to women. Brief, well-researched articles on personal finance, money management: saving, earning, investing, taxes, insurance and related subjects. Features on women's attitudes toward money and personal experiences in solving money management problems. Pays $75 for articles, on publication. Query with resume and writing sample.

609

NATIONAL BEAUTY SCHOOL JOURNAL—3839 White Plains Rd., Bronx, NY 10467. Mary Jane Tenerelli, Editor. Articles, 1,500 to 2,000 words, on running a cosmetology school, teaching techniques and problems, and new cosmetology procedures. All articles must be relevant to schools (not salons). Pays $150 for articles, $25 for crossword puzzles, $50 for cartoons, on publication.

NATIONAL FISHERMAN—21 Elm St., Camden, ME 04843. James W. Fullilove, Ed. Articles, 200 to 2,000 words, aimed at commercial fishermen and boat-builders. Pays from $2.50 per inch, extra for photos, on publication. Query preferred.

NATION'S BUSINESS—1615 H St., NW, Washington, DC 20062. Lively articles on business-related topics, including management advice and success stories. Pays negotiable rates, after acceptance. Query.

NEVADA BUSINESS JOURNAL—2375 E. Tropicana, Suite 270, Las Vegas, NV 89109. Henry C. Holcomb, Ed. Business articles, 1,000 to 3,000 words, on topics of interest to readers in Nevada: profiles of industries, companies, executives, and communities; how-to business articles; and articles of general business interest. Pays $150 to $300, on acceptance. Query first.

NEW BUSINESS—P.O. Box 3312, Sarasota, FL 33578. Business-related articles of regional/general interest. Pays $75 to $225, on publication. Query.

NEW CAREER WAYS NEWSLETTER—67 Melrose Ave., Haverhill, MA 01830. William J. Bond, Ed. How-to articles, 1,500 to 2,000 words, on new ways to succeed in business careers. Pays varying rates, on publication. Query with outline.

NORTHERN HARDWARE—2965 Broadmoor Valley Rd., Suite B, Colorado Springs, CO 80906. Edward Gonzales, Ed. Articles, 800 to 1,000 words, on unusual hardware and home center stores and promotions in Northwest and Midwest. Photos. Pays 8¢ a word, extra for photos, on publication. Query.

NURSINGWORLD JOURNAL—470 Boston Post Rd., Weston, MA 02193. Ira Alterman, Ed. Articles, 500 to 1,500 words, for nurses and nurse educators, on all aspects of nursing. Photos. Pays from 25¢ per column inch, on publication.

OPPORTUNITY MAGAZINE—6 N. Michigan Ave., Suite 1405, Chicago, IL 60602. Jack Weissman, Ed. Articles, 900 words, on sales psychology, sales techniques, self-improvement. Pays $20 to $40, on publication.

THE OSHA COMPLIANCE LETTER—See *The Safety Compliance Letter.*

THE OWNER BUILDER—1516 Fifth St., Berkeley, CA 94710. Pat Madsen, Ed. Articles of varying lengths on construction and building, for people building or remodeling their own homes. How-to pieces, profiles of owner builders, and materials and technique pieces. Queries are required. Pays on publication.

PAPERBOARD PACKAGING—7500 Old Oak Blvd., Cleveland, OH 44130. Mark Arzoumanian, Ed. Articles, any length, on corrugated containers, folding cartons and setup boxes. Pays on publication. Query with outline.

PC WEEK—800 Boylston St., Boston, MA 02199. David DeJean, Exec.

Ed. Features, 1,500 to 2,500 words, for volume buyers of PCs and related equipment and software within large organizations; corporate strategy profiles; reviews of PC-related products. Pays $500 to $1,000, on acceptance. Query required.

PERSONNEL ADMINISTRATOR—606 N. Washington St., Alexandria, VA 22314. Lynne A. Chiara, Ed. Articles on employment practices, compensation and benefits, health and safety, labor relations and general human resource management, 12 double-spaced pages, for human resource management professionals. Pays in copies.

PET BUSINESS—5400 N.W. 84th Ave., Miami, FL 33166. Linda Mills, Ed. News magazine format. Brief, documented articles on animals and products routinely found in pet stores. Of interest are research findings and legislative/regulatory actions. Pays $4 per column inch, extra for photos, on acceptance.

PETS/SUPPLIES/MARKETING—One E. First St., Duluth, MN 55802. David D. Kowalski, Ed. Articles, 1,000 to 1,200 words, with photos, on pet shops, and pet and product merchandising. Pays 10¢ a word, extra for photos. No fiction or news clippings. Query.

PHOENIX BUSINESS JOURNAL—1817 N. 3rd St., Suite 100, Phoenix, AZ 85004. Chambers Williams, Ed. Articles on leading and innovative businesses and business people in Arizona. Photos. Pays $2.75 to $3.50, per column inch, on publication.

PHOTO MARKETING—3000 Picture Pl., Jackson, MI 49201. Perry Washburn, Man. Ed. Business articles, 1,000 to 3,500 words, for owners and managers of camera stores or photo processing labs. Pays $150 to $500, extra for photos, on publication.

PHYSICIAN'S MANAGEMENT—7500 Old Oak Blvd., Cleveland, OH 44130. Bob Feigenbaum, Ed. Articles, about 2,500 to 3,000 words, on finance, investments, malpractice, and office management for primary care physicians. No clinical pieces. Pays $125 per printed page, on acceptance. Query.

P.O.B.—P.O. Box 810, Wayne, MI 48184. Jeanne M. Helfrick, Assoc. Ed. Technical and business articles, 1,000 to 4,000 words, for professionals and technicians in the surveying and mapping fields. Technical tips on field and office procedures and equipment maintenance. Pays $150 to $400, on acceptance.

POLICE PRODUCT NEWS—P.O. Box 847, Carlsbad, CA 92008. F. McKeen Thompson, Ed. Reviews of new products and equipment, and profiles of people in the law enforcement profession, 1,000 to 3,000 words. Pays from $100 to $300, on acceptance.

POOL & SPA NEWS—3923 W. Sixth St., Los Angeles, CA 90020. News articles on the swimming pool, spa, and hot tub industry. Photos are a plus. Pays 8¢ to 12¢ a word, extra for photos, on publication. Query first.

THE PRESS—302 Grote St., Buffalo, NY 14207. Mary Lou Vogt, Ed. Quarterly. Short profiles, 800 to 1,200 words, on cartoonists and industry and advertising personalities for advertising executives at newspapers and ad agencies. Pieces on unusual hobbies or occupations. Travel articles. Humor. Pays 10¢ a word, on acceptance.

PRIVATE PRACTICE—Box 12489, Oklahoma City, OK 73157. Cindy Wickersham, Asst. Ed. Articles, 1,500 to 2,000 words, on state or local legislation affecting medical field. Pays $250 to $350, on publication.

THE PROFESSIONAL—Office of Citizen Complaints, 850 Bryant St., San Francisco, CA 94103. Quarterly magazine for the San Francisco Police Dept. Articles advancing the cause of police professionalism, on the subject of professional standards, interpersonal contact and effective communications in difficult, stress-filled situations. Pays $250 to $500, for articles of 1,000 words.

PROFESSIONAL OFFICE DESIGN—111 Eighth Ave., New York, NY 10011. Tim Robinson, Ed. Articles, to 1,500 words, on space planning and design for offices in the fields of law, medicine, finance, accounting, advertising, and architecture/design. Pays competitive rates, on publication. Query required.

THE QUALITY CRAFTS MARKET—15 W. 44th St., New York, NY 10036. Marvin David, Ed. "The business magazine for craftspeople." Articles, information, and tips that will help professional craftspeople succeed at selling their crafts. "We especially need 220-word pieces on quality crafts shops and galleries, the types of crafts they want to buy, the price range they handle, and how they'll pay (cash or consignment)." Pays 10¢ a word, on publication.

RADIO ELECTRONICS—500-B Bi-County Blvd., Farmingdale, NY 11735. Art Kleiman, Ed. Dir. Technical articles, 1,500 to 3,000 words, on electronic equipment. Pays $50 to $500, on acceptance.

REAL ESTATE SALESPEOPLE—Suite 201, 2531 W. Dunlap, Phoenix, AZ 85021. Jeff Burger, Man. Ed. Articles, to 3,000 words, for American and Canadian sellers of residential real estate, giving real estate marketing tips and covering salesmanship success stories and homebuying trends—topics that help readers achieve career success. Pays competitive rates, on acceptance. Query.

REAL ESTATE TODAY—430 N. Michigan Ave., Chicago, IL 60611. Karin Nelson, Ed. Articles, 2,000 words, on residential, commercial-investment, and brokerage-management real estate, for members of the National Association of Realtors. Queries are required. Pays in copies.

RESORT & HOTEL MANAGEMENT—P.O. Box A, Del Mar, CA 92014. Articles, 1,000 to 1,500 words, on successful resort and hotel operation and management.

ROBOTICS ENGINEERING—174 Concord St., Peterborough, NH 03458. Stephanie Henkel, Ed. Tutorial pieces on robotics and automation and applications. Pays to $50 per published page, on publication.

THE ROOFER—P.O. Box 06253, Fort Myers, FL 33906. Shawn Holiday, Ed. Non-technical articles, 500 to 1,000 words, on roofing-related topics: new processes and products, energy savings, roofing concepts, etc., safety and medical pieces; interviews with contractors. Pays negotiable rates, on publication.

RV BUSINESS—29901 Agoura Rd., Agoura, CA 91301. Katherine Sharma, Exec. Ed. Articles, 1,500 to 2,500 words, on manufacturing, financing, selling and servicing recreational vehicles. Articles on legislative matters affecting the industry. Pays varying rates.

THE SAFETY COMPLIANCE LETTER (formerly *The OSHA Compliance Letter*)—24 Rope Ferry Rd., Waterford, CT 06386. Laurie Beth Roberts, Ed. Interview-based articles, 800 to 1,250 words, for safety professionals, on solving OSHA-related safety and health problems. Pays to 15¢ a word, on acceptance, after editing. Query.

612

SAILBOARD NEWS—P.O. Box 159, Two S. Park Pl., Fair Haven, VT 05743. Mark Gabriel, Ed. Interviews, articles, and how-to pieces on boardsailing and the boardsailing industry. Photos. Pays from $25, on publication.

SALES AND MARKETING MANAGEMENT—Bill Communications, Inc., 633 Third Ave., New York, NY 10017. Robert H. Albert, Ed. Short and feature articles for sales and marketing executives of medium to large corporations. Pays varying rates, on acceptance. Query required.

SAN FRANCISCO BUSINESS TIMES—325 Fifth St., San Francisco, CA 94107. Donald Keough, Ed. Articles, to about 20 column inches, on regional business topics; pieces for "Focus" section. Pays $75 to $100, on publication. Query required.

SECURITY MANAGEMENT—1655 N. Ft. Myer Dr., Suite 1200, Arlington, VA 22209. Mary Alice Crawford, Pub. Articles, 2,500 to 3,000 words, on legislative issues related to security; case studies of innovative security applications; management topics: employee relations, training programs, etc. Pays 10¢ a word, on publication. Query.

SELLING DIRECT—6255 Barfield Rd., Atlanta, GA 30328. Robert S. Rawls, Ed. Articles, 400 to 1,800 words, for independent salespersons selling to homes, stores, industries, and businesses. Pays 10¢ a word, on publication.

SNACK FOOD MAGAZINE—131 W. First St., Duluth, MN 55802. Jerry Hess, Ed. Articles, 600 to 1,500 words, on trade news, personalities, promotions, production in snack food manufacturing industry. Short pieces; photos. Pays 12¢ to 15¢ a word, extra for photos, on acceptance. Query.

SOFTWARE NEWS—1900 W. Park Dr., Westborough, MA 01581. Edward J. Bride, Ed. Technical features, 1,000 to 1,200 words, for computer literate audience, on how software products can be used. Pays about $150 to $200, on publication. Query preferred.

SOUVENIRS AND NOVELTIES—Suite 226-27, 401 N. Broad St., Philadelphia, PA 19108. Articles, 1,500 words, quoting souvenir shop managers on items that sell, display ideas, problems in selling, industry trends. Photos. Pays from $1 per column inch, extra for photos, on publication.

SUCCESSFUL FARMING—1716 Locust St., Des Moines, IA 50336. Loren Kruse, Ed. Articles, to 2,000 words, for farming families, on all areas of business farming: money management, marketing, machinery, soils and crops, livestock, and buildings. Pays from $300, on acceptance. Query required.

SYLVIA PORTER'S PERSONAL FINANCE MAGAZINE—380 Lexington Ave., New York, NY 10017. Articles on investing, taxes, financial planning, real estate, entrepreneurship. Also occasional pieces on careers, travel, and consumer issues. Queries only.

TEXTILE WORLD—4170 Ashford-Dunwoody Rd., N.E., Suite 420, Atlanta, GA 30319. L. A. Christiansen, Ed. Articles, 500 to 2,000 words, with photos, on manufacturing and finishing textiles. Pays varying rates, on acceptance.

TOURIST ATTRACTIONS AND PARKS—Suite 226-27, 401 N. Broad St., Philadelphia, PA 19108. Chuck Tooley, Ed. Articles, 1,500 words, on successful management of parks and leisure attractions. News items, 250 and 500 words. Pays 7¢ a word, on publication. Query.

TRAILER/BODY BUILDERS—1602 Harold St., Houston, TX 77006. Paul Schenck, Ed. Articles on engineering, sales, and management ideas for truck body and truck trailer manufacturers. Pays from $100 per printed page, on acceptance.

TRAINING, THE MAGAZINE OF HUMAN RESOURCES DEVELOP-MENT—50 S. Ninth St., Minneapolis, MN 55402. Jack Gordon, Ed. Articles, 1,000 to 2,500 words, for managers of training and development activities in corporations, government, etc. Pays to 15¢ a word, on acceptance. Query.

THE TRAVEL AGENT—2 W. 46th St., New York, NY 10036. Eric Friedheim, Ed. Articles, 1,500 words, with photos, on travel trade, for travel agents. Pays $50 to $75, on acceptance.

TRAVEL BUSINESS MANAGER—51 Monroe St., #1501, Rockville, MD 20850. Eleanor Alexander, Ed. Articles and features, 1,000 to 1,800 words, on management and strategic issues in the travel industry. Pays $200 to $500, on publication. Query required. Send SASE for guidelines.

TRAVELAGE SOUTHEAST—555 N. Birch Rd., Ft. Lauderdale, FL 33304. Marylyn Springer, Ed. Articles, 1,500 to 2,000 words, for travel agents and other travel industry personnel. Interviews. Pays $1.50 per column inch, on publication.

TRUCKERS/USA—P.O. Box 2029, Tuscaloosa, AL 35403. Claude Duncan, Ed. Features, 250 to 1,000 words, about incidents involving long-haul truck drivers, their families and others with whom they are involved. Not interested in pieces about safety, taxes, and road repair. Short humor directly related to trucking. Pays $10 to $50, on acceptance.

TRUCKS—20 Waterside Plaza, New York, NY 10010-2615. John Stevens, Ed. Bimonthly. Articles for long-haul, heavy duty truck drivers. Queries preferred. Pays $50 to $100 per published page, on publication.

VENDING TIMES—545 Eighth Ave., New York, NY 10018. Arthur E. Yohalem, Ed. Feature and news articles, with photos, on vending machines. Pays varying rates, on acceptance. Query.

VIEW—80 Fifth Ave., Suite 501, New York, NY 10011. Kathy Haley, Ed. Features and short pieces on trends in the business of television programming (network, syndication, cable and pay). Profiles. Pays to $400, after publication. Query.

VIRGINIA BUSINESS—600 E. Broad St., Richmond, VA 23219. James Bacon, Ed. Articles, 1,000 to 2,500 words, on business in Virginia. Pay rates negotiable, on acceptance. Queries are required.

WESTERN INVESTOR—400 S.W. Sixth Ave., Suite 1115, Portland, OR 97204. Business and investment articles, 800 to 1,200 words, about companies and their leaders listed in the *Western Investor* data section. Pays from $50, on publication. Query first.

WINES & VINES—1800 Lincoln Ave., San Rafael, CA 94901. Philip E. Hiaring, Ed. Articles, 1,000 words, on grape and wine industry, emphasizing marketing and production. Pays 5¢ a word, on acceptance.

WOMEN IN BUSINESS—9100 Ward Parkway, Box 8278, Kansas City, MO 64114. Publication of the American Business Women's Association. Margaret E. Horan, Ed. Features, 1,000 to 2,000 words, for career women from 25 to 55 years old; no profiles. Pays 15¢ a word, on acceptance. Query.

WOOD 'N ENERGY—P.O. Box 2008, Laconia, NH 03247. Jason Perry, Ed. Profiles and interviews, 1,000 to 2,500 words, with retailers and manufacturers of alternative energy equipment. Pays $150 to $250 for articles, on acceptance. Query.

WORLD OIL—Gulf Publishing Co., P.O. Box 2608, Houston, TX 77252. T. R. Wright, Jr., Ed. Engineering and operations articles, 3,000 to 4,000 words, on petroleum industry exploration, drilling or producing. Photos. Pays from $50 per printed page, on acceptance. Query.

WORLD SCREEN NEWS—80 Fifth Ave., Suite 501, New York, NY 10011. Claire Poole, Man. Ed. Features and short pieces on trends in international television programming (network, syndication, cable and pay). Pays to $500, after publication. Query.

WORLD WASTES—6255 Barfield Rd., Atlanta, GA 30328. Bill Wolpin, Pub. Case studies, 1,000 to 2,000 words, with photos, of refuse haulers, landfill operators, resource recovery operations and transfer stations, with solutions to problems in field. Pays from $100 per printed page, on publication. Query preferred.

YOUNG FASHIONS—370 Lexington Ave., New York, NY 10017. Marc Richards, Ed. Nuts-and-bolts, how-to pieces for retailers and manufacturers of children's clothing, 2,000 to 4,000 words. Pay varies, on acceptance. Queries are required.

COMPANY PUBLICATIONS

Company publications (also called house magazines or house organs) are excellent, well-paying markets for writers at all levels of experience. Hundreds of these magazines are published, usually by large corporations, to promote good will, familiarize readers with the company's services and products, and interest customers in these products. Always read a house magazine before submitting an article; write to the editor for a sample copy (offering to pay for it) and the editorial guidelines. Stamped, self-addressed envelopes should be enclosed with any query or manuscript. This list includes only a sampling of publications in this large market.

THE COMPASS—Mobil International Aviation and Marine Sales, Inc., 150 E. 42nd St., New York, NY 10017. R. G. MacKenzie, Ed. Articles, to 3,500 words, on the sea and deep sea trade. Photos. No fiction. Pays to $250, on acceptance. Query.

FRIENDS, THE CHEVY OWNERS' MAGAZINE—30400 Van Dyke, Warren, MI 48093. Herman Duerr, Exec. Ed. Feature articles 800 to 1,500 words, on automobile travel in the U.S.; celebrity profiles of Chevy owners; auto related humor; unusual uses of Chevrolet products; Chevrolet-sponsored events coverage. Pays $300, extra for photos, on acceptance. Query, by mail, with SASE.

THE FURROW—Deere & Company, John Deere Rd., Moline, IL 61265. George R. Sollenberger, Ed. Articles and humor, to 1,500 words; researched agricultural-technical features; rural social- and economic-trend features. Pays to $1,000, on acceptance.

INLAND—Inland Steel Co., 30 W. Monroe, Chicago, IL 60603. Sheldon A. Mix, Man. Ed. Imaginative articles, essays, commentaries, of any length, of special interest in Midwest. Pays varying rates, on acceptance.

THE MODERN WOODMEN—Modern Woodmen of America, Mississippi River at 17th St., Rock Island, IL 61201. Gloria Bergh, Manager, Public Relations. Family- and community-oriented, general-interest articles; some quality fiction. Photos. Pays from $40, on acceptance. Publication not copyrighted.

NEW HOLLAND INC.—New Holland, PA 17557. Gary Martin, Ed. Articles, to 1,000 words, with strong photo support, on production agriculture, research and rural human interest. Pays on acceptance. Query.

RAYTHEON MAGAZINE—141 Spring St., Lexington, MA 02173. Robert P. Suarez, Ed. Articles by assignment only. Pays $750 to $1,250, on acceptance, for articles 800 to 1,200 words. Query with writing sample.

ASSOCIATIONS, ORGANIZATIONS

CALIFORNIA HIGHWAY PATROLMAN—2030 V. St., Sacramento, CA 95818. Carol Perri, Ed. Articles, with photos, on transportation safety, California history, travel, consumerism, humor, general items, etc. Photos. Pays 2½¢ a word, extra for black-and-white photos, on publication.

CATHOLIC FORESTER—425 W. Shuman Blvd., Naperville, IL 60566. Barbara Cunningham, Ed. Official publication of the Catholic Order of Foresters, a fraternal life insurance company for Catholics. Articles and fiction that appeal to Middle America, to 2,000 words; no sex or violence. Pays 5¢ a word, on acceptance.

COLUMBIA—1 Columbus Plaza, New Haven, CT 06507-0901. Elmer Von Feldt, Ed. Journal of the Knights of Columbus. Articles, 2,500 to 3,500 words, on a wide variety of topics of interest to K. of C. members, their families, and the Catholic layman: current events, religion, education, art, etc. Must include substantial quotes from a variety of sources, and *must* be illustrated with color transparencies. Pays $600 to $750, on acceptance.

THE ELKS MAGAZINE—425 W. Diversey Pkwy., Chicago, IL 60614. William J. Balles, Exec. Ed. Articles, 3,000 words, on business, sports, and topics of current interest; for non-urban audience with above-average income. Informative or humorous pieces, to 2,500 words. Pays $150 to $500 for articles, on acceptance. Query.

FIREHOUSE—33 Irving Pl., New York, NY 10003. Elena Serocki, Exec. Ed. Articles, 500 to 2,000 words: on-the-scene accounts of fires, trends in firefighting equipment, controversial fire service issues, and life styles of firefighters. Humorous fillers to 100 words. Pays $100 to $200 for features, to $25 for fillers, on publication. Query.

GEOBYTE—P.O. Box 797, Tulsa, OK 74101. Ken Milam, Man. Ed. Quarterly publication of the American Association of Petroleum Geologists. Articles, to 20 typed pages, on computer applications in exploration and production of oil, gas, and energy minerals. Pays varying rates, on acceptance. Query first.

KIWANIS—3636 Woodview Trace, Indianapolis, IN 46268. Chuck Jonak, Exec. Ed. Serious and light articles on a variety of topics of interest to an intelligent male audience—current business; humanitarian, youth, and community issues; family relations; recreation; consumer trends; education; travel; etc. Readership is becoming increasingly international, and articles should reflect this, taking into account information from various regions of the world. Queries are preferred. Pays $400 to $1,000 for 2,000- to 3,000-word manuscripts, on acceptance.

THE LION—300 22nd St., Oak Brook, IL 60570. Robert Kleinfelder, Senior Ed. Official publication of Lions Clubs International. Articles, 800 to

2,000 words, and photo essays, on Club activities. Pays from $50 to $400, including photos, on acceptance. Query.

NRA NEWS—311 First St., N.W., Washington, DC 20001. Publication of the National Restaurant Association. Sylvia Rivchun, Ed. Articles, 5,000 words, on the food service and restaurant business. Pays $350 to $750, on acceptance. Query.

OPTIMIST MAGAZINE—4494 Lindell Blvd., St. Louis, MO 63108. James E. Braibish, Ed. Articles, to 1,500 words, on activities of local Optimist club, and techniques for personal and club success. Pays from $100, on acceptance. Query.

THE ROTARIAN—1600 Ridge Ave., Evanston, IL 60201. Willmon L. White, Ed. Articles, to 1,500 words, on international social and economic issues, business and management, human relationships, travel, sports, environment, science and technology; humor. Pays good rates, on acceptance. Query.

WOODMEN OF THE WORLD MAGAZINE—1700 Farnam St., Omaha, NE 68102. Leland A. Larson, Ed. Publication of the Woodmen of the World Life Insurance Society. Articles on history, travel, sports, do-it-yourself projects, science, etc. Photos. Pays 5¢ a word, extra for photos, on acceptance.

RELIGIOUS AND DENOMINATIONAL

ADVANCE—1445 Boonville Ave., Springfield, MO 65802. Gwen Jones, Ed. Articles, 1,200 words, slanted to ministers, on preaching, doctrine, practice; how-to-do-it features. Pays 3¢ to 4¢ a word, on acceptance.

AGLOW MAGAZINE—P.O. Box I, Lynnwood, WA 98046-1557. Gwen Weising, Man. Ed. First-person articles and testimonies, 1,000 to 2,000 words, that encourage, instruct, inform or entertain Christian women of all ages, and relate to the work of the Holy Spirit. Should deal with contemporary issues. Pays 10¢ a word, on acceptance.

AMERICA—106 W. 56th St., New York, NY 10019. George W. Hunt, S.J., Ed. Articles, 1,000 to 2,500 words, on current affairs, family life, literary trends. Pays $75 to $150, on acceptance.

AMERICAN BIBLE SOCIETY RECORD—1865 Broadway, New York, NY 10023. Clifford P. Macdonald, Man. Ed. Material related to work of American Bible Society: translating, publishing, distributing. Pays on acceptance. Query.

AMIT WOMAN—817 Broadway, New York, NY 10003. Micheline Ratzerdorfer, Ed. Articles, 1,000 to 2,000 words, of interest to Jewish women: Middle East, Israel, history, holidays, travel. Pays to $50, on publication.

ANNALS OF ST. ANNE DE BEAUPRÉ—P.O. Box 1000, St. Anne de Beaupré, Quebec, Canada G0A 3C0. Roch Achard, C.Ss.R., Ed. Articles, 1,100 to 1,200 words, on Catholic subjects and on St. Anne. Pays 2¢ to 4¢ a word, on acceptance.

BAPTIST LEADER—American Baptist Churches, USA, P.O. Box 851, Valley Forge, PA 19482-0851. L. Isham, Ed. Practical how-to or thought-provoking articles, 1,200 to 1,600 words, for local church education lay leaders and teachers. B & W photos a plus.

THE B'NAI B'RITH INTERNATIONAL JEWISH MONTHLY—1640 Rhode Island Ave., NW, Washington, DC 20036. Marc Silver, Ed. Original, lively articles, 500 to 3,000 words, on trends, politics, personalities, and culture of the Jewish community. Fiction, 1,000 to 4,000 words. Pays 10¢ to 25¢ a word, on publication. Query

BREAD—6401 The Paseo, Kansas City, MO 64131. Karen De Sollar, Ed. Church of the Nazarene. Devotional, Bible study and Christian guidance articles, to 1,200 words, for teen-agers. Religious short stories, to 1,500 words. Pays from 3¢ a word for prose, on acceptance.

BRIGADE LEADER—Box 150, Wheaton, IL 60189. Steve Neideck, Man. Ed. Inspirational articles, 1,000 to 1,800 words, for Christian men who help boys. Pays $60 to $150. Query only.

CATECHIST—2451 E. River Rd., Dayton, OH 45439. Patricia Fischer, Ed. Informational and inspirational articles, 1,200 to 1,500 words, for Catholic teachers, coordinators, and administrators in religious education programs. Pays $25 to $75, on publication.

CATHOLIC DIGEST—P.O. Box 64090, St. Paul, MN 55164. Address Articles Ed. Articles, 2,000 to 2,500 words, on Catholic and general subjects. Fillers, to 300 words, on instances of kindness rewarded, for "Hearts are Trumps"; accounts of good deeds, for "People Are Like That." Pays from $200 for original articles, $100 for reprints, on acceptance; $4 to $50 for fillers, on publication.

CATHOLIC LIFE—35750 Moravian Dr., Fraser, MI 48026. Robert C. Bayer, Ed. Articles, 600 to 1,200 words, on Catholic missionary work in Hong Kong, India, Latin America, Africa, etc. Photos. No fiction or poetry. Pays 4¢ a word, extra for photos, on publication.

CATHOLIC NEAR EAST MAGAZINE—1011 First Ave., New York, NY 10022. Michael Healy, Ed. Articles, 1,000 to 1,800 words, on places, people, religious history, sacred ritual, artistic heritage, living culture, and faith traditions of the Balkans, Near East, Middle East, and India. Special interest in Eastern rites of the church. Color photos illustrate all articles. Pays 10¢ a word, on publication. Query with SASE.

CATHOLIC TWIN CIRCLE—6404 Wilshire Blvd., Suite 900, Los Angeles, CA 90048. Mary Louise Frawley, Ed. Stories and interviews of interest to Catholics, 1,000 to 2,000 words, with photos. Strict attention to Catholic doctrine required. Enclose SASE. Pays 10¢ a word, on publication.

CHARISMA—190 N. Westmonte Dr., Altamonte Springs, FL 32714. Howard Earl, Sr. Ed. Charismatic Christian articles, 1,000 to 2,000 words, for developing the spiritual life. Photos. Pays varying rates, on publication. Query.

CHESAPEAKE SHALOM—P.O. Box 789, Severna Park, MD 21146. Lee Irwin, Ed. General interest articles, 300 to 1,200 words, on Jewish life and leisure in the Chesapeake Bay region, as well as pieces on Jewish issues and "heartwarming" anecdotes of Jewish-American life. Pays $5 to $15, $2 to $10 for poetry, on publication.

CHRISTIAN BOOKSELLER—190 N. Westmonte Dr., Altamonte Springs, FL 32714. Nancy Sabbag, Ed. Articles, 800 to 1,000 words, for Christian booksellers, on management, display, and promotion. Interviews with Christian authors. Photos. Pays $20 to $150, on publication. Query.

THE CHRISTIAN CENTURY—407 S. Dearborn St., Chicago, IL 60605. James M. Wall, Ed. Ecumenical. Articles, 1,500 to 2,500 words, with a religious angle, on political and social issues, international affairs, culture, the arts.

Poetry, to 20 lines. Photos. Pays about $25 per printed page, extra for photos, on publication.

CHRISTIAN HERALD—Chappaqua, NY 10514. Dean Merrill, Ed. Interdenominational. Articles, personal-experience pieces, to 1,500 words, on biblically-oriented topics. Short verse. Pays from 10¢ a word for full-length features, from $10 for short pieces, after acceptance. Query first.

CHRISTIAN LIFE MAGAZINE—396 E. St. Charles Rd., Wheaton, IL 60188. Janice Franzen, Exec. Ed. Articles, 1,500 to 2,500 words, on evangelical subjects, Christian living, and Christians in politics, sports, and entertainment. Photos. Fiction, 1,500 to 2,500 words, on problems faced by Christians. Pays to $150, on publication.

CHRISTIAN LIVING—850 N. Grove Ave., Elgin, IL 60102. Anne E. Dinnan, Ed. Weekly paper for evangelical and mainline Christian teens. Articles, and fiction, to 1,200 words, that challenge, interest, and inspire teens to spiritual growth. Taboos: obscenity, sexual scenes, heavy moralizing and preachiness. Pays 6¢ to 9¢ a word, on acceptance.

CHRISTIAN SINGLE—127 Ninth Ave. N., Nashville, TN 37234. Cliff Allbritton, Ed. Articles, 600 to 1,200 words, on leisure activities, inspiring personal experiences, for Christian singles. Humor. Pays 4¢ a word, on acceptance. Query. Send SASE for guidelines.

CHRISTIANITY TODAY—465 Gundersen Dr., Carol Stream, IL 60188. Harold Smith, Ed. Doctrinal, social issues and interpretive essays, 1,500 to 3,000 words, from evangelical Protestant perspective. Pays $300 to $500, on acceptance. Query required.

CHURCH ADMINISTRATION—127 Ninth Ave. N., Nashville, TN 37234. Gary Hardin, Ed. Southern Baptist. How-to articles, 1,500 to 1,800 words, on administrative planning, staffing, organization and financing. Pays 5¢ a word, on acceptance. Query.

CHURCH & STATE—8120 Fenton St., Silver Spring, MD 20910. Joseph L. Conn, Man. Ed. Articles, 600 to 2,600 words, on religious liberty and church-state relations issues. Pays varying rates, on acceptance. Query.

CHURCH EDUCATOR—Educational Ministries, 2861-C Saturn St., Brea, CA 92621. Robert G. Davidson, Ed. Articles, 200 to 3,000 words, with a "person-centered" approach to Christian education; articles on youth programs. How-to's for adult and juvenile Christian education. Pays 3¢ a word, on publication.

THE CHURCH HERALD—1324 Lake Drive S. E., Grand Rapids, MI 49506. John Stapert, Ed. Reformed Church in America. Articles, 500 to 1,500 words, on Christianity and culture, politics, marriage and home. Pays $40 to $125, on acceptance.

THE CHURCH MUSICIAN—127 Ninth Ave. N., Nashville, TN 37234. W. M. Anderson, Ed. Humorous fillers with a musical slant, for southern Baptist music leaders. No clippings. Pays about 4¢ a word, on acceptance. Same address and requirements for *Glory Songs* (for adults), and *Opus One* and *Opus Two* (for teen-agers).

THE CIRCUIT RIDER—P.O. Box 801, Nashville, TN 37202. Keith Pohli, Ed. Articles for United Methodist Pastors, 800 to 1,600 words. Pays $25 to $100, on acceptance. Query, with SASE, preferred.

COLUMBIA—Box 1670, New Haven, CT 06507. Elmer Von Feldt, Ed.

Knights of Columbus. Articles, 2,500 to 3,500 words, for Catholic families. Must be accompanied by color photos or transparencies. No fiction. Pays to $750 for articles and photos, on acceptance.

COMMENTARY—165 E. 56th St., New York, NY 10022. Norman Podhoretz, Ed. Articles, 5,000 to 7,000 words, on contemporary issues, Jewish affairs, social sciences, religious thought, culture. Serious fiction; book reviews. Pays on publication.

COMMONWEAL—15 Dutch St., New York, NY 10038. Peter Steinfels, Ed. Catholic. Articles, to 3,000 words, on political, religious, social and literary subjects. Pays 3¢ a word, on acceptance.

CONFIDENT LIVING (formerly *Good News Broadcaster*)—Box 82808, Lincoln, NE 68501. Norman A. Olson, Man. Ed. Articles, to 1,500 words, on relating biblical truths to daily living. Photos. Pays 4¢ a word, extra for photos, on acceptance. No simultaneous submissions or reprints. SASE required.

DAILY MEDITATION—Box 2710, San Antonio, TX 78299. Ruth S. Paterson, Ed. Inspirational nonsectarian articles, 650 to 2,000 words. Fillers, to 350 words; verse, to 20 lines. Pays ½¢ to 1½¢ a word for prose, 14¢ a line for verse, on acceptance.

DECISION—Billy Graham Evangelistic Association, 1300 Harmon Pl., Minneapolis, MN 55403. Roger C. Palms, Ed. Articles, Christian testimonials, 1,800 to 2,000 words. Poems, 4 to 20 lines, preferably free verse; narratives, 100 to 1,000 words. Pays varying rates, on publication.

THE DISCIPLE—Box 179, St. Louis, MO 63166. James L. Merrell, Ed. Disciples of Christ. Articles on Christian living; devotionals, 150 words. Poetry; short humor. Pays $10 to $25 for articles, $2 to $10 for poetry, on publication.

DISCOVERIES—6401 The Paseo, Kansas City, MO 64131. Middler Editor. Fiction for children, grades 3 to 6, 800 to 1,000 words, defining Christian experiences and demonstrating Christian values and beliefs. Pays 3½¢ a word for first rights, 2¢ a word for second rights, on acceptance. Query.

ENGAGE/SOCIAL ACTION MAGAZINE—100 Maryland Ave. N.E., Washington, DC 20002. Lee Ranck, Ed. Articles, 1,500 to 2,000 words, on social issues, for church-oriented audience. Pays $75 to $100, on publication.

THE EPISCOPALIAN—1201 Chestnut St., Philadelphia, PA 19107. Judy Foley, Man. Ed. Articles to 2,000 words, that show Episcopalians solving problems; action stories; profiles. Pays $25 to $100, on publication.

THE EVANGEL—901 College Ave., Winona Lake, IN 46590. Vera Bethel, Ed. Free Methodist. Personal–experience articles, 1,000 words. Short, devotional items, 300 to 500 words. Fiction, 1,200 words, on Christian solutions to problems. Serious poetry, 8 to 12 lines. Pays $25 for articles, $35 to $40 for fiction, $5 for poetry, on publication. Return postage required.

EVANGELICAL BEACON—1515 E. 66th St., Minneapolis, MN 55423. George Keck, Ed. Evangelical Free Church. Articles, 250 to 1,750 words, on religious topics; testimonials; pieces on current issues from an evangelical perspective; short inspirational and evangelistic devotionals. Pays 3¢ to 4¢ a word, on publication. Send SASE for writers' guidelines.

THE FUNDAMENTALIST JOURNAL—Langehorn Plaza, Lynchburg, VA 24514. Deborah Huff, Ed. Articles, 800 to 2,500 words, that examine matters of contemporary interest to all Fundamentalists: news articles, profiles, human-interest pieces; moral and religious issues; Bible stories. Pays 10¢ a word, on publication.

GLORY SONGS—See *The Church Musician.*

GOOD NEWS BROADCASTER—See *Confident Living.*

GUIDE—Review and Herald Publishing Co., 55 W. Oak Ridge Dr., Hagerstown, MD 21740. Stories and articles, 1,000 to 2,000 words, for Christian youth, ages 10 to 14. Pays 3¢ to 4¢ a word, on acceptance.

GUIDEPOSTS—747 Third Ave., New York, NY 10017. True first-person stories, 250 to 1,500 words, stressing how faith in God helps people cope with life. Anecdotal fillers, to 250 words. Pays $100 to $400, $10 to $25 for fillers, on acceptance.

HIS MAGAZINE—P.O. Box 1450, Downers Grove, IL 60515. Verne Becker, Ed. First-person stories, to 2,000 words, on Christian living in college, for a student audience. Pays 2¢ to 5¢ a word, on acceptance.

HOME LIFE—127 Ninth Ave. N., Nashville, TN 37234. Reuben Herring, Ed. Southern Baptist. Articles, preferably personal-experience, and fiction, to 2,000 words, on Christian marriage, parenthood, and family relationships. Human-interest pieces, 200 to 500 words; cartoons and short verse. Pays to 5¢ a word, on acceptance.

INSIDE—226 S. 16th St., Philadelphia, PA 19102. Jane Biberman, Ed. Articles, 1,500 to 3,000 words, and fiction, 2,000 to 3,000 words, of interest to Jewish men and women. Pays $100 to $500, on acceptance. Query.

INSIGHT—55 West Oak Ridge Dr., Hagerstown, MD 21740. Christopher Blake, Ed. Seventh-day Adventist. Personal-experience narratives, articles and humor, to 1,800 words, for high school and college students. Parables; shorts. Pays 10¢ to 15¢ a word, extra for photos, on acceptance. Query.

INTERACTION—1333 S. Kirkwood Rd., St. Louis, MO 63122. Martha S. Jander, Ed. Articles, 1,500 to 2,000 words; how-to pieces, to 2,000 words, for Lutheran Sunday School teachers. Pays $5 to $35, on publication. Limited freelance market.

KEY TO CHRISTIAN EDUCATION—8121 Hamilton Ave., Cincinnati, OH 45231. Virginia Beddow, Ed. Articles, on teaching methods, and success stories, for workers in Christian education. Pays varying rates, on acceptance.

LIBERTY MAGAZINE—6840 Eastern Ave. N.W., Washington, DC 20012. Roland R. Hegstad, Ed. Timely articles, to 2,500 words, and photo essays, on religious freedom and church-state relations. Pays 6¢ to 8¢ a word, on acceptance. Query.

LIGHT AND LIFE—901 College Ave., Winona Lake, IN 46590. Dave Disch, Ed. Ass't. Fresh, lively articles about practical Christian living, and sound treatments of vital issues facing the Evangelical in contemporary society. Pays 4¢ a word, on publication. Query.

LIGUORIAN—Liguori, MO 63057. Rev. Norman J. Muckerman, Ed. Francine O'Connor, Man. Ed. Catholic. Articles and short stories, 1,500 to 2,000 words, on Christian values in modern life. Pays 10¢ to 12¢ a word, on acceptance. Buys all rights.

LIVE—1445 Boonville Ave., Springfield, MO 65802. Kenneth D. Barney, Adult Ed. Sunday school paper for adults. Fiction, 1,500 to 2,000 words, and articles, 1,000 to 1,500 words, on applying Bible principles to everyday living. Pays 2¢ to 3¢ a word, on acceptance. Send SASE for guidelines first.

THE LIVING LIGHT—United States Catholic Conference, Dept. of Education, 1312 Massachusetts Ave. N.W., Washington, DC 20005. Berard L. Marthaler, Exec. Ed. Theoretical and practical articles, 1,500 to 4,000 words, on religious education, catechesis and pastoral ministry.

LIVING WITH CHILDREN—127 Ninth Ave. N., Nashville, TN 37234. SuAnne Bottoms, Ed. Articles, 800, 1,450 or 2,000 words, on parent-child relationships, told from a Christian perspective. Pays 5¢ a word, after acceptance.

LIVING WITH PRESCHOOLERS—127 Ninth Ave. N., Nashville, TN 37234. SuAnne Bottoms, Ed. Articles, 800, 1,450 to 2,000 words, and fillers, to 300 words, for Christian families. Pays 5¢ a word, on acceptance.

LIVING WITH TEENAGERS—127 Ninth Ave. N., Nashville, TN 37234. Articles told from a Christian perspective for parents of teenagers; first-person approach preferred. Poetry, 4 to 16 lines. Pays 5¢ a word, on acceptance.

THE LOOKOUT—8121 Hamilton Ave., Cincinnati, OH 45231. Mark A. Taylor, Ed. Articles, 1,000 to 1,500 words, on families and people overcoming problems by applying Christian principles. Inspirational or humorous shorts, 500 to 800 words; fiction. Pays 4¢ to 6¢ a word, on acceptance.

THE LUTHERAN—2900 Queen Ln., Philadelphia, PA 19129. Edgar R. Trexler, Ed. Articles, to 2,000 words, on Christian ideology, personal religious experiences, family life, church and community. Pays $90 to $360, on acceptance. Query.

LUTHERAN STANDARD—426 S. Fifth St., Box 1209, Minneapolis, MN 55440. Lowell G. Almen, Ed. Articles, 500 to 1,000 words, on personal, social, economic and political aspects of church and Christian living; human-interest items; personality profiles. Pays from 10¢ a word, on acceptance.

LUTHERAN WOMEN—2900 Queen Ln., Philadelphia, PA 19129. Terry Schutz, Ed. Articles, preferably with photos, on subjects of interest to Christian women. No recipes, homemaking hints. Fiction, 1,000 to 2,000 words, on personal growth and change. Short poems. Pays to $50 for articles, $35 to $40 for fiction, on publication.

MARRIAGE AND FAMILY LIVING—Division of Abbey Press, St. Meinrad, IN 47577. Kass Dotterweich, Man. Ed. Expert advice, personal–experience articles, 2,000 to 2,500 words, on marriage and family relationships. Family humor, 1,000 to 2,000 words. Pays 7¢ a word, on acceptance.

MATURE LIVING—127 9th Ave. N., Nashville, TN 37234. Jack Gulledge, Ed. General-interest pieces, travel articles, nostalgia and fiction, under 900 words, for Christian senior adults 60 years and older. Also, profiles recognizing a senior adult for an accomplishment or interesting or unusual experience, 25 lines; must include a B/W action photo. Brief, humorous items for "Cracker Barrel." Pays 5¢ a word, $10 for profiles, $5 for "Cracker Barrel," on acceptance. Buys all rights.

MATURE YEARS—201 Eighth Ave. S., Nashville, TN 37203. Daisy D. Warren, Ed. United Methodist. Articles on retirement or related subjects, 1,500 to 2,000 words. Humorous and serious fiction, 1,500 to 1,800 words, for adults. Poetry, to 14 lines. Pays 4¢ a word, 50¢ a line for poetry, on acceptance.

MESSENGER OF THE SACRED HEART—661 Greenwood Ave., Toronto,

Ont., Canada M4J 4B3. Write M. Pujolas. Articles and short stories, about 1,500 words, for American and Canadian Catholics. Pays from 2¢ a word, on acceptance.

MIDSTREAM—515 Park Ave., New York, NY 10022. Joel Carmichael, Ed. Jewish-interest articles and book reviews. Fiction, to 3,000 words, book excerpts, and poetry. Pays 5¢ a word, on publication.

THE MIRACULOUS MEDAL—475 E. Chelten Ave., Philadelphia, PA 19144. Robert P. Cawley, C.M., Edit. Director. Catholic. Fiction, to 2,400 words. Religious verse, to 20 lines. Pays from 2¢ a word for fiction, from 50¢ a line for poetry, on acceptance.

MODERN LITURGY—160 E. Virginia St., #290, San Jose, CA 95112. Ken Guentert, Ed. Creative material for Catholic worship services; religious parables, to 1,000 words; how-to's, essays on worship, 750 to 1,600 words. Plays. Poetry. Pays in copies.

MOMENT—462 Boylston St., Boston, MA 02116. Hester Kaplan, Man. Ed. Sophisticated articles and some fiction, 2,000 to 5,000 words, on Jewish topics. Pays $150 to $400, on publication.

MOMENTUM—National Catholic Educational Assn., Suite 100, 1077 30th St., NW, Washington, DC 20007-3852. Patricia Feistritzer, Ed. Articles, 500 to 1,500 words, on outstanding programs, issues and research in education. Book reviews. Pays 2¢ a word, on publication. Query.

MOODY MONTHLY—820 N. La Salle Dr., Chicago, IL 60610. Mike Umlandt, Man. Ed. Articles, 1,200 to 1,800 words, on the Christian experience in school, the home and the workplace. Pays 5¢ to 10¢ a word, on acceptance. Query.

THE NATIONAL CHRISTIAN REPORTER—See *The United Methodist Reporter.*

NEW ERA—50 E. North Temple, Salt Lake City, UT 84150. Brian Kelly, Ed. Articles, 150 to 3,000 words, and fiction, to 3,000 words, for young Mormons. Poetry; photos. Pays 5¢ to 10¢ a word, 25¢ a line for poetry, on acceptance. Query.

NEW WORLD OUTLOOK—475 Riverside Dr., Rm. 1351, New York, NY 10115. Arthur J. Moore, Ed. Articles, 1,500 to 2,500 words, on Christian missions, religious issues and public affairs. Poetry, to 16 lines. Pays on publication.

OBLATES MAGAZINE—15 S. 59th St., Belleville, IL 62222. Address Jacqueline Lowery Corn. Articles, 500 to 600 words, for middle-age to older Catholics, which inspire, uplift, and motivate through positive Christian values in relation to everyday life. Inspirational poetry, to 16 lines. Pays $75 for articles, $25 for poems, on acceptance. Guidelines.

OPUS ONE AND OPUS TWO—See *The Church Musician.*

OUR FAMILY—Box 249, Dept. E, Battleford, Sask., Canada S0M 0E0. Albert Lalonde, O.M.I., Ed. Articles, 1,000 to 3,000 words, for Catholic family readers, on modern society, family, marriage, current affairs. Fiction, 1,000 to 3,000 words; submissions should be addressed to John Gillese, 10450 144th St., Edmonton, Alb. T5N 2V4, Canada. Humor, verse. Pays 7¢ to 10¢ a word, for articles and fiction, 75¢ to $1 a line for poetry, on acceptance. Send SASE with *international reply coupons* for guidelines.

623

OUR SUNDAY VISITOR—Huntington, IN 46750. Robert Lockwood, Ed. In-depth features, 1,000 to 1,200 words, on the Catholic Church in America today. Pays $150 to $250, on acceptance.

PARISH FAMILY DIGEST—Noll Plaza, Huntington, IN 46750. Louis F. Jacquet, Ed. Articles, 750 to 900 words, fillers, and humor, for Catholic families and parishes. Pays 5¢ a word, on acceptance. Query.

PARTNERSHIP—Christianity Today, Inc., 465 Gunderson Dr., Carol Stream, IL 60188. Ruth Senter, Ed. Articles, 500 to 2,000 words, geared to the needs and interests of women in Christian leadership. Cartoons, humor. Fillers, to 50 words. Pays $50 to $300, on acceptance.

PENTECOSTAL EVANGEL—1445 Boonville Ave., Springfield, MO 65802. Richard Champion, Ed. Assemblies of God. Religious personal-experience and devotional articles, 500 to 1,500 words. Verse, 12 to 30 lines. Pays 3¢ to 4¢ a word, on publication.

THE PRESBYTERIAN SURVEY—341 Ponce de Leon Ave., NE., Atlanta, GA 30365. Vic Jameson, Ed. Articles, to 1,500 words, of interest to members of the Presbyterian Church or ecumenical individuals. Pays to $200, on acceptance. Query.

PRESENT TENSE—165 E. 56th St., New York, NY 10022. Murray Polner, Ed. Serious articles, 2,000 to 3,000 words, with photos, on news concerning Jews throughout the world; first-person encounters and personal-experience pieces. Literary-political reportage. Contemporary themes only. Pays $200 to $300, on publication. Query.

THE PRIEST—200 Noll Plaza, Huntington, IN 46750. Articles, to 2,500 words, in life and ministry of priests, current theological developments, etc., for priests, permanent deacons, and seminarians. Pays $35 to $100, on acceptance.

PURPOSE—616 Walnut Ave., Scottdale, PA 15683-1999. James E. Horsch, Ed. Articles, 350 to 1,200 words, on Christian discipleship themes, with good photos; pieces of history, biography, science, hobbies, from a Christian perspective. Fiction, 1,200 words, on Christian problem solving. Poetry, 3 to 12 lines. Pays to 5¢ a word, to $1 per line for poetry, extra for photos, on acceptance.

QUEEN—26 S. Saxon Ave., Bay Shore, NY 11706. James McMillan, S.M.M., Ed. Publication of Montfort Missionaries. Articles and fiction, 1,000 to 2,000 words, relating to the Virgin Mary. Pays varying rates on acceptance.

THE RECONSTRUCTIONIST—270 W. 89th St., New York, NY 10024. Dr. Jacob Staub, Ed. Articles and fiction, 2,000 to 3,000 words, relating to Judaism. Poetry. Pays $18 to $36, on publication.

ST. ANTHONY MESSENGER—1615 Republic St., Cincinnati, OH 45210. Norman Perry, O.F.M., Ed. Catholic. Articles, 2,500 to 3,500 words, on personalities, major movements, education, family, and social issues. Human-interest pieces. Humor. Fiction. Pays 12¢ a word, on acceptance. Query on nonfiction.

ST. JOSEPH'S MESSENGER—P.O. Box 288, Jersey City, NJ 07303. Sister Ursula Maphet, Ed. Inspirational articles, 500 to 1,000 words, and fiction, 1,000 to 1,500 words. Verse, 4 to 40 lines. Query first.

SCOPE—426 S. Fifth St., Box 1209, Minneapolis, MN 55440. Constance Lovaas, Ed. American Lutheran Church Women. Educational and inspirational articles for women in careers, the home, church, and community. Human-interest pieces, 500 to 1,000 words. Poetry and fillers. Pays moderate rates, on acceptance.

SEEK—8121 Hamilton Ave., Cincinnati, OH 45231. Eileen H. Wilmoth, Ed. Articles and fiction, to 1,200 words, on inspirational and controversial topics and timely religious issues. Christian testimonials. Pays up to 3¢ a word, on acceptance.

SHARING THE VICTORY—8701 Leeds Rd., Kansas City, MO 64129. Skip Stogsdill, Ed. Articles and profiles, to 800 words, for coed Christian athletes and coaches in high school and college. Pays from $35, on publication. Queries required.

SIGNS OF THE TIMES—P.O. Box 7000, Boise, ID 83707. Kenneth J. Holland, Ed. Feature articles on Christians who have performed community services; current issues from a Biblical perspective; health, home, marriage, human-interest pieces; inspirational articles, 500 to 2,000 words. Pays 12¢ to 15¢ a word, on acceptance. Seventh-day Adventists.

SISTERS TODAY—The Liturgical Press, St. John's Abbey, Collegeville, MN 56321. Sister Mary Anthony Wagner, O.S.B., Ed. Articles, 500 to 3,500 words, on Roman Catholic theology, religious issues for women and the Church. Poetry, to 34 lines. Pays $5 per printed page, $10 per poem, on publication. Send articles to Editor at St. Benedict's Convent, St. Joseph, MN 56374. Send poetry to Sister Audrey Synnott, R.S.M., 1437 Blossom Rd., Rochester, NY 14610.

SOCIAL JUSTICE REVIEW—3835 Westminster Pl., St. Louis, MO 63108. Rev. John H. Miller, C.S.C. Ed. Articles, 2,000 to 3,000 words, on social problems in light of Catholic teaching and current scientific studies. Pays 2¢ a word, on publication.

SPIRITUAL LIFE—2131 Lincoln Rd. N.E., Washington, DC 20002-1199. Christopher Latimer, O.C.D., and Steven Payne, O.C.D., Co-editors. Professional religious journal. Religious essays, 3,000 to 5,000 words, on spirituality in contemporary life. Pays from $50, on acceptance. Guidelines.

SPIRITUALITY TODAY—7200 W. Division St., River Forest, IL 60305. Richard Woods, O.P., Ed. Quarterly. Biblical, liturgical, theological, ecumenical, historical, and biographical articles of critical, probing kind, 4,000 words, about the challenges of contemporary Christian life. Pays from 1¢ a word, on publication. Guidelines.

STANDARD—6401 The Paseo, Kansas City, MO 64131. Address Ed. Articles, 300 to 1,500 words: true experiences; poetry to 20 lines; fiction, 800 to 1,700 words, with Christian emphasis but not preachy; fillers, puzzles, cryptograms of Scripture verses or inspiring quotes, cartoons in good taste. Pays 3½¢ a word, on acceptance.

SUNDAY DIGEST—850 N. Grove Ave., Elgin, IL 60120. Articles, to 1,500 words, on Christian faith in contemporary life; inspirational and how-to articles; free-verse poetry. Anecdotes, 500 words. Pays 10¢ a word, on acceptance.

SUNDAY SCHOOL COUNSELOR—1445 Boonville Ave., Springfield, MO 65802. Sylvia Lee, Ed. Articles, 1,000 to 1,500 words, on teaching and Sunday school people, for local Sunday school teachers. Pays 3¢ to 5¢ a word, on acceptance.

SUNSHINE MAGAZINE—Litchfield, IL 62056. Address Ed. Inspirational articles, to 600 words. Short stories, 1,000 words and juveniles, 400 words. No heavily religious material or "born-again" pieces. Pays varying rates, on acceptance.

TEENS TODAY—Church of the Nazarene, 6401 The Paseo, Kansas City, MO 64131. Karen De Sollar, Ed. Short stories that deal with teens demonstrating Christian principles, 1,200 to 1,500 words. Pays 3¢ a word, on acceptance.

THEOLOGY TODAY—Box 29, Princeton, NJ 08542. Hugh T. Kerr, Ed. Articles, to 3,500 words, or to 1,500 words, on theology, religion and related social issues. Literary criticism. Pays $50 to $100, on publication.

THE UNITED CHURCH OBSERVER—85 St. Clair Ave. E., Toronto, Ont., Canada M4T 1M8. Factual articles, 1,500 to 2,500 words, on religious trends, human problems, social issues. No poetry. Pays after publication. Query.

UNITED EVANGELICAL ACTION—P.O. Box 28, Wheaton, IL 60189. Kevin Piecuch, Man. Ed. National Assn. of Evangelicals. News-oriented expositions and editorials, 750 to 1,000 words, on current events of concern and consequence to the evangelical church. Pays about 7¢ to 10¢ a word, on publication. Query with writing samples required.

THE UNITED METHODIST REPORTER—P.O. Box 660275, Dallas, TX 75266-0275. Spurgeon M. Dunnam III, Ed. John Lovelace, Man. Ed. United Methodist. Religious features, to 500 words. Religious verse, 4 to 12 lines. Photos. Pays 4¢ a word, on acceptance. Send for guidelines. Same address and requirements for *The National Christian Reporter* (interdenominational).

UNITED SYNAGOGUE REVIEW—155 Fifth Ave., New York, NY 10010. Ruth M. Perry, Ed. Articles, 1,000 to 1,200 words, on issues of interest to the conservative Jewish community. Pays after publication. Query.

UNITY MAGAZINE—Unity School of Christianity, Unity Village, MO 64065. Pamela Yearsley, Ed. Inspirational and metaphysical articles, 500 to 2,500 words. Pays 4¢ to 7¢ a word, on acceptance.

VIRTUE—P.O. Box 850, Sisters, OR 97759. Articles for Christian women. Query only, except for pieces for "One Woman's Journal" and "In My Opinion."

VISTA—Box 2000, Marion, IN 46952. Articles and adult fiction, on current Christian concerns and issues. First-person pieces, 750 to 1,500 words. Opinion pieces from an Evangelical perspective, 500 to 750 words. Pays 2¢ to 3¢ a word, on acceptance.

THE YOUNG SALVATIONIST—The Salvation Army, 799 Bloomfield Ave., Verona, NJ 07044. Dorothy Hitzka, Ed. Articles, 1,000 to 1,200 words, teaching the Christian view to everyday living, for teen-agers. Short shorts, first-person testimonies, 600 to 800 words. Pays 3¢ to 5¢ a word, on acceptance. SASE required. Guidelines.

THE YOUNG SOLDIER—The Salvation Army, 799 Bloomfield Ave., Verona, NJ 07044. Dorothy Hitzka, Ed. For children 6 to 12. Must carry a definite Christian message, or teach a Biblical truth. Fiction, 800 to 1,000 words. Some poetry. Fillers, puzzles, etc. Pays 3¢ a word, $3 to $5 for fillers, puzzles, on acceptance. Guidelines.

YOUTHWORKER—1224 Greenfield Dr., El Cajon, CA 92021. Noel Becchetti, Ed. Articles, 2,500 to 3,000 words, for ministers of the Christian church who work with teens. Pays $100, on acceptance. Query.

HEALTH

ACCENT ON LIVING—P.O. Box 700, Bloomington, IL 61702. Raymond C. Cheever, Pub./Ed. Articles, 250 to 1,000 words, about physically disabled people—their careers, recreation and sports, self-help devices, and ideas that can make daily routine easier. Good photos a plus. Pays 10¢ a word, on publication. Query.

AEROBICS & FITNESS—15250 Ventura Blvd., Suite 310, Sherman Oaks, CA 91403. Peg Angsten, Ed. Articles, 500 to 1,500 words, on exercise, health, sports, nutrition, etc. Cartoons. Pays $60 to $120, 30 days after publication.

AMERICAN BABY—575 Lexington Ave., New York, NY 10022. Judith Nolte, Ed. Articles, 1,000 to 2,000 words, for new or expectant parents, on prenatal infant care. Pays varying rates, on acceptance.

AMERICAN HEALTH: FITNESS OF BODY AND MIND—80 Fifth Ave., Suite 302, New York, NY 10011. Address Editorial Dept. Features, 1,000 to 3,000 words, on recent developments in nutrition, exercise, medicine, and psychology. Shorter news items on similar topics: medical advances, consumer health, and life styles. Pays from $125 per manuscript page, on acceptance. Query required.

AMERICAN JOURNAL OF NURSING—555 W. 57th St., New York, NY 10019. Mary B. Mallison, R.N., Ed. Articles, 1,500 to 2,000 words, with photos, on nursing. Query.

BESTWAYS—1501 S. Sutro Terrace, P.O. Box 2028, Carson City, NV 89701. Barbara Bassett, Ed. Articles, 1,500 to 2,000 words, on health, food, life styles, exercise, nutrition. Pays from $75, on publication. Query.

CHILDBIRTH EDUCATOR—575 Lexington Ave., New York, NY 10022. Marsha Rehns, Ed. Articles, 2,000 words, on maternal and fetal health, child-care, child development, and teaching techniques for teachers of childbirth and baby care classes.Pays $450, on acceptance. Query with detailed outline.

DANCE EXERCISE TODAY—4501 Mission Bay Dr., Suite 2F, San Diego, CA 92109. Patricia Ryan, Ed. Practical articles, 1,000 to 3,000 words, on new programs, business tips, nutrition, sports medicine, and dance exercise techniques. Payment negotiable, on acceptance. Query preferred.

DAZZLE—1999 Shepard Rd., St. Paul, MN 55116. Quarterly for dental patients.Interesting, easy-to-read articles emphasizing the importance of proper dental care and preventive dentistry, 800 to 1,200 words. Fillers and humor, 400 to 800 words; must be dental-related, not deragatory. Query preferred. Pays $250 to $500.

EAST WEST JOURNAL—17 Station St., Box 1200, Brookline, MA 02147. Features, 1,500 to 2,500 words, on holistic health, natural foods, the environment, etc. Material for "Body," "Healing," "In the Kitchen," and "Beauty and Fitness." Interviews. Photos. Pays 7¢ to 12¢ a word, extra for photos, on publication.

EXPECTING—685 Third Ave., New York, NY 10017. Evelyn A. Podsiadlo, Ed. Articles, 700 to 1,800 words, for expectant mothers. Pays $150 to $350, on acceptance.

HEALTH—3 Park Ave., New York, NY 10016. Articles, 800 to 2,500 words, on medicine, nutrition, fitness, emotional and psychological well-being. Pays $200 to $1,000, on acceptance. Query.

627

HEALTH PROGRESS—4455 Woodson Rd., St. Louis, MO 63134. Michael F. McCauley, Ed. Journal of the Catholic Health Association. Features, 1,500 to 2,000 words, on hospital management and administration, medical-moral questions, technological developments and their impacts, and financial and human resource management. Pays by arrangement. Query.

HOSPITALS—211 E. Chicago Ave., Chicago, IL 60611. Frank Sabatino, Ed. Articles, 800 to 1,500 words, for hospital administrators, on financing, staffing, coordinating, and providing facilities for health care services. Pays varying rates, on acceptance. Query.

LET'S LIVE—444 N. Larchmont Blvd., Los Angeles, CA 90004. Keith Stepro, Man. Ed. Articles, 1,500 to 1,800 words, on preventive medicine and nutrition, alternative medicine, diet, exercise, recipes, and natural beauty. Pays $150, on publication. Query.

NEW BODY—888 Seventh Ave., New York, NY 10106. Norman Zeitchick, Ed. Well-researched, service oriented articles, 1,000 to 2,000 words, on exercise, nutrition, diet and health for men and women aged 18 to 35. Writers should have some background in or knowledge of the health field. Pays $250 to $500, on publication. Query; no recent report.

NONTOXIC AND NATURAL—Inverness, CA 94937. Debra Lynn Dadd, Ed. Articles, 500 to 2,500 words, on topics related to natural foods and products: allergies, chemical-sensitivity, medicine, organic and natural foods, etc. Pays $25, on publication. Guidelines.

NURSING 87—1111 Bethlehem Pike, Springhouse, PA 19477. Jeanmarie Coogan, Ed. Most articles are clinically oriented, and assigned to nursing experts. No poetry. Pays $25 to $350, on publication. Query.

NURSING HOMES—Centaur & Co., 5 Willowbrook Ct., Potomac, MD 20854. William D. Magnes, Ed.-in-Chief. Articles, 1,000 to 2,500 words, of interest to administrators, managers, and supervisory personnel in nursing homes; human-interest, academic and clinical pieces; book reviews, 250–300 words. Pays $50 for articles, $30 for reviews, on acceptance. Photos, graphics welcome.

NURSING LIFE—1111 Bethlehem Pike, Springhouse, PA 19477. Maryanne Wanger, Ed. Dir. Articles, 12 to 15 double-spaced pages, by nurses, lawyers, management consultants, psychologists, with practical advice for staff nurses. Pays negotiable rates, on publication. Query.

NURSINGWORLD JOURNAL—470 Boston Post Rd., Weston, MA 02193. Eileen Devito, Man. Ed. Articles, 500 to 1,500 words, for and by nurses and nurse-educators, on aspects of current nursing issues. Pays from 25¢ per column inch, on publication.

PATIENT CARE—16 Thorndal Circle, Darien, CT 06820. Clayton Raker Hasser, Ed. Articles on medical care, for physicians. Pays varying rates, on publication. Query; all articles assigned.

THE PHYSICIAN AND SPORTSMEDICINE—4530 W. 77th St., Minneapolis, MN 55435. Cindy Christian Rogers, Features Ed. News and feature articles, 500 to 3,000 words, on fitness, sport, and exercise. Medical angle necessary. Pays $150 to $900, on acceptance. Guidelines.

A POSITIVE APPROACH—P.O. Box 2179, S. Vineland, NJ 03860. Patricia M. Johnson, Ed. Articles, 500 to 1,000 words, on all aspects of the "positive thinking disabled/handicapped person's private and business life." Query with clips preferred. Pays 10¢ a word, extra for b&w photos, on publication.

RECOVERY—P.O. Box 31329, Seattle, WA 98103. Neil Scott, Ed. Articles, to 1,500 words, for recovering alcoholics, on how to meet the challenge of sobriety. First-person recovery stories, with helpful how-to's for others, 500 to 1,000 words. Send SASE for complete guidelines.

RN MAGAZINE—Oradell, NJ 07649. Articles, to 2,000 words, preferably by R.N.s, on nursing, clinical care, etc. Pays 10¢ to 15¢ a word, on acceptance. Query.

RX BEING WELL—800 Second Ave., New York, NY 10017. Mark Deitch, Ed. Articles, 500 to 2,000 words, providing authoritative information on prevention, fitness, nutrition, and current medical topics. No personal-experience pieces. Most articles co-authored by doctors. Pays $250 to $750, a few weeks after acceptance. Query with SASE.

RX HOME CARE—P.O. Box 2178, Santa Monica, CA 90406-2178. Dana Bigman, Ed. Articles, 1,500 to 2,000 words, on marketing aspects of home health care and rehabilitation equipment. Pays 10¢ a word, on acceptance. Query first.

SOUTH FLORIDA MEDICAL REVIEW—100 N.E. 7th St., Miami, FL 33132. News and features, 500 to 1,500 words, for doctors and health care administrators in Dade, Broward, and Palm Beach counties. Pays on publication. Query.

VEGETARIAN TIMES—P.O. Box 570, Oak Park, IL 60603. Paul Obis, Ed. Articles, 750 to 3,000 words, on nutrition, exercise and fitness, meatless food, etc. Personal experience and historial pieces, profiles. Pays $25 to $300, on publication.

VIBRANT LIFE—55 W. Oak Ridge Dr., Hagerstown, MD 21740. Features, 1,000 to 2,800 words, on total health: physical, mental, and spiritual. No disease-related articles or manuscripts geared to people over 50. Seeks upbeat articles on how to live happier and healthier lives; Christian slant. Pays $100 to $400, on acceptance.

VIM & VIGOR—2040 W. Bethany Home Rd., Suite 105, Phoenix, AZ 85015. Leo Calderella, Man. Ed. Positive articles, with accurate medical facts, on health and fitness, 1,200 words. Pays $250 to $300, on publication.

YOU AND YOUR HEALTH—Box AP, Los Altos, CA 94022. Janet Goodman, Ed. Articles, 200 to 1,000 words, on health care news and information. Pays $100 to $300, on publication.

YOUR HEALTH—1720 Washington Blvd., Box 10010, Ogden, UT 84409. Frank J. Cook, Ed. Articles, 1,200 words, on individual health care needs: prevention, treatment, fitness, nutrition, etc. Photos required. Pays 15¢ a word, after acceptance. Guidelines.

EDUCATION

AMERICAN EDUCATION—U.S. Dept. of Education, 400 Maryland Ave. S.W., Washington, DC 20202. Beverly P. Blondell, Ed. Articles, 2,000 to 3,000 words, on government policy, opinion, key issues, education programs or activities for all ages.

AMERICAN SCHOOL & UNIVERSITY—401 N. Broad St., Philadelphia, PA 19108. Dorothy Wright, Ed. Articles and case studies, 1,200 to 1,500 words, on design, construction, operation and management of school and college facilities. Payment varies.

AMERICAN SCHOOL BOARD JOURNAL—1680 Duke St., Alexandria, VA 22314. Bill Anderson, Managing Ed. Articles, 1,000 to 2,000 words, that examine how school districts have developed original solutions to problems shared by districts across the nation. Pay rates vary. Queries are preferred.

CAPSTONE JOURNAL OF EDUCATION—P.O. Box Q, University, AL 35486. Alexia M. Kartis, Asst. Ed. Articles, to 5,000 words, on contemporary ideas in educational research.

CHANGE—4000 Albemarle St. N.W., Suite 500, Washington, DC 20016. Reports, 1,500 to 2,000 words, on programs, people and institutions of higher education. Intellectual essays, 3,000 to 5,000 words, on higher education today. Payment varies.

CLASSROOM COMPUTER LEARNING—Peter Li, Inc., 19 Davis Dr., Belmont, CA 94002. Holly Brady, Ed. Articles, to 3,000 words, for teachers of grades K-12, related to uses of computers in the classroom: human-interest and philosophical articles, how-to pieces, software reviews, and hands-on ideas. Payment varies, on acceptance.

ELECTRONIC EDUCATION—Electronic Communications, 1311 Executive Center Dr., Suite 220, Tallahassee, FL 32301. Cindy Whaley, Man. Ed. Articles, to 1,000 words, for K-12 educators and administrators, on the uses of technology in education. Fillers. Query. Pays $100 to $200, on publication.

THE EXCEPTIONAL PARENT—605 Commonwealth Ave., Boston, MA 02215. Maxwell J. Schleifer, Ed. Articles, 600 to 3,000 words, with practical information for parents of disabled children. Pays on publication.

FOUNDATION NEWS—1828 L St. N.W., Washington, DC 20036. Arlie W. Schardt, Ed. Articles, to 2,000 words, on national or regional activities supported by, or of interest to, grant makers. Pays to $1,000, on acceptance. Query.

HOME EDUCATION MAGAZINE—P.O. Box 1083, Tonasket, WA 98855. Mark J. Hegener, Ed. Positive, informative articles, 1,500 words, for parents who teach their children at home. Fillers, poetry, artwork, photos, etc. Pays $5 per 500 words, after publication.

THE HORN BOOK MAGAZINE—Park Sq. Bldg., 31 St. James Ave., Boston, MA 02116. Anita Silvey, Ed. Articles, 600 to 2,800 words, on books for young readers, and related subjects, for librarians, teachers, parents, etc. Pays $25 per printed page, on publication. Query.

INDUSTRIAL EDUCATION—31600 Telegraph Rd., Suite 200, Birmingham, MI 48010. Kelley Harding, Ed. Educational and instructional articles, 1,000 to 1,500 words, for secondary and post-secondary technical education classes. Photos and drawings. Pays $30, on publication.

INSTRUCTOR—545 Fifth Ave., New York, NY 10017. Leanna Landsmann, Ed. How-to articles on elementary classroom teaching, and computers in the classroom, with practical suggestions and project reports. Pays varying rates, on acceptance.

JOURNAL OF CAREER PLANNING & EMPLOYMENT—62 Highland Ave., Bethlehem, PA 18017. Patricia A. Sinnott, Man. Ed. Articles, 2,000 to 4,000 words, on topics related to college career planning, placement, and recruitment. Pays $200 to $400, on acceptance. Query first with clips. Guidelines available.

KEY TO CHRISTIAN EDUCATION—8121 Hamilton Ave., Cincinnati, OH 45231. Virginia Beddow, Ed. Articles, 600 to 2,000 words, on Christian education; tips for teachers in the local church. Pays varying rates, on acceptance.

LEARNING 87/88—1111 Bethlehem Pike, Springhouse, PA 19477. Maryanne Wagner, Ed. How-to, why-to, and personal experience articles, to 3,000 words, for teachers of grades K-8. Tested classroom ideas for curriculum roundups, to 600 words. Pays to $300, on acceptance. Query.

MEDIA & METHODS—1511 Walnut St., Philadelphia, PA 19102. Michele Sokoloff, Ed. Articles, 1,200 to 1,500 words, on media, technologies, and methods used to enhance instruction and learning in junior and senior high school classrooms. Pays $25 to $75, on publication. Query.

THE MINORITY ENGINEER—44 Broadway, Greenlawn, NY 11740. James Schneider, Ed. Articles, 1,000 to 3,000 words, for college students, on career opportunities in engineering, scientific and technological fields; techniques of job hunting; developments in and applications of new technologies. Interviews. Profiles. Pays 10¢ a word, on publication. Query. Same address and requirements for *The Woman Engineer*.

PHI DELTA KAPPAN—8th and Union St., Box 789, Bloomington, IN 47402. Robert W. Cole, Jr., Ed. Articles, 1,000 to 4,000 words, on educational research, service, and leadership; issues, trends, and policy. Pays from $100, on publication.

SCHOOL ARTS MAGAZINE—50 Portland St., Worcester, MA 01608. David W. Baker, Ed. Articles, 800 to 1,000 words, on art education with special application to the classroom. Photos. Pays varying rates, on publication.

SCHOOL SHOP—Box 8623, Ann Arbor, MI 48107. Alan H. Jones, Exec. Ed. Articles, 1 to 10 double-spaced typed pages, for teachers and administrators in industrial, technical, and vocational educational fields, with particular interest in classroom projects and computer uses. Pays $25 to $100, on publication. Guidelines.

TEACHER UPDATE—P.O. Box 205, Saddle River, NJ 07458. Nick Roes, Ed. Original suggestions for classroom activities. Each page should have a unifying theme, preferably related to specific monthly issue. Pays $20 per published page, on acceptance. Readers are mostly preschool teachers.

TEACHING AND COMPUTERS—Scholastic, Inc., 730 Broadway, New York, NY 10003. Mary Dalheim, Ed. Articles, 300 to 500 words, for computer-using teachers in grades K-8. Payment varies, on acceptance.

TODAY'S CATHOLIC TEACHER—2451 E. River Rd., Suite 200, Dayton, OH 45439. Ruth A. Matheny, Ed. Articles, 600 to 800 words and 1,200 to 1,500 words, on Catholic education, parent-teacher relationships, innovative teaching techniques, etc. Pays $15 to $75, on publication.

WILSON LIBRARY BULLETIN—950 University Ave., Bronx, NY 10452. Milo Nelson, Ed. Articles, 2,500 to 3,000 words, on libraries, communications, and information systems. News, reports, features. Pays from $250, extra for photos, on acceptance.

THE WOMAN ENGINEER—See *The Minority Engineer*.

FARMING AND AGRICULTURE

ACRES USA—10008 E. 60 Terrace, Kansas City, MO 64133. Articles on biological agriculture. Pays 6¢ a word, on publication. Query required.

AMERICAN BEE JOURNAL—51 N. Second St., Hamilton, IL 62341. Joe M. Graham, Ed. Articles on beekeeping, for professionals. Photos. Pays 75¢ per column inch, extra for photos, on publication.

BEEF—1999 Shepard Rd., St. Paul, MN 55116. Paul D. Andre, Ed. Articles on beef cattle feeding, cowherds, stocker operations, and related phases of the cattle industry. Pays to $300, on acceptance.

BUCKEYE FARM NEWS—Ohio Farm Bureau Federation, 35 E. Chestnut St., Columbus, OH 43216. Keith M. Stimpert, Man. Ed. Articles and humor, to 1,000 words, related to agriculture. Pays on publication. Query.

COUNTRY PEOPLE—5400 S. 60th St., Greendale, WI 53129. Bob Ottum, Man. Ed. Rural/country-related, human-interest features, 300 to 1,000 words, and shorts, one-liners and up, with accent on humor. Pays $25 to $150, on acceptance. Queries preferred.

CRANBERRIES—P.O. Box 249, Cobalt, CT 06414. Bob Taylor, Ed. Articles of interest to cranberry growers, industry processors and agricultural researchers. Pays $15 to $40, extra for photos, on publication. Query.

THE EVENER—P.O. Box 7, 211 W. 6th St., Cedar Falls, IA 50613. Suzanne Seedorff, Man. Ed. How-to and feature articles, 300 to 2,500 words, related to draft horses, mules and oxen. Pays 3¢ to 10¢ a word, $5 to $25 for photos, on acceptance. Queries preferred.

FARM & RANCH LIVING—5400 S. 60th St., Greendale, WI 53129. Bob Ottum, Man. Ed. Articles, 2,000 words, on rural people and situations; nostalgia pieces; profiles of interesting farms and farmers, ranches and ranchers. Poetry. Pays $15 to $400, on acceptance and on publication.

FARM FUTURES—330 E. Kilbourn Ave., Milwaukee, WI 53202. Claudia Waterloo, Ed. Articles, to 1,500 words, on marketing of agricultural commodities, farm business issues, management success stories, and the use of commodity futures and options by agricultural producers. Query with outline.

FARM INDUSTRY NEWS—1999 Shepard Rd., St. Paul, MN 55116. Joe Degnan, Ed. Articles for farmers, on new products, buying, machinery, equipment, chemicals, and seeds. Pays $175 to $400, on acceptance. Query required.

FARM JOURNAL—Washington Sq., Philadelphia, PA 19105. Lane Palmer, Ed. Articles, 500 to 1,500 words, with photos, on the business of farming, for farmers. Pays 20¢ to 50¢ a word, on acceptance. Query.

FARM SUPPLIER—Mt. Morris, IL 61054. M. Sadler, Ed. Articles, 600 to 1,800 words, preferably with color photos, on retail farm trade products: feed, fertilizer, agricultural chemicals, etc. Photos. Pays abou 11¢ to 30¢ a word, on acceptance.

FARMSTEAD MAGAZINE—Box 111, Freedom, ME 04941. Heidi Brugger, Man. Ed. Articles, 500 to 2,500 words, on organic gardening; plant, fruit and vegetable varieties, soil building techniques, insects, cash crops, small-scale livestock, equipment, life styles, food, energy, etc. Must have country perspective. Pays 5¢ a word, on publication. Include SASE. Query preferred.

FLORIDA GROWER & RANCHER—723 E. Colonial Dr., Orlando, FL 32803. Frank H. Abrahamson, Ed. Articles and case histories on farmers, growers and ranchers. Pays on publication. Query; buys little freelance material.

THE FURROW—Deere & Company, John Deere Rd., Moline, IL 61265. George Sollenberger, Exec. Ed. Specialized illustrated articles on farming. Pays to $1,000, on acceptance.

GURNEY'S GARDENING NEWS—Gurney Seed and Nursery Co., 2nd and Capital, Yankton, SC 57079. Pattie Vargas, Ed. Practical articles on specific gardening topics and gardener profiles, 1,000 words. Children's section and "News from Gurney Gardeners." Pays 10¢ a word. Write for themes and guidelines first, then query.

HARROWSMITH—Camden House Publishing Ltd., Camden East, Ont., Canada K0K 1J0. James M. Lawrence, Ed./Pub. Articles, 100 to 5,000 words, on homesteading, husbandry, organic gardening and alternative energy with a Canadian slant. Pays $100 to $1,500 on acceptance. Query.

HARROWSMITH/USA—The Creamery, Ferry Rd., Charlotte, VT 05445. Tom Rawls, Man. Ed. Investigative pieces, 2,000 to 4,000 words, on ecology, energy, health, and the food chain. Short pieces for "Pantry Arts" (culinary arts and food preservation); "Benchmarks" (do-it-yourself projects); "Screed" (opinions); and "Gazette" (news briefs). Pays $500 to $1,500 for features, from $50 to $750 for department pieces, on acceptance. Query required. Send SASE for guidelines.

NORDEN NEWS—601 W. Cornhusker Hwy., Lincoln, NE 68501. Gary Svatos, Ed. Technical articles, 1,200 to 1,500 words, and clinical features, 500 words, on veterinary medicine. Photos. Pays $200 to $250, $100 for shorter pieces, extra for photos, on publication.

THE OHIO FARMER—1350 W. Fifth Ave., Columbus, OH 43212. Andrew L. Stevens, Ed. Articles on farming, rural living, etc., in Ohio. Pays $20 per column, on publication.

PEANUT FARMER—P.O. Box 95075, Raleigh, NC 27625. Sid Reynolds, Ed. Articles, 500 to 1,500 words, on production and management practices in peanut farming. Pays $50 to $350, on publication.

PENNSYLVANIA FARMER—704 Lisburn Rd., Camp Hill, PA 17011. John R. Vogel, Ed. Articles on farmers in PA, NJ, DE, MD, and WV; farm operations and successful management concepts. Pays $1 per column inch, on publication.

SHEEP! MAGAZINE—Box 329, Jefferson, WI 53549. Dave Thompson, Ed. Articles, to 1,500 words, on successful shepherds, woolcrafts, sheep raising and sheep dogs. B/W photos. Pays $2 per column inch, extra for photos, on publication.

SMALL ACREAGE MANAGEMENT—Rt. 1, Box 143, Silex, MO 63377. Kelly Klober, Ed. Articles, 500 to 800 words, on land uses for small farm owners. Pays 1¢ to 3¢ a word, on publication. Query.

SMALL FARMER'S JOURNAL, *featuring Practical Horse-Farming*— HC-81, Box 68, Reedsport, OR 97467. How-to's, humor, practical work horse information, livestock and produce marketing, and articles appropriate to the independent family farm. Pays negotiable rates, on publication. Query first.

SUCCESSFUL FARMING—1716 Locust St., Des Moines, IA 50336. Loren Kruse, Man. Ed. Articles on farm management, production, marketing, and machinery. Pays varying rates, on acceptance.

WALLACES FARMER—#501, 1501 42nd St., W. Des Moines, IA 50265.Monte Sesker, Ed. Features, 600 to 700 words, on farming in Iowa, methods and equipment; interviews with farmers. Pays 4¢ to 5¢ a word, on acceptance. Query.

THE WESTERN PRODUCER—Box 2500, Saskatoon, Saskatchewan, Canada S7K 2C4. Attn. Man. Ed. Articles, to 1,000 words, on agricultural and rural subjects, preferably with a Canadian slant. Photos. Pays from 10¢ a word, $15 for b&w photos and cartoons, on acceptance.

ENVIRONMENT, CONSERVATION, NATURAL HISTORY

ALASKA OUTDOORS—Box 8222, Fairbanks, AK 99708. Christopher Batin, Ed. Articles, 1,400 to 1,800 words, on outdoor recreational opportunities in Alaska. How-to's, fillers, humor, and investigative pieces on natural resource use. Pays $50 to $200, extra for photos, on publication. Query.

AMERICAN FORESTS—1319 18th St., N.W., Washington, DC 20036. Bill Rooney, Ed. Well-documented articles, to 2,000 words, with photos, on recreational, commercial and management uses of forests. Photos. Pays on acceptance.

AMERICAN LAND FORUM—5410 Grosvenor Ln., Bethesda, MD 20814. Sara Ebenreck, Ed. Well-researched articles on land issues, achievements, or leader profiles, 3,500 words; commentaries, 1,000 words. Pays $150 to $500, for articles, $75 for opinion pieces, on acceptance. Query first.

ANIMAL KINGDOM—New York Zoological Society, Bronx, NY 10460. Eugene J. Walter, Jr., Ed.-in-Chief. Articles, 1,000 to 2,500 words, with photos, on natural history, ecology and animal behavior, preferably based on original scientific research. No articles on pets. Pays $250 to $750, on acceptance.

THE ATLANTIC SALMON JOURNAL—1435 St. Alexandre, Suite 1030, Montreal, Quebec, Canada H3A 2G4. Joanne Eidinger, Ed. Material related to Atlantic salmon: Conservation, ecology, travel, politics, biology, etc. How-to's, anecdotes, cuisine. Articles, 1,500 to 3,000 words; short fillers and poetry, 50 to 100 words. Pays $100 to $350, on publication.

ENVIRONMENTAL ACTION—1525 New Hampshire Ave., NW, Washington, DC 20036. News and features, varying lengths, on a broad range of political and/or environmental topics: energy, toxics, self-sufficiency, etc. Book reviews; environmentally-related consumer goods. Pays 7¢ to 10¢ a word, extra for photos, on publication. Query required.

EQUINOX—7 Queen Victoria Rd., Camden East, Ont., Canada K0K 1J0. Frank Edwards, Exec. Ed. Articles, 4,000 to 8,000 words, on popular geography, biology, astronomy, sciences, the arts, industry, and adventure. Department pieces, 300 to 500 words, for "Nexus" (science and medicine) and "Habitat" (man-made and natural environment). Pays $1,000 to $2,000 for features, $100 to $200 for short pieces, on acceptance.

INTERNATIONAL WILDLIFE—See *National Wildlife*.

THE LOOKOUT—Seamen's Church Institute, 50 Broadway, New York, NY 10004. Carlyle Windley, Ed. Factual articles on the sea. Features, 200 to 1,500 words, on the merchant marines, sea oddities, etc. Photos. Pays $25 to $100, on publication.

NATIONAL GEOGRAPHIC—17th and M Sts. N.W., Washington, DC

20036. First-person, general-interest, illustrated articles on science, natural history, exploration, and geographical legions. No unsolicited manuscripts accepted; send 500-word query (with SASE) to Sr. Ass't. Ed. Study back issues and index before submitting. Pays on acceptance.

NATIONAL PARKS MAGAZINE—1015 31st St., NW, Washington, DC 20007. Michele Strutin, Ed. Articles, 1,000 to 2,000 words, on natural history, wildlife, outdoors activities, travel and conservation as they relate to national parks; illustrated features on the natural, historic and cultural resources of the National Park System. Pieces about legislation and other issues and events related to the parks. Pays $75 to $200, on acceptance. Query. Send for guidelines.

NATIONAL WILDLIFE AND INTERNATIONAL WILDLIFE—8925 Leesburg Pike, Vienna, VA 22184. Mark Wexler, Man. Ed., *National Wildlife*. Jon Fisher, Man. Ed., *International Wildlife*. Articles, 1,000 to 2,500 words, on wildlife, conservation, environment; outdoor how-to pieces. Photos. Pays market rates, on acceptance. Query.

NATURAL HISTORY—American Museum of Natural History, Central Park West at 79th St., New York, NY 10024. Alan Ternes, Ed.-in-Chief. Informative articles, to 3,000 words, by experts, on anthropology and natural sciences. Pays $750 for features, on acceptance. Query.

OCEAN REALM—6061 Collins Ave., Suite 19 C, Miami Beach, FL 33140. S. M. George, Ed. Articles, 1,200 to 1,800 words, on scuba diving and ocean science and technology. Department pieces: adventure; technology/medicine; instruction; photography and marine life. Photos. Short items, 100 to 500 words, for "FYI": up-to-date news items of interest to the diving community. Pays $100 per published page, $5 for FYI, on publication. Include SASE.

OCEANS—2001 W. Main St., Stamford, CT 06902. Michael Robbins, Ed. Articles, to 5,000 words, with photos, on marine life, oceanography, marine art, undersea exploration, seaports, conservation, fishing, diving, boating. Pays on acceptance. Query. Guidelines available.

OUTDOOR AMERICA—1701 N. Ft. Myer Dr., Suite 1100, Arlington, VA 22209. Quarterly publication of the Izaak Walton League of America. Articles, 1,500 to 2,000 words, on natural resource conservation issues and outdoor recreation; especially fishing, hunting and camping. Pays from 10¢ a word, for features, on publication. Query Articles Ed., with published clippings.

SIERRA—730 Polk St., San Francisco, CA 94109. James Keogh, Ed. Articles, 1,000 to 2,500 words, on environmental and conservation topics, hiking, backpacking, skiing, rafting, cycling. Book reviews and children's dept. Photos. Pays from $200, extra for photos, on acceptance. Query.

SMITHSONIAN—900 Jefferson Dr., Washington, DC 20560. Marlane A. Liddell, Articles Ed. Articles on history, art, natural history, physical science, etc. Query.

SOUTH CAROLINA WILDLIFE—P.O. Box 167, Columbia, SC 29202. John E. Davis, Ed. Articles, 1,000 to 3,000 words, with regional outdoors focus: conservation, natural history and wildlife, recreation. Profiles, how-to's. Pays on acceptance.

SPORTS AFIELD—250 W. 55th St., New York, NY 10019. Tom Paugh, Ed. Articles, 2,000 words, with quality photos, on hunting, fishing, natural history, personal experiences, new hunting/fishing spots. How-to pieces; humor. Pays top rates, on acceptance.

WASHINGTON WILDLIFE—c/o Washington State Game Dept., 600 N. Capital Way, Olympia, WA 98504. Janet O'Mara, Ed. Articles, 300 to 2,500 words, on fish and wildlife management and related recreational or environmental topics. Fillers, to 150 words. Photos. Pays in copies. Query.

WYOMING WILDLIFE—5400 Bishop Blvd., Cheyenne, WY 82002. Chris Madson, Ed. Articles, varying lengths, on western wildlife, scenerey, wildflowers, and outdoor recreation. Pays on acceptance. Query.

MEDIA AND THE ARTS

AHA! HISPANIC ARTS NEWS—Assoc. of Hispanic Arts, 200 East 87th St., New York, NY 10028. Dolores Prida, Ed. Interviews and book reviews with Hispanic authors, to 500 words. Pays on publication. Query required.

AIRBRUSH ACTION—P.O. Box 73, Lakewood, NJ 08701. Articles, 500 to 3,000 words, on airbrush and art-related topics. Pays $75 to $300, on publication. Query required.

THE AMERICAN ART JOURNAL—40 W. 57th St., 5th Floor, New York, NY 10019. Jane Van N. Turano, Ed. Quarterly. Scholarly articles, 2,000 to 10,000 words, on American art of the 17th through 20th centuries. Photos. Pays $200 to $400, on acceptance.

AMERICAN FILM—3 E. 54th St., New York, NY 10022. Peter Biskind, Ed. Feature articles, 2,500 to 3,000 words, on film and television. Profiles; news items; reports. Columns, 100 to 1,500 words. Photos. Pays from $50 to $1,000. Query preferred.

AMERICAN INDIAN ART MAGAZINE—7314 E. Osborn Dr., Scottsdale, AZ 85251. Roanne P. Goldfein, Man. Ed. Detailed, specific articles, 10 typed pages, on American Indian arts—painting, carving, bead work, basketry, textiles, ceramics, jewelry, etc. Pays varying rates for articles, on publication. Query.

AMERICAN THEATRE—355 Lexington Ave., New York, NY 10017. Jim O'Quinn, Ed. Features, 500 to 4,000 words, on the theatre and theatre-related subjects. Payment negotiable, on publication. Query.

ART GALLERY INTERNATIONAL—P.O. Box 52940, Tulsa, OK 74152. Debra Carter Nelson, Ed. Articles on artists and collecting, 1,000 to 1,500 words. Pays 10¢ a word, or $50 a page, on publication. Query first.

ART NEW ENGLAND—353 Washington St., Brighton, MA 02135. Carla Munsat, Stephanie Adelman, Eds. Features, 1,000 to 1,500 words, for artists, curators, gallery directors, collectors. Reviews and art criticism, 500 words. At least 2 photos must accompany article. Pays $15 for short reviews, $65 for longer pieces, on publication. Query.

ARTSATLANTIC—P.O. Box 848, Charlottetown, P.E.I., Canada C1A 7L9. Joseph Sherman, Ed. Articles, 800 to 2,500 words, on visual, performing and literary arts, crafts in Atlantic Canada. Also, "idea and concept" articles of universal appeal. Pays from 10¢ per word, on publication. Query.

ARTSLINE—2518 Western Ave., Seattle, WA 98121. Alice Copp Smith, Ed. Features, 1,800 to 2,400 words, on theatre, dance, music, and other performing or visual arts in the Northwest or the U.S.; arts-related humor; short pieces, 750 to 1,000 words, pay $75 to $100; longer pieces pay from $200, on acceptance. Query.

BLUEGRASS UNLIMITED—Box 111, Broad Run, VA 22014. Peter V. Kuykendall, Ed. Articles, to 3,500 words, on bluegrass and traditional country music. Photos. Pays 5¢ to 6¢ a word, extra for photos.

BROADCASTER—7 Labatt Ave., Toronto, Ont. Canada M5A 3P2. Colin J. Wright, Ed. Articles, 500 to 2,000 words, on communications business in Canada. Pays from $250, on publication. Query.

CHANNELS OF COMMUNICATIONS—19 West 44th St., New York, NY 10036. Les Brown, Ed.-in-Chief. Articles on developments in telecommunications and their impact on society (law, politics, religion, business, education and the arts). No personality profiles or reviews, unless related specifically to their effect on viewers. Pays on acceptance. Query required.

CLAVIER MAGAZINE—200 Northfield Rd., Northfield, IL 60093. Barbara Kreader, Ed. Practical articles, 2,000 words, for keyboard performers and teachers. Fiction and poetry. Pays $35 to $45 per column inch, on publication.

DANCE MAGAZINE—33 West 60th St., New York, NY 10023. William Como, Ed. Features on dance, personalities, and trends. Photos. Query; limited free-lance market.

DANCE TEACHER NOW—University Mall, Suite 2, 803 Russell Blvd., Davis, CA 95616. Martin A. David, Ed. Articles, 1,500 to 2,500 words, for professional dancers and dance teachers, on practical aspects of a dance teacher's professional life, and political or economic issues related to the dance profession. Profiles on teachers or schools. Must be thoroughly researched. Pays $100 to $300, on acceptance. Photos. Query first.

DARKROOM PHOTOGRAPHY—One Hallidie Plaza, Suite 600, San Francisco, CA 94102. Richard Senti, Ed. Articles on post-camera photographic techniques, 1,000 to 2,500 words, with photos, for all levels of photographers. Pays $100 to $500. Query.

DESIGN GRAPHICS WORLD—Communications Channels, 6255 Barfield Rd., Atlanta, GA 30328. James J. Maivald, Ed. Articles, 1,500 to 2,000 words, on news, trends, and current methods of engineering architecture, computer graphics, reprographics, and related design fields. Pays on publication. Query required.

THE DRAMA REVIEW—School of the Arts, New York Univ., 721 Broadway, New York, NY 10003. Richard Schechner, Ed. Quarterly journal of performance. Essays, interviews, letters, and editorials on all aspects of theatre, drawing from anthropology, performance theory, ethology, psychology, and politics. Pays 2¢ a word, on publication.

DRAMATICS—3368 Central Pkwy., Cincinnati, OH 45225. Don Corathers, Ed. Articles, 1,000 to 3,500 words, on the performing arts: theater, puppetry, dance, mime, one-act plays, etc. Pays $25 to $200, on acceptance.

THE ENGRAVERS JOURNAL—26 Summit St., Box 318, Brighton, MI 48116. Michael J. Davis, Man. Ed. Articles, varying lengths, on topics related to the engraving industry. Pays $60 to $175, on acceptance. Query first.

EXHIBIT—1776 Lake Worth Dr., Lake Worth, FL 33460. Mark Adams, Ed. Articles, to 800 words, with photos, on fine arts, new movements, techniques, profiles of artists. Query.

FILM QUARTERLY—Univ. of California Press, Berkeley, CA 94720. Ernest Callenbach, Ed. Film reviews, historical and critical articles, production projects, to 5,000 words. Pays on publication. Query.

FRETS—20085 Stevens Creek, Cupertino, CA 95014. Phil Hood, Ed. Articles, 750 to 3,000 words, for musicians, on acoustic string instruments, instrument making and repair, music theory and technique. Covers jazz, folk, bluegrass, classical, etc. Profiles of musicians and instruments. Pays $175 to $350, on acceptance. Query.

FUNCTIONAL PHOTOGRAPHY—210 Crossways Park Dr., Woodbury, NY 11797. David A. Silverman, Sr. Ed. Articles on use of photography and other imagemaking processes in science, medicine, research, etc. Photos. Pays varying rates, on publication. Query.

GUITAR PLAYER MAGAZINE—20085 Stevens Creek, Cupertino, CA 95014. Tom Wheeler, Ed. Articles, 1,500 to 5,000 words, on guitarists, guitars, and related subjects. Pays $75 to $300, on acceptance. Buys one-time and reprint rights.

HIGH FIDELITY—825 Seventh Ave., New York, NY 10019. Michael Riggs, Ed. Articles, 2,000 to 3,000 words, on stereo equipment, video equipment, and classical and popular recorded music. Pays on acceptance. Query.

HOME VIEWER MAGAZINE—Home Viewer Publications, 11 N. 2nd St., Philadelphia, PA 19106. Bruce Apar, Ed. Feature articles, reviews, celebrity interviews, commentary on home video-audio and all forms of popular entertainment. Pays to $100 for features, $35 for reviews, on publication. Query.

HORIZON—P.O. Drawer 30, Tuscaloosa, AL 35402. Articles, 1,500 to 3,500 words, on art, film, literature, photography, dance, music, theater, and other cultural happenings. Pays from $300, on publication. Query Senior Editor.

INDUSTRIAL PHOTOGRAPHY—50 W. 23rd St., New York, NY 10010-5292. Lynn Roher, Ed. Articles on techniques and trends in current professional photography; audiovisuals, etc., for industrial photographers and executives. Query.

INTERNATIONAL MUSICIAN—Suite 600, Paramount Bldg., 1501 Broadway, New York, NY 10036. Kelly L. Castleberry II, Ed. Articles, 1,500 to 2,000 words, for professional musicians. Pays varying rates, on acceptance. Query.

JAZZIZ—P.O. Box 8309, Gainesville, FL 32605. Michael Fagien, Editor-in-Chief. Feature articles on jazz, musicians, instruments, recordings and education, 1 to 8 double-spaced typed pages. Record, CD, video, cassette reviews, to 2 pages. Pays varying rates, on acceptance. Query.

KEYBOARD MAGAZINE—20085 Stevens Creek, Cupertino, CA 95014. Dominic Milano, Ed. Articles, 1,000 to 5,000 words, on keyboard instruments and players. Photos. Pays $125 to $500, on acceptance. Query.

MEDIA HISTORY DIGEST—c/o Editor & Publisher, 11 W. 19th St., New York, NY 10011. Hiley H. Ward, Ed. Articles, 1,500 to 2,000 words on the history of media for wide consumer interest. Puzzles and humor related to media history. Pays varying rates, on publication. Query.

MODERN DRUMMER—870 Pompton Ave., Cedar Grove, NJ 07009. Ronald L. Spagnardi, Ed. Articles, 500 to 2,000 words, on drumming; how-to's, interviews. Pays $50 to $500, on publication.

MODERN PERCUSSIONIST—870 Pompton Ave., Cedar Grove, NJ 07009. Rick Mattingly, Ed. Interviews, 4,000 to 5,000 words, with professional percussionists in all areas of music, for professional musicians. Pays $150 to $350, on publication. Query required.

MUSIC MAGAZINE—56 The Esplanade, Suite 202, Toronto, Ont., Canada M5E, 1A7. Articles, with photos, on musicians, conductors, and composers, for all classical music buffs. Pays $150 to $800, on publication. Query required.

MUSICAL AMERICA—825 Seventh Ave., New York, NY 10019. Shirley Fleming, Ed. Authoritative articles, 1,000 to 1,500 words, on classical music subjects. Pays around 15¢ a word, on acceptance.

NEW ENGLAND ENTERTAINMENT—P.O. Box 735, Marshfield, MA 02050. Paul J. Reale, Ed. News features and reviews on arts and entertainment in New England. Light verse. Pays $10 to $25, $1 to $2 for verse, on publication.

OPERA NEWS—The Metropolitan Opera Guild, 1865 Broadway, New York, NY 10023. Robert Jacobson, Ed. Articles, 600 to 2,500 words, on all aspects of opera. Pays 13¢ a word for articles, on publication. Query.

PERFORMANCE—1020 Currie St., Fort Worth, TX 76107. Don Waitt, Pub./Ed.-in-Chief. Reports on the touring industry: Concert promoters, booking agents, concert venues and clubs, as well as support services, such as lighting, sound and staging companies. Pays 35¢ per column line, on publication.

PETERSEN'S PHOTOGRAPHIC—8490 Sunset Blvd., Los Angeles, CA 90069. Bill Hurter, Ed. Articles and how-to pieces, with photos, on still, video, studio and darkroom photography, for beginners and advanced amateurs. Pays $60 per printed page, on publication.

PHOTOMETHODS—One Park Ave., New York, NY 10016. Lief Ericksenn, Ed. Articles, 1,500 to 3,000 words, on innovative techniques in imaging (still, film, video), working situations, and management. Pays from $75, on publication. Query.

PLAYBILL—71 Vanderbilt Ave., New York, NY 10169. Joan Alleman, Ed.-in-Chief. Sophisticated articles, 800 to 2,000 words, with photos, on theater and subjects of interest to theater-goers. Pays $100 to $500, on publication.

POPULAR PHOTOGRAPHY MAGAZINE—One Park Ave., New York, NY 10016. Sean Callahan, Ed. How-to articles, 500 to 2,000 words, for amateur and professional photographers. Query first with outline and photos.

PREVUE—P.O. Box 974, Reading, PA 19603. J. Steranko, Ed. Lively articles on films and filmmakers; entertainment features and celebrity interviews, 4 to 25 pages. Pays varying rates, on acceptance. Query with clips.

ROLLING STONE—745 Fifth Ave., New York, NY 10151. Articles on American culture, art, and politics. Query required. Rarely buys free-lance material.

SHOW-BOOK WEEK—*Chicago Sun-Times,* 401 N. Wabash Ave., Chicago, IL 60611. Henry Kisor, Ed. Articles, profiles and interviews, to 1,000 words, relating to fine arts or lively arts. Pays $75 to $100, on publication. Query.

SOAP OPERA DIGEST—254 W. 31st St., New York, NY 10001. Lynn Davey, Man. Ed. Features, to 1,500 words, for people interested in daytime and nighttime soaps. Pays from $200, on acceptance. Query.

SUN TRACKS—Box 2510, Phoenix, AZ 85002. Andy Van De Voorde, Music Ed. Music section of *New Times.* Long and short features, record reviews and interviews. Pays $15 to $150, on publication. Query.

TECHNICAL PHOTOGRAPHY—210 Crossways Park Drive, Woodbury, NY 11797. David A. Silverman, Sr. Ed. Features, 8 to 10 double-spaced pages, on applications and techniques of imaging for staff image producers. Some material on audio-visuals, film, and video. Pays varying rates, on publication. Query.

THEATRE CRAFTS MAGAZINE—135 Fifth Ave., New York, NY 10010. Patricia MacKay, Ed. Articles, 500 to 2,500 words, for professionals in the business, design, and production of theatre, film, video, and the performing arts. Pays on acceptance. Query.

TV GAME SHOW MAGAZINE—Serafini Publications, 211 E. 51st St., New York, NY 10022. Ken Carlton, Ed. Articles, 3 to 4 double-spaced, typed pages, related to television game shows. Pays $125, on publication. Query required.

VCR, THE HOME VIDEO MONTHLY—Box 385, Prospect, KY 40059. Kevin Nickols, Man. Ed. Articles on TV shows and movies available on video cassette. Pays $50 to $75 per printed page, on publication. Query required.

VIDEO—460 W. 34th St., New York, NY 10001. Doug Garr, Ed.-in-Chief. How-to and service articles on home video equipment and programming. Interviews and human-interest features related to non-broadcast television, from 800 to 2,500 words. Pays varying rates, on acceptance. Query.

VIDEO TIMES—3841 W. Oakton St., Skokie, IL 60076. Laurie Fortman, Ed. Articles, 1,500 to 3,000 words, about movies on videotape; reviews of current releases. Pays 15¢ a word, on acceptance. Query required. Guidelines available.

VIDEOGRAPHY—50 W. 23rd St., New York, NY 10010. John Rice, Ed. Articles, 1,000 to 3,000 words, on video production. Pays $50 to $250, on publication. Query required.

WHAT'S NEW—Multicom, Inc., 11 Allen Rd., Boston, MA 02135. Articles and news items, 150 to 3,000 words, with a heavy emphasis on music and entertainment, for readers in late teens to late twenties. Queries are required. Pays $25 to $250, on publication.

HOBBIES, CRAFTS, COLLECTING

AMERICAN CLAY EXCHANGE—P.O. Box 2674, La Mesa, CA 92041. Susan N. Cox, Ed. Articles, from 400 words, for collectors and/or dealers of American-made pottery, with an emphasis on antiques and collectibles. Photos. Pays from $5 for short items, to $100 for thoroughly-researched articles, on acceptance. Buys all rights.

ANTIQUE MONTHLY—P.O. Drawer 2, Tuscaloosa, AL 35402. Articles, 750 to 1,200 words, on the exhibition and sales (auctions, antique shops, etc.) of decorative arts and antiques more than 100 years old, with photos or slides. Pays $125, on publication. Query.

THE ANTIQUE TRADER WEEKLY—Box 1050, Dubuque, IA 52001. Kyle D. Husfloen, Ed. Articles, 1,000 to 2,000 words, on all types of antiques and collectors' items. Photos. Pays from $5 to $150, extra for photos, on publication. Query preferred. Buys all rights.

ANTIQUE WEEK—P.O. Box 90, Knightstown, IN 46148. Tom Hoepf, Ed. Articles, 500 to 1,000 words, on collectors' items; background on antiques, restorations, antique shops, genealogy. Auction and show reports. Photos. Pays from 50¢ an inch, $25 to $50 for in-depth articles, on publication. Query.

ANTIQUES DEALER—1115 Clifton Ave., Clifton, NJ 07013. Nancy Adams, Ed. Articles, 500 to 2,000 words, on trends, pricing, retailing hints, for antiques trade. Pays $75 to $135; b&w photos. Query.

AOPA PILOT—421 Aviation Way, Frederick, MD 21701. Magazine of the Aircraft Owners and Pilots Assn. Edward G. Tripp, Ed. Articles, to 2,500 words, with photos, on general aviation for beginning and experienced pilots. Pays to $750.

THE AUTOGRAPH COLLECTOR'S MAGAZINE—P.O. Box 55328, Stockton, CA 95205. Joe Kraus, Ed. Articles on all aspects of autograph collecting: special collections, personalities, preservation, etc., 100 to 1,500 words. Pays 5¢ a word, extra for b&w photos, on publication. Query preferred.

BIRD WATCHER'S DIGEST—P.O. Box 110, Marietta, OH 45740. Mary B. Bowers, Ed. Articles, 600 to 3,000 words, on bird-watching experiences and expeditions; information about rare sightings; updates on endangered species. Pays to $50, on publication.

THE BLADE MAGAZINE—P.O. Box 22007, Chattanooga, TN 37422. J. Bruce Voyles, Ed. Articles, 500 to 3,000 words: Historical pieces on knives and old knife factories, etc; interviews with knifemakers; how-to pieces. Pays from 5¢ a word, on publication.

CHESS LIFE—186 Route 9W, New Windsor, NY 12550. Larry Parr, Ed. Articles, 500 to 3,000 words, for members of the U.S. Chess Federation, on news, profiles, technical aspects of chess. Features on all aspects of chess— history, humor, puzzles, etc. Fiction, 500 to 2,000 words, related to chess. Photos. Pays varying rates, on acceptance. Query; limited freelance market.

COLLECTOR EDITIONS QUARTERLY—170 Fifth Ave., New York, NY 10010. Krystyna Poray Goddu, Man. Ed. Articles, 750 to 1,500 words, on collectibles: glass, porcelain, *objets d'art,* modern Americana, etc. Pays $150 to $350, within 30 days of acceptance. Query.

COUNTRY NEEDLECRAFT—Rt. 1, Box 414, Fountaintown, IN 46130. Denise Lohr-Stuckey, Ed. How-to and instructional needlework, crochet, cross stitch, traditional rug hooking and related folk art projects; interviews. Photos. Pays on publication.

CRAFTS 'N THINGS—14 Main St., Dept. W, Park Ridge, IL 60068. Nancy Tosh, Ed. How-to articles on all kinds of crafts projects, with instructions. Pays $35 to $200, on publication. Send manuscript with instructions and photograph of the finished item.

CREATIVE OHIO—Ohio Arts and Crafts Guild, 9 N. Main St., Mt. Vernon, OH 43050. Suzanne Cochran, Ed. Articles, 800 to 1,500 words, on business how-to's for the individual Ohio artist/craftsman. Pays 5¢ a word, on publication.

DOLLS, THE COLLECTOR'S MAGAZINE—170 Fifth Ave., New York, NY 10010. Krystyna Poray Goddu, Ed. Articles, 500 to 2,500 words, for knowledgeable doll collectors: sharply focused with a strong collecting angle, with concrete information: value, identification, dollmaking, restoration, etc. Pays $100 to $350, after acceptance. Query.

FINESCALE MODELER—1027 N. Seventh St., Milwaukee, WI 53233. How-to articles for people who make nonoperating scale models of aircraft, automobiles, boats, figures. Photos and drawings should accompany articles.

One-page model-building hints and tips. Pays from $30 per published page, on acceptance. Query preferred.

GAMBLING TIMES—1018 N. Cole Ave., Hollywood, CA 90038. Len Miller, Ed. Gambling-related articles, 1,000 to 6,000 words. Pays $100 to $150, on publication.

GAMES—1350 Ave. of the Americas, New York, NY 10019. Articles on games and puzzles. Quizzes, tests, brainteasers, etc. Photos. Pays varying rates, on acceptance.

GLASS CRAFT NEWS—See *Professional Stained Glass.*

GLASS STUDIO—Publication Development, Box 23383, Portland, OR 97223. Pay Jossy, Assoc. Ed. Feature articles, 1,500 to 2,500 words, for professional glass artists. Profiles, techniques, business tips, etc. pays $50 to $300 on publication. Query with SASE.

HANDS-ON ELECTRONICS—500-B Bi County Blvd., Farmingdale, NY 11735. Julian S. Martin, Ed. Features, 1,500 to 2,500 words, for the electronics activist. Pays from $250, on acceptance. Query.

HARRIS PUBLICATIONS—% Camille Pomaco, Ed., P.O. Box 1173, Inverness, FL 32651-1173. How-to and other feature articles on trends or activities in the needlework field, from 750 words, for quilting, crochet, and other needlework, with photos. Needlecraft designs, with instructions, and sample. Pays 6¢ a word, on publication. Query. Guidelines available.

THE HOME SHOP MACHINIST—2779 Aero Park Dr., Box 1810, Traverse City, MI 49685. Joe D. Rice, Ed. How-to articles, on precision metalworking and foundry work. Accuracy and attention to detail a must. Pays $40 per published page, extra for photos and illustrations, on publication. Send SASE for writer's guidelines.

HOMEBUILT AIRCRAFT—16200 Ventura Blvd., Suite 201, Encino, CA 91436. Steven Werner, Ed. Articles, to 2,500 words, on building and flying your own plane: pilot reports on specific aircraft; new designs in airplanes and airplane parts; news features; air show coverage; pilot experiences and proficiency. Photos. Pays $150 to $300.

JOEL SATER'S ANTIQUES & AUCTION NEWS—P.O. Box 500, Mount Joy, PA 17552. Weekly newspaper. Factual articles, 600 to 1,500 words, on antiques and collecting. Photos. Pays $12.50 to $15, on publication.

THE LEATHER CRAFTSMAN—Box 1386, Fort Worth, TX 76101. Nancy Sawyer, Prod./Cir. Man. Articles on leather crafters, helpful hints and projects of varying difficulty for readers. Pays $50 to $200, on publication.

LOOSE CHANGE—Mead Pub. Corp., 21176 S. Alameda St., Long Beach, CA 90810. Sue Boyce, Ed. Cover articles, 3,500 to 12,000 words, for collectors of antique gaming machines, slot machines, gambling as a hobby, etc. Shorter articles, 900 to 5,000 words, on related subjects. Pays $5 to $50, extra for photos, on acceptance. Buys all rights.

MINIATURE COLLECTOR—170 Fifth Ave., New York, NY 10010. Louise Fecher, Ed. Articles, 800 to 1,200 words, with photos, on outstanding miniatures and the people who make and collect them. Original, illustrated how-to projects for making miniatures. Pays varying rates, after acceptance. Query with photos.

MODEL RAILROADER—1027 N. Seventh St., Milwaukee, WI 53233.

Russ Larson, Ed. Articles, with photos of layout and equipment, on model railroads. Pays $66 per printed page, on acceptance. Query.

NEW SHELTER—See *Practical Homeowner.*

THE NEW YORK ANTIQUE ALMANAC—Box 335, Lawrence, NY 11559. Carol Nadel, Ed. Articles on antiques, shows, shops, museums, art, investments, collectibles, collecting suggestions, related humor. Photos. Pays $5 to $75, extra for photos, on publication.

NOSTALGIA WORLD—Box 231, North Haven, CT 06473. Bonnie Roth, Ed. Articles, 500 to 3,000 words, on collectibles. Pays $10 to $50, on publication.

NUTSHELL NEWS—Clifton House, Clifton, VA 22024. Bonnie Schroeder, Ed. Articles, 1,200 to 1,500 words, for miniature enthusiasts, collectors, craftspeople and hobbyists. Pays 10¢ a word, on publication. Query first.

THE OLD HOUSE JOURNAL—69A Seventh Ave., Brooklyn, NY 11217. Patricia Poore, Editor. Articles, 1,200 to 3,500 words, for do-it-yourself homeowners, on restoration, architecture, and building maintenance. Pays $100 per printed page, on acceptance. Query.

PAPERCUTTING WORLD—12439 Magnolia Blvd., Suite 111, N. Hollywood, CA 91607. Joseph W. Bean, Ed. Articles, 250 to 3,000 words, related to papercutting. Pays 4¢ a word, on publication. Query.

PLATE WORLD—9200 N. Maryland Ave., Niles, IL 60648. Alyson Sulaski Wyckoff, Ed. Articles on artists, collectors, manufacturers, retailers of limited-edition collector's plates. Internationally oriented. Pays varying rates, on acceptance. Query first.

POPULAR MECHANICS—224 W. 57th St., New York, NY 10019. Bill Hartford, Man. Ed. Articles, 300 to 2,000 words, on latest developments in mechanics, industry, science; features on hobbies with a mechanical slant; how-to's on home, shop and craft projects. Photos and sketches. Pays to $1,000, $25 to $100 for short pieces, on acceptance. Buys all rights.

PRACTICAL HOMEOWNER (formerly *New Shelter*)—33 E. Minor St., Emmaus, PA 18049. Do-it-yourself articles for suburban homeowners, 1,000 to 3,000 words, with photos, on innovative housing, alternative energy, water and resource conservation. Pays from 25¢ a word, extra for photos, on acceptance. Query preferred, with photos.

THE PROFESSIONAL QUILTER—Oliver Press, Box 4096, St. Paul, MN 55104. Jeannine M. Spears, Ed. Articles, 500 to 1,500 words, for women in small businesses related to the quilting field: business and marketing skills, personality profiles. Graphics, if applicable; no "how-to" quilt articles. Pays $25 to $75, on publication.

PROFESSIONAL STAINED GLASS (formerly *Glass Craft News*)—270 Lafayette St., Rm. 701, New York, NY 10012. Albert Lewis, Ed. Practical articles of interest to stained glass professionals. No historical articles. Pays $100 to $200, on publication. Query required.

THE QUALITY CRAFTS MARKET—15 West 44th St., New York, NY 10036. Marvin David, Editor. Articles for professional craftspeople, on business topics. Short, 220 words, pieces on needs of quality craft shops and galleries. Pays 10¢ a word, on publication. Query.

RAILROAD MODEL CRAFTSMAN—P.O. Box 700, Newton, NJ 07860.

William C. Schaumburg, Man. Ed. How-to articles on scale model railroading; cars, operation, scenery, etc. Pays on publication.

R/C MODELER MAGAZINE—P.O. Box 487, Sierra Madre, CA 91024. Patricia E. Crews, Ed. Technical and semi-technical how-to articles on radio-controlled model aircraft, boats and cars. Pays $25 to $450, 30 days after publication. Query.

THE ROBB REPORT—1 Acton Pl., Acton, MA 01720. Feature articles on investment opportunities, classic and collectible autos, art and antiques, home interiors, boats, travel, etc. Pays on publication. Query with SASE and published clips. Attn: Mary Frakes.

SCALE WOODCRAFT—P.O. Box 510, Georgetown, CT 06829. Richard C. West, Ed. In-depth, how-to articles, varying lengths, for serious scale woodworkers, carvers, modelers. Profiles. Pays varying rates, on publication. Query first.

SEVEN—Caesars World, Inc., 1801 Century Park E, Suite 2600, Los Angeles, CA 90067. Stewart Weiner, Ed. Resort-oriented, gaming articles, to 2,500 words. Pays $500 to $1,000, on acceptance. Query required.

73 AMATEUR RADIO—WGE Center, Peterborough, NH 03458. Perry Donham, Ed. Articles, 1,500 to 3,000 words, for electronics hobbyists and amateur radio operators. Pays $60 per printed page, on acceptance.

SEW NEWS—P.O. Box 1790, News Plaza, Peoria, IL 61656. Linda Turner Jones, Ed. Articles that teach a specific technique, inspire a reader to try new projects, or inform a reader about an interesting person, company, or project related to sewing, textiles, or fashion. "Our readers are beginning to advanced home sewers." Main emphasis is on fashion sewing; occasional articles on needlecrafts as related to clothing, sports sewing, and home decorating. Pays from $25 to $400, for articles to 3,000 words, on acceptance. Buys all rights. Query required.

TROPICAL FISH HOBBYIST—211 W. Sylvania Ave., Neptune City, NJ 07753. John R. Quinn, Ed. Articles, 500 to 3,000 words, for beginning and experienced tropical fish enthusiasts. Photos. Pays $35 to $100, on acceptance. Query.

VIDEOMAKER—P.O. Box 3015, Peterborough, NH 03458. Bradley Kent, Man. Ed. Authoritative articles, varying lengths, geared to hobbyist video camera users. Instructionals, innovative applications, tools and tips, industry developments, new products and equipment profiles, and promotion of video literacy. Pays varying rates, on publication. Query.

WESTART—Box 6868, Auburn, CA 95604. Martha Garcia, Ed. Features, 350 to 700 words, on fine arts and crafts. No hobbies. Photos. Pays 50¢ per column inch, on publication. SASE required.

WESTERN & EASTERN TREASURES—P.O. Box 1095, Arcata, CA 95521. Rosemary Anderson, Man. Ed. Illustrated articles, to 1,500 words, on metal detecting, treasure-hunting, rocks, and gems. Pays 2¢ a word, extra for photos, on publication.

THE WINE SPECTATOR—Opera Plaza Suite 2040, 601 Van Ness Ave., San Francisco, CA 94102. Harvey Steiman, Man. Ed. Features, 600 to 1,000 words, preferably with photos, on news and people in the wine world. Pays from $100, extra for photos, on publication. Query required.

WOODENBOAT—P.O. Box 78, Brooklin, ME 04616. Jonathan Wilson, Ed.

644

How-to and technical articles, 4,000 words, on construction, repair and maintenance of wooden boats; design, history and use of wooden boats; and profiles of outstanding wooden boat builders and designers. Pays $6 per column inch. Query preferred.

THE WOODWORKER'S JOURNAL—P.O. Box 1629, 517 Litchfield Rd., New Milford, CT 06776. Thomas G. Begnal, Man. Ed. Original plans for woodworking projects, with detailed written instructions and at least one B/W photo of finished product. Pays $80 to $120, per published page, on acceptance.

WORKBENCH—4251 Pennsylvania Ave., Kansas City, MO 64111. Jay Hedden, Ed. Articles on do-it-yourself home improvement and maintenance projects and general woodworking articles for beginning and expert craftsmen. Complete working drawings with accurate dimensions, step-by-step instructions, lists of materials, and photos of the finished product must accompany submission. Features on how to reduce energy consumption. Pays from $125 per published page, on acceptance.

YESTERYEAR—P.O. Box 2, Princeton, WI 54968. Michael Jacobi, Ed. Articles on antiques, collectibles, and nostalgia, for readers in Wisconsin, Illinois, Iowa, Minnesota and surrounding states. Photos. Will consider regular columns on collecting or antiques. Pays from $10, on publication.

ZYMURGY—Box 287, Boulder, CO 80306. Charles N. Papazian, Ed. Articles appealing to beer lovers and homebrewers. Pays $25 to $75, for pieces 750 to 2,000 words, on publication. Query.

POPULAR & TECHNICAL SCIENCE; COMPUTERS

AIR & SPACE—National Air & Space Museum, Washington, DC 20560. George Larson, Ed. General-interest articles, 1,000 to 3,500 words, on aerospace experience, past, present, and future. Pays varying rates on acceptance. Query first.

ANTIC, THE ATARI RESOURCE—524 2nd St., San Francisco, CA 94107. Nat Friedland, Ed. Programs and information for the Atari computer user/owner. Reviews of hardware and software, original programs, etc., 500 words. Game reviews, 400 words. Pays $50 per review, $60 per published page, on publication. Query.

ASTRONOMY—1027 N. Seventh St., Milwaukee, WI 53233. Richard Berry, Ed.-in-Chief. Articles on astronomy, astrophysics, space programs, research. Hobby pieces on equipment; short news items. Pays varying rates, on acceptance.

BIOSCIENCE—American Institute of Biological Science, 730 11th St., NW, Washington, DC 20001. Laura Tangley, Features Ed. Articles, 2 to 4 journal pages, on new developments in biology or science, for professional biologists. Pays $200 per journal page, on publication. Query required.

BYTE MAGAZINE—P.O. Box 372, Hancock, NH 03449. Philip Lemmons, Ed. Features on new technology, how-to articles, and reviews of computers and software, varying lengths, for sophisticated users of personal computers. Payment is competitive. Query.

COMPAQ—3381 Ocean Dr., Vero Beach, FL 32963. Paul Pinella, Man. Ed. Features, technicals, 2,000 to 3,500 words, for COMPAQ users. pays $250 to $700, after acceptance. Query required.

COMPUTE!—P.O. Box 5406, Greensboro, NC 27403. Lawrence Elko, Ed.

Timely articles on applications, tutorials, games and programs that address the needs of the consumer computer user, 500 to 6,000 words. Pays on acceptance.

COMPUTER AND SOFTWARE NEWS—425 Park Ave., New York, NY 10022. Charles J. Humphrey, Ed. Newsweekly for hardware and software retailers, distributors and suppliers. News items. Pays 15¢ per published word, on publication.

COMPUTING NOW!—Moorshead Publications, 1300 Don Mills Rd., Don Mills, Toronto, Ontario, Canada M3B 3M8. Steven Rimmer, Ed. Articles, from 2,000 to 4,000 words, for large audience, from beginners to business users. Pays 10¢ a word, on publication. Query.

DATAMATION—875 Third Ave., New York, NY 10022. Nancy Welles, Features Ed. Articles, varying lengths. Query first. Pays on publication.

DIGITAL REVIEW—800 Boylston St., Ste. 1390, Boston, MA 02199. Jonathan Cohler, Ed.-in-Chief. News stories, closer-look stories, surveys, and in-depth product reviews of DEC (Digital Equipment) computers and DEC-compatible market. Query required. Pays on acceptance. Write for guidelines.

DISCOVER—Time & Life Bldg., Rockefeller Ctr., New York, NY 10020. Frederic Golden, Asst. Managing Ed. "We are looking for well-written, thoughtful pieces that report or comment on some aspect of science of broad national interest. We've found that some of our most successful contributions have come from people who are writing in a field with which they've had professional or other experience because they bring a depth to the subject that all too often is missing from journalistic accounts. We especially favor articles that offer some new insight of perspective; obviously we don't want to repeat what our readers have seen in their daily newspapers and on television. We will read unsolicited manuscripts, but prefer to be queried first. We also like to see samples of past work. We have no particular length requirements, though most of our feature articles run to about 5,000 words. No subjects are taboo, but we do want material in good taste. Rates are negotiable, usually about $1.00 a word."

80 MICRO—Computer World Communications, 80 Pine St., Peterborough, NH 03458. Address Submissions Ed. Technical articles, programs and tutorials for Tandy and TRS-80 microcomputer; no general-interest articles. Pays $50 to $75 per printed page, on acceptance. Query.

ENVIRONMENT—4000 Albemarle St., N.W., Washington, DC 20016. Jane Scully, Ed. Factual articles, 2,500 to 5,000 words, on scientific, technological and environmental policy and decision-making issues. Pays $100 to $300. Query. Articles must be documented.

FOCUS—The Magazine of the North American Data General Users Group. Turnkey Publishing, 5332 Thunder Creek Rd., Austin, TX 78759. Greg Farman, Ed. Articles, 700 to 4,000 words, on Data General computers. Photos a plus. Pays to $100, on publication. Query required.

THE FUTURIST—World Future Society, 4916 Elmo Ave., Bethesda, MD 20814. Timothy Willard, Man. Ed. Features, 1,000 to 5,000 words, on subjects pertaining to the future: environment, education, science, technology, etc. Pays in copies.

GENETIC ENGINEERING NEWS—157 E. 86th St., New York, NY 10028. John Sterling, Man. Ed. Articles on all aspects of biotechnology; feature articles and news articles. Pays varying rates, on acceptance. Query.

GEOBYTE—P.O. Box 797, Tulsa, OK 74101. Ken Milam, Man. Ed. Quarterly publication of the American Association of Petroleum Geologists. Articles, to 20 typed pages, on computer applications in exploration and production of oil, gas, and energy minerals. Pays varying rates, on acceptance. Query first.

HAM RADIO—Greenville, NH 03048. Rich Rosen, Ed. Articles, to 2,500 words, on amateur radio theory and construction. Pays to $40 per printed page, on publication. Query.

HARDCOPY—Box 759, Brea, CA 92621. Dan Reese, Ed. Articles, 2,000 to 3,500 words, for manufacturers, users, and distributors of Digital Equipment Corp. (DEC): how-to pieces on product and system applications. Must have DEC tie-in. Pays $200 to $600, thirty days after acceptance. Query first.

INCIDER—1 Elm St., Peterborough, NH 03458. Articles for Apple II computer users: applications-oriented, state-of-the-art ready to type in program listings, and how-to pieces. Software and hardware reviews. Pays on acceptance. Query preferred.

LASERS & APPLICATIONS—23868 Hawthorne Blvd., Torrance, CA 90505. Tom Farre, Ed. Controlled-circulation publication for the laser electro-optics industry. News articles, 2 to 3 manuscript pages, with significant scientific content. Pays $100 per published page, on publication.

LINK-UP—143 Old Marlton Pike, Medford, NJ 08055. Bev Smith, Ed. Dir. How-to pieces and reviews for small-computer communications enthusiasts, 600 to 2,500 words. Photos are a plus. Pay runs from $80 to $200, on publication.

LOTUS—P.O. Box 9123, Cambridge, MA 01239-9123. Steven E. Miller, Ed. Articles, 1,500 to 2,000 words, on business and professional applications of Lotus software. Query with outline required. Pays varying rates, on acceptance.

MACWORLD—Editorial Proposals, 555 DeHaro St., San Francisco, CA 94107. How-to articles relating to Macintosh personal computers; varying lengths. Query or send outline with screenshots, if applicable. Pays from $300, on acceptance. Send SASE for writer's guidelines.

MICROAGE QUARTERLY—2308 S. 55th St., Tempe, AZ 85282. Linnea Maxwell, Ed. Distributed through MicroAge stores. Articles on technical subjects. Query first. Pays varying rates, on publication.

MINI-MICRO SYSTEMS—275 Washington St., Newton, MA 02158. George Kotelly, Ed. Technical monthly for computer system users, manufacturers, and integrators. How-to pieces, profiles, news items, etc. Pays $35 to $100 per printed page, on publication. Query.

MODERN ELECTRONICS—76 N. Broadway, Hicksville, NY 10081. Art Salsberg, Ed.-in-Chief. How-to features, technical tutorials, and construction projects related to latest consumer electronics circuits and products and personal computer equipment and software. Lengths vary. Query with outline required. Pays to $150, on acceptance.

NIBBLE—45 Winthrop St., Concord, MA 01742. David P. Szetela, Ed. Programs and programming methods, as well as short articles, reviews and general-interest pieces for Apple Computer users. Send short cover letter and sample program runs with manuscript. Pays $50 to $500 for articles, $20 to $250 for shorter pieces. Send SASE for writer's guidelines.

NIBBLE MAC—45 Winthrop St., Concord, MA 01742. David Szetela, Ed.

Articles and programs on programs and programming methods; product reviews, tutorials, and general-interest articles for Macintosh users. Pays $40 to $500, after acceptance. Programs must be submitted on disk. Send for guidelines.

OMNI—1965 Broadway, New York, NY 10023. Patrice Adcroft, Ed. Articles, 1,000 to 3,500 words, on scientific aspects of the future: space colonies, cloning, machine intelligence, ESP, origin of life, future arts, lifestyles, etc. Pays $800 to $3,000, $150 for short items, on acceptance. Query.

PC TECH JOURNAL—10480 Little Patuxent Pkwy., Ste. 800, Parkview, Columbia, MD 21044. Will Fastie, Ed. How-to pieces and reviews, for technically sophisticated computer professionals. Pays $100 to $1,000, on acceptance. Query required.

POPULAR SCIENCE—380 Madison Ave., New York, NY 10017. C. P. Gilmore, Ed. Articles, to 2,000 words, with photos, on developments in applied science and technology. Short illustrated articles on new inventions and products; photo essays, to 4 pages. Pays from $150 per printed page, on acceptance.

PORTABLE 100/200—Camden Communications, Inc., P.O. Box 250, Camden, ME 04843. Park Morrison, Ed. Programs and applications for users of Tandy portable computers, 2,000 to 4,000 words. Product reviews. Pays $100 to $400 for articles, $75 to $200 for reviews, on acceptance. Query.

THE RAINBOW—Falsoft, Inc., 9529 US Highway 42, Prospect, KY 40059. Jutta Kapfhammer, Submissions Ed. Articles and computer programs, for the Tandy Color computer. Pays on publication.

SEA FRONTIERS/SEA SECRETS—3979 Rickenbacker Causeway, Virginia Key, Miami, FL 33149. Jean Bradfisch, Ed. Illustrated articles, 500 to 3,000 words, on scientific advances related to the sea, biological, physical, chemical, or geological phenomena, etc., for lay readers. Send SASE for guidelines. Pays $50 to $300, on acceptance. Query.

SPACE WORLD—National Space Society, West Wing, Suite 203, 600 Maryland Ave., SW, Washington, DC 20024. Lively, non-technical features on all aspects of the international space program. Pays $150 per article, on publication. Query; guidelines available.

TECHNOLOGY REVIEW—Rm. 10-140, Massachusetts Institute of Technology, Cambridge, MA 02139. John Mattill, Ed. General-interest articles, and more technical features, 1,500 to 5,000 words, on technology, the environment and society. Payment varies, on publication. Query.

II COMPUTING—524 Second St., San Francisco, CA 94107. Anita Malnig, Ed. Articles, to 2,000 words, for home users of Apple II computers. Pays to 20¢ a word, on acceptance. Query; guidelines available

ANIMALS

CAT FANCY—P.O. Box 6050, Mission Viejo, CA 92690. Linda Lewis, Ed. Articles, from 1,500 to 3,000 words, on cat care, health, grooming, etc. Pays 5¢ a word, on publication.

CATS—P.O. Box 37, Port Orange, FL 32029. Address Eds. Articles, 1,000 to 2,000 words, with illustrations or photos, on cats: unusual anecdotes, medical pieces, humor, articles on cats in art, literature or science. Pays 5¢ a word, extra for illustrations, on publication. Replies in 8 weeks.

DOG FANCY—P.O. Box 6050, Mission Viejo, CA 92690. Linda Lewis, Ed. Articles, 1,500 to 3,000 words, on dog care, health, grooming, breeds, activities, events, etc. Photos. Pays 5¢ a word, on publication.

THE FLORIDA HORSE—P.O. Box 2106, Ocala, FL 32678. F. J. Audette, Publisher. Articles, 1,500 words, on Florida thoroughbred breeding and racing. Pays $100 to $150, on publication.

THE GREYHOUND REVIEW—National Greyhound Assn., Box 543, Abilene, KS 67410. Tim Horan, Man. Ed. Articles, 1,000 to 10,000 words, pertaining to the greyhound racing industry: how-to, historical nostalgia, interviews. Pays $40 to $150, on publication.

GUN DOG—1901 Bell Ave., Ste. 4, Des Moines, IA 50315. Bob Wilbanks, Man. Ed. Features, 1,000 to 2,500 words, with photos, on bird hunting: how-to's, where-to's, dog training, canine medicine, breeding strategy. Fiction. Humor. Fillers. Pays $50 to $150 for fillers and short articles, $150 to $350 for features, on acceptance.

HORSE & RIDER—Box 555, 41919 Moreno Rd., Temecula, CA 92390. Ray Rich, Ed. Articles, 500 to 3,000 words, with photos, on Western riding and general horse care: training, feeding, grooming, etc. Pays varying rates, before publication. Buys all rights.

HORSE ILLUSTRATED—P.O. Box 6050, Mission Viejo, CA 92690. Jill-Marie Jones, Ed. Articles, 1,500 to 2,500 words, on all aspects of owning and caring for horses. Photos. Pays 3¢ to 5¢ a word, on publication.

HORSEMAN—5314 Bingle Rd., Houston, TX 77092. David Gaines, Ed. Articles, to 2,500 words, with photos, primarily on western horsemanship. Pays from 10¢ a word, extra for photos, on publication.

HORSEMEN'S YANKEE PEDLAR—785 Southbridge St., Auburn, MA 01501. Nancy L. Khoury, Pub. News and feature-length articles, about horses and horsemen in the Northeast. Photos. Pays $2 per published inch, on publication. Query.

HORSEPLAY—Box 545, Gaithersburg, MD 20877. Cordelia Doucet, Ed. Articles, to 3,000 words, on eventing, show jumping, horse shows, dressage, driving and fox hunting, for horse enthusiasts. Pays 9¢ a word, after publication.

THE MORGAN HORSE—Senior Editor, Box 1, Westmoreland, NY 13490. Articles, from 500 to 3,500 words, on equestrian and Morgan topics. Pays from 5¢ a word, $5 to $25 for photos, on publication. Query.

PERFORMANCE HORSEMAN—Gum Tree Corner, Unionville, PA 19375. Miranda Lorraine, Articles Ed. Factual how-to pieces for the serious western rider, on training, improving riding skills, all aspects of care and management, etc. Pays from $300, on acceptance.

PRACTICAL HORSEMAN—Gum Tree Corner, Unionville, PA 19375. Miranda D. Lorraine, Articles Ed. How-to articles on English riding, training, and horse care. Pays on publication. Query.

SPUR MAGAZINE—P.O. Box 85, Middleburg, VA 22117. Address Ed. Dept. Articles, 300 to 5,000 words, on Thoroughbred racing and breeding. Profiles of people and farms. Historical and nostalgia pieces. Pays $50 to $250, on publication. Query.

THE WESTERN HORSEMAN—3850 N. Nevada Ave., Colorado Springs, CO 80933. Randy Witte, Ed. "We're a general-interest horse magazine, but our emphasis is on Western riding and Western lifestyles involving horses. We always have a need for good, in-depth pieces on horse training in which the reader can learn, step by step, how to teach a horse one particular movement or manner; and for equine health care pieces by writers who have either interviewed horse practitioners on specific subjects, or who have themselves knowledgeable, first-hand experience with some phase of horse care. Feature articles generally run 1,500 words; manuscripts should be accompanied by B&W photos or color slides. Pay varies, on acceptance."

CHILD CARE AND DEVELOPMENT

AMERICAN BABY—575 Lexington Ave., New York, NY 10022. Judith Nolte, Ed. Articles, about 2,000 words, for new or expectant parents; pieces on pregnancy and child care. No poetry. Pays on acceptance.

BABY TALK—185 Madison Ave., New York, NY 10016. Patricia Irons, Ed. Articles, 1,500 to 3,000 words, by mother or father, on babies, baby care, etc. Pays varying rates, on acceptance. SASE required.

CHILD—477 Madison Ave., 22nd Fl., New York, NY 10022. Nancy Clark, Features Ed. Articles for parents who want the best for their children, 1,500 to 2,000 words. Pays $500 to $1,000, on acceptance. Queries are preferred.

THE EXCEPTIONAL PARENT—605 Commonwealth Ave., Boston, MA 02215. Maxwell J. Schleifer, Ed. Articles, 600 to 3,000 words, with practical information for parents of disabled children. Pays on publication.

EXPECTING—685 Third Ave., New York, NY 10017. Evelyn A. Podsiadlo, Ed. Articles, 700 to 1,800 words, for expectant mothers. Pays $150 to $350, on acceptance.

GROWING CHILD/GROWING PARENT—22 N. Second St., Lafayette, IN 47902. Nancy Kleckner, Ed. Articles to 1,500 words on subjects of interest to parents of children under 6, with emphasis on the issues, problems, and choices of being a parent. No personal-experience pieces or poetry. Pays 8¢ to 15¢ a word, on acceptance. Query.

LIVING WITH CHILDREN—127 Ninth Ave. N., Nashville, TN 37234. SuAnne Bottoms, Ed. Articles, 800, 1,450 to 2,000 words, on parent-child relationships, told from a Christian perspective. Pays 5¢ a word, after acceptance.

LIVING WITH PRESCHOOLERS—127 Ninth Ave. N., Nashville, TN 37234. SuAnne Bottoms, Ed. Articles, 800, 1,450 or 2,000 words, and fillers, to 300 words, for Christian families. Pays 5¢ a word, on acceptance.

LIVING WITH TEENAGERS—127 Ninth Ave. N., Nashville, TN 37234. Articles, told from a Christian perspective for parents of teenagers; first-person approach preferred. Poetry, 4 to 16 lines. Photos. Pays 5¢ a word, on acceptance.

MARRIAGE & FAMILY LIVING—St. Meinrad, IN 47577. Kass Dotterweich, Man. Ed. Articles, to 2,000 words, on husband-wife and parent-child relationships. Pays 7¢ a word, on acceptance. Query.

NEW YORK FAMILY—420 E. 79th St., New York, NY 10021. Susan Ross, Ed. Articles on parenting in New York City. Pays $50 to $100, on publication.

PARENTS—685 Third Ave., New York, NY 10017. Elizabeth Crow, Ed.-in-

Chief. Articles, 2,000 to 3,000 words, on growth and development of infants, children, teens, family, women's issues, community, current research. Informal style with quotes from experts. Pays from $450, on acceptance. Query.

TODAY'S MARRIAGE—Dell Magazine Group, 245 E. 47th St., New York, NY 10017. Genevieve Landau, Edit. Dir. Articles, 2,000 to 3,000 words, on any aspect of married life, including pregnancy and infant care. Readers are young married women. Pay varies, on acceptance. Query with outline.

WORKING MOTHER—230 Park Ave., New York, NY 10169. Olivia Buehl, Ed. Well-thought-out articles, 1,500 to 2,000 words, for working mothers: child care, home management, the work world, single mothers, etc. Pays around $500, on acceptance. Query, with detailed outline.

WORKING PARENTS—441 Lexington Ave., New York, NY 10017. Janet Spencer King, Ed. Articles, to 1,800 words, on subjects of interest to parents with children to age six. Pay varies, on publication. Query first.

MILITARY

THE AMERICAN LEGION MAGAZINE—Box 1055, Indianapolis, IN 46206. Michael D. LaBonne, Ed. Articles, 750 to 1,800 words, on current world affairs, public policy, and subjects of contemporary interest. Pays $100 to $1,000, on acceptance. Query.

ARMY MAGAZINE—2425 Wilson Blvd., Arlington, VA 22201. L. James Binder, Ed.-in-Chief. Features, to 5,000 words, on military subjects. Essays, humor, history, news reports, first-person anecdotes. Pays 10¢ to 17¢ a word, $10 to $25 for anecdotes, on publication.

INFANTRY—P.O. Box 20005, Fort Benning, GA 31905-0605. Articles, 2,000 to 5,000 words, on military organization, equipment, tactics, foreign armies, etc., for U.S. infantry personnel. Pays varying rates, on publication; no payment made to U.S. Government employees. Query.

LEATHERNECK—Box 1775, Quantico, VA 22134. William V. H. White, Ed. Articles, to 3,000 words, with photos, on U.S. Marines. Pays $50 to $75 per printed page, on acceptance. Query.

LIFE IN THE TIMES—Army Times Publishing Co., Springfield, VA 22159-0200. Barry Robinson, Ed. Articles, to 3,000 words, on current military life. Pays $100 to $350, on acceptance.

MILITARY LIFESTYLE MAGAZINE—1732 Wisconsin Ave., N.W., Washington, DC 20007. Hope Daniels, Ed. Articles, 800 to 2,000 words, for military families in the U.S. and overseas, on lifestyles; pieces on issues of interest to military families; fiction. Pays $75 to $500, on publication. Query.

MILITARY REVIEW—U.S. Army Command and General Staff College, Fort Leavenworth, KS 66027. Frederick W. Timmerman, Ed.-in-Chief. Articles, 2,000 to 3,000 words, on tactics, national defense, military history and any military subject of current interest and importance. Pays $50 to $300, on publication.

NATIONAL GUARD—One Mass. Ave. N.W., Washington, DC 20001. Reid K. Beveridge, Ed. Articles, 2,000 to 4,000 words, with photos, of interest to National Guard members. Pays on publication.

OFF DUTY—3303 Harbor Blvd., Suite C-2, Costa Mesa, CA 92626. Informative, entertaining and useful articles, 900 to 1,800 words, for military service personnel and their dependents, on making the most of off duty time and getting the most out of service life: military living, travel, personal finance, sports, military people, American trends, etc. Military angle essential. Pays 13¢ to 16¢ a word, on publication. European and Pacific editions also. Guidelines available. Query required.

PROCEEDINGS—U.S. Naval Institute, Annapolis, MD 21402. Fred H. Rainbow, Ed. Articles, to 4,000 words, on naval and maritime subjects; article should come to grips with a problem and offer a solution. Opinion pieces, to 1,000 words. Anecdotes. Pays $60 to $150, per published page. Query.

THE RETIRED OFFICER MAGAZINE—201 N. Washington St., Alexandria, VA 22314. Address Manuscript Ed. Articles, 1,000 to 2,500 words, preferably with photos, of interest to military retirees and their families. Current affairs, contemporary military history and humor, and pieces on travel, hobbies, family living, and second-career job opportunities. Pays to $400, extra for photos, on acceptance. Query preferred. Send for writers guidelines.

VFW MAGAZINE—Broadway at 34th, Kansas City, MO 64111. Magazine for Veterans of Foreign Wars and their families. James K. Anderson, Ed. Articles, 1,000 words, on current issues, solutions to everyday problems, personalities, sports, etc. How-to and historical pieces. Photos. Pays 5¢ to 10¢ a word, extra for photos, on acceptance.

WESTERN

AMERICAN WEST—3033 N. Campbell Ave., Tucson, AZ 85719. Mae Reid-Bills, Man. Ed. Well-researched, illustrated articles, 1,000 to 3,000 words, on western America, past and present, in a lively style appealing to the intelligent general reader. Query required. Pays from $200, on acceptance.

OLD WEST—See *True West*.

PERSIMMON HILL—1700 N.E. 63rd St., Oklahoma City, OK 73111. Sara Dobberteen, Sr. Ed. Articles, 2,000 to 3,000 words, on Western history and art, rodeos, cowboys, ranching, and nature. Profiles, biographies. Pays from $150, on publication.

REAL WEST—Charlton Publications, Inc., Division St., Derby, CT 06418. Ed Doherty, Ed. True stories of the Old West, 1,000 to 4,000 words. Photos. Pays from 4¢ a word, on acceptance.

TRUE WEST—P.O. Box 2107, Stillwater, OK 74076. John Joerschke, Ed. True stories, 500 to 4,500 words, with photos, about the Old West to 1930. Some contemporary stories with historical slant. Source list required. Pays 3¢ to 8¢ a word, extra for B&W photos, after acceptance. Same address and requirements for *Old West*.

WESTWAYS—P.O. Box 2890, Terminal Annex, Los Angeles, CA 90051. Ann Fisher, Ed. Travel articles on where to go, what to see, and how to get there, 1,500 words. Domestic travel articles are limited to Western U.S., Canada, and Hawaii; foreign travel articles are also of interest. Quality color photos should be available. Pays 20¢ a word, 30 days before publication.

HISTORICAL

AMERICAN HERITAGE—60 Fifth Ave., New York, NY 10011. Byron Dobell, Ed. Articles, 750 to 5,000 words, on U.S. history and background of American life and culture. Pays from $300 to $1,500, on acceptance. Query.

652

AMERICAN HERITAGE OF INVENTION & TECHNOLOGY—60 Fifth Ave., New York, NY 10011. Frederick Allen, Ed. Articles, 2,000 to 3,500 words, on the history of technology in America, for the sophisticated general reader. Query. Pays on acceptance.

AMERICAN HISTORY ILLUSTRATED—2245 Kohn Rd., P.O. Box 8200, Harrisburg, PA 17105. Articles, 2,000 to 3,500 words, soundly researched. Style should be popular, not scholarly. Pays $300 to $500, on acceptance. Query required.

AMERICANA—29 W. 38th St., New York, NY 10018. Michael Durham, Ed. Articles, 1,000 to 2,500 words, with historical slant: restoration, crafts, food, collecting, travel, etc. Pays $400 to $750, on acceptance. Query.

BRITISH HERITAGE—P.O. Box 8200, Harrisburg, PA 17105. Well-researched articles, 1,000 to 2,000 words, blending travel with British history and culture (including the Empire and Commonwealth countries) for readers knowledgeable about Britain. Pays $100 per 1,000 words, on acceptance. Query with clips. Send SASE for guidelines.

CHICAGO HISTORY—Clark St. at North Ave., Chicago, IL 60614. Timothy C. Jacobson, Ed. Articles, to 4,500 words, on urban political, social and cultural history. Pays to $250, on publication. Query.

EARLY AMERICAN LIFE—Box 8200, Harrisburg, PA 17105. Frances Carnahan, Ed. Illustrated articles, 1,000 to 3,000 words, on early American life: arts, crafts, furnishings, architecture; travel features about historic sites and country inns. Pays $50 to $500, on acceptance. Query.

HISTORIC PRESERVATION—1785 Massachusetts Ave., N.W., Washington, DC 20036. Thomas J. Colin, Ed. Articles from published writers, 1,500 to 4,000 words, on historic preservation, maritime preservation and people involved in preservation. High-quality photos. Pays $300 to $850, extra for photos, on acceptance. Query required.

TIMELINE—1985 Velma Ave., Columbus, OH 43211-2497. Christopher Duckworth, Ed. Articles, 1,000 to 6,000 words, related to the history, prehistory, and natural history of Ohio; topics of regional and national focus will be considered. Shorter, sharply-focused vignettes, 500 to 1,000 words. Photos. Pays $100 to $900, on acceptance. Query. Guidelines.

COLLEGE, CAREERS

AMPERSAND'S COLLEGE ENTERTAINMENT GUIDE—303 N. Glenoaks Blvd., Ste. 600, Burbank, CA 91502. Charlotte Wolter, Ed. Lively, intelligent articles on current music, film, and humor personalities and trends, 1,000 to 2,000 words, for college students. Pays 15¢ to 20¢ a word, half on acceptance, half on publication. Queries are required.

THE BLACK COLLEGIAN—1240 S. Broad St., New Orleans, LA 70125. James Borders, Ed. Articles, to 2,000 words, on experiences of black students, careers, and how-to subjects. Pays on publication. Query.

CAMPUS LIFE—465 Gundersen Dr., Carol Stream, IL 60188. Gregg Lewis, Sr. Ed. Articles reflecting Christian values and world view, for high school and college students. Humor and general fiction. Photo essays, cartoons. Pays from $150, on acceptance. Limited free-lance market.

CAMPUS VOICE—505 Market St., Knoxville, TN 37902. Lively, in-depth articles, 2,500 to 3,000 words, of interest to college students. Department pieces, 1,500 to 2,000 words. Pays $300 to $2,000, on acceptance. Query required. Send SASE for guidelines.

COLLEGE WOMAN—303 N. Glenoaks Blvd., Ste. 600, Burbank, CA 91502. Charlotte Wolter, Ed. Articles, 1,500 words, of general interest to college women: controversial, on-campus issues, fashion, makeup, fitness, humor, and sports. Queries are required. Pays 15¢ to 20¢ a word, on acceptance.

JOURNAL OF CAREER PLANNING AND EMPLOYMENT—College Placement Council, Inc., 62 Highland Ave., Bethlehem, PA 18017. Patricia A. Sinnott, Man. Ed. Articles, 2,000 to 4,000 words, on topics related to career planning, placement, and recruitment. Pays $200 to $400, on acceptance. Query with clips. Editorial guidelines available.

ALTERNATIVE MAGAZINES

EAST WEST JOURNAL—17 Station St., Box 1200, Brookline, MA 02147. Features, 1,500 to 2,000 words, on holistic health, natural foods, the environment, etc. Material for "Body," "Healing," "In the Kitchen," and "Beauty and Fitness." Interviews. Photos. Pays 7¢ to 12¢ a word, on publication.

FATE—Clark Publishing Co., 500 Hyacinth Pl., Highland Park, IL 60035. Mary M. Fuller, Ed. Documented articles, to 3,000 words, on strange happenings. First-person accounts, to 300 words, of true psychic or unexplained experiences. Pays from 5¢ a word for articles, $10 for short pieces, on publication.

NEW AGE—342 Western Ave., Brighton, MA 02135. Articles for readers who take an active interest in social change and personal growth, health and contemporary social issues. Features run 2,000 to 4,000 words; columns, 750 to 1,500 words; short news items, 50 words; and first-person narratives, 750 to 1,500 words. Payment varies. Query first.

NEW REALITIES—680 Beach St., San Francisco, CA 94109. James Bolen, Ed. Articles on holistic health, personal growth, parapsychology, alternative lifestyles, new spirituality. Pays to $150, on publication. Query.

YOGA JOURNAL—2054 University Ave., Berkeley, CA 94704. Stephan Bodian, Ed. Articles, 1,200 to 3,000 words, on holistic health, spirituality, yoga, and transpersonal psychology; "new age" profiles; interviews. Pays $50 to $150, on publication.

OP-ED MARKETS

Op-ed pages in newspapers—those pages that run opposite the editorials— offer writers an excellent opportunity to air their opinions, views, ideas, and insights on a wide spectrum of subjects and in styles from the highly personal and informal essay to the more serious commentary on politics, foreign affairs, and news events. Humor and nostalgia often find a place here.

THE ANCHORAGE DAILY NEWS—Pouch 6616, Anchorage, AL 99502. Seeks articles, 800 to 900 words, that "balance the national and international orientation of the editorial page," on natural resources, local issues, humor, seasonal topics, oil, etc. Preference for local writers. Pays $50, on publication. Submit manuscript with SASE postcard.

THE ATLANTA CONSTITUTION—P.O. Box 4689, Atlanta, GA 30302. Peter Kent, Op-Ed Ed. Articles related to the Southeast, Georgia or the Atlanta metropolitan area, 200 to 800 words, on a variety of topics: law, economics, politics, science, environment, performing and manipulative arts, humor, education; religious, and seasonal topics. Pays $50 to $150, on publication. Submit complete manuscript.

THE BALTIMORE SUN—501 N. Calvert St., Baltimore, MD 21278. Harold Piper, Op-Ed Editor. Articles, 750 to 1,000 words, for Opinion Commentary page, on a wide range of topics: politics, education, foreign affairs, life styles, science, etc. Humor. Pays $75 to $125, on publication.

BOSTON HERALD—One Herald Sq., Boston, MA 02106. Shelly Cohen, Editorial Page Ed. Pieces, 600 to 800 words, on human-interest, political, regional, life style, and seasonal topics. Pays $50 to $75, on publication. Prefer submissions from regional writers.

THE CHICAGO TRIBUNE—435 N. Michigan Ave., Chicago, IL 60611. Richard Liefer, Op-Ed Ed. Pieces, 500 to 800 words, on politics, economics, education, environment, foreign and domestic affairs. Writers *must* have expertise in their fields. Pays $50 to $250, on publication.

THE CHRISTIAN SCIENCE MONITOR—One Norway St., Boston, MA 02115. Cynthia Hanson, Opinion Page Coordinator. Pieces, 600 to 700 words, for "Opinion and Commentary" page, on politics, domestic and foreign affairs. Humor. Payment varies. Query preferred.

THE CHRONICLE—901 Mission St., San Francisco, CA 94103. Ms. Lyle York, "This World" Ed. Articles, 1,500 to 2,500 words, on a wide range of subjects. Pays $50 to $100, on publication.

THE CLEVELAND PLAIN DEALER—1801 Superior Ave., Cleveland, OH 44114. William Henson, Deputy Ed. Dir. Pieces, 800 to 1,000 words, on politics, economics, foreign affairs, and regional issues. Pays $50 to $100, on publication.

DAILY NEWS—14539 Sylvan St., Van Nuys, CA 91411. Pieces, 800 words, with special interest in regional focus: politics, environment, law, and economics. Pays $50, on publication. Query first.

DALLAS MORNING NEWS—Communications Center, Dallas, TX 75265. Carolyn Berta, "Viewpoints" Ed. Pieces 750 words (1,000 words for Sunday issue), on politics, education, foreign and domestic affairs, seasonal and regional issues. Pays $75 to $100, on publication. SASE required.

DENVER POST—P.O. Box 1709, Denver, CO 80201. Fred Brown, Asst. Editorial Page Ed. Pieces, 500 to 700 words, on economics, environment, education, law, politics, and science; seasonal and regional issues. Humor. Pays $35 to $50, on publication.

DES MOINES REGISTER—715 Locust St., Des Moines, IA 50312. James Flansburg, "Opinion" Page Ed. Articles, 600 to 800 words, on all topics. Humor. Pays $25 to $250, on publication.

THE DETROIT FREE PRESS—321 W. Lafayette St., Detroit, MI 48231. Patricia C. Foley, Op-Ed Ed. Articles, 750 to 800 words, on topics of local interest, and opinion pieces. Pays varying rates, on publication.

THE DETROIT NEWS—615 Lafayette Blvd., Detroit, MI 48231. Jeffrey Hadden, Ed. Pieces, 500 to 900 words, on science, economics, foreign and domestic affairs, education, environment, regional topics, nostalgia, religion and politics. Humor. Pays varying rates, on publication.

THE HARTFORD COURANT—285 Broad St., Hartford, CT 06115. Elissa

Papirno, Deputy Ed. Page Ed. Opinionated articles, 750 words (1,000 for Sunday "Commentary" section), on science, environment, politics, economics, law, and domestic and foreign affairs; pieces of regional and season interest. Pays from $40, on publication.

THE LOS ANGELES HERALD EXAMINER—Box 2416, Terminal Annex, Los Angeles, CA 90051-0416. Mike Gordon, Deputy Editor, Editorial Page. Articles, to 800 words, on local topics not covered by syndicated columnists. Humor. Pays $75, on publication.

LOS ANGELES TIMES—Times Mirror Sq., Los Angeles, CA 90053. Commentary pieces, to 800 words, on all subjects. Pays $150 to $250, on publication.

LOUISVILLE COURIER-JOURNAL—525 W. Broadway, Louisville, KY 40202. Keith L. Runyon, Op-Ed Ed. Pieces, 400 to 800 words, on politics, economics, regional topics, life styles, law, education, environment, humor, nostalgia, foreign and domestic affairs, and seasonal topics. Pays varying rates, on publication.

THE MIAMI HERALD—One Herald Plaza, Miami, FL 33132-1693. Joanna Wragg, Op-Ed Ed. Informed opinion pieces, to 800 words, on all subjects. Pays $35 to $50, on publication.

MILWAUKEE JOURNAL—Box 661, Milwaukee, WI 53201. James P. Cattey, Op-Ed Ed. Occasional pieces, 600 words, on various subjects, and humor. Pays $30 to $35, on publication.

THE NEW YORK TIMES—229 W. 43rd St., New York, NY 10036. Robert Semple, Jr., Op-Ed Ed. Pieces, 750 words, on topics not covered by syndicated columnists. Pays $150, on publication.

NEWSDAY—Long Island, NY 11747. Ilene Barth, "Viewpoints" Ed. Pieces, 600 to 1,500 words, on foreign and domestic affairs, politics, economics, life styles, law, education, and the environment. Seasonal pieces. Prefer policy experts and local writers. Pays $75 to $300, on publication.

THE OAKLAND TRIBUNE—Box 24429, Oakland, CA 94623. Jonathan Marshall, Editorial Page Ed. Articles, 800 words, on a wide range of topics; no humor or life style material. Pays $20 to $35, on publication.

THE ORANGE COUNTY REGISTER—625 N. Grand Ave., Santa Ana, CA 92711. K. E. Grubbs, Jr., Ed. Articles on a wide range of local and national issues and topics. Pays $50, on publication.

PITTSBURGH POST GAZETTE—50 Blvd. of the Allies, Pittsburgh, PA 15222. Mike McGough, Editorial Page Ed. Articles, to 800 words, on politics, law, economics, life style, religion, foreign and domestic affairs. Pays varying rates, on publication. SASE required.

THE REGISTER—625 N. Grand Ave., Santa Ana, CA 92711. K. E. Grubbs, Editorial and Commentary Dir. Opinion pieces, humor, and satire; seasonal pieces. Pays $35 to $75, on publication.

THE REGISTER GUARD—975 High St., Eugene, OR 97401. Don Robinson, Editorial Page Ed. All subjects; regional angle preferred. Pays $10 to $25, on publication.

THE SACRAMENTO BEE—21st and Q, P.O. Box 15779, Sacramento, CA 95852. Peter Schrag, Editorial Page Editor. Op-Ed pieces, to 750 words; topics of regional interest preferred. Pays $100 to $200, on publication. Query.

ST. LOUIS POST DISPATCH—900 N. Tucker Blvd., St. Louis, MO 63101. Articles on economics, education, science, politics, foreign and domestic affairs, and the environment. Pays $50, on publication.

ST. PAUL PIONEER PRESS & DISPATCH—345 Cedar St., St. Paul, MN 55101. Robert J. R. Johnson, Ed. Uses occasional pieces, to 750 words, on topics related to Minnesota and Western Wisconsin. Pays $50, on publication. Query first.

ST. PETERSBURG TIMES—Box 1211, 490 First Ave., S., St. Petersburg, FL 33731. Daryl Frazell, "Perspective" Section Ed. Authoritative articles, to 2,000 words, on current political, economic, and social issues, for "Perspective" section. Payment varies, on publication. Query first.

SEATTLE POST-INTELLIGENCER—101 Elliott Ave., W., Seattle, WA 98119. Charles J. Dunsire, Editorial Page Ed. Current events articles, 800 to 1,000 words, with Pacific Northwest themes. Pays $75 to $100, on publication.

THE WALL STREET JOURNAL—World Financial Center, 200 Liberty St., New York, NY 10281. Tim Ferguson, Editorial Features Ed. Articles, 850 to 1,100 words, on politics, economics, life styles, law, education, environment, humor, nostalgia, science, foreign and domestic affairs, religion, human-interest, and seasonal topics. Submit manuscript with SASE.

ADULT MAGAZINES

CAVALIER—2355 Salzedo St., Coral Gables, FL 33134. Nye Willden, Man. Ed. Articles with photos, 1,500 to 3,000 words, for sophisticated young men. Pays to $400 for articles, on publication. Query for articles.

CHIC—2029 Century Park E., Suite 3800, Los Angeles, CA 90067. Tim Conaway, Exec. Ed. Articles, 4,500 words. Pays $750 for articles, on acceptance.

FORUM, THE INTERNATIONAL JOURNAL OF HUMAN RELATIONS—1965 Broadway, New York, NY 10023-5965. John Heidenry, Exec. Ed. Articles, 2,500 words; especially interested in true, first-person sexual adventures. Pays $800 to $1,000, on acceptance. Query.

GALLERY—800 Second Ave., New York, NY 10017. John Bensink, Ed.-in-Chief. Articles, investigative pieces, and men and women relationship pieces, to 3,000 words, for sophisticated men. Short humor, satire, service pieces. Photos. Pays varying rates, half on acceptance, half on publication. Query.

GEM—G&S Publications, 1472 Broadway, New York, NY 10036. Will Martin, Ed. Sex-related (not pornographic) articles, to 2,500 words. General articles on sports, fitness, cars, travel, food, etc., to 800 words. Humor, satire, and spoofs of sexual subjects. Pays $50 to $100, after acceptance. Also publishes *BUF,* A Magazine for Attractive Heavy Women. Short features, and humor. All submissions must be accompanied by SASE.

GENESIS—770 Lexington Ave., New York, NY 10021. J. J. Kelleher, Ed.-in-Chief. Articles, 2,500 to 3,500 words; celebrity interviews, 2,500 words. Photo essays. Pays 30 days after acceptance. Query.

HUSTLER—2029 Century Park E., Suite 3800, Los Angeles, CA 90067. Tim Conaway, Exec. Ed. Investigative articles and profiles, 4,500 words. Pays from $1,500, on acceptance. Query.

PENTHOUSE—1965 Broadway, New York, NY 10023. Peter Bloch, Ex. Ed. General-interest or investigative articles, to 5,000 words. Interviews, 5,000 words, with introductions. Satire, humor, and black comedy. Pays to 50¢ a word, on acceptance.

PLAYBOY—919 N. Michigan Ave., Chicago, IL 60611. James Morgan, Articles Ed. Alice K. Turner, Fiction Ed. Articles, 3,500 to 6,000 words, for urban men. Humor; satire. Pays to $5,000 for articles, on acceptance.

FICTION MARKETS

This list gives the fiction requirements of the general- and special-interest magazines, including those that publish detective and mystery, romance and confession, and science fiction and fantasy stories. Other good markets for short fiction are the little, literary, and college journals (listed on page 678). Though payment is modest—usually in copies only—publication here can help a beginning writer achieve recognition by editors at the larger magazines. Juvenile fiction markets are listed under *Juvenile, Teenage, and Young Adult Magazines*. Publishers of book-length fiction manuscripts are listed under *Book Publishers*.

All manuscripts must be typed double-space and submitted with self-addressed envelopes bearing postage sufficient for the return of the material. Use good white paper; onion skin or erasable bond is not acceptable. Always keep a copy of the manuscript, since occasionally a manuscript is lost in the mails. Magazines may take several weeks—often longer—to read and report on submissions. If an editor has not reported on a manuscript after a reasonable amount of time, write a brief, courteous letter of inquiry.

AIM MAGAZINE—P.O. Box 20554, Chicago, IL 60620. Ruth Apilado, Ed. Short stories, 800 to 1,000 words, geared to promoting racial harmony and peace. Pays from $15 to $25, on publication.

ALFRED HITCHCOCK'S MYSTERY MAGAZINE—380 Lexington Ave., New York, NY 10017. Cathleen Jordan, Ed. Well-plotted, plausible mystery, suspense, detection and crime stories, 1,000 to 14,000 words. Pays 3¢ to 8¢ a word, on acceptance.

ALOHA, THE MAGAZINE OF HAWAII—828 Fort Street Mall, Honolulu, HI 96813. Rita Arioyshi, Ed. Fiction to 4,000 words, on Hawaii and its ethnic groups. Pays 10¢ a word on publication. Query.

AMAZING STORIES—Box 110, Lake Geneva, WI 53147. Patrick L. Price, Ed. Science fiction and fantasy, to 15,000 words. Pays 4¢ to 7¢ a word, on acceptance.

AMERICAN TRUCKER MAGAZINE—P.O. Box 6366, San Bernadino, CA 92412. Carl Calvert, Assoc. Ed. Fiction, 1,200 to 2,500 words, for truck drivers and trucking industry personnel. Pays after publication.

ANALOG: SCIENCE FICTION/SCIENCE FACT—380 Lexington Ave., New York, NY 10017. Stanley Schmidt, Ed. Science fiction, with strong characters in believable future or alien setting: short stories, 2,000 to 7,500 words; novelettes, 10,000 to 20,000 words, serials, to 70,000 words. Pays 4¢ to 7¢ a word, on acceptance. Query on novels.

ARKANSAS TIMES—Box 34010, Little Rock, AR 72203. Mel White, Ed. Fiction, to 6,000 words: must have an Arkansas slant. Pays from $100, on acceptance.

THE ATLANTIC—8 Arlington St., Boston, MA 02116. William Whitworth, Ed. Short stories, 2,000 to 6,000 (occasionally, to 14,000) words, of highest literary quality. Pays on acceptance.

THE ATLANTIC ADVOCATE—P.O. Box 3370, Fredericton, N.B., Canada E3B 5A2. H. P. Wood, Ed. Fiction, 1,000 to 1,500 words, with regional angle. Pays to 10¢ a word, on publication.

THE ATLANTIC SALMON JOURNAL—1435 St. Alexandre, Suite 1030, Montreal, Quebec, Canada, H3A 2G4. Joanne Eidinger, Ed. Fiction, 1,500 to 2,500 words, related to the conservation of Atlantic salmon. Pays $100 to $400, on publication.

BANE K. WILKER'S TALES OF THE OLD WEST—PPG Publishing, Box 22866, Denver, CO 80222. Keith Olsen, Ed. Short stories, 500 to 5,000 words, and poetry, 3 to 100 lines, related to the Old West. Pays in copies. SASE required. Annual contest.

THE BOSTON GLOBE MAGAZINE—*The Boston Globe,* 135 Morrissey Blvd., Boston, MA 02107. Ande Zellman, Ed. Short stories, to 2,500 words. Include SASE. Pays on publication.

BOYS' LIFE—1325 Walnut Hill Lane, Irving, TX 75038-3096. W. E. Butterworth, IV, Fiction Ed. Publication of the Boy Scouts of America. Fiction, 1,000 to 2,000 words, for 8- to 18-year-old boys. Pays from $350, on acceptance.

BUFFALO SPREE MAGAZINE—Box 38, Buffalo, NY 14226. Johanna V. Shotell, Ed. Fiction and humor, to 1,500 words, for readers in the upstate New York region. Pays $75 to $100, on publication.

BURLINGTON MAGAZINE—444 S. Union St., Burlington, VT 05401. Tim Etchells, Ed. Fiction, varying lengths, related to the Burlington (VT) area. Payment varies, on acceptance.

CAMPUS LIFE—465 Gundersen Dr., Carol Stream, IL 60188. Gregg Lewis, Ed. Fiction and humor, reflecting Christian values (no overtly religious material), 1,000 to 4,000 words, for high school and college students. Pays from $150 to $400, on acceptance. Limited free-lance market.

CAPPER'S—616 Jefferson Ave., Topeka, KS 66607. Dorothy Harvey, Ed. Novel-length mystery and romance stories: no short stories. Pays $150 to $200. Query.

CAT FANCY—P.O. Box 6050, Mission Viejo, CA 92690. Linda W. Lewis, Ed. Fiction, to 3,000 words, about cats. Pays 3¢ a word, on publication.

CATHOLIC FORESTER—425 W. Shuman Blvd., Naperville, IL 60566. Barbara A. Cunningham, Ed. Official publication of the Catholic Order of Foresters. Fiction, to 3,000 words (prefer shorter). No sex or violence or "preachy" stories; religious angle not essential. Pays from 5¢ a word, on acceptance.

CAVALIER—2355 Salzedo St., Coral Gables, FL 33134. Maurice DeWalt,

Fiction Ed. Sexually-oriented fiction, to 3,000 words, for sophisticated young men. Pays to $300, on publication.

CHATELAINE—Maclean Hunter Bldg., 777 Bay St., Toronto, Ont., Canada M5W 1A7. Barbara West, Fiction Ed. Fiction, 2,500 to 4,000 words, on issues in contemporary women's lives: relationships, adventure, romance, humor. Canadian setting preferred. Pays from $1,500, on acceptance.

CHESAPEAKE BAY MAGAZINE—1819 Bay Ridge Ave., Annapolis, MD 21403. Betty Rigoli, Ed. Short stories, to 15 pages; must be related to Chesepeake Bay area. Pays $75 to $100, on publication.

CLUBHOUSE—Berrien Springs, MI 49103. Elaine Meseraull, Ed. Action-oriented Christian stories: features, 1,000 to 1,200 words. Children in stories should be wise, brave, funny, kind, etc. Pays $30 to $35, on acceptance.

COBBLESTONE—20 Grove St., Peterborough, NH 03458. Carolyn P. Yoder, Ed. Fiction, related to monthly theme, 500 to 1,200 words, for children aged 8 to 14 years. Pays 10¢ to 15¢ a word, on publication. Send SASE for editorial guidelines.

COMMENTARY—165 E. 56th St., New York, NY 10022. Marion Magid, Ed. Fiction, of high literary quality, on contemporary social or Jewish issues. Pays on publication.

THE COMPASS—Mobil International Aviation and Marine Sales, Inc., 150 E. 42nd St., New York, NY 10017. R. G. MacKenzie, Ed. Short stories, to 3,500 words, on the sea and sea trades. Pays to $250, on acceptance. Query.

CORVETTE FEVER—Box 44620, Ft. Washington, MD 20744. Pat Stivers, Ed. Corvette-related fiction, about 300 lines. Pays 10¢ a word, on publication.

COSMOPOLITAN—224 W. 57th St., New York, NY 10019. Betty Kelly, Fiction and Books Ed. Short shorts, 1,500 to 3,000 words, and short stories, 4,000 to 6,000 words, focusing on contemporary man-woman relationships. Solid, upbeat plots, sharp characterization; female protagonists preferred. Pays $300 to $600 for short shorts, from $1,000 for short stories. Payment negotiable.

CRICKET—Box 300, Peru, IL 61354. Marianne Carus, Ed.-in-Chief. Fiction, 200 to 1,500 words, for 6- to 12-year-olds. Pays to 25¢ a word, on publication.

DISCOVERIES—6401 The Paseo, Kansas City, MO 64131. Middler, Editor, Fiction, 800 to 1,000 words, for children grades 3 to 6, defining Christian experiences and values. Pays 3½¢ a word, on acceptance. Query.

DIVER MAGAZINE—Box 1312, Delta, BC, V4M 3Y8, Canada. Neil McDaniel, Ed. Fiction, related to diving/diving experiences. Humor. Pays $2.50 per column inch, on publication. Query.

DOG FANCY—P.O. Box 6050, Mission Viejo, CA 92690. Linda W. Lewis, Ed. Fiction, to 2,500 words: dog must be central element of the story; no "talking dog" stories. Pays 5¢ a word, on publication.

EASYRIDERS MAGAZINE—Box 52, Malibu, CA 90265. Lou Kimzey, Ed. Fiction, 3,000 to 5,000 words. Pays from 10¢ a word, on acceptance.

ELLERY QUEEN'S MYSTERY MAGAZINE—380 Lexington Ave., New York, NY 10017. Eleanor Sullivan, Ed. High-quality detective, crime, and mystery stories, 4,000 to 6,000 words. "First Stories" by unpublished writers. Pays 3¢ to 8¢ a word, on acceptance.

660

ENTERTAINER MAGAZINE—One Lytle Place, Suite 802, 621 Mehring Way, Cincinnati, OH 45202. Brian Baker, Ed. Fiction, 750 words, related to Cincinnati. Pays $15 and copies, on publication.

ESPIONAGE—Leo 11 Publications, P.O. Box 1184, Teaneck, NJ 07666. Jackie Lewis, Ed. Spy stories, 1,000 to 6,000 words: no horror, extreme violence, or explicit sex. Pays 3¢ to 8¢ a word, on publication.

ESQUIRE—2 Park Ave., New York, NY 10016. Rust Hills, Fiction Ed. Literary short stories only (no genre fiction), 1,000 to 7,000 words, for intelligent adult audience. Pays $1,000 to $1,500, on acceptance.

ESSENCE—1500 Broadway, New York, NY 10036. Susan L. Taylor, Ed.-in-Chief. Fiction, 1,500 to 3,000 words, for largely black, female readership. Pays varying rates, on acceptance.

FAMILY CIRCLE—488 Madison Ave., New York, NY 10022. Nicole Gregory, Books and Nonfiction Ed. No unsolicited manuscripts.

FAMILY MAGAZINE—P.O. Box 4993, Walnut Creek, CA 94596. Address Editors. Short stories, to 2,000 words, of interest to high school-educated military wives between 20 and 35. Pays from $100 to $300, on publication.

FARM WOMAN—P.O. Box 643, Milwaukee, WI 53201. Ruth C. Benedict, Man. Ed. Fiction, to 1,000 words, of interest to farm and ranch women. Pays $30 to $250, on publication.

FICTION INTERNATIONAL—English Dept., San Diego State Univ., San Diego, CA 92182. Harold Jaffe and Larry McCaffery, Eds. Post-modernist and politically committed fiction and theory.

THE FLYFISHER—1387 Cambridge Dr., Idaho Falls, ID 83401. Dennis Bitton, Ed. Serious or humorous fiction, 1,000 to 1,500 words, related to fly fishing. Pays from $50, after publication. Guidelines.

40+—Box 98120, Tacoma, WA 98498. Ila Russell, Ed. Short-shorts, romantic, or light, humorous fiction, 1,200 to 1,500 words, for women over age 40. Pays $200 to $300, on publication.

GALLERY—800 Second Ave., New York, NY 10017. Marc Lichter, Ed.-in-Chief. Fiction, to 4,000 words, for sophisticated men. Pays varying rates, half on acceptance, half on publication.

GENTLEMEN'S QUARTERLY (GQ)—350 Madison Ave., New York, NY 10017. Trish Rohrer, Sr. Ed. Fiction, to 3,000 words. Pays on acceptance. No unsolicited manuscripts.

GOLF DIGEST—5520 Park Ave., Trumbull, CT 06611. Jerry Tarde, Ed. Unusual or humorous stories, to 2,000 words, about golf; golf "fables," to 1,000 words. Pays 20¢ a word, on acceptance.

GOOD HOUSEKEEPING—959 Eighth Ave., New York, NY 10019. Naome Lewis, Fiction Ed. Short stories, 1,000 to 3,000 words, with strong identification figures for women, by published writers and "beginners with demonstrable talent." Novel condensations or excerpts. Pays top rates, on acceptance.

GROWING UP—5127 Summit Ave., Greensboro, NC 27405. Joe Benson, Ed. Some fiction, 2,500 to 4,000 words, for parents of children and adolescents. Pays from $25, on publication.

GUN DOG—1901 Bell Ave., Des Moines, IA 50315. Bob Wilbanks, Man.

Ed. Occasional fiction, humor related to gun dogs and bird hunting. Pays $100 to $300, on acceptance.

HANG GLIDING—U.S. Hang Gliding Assn., P.O. Box 66306, Los Angeles, CA 90066. Gilbert Dodgen, Ed. Fiction, 2 to 3 pages, related to hang gliding. Pays to $50. Query preferred.

HICALL—1445 Boonville Ave., Springfield, MO 65802. Jennifer J. Eller, Ed. Fiction, to 1,800 words, for 12- to 19-year olds with strong evangelical emphasis: believable characters working out their problems according to biblical principles. Pays 3¢ a word for first rights, on acceptance.

HIGHLIGHTS FOR CHILDREN—803 Church St., Honesdale, PA 18431. Kent L. Brown, Jr., Ed. Sports, humor, adventure, mystery, etc., stories, 900 words, for 9- to 12-year-olds. Easy rebus form, 200 to 250 words, and easy-to-read stories, to 600 words, for beginning readers. Pays from 6¢ a word, on acceptance. Buys all rights.

HIS—P.O. Box 1450, Downers Grove, IL 60515. Verne Becker, Ed. Fiction about college students who experience emotional and/or spiritual growth, to 2,000 words. No fantasy, parables, or Bible retellings. Pays 2¢ to 5¢ a word, on acceptance.

INSIDE RUNNING—9514 Bristlebrook Dr., Houston, TX 77083. Joanne Schmidt, Ed. Fiction, related to running. Pays $35 to $100, on acceptance.

IRISH AMERICA—34 E. 29th St., New York, NY 10016. Patricia Harty, Managing Ed. Fiction, 1,500 words, of interest to an Irish-American audience. Pays 7¢ a word, on publication.

ISAAC ASIMOV'S SCIENCE FICTION MAGAZINE—380 Lexington Ave., New York, NY 10017. Gardner Dozois, Ed. Short science fiction and fantasies, to 15,000 words. Pays 6¢ to 8¢ a word, on acceptance.

JACK AND JILL—Box 567, Indianapolis, IN 46206. Christine French Clark, Ed. Fiction, to 1,200 words, for early-elementary-age readers. Pays about 6¢ a word, on publication.

JUNIOR TRAILS—1445 Boonville Ave., Springfield, MO 65802. Fiction, 1,200 to 1,800 words, that presents believable characters working out their problems according to Bible principles, for children ages 9 to 10. Pays on acceptance. Guidelines.

LADIES' HOME JOURNAL—3 Park Ave., New York, NY 10016. Fiction with strong identification for women. Short stories and full-length manuscripts accepted *through agents only*.

LADYCOM—See *Military Lifestyle.*

LIVE—1445 Boonville Ave., Springfield, MO 65802. Kenneth D. Barney, Adult Ed. Fiction, 1,500 to 2,000 words, on applying Bible principles to everyday living. Send SASE for writers' guidelines (required). Pays 2¢ to 3¢ a word, on acceptance.

LOLLIPOPS—Good Apple Inc., P.O. Box 299, Carthage, IL 62321-0299. Jerry Aten, Ed. Short stories, to 1,200 words, with educational and/or moral value, teaching ideas and activities covering all areas of the curriculum for young children. Rates vary.

THE LOOKOUT—8121 Hamilton Ave., Cincinnati, OH 45231. Fiction Ed: Mark Taylor. Inspirational short-shorts, 1,000 to 1,800 words. Pays 4¢ to 6¢ a word, on acceptance.

LUTHERAN WOMEN—2900 Queen Lane, Philadelphia, PA 19129. Terry Schutz, Ed. Fiction, 1,000 to 2,000 words, demonstrating character growth and change. Pays $35 to $50, on publication. Include SASE.

MCCALL'S—230 Park Ave., New York, NY 10169. Helen DelMonte, Fiction Ed. Short stories, to 3,000 words. Short-shorts, 1,800 words: Contemporary themes with strong identification for intelligent women. Family stories, love stories, humor, suspense. Pays from $2,000 for stories, $1,500 for short-shorts, on acceptance.

MADEMOISELLE—350 Madison Ave., New York, NY 10017. Eileen Schnurr, Fiction Ed. Short stories, 2,500 to 4,500 words, of high literary quality. Pays from $1,000, on acceptance.

THE MAGAZINE OF FANTASY AND SCIENCE FICTION—Box 56, Cornwall, CT 06753. Edward Ferman, Ed. Fantasy and science fiction stories, to 10,000 words. Pays 4¢ to 6¢ a word, on acceptance.

MATURE LIVING—127 Ninth Ave. N., Nashville, TN 37234. Jack Gulledge, Ed. Zada Malugen, Ass't Ed. Fiction, 900 to 1,475 words, for senior adults. Must be consistent with Christian principles. Pays 5¢ a word, on acceptance.

MICHIGAN, THE MAGAZINE OF THE DETROIT NEWS—615 W. Lafayette Blvd., Detroit, MI 48231. Lisa Velders, Ed. Fiction, with *Michigan* slant, to 3,000 words. Pays $250 to $500, on publication.

MID-ATLANTIC COUNTRY—P.O. Box 246, Alexandria, VA 22313. Jim Scott, Ed. Fiction, related to the mid-Atlantic region, varying lengths. Pays $3.50 per column inch, on publication. Include SASE.

MIDSTREAM—515 Park Ave., New York, NY 10022. Joel Carmichael, Ed. Fiction on Jewish themes, to 3,000 words. Pays 5¢ a word, after publication.

MILITARY LIFESTYLE (formerly *Ladycom*)—1732 Wisconsin Ave., NW, Washington, DC 20007. Hope Daniels, Ed. Fiction, to 2,000 words, for military wives in the U.S. and overseas. Pays $75 to $200, on publication.

MOMENT—462 Boylston St., Boston, MA 02116. Leonard Fein, Ed. Short stories, 2,000 to 4,000 words, on Jewish themes. Pays $150 to $250, on publication.

MS.—119 W. 40th St., New York, NY 10018. Address Ed. Dept. Fiction. Short stories, to 3,000 words, on women's changing self-image and status. Pays varying rates, on acceptance. SASE required.

MY OWN MAGAZINE—3500 Western Ave., Highland Park, IL 60035. Carolyn Good Quattrocki, Ed. Short stories, 200 or 400 words, for children ages 3 to 6. Pays $150 for 200–word stories; $200 for 400-word stories, on acceptance. Guidelines.

NA'AMAT WOMAN (formerly *Pioneer Woman*)—200 Madison Ave., 18th fl., New York, NY 10016. Judith A. Sokoloff, Ed. Short stories, 2,500 words, with Jewish theme or of interest to women. Pays 8¢ a word, on publication.

NATIONAL RACQUETBALL—950 Milwaukee Ave., Suite 222, Glenview, IL 60025. Chuck Leve, Ed. Fiction, related to racquetball. Pays $25 to $150, on publication.

THE NEW BLACK MASK QUARTERLY—2006 Sumter St., Columbia, SC 29201. Matthew J. Bruccoli, Richard Layman, Eds. Mystery fiction, 3,000 to 6,000 words. Pays to 10¢ a word, on publication.

THE NEW YORKER—25 W. 43rd St., New York, NY 10036. Short stories, humor, and satire. Pays varying rates, on acceptance.

NORTHEAST MAGAZINE—*The Hartford Courant,* 285 Broad St., Hartford, CT 06115. Lary Bloom, Ed. Short stories, to 4,000 words; must have Connecticut tie-in, or be universal in theme and have non-specific setting. Pays $300 to $600, on acceptance. SASE required.

OMNI—1965 Broadway, New York, NY 10023-5965. Ellen Datlow, Fiction Ed. Strong, realistic science fiction, with real people as characters, to 9,000 words. Some contemporary hard-edged fantasy. Pays to $2,000, on acceptance.

OUR FAMILY—Box 249, Battleford, Sask., Canada S0M 0E0. A. Lalonde, O.M.I. Ed. Fiction, 1,000 to 3,000 words, on the struggle to live the Christian life in the face of modern-day problems. Pays 7¢ to 10¢ a word, on acceptance. Write for guidelines. Fiction submissions should be addressed to John Gillese, 10450-144th St., Edmonton, Alb., T5N 2V4, Canada. Enclose *international postal reply coupons* with SAE.

PENTHOUSE—1965 Broadway, New York, NY 10023. Address Fiction Department. Quality fiction, 4,000 to 6,000 words, on contemporary themes. Pays on acceptance. Query. No unsolicited manuscripts.

PIONEER WOMAN—See *Na'amat Woman.*

PLAYBOY—919 N. Michigan Ave., Chicago, IL 60611. Alice K. Turner, Fiction Ed. Quality fiction, 1,000 to 10,000 words (average 6,000): suspense, mystery, adventure and sports short stories; stories about contemporary relationships; science fiction. Active plots and strong characterization. Pays from $1,000 to $3,000, on acceptance.

PORTLAND MONTHLY—The Lafayette, 638 Congress St., Portland, ME 04102. Colin Sargent, Sr. Ed. Fiction, to 2,500 words, with regional slant. Pays $150, on publication.

PRIME TIMES—Suite 210, 2802 International Ln., Madison, WI 53704. Journal for the National Assn. for Retired Credit Union People. Joan Donovan, Assoc. Man. Ed. Fiction, 2,500 to 4,000 words; dynamic, upbeat, young themes. Pays varying rates, on publication. Query.

PULPSMITH—5 Beekman St., New York, NY 10038. Harry Smith, General Ed. Literary genre fiction; mainstream, mystery, SF, westerns. Short lyric poems, sonnets, ballads. Essays and articles. Pays $35 to $100 for fiction, $20 to $35 for poetry, on acceptance.

PURPOSE—616 Walnut Ave., Scottdale, PA 15683-1999. James E. Horsch, Ed. Articles, 350 to 1,200 words, on Christian themes, with good photos; pieces of history, biography, science, hobbies, from a Christian perspective. Fiction, 1,200 words, on problem solving from a Christian point of view. Poetry, 3 to 12 lines. Pays up to 5¢ a word, to $1 per line for poetry, extra for photos, on acceptance.

RANGER RICK MAGAZINE—1412 16th St., N.W., Washington, DC 20036. Betty Athey, Fiction Ed. Nature- and conservation-related fiction, for 7- to 12-year-olds. Maximum: 900 words. Pays to $350, on acceptance. Buys all rights.

REDBOOK—224 W. 57th St., New York, NY 10019. Deborah Purcell, Fiction Ed. Fresh, distinctive short stories, of interest to women, about love and relationships, friendship, careers, parenting, family dilemmas, confronting basic problems of contemporary life and women's issues. Pays $850 for short-shorts (about 9 manuscript pages), from $1,000 for short stories (to 20 pages). Allow 8 to 10 weeks for reply. Manuscripts without SASEs will not be returned. No unsolicited novellas or novels accepted.

RELIX MAGAZINE—Box 94, Brooklyn, NY 11229. Toni A. Brown, Ed. Rock- or sci-fi-related fiction, 1,200 words, with a tie-in to San Francisco and 60's rock music. Pays varying rates, after publication.

ROAD KING—P.O. Box 250, Park Forest, IL 60466. George Friend, Ed. Short stories, 1,200 to 1,500 words, for and/or about truck drivers. Pays to $400, on acceptance.

ROD SERLING'S THE TWILIGHT ZONE MAGAZINE—800 Second Ave., New York, NY 10017. Tappan King, Ed. Fiction, to 5,000 words: human-centered fantasies involving "ordinary people in extraordinary events." Avoid genre clichés. Pays about 5¢ a word, half on acceptance, half on publication.

ST. ANTHONY MESSENGER—1615 Republic St., Cincinnati, OH 45210. Norman Perry, Ed. Fiction that makes readers think about issues, lifestyles and values. Pays 12¢ a word, on acceptance. Query.

THE SATURDAY EVENING POST—1100 Waterway Blvd., Indianapolis, IN 46202. Rebecca Whitney, Fiction Ed. Upbeat short stories, 500 to 4,000 words, that lend themselves to illustration. Humor. Pays varying rates, on publication.

SCHOLASTIC SCOPE—Scholastic, Inc., 730 Broadway, New York, NY 10003. Fran Claro, Ed. Fiction for 15- to 18-year-olds, with 4th to 6th grade reading ability. Short stories, 500 to 1,000 words, on teen-age interests and relationships; family, job and school situations. Pays good rates, on acceptance.

SEA KAYAKER—1670 Duranleau St., Vancouver, BC, V6H 3S4 Canada. John Dowd, Ed. Fiction, to 1,000 words, related to ocean kayaking. Pays on publication. Include international reply coupons.

SEVENTEEN—850 Third Ave., New York, NY 10022. Bonni Price, Fiction Ed. High-quality fiction for young adults. Pays on acceptance.

SOUTHERN—P. O. Box 3418, 201 E. Markham, Suite 200, Little Rock, AR 72203. Linton Weeks, Ed. Short stories, 1,000 to 6,000 words, with a strong Southern angle, by Southern writers. Pays on acceptance.

SPLASH—458A N. Tamiami Trail, Osprey, FL 33559. Lisa D. Black, Ed. Dir. Short fiction, for sophisticated, contemporary readers. Pays after publication. Query; limited market.

SPORTS AFIELD—250 W. 55th St., New York, NY 10019. Tom Paugh, Ed. Fiction, on hunting, fishing, and related topics. Outdoor adventure stories. Humor. Pays top rates, on acceptance.

STRAIGHT—8121 Hamilton Ave., Cincinnati, OH 45231. Dawn Korth, Ed. Well-constructed fiction, 1,000 to 1,500 words, showing Christian teens using Bible principles in everyday life. Contemporary, realistic teen characters a must. Most interested in school, church, dating, and family life stories. Pays about 3¢ a word, on acceptance. Send SASE for guidelines.

SUNDAY DIGEST—850 N. Grove Ave., Elgin, IL 60120. Judy Couchman, Ed. Short shorts (500 words), short stories (1,000 to 1,500 words), and novel excerpts (1,000 to 1,500 words), with religious, evangelical slant. Pays 10¢ a word, on acceptance.

665

SUNSHINE MAGAZINE—Litchfield, IL 62056. Wholesome fiction, 900 to 1,200 words; short stories for youths, 400 to 700 words. Pays to $100, on acceptance.

SWANK—888 Seventh Ave., New York, NY 10106. Dave Trilby, Fiction Ed. Graphic erotic short stories, to 2,500 words. Pays on publication. Limited market.

'TEEN—8490 Sunset Blvd., Los Angeles, CA 90069. Address Fiction Dept. Short stories, 2,500 to 4,000 words: mystery, travel, adventure, romance, humor for teens. pays from $100, on acceptance.

TEENS TODAY—Nazarene Publishing House, 6401 The Paseo, Kansas City, MO 64131. Karen De Sollar, Ed. Short stories, 1,200 to 1,500 words, that deal with teens demonstrating Christian principles in real-life situations; adventure stories. Pays 3½¢ a word, on acceptance.

TORCH ROMANCES—P.O. Box 3307, McLean, VA 22103. Address Fiction Ed. Short-short love stories, 1,200 words. Romantic suspense short stories, 6,000 words, with sensual love scenes; avoid plots that contain murder, drugs, and excess violence. Pays flat rate or royalty. Top sheet available.

TQ/TEEN QUEST (formerly *Young Ambassador*)—Box 82808, Lincoln, NE 68501. Nancy Bayne, Man. Ed. Fiction, to 2,000 words, for Christian teens. Pays 4¢ to 10¢ a word, on acceptance.

VANITY FAIR—350 Madison Ave., New York, NY 10017. Patricia Towers, Fiction Ed. Fiction of high literary quality. Pays varying rates.

VIRTUE—Box 850, Sisters, OR 97759. Becky Durost, Ed. Fiction with a Christian slant. Pays 10¢ a word, on publication.

VOGUE—350 Madison Ave., New York, NY 10017. Amy Gross, Features Ed. No unsolicited manuscripts.

THE WASHINGTON POST MAGAZINE—1150 15th St. NW, Washington, DC 20071. Stephen Petranek, Man. Ed. Fiction, 3,000 words: fantasy, humor, mystery, historical, mainstream and science fiction. Pays $200 to $750, on acceptance.

WESTERN PEOPLE—Box 2500, Saskatoon, Sask., Canada S7K 2C4. Short stories, 1,000 to 2,500 words, on subjects or themes of interest to rural readers in Western Canada. Pays $40 to $150, on acceptance. *Enclose international postal reply coupons and SAE.*

WHAT'S NEW MAGAZINE—Multicom 7, Inc., 11 Allen Rd., Brighton, MA 02135. Bob Leja, Ed. Fiction, 150 to 3,000 words, for audience in their early to mid 20's. Pays varying rates, on publication. Limited market.

WILDFOWL—1901 Bell Ave., Suite #4, Des Moines, IA 50315. B. Wilbanks, Man. Ed. Occasional fiction, humor, related to duck hunters and wildfowl. Pays $100 to $300, on acceptance.

WOMAN'S DAY—1515 Broadway, New York, NY 10036. Eileen Herbert Jordan, Fiction Ed. Short fiction, humorous or serious. Pays top rates, on acceptance.

WOMAN'S WORLD—P.O. Box 6700, Englewood, NJ 07631. Elinor Nauen, Fiction Ed. Fast-moving short stories, about 4,500 words, with light romantic theme. Mini-mysteries, 1,500 words, with "whodunit" or "howdunit" theme. No science fiction, fantasy or historical romance. Pays $1,000 for short stories, $500 for mini-mysteries on acceptance. Submit manuscript with SASE.

WOMEN'S CIRCLE HOME COOKING—Box 198, Henniker, NH 03242. Susan Hankins Andrews, Ed. Humorous fiction, to 400 words. Pays 5¢ a word, on publication.

WOODMEN OF THE WORLD MAGAZINE—1700 Farnam St., Omaha, NE 68102. Leland A. Larson, Ed. Family-oriented fiction. Pays 5¢ a word, on acceptance.

WORKING MOTHER—230 Park Ave., New York, NY 10169. Maria Buhl, Assoc. Ed. Realistic short stories, 750 to 3,000 words, for working mothers. Pays $500 to $800, on acceptance.

YANKEE—Dublin, NH 03444. Judson Hale, Ed. Edie Clark, Fiction Ed. High-quality, literary short fiction, to 4,000 words, with setting in or compatible with New England. Pays $1,000, on acceptance.

YM—685 Third Ave., New York, NY 10017. Mary Kay Schilling, Fiction Ed. Fiction, to 3,500 words, for young women ages 15 to 19: stories must be complex and engaging, with strong characters, plot and dialogue; protagonist may be male or female. Study back issues before submitting. pays from $350, on acceptance.

YOUNG AMBASSADOR—See *TQ/Teen Quest.*

YOUNG AMERICAN—Box 12409, Portland, OR 97217. Kristina Linden, Ed. Fiction, to 1,000 words, for children ages 6 to 15. Pays 7¢ a word, on publication.

DETECTIVE AND MYSTERY

ALFRED HITCHCOCK'S MYSTERY MAGAZINE—380 Lexington Ave., New York, NY 10017. Cathleen Jordan, Ed. Well-plotted mystery, detective, suspense and crime fiction, 1,000 to 14,000 words. Submissions by new writers strongly encouraged. Pays 5¢ a word, on acceptance.

ARMCHAIR DETECTIVE—129 W. 56th St., New York, NY 10019. Michael Seidman, Ed. Articles on mystery and detective fiction; biographical sketches, reviews, etc. Pays in copies.

DETECTIVE DRAGNET—1440 St. Catherine W., Suite 625, Montreal, Quebec, Canada H3G 1S2. Domminick A. Merle, Ed. Well-researched true crime stories, 3,500 to 6,000 words, with photos, involving mystery, suspense and lots of human interest. No fiction. Include clippings describing the case, with date, location and names of victims and suspects. Pays $200 to $300, on acceptance. Same address and requirements for *Detective Cases, Detective Files, Headquarters Detective, Starting Detective,* and *True Police Cases.*

ELLERY QUEEN'S MYSTERY MAGAZINE—380 Lexington Ave., New York, NY 10017. Eleanor Sullivan, Ed. Detective, crime, mystery and spy fiction, 4,000 to 6,000 words. Suspense or straight detective stories. No sex, sadism or sensationalism. Particularly interested in new writers and "first stories." Pays 3¢ to 8¢ a word, on acceptance.

ESPIONAGE—35 Roberts Rd., Englewood Cliffs, NJ 07652. Jackie Lewis, Ed. Spy fiction, 1,000 to 6,000 words. No horror, extreme violence or explicit sex. Pays on publication.

FRONT PAGE DETECTIVE—See *Inside Detective.*

HEADQUARTERS DETECTIVE—See *Detective Dragnet.*

INSIDE DETECTIVE—Reese Communications, Inc., 460 W. 34th St., New York, NY 10001. Rose Mandelsberg, Ed. Timely, true detective stories, 5,000 to 6,000 words. No fiction. Pays $250, extra for photos, on acceptance. Query. Same address and requirements for *Front page Detective*.

MASTER DETECTIVE—460 W. 34th St., New York, NY 10001. Art Crockett, Ed. Detailed articles, 5,000 to 6,000 words, with photos, on current cases, emphasizing human motivation and detective work. Pays to $250, on acceptance. Query.

THE NEW BLACK MASK QUARTERLY—2006 Sumter St., Columbia, SC 29201. Matthew J. Bruccoli, Richard Layman, Eds. Mystery fiction, 3,000 to 6,000 words. Pays to 10¢ a word, on publication.

OFFICIAL DETECTIVE STORIES—460 W. 34th St., New York, NY 10001. Art Crockett, Ed. True detective stories, 5,000 to 6,000 words, on current investigations, strictly from the investigator's point of view. No fiction. Photos. Pays $250, extra for photos, on acceptance. Query.

STARTLING DETECTIVE—See *Detective Dragnet*.

TRUE DETECTIVE—460 W. 34th St., New York, NY 10001. Art Crockett, Ed. Articles, from 5,000 words, with photos, on current police cases, emphasizing detective work and human motivation. No fiction. Pays $250, extra for photos, on acceptance. Query.

TRUE POLICE CASES—See *Detective Dragnet*.

SCIENCE FICTION AND FANTASY

ABORIGINAL SF—P.O. Box 2449, Woburn, MA 01888-0849. Charles C. Ryan, Ed. Quality science fiction, 2,500 to 4,500 words. Pays $200, on acceptance.

AMAZING STORIES—Box 100, Lake Geneva, WI 53147. George Scithers, Ed. Science fiction and fantasy, to 15,000 words. Also general-interest science articles; query first on nonfiction. Pays 4¢ to 6¢ a word, on acceptance.

ANALOG SCIENCE FICTION/SCIENCE FACT—380 Lexington Ave., New York, NY 10017. Stanley Schmidt, Ed. Science fiction, with strong characters in believable future or alien setting: short stories, 2,000 to 7,500 words; novelettes, 10,000 to 20,000 words; serials, to 80,000 words. Also uses future-related articles. pays to 7¢ a word, on acceptance. Query on serials and articles.

THE ASYMPTOTICAL WORLD—P.O. Box 1372, Williamsport, PA 17703. Michael H. Gerardi, Ed. Psychodramas, fantasy, science fiction, experimental fiction, 1,500 to 2,500 words. Illustration, photographs. Pays 2¢ a word, on acceptance. Query required.

BIFROST—Southern Circle Press, P.O. Box 1180, Milford, DE 19963. Ann Wilson, Ed. Science fiction and fantasy, varying lengths. No x-rated material. Submit poetry to Cathie Whitehead, 4020 Woolslayer Way, Pittsburgh, PA 15224. Humor; jokes. Pays in copies. Send SASE for guidelines.

DIFFERENT WORLDS—2814-19th St., San Francisco, CA 94110. Tadashi Ehara, Ed. Articles, to 5,000 words, on role-playing games: reviews, variants, source materials, etc. Pays 1¢ a word, on publication. Query preferred.

DRAGON MAGAZINE—P.O. Box 110, Lake Geneva, WI 53147. Kim Mohan, Editor-in-Chief. Patrick L. Price, Fiction Ed. Articles, 1,500 to 10,000 words, on fantasy and SF role-playing games. Fiction, 1,500 to 8,000 words. Pays 4¢ to 6¢ a word for fiction, slightly lower for articles, on publication. Query.

EMPIRE FOR THE SF WRITER—1025 55th St., Oakland, CA 94608. Millea Kenin, Ed. Articles, 2,000 words preferred, on the craft of writing science fiction and fantasy. Cartoons, illustrations, poetry. Pays negotiable rates, on publication. Query. Send SASE for guidelines.

FANTASY BOOK—P.O. Box 60126, Pasadena, CA 91106. Nick Smith, Ed. Fantasy short stories, 2,000 to 10,000 words; poetry related to the fantastic. Pays 21/2¢ to 4¢ a word, before publication.

FANTASY REVIEW—College of Humanities, Florida Atlantic University, Boca Raton, FL 33431. Robert A. Collins, Ed. Articles and interviews, to 5,000 words. Fantasy and science fiction, poetry. Cartoons, photos, artwork. Pays varying rates. Query for nonfiction.

FOOTSTEPS—Box 75, Round Top, NY 12473. Bill Munster, Ed. Material related to horror, supernatural, or the weird tale: essays, reviews, profiles, fiction, to 3,500 words. Poetry to 40 lines. Pays in copies.

HAUNTS—Nightshade Publications, Box 3342, Providence, RI 02906. Joseph K. Cherkes, Ed. Short stories—horror, science-fantasy, and supernatural tales with strong characters—1,500 to 10,000 words. No explicit sexual scenes or gratuitous violence. Pays 1/4¢ to 1/3¢ a word, on publication. Query.

THE HORROR SHOW—Phantasm Press, 14848 Misty Springs Lane, Oak Run, CA 96069. David B. Silva, Ed. Contemporary horror fiction, to 4,000 words, with a style that keeps the reader's hand trembling as he turns the pages. Pays 1/2¢ a word, on acceptance. Send SASE for guidelines.

ISAAC ASIMOV'S SCIENCE FICTION MAGAZINE—380 Lexington Ave., New York, NY 10017. Gardner Dozois, Ed. Short, character-oriented science fiction and fantasy, to 15,000 words. Pays 4¢ to 7¢ a word, on acceptance. Send SASE for requirements.

THE MAGAZINE OF FANTASY AND SCIENCE FICTION—Box 56, Cornwall, CT 06753. Edward Ferman, Ed. Fantasy and science fiction stories, to 10,000 words. Pays 4¢ to 6¢ a word, on acceptance.

THE MAGE—The Colgate Science Fiction & Fantasy Assn., CUSA, Colgate Univ., Hamilton, NY 13346. Jeffrey V. Yule, Ed. Science fiction and fantasy stories, varying lengths. Articles, reviews, poetry. Pays in copies. Include SASE.

MAGICAL BLEND—Box 11303, San Francisco, CA 94101. Steven Spears, Literary Ed. Positive, uplifting articles on spiritual exploration, lifestyles, occult, white magic and fantasy. Fiction and features to 5,000 words. Poetry, 4 to 40 lines. Pays in copies.

NIGHT CRY—800 Second Ave., New York, NY 10017. Alan Rodgers, Ed. Horror fiction—short-shorts to novels. Horrific poetry. Some fantasy, mystery, and science fiction. Response time: two to six months. Pays 5¢ to 7¢ a word, half on acceptance, half on publication.

OMNI—1965 Broadway, New York, NY 10023-1965. Ellen Datlow, Ed. Strong, realistic science fiction, 2,000 to 9,000 words, with real people as characters. Some fantasy. No horror, ghost or sword and sorcery tales. Pays $1,250-$2,000, on acceptance.

OWLFLIGHT—1025 55th St., Oakland, CA 94608. Millea Kenin, Ed. Science fiction and fantasy, to 10,000 words. Science fiction/fantasy poetry, to 100 lines. Photographs, illustrations. Pays 1¢ a word, extra for illustrations, on publication. Send SASE for guidelines.

ROD SERLING'S TWILIGHT ZONE MAGAZINE—800 Second Ave., New York, NY 10017. Michael Blaine, Ed. Fiction, to 5,000 words: human-centered fantasies of horror, suspense and the supernatural involving "ordinary people in extraordinary events." Pays about 5¢ a word, half on acceptance, half on publication.

SCIENCE FICTION CHRONICLE—P.O. Box 4175, New York, NY 10163. Andrew Porter, Ed. News items, 100 to 400 words, for SF and fantasy readers, professionals, and collectors. Photos and short articles on authors' signings. Pays 3¢ a word, on publication.

SPACE AND TIME—138 W. 70th St., #4B, New York, NY 10023. Fantasy fiction, to 15,000 words; science fiction, supernatural, sword and sorcery; poetry. Pays ¼¢ a word for fiction, in copies for poetry, on acceptance.

THRESHOLD OF FANTASY—P.O. Box 70868, Sunnyvale, CA 94086. Randall D. Larson, Ed. Fiction (fantasy, horror, sci-fi), to 5,000 words; book reviews; interviews to 1,000 words. Pays .05¢ a word for fiction, $20 for interviews, copies for reviews and poetry, on acceptance and on publication.

THRUST: SCIENCE FICTION & FANTASY REVIEW—8217 Langport Terrace, Gaithersburg, MD 20877. D. Douglas Fratz, Ed. Articles, interviews, 2,000 to 6,000 words, for readers familiar with SF and related literary and scientific topics. Book reviews, 100 to 800 words. Pays ½¢ to 2¢ a word on publication. Query preferred.

CONFESSION AND ROMANCE

INTIMACY—355 Lexington Ave., New York, NY 10017. Judy Andrews, Ed. Fiction, 2,000 to 3,000 words, for women age 18 to 45. Must have interesting plot and contain two descriptive love scenes. Pays $75 to $100, after acceptance. *Jive* geared towards the younger woman, seeking adventure and romance.

JIVE—See *Intimacy.*

MODERN ROMANCES—215 Lexington Ave., New York, NY 10016. Jean Sharbel, Ed. Confession stories with reader-identification and strong emotional tone, 1,500 to 7,500 words. Articles for blue-collar, family-oriented women, 300 to 1,000 words. Light, romantic poetry, to 24 lines. pays 5¢ a word, after publication. Buys all rights.

SECRETS—215 Lexington Ave., New York, NY 10016. Jean Press Silberg, Ed. Realistic, emotional confession stories, 1,500 to 10,000 words, emphasizing family, home, and love relationships. Articles on subjects of interest to blue-collar, family-oriented women. Pays 3¢ a word, on publication. Buys all rights.

TRUE CONFESSIONS—215 Lexington Ave., New York, NY 10016. Barbara J. Brett, Ed. Timely, emotional, first-person stories, 2,000 to 10,000 words, on romance, family life, and problems of today's young blue-collar women. Love interest and love problems should be stressed. Articles, 300 to 700 words, for young wives and mothers. Pays 5¢ a word, a month after publication.

TRUE EXPERIENCE—215 Lexington Ave., New York, NY 10016. Paula

Misiewicz, Ed. Realistic first-person stories, 4,000 to 8,000 words (short shorts, to 2,000 words), on family life, love, courtship, health, religion, etc. Pays 3¢ a word, a month after publication.

TRUE LOVE—215 Lexington Ave., New York, NY 10016. Colleen Brennan, Ed. Fresh, true first-person stories, on young love, marital problems, and topics of current interest. pays 3¢ a word, a month after publication.

TRUE ROMANCE—215 Lexington Ave., New York, NY 10016. Susan Weiner, Ed. True, romantic first-person stories, 2,000 to 12,000 words. Love poems. Articles, 300 to 700 words, for young wives and singles. Pays 3¢ a word, a month after publication.

TRUE STORY—215 Lexington Ave., New York, NY 10016. Helen Vincent, Ed. First-person true stories, 3,000 to 12,000 words. Pays 5¢ a word, on publication.

POETRY MARKETS

Markets for both serious and light verse are included in the following list of magazines.

Although major magazines pay good rates for poetry, the competition to break into print is very stiff, since editors use only a limited number of poems in each issue. On the other hand, college, little, and literary magazines use a great deal of poetry, and though payment is modest—usually in copies—publication in these journals can establish a beginning poet's reputation, and lead to publication in the major magazines. (The listing of college, literary, and little magazines, which begins on page 678, includes requirements for poetry, fiction, and essays). Poets will find a number of competitions offering cash awards for unpublished poems in the *Literary Prize Offers* list, beginning on page 760.

Poets should also consider local newspapers as possible verse markets. Although they may not specifically seek poetry from free lancers, newspaper editors often print verse submitted to them, especially on holidays and for special occasions.

The market for book-length collections of poetry is extremely limited. Commercial publishers bring out few volumes of poetry. There are a number of university presses that publish poetry collections, however (see page 756), and many of them sponsor annual competitions. Consult the *Literary Prize Offers* list for more information about these contests.

ALCOHOLISM & ADDICTION MAGAZINE—P.O. Box 31329, Seattle, WA 98103. Neil Scott, Ed. Poetry, 4 to 15 lines, on recovery from chemical or other dependencies; humor. Pays $5 to $25, on publication. Guidelines available.

ALIVE! FOR YOUNG TEENS—Christian Board of Publication, Box 179, St. Louis, MO 63166. Short poems, for 12- to 15-year-olds. Pays 25¢ per line, on publication.

ALOHA, THE MAGAZINE OF HAWAII—828 Fort St. Mall, Suite 640,

Honolulu, HI 96813. Rita Ariyoshi, Ed. Poetry related to Hawaii. Pays $25 per poem, on publication.

AMAZING STORIES—Box 110, Lake Geneva, WI 53147. George Scithers, Ed. Serious and light verse, with SF/fantasy tie-in. Pays $1.00 per line for short poems, somewhat less for longer ones, on acceptance.

AMERICA—106 W. 56th St., New York, NY 10019. John Moffitt, Poetry Ed. Serious poetry of high quality, preferably in contemporary prose idiom, 10 to 30 lines. Half-rhyme, and occasional light verse. Pays $1.40 per line, on publication.

THE AMERICAN SCHOLAR—1811 Q St. N.W., Washington, DC 20009. Joseph Epstein, Ed. Highly original poetry, 10 to 32 lines, for college-educated, intellectual readers. pays $50, on acceptance.

THE ATLANTIC—8 Arlington St., Boston, MA 02116. Peter Davison, Poetry Ed. Poetry of highest quality. Limited market; only 3 to 4 poems an issue. Interest in young poets. Occasionally uses light verse. Pays excellent rates, on acceptance.

THE ATLANTIC ADVOCATE—P.O. Box 3370, Fredericton, N.B., Canada E3B 5A2. Poetry related to Canada'a Atlantic provinces. Pays to $5 per column inch, on publication.

AUGUSTA SPECTATOR—P.O. Box 3168, Augusta, GA 30904. Poetry. Submit to: Dr. John May, Dept. of Languages & Literature, Augusta College, 2500 Walton Way, August, GA 30910.

CAPE COD LIFE—P.O. Box 222, Osterville, MA 02655. Mary Shortsleeve, Ed. Poetry, all kinds, with special interest in nature or coastal themes. Pays on publication.

CAPPER'S—616 Jefferson St., Topeka, KS 66607. Dorothy Harvey, Ed. Traditional poetry and free verse, 4 to 16 lines. Submit up to 6 poems at a time, with SASE. Pays $3 to $5, on acceptance.

CHILDREN'S PLAYMATE—P.O. Box 567, Indianapolis, IN 46206. Elizabeth A. Rinck, Ed. Poetry for children, 5 to 7 years old, on good health, nutrition, exercise, safety, seasonal and humorous subjects. Pays from $10, on publication. Buys all rights.

THE CHRISTIAN SCIENCE MONITOR—One Norway St., Boston, MA 02115. Maggie Lewis, Ed., The Home Forum. Fresh, vigorous nonreligious poems of high quality, on various subjects. Short poems preferred. Pays varying rates, on acceptance. Submit no more than 5 poems at a time.

CLASS—27 Union Sq. West, New York, NY 10003. D. Alex Harris, Ed. Poetry, 8 to 10 lines, related to the Third World population in the U.S. Payment varies, after publication.

COBBLESTONE—20 Grove St., Peterborough, NH 03458. Carolyn P. Yoder, Ed. Poetry, to 100 lines, on monthly themes, for 8- to 14-year-olds. Pays varying rates, on publication. Send SASE for guidelines and themes.

COMMONWEAL—232 Madison Ave., New York, NY 10016. Rosemary Dean, Ed. Catholic. Serious and witty poetry of high quality. Pays 40¢ a line, on publication.

COMPLETE WOMAN—1165 N. Clark St., Chicago, IL 60610. Address Assoc. Ed. Poetry. Pays $10, on publication. SASE necessary for return of material.

COSMOPOLITAN—224 W. 57th St., New York, NY 10019. Karen Burke, Poetry Ed. Poetry about relationships, for young, active career women. Pays from $25, on acceptance.

DAILY MEDITATION—Box 2710, San Antonio, TX 78299. Ruth S. Paterson, Ed. Nonsectarian. Inspirational verse. Pays 14¢ a line to 16 lines, on acceptance.

DECISION—Billy Graham Evangelistic Assn., 1300 Harmon Pl., Minneapolis, MN 55403. Roger C. Palms, Ed. Poems, 5 to 20 lines, on devotional and other subjects; free verse. Pays on publication.

THE DISCIPLE—Box 179, St. Louis, MO 63166. James L. Merrell, Ed., Londia R. Darden, Poetry Ed. Journal of Disciples of Christ. Poetry, on religious, seasonal, and historical subjects. Pays $5 to $15, on publication.

THE EVANGEL—Dept. of Christian Education, Free Methodist Headquarters, 901 College Ave., Winona Lake, IN 46590. Vera Bethel, Ed. Free Methodist. Devotional or nature poetry, 8 to 16 lines. Pays $5, on publication.

EVANGELICAL BEACON—1515 E. 66th St., Minneapolis, MN 55423. George Keck, Ed. Denominational publication of Evangelical Free Church of America. Some poetry related to Christian faith. pays 4¢ a word, $2,50 minimum, on publication.

FAMILY CIRCLE—488 Madison Ave., New York, NY 10022. No unsolicited poetry.

FARM AND RANCH LIVING—5400 S. 60th St., Greendale, WI 53129. Bob Ottum, Ed. Poetry, to 20 lines, on rural people and situations. Photos. Pays $35 to $75, extra for photos, on acceptance and on publication. Query.

GEORGIA JOURNAL—Agee Publishers, P.O. Box 526, Athens, GA 30603. Janice Moore, Ed. Poetry, to 20 lines, related to Georgia. Pays on acceptance.

GOLF DIGEST MAGAZINE—5520 Park Ave., Trumbull, CT 06611-0395. Lois Hains, Ass't. Ed. Humorous golf-related verse, 4 to 8 lines. Pays $20 to $25, on acceptance. Send SASE.

GOOD HOUSEKEEPING—959 Eighth Ave., New York, NY 10010. Serious poetry, of interest to women; send to Rosemary Leonard, Poetry Ed. Light, humorous verse; send to Mary Ann Littell, Light Housekeeping Ed. Pays $5 a line, on acceptance.

GRIT—208 W. Third St., Williamsport, PA 17701. Joanne Decker, Assignment Ed. Traditional poetry and light verse, 4 to 16 lines, for readers in small-town and rural America. Pays $6 for poems up to 4 lines, 50¢ a line for each additional line, on acceptance.

HOME LIFE—127 Ninth Ave. N., Nashville, TN 37234. Reuben Herring, Ed. Southern Baptist. Short lyrical verse, humorous, marriage and family, seasonal, and inspirational. Pays to $24, on acceptance.

IRISH AMERICA—34 E. 29th St., New York, NY 10016. Patricia Harty, Managing Ed. Occasionally uses poetry, of interest to an Irish-American audience. Pays on publication.

LADIES' HOME JOURNAL—3 Park Ave., New York, NY 10016. No unsolicited poetry; submit through an agent only.

LAKE SUPERIOR PORT CITIES—325 Lake Ave., S., Meierhoff Bldg.,

Suite 510, Duluth, MN 55802. Paul Hayden, Ed. Occasional poetry related to Lake Superior region. Pays after publication.

LEATHERNECK—Box 1775, Quantico, VA 22134. W. V. H. White, Ed. Publication related to the U.S. Marine Corps. Marine-related poetry. Pays from $10, on acceptance. SASE required.

MCCALL'S MAGAZINE—230 Park Ave., New York, NY 10169. No longer considering unsolicited poetry.

MARRIAGE AND FAMILY LIVING—Abbey Press Publishing Div., St. Meinrad, IN 47577. Kass Dotterweich, Man. Ed. Verse, on marriage and family. Pays $15, on publication.

MATURE YEARS—201 Eighth Ave. S., Nashville, TN 37202. John P. Gilbert, Ed. United Methodist. Poetry, to 14 lines, on pre-retirement, retirement, seasonal subjects, aging. No saccharine poetry. Pays 50¢ to $1.00 per line.

MID-ATLANTIC COUNTRY—P.O. Box 246, Alexandria, VA 22313. Philip Hayward, Ed. Short poetry related to the mid-Atlantic region. Pays on publication.

MIDSTREAM—515 Park Ave., New York, NY 10022. Joel Carmichael, Ed. Poetry, of Jewish interest. Pays $25, on publication.

THE MIRACULOUS MEDAL—475 E. Chelten Ave., Philadephia, PA 19144. Robert P. Cawley, C.M., Ed. Catholic. Religious verse, to 20 lines. Pays 50¢ a line, on acceptance.

MODERN BRIDE—One Park Ave., New York, NY 10016. Mary Ann Cavlin, Man. Ed. Short verse of interest to bride and groom. Pays $25 to $35, on acceptance.

MODERN MATURITY—3200 E. Carson St., Lakewood, CA 90712. Ian Ledgerwood, Ed. Short verse, to 40 lines. Pays from $50, on acceptance.

MODERN ROMANCES—215 Lexington Ave., New York, NY 10016. Jean Sharbel, Ed. Light, romantic poetry, to 24 lines. Pays varying rates, after publication. Buys all rights.

MS.—119 W. 40th St., New York, NY 10018. Address Poetry Ed. Poetry of high quality, on feminist subjects. Pays $75, on acceptance.

THE NATION—72 Fifth Ave., New York, NY 10011. Grace Schulman, Poetry Ed. Poetry of high quality. Pays after publication.

NATIONAL ENGINEER—Lantana, FL 33464. Jim Allan, Asst. Ed. Short poems of a philosophical or amusing nature. Pays $20, on publication. Include SASE.

NEW ENGLAND ENTERTAINMENT DIGEST—P.O. Box 735, Marshfield, MA 02050. Paul J. Reale, Ed. Light verse, of any length, related to the entertainment field. Pays $1 to $2, on publication.

THE NEW REPUBLIC—1220 19th St., N.W., Washington, DC 20036. Richard Howard, Poetry Ed. Poetry, of interest to liberal, intellectual readers. Pays $75, after publication.

THE NEW YORKER—25 W. 43rd St., New York, NY 10036. First-rate poetry and light verse. Pays top rates, on acceptance. Include SASE.

NORTHWEST MAGAZINE—*The Oregonian,* 1320 SW Broadway, Portland, OR 97201. Traditional and experimental poetry, by Northwest poets only. Pays $5 on acceptance.

OBLATES MAGAZINE—15 S. 59th St., Belleville, IL 62222. Address Jacqueline Lowery Corn. Inspirational poetry, to 16 lines, for middle-age to older Catholics. Pays $25, on acceptance. Guidelines.

OUR FAMILY—Box 249, Dept. E., Battleford, Sask., Canada S0M 0E0. Rev. Albert Lalonde, O.M.I., Catholic. Verse, for family men and women. Pays 75¢ to $1.00 a line, on acceptance. Send self-addressed envelope with international reply coupons for guidelines.

PENTECOSTAL EVANGEL—1445 Boonville, Springfield, MO 65802. Richard G. Champion, Ed. Journal of Assemblies of God. Religious and inspirational verse, 12 to 30 lines. Pays to 40¢ a line, on publication.

PURPOSE—616 Walnut Ave., Scottdale, PA 15683-1999. James E. Horsch, Poetry Ed. Poetry, to 12 lines, with uplifting Christian discipleship angle. Pays 50¢ to $1 a line, on acceptance.

RECOVERY—P.O. Box 31329, Seattle, WA 98103. Poetry, of interest to those recovering from alcohol or drug dependency. Pays $5 to $25, after publication.

ST. JOSEPH'S MESSENGER—P.O. Box 288, Jersey City, NJ 07303. Sister Ursula Marie Maphet, Ed. Light verse and traditional poetry, 4 to 40 lines. Pays $5 to $15, on publication.

THE SATURDAY EVENING POST—1100 Waterway Blvd., Indianapolis, IN 46202. Address Post Scripts Ed. Light verse and humor. Pays $15, on publication.

SCORE, CANADA'S GOLF MAGAZINE—287 MacPherson Ave., Toronto, Ont., Canada M4V 1A4. Poetry, to 50 words, on the Canadian and U.S. golf scene. Pays to $20, on publication.

SEVENTEEN—850 Third Ave., New York, NY 10022. Poetry, to 40 lines, by teens. Submit up to 5 poems. Pays $15, after acceptance.

UNITED METHODIST REPORTER—P.O. Box 660275, Dallas, TX 75266-0275. Spurgeon M. Dunnam III, Editor. Religious verse, 4 to 16 lines. Pays $2, on acceptance.

WESTERN PEOPLE—P.O. Box 2500, Saskatoon, Sask., Canada S7K 2C4. Mary Gilchrist, Man. Ed. Short poetry, with Western Canadian themes. Pays on acceptance. Send SAE with International Reply Coupons.

YANKEE—Dublin, NH 03444. Jean Burden, Poetry Ed. Serious poetry of high quality, to 30 lines. Pays $35 per poem for all rights, $25 for first rights, on publication.

POETRY SERIES

The following university presses publish book-length collections of poetry by writers who have never had a book of poems published. Each has specific rules for submission, so before submitting any material, be sure to write well ahead of the deadline dates for further information. Some organizations sponsor competitions in which prizes are offered for book-length collections of poetry; see *Literary Prize Offers* list on page 760.

THE ALABAMA PRESS POETRY SERIES—Dept of English, Drawer A1, Univ. of Alabama, University, AL 35486. Address Thomas Rabbit or Dara Wier. Considers unpublished book-length collections of poetry for publication as part of the Alabama Press Poetry Series. Submissions accepted during the months of September, October, and November only.

UNIVERSITY OF GEORGIA PRESS POETRY SERIES—Athens, GA 30602. Poets who have never had a book of poems published may submit book-length poetry manuscripts for possible publication. Open during the month of September each year. Manuscripts from poets who have published at least one volume of poetry (chapbooks excluded) are considered during the month of January.

WESLEYAN UNIVERSITY PRESS—110 Mt. Vernon St., Middletown, CT 06547. Considers unpublished book-length poetry manuscripts, by poets who have never had a book published, for publication in the Wesleyan New Poets Series. There is no deadline. Submit manuscript and $15.00 reading fee.

GREETING CARD MARKETS

Greeting card companies often have their own specific requirements for submitting ideas, verse, and artwork. The National Association of Greeting Card Publishers, however, gives the following general guidelines for submitting material: Verses and messages should be typed, double-spaced, each one on 3 x 5 or 4 x 6 card. Use only one side of the card, and be sure to put your name and address in the upper left-hand corner. Keep a copy of every verse or idea you send. (It's also advisable to keep a record of what you've submitted to each publisher.) Always enclose a stamped, self-addressed envelope, and do not send out more than ten verse or ideas in a group to any one publisher.

The Greeting Card Association brings out a booklet for free lancers, *Artists and Writers Market List,* with the names, addresses, and editorial guidelines of greeting card companies. This may be obtained by sending a self-addressed stamped envelope and $5.00 to The Greeting Card Association at 1350 New York Ave., NW, Suite 615, Washington, DC 20005.

AMBERLEY GREETING CARD COMPANY—P.O. Box 36159, Cincinnati, OH 45236. Ned Stern, Ed. Humorous greeting card ideas, for birthday, illness, friendship, congratulations, miss you, thank you, retirement. Risque and non-risque humor. No seasonal cards. Pays $40. Buys all rights.

AMERICAN GREETING CORPORATION—10500 American Rd., Cleveland, OH 44144. Kathleen McKay, Free-lance Ed. Studio and light humor. Study catalogue and query before submitting.

ARTFORMS CARD CORP.—725 County Line Rd., Deerfield, IL 60015. Attn: Bluma Marder. Verse, suitable for Jewish and general market. Formal for holiday cards and humorous for get well, birthdays, etc. Pays $15 to $25.

BLUE MOUNTAIN ARTS, INC.—P.O. Box 4549, Boulder, CO 80306. Attn: Editorial Staff, Dept. TW. Poetry and prose: inspirational (non-religious) and sensitive. No artwork. No rhymed verse. Include SASE. Pays $150, on publication.

BRETT-FORER GREETINGS, INC.—105 E. 73rd St., New York, NY

10021. Ideas and designs for whimsical everyday and Christmas lines. Pays on acceptance.

H. GEORGE CASPARI—225 Fifth Ave., New York, NY 10010. Lucille Andriola, Ed. Verse for traditional, birthday, everyday, holiday, juvenile, informal, etc. Query letter required. Pays on acceptance.

CELEBRATION GREETINGS—Box 9500-WR, Boulder, CO 80301. Attn.: Edit. Ass't. Verse with a Christian theme, on strength, relationships, love. Sincerity a must. Pays $35 a verse, on publication. Query with SASE for guidelines first.

CRYSTAL GREETINGS—5315 NW 22nd Ave., Tamarac, FL 33309. Fred Richard, Ed. Verse for all occasions. Pays on publication. Query first.

DRAWING BOARD GREETING CARDS—8200 Carpenter Freeway, Dallas, TX 75222. Jimmie Fitzgerald, Edit. Director. General and studio card ideas. Pays to $100.

FRAVESSI-LAMONT, INC.—11 Edison Pl., Springfield, NJ 07081. Address Editor. Short verse, mostly humorous or sentimental; cards with witty prose. No Christmas material. Pays varying rates, on acceptance.

FREEDOM GREETING CARD COMPANY—P.O. Box 715, Bristol, PA 19007. Submit to Jay Levitt. Verse, traditional, humorous, and love message. Inspirational poetry for all occasions. Pays $1 a line, on acceptance. Query with SASE.

GALLANT GREETINGS CORPORATION—2654 West Medill, Chicago, IL 60647. Ideas for humorous and serious greeting cards. Pays $30 per idea, in 45 days.

GIBSON GREETINGS, INC.—2100 Selection Rd., Cincinnati, OH 45237. William Deveron, Freelance Ed. Highest quality contemporary, conversational prose for birthday and seasonal lines; no formula gags. Guidelines available for studio cards; writers must query first for conventional lines. Pays on acceptance.

HALLMARK CARDS, INC.—P.O. Box 580, Kansas City, MO 64141. No unsolicited material.

LEANIN' TREE PUBLISHING CO.—Box 9500, Boulder, CO 80301. Address Editorial Assistant. Verse with a western flavor or theme, friendship and inspirational verse, Christian verse for holiday and friendship cards, and short love poems of upbeat, contemporary nature. Pays $35, on publication. Send SASE for guidelines first (required).

THE MAINE LINE COMPANY—P.O. Box 418, Rockport, ME 04856. Attn. Perri Ardman. Untraditional cards for contemporary women. Send SASE with three first class stamps for guidelines. Pays $25 to $50 per card.

ALFRED MAINZER, INC.—27-08 40th Ave., Long Island City, NY 11101. Arwed H. Baenisch, Art Dir. Everyday, Christmas, Mother's Day, Father's Day, Valentine's Day, Easter verses, general and religious occasions. Rates vary. Query.

MARK I—1733 W. Irving Park Rd., Chicago, IL 60613. Overstocked.

OATMEAL STUDIOS—Box 138 TW, Rochester, VT 05767. Attn: Helene Lehrer. Humorous, clever, and funny ideas needed for birthday, anniversary, get well, etc., also, Valentine's Day, Christmas, Mother's Day, Father's Day, etc. Query with SASE.

OUTREACH PUBLICATIONS—P.O. Box 1010, Siloam Springs, AZ 72761. Roy Lessin, Ed. Verse for everyday, humorous, birthday, religious, and studio cards. Send for guidelines. Pays on acceptance.

PARAMOUNT CARDS INC.—Box 1225, Pawtucket, RI 02862. Attn: Dolores Riccio. Prose and verse for sensitivity, and general cards. Humorous cards to Duff Orlemann. Send SASE for guidelines. Pays varying rates, on acceptance.

RED FARM STUDIOS—P.O. Box 347, 334 Pleasant St., Pawtucket, RI 02862. Traditional cards, for graduations, weddings, birthdays, get-wells, anniversaries, friendship, new baby, Christmas, and sympathy. No studio humor. Pays varying rates. SASE required.

REED STARLINE CARD CO.—3331 Sunset Blvd., Los Angeles, CA 90026. Barbara Stevens, Ed. Short humorous studio card copy, conversational in tone, for sophisticated adults; no verse or jingles. Everyday copy, for birthday, friendship, get well, anniversary, thank you, travel, congratulations. Pays $40 per idea, on acceptance.

ROUSANA CARDS—28 Sager Pl., Hillside, NJ 07205. Attn: Ed Briscoe, Ed. Verse, prose, cutes, and humor for Everyday and all Seasonal lines.

SANDPIPER STUDIO—P.O. Box 1007, Boulder, CO 80306. Attn.: Editorial staff. Humorous writings for greeting cards: should be fresh, original, and funny, with a unique outlook. Query first with SASE for guidelines and submission format. Pays $150, on publication.

VAGABOND CREATIONS, INC.—2560 Lance Dr., Dayton, OH 45409. George F. Stanley, Jr., Ed. Greeting cards with graphics only on cover (no copy) and short tie-in copy punch line on inside page: birthday, everyday, Valentine, Christmas, and graduation. Mildly risqué humor with *double entendre* acceptable. Ideas for humorous buttons and illustrated theme stationery. Pays $15, on acceptance.

WARNER PRESS PUBLISHERS—1200 E. Fifth St., Anderson, IN 46012. Jane H. Wendt, Product Editor. Prose sensitivity, insp. poems, and verse card ideas, religious themes. Submit Christmas material in June and July. Pays $10 to $30 per verse, on acceptance. SASE for guidelines.

WILLIAMHOUSE-REGENCY, INC.—28 W. 23rd St., New York, NY 10010. Submit to Nancy Boecker. Captions for wedding invitations. Pays varying rates, on acceptance. Query with SASE.

COLLEGE, LITERARY AND LITTLE MAGAZINES

FICTION, NONFICTION, POETRY

The thousands of literary journals, little magazines, and college quarterlies being published today welcome work from novices and pros alike; editors are always interested in seeing traditional and experimental fiction, poetry, essays, reviews, short articles, criticism, and satire, and as long as the material is well-written, the fact that a writer is a beginner doesn't adversely affect his chances for acceptance.

Most of these smaller publications have small budgets and staffs, so they may be slow in their reporting time—several months is not unusual. In addition, they usually pay only in copies of the issue in which published work appears and some—particularly college magazines—do not read manuscripts during the summer.

Publication in the literary journals can, however, lead to recognition by editors of large-circulation magazines, who read the little magazines in their search for new talent. There is also the possibility of having one's work chosen for reprinting in one of the prestigious annual collections of work from the little magazines.

Because the requirements of these journals differ widely, it is always important to study recent issues before submitting work to one of them. Copies of magazines may be in large libraries, or a writer may send a postcard to the editor, and ask the price of a sample copy. When submitting a manuscript, always enclose a return envelope, with sufficient postage for its return.

For a complete list of literary and college publications and little magazines, writers may consult such reference works as *The International Directory of Little Magazines and Small Presses,* published annually by Dustbooks (P.O. Box 100, Paradise, CA 95969).

THE AGNI REVIEW—P.O. Box 660, Amherst, MA 01004. Sharon Dunn, Ed. Short stories and poetry. Pays in copies.

ALASKA QUARTERLY REVIEW—Dept. of English, Univ. of Alaska, 3211 Providence Dr., Anchorage, AK 99508. Address Eds. Short stories, novel excerpts, poetry (traditional and unconventional forms). Submit manuscripts between August 15 and May 15. Pays in copies.

AMELIA—329 E St., Bakersfield, CA 93304. Poetry, to 100 lines; critical essays, to 2,000 words; reviews, to 500 words; belles lettres, to 1,000 words; fiction, to 3,500 words; fine pen and ink sketches; photos. Pays $35 for fiction and criticism, $10 to $25 for other nonfiction and artwork, $2 to $25 for poetry. Annual awards.

THE AMERICAN BOOK REVIEW—P.O. Box 188, Cooper Sta., New York, NY 10003. Rochelle Ratner, Russell Hoover, Eds., Book reviews, 700 to 1,200 words. Pays $25 honorarium and copies.

THE AMERICAN POETRY REVIEW—1616 Walnut St., Rm. 405, Philadelphia, PA 19103. Address Eds. Highest-quality contemporary poetry. Responds in 8 weeks. SASE a must.

AMERICAN QUARTERLY—307 College Hall, Univ. of Pennsylvania, Philadelphia, PA 19104. Janice Radway, Ed. Scholarly essays, 5,000 to 10,000 words, on any aspect of U.S. culture. Pays in copies.

THE AMERICAN SCHOLAR—1811 Q St. N.W., Washington, DC 20009. Joseph Epstein, Ed. Articles, 3,500 to 4,000 words, on science, politics, literature, the arts, etc. Book reviews. Pays $450 for articles, $100 for reviews, on publication.

AMHERST REVIEW—Box 486, Sta. 2, Amherst, MA 01002. Ruth Abbe, Ed. Fiction, to 8,000 words, and poetry, to 160 lines. Photos and drawings. Pays in copies. Submit ms. Sept.-March.

ANEMONE—Box 656, Newburyport, MA 01950. Nanette Morin, Ed. Quarterly. Fiction, nonfiction, poetry. "We are life and individual oriented." Pays in copies and subscription.

ANOTHER CHICAGO MAGAZINE—Box 11223, Chicago, IL 60611. Ficton, essays on literature, and poetry. Pays $5 to $25, on acceptance.

ANTAEUS—18 W. 30th St., New York, NY 10001. Daniel Halpern, Ed. Short stories, essays, documents, parts-of-novels, poems. Pays on publication.

ANTIETAM REVIEW—Rm. 215, 33 W. Washington St., Hagerstown, MD 21740. Ann Knox, Ed.-in-Chief. Fiction and novel excerpts, to 5,000 words. Poetry; send 1 to 3 poems at a time. Regional magazine; accepts submissions from writers in MD, PA, WV, VA, DC only. Annual literary award for fiction. Pays $100 for fiction, $25 for poetry.

THE ANTIGONISH REVIEW—St. Francis Xavier Univ., Antigonish, N.S., Canada. George Sanderson, Ed. Poetry; short stories, essays, book reviews, 1,800 to 2,500 words. Pays in copies.

ANTIOCH REVIEW—P.O. Box 148, Yellow Springs, OH 45387. Robert S. Fogarty, Ed. Timely articles, 2,000 to 8,000 words, on social sciences, literature, and humanities. Quality fiction. Poetry. No inspirational poetry. Pays $10 per printed page, on publication.

APALACHEE QUARTERLY—Apalachee Press, P.O. Box 20106, Tallahassee, FL 32316. Monica Faeth, Barbara Hamby, and Elizabeth Woodsmall, Eds. Fiction, to 30 manuscript pages; poems (3 to 5). Pays in copies.

APOCALYPSO—673 Ninth Ave., New York, NY 10036. Articles and fiction, to 3,000 words. Poetry, any length. Archival material and graphics. Pays in copies.

ARIZONA QUARTERLY—Univ. of Arizona, Tucscon, AZ 85721. Albert F. Gegenheimer, Ed. Literary essays; regional material; general-interest articles. Fiction, to 3,500 words. Poetry (up to 30 lines)—any form or subject matter. Pays in copies.

THE ATAVIST—P.O. Box 5643, Berkeley, CA 94705. Robert Dorsett, Loretta Ko, Eds. Poetry and poetry criticism, varying lengths. Pays in copies. SASE required.

AURA LITERARY/ARTS REVIEW—P.O. Box 76, University Center Sta., Birmingham, AL 35294. Fiction and essays on literature, to 6,000 words. Poetry, photos and drawings. Pays in copies.

BALL STATE UNIVERSITY FORUM—Ball State Univ., Muncie, IN 47306. Bruce W. Hozeski and Frances Mayhew Rippy, Eds. Short stories and general-interest articles, 500 to 4,000 words. One-act plays. Poetry. Pays in copies.

BELLES LETTRES—Box 987, Arlington, VA 22216. Janet Mullaney, Ed. Reviews and essays, 250 and 1,500 words, on literature by women. Queries are required. Editorial guidelines available. Pays in copies.

THE BELLINGHAM REVIEW—932 Monitor Ave., Wenatchee, WA 98801. Randy Jay Landon, Ed. Fiction, to 5,000 words. Poetry of all kinds. Short dramas. Submit manuscripts between September 15 and May 1. Pays in copies plus subscription. Annual contest.

THE BELOIT FICTION JOURNAL—Box 11, Beloit College, Beloit, WI

53511. Clint McCown, Ed. Short fiction, 15 to 20 manuscript pages. Pays in copies. Submit Sept.–April only.

BELOIT POETRY JOURNAL—RFD 2, Box 154, Ellsworth, ME 04605. First-rate contemporary poetry, of any length or mode. Pays in copies. Send SASE for guidelines.

BELLOWING ARK—P.O. Box 45637, Seattle, WA 98154. Robert R. Ward, Managing Ed. Short stories, novels-in-progress (no set length). Poetry of varying lengths. "We publish poetry and fiction that explores the processes of conflict and affirmation in a human context. We are seeking only the highest quality material." Pays in copies.

BERKELEY POETS COOPERATIVE—P.O. Box 459, Berkeley, CA 94701. Charles Entrekin, Ed. Poetry, all forms; no restrictions. Submissions accepted from April 1 to August 1 and from October 1 to February 1. Pays in copies.

BIG TWO-HEARTED—Mid-Peninsula Library Cooperative, 424 Stephenson Ave., Iron Mountain, MI 49801. Gary Silver, Ed. Quarterly. Traditional or experimental fiction, to 2,500 words. Regional, local history of Michigan's upper peninsula, to 2,500 words. Poetry, traditional or experimental, any length. Filler material relating to public libraries. No obscenity. Pays in copies.

BITTERROOT—P.O. Box 489, Spring Glen, NY 12483. Menke Katz, Ed.-in-Chief. Poetry, to 50 lines; B&W camera ready drawings. Pays in copies. Annual contests. Send SASE for information.

BLACK MARIA—P.O. Box 25187, Chicago, IL 60625. Feminist. Short stories and experimental fiction, to 3,500 words. Poetry of any form. Articles; essays; B & W photos. Pays in copies.

BLACK RIVER REVIEW—855 Mildred Ave., Lorain, OH 44052. Poetry, short book reviews, short essays, cartoons. Pays in copies.

THE BLACK WARRIOR REVIEW—P.O. Box 2936, University, AL 35486. Lynn Domina, Ed. Serious and imaginative fiction; reviews and essays; poetry (no religious or haiku). Pays per printed page. Annual contest.

THE BLOOMSBURY REVIEW—P.O. Box 8928, Denver, CO 80201. Tom Auer, Ed.; Carol Arenberg, Senior Ed.; Ray Gonzalez, Poetry Ed. Book reviews, publishing features, interviews, essays, poetry, up to 800 words. Pays $5 to $25, on publication.

BLUELINE—Blue Mountain Lake, NY 12812. Alice Gilborn, Ed. Essays, fiction, to 2,500 words, on Adirondack region or similar areas. Poetry, to 44 lines. No more than 5 poems per submission. Pays in copies.

BOOK FORUM—38 E. 76th St., New York, NY 10021. Essays, 800 to 1,600 words, on books, writers, art, politics, etc. Interviews. Book reviews assigned. Pays $25 to $50, on acceptance. Query.

BOSTON REVIEW—33 Harrison Ave., Boston, MA 02111. Margaret Ann Roth, Ed.-in-Chief. Reviews and essays, 800 to 3,000 words, on literature, art, music, film, photography. Original fiction, to 5,000 words. Poetry. Pays $40 to $150.

BOTTOMFISH—De Anza College, 21250 Stevens Creek Blvd., Cupertino, CA 95014. Robert E. Brock, Ed. Short, contemporary fiction, to 3,500 words; poetry, prefer tight lyric. Pays in copies.

BUCKNELL REVIEW—Bucknell Univ., Lewisburg, PA 17837. Interdisciplinary journal in book form. Scholarly articles on arts, science, and letters. Pays in copies.

CAESURA—English Dept., Auburn Univ., Auburn, AL 36849. R. T. Smith, Managing Ed. Biannual. Short stories, to 3,000 words. Narrative and lyric poetry, in fixed forms or free verse, to 150 lines. Pays in copies.

CALLIOPE—Creative Writing Program, Roger Williams College, Bristol, RI 02809. Martha Christina, Ed. Short stories, to 2,500 words; poetry (query first to find out about thematic issues). Pays in copies. No submissions April through July.

CALYX, A JOURNAL OF ART & LITERATURE BY WOMEN—P.O. Box B, Corvallis, OR 97339. M. Donnelly, Man. Ed. Fiction, 5,000 words, reviews, 250 to 1,000 words; poetry, to 6 poems; poetry book reviews, to 1,000 words. Pays in copies. Include short bio and SASE. Send for guidelines.

CANADIAN FICTION MAGAZINE—Box 946, Sta. F., Toronto, Ontario, Canada M4Y 2N9. High-quality short stories, novel excerpts, and experimental fiction, to 5,000 words, by Canadians. Interviews with Canadian authors; translations. Pays $10 per page, on publication.

THE CAPILANO REVIEW—Capilano College, 2055 Purcell Way, North Vancouver, B.C., Canada V7J 3H5. Dorothy Jantzen, Ed. Fiction; poetry; drama; visual arts. Pays $10 to $40.

CAROLINA QUARTERLY—Greenlaw Hall 066A, Univ. of North Carolina, Chapel Hill, NC 27514. Emily Stockard, Ed. Fiction, to 7,000 words, by new or established writers. Poetry (no restrictions on length, though limited space makes inclusion of works of more than 300 lines impractical). Pays $3 per printed page for fiction, $5 per poem, on acceptance.

THE CENTENNIAL REVIEW—110 Morrill Hall, Michigan State Univ., East Lansing, MI 48824-1036. Linda Wagner, Ed. Articles, 3,000 to 5,000 words, on sciences and humanities. Poetry. Pays in copies and subscription.

THE CHARITON REVIEW—Northeast Missouri State Univ., Kirksville, MO 63501. Jim Barnes, Ed. Highest quality poetry and fiction, to 6,000 words. Modern and contemporary translations. Book reviews. Pays $5 per printed page for fiction and translations.

THE CHICAGO REVIEW—Univ. of Chicago, Chicago, IL 60637. Robert Sitko Ed. Essays; interviews; reviews; fiction; translations; poetry. Pays in copies plus subscription.

CIMARRON REVIEW—Oklahoma State Univ., Stillwater, OK 74078. Jeanne Adams Wray, Man. Ed. Articles, 1,500 to 2,500 words, on history, philosophy, political science, etc. Serious contemporary fiction. Pays in copies.

CINCINNATI POETRY REVIEW—Dept. of English, 069, Univ. of Cincinnati, Cincinnati, OH 45221. Poetry. Pays in copies.

CLOCK RADIO—3409 Tulane Dr., #1, Hyattsville, MD 20738. Jay Dougherty, Ed. Triannual. Short fiction and nonfiction, to 1,000 words. Poetry, traditional and experimental, any length. Pays in copies.

COLORADO REVIEW—English Dept., 322 Eddy, Colorado State Univ., Fort Collins, CO 80523. Fiction submissions accepted from August 1 to December 31; poetry from January 1 to April 30 every year. Poetry, fiction, translations, interviews, reviews, articles.

COLORADO-NORTH REVIEW—Univ. Center, Univ. of Northern Colorado, Greeley, CO 80639. Address Ed. Fiction, to 20 typed pages; poetry; graphic art. Include biographical sketch with submission. Pays in copies.

COLUMBIA, A MAGAZINE OF POETRY & PROSE—404 Dodge, Columbia Univ., New York, NY 10027. Address appropriate Ed. Articles and fiction, to 25 typed pages. Poetry. Pays in copies. Annual award. SASE *required*.

CONFRONTATION—Dept. of English, C. W. Post of L.I.U., Greenvale, NY 11548. Martin Tucker, Ed. Serious fiction, 750 to 6,000 words. Crafted poetry, 20 to 200 lines. Pays $5 to $50, on publication.

THE CONNECTICUT POETRY REVIEW—P.O. Box 3783, New Haven, CT 06525. J. Claire White and James Chichetto, Eds. Poetry, 5 to 20 lines, and reviews, 700 words. Pays $5 per poem, $10 for a review, on acceptance.

CONNECTICUT RIVER REVIEW—30 Burr Farms Rd., Westport, CT 06880. Peggy Heinrich, Ed. Poetry, to 40 lines. Pays in copies.

COTTON BOLL/THE ATLANTA REVIEW—P.O. Box 76757, Sandy Springs, Atlanta, GA 30358. Mary Hollingsworth, Ed. Literary short stories. to 3,500 words, and poetry, to 2 typed pages. Payment varies.

CRITICAL INQUIRY—Univ. of Chicago Press, Wieboldt Hall, 1050 E. 59th St., Chicago, IL 60637. W. J. T. Mitchell, Ed. Critical essays that offer a theoretical perspective on literature, music, visual arts, popular culture, etc. Pays in copies.

CROTON REVIEW—P.O. Box 277, Croton-on-Hudson, NY 10520. Quality short-short fiction (to 14 pages), poetry (to 75 lines), and literary essays. Submissions accepted from September to February only. Pays with copy and honorarium. Send SASE for guidelines.

CUMBERLAND POETRY REVIEW—P.O. Box 120128, Acklen Sta., Nashville, TN 37212. Address Eds. High-quality poetry and criticism; translations. No restrictions on form, style or subject matter. Pays in copies.

CUTBANK—English Dept., Univ. of Montana, Missoula, MT 59812. Pamela Uschuk, Ed. Biannual. Short stories, any length. Essays. Reviews, 1 to 1½ pages. Poetry (submit 3 to 5 at a time). Pays in copies.

DARING POETRY QUARTERLY—2020 Ninth St., S.W., Canton, OH 44706. Denise Reynolds, Ed. Quarterly. Poetry, all types, to 40 words. Pays in copies.

DENVER QUARTERLY—Univ. of Denver, Denver, CO 80208. David Milofsky, Ed. Literary, cultural essays, and articles; poetry; book reviews; fiction. Pays $5 per printed page, after publication.

DESCANT—Texas Christian Univ., T.C.U. Sta., Fort Worth, TX 76129. Betsy Colquitt and Stanley Trachtenberg, Eds. Fiction, to 6,000 words. Poetry to 40 lines. No restriction on form or subject. Pays in copies. Submit Sept.–May only.

EPOCH—245 Goldwin Smith Hall, Cornell Univ., Ithaca, NY 14853. Serious fiction and poetry. Submissions read between Sept. and June only. Pays $10 a page for prose; $1 a line for poetry.

EVENT—Douglas College, Box 2503, New Westminister, BC, Canada, V3L 5B2. Dale Zieroth, Ed. Short fiction; short plays; poetry. Pays modest rates, on publication.

683

EXPRESSIONS: FIRST STATE JOURNAL—P.O. Box 4064, Greenville, DE 19807. Joanne Pettrizzi, Ed. Contemporary, prose poems, and historical literary, regional, juvenile, and experimental poems. Submit up to 8 poems at a time. Pays in copies.

FARMER'S MARKET—P.O. Box 1272, Galesburg, IL 61402. Short stories, novel excerpts, and essays to 20 pages, and poetry, related to the Midwest. Pays in copies.

FAT TUESDAY—419 N. Larchmont Blvd., Ste. 104, Los Angeles, CA 90004. F. M. Cotolo, Ed. Annual. Short fiction, poetry, parts-of-novels, paragraphs, crystal thoughts of any dimension—up to 5 pages. Pays in copies.

FICTION INTERNATIONAL—English Dept., San Diego State Univ., San Diego, CA 92182. Harold Jaffe and Larry McCaffery, Eds. Post-modernist and politically committed fiction and theory. Pays in copies.

THE FIDDLEHEAD—Dept. of English, Univ. of New Brunswick, Fredericton, N.B., Canada E3B 5A3. Serious fiction, 2,500 words, preferably by Canadians. Pays about $10 per printed page, on publication.

FIELD—Rice Hall, Oberlin College, Oberlin, OH 44074. Stuart Friebert, David Young, Eds. Serious poetry, any length, by established and unknown poets; essays on poetics by poets. Translations by qualified translators. Pays $15 to $25 per page, on publication.

FINE MADNESS—P.O. Box 15176, Seattle, WA 98115. Address Eds. Poetry, any length. Pays in copies.

FOOTWORK—Cultural Affairs Office, Passiac Comm. College, College Blvd., Patterson, NJ 07509. Maria Gillan, Ed. High quality fiction, to 4 pages, and poetry, to 3 pages, any style. Pays in copies.

FORMATIONS—832 Chilton Lane, Wilmette, IL 60091. Jonathan Brent, Ed. Triannual. Fiction and essays, any length. Pays in copies.

THE GAMUT—1216 Rhodes Tower, Cleveland State Univ., Cleveland, OH 44115. Lively articles on general-interest topics concerned with the region or by regional writers, 2,000 to 6,000 words. Quality fiction and poetry. Photos. Pays $25 to $250, on publication. Send SASE for guidelines.

GARGOYLE—P.O. Box 30906, Bethesda, MD 20814. Richard Peabody, Ed. Poetry, average 10 to 35 lines. Fiction. Pays in copies.

THE GEORGIA REVIEW—Univ. of Georgia, Athens, GA 30602. Stanley W. Lindberg, Ed.; Stephen Corey, Asst. Ed. Short fiction; interdisciplinary essays on arts and the humanities; book reviews; poetry. No submissions in June, July, and August.

GRAIN—Box 1154, Regina, Sask., Canada, S4P 3B4. Brenda Riches, Ed. Short stories, to 30 typed pages. Songs, essays, and drama. Poems (send no more than 6). Pays $30 to $100 for prose; $20 per poem, on publication.

GREAT RIVER REVIEW—211 W. 7th St., Winona, MN 55987. Fiction and creative prose, 2,000 to 10,000 words. Quality contemporary poetry; send 4 to 8 poems. Special interest in Midwestern writers and themes.

THE GREENFIELD REVIEW—R.D. 1, Box 80, Greenfield Ctr., NY 12833. Contemporary poetry by established and new poets, and third world writers. Pays in copies.

GREEN'S MAGAZINE—P.O. Box 3236, Regina, Sask., Canada S4P 3H1.

David Green, Ed. Fiction for family reading, 1,500 to 4,000 words. Poetry, to 40 lines. Pays in copies.

THE GREENSBORO REVIEW—Univ. of North Carolina, Greensboro, NC 27412. Lee Zacharias, Ed. Semi-annual. Poetry and fiction. Submission deadlines: Sept. 15 and Feb. 15. Pays in copies.

THE HARBOR REVIEW—English Dept., U. Mass-Boston, Boston, MA 02125. Fiction, to 10 pages; poetry, 3 to 5 per submission; any length. Pays in copies.

THE HARVARD REVIEW—Byerly Hall 220, 8 Garden St., Cambridge, MA 02138. Nancy Bauer, Man. Ed. Quarterly. Seeks academic papers from graduate students, on all topics in the arts and sciences. Shorter essays, and book reviews, 1,000 to 2,000 words, on popular culture through an academic lens. Pays in copies. Query.

HAUNTS—Nightshade Publications, Box 3342, Providence, RI 02906. Joseph K. Cherkes, Ed. Quarterly. Short stories—horror, science-fantasy, and supernatural tales with strong characters—1,500 to 10,000 words. No explicit sexual scenes or gratuitous violence. Pays ¼¢ to ⅓¢ per word, on publication.

HAWAII REVIEW—Dept. of English, Univ. of Hawaii, 1733 Donaghho Rd., Honolulu, HI 96882. Quality fiction, poetry, interviews, and literary criticism reflecting both regional and universal concerns.

HELICON NINE, THE JOURNAL OF WOMEN'S ARTS AND LETTERS—P.O. Box 22412, Kansas City, MO 64113. Poetry and fiction about women. Include SASE.

HERESIES—Box 766, Canal St. Sta., New York, NY 10013. Biannual. Fiction and nonfiction, to 12 typed pages. Poetry. Feminist art/political magazine; each issue is centered on a specific theme. Query for details. Pays small honorarium.

HIGH COUNTRY NEWS—Box 1090, Paonia, CO 81428. C. L. Rawlins, Poetry Ed. Poetry, related to Western U.S. life and issues.

HOME PLANET NEWS—Box 415, Stuyvesant Sta., New York, NY 10009. Enid Dame, Donald Lev, Eds. Lively, energetic poetry, to 100 lines; shorter poems preferred. Pays in copies. Rarely accepts unsolicited manuscripts.

HUBBUB MAGAZINE—5344 S.E. 38th, Portland, OR 97202. Lisa Steinmen, Carlos Reyes, Eds. Poetry. Pays in copies. Rarely accepts unsolicited manuscripts.

IMAGINE, INTERNATIONAL CHICANO POETRY JOURNAL—645 Beacon St., Suite 7, Boston, MA 02215. Tino Villanueva, Ed. Articles, interviews, to 22 double-spaced pages; reviews; poetry. Pays $5.00 for articles and interviews, $3.00 for reviews, and 10¢ a line for poetry.

INDIANA REVIEW—316 N. Jordan Ave., Bloomington, IN 47405. Pamela Wampler, Jim Brock, Eds. Fiction with an emphasis on style. Poems that are well executed and ambitious. Pays $5 a page for poetry; poems and fiction are eligible for annual contest.

INLET—Dept. of English, Virginia Wesleyan College, Norfolk, VA 23502. Joseph Harkey, Ed. Short fiction, 500 to 3,000 words (short lengths preferred). Poems of 4 to 40 lines; all forms and themes. Submit between September and March 1st, each year. Pays in copies.

INTERNATIONAL POETRY REVIEW—Box 2047, Greensboro, NC 27402. Evalyn P. Gill, Ed. Contemporary poetry and translations (with original). Pays in copies.

INVISIBLE CITY—P.O. Box 2853, San Francisco, CA 94126. John McBride, Paul Vangelisti, Eds. Reviews, translations, especially contemporary European literature.

THE IOWA REVIEW—EPB 308, Univ. of Iowa, Iowa City, IA 52242. David Hamilton, Ed. Essays, poems, stories, reviews. Pays $10 a page for fiction and nonfiction, $1 a line for poetry, on publication

JAM TO-DAY—372 Dunstable Rd., Tyngsboro, MA 01879. Don Stanford and Judith Stanford, Eds. High-quality fiction and poetry, particularly from unknown and little-known writers. Pays $5 per printed page for fiction, $5 per poem, plus copies.

JAPANOPHILE—Box 223, Okemos, MI 48864. Earl R. Snodgrass, Ed. Fiction, to 10,000 words, with a Japanese setting. Each story should have at least one Japanese character and at least one non-Japanese. Pays to $20, on publication. Annual contest in December.

JOURNAL OF POPULAR CULTURE—Center for the Study of Popular Culture, Bowling Green State Univ., Bowling Green, OH 43403. Ray B. Browne, Ed. Articles. Pays in copies.

KANSAS QUARTERLY—Dept. of English, Denison Hall 122, Kansas State Univ., Manhattan, KS 66506. Literary criticism, art and history. Pays in copies. Query for articles and special topics.

KARAMU—Dept. of English, Eastern Illinois Univ., Charleston, IL 61920. John Guzlowski, Ed. Contemporary or experimental fiction. Poetry. Pays in copies.

LIGHT YEAR—Bits Press, Dept. of English, Case Western Reserve Univ., Cleveland, OH 44106. Robert Wallace, Ed. Annual. "The best funny, witty, or merely levitating verse being written." No restrictions on style or length. Pays $4 per poem plus 10¢ per line, on publication. Material will not be returned unless accompanied by SASE.

LILITH—250 W. 57th St., New York, NY 10019. Susan Weidman Schneider, Ed. Fiction, 1,500 to 2,000 words, on issues of interest to Jewish women. Pays in copies.

THE LION AND THE UNICORN—English Dept., Brooklyn College, Brooklyn, NY 11210. Geraldine DeLuca, Roni Natov, Eds. Articles, from 2,000 words, offering criticism of children's and young adult books, for teachers, librarians, scholars, artists, and parents. Query first for monthly themes. Pays in copies.

LITERARY MAGAZINE REVIEW—English Dept., Kansas State Univ., Manhattan, KS 66506. Reviews and articles concerning literary magazines, 1,000 to 1,500 words, for writers and readers of contemporary literature. Pays modest fees and copies. Query preferred.

THE LITERARY REVIEW—Fairleigh Dickinson Univ., 285 Madison Ave., Madison, NJ 07940. Martin Green, Harry Keyishian, Walter Cummins, William Zander, Eds. Serious fiction; poetry; translations; reviews; essays on literature. Pays in copies.

THE LITTLE BALKANS REVIEW—601 Grandview Heights Terrace, Pittsburg, KS 66762. Fiction, to 5,000 words; articles, to 6,000 words; and poetry (prefer Kansas slant). Illustrations. Pays in copies.

THE LONG STORY—11 Kingston St., N. Andover, MA 01845. Stories, 8,000 to 20,000 words; prefer committed fiction. Pays $1 a page, on publication. Poetry.

THE MAGAZINE OF SPECULATIVE POETRY—P.O. Box 564, Beloit, WI 53511. Mark Rich, Ed. Poetry, of any length. "We are looking for the best of the new poetry using the ideas, imagery, and approaches developed by speculative fiction. We welcome experimental techniques as well as the fresh employment of traditional form." Pays in copies.

THE MALAHAT REVIEW—Univ. of Victoria, P.O. Box 1700, Victoria, B.C., Canada V8W 2Y2. Constance Rooke, Ed. Fiction and poetry, including translations, and occasional articles. Pays from $10 to $15 per page, on acceptance.

THE MANHATTAN REVIEW—304 Third Ave., New York, NY 10010. Highest quality poetry. Pays in copies.

MASSACHUSETTS REVIEW—Memorial Hall, Univ. of Massachusetts, Amherst, MA 01003. Literary criticism; articles on public affairs, scholarly disciplines. Short fiction. Poetry. No submissions between June and October. Pays modest rates, on publication.

MEMPHIS STATE REVIEW—Dept. of English, Memphis State Univ., Memphis, TN 38152. Ed. Short stories, novel excerpts, to 4,500 words; poetry, to one page. Pays in copies. Annual award.

MENDOCINO REVIEW—Box 888, Mendocino, CA 95460-0888. Annual. All types of fiction and articles (no reviews), to 2,500 words; poetry. Pays in copies.

METROSPHERE—Metropolitan State College, 1006 11th St., Office of Publication, Box 57, Denver, CO 80204. Interviews and profiles of writers and artists, 1,200 words; fiction, to 1,500 words; and poetry, to 50 lines. Pays in copies.

MICHIGAN HISTORICAL REVIEW—Clark Historical Lib., Central Michigan Univ., Mt. Pleasant, MI 48859. Address Ed. Articles related to Michigan's political, social, economic, and cultural history. SASE.

MICHIGAN QUARTERLY REVIEW—3032 Rackham Bldg., Univ. of Michigan, Ann Arbor, MI 48109. Laurence Goldstein, Ed. Scholarly essays on all subjects; fiction; poetry. Pays $8 a page, on publication. Annual contest.

THE MICKLE STREET REVIEW—Box 1221, Haddonfield, NJ 08033. Annual. Articles, poems, and artwork related to Walt Whitman. Pays in copies.

MID-AMERICAN REVIEW—Dept. of English, Bowling Green State Univ., Bowling Green, OH 43403. Robert Early, Ed. High-quality fiction, poetry, articles, and reviews of contemporary writing. Fiction to 20,000 words. Reviews, articles, 500 to 2,500 words. Pays to $75, on publication.

MIDWEST QUARTERLY—Pittsburg State Univ., Pittsburg, KS 66762. James B. Schick, Ed. Scholarly articles, 2,500 to 5,000 words, on contemporary issues. Pays in copies.

MILKWEED CHRONICLE—Box 24303, Minneapolis, MN 55424. Emilie Buchwald, Ed. Poems that reflect a unique voice. No overly religious or political material. Pays $15 per poem, $50 to $100 for essays (1,200 to 3,000 words), on publication.

MIND IN MOTION—P.O. Box 1118, Apple Valley, CA 92307. Celeste

Goyer, Ed. Poetry, to 45 lines, that stimulates the intellect through liberal use of inventive figues and free association and encourages envisioning familiar realities in new ways. Emphasis should be upon universal concerns artfully directed toward the everyday and esoteric. Fiction, 500 to 2,500 words—allegory, fable, surrealism, parody, psychology. Pays in copies.

THE MINNESOTA REVIEW—Dept. of English, SUNY, Stony Brook, NY 11794. Michael Sprinker, Ed. Poetry, fiction, essays, reviews. Pays in copies.

MISSISSIPPI REVIEW—Center for Writers, Univ. of Southern Mississippi, Southern Sta., Box 5144, Hattiesburg, MS 39406. Serious fiction, poetry, criticism, interviews.

THE MISSISSIPPI VALLEY REVIEW—Dept. of English, Western Illinois Univ., Macomb, IL 61455. Forrest Robinson, Ed. Short fiction, to 20 typed pages. Poetry; send 3 to 5 poems. Pays in copies.

THE MISSOURI REVIEW—Dept. of English, 231 Arts & Science, Univ. of Missouri-Columbia, Columbia, MO 65211. Greg Michalson, Man. Ed. Poems, of any length. Fiction and essays. Pays $5 to $10 per printed page, on publication.

MODERN HAIKU—P.O. Box 1752, Madison, WI 53701. Robert Spiess, Ed. Haiku and articles about haiku. Pays $1 a haiku, $5 a page for articles.

MONTHLY REVIEW—155 W. 23rd St., New York, NY 10011. Paul M. Sweezy, Harry Magdoff, Eds. Serious articles, 5,000 words, on politics and economics, from independent socialist viewpoint. Pays $50, on publication.

THE MOVEMENT—P.O. Box 19458, Los Angeles, CA 90019. Roberts C. Taylor, Ed. Articles dedicated to spiritual/transformational interests, 1,000 words. Pays in copies. Must include SASE.

MOVING OUT—P.O. Box 21249, Detroit, MI 48221. Quality poetry, fiction, articles and art by women; submit 4 to 6 poems at a time. Pays in copies.

MSS—State Univ. of New York, Binghamton, NY 13901. L. M. Rosenberg, Joanna Higgins, Eds. Short stories, novellas, essays, poems, illustrations, any length. Tri-quarterly. Pays negotiable rates. No submissions May 1-Aug. 1.

MUNDUS ARTIUM—Univ. of Texas at Dallas, Box 688, Richardson, TX 75080. Rainer Schulte, Ed. Short fiction, poetry, translations, interdisciplinary essays on the humanities. Pays in copies.

NATIONAL POETRY JOURNAL—177 S. Front St., Souderton, PA 18964. W. Bruce Fenstermacher, Ed. Quarterly. Poetry, any length, by new poets. Pays in copies.

NEBO—Dept. of English, Arkansas Tech. Univ., Russellville, AR 72801. Mainstream fiction, to 20 pages; critical essays, to 10 pages; poetry, 5 poems per submission. Pays in copies.

NEGATIVE CAPABILITY—6116 Timberly Rd. N., Mobile, AL 36609. Sue Walker, Ed. Poetry, any length; fiction, essays, art. Pays in copies. Annual Eve of St. Agnes poetry competition.

THE NEW CRITERION—850 Seventh Ave., New York, NY 10019. Robert Richman, Poetry Ed. Poems of varying lengths. Pays in copies.

NEW ENGLAND ENTERTAINMENT DIGEST—P.O. Box 735, Marshfield, MA 02050. Paul J. Reale, Ed. Light verse, of any length, related to the entertainment field. Pays $1 to $2, on publication.

NEW JERSEY POETRY JOURNAL—Dept. of English, Monmouth College, W. Long Beach, NJ 07764. Poetry. Pays in copies.

NEW LETTERS—Univ. of Missouri-Kansas City, Kansas City, MO 64110. Short fiction and poetry. Personal or scholarly essays. Annual contest.

NEW MEXICO HUMANITIES REVIEW—Box A, New Mexico Tech, Socorro, NM 87801. Poetry, any length, any themes; southwestern and native American themes welcome. Pays with subscription.

NEW ORLEANS REVIEW—Loyola Univ., New Orleans, LA 70118. John Mosier, Ed. Literary or film criticism, to 6,000 words. Serious fiction and poetry.

THE NEW SOUTHERN LITERARY MESSENGER—400 S. Laurel St., Richmond VA 23220. Charles Lohmann, Ed. Ingraham Kirkland, Fiction Ed. Quarterly. Short stories, satire, science fiction, contemporary history, 1,000 to 5,000 words. One-act plays and short film scripts. Pays $5 for one-time reprint rights, plus one copy, on publication. Send for guidelines.

NEXUS—Wright State Univ., 006 U.C., Dayton, OH 45431. High quality short stories, to 2,000 words; poetry, to 50 lines. Book reviews and recent releases, to 1,500 words.

NIMROD—2210 S. Main St., Tulsa, OK 74114. Quality poetry and fiction, experimental and traditional. Pays in copies. Annual awards for poetry and fiction. Send for guidelines.

THE NORTH AMERICAN REVIEW—University of Northern Iowa, Cedar Falls, IA 50614. Peter Cooley, Poetry Ed. Poetry of high quality. Fiction, of highest quality (address Fiction Ed. Submissions accepted Jan.-March only). Pays 50¢ a line for poetry, $10 per published page for fiction, on acceptance.

THE NORTH DAKOTA QUARTERLY—Box 8237, Univ. of North Dakota, Grand Forks, ND 58202. Nonfiction essays in the humanities. Some fiction, reviews, graphics and poetry. Limited market. Pays in copies.

NORTHWEST REVIEW—369 PLC, Univ. of Oregon, Eugene, OR 97403. John Witte, Ed. Serious fiction, commentary, and poetry. Reviews. Pays in copies.

NYCTICORAX—P.O. Box 844 4, Asheville, NC 28814. John A. Youril, Ed. Triannual. Short-short fiction and poetry (submit 4 to 8 poems at a time). Theme and style are open. Query about essays on literary criticism. Pays in copies.

OAK SQUARE—Box 1238, Allston, MA 02134. Philip Borenstein, Ed. Experimental and traditional short stories, about 2,500 words. Genre fiction (westerns and gothics, for instance) are of interest. Nonpolitical essays and interviews (query first). Some poetry. Pays in copies.

OBSIDIAN—Dept. of English, Wayne State Univ., Detroit, MI 48202. Alvin Aubert, Ed. Short fiction, poetry and plays by blacks, interviews, reviews, scholarly articles, on black authors and their work. Pays in copies.

THE OHIO JOURNAL—164 W. 17th Ave., Columbus, OH 43210. David Citino, Ed. Short stories, poetry, book reviews. No submissions during the summer. Pays in copies.

OHIO RENAISSANCE REVIEW—P.O. Box 804, Ironton, OH 45638. James R. Pack, Ed. Ron Houchin, Poetry Ed. Science fiction, fantasy, and mystery stories, 400 to 3,000 words. Contemporary, avant-garde poetry, any length. Pays $2.50 per column for fiction, 25¢ a line for poetry, on publication. Include bio and SASE.

THE OHIO REVIEW—Ellis Hall, Ohio Univ., Athens, OH 45701-2979. Short stories, poetry, essays, reviews. Pays from $5 per page, plus copies, on publication.

OLD HICKORY REVIEW—P.O. Box 1178, Jackson, TN 38302. Joe De-Vitis, Edna Lackie, Eds. Biannual. Fiction and nonfiction, humorous articles, 2,500 to 3,000 words. Poetry, all forms—blank verse, free verse, haiku, avant-garde, traditional forms, light and serious verse. Avoid sentimental and mawkishly religious submissions. Length: 40 lines maximum. Pays in copies.

THE ONTARIO REVIEW—9 Honey Brook Dr., Princeton, NJ 08540. Raymond J. Smith, Ed. Poetry and fiction. No unsolicited manuscripts.

ORPHEUS—P.O. Box 67807, Los Angeles, CA 90067. P. Schneidre, Ed. Poetry. Pays from $5, on publication.

ORPHIC LUTE—1675A 16th St., Los Alamos, NM 87544. Patricia Doherty Hinnebusch, Ed. Quarterly. Lyric poetry, traditional and contemporary. A lyric poem should be a distillation of an event to communicate its significance, not a statement of what happened and how poet reacted. Send up to 4 poems at a time. Pays in copies.

OTHER VOICES—820 Ridge Rd., Highland Park, IL 60035. Dolores Weinberg, Ed. Semiannual. Short stories and novel excerpts, to 5,000 words. Pays in copies.

PACIFIC REVIEW—Dept. of English and Comp. Lit., San Diego State Univ., San Diego, CA 92181. High quality fiction, essays, reviews, and poetry. Pays in copies.

PANDORA—Empire Books, P.O. Box 625, Murray, KY 42071. Science fiction and speculative fantasy stories, to 5,000 words. Pays 1¢ a word, on acceptance. SASE for guidelines.

PARABOLA—150 Fifth Ave., New York, NY 10011. Lorraine Kisly, Ed. Non-academic articles, 3,000 to 5,000 words, on mythology, comparative religion, the arts, in relation to contemporary life. Book reviews. Some poetry and fiction. Pays varying rates, on publication. Query.

PARAGRAPH—Oat City Press, P.O. Box 375, Haydenville, MA 01039. Walker Rumble, Ed. Triannual. Fiction and nonfiction, to 200 words. Innovations with form invited, but not essential. Pays in copies.

PARIS REVIEW—541 E. 72nd St., New York, NY 10021. Address Fiction and Poetry Eds. Fiction and poetry of high literary quality. Pays on publication.

PARNASSUS—205 W. 89th St., New York, NY 10024. Herbert Leibowitz, Ed. Critical essays and reviews on contemporary poetry. International scope. Pays in cash and copies.

PARTISAN REVIEW—Boston Univ., 141 Bay State Rd., Boston, MA 02215. William Phillips, Ed. Serious fiction, poetry and essays. Payment varies.

PASSAGES NORTH—William Bonifas Fine Arts Center, Escanaba, MI 49829. Elinor Benedict, Ed. Quality short fiction and contemporary poetry. Pays in copies, occasional prizes and honoraria. Contest.

THE PENNSYLVANIA REVIEW—Dept. of English, 526 Cathedral of Learning, Univ. of Pittsburgh, Pittsburgh, PA 15260. Articles and fiction, to

5,000 words, and poetry (send as many as six at one time). Pays $5 a page for prose, $3 for poetry.

PERMAFROST—Engl. Dept., UAF, Fairbanks, AK 99775. Poetry, fiction, essays, translations, reviews, b&w art. Pays in copies.

PIEDMONT LITERARY REVIEW—P.O. Box 3656, Danville, VA 24543. Fiction, to 4,000 words. Poems, of any length and style. Special interest in young poets. Pays in copies. Submit up to 5 poems.

PIG IRON—P.O. Box 237, Youngstown, OH 44501. Rose Sayre, Jim Villani, Eds. Fiction and nonfiction, to 8,000 words. Poetry, to 100 lines. Pays $2 per published page, on publication.

PINCHPENNY—4851 Q St., Sacramento, CA 95819. Tom Miner, Elisabeth Goossens, Ed. Prose poems and tiny poems. New writers welcome. Pays in copies.

PLAINS POETRY JOURNAL—Box 2337, Bismarck, ND 58502. Jane Greer, Ed. Poetry using traditional conventions in vigorous, compelling ways; no "greeting card" -type verse. No subject is taboo. Pays in copies.

PLOUGHSHARES—Box 529, Dept. M, Cambridge, MA 02139. Address Fiction or Poetry Ed. Serious fiction, to 7,000 words. Poetry. Pays $10 to $50, on publication. Query.

POEM—c/o English Dept., U.A.H., Huntsville, AL 35899. Nancy Dillard, Ed. Serious poetry, any length. Pays in copies.

THE POET—P.O. Box 44021, Shreveport, LA 71134-4021. Quarterly. Peggy Cooper, Ed. Poetry, all types and forms. No length limit. Pays in copies.

POET AND CRITIC—203 Ross Hall, Iowa State Univ., Ames, IA 50011. Michael Martone, Ed. Poetry, essays on contemporary poetry. Pays in copies.

POET LORE—4000 Albemarle St. N.W., Washington, DC 20016. Ed Taylor, Man. Ed. Original poetry, all kinds. Translations, reviews. Pays in copies. Annual contest.

POETIC JUSTICE—8220 Rayford Dr., Los Angeles, CA 90045. Alan Engebretsen, Ed. Quarterly. Poetry, 4 to 70 lines. Pays in copies.

POETRY—P.O. Box 4348, 601 S. Morgan St., Chicago, IL 60680. Joseph Parisi, Ed. Poetry of highest quality. Pays $1 a line, on publication.

POETRY NEWSLETTER—Dept. of English, Temple Univ., Philadelphia, PA 19122. Richard O'Connell, Ed. Quarterly. Poetry and translations. Pays in copies.

POETS ON:—Box 255, Chaplin, CT 06235. Ruth Daigon, Ed. Semiannual. Poetry; each issue focuses on specific theme. Query first. Pays in copies.

THE PORTABLE LOWER EAST SIDE—463 West St., #344, New York, NY 10014. Kurt Hollander, Ed. Quality, experimental fiction, to 15 pages; poetry, to 3 pages. Articles related to the Lower East Side of New York City. Pays in copies.

PRAIRIE SCHOONER—201 Andrew Hall, Univ. of Nebraska, Lincoln, NE 68588. Hugh Luke and Hilda Raz, Eds. Short stories, poetry and essays, to 6,000 words. Pays in copies.

PRIMAVERA—1212 E. 59th St., Chicago, IL 60637. Stories, poems and personal essays, to 30 typed pages, by or about women. Send no more than 6 poems at a time. Pays in copies.

PRISM INTERNATIONAL—E459-1866 Main Mall, Dept. of Creative Writing, Univ. of British Columbia, Vancouver, B.C., Canada V6T 1W5. Steve Noyes, Ed.-in-Chief. Chris Petty, Fiction Ed. Sara Gaddes, Drama Ed. High-quality fiction, poetry, drama, and literature in translation. Pays $25 per published page, on publication. Quarterly.

PROOF ROCK—P.O. Box 607, Halifax, VA 24558. Don Conner, Ed. Fiction, to 2,500 words. Poetry, to 32 lines. Reviews. Pays in copies. Sample copies available.

PUDDING—2384 Hardesty Dr. South, Columbus, OH 43204. Jennifer Welch Bosveld, Ed. Poems—especially free verse and experimental—with fresh language, concrete images, and specific detail. Short articles about poetry in human services.

PUERTO DEL SOL—New Mexico State Univ., Box 3E, Las Cruces, NM 88003. Kevin McIlvoy, Ed. Short stories, to 30 pages; novel excerpts, to 65 pages; articles, to 45 pages, related to the Southwest; and reviews, to 15 pages. Poetry, photos. Pays in copies.

PULPSMITH—5 Beekman St., New York, NY 10038. Harry Smith, General Ed. Literary genre fiction; mainstream, mystery, SF, westerns. Short lyric poems, sonnets, ballads. Essays and articles. Pays $35 to $100 for fiction, $15 to $35 for poetry, on acceptance.

QUEEN'S QUARTERLY—Queens Univ., Kingston, Ont., Canada K7L 3N6. Articles, to 6,000 words, on a wide range of topics, and fiction, to 5,000 words. Poetry; send no more than 6 poems. Pays to $150, on publication.

RACCOON—3387 Poplar Ave., #205, Memphis, TN 38111. David Spicer, Ed. Poetry and poetic criticism, varying lengths. Pays in copies.

RAMBUNCTIOUS REVIEW—1221 W. Pratt Ave., Chicago, IL 60626. Mary Dellutri, Richard Goldman, Eds. Fiction, poetry, short drama. Pays in copies. Submit material Sept.-May.

REAR VIEW MIRROR—307 Louise Ave., Dowagiac, MI 49047. Scott Topping, Ed. Humorous articles and short stories, to 1,500 words. Pays in copies. SASE for guidelines.

RED CEDAR REVIEW—Dept. of English, Morrill Hall, Michigan State Univ., East Lansing, MI 48825. Fiction, 4,000 to 8,000 words. Poetry (5 per submission). Interviews, book reviews, graphics. Pays in copies. Query.

RHINO—3915 Foster St., Evanston, IL 60203. Laurie Buehler, Ed. Annual. Fiction, to 3 pages. Poetry, all lengths. Seeking authentic emotion in well-crafted forms using fresh images. Pays in copies.

RIVERSIDE QUARTERLY—P.O. Box 833-044, Richardson, TX 75083. Science fiction and fantasy (to 3,500 words); criticism, reviews. Send fiction to Redd Boggs, Box 1111, Berkeley, CA 94701; poetry to Sheryl Smith. Pays in copies.

ROANOKE REVIEW—Roanoke College, Salem, VA 24153. Robert R. Walter, Ed. Quality short fiction, to 10,000 words, and poetry, to 100 lines. Pays in copies.

SAN FERNANDO POETRY JOURNAL—18301 Halstead St., Northridge, CA 91325. Richard Cloke, Ed. Quality poetry, 20 to 100 lines, with social content; scientific, philosophic and historical themes. Pays in copies.

SAN JOSE STUDIES—San Jose State Univ., San Jose, CA 95192. Fauneil J. Rinn, Ed. Poetry, fiction, and essays on interdisciplinary topics. Pays in copies. Annual awards.

SANDS—P.O. Box 638, Addison, TX 75001. Susan C. Baugh, Ed. Quality fiction, poetry. Pays in copies.

SANSKRIT—Bonnie Cone Center, University of North Carolina, Charlotte, NC 28223. Laura Trahan-Priko, Business Ed. Short fiction and poetry. Limit of five double-spaced pages. Enclose short biographical note. Pays in copies.

SCANDINAVIAN REVIEW—127 E. 73rd St., New York, NY 10021. Essays on contemporary Scandinavia. Fiction and poetry, translated from Scandinavian. Pays to $100, on publication.

SCRIVENER—McGill Univ., 853 Sherbrooke St. W., Montreal, Quebec, Canada H3A 2T6. Andrew Burgess, Ed. Biannual. Poetry, 5 to 15 poems; prose, to 15 pages; reviews, to 3 pages; essays, to 8 pages. Photography and graphics. Pays in copies.

THE SEATTLE REVIEW—Padelford Hall, GN-30, Univ. of Washington, Seattle, WA 98195. Donna Gerstenberger, Ed. Short stories and poetry, to 2 pages. Pays in copies.

SENECA REVIEW—Hobart & William Smith Colleges, Geneva, NY 14456. Poetry. Pays in copies.

SEVEN—3630 N.W. 22, Oklahoma City, OK 73107-2893. James Neill Northe, Ed. Serious poetry, in any form. Pays $5, on acceptance. Query. Guidelines available.

SEWANEE REVIEW—Sewanee, TN 37375. George Core, Ed. Fiction, to 7,500 words. Serious poetry, to 40 lines, of highest quality. Pays about $12 per printed page for fiction, 60¢ per line for poetry, on publication. Send cover letter and SASE.

SHENANDOAH—Washington and Lee Univ., P.O. Box 722, Lexington, VA 24450. James Boatwright, Ed. Richard Howard, Poetry Ed. Highest quality fiction, poetry, criticism, essays and interviews.

THE SHORT STORY REVIEW—P.O. Box 882108, San Francisco, CA 94188. Dwight Gabbard, Ed. Short stories, to 3,500 words. Book reviews of short story collections (not anthologies), 600 words. Interviews with authors known primarily for their short stories, 10 double-spaced pages. Pays $180 for interviews, in copies for reviews and short stories. Queries required for interviews and reviews. Send SASE for guidelines.

SIDEWINDER—Dept. of Arts and Humanities, College of the Mainland, Texas City, TX 77591. Thomas Poole, Ed. Biannual. Fiction and poetry, any length. Pays in copies. Submit complete manuscripts; no queries.

SING HEAVENLY MUSE! WOMEN'S POETRY & PROSE—P.O. Box 13299, Minneapolis, MN 55414. Short stories and essays, to 5,000 words. Poetry. Pays $25, plus copies, on publication.

SINISTER WISDOM—P.O. Box 1308, Montpelier, VT 05602. Melanie Kaye/Kantrowitz, Ed. Articles, fiction, poetry, reviews, and plays, from feminist and lesbian perspective, varying lengths. Pays in copies.

SLIPSTREAM—Box 2071, New Market Sta., Niagara Falls, NY 14301. Fiction, 2 to 25 pages, and contemporary poetry, any length. Pays in copies. Query for themes.

SLOW DANCER—Box 149A, RFD 1, Lubec, ME 04652. Alan Brooks, Assoc. American Ed. Poetry. Pays in copies.

SMALL PRESS REVIEW—Box 100, Paradise, CA 95969. Len Fulton, Ed. News pieces and reviews, to 250 words, about small presses and little magazines. Pays in copies.

SNAPDRAGON—English Dept., Univ. of Idaho, Moscow, ID 83843. Ron McFarland, Ed. Fiction and articles, 2,000 to 4,000 words, and poetry. Pays in copies.

SNOWY EGRET—205 S. Ninth St., Williamsburg, KY 40769. Humphrey A. Olsen, Alan Seaburg, Eds. Poetry to 10,000 words, related to natural history. Fiction and nonfiction, about 3,000 words, related to natural history. Pays $2 per page, on publication. Send fiction and poetry to Alan Seaburg, Ed., 67 Century St., W. Medford, MA 02155.

SONORA REVIEW—Dept. of English, Univ. of Arizona, Tucson, AZ 85721. Scott Wigton and Alison Hicks, Eds. Fiction, poetry, reviews. Pays in copies. Annual prizes for fiction and poetry.

SOUTH CAROLINA REVIEW—c/o Dept. of English, Clemson Univ., Clemson, SC 29631. Martin Jacobi, Man. Ed. Short stories, 3,000 to 5,000 words. Poetry. Criticism. Pays in copies.

SOUTH DAKOTA REVIEW—Box 111, Univ. Exchange, Vermillion, SD 57069. John R. Milton, Ed. Exceptional fiction, 3000 to 5,000 words, and poetry, 10 to 25 lines. Critical articles, especially on American literature, Western American literature, theory and esthetics, 3,000 to 5,000 words. Pays in copies.

SOUTHERN HUMANITIES REVIEW—9088 Haley Center, Auburn Univ., AL 36849. Thomas L. Wright and Dan R. Latimer, Eds. Short stories, essays, and criticism, 3,500 to 5,000 words; poetry, to 2 pages.

SOUTHERN POETRY REVIEW—Dept. of English, Univ. of North Carolina, Charlotte, NC 28223. Robert W. Grey, Ed. Poems. No restrictions on style length or content. Annual contest.

SOUTHERN REVIEW—43 Allen Hall, Louisiana State Univ., Baton Rouge, LA 70803. Lewis P. Simpson, James Oleny, Eds. Fiction, and essays, 4,000 to 8,000 words. Serious poetry of highest quality. Pays $12 a page for prose, $20 a page for poetry, on publication. Annual contest.

SOUTHWEST REVIEW—Southern Methodist Univ., Dallas, TX 72575. Willard Spiegelman, Ed. Short stories, book reviews and articles, 3,000 to 7,500 words. Poetry. Payment and gratis copies.

SOU'WESTER—Dept. of English, Southern Illinois Univ. at Edwardsville, Edwardsville, IL 62026. Dickie Spurgeon, Ed. Fiction, to 10,000 words. Poetry, especially poems over 100 lines. Pays in copies.

SPECTRUM—U.C.S.B., Box 14800, Santa Barbara, CA 93106. Short stories, articles on literature, memoirs. Poetry. Pays in copies and awards. Annual contest.

THE SPIRIT THAT MOVES US—P.O. Box 1585 TW, Iowa City, IA 52244. Morty Sklar, Ed. Biannual. Fiction, poetry, that is expressive rather than formal or sensational. Each issue focuses on a specific theme—query. Pays in copies.

STONE COUNTRY—P.O. Box 132, Menemsha, MA 02552. Judith Neeld,

Ed. High-quality contemporary poetry in all genres. Pays in copies. Semi-annual award. SASE required.

STONY HILLS: NEWS & REVIEWS OF THE SMALL PRESS—Weeks Mills, New Sharon, ME 04955. Diane Kruchkow, Ed. Reviews of small press books and magazines nationwide, to 500 words. Some short poetry. Pays in copies. Query on nonfiction preferred.

STORYQUARTERLY—P.O. Box 1416, Northbrook, IL 60065. Short stories and interviews. Pays in copies.

STUDIES IN AMERICAN FICTION—English Dept., Northeastern Univ., Boston, MA 02115. James Nagel, Ed. Reviews, 750 words; scholarly essays, 2,500 to 6,500 words, on American fiction. Pays in copies.

SUN DOG—English Dept. Florida State Univ., Tallahassee, FL 32306. Short fiction. Annual contest.

SUNRUST—P.O. Box 58, New Wilmington, PA 16142. James Ashbrook Perkins, Nancy Esther James, Eds. Nonfiction, to 2,000 words, and poetry, to 75 lines, about rural life, nature, memories of the past, and small communities. Pays in copies.

TAR RIVER POETRY—Dept. of English, East Carolina Univ., Greenville, NC 27834. Peter Makuck, Ed. Poems, all styles. Submit between September and May. Pays in copies.

TAURUS—Box 28, Gladstone, OR 97027. Bruce Combs, Ed. Quarterly. Fresh, earnest, and energetic poetry. Pays in copies.

TERRA POETICA—Dept. of Modern Languages and Literatures, SUNY at Buffalo, Buffalo, NY 14260. Jorge Guitart, Ed. Poetry: originals in all languages, and English translations. Pays in copies. Query preferred.

THE TEXAS REVIEW—English Dept., Sam Houston State Univ., Huntsville, TX 77341. Paul Ruffin, Ed. Fiction, poetry, articles, to 20 typed pages. Reviews. Pays in copies.

13TH MOON—Box 309, Cathedral Sta., New York, NY 10025. Marilyn Hacker, Ed. Poetry, literary criticism, and fiction by women. Pays in copies. No unsolicited manuscripts May–Sept.

THE THREEPENNY REVIEW—P.O. Box 9131, Berkeley, CA 94709. Wendy Lesser, Ed. Fiction, to 5,000 words. Poetry, to 40 lines. Essays, on books, theater, film, dance, music, art, television, and politics, 1,500 to 3,000 words. Pays $25 to $50, on publication. Limited market. Query first.

TOUCHSTONE—P.O. Box 42331, Houston, TX 77042. Bill Laufer, Pub. Quarterly. Fiction, 750 to 2,000 words: mainstream, experimental. Interviews, essays, reviews. Poetry, to 40 lines. Pays in copies.

TRANSLATION—The Translation Center, 307A Mathematics Bldg., Columbia Univ., New York, NY 10027. Frank MacShane, Dir. Diane G. H. Cook, Man. Ed. Semiannual. New translations of contemporary foreign poetry and prose.

TRIQUARTERLY—1735 Benson Ave., Northwestern Univ., Evanston, IL 60201. Serious, aesthetically informed and inventive poetry and prose, for an international and literate audience. Pays $10 per page.

THE UNIVERSITY OF PORTLAND REVIEW—Univ. of Portland, Portland, OR 97203. Thompson H. Faller, Ed. Scholarly articles and contemporary fiction, 500 to 2,500 words. Poetry. Book reviews. Pays in copies.

UNIVERSITY OF WINDSOR REVIEW—Dept. of English, Univ. of Windsor, Windsor, Ont., Canada N9B 3P4. Eugene McNamara, Ed. Short stories, poetry, criticism, reviews. Pays $10 to $25, on publication.

THE VILLAGER—135 Midland Ave., Bronxville, NY 10708. Amy Murphy, Ed. Fiction, 900 to 1,500 words: mystery, adventure, humor, romance. Short, preferably seasonal poetry. Pays in copies.

VIRGINIA QUARTERLY REVIEW—One W. Range, Charlottesville, VA 22903. Quality fiction and poetry. Serious essays and articles, 3,000 to 6,000 words, on literature, science, politics, economics, etc. Pays $10 per page for prose, $1 per line for poetry, on publication.

WASCANA REVIEW—c/o Dept. of English, Univ. of Regina, Regina, Sask., Canada S4S 0A2. Joan Givner, Ed. Short stories, 2,000 to 6,000 words; critical articles; poetry. Pays $3 per page, after publication.

WASHINGTON REVIEW—P.O. Box 50132, Washington, DC 20004. Mary Swift, Ed. Poetry; articles on literary, performing and fine arts in the Washington, D.C. area, 1,000 to 2,500 words. Fiction, to 1,000 words. Area writers preferred. Pays in copies.

WAVES—79 Denham Dr., Richmond Hill, Ont., L4C 6H9, Canada. Excerpts and short stories, 500 to 5,000 words. Haiku; poetry to 500 lines. Reviews of and interviews with Canadian writers. Pays $6.50 per printed page, on publication. Include international reply coupons.

WEBSTER REVIEW—Webster Univ., 470 E. Lockwood, Webster Groves, MO 63119. Nancy Schapiro, Ed. Fiction; poetry; interviews; essays; translations. pays in copies.

WEST BRANCH—English Dept., Bucknell Univ., Lewisburg, PA 17837. Karl Patten, Robert Taylor, Eds. Poetry and fiction. Pays in copies and subscriptions.

WESTERN HUMANITIES REVIEW—Univ. of Utah, Salt Lake City, UT 84112. Jack Garlington, Ed. Articles on the humanities; fiction; poetry, book and film reviews. Pays $150 for fiction, to $50 for poems, on acceptance.

WIDE OPEN—326 I St., Eureka, CA 95501. Clif Simms, Ed. Fiction, to 2,500 words. Nonfiction, to 2,500 words. Poetry, to 16 lines. Humor, to 2,500 words. "We are looking for nonfiction that logically presents solutions to problems current in the world. In fiction, we want solid plots, with characters facing current problems and solving these problems themselves. We will consider poetry in all styles and forms, and on any subject matter." Pays $5 to $25 for fiction and nonfiction; in copies for poetry.

THE WINDLESS ORCHARD—Dept. of English, Indiana-Purdue Univ., Ft. Wayne, IN 46805. Robert Novak, Ed. Contemporary poetry. Pays in copies.

WISCONSIN REVIEW—Box 158, Radford Hall, Univ. of Wisc., Oshkosh, WI 54901. Patricia Haebig, Ed. Fiction, to 3,000 words, poetry, all forms. Pays in copies.

WITHOUT HALOS—P.O. Box 1342, Point Pleasant Beach, NJ 08742. Wayne R. Toensmann, Assoc. Ed. Poetry. Accepts submissions from January 1 through May 31. Pays in copies.

WOMAN OF POWER—Box 827, Cambridge, MA 02238-0827. Linda Roach, Ed. Quarterly. Fiction, and nonfiction, to 3,500 words. Poetry, of varying length; submit 3 to 5 poems at a time. Main commitment of the magazine is to promote awareness of feminist and radical feminist principles. Each issue focuses on specific theme; write for guidelines. Pays in copies.

WRITERS FORUM—Univ. of Colorado, Colorado Springs, CO 80933-7150. Alex Blackburn, Ed. Annual. mainstream and experimental fiction, 1,000 to 10,000 words. Poetry (1 to 5 poems per submission). Emphasis on Western themes and writers. Send material October through May. Pays in copies.

WYOMING, THE HUB OF THE WHEEL—Box 9, Saratoga, WY 82331. Lenore A. Senior, Managing Ed. Fiction, to 2,500 words. Nonfiction, to 2,500 words. Poetry, to 80 lines. Material should relate in some way to the following themes: peace, the human race, positive relationships, the human spirit and possibilities. Queries are preferred. Pays in copies. Annual awards. Send SASE for guidelines.

YALE REVIEW—1902A Yale Sta., New Haven, CT 06520. Kai Erikson, Ed. Serious poetry, to 200 lines and fiction, 3,000 to 5,000 words. Pays nominal sum.

HUMOR, FILLERS, AND SHORT ITEMS

Magazines noted for their excellent filler departments, plus a cross-section of publications using humor, short items, jokes, quizzes, and cartoons, follow. However, almost all magazines use some type of filler material, and writers can find dozens of markets by studying copies of magazines at a library or newsstand.

Many magazines do not acknowledge or return filler material, and in such cases, writers may assume that after 90 days have passed from the time of submission, a filler may be submitted to another market.

ALCOHOLISM & ADDICTION MAGAZINE—P.O. Box 31329, Seattle, WA 98103. "Coffee Break Page": short, true experience pieces, jokes and anecdotes relating to alcoholism and chemical dependency for professionals in the treatment field and recovering persons. Nominal payment.

ALIVE! FOR YOUNG TEENS—Christian Board of Publication, P.O. Box 179, St. Louis, MO 63166. Mike Dixon, Ed. Puzzles, riddles, daffy definitions; poetry, to 20 lines. Pays to $10, 25¢ a line for poetry, on publication.

AMERICAN CLAY EXCHANGE—P.O. Box 2674, La Mesa, CA 92041. Short items on American-made pottery. Pays $5, on acceptance.

THE AMERICAN FIELD—222 W. Adams St., Chicago, IL 60606. W. F. Brown, Ed. Short fact items and anecdotes on hunting dogs, and field trials for bird dogs. Pays varying rates, on acceptance.

THE AMERICAN LEGION MAGAZINE—Box 1055, Indianapolis, IN 46206. Parting Shots Page: short humorous anecdotes, appealing to military veterans and their families. General humor: no sex, religion, ethnic humor or political satire. Pays $12.50 for definitions, $15 for anecdotes and gags, on acceptance. No fillers.

THE AMERICAN NEWSPAPER CARRIER—P.O. Box 15300, Winston-Salem, NC 27103. Short, humorous pieces, to 1,000 words, for pre-teen and teen-age newspaper carriers. Pays to $25, on publication.

AMPERSAND—303 N. Glenoaks Blvd., Burbank, CA 91502. Short items, 500 words, of interest to college students. Pays 15¢ a word, on acceptance.

ARMY MAGAZINE—2425 Wilson Blvd., Arlington, VA 22201. L. James Binder, Ed.-in-Chief. True anecdotes on military subjects. Pays $10 to $35, on publication.

ARTS LINE—2518 Western Ave., Seattle, WA 98121. Arts-related fillers. pays on acceptance.

THE ATLANTIC—8 Arlington St., Boston, MA 02116. Sophisticated humorous or satirical pieces, 1,000 to 3,000 words. Some light poetry. Pays from $750 for prose, on acceptance.

ATLANTIC SALMON JOURNAL—1435 St-Alexandre, Suite 1030, Montreal, Quebec, Canada H3A 2G4. Joanne Eidinger, Ed. Fillers, 50 to 100 words on salmon politics, conservation, and nature. Cartoons. Pays on publication.

THE AUTOGRAPH COLLECTOR'S MAGAZINE—P.O. Box 55328, Stockton, CA 95205. Joe Kraus, Ed. Brief news items about autograph collecting. Pays 5¢ a word, on publication.

BASSMASTER MAGAZINE—B. A. S. S. Publications, Box 17900, Montgomery, AL 36141. Dave Precht, Ed. Anecdotes, short humor and news breaks related to bass fishing, 250 to 500 words. Pays $50 to $100, on acceptance.

BICYCLING—33 E. Minor Rd., Emmanus, PA 18049. Anecdotes and other items for "People and Places" section, 150 to 250 words. Pays $15 to $35, on publication.

BIKE REPORT—Bikecentennial, P.O. Box 8308, Missoula, MT 59807. Daniel D'Ambrosio, Ed. News shorts from the bicycling world for "In Bicycle Circles." Pays $5 to $10, on publication.

BIRD WATCHER'S DIGEST—P.O. Box 110, Marietta, OH 45750. Mary Bowers, Ed. Cartoons. Pays $10, on publication.

BOYS' LIFE—1325 Walnut Hill Lane, Irving, TX 75062. William B. McMorris, Exec. Ed. How-to features, to 400 words, with photos, on hobbies, crafts, science, out-door skills, etc. Pays from $150.

BUSINESS LIFE—8100 Penn Ave., S., Minneapolis, MN 55431. Terry White, Ed. Fillers, anecdotes, case studies, and cartoons for Christian businesses and professional people. Pays 10¢ a word, on publication.

BUSINESS VIEW OF SOUTHWEST FLORIDA—P.O. Box 9859, Naples FL 33941. Business- or economic-related shorts, 100 to 300 words. Pays $10 to $25, on publication.

CAPPER'S—616 Jefferson St., Topeka, KS 66607. Dorothy Harvey, Ed. Household hints, recipes, jokes. Pays varying rates, on publication.

CASCADES EAST—716 N.E. 4th St., P.O. Box 5784, Bend, OR 97708. Geoff Hill, Ed. Fillers, related to travel and recreation in Central Oregon. pays 3¢ to 10¢ a word, on publication.

CASHFLOW—1807 Glenview, Glenview, IL 60025. Vince DiPaolo, Ed. Fillers, to 1,000 words, on varied aspects of treasury financial management, for treasury managers in public and private institutions. Pays on publication. Query.

CATHOLIC DIGEST—P.O. Box 64090, St. Paul, MN 55164. Features, to 300 words, on instances of kindness rewarded, for "Hearts Are Trumps." Stories about conversions, for "Open Door." Reports of tactful remarks or actions, for "The Perfect Assist." Accounts of good deeds, for "People Are Like That." Humorous pieces on parish life, for "In Our Parish." Amusing signs, for "Signs of the Times." Jokes; fillers. Pays $4 to $50, on publication.

CHEVRON USA ODYSSEY—P.O. Box 6227, San Jose, CA 95150. Mark Williams, Ed. Quarterly. True, previously unpublished, humorous anecdotes with a travel tie-in, 200 words. Pays $25, on publication.

CHIC—2029 Century Park E., Suite 3800, Los Angeles, CA 90067. Visual fillers, short humor with visuals, 100 to 200 words, for "Odds and Ends" section. Pays on acceptance.

CHICKADEE—59 Front St. E., Toronto, Ont., Canada M5E 1B3. Humorous poetry about animals and nature, for children, 10 to 15 lines. Pays on publication.

CHILD LIFE—P.O. Box 567, Indianapolis, In 46206. Steve Charles, Ed. Puzzles, games, mazes, and rebuses, on health or safety-related subjects, for children 7 to 9 years. Pays $10 to $15, on publication.

CHILDREN'S PLAYMATE—1100 Waterway Blvd., P.O. Box 567, Indianapolis, IN 46206. Elizabeth Rinck, Ed. Puzzles, games, mazes for 5- to 7-year-olds, emphasizing health, safety, nutrition. Pays about 6¢ a word (varies on puzzles), on publication.

CHRISTIAN HERALD—40 Overlook Dr., Chappaqua, NY 10514. Dean Merrill, Ed. Poetry and true anecdotes, to 24 lines, on Christian/church themes. pays $5 to $15, after acceptance.

CHRISTIAN LIFE—396 E. St. Charles Rd., Wheaton, IL 60188. Pat Kampert, Man. Ed. News items, to 200 words, on trends, ideas, unique personalities/ministries, and events of interest to Christians. Photos. Pays $5 to $15, on publication.

THE CHURCH MUSICIAN—127 Ninth Ave., N., Nashville, TN 37234. W. M. Anderson, Ed. For Southern Baptist music leaders. Humorous fillers with a music slant. No clippings. Pays around 4¢ a word, on acceptance. Same address and requirements for *Glory Songs* (for adults), and *Opus One* and *Opus Two* (for teen-agers).

CLAVIER MAGAZINE—200 Northfield Rd., Northfield, IL 60093. Barbara Kreader, Ed. Fillers, humor, and jokes of interest to keyboard performers and teachers. Pay varies, on publication.

COLLEGE WOMAN—303 N. Glenoaks Blvd., Ste. 600, Burbank, CA 91502. Charlotte Wolter, Ed. Fillers, to 500 words, of interest to college women. Pays on acceptance.

COLORADO OUTDOOR JOURNAL—P.O. Box 432, Florence, CO 81226. Galen Geer, Exec. Ed. Fillers, with a Colorado tie-in, for outdoors enthusiasts. Pays $1.50 per column inch, on publication.

COLUMBIA—Box 1670, New Haven, CT 06507. Elmer Von Feldt, Ed.

Journal of the Knights of Columbus. Catholic family magazine. Humor and satire, to 1,000 words; captionless cartoons. Pays $200, $25 for cartoons, on acceptance.

COLUMBIA JOURNALISM REVIEW—700 Journalism Bldg., Columbia Univ., New York, NY 10027. Gloria Cooper, Man. Ed. Amusing mistakes in news stories, headlines, photos, etc. (original clippings required), for "Lower Case." Pays $10, on publication.

COUNTRY PEOPLE—5400 S. 60th St., Greendale, WI 53129. Fillers, 50 to 200 words, for rural audience. Pays on publication. Address: Dan Johnson.

CYCLE WORLD—1499 Monrovia Ave., P.O. Box 1757, Newport Beach, CA 92663. Paul Dean, Ed. News items on motorcycle industry, legislation, trends. pays on acceptance.

DALLAS CITY—*The Dallas Times Herald,* 1101 Pacific Ave., Dallas, TX 75202. Dallas-oriented humor essays, 500 to 1,000 words. Pays $250, on publication.

DANCE TEACHER NOW—University Mall, Suite 2, 803 Russell Blvd., Davis, CA 95616. Martin A. David, Ed. Fillers—short, humorous pieces. Pays on acceptance. Buys all rights.

DAZZLE—1999 Shepard Rd., St. Paul, MN 55116. Quarterly for dental patients. Fillers and humor, 400 to 800 words; must be dental-related, not derogatory.

DOWN EAST—Camden, ME 04843. Anecdotes about Maine, to 1,000 words, for "I Remember." Humorous anecdotes, to 300 words, for "It Happened Down East." Pays $10 to $50, on acceptance.

EBONY—820 S. Michigan Ave., Chicago, IL 60605. Charles L. Sanders, Man. Ed. "Speaking of People," short features, to 200 words, on blacks in traditionally non-black jobs. Cartoons. Pays $75 for cartoons, on publication.

ELECTRONIC EDUCATION—1311 Executive Center Dr., Ste. 220, Tallahassee, FL 32301. Sharon Lobello, Ed. Fillers of interest to educators. Pays on publication.

THE ELKS MAGAZINE—425 W. Diversey Pkwy., Chicago, IL 60614. Judith Keogh, Ed. Humor, 1,500 to 3,000 words, for a family audience. No fillers. Query only; send SASE for guidelines. Pays from $150, on acceptance.

ESSENCE—1500 Broadway, New York, NY 10036. Susan L. Taylor, Ed.-in-Chief. Short items, 500 to 750 words, on work and health, of interest to black women. Pays on acceptance.

THE EVENER—P.O. Box 7, Cedar Falls, IA 50613. Anecdotes and newsbreaks, 100 to 750 words, related to draft horse, mule and oxen industry. Pays 3¢ to 10¢ a word, on acceptance.

EXPECTING—685 Third Ave., New York, NY 10017. E. Podsiadlo, Ed. Anecdotes about pregnancy, for "Happenings." Pays $10, on publication.

FACES—20 Grove St., Peterborough, NH 03458. Carolyn Yoder, Ed. Puzzles, mazes, crosswords, and picture puzzles, related to monthly themes, for children. Send SASE for list of themes before submitting.

FAMILY CIRCLE—Box 2822, Grand Central Sta., New York, NY 10017. Ideas or suggestions on homemaking and community betterment, for "Readers' Idea Exchange." Pays $50. Unpublished entries cannot be returned or acknowledged. Query.

FARM AND RANCH LIVING—5400 S. 60th St., Greendale, WI 53129. Bob Ottum, Man. Ed. Fillers on rural people and living, 200 words. Pays from $15, on acceptance and on publication.

FARM WOMAN—P.O. Box 643, Milwaukee, WI 53201. Ruth C. Benedict, Man. Ed. Short verse, 4 to 20 lines, and fillers, to 250 words, on the rural experience. Pays from $40, on acceptance.

FATE—500 Hyacinth Pl., Highland Park, IL 60035. Mary Margaret Fuller, Ed. Factual fillers, to 300 words, on strange or psychic happenings. True stories, to 300 words, on psychic or mystic personal experiences. Pays $2 to $15.

FIELD & STREAM—1515 Broadway, New York, NY 10036. Duncan Barnes, Ed. Fillers on hunting, camping, fishing, etc., 500 to 1,000 words, for "How It's Done," and "Did You Know?" Cartoons. Pays $250 for "How It's Done," $350 for "Did You Know?," $100 for cartoons, on acceptance.

FIREHOUSE—33 Irving Pl., New York, NY 10003. Humorous fillers, to 100 words, for professional firefighters. Pays $25, on publication.

FLARE—777 Bay St., Toronto, Ont., Canada M5W 1A7. Dianne Rinhart, Man. Ed. Career-related items, profiles, 100 to 150 words, for young Canadian working women aged 18 to 34. Pays on acceptance. Query.

FLY FISHERMAN—Harrisburg, PA 17105. Jack Russell, Assoc. Ed. Fillers, 100 words, on equipment tackle tips, knots, and fly-tying tips. Pays from $35, on acceptance.

FORD TIMES—One Illinois Center, 111 E. Wacker Dr., Suite 1700, Chicago, IL 60601. Thomas A. Kindre, Ed. Travel and dining anecdotes for "Road Show" and "Glove Compartment." Pays $50, on publication.

GALLERY—800 Second Ave., New York, NY 10017. John Bensink, Ed.-in-Chief; Marc Lichter, Man. Ed. Short humor, satire, and short service features for men. Pays varying rates, on acceptance and on publication. Query.

THE GENERAL LEDGER—78 Wethersfield St., Rowley, MA 01969. Shirley E. Doherty, Ed. Fillers and short humor, to 50 words, on bookkeeping, accounting, and the office environment. Pays $5, on acceptance.

GEOFFREY'S TOYS "R" US—1220 Mound Ave., Racine, WI 53404. Don Lesinski, Ed. Fillers, humor, jokes, and puzzles for children ages 6 to 12. Pays on acceptance.

GLAMOUR—350 Madison Ave., New York, NY 10017. Articles, 1,000 words, for "Viewpoint" section: opinion pieces for women. Pays $500, on acceptance. Send SASE.

GOLF DIGEST—5520 Park Ave., Trumbull, CT 06611. Lois Hains, Asst. Ed. Short fact items, anecdotes, quips, jokes, light verse related to golf. True humorous or odd incidents, to 200 words. Pays from $25, on acceptance.

GOLF ILLUSTRATED—3 Park Ave., New York, NY 10016. Golf-related fillers; one- to two-paragraph news snippets, preferably of humorous or offbeat nature. Pays $25 to $100, on acceptance.

GOLF MAGAZINE—380 Madison Ave., New York, NY 10017. Desmond Tolhurst, Sr. Ed. Fillers to 750 words, on golf. Pays from $50, on acceptance.

GOOD HOUSEKEEPING—959 Eighth Ave., New York, NY 10019. Rosemary Leonard, Asst. Ed. Light verse and very short humorous prose. Pays from $10 to $100, and from $5 a line for verse.

GRIT—208 W. Third St., Williamsport, PA 17701. Joanne Decker, Assignment Ed. Brief anecdotal features, from 30 words, on interesting, amusing, heartwarming, and inspiring subjects. Humorous verse. Pays 12¢ a word for prose, $6 for four lines of verse.

GUIDEPOSTS—747 Third Ave., New York, NY 10017. Inspirational anecdotes, to 250 words. Pays $10 to $50, on acceptance.

HARROWSMITH—Camden House Publishing, Camden East, Ont., Canada K0K 1J0. James H. Lawrence, Ed./Pub. Short essays, to 750 words, expressing an opinion on pieces appearing in the magazine. Pays $25, on acceptance.

HARROWSMITH/USA—The Creamery, Ferry Rd., Charlotte, VT 05445. Rux Martin, Assoc. Ed. News briefs for "Gazette." Pays $50 to $150, on acceptance.

HICALL—1445 Boonville Ave., Springfield, MO 65802. Jennifer J. Eller, Ed. Brief fillers, to 300 words, with a strong evangelical emphasis, of interest to readers ages 15 to 17. Pays on acceptance.

HOME LIFE—127 Ninth Ave. N., Nashville, TN 37234. Reuben Herring, Ed. Southern Baptist. Personal-experience pieces, 100 to 500 words, on Christian marriage, and family relationships. Pays 4¢ a word, on acceptance.

HOME MECHANIX—1515 Broadway, New York, NY 10036. Joseph R. Provey, Ed. Single photos with captions and tips for shortcuts in shop, garage or home. Pays $50 to $75, on acceptance.

THE INTERNATIONAL AMERICAN—201 E. 36th St., New York, NY 10016. Alison R. Lanier, Ed. Short pieces, 200 to 300 words, by writers who have lived abroad, with advice, suggestions, warnings and information for Americans who are now living overseas. No travel tips, or stories of personal interest. Pays $35, on acceptance.

JACK & JILL—1100 Waterway Blvd., P.O. Box 567, Indianapolis, IN 46206. Christine French Clark, Ed. Poems, puzzles, games, science and craft projects, for 6- to 8-year olds, with health or holiday themes. Instructions for activities should be clearly written, accompanied by diagrams and a list of needed materials. Pays varying rates, on publication.

KEY TO CHRISTIAN EDUCATION—8121 Hamilton Ave., Cincinnati, OH 45231. Virginia Beddow, Ed. Short pieces, 50 to 250 words, for "This is How We Did It" (personal experience) column. Pays $5 to $10, on acceptance.

LADIES' HOME JOURNAL—"Last Laughs," Three Park Ave., New York, NY 10016. Brief anecdotes and poems about the funny business of being a woman today. Pays $25. Submissions cannot be acknowledged or returned.

LAUGH FACTORY—400 S. Beverly Dr., #214, Beverly Hills, CA 90212. Jamie Masada, Pub. Quick, hilarious pieces, to 600 words, jokes, cartoons, belly laugh material. Pays varying rates, on publication.

MAD MAGAZINE—485 Madison Ave., New York, NY 10022. Humorous pieces on a wide variety of topics. No straight text pieces. Query with proposal and SASE. Pays top rates, on acceptance.

MAGAZINE DESIGN & PRODUCTION—P.O. Box 7926, Overland Parks, KS 66207. Items, 500 words, for "Tip Sheet," on improving magazine design or being more cost-effective in production management. Pays $50.

MANUFACTURED HOMES MAGAZINE—P.O. Box 354, Bremerton, WA 98310. Sandra E. Haven, Editorial Dir. For "Readers Projects," 200- to 500-word description of how a homeowner customized a manufactured home after purchase. Pays on acceptance.

MANUFACTURING SYSTEMS—Hitchcock Publishing Co., Hitchcock Bldg., Wheaton, IL 60188. Fillers, related to computers in industry. Pay varies, on acceptance.

MATURE LIVING—127 Ninth Ave. N., MSN 140, Nashville, TN 37234. Nostalgia, 875 words, for "I Remember When . . ." Brief, humorous, original items. Profiles of senior adults, 25 lines with photos. Pays after acceptance. Send SASE for guidelines.

MATURE YEARS—201 Eighth Ave. S., Nashville, TN 37202. Daisy D. Warren, Ed. Poems, cartoons, puzzles, jokes, anecdotes, to 300 words, for older adults. Pays 4¢ a word, on acceptance.

MBM: MODERN BLACK MEN—1123 Broadway, Ste. 802, New York, NY 10010. Fillers, 100 to 1,000 words, of interest to black men. Pays from $15, on publication.

MIAMI/SOUTH FLORIDA MAGAZINE—P.O. Box 34008, Coral Gables, FL 33114. Rick Eyerdam, Man. Ed. Short, localized, "bright" items, 200 to 400 words, for the "Big Orange" section. Pays 15 days before publication.

MID-WEST OUTDOORS—111 Shore Dr., Hinsdale, IL 60521. Gene Laulunen, Ed. Where to and how to fish in the Midwest, 200 to 1,500 words, with 2 photos. Pays $15 to $35, on publication.

MODERN BRIDE—One Park Ave., New York, NY 10016. Mary Ann Cavlin, Man. Ed. Humorous pieces, 500 to 1,500 words, for brides. Pays on acceptance.

MODERN MATURITY—3200 E. Carson St., Lakewood CA 90712. Ian Ledgerwood, Ed. Money-saving ideas and how-to-items; jokes; quizzes; graphic puzzles; narrative math problems, etc. Submit seasonal material 6 months in advance. Pays from $50, on acceptance. Query.

MODERN PHOTOGRAPHY—825 Seventh Ave., New York, NY 10019. Julia Scully, Ed. How-to pieces, 200 to 300 words, with photos, on photography. Pays $50 to $500, on acceptance.

MODERN ROMANCES—215 Lexington Ave., New York, NY 10016. Short items, to 300 words, for "Little Things (That Say 'I Love You')" and "My Most Treasured Possession." Pays $25, thirty days after month of publication.

MOTHER JONES—1663 Mission St., San Francisco, CA 94103. Michael Moore, Ed. For "Frontlines" section of short items: amazing statistics, quotations from public figures, news items under-reported by the conventional press, etc. Pays $50 to $250.

NATIONAL BEAUTY SCHOOL JOURNAL—3839 White Plains Rd., Bronx, NY 10467. Mary Jane Tenerelli, Ed. Crossword puzzles of interest to cosmetology school owners and instructors. Pays $25, on publication.

NATIONAL ENQUIRER—Lantana, FL 33464. Jim Allan, Asst. Ed. Short, humorous fillers, witticisms, anecdotes, tart comments. Original items preferred, but others considered if source and date given. Short poems of a philosophical or amusing nature. Pays $20, on publication. SASE required.

NATIONAL REVIEW—150 E. 35th St., New York, NY 10016. William F. Buckley, Ed. Satire, to 900 words. Short, satirical poems. Pays $35 to $100, on publication.

NEW ENGLAND MONTHLY—P.O. Box 466, Haydenville, MA 01039. Daniel Okrent, Ed. Shorts, 400 to 1,000 words, on various aspects of life and culture in the six New England states. Pays $75 to $250, on acceptance.

NEW JERSEY MONTHLY—7 Dumont Pl., Morristown, NJ 07960. Patrick Sarver, Man. Ed. Short pieces related to life in New Jersey. Pays $35 to $75, on acceptance.

NEW YORK—755 Second Ave., New York, NY 10017. Nancy McKeon, Sr. Ed. Short, lively pieces, to 400 words, highlighting events and trends in New York City for "Fast Track." Profiles to 300 words for "Brief Lives." Pays $25 to $150, on publication. Include SASE.

NEW YORK'S NIGHTLIFE MAGAZINE—1770 Deer Park Ave., Deer Park, NY 11729. Bill Ervolino, Ed. Topical humor, 1,000 to 2,000 words, on entertainment, leisure, personalities in New York. Pays from $50, on publication. Query preferred.

THE NEW YORKER—25 W. 43rd St., New York, NY 10036. Amusing mistakes in newspapers, books, magazines, etc. Pays from $10, extra for headings and tag lines, on acceptance.

NONTOXIC AND NATURAL—Inverness, CA 94937. Debra Lynn Dadd, Ed. Short fillers on natural foods, products, etc. Pays on publication.

NORTHWEST LIVING—130 Second Ave. S., Edmonds, WA 98020. Archie Satterfield, Ed. Shorts, 100 to 400 words, related to the natural resources of the Northwest. Must be illustrated with color transparencies. Query first with SASE. Pays on acceptance.

OHIO FISHERMAN—1570 Fishinger Rd., Columbus, OH 43221. Short, do-it-yourself fishing-related tidbits, 250 to 500 words. Pays varying rates, on acceptance.

OMNI—1965 Broadway, New York, NY 10023. Douglas Colligan, Senior Ed. Humorous and satirical pieces, to 800 words, on aspects of the future: science and technology, the arts, lifestyles. Pays from $750, on acceptance.

OPUS ONE and **OPUS TWO**—See *The Church Musician*

ORBEN'S CURRENT COMEDY—1200 N. Nash St., #1122, Arlington, VA 22209. Robert Orben, Ed. Original, funny, performable one-liners and brief jokes on news, fads, topical subjects, etc. Openings, jokes, roast material, etc., for speakers. Pays $8, after publication. SASE required.

OUTDOOR AMERICA—Suite 1100, 1701 N. Ft. Myer Dr., Arlington, VA 22209. Humor, 1,500 words, on fishing, hunting, boating. Pays from 10¢ a word, on publication.

OUTDOOR LIFE—380 Madison Ave., New York, NY 10017. Clare Conley, Ed. Short instructive items and 1-pagers on hunting, fishing, camping gear, boats, outdoor equipment. Photos. Pays on acceptance.

PAPERCUTTING WORLD—12439 Magnolia Blvd., Ste. 111, N. Hollywood, CA 91607. Joseph W. Bean, Ed. Brief fillers, humor and jokes. Pays 4¢ a word, on publication.

PARENTS—685 Third Ave., New York, NY 10017. Short items on solutions of child care-related problems for "Parents Exchange." Pays $20, on publication.

PARISH FAMILY DIGEST—200 Noll Plaza, Huntington, IN 46750. Louis F. Jacquet, Ed. Family- or parish-oriented humor. Anecdotes, 250 words, of unusual parish experiences, for "Our Parish." Pays $5 to $12.50, on acceptance.

PENNYWHISTLE PRESS—Box 500-P, Washington, DC 20044. Anita Sama, Ed. Short fillers, puzzlers, word games, humorous stories, for 6- to 12-year-olds. Pays varying rates, on acceptance.

PENTHOUSE—1965 Broadway, New York, NY 10023. Peter Bloch, Articles Ed. Satire, humor, black comedy. Pays to 50¢ a word, on acceptance.

PEOPLE IN ACTION—P.O. Box 10010, Ogden, UT 84409. Profiles, 500 to 700 words, on accomplished cooks, for "Celebrity Chief." Must be accompanied by recipe and color transparency. Query. Pays 15¢ a word, extra for photos, on acceptance.

PGA MAGAZINE—100 Ave. of the Champions, Palm Beach Gardens, FL 33410. Humorous pieces related to golf, to 1,500 words. Pays to $300, on acceptance.

PLAYBOY—919 N. Michigan Ave., Chicago, IL 60611. Address Party Jokes Editor or After Hours Editor. Jokes; short original material on new trends, lifestyles, personalities; humorous news items. Pays $50 for jokes, on acceptance; $50 to $350 for "After Hours" items, on publication.

POPULAR MECHANICS—224 W. 57th St., New York, NY 10019. Bill Hartford, Man. Ed. How-to pieces, from 300 words, with photos and sketches, on home improvement and shop and craft projects. Pays $25 to $200, on acceptance. Buys all rights.

POPULAR SCIENCE—380 Madison Ave., New York, NY 10017. A. W. Lees, Group Ed. One-column fillers, 350 words, with photo or sketch if demo necessary; general workshop ideas, maintenance tips for home and car. Pays from $100; $50 for ideas for "Taking Care of Your Car" and "Wordless Workshop," on acceptance.

PROCEEDINGS—U.S. Naval Institute, Annapolis, MD 21402. Fred H. Rainbow, Ed. Short humorous anecdotes of interest to Navy, Marine Corps, and Coast Guard professionals. Pays $25, on acceptance.

THE QUALITY CRAFTS MARKET—15 W. 44th St., New York, NY 10036. Marvin David, Ed. Pieces of 220 words on quality crafts shops and galleries, the types of crafts they want to buy, the price range they handle, and how they'll pay (cash or consignment). Pays 10¢ a word, on publication.

THE RAINBOW—9529 US Hwy. 42, Prospect, KY 40059. Jutta Kapfhammer, Asst. Edit. Dir. Fillers about Tandy Color Computers, to ¼ page. Pays on publication.

READER'S DIGEST—Pleasantville, NY 10570. Anecdotes for "Life in These United States," "Humor in Uniform," "Campus Comedy" and "All in a Day's Work." Pays $300, on publication. Short items for "Toward More Picturesque Speech." Pays $50. Anecdotes, fillers, for "Laughter, the Best Medicine," "Personal Glimpses," etc. Pays $20 per two-column line. No submissions acknowledged or returned. Consult anecdotes page in each issue for additional guidelines.

REAL ESTATE SALESPEOPLE—Suite 201, 2531 W. Dunlap, Phoenix, AZ 85021. Jeff Burger, Man. Ed. Fillers, 50 to 200 words, of interest to American sellers of residential real estate. Pays on acceptance.

RECOVERY—P.O. Box 31329, Seattle, WA 98103. Poetry and fillers of interest to those recovering from alcohol and drug dependencies. Pays $5 to $25, after publication.

ROAD KING—P.O. Box 250, Park Forest, IL 60466. Address Features Ed. Trucking-related cartoons for "Loads of Laughs"; anecdotes to 200 words, for "Trucker's Life." Pays $25 for cartoons, $25 for anecdotes, on publication. SASE required.

SACRAMENTO—P.O. Box 2424, Sacramento, CA 95811. "City Lights," interesting and unusual people, places, and behind-the-scenes news items, 75 to 250 words. All material must have Sacramento tie-in. Pays on acceptance.

THE SATURDAY EVENING POST—1100 Waterway Blvd., Indianapolis, IN 46202. Jack Gramling, Post Scripts Ed. Humor and satire, to 300 words; cartoons, jokes, for "Post Scripts." Pays $15, on publication.

SCHOOL SHOP—Prakken Publishing, Box 8623, 416 Longshore Dr., Ann Arbor, MI 48107. Alan H. Jones, Exec. Ed. Puzzles and cartoons of interest to technology and industrial education teachers and administrators. Pay varies, on publication.

SCORE, CANADA'S GOLF MAGAZINE—287 MacPherson Ave., Toronto, Ont., Canada M4V 1A4. Lisa A. Leighton, Man. Ed. Fillers, 50 to 100 words, related to Canadian golf scene. Pays $10 to $25, on publication. Include international reply coupons.

SKI MAGAZINE—380 Madison Ave., New York, NY 10017. Dick Needham, Ed. Short 100 to 300 word items on events and people in skiing, for "Ski Life" department. Humor, to 2,000 words, related to skiing. Pays on acceptance.

SKIING MAGAZINE—One Park Ave., New York, NY 10016. Bill Grout, Ed.-in-Chief. Articles, to 600 words, on skiing; humorous vignettes, fillers on skiing oddities. Pays from 15¢ a word, on acceptance.

SNOWMOBILE—11812 Wayzata Blvd., Ste. 100, Minnetonka, MN 55343. Dick Hendricks, Ed. Short humor and cartoons on snowmobiling and winter "Personality Plates" sighted. Pays varying rates, on publication.

SOUTH FLORIDA MEDICAL REVIEW—100 NE 7th St., Miami, FL 33132. Avram Goldstein, Ed. Opinion pieces and feature stories about American health care system; puzzles, cartoons of interest to doctors and health care administrators. Pays on publication. Include SASE

SOUTHERN EXPOSURE—P.O. Box 531, Durham, NC 27702. Ashaki M. Binta, Ed. Fillers on civil rights, black politics, nuclear power, utility reform, land use, southern people, etc. Pays from $50, on publication.

SOUTHERN OUTDOORS—1 Bell Rd., Montgomery, AL 36117. Larry Teague, Ed. Humor, 1,000 words, related to the outdoors. Pays 15¢ to 20¢ a word, on acceptance.

SPORTS AFIELD—250 W. 55th St., New York, NY 10019. Unusual, useful tips, 100 to 500 words, for "Almanac" section: hunting, fishing, camping, boating, etc. Photos. Pays $10 per column inch, on publication.

SPUR—Box 85, Middleburg, VA 22117. Anecdotes and short humor, 100 to

500 words, related to the thoroughbred horse industry. Pays $50 to $75, on publication.

THE STATE: DOWN HOME IN NORTH CAROLINA—P.O. Box 2169, Raleigh, NC 27602. W. B. Bright, Ed. Short fillers. Pays on acceptance.

TEACHING AND COMPUTERS—730 Broadway, New York, NY 10003. Mary Dalheim, Ed. Short computer ideas or programs of 50 words or so for teachers of grades K through 8. Pays on acceptance.

TENNIS—495 Westport Ave., P.O. Box 5350, Norwalk, CT 06856. Short articles and humor, 750 to 1,000 words, on personal experiences in the game. Pays to $300, on publication.

TEXAS REAL ESTATE—4665 Sweetwater Blvd., Suite 100, Sugar Land, TX 77479. Short 150 to 500 word developer briefs, real estate short stories, pieces on architecture, brokerage, finance, personalities, and short interviews. Pays $50 to $150, after acceptance.

TOUCH—Box 7259, Grand Rapids, MI 49510. Carol Smith, Man. Ed. Fillers, Bible puzzles from NIV version, for Christian girls aged 8 to 14. Pays 2¢ a word, on acceptance.

TRAILER BOATS—P.O. Box 2307, Gardena, CA 90248. Jim Youngs, Ed. Fillers and humor, preferably with illustrations, on boating and related activities. Pays 7¢ to 10¢ a word, on publication.

TRAVEL SMART—Dobbs Ferry, New York 10522. Interesting, unusual or helpful travel-related tips, vacation or business-travel information, to 1,000 words. Pays $5 to $100, on publication. Query.

TRUE CONFESSIONS—215 Lexington Ave., New York, NY 10016. Barbara J. Brett, Ed. Warm, inspirational first-person fillers, 300 to 700 words, about love, marriage and family life for "The Feminine Side of Things." Pays after publication. Buys all rights.

VIDEOMAKER—P.O. Box 3015, Peterborough, NH 03458. Bradley Kent, Managing Ed. Fillers, humor, jokes, and puzzles pertaining to videomaking. Pay varies, on publication.

THE VIRGINIAN—P.O. Box 8, New Hope, VA 24469. Hunter S. Pierce, IV, Ed. Dir. Fillers, relating to Virginia and adjacent region of the South. Anecdotes and nostalgic pieces preferred. Pays varying rates, on publication.

VOLKSWAGEN'S WORLD—Volkswagen of America, Troy, MI 48099. Ed Rabinowitz, Ed. Anecdotes, to 100 words, about Volkswagen owners' experiences; humorous photos of Volkswagens. Pays from $15 to $40, on acceptance.

WASHINGTON'S ALMANAC—1500 Eastlake Ave., E., Seattle, WA 98102. David Fuller, Managing Editor. Annual publication of *Washington* Magazine. Fillers and short items related to Washington State. Payment varies, on publication.

WESTART—Box 6868, Auburn, CA 95604. Martha Garcia, Ed. Features and current news items, 350 to 500 words, on fine arts. No hobbies. Pays 50¢ per column inch, on publication.

THE WESTERN HORSEMAN—3850 N. Nevada Ave., Colorado Springs, CO 80933. Randy Witte, Ed. For "Here's How," short, handy hints for horsemen (past items have included "horse-proof" corral gate latches, emergency equipment repair, how to remove a halter from a horse safely).

WINES OF THE AMERICAS—P.O. Box 498, Geyserville, CA 95411. Fillers, related to the wine-making industry. Pays on publication. Address Mildred Howie.

WINNING—15115 S. 76 E. Ave., Bixby, OK 74008. Short pieces, 400 to 600 words, on winning contests, sweepstakes, lotteries, games shows, bingo, Vegas-style gambling, etc. Pays 5¢ a word, on publication.

WISCONSIN TRAILS—P.O. Box 5650, Madison, WI 53705. Short fillers about Wisconsin: places to go, things to see, etc., 500 words. Pays $100, on publication.

WOMAN—1115 Broadway, New York, NY 10010. Sherry Amatenstein, Ed. Short newsbreaks on medical and legal advances for women for "Let's Put Our Heads Together." Pays on acceptance. Query.

WOMAN'S DAY—1515 Broadway, New York, NY 10036. Heart-warming or funny, true, anecdotes about a "good neighbor"; creative solutions to community problems; reader versions of a *Woman's Day*-inspired craft (including photo); For "Tips to Share": short pieces of personal instructive family experiences, practical suggestions for homemakers. Pays $50, on publication.

WOMEN'S SPORTS AND FITNESS—310 Town and Country Village, Palo Alto, CA 94301. Short pieces, 500 to 3,000 words, on nutrition, beauty, health, and new products for the active woman; profiles of up-and-coming female athletes or other female sports figures; book reviews; opinion pieces. Pays from $50, on publication.

WOOD 'N ENERGY—P.O. Box 2008, Laconia, NH 03247. Jason Perry, Ed. Short pieces for columns: "Reports" (energy news); "Regulations" (safety and standard news); and "Retailers Corner" (tips on running a retail shop). Pieces run from 150 to 500 words. Pays to $50, on publication.

WOODENBOAT MAGAZINE—Box 78, Brooklin, ME 04616. Jon Wilson, Ed. Short items and information on wooden boat related events, projects, workshop activities, 250 to 1,000 words, for "On the Waterfront" Pays $5 to $25, on publication.

YM—685 Third Ave., New York, NY 10017. First-person, humorous fillers, to 850 words, on any aspect of adolescence: early or late blooming, boy-girl relationships, school, part-time jobs, getting along with siblings, dieting, etc. Serious fillers, to 850 words, on such teen concerns as shyness, loneliness, popularity, self-confidence, etc. Teen quotes. Professional advice. Pays on acceptance.

JUVENILE, TEENAGE, AND YOUNG ADULT MAGAZINES

JUVENILE MAGAZINES

ACTION—Dept of Christian Education, Free Methodist Headquarters, 901 College Ave., Winona Lake, IN 46590. Vera Bethel, Ed. Stories, 1,000 words, for 9- to 11-year olds. How-to features, 200 to 500 words. Verse. Seasonal material. Pays $25 for stories, $15 for features with photos or sketch, $5 for poetry, on publication.

CHICKADEE—The Young Naturalist Foundation, 59 Front St., E. Toronto, Ont., Canada M5E 1B3. Janis Nosbakken, Ed. Animal and adventure stories, 200 to 800 words, for children aged 3 to 8. Also, puzzles, activities and observation games, 50 to 300 words. Humorous poems, 10 to 15 lines, about animals and nature. Pays varying rates, on publication. Send complete manuscript and International postal coupons. No outlines.

CHILD—477 Madison Ave., 22nd Fl., New York, NY 10022. Nancy Clark, Features Ed. Articles for parents who want the best for their children, 1,500 to 2,500 words. Pays $500 to $1,000, on acceptance. Queries are preferred.

CHILD LIFE—1100 Waterway Blvd., P.O. Box 567, Indianapolis, IN 46206. Steve Charles, Ed. Articles, 500 to 1,200 words, for 7- to 9-year olds. Fiction and humor stories, to 1,600 words. Puzzles. Photos. Pays about 6¢ a word, extra for photos, on publication. Buys all rights.

CHILDREN'S DIGEST—1100 Waterway Blvd., P.O. Box 567, Indianapolis, IN 46202. Elizabeth Rinck, Ed. Health publication for children aged 8 to 10. Informative articles, 500 to 1,200 words, and fiction (especially realistic, adventure, mystery, and humorous), 500 to 1,800 words, with health, safety, exercise, nutrition, or hygiene as theme. Historical and biographical articles. Poetry. Pays 6¢ a word, from $7 for poems, on publication. Buys all rights.

CHILDREN'S PLAYMATE—Editorial Office, 1100 Waterway Blvd., P.O. Box 567, Indianapolis, IN 46206. Elizabeth Rinck, Ed. Humorous and health-related short stories, 500 to 800 words, for 5- to 7-year-olds. Simple science articles and how-to crafts pieces with brief instructions. "All About" features, about 500 words, on health, nutrition, safety, and exercise. Poems. Pays about 6¢ a word, $7 minimum for poetry, on publication.

CLUBHOUSE—Berrien Springs, MI 49103. Elaine Meseraull, Ed. Action-oriented Christian stories: features, 1,000 to 1,200 words; "Story Cubes" and "Thinker Tales" (parables), about 800 words. Children in stories should be wise, brave, funny, kind, etc. Pays to $35 for features, $30 for parables and nonfeatures, on acceptance.

COBBLESTONE—20 Grove St., Peterborough, NH 03458. Carolyn Yoder, Ed. Theme-related biographies, and short accounts of historical events, to 1,200 words, for children aged 8 to 14 years. Fiction, 500 to 1,200 words. Poetry, to 100 lines. Photos. Pays 10¢ to 15¢ a word for prose, varying rates for poetry, on publication. Send SASE for editorial guidelines with monthly themes.

COUNSELOR—P.O. Box 632, Glen Ellyn, IL 60138. Grace Anderson, Ed. Articles, 800 to 1,200 words, for children 8 to 11 years, that glorify God and His teachings. Pays 4¢ to 10¢ a word. Query required.

CRICKET—Box 100, La Salle, IL 61301. Marianne Carus, Ed.-in-Chief. Articles and fiction, 200 to 1,500 words, for 6- to 12-year-olds. Poetry, to 30 lines. Pays to 25¢ a word, to $3 a line for poetry, on publication. Send SASE for guidelines. Overstocked.

DISCOVERIES—6401 The Paseo, Kansas City, MO 64131. Libby Huffman, Ed. Stories, 800 to 1,000 words, for 3rd to 6th graders, with Christian emphasis. Poetry, 4 to 20 lines. Cartoons. Pays 3.5¢ a word (2¢ a word for reprints), 25¢ a line for poetry (minimum of $2), on acceptance.

THE DOLPHIN LOG—The Cousteau Society, 8440 Santa Monica Blvd., Los Angeles, CA 90069. Articles, 500 to 1,200 words, on a variety of topics related to our global water system: marine biology, ecology, natural history, and water-related stories, for children ages 7 to 15. Pays $25 to $150, on publication. Query.

ELECTRIC COMPANY MAGAZINE—See *3-2-1 Contact*.

THE FRIEND—50 E. North Temple, 23rd Fl., Salt Lake City, UT 84150. Vivian Paulsen, Man. Ed. Stories and articles, 1,000 to 1,200 words. "Tiny tot" stories, to 250 words. Pays from 8¢ a word, from $15 per poem, on acceptance.

GEOFFREY'S TOYS "R" US—1220 Mound Ave., Racine, WI 53404. Don Lesinski, Ed. Fiction and articles, 500 to 1,000 words, for children 6 to 12. Poetry, fillers, humor, jokes, and puzzles. Pays $100 to $2,000, on acceptance. Queries are preferred.

HIGHLIGHTS FOR CHILDREN—803 Church St., Honesdale, PA 18431. Kent L. Brown, Ed. Fiction and articles, to 900 words, for 2- to 12-year-olds. Fiction should have strong plot, believable characters, story that holds reader's interest from beginning to end. No crime or violence. For articles, cite references used and qualifications. Easy rebus-form stories. Easy-to-read stories, 400 to 600 words, with strong plots. Pays from 6¢ a word, on acceptance.

HUMPTY DUMPTY'S MAGAZINE—1100 Waterway Blvd., P.O. Box 567, Indianapolis, In 46202. Christine French Clark, Ed. Health publication for children ages 4 to 6. Easy-to-read fiction, to 600 words, some with health and nutrition, safety, exercise, or hygiene as theme; humor and light approach preferred. Crafts with clear, brief instructions. Short poems. Stories-in-rhyme. Pays about 6¢ a word, from $7 for poems, on publication. Buys all rights.

JACK AND JILL—Box 567, Indianapolis, IN 46206. Christine French Clark, Ed. Articles, 500 to 1,000 words, for 6- to 8-year-olds, on sports, nature, science, health, safety, exercise. Features 1,000 to 1,200 words, on history, biography, life in other countries, etc. Fiction, to 1,200 words. Short poems, games, puzzles, projects. Photos. Pays about 6¢ a word, extra for photos, varying rates for fillers, on publication.

LOLLIPOPS—Good Apple, Inc., P.O. Box 299, Carthage, IL 62321-0299. Short stories, 500 to 1,200 words, for children, preschool to 7; poetry, fillers. Pays varying rates, on publication. Query.

NATIONAL GEOGRAPHIC WORLD—1145 17th N.W., Washington, DC 20036. Pat Robbins, Ed. Original games and puzzles for readers age 8 and older. Proposals for picture stories (accompanied by samples of photographic work). Pays $25.

ODYSSEY—625 E. St. Paul Ave., Milwaukee, WI 53202. Nancy Mack, Ed. Features, 600 to 1,500 words, on astronomy and space science for 8- to 12-year-olds. Short experiments, projects, and games. Pays $100 to $350, on publication. Query.

ON THE LINE—616 Walnut, Scottdale, PA 15683-1999. Virginia A. Hostetler, Ed. Nature and how-to articles, 500 to 750 words, for 10- to 14-year-olds. Fiction, 800 to 1,200 words. Poetry, puzzles, cartoons. Pays to 4¢ a word, on acceptance.

OWL—The Young Naturalist Foundation, 59 Front St., E. Toronto, Ont., Canada M5E 1B3. Sylvia Funston, Ed. Articles, 500 to 1,000 words, for children aged 8 to 12, on animals, science, people, places, experiments, etc.

Should be informative but not preachy. Pays varying rates, on publication. Send brief outline and International reply coupons.

PENNYWHISTLE PRESS—Box 500-P, Washington, DC 20044. Anita Sama, Ed. Short fiction, 850 words for 8- to 12-year-old children, 400 words for 5- to 8-year-olds. Puzzles and word games. Payment varies, on publication.

PLAYS, THE DRAMA MAGAZINE FOR YOUNG PEOPLE—120 Boylston St., Boston, MA 02116. Elizabeth Preston, Man. Ed. Needs one-act plays, programs, skits, creative dramatic material, suitable for school productions at junior high, middle and lower grade levels. Plays with one set preferred. Uses comedies, dramas, satires, farces, melodramas, dramatized classics, folktales and fairy tales, puppet plays. Pays good rates, on acceptance. Send SASE for manuscript specification sheet. Buys all rights.

POCKETS—1908 Grand Ave., Box 189, Nashville, TN 37202. Shirley Paris, Assistant Ed. Ecumenical magazine for children ages six through twelve. Material that will help children experience a Christian lifestyle: 600- to 1,500-word contemporary fiction and scripture stories; short poems; and 400- to 600-word articles about the Bible, church history, holidays, etc. Pay starts at 7¢ a word, on acceptance; $25 to $50 for poetry. Writers guidelines are available; send SASE.

RADAR—8121 Hamilton Ave., Cincinnati, OH 45231. Margaret Williams, Ed. Articles, 400 to 650 words, on nature, hobbies, crafts. Short stories, 900 to 1,100 words: mystery, sports, school, family, with 12-year-old as main character; serials of 2,000 words. Christian emphasis. Poems to 12 lines. Pays to 3¢ a word, to 40¢ a line for poetry, on acceptance.

RANGER RICK—8925 Leesburg Pike, Vienna, VA 22184. Trudy Farrand, Ed. Articles, to 900 words, on wildlife, conservation, natural sciences, and kids in the outdoors, for 6- to 12-year-olds. Nature-related fiction and science fiction welcome. Games, crafts, poems, and puzzles. Pays to $350, on acceptance.

SESAME STREET MAGAZINE—See *3-2-1 Contact*.

SHOFAR—43 Northcote Dr., Melville, NY 11747. Alan A. Kay, Exec. Ed. Short stories, 500 to 750 words; articles, 250 to 750 words; poetry, to 50 lines; and short fillers, games, puzzles, and cartoons, for Jewish children, 8 to 13. All material must have a Jewish theme. Pays 10¢ a word, on publication. Submit holiday pieces at least three months in advance.

STONE SOUP, THE MAGAZINE BY CHILDREN—Box 83, Santa Cruz, CA 95063. Gerry Mandel, Ed. Stories, poems, plays, book reviews by children under 14. Pays in copies.

STORY FRIENDS—Mennonite Publishing House, Scottdale, PA 15683. Marjorie Waybill, Ed. Stories, 350 to 800 words, for 4- to 9-year-olds on Christian faith and values in everyday experiences. Quizzes, riddles. Poetry. Pays to 5¢ a word, to $5 per poem, on acceptance.

3-2-1 CONTACT—Children's Television Workshop, 1 Lincoln Plaza, New York, NY 10023. Jonathan Rosenbloom, Ed. Entertaining and informative articles, 600 to 1,000 words, for 8- to 14-year-olds, on all aspects of science, computers, scientists, and children who are learning about or practicing science. Pays $75 to $400, on acceptance. No fiction. Query. Also publishes *Electric Company Magazine* and *Sesame Street Magazine*.

TOUCH—Box 7244, Grand Rapids, MI 49510. Carol Smith, Man. Ed. Upbeat fiction and features, 1,000 to 1,500 words, for Christian girls age 8 to 14;

personal life, nature, crafts. Poetry; fillers, puzzles. Pays 2¢ a word, extra for photos, on acceptance. Query for theme with SASE.

TURTLE MAGAZINE FOR PRESCHOOL KIDS—1100 Waterway Blvd., Box 567, Indianapolis, IN 46206. Beth Wood Thomas, Ed. Stories about safety, exercise, health, and nutrition, for preschoolers. Humorous, entertaining fiction, 600 words. Simple poems. Stories-in-rhyme; easy-to-read stories, to 500 words, for beginning readers. Pays about 6¢ a word, on publication. Buys all rights. Send SASE for guidelines.

WEE WISDOM—Unity Village, MO 64065. Verle Belle, Ed. Character-building stories, to 800 words, for 3- to 12-year-olds. Pays 3¢ to 4¢ per word, on acceptance.

WONDER TIME—6401 The Paseo, Kansas City, MO 64131. Evelyn J. Beals, Ed. Stories, 200 to 600 words, for 6- to 8-year-olds, with Christian emphasis to correlate with Sunday school curriculum. Features, to 300 words, on nature, crafts, etc. Poetry, 4 to 12 lines. Pays 3½¢ a word, from 25¢ a line for verse, $2.50 minimum, on acceptance.

YABA WORLD—5301 S. 76th St., Greendale,WI 53129. Paul Bertling, Ed. Articles, 1,500 words, on Young American Bowling Alliance league or tournament bowling. Profiles; how-to's. Photos. Pays $25 to $100, extra for photos, on acceptance. Query preferred.

YOUNG AMERICAN—Box 12409, Portland, OR 97217. Kristina Linden, Ed. Stories—fantasy, humor, true to life—to 1,000 words, for 5th-grade reading level. Articles about kids, science, computers, health, news, 350 words. Light verse. Readers are ages 6 to 15. All material must have a positive focus; no religious material, sex, or violence. Submit complete manuscripts. Pays 7¢ a word, on publication.

YOUNG JUDAEAN—50 W. 58th St., New York, NY 10019. Mordecai Newman, Ed. Articles, 500 to 1,000 words, with photos, for 9- to 12-year-olds, on Israel, Jewish holidays, Jewish-American life, Jewish history. Fiction, 800 to 1,500 words, on Jewish themes. Poetry, from 8 lines. Fillers, humor, reviews. Pays $20 per printed page.

THE YOUNG SALVATIONIST—The Salvation Army, 700 Bloomfield Ave., Verona, NJ 07044. Capt. Dorothy Hitzka, Ed. Articles for teens, 800 to 1,200 words with Christian perspective; fiction, 1,000 to 1,200 words; short fillers. Young Soldier Section: Fiction: 600 to 800 words; games and puzzles for children. Pays 3¢ a word, on acceptance.

TEENAGE AND YOUNG ADULT

ALIVE NOW!—P.O. Box 189, Nashville, TN 37202. Mary Ruth Coffman, Ed. Short essays, 250 to 400 words, with Christian emphasis. Poetry, one page. Photos. Pays $5 to $20, on publication.

AMERICAN NEWSPAPER CARRIER—P.O. Box 15300, Winston-Salem, NC 27013. Marilyn Rollins, Ed. Light fiction, 1,000 words, for teenage newspaper carriers; mystery, adventure, etc. Inspiration articles, editorials. Pays $25, on acceptance.

BOP—7060 Hollywood Blvd., Suite 720, Hollywood, CA 90028. Julie Laufer, Ed. Interviews and features, 500 to 1,000 words, for teenage girls, on stars popular with teenagers. Photos. Pays varying rates, on acceptance. Query preferred.

BOYS' LIFE—1325 Walnut Hill Lane, Irving, TX 75038-3096. William B. McMorris, Exec. Ed. Publication of Boy Scouts of America. Articles, 300 to 1,500 words, and fiction, 1,000 or 2,500 to 3,200 words, for 8- to 18-year-old boys. Photos. Pays from $250 for articles, from $350 for fiction, on acceptance. Query for articles.

CAMPUS LIFE—465 Gundersen Dr., Carol Steam, IL 60188. Gregg Lewis, Sr. Ed. Articles reflecting Christian values and world view, for high school and college students. Humor and general fiction. Photo essays, cartoons. Pays from $150, on acceptance. Limited free-lance market.

CAMPUS VOICE—505 Market St., Knoxville, TN 37902. Lively, in-depth articles, 2,500 to 3,000 words, of interest to college students. Department pieces, 1,500 to 2,000 words. Pays $300 to $2,000, on acceptance. Query required. Send SASE for guidelines.

THE CHRISTIAN ADVENTURER—P.O. Box 850, Joplin, MO 64802. Rosmarie Foreman, Ed. Fiction, 1,500 to 1,800 words, for 13- to 19-year-olds, on Christian living. Fillers. Pays 1.5¢ a word, quarterly.

CHRISTIAN LIVING FOR SENIOR HIGH—850 N. Grove, Elgin, IL 60120. Anne E. Dinnan, Ed. Articles and fiction, 1,000 to 1,500 words, of interest to Christian teens. Don't preach. Pays 10¢ a word, on acceptance.

CURRENT CONSUMER & LIFESTUDIES—3500 Western Ave., Highland Park, IL 60035. Carol Rubenstein, Sr. Assoc. Ed. Practical, well-researched articles, 1,000 to 1,200 words, for high school students, on family living, interpersonal relationships, and consumer topics. Pays $100, on publication. Queries only; no unsolicited manuscripts accepted.

DISCOVERY MAGAZINE—1420 Centre Ave., Suite 804, Pittsburgh, PA 15219. Articles for teens on drug and alcohol abuse; interviews with nationally-known celebrities who take strong positions against substance abuse. Pays 10¢ a word, on publication, for articles of 1,000 to 5,000 words. Fillers, 50 to 250 words. Queries are preferred. B&W and color photos.

EXPLORING—1325 Walnut Hill Ln., Irving, TX 75038-3096. Scott Daniels, Exec. Ed. Publication of Boy Scouts of America. Articles, 500 to 1,800 words, for 15- to 21-year-olds, on education, careers, Explorer post activities (hiking, canoeing, camping), and program ideas for Explorer post meetings. No controversial subjects. Pays $150 to $400, on acceptance. Query. Send SASE for guidelines.

FREEWAY—Box 632, Glen Ellyn, IL 60138. Cindy Atoji, Ed. First-person true stories, personal experience, how-to's, fillers, and humor, to 1,000 words, with photos, for 13- to 22-year-olds. Christian emphasis. Pays to 8¢ a word.

GRIT—Williamsport, PA 17701. Joanne Decker, Assignment Ed. Articles, 300 to 500 words, with photos, on young people involved in unusual hobbies, occupations, athletic pursuits, and personal adventures. Pays 12¢ a word, extra for photos, on acceptance.

HICALL—1445 Boonville Ave., Springfield, MO 65802. Jennifer J. Eller, Ed. Fiction, 1,200 to 1,800 words, with believable characters working out their problems according to Bible principles: down-to-earth articles emphasizing some phase of Christian living, as well as biographical, historical, and scientific pieces, 500 to 700 words; and brief fillers, to 300 words, with a strong evangelical emphasis. Readers are 15 to 17. Payment varies, on acceptance.

IN TOUCH—Box 2000, Marion, IN 46952. Articles, 1,200 to 1,500 words, on contemporary issues, athletes and singers from conservative Christian perspective, for 13- to 18-year-olds. Pays 2¢ to 3¢ a word. Send SASE for guidelines. No queries.

JUNIOR TRAILS—1445 Boonville Ave., Springfield, MO 65802. John Maempa, Ed. Short stories (contemporary) with a moral emphasis, 1,000 to 1,800 words. Articles, 500 to 1,000 words, on science, nature, biography. Poetry of varying lengths. Pays 3¢ a word, on acceptance.

KEYNOTER—3636 Woodview Trace, Indianapolis, IN 46268. Jack Brockley, Exec. Ed. Articles, 1,000 to 2,500 words, for high school leaders: general-interest features; self-help; pieces on contemporary teenage problems. Photos. Pays $75 to $250, extra for photos, on acceptance. Query preferred.

LIGHTED PATHWAY—922 Montgomery Ave., Cleveland, TN 37311. Marcus V. Hand, Ed. Human-interest and inspirational articles, 1,200 to 1,600 words, for teenagers. Short pieces, 600 to 800 words. Fiction, 1,500 to 1,800 words. Pays 2¢ to 4¢ a word, on acceptance.

THE NATIONAL FUTURE FARMER—Box 15160, Alexandria, VA 22309. Wilson W. Carnes, Ed.-in-Chief. Articles, to 1,000 words, preferably with photos, for agriculture students aged 14 to 21, on activities of Future Farmers of America, new developments in agriculture, and general-interest subjects. Pays from 6¢ a word, on acceptance. Query.

NEW ERA—50 E. North Temple, Salt Lake City, UT 84150. Brian Kelley, Ed. Articles, 150 to 3,000 words, and fiction, to 3,000 words, for young Mormons. Poetry. Photos. Pays 3¢ to 10¢ a word, 25¢ a line for poetry, on acceptance. Query.

PROBE—1548 Poplar Ave., Memphis, TN 38104. Michael S. Day, Ed. Southern Baptist. Articles, to 1,500 words, for 12- and 17-year-old boys, on teen problems, current events. Photo essays on Baptist sports personalities. Pays 3½¢ a word, extra for photos, on acceptance.

SCHOLASTIC SCOPE—730 Broadway, New York, NY 10003. Fran Claro, Ed. For 15- to 18-year-olds with 4th to 6th grade reading ability. Realistic fiction, 400 to 1,200 words, and plays, to 6,000 words, on teen problems. Profiles, 400 to 800 words, of interesting teenagers, with black and white photos. Pays $125 for 500- to 600-word articles, from $200 for plays and short stories, from $150 for longer pieces, on acceptance.

SEVENTEEN—850 Third Ave., New York, NY 10022. Articles, to 2,500 words, on subjects of interest to teens. Sophisticated, well-written fiction, 1,500 to 3,500 words, for young adults. Poetry, to 40 lines, by teens. Short news and features, to 750 words, for "Mini-Mag." Articles, 1,000 words, by teens, for "Your Words." Pays varying rates, on acceptance.

SPLICE—10 Columbus Circle, Ste. 1300, New York, NY 10019. Bob Woods, Ed. Bimonthly on the teen movie and entertainment scene. Personality profiles and behind-the-scenes articles, 1,000 words. Music articles, as long as they relate to movies and music videos. Queries are preferred. Payment is negotiable, on publication.

SPRINT—850 N. Grove Ave., Elgin, IL 60120. Paul Woods, Ed. Feature articles from Christian perspective, 800 to 1,000 words, for junior high Sunday school students, on current teen problems, and Christian personalities. Fiction, 1,000 to 1,200 words, with realistic characters and dialogue. Poetry. Photos. Pays to $100, extra for photos, on acceptance. Submit seasonal material one year in advance. Buys all rights. Query for nonfiction.

STRAIGHT—8121 Hamilton Ave., Cincinnati, OH 45231. Dawn Brett-schneider Korth, Ed. Devotional pieces, features on current situations and issues, humor, for Christian teens. Well-constructed fiction, 1,000 to 1,200 words, showing teens using Christian principles. Poetry, by teen-agers. Photos. Pays about 2¢ a word, on acceptance. Guidelines.

TEEN POWER—Box 632, Glen Ellyn, IL 60138. Pam Campbell, Ed. First person (as told to), true teen experience stories with Christian insights and conclusion, 700 to 1,000 words. Include photos. Pays 4¢ to 7¢ a word, extra for photos, on acceptance.

TEENAGE—175 Middlesex Tpke., Bedford, MA 01730. Andrew Calkins, Ed.-in-Chief. Articles, profiles, interviews, short news reports, essays, humor, celebrity interviews, 500 to 2,000 words, on topics of vital interest to sophisticated young women, ages 14 to 18: sex, relationships, college, careers, sports and fitness, dating, health, money, computers, drugs and alcohol, examples of achievement and leadership among peers, advice on "making it" in the adult world. Some preference given to high school and college-age writers; fiction accepted only from students. Pays $100 to $1,000, on publication.

TEENS TODAY—Nazarene Publishing House, 6401 The Paseo, Kansas City, MO 64131. Gary Sivewright, Ed. Short stories, 1,200 to 1,500 words, dealing with teens demonstrating Christian principles in real-life situations. Adventure stories; stories about relationships and ethics. Pays 3½¢ a word, on acceptance.

TIGER BEAT—105 Union Ave., Cresskill, NJ 07626. Diane Umansky, Ed. Articles, to 4 pages, on young people in show business and music industry. Teen romance fiction, to 1,000 words. Self-help articles. Pays varying rates, on acceptance. Query. Unsolicited manuscripts sent without SASE will not be returned.

TIGER BEAT STAR—105 Union Ave., Cresskill, NJ 07626. Lisa Arcella, Ed. Light celebrity fan pieces and interviews (pop/rock, movies, and TV) and occasional serious articles on topics of interest to teens, ages 12 to 16 years old. Pays $50 per published for articles of 300 words, on publication. Query.

WRITING!—3500 Western Ave., Highland Park, IL 60035. Alan Lenhoff, Ed. Interviews, 1,200 words, for "Writers at Work" department, for high school students. Pays $100, on publication. Query.

YM—685 Third Ave., New York, NY 10017. Lively articles, 1,500 to 2,500 words, on topics of concern to young women ages 12–18; material should be based on thorough research and interviews with experts, and should strongly represent teenagers' feelings. Fillers, 750 to 1,000 words; short stories, 3,000 to 3,500 words, with romantic themes. Pays from $250 for features, from $350 for fiction, and from $75 for fillers, on acceptance. Query first for articles and fillers.

YOUNG AMBASSADOR—Box 82808, Lincoln, NE 68501. Nancy Bayne, Ed. Articles, to 1,800 words, and well-crafted fiction, to 2,500 words, for conservative Christian teens. B/W photos and color slides. Pays 4¢ to 10¢ a word, extra for photos, on publication.

YOUNG AND ALIVE—4444 S. 52nd St., Lincoln, NE 68506. Richard Kaiser, Ed. Feature articles, 800 to 1,400 words, for blind and visually impaired young adults, on adventure, biography, camping, health, hobbies, and travel. Photos. Pays 3¢ to 5¢ a word, extra for photos, on acceptance. Write for guidelines.

YOUTH!—P.O. Box 801, Nashville, TN 37202. Sidney Fowler, Ed. Articles and fiction, 700 to 2,000 words, that help teenagers develop a Christian identity and faith in contemporary culture. Photos. Pays 4¢ a word, on acceptance.

THE DRAMA MARKET

REGIONAL AND UNIVERSITY THEATERS

Community, regional and civic theaters and college dramatic groups offer the best opportunities today for playwrights to see their plays produced, whether for staged production, or for dramatic readings. Indeed, aspiring playwrights who can get their work produced by any of these have taken an important step toward breaking into the competitive dramatic field—many well-known playwrights received their first recognition in the regional theaters. Payment is generally not large, but regional and university theaters usually buy only the right to produce a play, and all further rights revert to the author. Since most directors like to work closely with the authors on any revisions necessary, theaters will often pay for the playwright's expenses while in residence during rehearsals. The thrill of seeing your play come to life on the stage is one of the pleasures of being on hand for rehearsals and performances.

Aspiring playwrights should query college and community theaters in their region to find out which ones are interested in seeing original scripts. Dramatic associations of interest to playwrights include the Dramatists Guild (234 W. 44th St., New York, NY 10036), Theatre Communications Group, Inc. (355 Lexington Ave., New York, NY 10017), which publishes the annual *Dramatists Sourcebook,* and The International Society of Dramatists, publishers of *The Dramatist's Bible* (P.O. Box 3470, Fort Pierce, FL 33448).

Some of the theaters on the following list require that playwrights submit all or some of the following with scripts—cast list, synopsis, resumé, recommendations, return postcard—and with scripts and queries, self-addressed, stamped envelopes (SASE) must *always* be enclosed. Playwrights may also wish to register their material with the U.S. Copyright Office. For additional information about this, write Register of Copyrights, Library of Congress, Washington, DC 20559.

ACADEMY OF MEDIA & THEATRE ARTS—Fort Mason Center, San Francisco, CA 94123. Phyllis Ruskin, Art. Dir. Children's plays, adaptations; simple sets. Query with synopsis, resumé, recommendations, cast list, and SASE. Pays per performance.

ACADEMY THEATRE—1137 Peachtree St., N.E., Atlanta, GA 30309. Frank Wittow, Artistic Dir. One-act and full-length dramas, and adaptations with new approaches that go beyond the conventions of naturalism; 6 to 8 cast members unless actors can play multiple roles. Simple sets. Pays negotiable rates. Query first.

ACTORS THEATRE OF LOUISVILLE—316 W. Main St., Louisville, KY 40202. Jon Jory, Artistic Dir. One-act and full-length dramas and comedies.

Send manuscript, cast list, and SASE to "New Play Program." Reports in 6 to 9 months. Pays royalty, on production. Full-length scripts accepted through agents only.

ALASKA REPERTORY THEATRE—705 W. 6th Ave., Suite 201, Anchorage, AK 99501. Robert Farley, Artistic Dir. Full-length dramas, comedies, and adaptations. Queries only; include SASE.

ALLEY THEATRE—615 Texas Ave., Houston, TX 77002. Edwin Carl Erwin, Lit. Assoc. No unsolicited scripts. Scripts are accepted on the basis of query letters (with synopsis), agent submissions, or professional recommendation. Full length and one-act comedies, dramas, and translations.

ALLIANCE THEATRE COMPANY—1280 Peachtree St. N.E., Atlanta, GA 30309. Sandra Deer, Lit. Man. No unsolicited manuscripts.

AMERICAN JEWISH THEATRE—1395 Lexington Ave., New York, NY 10128. Stanley Brechner, Art. Dir. Full-length comedies and dramas, reflecting Jewish themes. Submit script with SASE to Susan Nanus. Standard contract.

AMERICAN PLACE THEATRE—111 W. 46th St., New York, NY 10036. Chris Breyer, Lit. Man. Full-length plays. Do not prefer commercial comedies; favor plays innovative in both form and content. Send play with SASE. Allow 3 to 5 months for reply.

AMERICAN REPERTORY THEATRE—64 Brattle St., Cambridge, MA 02138. Johnathan Marks, Lit. Man. No unsolicited manuscripts. Submit one-page description of play, 10 page sample, and SASE.

AMERICAN STAGE COMPANY—P.O. Box 1560, St. Petersburg, FL 33731. Victoria Holloway, Artistic Dir. Full-length comedies and dramas. Send synopsis with short description of cast and production requirements with self-addressed postcard. Pays negotiable rates. Submit material September through January.

AMERICAN THEATRE ARTS—11305 Magnolia Blvd., N. Hollywood, CA 91601. Pamela Bohnert, Play Dev. Dir. Submit synopsis, cast list, set requirements, resumé, and SASE. Responds in 8 to 10 weeks.

THE APPLE CORPS.—336 W. 20th St., New York, NY 10011. Bob Del Pazzo, Coordinator. All types of one-act and full-length plays. Send bio, synopsis with SASE. Allow 4 to 6 months for response. Payment varies. No phone calls.

ARENA STAGE—6th and Maine Ave., S.W., Washington, DC 20024. Full-length comedies, dramas, musicals and adaptations. David Copelin, Dir. of Play Development. Submit one-page synopsis, first 10 pages of dialogue, resumé and professional recommendations. No unsolicited manuscripts. Pays varying rates. Workshops and readings offered. Allow 2 to 4 months for reply.

ARKANSAS ARTS CENTER CHILDREN'S THEATRE—Box 2137, Little Rock, AR 72203. Bradley Anderson, Art. Dir. Seeks solid, professional (full length or one-act) scripts. Original, and, particularly, adapted work from contemporary and classic literature. Pays flat rate.

ARTREACH TOURING THEATRE—2926 Millsbrae Ave., Cincinnati, OH 45209. Kathryn Schultz Miller, Art. Dir. One-act dramas and adaptations for touring children's theatre; cast to 4, simple sets. Submit script with synopsis, cast list, resumé, recommendations and SASE. Payment varies.

ASOLO STATE THEATRE—P.O. Drawer E., Sarasota, FL 33578. John

Ulmer, Artistic Dir. Full-length dramas, comedies, musicals, and children's plays. Small stage. Pays royalty or varying rates. Readings and workshops offered. No unsolicited manuscripts. Submit synopsis and letter of inquiry.

AT THE FOOT OF THE MOUNTAIN—2000 S. 5th St., Minneapolis, MN 55454. Kim Hines, Lit. Man. Full-length, one-act and musical plays of all types by and about women, with particular interest in scripts by women of color. Submit manuscript with synopsis, return postcard, and SASE: best time to submit is early spring. Reports in 4 to 6 months. Royalty basis.

BACK ALLEY THEATRE—15231 Burbank Blvd., Van Nuys, CA 91411. Laura Zucker, Producing Dir. Full-length plays. Submit manuscript with SASE and resumé. Reports in 2–3 months. Pays $500, and travel/expenses for playwright to attend rehearsals.

BARTER THEATER—P.O. Box 867, Abingdon, VA 24210. Rex Partington, Producing Dir. Full-length dramas, comedies, adaptations, musicals and children's plays. Full workshop and reading productions. Allow 6 to 8 months for report. Payment rates negotiable.

BERKSHIRE THEATRE FESTIVAL—Box 797, Stockbridge, MA 02162. Josephine Abady, Art. Dir. Full-length comedies, musicals and dramas; cast to 8. Submit through agent only.

BEVERLY HILLS PLAYHOUSE/SKYLIGHT THEATRE—254 S. Robertson Blvd., Beverly Hills, CA 90212. Full-length and one-act comedies, dramas, and musicals; simple sets. Submit scripts with synopsis, recommendations, and SASE. Reports in 8 weeks. No payment.

BOARSHEAD: MICHIGAN PUBLIC THEATRE—425 S. Grand Ave., Lansing, MI 48933. John Peakes, Artistic Dir. Full-length and one-act comedies and dramas. Midwestern origin/theme preferred. Pays negotiable rates. Include SASE.

CENTER STAGE—700 N. Calvert St., Baltimore, MD 21202. Full-length and one-act comedies, dramas, musicals, adaptations. No unsolicited manuscripts. Send synopsis, resumé, cast list, recommendations and production history, with return postcard and SASE. Pays varying rates. Allow 2 to 6 weeks for reply.

CHOCOLATE BAYOU THEATRE CO.—Box 270363, Houston, TX 77277. Attn. John R. Pearson. Preston Jones New Plays Symposium. Four-week residency to develop work with cast and director. Write for details. Other plays accepted through agents only.

CIRCLE REPERTORY COMPANY—161 Ave. of the Americas, New York, NY 10013. B. Rodney Marriott, Assoc. Art. Dir. Full-length comedies and dramas. Send manuscript, cast list, and SASE.

CLASSIC STAGE COMPANY—136 East 13th St., New York, NY 10003. Carol Ostrow, Prod. Dir. Full-length adaptations and translations of existing classic literature. Submit synopsis with cast list and SASE, Sept.–May. Offers workshops and readings. Pays on royalty basis.

CLEVELAND PLAYHOUSE—8500 Euclid Ave., P.O. Box 1989, Cleveland, OH 44106. Wayne S. Turney, Dramaturg. Full-length dramas, comedies, adaptations, and musicals. Query with synopsis and sample dialogue. Pays on royalty basis.

A CONTEMPORARY THEATRE—100 West Roy St., Seattle, WA 98119.

Address Barry Pritchard. Full-length plays of all kinds. Small musicals. Pays on royalty basis.

CREATIVE THEATRE UNLIMITED—33 Mercer St., Princeton, NJ 08540. Pam Hoffman, Troupe Dir. One-act participatory plays and adaptations for children; cast to 5; arena stage. Submit manuscript with synopsis and cast list in the spring. Pays $200.

CROSSROADS THEATRE CO.—320 Memorial Pkwy., New Brunswick, NJ 08901. Lee Richardson, Art. Dir. Full-length and one-act dramas, comedies, musicals and adaptations; experimental pieces; one man/one woman shows. Queries only, with synopsis, cast list, resumé and SASE.

DALLAS THEATER CENTER—3636 Turtle Creek, Dallas, TX 75219. Address Kimberly Cole. Full-length comedies and dramas. Pays percentage of box office receipts. Reporting time: 12 to 16 weeks.

DELAWARE THEATRE COMPANY—P.O. Box 516, Wilmington, DE 19899. Cleveland Morris, Art. Dir. Full-length comedies, dramas, musicals, and adaptations, with cast to 10; prefer single set. Send cast list, synopsis, and SASE. Reports in 6 months. Pays royalty.

DENVER CENTER THEATRE COMPANY—1050 13th St., Denver, CO 80204. Donovan Markey, Art. Dir. Full-length comedies and dramas; 12 characters max. Send manuscript with resumé, return postcard and SASE. Pays negotiable rates. Special interest in regional material.

DETROIT REPERTORY THEATRE—13103 Woodrow Wilson Ave., Detroit, MI 48238. Barbara Busby, Lit. Man. Full-length comedies, and dramas. Enclose SASE. Pays royalty. Annual contest.

DORSET THEATRE FESTIVAL—Box 519, Dorset, VT 05251. Jill Charles, Art. Dir. Full-length comedies, musicals, dramas, and adaptations; cast to 8; simple set preferred. Query with synopsis, cast list, 5 to 10 pages of dialogue, resumé and return postcard. No unsolicited manuscripts. Pays varying rates.

EAST WEST PLAYERS—4424 Santa Monica Blvd., Los Angeles, CA 90029. Full-length comedies, dramas and musicals, dealing with Asian American issues and/or including important roles for Asian actors. Cast up to 15. Send manuscript with synopsis, cast list, resumé and SASE. Pays varying rates. Offers workshops and readings. Allow 3 months for reply.

EMPIRE STATE INSTITUTE FOR THE PERFORMING ARTS—Empire State Plaza, Albany, NY 12223. Barbara R. Maggio, Lit. Man. Full-length and one-act plays and musicals (preferably unproduced) on any subject, particularly for family audiences. Submit manuscript and synopsis. Pays negotiable rates.

THE EMPTY SPACE THEATRE—95 S. Jackson St., Seattle, WA 98104. Tom Creamer, Lit. Man. Unsolicited scripts accepted only from WA, OR, WY, MT, and ID. Annual new play conference for writers from same states: send for brochure. Outside five-state NW region: scripts accepted through agents or established theater groups only.

ENSEMBLE STUDIO THEATRE—549 W. 52nd St., New York, NY 10019. D.S. Moynihan, Lit. Man. Full-length and one-act dramas and comedies, for cast of up to 12; small stage. Send manuscript with cast list, and SASE. Pays $1,000 for full-length, $200 for one-acts.

THE FAMILY REPERTORY CO.—9 Second Ave., New York, NY 10003.

Marvin F. Camillo, Art. Dir. Contemporary, social works on variety of topics. Full-length dramas and musicals for young people and adults. Submit manuscript with synopsis, resume, and return postcard. Pays small fee.

FLORIDA STUDIO THEATRE—1241 N. Palm Ave., Sarasota, FL 33577. Jeff Mousseau, New Play Development. Innovative smaller cast plays that are pertinent and contemporary. Query first. Pays varying rates.

FOLGER THEATRE—301 E. Capitol St., S.E., Washington, DC 20003. Genie Barton, Dramaturg. New versions or adaptations of classics. Payment rates negotiable. Query with SASE.

FULTON OPERA HOUSE—Box 1865, 12 N. Prince, Lancaster, PA 17603. Kathleen Collins, Art. Dir. One-act and full-length children's plays for family theatre. Cast to 10; unit set. Query with synopsis and return postcard.

WILL GEER THEATRICUM BOTANICUM—Box 1222, Topanga, CA 90290. All types of scripts for outdoor theater, with large playing area. Submit manuscript with SASE. Pays varying rates.

GEORGE STREET PLAYHOUSE—9 Livingston Ave., New Brunswick, NJ 08901. Alexis Greene, Lit. Man. Full-length comedies and dramas; simple sets, cast to 8. Submit script with SASE. Payment varies. Offers workshops and readings.

GEVA THEATRE—75 Woodbury Blvd., Rochester, NY 14607. Ann Patrice Carrigan, Lit. Dir. Full-length dramas, comedies, and musicals. Query with synopsis and cast list. Pays on percentage basis.

EMMY GIFFORD CHILDREN'S THEATRE—3504 Center St., Omaha, NE 68105. Bill Kirk, Dramaturg. Previously produced one-act children's plays, especially adaptations from books or classic tales. Include return postcard. Pays $250 to $1,000.

THE GOODMAN THEATRE—200 S. Columbus Dr., Chicago, IL 60603. No unsolicited manuscripts. Query Literary Dept. with synopsis, resumé, cast list, and SASE only.

THE GROUP THEATRE—3940 Brooklyn NE, Seattle, WA 98105. Attn. Tim Bond. Full-length comedies and dramas, suitable for multi-ethnic casts of up to 10 players; unit set. Submit synopsis and sample pages of dialogue, with recommendations. Pays negotiable rates. Annual contest.

THE GUTHRIE THEATRE—725 Vineland Pl., Minneapolis, MN 55403. Mark Bly, Lit. Man. Full-length comedies, dramas, and adaptations. Manuscripts accepted only from recognized theatrical agents. Query with detailed synopsis, cast size, resumé, return postcard and recommendations. Pays negotiable rates, and travel/residency expenses. Offers readings. Reports in 1 to 2 months.

HARTFORD STAGE COMPANY—50 Church St., Hartford, CT 06103. Constance Congdon, Lit. Man. Full-length plays of all types, for cast up to 12. No unsolicited manuscripts; submit through agent or send synopsis. Pays varying rates.

THE HARTMAN THEATER—307 Atlantic St., Stamford, CT 06901. Margaret Booker, Artistic Dir. Full-length comedies, dramas and musicals. No unsolicited manuscripts. Query with synopsis, outline, return postcard and SASE. Reports in 3 to 4 months.

HIPPODROME STATE THEATRE—25 S.E. Second Place, Gainesville,

FL 32601. Gregory Hausch, Artistic Director. Full-length plays, with unit sets and casts up to 15. Submit in summer and fall. Enclose return postcard and synopsis.

HOLLYWOOD ACTORS THEATRE—P.O. Box 27429, Los Angeles, CA 90027. Ron Bastone, Art. Dir. Full-length comedies and dramas, for cast of 6 to 8 actors; single or unit set preferred. Send manuscript with synopsis, cast list, resumé, and SASE. Pays 20% of gross receipts.

HONOLULU THEATRE FOR YOUTH—Box 3257, Honolulu, HI 96801. John Kauffman, Art. Dir. Plays, 60 to 90 minutes playing time, for young people/family audiences. Adult casts. Contemporary issues, Pacific themes, etc. Unit sets, small cast. Query or send manuscript with synopsis, cast list and SASE. Royalties negotiable.

HUNTINGTON THEATRE CO.—264 Huntington Ave., Boston, MA 02115. Gary Mitchell, Asst. to the Prod. Dir. Full-length comedies and dramas. Query with synopsis, cast list, resumé, recommendations, and return postcard.

THE ILLUSION THEATER—528 Hennepin Ave., Minneapolis, MN 55403. Michael Robbins, Producing Dir. Seeks writers to collaborate on new plays with the acting company. Submit resumé and synopsis. Pays varying rates.

INDIANA REPERTORY THEATRE—140 W. Washington St., Indianapolis, IN 46204. Janet Allen, Dramaturg. Full-length comedies, dramas, musicals, and adaptations. Single sets preferred, as are casts of no more than eight. Query with resume, synopsis, and SASE; response time for queries is a month; for scripts, two to three months. Pays on percentage basis. Produces up to three new plays each season.

INVISIBLE THEATRE—1400 N. First Ave., Tucson, AZ 85719. Susan Claassen, Lit. Man. Full-length comedies, dramas, musicals and adaptations, for cast to 10; simple set. Send synopsis with cast list. Pays on percentage basis.

JACKSONVILLE UNIVERSITY THEATRE—Jacksonville Univ., Jacksonville, FL 32211. Davis Sikes, Artistic Dir. Unproduced full-length and one-act dramas and comedies. Send manuscript with synopsis, cast list, return postcard, and SASE. Pays $1,000 and production. Annual contest.

JEWISH REPERTORY THEATRE—344 E. 14th St., New York, NY 10003. Ran Avni, Artistic Dir. Full-length comedies, dramas, musicals, children's plays and adaptations, with cast to 10, relating to the Jewish experience. Pays varying rates. Enclose return postcard.

THE JULIAN THEATRE—953 DeHaro St., San Francisco, CA 94107. Address New Plays. Full-length comedies and dramas with a social statement. Send 5 to 10 page scene, synopsis, cast description, and SASE. Pays on contractual basis. Allow 2 to 9 months for reply. Workshops and readings offered. No recent report.

LAGUNA MOULTON PLAYHOUSE—606 Laguna Canyon Rd., Laguna Beach, CA 92651. Douglas Rowe, Art. Dir. Original plays. Submit manuscript with SASE and return postcard. Payment varies.

LAMB'S PLAYERS THEATRE—500 Plaza Blvd., P.O. Box 26, National City, CA 92050. Address Script Search Committee. All types of full-length plays, for small cast; arena staging. Send manuscript with cast list and synopsis. Pays $500 to $1,000. Sponsors readings and annual contest.

LITTLE BROADWAY PRODUCTIONS—% Jill Shawn, 20247 Lorenzana Dr., Woodland Hills, CA 91364. Musicals and other plays for children; 55

721

minutes, no intermission. Submit manuscript with synopsis, return postcard, resumé, and SASE. Pays negotiable rates.

LONG ISLAND STAGE—Box 190, Hempstead, NY 11550. Clinton J. Atkinson, Art. Dir. Full-length dramas and adaptations. Query with SASE in late spring/early summer. Pays varying rates.

LOOKING GLASS THEATRE—175 Matthewson St., Providence, RI 02903. Pamela Messore, Artistic Dir. One-act, participation style children's plays, with cast to 5. Send manuscript with return postcard and SASE. Pays negotiable rates. Allow 6 weeks for reply. No recent report.

LOS ANGELES THEATER UNIT—P.O. Box 429, Hollywood, CA 90078. Lanny Thomas, Lit. Dir. One-act and full-length original scripts, with special interest in plays with larger casts and several roles for women, "but please no elaborate sets or elephants." Submit script with synopsis and cast list. Pays on performance.

LOS ANGELES THEATRE CENTER—514 S. Spring St., Los Angeles, CA 90013. Mame Hunt, Lit. Man. Full-length comedies, dramas, musicals, and adaptations. Special interest in scripts with social/political content; and by women and ethnic minorities. Query with synopsis, 10 pages of text, and SASE. Pays advance against royalty, on production, and travel and residence expenses.

MCCADDEN PLACE THEATRE—1157 N. McCadden Place, Los Angeles, CA 90038. Address Joy Rinaldi, Artistic Dir. Full-length and one-act comedies, dramas and adaptations. Send manuscript with cast list, synopsis, resumé, return postcard and SASE.

MCCARTER THEATRE COMPANY—91 University Pl., Princeton, NJ 08540. Robert Lanchester, Assoc. Art. Dir. Full-length and one-act comedies, dramas and adaptations. Submit script with SASE, synopsis, resumé, cast list, and recommendations. Pays negotiable rates.

MANHATTAN PUNCH LINE—410 W. 42nd St., New York, NY 10036. Steve Kaplan, Art. Dir. Comedies. Showcase contract. SASE required.

MANHATTAN THEATRE CLUB—453 W. 16th, New York, NY 10011. Address Molly Fowler. Full-length and one-act comedies, dramas and musicals. No unsolicited manuscripts. Send synopsis with cast list, resumé, recommendations and return postcard. Pays negotiable rates. Allow 6 months for reply. Offers workshops and readings.

MEGAW THEATRE, INC.—17601 Saticoy St., Northridge, CA 91325. Full-length comedies and dramas, with cast of 6 to 8, and unit set. Send manuscripts with synopsis, cast list, resumé, recommendations, return postcard and SASE. Pays on contractual basis. Offers readings.

MIDWEST PLAYLABS—% The Playwrights' Center, 2301 Franklin Ave. E., Minneapolis, MN 55406. Full-length previously unproduced scripts (no musicals). Query. Pays stipend, room and board, and travel for 2-week August conference.

MILL MOUNTAIN THEATRE—Center in the Square, One Market Sq., Roanoke, VA 24011. Jo Weinstein, Lit. Man. Full-length and one-act original comedies, dramas, musicals, and adaptations; small casts and simple sets preferred. Submit manuscript with cast list, resumé, return postcard and SASE. Pays varying rates. Readings and workshops.

MISSOURI REPERTORY THEATRE—4949 Cherry St., Kansas City, MO

64110. Felicia Londre, Dramaturg. Full-length comedies and dramas. Query with synopsis, cast list, resumé, and return postcard. Pays standard royalty.

MUSIC THEATRE GROUP/LENOX ARTS CENTER—735 Washington St., New York, NY 10014. Innovative musicals, to 1½ hours; cast to 10. Query only, with synopsis and return postcard; address Vanessa Palmer. Best submission time: Sept.–Dec.

MUSICAL THEATRE WORKS—133 Second Ave., New York, NY 10003. Mark Herko, Lit. Dir. Full-length musicals; cast to 10; simple sets. Submit manuscript with SASE and cassette score. No payment.

THE NEGRO ENSEMBLE COMPANY—165 W. 46th St., Suite 800, New York, NY 10036. Douglas Turner Ward, Art. Dir. Full-length comedies, dramas, musicals and adaptations pertaining to Black life and the Black experience. Submit March through May. Pays on royalty basis. Enclose return postcard.

NEW ARTS THEATRE—702 Ross Ave., Dallas, TX 75202. Stephen Hollis, Art. Dir. Full-length dramas and comedies. Cast to 8. Submit manuscript with return postcard and resumé. Reports in 3 months. Pays percentage.

NEW DRAMATISTS—424 W. 44th St., New York, NY 10036. Workshop for member playwrights. Write Liz Wright, Assoc. Lit. Dir. for membership information.

NEW TUNERS/PERFORMANCE COMMUNITY—1225 W. Belmont Ave., Chicago, IL 60657. George H. Gorham, Dramaturg. Full-length musicals only, for cast to 15; no wing/fly space. Send manuscript with cassette tape of score, cast list, resumé and return postcard. Pays on a royalty basis. No recent report.

NEW YORK SHAKESPEARE FESTIVAL/PUBLIC THEATER—425 Lafayette St., New York, NY 10003. Gail Merrifield, Dir. of Plays and Musicals. Bill Hart, Lit. Man. Plays and musical works for the theater, translations, and adaptations. Submit manuscript, synopsis, character breakdown, cassette (with musicals), and SASE.

NORTHLIGHT THEATRE—2300 Green Bay Rd., Evanston, IL 60201. Jimmy Bickerstaff, Asst. Art. Dir. Full-length plays, music theatre, translations, and adaptations for cast to 10; small theatre. Synopses only. Royalties, fees and compensations negotiable.

ODYSSEY THEATRE ENSEMBLE—12111 Ohio Ave., Los Angeles, CA 90025. Ron Sossi, Artistic Dir. Full-length comedies, dramas, musicals, and adaptations: provocative subject matter, or plays that stretch and explore the form and possibilities of theatre. Query with synopsis and return postcard. Pays variable rates. Allow 2 to 6 months for reply. Workshops and readings offered.

OLD GLOBE THEATRE—Simon Edison Center for the Performing Arts, Box 2171, San Diego, CA 92112. Address Robert Berlinger. Full-length comedies and dramas. No unsolicited manuscripts. Submit query with synopsis.

ONE ACT THEATRE COMPANY OF SAN FRANCISCO—430 Mason St., San Francisco, CA 94102. Fredericka Bernhardt, Lit. Man. One-act comedies and dramas. Submit synopsis, 2–5 pages of sample dialogue with SASE. Pays negotiable rates.

EUGENE O'NEILL THEATER CENTER—Suite 901, 234 W. 44th St., New York, NY 10036. Annual competition to select new stage and television plays for development at organization's Waterford, Ct. location. Submit entries between Sept. 15 and Dec. 1, 1987, for 1988 conference. Send SASE for rules to

National Playwright's Conference, % above address. Pays stipend, plus travel/living expenses during conference.

PAPER MILL PLAYHOUSE—Brookside Dr., Millburn, NJ 07041. Jeffrey Solis, Dramaturg. Full-length musicals only; simple sets. Submit synopsis and resumé; report in 6 to 8 weeks. Pays Dramatists Guild contract. No recent report.

PENGUIN REPERTORY THEATRE—Box 91, Stony Point, NY 10980. Joe Brancato, Art. Dir. Full-length comedies and dramas; cast to 8. Submit manuscript, synopsis, resumé and SASE. Pays varying rates, on production.

PENNSYLVANIA STAGE COMPANY—837 Linden St., Allentown, PA 18101. Pam Pepper, Lit. Man. Full-length plays with cast to 8; one set. Full-length musicals, with unit set and cast to 18. Send synopsis, cast list and return postage. Pays negotiable rates. Allow 6 months for reply. Offers readings.

PEOPLE'S LIGHT AND THEATRE COMPANY—39 Conestoga Rd., Malvern, PA 19355. Alda Cortese, Lit. Man. Full-length and one-act comedies and dramas, for cast to 10; unit set preferred. Query first.

PHILADELPHIA FESTIVAL FOR NEW PLAYS—3900 Chestnut St., Philadelphia, PA 19104. Hilary Missan, Program Coordinator. Full-length and one-act comedies, dramas; must be unproduced. Query first.

PLAYHOUSE ON THE SQUARE—51 S. Cooper, Memphis, TN 38104. Jackie Nichols, Artistic Dir. Full-length comedies, dramas, and musicals, with unit or single set, and cast to 15. Send manuscript with resumé, return postcard and SASE. Pays $500. Workshops or readings offered.

THE PLAYWRIGHTS FUND OF NORTH CAROLINA, INC.—P.O. Box 646, Greenville, NC 27835-0646. Jeffrey Scott Jones, Lit. Dir. One-act comedies and dramas, from SE playwrights. Submit manuscript with SASE. Pays small honorarium. Readings, workshops, and annual contest.

PLAYWRIGHTS HORIZONS—416 W. 42nd St., New York NY 10036. Address Literary Dept. Full-length, original comedies, dramas, and musicals. Send synopsis and SASE. Pays varying rates.

PLAYWRIGHTS' PLATFORM—Box 392, Boston, MA 02117. Patrick Flynn, Pres. Script development workshops and public readings for New England playwrights only. Full-length and one-act plays of all kinds. Residents of New England send scripts with short synopsis, resumé, return postcard and SASE.

PORTLAND STAGE COMPANY—Box 1458, Portland, ME 04112. Barbara Rosoff, Art. Dir. Full-length comedies, dramas, and musicals, for cast to 8. Send synopsis with return postcard. Pays fee, travel, and board for 4-week residency if play is produced.

THE REPERTORY THEATRE OF ST. LOUIS—Box 28030, St. Louis, MO 63119. James Nicholson, Scripts. Full-length dramas. Query with resumé first. Payment negotiable.

THE ROAD COMPANY—Box 5278 EKS, Johnson City, TX 37603. Robert H. Leonard, Artistic Dir. Full-length and one-act comedies, dramas with social/political relevance to small town audiences. Send synopsis, cast list, and production history, if any. Pays negotiable rates. Reports in 6 to 12 months.

ROUND HOUSE THEATRE—12210 Bushey Dr., Silver Spring, MD 20902. Diane Ruscher, Production Office Man. Full-length comedies, dramas, musicals, and adaptations; cast to 15; prefer simple set. No unsolicited manuscripts.

RICHMOND SHEPARD THEATRE STUDIOS—6476 Santa Monica Blvd., Hollywood, CA 90038. Richmond Shepard, Art. Dir. Full-length comedies and dramas; cast to 8; prefer one set. Submit manuscript or synopsis with SASE. Pays varying rates.

SOCIETY HILL PLAYHOUSE—507 S. 8th St., Philadelphia, PA 19147. Walter Vail, Dramaturg. Full-length dramas and comedies; cast to 10; simple set. Submit synopsis and SASE. Reports in 6 months. Nominal payment.

SOHO REPERTORY THEATRE—80 Varick St., New York, NY 10013. Jerry Engelbach, Artistic Dir. Full-length dramas, musicals, adaptations and mixed media works for thrust stage. No unsolicited manuscripts. Send brief precis, cast list, and resumé. Send for guidelines. Pays $100. Readings offered.

SOUTH COAST REPERTORY—655 Town Center Dr., Box 2197, Costa Mesa, CA 92626-1197. Jerry Patch, Dramaturg. Full-length comedies and dramas. Query with synopsis, resumé and return postcard. Pays percent of gross, and travel/living expenses.

SPOKANE INTERPLAYERS ENSEMBLE—P.O. Box 1691, Spokane, WA 99210. Robert A. Welch, Art. Dir. Full-length and one-act comedies, dramas, and adaptations; cast to 10; simple set preferred. Send synopsis, cast list, resumé, and return postcard. Payment negotiable.

STAGE ONE: THE LOUISVILLE CHILDREN'S THEATRE—721 W. Main St., Louisville, KY 40202. Moses Goldberg, Artistic Director. Children's plays for adult actors to perform. Pays varying rates. Allow 3 to 4 months for reply. Enclose SASE.

STAGES—3201 Allen Parkway, Houston, TX 77019. Brenda Dubay, Prod. Dir. Full-length and one-act comedies, dramas, and children's scripts, especially from Texan playwrights; cast to 12; simple set. Submit script, synopsis and resumé.

STUDIO ARENA THEATRE—710 Main St., Buffalo, NY 14202. Kathryn Long, Dramaturg. Full-length dramas, comedies, and adaptations. Query with synopsis. Pays negotiable rates.

TAKOMA THEATRE—6833 4th St., NW, Washington, DC 20012. Milton O. McGinty, Art. Dir. Realistic, full-length dramas, comedies and musicals; special interest in scripts involving Black people. Submit manuscript with SASE; reports in 3 months. Payment negotiable.

MARK TAPER FORUM—135 N. Grand Ave., Los Angeles, CA 90012. Plays, preferably full-length, on any subject, for production in thrust theater or flexible theater. Pays on royalty basis. Query first.

THEATRE AMERICANA—Box 245, Altadena, CA 91001. Full-length comedies and dramas, preferably with American theme. Send manuscript with cast list and SASE. No payment. Allow 3 to 6 months for reply.

THEATRE BY THE SEA—125 Bow St., Portsmouth, NH 03801. Janet Wade, Man. Dir. Full-length comedies, dramas, musicals, and adaptations, with casts up to 15. Payment rates negotiable. Enclose resumé, cast list, and synopsis.

THEATRE/TEATRO—Bilingual Foundation for the Arts, 421 N. Ave., #19, Los Angeles, CA 90031. Margarita Galban, Art. Dir. Full-length plays about Hispanic experience; small casts. Submit manuscript with return postcard. Pays negotiable rates.

THEATRE THREE—2800 Routh St., Dallas, TX 75201. Sharon Bunn, Lit. Man. Full-length and one-act comedies and dramas for Festival of New Plays.

THEATREWORKS/USA—131 W. 86th St., New York, NY 10024. Barbara Pasternak, Lit. Man. Musicals or plays with music: Historical biographies, issue-oriented works, fantasies and adaptations of literary classics for young people; one hour in length; cast to 6 (can double). Include SASE. Pays varying rates.

UNIVERSITY OF ALABAMA THEATRE—115 Music and Speech Bldg., P.O. Box 6386, University, AL 35486. Dr. Richard France, Art. Dir. Full-length and one-act comedies, dramas, and musicals. Send manuscript with SASE. Payment varies. Reports in 2 to 3 months.

WISDOM BRIDGE THEATRE—1559 W. Howard St., Chicago, IL 60626. Address Douglas Finlayson. Full-length and one-act dramas, comedies, adaptations, and translations. Query with synopsis and SASE. Pays negotiable rates.

WOOLLY MAMMOTH THEATRE COMPANY—1317 G St. N.W., Washington, D.C. 20005. Neil Steyskal, Lit. Man. Very unusual scripts for full-length plays; cast to 8. Unusual, small-scale musicals. Submit synopsis with SASE. Pays on performance.

GARY YOUNG MIME THEATRE—9613 Windcroft Way, Rockville, MD 20854. Gary Young, Artistic Director. Comedy monologues and two person vignettes, for children and adults, 1 minute to 90 minutes in length; casts of 1 or 2, and portable set. Pays varying rates. Enclose return postcard, resumé, recommendations, cast list and synopsis.

RADIO THEATERS

R. BEAN'S VOICE THEATRE—223 N. Baldwin, Madison, WI 53703. Gene Becker, Prod. Radio Theatre. Half-hour radio scripts: mysteries, comedies, adventure, drama, etc.; 10- to 15-minute children's scripts. Pays varying rates. Send SASE for "Writers' Format."

CHILDREN'S RADIO THEATRE—1314 14th St., NW, Washington, DC 20005. Joan Bellsey, Art. Dir. Children's radio plays. No unsolicited material. Query with resumé and SASE required.

TIC RADIO THEATRE WORKSHOP—Library Plaza, Marshfield, MA 02050. Alberta Fahanley, Dir. Creative Develop. Accepts 30-minute radio scripts to be aired on closed circuit for the visually impaired. Pays in copy of master tape. Send SASE for guidelines.

PLAY PUBLISHERS

ART CRAFT PLAY COMPANY—Box 1058, Cedar Rapids, IA 52406. Three-act comedies, mysteries, and farces, and one-act comedies or dramas, with one set, for production by junior and senior high schools. Pays on royalty basis or by outright purchase.

WALTER H. BAKER COMPANY (Incorporating *Performance Publishing*)—100 Chauncy St., Boston, MA 02111. Scripts for amateur production: one-act plays for competition, children's plays, musicals, religious drama, full-length plays for high school production. Three- to four-month reading period. Include SASE.

CHILD LIFE MAGAZINE—P.O. Box 567, Indianapolis, IN 46206. Plays,

700 and 1,000 words, for classroom or living-room production by children 8 to 11 years. Pays about 6¢ a word, on publication. Buys all rights.

CHILDREN'S PLAYMATE MAGAZINE—1100 Waterway Blvd., P.O. Box 567, Indianapolis, IN 46206. Elizabeth A. Rinck, Ed. Plays, 200 to 600 words, for children aged 5 to 7; special emphasis on health, nutrition, exercise, and safety. Pays about 6¢ a word, on publication.

CONTEMPORARY DRAMA SERVICE—Meriwether Publishing, Ltd., Box 7710, 885 Elkton Dr., Colorado Springs, CO 80933. Arthur Zapel, Ed. Easy-to-stage comedies, skits, one-acts, musicals, puppet scripts, full-length plays for schools and churches. Adaptations of classics, and improvisational material for classroom use. Comedy monologues and duets. Chancel drama for Christmas and Easter church use. Enclose synopsis. Pays by fee arrangement or on royalty basis.

THE DRAMATIC PUBLISHING COMPANY—311 Washington St., P.O. Box 109, Woodstock, IL 60098. Full-length and one-act plays, musical comedies for amateur, children, and stock groups. Must run at least thirty minutes. Pays on royalty basis. Address Sally Fyfe. Reports within 10 to 14 weeks.

DRAMATICS—3368 Central Pkwy., Cincinnati, OH 45225. Don Corathers, Ed. One-act and full-length plays, for high school production. Pays $50 to $200, on acceptance.

ELDRIDGE PUBLISHING COMPANY—P.O. Box 216, Franklin, OH 45005. Nancy Vorhis, Edit. Dept. One-, two- and three-act plays and operettas for schools, churches, community groups, etc. Special interest in comedies and Christmas plays. Include SASE. Pays varying rates.

SAMUEL FRENCH, INC.—45 W. 25th St., New York, NY 10010. Lawrence R. Harbison, Ed. Full-length plays for dinner, community, stock, college and high school theatres. One-act plays (30 to 45 minutes). Children's plays, 45 to 60 minutes. Pays on royalty basis.

HEUER PUBLISHING COMPANY—Drawer 248, Cedar Rapids, IA 52406. C. Emmett McMullen, Ed. One-act comedies and dramas for contest work; three-act comedies, mysteries or farces, with one interior setting, for high school production. Pays on acceptance.

INSTRUCTOR—545 Fifth Ave., New York, NY 10017. Leanna Landsmann, Ed. Plays, 700 to 2,000 words, for elementary school children. Holiday and seasonal plays only. Send six months in advance. Pays $50 to $100, on acceptance.

PERFORMANCE PUBLISHING—See *Walter H. Baker Co.*

PIONEER DRAMA SERVICE—P.O. Box 22555, Denver, CO 80222. Patrick Dorn, Asst. Ed. Full-length and one-act plays for young audiences: musicals, melodramas, religious scripts. No unproduced plays, plays with largely male casts or multiple sets. Query. Pays royalty or outright purchase.

PLAYS, THE DRAMA MAGAZINE FOR YOUNG PEOPLE—120 Boylston St., Boston, MA 02116. Elizabeth Preston, Man. Ed. One-act plays, with simple settings, for production by young people, 7 to 17; holiday plays, comedies, dramas, skits, dramatized classics, farces, puppet plays, melodramas, dramatized folktales, and creative dramatics. Maximum lengths: lower grades, 10 double-spaced pages; middle grades, 15 pages; junior and senior high, 20 pages. Casts may be mixed, all-male or all-female; plays with one act preferred. Manuscript specification sheet available on request. Queries suggested for adaptations. Pays good rates, on acceptance. Buys all rights.

727

SCHOLASTIC SCOPE—730 Broadway, New York, NY 10003. Fran Claro, Ed. For ages 15 to 18 with 4th to 6th grade reading ability. Plays, to 6,000 words, on problems of contemporary teenagers, relationships between people in family, job and school situations. Some mysteries, comedies, and science fiction; plays about minorities. Pays good rates, on acceptance.

THE TELEVISION MARKET

The almost round-the-clock television offerings available for viewers on commercial and educational television stations—greatly expanded by the mushrooming cable TV offerings—may understandably lead free-lance writers to believe that opportunities to sell scripts or program ideas are infinite.

But unfortunately the realities of the television marketplace are generally quite different from this fantasy. With few exceptions, direct submissions of scripts, no matter how good they are, are not considered by producers or programmers, and in general free-lance writers can achieve success in this almost-closed field by concentrating on getting their fiction (short and in novel form) and nonfiction published in magazines or books, combed diligently by television producers for possible adaptations. A large percentage of the material offered over all types of networks (in addition to the motion pictures made in Hollywood or especially for TV) is in the form of adaptations of what has appeared in print.

Writers who want to try their hand at writing directly for this very limited market should be prepared to learn the special techniques and acceptable format of script writing. Also, experience in playwriting and a knowledge of dramatic structure gained through working in amateur, community, or professional theatres can be helpful, though TV is a highly specialized and demanding field, with unique requirements and specifications.

This section of the *Handbook* includes the names of TV shows scheduled for broadcast during the 1986–87 season, and names and addresses of the production companies responsible for these shows. The lists should not be considered either complete or permanent. A more complete list of shows and production companies may be found in *Ross Reports Television,* published monthly by Television Index, Inc., 40-29 27th St., Long Island City, NY 11101. The cost is $3.73 ($4.00 for New York residents) prepaid for each issue (including first-class postage).

Because virtually all of the producers of these shows tell us that they will read only scripts (and queries) submitted through recognized agents, we've included a list of agents who have indicated to us that they are willing to read queries from writers about television scripts. The names and addresses of other literary and dramatic agents can be found in *Literary Market Place* (Bowker), available in most libraries. A list of agents can also be obtained by sending a self-addressed, stamped envelope to Society of Authors' Representatives, 39½ Washington Sq. S., New York, NY 10012. Before submitting scripts to producers or to agents, authors should query to learn whether they prefer to see the material in television script form, or as an outline or summary.

Writers may wish to register their story, treatment, series format, or script with the Writers Guild of America. This registration doesn't confer statutory rights, but it does supply evidence of authorship which is effective for five years (and is renewable after that). To register material a writer should send one copy of his work, along with a $10 fee, to the Writers Guild of America Registration Service, 8955 Beverly Blvd., Los Angeles, CA 90048. Writers can also register dramatic material with the U.S. Copyright Office—for further information, write Register of Copyrights, Library of Congress, Washington, DC 20559. The Copyright Office is mainly used for book manuscripts, plays, music or lyrics, which the Writer's Guild will not register.

TELEVISION SHOWS

THE "A" TEAM (NBC)—Stephen J. Cannell Productions.

ALF (NBC)—Alien Productions/MGM Studios.

ALL MY CHILDREN (ABC)—ABC-TV.

AMEN (NBC)—Carson Productions.

ANOTHER WORLD (NBC)—Proctor & Gamble.

AS THE WORLD TURNS (CBS)—Joe Willmore, Exec. Prod.

BETTER DAYS (CBS)—Lorimar-Telepictures Productions.

THE ELLEN BURSTYN SHOW (ABC)—Ellen Burstyn Prod./Touchstone Films/ABC Studios

CAGNEY & LACEY (CBS)—Barney Rosenzweig Prod./Orion Television.

CAPITOL (CBS)—John Conboy Prod.

CHEERS (NBC)—Charles-Burrows-Charles Prod./Paramount Television.

THE COSBY SHOW (NBC)—Carsey-Werner Prod.

CRIME STORY (NBC)—Michael Mann Co., Inc./New World Television.

DALLAS (CBS)—Lorimar-Telepictures Prod.

DAYS OF OUR LIVES (NBC)—Corday Prod./Columbia Pictures Television.

DESIGNING WOMEN (CBS)—Bloodworth/Thomason Mozark Prod. with Columbia Pictures Television.

DOWNTOWN (CBS)—Ron Samuels Prod./Tri-Star Television.

DYNASTY (ABC)—Richard and Esther Shapiro Prod./Aaron Spelling Prod.

DYNASTY II: THE COLBYS (ABC)—Richard and Esther Shapiro Prod./Aaron Spelling Prod.

EASY STREET (NBC)—Viacom Prod.

THE EQUALIZER (CBS)—Universal Television.

THE FACTS OF LIFE (NBC)—Embassy Communications.

FALCON CREST (CBS)—Lorimar–Telepictures Productions.

FAMILY TIES (NBC)—Paramount Television/UBU Productions.

GENERAL HOSPITAL (ABC)—ABC-TV.

GIMME A BREAK (NBC)—Mort Lachman & Assoc./Reeves Entertainment Group.

THE GOLDEN GIRLS (NBC)—Witt-Thomas-Harris Prod./Sunset Gower.

GOOD MORNING AMERICA (ABC)—ABC Entertainment.

GROWING PAINS (ABC)—Warner Bros. Television.

THE GUIDING LIGHT (CBS)—Joe Willmore, Exec. Prod.

HEAD OF THE CLASS (ABC)—Eustis/Elias Prod./Warner Bros. Television.

HEART OF THE CITY (ABC)—Michael Zinberg and American Flyer Television/20th-Century Fox Television.

HIGHWAY TO HEAVEN (NBC)—Michael Landon Prod./MGM-UA Studios.

HILL STREET BLUES (NBC)—MTM Enterprises.

HOTEL (ABC)—Aaron Spelling Productions.

HUNTER (NBC)—Stephen J. Cannell Productions.

JACK AND MIKE (ABC)—MGM-UA/David Gerber Prod.

KATE & ALLIE (CBS)—Mort Lachman/Reeves Entertainment Group.

KNOT'S LANDING (CBS)—Lorimar-Telepictures Prod.

L.A. LAW (NBC)—20th Century Fox Television.

THE LAST ELECTRIC KNIGHT (ABC)—Motown Prod./Walt Disney Prod.

LATE NIGHT WITH DAVID LETTERMAN (NBC)—NBC-TV.

MACGYVER (ABC)—Winkler/Rich Productions.

MAGNUM, P.I. (CBS)—Bellisarius—Glen A. Larson Prod./Universal Television.

MATLOCK (NBC)—Viacom Prod./InterMedia and Strathmore Prod.

MIAMI VICE (NBC)—Universal Television.

MR. BELVEDERE (ABC)—Lazy B/F.O.B. Prod./20th Century Fox Television.

MOONLIGHTING (ABC)—Picturemaker Prod./ABC Circle Films.

MURDER, SHE WROTE (CBS)—Universal Television.

MY SISTER SAM (CBS)—Warner Bros. Television/Pony Prod.

NBC'S SATURDAY NIGHT LIVE (NBC)—NBC-TV.

THE NEW MIKE HAMMER (CBS)—J. Bernstein Prod./Columbia Pictures Television.

NEWHART (CBS)—MTM Enterprises.

NIGHT COURT (NBC)—Starry Night Prod./Warner Bros. Television.

O'HARA (ABC)—Brian Grazer Prod./Warner Bros. Television.

ONE LIFE TO LIVE (ABC)—ABC-TV.

OUR HOUSE (NBC)—Lorimar-Telepictures Prod.

PERFECT STRANGERS (ABC)—Lorimar-Telepictures Prod.

RYAN'S HOPE (ABC)—ABC-TV.

ST. ELSEWHERE (NBC)—MTM Enterprises.

SANTA BARBARA (NBC)—Dobson Productions.

SCARECROW AND MRS. KING (CBS)—Warner Bros. Television/Shoot the Moon Enterprises.

SEARCH FOR TOMORROW (NBC)—Benton & Bowles.

SHELL GAMES (CBS)—Warner Bros. Television.

SILVER SPOONS (Synd.)—Embassy Communications/Sunset Gower.

SIMON & SIMON (CBS)—Universal Television.

SLEDGE HAMMER! (ABC)—New World Television.

SPENSER: FOR HIRE (ABC)—Jadda Prod./Warner Bros. Television.

STARMAN (ABC)—Michael Douglas/Henerson-Hirsh Prod./Columbia Pictures Television.

REMINGTON STEELE (NBC)—MTM Enterprises.

TODAY (NBC)—NBC-TV.

TOGETHER WE STAND (CBS)—Al Burton Prod./Universal Television.

THE TWILIGHT ZONE (CBS)—CBS Entertainment.

227 (NBC)—Embassy Communications.

VALERIE (NBC)—Lorimar-Telepictures Prod.

WEBSTER (ABC)—Georgian Bay, Ltd./Paramount Television.

WHO'S THE BOSS (ABC)—Embassy Communications/Sunset Gower Studios.

WIZARD OF ELM STREET (CBS)—BSR Prod./20th Century Fox Television.

YOU AGAIN? (NBC)—Taft Entertainment/Lawson Group/Sweater Prod.

THE YOUNG AND THE RESTLESS (CBS)—Columbia Pictures Television/Bell Phillip TV/Corday Prod.

TELEVISION PRODUCERS

ABC CIRCLE FILMS—9911 W. Pico Blvd., Los Angeles, CA 90067.

ABC ENTERTAINMENT—1965 Broadway, New York, NY 10023.

ABC PRODUCTIONS—101 W. 67th St., New York, NY 10023.

ABC-TV—1330 Ave. of the Americas, New York, NY 10019.

BELL-PHILLIP TELEVISION—Colgems Sq., Burbank, CA 91505.

BENTON & BOWLES, INC.—909 Third Ave., New York, NY 10022.

STEPHEN J. CANNELL PRODUCTIONS—7083 Hollywood Blvd., Hollywood, CA 90028.

CBS ENTERTAINMENT—51 W. 52nd St., New York, NY 10019.

CARSEY-WERNER PRODUCTIONS—NBC Studios, 1268 E. 14th St., Brooklyn, NY 11230.

CARSON PRODUCTIONS—10045 Riverside Dr., Toluca Lake, CA 91602.

COLUMBIA PICTURES TELEVISION—Columbia Plaza, Burbank, CA 91505.

JOHN CONBOY PRODUCTIONS—CBS-TV, 7800 Beverly Blvd., Los Angeles, CA 90036.

CORDAY PRODUCTIONS, INC.—Colgems Sq., Burbank, CA 91505.

731

WALT DISNEY TELEVISION—500 S. Buena Vista, Burbank, CA 91505.

DOBSON PRODUCTIONS—NBC Studio 11, 3000 W. Alameda Ave., Burbank, CA 91523.

DRAMATIC CREATIONS—320 W. 66th St., New York, NY 10023.

EMBASSY COMMUNICATIONS—1438 N. Gower, Los Angeles, CA 90028.

DAVID GERBER PRODUCTIONS—10202 W. Washington Blvd., Culver City, CA 90230.

MORT LACHMAN & ASSOCIATES—3500 W. Olive Blvd., Burbank, CA 91505.

LORIMAR-TELEPICTURES PRODUCTIONS—3970 Overland Ave., Culver City, CA 90230.

MGM-UA TELEVISION—10202 W. Washington Blvd., Culver City, CA 90230.

MTM ENTERPRISES—4024 Radford Ave., Studio City, CA 91604.

NBC PRODUCTIONS—NBC-TV, 3000 W. Alameda Ave., Burbank, CA 91523.

NBC-TV—30 Rockefeller Plaza, New York, NY 10020.

ORION ENTERPRISES—1875 Century Park East, Los Angeles, CA 90067.

PARAMOUNT TELEVISION—5555 Melrose Ave., Los Angeles, CA 90038.

REEVES ENTERTAINMENT GROUP—3500 W. Olive Ave., Suite 500, Burbank, CA 91505.

AARON SPELLING PRODUCTIONS—1041 Formosa Ave., Hollywood, CA 90046.

SUNSET GOWER STUDIOS—1438 N. Gower, Hollywood, CA 90028.

20TH CENTURY FOX TELEVISION—10201 W. Pico Blvd., Los Angeles, CA 90064.

UNIVERSAL TELEVISION—100 Universal City Plaza, Universal City, CA 91608.

VIACOM ENTERPRISES—10900 Wilshire Blvd., Los Angeles, CA 90024.

WARNER BROTHERS TELEVISION—4000 Warner Blvd., Burbank, CA 91522.

JOE WILLMORE, PRODUCER—221 W. 26th St., New York, NY 10001.

WITT-THOMAS-HARRIS PRODUCTIONS—1438 Gower, Los Angeles, CA 90028.

TELEVISION SCRIPT AGENTS

ACT 48 MANAGEMENT—1501 Broadway, Suite 705, New York, New York 10036. Address Literary Dept. Reads synopses of scripts for feature films, TV movies, and stage plays, with SASE.

HOWARD T. BRODY AGENCY—P.O. Box 291423, Davie FL 33329. Milton Risblah, Script Consultant. Reads queries and scripts with SASEs.

732

THE CALDER AGENCY—4150 Riverside Dr., Burbank, CA 91505. Reads queries and synopses for features only; no television material.

BILL COOPER ASSOCIATES—224 W. 49th St., New York, NY 10019. Will look at developed ideas for comedies, dramas, theatre, and motion pictures.

HOLLYWOOD TALENT AGENCY—478 Brownridge Dr., Thornhill, Ont., Canada, L4J 3X9. Reads queries, scripts, treatments, and manuscripts.

SCOTT C. HUDSON TALENT REPRESENTATION—215 E. 76th St., New York, NY 10021. Reads queries and treatments, with SASEs.

WILLIAM KERWIN AGENCY—1605 N. Cahuenga Blvd., #202, Hollywood, CA 90028. Reads queries for originals only. No unsolicited manuscripts.

ARCHER KING, LTD.—1440 Broadway, #2100, New York, NY 10018. Reads queries and treatments. No TV sitcoms.

OTTO R. KOZAK LITERARY AGENCY—P.O. Box 152, Long Beach, NY 11561. Query.

L. HARRY LEE LITERARY AGENCY—Box 203, Rocky Point, NY 11778. Reads queries accompanied by SASE only. No episodic scripts or sit-coms.

LONDON STAR PROMOTIONS—7131 Owensmouth Ave., #C116, Canoga Park, CA 91303. Reads queries and synopses.

HAROLD MATSON CO., INC.—276 Fifth Ave., New York, NY 10001. Handles writers on recommendation only.

WILLIAM MORRIS AGENCY—1350 Ave. of the Americas, New York, NY 10019. Reads queries with SASEs.

SUZANNE SHELTON—CNA Associates, 8721 Sunset Blvd., #202, Los Angeles, CA 90069. Reads queries accompanied by SASEs only. No episodic scripts. New series ideas or MFT only.

JACK TANTLEFF—c/o the Tantleff Office, 360 W. 20th St., New York, NY 10011. Reads queries.

VAMP TALENT AGENCY—713 E. La Loma, #1, Somis, CA 93066. Reads queries, treatments and scripts, accompanied by SASEs.

DAN WRIGHT—c/o Ann Wright Representatives, Inc., 136 E. 57th St., New York, NY 10022. Reads queries. Specializes in motion pictures.

BOOK PUBLISHERS

The following list includes the major publishers of trade books (adult and juvenile fiction and nonfiction) and a representative number of small publishers from across the country. All companies in the list publish both hardcover and paperback books, unless otherwise indicated.

Before sending a complete manuscript to an editor, it is advisable to send a brief query letter describing the proposed book. The letter should also include information about the author's special qualifications for dealing with a particular topic and any previous publication credits. An outline of the book (or a synopsis for fiction) and a sample chapter may also be included.

It is common practice to submit a book manuscript to only one publisher at a time, although it is becoming more and more acceptable for writers, even those without agents, to submit the same query or proposal to more than one editor at the same time.

Book manuscripts may be wrapped in typing paper boxes (available from a stationer) and sent by first-class mail, or, more common and less expensive, by "Special Fourth Class Rate-Manuscript." For rates, details of insurance, and so forth, inquire at your local post office. With any submission to a publisher, be sure to enclose sufficient postage for the manuscript's return.

Royalty rates for hardcover books usually start at 10% of the retail price of the book, and increase after a certain number of copies have been sold. Paperbacks generally have a somewhat lower rate, about 5% to 8%. It is customary for the publishing company to pay the author a cash advance against royalties when the book contract is signed or when the finished manuscript is received. Some publishers pay on a flat fee basis.

ABBEY PRESS—St. Meinrad, IN 47577. Rev. Keith McClellan, Pub. Nonfiction Christian materials on marriage and family living. Royalty basis. Query with table of contents and writing sample.

HARRY N. ABRAMS, INC. (Subsidiary of *Times Mirror Co.*)—100 Fifth Ave., New York, NY 10011. Paul Gottlieb, Ed-in-Chief. Art and other heavily illustrated books. Pays varying rates. Query.

ACADEMIC PRESS—Harcourt, Brace, Jovanovich, Inc., Orlando, FL 32887. Blake Vance, Ed. Dir. Scientific books for professionals; college science texts. Royalty basis. Query.

ACADEMY CHICAGO, PUBLISHERS—425 N. Michigan Ave., Chicago, IL 60601. Anita Miller, Ed. General quality fiction; mysteries. History; biographies, travel; books by and about women. Royalty basis. Query with three sample chapters. SASE required.

ACCENT BOOKS—Box 15337, 12100 W. 6th Ave., Denver, CO 80215. Mary Nelson, Man. Ed. Fiction and nonfiction from evangelical Christian perspective. Query with sample chapters. Royalty basis. Paperback only.

ACE BOOKS (Imprint of *Berkley Publishing Group*)—200 Madison Ave., New York, NY 10016. Susan Allison, V.P., Ed.-in-Chief. Science fiction and fantasy. Royalty basis. No unsolicited manuscripts.

ADAMA BOOKS—306 W. 38th St., New York, NY 10018. Esther Cohen, Ed. Adult nonfiction. Juvenile fiction, nonfiction, picture books. Query with outline and sample chapters. Royalty.

ADDISON-WESLEY PUBLISHING CO.—Reading, MA 01867. General Publishing Group: Adult nonfiction on current topics: education, health, psychology, computers, professions, human resources, business, etc. Royalty basis.

ALASKA NORTHWEST PUBLISHING CO.—130 2nd Ave. S., Edmonds, WA 98020. Ethel Dassow, Sr. Book Ed. Nonfiction, some fiction, 10,000 to 100,000 words, with an emphasis on natural resources and history of Alaska, Northwestern Canada, and Pacific Northwest: how-to books; biographies; cookbooks; gardening; humor; nature; guidebooks. Send query or sample chapters with outline. Limited market.

AMERICAN BOOK COMPANY—See *D.C. Heath.*

THE AMERICAN PSYCHIATRIC PRESS—1400 K St., NW, Washington, DC 20005. Tim Clancy, Man. Ed. Books that interpret scientific and medical aspects of psychiatry for a lay audience, and that address specific psychiatric problems. Query required. Royalty.

APPLE BOOKS—See *Scholastic, Inc.*

ARBOR HOUSE PUBLISHING CO.—235 E. 45th St., New York, NY 10017. Eden Collinsworth, Pub. Ann Harris, Ed.-in-Chief. General fiction and nonfiction. Royalty basis. Query.

ARCHWAY PAPERBACKS (Imprint of *Pocket Books*)—1230 Ave. of the Americas, New York, NY 10020. Fiction for young adults age 11 and up. Query first with outline and stamped, self-addressed envelope. No unsolicited manuscripts. Pays on a royalty basis. Paperback only.

ARCO PUBLISHING *(Prentice Hall Press*/a div. of *Simon & Schuster)*—Gulf + Western Bldg., One Gulf & Western Plaza, New York, NY 10023. William Mlawer, Ed.-in-Chief. Nonfiction, originals and reprints, from 50,000 words. Career guides, test preparation, how-to's, young adult science, needlecraft. No fiction, poetry, humor, history, biography, personal accounts. Pays on royalty basis. Query with outline. Return postage required.

ARCSOFT PUBLISHERS—P.O. Box 132, Woodsboro, MD 21798. Anthony Curtis, Pres. Nonfiction hobby books for beginners, personal computing, space science, journalism, and hobby electronics, for laymen, general and public consumers, beginners and novices. Outright purchase and royalty basis. Query. Paper only.

ATHENEUM PUBLISHERS (Subsidiary of *Macmillan Publishing Co.)*—115 Fifth Ave., New York, NY 10003. Susan Ginsburg, Ed.-in-Chief. General nonfiction, biography, history, current affairs, belles-lettres. Send complete manuscript or sample chapters and outline. No unsolicited adult fiction. Royalty.

THE ATLANTIC MONTHLY PRESS—420 Lexington Ave., New York, NY 10017. Gary Fisketjon, Edit. Dir. Fiction, biography, history, belles-lettres, poetry, general nonfiction, children's books. Royalty basis. Query.

AUGSBURG PUBLISHING HOUSE—Box 1209, 426 S. Fifth St., Minneapolis, MN 55440. Roland Seboldt, Dir. of Book Development. Fiction and nonfiction, for adults, children and teens, on Christian themes. Royalty basis.

AVON BOOKS—1790 Broadway, New York, NY 10019. Susan Jaffe, Ed.-in-Chief. Modern fiction; mysteries, historical romances; general nonfiction, 60,000 to 200,000 words. Science fiction, 75,000 to 100,000 words. Royalty basis. Query with synopsis, sample chapters, and SASE. *Camelot Books:* Ellen Krieger, Ed. Fiction and nonfiction for 7- to 10-year-olds. Pays on royalty basis. Query. *Flare Books:* Ellen Krieger, Ed. Fiction and nonfiction for 12-year-olds and up. Royalty basis. Query. Paperback only.

BACKCOUNTRY PUBLICATIONS, INC.—P.O. Box 175, Woodstock, VT 05091. Christopher Lloyd, Ed. Regional guidebooks, 150 to 300 manuscript pages, on hiking, walking, canoeing, bicycling, and fishing. Royalty basis. Query first.

BAEN BOOKS—Baen Enterprises, 260 Fifth Ave., New York, NY 10001. Elizabeth Mitchell, Sr. Ed. Jim Baen, Pres. High-tech science fiction; innovative fantasy. Query with synopsis and sample chapters. Royalty.

BAKER BOOK HOUSE—P.O. Box 6287, Grand Rapids, MI 49506. Dan Van't Kerkhoff, Ed., general trade and professional books. Allan Fisher, Ed., academic and reference books. Religious nonfiction. Royalty.

BALLANTINE BOOKS—201 E. 50th St., New York, NY 10022. Robert Wyatt, Ed.-in-Chief. General fiction and nonfiction. Query.

BALSAM PRESS—122 E. 25th St., New York, NY 10010. Barbara Krohn, Exec. Ed. General and illustrated adult nonfiction. Royalty basis. Query.

BANTAM BOOKS, INC.—666 Fifth Ave., New York, NY 10103. Lou Aronica, Publishing Dir., Bantam Science Fiction/Fantasy. Judy Gitenstein, Ed. Dir., Young Readers Books. Carolyn Nichols, *Loveswept*. Steve Rubin, Ed. Dir., Adult Fiction and Nonfiction. General and educational fiction and nonfiction, 75,000 to 100,000 words. No unsolicited manuscripts.

BEACON PRESS—25 Beacon St. Boston, MA 02108. Joanne Wyckoff, Carol Birdsall, Sr. Eds. General nonfiction: world affairs, sociology, psychology, women's studies, political science, art, literature, history, philosophy, religion. No fiction or poetry. Royalty basis. Query. Return postage required.

BEAUFORT BOOKS—9 E. 40th St., New York, NY 10016. Susan Suffes, Ed. Fiction and nonfiction. Query with outline and sample chapters for nonfiction; complete manuscripts (no first novels) for fiction. Royalty basis.

BEECH TREE BOOKS (Imprint of *William Morrow and Co., Inc.*)—105 Madison Ave., New York, NY 10016. James Landis, Pub. and Ed.-in-Chief. Adult fiction and nonfiction. No unsolicited manuscripts.

BERKLEY PUBLISHING GROUP—200 Madison Ave., New York, NY 10016. Roger Cooper, Pub. and Ed. Dir. General-interest fiction and nonfiction: science fiction; suspense and espionage novels; romance. Submit through agent only. Publishes both reprints and originals. Paper only.

BETHANY HOUSE PUBLISHERS—6820 Auto Club Rd., Minneapolis, MN 55438. Address Ed. Dept. Fiction, nonfiction. Religious. Royalty basis. Query required.

BETTER HOMES AND GARDENS BOOKS—See *Meredith Corporation*.

BINFORD & MORT PUBLISHING—1202 NW 17th Ave., Portland, OR 97209. J. F. Roberts, Ed. Books on subjects related to the Pacific Coast and Northwest. Lengths vary. Royalty. Query first.

JOHN F. BLAIR, PUBLISHER—1406 Plaza Dr., Winston-Salem, NC 27103. Gail Lathey Warner, Ed. Dept. Biography, history, fiction, travel and guidebooks, with North Carolina tie-in. Length: at least 75,000 words. Royalty. Query.

BLUEJAY BOOKS—1123 Broadway, Suite 306, New York, NY 10010. James Frenkel, Ed. Science fiction, fantasy, and related nonfiction. Royalty. Query with SASE required.

THOMAS BOUREGY & CO., INC.—401 Lafayette St., New York, NY 10003. Rita Brenig, Ed. Light, wholesome, well-plotted romances, modern Gothics, westerns, and nurse romances, 50,000 words. Send one-page synopsis. SASE required. Hardcover only.

BRADBURY PRESS, INC. (An affiliate of *Macmillan, Inc.*)—866 Third Ave., New York, NY 10022. Richard Jackson, Ed.-in-Chief. Picture books; juvenile and young adult fiction. Royalty basis. Hardcover only.

BRANDEN PRESS—17 Station St., Box 843, Brookline Village, MA 02147.

Adolph Caso, Ed. Novels and biographies, 250 to 350 pages. Query with SASE required. Royalty.

GEORGE BRAZILLER, INC.—60 Madison Ave., Suite 1001, New York, NY 10010. Literature, history, philosophy, science, art, social science; fiction. Royalty basis. No unsolicited manuscripts. Query with SASE required.

BROADMAN PRESS—127 Ninth Ave. N., Nashville, TN 37234. Harold S. Smith, Supervisor. Religious and inspirational fiction and nonfiction. Royalty basis. Query.

CANDELIGHT ECSTASY ROMANCES (Imprint of *Dell Publishing Co.*)— 245 E. 47th St., New York, NY 10017. Lydia E. Paglio, Sr. Ed. Sensuous, realistic contemporary romantic novels, 50,000 to 60,000 words, set in the United States. *Candlelight Supremes:* 85,000 to 100,000 words, with more complex plots, more fully developed characterizations; not necessarily confined to the United States. Query with letter and 2- to 4-page synopsis only. Softcover.

CAROLRHODA BOOKS—241 First Ave. N., Minneapolis, MN 55401. Beverly Charette, Ed. Dir. Picture books, fiction, nonfiction for elementary children. Outright purchase. Overstocked. Hardcover only.

CARROLL AND GRAF PUBLISHERS, INC.—260 Fifth Ave., New York, NY 10001. Kent E. Carroll, Exec. Ed. General fiction and nonfiction. Royalty basis. Query with SASE.

CBI PUBLISHING CO.—See *Van Nostrand Reinhold Co., Inc.*

CELESTIAL ARTS (Subsidiary of *Ten Speed Press*)—P.O. Box 7327, Berkeley, CA 94707. Nonfiction, 25,000 to 80,000 words, on all subjects. No fiction or poetry. Query Paul Reed. Royalty basis.

CHARTER BOOKS (Imprint of *Berkley Publishing Group*)—200 Madison Ave., New York, NY 10016. Roger Cooper, Pub. Adventure, espionage and suspense fiction, women's contemporary fiction, family sagas, and historical novels. Westerns, male action/adventure, and cartoon books. No unsolicited manuscripts. Royalty basis or outright purchase. Paperback.

CHATHAM PRESS—P.O. Box A, Old Greenwich, CT 06807. Roger H. Lourie, Man. Dir. Books on the Northeast coast, New England and the ocean. Royalty basis. Query with outline, sample chapters, illustrations and SASE large enough for return of material.

CHELSEA GREEN PUBLISHING CO.—P.O. Box 283, Chelsea, VT 05038. Ian Baldwin, Jr., Ed. Fiction and nonfiction on rural life, natural history, biography, history, politics, travel, and regional themes. Query with outline and sample chapter. Royalty.

CHILDRENS PRESS—1224 W. Van Buren St., Chicago, IL 60607. Fran Dyra, Ed. Dir. Juvenile nonfiction: science, biography, 10,000 to 25,000 words, for supplementary use in classrooms. Query first. Picture books, 50 to 1,000 words. Royalty basis or outright purchase.

CHILTON BOOK CO.—201 King of Prussia Rd., Radnor, PA 19089. Alan F. Turner, Edit. Dir. Business, crafts and hobbies, automotive. Royalty basis. Query with outline, sample chapter, and return postage.

CHRONICLE BOOKS—One Hallidie Plaza, Suite 806, San Francisco, CA 94102. Larry L. Smith, Ed. Nonfiction: West Coast regional recreational guides, regional histories—natural history, food, photography, art and architecture. Royalty basis.

CITADEL PRESS—See *Lyle Stuart, Inc.*

CLARION BOOKS (Juvenile imprint of *Ticknor & Fields*, a *Houghton Mifflin* company)—52 Vanderbilt Ave., New York, NY 10017. James C. Giblin, Ed. Juvenile fiction and nonfiction, picture books, for ages 4 and up. Royalty basis. Query preferred on manuscripts of more than 20 pages. SASE required. Publishes approximately 30–35 hardcover titles a year.

CLOVERDALE PRESS—133 Fifth Ave., New York, NY 10003. Book packager. Adult and juvenile series fiction and nonfiction: young adult romances, westerns, war, women's fiction. Send query letter, synopsis, and two sample chapters. Send SASE for guidelines. No manuscripts returned without SASE. Paperback only.

COMPUTE! PUBLICATIONS, INC.—324 W. Wendover, Suite 200, Greensboro, NC 27408. How-to computer books; specializes in machine specific publications. Query preferred. Royalty basis.

CONCORDIA PUBLISHING HOUSE—3558 S. Jefferson Ave., St. Louis, MO 63118. Practical nonfiction with moral or religious values. Very little fiction. No poetry. Royalty basis. Query.

CONTEMPORARY BOOKS—180 N. Michigan Ave., Chicago, IL 60601. Nancy Crossman, Vice President. General nonfiction: health, fitness, nutrition, sports, real estate, business, popular culture, humor, biographies. Query with outline and sample chapters. Royalty.

DAVID C. COOK PUBLISHING CO.—850 N. Grove Ave., Elgin, IL 60120. David Orris, Book Division Dir.; Catherine L. Davis, Man. Ed./Books. Religious children's/juveniles only. Royalty and work-for-hire basis. Query with chapter-by-chapter synopsis and two sample chapters. Unsolicited manuscripts returned unopened. Label envelope "query." SASE required.

COPLEY BOOKS—7776 Ivanhoe Ave., La Jolla, CA 92037. Jean I. Bradford, Ed. Nonfiction, with photos/illustrations, on history of California (and Baja) and the southwest, geared to the general reader. Query with synopsis and SASE. Royalty. Hardcover.

COWARD, McCANN (Div. of *Putnam Publishing Group*)—200 Madison Ave., New York, NY 10016. Fiction and nonfiction through agents only.

CRAFTSMAN BOOK COMPANY—6058 Corte del Cedro, P.O. Box 6500, Carlsbad, CA 92008-0992. Laurence D. Jacobs, Ed. How-to construction manuals for builders, 450 pages. Royalty basis. Query. Softcover only.

CREATIVE EDUCATION—P.O. Box 227, Mankato, MN 56001. Nonfiction for children aged 5 to 12. No textbooks. Mostly flat fee, some royalty.

THE CROSSING PRESS—P.O. Box 207, Freedom, CA 95019. Elaine Gill, John Gill, Pubs. How-to books; feminist; gay; cookbooks. Fiction. Royalty basis.

THOMAS Y. CROWELL—See *Harper Junior Books Group.*

CROWN PUBLISHERS, INC.—225 Park Ave. S., New York, NY 10003. Fiction and general nonfiction. Royalty basis. Query letters only: Address Ed. Dept.; no unsolicited manuscripts. SASE required.

DATAMOST—21040 Nordhoff St., Chatsworth, CA 91311. Lorraine Coffey, Man. Ed. Computer technical manuals, 300 pages double-spaced. Send outline with sample chapter and SASE. Royalty.

JONATHAN DAVID PUBLISHERS, INC.—68-22 Eliot Ave., Middle Village, NY 11379. Alfred J. Kolatch, Ed.-in-Chief. General nonfiction—how-to, sports, cooking and food, self-help, etc.—and nonfiction on Judaica. Royalty basis or outright purchase. Query with outline, sample chapter, and resume.

DAW BOOKS, INC.—1633 Broadway, New York, NY 10019. Elizabeth R. Wollheim, Ed.-in-Chief. "We are especially interested in developing new authors, and publish at least two first novels a year, but frequently more." Needs include science fiction and fantasy books, 60,000 to 120,000 words (occasionally longer). Will consider more than one work from an author at a time. Royalty basis.

DEL REY BOOKS (a division of *Random House*)—201 East 50th St., New York, NY 10022. Shelly Shapiro, Ed. Science fiction and fantasy, 60,000 to 120,000 words. "Science fiction runs the gamut from hard science to sociological science fiction to space opera adventures. For fantasy, we require that magic be intrinsic to the plot." Query with detailed outline and first three chapters or complete manuscript. Pays competitive rates.

DELACORTE PRESS (Div. of *Dell Publishing Co., Inc.*)—245 E. 47th St., New York, NY 10017. Jackie Farber, Ed. Adult fiction and nonfiction. George Nicholson, *Books for Young Readers* Ed. Contemporary fiction for students through secondary school. Royalty basis. Query with outline; no unsolicited manuscripts.

DELL PUBLISHING CO., INC.—245 E. 47th St., New York, NY 10017. *Dell Books:* family sagas, historical romances, sexy modern romances, war action, occult/horror/psychological suspense, true crime, men's adventure. *Delta:* General-interest nonfiction, psychology, feminism, health, nutrition, child care, science. Juvenile Books: *Yearling* (kindergarten through 6th grade; no unsolicited manuscripts); and *Laurel-Leaf* (grades 7 through 12; no unsolicited manuscripts). Submissions policy for *Dell Books:* Send four-page narrative synopsis for fiction, or an outline for nonfiction. Enclose SASE. Don't send any sample chapters, artwork, or manuscripts. Address submissions to the appropriate Dell division and add Editorial Dept.—Book Proposal.

DELTA BOOKS—See *Dell Publishing Co.*

DEMBNER BOOKS—80 Eighth Ave., New York, NY 10011. S. Arthur Dembner, Pres. Self-help, life style, reference and other nonfiction; good fiction. Royalty basis. Query with outline, sample chapters, and SASE large enough for return of material.

DEVIN-ADAIR PUBLISHERS, INC.—6 N. Water St., Greenwich, CT 06830. C. de la Belle Issue, Pub. J. Andrassi, Ed. Books on conservative affairs, Irish topics, Americana, computers, self-help, health, ecology. Royalty. Query with outline, sample chapters, and SASE. Hardcover only.

DIAL BOOKS FOR YOUNG READERS—2 Park Ave., New York, NY 10016. Picture books; Easy-to-Read Books; middle-grade readers; young adult fiction and nonfiction. Submit complete manuscript for fiction; outline and sample chapters for nonfiction. Enclose SASE. Royalty. Hardcover only.

DILLON PRESS—242 Portland Ave. S., Minneapolis, MN 55415. Uva Dillon, Ed.-in-Chief. Janet Mills, Fiction Ed. Tom Schneider, Nonfiction Ed. Juvenile nonfiction: foreign countries, contemporary biographies for elementary and middle grade levels, unusual approaches to science topics for primary grade readers, wildlife, craft/outdoor activities, contemporary issues of interest to young people. Royalty and outright purchase. Query with outline and sample chapter. SASE required. *Gemstone Books:* Fiction for grades 3-9: mystery, adventure, romance, science fiction, contemporary problems, historical, girls' sports stories. Royalty and outright purchase. Hardcover only.

DODD, MEAD & CO.—79 Madison Ave., New York, NY 10016. Allen Klots, Jerry Gross, Cynthia Vartan, Margaret Norton, Sr. Eds. Joe Ann Daly, Dir., Children's Books. General fiction and nonfiction: biography, history, belles-lettres, travel, mystery, social issues, current events. Juveniles. Royalty basis. Query.

DOUBLEDAY AND CO., INC.—245 Park Ave., New York, NY 10167. Hardcover: Mystery/suspense fiction, romance, science fiction, 70,000 to 80,000 words. Submit complete manuscript to appropriate editor: Crime Club, Starlight Romance, or Science Fiction. SASE required. Paperback: Loretta Barrett, V.P., Exec. Ed. Adult trade books: fiction, sociology, psychology, philosophy, women's, etc. Query.

DOWN EAST BOOKS—Box 679, Camden, ME 04843. Mostly nonfiction about New England. Query with sample chapters and outline. Royalty.

THOMAS DUNNE BOOKS (Imprint of *St. Martin's Press*)—175 Fifth Ave., New York, NY 10010. Thomas L. Dunne, Ed. Adult fiction (mysteries, trade, sci-fi, etc.) and nonfiction (history, biographies, how-to, etc.). Query with outline and sample chapters and SASE. Royalty.

E.P. DUTTON (Div. of *New American Library*)—2 Park Ave., New York, NY 10016. General fiction, nonfiction; query with outline and sample chapters. *Lodestar Books,* Virginia Buckley, Ed. Dir. Young adult fiction and nonfiction— submit proposals for nonfiction, complete manuscripts for fiction. Royalty basis. Send queries to Adult or Juvenile Editorial Dept.

EAST WOODS PRESS (A subsidiary of *The Globe Pequot Press*)—429 E. Kingston Ave., Charlotte, NC 28203. Sally McMillan, Sr. Ed. Outdoor and travel books; cookbooks; self-help and how-to books; natural science; regional history; sports; trail guides; and gardening topics. Royalty basis. Query first.

WM. B. EERDMANS PUBLISHING COMPANY, INC.—255 Jefferson Ave., S.E., Grand Rapids, MI 49503. Jon Pott, Ed.-in-Chief. Protestant theological nonfiction; American history; some fiction. Royalty basis.

EMC CORP.—300 York Ave., St. Paul, MN 55101. Eileen Slater, Ed. Vocational, career, and consumer education textbooks. Royalty. No unsolicited manuscripts.

ENSLOW PUBLISHERS—Bloy St. & Ramsey Ave., Box 777, Hillside, NJ 07205. R. M. Enslow, Jr., Ed./Pub. Specialized nonfiction. Children's nonfiction. Royalty basis. Query first.

PAUL S. ERIKSSON, PUBLISHER—208 Battell Bldg., Middlebury,VT 05753. General nonfiction; some fiction. Royalty basis. Query with outline and sample chapters.

M. EVANS & CO., INC.—216 E. 49th St., New York, NY 10017. Books on health, self-help, popular psychology, and cookbooks. Commercial fiction for adults. Query with outline and sample chapter. Royalty basis.

FACTS ON FILE PUBLICATIONS—460 Park Ave. S., New York, NY 10016. John Thornton, Edit. Dir. Reference and trade books on business, science, consumer affairs, the performing arts, etc. Query with outline and sample chapter. Royalty basis. Hardcover.

FARRAR, STRAUS & GIROUX—19 Union Sq. W., New York, NY 10003. General fiction, nonfiction, juveniles. Address queries to Editorial Dept.

FAWCETT BOOKS—Ballantine Books, 201 E. 50th St., New York, NY 10022. Leona Nevler, Ed.-in-Chief. Fiction and nonfiction. Query. Softcover only.

FREDERICK FELL PUBLISHERS, INC.—2500 Hollywood Blvd., Hollywood, FL 33020. Bryce Webster, Ed. Nonfiction: how-to's, especially business and health. Query with letter or outline and sample chapter and SASE. Royalty.

THE FEMINIST PRESS AT THE CITY UNIVERSITY OF NEW YORK—311 E. 94th St., New York, NY 10128. Reprints of significant lost fiction or autobiographies by women; reprints of other classic feminist texts; feminist biography; women's studies for classroom adaptation. Royalty.

DONALD I. FINE, INC.—128 E. 36th St., New York, NY 10016. Deborah Wilburn, V.P. Literary and commercial fiction. General nonfiction, to 90,000 words. Query with sample chapters. Advance royalty basis. Prefer agent submissions.

FIREBRAND BOOKS—141 The Commons, Ithaca, NY 14850. Nancy K. Bereano, Ed. Feminist and lesbian fiction and nonfiction. Royalty basis. Softcover.

FIRESIDE BOOKS (Imprint of *Simon & Schuster*)—1230 Ave. of the Americas, New York, NY 10020. General nonfiction. Royalty basis or outright purchase. Submit outline and one chapter. Softcover only.

FLARE BOOKS—See *Avon Books*.

FLEET PRESS CORPORATION—160 Fifth Ave., New York, NY 10010. S. Nueckel, Ed. General nonfiction; sports and how-to. Royalty basis. Query; no unsolicited manuscripts.

FORTRESS PRESS—2900 Queen Lane, Philadelphia, PA 19129. Harold W. Rast, Th.D., Dir. Serious, nonfiction works, from 100 pages, on theology and religion, for the academic or lay reader. Royalty basis. Query preferred.

FOUR WINDS PRESS (An imprint of *Macmillan Publishing Co.*)—866 Third Ave., New York, NY 10022. Juveniles: picture books, fiction for all ages. Nonfiction for young children. Query with SASE required. Hardcover only.

THE FREE PRESS—See *Macmillan Publishing Co.*

GAMUT BOOKS (Imprint of *Dodd, Mead*)—79 Madison Ave., New York, NY 10016. Trade paperbacks. How-to and self-help nonfiction: business and careers, emphasizing entrepreneurship; inspiration/motivation; guides for success in work and life; popular psychology, marriage, parapsychology and social issues; holistic health. Royalty basis.

GARDEN WAY PUBLISHING COMPANY—Storey Communications, Schoolhouse Rd., Pownal, VT 05261. Deborah Burns, Ed. How-to books on gardening, cooking, building, etc. Royalty basis or outright purchase. Query with outline and sample chapter.

GEMSTONE BOOKS—See *Dillon Press*.

THE K. S. GINIGER CO., INC.—235 Park Ave. S., New York, NY 10003. General nonfiction; reference and religious. Royalty basis. Query with SASE; no unsolicited manuscripts.

THE GLOBE PEQUOT PRESS—Old Chester Rd., Box Q, Chester, CT 06412. Eric Newman, Man. Ed. Nonfiction about New England and the Northeast; cookbooks with natural focus; journalism and media. Travel guidebooks a specialty. Royalty basis. Query with a sample chapter, contents, and one-page synopsis. SASE a must.

GOLD EAGLE BOOKS (Imprint of *Harlequin Books*)—225 Duncan Mill Rd., Don Mills, Ont., Canada M3B 3K9. Mark Howell, Exec. Ed. Action adventure series novels; thrillers, espionage and suspense novels. Query. Paperback.

GOLDEN PRESS—See *Western Publishing Co., Inc.*

THE STEPHEN GREENE PRESS, INC. (An imprint of *Viking*)—15 Muzzey St., Lexington, MA 02173. Thomas L. Begner, Ed. Nonfiction, with heavy emphasis on sports, health and wellness, nature, cooking, popular psychology, and regional (New England) titles. Submit query with synopsis, sample chapters, and SASE. Manuscripts should be at least 60,000 words. No fiction. Royalty basis.

GREENWILLOW BOOKS (Imprint of *William Morrow and Co., Inc.*)—105 Madison Ave., New York, NY 10016. Susan Hirschman, Ed.-in-Chief. Children's books for all ages. Picture books. Query.

GROSSET AND DUNLAP, INC. (Div. of *Putnam Publishing Group*)—51 Madison Ave., New York, NY 10010. Material accepted through agents only.

GROVE PRESS—920 Broadway, New York, NY 10010. Aaron Asher, Ed. Query first.

HAMMOND INCORPORATED—Maplewood, NY 07040. Dorothy Bacheller, Ed. Nonfiction: reference, travel. Payment varies. Query with outline and sample chapters. SASE required.

HANCOCK HOUSE—1431 Harrison Ave., Blaine, WA 98230. David Hancock, Ed. Nonfiction: cookbooks, gardening, outdoor guides, Western history, American Indians, sports, real estate, and investing. Royalty basis.

HARCOURT BRACE JOVANOVICH—1250 Sixth Ave., San Diego, CA 92101. Adult trade nonfiction and fiction. *Books for Professionals:* test preparation guides and other student self-help materials. *Miller Accounting Publications, Inc.:* professional books for practitioners in accounting and finance; college accounting texts. Juvenile fiction and nonfiction for beginning readers through young adults, especially contemporary young adult novels and nonfiction with commercial appeal. Nonfiction paperback originals. Query Maria Modugno, Man./Children's Books. Query; unsolicited manuscripts accepted.

HARLEQUIN BOOKS/CANADA—225 Duncan Mill Rd., Don Mills, Ont., Canada M3B 3K9. *Harlequin Romance:* Maryan Gibson, Sr. Ed. Contemporary romance novels, 50,000 to 60,000 words, any setting, ranging in plot from the traditional and gentle to the more sophisticated and sensuous. Query first. *Harlequin Presents:* Maryan Gibson, Sr. Ed. Romantic novels, 50,000 to 60,000 words, any setting. Query first. *Harlequin Superromance:* Laurie Bauman, Sr. Ed. Contemporary romances, 85,000 words, with North American or foreign setting. New writers: query first. Published writers: manuscripts and synopsis plus copy of published work. *Harlequin Temptation:* Margaret Carney, Sr. Ed. Sensually charged contemporary romantic fantasies, 60,000 to 65,000 words. Send for tip sheets.

HARLEQUIN BOOKS/U.S.—300 E. 42nd St., 6th Fl., New York, NY

10017. *Harlequin American Romance:* Debra Matteucci, Sr. Ed. Contemporary romances, 70,000 to 75,000 words, with American setting and American characters. *Harlequin Gothic Romances:* Reva Kindser, Ed. Modern or period romances, 50,000 to 60,000 words, with element of foreboding or hidden evil. *Harlequin Regency Romances:* Reva Kindser, Ed. Romances, 50,000 to 60,000 words, set in England between 1811 and 1820. Query. *Harlequin Romantic Intrigue:* Reva Kindser, Ed. Contemporary romances, 70,000 to 75,000 words, with suspense and adventure. Query. Tip sheets. Paperback only.

HARPER & ROW—10 E. 53rd St., New York, NY 10022. Fiction, nonfiction, biography, economics, etc.: address Trade Dept. College texts: address College Dept. Nonfiction paperback originals: address Paperback Dept. Religion, theology, etc.: address Religious Books Dept., Ice House One, 151 Union St., San Francisco, CA 94111. No unsolicited manuscripts; query only. Royalty basis.

HARPER JUNIOR BOOKS GROUP—10 E. 53rd St., New York, NY 10022. Juvenile fiction, nonfiction and picture books. Imprints include *Thomas Y. Crowell Co., Publishers:* juveniles, etc.; *J. B. Lippincott Co.:* juveniles, picture books, etc.; *Harper & Row:* juveniles, picture books, etc.; *Trophy Books:* paperback juveniles. All publish from preschool to young adult titles. Query. Royalty basis.

HARVEST HOUSE PUBLISHERS—1075 Arrowsmith, Eugene, OR 97402. Eileen L. Mason, Ed. Nonfiction—how-to's, educational, health—with evangelical theme. No biographies, history or poetry. Query first. SASE required.

HASTINGS HOUSE, PUBLISHERS—260 Fifth Ave., New York, NY 10001. Raphaela Seroy, Edit. Consultant. Nonfiction and juveniles. Query with outline and sample chapters. Royalty basis.

HEALTH PLUS PUBLISHERS—Box 22001, Phoenix, AZ 85028. Karen M. Jensen, Ed. Books on health and fitness. Send query with outline and sample chapters. Pays on royalty basis.

HEARST BOOKS—See *William Morrow and Co.*

D. C. HEATH & COMPANY (Incorporating *American Book Company*)—125 Spring St., Lexington, MA 02173. Textbooks for schools and colleges. Professional books (*Lexington Books* division). Software and related educational material. Query Bruce Zimmerli, College; Albert Bursma, School; Robert Bovenschulte, Lexington Books; Thomas Haver, Collamore Educational Publishing.

HERALD PRESS—616 Walnut Ave., Scottdale, PA 15683. Paul M. Schrock, General Book Editor. Christian books for adults and children (age 9 and up): inspiration, Bible study, self-help, devotionals, current issues, peace studies, church history, missions and evangelism, family life. Send one-page summary and sample chapter. Royalty basis.

HOLIDAY HOUSE, INC.—18 E. 53rd St., New York, NY 10022. Margery S. Cuyler, Vice Pres. General juvenile and young adult fiction and nonfiction. Royalty basis. Query with outline and sample chapter. Hardcover only.

HENRY HOLT AND CO.—521 Fifth Ave., New York, NY 10175. John Macrae, Ed.-in-Chief. No unsolicited material.

HOUGHTON MIFFLIN COMPANY—2 Park St., Boston, MA 02108. Fiction: literary, mainstream, historical, suspense and science fiction. Nonfiction: history, biography. Query Submissions Dept. with SASE. Children's Book

Division, address Walter Lorraine: picture books, fiction and nonfiction for all ages. Query. Royalty basis.

H.P. BOOKS—P.O. Box 5367, Tucson, AZ 85703. Rick Bailey, Pub. Illustrated how-to's, 50,000 to 80,000 words, on cooking, gardening, photography, health & fitness, etc. Royalty basis. Query.

IDEALS PUBLISHING—Nelson Place at Elm Hill Pike, P.O. Box 1410000, Nashville, TN 37214-1000. Patricia Pingry, V.P./Ed. Children's books; cookbooks. Flat fee or royalty. Query with SASE. Hardcover only.

IMPACT BOOKS (Imprint of *Sterling Publishing Company*)—Two Park Ave., New York, NY 10016. Jonathan Eisen, Ed. Dir. "We are interested mostly in books that could have a major social or political—or scientific—impact. Hence the name of our imprint. We would like to see books on world affairs, science, consumer issues, and how-to topics. We have no length requirements; books tend to seek their own length." Query first. Pays on royalty basis.

INTERNATIONAL MARINE—21 Elm St., Camden, ME 04843. Jonathan Eaton, Editor. Nonfiction books on nautical topics (20,000 to 100,000 words). Nautical fiction, 25,000 to 60,000 words. Submit outline and sample chapters. Royalty basis.

IVY BOOKS—Cloverdale Press, Inc., 133 Fifth Ave., New York, NY 10003. Book packager. Women's contemporary romances, generational sagas, inspirational romances, westerns, male action adventure, medical fiction, and young adult fiction. Historicals, suspense, and other fiction categories suitable for a mass market audience. Pays on a flat fee basis. Send queries and resumés; ask for guidelines. Address young adult queries to Caryn Jenner, adult queries to Lisa Howell.

JAMESON BOOKS/GREENHILL PUBLISHERS—722 Columbus St., Ottawa, IL 61350. J. G. Campaigne, Pres. Early American fiction for "Frontier Library" series. Query with outline and sample chapters. Royalty basis.

JOHNSON BOOKS, INC.—1880 S. 57th Ct., Boulder, CO 80301. Michael McNierney, Ed. Nonfiction: western history and archaeology, nature, outdoor recreation, fly fishing, regional. Royalty basis. Query.

JOVE BOOKS—200 Madison Ave., New York, NY 10016. Fiction and nonfiction. No unsolicited manuscripts.

KEATS PUBLISHING, INC.—27 Pine St., Box 876, New Canaan, CT 06840. An Keats, Ed. Nonfiction: health, inspiration, how-to. Royalty basis. Query.

ROBERT R. KNAPP, PUBLISHER—Box 7234, San Diego, CA 92107. Professional reference and textbooks in the humanities and social sciences. Royalty basis. Query.

ALFRED A. KNOPF, INC.—201 E. 50th St., New York, NY 10022. Ashbel Green, Vice-Pres. and Senior Ed. Frances Foster, Juvenile Ed. Distinguished fiction and general nonfiction. Juvenile fiction and nonfiction, 3,000 to 5,000 words. Picture books. Royalty basis. Query.

JOHN KNOX PRESS—341 Ponce de Leon Ave., N.E., Atlanta, GA 30365. Walter Sutton, Ed. Dir. Books that inform, interpret, challenge and encourage Christian faith and living. Royalty. Send SASE for "Guidelines for a Book Proposal."

LAUREL-LEAF BOOKS—See *Dell Publishing Co.*

LEISURE BOOKS—Dorchester Publishing Co., 6 E. 39th St., New York, NY 10016. Jane Thornton, Ed. Dir. Historical romance novels, from 100,000 words; contemporary women's fiction, from 90,000 words; historical romantic suspense novels, from 80,000 words. Submit query, synopsis, and sample chapters. Royalty or flat fee basis.

HAL LEONARD BOOKS—Box 13819, 8112 W. Bluemound Rd., Milwaukee, WI 53213. Glenda Herro, Ed. Adult nonfiction; juvenile nonfiction, picture books, and young adult. Prefer subjects related to music and entertainment. Query first. Pays on royalty or flat fee basis.

LEXINGTON BOOKS—See *D. C. Heath & Co.*

J.B. LIPPINCOTT COMPANY—See *Harper Junior Books Group.*

LITTLE, BROWN AND COMPANY—34 Beacon St., Boston, MA 02106. Address Ed. Dept., Trade Division or Children's Books, Trade Division. Fiction, general nonfiction, sports books, juveniles; divisions for law, medical and college texts. Royalty basis. Submissions only from authors who have previously published in professional or literary journals, newspapers or magazines. Query first.

LODESTAR BOOKS—See *E. P. Dutton.*

LOTHROP, LEE & SHEPARD CO.(Imprint of *William Morrow & Co., Inc.*)—105 Madison Ave., New York, NY 10016. Dorothy Briley, Ed.-in-Chief. Juvenile fiction and nonfiction. Royalty basis. Query.

LOVESWEPT (Imprint of *Bantam Books*)—666 Fifth Ave., New York, NY 10019. Elizabeth Barrett, Assoc. Ed. Highly sensual, adult contemporary romances, approx 55,000 words. Study field before submitting. Query required. Paperback only.

MARGARET K. McELDERRY BOOKS—Atheneum Publishers, 115 Fifth Ave., New York, NY 10003. Margaret K. McElderry, Dir. Fiction and nonfiction for preschoolers through 16-year-olds. Picture books. Query with SASE. Guidelines available. Hardcover.

MCGRAW-HILL BOOK CO.—1221 Ave. of the Americas, New York, NY 10020. Fiction and nonfiction. No unsolicited manuscripts. Queries only.

DAVID MCKAY COMPANY—2 Park Ave., New York, NY 10016. Richard T. Scott, Pub. Nonfiction. Unsolicited manuscripts neither acknowledged or returned.

MACMILLAN PUBLISHING CO., INC.—866 Third Ave., New York, NY 10022. General Books Division: General and genre fiction, general nonfiction— how-to, current affairs, biography, business, religious, and juveniles. Paperbacks, *Collier Books.* College texts and professional books in social sciences, humanities, address *The Free Press.* Royalty basis.

MADRONA PUBLISHERS, INC.—P.O. Box 22667, Seattle, WA 98122. Sara Levant, Acquisitions Ed. General-interest nonfiction trade books (no poetry, children's books or fiction). Royalty basis.

MEADOWBROOK PRESS—18318 Minnetonka Blvd., Deephaven, MN 55391. Marge Hughes, Ed. Dir. Books on infant and child care; maternity; health; travel; consumer interests. Fiction: juvenile mysteries. Royalty basis and outright purchase. Query. SASE required. No recent report.

MENTOR BOOKS—See *New American Library.*

MERCURY HOUSE—P.O. Box 640, Forest Knolls, CA 94933. Mrs. Alev Lytel, Exec. Ed. Adult fiction and nonfiction, 250 to 350 pages. Query with outline and sample chapters. Royalty basis.

MEREDITH CORP., BOOK GROUP *(Better Homes and Gardens Books)*—1716 Locust St., Des Moines, IA 50336. Gerald M. Knox, Ed. Address The Editors. Books on gardening, crafts, health, decorating, etc. Outright purchase. Query with outline and sample chapter.

JULIAN MESSNER (Div. of *Simon & Schuster*)—1230 Ave. of the Americas, New York, NY 10020. Jane Steltenpohl, Exec. Ed. High-interest, curriculum-oriented nonfiction. General nonfiction for junior and senior high, about 30,000 words. Royalty basis.

MILLER ACCOUNTING PUBLICATIONS, INC.—See *Harcourt Brace Jovanovich.*

MOREHOUSE-BARLOW CO., INC.—78 Danbury Rd., Wilton, CT 06897. Stephen S. Wilburn, Ed. Dir. Theology, pastoral care, church administration, spirituality, Angelican studies, history of religion, etc. Royalty basis or outright purchase. Query with outline, contents, and sample chapter.

WILLIAM MORROW AND CO., INC.—105 Madison Ave., New York, NY 10016. Sherry Arden, Pub. Adult fiction and nonfiction. No unsolicited manuscripts. *Morrow Junior Books:* David Reuther, Ed.-in-Chief. Children's books for all ages. *Hearst Marine Books:* Jake Whiting, Ed. *Hearst Books:* Joan B. Nagy, Ed. Dir. General nonfiction. No unsolicited manuscripts.

MORROW QUILL PAPERBACKS (Div. of *William Morrow*)—105 Madison Ave., New York, NY 10016. Alison Brown-Cerier, Man. Ed. Trade paperbacks. Adult nonfiction. No unsolicited manuscripts.

THE MOUNTAINEERS BOOKS—306 Second Ave. W., Seattle, WA 98119. Ann Cleeland, Man. Ed. Nonfiction on mountaineering, backpacking, canoeing, kayaking, bicycling, skiing. Field guides, regional histories, biographies of mountaineers; accounts of expeditions. Nature books. Royalty basis. Submit sample chapters and outline.

JOHN MUIR PUBLICATIONS—P.O. Box 613, Santa Fe, NM 87501. Richard Harris, Project Coordinator. General nonfiction: current interest, gardening, how-to, travel, automotive, etc. Royalty basis. Query with outline and sample chapters. Softcover only.

MULTNOMAH PRESS—10209 SE Division St., Portland, OR 97266. Roger L. Morris, Ed. Man. Conservative, evangelical nonfiction. Send outline and sample chapters. Royalty basis.

THE MYSTERIOUS PRESS—129 W. 56th St., New York, NY 10019. William Malloy, Man. Ed. Mystery/suspense novels. Query with synopsis, SASE.

NAL BOOKS (Div. of *New American Library*)—1633 Broadway, New York, NY 10019. Michaela Hamilton, Ed. Dir. Fiction and nonfiction books. Manuscripts and proposals accepted only from agents or upon personal recommendation.

NATUREGRAPH PUBLISHERS—P.O. Box 1075, Happy Camp, CA 96039. Barbara Brown, Gary M. Kunkle, Eds. Nonfiction: Native American culture, natural history, outdoor living, land and gardening, holistic learning and health, Indian lore, crafts and how-to. Royalty basis. Query.

THOMAS NELSON INC.—Nelson Place at Elm Hill Pike, Nashville, TN 37214. Bruce A. Nygren, Ed. Dir. Religious adult nonfiction. Royalty basis. Query with outline and sample chapters.

NEW AMERICAN LIBRARY—1633 Broadway, New York, NY 10019. Pat Taylor, Ed. *Signet Books:* Commercial fiction; historicals, sagas, thrillers, action/adventure, mysteries. Nonfiction: self-help, how-to, etc. *Plume Books:* Nonfiction: hobbies, business, health, cooking, child care, psychology, etc. *Mentor Books:* Nonfiction originals for high school and college market. Royalty basis. No unsolicited manuscripts.

NEW REPUBLIC BOOKS/HENRY HOLT AND CO.—1220 19th St., N.W., Washington, DC 20036. Steve Wasserman, Ed.-in-Chief. Books on politics, Washington affairs, culture, the arts. Royalty basis. Query. Hardcover only.

NEW YORK GRAPHIC SOCIETY BOOKS/LITTLE, BROWN AND CO.—34 Beacon St., Boston, MA 02108. Books on fine arts and photography. Query with outline or proposal and vita. Royalty basis.

W. W. NORTON & COMPANY, INC.—500 Fifth Ave., New York, NY 10110. H. Hinzmann, Assoc. Ed. Fiction and nonfiction. Royalty basis. Query with synopsis, 2 to 3 chapters, and resumé. SASE required.

OAK TREE PUBLICATIONS—9601 Aero Dr., San Diego, CA 92123. Juvenile books for ages preschool to 11: picture books, pop-ups, unique craft, activity, adventure and science books for children. Royalty basis. Query with synopsis, outline, illustrations and credentials. SASE required.

101 PRODUCTIONS—834 Mission St., San Francisco, CA 94103. Jacqueline Killeen, Ed. Nonfiction: gardening, domestic arts, travel. Royalty basis. Query; no unsolicited manuscripts. Softcover only.

OPEN COURT PUBLISHING COMPANY—Box 599, Peru, IL 61354. Scholarly books. Elementary textbooks. Royalty basis. Query.

ORCHARD BOOKS (Imprint of *Franklin Watts*)—387 Park Ave. South, New York, NY 10016. Children's hardcover picture books and fiction. Fiction for young adults. Complete manuscripts. Royalty basis.

OSBORNE/McGRAW-HILL—2600 Tenth St., Berkeley, CA 94710. Cynthia Hudson, Ed.-in-Chief. Microcomputer books for a general audience. Query. Royalty basis.

OXFORD UNIVERSITY PRESS—200 Madison Ave., New York, NY 10016. Authoritative books on literature, history, philosophy, etc.; college textbooks, medical, and reference books; paperbacks. Royalty basis. Query.

OXMOOR HOUSE, INC.—Box 2262, Birmingham, AL 35201. John Logue, Ed. Nonfiction: art, photography, gardening, decorating, cooking and crafts. Royalty basis.

PACER BOOKS FOR YOUNG ADULTS (Imprint of the *Berkley Publishing Group*)—200 Madison Ave., New York, NY 10016. Fiction: adventure, fantasy, humor, and non-formula romance. No unsolicited manuscripts; queries only. Address Hillary Cige. Softcover only.

PACER BOOKS FOR YOUNG ADULTS (Imprint of the *Putnam Publishing Group*)—51 Madison Ave., New York, NY 10010. Fiction: adventure, fantasy, humor and non-formula romance. Query: attn. Anne O'Connell. Hardcover only.

PACIFIC SEARCH PRESS—222 Dexter Ave. N., Seattle, WA 98109. Carolyn Threadgill, Dir. of Books. Crafts, natural history, travel, outdoor recreation, cooking. Royalty basis. Query; no unsolicited manuscripts.

PANTHEON BOOKS (Div. of *Random House*)—201 E. 50th St., New York, NY 10022. Address Daniel Cullen or Helena Franklin. Nonfiction: academic level for general reader on history, political science, sociology, etc.; picture books; folklore. Some fiction. Royalty basis. Query; no unsolicited manuscripts.

PARENTING PRESS—7744 31st Ave., NE, Seattle, WA 98115. Shari Steelsmith, Ed. Parenting/child guidance books, 78,000 words, and social skills building books for children, 600 to 1,000 words. Query required. Send SASE for guidelines and catalogue.

PARKER PUBLISHING COMPANY, INC.—West Nyack, NY 10994. James Bradler, Pres. Self-help and how-to books, 65,000 words: health, money opportunities, business, etc. Royalty basis.

PEACHTREE PUBLISHERS, LTD.—494 Armour Circle, N.E., Atlanta, GA 30324. Chuck Perry, Exec. Ed. Fiction and nonfiction of Southern interest. Humor, cooking, gardening, health, how-to, travel, sports and recreation. Query, with sample chapters and an outline for nonfiction, complete manuscript for fiction.

PELICAN PUBLISHING CO., INC.—1101 Monroe St., Gretna, LA 70053. James L. Calhoun, Exec. Ed. General nonfiction: Americana, regional, architecture, how-to, travel, cookbooks, inspiration, motivation, music, parenting, etc. Juvenile fiction. Royalty basis.

PELION PRESS—See *The Rosen Publishing Group.*

PENGUIN BOOKS (Div. of *Viking/Penguin, Inc.*)—40 W. 23rd St., New York, NY 10010. Kathryn Court, Ed.-in-Chief. Adult fiction and nonfiction. No original poetry or juveniles, Royalty basis. No unsolicited material.

PERSEA BOOKS—225 Lafayette St., New York, NY 10012. Address Editorial Dept. Literary fiction; nonfiction; women's studies, visual books. Royalty basis. Query only.

PHALAROPE BOOKS—Prentice Hall Press, Gulf and Western Bldg., New York, NY 10023. Mary E. Kenan, Ed. Series in natural history; Frontiers of Science; science. Royalty basis. Query with partial or detailed outline and SASE.

PHILOMEL BOOKS (Div. of *Putnam Publishing Group*)—51 Madison Ave., New York, NY 10010. Query Victoria Rock. General fiction, nonfiction, picture books for juveniles.

THE PILGRIM PRESS/UNITED CHURCH PRESS—132 W. 31 St., New York, NY 10001. Larry K. Kalp, Pub. Religious and general-interest nonfiction. Royalty basis. Query with outline and sample chapters.

PINEAPPLE PRESS—P.O. Box 314, Englewood, FL 33533. June Cussen, Ed. Serious fiction and nonfiction; books on nature, 60,000 to 125,000 words. Query with outline and sample chapters. Royalty basis.

PLENUM PUBLISHING CORP.—233 Spring St., New York, NY 10013. Linda Greenspan Regan, Ed. Nonfiction, 200 to 300 pages, on scientific and social scientific topics. Royalty basis. Query required.

PLUME BOOKS—See *New American Library.*

POCKET BOOKS (Div. of *Simon and Schuster*)—1230 Ave. of the Americas, New York, NY 10020. William R. Grose, Ed. Dir. Some original fiction and nonfiction. Query with outline; no unsolicited manuscripts. Royalty basis.

POINT BOOKS—See *Scholastic, Inc.*

POSEIDON PRESS (Imprint of *Pocket Books*)—1230 Ave. of the Americas, New York, NY 10020. Ann Patty, V.P. & Pub. General fiction and nonfiction. Royalty basis. No unsolicited material.

CLARKSON N. POTTER, INC.—225 Park Ave. S., New York, NY 10003. Carol Southern, Ed. Dir. General trade books. Submissions accepted through agents.

PRAEGER PUBLISHERS (Div. of *Greenwood Press*)—521 Fifth Ave., New York, NY 10175. Ron Chambers, Pub. General nonfiction; scholarly and reference books. Royalty basis. Query with outline.

PRENTICE HALL PRESS (Div. of *Simon and Schuster*)—Gulf + Western Bldg., New York, NY 10023. General fiction and nonfiction. Queries only. Address Editorial Dept. Royalty basis.

PRESIDIO PRESS—31 Pamaron Way, Novato, CA 94947. Nonfiction: contemporary military history, from 50,000 words. Selected fiction of a military nature. Royalty basis. Query.

PRICE/STERN/SLOAN PUBLISHERS, INC.—410 N. La Cienega Blvd., Los Angeles, CA 90048. Short, humorous "non-books." Royalty basis or outright purchase. Query only.

PRUETT PUBLISHING COMPANY—2928 Pearl, Boulder, CO 80301. Gerald Keenan, Man. Ed. Nonfiction: railroadiana, Western Americana, recreational guides with Western orientation. Royalty basis. Query. Submit sample chapters with outline; no complete manuscripts.

PUFFIN BOOKS (Div. of *Viking/Penguin*)—40 W. 23rd St., New York, NY 10010. Some original juvenile paperbacks.

G. P. PUTNAM'S SONS (Div. of *Putnam Publishing Group*)—200 Madison Ave., New York, NY 10016. General fiction and nonfiction. No unsolicited manuscripts or queries.

QUEST BOOKS (Imprint of *The Theosophical Publishing House*)—396 W. Geneva Rd., P.O. Box 270, Wheaton, IL 60189-0270. Shirley Nicholson, Senior Ed. Nonfiction books on Eastern and Western religion and philosophy, holism, healing, meditation, yoga, astrology. Royalty basis. Query.

QUINLAN PRESS—131 Beverly St., Boston, MA 02114. Sandra E. Bielawa, Exec. Ed. General nonfiction. Query with SASE required. Royalty.

RAINTREE PUBLISHERS INC.—310 W. Wisconsin Ave., Milwaukee, WI 53203. Address Ed. Dept. Juveniles: information and reference books; nonfiction and fiction picture books. Outright purchase or royalty basis. Query.

RAND MCNALLY & COMPANY—Editorial Dept., Box 7600, Chicago, IL 60680. Informational reference; rated publications; atlas supplementary material. Royalty or outright purchase. Query with SASE required.

RANDOM HOUSE, INC.—201 E. 50th St., New York, NY 10022. Howard Kaminsky, Pub. Jason Epstein, Ed.-in-Chief. J. Schulman, Ed.-in-Chief, Juvenile Books; Stuart Flexner, Ed.-in-Chief, Reference Books. General fiction and nonfiction; reference and college textbooks; juvenile fiction and nonfiction, picture books, easy-to-read material. Royalty basis. Query with three chapters and outline for nonfiction; complete manuscript for fiction.

RAWSON ASSOCIATES—(Div. of *The Scribner Book Cos.*)—115 Fifth Ave., New York, NY 10003. Kennett L. Rawson, Pres. General nonfiction. Royalty basis. Query.

REGNERY GATEWAY—950 North Shore Dr., Lake Bluff, IL 60044. Nonfiction, average of 70,000 words in length: politics, business, religion, science, etc. Royalty basis. Query first.

RENAISSANCE HOUSE—541 Oak St., P.O. Box 177, Frederick, CO 80530. Eleanor H. Ayer, Ed. Western Americana, World War II, and Rocky Mountain West; biographies and historical books. Submit outline, two sample chapters, and short bio. Pays on royalty basis.

FLEMING H. REVELL COMPANY—Old Tappan, NJ 07675. Gary A. Sledge, V.P. and Ed.-in-Chief. Inspirational and devotional religious books. Royalty basis. Query required.

REWARD BOOKS (Imprint of *Prentice-Hall*)—Englewood Cliffs, NJ 07632. Ted Nardin, Manager. Nonfiction: self-help, real estate, selling, business, health, etc. Royalty basis. Softcover only.

RODALE PRESS, BOOK DIVISION—33 E. Minor St., Emmaus, PA 18049. Thomas Woll, Pub. Nonfiction: health, nutrition, alternative energy, gardening, sports, fitness, etc. Royalty basis or outright purchase. Query.

THE ROSEN PUBLISHING GROUP, INC.—29 E. 21st St., New York, NY 10010. Roger Rosen, Pres. Ruth C. Rosen, Ed. Young adult books, to 40,000 words, on vocational guidance, journalism, theater, etc. *Pelion Press:* music, art, history. Pays varying rates.

ST. MARTIN'S PRESS—175 Fifth Ave., New York, NY 10010. General adult fiction and nonfiction. Royalty basis. Query first.

SCHOCKEN BOOKS—62 Cooper Sq., New York, NY 10003. David I. Rome, Pres. General nonfiction: history, Judaica, women's studies, etc. Royalty basis. Query.

SCHOLASTIC, INC.—730 Broadway, New York, NY 10003. *Point:* Brenda Bowen, Ed. Young adult fiction for readers age 12 and up. *Apple Books:* Brenda Bowen, Ed. Fiction for readers ages 9 to 12. Submit complete manuscript with cover letter and SASE. Royalty basis. Romance lines for girls 12 to 15 years, 40,000 to 45,000 words. Ann Reit, Ed.: *Wildfire,* realistic problems of girls in first or early relationships; *Sunfire,* American historical romances, 55,000 words. Query with outline and three sample chapters. Write for tip sheets.

SCOTT, FORESMAN & COMPANY—1900 E. Lake Ave., Glenview, IL 60025. Richard T. Morgan, Pres. Elementary, secondary, and college textbooks and materials. Royalty basis.

CHARLES SCRIBNER'S SONS—115 Fifth Ave., New York, NY 10003. Christine Pevitt, Ed.-in-Chief. Fiction; general nonfiction, especially science, business, health. Royalty basis. Query first.

SEAVER BOOKS—333 Central Park W., New York, NY 10025. Jeannette W. Seaver, Pub. Trade fiction, nonfiction. Accepts no unsolicited manuscripts. Royalty basis. Query.

SECOND CHANCE AT LOVE (Imprint of *Berkley Publishing Group*)—200

Madison Ave., New York, NY 10016. Ellen Edwards, Sr. Ed. Contemporary category romances, 55,000 words, with mature, experienced heroines, whose previous relationships/marriages have ended and who find true love with their second chance. Originality a must. Humor popular. Royalty basis. Query with synopsis. Tip sheet. Softcover only.

SERENADE AND SERENADE/SAGA ROMANCES (Imprints of *Zondervan Publishing House*)—1414 Lake Dr. S.E., Grand Rapids, MI 49506. Inspirational romances, 60,000 words, for Christian readers. *Serenade:* Contemporary. *Serenade/Saga, Serenade SuperSaga:* historical. Royalty basis. Send sample chapter, outline, synopsis and biographical sketch. Send SASE for tip sheet.

SEVEN SEAS PRESS—Box 100, Newport, RI 02840. James R. Gilbert, Ed. Books on sailing. Query first. Royalty basis.

SIERRA CLUB BOOKS—730 Polk St., San Francisco, CA 94109. Nonfiction: environment, natural history, the sciences; outdoors and regional guidebooks; juvenile fiction and nonfiction. Royalty basis. Query with SASE.

SIGNET VISTA (Imprint of *New American Library*)—1633 Broadway, New York, NY 10019. Susan Donavan, Ed. Contemporary teen fiction and nonfiction, 45,000 to 50,000 words. No tip sheet. No unsolicited manuscripts. Royalty. Paperbacks only.

SILHOUETTE BOOKS—300 E. 42nd St., New York, NY 10017. Karen Solem, Ed.-in-Chief. *Silhouette Romances:* Mary Tara Hughes, Sr. Ed. Contemporary romances, 53,000 to 58,000 words. *Special Edition:* Roz Noonan, Sr. Ed. Sophisticated contemporary romances, 70,000 to 80,000 words. *Intimate Moments:* Leslie Wainger, Sr. Ed. Sensuous, sophisticated contemporary romances, 80,000 to 85,000 words. *First Love:* Nancy Jackson, Sr. Ed. Contemporary romances for 11- to 16-year-old girls, 40,000 words. Submit complete manuscript for young adult. For adult lines, query with synopsis and SASE to appropriate editor.

SILVER BURDETT—250 James St., Morristown, NJ 07960. Walter Kossman, Product Development Ed. Fiction and nonfiction for children, preschool through twelfth grade. Query required. Royalty basis.

SIMON & SCHUSTER—Gulf & Western Bldg., One Gulf & Western Plaza, New York, NY 10023. No unsolicited material.

SLAWSON COMMUNICATIONS—3719 Sixth Ave., San Diego, CA 92103. Leslie S. Smith, Ed. *Avant Books:* Business; health and fitness. *Microtrend:* computer topics. *Mad Hatter Press:* Children's books with emphasis on the preschool market. Query with SASE. Royalty basis.

GIBBS M. SMITH, INC./PEREGRINE SMITH BOOKS—P.O. Box 667, Layton, UT 84041. James Thomas, Trade Ed. Adult and juvenile fiction and nonfiction. Query. Royalty basis.

SOS PUBLICATIONS—4223–25 W. Jefferson Blvd., Los Angeles, CA 90016. S. Paul Bradley, Pub. Carla O. Glover, Ed. Novels, mystery, romance, and adventure, from 85,000 words, for "Mini-Bound" series. Royalty basis.

SPECTRA BOOKS (Imprint of *Bantam Books*)—666 Fifth Ave., New York, NY 10103. Lou Aronica, Sr. Ed. Science fiction and fantasy, with emphasis on storytelling and characterization. Query; no unsolicited manuscripts. Advance royalty basis.

STANDARD PUBLISHING—8121 Hamilton Ave., Cincinnati, OH 45231. Address Mark Plunkett. Fiction: juveniles; based on Bible or with moral tone.

Nonfiction: biblical, Christian education. Conservative evangelical. Query preferred.

STEIN AND DAY—Scarborough House, Briarcliff Manor, NY 10510. Address Editorial Dept. Adult general fiction and nonfiction. Royalty basis. Query with outline and sample chapter for nonfiction; descriptive letter, up to two pages, for fiction. No unsolicited manuscripts. SASE required.

STEMMER HOUSE—2627 Caves Rd., Owings Mills, MD 21117. Barbara Holdridge, Ed. Adult and juvenile fiction and nonfiction. Royalty basis. Query.

STERLING PUBLISHING CO., INC.—Two Park Ave., New York, NY 10016. Burton Hobson, Pres. Jonathan Eisen, Edit. Dir. How-to, self-help, hobby, woodworking, health, craft, and sports books. Royalty and outright purchase. Query with outline, sample chapter, and sample of illustration. *Impact Books:* world affairs, science, consumer issues, and how-to topics, with social, political or scientific impact. Query first. Royalty basis.

STONE WALL PRESS—1241 30th St., N.W., Washington, DC 20007. Nonfiction on hunting, fishing, outdoors, conservation, 200 to 300 pages. Pays on royalty basis. Query first.

STRAWBERRY HILL PRESS—2594 15th Ave., San Francisco, CA 94127. Carolyn Soto, Ed. Nonfiction: biography, autobiography, history, cooking, health, how-to, philosophy, performance arts, and Third World. Query first with sample chapters, outline, and SASE. Royalty.

LYLE STUART, INC.—120 Enterprise Ave., Secaucus, NJ 07094. Allan J. Wilson, Ed. General fiction and nonfiction. *Citadel Press* division: biography, film, history, limited fiction. Royalty basis. Query; no unsolicited manuscripts. *Irma Heldman Books:* Submit to Irma Heldman, 275 Central Park West, New York, NY 10024. Mystery and suspense fiction, mainstream fiction, and nonfiction, from 65,000 words. Submit query for nonfiction, complete manuscripts for fiction. Royalty basis.

SUMMIT BOOKS—1230 Ave. of the Americas, New York, NY 10020. General-interest fiction and nonfiction of high literary quality. No category books. Royalty basis. Query with outline for nonfiction; query with several chapters for fiction.

SUNFIRE—See *Scholastic, Inc.*

SWALLOW PRESS—P.O. Box 2080, Chicago, IL 60690. Self-help, history, biography. Contemporary novels. Western Americana. No unsolicited poetry or fiction. Royalty basis.

TAB BOOKS INC.—Blue Ridge Summit, PA 17214. Raymond A. Collins, Vice-Pres., Edit. Dept. Nonfiction: electronics, computer, how-to, aviation, business, solar and energy, science and technology, back to basics, automotive, marine and outdoor life. Royalty basis or outright purchase. Query.

TAPLINGER PUBLISHING CO.—132 W. 22nd St., New York, NY 10011. Bobs Pinkerton, Roy Thomas, Eds. Serious literary fiction. General nonfiction: history, art, etc. Royalty basis.

JEREMY P. TARCHER, INC.—9110 Sunset Blvd., Los Angeles, CA 90069. Jeremy P. Tarcher, Ed.-in-Chief. General nonfiction: psychology, personal development, health and fitness, women's concerns, science for the layperson, etc. Royalty basis. Query with outline, sample chapter and SASE.

TAYLOR PUBLISHING CO.—1550 W. Mockingbird Lane, Dallas, TX 75235. Robert Frese, Sr. Ed. Nonfiction: fine arts, regional, biography, cooking, gardening, sports and recreation, art/photo, and lifestyle. Query with sample chapters, SASE, and outline required. Pays on royalty basis.

TEN SPEED PRESS—P.O. Box 7123, Berkeley, CA 94707. Kim Knutson, Ed. Self-help and how-to books on careers, recreation, etc.; natural science, history, cookbooks. Query with outline and sample chapters. Royalty basis. Softcover only.

TEXAS MONTHLY PRESS—Box 1569, Austin, TX 78767. Scott Lubeck, Dir. Fiction, nonfiction, related to Texas or the Southwest: 60,000 words. Royalty basis.

THUNDER'S MOUTH PRESS—Box 780, New York, NY 10025. Neil Ortenberg, Ed. Literary fiction and poetry collections; books on historical and political topics. Query first. Length requirements: poetry, 96 pages; fiction, to 200 pages. Royalty basis.

TICKNOR & FIELDS (Subsidiary of *Houghton Mifflin Company*)—52 Vanderbilt Ave., New York, NY 10017. General nonfiction and fiction. Royalty basis.

TIMBRE BOOKS (Imprint of *Arbor House*)—235 E. 45th St., New York, NY 10017. Address Editorial Dept. Nonfiction: business, sports, humor, health, music, finance, etc. Biographies, essays, reference books. Query with detailed outline or submit complete manuscripts. Advance royalty basis. Softcover only.

TIMES BOOKS (Div. of *Random House, Inc.*)—201 E. 50th St., New York, NY 10022. Jonathan B. Segal, Ed. Dir. General nonfiction. No unsolicited manuscripts or queries accepted.

TOR BOOKS—49 W. 24th St., New York, NY 10010. Beth Meacham, Ed.-in-Chief: Science fiction and fantasy. Michael Seidman, Exec. Ed.: Thrillers, espionage, and mysteries. Melissa Ann Singer, Ed.: Horror and dark fantasy. Wanda June Alexander, Asst. Ed.: Historicals. Length: 60,000 words. Query with outline and sample chapters. Royalty basis.

TROLL ASSOCIATES—320 Rt. 17, Mahwah, NJ 07430. M. Francis, Ed. Juvenile fiction and nonfiction. Royalty basis or outright purchase. Query preferred.

TROUBADOR PRESS—One Sutter St., Suite 205, San Francisco, CA 94104. Juvenile illustrated games, activity, paper doll, coloring and cut-out books. Royalty basis or outright purchase. Query with outline and SASE.

TYNDALE HOUSE—336 Gundersen Dr., Box 80, Wheaton, IL 60189. Wendell Hawley, Ed.-in-Chief. Christian. Juvenile and adult fiction and nonfiction on subjects of concern to Christians. Submit complete manuscripts. Royalty basis.

UNIVERSE BOOKS—381 Park Ave. S., New York, NY 10016. Louis Barron, Vice-Pres. and Ed. Dir. Art, anthropology, ballet, history, music, natural history, biographies, crafts, linguistics, design, social science, etc. Royalty basis. Query with SASE.

VAN NOSTRAND REINHOLD, INC.—115 Fifth Ave., New York, NY 10003. John Connolly, Pres. Business, professional, scientific, and technical publishers of applied reference works. *CBI Publishing Co.*: Food service and hospitality books. Royalty.

THE VANGUARD PRESS, INC.—424 Madison Ave., New York, NY 10017. Bernice Woll, Ed. Adult and juvenile fiction and nonfiction. Royalty basis. Query with sample chapters.

VIKING PENGUIN, INC.—40 W. 23rd St., New York, NY 10010. *The Viking Press:* Adult fiction and nonfiction. *Viking Junior Books:* Juveniles. *Penguin Books:* Paperback reprints and originals. *Viking Kestrel:* juveniles. *Puffin:* Juvenile paperback reprints and originals. Royalty basis. No unsolicited material.

WALKER AND COMPANY—720 Fifth Ave., New York, NY 10019. Fiction: mysteries, men's action, westerns, Regency romance, romantic suspense, science fiction and fantasy, and espionage. Nonfiction: Americana, biography, history, how-to, science, and natural history, medicine, psychology, parenting, sports, outdoors, reference, popular science, self-help. Juveniles. Royalty basis. Query with synopsis.

WALLACE-HOMESTEAD—580 Waters Edge, Lombard, IL 60148. William N. Topaz, General Manager. Books on quilting, antiques and collectibles. Cookbooks. Submit outline with sample chapters. Pays on a royalty basis.

WANDERER BOOKS (Div. of *Simon & Schuster, Inc.*)—Gulf and Western Plaza, New York, NY 10023. Ron Buehl, Pub. General-interest juveniles, for 8- to 14-year-olds: Nonfiction, series fiction. Flat fee and royalty basis. Query with outline and sample chapter for nonfiction.

WARNER BOOKS—666 Fifth Ave., New York, NY 10103. Bernard Shir-Cliff, Ed.-in-Chief. Fiction: historical romance, contemporary women's fiction, unusual big-scale horror and suspense. Nonfiction: business books, health and nutrition, self-help and how-to books. Royalty basis. Query with sample chapters. Also publishes trade paperbacks and hardcover titles.

FRANKLIN WATTS, INC.—387 Park Ave. S., New York, NY 10016. Jeanne Vestal, Edit. Dir. Juvenile nonfiction. Royalty basis. Query. SASE required.

PETER WEED BOOKS (Imprint of *Beaufort Books*)—9 E. 40th St., New York, NY 10016. Peter Weed, Ed. Fiction and serious nonfiction. Queries only; no unsolicited manuscripts. Royalty basis.

WESTERN PUBLISHING CO., INC.—850 Third Ave., New York, NY 10022. Doris Duenewald, Pub., Children's Books; Jonathan B. Latimer, Pub., Adult Books; Rosanna Hanson, Ed.-in-Chief, Children's Books. Adult nonfiction: Field guides, cookbooks, etc. Children's books, fiction and nonfiction: picture books, storybooks, concept books, novelty books. Royalty basis and outright purchase. Query. Same address and requirements for *Golden Press.*

ALBERT WHITMAN & COMPANY—5747 W. Howard St., Niles, IL 60648. Kathleen Tucker, Ed. Children's books, for preschool through eighth grade. Picture books (short, simple ones for children two to four and longer stories for children five through eight); short and long novels for middle-grade readers; biographies; mysteries; and general nonfiction. Submit complete manuscripts for picture books, and three chapters and an outline for longer fiction. Query letter for nonfiction. Royalty basis.

WILDERNESS PRESS—2440 Bancroft Way, Berkeley, CA 94704. Thomas Winnett, Ed. Sports, recreation, and travel in the western U.S. Royalty.

WILDFIRE—See *Scholastic, Inc.*

JOHN WILEY & SONS—605 Third Ave., New York, NY 10158. David Sobel, Ed. Health, business and management, computing, home reference, and other general nonfiction areas. For *Wiley Science Editions,* books on science and technology. Submit a cover letter describing overall concept, package and intended audience, giving a detailed account of competing titles, to the best of the author's knowledge. Provide a current biography and bibliography of the author, along with chapter-by-chapter outline and at least one but not more than two sample chapters. Do not submit complete manuscripts.

WILSHIRE BOOK COMPANY—12015 Sherman Rd., North Hollywood, CA 91605. Specialized nonfiction: Inspirational, self-help, entrepreneurship, business, advertising, mail order, sports, health, horses, etc. Royalty basis. Query with synopsis or outline. SASE required.

WINCHESTER PRESS—220 Old New Brunswick Rd., CN 1332, Piscataway, NJ 08854. Robert Elman, Consulting Ed. Nonfiction: outdoors, how-to, etc. Royalty basis. Query.

WINGBOW PRESS—2929 Fifth St., Berkeley, CA 94710. Randy Fingland, Ed. Nonfiction: travel/guidebooks for Northern California, San Francisco Bay area, women's interests, health, psychology, how-to. Query or sample chapter and outline preferred. Royalty basis.

WOODBINE HOUSE—10400 Connecticut Ave., Suite 512, Kensington, MD 20895. Marshall S. Levin, Ed. Full-length original works of both fiction and nonfiction of interest to a wide audience. Submit outline, sample chapter, and short biography. Pays either royalty or flat fee.

WORKMAN PUBLISHING CO., INC.—1 W. 39th St., New York, NY 10018. General nonfiction. Normal contractual terms based on agreement.

YANKEE BOOKS—Main St., Dublin, NH 03444. Sandra Taylor, Acquisitions Ed. Books relating to Northeastern U.S. Cooking, crafts, photographs, maritime subjects, travel, gardening, nature, nostalgia, humor, folklore and popular history. No scholarly history, highly technical work, or off-color humor. Regional New England fiction considered. Royalty basis. Query or send proposal.

YEARLING BOOKS—See *Dell Publishing Co., Inc.*

ZEBRA BOOKS—475 Park Ave. S., New York, NY 10016. Leslie Gelbman, Fiction Ed. Wendy McCurdy, Nonfiction Ed. Biography, how-to, humor, self-help. Fiction: adventure, regency, mainstream fiction, historical romance, gothic, historical, horror, etc. Query required. Softcover only.

CHARLOTTE ZOLOTOW BOOKS (Imprint of *Harper & Row*)—10 E. 53rd St., New York, NY 10022. Juvenile fiction and nonfiction "with integrity of purpose, beauty of language, and an out-of-ordinary look at ordinary things." Royalty basis. Hardcover only.

THE ZONDERVAN CORPORATION—1415 Lake Dr., S.E., Grand Rapids, MI 49506. Pamela Jewell, Manuscript Review Ed. Nonfiction books with an evangelical Christian viewpoint: self-help; general nonfiction; Bible study; devotional and gift. Fiction, with a religious theme. Royalty basis. Query with outline, sample chapter, and SASE.

UNIVERSITY PRESSES

University presses generally publish books of a scholarly nature or of specialized interest by authorities in a given field. A few publish fiction and poetry. Many publish only a handful of titles a year. Always query first. Do not send any manuscripts until you have been invited to do so by the editor.

BRIGHAM YOUNG UNIVERSITY PRESS—209 University Press Bldg., Provo, UT 84602.

BUCKNELL UNIVERSITY PRESS—Lewisburg, PA 17837.

CAMBRIDGE UNIVERSITY PRESS—32 East 57th St., New York, NY 10022.

THE CATHOLIC UNIVERSITY OF AMERICA PRESS—620 Michigan Ave., N.E., Washington, DC 20064.

COLORADO ASSOCIATED UNIVERSITY PRESS—University of Colorado, 1424 15th St., Boulder, CO 80302.

COLUMBIA UNIVERSITY PRESS—562 West 113th St., New York, NY 10025.

DUKE UNIVERSITY PRESS—Box 6697, College Station, Durham, NC 27708.

DUQUESNE UNIVERSITY PRESS—101 Administration Bldg., Pittsburgh, PA 15219.

FORDHAM UNIVERSITY PRESS—Box L, Bronx, NY 10458.

GEORGIA STATE UNIVERSITY, SCHOOL OF BUSINESS ADMINISTRATION, PUBLISHING SERVICES DIVISION—University Plaza, Atlanta, GA 30303.

HARVARD UNIVERSITY PRESS—79 Garden St., Cambridge, MA 02138.

INDIANA UNIVERSITY PRESS—10th and Morton Sts., Bloomington, IN 47401.

THE JOHNS HOPKINS UNIVERSITY PRESS—Baltimore, MD 21218.

KENT STATE UNIVERSITY PRESS—Kent, OH 44242.

LOUISIANA STATE UNIVERSITY PRESS—Baton Rouge, LA 70803.

LOYOLA UNIVERSITY PRESS—3441 North Ashland Ave., Chicago, IL 60657.

MEMPHIS STATE UNIVERSITY PRESS—Memphis, TN 38152.

MICHIGAN STATE UNIVERSITY PRESS—1405 South Harrison Rd., East Lansing, MI 48824.

THE M.I.T. PRESS—28 Carleton St., Cambridge, MA 02142.

NEW YORK UNIVERSITY PRESS—Washington Sq., New York, NY 10003.

OHIO STATE UNIVERSITY PRESS—Hitchcock Hall, Rm. 316, 2070 Neil Ave., Columbus, OH 43210.

OHIO UNIVERSITY PRESS—Scott Quadrangle, Athens, OH 45701.

OREGON STATE UNIVERSITY PRESS—101 Waldo Hall, Corvallis, OR 97331.

THE PENNSYLVANIA STATE UNIVERSITY PRESS—215 Wagner Bldg., University Park, PA 16802.

PRINCETON UNIVERSITY PRESS—Princeton, NJ 08540.

RUTGERS UNIVERSITY PRESS—30 College Ave., New Brunswick, NJ 08903.

SOUTHERN ILLINOIS UNIVERSITY PRESS—Box 3697, Carbondale, IL 62901.

SOUTHERN METHODIST UNIVERSITY PRESS—Dallas, TX 75275.

STANFORD UNIVERSITY PRESS—Stanford, CA 94305.

STATE UNIVERSITY OF NEW YORK PRESS—State Univ. Plaza, Albany, NY 12246.

SYRACUSE UNIVERSITY PRESS—1011 East Water St., Syracuse, NY 13210.

TEMPLE UNIVERSITY PRESS—Broad and Oxford Sts., Philadelphia, PA 19122.

UNIVERSITY OF ALABAMA PRESS—Drawer 2877, University, AL 35486.

UNIVERSITY OF ARIZONA PRESS—Box 3398, College Station, Tucson, AZ 85722.

UNIVERSITY OF CALIFORNIA PRESS—2223 Fulton St., Berkeley, CA 94720.

UNIVERSITY OF CHICAGO PRESS—5801 Ellis Ave., Chicago, IL 60637.

UNIVERSITY OF GEORGIA PRESS—Athens, GA 30602.

UNIVERSITY OF ILLINOIS PRESS—Urbana, IL 61801.

UNIVERSITY OF MASSACHUSETTS PRESS—Box 429, Amherst, MA 01002.

UNIVERSITY OF MICHIGAN PRESS—Ann Arbor, MI 48106.

UNIVERSITY OF MINNESOTA PRESS—2037 University Ave., S.E., Minneapolis, MN 55455.

UNIVERSITY OF MISSOURI PRESS—107 Swallow Hall, Columbia, MO 65201.

UNIVERSITY OF NEBRASKA PRESS—901 North 17th St., Lincoln, NE 68588.

UNIVERSITY OF NEW MEXICO PRESS—Albuquerque, NM 87131.

UNIVERSITY OF NOTRE DAME PRESS—Notre Dame, IN 46556.

UNIVERSITY OF OKLAHOMA PRESS—1005 Asp Ave., Norman, OK 73019.

UNIVERSITY OF PITTSBURGH PRESS—127 North Bellefield Ave., Pittsburgh, PA 15260.

UNIVERSITY OF SOUTH CAROLINA PRESS—USC Campus, Columbia, SC 29208.

UNIVERSITY OF TENNESSEE PRESS—Communications Bldg., Knoxville, TN 37916.

UNIVERSITY OF UTAH PRESS—Bldg. 513, Salt Lake City, UT 84112.

UNIVERSITY OF WASHINGTON PRESS—Seattle, WA 98195.

UNIVERSITY OF WISCONSIN PRESS—Box 1379, Madison, WI 53701.

THE UNIVERSITY PRESS OF KENTUCKY—Lafferty Hall, Lexington, KY 40506.

UNIVERSITY PRESS OF MISSISSIPPI—3825 Ridgewood Rd., Jackson, MS 39211.

THE UNIVERSITY PRESS OF NEW ENGLAND—Box 979, Hanover, NH 03755.

THE UNIVERSITY PRESS OF VIRGINIA—Box 3608, University Sta., Charlottesville, VA 22903.

THE UNIVERSITY PRESS OF FLORIDA—15 N.W. 15th St., Gainesville, FL 32603.

WAYNE STATE UNIVERSITY PRESS—5959 Woodward Ave., Detroit, MI 48202.

WESLEYAN UNIVERSITY PRESS—55 High Street, Middletown, CT 06457.

YALE UNIVERSITY PRESS—302 Temple St., New Haven, CT 06511.

SYNDICATES

Syndicates are business organizations that publish nothing themselves, but buy material from writers and artists to sell to newspapers all over the country and the world. Authors are paid either a percentage of the gross proceeds or an outright fee.

Of course, features by people well known in their fields have the best chance of being syndicated. In general, syndicates want columns that have been popular in a local newspaper, perhaps, or magazine. Since most syndicated fiction has been published previously in magazines or books, beginning fiction writers should try to sell their stories to magazines before submitting them to syndicates.

Always query syndicates before sending manuscripts—their needs change frequently—and be sure to enclose self-addressed, stamped envelopes with queries and manuscripts.

BUSINESS FEATURES SYNDICATE—P.O. Box 9844, Ft. Lauderdale, FL 33310. Dana K. Cassell. How-to articles on small business; articles for the independent retailer or small service business owner on any of the following topics: marketing, security, personnel, merchandising, general management. Length: 1,500 to 2,000 words. Proceeds from sales split ⁵⁰/₅₀ between author and syndicate.

CANADA WIDE FEATURE SERVICE—Box 345, Station A, Toronto, Ontario, M5A 3W7, Canada. Glenn-Stewart Garnett, Ed. Interviews with well-known celebrities and international political figures, 1,500 to 2,000 words with photos. Pays 50% of gross, on publication.

CONTEMPORARY FEATURES SYNDICATE—P.O. Box 1258, Jackson, TN 38301. Lloyd Russell, Ed. Articles, 1,000 to 3,000 words: how to-, back-to-nature, money-savers, travel, business, etc. Self-help pieces, 1,000 to 10,000 words. Pays from $25, on acceptance.

FICTION NETWORK—Box 5651, San Francisco, CA 94101. Fiction, to 2,500 words. One submission per author; submit manuscript unfolded. SASE required. Pays royalty basis. Allow 12 weeks for response.

HARRIS & ASSOCIATES FEATURES—5353 La Jolla Blvd., #34, La Jolla, CA 92037. Dick Harris, Ed. Sports and family-oriented features, to 1,200 words; fillers and short humor, 500 to 800 words. Queries preferred. Pays varying rates.

HERITAGE FEATURES SYNDICATE—214 Mass. Ave., NE, Washington, DC 20002. Andy Seamans, Man. Ed. Public policy news features; syndicates weekly by-lined columns and editorial cartoons. Query with SASE a must.

HISPANIC LINK NEWS SERVICE—1420 N St., NW, Washington, DC 20005. Hector Ericksen-Mendoza, Ed. Trend articles, general features, Hispanic focus, 650 to 700 words; editorial cartoons. Pays $25 for op/ed column and cartoons, on acceptance. Send SASE for writers' guidelines.

THE HOLLYWOOD INSIDE SYNDICATE—Box 49957, Los Angeles, CA 90049. John Austin, Director. Feature material, 750 to 1,000 words, on TV and motion picture personalities. Story suggestions for 3-part series. Pieces on unusual medical and scientific breakthroughs. Pays on percentage basis for features, negotiated rates for ideas, on acceptance.

INTERNATIONAL ECO FEATURES SYNDICATE—Box 69193, W. Hollywood, CA 90069. Articles, 750 to 2,000 words. Query required. Pays on publication.

INTERNATIONAL MEDICAL TRIBUNE SYNDICATE—257 Park Ave. S., 19th fl., New York, NY 10010. Health and medical news, features, 250 to 1,000 words; technical accuracy and clarity a must. Pays 15¢ to 20¢ a word.

KING FEATURES SYNDICATE—235 E. 45th St., New York, NY 10017. James D. Head, Ed. Columns, comics; most contributions on contract for regular columns. Feature articles for newspaper supplement "Sunday Woman Plus"; query Merry Clark.

LOS ANGELES TIMES SYNDICATE—Times Mirror Sq., Los Angeles, CA 90053. Cartoons, comics, features and columns. Query for articles, either one-shots or series.

NATIONAL CATHOLIC NEWS SERVICE—1312 Massachusetts Ave. N.W., Washington, DC 20005. Richard W. Daw, Director and Ed.-in-Chief. Articles on the Catholic Church and Catholic issues; photos. Pays to 5¢ a word, after publication.

NATIONAL NEWS BUREAU—2019 Chancellor St., Philadelphia, PA 19103. Articles, 500 to 800 words, interviews, consumer news, how-to's, travel pieces, reviews, entertainment pieces, features, etc. Pays on publication.

NEW YORK TIMES SYNDICATION SALES—130 Fifth Ave., New York, NY 10011. Paula Reichler, V.P./Ed. Dir. Previously published articles only, to 2,000 words. Query with published article or tear sheet. Pays 40%, on publication.

NEWS AMERICA SYNDICATE—1703 Kaiser Ave., Irvine, CA 92714. Tom Reinken, Exec. Ed. Columns, comic strips, panel cartoons, serials.

NEWSPAPER ENTERPRISE ASSOCIATION, INC.—200 Park Ave., New York, NY 10166. David Hendin, Sr. Vice Pres. and Ed. Director. Ideas for new concepts in syndicated columns, comic strips, and panels. No single stories or stringers. Payment by contractual arrangement.

OCEANIC PRESS SERVICE—P.O. Box 6538, Buena Park, CA 90622-6538. Nat Carlton, General Manager. Buys reprint rights for foreign markets, on previously published novels, self-help, and how-to books; interviews with celebrities; illustrated features on celebrities, family, health, beauty, personal relations, etc.; cartoons, comic strips. Pays on acceptance. Query.

RELIGIOUS NEWS SERVICE—104 W. 56th St., New York, NY 10019. Judy Weidman, Ed. and Director. Religious news stories and features. Photos on religious subjects. Query first.

SELECT FEATURES OF NEWS AMERICA SYNDICATE—1703 Kaiser Blvd., P.O. Box 19620, Irvine, CA 92714. Anita Medeiros, Asst. Man., Select Features. Articles and series dealing with lifestyle trends, psychology, health, beauty, fashion, finance, jobs; personality profiles. Query or send complete manuscript. Pays varying rates, on publication.

SINGER COMMUNICATIONS INC.—3164 W. Tyler Ave., Anaheim, CA 92801. Kurt D. Singer, Ed. U.S. and/or foreign reprint rights to romantic short stories, historical and romantic novels, published during last 25 years. Biography, women's-interest material, all lengths. Home repair, real estate, crosswords. Interviews with celebrities. Illustrated columns, humor, cartoons, comic strips. Pays on percentage basis or by outright purchase.

TRANSWORLD FEATURE SYNDICATE, INC.—2 Lexington Ave., Suite 1021, New York, NY 10010. Thelma Brown, Syndication Manager. Feature material for North American and overseas markets. Query required.

TRIBUNE MEDIA SERVICES—64 E. Concord St., Orlando, FL 32801. Michael Argirion, Ed. Continuing columns, comic strips, features, electronic data bases.

UNITED FEATURE SYNDICATE—200 Park Ave., New York, NY 10166. David Hendin, Sr. Vice President/Ed. Dir. Creative, professional columns and comics. No one-shots or series. Payment by contractual arrangement.

UNITED PRESS INTERNATIONAL—1400 Eye St., NW, Washington, DC 20005. Ron Cohen, Man. Ed. Seldom accepts free-lance material.

LITERARY PRIZE OFFERS

Each year many important prize contests are open to free-lance writers. The short summaries given below are intended merely as guides. Closing dates, requirements, and rules are tentative. No manuscript should be submitted to any competition unless the writer has first checked with the Contest Editor and received complete information about a particular contest.

Send a stamped, self-addressed envelope with all requests for contest rules and application forms.

ACADEMY OF AMERICAN POETS—177 E. 87th St., New York, NY 10128. Offers Walt Whitman Award: Publication and $1,000 cash prize for a book-length poetry manuscript by a poet who has not yet published a volume of poetry. Closes in November.

ACTORS THEATRE OF LOUISVILLE—316 W. Main St., Louisville, KY 40202. Conducts the National One-Act Play Contest, with a prize of $1,000 for a one-act, previously unproduced play. Closes in April.

THE AMERICAN ACADEMY AND INSTITUTE OF ARTS AND LETTERS—633 W. 155th St., New York, NY 10032. Offers Richard Rodgers Production Award, which consists of subsidized production in New York City by a non-profit theater for a musical, play with music, thematic review, or any comparable work other than opera. Closes in November.

AMERICAN HEALTH MAGAZINE—80 Fifth Ave., New York, NY 10011. Offers prize of $2,000 for short story about an intense physical experience. Closes in April.

ASSOCIATED WRITING PROGRAMS—Old Dominion University, Norfolk, VA 23508. Conducts Annual Award Series in Short Fiction, the Novel, and Nonfiction. In each category the prize is book publication and a $1,000 honorarium. Closes in December. Offers the Edith Shiffert Prize in Poetry: $1,000 cash prize and publication by the University Press of Virginia for an unpublished book-length collection of poetry. Closes in December.

ASSOCIATION OF JEWISH LIBRARIES—15 Goldsmith St., Providence, RI 02906. Address Lillian Schwartz, Secretary. Conducts Sydney Taylor Manuscript competition for best fiction manuscript for readers age 8 to 12. Prize is $1,000. Closes in December.

BEVERLY HILLS THEATRE GUILD—JULIE HARRIS PLAYWRIGHT AWARD—2815 N. Beachwood Dr., Los Angeles, CA 90068. Address Marcella Meharg. Offers prize of $5,000, plus $2,000 for production in Los Angeles area, for a previously unproduced and unpublished full-length play. Closes in November.

THE CHICAGO TRIBUNE—435 N. Michigan Ave., Chicago, IL 60611. Sponsors Nelson Algren Awards for Short Fiction, with a first prize of $5,000 and three runners-up prizes of $1,000 for outstanding unpublished short stories of 10,000 words or less, by American writers. Closes in February.

COURT THEATRE—The University of Chicago, 5706 S. University Ave., Chicago, IL 60637. Offers Sergel Drama Prize: $1,500 for full-length unpublished and unproduced play. Closes in June of odd-numbered years.

EUGENE V. DEBS FOUNDATION—Dept. of History, Indiana State University, Terre Haute, IN 47809. Offers Bryant Spann Memorial Prize of $750 for published or unpublished article or essay on themes relating to social protest or human equality. Closes in April.

DELACORTE PRESS—Dept. BFYR, 1 Dag Hammarskjold Plaza, New York, NY 10017. Sponsors Delacorte Press Prize for an outstanding first young adult novel. The prize consists of one Delacorte hardcover and Dell paperback contract, an advance of $4,000 on royalties, and a $1,000 cash prize. Closes in December.

761

FOREST A. ROBERTS-SHIRAS INSTITUTE—Forest Roberts Theatre, Northern Michigan Univ., Marquette, MI 49855. Dr. James A. Panowski, Dir. Conducts annual Playwriting Competition, with prize of $1,000, plus production, for an original, full-length, previously unproduced and unpublished play. Closes in November.

THE FOUNDATION OF THE DRAMATISTS GUILD—234 W. 44th St., New York, NY 10036. Sponsors Young Playwrights Festival. Playwrights under 19 years of age may submit scripts; winning plays will be given full stage productions or staged readings. Closes in October.

FULCRUM, INC.—350 Indiana St., Ste. 510, Golden, CO 80401. Offers Fulcrum American Writing Award for a book of nonfiction or fiction by an American writer on environmental, resource, and social issues. The prize is $2,500, plus publication. Closes in November.

HIGHLIGHTS FOR CHILDREN—803 Church St., Honesdale, PA 18431. Conducts Contest for Juvenile Fiction, with cash prizes and publication for short stories. Closes in March.

HONOLULU MAGAZINE—36 Merchant St., Honolulu, HI 96813. Sponsors an annual fiction contest, with a cash prize of $500, plus publication in *Honolulu*, for an unpublished short story with a Hawaiian theme, setting, and/or characters. Closes in September.

HOUGHTON MIFFLIN COMPANY—2 Park St., Boston, MA 02108. Offers Literary Fellowship for fiction or nonfiction project of exceptional literary merit written by American author. Work under consideration must be unpublished and in English. Fellowship consists of $10,000, of which $2,500 is an outright grant and $7,500 is an advance on royalties. There is no deadline.

HUMBOLDT STATE UNIVERSITY—English Dept., Arcata, CA 95521. Sponsors the Raymond Carver Short Story Contest, with a prize of $250, plus publication in the literary journal *Toyon*, for an unpublished short story by a writer living in the U.S. Closes in December.

ILLINOIS STATE UNIVERSITY—Dept. of Theatre, Illinois State Univ., Normal, IL 61761. Address John W. Kirk. Sponsors Fine Arts Competition, with prize of $1,000, plus production, for previously unpublished and unproduced full-length play. Closes in October.

INDIANA UNIVERSITY—PURDUE UNIVERSITY AT INDIANAPOLIS—IUPUI Univ. Theatre, 525 N. Blackford St., Indianapolis, IN 46202. Conducts National Children's Theatre Playwriting Competition, with a prize of $2,000 for an original, previously unproduced one-act children's play. Closes in November.

INTERNATIONAL SOCIETY OF DRAMATISTS—Fulfillment Center, Box 3470, Ft. Pierce, FL 33448. Sponsors Adriatic Award: a prize of $10,000 for a full-length play. Closes in November.

JACKSONVILLE UNIVERSITY—Annual Playwriting Contest, Dept. of Theatre Arts, College of Fine Arts, Jacksonville Univ., Jacksonville, FL 32211. Davis Sikes, Dir. Conducts playwriting contest, with prize of $1,000 and production, for original, previously unproduced script (full-length or one-act). Closes in January.

JEWISH COMMUNITY CENTER THEATRE—3505 Mayfield Rd., Cleveland Heights, OH 44118. Dorothy Silver, Dir. of Cultural Arts. Offers cash award of $1,000 and a staged reading for an original, previously unproduced full-length play on some aspect of the Jewish experience. Closes in December.

CHESTER H. JONES FOUNDATION—P.O. Box 43033, Cleveland, OH 44143. Conducts the National Poetry Competition, with more than $1,800 in cash prizes (including a first prize of $1,000) for original, unpublished poems. Closes in March.

LAMB'S PLAYERS THEATRE—P.O. Box 1315, National City, CA 92050. Offers Fieldstead New Plays Award, consisting of a $5,000 prize, plus production, and a two-week residency, for a full-length play by an American. Closes in August.

LINCOLN COLLEGE—Lincoln, IL 62656. Address Janet Overton. Offers Billee Murray Denny Poetry Award for original poem by poet who has not previously published a volume of poetry. First prize of $1,000, 2nd prize of $450, and 3rd prize of $200 are offered. Closes in May.

MADEMOISELLE MAGAZINE—350 Madison Ave., New York, NY 10017. Sponsors Fiction Writers Contest, with first prize of $1,000, plus publication, and second prize of $500, for short fiction. Closes in March.

MS. MAGAZINE—119 W. 40th St., New York, NY 10018. Sponsors annual Fiction Contest for short story. Prize is publication and electronic typewriter. Closes in August.

MSS PRESS—SUNY Binghamton, Binghamton, NY 13901. Sponsors MSS/Gardner Poetry Award for an unpublished book-length manuscript of poetry. A prize of $1,000, plus publication, is offered. Closes in October.

NATIONAL ENDOWMENT FOR THE ARTS—Washington, DC 20506. Address Director, Literature Program. The National Endowment for the Arts offers fellowships to writers of poetry, fiction, scripts, and other creative prose. Deadlines vary; write for guidelines.

NATIONAL PLAY AWARD—P.O. Box 71011, Los Angeles, CA 90071. National Play Award consists of a $7,500 cash prize, plus $5,000 for production, for an original, previously unproduced play. Sponsored by National Repertory Theatre Foundation. Closes in October of odd-numbered years.

NATIONAL POETRY SERIES—18 W. 30th St., New York, NY 10001. Sponsors Annual Open Competition for unpublished, book-length poetry manuscript. The prize is publication. Closes in February.

THE NEW ENGLAND THEATRE CONFERENCE—50 Exchange St., Waltham, MA 02154. First prize of $500 and second prize of $250 are offered for unpublished and unproduced one-act plays in the John Gassner Memorial Playwriting Award Competition. Closes in June.

NEW VOICES—551 Tremont St., Boston, MA 02116. Conducts Clauder Competition for a full-length play by a New England writer. The prize is $3,000 and workshop production. Closes in June.

NORTHEASTERN UNIVERSITY PRESS—English Dept., 406 Holmes, Northeastern University, Boston, MA 02115. Guy Rotella, Chairman. Offers Samuel French Morse Poetry Prize—publication of a full-length poetry manuscript—by a U.S. poet who has published no more than one book of poems. Closes in September.

O'NEILL THEATER CENTER—234 W. 44th St., Suite 901, New York, NY 10036. Offers stipends, staged readings, and room and board at the National Playwrights Conference, for new stage and television plays. Closes in December.

THE PARIS REVIEW—541 E. 72nd St., New York, NY 10021. Sponsors Aga Khan Prize for Fiction: $1,000, plus publication, for previously unpublished short story. Closes in June. Offers Bernard F. Connors Prize: $1,000, plus publication, for previously unpublished poem. Closes in May. Offers John Train Humor Prize: $1,500, plus publication, for unpublished work of humorous fiction, nonfiction, or poetry. Closes in March.

PEN AMERICAN CENTER—568 Broadway, New York, NY 10012. Sponsors PEN/Nelson Algren Award: stipend of $1,000, plus one-month residency at Edward Albee Foundation's summer residence on Long Island, for uncompleted novel or collection of short stories by an American writer who needs assistance to complete the work. Closes in November. Sponsors Renato Poggioli Translation Award: $3,000 grant for a translator working on his or her first book-length translation from Italian into English. Closes in February.

PLAYBOY MAGAZINE—919 N. Michigan Ave., Chicago, IL 60611. Sponsors college fiction contest, with first prize of $3,000 and publication in *Playboy,* for a short story by a college student. Closes in January.

POETRY SOCIETY OF AMERICA—15 Gramercy Park, New York, NY 10003. Conducts annual contests—The Celia B. Wagner Memorial Award, the John Masefield Memorial Award, and the Elias Lieberman Student Poetry Award—in which cash prizes are offered for unpublished poems. Contests close in December.

RADIO DRAMA AWARDS—3319 W. Beltline Hwy., Madison, WI 53713. Norman Michie, Exec. Producer. Wisconsin Public Radio conducts annual Radio Drama Awards competition for original scripts by writers in Illinois, Iowa, Michigan, Minnesota, and Wisconsin. Prizes for thirty-minute radio scripts are professional production and cash awards of $500 (first prize), $300 (second), and $200 (third). Closes in January.

REDBOOK MAGAZINE—224 W. 57th St., New York, NY 10019. Conducts Short Story Contest for original fiction. First prize is $1,000, plus publication. Second prize of $500 and third prize of $300 are also offered. Closes in May.

SAN JOSE STATE UNIVERSITY—One Washington Square, San Jose, CA 95192. Address Dr. Howard Burman, Theatre Arts Dept. Sponsors Harold C. Crain Playwriting Contest, with a prize of $500, plus production, for a previously unproduced full-length play. Closes in November.

SEVENTEEN—850 Third Ave., New York, NY 10022. Conducts *Seventeen*/Dell Fiction Contest for original unpublished fiction by writers aged 13 to 20. A first prize of $2,000, second prize of $1,200, and third prize of $700 will be awarded. Winning entries will be considered for publication in *Seventeen* and future publications of Dell Publishing. Closes in January.

SIERRA REPERTORY THEATRE—P.O. Box 3030, Sonora, CA 95370. Offers Cummings/Taylor Award of $350, plus production, for original, previously unpublished, unproduced full-length play or musical. Closes in May.

SUNSET CENTER—P.O. Box 5066, Carmel, CA 93921. Richard Tyler, Director. Offers prize of up to $2,000 for an original, unproduced full-length play in its annual festival of Firsts Playwriting Competition. Closes in August.

SYRACUSE UNIVERSITY PRESS—1600 Jamesville Ave., Syracuse, NY 13210. Address Director. Sponsors John Ben Snow Prize: $1,500, plus publication, for unpublished book-length manuscript about New York State, especially upstate or central New York. Closes in December.

THEATRE MEMPHIS—630 Perkins Extended, Memphis, TN 38117. Conducts New Play Competition for a full-length play or related one-acts. The prize is $3,000 and production. Closes in September.

UNICORN THEATRE—3514 Jefferson, Kansas City, MO 64111. Sponsors National Playwright Competition, with a first prize of $1,000, plus travel and residency while in production, for an original, unpublished and unproduced full-length play. Closes in May.

U.S. NAVAL INSTITUTE—Annapolis, MD 21402. Address Membership Department. Conducts Arleigh Burke Essay Contest, with prizes of $2,000, $1,000, and $750, plus publication, for essays on the advancement of professional, literary, and scientific knowledge in the naval and maritime services, and the advancement of the knowledge of sea power. Closes in December.

UNIVERSITY OF ALABAMA AT BIRMINGHAM—Dept. of Theatre and Dance, University Sta., Birmingham, AL 35294. Rick J. Plummer, Director. Conducts Ruby Lloyd Apsey Playwriting Competition, with $500 cash prize, plus production and travel expenses, for previously unproduced full-length play. Closes in January.

UNIVERSITY OF GEORGIA PRESS—Athens, GA 30602. Offers Flannery O'Connor Award for Short Fiction: a prize of $500, plus publication, for a book-length collection of short fiction. Closes in July.

UNIVERSITY OF HAWAII—Kennedy Theatre, Univ. of Hawaii, 1770 East-West Rd., Honolulu, HI 96822. Conducts annual Kumu Kahua Playwriting Contest with cash prizes for original plays dealing with some aspect of Hawaiian experience. Close in January.

UNIVERSITY OF HAWAII PRESS—2840 Kolowalu St., Honolulu, HI 96822. Sponsors Pacific Poetry Series competition, with prize of publication and royalty contract, for unpublished book-length poetry manuscript by a writer who has not previously published a volume of poetry. Closes in March of odd-numbered years.

UNIVERSITY OF IOWA—Iowa School of Letters Award, Dept. of English, English-Philosophy Bldg., Univ. of Iowa, Iowa City, IA 52242. Offers Iowa School of Letters Award—$1,000, plus publication—for a book-length collection of short stories by writer who has not yet had a book published. Closes in September.

UNIVERSITY OF MASSACHUSETTS PRESS—Juniper Prize, Univ. of Massachusetts Press, % Mail Rm., Amherst, MA 01003. Offers Juniper Prize of $1,000, plus publication, for book-length manuscript of poetry. Closes in October.

UNIVERSITY OF PITTSBURGH PRESS—Pittsburgh, PA 15260. Sponsors Drue Heinz Literature Prize—$5,000, plus publication and royalty contract—for unpublished collection of short stories. Closes in August. Also sponsors Agnes Lynch Starrett Poetry Prize—$1,000, plus publication and royalty contract—for book-length collection of poems by poet who has not yet published a volume of poetry. Closes in April.

UNIVERSITY OF WISCONSIN-PARKSIDE—Fine Arts Division, Univ. of Wisconsin-Parkside, Box 2000, Kenosha, WI 53141. Address Judith Tucker Snider. Offers award of $1,000, plus production, for an unpublished, unproduced, full-length original play or musical. Closes in December.

UNIVERSITY OF WISCONSIN PRESS—Poetry Series, 114 N. Murray

St., Madison, WI 53715. Ronald Wallace, Admin. Offers Brittingham Prize in Poetry: $500 plus publication, for unpublished book-length poetry manuscript. Closes in September.

WALT WHITMAN CENTER FOR THE ARTS AND HUMANITIES—2nd and Cooper Sts., Camden, NJ 08102. Sponsors the annual Camden Poetry Award: $1,000, plus publication, for an unpublished book-length collection of poetry. Closes in November.

WORD WORKS—P.O. Box 42164, Washington, DC 20015. Offers the Washington Prize of $1,000 for unpublished poem by American poet. Closes in November.

YALE UNIVERSITY PRESS—Box 92A, Yale Sta., New Haven, CT 06520. Address Editor, Yale Series of Younger Poets. Conducts Yale Series of Younger Poets Competition, in which the prize is publication of a book-length manuscript of poetry, written by a poet under 40 who has not previously published a volume of poems. Closes in February.

WRITERS COLONIES

A writers colony offers isolation and freedom from everyday distractions to writers who want a quiet place to concentrate on their work. Though some colonies are quite small, with space for just three or four writers at a time, others can provide accommodations for as many as thirty or forty. The length of a residency may vary, too—from a couple of weeks to five or six months. These programs have strict admissions policies, and writers must submit a formal application or letter of intent, a resume, writing samples, and letters of recommendation. Write for application information first, enclosing a stamped, self-addressed envelope (SASE).

CENTRUM FOUNDATION—The Centrum Foundation sponsors residencies of two to three months at Fort Worden State Park, a Victorian fort on the Strait of Juan De Fuca in Washington. Nonfiction, fiction, and poetry writers may apply for residency awards, which include stipend of $600 a month. Application deadline is in early December; send letter explaining the project, short biographical note, and sample of published work. For details, send SASE in fall, to Carol Jane Bangs, Director of Literature Programs, Centrum Foundation, Fort Worden State Park, P.O. Box 1158, Port Townsend, WA 98368.

CUMMINGTON COMMUNITY OF THE ARTS—Residencies of one month or more in the Berkshires. Quarterly deadlines. For more information, send SASE to Cummington Community of the Arts, Cummington, MA 01026.

DORLAND MOUNTAIN COLONY—Novelists, playwrights, and poets may apply for residencies at the Dorland Preserve of the Nature Conservancy in the Palomar Mountains of Southern California. Cottages, firewood, and kerosene are provided. Application deadlines are March 1 and September 1. For further information and application forms, send SASE to Resident Director, Dorland Mountain Colony, P.O. Box 6, Temecula, CA 92390.

DORSET COLONY HOUSE—Writers and playwrights are offered low-cost room with kitchen facilities at the Colony House in Dorset, Vermont. Periods of residency are 3 to 6 weeks, and are available between October 1 and June 1. Application deadlines are September 15, December 15, and February 15 for the periods immediately following the deadlines. For more information, send SASE to John Nassivera, Director, Dorset Colony House, Dorset, VT 05201.

FINE ARTS WORK CENTER IN PROVINCETOWN—Fellowships including living and studio space and monthly stipends at the Fine Arts Work Center on Cape Cod, for writers to work independently. Residencies are for seven months only; apply before the February 1 deadline. For details, send SASE to Jim Potter, Dir., Fine Arts Work Center, P.O. Box 565, 24 Pearl St., Provincetown, MA 02657.

THE HAMBIDGE CENTER—Two-week to two-month residencies are offered to writers at the Hambidge Center in the Northeast Georgia mountains. Send SASE for application form to Director, Residency Program, The Hambidge Center, P.O. Box 33, Rabun Gap, GA 30568.

THE MACDOWELL COLONY—Studios, room and board at the MacDowell Colony of Peterborough, New Hampshire, for writers to work without interruption in semi-rural woodland setting. Selection is competitive. Apply at least six months in advance of season desired; residencies average 5 to 6 weeks. For details and admission forms, send SASE to Admissions Coordinator, The MacDowell Colony, 100 High St., Peterborough, NH 03458.

THE MILLAY COLONY FOR THE ARTS—At Steepletop in Austerlitz, New York—former home of Edna St. Vincent Millay—studios, living quarters, and meals are provided to writers at no cost. Residencies are for one month. Application deadlines are February 1, May 1, and September 1. To apply, send SASE to The Millay Colony for the Arts, Inc., Steepletop, Austerlitz, NY 12017.

MONTALVO CENTER FOR THE ARTS—Three-month, low-cost residencies at the Villa Montalvo in the foothills of the Santa Cruz Mountains south of San Francisco, for writers working on specific projects. There are a few small fellowships available to writers with demonstrable financial need. Send self-addressed envelope and 39¢ stamp for application forms to Montalvo Residency Program, P.O. Box 158, Saratoga, CA 95070.

UCROSS FOUNDATION—Residencies, two weeks to four months, at the Ucross Foundation in the foothills of the Big Horn Mountains in Wyoming, for writers to concentrate on their work without interruptions. Residencies are available from August through May. The application deadline is October 1; for more information, send SASE to Director, Residency Program, Ucross Foundation, Ucross Route, Box 19, Clearmont, WY 82835.

VIRGINIA CENTER FOR THE CREATIVE ARTS—Residencies of one to three months at the Mt. San Angelo Estate in Sweet Briar, Virginia, for writers to work without distraction. Apply at least three months in advance. A limited amount of financial assistance is available. For more information, send SASE to William Smart, Director, Virginia Center for the Creative Arts, Sweet Briar, VA 24595.

HELENE WURLITZER FOUNDATION OF NEW MEXICO—Rent-free and utility-free studios at the Helene Wurlitzer Foundation in Taos, New Mexico, are offered to creative writers and other artists. Length of residency varies from three to six months. The Foundation is closed from October 1 through March 31 annually. For details, send SASE to Henry A. Sauerwein, Jr.,

Exec. Dir., The Helene Wurlitzer Foundation of New Mexico, Box 545, Taos, NM 87571.

YADDO—Artists, writers, and composers are invited for short-term residencies at the Yaddo estate in Saratoga Springs, New York. Although there is no fixed charge, voluntary contributions are encouraged. Requests for applications should be sent with SASE before January 15 or August 1 to Curtis Harnack, Exec. Director, Yaddo, Box 395, Saratoga Springs, NY 12866. An application fee of $10.00 is required.

WRITERS CONFERENCES

Each year, hundreds of writers conferences are held across the country. The following list, arranged geographically, represents a sampling of conferences; each listing includes the location of the conference, the month during which it is usually held, and the name of the person from whom specific information can be received. Additional conferences are listed annually in the May issue of *The Writer* Magazine.

ARKANSAS

ARKANSAS WRITERS' CONFERENCE—North Little Rock, AR. June. Write Clovita Rice, 1115 Gillette Dr., Little Rock, AR 72207.

CALIFORNIA

ANNUAL WRITERS CONFERENCE IN CHILDREN'S LITERATURE—Los Angeles, CA. August. Write Lin Oliver, Dir., SCBW, PO Box 296, Mar Vista Station, Los Angeles, CA 90066.

CABRILLO SUSPENSE WRITERS CONFERENCE—Mills College, Oakland, CA. July. Write Dr. Timothy Welch, Dir., PO Box 851, Aptos, CA 95001.

SQUAW VALLEY COMMUNITY OF WRITERS—Olympic Valley, CA. August. Write Carolyn Doty, PO Box 2352, Olympic Valley, CA 95730.

STANFORD PUBLISHING COURSE—Stanford, CA. July. Write Dir., Alumni Assoc., Bowman House, Stanford Univ., Stanford, CA 94305.

COLORADO

ASPEN WRITERS CONFERENCE—Aspen, CO. August. Write Dir., Box 7726 D, Aspen, CO 81612.

CONNECTICUT

WESLEYAN WRITERS CONFERENCE—Middletown, CT. July. Write Anne Greene, Wesleyan Writers Conference, Wesleyan Univ., Middletown, CT 06457.

DEAF PLAYWRIGHT CONFERENCE—Chester, CT. June. Write Shanny Mow, Dir., National Theatre of the Deaf, Chester, CT 06412.

FLORIDA

FLORIDA SUNCOAST WRITERS' CONFERENCE—St. Petersburg, FL. January. Write Writers' Conference, Univ. of Southern Florida/St. Petersburg, 830 First St., South, St. Petersburg, FL 33701.

GEORGIA

DIXIE COUNCIL OF AUTHORS AND JOURNALISTS INC.—St. Simonds Island, GA. June. Dr. James C. Bryant, Dir. Write Leara Rhodes, 1041 Latham Rd., Decatur, GA 30033.

ILLINOIS

INTERNATIONAL BLACK WRITERS—Chicago, IL. June. Write Mable J. Terrell, PO Box 1030, Chicago, IL 60617.

ILLINOIS WESLEYAN UNIVERSITY WRITERS' CONFERENCE—Bloomington, IL. July–August. Write Illinois Wesleyan Univ. Writers' Conference, Illinois Wesleyan Univ., PO Box 2900, Bloomington, IL 61702.

MISSISSIPPI VALLEY WRITERS CONFERENCE—Augustana College, Rock Island, IL. June. Write David R. Collins, 3403 45th St., Moline, IL 61265.

ANNUAL CHRISTIAN WRITERS INSTITUTE CONFERENCE AND WORKSHOPS—Wheaton College, Wheaton, IL. June. Write June Eaton, Dir., CWI, 396 E. St. Charles Rd., Wheaton, IL 60188.

INDIANA

OHIO RIVER WRITERS' CONFERENCE—Evansville, IN. October. Write Carol D. Gottliebsen, Program Coord., Evansville Arts & Education Council, 16½ SE Second St., Suite 210, Evansville, IN 47708.

INDIANA UNIVERSITY WRITERS' CONFERENCE—Bloomington, IN. June. Write Sharon Shaloo, Ballantine Hall 464, Indiana Univ., Bloomington, IN 47405.

KENTUCKY

JESSE STUART WRITERS WORKSHOP—Murray State Univ., KY. June. Write Kent Forrester, English Dept., Murray State Univ., Murray, KY 42071.

ANNUAL APPALACHIAN WRITERS WORKSHOP—Hindman, KY. August. Write Mike Mullins, Box 844, Settlement School, Hindman, KY 41822.

WRITING WORKSHOP FOR PEOPLE OVER 57—Lexington, KY. August. Write Roberta H. James, Council on Aging, Ligon House, Univ. of Kentucky, Lexington, KY 40506-0442.

CREATIVE WRITING CONFERENCE—Richmond, KY. June. Write William Sutton, Dept. of English, Eastern Kentucky Univ., Richmond, KY 40475.

LOUISIANA

ANNUAL LOUISIANA WRITERS CONFERENCE—Centenary College, Shreveport, LA. June. Write Dr. David Jackson, Co-Dir., PO Box 4633, Shreveport, LA 71134-0633.

MAINE

STONECOAST WRITERS' CONFERENCE—Univ. of Southern Maine, Gorham, ME. July. Write Kenneth Rosen, English Dept., USM, Portland, ME 04038.

MAINE WRITERS WORKSHOP—Oceanville, ME. July and August. Write George F. Bush, Dir., PO Box 905W, Stonington, ME 04681.

STATE OF MAINE WRITERS CONFERENCE—Ocean Park (Old Orchard Beach), ME. August. Write Richard F. Burns, Box 296, Ocean Park, ME 04063.

MARYLAND

THE JOHNS HOPKINS UNIVERSITY SUMMER WRITERS' CONFERENCE—Baltimore, MD. June. Write Summer Writers' Conference, The Johns Hopkins Univ., School of Continuing Studies, 102 Macaulay Hall, Baltimore, MD 21218.

MASSACHUSETTS

HARVARD SUMMER WRITING PROGRAM—Cambridge, MA. June–August. Write Harvard Summer School, 20 Garden Street, Dept. 274, Cambridge, MA 02138.

EASTERN WRITERS' CONFERENCE—Salem, MA. June. Write Claire Keyes, English Dept., Salem State College, Salem, MA 01970.

CAPE COD WRITERS' CONFERENCE—Craigville, MA. August. Write Marion Vuilleumier, Box 111, West Hyannisport, MA 02672.

NEW ENGLAND WRITERS' WORKSHOP AT SIMMONS COLLEGE—Boston, MA. July. Write Theodore Vrettos, Dir., Simmons College, 300 The Fenway, Boston, MA 02115.

MICHIGAN

CLARION SCIENCE FICTION AND FANTASY WRITERS' WORKSHOP—East Lansing, MI. June–August. Write David Wright, E-35 Holmes Hall, Lyman Briggs School, MSU, E. Lansing, MI 48854.

ANNUAL BAY DE NOC WRITERS' CONFERENCE—Escanaba, MI. June. Write Larry Leffel, Bay de Noc Community College, Escanaba, MI 49829.

MINNESOTA

MISSISSIPPI RIVER CREATIVE WRITING WORKSHOP IN POETRY AND FICTION—St. Cloud, MN. June. Write Bill Meissner, St. Cloud State Univ., Dept. of English, St. Cloud, MN 56301.

DECISION MAGAZINE'S SCHOOL OF CHRISTIAN WRITING—Roseville, MN. August. Write Lori J.P. Sorensen, Dir., Box 779, Minneapolis, MN 55440.

ANNUAL UPPER MIDWEST WRITERS' CONFERENCE—Bemidji, MN. July. Write Dr. William D. Elliott, Box 48, Hagg-Sauer Hall, Bemidji State Univ., Bemidji, MN 56601.

Missouri

AVILA COLLEGE WRITERS CONFERENCE—Kansas City, MO. August. Write Marcy Caldwell, Dept. of Cont. Ed., Avila College, 11901 Wornall Rd., Kansas City, MO 64145.

New Hampshire

ANNUAL SEACOAST WRITERS CONFERENCE—Portsmouth, NH. September. Write Alice Currie, Box 704, Kennebunkport, ME 04046.

MILDRED I. REID WRITERS CONFERENCE—Contoocook, NH. July–August. Write Mildred I. Reid, Writers Colony, Penacook Rd., Contoocook, NH 03229.

New York

WRITERS WORKSHOP—Univ. of Rochester, NY. July. Write Anne Ludlow, Writers Workshop, 127 Lattimore Hall, Univ. of Rochester, Rochester, NY 14627.

SOUTHAMPTON WRITERS' CONFERENCE—Southampton, NY. July. Write William Roberson, Library, Southampton Campus/LIU, Southampton, NY 11968.

THE TECHNICAL WRITERS INSTITUTE—Troy, NY. June. Write Dr. C. Lee Odell, Sage Bldg., Office of Cont. Studies, RPI, Troy, NY 12180-3590.

CORNELL UNIVERSITY WRITERS PROGRAM—Ithaca, NY. June–August. Write Dean Charles W. Jermy, Jr., Dir., B12L Ives Hall, Cornell Univ., Ithaca, NY 14853.

HOFSTRA UNIVERSITY'S ANNUAL WRITERS' CONFERENCE—Hempstead, NY. July. Write Dr. James J. Kolb, Dir., 017 Weller Hall, Hofstra Univ., Hempstead, NY 11550.

VASSAR INSTITUTE OF PUBLISHING AND WRITING: CHILDREN'S BOOKS IN THE MARKETPLACE—Poughkeepsie, NY. June. Write Publishing Institute, Box 300, Vassar College, Poughkeepsie, NY 12601.

IWWG WOMEN'S WRITING CONFERENCE—Skidmore Coll., Saratoga Springs, NY. July. Write Hannelore Hahn, Exec. Dir., International Women's Writing Guild, PO Box 810, Gracie Station, New York, NY 10028.

North Carolina

DUKE UNIVERSITY WRITERS' CONFERENCE—Durham, NC. June. Write Joe Porter, Office of Cont. Ed., The Bishop's House, Duke University, Durham, NC 27708.

BLUE RIDGE CHRISTIAN WRITERS CONFERENCE—Black Mountain, NC. July–August. Write Yvonne Lehman, PO Box 188, Black Mountain, NC 28711.

Ohio

ANNUAL QUEEN CITY WRITERS' SEMINAR—Cincinnati, OH. May. Write Juanita K. Pence, Pres., Queen City Writers, 8413 Flamingo Ln., Cincinnati, OH 45239.

ANTIOCH WRITERS WORKSHOP—Yellow Springs, OH. July. Write Antioch Writers Workshop, Antioch Univ., Yellow Springs, OH 45387.

Oklahoma

ANNUAL WRITERS OF CHILDREN'S LITERATURE CONFERENCE—Lawton, OK. June 7. Write Dr. George E. Stanley, PO Box 16355, Cameron Univ. Station, Lawton, OK 73505.

Oregon

HAYSTACK PROGRAM IN THE ARTS—Cannon Beach, OR. June–August. Write Steve Reischman, PO Box 1491, Portland State Univ., Portland, OR 97207.

Pennsylvania

ST. DAVIDS CHRISTIAN WRITERS—St. Davids, PA. June. Write Shirley Eaby, Registrar, 1775 Eden Rd., Box W, Lancaster, PA 17601.

ANNUAL OUTDOOR WRITERS ASSOCIATION OF AMERICA CONFERENCE—Harrisburg, PA. June. Write Sylvia G. Bashline, 2017 Cato Ave., Suite 101, State College, PA 16801. For members only.

ANNUAL PHILADELPHIA WRITERS' CONFERENCE—Philadelphia, PA. June. Send SASE to H. Patricia Brown, Registrar-W, PO Box 392, Drexel Hill, PA 19026.

Tennessee

CHRISTIAN WRITERS' GRAND OLE WORKSHOP—Nashville, TN. June. Write Dr. John Warren Steen, 6511 Currywood Dr., Nashville, TN 37205.

Texas

SOUTHWEST WRITER'S CONFERENCE—Houston, TX. July. Write Patricia Robinson, Coordinator, Univ. of Houston, Cont. Ed., 4800 Calhoun Rd., Houston, TX 77004.

Vermont

BENNINGTON WRITING WORKSHOPS—Bennington, VT. June–July. Write Dir., Box H, Bennington College, Bennington, VT 05201.

BREAD LOAF WRITERS' CONFERENCE—Middlebury, VT. August. Write Mrs. Carol Knauss, Bread Loaf Writers' Conference, Middlebury College–TW, Middlebury, VT 05753.

Virginia

ANNUAL HIGHLAND SUMMER CONFERENCE—Radford, VA. June. Write Dr. Grace Toney Edwards, Box 5917, Radford Univ., Radford, VA 24142.

772

WASHINGTON

PACIFIC NORTHWEST WRITERS' CONFERENCE—Tacoma, WA. July. Write Gladys Johnson, Exec. Secretary, PNWC, 1811 NE 199th, Seattle, WA 98155.

PORT TOWNSEND WRITERS' CONFERENCE—Port Townsend, WA. July. Write Carol Jane Bangs, CENTRUM, PO Box 1158, Port Townsend, WA 98368.

SEATTLE PACIFIC CHRISTIAN WRITERS' CONFERENCE—Seattle, WA. June. Write Rose Reynoldson, Humanities Dept., Seattle Pacific Univ., Seattle, WA 98119.

WISCONSIN

SCHOOL OF ARTS AT RHINELANDER—Rhinelander, WI. July. Write Genevieve Lewis, Admin. Coord., School of Arts at Rhinelander, 610 Langdon Street, Rm. 722, Madison, WI 53703.

MIDWEST WRITERS' CONFERENCE—River Falls, WI. June. Write Michael Norman, Dir., Midwest Writers' Conference, Univ. of Wisconsin-River Falls, River Falls, WI 54022.

WYOMING

WYOMING WRITERS' ANNUAL CONFERENCE—Douglas, WY. June. Write Lee Ann Siebken, Conference Chairman, PO Box 155, Douglas, WY 82633.

CANADA

MARITIME WRITERS' WORKSHOP—Fredericton, NB. July. Write Sheetagh Russell-Brown, % Dept. of Extension and Summer Session, University of New Brunswick, Box 4400, Fredericton, NB E3B 5A3.

SASKATCHEWAN SCHOOL OF THE ARTS—Ft. Sam, Sask. June–August. Write Ann Hewat, Dir., 2550 Broad St., Regina, Sask. S4P 3V7.

INTERNATIONAL

SUMMER WRITING WORKSHOP—Dublin, Ireland. July. Write James McAuley, English Dept., Mail Stop 25, Eastern Washington Univ., Cheney, WA 99004.

WRITERS WORKSHOP IN LONDON—London, England. July. Write Suzanne Robblee, College of Arts and Sciences, Northeastern Univ., Boston, MA 02115.

SCREENPLAY WRITING IN LONDON—London, England. July. Write Lynne Kaufman, Public Information Office, UC Extension, 2223 Fulton St., Berkeley, CA 94720.

ANNUAL WRITERS' SUMMER SCHOOL—Derbyshire, England. August. Write Philippa Boland, The Red House, Mardens Hill, Crowborough, Sussex, TN6 1XN, England.

STATE ARTS COUNCILS

State Arts Councils sponsor grants, fellowships, and other programs for writers. To be eligible for funding, a writer *must* be a resident of the state in which he is applying. For more information, write to the addresses listed below.

ALABAMA STATE COUNCIL ON THE ARTS AND HUMANITIES
Albert B. Head, Exec. Director
323 Adams Ave.
Montgomery, AL 36130

ALASKA STATE COUNCIL ON THE ARTS
Christine D'Arcy, Director
619 Warehouse Ave., Suite 220
Anchorage, AK 99501

ARIZONA COMMISSION ON THE ARTS
Shelley Cohn, Executive Director
417 W. Roosevelt
Phoenix, AZ 85003

OFFICE OF ARKANSAS STATE ARTS AND HUMANITIES
Amy Aspell, Executive Director
The Heritage Center, Suite 200
225 E. Markham
Little Rock, AR 72201

CALIFORNIA ARTS COUNCIL
JoAnn Anglin, Public Information Officer
1901 Broadway, Suite A
Sacramento, CA 95818-2492

COLORADO COUNCIL ON THE ARTS AND HUMANITIES
T. Ellen Sollod, Executive Director
770 Pennsylvania St.
Denver, CO 80203

CONNECTICUT COMMISSION ON THE ARTS
John Ostrout, Deputy Director
190 Trumbull St.
Hartford, CT 06103

DELAWARE STATE ARTS COUNCIL
Cecelia Fitzgibbon, Administrator
Carvel State Building
820 N. French St.
Wilmington, DE 19801

FLORIDA ARTS COUNCIL
Chris Doolin
Dept. of State
Div. of Cultural Affairs
The Capitol
Tallahassee, FL 32399-0250

GEORGIA COUNCIL FOR THE ARTS
2082 E. Exchange Place, Suite 100
Tucker, GA 30084

774

HAWAII STATE FOUNDATION ON CULTURE AND THE ARTS
Sarah M. Richards, Executive Director
335 Merchant St., Rm. 202
Honolulu, HI 96813

IDAHO COMMISSION ON THE ARTS
304 W. State St.
Boise, ID 83720

ILLINOIS ARTS COUNCIL
Bill Seeback, Director, Performing & Communication Arts Programs
State of Illinois Center
100 W. Randolph, Suite 10-500
Chicago, IL 60601

INDIANA ARTS COMMISSION
Geoff Gephart, Program Specialist, Literature
32 E. Washington St., 6th Fl.
Indianapolis, IN 46204

IOWA STATE ARTS COUNCIL
Marilyn Parks, Technical Assistance/Grants Officer
State Capitol Complex
Des Moines, IA 50319

KANSAS ARTS COMMISSION
John Austin Carey, Executive Director
700 Jackson, Suite 1004
Topeka, KS 66603-3714

KENTUCKY ARTS COUNCIL
Roger L. Paige, Director
Berry Hill, Louisville Rd.
Frankfort, KY 40601

LOUISIANA COUNCIL FOR MUSIC AND PERFORMING ARTS, INC.
Literature Program Associate
7524 St. Charles Ave.
New Orleans, LA 70118

MAINE ARTS COMMISSION
Stuart Kestenbaum
State House, Station 25
Augusta, ME 04330

MARYLAND STATE ARTS COUNCIL
Linda Vlasak, Program Director
Artists-in-Education and Poets-in-the-Schools
15 W. Mulberry St.
Baltimore, MD 21201

MASSACHUSETTS COUNCIL ON THE ARTS AND HUMANITIES
Pat Dixon, Literature Program Director
80 Boylston St., 10th Fl.
Boston, MA 02116

MICHIGAN COUNCIL FOR THE ARTS
Barbara K. Goldman, Executive Director
1200 Sixth Ave.
Detroit, MI 48226

COMPAS: WRITERS IN THE SCHOOLS
Molly LaBerge, Executive Director
Randy Jennings, Program Director
308 Landmark Center
75 W. 5th St.
St. Paul, MN 55102

MINNESOTA STATE ARTS BOARD
Karen Mueller
Artist Assistance Program Associate
432 Summit Ave.
St. Paul, MN 55102

MISSISSIPPI ARTS COMMISSION
Marian Bordeaux, Program Administrator
301 N. Lamar St., Suite 400
Jackson, MS 39201

MISSOURI ARTS COUNCIL
Teresa Goettsch, Program Administrator for Literature
Wainwright Office Complex
111 N. 7th St., Suite 105
St. Louis, MO 63101

MONTANA ARTS COUNCIL
Program Director, Artist Services
35 S. Last Chance Gulch
Helena, MT 59620

NEBRASKA ARTS COUNCIL
Douglas D. Elliott, Associate Director/Programs
1313 Farnam On-the-Mall
Omaha, NE 68102-1873

NEVADA STATE COUNCIL ON THE ARTS
William L. Fox, Executive Director
329 Flint St.
Reno, NV 89501

NEW HAMPSHIRE STATE COUNCIL ON THE ARTS
Phenix Hall, 40 N. Main St.
Concord, NH 03301

NEW JERSEY STATE COUNCIL ON THE ARTS
Noreen M. Tomassi, Literary Arts Coordinator
109 W. State St.
Trenton, NJ 08625

NEW MEXICO ARTS DIVISION
Santa Fe Poets-in-the Schools Program
224 E. Palace Ave.
Santa Fe, NM 87501

NEW YORK STATE COUNCIL ON THE ARTS
Gregory Kolovakos, Director, Literature Program
915 Broadway
New York, NY 10010

NORTH CAROLINA ARTS COUNCIL
Jean W. McLaughlin, Literature Program
Dept. of Cultural Resources
Raleigh, NC 27611

NORTH DAKOTA COUNCIL ON THE ARTS
Donna Evenson, Exec. Director
Black Building, Suite 606
Fargo, ND 58102

OHIO ARTS COUNCIL
727 E. Main St.
Columbus, OH 43205

STATE ARTS COUNCIL OF OKLAHOMA
Ellen Binkley, Assistant Director
Jim Thorpe Bldg., Rm. 640
Oklahoma City, OK 73105

OREGON ARTS COMMISSION
835 Summer St., N.E.
Salem, OR 97301

PENNSYLVANIA COUNCIL ON THE ARTS
Peter Carnahan, Literature and Theatre Programs
Mack Granderson, Artists-in-Education Program
Room 216, Finance Bldg.
Harrisburg, PA 17120

RHODE ISLAND STATE COUNCIL ON THE ARTS
Iona B. Dobbins, Executive Director
312 Wickenden St.
Providence, RI 02903

SOUTH CAROLINA ARTS COMMISSION
Steve Lewis, Director, Literary Arts Program
1800 Gervais St.
Columbia, SC 29201

SOUTH DAKOTA ARTS COUNCIL
108 W. 11th St.
Sioux Falls, SD 57102

TENNESSEE ARTS COMMISSION
320 Sixth Ave. N., Suite 100
Nashville, TN 37219

TEXAS COMMISSION ON THE ARTS
P.O. Box 13406, Capitol Station
Austin, TX 78711

UTAH ARTS COUNCIL
G. Barnes, Literary Arts Coordinator
617 East South Temple
Salt Lake City, UT 84102

VERMONT COUNCIL ON THE ARTS
Geof Hewitt, Grants Coordinator
136 State St.
Montpelier, VT 05602

777

VIRGINIA COMMISSION FOR THE ARTS
Peggy J. Baggett, Executive Director
James Monroe Bldg., 17th Floor
101 N. 14th St.
Richmond, VA 23219

WASHINGTON STATE ARTS COMMISSION
Lee Bassett, Artists-in-Residence Program
110 9th and Columbia Bldg., MS GH-11
Olympia, WA 98504

WEST VIRGINIA DEPT. OF CULTURE AND HISTORY
Arts and Humanities Division
The Cultural Center, Capitol Complex
Charleston, WV 25305

WISCONSIN ARTS BOARD
107 S. Butler St.
Madison, WI 53703

WYOMING COUNCIL ON THE ARTS
Joy Thompson, Executive Director
Capitol Complex
Cheyenne, WY 82001

ORGANIZATIONS FOR WRITERS

THE ACADEMY OF AMERICAN POETS
117 E. 87th St.
New York, NY 10128
Mrs. Hugh Bullock, *President*
   Founded in 1934 to "encourage, stimulate and foster the art of poetry," the AAP sponsors a series of poetry readings in New York City and numerous annual awards. Membership is open to all: $35 annual fee includes subscription to the monthly newsletter, admission to sponsored readings, and free copies of prize book selection.

AMERICAN MEDICAL WRITERS ASSOCIATION
5272 River Rd., Suite 410
Bethesda, MD 20816
Lillian Sablack, *Executive Director*
   Members of this association are engaged in communication about medicine and its allied professions. Any person actively interested in or professionally associated with any medium of medical communication is eligible for membership. The annual dues are $55.

AMERICAN SOCIETY OF JOURNALISTS AND AUTHORS, INC.
1501 Broadway, Suite 1907
New York, NY 10036
Alexandra Cantor, *Executive Secretary*
   A nationwide organization dedicated to promoting high standards of non-

fiction writing through monthly meetings, annual writers' conferences, etc., ASJA offers extensive benefits and services including referral service, group health insurance, and the opportunity to explore professional issues and concerns with other writers. Members also receive a monthly newsletter. Membership is open to qualified professional free-lance writers of nonfiction; qualifications are judged by Membership Committee. Initiation fee: $50; annual dues: $95.

THE AUTHORS LEAGUE OF AMERICA, INC.
(The Authors Guild and The Dramatists Guild)
234 W. 44th St., New York, NY 10036

The Authors League of America is a national organization of over 12,000 authors and dramatists, representing them on matters of joint concern, such as copyright, taxes, and freedom of expression. Membership in the league is restricted to authors and dramatists who are members of The Authors Guild and The Dramatists Guild. Matters such as contract terms and subsidiary rights are in the province of the two guilds.

A writer who has published a book in the last seven years with an established publisher, or one who has published several magazine pieces with periodicals of general circulation within the last eighteen months, may be eligible for active voting membership in The Authors Guild. A new writer may be eligible for associate membership on application to the Membership Committee. Dues: $60 a year.

The Dramatists Guild is a professional association of playwrights, composers, and lyricists, established to protect dramatists' rights and to improve working conditions. Services include use of the Guild's contracts, business counseling, publications, and symposia in major cities. All theater writers (produced or not) are eligible for membership.

THE INTERNATIONAL SOCIETY OF DRAMATISTS
Box 1310
Miami, FL 33153

Open to playwrights, agents, producers, novelists, and others involved in the theater. Publishes *Dramatist's Bible,* a directory of script opportunities, and *The Globe,* a newsletter, with information and news of theaters across the country. Also provides referral service for playwrights.

MYSTERY WRITERS OF AMERICA, INC.
236 W. 27th St.
New York, NY 10001
Mary A. Frisque, *Executive Secretary*

The MWA exists for the purpose of raising the prestige of mystery and detective writing, and of defending the rights and increasing the income of all writers in the field of mystery, detection, and fact crime writing. Each year, the MWA presents the Edgar Allan Poe Awards for the best mystery writing in a variety of fields. The four classifications of membership are: *active* (open to any writer who has made a sale in the field of mystery, suspense, or crime writing); *associate* (for nonwriters, allied to the mystery field); *corresponding* (writers living outside the U.S.); *affiliate* (for unpublished writers and mystery enthusiasts). Annual dues: $50; $25 for corresponding members.

NATIONAL ASSOCIATION OF SCIENCE WRITERS, INC.
P.O. Box 294
Greenlawn, NY 11740

The NASW promotes the dissemination of accurate information regarding science through all media, and conducts a varied program to increase the flow of news from scientists, to improve the quality of its presentation, and to communicate its meaning to the reading public.

Anyone who has been actively engaged in the dissemination of science information for two years is eligible to apply for membership. Active members must be principally involved in reporting on science through newspapers, magazines, TV, or other media that reach the public directly. Associate members report on science through limited-circulation publications and other media. Annual dues: $45.

THE NATIONAL WRITERS CLUB
1450 S. Havana, Suite 620
Aurora, CO 80012
James Lee Young, *Assoc. Dir.*

New and established writers, poets, and playwrights throughout the U.S. and Canada may become members of The National Writers Club, a nonprofit representative organization. Membership includes bimonthly newsletter, *Authorship.* Dues: $50 annually, plus a $15 initiation fee.

NATIONAL WRITERS UNION
13 Astor Pl., 7th Fl.
New York, NY 10003

Any writer who has published one book, play, short story, or three articles, five poems or the equivalent in unpublished work is eligible to join The National Writers Union. The NWU offers advice on contracts, discounts, insurance, and sponsors events across the country. Annual dues range from $35 to $115.

OUTDOOR WRITERS ASSOCIATION OF AMERICA, INC.
2017 Cato Ave., Suite 101
State College, PA 16801
Sylvia G. Bashline, *Executive Director*

The OWAA is an organization for professional print and broadcast journalists who report on outdoor recreational activities and concerns. Membership (by nomination only) includes a monthly publication, *Outdoors Unlimited;* annual conference; members' directory; and contests. Also provides scholarships.

PEN AMERICAN CENTER
568 Broadway
New York, NY 10012

PEN American Center is one of 80 centers that comprise International PEN, a worldwide association of literary workers, offering conferences, writing programs, financial and educational assistance. Membership is open to writers who have published two books of literary merit, as well as editors, agents, playwrights, and translators who meet specific standards (apply to nomination committee). PEN sponsors annual awards and grants and publishes the quarterly *Pen Newsletter.*

THE POETRY SOCIETY OF AMERICA
15 Gramercy Park
New York, NY 10003
Dennis Stone, *Administrative Director*

Founded in 1910, The Poetry Society of America seeks through a variety of programs to gain a wider audience for American poetry. The Society offers 17 annual prizes for poetry (with many contests open to non-members as well as members), and sponsors workshops, free public poetry readings, and publications (including the semiannual *The Poetry Review*). Dues: $30 annually.

POETS AND WRITERS, INC.
201 W. 54th St.
New York, NY 10019
Elliot Figman, *Executive Director*
Poets & Writers, Inc. was founded in 1970 to foster the development of poets and fiction writers and to promote communication throughout the literary community. A non-membership organization, it offers a nationwide information center for writers; *Coda, Poets & Writers Newsletter* and other publications; as well as sponsored readings and workshops.

PRIVATE EYE WRITERS OF AMERICA
1873 Crowley Circle East
Longwood, FL 32779
Robert J. Randisi, *Executive Director*
Private Eye Writers of America is a national organization that seeks to promote a wider recognition and appreciation of private eye literature. Writers who have published a work of fiction—short story, novel, TV script, or movie screenplay—with a private eye as the central character are eligible to join as active members. Serious devotees of the P.I. story may become associate members. Dues: $20 (active), $10 (associate). Annual Shamus Award for the best in P.I. fiction.

ROMANCE WRITERS OF AMERICA
5206 FM 1960 West, #207
Houston, TX 77069
Pat Hudgins, Executive Secretary
The RWA is a national organization with over 80 local chapters across the U.S., open to any writer, published or unpublished, interested in the field of romantic fiction. Annual dues of $35; benefits include annual conference, contest, market information, and bimonthly newsmagazine, *Romance Report*.

SCIENCE FICTION WRITERS OF AMERICA
P.O. Box H
Wharton, NJ 07885
Peter D. Pautz, *Executive Secretary*
The purpose of the SFWA, a professional organization of science fiction and fantasy writers, is to foster and further the interests of writers of fantasy and science fiction. SFWA presents the Nebula Award annually for excellence in the field and publishes the *Bulletin* for its members.
Any writer who has sold a work of science fiction or fantasy is eligible for membership. Dues: $50 per year for active members, $35 for affiliates, plus $10 installation fee; send for application and information. The *Bulletin* is available to nonmembers for $10 (four issues).

SOCIETY FOR TECHNICAL COMMUNICATION
815 15th St., NW
Washington, DC 20005
William C. Stolgitis, *Executive Director*
The Society for Technical Communication is a professional organization dedicated to the advancement of the theory and practice of technical communication in all media. The almost 10,000 members in the U.S. and other countries include technical writers and editors, publishers, artists and draftsmen, reseachers, educators, and audiovisual specialists.

SOCIETY OF AMERICAN TRAVEL WRITERS
1120 Connecticut Ave., Suite 940
Washington, DC 20036
Ken Fischer, *Administrative Coordinator*

The Society of American Travel Writers represents writers and other professionals who strive to provide travelers with accurate reports on destinations, facilities, and services.

Membership is by invitation. Active membership is limited to salaried travel writers and others employed as free lancers, who have a steady volume of published or distributed work about travel. Initiation fee for active members is $150, for associate members $300. Annual dues: $90 (active); $170 (associate).

SOCIETY OF CHILDREN'S BOOK WRITERS
P.O. Box 296
Mar Vista Station
Los Angeles, CA 90066
Lin Oliver, *Executive Director*

This national organization of authors, editors, publishers, illustrators, librarians, and educators offers a variety of services to people who write for or share an interest in children's literature. Full memberships are open to those who have had at least one children's book or story published. Associate memberships are open to all those with an interest in children's literature. Yearly dues are $30.

WESTERN WRITERS OF AMERICA
1753 Victoria
Sheridan, WY 82801
Barbara Ketcham, *Secretary/Treasurer*

Writers of fiction, nonfiction, and poetry pertaining to the traditions, legends, development, and history of the American West may join the nonprofit Western Writers of America. Its chief purpose is to promote a more widespread distribution, readership, and appreciation of the West and its literature. Dues are $40 a year. Sponsors annual Spur Awards.

WRITERS GUILD OF AMERICA, EAST, INC.
555 W. 57th St.
New York, NY 10019
Mona Mangan, *Executive Director*

WRITERS GUILD OF AMERICA, WEST, INC.
8955 Beverly Blvd.
Los Angeles, CA 90048
Brian Walton, *Executive Director*

The Writers Guild of America (East and West) represents writers in the fields of radio, television and motion pictures.

In order to qualify for membership a writer must fulfill current requirements for employment or sale of material in one of these three fields.

The basic dues are $25 a quarter for the Writers Guild West and $12.50 a quarter in the case of Writers Guild East. In addition, there are quarterly dues based on a percentage of the member's earnings in any one of the fields over which the Guild has jurisdiction. The initiation fee is $1,000 for Writers Guild East and $1,500 for Writers Guild West. (Writers living east of the Mississippi join Writers Guild East, and those living west of the Mississippi, Writers Guild West.)

AMERICAN LITERARY AGENTS

Most literary agents do not usually accept new writers as clients. Since the agent's only income is a percentage—10% to 20%—of the amount he receives from the sales he makes for his clients, he must have as clients writers who are selling fairly regularly to good markets. Always query an agent first. Do not send any manuscripts until the agent has asked you to do so. The following list is only a partial selection of representative agents. Addresses which include zip codes in parentheses are located in New York City (the majority of agents in this list are in New York). A list of agents can also be obtained by sending a stamped, self-addressed envelope to Society of Authors' Representatives, 39½ Washington Square South, New York, NY 10012 or Independent Literary Agents Assn., Inc., 21 W. 26th St., New York, NY 10010.

BRET ADAMS, LTD., 448 W. 44th St. (10036)

JULIAN BACH LITERARY AGENCY, INC., 747 Third Ave. (10017)

LOUIS BERMAN, The Little Theatre Bldg., 240 W. 44th St. (10036)

GEORGES BORCHARDT, INC., 136 E. 57th St. (10022)

BRANDT & BRANDT LITERARY AGENTS, INC., 1501 Broadway (10036)

THE HELEN BRANN AGENCY, INC., 157 W. 57th St. (10019)

CURTIS BROWN, LTD., 10 Astor Place (10003)

KNOX BURGER ASSOCIATES, LTD., 39½ Washington Square South (10012)

COLLIER ASSOCIATES, 875 Sixth Ave., #1003 (10001)

DON CONGDON ASSOCIATES, INC., 111 5th Ave. (10003)

JOAN DAVES, 59 E. 54th St. (10022)

ANITA DIAMANT, 310 Madison Ave., #1508 (10017)

CANDIDA DONADIO & ASSOCIATES, INC., 231 W. 22nd St. (10011)

THE DORSET GROUP, 820 W. Belmont Ave., Chicago, IL 60657

ANN ELMO AGENCY, INC., 60 E. 42nd St. (10165)

JOHN FARQUHARSON, LTD., Suite 1914, 250 W. 57th St. (10107)

THE FOX CHASE AGENCY, INC., 419 E. 57th St. (10022)

ROBERT A. FREEDMAN DRAMATIC AGENCY, INC., 1501 Broadway, #2310 (10036)

SAMUEL FRENCH, INC., 45 W. 25th St. (10010)

GRAHAM AGENCY, 311 W. 43rd St. (10036)

BLANCHE C. GREGORY, INC., Two Tudor City Place (10017)

HELEN HARVEY, 410 W. 24th St. (10019)

INTERNATIONAL CREATIVE MANAGEMENT, INC., 40 W. 57th St. (10019)

JCA LITERARY AGENCY, INC., 242 W. 27th St., No. 4A (10001)

LUCY KROLL AGENCY, 390 West End Ave. (10024)

PINDER LANE PRODUCTIONS, LTD., 159 W. 53rd St. (10019)

THE LANTZ OFFICE, 888 Seventh Ave. (10106)

LESCHER & LESCHER, LTD., 155 E. 71st St. (10021)

ELLEN LEVINE LITERARY AGENCY, 432 Park Ave. S., #1205 (10016)

LITERISTIC, LTD., 264 Fifth Ave. (10001)

THE STERLING LORD AGENCY, INC., 660 Madison Ave. (10021)

ELISABETH MARTON, 96 Fifth Ave. (10011)

HAROLD MATSON COMPANY, INC., 276 Fifth Ave. (10001)

GERARD MCCAULEY AGENCY, INC., 141 E. 44th St. #208 (10017)

MCINTOSH & OTIS, INC., 475 Fifth Ave. (10017)

HELEN MERRILL, 361 W. 17th St. (10011)

WILLIAM MORRIS AGENCY, INC., 1350 Ave. of the Americas (10019)

HAROLD OBER ASSOCIATES, INC., 40 E. 49th St. (10017)

FIFI OSCARD ASSOCIATES, INC., 19 W. 44th St. (10036)

RAINES & RAINES, 71 Park Ave. (10016)

PAUL R. REYNOLDS, INC., 71 W. 23rd St. (10011)

FLORA ROBERTS, INC., Penthouse A, 157 W. 57th St. (10019)

MARIE RODELL-FRANCES COLLIN LITERARY AGENCY, Suite 2004, 110 W. 40th St. (10018)

ROSENSTONE/WENDER, 3 E. 48th St. (10017)

RUSSELL & VOLKENING, INC., 50 W. 29th St. (10001)

JOHN SCHAFFNER ASSOCIATES, INC., 114 E. 28th St. (10016)

JAMES SELIGMANN AGENCY, 175 Fifth Ave., #1101 (10010)

CHARLOTTE SHEEDY LITERARY AGENCY, INC., 145 W. 86th St. (10024)

THE SHUKAT COMPANY, LTD., 340 W. 55th St., #1A (10019)

PHILIP G. SPITZER LITERARY AGENCY, 111-25 76th Ave., Flushing, NY 11375.

ROSLYN TARG LITERARY AGENCY, INC., 105 W. 13th St., #15E (10011)

WALLACE & SHEIL AGENCY, INC., 177 E. 70th St. (10021)

RHODA WEYR LITERARY AGENCY, 322 Central Park West (10025)

MARY YOST ASSOCIATES, INC., 59 E. 54th St., No. 52 (10022)